Graphic Novels

Recent Titles in
Genreflecting Advisory Series

Diana Tixier Herald, Series Editor

Primary Genreflecting: A Guide to Picture Books and Easy Readers
Susan Fichtelberg and Bridget Dealy Volz

Teen Genreflecting 3: A Guide to Reading Interests
Diana Tixier Herald

Urban Grit: A Guide to Street Lit
Megan Honig

Historical Fiction for Teens: A Genre Guide
Melissa Rabey

Graphic Novels for Young Readers: A Genre Guide for Ages 4–14
Nathan Herald

Make Mine a Mystery II: A Reader's Guide to Mystery and Detective
Fiction
Gary Warren Niebuhr

Mostly Manga: A Genre Guide to Popular Manga, Manhwa, Manhua,
and Anime
Elizabeth Kalen

Romance Fiction: A Guide to the Genre, Second Edition
Kristin Ramsdell

Reality Rules II: A Guide to Teen Nonfiction Reading Interests
Elizabeth Fraser

Genreflecting: A Guide to Popular Reading Interests, Seventh Edition
Cynthia Orr and Diana Tixier Herald, Editors

Women's Fiction: A Guide to Popular Reading Interests
Rebecca Vnuk and Nanette Donohue

Encountering Enchantment: A Guide to Speculative Fiction for Teens,
Second Edition
Susan Fichtelberg

Graphic Novels

A Guide to Comic Books, Manga, and More

Second Edition

Michael Pawuk and David S. Serchay

Genreflecting Advisory Series

Diana Tixier Herald, Series Editor

LIBRARIES UNLIMITED™

An Imprint of ABC-CLIO, LLC

Santa Barbara, California • Denver, Colorado

Library of Congress Cataloging-in-Publication Data

Names: Pawuk, Michael, author. | Serchay, David S., 1971– author.
Title: Graphic novels : a guide to comic books, manga, and more /
    Michael Pawuk and David Serchay.
Description: Second edition. | Santa Barbara, California : Libraries
    Unlimited, an imprint of ABC-CLIO, LLC, [2017] | Series: Genreflecting
    advisory series | Includes bibliographical references and indexes.
Identifiers: LCCN 2017020105 (print) | LCCN 2017002418 (ebook) |
    ISBN 9781440851360 (ebook) | ISBN 9781598847000 (acid-free paper)
Subjects: LCSH: Comic books, strips, etc.—Bibliography. | Comic books,
    strips, etc.—Themes, motives.
Classification: LCC Z5956.C6 (print) | LCC Z5956.C6 P38 2017 PN6710
    (ebook) | DDC 016.7415/9—dc23
LC record available at https://lccn.loc.gov/2017020105

ISBN: 978-1-59884-700-0
EISBN: 978-1-4408-5136-0

21 20 19 18 17   1 2 3 4 5

This book is also available as an eBook.

Libraries Unlimited
An Imprint of ABC-CLIO, LLC

ABC-CLIO, LLC
130 Cremona Drive, P.O. Box 1911
Santa Barbara, California 93116-1911
www.abc-clio.com

This book is printed on acid-free paper ∞

Manufactured in the United States of America

Dedicated in loving memory of my father, Stephen Gregory Pawuk (1943–2015). You always were my favorite super-hero.

—Mike Pawuk

Dedicated to my darling daughters, Kara and Wendy

—David S. Serchay

Contents

Acknowledgments.. xi
Introduction.. xxix

Chapter 1—Super-Heroes.. 1
   Super-Hero Icons 2
   Other Classic and Contemporary Crime Fighters.................................... 24
   Cosmic Heroes.. 69
   Super-Hero Teams 76
   Team-Ups and Epic Events.. 103
   Villains: Archenemies and Rogues Galleries 116
   Alternate Time Lines, Elseworlds, and What-If Worlds 122
   Slice-of-Life/Common Man Perspectives.. 126
   Anthologies 130

Chapter 2—Action and Adventure 133
   Prehistoric Adventure 135
   Heroic Adventure... 143
   Adventurers, Explorers, Pirates, and Soldiers of Fortune........................ 148
   Fists of Fury and Sword of Steel—Fighting Adventure Stories 157
   War Stories.. 162
   Far East Adventure—Code of the Warrior: Samurai, Ninja, and Other Asian
      Influences 172
   Spies/Espionage 188
   Westerns.. 193
   Western Genre Blends: The Weird West... 197

Chapter 3—Science Fiction.. 201
   Space Opera/Space Fantasy 201
   Space Exploration 221
   Science Action 227
   New Wave Science Fiction 241
   Aliens from Outer Space.. 243
   Alternate Worlds, Time Travel, and Dimensions 248
   Dystopian and Utopian Worlds... 256
   Post-Apocalypse 261
   Computers and Artificial Intelligence.. 267
   Psychic Powers and Mind Control.. 268
   Robots, Androids, and Cyborgs 270
   Science Fiction Anthologies 288

Chapter 4—Fantasy 291
    Sword and Sorcery Fantasy 291
    Fairy Tales and Folklore 316
    Mythological Fantasy..326
    Magic Portal Fantasy/Parallel Worlds 336
    Contemporary Fantasy 347
    Dark Fantasy 356

Chapter 5—Horror 367
    Supernatural Heroes...368
    A Beastiary...380
    Ghosts and Spirits 402
    Demonic Possession, Black Magic, Witches, and the Occult.................410
    Slasher/Thriller 417
    Anthologies and Short Story Collections..419

Chapter 6—Crime and Mysteries 423
    Detectives...423
    Crime and the Criminal Underworld 443
    True Crime 451

Chapter 7—General Fiction...457
    Romance 457
    Coming of Age/Slice of Life...468
    Sports 487
    Food 490
    Historical Fiction 498
    Short Stories and Anthologies 506

Chapter 8—Humor...511
    General Humor..511
    Cartoons, Animation, and Media Tie-Ins 522
    Funny Animals..541
    Black Humor/Satire 553
    Genre Blends...556

Chapter 9—Non-Fiction...603
    Art—Comics, Comic Books, and Graphic Novels 603
    Biography/Autobiography/Memoir 605
    History..623
    Science and Math 629
    Miscellaneous Non-Fiction...639

Appendix I—Recommended Additional Book Sources 643
Appendix II—Publishing Companies on the Internet 649
Appendix III—Other Online Sources 655
Creator Index 659
Title Index 677
Subject Index 713

Acknowledgments

From Mike:

We would like to thank the following for their assistance and support for this book: editor Barbara Ittner, and the staff at Libraries Unlimited for all their input, advice, and patience; the fellow librarian/graphic novel specialists for their invaluable assistance and support including, but not limited to, Polykarpos Panos, Kat Kan, Robin Brenner, Eva Volin, Dawn Rutherford, Scott Robbins, Steve Weiner, Steve Raiteri, and Snow Wildsmith; the members of the Graphic Novels for Libraries listserv (GN4LIB) for their input and advice; a special thank you also to all the individual creators including Kazu Kibuishi, Gene Luen Yang, Jenni Holm, Chris Schweizer, Raina Telgemeier, Ben Hatke, David Roman, John Green, Nathan Hale, and too many others here to list who have been supportive of libraries and have helped to inspire me to write a second book; all the graphic novel publishers, and distributors including Marvel Comics, Dark Horse Comics, DC Comics, Image Comics, IDW Publishing, First Second Books, Scholastic, Random House, VIZ Media, Cartoon Books, Candlewick Press, Disney Press, Lucasfilm LTD, Kid Can Press, Top Shelf Productions, and countless others who gave me copyright permission for this publication and those who were able to send me review copies of their titles for this publication; the YALSA Great Graphic Novels for Teens committee members throughout the years for all their selections; John Dudas of Carol & John's Comic Book Shop and John Gavin of York Comics & Cards for supplying me with the graphic novel titles I purchased for research; Sean Kollar for his illustrations in the comic book section of this collection; my twin brother Paul who has shared my love for comic books ever since we were kids; and most importantly this couldn't have been done without the support of my parents Greg and Ludmilla Pawuk who were supportive of my love for comic books ever since I was a child. A special thanks to my children Nathan and Lilia, who have missed a lot of daddy time while I was hunkered down late at night and weekends for far too long writing instead of having fun with the both of you. Lastly, I'd like to thank my wife, Laurie, who has been supportive of this hobby of mine and this sequel project since day one. I love you with all my heart. I owe you a great deal of date nights.

From David:

Thanks again to the librarians, creators, and publishers listed earlier. Thanks with love to my parents, my family, my daughters, Kara and Wendy, and my wonderful wife Bethany for all of your love and support over the years. And a special thank you to Mike for asking me to be a part of this project. Here's to more collaborations in the future.

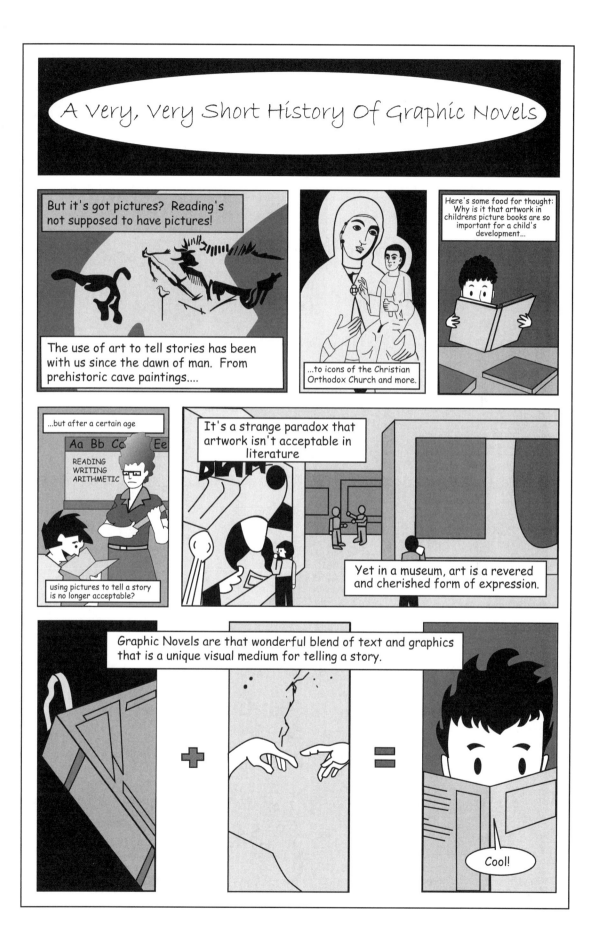

Comic Books, Trade Paperbacks and Graphic Novels

What's the difference between comic books, trades and graphic novels?

Are they just the same but different?

Oh yeah!

Well most of us are familiar with a comic book.

It's typically a 32-page pamphlet-sized publication. It can be a self contained or part of an ongoing plot.

Here we have an example of the comic book "Ultimate Spider-Man" published by Marvel Comics.

The single issues were collected and reprinted as a trade paperback

A trade paperback is a collection of comic books that were once sold as individual single issues. It can come in paperback or hardcover.

You can usually tell from the table of contents section of a book if it's a trade or not. For example the USM book says the following: "Originally published as USM #1-7, (c) 2002."

A graphic novel is a self-contained publication by the publisher. It was never done in a comic book format and it was only printed just like the way you're seeing it now.

It can feature all-new characters or feature familiar characters such as Batman and Spider-Man.

Comic veteran Will Eisner coined the term as a way to have his work stand out from the standard super-hero titles of the day.

The term has stuck, for better or for worse, as an all-encompassing term for both trades and graphic novels.

Graphic Novels Are More Than What?

One of the concerns you might have for your readers is that unlike a novel, graphic novels visually show the reader events that are happening.

BETTER THIS WAY. QUICK. CLEAN. FINAL.

Jean, No DON'T

SCOTT!

Is it called a "graphic novel" because it has a lot of pictures of naked people?

Nope.

All it means is is that it's a visual novel.

Here's an example of prose vs. a graphic novel.

It's a small segment from Homer's classic epic poem The Odyssey to show how describing a scene and visually showing it can be portrayed.

Wow- I feel like I'm in High School again! Toga! Toga! Toga!

"When my men and I were sure that he was asleep, we took our weapon, which was a very long, and thick stick of wood, put the point into the still burning fire, crept up on the sleeping Cyclops, and then we thrust into the Cyclops eye. He screamed, and yelled so loudly that all the other Cyclops' came running to see what had happened.

Now we wait, AND WAIT, as Sean draws this in page form.

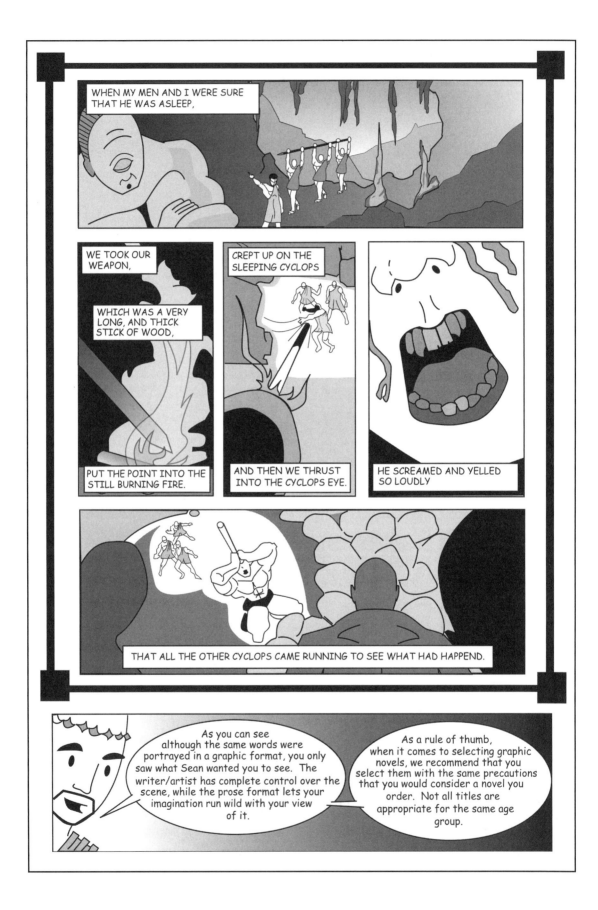

Introduction

Graphic novels have continued to be a growing part of the collections of public libraries, bookstores, schools, and more. Readers of all ages have embraced the format, and today there have never been such a wide variety of titles available for children, teens, and adults. In the 10+ years since the first edition of this book, the graphic novel explosion can be credited in part to the still-increasing diversity of the publishing companies in North America today as well as the influx of titles originally published in Asia that have been embraced by North American culture. Even in the library world, graphic novels have found a place of respectability with graphic novels becoming more and more a common medium in libraries for not only children's and teen departments, but adult departments as well. Graphic novels now also frequently appear on library selection lists in their own category—such as YALSA's Great Graphic Novels for Teens selection list, but have also been recognized on other American Library Association awards, including the Michael L. Prinz (winner for Gene Luen Yang's *American Born Chinese* and honor book for *This One Summer* by Jillian and Mariko Tamaki); the Newbery Award honor book (Cece Bell's *El Deafo*), a Caldecott honor book (Jillian and Mariko Tamaki's *This One Summer*), and many others.

According to the weekly listing of graphic novels released each Wednesday in comic book shops across North America, in 2015–2016, there were approximately 230–250 graphic novel titles published each month—that's approximately 2,800–3,000 graphic novels per year. The titles included new graphic novels published in North America, reprints, as well as titles originally published in Asia and Europe.

Purpose and Audience

This guide is intended to help readers and readers' advisors find the graphic novels readers enjoy most for all age groups. As with the first edition of this publication, the span of titles that appear in the publication may appeal to all age ranges. This publication organizes and describes more than 3,000 original graphic novel titles and collected graphic novels series by genre and subgenre. Original graphic novels are defined as graphic novel titles that were created solely in a bound format and were never before originally published as a comic book. Collected graphic novels (also referred to as a trade paperback by many comic book publishers) were previously published as a monthly comic book and, after a period of time, were repackaged in a collected paperback or hardcover format. For brevity's sake, the titles are all referred to as graphic novels in this publication.

The annotations listed herein include a wide variety of publishers of graphic novels, including mainstream comic book publishers such as DC Comics, Marvel Comics, Dark Horse Comics, Image Comics, IDW Publishing, Boom! Studios, Valiant Entertainment, Dynamite Entertainment, and more. Also included are independent publishers including Drawn + Quarterly, Top Shelf, Fantagraphics Books, Top Shelf Productions, NBM Publishing, Oni Press, as well as mainstream book publishers who have also ventured into publishing graphic novels including Random House's Pantheon Press, Macmillan's First

Second Books, Scholastic's Graphix, Amulet Books; as well as a wide variety of Asian publishers including VIZ Media, Kodansha Comics, Seven Seas Entertainment, and more.

This guide is by no means a comprehensive overview of titles by specific writers and illustrators. It is not intended to serve as a guide to what could be considered as "safe" or "clean" graphic novels, or even what can be considered as "best of" graphic novels for the last decade. Instead, it is hoped that this guide will help readers' advisors and readers build their graphic novel collections and find graphic novel titles that will appeal to the adult and teen readers they serve. It is also hoped that public librarians, school librarians, educators, booksellers, and others who work with readers of all ages will find this to be a valuable and useful aid.

This book is also not intended as a beginner's introduction to graphic novels. Though it was briefly covered in the illustrated introduction of this book, there are many wonderful works written by fellow librarians and comic book historians that focus on the origin and history of the comic book and graphic novel. Featured titles as well as recommended web sites are listed in the Appendix section.

Like prose fiction, new titles, authors, publishing companies, and subgenre fields appear constantly, and it is impossible for a book such as this one to remain completely up to date. Readers of this book looking for further graphic novel titles of interest should supplement this guide with book reviews, visiting your local comic book shop, library, or bookstore that carries graphic novels to browse the latest releases, and try speaking with fans of the medium for titles they recommend.

Scope, Selection Criteria, and Methodology

This book lists all major genres published by graphic novel publishers and includes publications written for children, teens, and adults. The majority of the titles listed in this second edition were published within the last 10 years, but on occasion older titles prior to that date are included in this publication. Older titles are included in this edition only if they were key volumes in an ongoing series, a select book that received significant recognition after originally being included in the first edition of this book; the book/series is a significant core title that has stood the test of time, or a core title/series that received a significantly new printing of the original series within the last 10 years. The selections include titles popular with readers, as well as critically acclaimed and award-winning titles, and those that have stood the test of time and have helped to define the medium.

Unlike most prose fiction where the readers often look for what is new for their respective age group, graphic novels tend to transcend this age. Similar to the appeal of other popular culture mediums including motion pictures, music, animation, and video games, most graphic novels, regardless of when they were originally published, can still find themselves in the arms of a reader. Many graphic novel titles originally published decades earlier can still be as relevant today despite the age of the story. In fact, this trend can be clearly seen with the hit Japanese manga (manga loosely translates as the Japanese word for "humorous pictures") titles that are current hits with readers, particularly teens. Despite the fact that many of the manga and other Asian titles are currently popular in North America today, many of them were originally published several decades or less ago and have recently been retranslated for an English-speaking audience.

Many of the authors and illustrators who are featured in this guide are well known to fans of the medium but may not be to the average reader. If you are an avid reader, librarian, or readers' advisor familiar with minimal knowledge of graphic novel creators, then names such as Neil Gaiman, Alan Moore, Jeff Smith, Stan Lee, Art Spiegelman, Jack Kirby, Daniel Clowes, Frank Miller, Will Eisner, Brian Michael Bendis, Rumiko Takahashi, Brian K. Vaughan, and many more creators may already be familiar to you. Their works are featured in this collection. Also included in this guide are a wide variety of creators who have helped shape graphic novels for decades including creators such as Chuck Dixon, Mark Waid, Kurt Busiek, Walter Simonson, John Ostrander, Arthur Adams, as well as new up-and-coming creators of graphic novels such as Craig Thompson, Bryan Lee O'Malley, Jill Thompson, Raina Telgemeier, Kazu Kibuishi, Jenni Holm, Josh Howard, and countless others. Through this guide, we hope that you become as intimately familiar with the creators as we, along with many other graphic novel readers, have.

All titles listed in this guide were reviewed by either of both authors with the exception of multiple volumes in series collections and anthologies. For series titles and anthologies, a sample title from the collection was read, reviewed, and deemed appropriate for inclusion in this guide. As with other literature, it is advised that educators always read a graphic novel before recommending to young readers.

The following is a listing of what we have included in the book and what we have left out:

Included:

Original graphic novels—stories published exclusively in the graphic novel format

Collected graphic novels—book-sized reprints of a comic book

Excluded:

Collections of newspaper, magazine strips, and web comics (aside from those published by comic book publishers; see *Chapter 8: Humor* for a brief list)

Children's picture books

Non-English-language material

Sketchbooks and art books

Fotonovelas and Cinestories

Single-issue comic books

Hybrid novels

This publication features titles published throughout the world with a focus mainly on North American publishers and Asian publishers, although some foreign language titles from Europe are listed as well. A good portion of the book features Asian titles, mostly due in part to the "manga explosion" which has reinvigorated the graphic novel field with the influx of titles now available for many readers that North American publishers typically have ignored: girls. We have included a brief content indicator after the age rating if a title was originally published in Japan, Korea, China, or a North American publication mimicking the format. The content indicators are as follows:

Japanese manga = Asian graphic novel titles published originally in Japan. Manga is the general name given to comic books published in Japan. Popular publisher examples in North America include VIZ Media, Kodansha, Seven Seas Entertainment, Vertical, and others.

To lesser extent, we also listed the other main formats of graphic novels:

Korean manhwa = Asian graphic novel titles published originally in Korea.

Chinese manhua = Asian graphic novel titles published originally in China.

Neo-manga = North American graphic novels made to appear almost identical to the Japanese manga format. Popular publisher examples of these titles include Antarctic Press, and Seven Seas Entertainment. Thanks to manga and anime specialist Gilles Poitras for the title suggestion the majority of Asian comic books republished today for the North American market are mainly Japanese manga, though there are exceptions.

There are many recently published and forthcoming books on the subject of the influx of Asian titles and of their own comic book history in Asia. Recommended titles on the subject are listed in the Appendix.

Like many other popular culture mediums such as film, television, and music, comic books and graphic novels also have awards and honors recognizing best works in the industry. The following are the awards and recognitions given for graphic novels listed in this publication:

Will Eisner Comic Industry Award—Started in 1988, the award is one of the highest honors in North America for comic book professionals and is named in honor of the pioneering writer/artist Will Eisner. The awards are given each year at the San Diego Comic Con and are known in the industry as the "Eisners." Due to spacing concerns, not all Eisner Award winners are listed in this publication. Award categories of note listed throughout the book include the following: Best Single Issue/Single Story, Best Short Story, Best Serialized Story, Best Continuing Series, Best Finite/Limited Series, Best New Series, Best Title for Younger Readers/ Best Comics Publication for a Younger Audience, Best Anthology, Best Graphic Album—New, Best Graphic Album: Reprint, Best Writer, Best Artist, Best Writer/ Artist, Best Artist/Penciller/Inker or Penciller/Inker Team, and Talent Deserving of Wider Recognition.

Harvey Kurtzman Award—Started in 1988, the award is voted on by comic book professionals and is named after the pioneering artist and editor Harvey Kurtzman. The awards are also known as the "Harveys." Due to spacing concerns not all Harvey Award winners are included in this book. Some categories listed in this book include: Best Writer, Best Artist, Best Cartoonist (Writer/Artist), Best New Series, Best Continuing or Limited Series, Best Graphic Album of Original Work, Best Graphic Album of Previously Published Work, and Best American Edition of Foreign Material.

Ignatz Award—Started in 1997, the award recognizes outstanding achievement in the industry and is awarded at the Small Press Expo each year. The award is named in honor of the character Ignatz Mouse from Mouse from George Herriman's classic comic strip *Krazy Kat*. Due to spacing concerns, not all Ignatz Award titles are listed in this publication. Titles listed in this publication include Ignatz winners in categories including Outstanding Graphic Novel, Outstanding Series, and Promising New Talent.

Over the years a variety of graphic novels have been selected by the book selection committees of the American Library Association (ALA). The majority of titles have been recognized by the Young Adult Library Services Association (YALSA), a division with some titles recognized by the Association for Library Service to Children (ALSC). The following notable book selection committees have listed graphic novels in their selection lists and awards. The YALSA recognized-works are listed throughout this publication and are for the majority listed in the following recognition awards.

Quick Picks for Reluctant Young Adult Readers

Best Books for Young Adults

Popular Paperbacks for Young Adults

Great Graphic Novels for Teens

To lesser extent, other ALA awards, including but not limited to the YALSA's Michael L. Printz award and ALSC's Newbury and Caldecott awards, as well as others are listed in this publication.

In order to better recognize graphic novel titles that have won awards or have been recognized, We have included the symbol 🏆 following the content indicator listed after the age rating if a title has received recognition from within the comic book industry or by the ALA.

Other icons are also used throughout the book to denote graphic novels that have tie-ins with film, television, gaming, Japanese anime, as well as core collection titles.

◎ (((CORE)))

🎬 (((FILM)))

🖵 (((TELEVISION)))

🎮 (((GAMING))) and

あ (((ANIME)))

Organization and Features

As previously mentioned, this guide organizes titles according to genre, subgenre, and theme, and sorts them into similar groups for the readers and readers' advisors to find similar titles. There may be some debate or questions among the readers as to whether a specific title belongs to a specific chapter and not in another. The decisions were reached by consulting publishers, asking colleagues, and reading reviews on the ideal genre for specific titles. However, genre labels are always somewhat subjective and in the end, the final decision was decided by both authors.

Books featured in the chapters in the appropriate subgenres are listed alphabetically according to the main title of the graphic novel, a graphic novel series, or in some cases (such as the Super-Hero chapter) by the name of the featured character. Unlike prose fiction, with graphic novels the focus is not always on the creators (i.e., writers and artists), but on the particular characters featured in the title or series. Many readers may not know creators such as writer Stan Lee and illustrator Steve Ditko, but they are most definitely aware of the hero Spider-Man, whom they both created. For that reason, the titles in this guide are listed not in alphabetical order by the writer's last name, but by the title of the graphic novel, graphic novel series, or featured character. Due to space concerns, no contributors to a graphic novel outside of the writer and artist are included in this publication. This includes inkers, colorists, editors, translators, and more. We fully recognize that comic book and graphic novels are more than only the talents of a writer and artist, and we apologize if we have left out any creators who have also played a role in the creation of a series outside of the writer and artist.

All graphic novel titles covered by this guide include the title of the book or series, the writer and illustrator for the book, publisher, publication year, ISBN-13, as well as a brief description. All graphic novel series title listings are sorted by the volume number, and collections featuring specific characters or series titles are sorted according to specific themes that help to distinguish the titles from other books. Featured sections in the chapters focusing on specific characters (such as Batman) or series titles (such as <u>Star Wars</u>) include brief descriptions of the overall subject, followed by short annotations highlighting the specific titles in the sections. Also, unless specifically noted, titles are published in softcover. Titles published in hardcover are noted in the annotations.

Also included in the guide following the year of publication is an age indicator of recommended reading levels. The designations used are as follows:

A = All ages

Y = Youth ages 7–12

T = Teens 13–15

O = Older teens 16+

M = Mature readers 18+

These designations are based on the ratings assigned by the respective publishing companies, recommendations by fellow librarians, readers, as well as based on personal reviews of the titles. Readers should keep in mind that these ratings are subjective. We can't overemphasize that readers should read what they are comfortable with and find exciting, regardless of a designated age range.

Please note that graphic novel titles that some may consider to be appropriate for mature readers (typically a rating set for ages 18+) due to content can very well be enjoyed and appreciated by younger readers. What constitutes a "mature reader" can be very subjective and is not limited only to a set age of 18. We have known many younger readers who can handle mature content better than many adult readers. In fact certain titles including *Swamp Thing*, *John Constantine: Hellblazer*, and *Sandman*—all published by DC Comics' mature readers imprint Vertigo—were titles that we ourselves began to read as teenagers.

By that same token, we have also listed titles in this publication that are for young readers. What is interesting about graphic novels is that they share very similar qualities in their all-ages appeal to other popular culture mediums such as movies, where films ranging from features such as a Disney•PIXAR animated film to *Star Wars* movies have great appeal for all ages. Just because a graphic novel was created for a specific age group does not mean an audience younger or older than the target audience cannot enjoy it. In fact, many popular series, such as Jeff Smith's award-winning *Bone* (listed in the Fantasy Chapter), was written in mind for a target audience of a comic book reader in his or her 20s–30s, yet librarians have hailed the series as an ideal title for middle-school children and Scholastic Books' graphic novel imprint, Graphix, featured the series as one of its biggest launch titles for its imprint.

The annotations listed in the chapters are specifically designed to be descriptive rather than critical due to the philosophy of the book to support readers in their choices of books as opposed to point out what we consider to be good literature. The annotations focus mainly on the storyline, details on the main protagonist, main plot points, and other basic descriptions. The same philosophy holds in regards to why content indicators such as violence, sex, language, and others are not included.

How to Use This Guide

This guide can be used in a number of ways. Firstly, it can be used as a source for readers' advisory and to help patrons find real-alike titles. Since the titles are broken down according to a wide variety of genres and subgenres, the readers' advisor need to only consult the similar works on the page to find like titles.

Librarians can use this publication to build more genre-specific collections and to browse titles that may be more popular for their specific collection.

This book can also be used as a genre guide to graphic novel literature for those unfamiliar with the medium or just looking for another good book or hidden treasure to read.

As mentioned previously, this book examines just a small fraction of the variety of graphic novels being published today. We have attempted to include major works for each genre as well as significant works by a wide variety of authors and illustrators, but many titles are not listed due to space constraints. Many of the titles listed in this book have gone out of print or may have recently been reprinted. With over 2,600 titles published in the span of just one year, there are many titles that could not be listed and accordingly, many new wonderful titles are appearing on the horizon. We apologize if we have excluded a favorite title of you, the reader.

Regardless of how you wish to use this book it is our hope that this book is used to spread the love of reading and enjoying graphic novels. Happy reading.

Mike Pawuk and David S. Serchay

Chapter 1

Super-Heroes

The Super-Hero genre has continued to be one of the most popular and enduring genres of the comic book and graphic novel in the United States. The genre's popularity began with the first appearance of Superman, in the pages of DC Comics' *Action Comics* #1 in 1938. As the popularity of Superman soared, DC Comics and many other publishers introduced other super-powered characters to the industry's pantheon of heroes, and a genre was born. Most super-hero characters do tend to exhibit certain universal traits including strong moral ideals, a willingness to confront and battle evil in the world, a heroic-sounding codename to hide their secret identity, a brightly colored costume with optional mask, and extraordinary powers that help to make the hero stand out. The powers can include flight, heat vision, or speed, as well as countless others. Some characters, such as Batman, do not have any superpowers, per se, but have honed their bodies to the peak of human perfection. Other traits of the genre include unique weapons and gadgets, a large cast of supporting characters and loved ones, an arch-nemesis or rogues gallery for the hero, as well as the occasional sidekick.

The genre has a lot in common with the genres of Action/Adventure, Science Fiction, and Fantasy, where many of the titles that follow could easily be placed. Due to the flexible nature of the super-hero tales, many times the titles can also cross over into many other genres including Romance, Drama, Humor, Science Fiction, Horror, Adventure, and more action-oriented genres. Listed below are examples of highlights of the Super-Hero genre from approximately the last 10 years from a wide variety of publishers. The titles include tales of heroics from the most popular heroes of today, classic heroes of yesterday, super-teams, villains, deconstructionist works on the genre, and many more titles. Please note that super-hero titles featuring a healthy dosage of humor are listed in the "Genre Blends" section of the humor chapter. The titles in this chapter are listed by the main codename of the hero or super-hero team, and listings with more than one title featuring the characters are listed below the heroes' codename if applicable. Titles that do not have a featured hero or team are listed according to the main title of the graphic novel.

Super-Hero Icons

Superman, Batman, and Spider-Man are some of the most recognizable super-hero characters in the world today and have set the standard for the plethora of heroes that have published over the decades. Television series, movies, and merchandising have also helped to make these protagonists the best-known characters ever published in comic books. Listed below is a wide range of titles that represent a small sample of graphic novel collections of these super-hero icons. Note that the iconic characters appear elsewhere in this chapter including sections on team-ups, epic events that typically involve a multitude of super-heroes, as well as tales of alternative histories that can feature the iconic heroes reinterpreted in a whole new light.

Superman

Created by Jerry Siegel and **Joe Shuster**. DC Comics, 1993–. ▮ ▢ ⚔

Created by Clevelanders Jerry Siegel and Joe Shuster in 1938, Superman has become one of the best-recognized characters in fiction worldwide. His first appearance in *Action Comics* #1 helped to usher in the age of the super-heroes. Born as Kal-El on the doomed planet Krypton, he was sent to Earth in a rocketship by his Kryptonian parents Jor-El and Lara before the planet was destroyed. The last survivor of Krypton, he crash-landed in Smallville, Kansas, and he was taken in by John and Martha Kent who named him Clark. The yellow sun of Earth, much different from the red sun that Krypton orbited, results in Clark Kent's having powers beyond those of men from Earth: flight, super-strength, invulnerability, X-ray vision, heat vision, acute hearing, and super-breath. He uses these gifts to fight the never-ending battle for truth and justice as the hero known as Superman. As Clark Kent, he works as a reporter in the city of Metropolis while as Superman he faces adversaries from his rogues gallery including Lex Luthor, Doomsday, Brainiac, Bizarro, Mr. Mxyzptlk, Metallo, the Parasite, and many more. Superman has also proved to be a franchisable character and has appeared in feature films, television shows, animated cartoons, video games, and many more. In January 2011, DC Comics relaunched its main comics as its "New 52" lineup including an alternate take on Superman with a slightly revised history. Additional changes were made after the 2016 Rebirth event. Below are listed popular collected comic book stories and graphic novel collections of the greatest American hero. Please note that many more *Superman* titles have been published but are not included in this list. Visit DC Comics' web site at http://www.dccom ics.com for more titles.

Collected Comic Book Titles Featuring Superman. T

Listed below are recommended Superman stories that were originally published in the variety of monthly comic book titles published by DC Comics as part of its recent New 52 lineup as well as pre-New 52 titles. The titles are collected editions of the various

Superman monthly comic books titles, including *Superman* and *Action Comics* as well as stand-alone graphic novels.

The Death and Return of Superman/Superman vs. Doomsday Collections. Written by **Dan Jurgens**, **Jerry Ordway**, **Louise Simonson**, and **Roger Stern**. Illustrated by **Dan Jurgens**, **Jon Bogdanove**, **Tom Grummett**, and **Jackson Guice**. 1993–2013. T ◎ ▟

© 2016 DC Comics

Superman has faced many villains and evildoers, but what happens when the Man of Steel dies? After confronting Doomsday, a behemoth beast from Krypton that has been buried deep in the Earth and is now rampaging across the United States, Superman must make the ultimate sacrifice to defeat his greatest foe. As the citizens around the world mourn Superman and his sacrifice, four mysterious heroes are claiming to be Superman—a man in forged armor, a teenage clone of Superman, a cyborg Superman, and a dark and brooding vigilante who closely resembles Superman. Can any of the four heroes really be Superman back from the dead? When the archvillain Mongul plans to invade Earth, secret enemies are revealed and once again the real Superman proves that not even death can stop justice. *Hunter/Prey* and *The Doomsday Wars*, *The Return of Doomsday*, and *Reign of Doomsday* continue Superman's struggles against the diabolical Doomsday, and *Day of Doom* recounts the anniversary of the day Metropolis's favorite son died to save the world. *The Death of Superman* storyline was originally published in 1993, and its reverberations into Superman's popularity to this day are still stronger than ever. The storyline also was adapted as an animated film in 2007, and the character of Doomsday, who first appeared in the storyline, has even transitioned into the big screen with his debut in the 2016 film *Batman v Superman: Dawn of Justice*.

The Death of Superman, 2nd edition. 2013. 168pp. 978-1-4012-4182-7.
World Without a Superman. 1993. 240pp. 978-1-56389-118-2.
The Return of Superman. 1993. 480pp. 978-1-56389-149-6.
The Doomsday Wars. 1999. 142pp. 978-1-56389-562-3.
Day of Doom. 2003. 96pp. 978-1-4012-0086-2.
Superman/Doomsday Omnibus. 2006. 416pp. 978-1-4012-1107-3.
Superman: The Return of Doomsday. 2011. 144pp. 978-1-4012-3253-5.
The Death and Return of Superman Omnibus. 2013. 1124pp. 978-1-4012-3864-3, hardcover.
Superman: Reign of Doomsday. 2013. 200pp. 978-1-4012-3688-5.

Pre-New 52 Continuity

Superman stories published before the 2011 "New 52" relaunch of Superman. Though many of the plot elements aren't considered to be in canon with the current story arcs, the stories are still highly recommended.

Superman. Written by **Kurt Busiek**, **Geoff Johns**, and **Fabian Nicieza**. Illustrated by **Pete Woods** and **Renato Guedes**. DC Comics, 2006–2007.

> After the storyline called Infinite Crisis, a depowered Superman is gone and the world copes without its greatest hero. Meanwhile, Clark Kent still carries on his battle for truth and justice the only way he knows how. Collected from the monthly issues.
>
> *Up Up and Away*. 2006. 192pp. 978-1-4012-0954-4.
> *Back in Action*. 2007. 144pp. 978-1-4012-1263-6.

Superman: Emperor Joker. Written by various. Illustrated by various. DC Comics, 2016. 244pp. 978-1-4012-6213-6. T

> When Batman's arch-nemesis the Joker steals the powers of Superman's adversary Mr. Mxyzptlk, the world becomes as mad as the Clown Prince of Crime himself! The Joker has turned the world in his image, and each day repeats over and over again culminating with the Joker killing Batman each day and then bringing him back to life. Superman must find a way to break free of the time loop and save the day.

Superman: Ending Battle. Written by **Geoff Johns**, **Joe Kelly**, **Joe Casey**, and **Mark Schultz**. Illustrated by various. DC Comics, 2009. 192pp. 978-1-4012-2259-8. T

> Superman's secret identity has been revealed, and super-villains are striking back at him the only way they can: by attacking his loved ones. Also included is one of the best single issues of *Action Comics #775* in which Superman must prove against a bombastic super-hero team that he's as relevant as ever.

Superman: The Last Son of Krypton. Written by **Geoff Johns** and **Richard Donner**. Illustrated by **Adam Kubert** and **Gary Frank**. DC Comics, 2013. 288pp. 978-1-4012-3779-0. T

> Co-plotted by 1978 Superman movie director Richard Donner, Superman finds out he's not the only Kryptonian when a young boy from Krypton is discovered in a spacecraft near Metropolis and seized by the government. Superman breaks the young boy out of jail and gives him an identity of Christopher Kent (a nod to the late Superman actor Christopher Reeve). When the parent of Christopher comes to play, Superman will have his hands full against one of his greatest enemies: General Zod.

Superman: Secret Origin. Written by **Geoff Johns**. Illustrated by **Gary Frank**. DC Comics, 2011. 224pp. 978-1-4012-3299-3. T

> An origin tale showing the Man of Steel from his roots in Smallville, Kansas, and what makes him the hero he is today. The collection also features appearances by Lex Luthor, the Legion of Super-Heroes, and many other characters from Superman's history.

Post-New 52 Continuity

Stories featuring Superman published after DC Comics' revised continuity from 2011.

Superman. Written by **George Pérez**, **Scott Lobdell**, and **Geoff Johns**. Illustrated by **Jesus Marino**, **Kenneth Rocafort**, and **John Romita Jr**. DC Comics, 2013–2015.

> The Superman relaunch from DC Comics in 2011, the core of the hero remains the same, but with a slightly revised continuity, costume, and relationships with his friends.
>
> *Vol. 1: What Price Tomorrow?* 2013. 144pp. 978-1-4012-3686-1.
> *Vol. 2: Secrets and Lies*. 2014. 176pp. 978-1-4012-4257-2.

Vol. 3. Fury at World's End. 2014. 144pp. 978-1-4012-4622-8.

Vol. 4: Psi-War. 2015. 224pp. 978-1-4012-5094-2.

Vol. 5: Under Fire. 2015. 176pp. 978-1-4012-5542-8.

Vol. 6: The Men of Tomorrow. 2015. 256pp. 978-1-4012-5239-7.

Superman: Action Comics. Written by **Grant Morrison, Scott Lobdell, Greg Pak, and various.** Illustrated by **Rags Morales**, **Adam Kubert, Cliff Richards, and others**. DC Comics, 2013–2014. T

The kickoff title of DC Comics' "New 52" relaunch of Superman by fan-favorite author Grant Morrision, with art by Rags Morales and Adam Kubert. The series takes place approximately five years in the past when Clark Kent is making a name for himself as a super-hero and Metropolis has never heard of Superman. Starting with volume four, new creative teams took over and the setting was moved to the present. Collections of stories from *Action Comics* after the events of DC's 2016 "Rebirth" storyline began to appear in 2017.

Vol. 1: Superman and the Men of Steel. 2013. 256pp. 978-1-4012-35468, hardcover. 978-1-4012-3547-5.

Vol. 2: Bulletproof. 2013. 224pp. 978-1-4012-4101-8, hardcover. 978-1-4012-4254-1.

Vol. 3: At the End of Days. 2013. 224pp. 978-1-4012-4232-9, hardcover. 978-1-4012-4606-8.

Vol. 4: Hybrid. 2014. 200pp. 978-1-4012-4632-7, hardcover. 978-1-4012-5077-5.

Vol. 5: What Lies Beneath. 2014. 160pp. 978-1-4012-4947-2, hardcover. 978-1-4012-5488-9.

Vol. 6: Superdoom. 2015. 200pp. 978-1-4012-5489-6, hardcover. 978-1-4012-5865-8.

Vol. 7: Under the Skin. 2015. 160pp. 978-1-4012-5866-5, hardcover. 978-1-4012-6262-4.

Vol. 8: Truth. 2016. 192pp. 978-1-4012-6263-1, hardcover. 978-1-4012-6920-3.

Vol. 9: Last Rites. 2016. 144pp. 978-1-4012-6919-7, hardcover. 978-1-4012-7410-8.

Superman. Written by **Gene Luen Yang**. Illustrated by **John Romita Jr**. DC Comics, 2016. ◉

Superstar writer Gene Luen Yang took over writing the monthly Superman comic book in 2015. The first story arc features the reveal of Superman's secret identity to the world by Lois Lane and how Clark Kent must deal with everyone knowing his true identity. Also, Superman must deal with his new-found ability and the repercussions of it that leave him temporarily depow-ered. Following DC's 2016 "Rebirth" event, Yang, along with artist Viktor Bodganovic, began work on *New Super Man* about a Chinese Teenager who gains a portion of Superman's power. These volumes continue the collection of the post-52 titles listed earlier. Collections of the post-"Rebirth" *Superman* comic as well as *New Super Man* began in 2017.

Vol. 1: Before Truth. 2016. 224pp. 978-1-4012-5981-5, hardcover. 978-1-4012-6510-6.

Vol. 2: Return to Glory. 2016. 168pp. 978-1-4012-6511-3, hardcover. 978-1-4012-6830-5.

Superman Miniseries and Graphic Novel Titles. T

Listed below are recommended Superman stories that were originally published as a comic book miniseries or as an original graphic novel title published by DC Comics.

All-Star Superman. Written by **Grant Morrison**. Illustrated by **Frank Quitely**. DC Comics, 2007–2011. ◎ 🏵

© 2016 DC Comics

A reinterpretation of Superman by DC Comics by the creative team of Grant Morrison and Frank Quitely, the series was met with critical acclaim and is regarded as one of the best Superman stories created. The first volume also received recognition in 2008 for YALSA's Great Graphic Novels for Teens selection list, and the series as a whole received several Eisner Awards for Best New Series and Best Continuing Series in 2006, 2007, and 2009. It also won a Harvey Award in 2008 for Best Artist and Best Single Issue. The series was also adapted into an animated film by DC Comics and Warner Bros. Animation in 2011.

Vol. 1. 2007. 160pp. 978-1401209148, hardcover; 2008. 160pp. 978-1-4012-1102-8.
Vol. 2. 2009. 160pp. 978-1401218379, hardcover; 2010. 160pp. 978–1401218607.
Omnibus Edition. 2011. 320pp. 978-1-4012-3205-4.
Absolute Edition. 2011. 320pp. 978-1-4012-2917-7, hardcover.

Superman: Brainiac. Written by **Geoff Johns**. Illustrated by **Gary Frank**. 2009. 128pp. 978-1-4012-2087-7, hardcover. T 🏵

Superman has fought against the terror of Brainiac countless times—but little does he realize he's fought against mere duplicates of him—precursors to the real villain. Now for the first time Superman faces the terror of Brainiac, and the Man of Steel will never be the same. The stand-alone story was recognized by YALSA as a Great Graphic Novel for Teens in 2010.

Superman Adventures. Written by **Scott McCloud**. Illustrated by **Rick Burchett**. 2015– . A

© 2016 DC Comics

Originally published by DC Comics from 1996 to 2002, the series is written in the style and continuity of the highly regarded *Superman: The Animated Series* show which originally aired from 1996 to 2000. The storylines are streamlined for younger readers but enjoyable by old fans as well.

Vol. 1. 2015. 240pp. 978-1-4012-5867-2.
Vol. 2. 2016. 240pp. 978-1-4012-6094-1.
Vol. 3. 2017. 240pp 978-1-4012-7242-5.

Batman

Created by **Bill Finger** and **Bob Kane**. DC Comics, 2003– .

Since his first appearance in Detective Comics #27 in 1939, Batman has continued to be one of the most popular comic book characters ever, branching out into hit movies, television shows, cartoons, action figures, and more. Billionaire Bruce Wayne spends his nights as the Dark Knight Detective called Batman. Although he does not have superpowers per se, he is a highly skilled detective and crime fighter, and night after night Batman fights the never-ending battle trying to save his beloved Gotham City from the rampant crime that took his parents away from him at a young age. Vowing after the brutal death of his parents to strike fear into the hearts of criminals, he trained for years in a variety of martial arts and detective skills, but all that talent still lacked the ability to instill fear in the cowardly and superstitious criminals. After an encounter with a bat, Bruce found just what he needed to fight against crime and the Batman was born. Draped in a long dark cape, bat-eared mask concealing his face, a matching black and gray costume, and a belt carrying an amazing array of gadgets and weapons, including gas bombs, Batarangs, and grapple guns, Bruce now found the right costume to instill fear in the criminals of Gotham City. Benefiting from a large bat cave located beneath his mansion, Bruce also had his own lair to run a state-of-the-art crime lab with the aid of his trusted butler, Alfred Pennyworth. Batman's war on crime has also expanded to include allies including Robin, Nightwing, Huntress, Batgirl, and others including the Gotham City Police Department. Together with Batman, they're out to save Gotham City from common criminals and Batman's rogues gallery including such adversaries as the Joker, Mr. Freeze, Clayface, the Ventriloquist, Two-Face, the Penguin, the Riddler, and Catwoman. In 2011, DC Comics relaunched all of its comic books with new number one issues with the New 52 continuity and discarded many plotlines that were previously considered to have "happened." Additional changes were made after 2016's "Rebirth." Many more excellent Batman titles have been published over the years but are not included in this list and can be found at DC Comics' web site at http://www.dccomics.com.

Collected Comic Book Titles Featuring Batman

Listed below are recommended Batman stories that were originally published in the variety of monthly comic book titles published by DC Comics. The titles are collected editions of the ongoing Batman comic books including *Batman*, *Detective Comics*, and more. The collections are listed by title.

Batman, 1st series. Written by **Grant Morrison**. Illustrated by **Andy Kubert**. DC Comics, 2008–2012. T

Famed comic book writer Grant Morrison, no stranger to writing Batman over the years in other series, finally took over the monthly flagship *Batman* title beginning in 2006. With his first story arc, he introduced Bruce Wayne/Batman's son Damian Wayne into the Batman mythos. Damian

ultimately became the new Robin in the book, and he continues to be a popular hero today.

Batman and Son (new edition). 2014. 384pp. 978-1-4012-4402-6.
The Black Glove. 2008. 176pp. 978-1-4012-1909-3, hardcover; 2011. 176pp. 978-1-4012-1945-1.
Batman R.I.P. 2009. 208pp. 978-1-4012-2090-7, hardcover; 208pp. 978-1-4012-2576-6.
Time and the Batman. 2011. 128pp. 978-1-4012-2989-4, hardcover; 2012. 978-1-4012-2990-0.

***Batman and Robin**, 1st series*. Written by **Grant Morrison** and **Peter J. Tomasi**. Illustrated by **Frank Quitely** and **Patrick Gleason**. DC Comics, 2010–2013. T

Though they appear frequently as hero and sidekick since Robin's first introduction in the pages of 1940's *Detective Comics #38*, their first series focusing purely as a team book was not released in 2009 following the events of *Batman: R.I.P.* in which Bruce Wayne had "died." The series featured original Robin Dick Grayson in the role of Batman and Damian Wayne as Robin.

Vol. 1: Reborn. 2010. 168pp. 978-1-4012-2566-7, hardcover; 2011. 168pp. 978-1-4012-2566-7.
Vol. 2: Batman vs. Robin. 2010. 168pp. 978-1-4012-2833-0, hardcover; 2011. 168pp. 978-1-4012-3271-9.
Vol. 3: Batman and Robin Must Die. 2011. 168pp. 978-1-4012-3091-3, hardcover; 2012. 168pp. 978-1-4012-3508-6.
Vol. 4: Dark Knight, White Knight. 2012. 208pp. 978-1-4012-3373-0, hardcover.
Absolute Batman and Robin: Batman Reborn. Written by Grant Morrison. Illustrated by various. 2013. 488pp. 978-1-4012-3737-0.

Batman and Robin, 2nd series. Written by **Peter J. Tomasi**. Illustrated by **Patrick Gleason**. DC Comics, 2012–2015. T ◎

After the departure of writer Grant Morrison, DC Comics continued the popularity of the series by having Bruce Wayne once again in the role of Batman and his son, Damian Wayne, as Robin. Batman must teach his son how to unlearn his dark past under the League of Assassins and to be a hero worthy of the mantle of Robin. The series is regarded by many as one of the best ongoing monthly comic books published by DC Comics.

Vol. 1: Born to Kill. 2012. 192pp. 978-1-4012-3487-4, hardcover; 2013. 192pp. 978-1-4012-3838-4.
Vol. 2: Pearl. 2013. 176pp. 978-1-4012-4089-9, hardcover; 2013. 176pp. 978-1-4012-4267-1.
Vol. 3: Death of the Family. 2013. 160pp. 978-1-4012-4268-8, hardcover; 2014. 160pp. 978-1-4012-4617-4.

Vol. 4: Requiem for Damien. 2014. 176pp. 978-1-4012-4618-1, hardcover; 2014. 176pp. 978-1-4012-5058-4.

Vol. 5: The Big Burn. 2014. 176pp. 978-1-4012-5059-1, hardcover; 2015. 176pp. 978-1-4012-5333-2.

Vol. 6: The Hunt for Robin. 2015. 192pp. 978-1-4012-5334-9, hardcover; 2015. 192pp. 978-1-4012-5800-9.

Vol. 7: Robin Rises. 2015. 240pp. 978-1-4012-5677-7, hardcover; 2016. 240pp. 978-1-4012-6114-6.

Batman: A Death in the Family. Written by **Jim Starlin**. Illustrated by **Jim Aparo**. DC Comics, 2011. 272pp. 978-1-4012-3274-0. T

A gripping tale originally published in 1989 that culminates with the death of Jason Todd, the second teen hero to take on the mantle of Robin. When Jason's mother is kidnapped by the Joker, Jason heads to rescue her but instead is captured and beaten, bruised, and ultimately killed by the Joker. Batman, after finding his partner's tattered corpse, vows that the Joker will pay, with his life if need be. The expanded collection also includes the first appearance of Tim Drake, who would become the next Robin. Jason would later return to life and become the Red Hood.

Batman: Hush. Written by **Jeph Loeb**. Illustrated by **Jim Lee**. DC Comics, 2009–2011. T ◉

Someone is out to toy with Batman, someone who knows his deepest, darkest secrets and has hired a legion of Batman's enemies to push the Dark Knight over the edge. Killer Croc, the Joker, the Riddler, Poison Ivy, Ra's al Ghul, and even Superman are out to stop him. Who is this mysterious foe named Hush, and what vendetta does he have against Batman? Will he succeed in bringing Bruce Wayne his biggest defeat? The story originally was published in the monthly *Batman* comic book issues #609–619 and is regarded as one of the best Batman stories made. The *Absolute Hush Edition* collects both volumes in a deluxe format, including extra features including sketch artwork, scripts, and more. The *Unwrapped Deluxe Edition* reprints the book, but the pencils of artist Jim Lee are the focus of the book.

Batman: Hush. 2009. 320pp. 978-1-4012-2317-5.

Absolute Hush Edition. 2011. 372pp. 978-1-4012-0426-6, hardcover.

Unwrapped Deluxe Edition. 2011. 978-1-4012-2992-4, hardcover.

Batman: The Man Who Laughs. Written by **Ed Brubaker**. Illustrated by **Doug Mahnke**. DC Comics, 2008–2009. 2008. 144pp. 978-1-4012-1622-1, hardcover; 2009. 144pp. 978-1-4012-1626-9. T

The first tale of Batman's encounter with the Joker is finally told! When a maniac is murdering prominent people of Gotham City and leaving them with a sickening grim on the victims' faces, Batman must do whatever he can to stop the rampage of the Joker! The title of the book is a nod to the inspiration for the look of the Joker—an actor named Conrad Veidt who starred in the 1928 movie *The Man Who Laughs*.

Batman: The Return of Bruce Wayne. Written by **Grant Morrison**. Illustrated by **Chris Sprouse**, **Ryan Sook**, and various. DC Comics, 2012. 232pp. 978-1-4012-2968-9.

Batman/Bruce Wayne was thought to have died at the hands of Darksied (as told in the *Final Crisis* storyline), but instead he was sent back in time and set up by Darkseid to be pawn in his game of destruction. Batman travels from era to era, finding himself in the age of cavemen, at the Salem witch trials, on the high seas with pirates, and more, all in a bid to return home and defeat Darkseid.

Batman Incorporated. Written by **Grant Morrison**. Illustrated by **Yanick Paquette**, **Cameron Stewart**, **Scott Clark**, and **Chris Burnham**. DC Comics, 2012–2014. T

Writer Grant Morrison created Batman Incorporated series as a way of looking at Batman's inspiration on a global level. After the events of *Batman: The Return of Bruce Wayne*, Bruce Wayne sets up a global Batman team to combat threats around the world. Batman works alongside many other Bat-themed heroes across the globe, including Knight and Squire (Great Britain), El Gaucho (Argentina), Nightrunner (France), Batwing (Tinasha), Blackbat (Hong Kong), Dark Ranger (Australia), and Ravil (Russia). The series was set during and after the events of the New 52 continuity reboot, but changes to the series were minimal. The *Gotham's Most Wanted* collection is notable since it features Grant Morrison's final issue in which he kills off Damian Wayne (aka Robin).

Batman Incorporated, Vol. 1. 2012. 264pp. 978-1-4012-3212-2, hardcover; 2013. 264pp. 978-1-4012-3827-8.
Vol. 1: Demon Star (New 52). 2013. 176pp. 978-1-4012-3888-9, hardcover; 2013. 176pp. 978-1-4012-4263-3.
Vol. 2: Gotham's Most Wanted (New 52). 2013. 240pp. 978-1-4012-4400-2, hardcover; 2013. 240pp. 978-1-4012-4697-6, hardcover.

Batman: The Resurrection of Ra's Al Ghul. Written by **Grant Morrison** and **Paul Dini**. Illustrated by various. DC Comics, 2009. 256pp. 978-1-4012-2032-7. T

Following the apparent demise of Batman's ancient foe, Batman learns that true evil can never die as the demon's head is brought back to the land of the living.

Batman: Streets of Gotham. Written by **Paul Dini**. Illustrated by **Dustin Nguyen**. DC Comics, 2010–2011. T

A Batman series closely tied into the Batman and Robin first series by Grant Morrison, the series featured Dick Grayson as Batman. As the title applied to the series invokes, the series focused on the grittier action on the streets of Gotham City with other characters providing the narrative with Batman as the main character. The series' third volume, *The House of Hush*, was highly regarded by fans as being a worthy successor to the popular Batman: Hush series originally published in 2001–2002.

Vol. 1: Hush Money. 2010. 144pp. 978-1-4012-2721-0.
Vol. 2: Leviathan. 2010. 160pp. 978-1-4012-2905-4.
Vol. 3: The House of Hush. 2011. 192pp. 978-1-4012-3129-3.

Batman: Whatever Happened to the Caped Crusader? Written by **Neil Gaiman**. Illustrated by **Adam Kubert**. 2010. 128pp. 978-1-4012-2724-1. T

Acclaimed author Neil Gaiman teams up with popular illustrator Adam Kubert and tells a story after Batman is presumed dead and his supporting cast of heroes and villains all pay their respects to the late Dark Knight. A love letter to Batman.

Detective Comics

Written by **Paul Dini**. Illustrated by **J.H. Williams III**, **Dustin Nguyen**, and various. DC Comics, 2007–2008. T

Fan-favorite writer Paul Dini's short story collections from the pages of *Detective Comics*. The stories are intended to be concise mysteries which showcase Batman's actual detective skills as he solves murders and mysteries in the gloomy darkness of Gotham City.

Batman: Death and the City. 2007. 192pp. 978-1-4012-1575-0.
Batman: Detective. 2007. 144pp. 978-1-4012-1239-1.
Batman: Private Casebook. 2008. 160pp. 978-1-4012-2015-0.

Post-New 52 Continuity

Stories featuring Batman published after DC Comics' revised continuity from 2011.

Batman, 2nd series (New 52). Written by **Scott Snyder**. Illustrated by **Greg Capullo**. DC Comics, 2012–2016. T 🎗 ◎

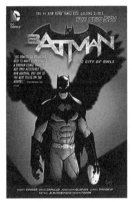

© 2016 DC Comics

Following the departure of Grant Morrison, Scott Snyder took over the main *Batman* monthly comic book, collected in the volumes listed below. The series has introduced many new storylines which are still being played out in the comics today including the introduction of the sinister organized crime group called the Court of Owls, the deadly gambit against the Joker in the *Death of the Family* storyline, and even a temporary takeover of the Batman role by Gotham City police commissioner James Gordon wearing an armored Batsuit. Never fear though—Bruce Wayne returned to the familiar cape and cowl soon thereafter. The collection *The Court of Owls* was recognized by YALSA's Great Graphic Novels for Teens selection list in 2013. Beginning in 2016, DC Comics revitalized its hero lineup and discontinued the *New 52* series for a new direction. The new main-titled Batman series is written by Tom King with art by David Finch.

Vol. 1: The Court of Owls. 2012. 176pp. 978-1-4012-3541-3, hardcover; 2013. 176pp. 978-1-4012-3542-0.
Vol. 2: The City of Owls. 2013. 208pp. 978-1-4012-3777-6, hardcover; 2013. 208pp. 978–9351116615.
Vol. 3: Death of the Family. 2013. 176pp. 978-1-4012-4234-3, hardcover; 2014. 978-1-4012-4602-0.
Vol. 4: Zero Year—Secret City. 2014. 176pp. 978-1-4012-4508-5, hardcover; 2014. 176pp. 978-1-4012-4933-5.
Vol. 5: Zero Year—Dark City. 2014. 256pp. 978-1-4012-4885-7, hardcover. 2015. 256pp. 978-1-4012-5335-6.
Vol. 6: Graveyard Shift. 2015. 224pp. 978-1-4012-5230-4, hardcover; 2015. 978-1-4012-5753-8.

Vol. 7: Endgame. 2015. 192pp. 978-1-4012-5689-0, hardcover; 2016. 192pp. 978-1-4012-6116-0.

Vol. 8: Superheavy. 2016. 176pp. 978-1-4012-5969-3, hardcover. 978-1-4012-6630-1.

Vol. 9: Bloom. 2016. 192pp. 978-1-4012-6923-4, hardcover. 978-1-4012-6922-7.

Vol. 10: Epilogue. 2016. 144pp. 978-1-4012-6773-5, hardcover. 978-1-4012-6832-9.

Batman, 3rd series (Rebirth). Written by **Tom King**. Illustrated by **Greg Capullo**. DC Comics, 2012–2016. T 🏍 ◎

Beginning in 2016, DC Comics discontinued the New 52 settings and characters and returned to what is called the Rebirth era where continuity has reverted for the most part prior to the New 52 era with some elements of the New 52. In the Rebirth continuity Bruce Wayne is still Batman and has an ally in Duke Thomas, a black teenager who joins Batman's war on crime as well as Nightwing, Batgirl, and others.

Vol. 1: I am Gotham. 2017. 192pp. 978-1-4012-6777-3.

Vol. 2: I am Suicide. 2017. 168pp. 978-1-4012-6854-1.

Vol. 3: I am Bane. 2017. 144pp. 978-1-4012-7131-2.

Batman: The Dark Knight (New 52). Written by **David Finch**, **Paul Jenkins**, **Joe Harris**, **Judd Winick**, and **Gregg Hurwitz**. Illustrated by **David Finch**, **Ed Benes**, and **Ethan Van Sciver**. DC Comics, 2011–2014. T

One of the first of the revised continuity Batman stories, the series originally featured artist/illustrator David Finch, with crime novelist Gregg Hurwitz and fan-favorite artist Ethan Van Sciver taking over the series with Volume 3.

Vol. 1: Knight Terrors. 2012. 208pp. 978-1-4012-3543-7, hardcover; 2013. 208pp. 978-1-4012-3711-0.

Vol. 2: Cycle of Violence. 2013. 160pp. 978-1-4012-4074-5, hardcover; 2014. 160pp. 978-1-4012-4282-4.

Vol. 3: Mad. 2014. 176pp. 978-1-4012-4247-3, hardcover; 2014. 176pp. 978-1-4012-4619-8.

Vol. 4: Clay. 2014. 176pp. 978-1-4012-4620-4, hardcover; 2015. 176pp. 978-1-4012-4930-4.

Batman: Detective Comics (New 52). Written by **Tony S. Daniel**, **John Layman**, **Francis Manapul**, **Brian Buccellato**, and **Peter J. Tomasi**. Illustrated by **Tony S. Daniel**, **Jason Fabok**, and **Francis Manapul**. DC Comics, 2012–2016. T

With the relaunch of the new DC Comics' continuity with its New 52 core titles, Detective Comics, one of the longest-published monthly comic book titles, was relaunched again with issue #1 in 2011. The series serves as the main secondary core title to the monthly Batman series. The series has had several creative team changes since the series was relaunched. In 2016 it returned to its old numbering.

Vol. 1: Faces of Death. 2012. 176pp. 978-1-4012-3466-9, hardcover; 2013. 176pp. 978-1-4012-3467-6.

Vol. 2: Scare Tactics. 2013. 232pp. 978-1-4012-3840-7, hardcover; 2013. 232pp. 978-14012-4265-7.

Vol. 3: Emperor Penguin. 2013. 192pp. 978-1-4012-4266-4, hardcover; 2014. 192pp. 978-1-4012-4634-1.

Vol. 4: The Wrath. 2014. 264pp. 978-1-4012-4633-4, hardcover; 2014. 264pp. 978-1-4012-4997-7.

Vol. 5: Gothtopia. 2014. 176pp. 978-1-4012-4998-4, hardcover; 2015. 176pp. 978-1-4012-5466-7.

Vol. 6: Icarus. 176pp. 2015. 978-1-40125-442-1, hardcover; 978-1-4012-5802-3.

Vol. 7: Anarchy. 2016. 176pp. 978-1-4012-5749-1, hardcover; 978-1-4012-6354-6.

Vol. 8: Blood of Heroes. 2016. 192pp. 978-1-4012-6355-3, hardcover; 978-1-4012-6924-1.

Vol. 9: Gordon at War. 2016. 176pp. 978-1-4012-6923-4, hardcover. 978-1-4012-7411-5.

Batman: Detective Comics (Rebirth). Written by **James Tynion IV**. Illustrated by **Eddy Barrows** and **Alvaro Martinez**. DC Comics, 2017– . T

DC Comics revised its own continuity in 2016 with the launch of the Rebirth story arc. It was a way of winning back longtime readers as well as fans of the New 52 continuity. The new Detective Comics series debuted in 2016 and features Batman alongside a group of allies including Tim Drake, aka Red Robin. Stephanie Brown, aka Spoiler. Cassandra Cain, aka the Orphan as well as reformed criminal Basil Karlo, aka Clayface. These are the shock troops in Batman and Batwoman's war.

Vol. 1: Rise of the Batmen. 2017. 176pp. 978-1-4012-6799-5.
Vol. 2: The Victim Syndicate. 2017. 168pp. 978-1-4012-6891-6.

Batman Eternal/Batman and Robin Eternal. Written by **Scott Snyder**, **Tim Seeley**, **Ray Fawkes**, **John Layman**, and **James Tynion IV**. Illustrated by **Jason Fabok**, **Joe Quinones**, **Andrea Mutti**, **Fernando Blanco**, and various. 2014–2016. T

One of the most ambitious Batman-related projects, the series was published in single issue comics each week for 52 weeks. The sequel, Batman & Robin Eternal, was published for 26 weeks straight. Both storylines are epic in nature and feature Batman and his Batman family of heroes against a city out of control. A mysterious puppet master is pulling the strings as the city buckles under the strain of violence and destruction from gang warfare and Batman's rogues gallery gone amok.

Batman Eternal. 2014–2015.

Vol. 1. 2014. 480pp. 978-1-4012-5173-4.
Vol. 2. 2015. 448pp. 978-1-4012-5231-1.
Vol. 3. 2015. 424pp. 978-1-4012-5752-1.

Batman and Robin Eternal. 2016.

Vol. 1. 272pp. 978-1-4012-5967-9.
Vol. 2. 2016. 272pp. 978-1-4012-6248-8.

All-Star Batman. Written by **Scott Snyder**. Illustrated by **John Romita Jr**. DC Comics, 2017–. T.

After Scott Snyder's stint as the writer for the main DC Comics flagship Batman title during the New 52 era, Snyder has returned to tell new adventures of the Dark Knight alongside legendary illustrator John Romita Jr. The new series features Batman out of his element and on the run with Two-Face by his side.

Vol. 1: My Own Worst Enemy. 2017. 192pp. 978-1-4012-6978-4, hardcover.

Batman: Arkham Asylum Video Game Tie-In Titles. 🐗 ◎

In 2009, the video game *Batman: Arkham Asylum* was released by Warner Bros. Interactive Entertainment and developed by Rocksteady Studios. The video game was highly regarded by comic book fans and video gamers alike and was written by fan-favorite writer Paul Dini as well as Paul Crocker and Sefton Hill. Two direct sequels were also released by Rocksteady Studios, *Arkham City* (2011) and *Arkham Knight* (2015), as well as a prequel game *Arkham Origins* (2013) by Warner Bros. Games Montreal. More in the series are expected in the coming years for the Xbox One, Playstation 4, and PC. The popularity of the video game has crossed over into comic books as well, telling the continuing tales of Batman in the world of this dark video game series.

Batman: Arkham City. Written by **Paul Dini**. Illustrated by **Carlos D'Anda**. 2011. 168pp. 978-1-4012-3255-9, hardcover; 2012. 978-1-4012-3493-5.

© 2016 DC Comics

*Batman: Arkham Unhinge*d. Written by **Derek Fridolfs**. Illustrated by **Dave Wilkins**.

Vol. 1. 2013. 160pp. 978-1-4012-3749-3, hardcover; 2013. 978-1-4012-4018-9.
Vol. 2. 2014. 160pp. 978-1-4012-4283-1, hardcover; 2014. 978-1-4012-4283-1.
Vol. 3. 2014. 232pp. 978-1-4012-4680-8, hardcover; 2014. 978-1-4012-4680-8.
Vol. 4. 2014. 168pp. 978-1-4012-4681-5, hardcover; 2015. 978-1-4012-5042-3.

Batman: Arkham Origins. Written by **Adam Beechen** and **Doug Wagner**. Illustrated by **Christian Duce**. 2014. 160pp. 978-1-4012-4886-4, hardcover; 2015. 160pp. 978-1-4012-5465-0.

Batman: Arkham Knight. Written by **Peter J. Tomasi**. Illustrated by **Viktor Bogdanovic**. 2015–2016.

Vol. 1. 2015. 140pp. 978-1-4012-5804-7, hardcover.
Vol. 2. 2016. 140pp. 978-1-4012-6067-5, hardcover.
Vol. 3. 2016. 144pp. 978-1-4012-6339-3, hardcover.
Arkham Knight: Genesis. 2016. 140pp. 978-1-4012-6066-8, hardcover.

Batman Miniseries and Graphic Novel Titles

Listed below are recommended Batman stories that were originally published as a comic book miniseries or as an original graphic novel title published by DC Comics.

Batman: Birth of the Demon. Written by **Mike W. Barr** and **Dennis O'Neil**. Illustrated by **Jerry Bingham**, **Tom Grindberg**, and **Norm Breyfogle**. DC Comics, 2012. 296pp. 978-1-4012-3381-5. T

The history of Batman's villain Ra's al Ghul is featured in three stand-alone stories collected for the first time. The origin of Ra's and his motivations for world domination are revealed as well as the origins of Batman's son Damian, grandson to Ra's.

Batman: Black and White. Written and Illustrated by various. DC Comics, 2003–2015. T 🎬 ◎

Short stories by a variety of writers and artists including Neil Gaiman, Simon Bisley, Walter Simonson, Paul Dini, Chris Claremont, Alex Ross, Jim Lee and Tim Sale as they each reinterpret Batman in a unique way: through stories that are only told in black and white. The short story "Heroes" written by the late Archie Goodwin and illustrated by Gary Gianni won an Eisner Award for Best Short Story in 1997 and appears in Volume 1. Volume 2 received an Eisner Award in 2003 for Best Graphic Album: Reprint. Volume 1 also received a Harvey Award in 1998 for Best Graphic Album of Previously Published Work.

Vol. 1, new printing. 2007. 232pp. 978-1-4012-1589-7.
Vol. 2, new printing. 2003. 176pp. 978-1-56389-828-0.
Vol. 3. 2008. 288pp. 978-1-4012-13541.
Vol. 4. 2015. 288pp. 978-1-4012-5062-1.

Batman: The Dark Knight Returns/Batman: The Dark Knight Strikes Again. Written and Illustrated by **Frank Miller**. DC Comics, 2015–2016. ◎ 🎬) O

© 2016 DC Comics

Set 10 years after Batman has retired, the world's heroes save for Superman have all but left, and Bruce Wayne is haunted by the death of Robin (Jason Todd). As Gotham City further plunges into despair with the rise of a mutant gang and Batman's old foes still running loose in the city, Bruce Wayne must don the cape and cowl and the Dark Knight returns again. Striking fear into the criminals once again and allied with a new Robin (Carrie Kelly), Batman must face Two-Face, the leader of the Mutants, vengeful Joker, and a government-sanctioned Superman. One of the most highly regarded Batman stories ever told, the story was adapted into a two-part, direct-to-DVD animated film in 2012 and 2013. The book has also inspired many of the Batman movies, including the 2016 film *Batman v Superman: Dawn of Justice*. A sequel to the original, called *Batman: The Dark Knight Strikes Again,* was released in 2001 and continues the story of Batman and Catgirl (a renamed Carrie Kelly) and their struggle to fight corruption. The second story is collected in *The Dark Knight Saga Deluxe Edition* published in 2015. A third, eight-issue limited series The Dark Knight Returns III: The Master Race, began in 2015, co-written by Brian Azzarello and illustrated by Miller, Andy Kubert, and Klaus Janson.

Batman: The Dark Knight Returns, 30th anniversary edition. 2016. 224pp. 978-1-4012-6311-9. O

The Dark Knight Saga Deluxe Edition. 2015. 512pp. 978-1-4012-5691-3, hardcover.

Batman: The Dark Knight Returns: The Last Crusade. Written by **Frank Miller** and **Brian Azzarello**. Illustrated by **John Romita Jr**. and **Klaus Janson**. DC Comics, 2016. 64pp. 978-1-4012-6506-9. O

A prequel to the classic graphic novel story, *The Dark Knight Returns*. The story focuses on the final days of Batman's crime-fighting career before the events in *The Dark Knight Returns*.

Batman: Ego and Other Tales. Written and Illustrated by **Darwyn Cooke**. DC Comics, 2007. 200pp. 978-1-4012-1359-6. T ◉

The late, great creator Darwyn Cooke was no stranger to Batman. He worked as an animator on the popular *Batman: The Animated Series* cartoon and also a comic book writer and illustrator. Collected are various Batman stories including *Batman: Ego*, the 1950's crime-inspired story *Catwoman: Selina's Book Score*, and stories from *Batman: Gotham Knights* #23, 33, and *Solo* #1.

Batman: The Killing Joke, Deluxe Edition. Written by **Alan Moore**. Illustrated by **Brian Bolland**. DC Comics, 2008. 64pp. 978-1-4012-1667-2. O 🏃 ◉ 🎬

The Joker, Batman's insane arch-nemesis, goes on a rampage across Gotham City in a bid to drive Commissioner Gordon insane. After shooting and crippling Barbara Gordon (Batgirl) and kidnapping the commissioner, the Dark Knight seeks to put an end to the Joker's madness before they both kill themselves in the process. All the while, the origin of the Joker is revealed as a young man who takes a plunge into toxic waste and has never stopped maniacally laughing ever since. The powerful short story won many awards in the comic book industry in 1989, including three Eisner Awards for Best Graphic Album, Best Writer, and Best Artist/Penciller/Inker; as well as Harvey Awards for Best Artist or Penciller, Best Single Issue or Story, and Best Graphic Album. A deluxe version of the short story was published in 2008, and a black and white "Batman Noir" edition came out in 2016. An animated film based on the story was released in 2016.

Batman: Noel. Written and Illustrated by **Lee Bermejo**. DC Comics, 2011. 112pp. 978-1-4012-3213-9, hardcover. T 🏃

A unique retelling of Charles Dickens's classic tale A Christmas Carol featuring the Dark Knight. Batman must confront his past, present, and future as he takes on villains from the campy 1960s' era to the brooding villains of today. The book is filled with heroes and villains playing familiar roles to anyone familiar with the original Christmas tale. The graphic novel was recognized by YALSA's Great Graphic Novels for Teens selection list in 2013.

Batman: Year One, Deluxe Edition. Written by **Frank Miller**. Illustrated by **David Mazzucchelli**. DC Comics, 2007. 136pp. 978-1-4012-0752-6. T ◉ 🎬

A young Bruce Wayne traveled the world after the death of his parents, seeking to learn all the martial arts and detective skills he could to become the man he is today. After he returns to Gotham City, a fight with street criminals nearly takes his life, but he knows that something's wrong with his approach: the criminals don't fear him. He adopts the identity of the Batman, but he has a long way to go to become the feared vengeance of the night. Then he forges a friendship of sorts with police officer James Gordon, and together they fight to bring down the corruption that's rampant in Gotham City. Batman has taken his first steps as the protector of Gotham City. The basis for the story also served as the inspiration for the 2006 film *Batman Begins*. The story was also adapted into an animated film in 2011.

Batman: Year 100. Written and Illustrated by **Paul Pope**. DC Comics, 2013–2015. T 🎖

Set in the year 2039 (100 years since Batman's first appearance in comic books in 1939), a federal agent has been murdered and the suspect seems to be a forgotten icon from the past—the legendary Batman. Gotham City Police Department detective Gordon, grandson to the former commissioner, is on the case. If Batman is just a myth from days gone by, then is the man they're chasing the original Batman and did he commit the murder? In 2007, the series won two Eisner Awards for Best Limited Series and Best Writer/Artist.

Batman: Year 100. 2013. 232pp. 978-1-4012-1192-9.
Batman: Year 100 and Other Tales, Deluxe Edition. 2015. 240pp. 978-1-4012-5807-8, hardcover.

Batman-Animated Tie-Ins

Batman has translated well to other mediums, especially in the world of animation. Below are listed several translations of popular Batman cartoons to comic books that are accessible to Batman fans of all ages.

Batman Adventures/Batman and Robin Adventures. Written by **Kelley Puckett, Paul Dini, and various**. Illustrated by **Ty Templeton** and **Mike Parobeck**. 2014– . A ◎ ▭

© 2016 DC Comics

In 1992, Warner Bros. animation ventured to tell the tales of the Dark Knight in the instant cult-hit show *Batman: The Animated Series* created by Bruce Timm and Paul Dini. Mixing solid writing with a 1930s-styled artwork, it become an instant classic and has been considered by fans to be the definitive version of Batman on television. The show's enduring popular spawned a successful comic book series, as well as introduced the character of Harley Quinn to the regular DC Comics continuity. Listed below are the various collections of titles inspired by the animated style of the series and recently reprinted by DC Comics. Beginning in 2017 the second collection of comics, *Batman and Robin Adventures,* was released.

Batman Adventures, 2014–2016.

Vol. 1. 2014. 240pp. 978-1-4012-5229-8.
Vol. 2. 2015. 240pp. 978-1-4012-5463-6.

Vol. 3. 2015. 208pp. 978-1-4012-5872-6.
Vol. 4. 2016. 256pp. 978-1-4012-6061-3.
Batman and Robin Adventures, 2016-2017.
Vol. 1. 2016. 240pp. 978-1-4012-6783-4.
Vol. 2. 2017. 240pp. 978-1-4012-7405-4.

Batman: The Brave and the Bold*.* Written by **Matt Wayne**, **J. Torres**, **Landry Q. Walker**, and **Sholly Fisch**. Illustrated by **Eric Jones**, **Rick Burchett**, and **Dan Davis**. DC Comics, 2010–2013. A ▢

From 2009 to 2012, Warner Bros. animation studio released a popular animated series called Batman: The Brave and the Bold. Taking the title from the old comic book series of the same name, the series featured a more light-hearted tone than previous incarnations of Batman cartoons. The series focused on team-up adventures with a rotating cast of heroes fighting alongside Batman. The comic book series of the same name also features many of the same quirky nods to Batman's campier days, but still features light-hearted but fun stories of the Dark Knight Detective. The series had a title change to All-New Batman: The Brave and the Bold after the third volume.

Batman: Brave and the Bold*.* 2010–2011.

Vol. 1: The Brave and the Bold. 2010. 128pp. 978-1-4012-2650-3.
Vol. 2: The Fearsome Fangs Strike Again. 2010. 128pp. 978-1-4012-2896-5.
Vol. 3: Emerald Knight. 2011. 128pp. 978-1-4012-3143-9.

The All-New Batman: Brave and the Bold*.* 2011–2013.

Vol. 1. 2011. 128pp. 978-1-4012-3272-6.
Vol. 2: Help Wanted. 2012. 128pp. 978-1-4012-3524-6.
Vol. 3: Small Miracles. 2013. 128pp. 978-1-4012-3852-0.

Spider-Man

Created by Stan Lee and Steve Ditko. Marvel Comics, 2002– .

When teenage junior scientist and bookworm Peter Parker was bitten by a radioactive spider during a high school field trip, little did he know that he would gain the proportionate strength of a spider, the ability to climb walls, and a kind of "spider-sense" able to warn him of coming danger. Peter also created his own spider-web cartridges and a red and blue costume with a mask that completely covered his face and with that the wise-cracking wall-crawler, Spider-Man, was born! After losing his beloved Uncle Ben to a common thief that Peter had failed to stop, he has vowed to remember his uncle's words that "with great power there must also come great responsibility," and he will always protect the streets of New York City from common criminals as well as super-powered villains including the Green Goblin, Doctor Octopus, Venom, the Lizard, and Electro. Since his first appearance in 1962, Spider-Man has continued to be one of the most popular super-hero characters ever created. The listings below include collections featuring Peter Parker as well as the new Spider-Man named Miles Morales who is from an alternate universe but is now a part of Marvel continuity.

Amazing Spider-Man. Written by **Dan Slott**, **Mark Waid**, and various. Illustrated by **Humberto Ramos**, various. Marvel Comics, 2008–2013. T 🎗 ◎

Beginning in 2008, the <u>Amazing Spider-Man</u> monthly comic book series was relaunched with the "Brand New Day" story arc—a way to reinvigorate Spider-Man/Peter Parker where he was no longer married, new cast members, and villains as well. Writer Dan Slott took over the main writing for the series with the publication of the Big Time collection and has been writing <u>Amazing Spider-Man</u> up to the time of this book's publication. The series was well received by fans despite alienating those who missed when Peter Parker was married to Mary Jane Watson. For a brief time, listed elsewhere in this section, the series was briefly renamed as <u>The Superior Spider-Man</u> to feature the story arc where longtime Spider-Man foe, Otto Octavius (aka Doctor Octopus), temporarily takes over Spider-Man's brain.

Brand New Day. Vol. 1. 2008. 200pp. 978-0-7851-2845-8.
Brand New Day. Vol. 2. 2008. 168pp. 978-0-7851-2846-5.
Brand New Day. Vol. 3. 2009. 120pp. 978-0-7851-3242-4.
Crime and Punisher. 2009. 136pp. 978-0-7851-3417-6.
Death and Dating. 2009. 192pp. 978-0-7851-3418-3.
Kraven's First Hunt. 2009. 112pp. 978-0-7851-3243-1.
New Ways to Die. 2009. 192pp. 978-0-7851-3244-8.
American Son. 2010. 136pp. 978-0-7851-4083-2.
Died in Your Arms Tonight. 2010. 184pp. 978-0-7851-4485-4.
Election Day. 2010. 184pp. 978-0-7851-3419-0.
The Gauntlet, Book 1—Electro and Sandman. 2010. 176pp. 978-0-7851-3871-6.
The Gauntlet, Book 2—Rhino and Mysterio. 2010. 160pp. 978-0-7851-3872-3.
The Gauntlet, Book 3—Vulture and Morbius. 2010. 136pp. 978-0-7851-4612-4.
The Gauntlet, Book 4—Juggernaut. 2010. 152pp. 978-0-7851-4614-8.
The Gauntlet, Book 5—Lizard. 2010. 128pp. 978-0-7851-4616-2.
Grim Hunt. 2010. 192pp. 978-0-7851-4618-6.
Red-Headed Stranger. 2010. 128pp. 978-0-7851-3869-3.
Return of the Black Cat. 2010. 168pp. 978-0-7851-3868-6.
24/7. 2010. 176pp. 978-0-7851-3420-6.
Big Time. 2011. 144pp. 978-0-7851-4624-7.
Matters of Life and Death. 2011. 224pp. 978-0-7851-5103-6.
One Moment in Time. 2011. 152pp. 978-0-7851-4620-9.
Origin of the Species. 2011. 232pp. 978-0-7851-4622-3.
The Fantastic Spider-Man. 2012. 160pp. 978-0-7851-5107-4.
Flying Blind. 2012. 120pp. 978-0-7851-6001-4.
The Return of Anti-Venom. 2012. 120pp. 978-0-7851-5109-8.
Spider-Island. 2012. 376pp. 978-0-7851-5105-0.
Danger Zone. 2013. 160pp. 978-0-7851-6010-6.
Dying Wish. 2013. 136pp. 978-0-7851-6524-8.
Ends of the Earth. 2013. 192pp. 978-0-7851-6006-9.
Lizard—No Turning Back. 2013. 112pp. 978-0-7851-6008-3.
Trouble on the Horizon. 2013. 112pp. 978-0-7851-6003-8.

Amazing Spider-Man, 2nd series. Written by **Dan Slott** with **Gerry Conway**. Illustrated by **Humberto Ramos** and various. Marvel Comics, 2014–2015. T

© 2016 Marvel Comics

Following the events chronicled in the <u>Superior Spider-Man</u> series (see listing in this chapter until the Villains heading), Peter Parker is back and given a second chance at life! Now the head of Parker Industries, he's got a billion-dollar company to run as well as new problems to worry about. Who is the mysterious woman called Silk and what is her connection to Spider-Man? Plus, multiple Spider-Men from various parallel universes must team up to fight a threat that is in danger of killing every spider-powered hero from every universe!

Vol. 1: The Parker Luck. 2014. 152pp. 978-0-7851-6676-4.
Vol. 2: Spider-Verse Prelude. 2015. 120pp. 978-0-7851-8798-1.
Vol. 3: Spider-Verse. 2015. 168pp. 978-0-7851-9234-3.
Vol. 4: Graveyard Shift. 2015. 104pp. 978-0-7851-9338-8.
Vol. 5: Spiral. 2015. 112pp. 978-0-7851-9316-6.

Amazing Spider-Man, 3rd series. Written by **Dan Slott**. Illustrated by **Giuseppe Camuncoli** and **Matteo Buffagni**. Marvel Comics, 2016– .

After the events of the 2015 <u>Secret Wars</u> series, the <u>Amazing Spider-Man</u> series relaunched with a new number one issue in comics and set up the status quo that Peter Parker and Miles Morales are both Spider-Man in the same universe, and Peter Parker has used his science skills to expand the Parker Industries, and Spider-Man is his "bodyguard" as Parker travels the globe. A new direction for the <u>Amazing Spider-Man</u> has begun!

Vol. 1: Worldwide. 2016. 112pp. 978-0-7851-9942-7.
Vol. 2: Worldwide. 2016. 136pp. 978-0-7851-9943-4.
Vol. 3: Worldwide. 2016. 112pp. 978-0-7851-9944-1.
Vol. 4: Worldwide. 2017. 120pp. 978-1-3029-0237-7.
Vol. 5: Worldwide. 2017. 144pp. 978-1-3029-0238-4.
Vol. 6: Worldwide. 2017. 160pp. 978-13029-0293-3.

Spider-Men. Written by **Brian Michael Bendis**. Illustrated by **Sara Pichelli**. Marvel Comics, 2012. 128pp. 978-0-7851-6533-0, hardcover. T ◉

When Mysterio, the Master of Illusions, threatens both universes, both Spider-Men will never be the same. The story is the first-ever meeting of Peter Parker with Miles Morales—the new Spider-Man from the Ultimate universe.

Spider-Verse. Written by **Dan Slott**, **Gerard Way**, **Christos Gage**, **Michael Costa**, **Peter David**, **David Hine**, **Katie Cook**, and various. Illustrated by **Humberto Ramos**, **Greg Land**, **Richard Isanove**, and various. Marvel Comics, 2015–2015. T

The Evil Morlun and his family, the Inheritors, are traveling the dimensions killing all of the "Spider-Totems," mainly version of Spider-Man. To stop them, Spider-folk from all worlds must team up. Besides the regular Peter Parker Spider-Man, others include the Spider-Man of 2099, Spider-Girl, multiple versions of Spider-Woman,

© 2016 Marvel Comics

and even Peter Porker, the Spectacular Spider-Ham. Spider-Men from other previously seen alternate worlds and even TV shows also appear. This crossover storyline also introduced the alternate Gwen Stacy Spider-Woman (aka Spider-Gwen), who later received her own title.

Amazing Spider-Man: Edge of Spider-Verse. 2015. 112pp. 978-0-7851-9728-7.

Amazing Spider-Man: Spider-Verse. 2015. 168pp. 978-0-7851-9234-3.

Amazing Spider-Man: Spider-Verse Prelude. 2015. 120pp. 978-0-7851-8798-1.

Spider-Verse. 648pp. 978–0785190356, hardcover.

Ultimate Spider-Man. Written by **Brian Michael Bendis**. Illustrated by **Mark Bagley**. Marvel Comics, 2002–2011. T ◎

© 2016 Marvel Comics

In 2001, Marvel Comics reimagined the world of the Marvel Universe with its "Ultimate" line of titles that reinterprets some of its most popular characters for a new generation and starts them back to the basics. In *Ultimate Spider-Man*, good teen characterization and plenty of web-swinging action go hand in hand as Peter Parker, an awkward teenager, deals with school bullies, homework problems, and first-love woes. After a bite by a super-spider at Osborn Labs has given him spider-like powers, he's learned the importance of being responsible with his great power and is out to protect New York City as the costumed hero Spider-Man. But life isn't easy of the young teen. He's trying to hold onto a secret identity (though his girlfriend, Mary Jane Watson, knows) and work a part-time job at the Daily Bugle, and he's the target of villains, including the Green Goblin, Doctor Octopus, Venom and Carnage. The collections featured below are in paperback format except for those listed as hardcover. Multiple volumes have received recognition by YALSA, including the Popular Paperbacks for Young Adults committee in 2002 and 2003 for Volumes 1 and 3, respectively, as well as Quick Picks for Reluctant Readers in 2002 and 2004 for Volumes 1 and 2, respectively. It should also be noted that after the events of the *Death of Spider-Man* volume, Peter Parker was killed off in the "Ultimate" universe and a new Spider-Man has taken over the role—an Afro-Hispanic teen by the name of Miles Morales. In 2015 the "Ultimate" universe was phased out and Miles Morales is Spider-Man in current mainstream Marvel continuity alongside an adult Peter Parker.

Vol. 1: Power and Responsibility, 2nd printing. 2009. 192pp. 978-0-7851-3940-9.

Vol. 2: Learning Curve. 2002. 192pp. 978-0-7851-0820-7.

Vol. 3: Double Trouble. 2002. 176pp. 978-0-7851-0879-5.

2

3

4

5

6

7

8

9

Vol. 4: Legacy. 2002. 160pp. 978-0-7851-0968-6.
Vol. 5: Public Scrutiny. 2003. 120pp. 978-0-7851-1087-3.
Vol. 6: Venom. 2003. 168pp. 978-0-7851-1094-1.
Vol. 7: Irresponsible. 2003. 144pp. 978-0-7851-1092-7.
Vol. 8: Cats and Kings. 2004. 152pp. 978-0-7851-1250-1.
Vol. 9: Ultimate Six. 2004. 208pp. 978-0-7851-1312-6.
Vol. 10: Hollywood. 2004. 144pp. 978-0-7851-1402-4.
Vol. 11: Carnage. 2005. 144pp. 978-0-7851-1403-1.
Vol. 12: Superstars. 2005. 144pp. 978-0-7851-1629-5.
Vol. 13: Hobgoblin. 2005. 144pp. 978-0-7851-1647-9.
Vol. 14: Warriors. 2005. 168pp. 978-0-7851-1680-6.
Vol. 15: Silver Sable. 2006. 168pp. 978-0-7851-1681-3.
Vol. 16: Deadpool. 2006. 144pp. 978-0-7851-1927-2.
Vol. 17: Clone Saga. 2007. 168pp. 978-0-7851-1928-9.
Vol. 18: Ultimate Knights. 2007. 144pp. 978-0-7851-2136-7.
Vol. 19: Death of the Goblin. 2008. 144pp. 978-0-7851-2137-4.
Vol. 20: And His Amazing Friends. 2008. 120pp. 978-0-7851-2961-5.
Vol. 21: War of the Symbiotes. 2009. 144pp. 978-0-7851-2962-2.
Vol. 22: Ultimatum. 2010. 160pp. 978-0-7851-3845-7.
Ultimatum: Requiem. 2010. 152pp. 978-0-7851-3926-3.

Ultimate Comics: Spider-Man, First Series

Vol. 1: The World According to Peter Parker. 2010. 152pp. 978-0-7851-4011-5, hardcover; 2010. 978-0-7851-4099-3.
Vol. 2: Chameleons. 2011. 200pp. 978-0-7851-4012-2, hardcover; 978-0-7851-4100-6.
Vol. 3: The Death of Spider-Man Prelude. 2011. 112pp. 978-0-7851-4639-1, hardcover; 978-0-7851-4639-1.
Vol. 4: The Death of Spider-Man. 2011. 128pp. 978-0-7851-5274-3, hardcover; 978-0-7851-5275-0.
Vol. 5: The Death of Spider-Man—Fallout. 2011. 126pp. 978-0-7851-5912-4.

Miles Morales Spider-Man

Beginning in 2011, Marvel Comics relaunched its Ultimate Comics brand—which featured a reimagined Marvel Comics universe parallel to the main "real" universe that reimagines the characters. After the death of Peter Parker, a new Spider-Man takes over as the protector of New York City, and Afro-Hispanic teenager named Miles Morales. Bitten by a radioactive spider similar to the one that transformed the original Spider-Man, Miles reluctantly at first takes on the mantle of Spider-Man, but soon finds himself facing the hard truths like Peter Parker did that with great power comes great responsibility. The series had several title changes, most recently with the reintroduction of Miles Morales into the mainstream Marvel Comics universe alongside Peter Parker. The new series is titled Spider-Man: Miles Morales and features Miles as the Spider-Man of New York City, and serving as a member of the Avengers as well. The first collection, *Who Is Miles Morales?* was recognized by YALSA's Great Graphic Novels for Teens selection list in 2013. In some cases, collections of Miles's original series are listed as *Ultimate Comics Spider-Man by Brian Michael Bendis.* In 2017 it was announced that an animated feature film with Miles as Spider-Man was in production.

Ultimate Comics: Spider-Man, 2nd series. Written by **Brian Michael Bendis**. Illustrated by **Sara Pichelli** and **David Marquez**. 2012–2015. T ◉ 🎗

© 2016 Marvel Comics

Vol. 1: Who Is Miles Morales? 2012. 136pp. 978-0-7851-5712-0, hardcover; 978-0-7851-5713-7.
Vol. 2: Scorpion. 2012. 112pp. 978-0-7851-5714-4, hardcover; 2012. 112pp. 978-0-7851-5715-1.
Vol. 3: Divided We Fall, United We Stand. 2013. 184pp. 978-0-7851-6175-2, hardcover; 2013. 184pp. 978-0-7851-6176-9.
Vol. 4: Venom War. 2013. 112pp. 978-0-7851-6503-3, hardcover; 2014. 112pp. 978-0-7851-6504-0.
Vol. 5. 2014. 136pp. 978-0-7851-6802-7, hardcover; 2015. 136pp. 978-0-7851-6706-8.
Ultimate Collection, Vol. 1. 2015. 400pp. 978-0-7851-9778-2.
Ultimate Collection, Vol. 2. 2015. 386pp. 978-0-7851-9779-9.
Ultimate Collection, Vol. 3. 2015. 360pp. 978-0-7851-9780-5.

Miles Morales: Ultimate Spider-Man. Written by **Brian Michael Bendis**. Illustrated by **Sara Pichelli**. Marvel Comics, 2014–2015.

Vol. 1: Revival. 2014. 144pp. 978-0-7851-5417-4.
Vol. 2: Revelations. 2015. 112pp. 978-0-7851-5418-1.

Spider-Man: Miles Morales. Written by **Brian Michael Bendis**. Illustrated by **Sara Pichelli**. 2016– .

Vol. 1. 2016. 112pp. 978-0-7851-9961-8.
Vol. 2. 2017. 136pp. 978-07851-9962-5.

Spider-Man 2099. Written by **Peter David**. Illustrated by **Rick Leonardi** and **William Sliney**. Marvel Comics. 2013– . T 🖵 🐾

In the year 2099, Miquel O'Hara is a geneticist who was attempting to re-create the same formula which gave the original Spider-Man his powers, but accidentally has his own DNA written so that he's genetically 50 percent a spider. He survives the process, but realizes he now has spider-related powers, including sharp claws, the proportionate strength, speed, and agility of a spider. He is the first Hispanic Spider-Man and has his costume based off of a Day of the Dead spider-themed costume. The original series, reprinted as Spider-Man 2099, was originally released in 1992. A new series debuted in 2015 and features a time-displaced Spider-Man 2099 who is now stuck in the present. He's still an ally of Peter Parker and Miles Morales and has frequently teamed up with them for special events such as the Spider-Verse crossover event. Spider-Man 2099 has also frequently appeared as a playable character in various Spider-Man video games as well as appearing in various animated series over the years.

Spider-Man 2099 Classic. 2013.

Vol. 1. 2013. 240pp. 978-0-7851-8478-2.
Vol. 2. 2013. 240pp. 978-0-7851-8537-6.
Vol. 3: Fall of the Hammer. 2013. 296pp. 978-0-7851-9302-9.

Spider-Man 2099 (***2nd series and 3rd series***). 2015.

> *Vol. 1: Out of Time.* 2015. 120pp. 978-0-7851-9079-0.
> *Vol. 2: Spider-Verse.* 2016. 160pp. 978-0-7851-9080-6.
> *Vol. 3: Smack to the Future.* 2016. 120pp. 978-0-7851-9963-2.
> *Vol. 4: Gods and Women.* 2016. 112pp. 978-0-7851-9964-9.
> *Vol. 5: Civil War II.* 2017. 136pp. 978-1-3029-0281-0.
> *Vol. 6.* 2017. 112pp. 978-1-3029-0282-7.

Other Classic and Contemporary Crime Fighters

Since their first appearances in the late 1930s, super-heroes have come in all shapes and sizes. Included below are a variety of heroes and their respective collected editions of their stories available from publishers within approximately the last 10 years. The list features heroes that have been popular for decades up to modern heroes of today, and the main listings are sorted by the name of the character. Please note that many of the titles featuring the characters are from the collected editions of the character's serial comic book titles. Due to spacing concerns, not every volume featuring a character has been annotated. Unless otherwise noted, each main listing features a brief write-up of the character, the recommended titles from the collected comic book series, and specific graphic novel titles.

Angel Catbird. Written by **Margaret Atwood**. Illustrated by **Johnnie Christmas**. Dark Horse, 2016– . A

> Written by award-winning author Margaret Atwood, the three-part Angel Catbird tells the story of Strig Feleedus, a genetic engineer whose experiment goes wrong, merging his own DNA with that of a cat and an owl. Strig uses his new abilities to become a super-hero. This story, which among other things, pays tribute to classic pulp adventures, is published in tandem with Keep Cats Safe and Save Bird Lives, an initiative led by the conservation charity, Nature Canada.
>
> *Vol. 1.* 2016. 112pp. 978-1-5067-0063-2.
> *Vol. 2: To Castle Catula.* 2017. 80pp. 978-1-5067-0127-1.

Ant-Man. Written by **Nick Spencer**. Illustrated by **Ramon Rosanas** and **Jordan Boyd**. Marvel Comics, 2015– . T 🎬 🐜

> Scott Lang has a second chance to get things right—a reformed thief, he's recruited by Iron Man to turn his life around and be the hero he's always wanted to be (see Ant-Man: Scott Lang, 2015). Though he's the second Ant-Man (the original one was Hank Pym, founder of the Avengers and the creator of Ultron), he's out to prove he's the best at becoming really tiny and able to talk to ants. But nevertheless, he's going to be the best micro-hero possible! Ant-Man also made the transition to a feature-length movie in 2016 starring Paul Rudd as Ant-Man/Scott Lang. The collection Second-Chance Man received recognition from YALSA on its 2016 Great Graphic Novels for Young Adults selection list.
>
> *Ant-Man: Second-Chance Man.* 2015. 120pp. 978-0-7851-9387-6.
> *Astonishing Ant-Man,* 2016-
> *Vol. 1: Everybody Loves Team-Ups.* 2016. 144pp. 978-0-7851-9948-9.
> *Vol. 2: Small-Time Criminal.* 2016. 136pp. 978-0-7851-9949-6.
> *Vol. 3: The Trial of Ant-Man.* 2017. 120pp. 978-0-7851-9952-6.

Aquaman

DC Comics. 🎬 🕹 🖥

DC's King of the Seven Seas has been around for a long time, showing that breathing underwater and talking to aquatic life is enough to fight alongside Superman and Wonder Woman. Created by Paul Norris and Mort Weisinger in the pages of *More Fun Comics #73* in 1941, Aquaman has been the star of a number of ongoing series since the 1960s, with some of the material from the 1960s, 1970s, and 1980s collected in various places. Issues from the 2003 series by Will Pfeifer and Patrick Gleason have recently been collected in new editions, telling the storyline in which San Diego sinks beneath the Pacific Oceans with its inhabitants becoming water breathers. In the "New 52" Universe Aquaman's history (half human, half-Atlantian, occasional King of Atlantis) is generally the same, including his being a founding member of the Justice League. In addition, it has been shown that early in his career he was a member of a team called The Others. Creators on this title include Geoff Johns, Ivan Reis, Paul Pelletier, and Jeff Parker. A third Aquaman series began in 2016, with collections beginning in 2017. Aquaman has appeared in various animated programs including *Super Friends*. Though the character over time has been perceived as more hokey than heroic, that's definitely not the case. His playable character, most notably in the hit video game *Injustice: Gods Among Us,* proves to the players just how powerful Aquaman is and that he isn't to be trifled with. On the big screen, Aquaman is part of the new DC Extended Universe debuting in *Batman v Superman: Dawn of Justice* where he is played by Jason Momoa, and starring in his own film in 2018.

Aquaman, 1st series. Written by **Rick Veitch** and **Will Pfeifer**. Illustrated by **Patrick Gleason**. DC Comics, 2013–2016. T

> *The Waterbearer*. 2003. 128pp. 978-0062-21003-6.
> *Sub Diego*. 2015. 192pp. 978-1-4012-5510-7.
> *To Serve and Protect*. 2016. 224pp. 978-1-4012-6382-9.

Aquaman, 2nd series (New 52). Written by **Geoff Johns**. Illustrated by **Ivan Reis** and **Joe Prado**. DC Comics, 2013– . T

> *Vol. 1: The Trench*. 2013. 144pp. 978-1-4012-3710-3.
> *Vol. 2: The Others*. 2013. 160pp. 978-1-4012-4295-4.
> *Vol. 3: Throne of Atlantis*. 2013. 176pp. 978-1-4012-4695-2.
> *Vol. 4: Death of a King*. 2014. 192pp. 978-1-4012-4995-3.
> *Vol. 5: Sea of Storms*. 2014. 208pp. 978-1-4012-544-0.
> *Vol. 6: Maelstrom*. 2015. 240pp. 978-1-4012-6096-5.
> *Vol. 7: Exiled*. 2016. 200pp. 978-1-4012-6098-9.
> *Vol. 8: Out of Darkness*. 2016. 176pp. 978-1-4012-6475-8.

2

3

4

5

6

7

8

9

Aquaman and the Others. Written by **Dan Jurgens**. Illustrated by **Manuel Garcia**. 2015. DC Comics, 2015.

> *Vol. 1: Legacy of Gold.* 2015. 176pp. 978-1-4012-5038-6.
> *Vol. 2: Alignment: Earth.* 2015. 176pp. 978-1-4012-5331-8.

Batgirl

DC Comics, 2013– . T 🏆

> Batman and Robin aren't the only heroes who protect Gotham City at night. Barbara Gordon first appeared in 1967 in the pages of Detective Comics, #359. She is the daughter of Gotham police commissioner Jim Gordon. A mild-mannered college student by day, she fights crime at night as Batgirl. Recommended titles featuring Barbara Gordon as the masked heroine are listed below. The first New 52 collection *The Darkest Reflection* as well as the collection *The Batgirl of Burnside* and Family Business were recognized by YALSA's Great Graphic Novels for Teens selection list in 2013, 2016 and 2017, respectively.

Batgirl, 1st series. Written by **Gail Simone**. Illustrated by **Ardian Syaf**, **Fernando Pasarin**, and **Ed Benes**. DC Comics, 2013–2015.

> The series was relaunched in 2011 with Barbara Gordon once again in the role of the popular hero. Though she was wounded with a spinal injury by the Joker following the events of the graphic novel *Batman: The Killing Joke* and was known as the wheelchair-bound computer expert Oracle, she served as a member of the Birds of Prey team as well as assisting Batman and the Batman family of heroes. In the New 52 continuity, Barbara's injury has been healed and while she still suffers PTSD from the encounter, she doesn't let it impinge her skills as a fighter and expert detective.

> *Vol. 1: The Darkest Reflection.* 2013. 144pp. 978-1-4012-3814-8.
> *Vol. 2: Knightfall Descends.* 2013. 192pp. 978-1-4012-3817-9.
> *Vol. 3: Death of the Family.* 2014. 224pp. 978-1-4012-4628-0.
> *Vol. 4: Wanted.* 2014. 192pp. 978-1-4012-5040-9.
> *Vol. 5: Deadline.* 2015. 256pp. 978-1-4012-5511-4.

Batgirl, 2nd series. Written by **Brenden Fletcher** and **Cameron Stewart**. Illustrated by **Babs Tarr**. DC Comics, 2015–2016. T

© 2016 DC Comics

> A relaunch of the Batgirl series, relocating Barbara Gordon to Burnside, a hip Gotham borough with new roommate named Frankie, who has plenty of secrets herself. The series has a lighter tone than previous incarnations of the book with a focus on adventure and fun without most of the angst common in most Batman-related titles. The series was also highly praised for adding artist Babs Tarr, whose redesign of Batgirl's costume was beloved by many Internet followers. Volume 2 was on YALSA's 2017 Great Graphic Novels for Teens selection list. In 2016, a new Batgirl series began as well as <u>Batgirl and the Birds of Prey</u>. Collections for both titles began in 2017.

> *Vol. 1: The Batgirl of Burnside.* 2015. 176pp. 978-1-4012-5332-5, hardcover; 978-1-4012-5798-9.
> *Vol. 2: Family Business.* 2016. 176pp. 978-1-4012-5966-2.
> *Vol. 3: Mindfields.* 2016. 168pp. 978-1-4012-6269-3.

Batgirl/Robin: Year One. Written by **Chuck Dixon** and **Scott Beatty**. Illustrated by **Marcos Martin**. DC Comics, 2013. 424pp. 978-1-4012-4033-2. T ◉

> Collected together are the first adventures of Dick Grayson as the original Robin and Barbara Gordon as they don their costumes and fight crime for the first time!

Batman Beyond. Written by **Adam Beechen**, **Kyle Higgins**, **Dan Jurgens**, and **Christos Gage**. Illustrated by **Thony Silas** and **Norm Breyfogle**. DC Comics, 2012–2016. T ▭

> Based off the animated series which originally aired from 1999 to 2001, the series is set in the near-future and focuses on Terry McGinnis, a young man who inherits the Batman role after Bruce Wayne is retired and now an old man. The show inspired a new DC Comics series which introduced Terry McGinnis to the mainstream comic book continuity. After the events of the New 52: Future's End storyline in 2015, former Robin Tim Drake took over the mantle of the Batman of the future following Terry McGinnis's apparent death. As is often the case, Terry turns out to be alive, and has resumed the role for a new series that began in 2016. Three volumes of Justice League Beyond and one of Superman Beyond have also come out.

> *Hush Beyond*. 2011. 144pp. 978-1-4012-2988-7.
> *Industrial Revolution*. 2012. 176pp. 978-1-4012-3374-7.
> *10,000 Clowns*. 2013. 200pp. 978-1-4012-4034-9.
> *Batgirl Beyond*. 2014. 168pp. 978-1-4012-4753-9.
> *Rewired*. 2014. 176pp. 978-1-4012-5060-7.
> *Justice Lords Beyond*. 2015. 176pp. 978-1-4012-5464-3.
> *Mark of the Phantasm*. 2015. 176pp. 978-1-4012-5801-6.
> *Brave New Worlds*. 2016. 152pp. 978-1-4012-6191-7.
> *City of Yesterday*. 2016. 128pp. 978-1-4012-6470-3.
> *Wired For Death*. 2017. 136pp. 978-1-4012-7039-1.

Batwoman. Written by **Greg Rucka**, **J.H. Williams III**, **Haden Blackman**, and **Marc Andreyko**. Illustrated by **J.H. Williams III** and **Jeremy Haun**. DC Comics, 2010–2015. T 🎖

> Inspired by her own brush with Batman after she defeats a mugger on her own, a wealthy Gotham socialite uses her own military training and expertise to wage war upon the criminals of Gotham as Batwoman. The character received much praise in the gay community for her proud declaration of being a lesbian, but has more than enough training in combat to give the criminals of Gotham something to worry about at night other than the Dark Knight. The first collection, Elegy, was recognized by YALSA as a Great Graphic Novels for Teens selection list recipient in 2011.

> *Elegy*. 2010. 192pp. 978-1-4012-3146-0.
> *Vol. 1: Hydrology*. 2013. 144pp. 978-1-4012-3784-4.
> *Vol. 2: To Drown the World*. 2013. 144pp. 978-1-4012-3792-9.
> *Vol. 3: World's Finest*. 2014. 168pp. 978-1-4012-4610-5.
> *Vol. 4: This Blood Is Thick*. 2014. 144pp. 978-1-4012-4999-1.
> *Vol. 5: Webs*. 2014. 272pp. 978-1-4012-5082-9.
> *Vol. 6: The Unknowns*. 2015. 208pp. 978-1-4012-5468-1.

Battling Boy. Written and Illustrated by **Paul Pope**. First Second, 2013– . T ◎

© 2016 Paul Pope and
First Second Books

The city of Acropolis is under the threat of gangs of monsters and demons that have been kidnapping children. In the past, the city was protected by the great hero Haggard West, but he is no more. However, help comes in the form of Battling Boy, a young man with superpowers from another dimension sent to learn how to become a hero. Also trying to help is Haggard's daughter Aurora who is the main character in two prequels in which she is trying to find her mother's killer.

Battling Boy. 2013. 208pp. 978-1-5964-3145-4.
The Rise of Aurora West. 2014. 160pp. 978-1-6267-2009-1.
The Fall of the House of West. 2015. 160pp. 978-1-6267-2010-7.

Black Canary. Written by **Brenden Fletcher**. Illustrated by **Annie Wu**. DC Comics, 2016. T 🎭

A relaunch by DC Comics of the black-clad siren Dinah Lance, aka the Black Canary. After striking out on her own, Dinah joins a rock band called Black Canary and together with her new band mates, trouble is sure to follow them anywhere they go on the road. Volume 1 was on YALSA's 2017 Great Graphic Novels for Teens selection list.

Vol. 1: Kicking and Screaming. 2016. 148pp. 978-1-4012-6117-7.
Vol. 2: New Killer Star. 2016. 144pp. 978-1-4012-6527-4.

Black Panther

Marvel Comics, 2015– . T 🎭 🎬

The ruler of the African kingdom of Wakanda, T'Challa, has served as the guardian hero for his kingdom in the guise of the Black Panther after ingesting a mystical heart-shaped herb that has given him enhanced strength. His costume is woven with Vibranium, a special metal that comes from his country. It makes his costume bulletproof and allows T'Challa to absorb the impact from falling from tall heights as well as the ability to run up walls. A leader, hero, and scientist, under T'Challa's rule, Wakanda has become one of the most technologically advanced nations on the planet. Black Panther has served as an Avenger, but his heart and his home are in Wakanda. Black Panther appeared also for the first time in the movies in 2016's *Captain America: Civil War* and will have his own feature film in 2018. A new series from Ta-Nehisi Coates and Brian Stelfreeze began in 2016 and was on the YALSA's top 10 list of the 2017 Great Graphic Novels for Teens list.

Black Panther The Complete Collection. Written by **Christopher Priest**. Illustrated by **Mark Texeira**.

Vol. 1. 2015. 416pp. 978-0-7851-9267-1.
Vol. 2. 2015. 448pp. 978-0-785-1-9811-6.
Vol. 3. 2016. 456pp. 978-0-785-1-9508-5.
Vol. 4. 2016. 416pp. 978-1-302-90058-8.

Black Panther Who Is the Black Panther? Written by **Reginald Hudlin**. Illustrated by **John Romita Jr**. 2015. 200pp. 978-0-7851-9799-7.

Black Widow. Marvel Comics, 2010– . O 📽

© 2016 Marvel Comics

Natasha Romanov, aka the Black Widow, is one of the deadliest spies. She first appeared in *Tales of Suspense #52* in April 1964. Originally introduced as a Russia spy and antagonist for Tony Stark/Iron Man, she defected to the United States and soon proved her worth as a hero and became a member of the Avengers. The Black Widow also one of the most recognizable female heroes since her character played by actress Scarlet Johansson appeared in the films *Iron Man 2* (2010), *Marvel's The Avengers* (2012), *Captain America: The Winter Soldier* (2014), and *Avengers: Age of Ultron* (2015) and in *Captain America: Civil War* (2016). A new Black Widow series by Mark Waid and Chris Samnee began in 2016. The character also appears in a series of Young Adult novels.

Black Widow: Deadly Origin. 2010. Written by **Paul Cornell**. Illustrated by **Tom Raney**. 2010. 112pp. 978-0-7851-4402-1.

Black Widow: Web of Intrigue. 2010. Written by various. Illustrated by various. 176pp. 978-0-7851-4474-8.

Black Widow: The Name of the Rose. Written by **Marjorie Liu**. Illustrated by **Daniel Acuña**. 2011. 144pp. 978-0-7851-4354-3.

Black Widow: Kiss or Kill. Written by **Duane Swierczynski**. Illustrated **Manuel Garcia**. 2011. 96pp. 978-0-7851-4701-5.

Black Widow: Itsy-Bitsy Spider. Written by **Devin Grayson** and **Greg Rucka**. Illustrated by **J.G. Jones**. 2011. 152pp. 978-0-7851-5827-1, hardcover; 2016. 978-0-7851-9602-0.

Black Widow (current series). Written by **Nathan Edmondson**. Illustrated by **Phil Noto**. 2014–2015.

>*Vol. 1: The Finely Woven Thread*. 2014. 142pp. 978-0-7851-8819-3.
>*Vol. 2: The Tightly Tangled Web*. 2015. 160pp. 978-0-7851-8820-9.
>*Vol. 3: Last Days*. 2015. 160pp. 978-0-7851-9253-4.

Captain America

Created by **Joe Simon** and **Jack Kirby**. Marvel Comics, 2010– . T

During World War II, Steve Rogers was a scrawny would-be soldier who was unfit to serve in the military, but instead served his country as a volunteer for the Operation: Rebirth Super-Soldier program. When injected with the Super-Soldier serum, he was transformed into the ultimate human, gaining enhanced muscle mass, strength, physical endurance, and a keen sense of agility. After months of training in hand-to-hand combat, military strategy, gymnastics, and more, Rogers was given a red, white, and blue light-weight chain-mail uniform, and was christened as Captain America, the symbolic leader of the United States. His only weapon is his shield, a disc forged from Vibranium-Adamantium, making it one of the hardest-known substances on Earth. At the end of the war he was trapped in suspended animation, and not revived, still young, until decades later. He is still a hero today as he was in World War II, and the Sentinel of Liberty from the Greatest Generation continues to fight for freedom on his own, partnered with the winged ally the Falcon, or as an Avenger in his battle against villains including his arch-nemesis the Red Skull, Baron Zemo, and foreign terrorists that threaten America. Long after his 1941 debut, Captain America is still a leading symbol for democracy and one of the most recognized and noble of Marvel Comics' heroes and has appeared regularly in video games and television. Captain America is also one of the most recognizable movie heroes from Marvel Comics since the hero, played by actor Chris Evans, has appeared in the Marvel Studio/Disney films *Captain America: The First Avenger* (2011), *Marvel's The Avengers* (2012), *Captain America: The Winter Soldier* (2014), *Avengers: Age of Ultron* (2015) and *Captain America: Civil War* (2016). In 2015, when Steve Rogers was no longer able to fill the role of Captain America, his longtime friend Sam Wilson (the Falcon) took over the role of Captain America. Recently, both Sam Wilson and a rejuvenated Steve Rogers have resumed the role of Captain America, with both heroes serving as the hero in differing capacities. Listed below are a variety of recommended *Captain America* titles from the various recommended monthly series collected and more.

Captain America, 1st series. Written by **Ed Brubaker**. Illustrated by **Steve Epting**, with **Alan Davis**, **Steve McNiven**, **Scot Eaton**, **James Asmus**, and various. Marvel Comics, 2005–2013. T ◎ 🎯

© 2016 Marvel Comics

Ed Brubaker's run on Captain America has been considered by many to be one of Marvel's best Captain America stories. The main writer on the series from November 2004 to October 2012, the series features many memorable storylines, most notable is the reintroduction of James "Bucky" Barnes into the series as the character the Winter Soldier. The story was adapted into the feature film *Captain America: The Winter Soldier* in 2014. Also one of the major story arcs featured the death—and eventually return—of Steve Rogers. While Steve was dead, James Barnes filled in the role of Captain America, but eventually the mantle of Captain America reverted to Steve Rogers. Collected below is the entire run of Ed Brubaker and Steve Epting's Captain America stories in chronological order. Ed Brubaker received multiple Eisner Awards for Best Writer for the years 2007, 2008, and 2010 and a Harvey Award for Best Writer in 2007. The series can be broken down into specific story arcs listed below.

Chapter I

Vol. 1: Winter Soldier Ultimate Collection. 2010. 304pp. 978-0-7851-4341-3.
Vol. 2: The Red Menace Ultimate Collection. 2011. 216pp. 978-0-7851-5617-8.

Chapter II

The Death of Captain America: The Complete Collection. 2013. 568pp. 978-0-7851-8379-2.
The Man with No Face. 2009. 144pp. 978-0-7851-3163-2.
Road to Reborn. 2010. 176pp. 978-0-7851-4175-4.
Reborn. 2010. 232pp. 978-0-7851-4073-3.

Chapter III

Two Americas. 2010. 128pp. 978-0-7851-4511-0.
No Escape. 2011. 120pp. 978-0-7851-4513-4.
The Trial of Captain America. 2011. 144pp. 978-0-7851-5120-3.
Prisoner of War. 2012. 200pp. 978-0-7851-5122-7.

Chapter IV

Steve Rogers, Super-Soldier. 2011. 152pp. 978-0-7851-4879-1.
Secret Avengers, Vol. 1: Mission to Mars. 2011. 168pp. 978-0-7851-4600-1.
Secret Avengers, Vol. 2: Eyes of the Dragon. 2012. 168pp. 978-0-7851-4602-5.

Chapter V

Captain America, Vol. 1. 2012. 120pp. 978-0-7851-5709-0.
Captain America, Vol. 2. 2012. 112pp. 978-0-7851-5711-3.
Captain America, Vol. 3. 2013. 112pp. 978-0-7851-6076-2.
Captain America, Vol. 4. 2013. 112pp. 978-0-7851-6078-6.
Captain America and Bucky: The Life Story of Bucky Barnes. 2012. 112pp. 978-0-7851-5124-1.
Captain America and Bucky: Old Wounds. 2012. 128pp. 978-0-7851-6084-7.

Omnibus Collections, 2007–2015.

Captain America Omnibus. 2007. 744pp. 978-0-7851-2866-3, hardcover.
The Death of Captain America Omnibus. 2009. 464pp. 978-0-7851-3806-8, hardcover.
Captain America Lives Omnibus. 2011. 560pp. 978-0-7851-4514-1, hardcover.
The Trial of Captain America Omnibus. 2014. 928pp. 978-0-7851-9272-5, hardcover.
Return of the Winter Solider Omnibus. 2015. 752pp. 978-0-7851-9271-8, hardcover.

Captain America, 2nd series. Written by **Rick Remender**. Illustrated by **John Romita Jr.**, **Carlos Pacheco**, and various. Marvel Comics, 2014–2015. T
Following Ed Brubaker's run, the series was turned into a pulp sci-fi series. Captain America is trapped in another dimension by his enemy, the bizarre Arnim Zola. What can the Sentinel of Liberty fight for when he no longer has a country to defend? The series concluded with Captain America passing on the mantle to his longtime friend, Sam Wilson.

Vol. 1: Castaway in Dimension Z, part 1. 2013. 136pp. 978-0-7851-6655-9.
Vol. 2: Castaway in Dimension Z, part 2. 2014. 136pp. 978-0-7851-6656-6.
Vol. 3: Loose Nuke. 2014. 136pp. 978-0-7851-8952-7.
Vol. 4: The Iron Nail. 2015. 144pp. 978-0-7851-8954-1.
Vol. 5: The Tomorrow Soldier. 2015. 978-0-7851-8956-5.

Captain America, 3rd series. Written by **Rick Remender** and **Nick Spencer**. Illustrated by **Stuart Immonen**, **Jesus Saiz**, and **Paul Renaud**. Marvel Comics, 2016– . T
No longer fit enough to serve as Captain America, Steve appoints his longtime friend, Sam Wilson, the hero who has faithfully served alongside him as the Falcon, as the new Captain America. Though Sam wears the colors

HYDRA ASCENDANT

© 2016 Marvel Comics

of the American flag, his costume is more in line with his Falcon design. Originally the series was named <u>All-New Captain America</u> but was relaunched as <u>Captain America: Sam Wilson</u> not long afterwards. Soon after, *Captain America: Steve Rogers* began a run alongside it.

***All-New Captain America*, 2016.**

Vol. 1: Hydra Ascendant. 2015. 136pp. 978-0-7851-9232-9.
Vol. 2: Fear Him. 2015. 136pp. 978-0-7851-9258-9.

***Captain America: Sam Wilson*, 2016– .**

Vol. 1: *Not My Captain America.* 2016. 136pp. 978-0-7851-9640-2.
Vol. 2: Standoff. 2016. 152pp. 978-0-7851-9641-9.
Vol. 3: Civil War II. 2017. 112pp. 978-1-3029-0319-0.

***Captain America: Steve Rogers*, 2016– .**

Vol. 1: Hail Hydra. 2016. 152pp. 978-1-3029-0112-7.
Vol. 2: The Trial of Maria Hill. 2017. 120pp. 978-1-3029-0113-4.

Captain America: Man out of Time. Written by **Mark Waid**. Illustrated by **Jorge Molina**. Marvel Comics, 2011. 144pp. 978-0-7851-5129-6. T

Steve Rogers is a man out of time. Revived from being trapped in ice after seemingly sacrificing himself on a dangerous mission during World War II, he's lost without his partner, Bucky, whom he believes to have died on the mission. Feeling trapped in this new age of an America that he hardly recognizes, when Cap discovers the Avengers have access to a time machine, he decides to use it and go back in time to save Bucky's life—but the Avengers must do everything they can to prevent that from happening!

Captain America: White. Written by **Jeph Loeb**. Illustrated by **Tim Sale**. Marvel Comics, 2016. 160pp. 978-0-7851-9419-4, hardcover. T

Set during the height of World War II, the Howling Commandoes want to kick back and relax, but Captain America and Bucky have a special assignment in mind and they need the help from the best fighting team for a dangerous mission!

Captain Marvel/Shazam

Created by **C.C. Beck** and **Bill Parker**. DC Comics, 2009–2013.

The young boy Billy Batson was given the powers of ancient biblical and mythological heroes by an ancient wizard called Shazam. When he says aloud the wizard's name "SHAZAM!" a bolt of magic lightning strikes and he's transformed into the caped red and gold-costumed hero Captain Marvel. With super-speed, great strength, flight, and more, he's one of the most powered heroes in the universe, but with the mind of a boy in the body of an adult. Billy is also joined on his adventures by some other of his Marvel Family including his twin sister Mary (Mary Marvel), as well as crippled newsboy Freddie Freeman (Captain Marvel Jr.). Captain Marvel's most popular villains include Black Adam, Dr. Sivana, and Mister Mind. The hero was originally created by Fawcett Comics in 1940 in *Whiz Comics* #2 and was one of the most popular heroes in the 1940s–1950s. Due to a copyright infringement suit by DC Comics, the series ended in 1953, and DC Comics later began publishing Captain Marvel's adventures in the 1970s. Due to the fact that Marvel Comics owns the trademark to the title Captain Marvel (see the "Cosmic Heroes" section of this chapter) all of DC Comics' titles featuring Captain Marvel cannot be titled by the heroes' name. Due to the copyright embargo, most titles featuring Captain Marvel tend to use the word "Shazam" in the publication title. In fact DC Comics, with the creation of its New 52 line of titles, now has officially changed the hero's name to Shazam.

Shazam!: The Monster Society of Evil. Written and Illustrated by **Jeff Smith**. DC Comics, 2009. 208pp. 978-1-4012-0974-2. A

© 2016 DC Comics

Jeff Smith, creator of *Bone,* grew up reading Captain Marvel comics. A labor of love for the creator, the collection tells of Billy Batson and how he has to thwart an alien invasion as well as stop the Monster Society of Evil lead by Dr. Sivana from taking over the world!

Shazam! Written by **Geoff Johns**. Illustrated by **Gary Frank**. DC Comics, 2014. 192pp. 978-1-4012-4699-0. T

A new retelling of the origin of how teenager Billy Batson is granted with the power of Shazam, a magical-based hero with the combined powers of Solomon, Hercules, Atlas, Zeus, Achilles, and Mercury! Billy must battle against the foe Black Adam.

Catwoman

DC Comics, 2012– .T-O

Femme fatale Selena Kyle has forever been a thorn in Batman's side since her first appearance in the comic book *Batman #1* in 1940. Walking a fine line and playing neither hero or villain, Catwoman is a talented thief and occasional lover of Batman who is out to make it rich, looking out for what matters most: herself. Following a rough upbringing and a life of crime, Selena became enamored with Batman and the other costumed characters and adopted her own identity as Catwoman. Rich from her thefts, Selena became well known as a wealthy socialite, but as Catwoman, she robs from the rich and gives to herself. Now a little older and wiser, Selena has become a guardian of sorts in Gotham City for those in need, living outside the law and helping those society has cast off, who remind of herself when she was a lost teenage girl.

Catwoman, 1st series. Written by **Ed Brubaker**, **Will Pfeifer**, and **Darwyn Cooke**. Illustrated by **Darwyn Cooke**, **Paul Gulacy**, **Jimmy Palmiotti**, and various. 2012– . T ◉

© 2016 DC Comics

Originally published from 2001 to 2004, writers Ed Brubaker and Darwyn Cooke redefined Selina Kyle and her supporting cast in this well-received series. The first volume also reprints Darwyn Cooke's acclaimed graphic novel *Selina's Big Score,* which is a tribute to the pulp crime novels and heist movies of the 1950s like *Ocean's Eleven.*

Vol. 1: The Dark End of the Street. 2012. 336pp. 978-1-4012-3384-6.
Vol. 2: No Easy Way Down. 2013. 400pp. 978-1-4012-4037-0.
Vol. 3: Under Pressure. 2014. 312pp. 978–1401245924.
Vol. 4: The One That You Love. 2015. 240pp. 978-1-4012-5832-0.
Vol. 5: Backward Masking. 2016. 232pp. 978-1-4012-6073-6.
Vol. 6: Final Jeopardy. 2016. 200pp. 978-1-4012-6558-8.

Catwoman, 2nd series (New 52). Written by **Judd Winick**, **Ann Nocenti**, and **Genevieve Valentine**. Illustrated by **Guillem March**, **Rafa Sandoval**, **David Messina**, and **Garry Brown**. DC Comics, 2012–2016. O

Below are listed the currently published collected titles from the monthly Catwoman comic book series since the series' relaunch in 2011. In *Volume 6,* a new creative writer came on, Genevieve Valentine, and made Selina that heir apparent of a crime family in Gotham City. Now Selina wants to reunite the mob families, but others may have different opinions.

Vol. 1: The Game. 2012. 144pp. 978-1-4012-3464-5.
Vol. 2: Dollhouse. 2013. 144pp. 978-1-4012-3839-4.
Vol. 3: Death of the Family. 2013. 176pp. 978-1-4012-4272-5.
Vol. 4: Gotham Underground. 2014. 208pp. 978-1-4012-4627-3.
Vol. 5: Race of Thieves. 2014. 232pp. 978-1-4012-5063-8.
Vol. 6: Keeper of the Castle. 2015. 192pp. 978-1-4012-5469-8.
Vol. 7: Inheritance. 2016. 152pp. 978-1-4012-6118-4.
Vol. 8: Run Like Hell. 2016. 144pp. 978-1-4012-6486-4.

Catwoman: A Celebration of 75 Years. Written and Illustrated by various. DC Comics, 2015. 408pp. 978-1-4012-6006-4, hardcover. T

Features highlights of Catwoman's long history in comic books. The collection includes works by such comic book legends as Bob Kane, Bill Finger, Dennis O'Neil, Dick Giordano, Len Wein, Kurt Schaffenberger, Chuck Dixon, Ed Brubaker, Cameron Stewart, Darwyn Cooke, Tim Sale, Paul Dini, and Guillem March.

Codename: Sailor V. Written and Illustrated by **Naoko Takeuchi**. Kodansha Comics, 2011. T Japanese manga.

What would a teenage girl do if she was destined to save the world from soul-eating bad guys? Everything a normal 13-year-old would do! Minako Aino chases boys, goes to concerts, and likes to go shopping all while fighting the monster of the week. Even though Minako became Sailor V, a Pretty Guardian sailor scout, has a talking cat and fights the dark agency, she does it all without breaking a nail.

Codename: Sailor V is the precursor to Ms. Takeuchi's popular manga series Sailor Moon.

Vol. 1. 2011. 272pp. 978-1-935429-77-7.
Vol. 2. 2011. 296pp. 978-1-935429-78-4.

Daredevil

Marvel Comics, 2012– . T 🖳

Matt Murdock always had a life that was full of challenges. Growing up in Hell's Kitchen in New York City was tough enough, but Matt learned to roll with the punches. As a young boy, he was blinded by a canister of nuclear waste. The substance, though it stole his vision, gave the boy a heightened sense akin to super-radar, and Matt was forever changed. He was trained by a mysterious man named Stick and was able to use his heightened skills to his advantage. He also went to college where he got his law degree. He fell in love with Elektra Natchios, but after she disappeared and his boxer father was killed, Matt lost faith in the judicial system and decided to take matters into his own hands. By day he serves as a lawyer for those less fortunate, and by night he protects Hell's Kitchen when the law can't and is known as the masked crimson hero called Daredevil. Included are the classic works of Frank Miller, who was instrumental in redefining the character in the 1980s, the works of Ann Nocenti from the late 1980s, and the latest writings by Brian Michael Bendis, David Mack, Kevin Smith, and Jeph Loeb, who have all been influenced by Frank Miller's storytelling. Daredevil has also been adapted into a live-action series on Netflix by Marvel Comics. The series debuted in 2015 and stars actor Charlie Cox as Matt Murdock. The series also features many familiar characters from the comic books, including Matt's business partner Foggy Nelson, Karen Page, Elektra, the Punisher, and the Kingpin.

Frank Miller's Daredevil. T ◎

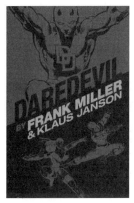

Writer/artist Frank Miller has been credited for reviving interest in Daredevil after taking over the title in the late 1970s. Through his art and writing he infused a noir style to the series and introduced popular characters including Elektra Natchios, a love interest of Matt Murdock as well as a highly trained assassin, as well as introducing Matt Murdock's mentor, Stick. Miller also revived classic Marvel characters such as the Kingpin and Bullseye into top-class villains, and his influence is still felt today. Below are listed all of Frank Miller's collected tales of Daredevil published by Marvel Comics.

© 2016 Marvel Comics

Daredevil by Frank Miller & Klaus Janson Omnibus. Written by **Frank Miller** and various. Illustrated by **Frank Miller**. 2016. 840pp. 978-0-7851-9536-8, hardcover.

Daredevil by Frank Miller Omnibus Companion. Written by **Frank Miller**. Illustrated by **Frank Miller**, **John Romita Jr.**, **David Mazzucchelli**, **John Buscema**, and **Bill Sienkiewicz**. 2016. 608pp. 978-0-7851-9538-2, hardcover.

Daredevil by Frank Miller & Klaus Janson. 2008–2009.

> *Vol. 1*. 2008. 336pp. 978-0-7851-3473-2.
> *Vol. 2*. 2008. 328pp. 978-0-7851-3474-9.
> *Vol. 3*. 2009. 320pp. 978-0-7851-3475-6.

Daredevil: Born Again. Written by **Frank Miller**. Illustrated by **David Mazzucchelli**. 2010. 248pp. 978-0-7851-3481-7.

Daredevil: The Man without Fear. Written by **Frank Miller**. Illustrated by **John Romita Jr**. 2010. 224pp. 978-0-7851-3479-4.

Daredevil (recent collections). 2010– . T 🏵 ◎

Inspired and heavily influenced by Frank Miller's take on Daredevil, many other writers have continued to work in the playground that Miller created and used it as a springboard for more adventures of Matt Murdock. Writer Brian Michael Bendis wrote a memorable run on the series in 2001 that lasted until 2006. Following Bendis's run, Ed Brubaker took over the series from 2006 to 2009. The recent *Daredevil* stories written by Mark Waid and Chris Samnee, which have taken a much lighter approach to the hero, has also been highly praised as well. Ed Brubaker has won numerous Eisner Awards and Harvey Awards for Best Writer, and Mark Waid won an Eisner Award as well for the stand-alone story from Daredevil #7 (reprinted in volume 2) as well as an Eisner for Best Continuing Series. Waid's <u>Daredevil</u> series was also honored by YALSA as a Great Graphic Novel for Teens in 2013. The Waid series was followed in 2016 by a new series by Charles Soule and Ron Garney.

Daredevil by Brian Michael Bendis & Alex Maleev Ultimate Collection. Written by **Brian Michael Bendis**. Illustrated by **Alex Maleev**. Marvel Comics, 2010.

> *Vol. 1*. 2010. 480pp. 978-0-7851-4388-8.
> *Vol. 2*. 2010. 512pp. 978-0-7851-4950-7.
> *Vol. 3*. 2010. 512pp. 978-0-7851-4951-4.

Daredevil by Ed Brubaker & Michael Lark Ultimate Collection. Written by **Ed Brubaker**. Illustrated by **Michael Lark**. Marvel Comics, 2012.

> *Vol. 1*. 2012. 304pp. 978-0-7851-6334-3.
> *Vol. 2*. 2012. 304pp. 978-0-7851-6335-0.
> *Vol. 3*. 2012. 384pp. 978-0-7851-6336-7.

Daredevil, 2011 and 2014 series. Written by **Mark Waid**. Illustrated by **Javier Rodriguez**, **Chris Samnee**, and various. Marvel Comics, 2012–2015.

> *Vol. 1*. 2012. 152pp. 978-0-7851-5237-8, hardcover; 978-0-7851-5238-5.
> *Vol. 2*. 2012. 136pp. 978-0-7851-5239-2, hardcover; 978-0-7851-5240-8.
> *Vol. 3*. 2012. 160pp. 978-0-7851-6100-4, hardcover; 978-0-7851-6101-1.
> *Vol. 4*. 2013. 136pp. 978-0-7851-6102-8, hardcover; 978-0-7851-6103-5.
> *Vol. 5*. 2013. 144pp. 978-0-7851-6104-2, hardcover; 978-0-7851-6105-9.

Vol. 6. 2013. 112pp. 978-0-7851-8480-5, hardcover; 978-0-7851-6679-5.
Vol. 7. 2014. 136pp. 978-0-7851-5442-6, hardcover; 978-0-7851-8961-9.
Vol. 1: Devil at Bay. 2014. 978-0-7851-5411-2.
Vol. 2: West-Case Scenario. 2015. 978-0-7851-5412-9.
Vol. 3: The Devil You Know. 2015. 112pp. 978-0-7851-9228-2.
Vol. 4: The Autobiography of Matt Murdock. 2015. 104pp. 978-0-7851-9802-4.

Daredevil **(2016) series**. Written by **Charles D. Soule**. Illustrated by **Ron Garney** and **Goran Sudžuka**. Marvel Comics 2016– .

Back in Black Vol. 1: Chinatown. 2016. 120pp. 978-0-7851-9645-7.
Back in Black Vol. 2: Supersonic. 2016. 120pp. 978-0-7851-9645-7.
Back in Black Vol. 3: Dark Art. 2017. 112pp.1 978-1-302-90297-1.
Back in Black Vol. 4: Identity. 2017. 136pp. 978-1-302-90562-0.

Deadpool

Marvel Comics, 2008– . 🎬 🐾 O-M

When Marvel's "Merc With a Mouth" was first introduced, it seemed he was just latest foe for the various X-teams. But with his 1997 ongoing series, this anti-hero grew in popularity with his occasionally goofy antics which included breaking the fourth wall. The <u>Deadpool Classic</u> series of books has collected the original series as well as a number of spin-off series, limited series, and one-shots. The <u>Max</u> series by writer David Lapham is from Marvel's explicit line and for mature readers. The 2008 and 2013 ongoing series have been collected in various volumes as well, and a new ongoing Deadpool book began in 2016. Writers and artists over the years have included Joe Kelly, Ed McGuinness, Gail Simone, Christopher Priest, Fabian Nicieza, Daniel Way, Paco Medina, Brian Posehn, and Gerry Duggan. Deadpool has also been featured in the world of video games, including the Marvel vs. Capcom 3 video game and his own self-titled console game released by Activision 2013. In 2016 a *Deadpool* feature film was released in theaters starring Ryan Reynolds and garnered positive reviews, box-office success, and a heavy R-rating. Listed below are just a short sampling of some of the more popular Deadpool volumes available. Many more can be found on Marvel Comics' web site.

Deadpool Classic. Written by **Fabian Nicieza, Mark Waid, Joe Kelly, Gail Simone, Cullen Bunn**, and various. Illustrated by **Rob Liefeld, Ed McGuinness, Joe Madureira, UDON Studios**, and various. Marvel Comics, 2008– . O

Vol. 1. 2008. 264pp. 978-0-7851-3124-3.
Vol. 2. 2009. 256pp. 978-0-7851-3731-3.
Vol. 3. 2009. 280pp. 978-0-7851-4244-7.
Vol. 4. 2011. 296pp. 978-0-7851-5302-3.
Vol. 5. 2011. 272pp. 978-0-7851-5519-5.

© 2016 Marvel Comics

Vol. 6. 2012. 312pp. 978-0-7851-5941-4.
Vol. 7. 2012. 272pp. 978-0-7851-6238-4.
Vol. 8. 2013. 272pp. 978-0-7851-6732-7.
Vol. 9. 2014. 200pp. 978-0-7851-8513-0.
Vol. 10. 2014. 272pp. 978-0-7851-9046-2.
Vol. 11: Merc With a Mouth. 2015. 376pp. 978-0-7851-9730-0.
Vol. 12: Deadpool Corps. 2015. 448pp. 978-0-7851-9731-7.
Vol. 13: Deadpool Team-Up. 2015. 448pp. 978-0-7851-9732-4.
Vol. 14: Suicide Kings. 2015. 392pp. 978-0-7851-9733-1.
Vol. 15: All the Rest. 2016. 360pp. 978-0-7851-9690-7.
Vol. 16: Killogy. 2016. 280pp. 978-0-7851-9541-2.
Vol. 17: Headcannon. 2017. 384pp. 978-1-302-90430-2.
Deadpool Classic Omnibus, Vol. 1. 2016. 1304pp. 978-0-7851-9674-7.
Deadpool Classic Companion. 2015. 384pp. 978-0-7851-9294-7.

Deadpool, 2nd series. 2008–2012.

Deadpool by Daniel Way: The Complete Collection. Written by **Daniel Way**. Illustrated by **Paco Medina**. 2013–2014.

Vol. 1. 2013. 472pp. 978-0-7851-8532-1.
Vol. 2. 2013. 464pp. 978-0-7851-8547-5.
Vol. 3. 2014. 448pp. 978-0-7851-8888-9.
Vol. 4. 2014. 328pp. 978-0-7851-6012-0.

Deadpool Max. Written by **David Lapham**. Illustrated by **Kyle Baker** and **Shawn Crystal**. MAX/Marvel Comics, 2011–2012. M

Vol. 1: Nutjob. 2011. 144pp. 978–0-7851-4851-7.
Vol. 2: Involuntary Armageddon. 2011. 144pp. 978–0-7851-4853-1.
Vol. 3: Second Cut. 2013. 160pp. 978–0-7851-5923-0.
Omnibus. 2012. 440pp. 978-0-7851-5707-6.

Deadpool, 3rd series. Written by **Gerry Duggan** and **Brian Posehn**. Illustrated by **Tony Moore**, **Scott Koblish**, and **Mike Hawthorne**. Marvel Comics, 2014–2015. O

Vol. 1. 2014. 280pp. 978-0-7851-5446-4, hardcover.
Vol. 2. 2015. 296pp. 978-0-7851-9792-8, hardcover.
Vol. 3. 2015. 312pp. 978-0-7851-9825-3, hardcover.
Vol. 4. 2015. 312pp. 978-0-7851-9826-0, hardcover.

Deadpool: Bad Blood. Written by **Chris Sims** and **Chad Bowers**. Illustrated by **Rob Liefeld**. Marvel Comics, 2016. 112pp. 978-1-309-90153-0.

Deadpool: World's Greatest, 4th series. Written by **Gerry Duggan** and various. Illustrated by **Mike Hawthorne**. Marvel Comics, 2016– .

Vol. 1: Millionaire with a Mouth. 2016. 112pp. 978-0-7851-9617-4.
Vol. 2. 2016. 128pp. 978-0-7851-9618-1.
Vol. 3. 2016. 112pp. 978-0-7851-9619-8.
Vol. 4. 2016. 112pp. 978-1-309-90091-5.
Vol. 5: Civil War II. 2016. 112pp. 978-1-309-90148-6.
Vol. 6. 2017. 136pp. 978-1-302-90243-8.

Dial H: The Deluxe Edition. Written by **China Miéville**. Illustrated by **Alberto Ponticelli** and **Mateus Santolouco**. DC Comics, 2015. 368pp. 978-1-4012-5520-6, hardcover. T

> What would you do if you could become a super-hero with a push of a button and could instantly have the power of flight, X-ray vision, super-strength, and more? When overweight, unemployed slacker Nelson Jent finds an abandoned old pay phone, he discovers that every time you turn the dial on the pay phone to the numbers 4-3-7-6 (HERO) you receive a brand-new superpower complete with a costume, too! Will this newfound ability turn Nelson into a real hero? The series was inspired by the "Dial H for Hero" stories of the 1960s and 1980s.

Ex Machina. Written by **Brian K. Vaughan**. Illustrated by **Tony Harris**. Vertigo/DC Comics, 2014–2015. M 🏃 ◎

> In a world where super-heroes are only make-believe, civil engineer Mitchell Hundred received the amazing power to control machinery in an accident and became New York City's first super-hero. Calling himself the Great Machine, Mitchell soon grows tired of risking his life vigilante-style and does the unthinkable: he runs for mayor of New York City and wins in a landslide. Now Mitchell has traded in one dangerous job for another. When snowplow drivers are being murdered during the biggest snowstorm of the century and controversial decisions must be made, it's time for Mitchell Hundred to save the day. The series won several Eisner Awards in 2005, including Best New Series and Best Writer for Vaughan's body of work. The series was originally published from 2004 to 2010.

> *Deluxe Edition Book 1*. 2014. 272pp. 978-1-4012-4498-9.
> *Deluxe Edition Book 2*. 2014, 272pp. 978-1-4012-4691-4.
> *Deluxe Edition Book 3*. 2015. 272pp. 2015, 978-1-4012-5003-4.
> *Deluxe Edition Book 4*. 2015, 272pp. 978-1-4012-5002-7.
> *Deluxe Edition Book 5*. 2015. 320pp. 978-1-4012-5422-3.

The Flash

DC Comics, 2010– . T 🖥 🎬 🐾

> Since 1940 a series of "Fastest Men Alive" have protected the DC Universe. Jay Garrick was the first, but it was the 1956 debut of Barry Allen as the Flash that most consider to be the beginning of the Silver Age of Comics. He had a long career, becoming a founder of the Justice League and fighting such enemies as Captain Cold, Pied Piper, and Captain Boomerang. After Barry died saving the world in the Crisis on Infinite Earths, the role was taken on by Wally West, the former Kid Flash. Wally was the Flash for over 20 years often working with other speedsters including the semi-retired Jay Garrick, Max Mercury the "Zen Master of Speed" who introduced Wally to the concept of the "Speed Force," and Bart Allen, Barry's future-born grandson who came to the present and became Impulse (and later Kid Flash, and for a short time, the Flash).

> Barry returned in 2009, but a time-traveling enemy changed the past so that Barry's father was now in jail for killing his wife when Barry was young. Barry's attempt to prevent this led to the "Flashpoint Universe," which then led to the "New 52" DC Universe. In this universe, Barry is the Flash but many

of the supporting characters no longer existed or were altered. A new <u>Flash</u> series with Barry began in 2016 following the events of "Rebirth." Collections of this series began in 2017. The Wally West incarnation appeared on the Justice League cartoon, while Barry appeared in a 1990–1991 TV series and a second series that debuted in 2014 (with the actor from the 1990 show playing the father of the new Flash). A Barry Allen flash will be appearing in several films, including a self-titled 2018 film. The hero has also appeared in numerous video games including the *LEGO Batman* video game series as well as *Injustice: Gods and Monsters* fighting game.

The Flash, 2nd series.

A collection of recommend stories focusing on Wally West, the third- generation Flash and nephew of Barry Allen, the second Flash.

The Flash by Grant Morrison & Mark Millar. Written by **Grant Morrison** and **Mark Millar**. Illustrated by **Paul Ryan**. DC Comics, 2016. 256pp. 978-1-4012-6102-3.

When Wally West, the third-generation Flash, is wheelchair bound after an accident, how can he defeat a villain without the aid of his legs?

The Flash Omnibus by Geoff Johns. DC Comics, 2011–2012.

Vol. 1. 2011. 448pp. 978-1-4012-3068-5, hardcover.
Vol. 2. 2012. 648pp. 978-1-4012-3391-4, hardcover.
Vol. 3. 2012. 656pp. 978-1-4012-3717-2, hardcover.

The Flash by Mark Waid. Written by **Mark Waid**. Illustrated by **Mike Wieringo** and various. DC Comics, 2016. T

Vol. 1. 2016. 448pp. 978-1-4012-6735-3.
Vol. 2. 2017. 432pp. 978-1-4012-6844-2.

The Flash, 3rd series. 2010–2011.

A collection of stories once again starring Barry Allen as the Flash after his resurrection from the dead.

The Flash. Written by **Geoff Johns**. Illustrated by **Ethan Van Sciver**. 2010–2011.

Rebirth. 2010. 168pp. 978-1-4012-2568-1.
Vol. 1: The Dastardly Death of the Rogues. 2011. 228pp. 978-1-4012-2970-2.
Vol. 2: The Road to Flashpoint. 2011. 128pp. 978-1-4012-3279-5.

The Flash, current series (The New 52).

Featuring the new adventures of Barry Allen in the post-New 52 world.

The Flash. Written by **Francis Manapul**, **Brian Buccellato**, **Robert Venditti**, and **Van Jensen**. Illustrated by **Brett Booth** and **Francis Manapul**. DC Comics, 2012– . T

> *Vol. 1: Move Forward*. 2012. 192pp. 978-1-4012-3553-6, hardcover. 978-1-4012-3554-3.
> *Vol. 2: Rogues Revolution*. 2013. 176pp. 978-1-4012-4031-8, hardcover. 978-1-4012-4273-2.
> *Vol. 3: Gorilla Warfare*. 2014. 176pp. 978-1-4012-4274-9, hardcover. 978-1-4012-4712-6.
> *Vol. 4: Reverse*. 2014. 176pp. 978-1-4012-47133, hardcover. 978-1-4012-4949-6.
> *Vol. 5: History Lessons*. 2015. 144pp. 978-1-4012-49502 hardcover. 978-1-4012-5772-9.
> *Vol. 6: Out of Time*. 2015. 208pp. 978-1-4012-5427-8, hardcover. 978-1-4012-5772-9.
> *Vol. 7: Savage World*. 2016. 144pp. 978-1-4012-5875-7, hardcover. 978-1-4012-6365-2.
> *Vol. 8: Zoom*. 2016. 224pp. 978-1-4012-6366-9, hardcover. 978-1-4012-6926-5.
> *Vol. 9: Full Stop*. 2016. 224pp. 978-1-4012-69258, hardcover. 978-1-4012-7412-2.

The Flash: A Celebration of 75 Years. Written and Illustrated by various. DC Comics, 2015. 400pp. 978-1-4012-5178-9, hardcover. T

A compilation of the greatest Flash stories told in the last 75 years of DC Comics history.

Grayson. Written by **Tim Seeley** and **Tom King**. Illustrated by **Mikel Janín** and **Stephen Mooney**. DC Comics, 2015–2017. T

© 2016 DC Comics

As Batman's protégé and sidekick, Dick Grayson learned from the best. When he became Nightwing (see entry, later in this chapter), he went on his own path and became a hero in his own right. Now, after seemingly dying to save the world, Dick Grayson has a new path ahead of him—the perfect recruit to the super-spy organization called Spyral. The organization's mission is to hunt down and locate the missing shards of a deceased god called Paragon, whose body parts each can be considered a weapon of mass destruction. Spyral has another plan too: to reveal the secret identities of all costumed heroes. As Batman's inside mole in a super-spy organization, Dick must balance becoming a dual agent and must find where his true loyalties lie.

> *Vol. 1: Agents of Spyral*. 2015. 160pp. 978-1-4012-5234-2, hardcover; 2016. 978-1-4012-5759-0.
> *Vol. 2: We All Die at Dawn*. 2016. 160pp. 978-1-4012-5760-6.
> *Vol. 3: Nemesis*. 2016. 160pp. 978-1-4012-6276-1.
> *Vol. 4: A Ghost in the Tomb*. 2016. 184pp. 978-1-4012-6762-9.
> *Vol. 5: Spyral's End*. 2017. 168pp. 978-1-4012-6825-1.

Green Arrow

DC Comics, 2008– . T

© 2016 DC Comics

For his first few decades, Green Arrow was very similar to Batman—millionaire, boy ward/sidekick, paraphernalia with the prefix "Arrow," and so on. But after losing his fortune he was different with a new costume and a more liberal viewpoint. During this period he traveled across America with Green Lantern and, in one notable story, learned that his sidekick Speedy was a drug addict. In the mid-1980s, Mike Grell wrote the limited series <u>Green Arrow: The Longbow Hunters</u>, which led to an ongoing series originally written by Grell. In the new series Green Arrow and his girlfriend Black Canary move to Seattle, where, among other things, Green Arrow stops wearing his mask. Later in the run, he met his previously unknown son Connor Hawke, who took over the role when Green Arrow was killed in an explosion.

However, like many of his allies Green Arrow was restored to life in a new series originally written by writer/director Kevin Smith with art by Phil Hester and Ande Parks. Later writers of the series included author Brad Meltzer and Judd Winick, while a revised origin story—putting a new twist on the old origin of the rich Oliver Queen being stranded on an island where he stops criminals—was written by Andy Diggle. After many years Green Arrow finally married the Black Canary and they shared a book as well. Other events in the DC Universe caused various problems for the "Emerald Archer."

In the "New 52" Green Arrow has been totally rebooted, making a number of changes to the character. The new series was originally written by J.T. Krul, who has been succeeded by several writers including Keith Giffen, Dan Jurgens, Ann Nocenti, and Jeff Lemere, with art by various creators including Andrea Sorrentino. Some of the older aspects of the character, including a relationship with Black Canary, were restored for the new series that began in 2016. Green Arrow was a regular character on the latter seasons of Smallville and was the lead in the show Arrow which debuted in 2012 (though it took several seasons for the character to take the Green Arrow name). Several characters and concepts from Arrow have made their way into the New 52–era comics.

Green Arrow, 1st series. Written by **Mike Grell**. Illustrated by **Mike Grell** and various. DC Comics, 2012–2016. T

Originally published from the late 1980s to the early 1990s, Mike Grell focused on a grittier side of the Green Arrow mixed in with martial arts elements too. An aging Oliver Queen relocates to Seattle with Dinah Lance, the heroine known as Black Canary. There they take on drug lords, serial killers, and a Japanese assassin known as Shado. *The Longbow Hunters* collection is a darker in tone departure from Green Arrow stories in the past and features a well-rounded complex hero reevaluating his role in the world.

Green Arrow: The Longbow Hunters. 2012. 160pp. 978-1-4012-3862-9.
Vol. 1: Hunters Moon. 2013. 160pp. 978-1-4012-4326-5.
Vol. 2: Here There Be Dragons. 2014. 160pp. 978-1-4012-5133-8.
Vol. 3: The Trial of Oliver Queen. 2015. 208pp. 978-1-4012-5523-7.

Vol. 4: Blood of the Dragon. 2016. 208pp. 978-1-4012-5822-1.
Vol. 5: Black Arrow. 2016. 312pp. 978-1-4012-6079-8.
Vol. 6: Last Action Hero. 2016. 328pp. 978-1-4012-6457-4.
Vol. 7: Homecoming. 2017. 320pp. 978-1-4012-6574-8.
Vol. 8: The Hunt for the Red Dragon. 2017. 256pp. 978-1-4012-6903-6.

Green Arrow/Black Canary. Written by **J. Torres** and **Andrew Kreisberg**. Illustrated by **Nicola Scott** and **Mike Norton**. DC Comics, 2008–2010.

Dinah Lance (Black Canary) has had an on-again/off-again relationship with Oliver Queen. Collected here is the series from the late 2000s, with them fighting alongside together as well as preparing for their wedding.

Road to the Altar. 2008. 144pp. 978-1-4012-1863-8.
Enemies List. 2009. 144pp. 978-1-4012-2498-1.
Family Business. 2009. 128pp. 978-1-4012-2016-7.
A League of Their Own. 2009. 128pp. 978-1-4012-2250-5.
The Wedding Album. 2009. 176pp. 978-1-4012-2219-2.
Big Game. 192pp. 2010. 978-1-4012-2709-8.
Five Stages. 128pp. 2010. 978-1-4012-2898-9.

Green Arrow, 2nd series (The New 52). Written by **J.T. Krul**, **Ann Nocenti**, **Jeff Lemire**, and **Benjamin Percy**. Illustrated by **Harvey Tolibao**, **Freddie E. Williams**, **Andrea Sorrentino**, and **Patrick Zircher**. DC Comics, 2012–2016. T

Featuring the new adventures of Oliver Queen in the post-New 52 era of continuity. The most recent creative team is acclaimed horror writer Benjamin Percy and illustrator Patrick Zircher.

Vol. 1: The Midas Touch. 2012. 144pp. 978-1-4012-3486-0.
Vol. 2: Triple Threat. 2013. 160pp. 978-1-4012-3842-1.
Vol. 3: Harrow. 2013. 144pp. 978-1-4012-4405-7.
Vol. 4: The Kill Machine. 2014. 208pp. 978-1-4012-4690-7.
Vol. 5: The Outsiders War. 2014. 176pp. 978-1-4012-5044-7.
Vol. 6: Broken. 2015. 128pp. 978-1-4012-5474-2.
Vol. 7: Kingdom. 2015. 144pp. 978-1-4012-3528-4.
Vol. 8: The Nightbirds. 2016. 144pp. 978-1-4012-6255-6.
Vol. 9: Outbreak. 2016. 200pp. 978-1-4012-7002-5.
Green Arrow by Jeff Lemire and Andrea Sorrentino Deluxe Edition. 2016. 464pp. 978-1-4012-5761-3, hardcover.

Green Arrow: A Celebration of 75 Years. 2016. 400pp. 978-1-4012-6386-7, hardcover. T

A collection of highlights of Oliver Queen's 75-year history with DC Comics.

Green Arrow: Year One. Written by **Andy Diggle**. Illustrated by **Jock**. DC Comics, 2009. 160pp. 978-1401217433. T 🏆

A look back at the early career of Oliver Queen and what made him the hero he is today. Queen, a young and frivolous playboy, gets double-crossed and marooned on a jungle island. Now the spoiled boy must learn to fend for himself on an island and seek revenge. The story was the inspiration for the hit TV series <u>Arrow</u> starring Stephen Amell. The book was recognized by YALSA in 2009 as a Great Graphic Novel for Teens.

Green Lantern

DC Comics, 2006– . T 🎬 ◎ 📷 🖥 🎮

© 2016 DC Comics

The original Green Lantern, Allan Scott, had a magic ring, but the Silver Age version had his origins in science fiction. Test pilot Hal Jordan is chosen by a dying alien to become a Green Lantern, one of 3,600 beings across the cosmos, working for the Guardians of the Universe fighting evil with their power rings. Over the years Green Lantern fought many different foes, working both solo and with others including other members of the Green Lantern Corps, the Justice League of America, and notably, in some classic stories, with Green Arrow. "Back Up" Lanterns Guy Gardner and John Stewart took on the role at times, later working simultaneously with Jordan. When Jordan appeared to go mad and become the evil Parallax, he was succeeded by artist Kyle Rayner. Jordan eventually died, took on the role of the Spectre, and came back to life.

During the 2000s there was not only a Green Lantern title but others including Green Lantern Corps which featured all four human Lanterns and a number of the alien ones. During this time possessors of other rings were introduced as both friends and foes of the Will-based Green Lanterns. These included The Sinestro Corps and their fear-based Yellow rings who were led by Jordan's old foe Sinestro, himself a former Green Lantern; the rage-based Red Lanterns; the love-based Star Sapphires with love-based powers, whose number included Jordan's occasional girlfriend Carol Ferris; and Larfleeze, possessor of the Orange Ring which reflects his avarice. There were several major events during this period, including The Blackest Night, a DC-wide event in which the dead came back to life with their black rings, who were defeated with the life-based powers of the new White Lanterns.

The "New 52" reboot kept much of the old stories in continuity with four regular series that also introduced new Lanterns, of multiple colors, both alien and human, including new Earth Green Lantern Simon Baz. Many of their storylines crossed over, with issues being collected both in the volumes for a particular series. Green Lantern has appeared in video games, film and television including a 2011 feature film, and an animated series that had a comic book tie-in.

Pre-New 52 Continuity

Stories featuring Green Lantern published before the DC Comics' revised continuity from 2011.

Green Lantern. Written by **Geoff Johns**. Illustrated by **Ethan Van Sciver**, **Ivan Reis**, and various. 2006–2013. T 🎬

Listed below are highlights of recommended *Green Lantern* titles written by fan-favorite Geoff Johns that have been collected by DC Comics from the original comic book issues from 2006 to the New 52 reboot in 2011. They feature the return of Hal Jordan as a Green Lantern member and the rise of the many colors of lanterns. The *Sinestro*

Corps War title was recognized as a Great Graphic Novels for Teens selection list recipient in 2009. The Omnibus editions reprints many of the volumes listed below in one voluminous collection spread over three volumes so far.

Rebirth. 2010. 192pp. 978-1-4012-2755-5.
No Fear. 2008. 176pp. 978-1-4012-1058-8.
Revenge of the Green Lanterns. 2008. 176pp. 978-1-4012-0960-5.
Wanted: Hal Jordan. 2009. 144pp. 978-1-4012-1590-3.
Agent Orange. 2010. 128pp. 978-1-4012-2420-2.
Rage of the Red Lanterns. 2010. 176pp. 978-1-4012-2302-1.
Blackest Night. 2011. 272pp. 978-1-4012-2952-8.
Secret Origin. 2011. 192pp. 978-1-4012-3086-9.
Sinestro Corps War. 2011. 336pp. 978-1-4012-3301-3.
Brightest Day. 2012. 256pp. 978-1-4012-3141-5.
War of the Green Lanterns. 2012. 272pp. 978-1-4012-3452-2.
War of the Green Lanterns: Aftermath. 2013. 208pp. 978-1-4012-35383.
Green Lantern by Geoff Johns Omnibus, 2015–2016.
Vol. 1. 2015. 1232pp. 978-1-4012-5134-5, hardcover.
Vol. 2. 2015. 1040pp. 978-1-4012-5526-8, hardcover.
Vol. 3. 2016. 1104pp. 978-1-4012-5820-7, hardcover.

Post-New 52 Continuity

Stories featuring Green Lantern published after DC Comics' revised continuity from 2011. After the New 52 Reboot, DC began four different titles featuring past Green Lanterns (Hal Jordan, John Stewart, Guy Gardner, and Kyle Rayner), new Lanterns (Simon Baz) new and old alien Green Lanterns, and Lanterns of other colors—including Yellow, Orange, Blue, Purple, and Red, the latter of which was rage based and got their own book. Several storylines crossed over and were featured in separate volumes, though the relevant issues were also collected in the respective titles. Following the DC Comics "Rebirth" event in 2016, the two Green Lantern titles were *Green Lanterns,* written by Sam Humphries, and *Hal Jordan & the Green Lantern Corps* by Robert Venditti.

Green Lantern (New 52). Written by **Geoff Johns** and **Robert Venditti**. Illustrated by **Doug Mahnke** and **Billy Tan**. DC Comics, 2012–2016. T

Vol. 1: Sinestro. 2012. 160pp. 978-1-4012-3454-6, hardcover. 978-1-4012-3455-3.
Vol. 2: Revenge of the Black Hand. 2013. 192pp. 978-1-4012-3766-0, hardcover. 978-1-4012-3767-7.
Vol. 3: The End. 2013. 224pp. 978-1-4012-4408-8, hardcover. 978-1-4012-4684-6.
Vol. 4: Dark Days. 2014. 200pp. 978-1-4012-4744-7, hardcover. 978-1-4012-4942-7.
Vol. 5: Test of Wills. 2014. 256pp. 978-1-4012-5089-8, hardcover. 978-1-4012-5416-2.
Vol. 6: The Life Equation. 2015. 184pp. 978-1-4012-5476-6, hardcover. 978-1-4012-5846-7.
Vol. 7: Renegade. 2016. 208pp. 978-1-4012-6125-2, hardcover. 978-1-4012-6522-9.
Vol. 8: Reflections. 2016. 200pp. 978-1-4012-6523-6 hardcover. 978-1-4012-7249-4.
Rise of the Third Army. 2013. 416pp. 978-1-4012-4613-6.
Lights Out. 2014. 192pp. 978-1-4012-4943-4.
Wrath of the First Lantern. 2014. 416pp. 978-1-4012-4693-8.

Green Lantern Corps (New 52). Written by **Peter J. Tomasi**. Illustrated by **Fernando Pasarin**. 2012–2015. T

Vol. 1: Fearsome. 2012. 160pp. 978-1-4012-370l1, hardcover. 978-1-4012-3702-8.
Vol. 2: Alpha War. 2013. 192pp. 978-1-4012-4012-7, hardcover. 978-1-4012-4294-7.
Vol. 3: Willpower. 2013. 256pp. 978-1-4012-4407-1, hardcover. 978-1-4012-4766-9.
Vol. 4: Rebuild. 2014. 208pp. 978-1-4012-4745-4.
Vol. 5: Uprising. 2015. 264pp. 978-1-4012-5087-4.
Vol. 6: Reckoning. 2015. 144pp. 978-1-4012-5475-9.

Green Lantern Corps: The Lost Army. Written by **Cullen Bunn**. Illustrated by **Jesus Saiz**, **Javier Pina**, and **Cliff Richards**. DC Comics, 2016. 152pp. 978-1-4012-6126-9.

Green Lantern: New Guardians. Written by **Tony Bedard** and **Justin Jordan**. Illustrated by **Tyler Kirkham**, **Aaron Kuder**, and **Brad Walker**. DC Comics, 2012–2015. T

Vol. 1: The Ring Bearer. 2012. 160pp. 978-1-4012-3707-3, hardcover. 978-1-4012-3708-0.
Vol. 2: Beyond Hope. 2013. 144pp. 978-1-4012-4077-6, hardcover. 978-1-4012-4293-0.
Vol. 3: Love & Death. 2014. 288pp. 978-1-4012-4406-4, hardcover. 978-1-4012-4710-2.
Vol. 4: Gods and Monsters. 2014. 200pp. 978-1-4012-4746-1.
Vol. 5: Godkillers. 2015. 200pp. 978-1-4012-5477-3.
Vol. 6: Storming the Gates. 2015. 160pp. 978-1-4012-5477-3.

Red Lanterns. Written by **Peter Milligan** and **Charles Soule**. Illustrated by **Ed Benes**, **Miguel Sepulveda**, and **Tony Bedard**. DC Comics, 2012–2015. T

Vol. 1: Blood and Rage. 2012. 144pp. 978-1-4012-3491-1.
Vol. 2: Death of the Red Lanterns. 2013. 144pp. 978-1-4012-3847-6.
Vol. 3: The Second Prophecy. 2013. 272pp. 978-1-4012-4414-9.
Vol. 4: Blood Brothers. 2014. 176pp. 978-1-4012-4742-3.
Vol. 5: Atrocities. 2014. 272pp. 978-1-4012-5090-4.
Vol. 6: Forged in Blood. 2015. 160pp. 978-1-4012-5484-1.

Green Lantern: A Celebration of 75 Years. 2015. 400pp. 978-1-4012-5819-1, hardcover.
A collection of Green Lantern stories throughout the 75-year history of DC Comics from the earliest adventures of the first Green Lantern, Alan Scott, to the tales of Hal Jordan from today.

Harley Quinn

Created by **Paul Dini** and **Bruce Timm**. DC Comics, 2011– . T
Created originally as a comedic henchman for the Joker in the classic *Batman: The Animated Series* cartoon, Harley Quinn first appeared in the 1992 episode called *The Joker's Favor* as a walk-on character. Her appearance proved popular, and she eventually got an origin story in the 1994 comic book tie-in to the *Batman: The Animated Series* called *Mad Love*. Written and drawn by Dini and Timm, the story received wide praise from fans and received the Eisner and Harvey Awards for Best Single Issue Comic of the Year. Dr. Harleen Quinzel was an Arkham Asylum psychiatrist who falls for the Joker and becomes his accomplice and on-again, off-again sidekick. A frequent partner with Poison Ivy, she has an immunity to poison (thanks to Poison Ivy) and is a skilled gymnast. By 1997 Harley Quinn was so popular that she was

introduced into the mainstream DC Comics line in the *Batman: Harley Quinn* special issue. Her first comic book series was collected in four volumes and was originally published from 2001 to 2003. Her second and currently ongoing series was released in comic book form 2013 under the New 52 line of titles written by Jimmy Palmiotti and illustrated by his wife Amanda Conner. An additional Harley Quinn series began in 2016, the same year the character appeared in the film *Suicide Squad*. Below are listed the various key books featuring the character over her history.

Batman: The Animated Series Tie-In Books
Stories featuring Harley Quinn based on the *Batman: The Animated Series* show.

Batman Adventures: Mad Love Deluxe Edition. Written by **Paul Dini**. Illustrated by **Bruce Timm**. DC Comics, 2015. 144pp. 978-1-4012-5512-1, hardcover. 🎖 T

Harley and Ivy: Deluxe Edition. Written by **Paul Dini**. Illustrated by **Bruce Timm**. DC Comics, 2016. 144pp. 978-1-4012-6080-4.

Mainstream DC Comics titles

Stories featuring Harley Quinn which are based in the mainstream DC Comics continuity and not tied into the *Batman: The Animated Series* show.

© 2016 DC Comics

Batman: Harley Quinn. Written by **Paul Dini** and various. Illustrated by **Neil Googe** and various. 2015. 200pp. 978-1-4012-5517-6. T
The original story from DC Comics introducing Harley Quinn to the DC Comics Universe is reprinted as well as a variety of comic book appearances over the years.

Harley Quinn*, *1st series. Written by **Karl Kesel** and **A.J. Lieberman**. Illustrated by **Terry Dodson**, **Rachel Dodson**, and **Charlie Adlard**. DC Comics, 2009–2014. T

   Vol. 1: Preludes and Knock-Knock Jokes. 2009. 192pp. 978-1-4012-1657-3.
   Vol. 2: Night and Day. 2013. 192pp. 978-1-4012-4041-7.
   Vol. 3: Welcome to Metropolis. 2014. 288pp. 978-1-4012-4595-5.
   Vol. 4: Vengeance Unlimited. 2014. 288pp. 978-1-4012-5068-3.

Harley Quinn*, *2014 series. Written by **Jimmy Palmiotti** and **Amanda Conner**. Illustrated by **Chad Hardin** and various. DC Comics, 2014–2017. 🎖
The 2014 relaunch of the Harley Quinn series with the New 52 label brought on board the husband and wife team of Jimmy Palmiotti and Amanda Conner. They brought a new sense of humor to the series and totally redesigned Harley Quinn's signature costume and look. The recent collection *Hot in the City*

© 2016 DC Comics

was recognized by YALSA as a Great Graphic Novel for Teens. Palmiotti and Conner are also the writers of the post-Rebirth 2016 series.

Vol. 1: Hot in the City. 2014. 224pp. 978-1-4012-4892-5, hardcover; 2015. 978-1-4012-5415-5.
Vol. 2: Power Outage. 2015. 208pp. 978-1-4012-5478-0, hardcover; 2016; 978-1-4012-5763-7.
Vol. 3: Kiss Kiss Bang Stab. 2015. 208pp. 978-1-4012-5764-4, hardcover; 2016. 978-1-4012-6252-5.
Vol. 4: A Call to Arms. 2016. 176pp. 978-1-4012-6253-2, hardcover. 978-140126929-6.
Vol. 5: The Joker's Last Laugh. 2016. 200pp. 978-1-4012-6928-9, hardcover. 978-1-4012-7199-2.
Vol. 6: Black and White and Red All Over. 2017.144pp. 978-1-4012-7198-5 hardcover. 978-1-4012-7259-3.

Team-Up Books Featuring Harley Quinn
Harley recently has teamed up with Catwoman and Poison Ivy for the Gotham City Sirens miniseries as well as the super-hero Power Girl.

Gotham City Sirens. Written by **Paul Dini** and **Tony Bedard**. Illustrated by **Guillem March**. DC Comics, 2014–2015. T

> *Book One.* 2014. 322pp. 978-1-4012-5175-8.
> *Book Two.* 2015. 304pp. 978-1-4012-5412-4.

Harley Quinn and Power Girl. Written by **Amanda Conner** and **Jimmy Palmiotti**. Illustrated by **Stephane Roux**. DC Comics, 2016. 144pp. 978-1-4012-5974-7. T

Hawkeye. Written by **Matt Fraction**. Illustrated by **David Aja**, **Javier Pulido**, **Annie Wu**, **Francesco Francavilla**, and **Ramon Perez**. Marvel Comics, 2013–2015. T ◎ 🏃 🎞 🖥

© 2016 Marvel Comics

When he debuted in 1964, Clint Barton, aka Hawkeye, the bow-wielding hero, was actually a bad guy. But by the following year he was a member of the Avengers, working with the team on and off over the years and even leading the West Coast Avengers branch. After various limited series, and one short-lived title, an Eisner Award–winning series by Matt Fraction and David Aja was released in 2012 featuring both the original, Clint Barton, and a new Hawkeye named Kate Bishop who took on the role when Barton was briefly dead (like many comic characters, he got better). Collected below in its entirety is the excellent series by Matt Fraction, which focuses on Clint when he's not on active duty with the Avengers. The character has also appeared in various animated series and in the Marvel Cinematic Universe where he is played by actor Jeremy Renner. The 2012 series was followed by two consecutive 2015 titles called All-New Hawkeye which were collected and the fifth and sixth volumes. These volumes were on YALSA's 2017 Great Graphic Novels for Teens selection list.

Vol. 1: My Life as a Weapon. 2013. 136pp. 978-0-7851-6562-0.
Vol. 2: Little Hits. 2013. 136pp. 978-0-7851-6563-7.
Vol. 3. L.A. Woman. 2014. 120pp. 978-0-7851-8390-7.
Vol. 4: Rio Bravo. 2015. 160pp. 978-0-7851-8531-4.
Vol. 5: All-New Hawkeye. 2015. 112pp. 978-0-7851-9403-3.
Vol. 6: Hawkeyes. 2016, 136pp. 978-0-7851-9946-5.
Omnibus. 2015. 552pp. 978-0-7851-9219-0, hardcover.

The Hulk

Created by **Stan Lee** and **Jack Kirby**. Marvel Comics, 2005– . 🎞 🖥
Irradiated with gamma ray particles after being exposed to a gamma bomb, Doctor Bruce Banner miraculously survived the gamma ray atomic blast and was amazingly transformed into something less than human but phenomenally strong. Nicknamed the "Hulk" by the military, Banner transforms into the green-skinned monster whenever he releases his repressed rage, making him one of the most powerful forces on the planet able to leap great distances and crush anything that stands in his way. At various times Banner's transformation into the Hulk has created variations of Hulks, each with a different psyche of sorts. Sometimes Banner's transformation releases a mindless brute with the mind of a child, a gray-colored "Joe Fixit" Hulk that is a semi-intelligent tough guy, as well as an intelligent "Professor" Hulk that retains Banner's intelligence. Though not a team player, the Hulk has been known to be an occasional member of such super-teams as the Avengers and the Defenders. The Hulk has been adapted many times in various video games, several animated series, and the hit series of live-action Marvel films in which the character of Bruce Banner is portrayed by Mark Ruffalo in the live-action films *The Avengers* (2012), *Avengers: Age of Ultron* (2015), and *Thor: Ragnarok* (2017).

Hulk Visionaries: Peter David. Written by **Peter David**. Illustrated by **Todd McFarlane**, **Erik Larsen**, **Gary Frank**, **Dale Keown**, and various. 2005–2011. T 🏃 ◎
A collection highlighting writer Peter David's contribution to the Jade Giant from his run on the monthly <u>Incredible Hulk</u> comic book series from 1986 to 1998. The collections also feature the artwork of Todd McFarlane, Gary Frank, Dale Keown, and more, and Peter David's stories have been regarded by many fans as the definitive treatment of the Hulk. In 1992, the work by Peter David and artist Dale Keown won an Eisner Award for Best Writer/Artist.

Vol. 1. 2005. 224pp. 978-0-7851-1541-0.   *Vol. 5.* 2008. 248pp. 978-0-7851-2757-4.
Vol. 2. 2005. 232pp. 978-0-7851-1878-7.   *Vol. 6.* 2009. 232pp. 978-0-7851-3762-7.
Vol. 3. 2006. 192pp. 978-0-7851-2095-7.   *Vol. 7.* 2010. 108pp. 978-0-7851-4457-1.
Vol. 4. 2007. 232pp. 978-0-7851-2096-4.   *Vol. 8.* 2011. 256pp. 978-0-7851-5603-1.

Incredible Hulk: Planet Hulk/World War Hulk/Incredible Hulks. Written by **Greg Pak**. Illustrated by **Carlo Pagulayan**, **Aaron Lopresti**, **Juan Santacruz**, **John Romita Jr.**, and various. Marvel Comics, 2007–2011.
A multi-arc storyline by writer Greg Pak that began with Planet Hulk is one of the most popular recent Hulk storylines. When the Hulk was deemed to

© 2016 Marvel Comics

be too dangerous to remain on Earth, he was transported outside the solar system by a rocket, but the ship accidentally crashed on a foreign planet named Sakaar. There the Hulk is enslaved and forced to fight in gladiator battles for the planet's leader, the Red King. The Hulk leads a rebellion against the Red King and falls in love with a warrior named Caiera, but before they can be happy, she dies in a nuclear explosion and the Hulk returns to Earth to seek revenge. Along the way the Hulk discovers that he had two sons from Caiera born out of the womb after she died, one a green Hulk-like beast named Skaar and one dark son named Hiro-Kala. As the Hulk's family grows, their problems get just as big as ever. Can the Hulks alongside She-Hulk—a daughter from a different dimension named Lyra—and Rick Jones defeat Hiro-Kala? No one said having a family would be easy!

Planet Hulk. 2008. 416pp. 978-0-7851-2012-4.
World War Hulk. 2008. 304pp. 978-0-7851-2596-9.
Skaar, Son of Hulk. 2009. 200pp. 978-0-7851-2714-7.
Planet Skaar. 2010. 192pp. 978-0-7851-2821-2.
Son of Banner. 2010. 144pp. 978-0-7851-4251-5.
Dark Son. 2011. 160pp. 978-07851-5001-5.
Heart of the Monster. 2011. 144pp. 978-0-7851-5631-4.
Planet Savage. 2011. 112pp. 978-0-7851-5159-3.
World War Hulks. 2011. 112pp. 978-0-7851-4548-6.
Fall of the Hulks. 2012. 512pp. 978-0-7851-6211-7.

Hulk: Future Imperfect. Written by **Peter David**. Illustrated by **George Pérez**. Marvel Comics, 2015. 160pp. 978-0-7851-9746-1. T ◉

© 2016 Marvel Comics

The Hulk is sent to the far future by his longtime friend Rick Jones to battle against the toughest foe he's ever faced: himself. The heroes of the world are long gone and the future is ruled by the psychotic but familiar green-skinned beast called the Maestro. When it comes to a battle of brawn and brains, the Hulk has finally met his match. How can the Hulk defeat the only person who knows himself better that he does? Also included is the short story "The End" where after mankind is extinct, the Hulk is the last remaining human on the planet and must confront his ultimate nemesis.

Immortal Iron Fist: The Complete Collection. Written by **Matt Fraction** and **Ed Brubaker** (Collection 1) and **Duane Swierczynski** (Collection 2). Illustrated by **David Aja** and various. Marvel Comics, 2013–2014. T 🏃📖

Danny Rand is a martial artist and wielder of a powerful mystical force called the Iron Fist, which allows him to focus his chi. In this popular series, the origin of the Iron Fist is revealed as Danny receives a sacred text called the Book of the Iron Fist by his predecessor before his is killed. Meanwhile, corruption is afoot as the Seven Cities of Heaven plan a secret attack on K'un-Lun, the mystical location where Danny received his Iron Fist powers. As Danny discovers more about the secret history of the Iron Fist power, the more his life is in danger from enemies all around him. The series won Ed Brubaker an Eisner for Best Writer in 2008. In the past, Iron Fist teamed up with Luke Cage (aka Power Man) as part of the Heroes for Hire (see later in this chapter). Some of his earliest appearances can be found in 2015's *Iron Fist Epic Collection: The Fury of Iron Fist* (978-0-7851-9164-3). Iron Fist appeared also in his own Netflix series in 2017 where he was played by Finn Jones.

Collection 1. 2013. 496pp. 978-0-7851-8542-0.
Collection 2. 2014. 496pp. 978-0-7851-8890-2.

Invincible. Written by **Robert Kirkman**. Illustrated by **Cory Walker** and **Ryan Ottley**. Image Comics, 2003– . T 🏅 ◎

© 2016 Robert Kirkman and Cory Walker

Mark Grayson, average teenage son, is going through some changes. His voice is changing, he's starting to get interested in girls, and . . . he's gained his father's super-hero powers! Just what can you do when you're the son of Omni-Man, the most powerful hero in the universe? Anything! Now he's following in his dad's footsteps living the life of schoolbooks, super-villains, and plenty of action as the hero known as Invincible. Soon after he learns that while his father is, as he told him, a "strange visitor from another planet," he is also helping to weaken Earth for a takeover by the Viltrumite race. Mark rejects his father and becomes a great hero saving the world from various menaces both alone and with other heroes. *Invincible* was briefly adapted into an animated TV show. The series has been collected into over 20 volumes (in which most of the subtitles are the names of television shows), a number of Ultimate Collections, three "Complete Libraries," and two Compendiums of over 1,000 pages each. Several related titles tied into the Invincible series have also been listed below. The collection *Invincible: The Ultimate Collection, Vol. 1* received recognition by YALSA's Quick Picks for Reluctant Readers committee in 2006.

Vol. 1: Family Matters. 2006. 120pp. 978-1-58240-711-1.
Vol. 2: Eight Is Enough. 2004. 128pp. 978-1-58240-347-2.
Vol. 3: Perfect Strangers. 2008. 144pp. 978-1-58240-793-7.
Vol. 4: Head of the Class. 2007. 168pp. 978-1-58240-778-4.
Vol. 5: The Facts of Life. 2005. 176pp. 978-1-58240-554-4.
Vol. 6: A Different World. 2006. 168pp. 978-1-58240-579-7.
Vol. 7: Three's Company. 2006. 144pp. 978-1-58240-656-5.
Vol. 8: My Favorite Martian. 2013. 128pp. 978-1-582-40683-1.
Vol. 9: Out of This World. 2008. 144pp. 978-1-582-40827-9.
Vol. 10: Who's the Boss? 2009. 160pp. 978-1-607-06013-0.
Vol. 11: Happy Days. 2009. 168pp. 978-1-607-06062-8.
Vol. 12: Still Standing. 2010. 168pp. 978-1-607-06166-3.
Vol. 13: Growing Pains. 2010. 144pp. 978-1-607-06251-6.

Vol. 14: The Viltrumite War. 2011. 196pp. 978-1-607-06367-4.
Vol. 15: Get Smart. 2012. 144pp. 978-1-607-06498-5.
Vol. 16: Family Ties. 2012. 136pp. 978-1-607-06579-1.
Vol. 17: What's Happening? 2013. 144pp. 978-1-607-06662-0.
Vol. 18: The Death of Everyone. 2013. 160pp. 978-160-706762-7.
Vol. 19: The War at Home. 2014. 144pp. 978-1-607-06856-3.
Vol. 20: Friends. 2014. 152pp. 978-1-6321-5043-1.
Vol. 21: Modern Family. 2015. 152pp. 978-1-63215-318-0.
Vol. 22: Reboot. 2016. 152pp. 978-1-63215-626-6.
Vol. 23: Full House. 2017. 152pp. 978-1-63215-888-8.

Ultimate Collection, 2005– .

Vol. 1. 2005. 400pp. 978-1-58240-500-1, hardcover.
Vol. 2. 2006. 352pp. 978-1-58240-594-0, hardcover.
Vol. 3. 2007. 336pp. 978-1-58240-763-0, hardcover.
Vol. 4. 2009. 336pp. 978-1-58240-989-4, hardcover.
Vol. 5. 2010. 336pp. 978-1-60706-116-8, hardcover.
Vol. 6. 2011. 336pp. 978-1-60706-360-5, hardcover.
Vol. 7. 2012. 384pp. 978-1-60706-509-8, hardcover.
Vol. 8. 2013. 336pp. 978-1-60706-680-4, hardcover.
Vol. 9. 2014. 336pp. 978-1-63215-032-5, hardcover.
Vol. 10. 2015. 336pp. 978-1-63215-494-1, hardcover.
Vol. 11. 2017. 336pp. 978-1-5343-0045-3. hardcover.

Complete Invincible Library, 2007– .

Vol. 1. 2007. 768pp. 978-1-58240-718-0, hardcover.
Vol. 2. 2010. 768pp. 978-1-60706-112-0, hardcover.
Vol. 3. 2011. 768pp. 978-1-60706-421-3, hardcover.

Invincible Compendium, 2011– .

Vol. 1. 2011. 1024pp. 978-1-60706-411-4.
Vol. 2. 2013. 1024pp. 978-1-60706-772-6.

Invincible Presents: Atom Eve & Rex Splode. Written by **Benito Cereno**. Illustrated by **Nate Bellegarde**. 2010. 144pp. 978-1-60706-255-4.

Invincible Universe. Written by **Phil Hester**. Illustrated by **Todd Nauck**. Image Comics, 2013–2014.

Vol. 1: On Deadly Ground. 2013. 144pp. 978-160-706-820-4.
Vol. 2. 2014. 144pp. 978-1-60-706-986-7.

Iron Man

Created by **Stan Lee**, **Jack Kirby**, and **Don Heck**. Marvel Comics, 1990– . T 🎬 🖥 🐾
Tony Stark has been known to be many things to many people, including billionaire, ladies' man, inventor, and owner of Stark Industries, the leading provider of some of the greatest technologies the world has even seen. Unknown to most, however, he is secretly best known as the golden-plated armored Avenger called Iron Man. Tony Stark suffered a severe chest injury during a kidnapping in which his captors

attempted to force him to build a weapon of mass destruction. Instead, Tony created an exoskeletal suit of armor that would help sustain his damaged heart and to free himself from captivity—and the high-tech hero Iron Man was born! Tony Stark created a front for a time that Iron Man was his own private bodyguard, but has since embraced his role. Recently going public with his identity, Tony Stark has entered a new world as one of the only heroes to reveal his identity to the world at large. Tony as Iron Man has served as one of the founding members of the super-team called the Avengers and to this day fights against high- and low-tech villains including the Mandarin, the dragon Fing-Fang-Foom, and Ultimo. Iron Man has been adapted many times in various video games, several animated series, and the hit series of live-action Marvel film where the character of Tony Stark is portrayed by Robert Downey Jr. in the live-action films *Iron Man* (2008), *Iron Man 2* (2010), *Iron Man 3* (2013), *The Avengers* (2012), *Avengers: Age of Ultron* (2015), and *Captain America: Civil War* (2016).

Iron Man

Marvel Comics, 2013– . T

Below are listed a variety of trade collections of the monthly Marvel Comics Iron Man series. *Stark Wars* collects the classic storyline where Tony learns his technology has been stolen against his knowledge and seeks to dismantle it even if it means fighting against the government. *Extremis* introduces a new danger to Iron Man which was also the focal point of the *Iron Man 3* film, and *Reboot* showcases the new Iron Man after the 2015 Secret Wars series.

Iron Man Epic Collection: Stark Wars. Written by **David Michelinie**. Illustrated by **Bob Layton**. Marvel Comics, 2015. 496pp. 978-0785192909.

Invincible Iron Man, Vol. 1: Reboot. Written by **Brian Michael Bendis**. Illustrated by **David Marquez**. Marvel Comics, 2016. 112pp. 978-0-7851-9520-7, hardcover.

Iron Man: Extremis. Written by **Warren Ellis**. Illustrated by **Adi Granov**. Marvel Comics, 2013. 160pp. 978-0-7851-8378-5.

Invincible Iron Man. Written by **Matt Fraction**. Illustrated by **Salvador Larroca**. Marvel Comics, 2008–2015. T 🎖 ◎

© 2016 Marvel Comics

Matt Fraction was the writer of the monthly comic book series The Invincible Iron Man from 2008 to 2012. The series received an Eisner Award in 2008 for Best New Series as well as recognition from YALSA on its Great Graphic Novels for Teens selection list in 2010.

Vol. 1: The Five Nightmares. 2008. 184pp. 978-0-7851-3460-2, hardcover; 2009. 184pp. 978-0-7851-3412-1.

Vol. 2: World's Most Wanted, part 1. 2009. 152pp. 978-0-7851-3828-0, hardcover; 2010. 152pp. 978-0-7851-3413-8.

Vol. 3: World's Most Wanted, part 2. 2010. 160pp. 978–0785139355, hardcover; 2011. 160pp. 978-0-7851-3685-9.

Vol. 4: Stark Disassembled. 2010. 136pp. 978-0-7851-4554-7; 2011. 136pp. 978-0-7851-3686-6.

Vol. 5: Stark Resilient, Book 1. 2010. 128pp. 978-0-7851-4555-4, hardcover; 2011. 128pp. 978-0-7851-4556-1.

Vol. 6: Stark Resilient, Book 2. 2011. 136pp. 978-0-7851-4834-0; 2011. 136pp. 978-0-7851-4835-7.

Vol. 7: My Monsters. 2011. 168pp. 978-0-7851-4836-4, hardcover; 2011. 168pp. 978-0-7851-4837-1.

Vol. 8: The Unfixable. 2011. 120pp. 978-0-7851-5322-1, hardcover; 2012. 120pp. 978-0-7851-5323-8.

Fear Itself. 2012. 144pp. 978-0-7851-5773-1, hardcover; 2012. 144pp. 978-0-7851-5774-8.

Vol. 9: Demon. 2012. 144pp. 978-0-7851-6046-5, hardcover; 2013. 144pp. 978-0-7851-6047-2.

Vol. 10: Long Way Down. 2012. 120pp. 978-0-7851-6048-9, hardcover; 2013. 120pp. 978-0-7851-6049-6.

Vol. 11: The Future. 2013. 152pp. 978-0-7851-6521-7, hardcover; 2013. 152pp. 978-0-7851-6522-4.

Omnibus, Vol. 1. 2010. 344pp. 978-0-7851-4295-9, hardcover.

Omnibus, Vol. 2. 2012. 408pp. 978-0-7851-4553-0, hardcover.

Longshot

Marvel Comics, 2013– .

On the run and with no memory of his identity at all, a blonde-haired hero, innocent in mind and heart, seems to also have a talent for luck. Nicknamed "Longshot" by those around him, he has the ability to read items and get a mental imprint of them as well as athletic skills of an acrobat. Little by little Longshot remembers part of his past and discovers that he's an artificially created being and a pawn of a ruthless spineless ruler named Mojo. With the aid of other heroes including Quark, Ricochet Rita, and the Sorcerer Supreme Doctor Strange, Longshot is out to take the fight back to Mojo to save the Earth and his own world no matter what it takes! In the book *Longshot Saves the Marvel Universe*, Longshot is over his head when he's targeted for death, but can Longshot turn his luck around and save the world when no one else can?

Longshot. Written by **Ann Nocenti**. Illustrated by **Arthur Adams**. Marvel Comics, 2013. 208pp. 978-0-7851-6711-2. T

© 2016 Marvel Comics

Longshot Saves the Marvel Universe. Written by **Christopher Hastings**. Illustrated by **Jacopo Camagni** and **Victor Calderon-Zurita**. Marvel Comics, 2014. 96pp. 978-0-7851-9012-7. T

Luke Cage

Power Man 🖥

One of the first African American super-heroes, Luke Cage was created at a time when the "Blaxploitation" genre was appearing in films. When Carl Lucas was wrongly sent to prison, he volunteered for a scientific experiment in order to get parole. When a racist guard sabotaged the experiment, there was an explosion and Lucas found himself with super-strength and steel-hard skin. Escaping, he made his way to New York City where he changed his name to Luke Cage and started a business of Hero for Hire (in the 1980s, actor and comics fan Nicholas Coppola would take "Cage" as his stage name after the character). He later teamed up with Iron Fist (see earlier in this chapter) in a shared book. Over the years Cage, going both by Power Man and by Luke Cage, has appeared in comics both solo and in the various incarnations of Heroes for Hire. Cage also has been on several Avengers teams, leading one of them. Cage is married to super-hero-turned-investigator Jessica Jones, and they have a daughter. Mike Colter played Luke Cage on the Jessica Jones television series and spun off into his own program in 2016. Below are various collections featuring Luke Cage over the years.

Marvel Masterworks Luke Cage: Hero for Hire, Vol. 1. Written by **Steve Englehart** and **Archie Goodwin**. Illustrated by **Billy Graham** and **George Tuska**. 2015. 336pp. 978-0-7851-9180-3. T

Power Man & Iron Fist Epic Collection. Written by **Jo Duffy**, **Chris Claremont**, and various. Illustrated by **Trevor Von Eeden**, **Kerry Gammill**, **John Byrne**, and various. T

> *Heroes for Hire*. 2015. 448pp. 978-0-7851-9296-1.
> *Revenge*. 2016. 472pp. 978-1-309-90013-7.

Luke Cage: Second Chances. Written by **Marc McLauirn** and various. Illustrated by **Gordon Purcell**, **Dwayne Turner**, and various. Marvel Comics. T

> *Vol. 1*. 2015. 978-0-7851-9298-5.
> *Vol. 2*. 2016. 978-0-7851-95007-8.

Luke Cage, Iron Fist, & The Heroes for Hire. Written by **John Ostrander**, **James Felder**, and **Jamie Campos**. Illustrated by **Joe Bennett** and **Pasqual Ferry**. Marvel Comics, 2016. 312pp. 978-1-309-90194-3. T

Power Man and Iron Fist Vol. 1: The Boys Are Back in Town. Written by **David Walker**. Illustrated by **Sandford Greene**. 2016. 136pp. 978-1-309-90114-1. T

Miracleman. Written by **Alan Moore** (*Books 1–3*) and **Neil Gaiman** (*Book 1: The Golden Age*). Illustrated by **Alan Davis**, **Rick Veitch**, **Chuck Austen**, **John Totleben**, and **Mark Buckingham**. Marvel Comics, 2014– . M ◎

> One of the classic series from acclaimed writer Alan Moore. Reporter Michael Moran discovers that he's destined for much more as once again he is imbued with the powers of a god and once again becomes the hero known as Miracleman. Originally published in the United Kingdom in 1954 as Marvelman by creator Mick Anglo, Marvelman was made as a knock-off Fawcett Comics Captain Marvel series (see the section of *Shazam* in this chapter). Instead of shouting "Shazam!" the hero Micky Moran would say the word "Kimota" to transform into Marvelman. The cast was also similar, featuring Young Marvelman and Kid Marvelman instead of Captain Marvel's Captain Marvel Jr.

© 2016 Marvel Comics

and Mary Marvel. The story was revised with a name change to Miracleman as a dark post-modern deconstructionist look at super-heroes by Moore and later by Neil Gaiman. The series was long out of print for over two decades but finally reissued by Marvel Comics. Writer Neil Gaiman took over the series, and his story arc has never been completed until now. The series is still being reprinted by Marvel Comics. At Moore's request, he is listed as "The Original Writer" in the credits of the book, and it is shown that way in Worldcat and other library catalogs.

Book 1: A Dream of Flying. 2014. 176pp. 978-0-7851-5462-4, hardcover.
Book 2: The Red King Syndrome. 2014. 224pp. 978-0-7851-5464-8, hardcover.
Book 3: Olympus. 2015. 328pp. 978-0-7851-5466-2, hardcover.
Book 1: The Golden Age. 2016. 192pp. 978-0-7851-9055-4, hardcover.

Mockingbird. Written by **Roy Thomas**, **Mike Friedrich**, **Steven Grant**, **Mark Gruenwald,** and **Chelsea Cain**. Illustrated by **Herb Trimpe**, **Barry Windsor-Smith**, **John Buscema**, **Gil Kane**, and **Kate Niemczyk**. Marvel Comics, 2016– . T 🎖

Bobbi Morse is a special agent of SHIELD—codename Mockingbird, she's a brilliant scientific intellect as well as training in the martial arts, she's a force to be reckoned with. A former Avenger as well, there's nothing that Bobbi can't do with the aid of her battle staves. The collection *Mockingbird: Bobbi Morse, Agent of S.H.I.E.L.D* includes her first appearance and key adventures since the 1971 to today. The new series collection *I Can Explain* by writer Chelsea Cain and illustrator Kate Niemczyk was recognized by YALSA as a Great Graphic Novel for Teens in 2017. Please feel free to ask her about her feminist agenda. The character of Bobbi Morse is portrayed by Adrianne Palicki in the *Agents of S.H.I.E.L.D*. TV series.

Mockingbird: Bobbi Morse, Agent of S.H.I.E.L.D. 2016. 440pp. 978-1-302-90086-1, hardcover.
Vol. 1: I Can Explain. 2016. 136pp. 978-1-302-90122-6.
Vol. 2: My Feminist Agenda. 2017. 112pp. 978-1-302-90123-3.

Ms. Marvel. Written by **G. Willow Wilson**. Illustrated by **Jacob Wyatt**, **Adrian Alphona**, and **Takeshi Miyazawa**. Marvel Comics, 2014– . T 🎖 ◎

© 2016 Marvel Comics

When transforming Terragen Mists are released in the air with the intent to release long-dormant Inhuman powers, a Muslim American teenager named Kamala Khan finds that she has shape-shifting abilities after she was exposed. A fan of Carol Danvers, the original Ms. Marvel (and recently renamed Captain Marvel, see later in this chapter), she takes on the Ms. Marvel identity as homage to her favorite hero. Now all Kamala has to do is to balance school, family, and a super-hero gig on the side as well! The original 2014 series has been very popular and won the Hugo Award. The first five volumes have also been recognized by YALSA selection lists as Great Graphic Novels for Teens in 2015, 2016, and 2017. Volume 5 marks the start of the 2016 series. The hardcover collections collect the first four volumes of the series so far.

Vol. 1: No Normal. 2014. 120pp. 978-0-7851-9021-9.
Vol. 2: Generation Why. 2015. 136pp. 978-0-7851-9022-6.
Vol. 3: Crushed. 2015. 112pp. 978-0-7851-9227-5.
Vol. 4: Last Days. 2015. 120pp. 978-0-7851-9736-2.
Vol. 5: Super Famous. 2016. 136pp. 978-0-7851-9611-2.
Vol. 6: Civil War II. 2016. 136pp. 978-0-7851-9612-9.
Vol. 1. 2015. 256pp. 978-0-7851-9828-4, hardcover.
Vol. 2. 2016. 232pp. 978-0-7851-9836-9, hardcover.
Vol. 3. 2017. 272pp. 978-1-302-90361-9, hardcover.
Ms. Marvel Omnibus, Vol. 1. 2016. 488pp. 978-1-4215-9347-0, hardcover.

Mudman. Written and Illustrated by **Paul Grist**. Image Comics, 2012. 144pp. 978-1-60706-580-7. T

High school student Owen has discovered he's one of the messiest super-heroes in all of England when he gets mud-based powers tied into his seaside town off the coast of the United Kingdom. Owen's police detective dad might just need Owen's help too as a simple investigation of an abandoned home off the coast discovers that it is really a sanctuary for high-profile bank robbers. Can Owen adjust to the weirdest powers of all and also find a way to help his dad?

Nightwing. Written by **Kyle Higgins**. Illustrated by **Eddy Barrows**. DC Comics, 2011–2014. T

© 2016 DC Comics

Dick Grayson was the first person to take up the role of Robin, the light-hearted sidekick of Batman. After years of following in the Dark Knight's footsteps, a now grown-up Dick Grayson has gone on to be known as Nightwing. In the New 52 reset, Dick Grayson still fights crime in Gotham City. When the Haley's Circus tour comes to Gotham, Dick decides to go back to his roots as a boy and rejoins the circus that he and his parents once called home. Known as The Flying Graysons, Dick and his parents were trapeze artists until their lives were cut short and Dick was taken in by Bruce Wayne as his ward. Now Dick rejoins the circus and discovers there's an air of mystery and intrigue that awaits him even at his old home. Soon after, Dick relocated to Chicago where he discovers the man who killed his parents is still alive and under a new identity. The series ended in 2014 in comic book form with a new series titled Grayson in which Dick Grayson goes undercover for Batman as a secret agent spy for the organization known as Spyral (see Grayson series in this chapter). A new Nightwing series began in 2016, with collections beginning in 2017.

Vol. 1: Traps and Trapezes. 2012. 160pp. 978-1-4012-3705-9.
Vol. 2: Night of the Owls. 2013. 144pp. 978-1-4012-4027-1.
Vol. 3: Death of the Family. 2013. 176pp. 978-1-4012-4413-2.
Vol. 4: Second City. 2014. 144pp. 978-14012-4630-3.
Vol. 5: Setting Son. 2015. 200pp. 978-1-4012-5011-9.

Patsy Walker, A.K.A. Hellcat. Written by **Kate Leth**. Illustrated by **Brittney Williams**. Marvel Comics, 2016– . T 🎋 🖥

Patsy Walker's life is definitely anything but boring. A natural talent at gymnastics, she longed to be a superhero. Serving both as a member of the Avengers and Defenders, Patsy wears an ability-enhancing costume that formerly belonged to Greer Grant Nelson, the former masked adventuress the Cat, and Walker took on the name of Hellcat. The current series is light-hearted in tone and features Patsy as she tries to establish a job agency for superpowered people while trying to juggle a dating life, a secret identity, and barely being able to pay the rent. The first volume was recognized by YALSA as a Great Graphic Novel for Teens title in 2017. Rachael Taylor plays a version of the character, Trish Walker, in the Netflix original series *Jessica Jones* which premiered in 2015.

Vol. 1. Hooked on a Feline. 2016. 136pp. 978-1-302-90035-9.
Vol. 2: Don't Stop Me-Ow. 2017. 136pp. 978-1-302-90036-6.
Vol. 3: Careless Whisker(s). 2017. 112pp. 978-1-302-90662-7.

Phantom Jack: The Nowhere Man Agenda. Written by **Mike SanGiacomo**. Illustrated by various. IDW Publishing, 2010. 114pp. 978-1-60010-710-8. O

Jack Baxter is a news reporter like no other—he has the secret power to turn himself invisible. Using his "fade" powers for personal gain, he's risen to the top of the newspaper world winning accolades for his daring reporting, when in actuality he's had an upper hand all along. Reluctant to play the role of hero, he must see if he's up to the task fighting against the adversary called the Nowhere Man.

The Punisher

Marvel Comics, 2011– . T-M 🖥

The vigilante anti-hero of the Marvel Comics universe. Originally created in 1974, he has remained an enduring character in the Marvel Comics universe. Special Black Ops specialist Frank Castle lost his entire family when they were assassinated after witnessing a Mafia-issued murder in Central Park. The only one to survive the experience, the former Vietnam vet fell back on his wartime experience as a Marine Captain, focusing his rage in order to seek revenge on organized crime for the death of his wife and his children. Frank created a vigilante identity called the Punisher, a fearful vigilante that shows no mercy on the criminals. Swearing a bloody vengeance on organized crime, Frank now wears an all-black Kevlar uniform with a large image of a skull on his chest and is a master in armed and unarmed combat. Armed to the teeth with the latest high-tech weaponry and utilizing the deadliest of force, the Punisher will never rest until he's killed those responsible for his family's death. Note that some of the titles are for more mature readers due to extreme content. Though the Punisher has appeared in mostly forgettable films, recently the character has appeared in the Netflix <u>Daredevil</u> series' 2016 second season which led to his own show in 2017. A new Punisher series began in 2016 by Becky Cloonan and Steve Dillon.

Punisher: Circle of Blood. Written by **Steven Grant**. Illustrated by **Mike Zeck**. 2011. 176pp. 978-0-7851-5785-4. T

The Punisher: Welcome Back, Frank. Written by **Garth Ennis**. Illustrated by **Steve Dillon**. 2011. 288pp. 978-0-7851-5716-8. O ◎

Punisher MAX: The Complete Collection. Written by **Garth Ennis**. Illustrated by **Darick Robertson**, **Lewis Larosa**, and **Leandro Fernandez**. 2016– . M

Vol. 1. 2016. 424pp. 978-1-302-90015-1.
Vol. 2. 2016. 440pp. 978-1-302-90016-8.
Vol. 3. 2016. 448pp. 978-1-309-90187-5.

The Punisher (2014 series). Written by **Nathan Edmondson**. Illustrated by **Mitch Gerads**. 2014–2015. O

Vol. 1: Black and White. 2014. 136pp. 978-0-7851-5443-3.
Vol. 2: Border Crossing. 2015. 160pp. 978-0-7851-5444-0.
Vol. 3: Last Days. 2015. 176pp. 978-0-7851-9254-1.

Robin

The Boy Wonder. 2006– . 🎬 🎮 🖥

The Boy Wonder sidekick to Batman, the mantle of Robin has been worn by many young men and a few good women, too. Dick Grayson, Jason Todd, Tim Drake, and most recently Damian Wayne have all taken on the responsibility of wearing the mask, sometimes at the cost of their very lives. The main focus of this listing here is on the third and fourth Robin, Tim Drake and Damian Wayne, the son of Bruce Wayne/Batman, as they fight crime in Gotham City alongside Batman while tackling homework and a teenage social life. The heroes have appeared in numerous spin-off movies and TV shows as well as video games over the years, including titles such as LEGO Batman series of games and the Batman: Arkham Asylum series of titles.

Robin the Boy Wonder. DC Comics, 2006– . T

There have been many who have taken up the mantle of Robin, the Boy Wonder and crime-fighting sidekick to Batman; Tim Drake was the first to feature his own stand-alone series and is a fan favorite. The collections were published by DC Comics and appeared as miniseries collections and from the ongoing monthly comic book series, too. Collections are highlights from the first books in the series as well as other recommended stories published after 2006 through the New 52 revamp in 2011. Tim Drake has also used the name Red Robin in his quest to find Batman who had been lost in time.

Robin, 1st series. Written by **Chuck Dixon** and **Alan Grant**. Illustrated by **Norm Breyfogle** and **Tom Lyle**. DC Comics, 2015– . T ◎

© 2016 DC Comics

Originally published in 1989, Tim Drake became Robin shortly following the "death" of Jason Todd, the second Robin. The collections listed here reprint the original issues of Tim Drake's introduction and his eventual training by Batman as well as other martial arts schools to hone his training. The series was light in tone and was regarded by many at the time to be the best book featuring a young super-hero. DC Comics has recently republished the books in 2015.

Vol. 1: Reborn. 2015. 296pp. 978-1-4012-5857-3.
Vol. 2: Triumphant. 2016. 360pp. 978-1-4012-6089-7.
Vol. 3: Solo. 2016. 304pp. 978-1-4012-6362-1.

Robin titles from 2006 to 2012.
Included here are the Tim Drake *Robin* titles featured after those listed in the first edition of this book. The series eventually was renamed <u>Red Robin</u> but still featured Tim Drake in the lead role as he searched for clues to find a missing Batman/Bruce Wayne who had been lost in time.

Robin (2006–2009). Written by **Bill Willingham**, **Adam Beechen**, **Fabian Nicieza**, and **Chuck Dixon**. Illustrated by **Damion Scott**, **Giuseppe Camuncoli**, **Scott McDaniel**, **Pop Mhan**, and **Freddie Williams**. DC Comics, 2006–2009.

© 2016 DC Comics

Days of Fire and Madness. 2006. 144pp. 978-1-4012-0911-7.
To Kill a Bird. 2006. 144pp. 978-1-4012-0909-4.
Teenage Wasteland. 2007. 208pp. 978-1-4012-1480-7.
Wanted. 2007. 144pp. 978-1-4012-1225-4.
The Big Leagues. 2008. 128pp. 978-1-4012-1673-3.
Violent Tendencies. 2008. 160pp. 978-1-4012-1988-8.
Search for a Hero. 2009. 208pp. 978-1-4012-2310-6.

Red Robin. Written by **Christopher Yost** and **Fabian Nicieza**. Illustrated by **Ramon Bachs**, **Marcus To**, and **Ray McCarthy**. DC Comics, 2010–2012.

Vol. 1: The Grail. 2010. 128pp. 978-1-4012-2619-0.
Vol. 2: Collision. 2010. 192pp. 978-1-4012-2883-5.
Vol. 3: Hit List. 2011. 128pp. 978-1-4012-3165-1.
Vol. 4: 7 Days of Death. 2012. 208pp. 978-1-4012-3364-8.

Robin: Son of Batman, 2nd series. Written and Illustrated by **Patrick Gleason**. DC Comics, 2016. T

Damian Wayne, the current Robin, has a dark past. The son of Batman and Talia al Ghul, he was raised by his mother to lead the vicious League of Assassins—a ruthless army created to help usher in world domination. Now, Damian is free of his past and ready to atone for his past sins by righting the wrongs of his vicious past. For other stories featuring Damian Wayne, please look at the Batman section of this chapter under the listings for Grant Morrison's *Batman* stories and the <u>Batman and Robin</u> series by Grant Morrison and Peter Tomasi.

Vol. 1: Year of Blood. 2016. 176pp. 978-1-4012-6155-9, hardcover. 978-1-4012-6479-6.

Vol. 2: Dawn of the Demons. 2016. 176pp. 978-1-4012-6481-9, hardcover. 978-1-4012-6789-6.

We Are Robin. Written by **Lee Bermejo**. Illustrated by **Rob Haynes** and **Khary Randolph**. DC Comics, 2016. T 🎗

When Gotham City needs them, teenagers from the city rise to the call and keep the peace. Adopting the "R" they are all Robins and together they are ready to make a difference. The first volume was recognized by YALSA's Great Graphic Novels for Teens 2017 selection list.

Vol. 1: The Vigilante Business. 2016. 160pp. 978-1-4012-5982-2.
Vol. 2. Jokers. 2016. 152pp. 978-1-4012-6490-1.

The Rocketeer

Written and Illustrated by **Dave Stevens** and various. IDW Publishing, 2009– . T 🎬

© 2016 Dave Stevens & IDW Publishing

Set in the late 1930s, test pilot Cliff Secord discovered a top-secret experimental bullet-shaped jetpack hidden in the seat of his stunt plane. The engine can go over 200 miles per hour and seems like manna from Heaven as an answer to Cliff's prayers for the upcoming stunt show. With his pal Peevy, he designs a futuristic helmet, and the Rocketeer is born. Now a daring-do hero with a heart of gold and a nifty jetpack, Cliff dons the rocketpack into harm's way no matter what the cost. The original series was created by the late Dave Stevens. Since then, IDW Publishing has relaunched a new <u>Rocketeer</u> series inspired by Dave Stevens's work and written and illustrated by some of the best in the comic book industry, including Mark Waid, Stan Sakai, and Peter David. Highlights include the story *Cargo of Doom* which is an unofficial tie-in to the classic 1933 *King Kong* film and the *Rocketeer/Spirit* crossover. The graphic novel inspired the 1991 Disney cult movie.

The Rocketeer: The Complete Adventures. Written and Illustrated by **Dave Stevens**. 2009. 144pp. 978-1-60010-538-8, hardcover; 2015. 148pp. 978-1-63140-227-2.

Rocketeer Adventures. Written and Illustrated by various. 2011–2012.

Vol. 1. 2011. 128pp. 978-1-61377-034-4.
Vol. 2. 2012. 136pp. 978-1-61377-401-4.

Cargo of Doom. Written by **Mark Waid**. Illustrated by **Chris Samnee**. 2013. 136pp. 978-1-61377-565-3.

Hollywood Horror. Written by **Roger Landridge**. Illustrated by **J. Bone**. 2013. 104pp. 978-1-61377-686-5.

Rocketeer/Spirit: Pulp Friction. Written by **Mark Waid**. Illustrated by **Paul Smith**. 2014. 104pp. 978-1-61377-881-4.

At War! Vol. 1. Written by **Marc Guggenheim**. Illustrated by **Dave Bullock**. 2016. 132pp. 978-1-63140-584-6.

The Shadow Hero. Written by **Gene Luen Yang**. Illustrated by **Sonny Liew**. First Second Books, 2014. 176pp. 978-1-59643-697-8. T 🎖 ◎

© 2016 Gene Luen Yang/
First Second Books

The secret origin of one of the first Chinese super-heroes called the Green Turtle. Created in 1944 by artist Chu Hing, the Green Turtle first appeared in the pages of Rural Home Publishing's Blazing Comics. Now decades later, witness the origin of the costumed hero. Hank Chu is a mild-mannered Chinese American teenager growing up in a fictional 1930s Chinatown. Hank wants nothing more than to work in his family's grocery store, but his mother has more ambitious plans. She wants him to embody the excitement of their new country: she wants him to become a super-hero. When tragedy strikes, Hank finds that he may be a reluctant hero, but destiny has something else in store for him! The book was recognized by YALSA as a Great Graphic Novels for Teens title in 2015 as well as a Popular Paperback for Young Adults title in 2016.

Silk. Written by **Robbie Thompson**. Illustrated by **Stacey Lee**. Marvel Comics, 2015– . T
The day that Peter Parker was bitten by a radioactive spider, little did anyone realize that the spider also bit one more individual—a girl named Cindy Moon. Bitten on her leg by the dying spider, she also gained superhuman strength, speed, agility, and the ability to spin webs. Now free from a bunker that was to protect her from the villainous Morlun, she is out on her own taking down bad guys and making a name for herself as Silk whether Peter Parker (aka Spider-Man) approves or her tactics or not!
Vol. 0: The Life and Times of Cindy Moon. 2015. 160pp. 978-0-7851-9704-1.
Vol. 1: Sinister. 2016. 144pp. 978-0-7851-9957-1.
Vol. 2: The Negative. 2017. 136pp. 978-0-7851-9958-8.
Vol. 3: The Clone Conspiracy. 136pp. 978-1-302-90593-4.

Spider-Girl. Written by **Tom DeFalco**. Illustrated by **Pat Olliffe** and **Ron Frenz**. Marvel Comics, 2004–2010. T
Set in an alternate future in which May "Mayday" Parker, the daughter of Peter Parker and Mary Jane Watson-Parker, finds that she's inherited her father's powers and sets out to save the day as Spider-Girl. Like her father before her, May finds that her great powers come at a great price as she's constantly under threat by the next generation of

Spider-Man foes including Ladyhawk, the Kingpin of Crime, Lady Octopus, Mr. Nobody, and Crazy Eight. How will May be able to balance school, a social life, and a night life of fighting villains and worst enemies of all—her parents.

Vol. 1: Legacy. 2004. 144pp. 978-0-7851-1441-3.
Vol. 2: Like Father, Like Daughter. 2004. 144pp. 978-0-7851-1657-8.
Vol. 3: Avenging Allies. 2005. 152pp. 978-0-7851-1658-5.
Vol. 4: Turning Point. 2005. 152pp. 978-0-7851-1871-8.
Vol. 5: Endgame. 2006. 144pp. 978-0-7851-2034-6.
Vol. 6: Too Many Spiders!. 2006. 144pp. 978-0-7851-2156-5.
Vol. 7: Betrayed. 2006. 144pp. 978-0-7851-2157-2.
Vol. 8: Duty Calls. 2007. 144pp. 978-07851-2495-5.
Vol. 9: Secret Lives. 2007. 160pp. 978-07851-2602-7.
Vol. 10: Season of the Serpent. 144pp. 2009. 978-0-7851-3213-4.
Vol. 11: Marked for Death. 2009. 144pp. 978-0-785137412.
Vol. 12: Games Villains Play. 2010. 136pp. 978–0785144823.

Amazing Spider-Girl

Vol. 1: Whatever Happened to the Daughter of Spider-Man? 2007. 160pp. 978-0-7851-2341-5.
Vol. 2: Along Comes Carnage. 2007. 136pp. 978-0785123422.
Vol. 3: Mind Games. 2008. 160pp. 978-0785125587.
Vol. 4: Brand New May. 2008. 136pp. 978-0-7851-2974-5.
Vol. 5: Maybreak. 2009. 160pp. 978-0-7851-3187-8.

Spectacular Spider-Girl, 2010.

Vol. 1: Who Killed Gwen Reilly? 2010. 216pp. 978-0-7851-4319-2.
Vol. 2: The Last Stand. 2010. 200pp. 978-0-7851-4899-9.

Spider-Gwen. Written by **Jason Latour**. Illustrated by **Robbi Rodriguez**. Marvel Comics, 2015– . T

Peter Parker's first love Gwen Stacy may have died at the hands of the Green Goblin in the real Marvel Comics universe, but this Gwen isn't like the Gwen of old! On the alternate Earth-65, Peter Parker was never bitten by a radioactive spider, and instead it was Gwen who was bitten and who uses her newfound abilities to fight crime as the Spider-Woman of her dimension!

Vol. 0: Most Wanted? 2015. 112pp. 978-0-7851-9773-7.
Vol. 1: Greater Power. 2016. 136pp. 978-0-7851-9959-5.
Vol. 2: Castle. 2016. 136pp. 978-0-7851-9960-1.
Vol. 3: Long Distance. 2017. 112pp. 978-1-302-90310-7.

Starman. Written by **James Robinson**. Illustrated by **Tony Harris** et al. DC Comics, 1996–2013. T 🎎 ◎

© 2016 DC Comics

Jack Knight is the younger son of the Golden Age hero known as Starman, but he couldn't care less about his father's alter-ego and proud history. He wants nothing to do with his father's legacy and considers it a job for his older brother, David. When David is killed by the son of an old foe of his father called The Mist, Jack takes up his father's cosmic rod and in time learns to proudly carry on his family's legacy as the guardian of Opal City. The series also boasts a rich supporting cast that includes others who bore the Starman identity and villain turned occasional anti-hero the Shade. The Omnibuses collect the entire series as well as several related comic books include the original Shade limited series. A second Shade limited series has also been collected. The older collection *Volume 3: A Wicked Inclination* includes the 1997 Best Serialized Story Eisner Award–winning story "Sand & Stars" (reprinted in *Omnibus, Vol. 2*) and the collection *Volume 1: Sins of the Father* (reprinted in *Omnibus, Vol. 1*) received recognition by YALSA's Popular Paperbacks for Young Adults committee in 2004.

Omnibus, Vol. 1. 2008. 448pp. 978-1-4012-1699-3, hardcover.
Omnibus, Vol. 2. 2009. 416pp. 978-1-401221942, hardcover.
Omnibus, Vol. 3. 2009. 432pp. 978-1-401222840, hardcover.
Omnibus, Vol. 4. 2010. 432pp. 978-1-401225964, hardcover.
Omnibus, Vol. 5. 2010. 464pp. 978-1-401228897, hardcover.
Omnibus, Vol. 6. 2011. 544pp. 978-1-4012-3044-9, hardcover.
The Shade. 2013. 280pp. 978-1-4012-3782-0.

Supergirl

DC Comics, 2012– . T 🖥

© 2016 DC Comics

Kara Zor-El, the true cousin of Superman, came to Earth as a young adult. Gifted with powers similar to Superman due to the proximity to a yellow sun, Supergirl has adopted Earth as her home. Her first appearance in comic books was in *Action Comics #252* in 1959 and is now more popular than ever thanks in part to a new TV series starring Melissa Benoist that debuted in 2015. The hero had a slightly tweaked origin story after the debut of the New 52 relaunch of all their main titles in 2011. Some volumes of the 2011 series tie in with the Red Lanterns series (see later in this chapter). After the 2016 "Rebirth" event, the series was relaunched yet again from creators Steve Orlando and Brian Ching. Other collections with various incarnations of Supergirl also came out in 2016.

Supergirl (2005 series). Written by **Jeph Loeb**, **Joe Kelly**, and various. Illustrated by **Michael Turner, Adam Archer**, and various.

Vol. 1: The Girl of Steel. 2016. 302pp. 978-1-4012-6093-4.
Vol. 2: Breaking the Chain. 2016. 727pp. 978-1-4012-6467-3.

Supergirl (New 52, 2011 series). Written by **Michael Green, Michael Alan Nelson Mike Johnson and various**. Illustrated by **Mahmud Asrar and others**. 2012–2015.

Vol. 1: Last Daughter of Krypton. 2012. 160pp. 978-1-4012-3680-9.
Vol. 2: Girl in the World. 2013. 144pp. 978-1-4012-4087-5.
Vol. 3: Sanctuary. 2014. 192pp. 978-1-4012-4318-0.
Vol. 4: Out of the Past. 2014. 168pp. 978-1-4012-4700-3.
Vol. 5: Red Daughter of Krypton. 2015. 256pp. 978-1-4012-5051-5.
Vol. 6: Crucible. 2015. 192pp. 978-1-4012-5541-1.

Tiger & Bunny. Written by **Sunrise** and **Masakazu Katsura**. Illustrated by **Mizuki Sakakibara**. VIZ Media, 2013–2015. 🏃 T. Japanese manga. あ

Based on the popular anime series, *Tiger & Bunny* is about two corporate-owned super-heroes, the veteran Kotetsu T. "Wild Tiger" Kaburagi and the rookie Barnaby "Bunny" Brooks Jr., who are forced by their sponsors to work together. This was selected as one of YALSA's Great Graphic Novels for Teens. The Comic Anthology collections collect a wide variety of humorous short stories by a wide variety of manga creators. The Beginning collections adapt the first anime film.

Vol. 1. 2013. 168pp. 978-1-4215-5561-4.
Vol. 2. 2013. 200pp. 978-1-4215-5562-1.
Vol. 3. 2013. 180pp. 978-1-4215-5563-8.
Vol. 4. 2014. 180pp. 978-1-4215-6235-3.
Vol. 5. 2014. 192pp. 978-1-4215-6946-8.
Vol. 6. 2015. 162pp. 978-1-4215-7680-0.
Vol. 7. 2015. 178pp. 978-1-4215-7903-0.
Vol. 8. 2015. 154pp. 978-1-4215-8173-6.
Vol. 9. 2016. 176pp. 978-1-4215-8958-9.
The Beginning, Side A. 2013. 160pp. 978-1-4215-6075-5.
Comic Anthology, Vol. 1. 2013. 324pp. 978-1-4215-5559-1.
Comic Anthology, Vol. 2. 2013. 372pp. 978-1-4215-5560-7.

Winter Soldier: The Complete Collection. Written by **Ed Brubaker**. Illustrated by **Butch Guice** and **Michael Lark**. Marvel Comics, 2014. 344pp. 978-0-7851-9065-3. T

Once he was known as Bucky, youthful sidekick to Captain America, but now James Buchanan Barnes is back in the role of the super-spy known as the Winter Soldier. The Winter Solider teams up with the Black Widow to track down ex-Russian sleeper agents that have awakened and are threatening to cause an all-out war with Latveria, the country ruled by Doctor Doom. Played by Sebastian Stan, the character has appeared in several movies including *Captain America: The Winter Solider* and *Captain America: Civil War.*

© 2016 Marvel Comics

Wolverine

Marvel Comics, 2006– . T 🏃 🎬 🖥 🎮

The enigmatic anti-hero known as Wolverine first appeared in the pages of *The Incredible Hulk* #181 in 1974 and since that time has become one of the

© 2016 Marvel Comics

most popular comic book characters ever. One of the toughest mutants on the planet, the man known as Logan is the best at what he does, but what he does isn't very nice. Born as James Howlett in the late 19th century, he's been gifted with a mutant healing factor and sharp retractable claws, and his entire bone structure is laced with adamantium, the hardest-known metal substance on the planet. All three of these factors help to make Wolverine a one-mutant fighting force. One of the most popular of the X-Men characters, he has appeared in a significant number of titles, both as the lead and as a team member. As of 2016, Logan was killed off in the series The Death of Wolverine, included below. Currently a female clone of Logan, known as X-23, has taken over the mantle of Wolverine . . . for now. Also, a time-displaced Logan from the future is stuck in the present as well in the new Old Man Logan series. Wolverine has appeared in many X-Men-related animated series as well as multiple video games. Actor Hugh Jackman has played the hero in many X-Men live-action films as well as three Wolverine movies. Listed below are recommended collections of graphic novel titles featuring the famous X-Man and Avenger. The titles tend to be collected editions of a variety of storylines from the ongoing Wolverine comic book series and various miniseries and are sorted by release date of the graphic novels. There have been many fantastic Wolverine stories published, and many others can be found at Marvel Comics' web site.

All-New Wolverine. Written by **Tom Taylor**. Illustrated by **David Lopez**. Marvel Comics, 2016– . T

Once she was known as X-23, created to be a killing machine. Thanks to her training with her master, the late Logan, Laura is out of that dark place. Now that Logan is dead, Laura takes up the mantle of Wolverine in this first collection of an ongoing series. Volume one was on YALSA's 2017 Great Graphic Novels for Teens selection list.

Vol. 1: The Four Sisters. 2016. 136pp. 978-0-7851-9652-5.
Vol. 2: Civil War II. 2016. 136pp. 978-0-7851-9653-2.
Vol. 3: Enemy of the State II. 2017.136pp. 978-1-302-90290-2.

Wolverine. Written by **Chris Claremont**. Illustrated by **Frank Miller**. 2013, revised edition. 144pp. 978-0-7851-8383-9. ◉

In the first-ever Wolverine miniseries, Logan travels to Japan to protect Lady Mariko Yashida, a daughter of a crime lord and the woman he loves. As his honor is tested, Logan must follow the code of the Samurai and protect Mariko from the attacks of the Hand, a secret society of ninja.

Wolverine by Jason Aaron: The Complete Collection. Written by **Jason Aaron**. Illustrated by **Esad Ribic**, **Yanick Paquette**, **C.P. Smith**, **Ron Garney**, and various. Marvel Comics, 2013–2014. O

Writer Jason Aaron's run from the Wolverine monthly series from the mid-2000s is collected in a massive complete collection.

Vol. 1. 2013. 392pp. 978-0-7851-8541-3.
Vol. 2. 2014. 320pp. 978-0-7851-8576-5.
Vol. 3. 2014. 456pp. 978-0-7851-8908-4.
Vol. 4. 2014. 408pp. 978-0-7851-8909-1.

Wolverine by Larry Hama and Marc Silvestri. Written by **Larry Hama** with **Walter Simonson** and **Peter David**. Illustrated by **Marc Silvestri** with **Mike Mignola**. Marvel Comics, 2013–2014. T

A collection of the extremely popular collection of stories by fan-favorite writer Larry Hama and illustrator Marc Silvestri featuring Wolverine against some of his deadliest opponents. The collection also features a short story by Walter Simonson and Mike Mignola.

Vol. 1. 2013. 280pp. 978-0-7851-8451-5.
Vol. 2. 2014. 280pp. 978-0-7851-8871-1.

Wolverine by Mark Millar Omnibus. Written by **Mark Millar**. Illustrated by various. Marvel Comics, 2013. 576pp. 978-0-7851-6796-9, hardcover.

© 2016 Marvel Comics

A collection featuring the popular writer Mark Millar. When Wolverine is brainwashed to be an agent of evil, he's a force to be reckoned with. When Wolverine is finally captured and deprogrammed, Wolverine declares vengeance on those who tormented him. Also the collection includes the original *Old Man Logan* story created by Mark Millar where a Logan 50 years in the future lives in a world where the heroes have all but died.

Wolverine: Old Man Logan. Written by **Jeff Lemire**. Illustrated by **Andrea Sorrentino**. Marvel Comics, 2015– . O

After the year-long epic *Secret Wars* crossover event, a Logan from 50 years in the future has become stuck in the new mainstream Marvel Universe. From a horrible future where the villains had teamed up to defeat the heroes of tomorrow, Logan sets out to ensure that horrible future never happens.

Vol. 0: Warzones. 2015. 136pp. 978-0-7851-9893-2.
Vol. 1: Berzerker. 2016. 144pp. 978-0-7851-9620-4.
Vol. 2: Bordertown. 2016. 112pp. 978-0-7851-9621-1.
Vol. 3: The Last Ronin. 2017. 112p. 978-1-302-90314-5.

Wolverine: Origin. Written by **Paul Jenkins** and **Kieron Gillen**. Illustrated by **Andy Kubert**. Marvel Comics, 2013–2014. T 🎖 ◎

Presenting for the first time the true origin of one of Marvel's most popular mutants: Wolverine! Born James Howlett in Canada in the late 19th century, the boy who would become Wolverine was born sick and frail, and was constantly hindered by his allergies while growing up. His mutant powers manifested themselves early in life while protecting his mother shortly after his father was killed by Thomas Logan, an alcoholic groundskeeper. After fleeing to British Columbia with a red-haired girl he adored called Rose, James adopts the name Logan to conceal his identity, but evil never does sleep. The sequel was released in 2014. The original collection received recognition by YALSA's Quick Picks for Reluctant Readers committee in 2003.

Origin. 2013. 208pp. 978-0785183846, hardcover.
Origin II. 2014. 128pp. 978-0-7851-8481-2, hardcover.

Death of Wolverine. Written by **Charles Soule**. Illustrated by **Steve McNiven**. 2015. 144pp. 978-0-7851-9351-7, hardcover; 2016. 144pp. 978-0-7851-9163-6. O

All roads come to an end, and its curtain calls for Logan (for now) as Wolverine dies after taking down his foes even while his healing factor is taken away from him and he can't heal. Rest assured he'll be back in comics where people come back from death all the time, but Logan goes out in a blaze of glory.

Wonder Woman. Written by **Brian Azzarello** and **Meredith Finch**. Illustrated by **Cliff Chiang** and **David Finch**. DC Comics, 2013–. T

© 2016 DC Comics

Princess Diana is from the Amazon tribe of female warriors who reside on the magical Greek island of Themyscira. She is the goddess daughter of Queen Hippolyta and Zeus, king of the Greek Gods. She was blessed with this union as a demi-god with great powers to combat many foes including flight, great strength, and super-speed. She also carries a magic lasso of truth that was made from the girdle of Gaia and will force a fiend to tell the truth when in its grasp. The ambassador of her culture to the world, she earned the moniker of "Wonder Woman" by the press when she first appeared and to this day is an ally of Superman, Batman, and the Justice League of America. A new series began in 2016. Wonder Woman also has transitioned to feature films—making her first appearance in the 2016 film *Batman v Superman: Dawn of Justice*. She's played by actress Gal Gadot. A feature film *Wonder Woman* film was be released in 2017.

Vol. 1: Blood. 2013. 160pp. 978-1-4012-3562-8, hardcover. 978-1-302-90314-5.
Vol. 2: Guts. 2013. 144pp. 978-1-4012-3809-4. hardcover. 978-1-4012-3810-0.
Vol. 3: Iron. 2014. 176pp. 978-1-4012-4261-9, hardcover. 978-1-4012-4607-5.
Vol. 4: War. 2014. 144pp. 978-1-4012-4608-2, hardcover. 978-1-4012-4954-0.
Vol. 5: Flesh. 2015. 176pp. 978-1-4012-5097-3, hardcover. 978-1-4012-5349-3.
Vol. 6: Bones. 2015. 160pp. 978-1-4012-5350-9, hardcover. 978-1-4012-5775-0.
Vol. 7: War Torn. 2016. 160pp. 978-1-4012-5679-1, hardcover. 978-1-4012-6163-4.
Vol. 8: A Twist of Fate. 2016. 184pp. 978-1-4012-6164-1, hardcover. 978-1-4012-6583-0.
Vol. 9: Resurrection. 2017 176. 978-1-4012-6584-7, hardcover. 978-1-4012-6805-3.

Wonder Woman: The True Amazon. Written and Illustrated by **Jill Thompson**. DC Comics, 2016. 128pp. 978-1-4012-4901-4, hardcover. T

Beloved by the Amazon people, Princess Diana soon becomes spoiled and ungrateful. After tragedy strikes, young Diana must learn to grow up and learn the error of her ways

© 2016 DC Comics

and embrace her destiny. Beautifully illustrated by Jill Thompson, see the origins of young Diana, the Amazon princess, as she develops into the hero we know and love.

Wonder Woman Omnibus by George Perez. Written by **Len Wein**. Illustrated by **George Perez**.

No artist in Wonder Woman's history has had such an impact on the hero than George Perez. Collected is the entire collection of Perez's amazing artwork featuring the hero of the Amazons. This material from the 1980s has also begun to be collected in a series of smaller volumes titled *Wonder Woman by George Perez*.

Vol. 1. 2015. 640pp. 978-1-4012-5547-3, hardcover.
Vol. 2. 2017. 500pp. 978-1-4012-7238-8, hardcover

Cosmic Heroes

Of the many heroes published by the comic book industry, many tales feature heroes whose powers and origins are derived from outer space. The hero may be an alien from outer space or have powers that originate from a cosmic source that is not from Earth.

Captain Marvel

Ms. Marvel, 1st series. Marvel Comics, 2007– . 🌹

© 2016 Marvel Comics

Carol Danvers gained the powers of super-strength, invulnerability, and flight when she was caught in an explosion near the alien Kree hero called Captain Marvel. One of the most powerful heroes, Carol Danvers took on the super-hero name Ms. Marvel and soon became a regular member of the Avengers. She had her own comic book series in 1978, but a new Ms. Marvel series was released in 2006. In 2012, Carol changed the name of her super-hero moniker to Captain Marvel in honor of the original hero whose powers she inherited. A Captain Marvel live-action film is planned for 2019, with award-winning actress Brie Larson in the title role. A fifth Captain Marvel series began in 2016, written by Tara Butters and Michele Fazekas, who were writers and producers on the Marvel's Agent Carter television series. In 2017 YALSA's Great Graphic Novels for Teens recognized the volume Rise of Alpha Flight on their annual selection list.

Ms. Marvel, 1st series. 2007.

Essential Ms. Marvel. Written by **Gerry Conway** and **Archie Goodwin**. Illustrated by **John Buscema** and various. 2007. 512pp. 978-0-7851-2499-3.

Ms. Marvel, 2nd series. Written by **Brian Reed**. Illustrated by **Roberto De La Torre**. 2006–2010. T

> *Vol. 1: Best of the Best*. 2006. 136pp. 978-0-7851-1996-8.
> *Vol. 2: Civil War*. 2007. 136pp. 978-0-7851-2305-7.
> *Vol. 3: Operation Lightning Storm*. 2007. 160pp. 978-0-7851-2449-8.
> *Vol. 4: Monster Smash*. 2008. 168pp. 978-0-7851-2813-7.
> *Vol. 5: Secret Invasion*. 2008. 160pp. 978-0-7851-3299-8.
> *Vol. 6: Ascension*. 2009. 160pp. 978-0-7851-3178-6.
> *Vol. 7: Dark Reign*. 2009. 176pp. 978-0-7851-3839-6.
> *Vol. 8: War of the Marvels*. 2009. 120pp. 978-0-7851-3841-9.
> *Vol. 9: Best You Can Be*. 2010. 112pp. 978-0-7851-4574-5.

Captain Marvel, 3rd series. Written by **Kelly Sue Deconnick**. Illustrated by **Dexter Soy** and **Emma Rios**. Marvel Comics, 2013.

> *Vol. 1: In Pursuit of Flight*. 2013. 136pp. 978-0785165491.
> *Vol. 2: Down*. 2013. 136pp. 978-0785165507.

Captain Marvel, 4th series. Written by **Kelly Sue Deconnick**. Illustrated by **David Lopez**. Marvel Comics, 2014–2015. T

> *Vol. 1: Higher, Further, Faster, More*. 2014. 136pp. 978-0-7851-9013-4.
> *Vol. 2: Stay Fly*. 2015. 120pp. 978-0-7851-9014-1.
> *Vol. 3: Alis Volat Propriis*. 2015. 96pp. 978-0-7851-9841-3.

Captain Marvel, 5th series. Written by **Tara Butters** and **Michelle Fazekas**. Illustrated by **Kris Anka** and **Felipe Smith**. Marvel Comics, 2016– . T

> *Vol. 1: Rise of Alpha Flight*. 2014. 112pp. 978-0-7851-9642-6.
> *Vol. 2: Civil War II*. 2017. 120pp. 978-0-7851-9643-3.

Guardians of the Galaxy

Marvel Comics, 2000. T 🎬 🖥 🐾

The Guardians of the Galaxy is the name of two space-oriented teams in the Marvel Universe. The first originally appeared in Marvel Super-Heroes #18 in 1969 and is set in the far future in the 31st century. The second team is set in the present day and is made up of both humans and aliens. Both teams have interacted with the major heroes of the Marvel Universe, with the newer team taking part in several of the more "cosmic" events as listed in this chapter. That second team was also the basis of the highly successful 2014 film. Solo adventures of some of the Guardians team members are also included here, while others, such as Gamora and Drax, can be found in some

© 2016 Marvel Comics

of the titles in the Thanos entry. Additional titles featuring various incarnations of the teams, as well as solo adventures of its members, came out in 2016, along with the first collected volume of the third modern era series. Some of the solo adventures are listed later in this section.

Original Guardians of the Galaxy

Collects the earliest adventures of the original *Guardians* stories set in the present and the far future in the 31st century. The stories include appearances by The Avengers, The Defenders, Spider-Man, and others.

Guardians of the Galaxy: Tomorrow's Avengers. Written by **Steve Gerber**, **Chris Claremont**, **Roger Stern**, and various. Illustrated by various. Marvel Comics, 2013.

> *Vol. 1.* 2013. 368pp. 978-0-7851-6687-0.
> *Vol. 2.* 2013. 376pp. 978-0-7851-6755-6.

Guardians of the Galaxy. Written and Illustrated by **Jim Valentino** and various. Marvel Comics, 2014.

> *Vol. 1.* 2014. 328pp. 978-0-7851-8420-1.
> *Vol. 2.* 2014. 336pp. 978-0-7851-8563-5.
> *Vol. 3.* 2015. 312pp. 978-0-7851-9812-3.

Guardians of the Galaxy, Modern Era

Guardians of the Galaxy by Abnett & Lanning: The Complete Collection. Written by **Dan Abnett** and **Andy Lanning**. Illustrated by **Paul Pelletier**, **Wes Craig**, **Brad Walker**, and various. Marvel Comics, 2014.

These collect the 2008 Guardians series, which served as the inspiration for the feature film. The material originally was collected in four volumes from 2008 to 2010. The team consists of a rotating roster of heroes, which includes Star-Lord, Gamora, Rocket Raccoon, Groot, Adam Warlock, Drax the Destroyer, Bug, Major Victory, Mantis, and Phyla-Vell.

Vol. 1. 296pp. 978-0-7851-9064-6.
Vol. 2. 312pp. 978-0-7851-9063-9.

Guardians of the Galaxy, 2nd series. Written by **Brian Michael Bendis**. Illustrated by **Steve McNiven**, **Sara Pichelli**, and various. 2013–2015.

The second series with the modern-day team. The team in this current group includes Rocket Raccoon, Agent Venom, Drax the Destroyer, Groot, Gamora, Angela, and Peter Quill.

Vol. 1: Cosmic Avengers. 2013. 144pp. 978-0-7851-6607-8.
Vol. 2: Angela. 2014. 168pp. 978-0-7851-6829-4.

Guardians of the Galaxy/All-New X-Men: The Trial of Jean Grey. 2014. 144pp. 978-0-7851-6830-0, hardcover.

Vol. 3: Guardians Disassembled. 2014. 160pp. 978-0-7851-5479-2, hardcover; 2015. 160pp. 978-0-7851-8967-1.

Vol. 4: Original Sin. 2015. 168pp. 978-0-7851-9245-9, hardcover; 2015. 136pp. 978-0-7851-9246-6.

Guardians of the Galaxy & X-Men: The Black Vortex. 2015. 312pp. 978-0-7851-9770-6, hardcover; 2016. 312pp. 978-0-7851-9909-0.

Guardians of the Galaxy, 3rd series. Written by **Brian Michael Bendis**. Illustrated by **Valerio Schiti**. 2015– .

The third series adds some members to the team including The Thing from the Fantastic Four and the X-Men's Kitty Pryde.

Vol. 1: New Guard—Emperor Quill. 2016. 112pp. 978-0-7851-9518-4, hardcover. 978-0-7851-9950-2.

Vol. 2: New Guard—Wanted. 2016. 136pp. 978-0-7851-9519-1, hardcover. 978-0-7851-9951-9.

Vol. 3: New Guard—Civil War II. 2017. 136pp 978-1-302-90301-5, hardcover.

Vol. 4: New Guard—Grounded. 2017. 136pp. 978-1-302-90669-6, hardcover.

Annihilation/Annihilation: Conquest. Written by **Keith Giffen**, **Dan Abnett**, **Andy Lanning**, and various. Illustrated by various. Marvel Comics, 2007–2014. T

The Universe is faced with destruction by a force from another dimension. The story was mainly told through a series of limited series, several one-shots, and some crossovers with ongoing titles. The events led into the creation of the new Guardians of the Galaxy team. Other collections include *Annihilation Classic* in which several of the stories are also collected in other volumes in this collection.

Annihilation, 2007–2014.

Book 1. 2007. 256pp. 978-0-7851-2511-2, hardcover; 2007. 256pp. 978-0-7851-2901-1.

Book 2. 2007. 320pp. 978-0-7851-2512-9, hardcover; 2007. 320pp. 978-0-7851-2902-8.

Book 3. 2007. 304pp. 978-0-7851-2513-6, hardcover; 2007. 304pp. 978-0-7851-2903-5.

Annihilation Omnibus. 2014. 880pp. 978-0-7851-8889-6, hardcover.

Annihilation: Conquest, 2008–2009.

Book One. 2008. 272pp. 978-07851-2782-6, hardcover; 2008. 272pp. 978-0-7851-2783-3.

Book Two. 2008. 352pp. 978-0-7851-2716-1, hardcover; 2009. 352pp. 978-0-7851-2717-8.

Annihilation: Conquest Omnibus. 2015. 872pp. 978-0-7851-9270-1, hardcover.

War of Kings/Realm of Kings. Written by **Dan Abnett**, **Andy Lanning**, **Greg Pak**, and **C.B. Cebulski**. Illustrated by **Paul Pelletier** and **Bong Dazo**, **Scott Reed**, and **Kev Walker**. Marvel Comics, 2009–2010. T

The Guardians are among those characters that get caught up in a war between several alien races and the aftereffects that threaten Earth and other worlds.

War of Kings, 2009–2010.

Vol. 1: War of Kings. 2009. 256pp. 978-0-7851-9066-0.

Vol. 2: War of Kings: Warriors. 2010. 248pp. 978-0-7851-4368-0.

Omnibus Edition. 2009. 432pp. 978-0-7851-4293-5, hardcover.

Realm of Kings. 2010. 368pp. 978-0-7851-4809-8, hardcover; 2014. 368pp. 978-0-7851-9066-0.

Solo Adventures of the Guardians of the Galaxy

Star-Lord

Peter Quill was human with mixed-race parents—half alien and half human, he was an astronaut in training but was rescued in space by a pirate group known as the Ravagers and learned the life of piracy and eventually took up the mantle of Star-Lord. His original adventures have been collected as has a new ongoing series. A new series debuted in 2014 and was published in two volumes, but a new series was issued in 2015 and retells of Star-Lord's origins (though the volume numbering continued). Another Star-Lord series began in 2017.

Star-Lord: Guardian of the Galaxy. Written by **Chris Claremont**, **Steve Englehart**, and **Doug Moench**. Illustrated by **Steve Gan**, **John Byrne**, **Carmine Infantino**, and **Bill Sienkiewicz**. 2014. 424pp. 978-0-7851-5449-5. T

Legendary Star-Lord. Written by **Sam Humphries**. Illustrated by **Paco Medina**, **Freddie Williams**, and **Javier Garron**. 2015–2016.

> *Vol. 1: Face It, I Rule*. 2015. 112pp. 978-0-7851-9159-9.
> *Vol. 2: Rise of the Black Vortex*. 2015. 136pp. 978-0-7851-9160-5.
> *Vol. 3: First Flight*. 2016. 112pp. 978-0-7851-9624-2.
> *Vol. 4: Out of Orbit*. 2016. 128pp. 978-0-7851-9625-9.

Rocket Raccoon and Groot 🎗

A gun-wielding Raccoon-like creature and a walking-tree with a three-word vocabulary have become two of the breakout characters of the Guardians series as well as the movies. The pair has also appeared in children's books. Fellow Guardians Gamora and Drax have also received ongoing series and as well as collections of their earlier appearances. The self-titled 2016 *Groot* graphic novel was recognized by YALSA's Great Graphic Novels for Teens 2017 selection list.

Rocket Raccoon and Groot: The Complete Collection. Written by **Bill Mantlo**, **Dan Abnett**, and **Andy Lanning**. Illustrated by **Jack Kirby**, **Sal Buscema**, **Mike Mignola**, and various. 2013. 264pp. 978-0-7851-6713-6.

> The pair's earliest appearances including Rocket's debut in the pages of *The Incredible Hulk* and his goofy 1980s limited series. Many of the stories in this volume have been reprinted elsewhere.

Rocket Raccoon. Written by **Skottie Young**. Illustrated by **Skottie Young**, **Filipe Andrade**, and **Jake Parker**. Marvel Comics, 2015– .

> *Vol. 1: A Chasing Tale*. 2015. 136pp. 978-0-7851-9389-0, hardcover; 2015. 136pp. 978-0-7851-9045-5.

© 2016 Marvel Comics

Rocket Raccoon and Groot. Written by **Skottie Young**. Illustrated by **Filipe Andrade**. Marvel Comics, 2016– . T

> *Vol. 1: Tricks of the Trade* 2016. 112pp. 978-0-7851-9973-1.
> *Vol. 2: Civil War II*. 2016. 112pp. 978-0-7851-9974-8.

Groot. Written by **Jeff Loveness**. Illustrated by **Brian Kessinger**. Marvel Comics, 2016. 136pp. 978-0-7851-9552-8, hardcover. T 🎋

Nova

Marvel Comics, 2007–2015. T 🐾 🖵

Nova is a member of a larger group of galaxy policemen known as the Nova Corps. They wear a special helmet and flight suit tied into a mysterious power called the Nova Force that gives the wearer superhuman strength, flight, and the resistance to injury. Several Earth heroes have been members of the Nova Corps and have worn the mantle of Nova—Richard Rider and Sam Alexander. The character has appeared in many animated shows as well as in video games including Disney Infinity 2.0.

Richard Rider as Nova, 2007–2014

Richard Rider is a human who was given the power of the Nova Corps suit by a dying alien. He first appeared in 1977 with a monthly comic book series originally published from 1977 to 1979. Afterward he was a member of the team of heroes known as the New Warriors, and eventually a member of the Nova Corps and a part-time Avenger. He frequently has appeared in cosmic-related stories alongside the Guardians of the Galaxy.

Nova Classic. Written by **Marv Wolfman** and **Len Wein**. Illustrated by **John Buscema**, **Sal Buscema**, **Carmine Infantino**, and **Ross Andru**. Marvel Comics, 2013– .

> *Vol. 1*. 2013. 240pp. 978-0-7851-6028-1.
> *Vol. 2*. 2013. 264pp. 978-0-7851-8544-4.
> *Vol. 3*. 2014. 304pp. 978-0-7851-8552-9.

Nova, 2nd series. Written by **Dan Abnett** and **Andy Lanning**. Illustrated by **Wellington Alves** and various. 2007–2010.

Vol. 2: Storytailer. 2015. 136pp. 978-0785193906, hardcover; 2016. 136pp. 978-0-7851-9167-4.

Vol. 1: Annihilation: Conquest. 2007. 168pp. 978-0-7851-2631-7.
Vol. 2: Knowhere. 2008. 160pp. 978-0-7851-2632-4.
Vol. 3: Secret Invasion. 2009. 144pp. 978-0-7851-2662-1.
Vol. 4: Nova Corps. 2009. 144pp. 978-0-7851-3188-5.
Vol. 5: War of Kings. 2009. 144pp. 978-0-7851-4066-5.
Vol. 6: Realm of Kings. 2010. 192pp. 978-0-7851-4067-2.

Sam Alexander as Nova, 2013– .

The third and fourth <u>Nova</u> series focuses on another member of the Nova Corps, a young Hispanic hero named Sam Alexander who takes on the mantle from his dad who was once a member of the Nova Corps.

Nova, 3rd series. Written by **Jeph Loeb** and **Gerry Duggan**. Illustrated by **Ed McGuinness**, **David Baldeon**, and **Paco Medina**. Marvel Comics, 2013– .

© 2016 Marvel Comics

Vol. 1: Origin. 2014. 160pp. 978-0-7851-6605-4.
Vol. 2: Rookie Season. 2014. 136pp. 978-0-7851-6839-3.
Vol. 3: Nova Corpse. 2014. 152pp. 978-0-7851-8957-2.
Vol. 4: Original Sin. 2015. 136pp. 978-0-7851-8958-9.
Vol. 5: Axis. 2015. 120pp. 978-0-7851-9241-1.
Vol. 6: Homecoming. 2015. 128pp. 978-0-7851-9375-3.

Nova: The Human Rocket. Written by **Sean Ryan**. Illustrated by **Cory Smith** and **John Timms**.

Vol. 1: Burn Out. 2016. 136pp. 978-0-7851-9650-1.
Vol. 2: After Burn. 2016. 112pp. 978-0-7851-9651-8.

Orion Omnibus. Written and Illustrated by **Walter Simonson**. DC Comics, 2015. 752pp. 978-1-4012-5535-0, hardcover. T

The adventures of Orion, the son of the evil despot Darkseid, the dark ruler of the planet Apokolips. A warrior since his birth, Orion has lived on the peaceful planet of New Genesis in the company of the race of beings called the New Gods and has renounced his family's dark past. When Darkseid discovers an ultimate power in the form of the Anti-Life Equation, Orion must find a way to defeat his unbeatable father while the fate of the universe hangs in the balance. See also the entry for *Jack Kirby's Fourth World Omnibus* later in this chapter.

Silver Surfer

Created by **Stan Lee** and **Jack Kirby**. Marvel Comics. T

© 2016 Marvel Comics

The silver-skinned man known as Norrin Radd from the utopian planet of Zenn-La saved his planet from the ravages of the planet-devouring Galactus by becoming his herald. Powered by the awesome might of Galactus's Power Cosmic, the Silver Surfer soars the spaceways on his cosmic surfboard trying to redeem himself for his crimes against the universe for serving Galactus and inadvertently causing the deaths of billions of lives across the universe. The Silver Surfer has also been a powerful ally with the Fantastic Four and other Marvel heroes in times of crisis. The Silver Surfer was created by Stan Lee and Jack Kirby and first appeared in the pages of *Fantastic Four* #48 from 1965. The short story *Parable* by Stan Lee and Moebius won an Eisner Award in 1989 for Best Short Story and tells of a futuristic tale when the Silver Surfer comes out of retirement to combat the threat of Galactus once more. The titles featuring the galactic hero are listed below by publication date.

Silver Surfer: Parable. Written by **Stan Lee**. Illustrated by **Moebius**. 2012. 168pp. 978-0-7851-6209-4, hardcover.

Silver Surfer: Requiem. Written by **J. Michael Straczynski**. Illustrated by **Esad Ribic**. 2007. 104pp. 978-0-7851-2848-9, hardcover.

Silver Surfer Epic Collection. Written by **Stan Lee**, **John Byrne**, and **Steve Englehart**. Illustrated by **Jack Kirby**, **Marshall Rogers**, **John Buscema**, and various. 2014–2015.

> *Vol. 1: When Calls Galactus*. 2014. 320pp. 978-0-7851-9002-8.
> *Vol. 2: Freedom*. 2015. 488pp. 978-0-7851-9903-8.

Silver Surfer: Rebirth of Thanos. Written by **Jim Starlin**. Illustrated by **Ron Lim**. 2010. 224pp. 978-0-7851-4478-6, hardcover.

Silver Surfer (current series). Written by **Dan Slott**. Illustrated by **Michael Allred**. Marvel Comics, 2014– . T

> The new Silver Surfer series was originally published beginning in 2014. The series features the Silver Surfer and his traveling companion, a human named Dawn Greenwood who challenges the Surfer to show her the beauty and uniqueness of the galaxy. The third volume collects the story "Never After" which was recognized by an Eisner Award in 2016 for the category of Best Single Issue/One Shot.
>
> *Vol. 1: New Dawn*. 2014. 128pp. 978-0-7851-8878-0.
> *Vol. 2: Worlds Apart*. 2015. 128pp. 978-0-7851-8879-7.
> *Vol. 3: Last Days*. 2016. 128pp. 978-0-7851-9737-9.
> *Vol. 4: Citizen of Earth*. 2016. 144pp. 978-0-7851-9969-4.
> *Vol. 5: The Man Who Lived Twice*. 2017. 176pp. 978-0-7851-9970-0.

Super-Hero Teams

Though many super-heroes fight crime individually, there are many super-hero teams. A staple in comic book history since the formation of DC Comics' Justice Society of

America back in 1940's *All-Star Comics #3*, they have continued to be popular to this day. The teams can be made up of heroes who have common origins such as the Fantastic Four and X-Men, or be comprised of a group of heroes from various origins such as the Justice League of America and the Avengers. Below are listed a variety of super-hero teams from a wide range of publishers including DC Comics, Marvel Comics and Image Comics.

A-Force. Written by **G. Willow Wilson** and **Marguerite Bennett**. Illustrated by **Jorge Molina**. Marvel Comics, 2015– . T

Originally created as part of the special *Secret Wars* event from 2015, A-Force is the first all-female Avengers team. Originally founded in an alternate reality by She-Hulk and part of a matriarchal society from the kingdom of Arcadia, she's joined by many others including Dazzler, Captain Marvel, Ms. Marvel and Singularity, to help defend their borders from the threat of Loki. After the *Secret Wars* event, the team is reformed once again when the hero called Singularity finds herself lost after the Secret Wars and searches to reunite her teammates who don't remember her. Also available is *A-Force Presents* (2015– .), each volume of which collects a corresponding issue of a series with a female lead, including *Thor, Captain Marvel,* and *She-Hulk*.

Vol. 0: Warzones. 2015. 112pp. 978-0-7851-9861-1.
Vol. 1: Hypertime. 2016. 112pp. 978-0-7851-9605-1.
Vol. 2 Rage Against the Dying of the Light. 2017. 136pp. 978-0-7851-9606-8.

The Avengers

Created by **Stan Lee** and **Jack Kirby**. Marvel Comics, 2006– .

© 2016 Marvel Comics

The Avengers are one of Marvel Comics' best-known super-hero teams and first appeared in 1963's *The Avengers, #1*. The team over the last 50-plus years has consisted of some of the best-known and most popular super-heroes from Marvel Comics, including Captain America, Thor, Iron Man, The Wasp, Giant-Man, Vision, Hawkeye and Wonder Man. Working with the full support of the U.S. government, they're one of the best fighting forces America has, battling against common foes including Ultron, Kang, and other forces of evil. The Avengers have been a part of video games for a long time as well as the popular Disney Avengers—series of Marvel Comics movies culminating with the *Avengers* and *Avengers: Age of Ultron* feature films and their solo Marvel movie films. Below are listed highlights of *Avengers* titles over the last 10 years in alphabetical order.

All-New, All-Different Avengers. Written by **Mark Waid**. Illustrated by **Adam Kubert** and **Mahmud Asrar**. Marvel Comics, 2016– . T

Launched after the events from the Secret Wars series, a new Avengers team is united under the leadership of Captain America (Sam Wilson). The team is made up of Thor (Jane Foster), Iron Man, Vision, Nova, Ms. Marvel, and Spider-Man (Miles Morales).

Vol. 1: The Magnificent Seven. 2016. 168pp. 978-0-7851-9967-0.
Vol. 2: Family Business. 2016. 144pp. 978-0-7851-9968-7.
Vol. 3: Civil War II. 2017. 112pp. 978-1-3029-0236-0.

The Avengers, 4th series. Written by **Brian Michael Bendis**. Illustrated by **John Romita Jr.**, **David Finch**, **Walter Simonson**, and **Brandon Peterson**. Marvel Comics, 2011–2013. T
The fourth team was published in the monthly comic books from 2011 to 2013 and featured Thor, Hawkeye, Spider-Man, Wolverine, Captain America, Spider-Woman, Iron Man, team leader Maria Hill, and the Red Hulk.

Vol. 1. 2011. 160pp. 978-0-7851-4501-1.
Vol. 2. 2011. 176pp. 978-0-7851-4505-9.
Vol. 3. 2012. 168pp. 978-0-7851-5117-3.
Vol. 4. 2013. 136pp. 978-0-7851-6080-9.
Vol. 5. 2013. 176pp. 978-0-7851-6082-3.

The Avengers, 5th series. Written by **Jonathan Hickman**. Illustrated by **Jerome Opena**, **Nick Spencer**, **Mike Deodato**, **Stefano Caselli**, **Leinil Francis Yu**, and various. Marvel Comics, 2013–2015. T
Writer Jonathan Hickman took over the main series from 2013 through 2015. The series features a more cosmic role and serves as a prequel to the 2015 Secret Wars series where the Avengers must try to prevent the multiverses from collapsing.

Vol. 1: Avengers World. 2014. 152pp. 978-0-7851-6652-8.
Vol. 2: The Last White Event. 2014. 136pp. 978-0-7851-6653-5.
Vol. 3: Prelude to Infinity. 2014. 152pp. 978-0-7851-6654-2.
Vol. 4: Infinity. 2014. 168pp. 978-0-7851-8414-0.
Vol. 5: Adapt or Die. 2015. 136pp. 978-0-7851-8921-3.
Vol. 6: Infinite Avengers. 2015. 152pp. 978-0-7851-8922-0.
Vol. 7: Time Runs Out, Vol. 1. 2015. 978-0-7851-9341-8.
Vol. 8: Time Runs Out, Vol. 2. 2015. 978-0-7851-9372-2.
Vol. 9: Time Runs Out, Vol. 3. 2015. 978-0-7851-9222-0.
Vol. 10: Time Runs Out, Vol. 4. 2015. 978-0-7851-9224-4.

Mighty Avengers. Written by **Brian Michael Bendis** and **Al Ewing**. Illustrated by **Frank Cho**, **Greg Land**, and various. Marvel Comics, 2008–2015. T

Set up as a government-run version of the Avengers, the original team comprised of all federal-registered super-heroes. The first team included Iron Man, Wonder Man, Black Widow, Sentry, Ares, and Ms. Marvel. The team has changed rosters over the years with some other members including Luke Cage, Spider-Man, Falcon, White Tiger, Ronin, Blue Marvel, Power Man, and the She-Hulk. The series that was originally published in comic book form from 2007 to 2015 has concluded for the time being, with the short-lived series Captain America and the Mighty Avengers ending in 2015.

Mighty Avengers, Volume 1: 2008–2010.

Vol. 1: The Ultron Initiative. 2008. 978-0-7851-2368-2.
Vol. 2: Venom Bomb. 2008. 978-0-7851-2369-9.

Vol. 3: Secret Invasion, Book 1. 2009. 978-0-7851-3010-9.
Vol. 4: Secret Invasion, Book 2. 2009. 978-0-7851-3650-7.
Vol. 5: Earth's Mightiest. 2009. 978-0-7851-3746-7.
Vol. 6: The Unspoken. 2010. 978-0-7851-3747-4.
Vol. 7: Siege. 2010. 978-0-7851-4800-5.

Mighty Avengers, Volume 2: 2014.

Vol. 1: No Single Hero. 2014. 112pp. 978-0-7851-8874-2.
Vol. 2: Family Bonding. 2014. 112pp. 978-0-7851-8875-9.
Vol. 3: Original Sin—Not Your Father's Avengers. 2014. 96pp. 978-0-7851-9072-1.

Mighty Avengers, Volume 3: 2015.

Captain America and the Mighty Avengers. Vol. 1: Open for Business. 2015. 160pp. 978-0-7-851-9382-1.
Captain America and the Mighty Avengers. Vol. 2: Last Days. 2015. 112pp. 978-0-7851-9803-1.

New Avengers. Written by **Brian Michael Bendis**, **Jonathan Hickman**, and **Al Ewing**. Illustrated by **David Finch**. Marvel Comics, 2005–2015. T ◎

After the fallout from the *Avengers: Disassembled* storyline, a new Avengers team is formed and now includes veterans Captain America and Iron Man, joined by Spider-Man, Luke Cage, Spider-Woman, Wolverine, Sentry, and a new mysterious hero called Ronin. The overall series lasted through 2015 in various forms as the team became the counterpoint to Iron Man's Mighty Avengers government-sanctioned team. Though the roster has changed dramatically over the years, the core belief of the team remains to protect those that need protecting and to avenge those who have been wronged. In 2016, a brand-new version of the New Avengers was created. The team is led by former New Mutants member Sunspot and includes past members of the Young Avengers and Thunderbolts including Wiccan, Hulkling, White Tiger, Squirrel Girl, Pod, Power Man, and Hawkeye. A.I.M. (Advanced Idea Mechanics), a former super-villain group, has been rebranded as the Avengers Idea Mechanics. The new series is written by Al Ewing and illustrated by Gerardo Sandoval.

© 2016 Marvel Comics

New Avengers, Volume 1: 2006–2010.

Vol. 1: Breakout. 2006. 160pp. 978-0-7851-1479-6.
Vol. 2: Sentry. 2006. 152pp. 978-0-7851-1672-1.
Vol. 3: Secrets and Lies. 2006. 128pp. 978-0-7851-1706-3.
Vol. 4: The Collective. 2007. 128pp. 978-0-7851-1987-6.
Vol. 5: Civil War. 2007. 120pp. 978-0-7851-2446-7.
Vol. 6: Revolution. 2007. 144pp. 978-0-7851-2468-9.
Vol. 7: The Trust. 2008. 184pp. 978-0-7851-2503-7.

Vol. 8: Secret Invasion, Book 1. 2009. 120pp. 978-0-7851-2947-9.
Vol. 9: Secret Invasion, Book 2. 2009. 128pp. 978-0-7851-2949-3.
Vol. 10: Power. 2009. 120pp. 978-0-7851-3560-9.
Vol. 11: Search for the Sorcerer Supreme. 2009. 120pp. 978-0-7851-3690-3.
Vol. 12: Powerloss. 2010. 144pp. 978-0-7851-4576-9.
Vol. 13: Siege. 2010. 224pp. 978-0-7851-4578-3.

New Avengers, Volume 2: 2010–2012.

Vol. 1. 2011. 160pp. 978-0785148722, hardcover.
Vol. 2. 2012. 168pp. 978-0-7851-4875-3.

Avengers: Fear Itself. 2012. 184pp. 978-0-7851-6349-7.

Vol. 3. 2012. 184pp. 978-0-7851-5180-7.
Vol. 4. 2013. 160pp. 978-0-7851-6156-1.
Vol. 5. 2013. 112pp. 978-0-7851-6159-2.

New Avengers, Volume 3: 2013–2015.

Vol. 1: Everything Dies. 2014. 152pp. 978-0-7851-6661-0.
Vol. 2: Infinity. 2014. 152pp. 978-0-7851-6837-9.
Vol. 3: Other Worlds. 2015. 136pp. 978-0-7851-5484-6.
Vol. 4: A Perfect World. 2015. 144pp. 978-0-7851-5485-3.
Time Runs Out, Vol. 1. 2015. 144pp. 978-0-7851-9341-8.
Time Runs Out, Vol. 2. 2015. 136pp. 978-0-7851-9372-2.
Time Runs Out, Vol. 3. 2015. 136pp. 978-0-7851-9222-0.
Time Runs Out, Vol. 4. 2015. 152pp. 978-0-7851-9224-4.

New Avengers, Volume 4: 2016.

Vol. 1: Everything Is New. 2016. 144pp. 978-0-7851-9648-8.
Vol. 2: Standoff. 2016. 112pp. 978-0-7851-9649-5.
Vol. 3: Civil War II. 2016. 112pp. 978-1-309-90235-3.

Secret Avengers. Written by **Ed Brubaker, Cullen Bunn, Nick Spencer, Warren Ellis, Ales Kot**, and **Rick Remender**. Illustrated by **Mike Deodato, Scot Eaton, Gabriel Hardman, Peter Nguyen, Michael Walsh,** and various. Marvel Comics, 2011–2015. T

Originally created by Steve Rogers (Captain America), the group is an elite black ops team of heroes who are sent on missions vital to S.H.I.E.L.D. The original team members were Beast, War Machine, Valkyrie, Moon Knight, Nova, Black Widow, Sharon Carter, and Ant-Man, and led by Steve Rogers. Over the next variations of the series, the team and their jurisdictions changed. The last version of the team was comprised of Nick Fury Jr., Black Widow, Phil Coulson, Hawkeye, and Spider-Woman.

Secret Avengers, Volume 1: 2011–2012.

Vol. 1: Mission to Mars. 2011. 168pp. 978-0785146001.
Vol. 2: Eyes of the Dragon. 2012. 168pp. 978-0785146025.
Fear Itself: Secret Avengers. 2012. 112pp. 978-0-7851-5178-4.
Vol. 3: Run the Mission, Don't Get Seen, Save the World. 2012. 144pp. 978-0-7851-5256-9.

Secret Avengers, Volume 2: 2013.

> *Vol. 1: The Descendants.* 2013. 112pp. 978-0-7851-6119-6.
> *Vol. 2: Avengers vs. X-Men.* 2013. 384pp. 978-0-7851-6318-3.
> *Vol. 3: Rise of the Descendants.* 2013. 112pp. 978-0-7851-6123-3.

Secret Avengers, Volume 3: 2013–2014.

> *Vol. 1: Reverie.* 2013. 120pp. 978-0-7851-6688-7.
> *Vol. 2: Iliad.* 2014. 136pp. 978-0-7851-6689-4.
> *Vol. 3: How to MA.I.M. a Mockingbird.* 2014. 112pp. 978-0-7851-8482-9.

Secret Avengers, Volume 4: 2014–2015.

> *Vol. 1: Let's Have a Problem.* 2014. 144pp. 978-0-7851-9052-3.
> *Vol. 2: The Labyrinth.* 2015. 112pp. 978-0-7851-9053-0.
> *Vol. 3: God Level.* 2015. 112pp. 978-0-7851-9710-2.

Uncanny Avengers. Written by **Rick Remender** and **Gerry Duggan**. Illustrated by **John Cassaday**, **Olivier Coipel**, **Daniel Acuña**, **Adam Kubert**, **Salvador Larroca**, **Ryan Stegman**, and **Steve McNiven**. Marvel Comics, 2013– . T

© 2016 Marvel Comics

After the crossover event called Avengers vs. X-Men from 2012, a new team of Avengers were created featuring members of both the Avengers and X-Men teams. The mixed hero team was officially named the Avengers Unity Squad but recently has been renamed the Avengers Unity Division. The members of the first team were comprised of Captain America, Havok, Rogue, the Scarlet Witch, Thor, and Wolverine. The team is currently in flux, and a new team debuted in 2016 in the *Lost Future* collection. Volumes for the third series contain the subtitle "Unity" as well as the volume's subtitle.

Uncanny Avengers, Volume 1: 2013–2015.

> *Vol. 1: The Red Shadow.* 2013. 136pp. 978-0-7851-6844-7, hardcover. 978-0-7851-92374.
> *Vol. 2: The Apocalypse Twins.* 2013. 160pp. 978-0-7851-68454, hardcover. 978-0-7851-6604-7.
> *Vol. 3: Ragnarok Now.* 2014. 136pp. 978-0-7851-84836, hardcover. 978-0-7851-8484-3.
> *Vol. 4: Avenge the Earth.* 2014. 136pp. 978-0-7851-54235, hardcover, 978-0-7851-5424-2.
> *Vol. 5: AXIS Prelude.* 2015. 144pp. 978–0-7851-54259, hardcover.
> *Uncanny Avengers Omnibus.* 2015. 672pp. 978-0-7851-9394-4, hardcover.

Uncanny Avengers, Volume 2: 2015.

> *Counter-Evolutionary.* 2015. 112pp. 978-0-7851-9237-4.

Uncanny Avengers, Volume 3: 2015.

> *Vol. 1: Lost Future.* 2016. 144pp. 978-0-7851-9615-0, hardcover, 978-0-7851-96150.

Vol. 2: The Man Who Fell to Earth. 2016. 136pp. 978-0-7851-9616-7.
Vol. 3: Civil War II. 2017. 112p. 978-1-302-90234-6.
Vol. 4: Red Skull. 2017. 136pp. 978-1-302-90644-3.

Big Hero 6. Written and Illustrated by **Haruki Ueno**. Yen Press, 2014–2015. Y Japanese manga.

© 2015 Disney

Though he was born a genius, Hiro Hamada was always a shy and awkward boy who preferred to work with his inventions instead of people. His brother Tadashi, already an inventor himself, created a home health-care robot named Baymax, and soon Hiro finds the unlikeliest of friends in the cuddly robot. When tragedy strikes, Hiro uses his own technological skills to upgrade Baymax as well as four of Tadashi's inventor college friends into homemade high-tech super-heroes! Now Hiro, alongside Baymax, Honey Lemon, Wasabi, GoGo, and Fred, are out to find the identity of the mysterious masked man named Yokai who is threatening the city of San Fransokyo. Who is the real identity of Yokai and what is his connection with Hiro's brother Tadashi? An adaptation of the hit 2014 Disney animated film, which was based on a 1998 Marvel Comics limited series.

Vol. 1. 2014. 192pp. 978-0-316-26389-4.
Vol. 2. 2015. 192pp. 978-0-316-26390-0.

Birds of Prey. Written by **Duane Swierczynski** and **Christy Marx**. Illustrated by various. DC Comics, 2012–2015. T

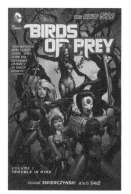

© 2016 DC Comics

Batman's not the only hero of Gotham City. When the Black Canary is falsely accused of a murder, she seeks aid from new hero Starling—who is on the run from her past. Along the way they team up with Batgirl, Katana, and the villain Poison Ivy to right the wrongs in Gotham City and to take out the bad guys no one else can. The team features a rotating cast of female heroes (and the occasional villain) as they serve as the covert-ops team of Gotham City. New collections of the 1990s incarnation of the series began to come out in 2015. A new series Batgirl and the Birds of Prey began in 2016.

Vol. 1: Trouble in Mind. 2012. 160pp. 978-1-4012-3699-5.
Vol. 2: Your Kiss Might Kill. 2013. 144pp. 978-1-4012-3813-1.
Vol. 3: A Clash of Daggers. 2013. 160pp. 978-1-4012-4404-0.
Vol. 4: The Cruelest Cut. 2014. 200pp. 978-1-4012-4635-8.
Vol. 5: Soul Crisis. 2015. 232pp. 978-1-4012-5083-6.

Fantastic Four

Created by **Stan Lee** and **Jack Kirby**. Marvel Comics, 1992– . T

Created in 1961 by Stan Lee and Jack Kirby, the Fantastic Four was the original dawn of the Marvel Age of comics. When an experimental flight into outer space is bombarded by cosmic rays, Reed Richards, genius scientist and the leader of the four-person crew, knew there would be risks involved in the flight. But when the crew crashes safely back to Earth, they find that each of them has been transformed by the cosmic rays into something a little more than human. Reed Richards discovers that he now has the ability to stretch his skin into any shape and calls himself "Mr. Fantastic." Reed's girlfriend, Susan Storm, finds that she can become invisible and can project invisible force bubbles and calls herself the "Invisible Woman." Her younger brother, the hot-headed Johnny Storm, now controls the power of fire and calls himself the "Human Torch." And Ben Grimm, the pilot of the crew, has gained super-strength as well as a thick rock-like skin covering him and aptly calls himself "The Thing." Together the super-powered family use their unique gifts to explore the unknown and to protect New York City, the Earth, and beyond from the forces of evil including Reed's arch-nemesis, the metal-armored villainous dictator of the country of Latveria, Doctor Doom, the world-eating devourer Galactus, and Annihilus from the Negative Zone. Below are listed recent collections of the series published in the last 10 years reprinting old and new adventures of Marvel's first family of super-heroes.

Fantastic Four. Marvel Comics, 2009–2015. T ◉ ◎

Listed below are the currently published Fantastic Four titles that were originally published as comic books. The collections feature the well-received run by older creative teams as well as the most recent volumes by Mark Millar, Jonathan Hickman, and James Robinson.

© 2016 Marvel Comics

Epic Collection: Into the Time Stream. Written by **Walter Simonson**, **Louise Simonson**, and **Chris Claremont**. Illustrated by **Walter Simonson** and **Arthur Adams**. 2014. 504pp. 978-0-7851-8895-7.

> *Fantastic Four*. Written by **Mark Millar**. Illustrated by **Bryan Hitch**. 2009–2010.
>
>> *World's Greatest*. 2009. 200pp. 978-0785125556.
>> *The Masters of Doom*. 2010. 248pp. 978-0785129677.
>
> *Fantastic Four*. Written by **Jonathan Hickman**. Illustrated by **Dale Eaglesham**, **Ron Garney**, **Mike Choi**, and various. 2010–2013.
>
>> *Vol. 1*. 2010. 144pp. 978-07851-3688-0.
>> *Vol. 2*. 2010. 112pp. 978-0-7851-4541-7.
>> *Vol. 3*. 2011. 112pp. 978-0-7851-4718-3.
>> *Vol. 4*. 2011. 184pp. 978-0-7851-5143-2.
>> *Vol. 5*. 2013. 208pp. 978-0-7851-6153-8.
>> *Vol. 6*. 2013. 184pp. 978-0-7851-6155-4.
>
> *Fantastic Four*. Written by **Matt Fraction**. Illustrated by **Mark Bagley**. 2013–2014.
>
>> *Vol. 1: New Departure, New Arrivals*. 2013. 144pp. 978-0-7851-6659-7.
>> *Vol. 2: Road Trip*. 2013. 136pp. 978-0785166602.
>> *Vol. 3: Doomed*. 2014. 184pp. 978-0785188835.

Fantastic Four. Written by **James Robinson**. Illustrated by **Leonard Kirk** and **Tom Grummett**. 2014–2015.

> *Vol. 1: The Fall of the Fantastic Four*. 2014. 128pp. 978-0-7851-5474-7.
> *Vol. 2: Original Sin*. 2014. 112pp. 978-0-7851-5475-4.
> *Vol. 3: Back in Blue*. 2015. 120pp. 978-0-7851-9220-6.
> *Vol. 4: The End Is Fourever*. 2015. 144pp. 978-0-7851-9744-7.

Fantastic Four by John Byrne Omnibus. Written and Illustrated by **John Bryne**. Marvel Comics, 2011–2013. Y

Collects the highly popular run by writer/illustrator **John Byrne** that was originally published from 1981 through 1986 and included the trial of Galactus, the loss of Reed and Sue's second child, the introduction of the She-Hulk as a Fantastic Four team member, and a classic battle between Galactus's former heralds Terrax and the Silver Surfer that was manipulated by Doctor Doom.

Vol. 1. 2011. 1096pp. 978-0-7851-5824-0, hardcover.
Vol. 2. 2013. 1224pp. 978-0-7851-8543-7, hardcover.

Fantastic Four Omnibus. Written by **Stan Lee**. Illustrated by **Jack Kirby**. Marvel Comics, 2013–2015. Y

A collection of all of the early original Fantastic Four books by Stan Lee and Jack "King" Kirby. The hardcover omnibus collections showcase the origin of the Fantastic Four, the first meeting of Doctor Doom, and the first appearances of the Silver Surfer and the coming of Galactus.

Vol. 1. 2013. 848pp. 978-0-7851-8566-6, hardcover.
Vol. 2. 2013. 832pp. 978-0-7851-8567-3, hardcover.
Vol. 3. 2015. 952pp. 978-0-7851-9174-2, hardcover.

© 2016 Marvel Comics

The Incredibles. Written by **Mark Waid** and **Landry Walker**. Illustrated by **Marcio Takara** and **Ramanda Kamarga**. Boom Kids, 2009–2011. Y 🎬

A continuation of the hit 2004 Disney•Pixar film created and directed by Brad Bird. Set in a world where super-heroes once thrived, Bob Parr and his wife Helen aren't like all the other suburban families: they're super-heroes known as Mr. Incredible and Elasta-Girl! Now the parents of three super-powered siblings, Violet, Dash, and infant Jack-Jack, each of them is powerful in their own right, but together they are the super-hero family known as the Incredibles! A sequel to the movie will be released in 2019.

Family Matters. 2009. 128pp. 978-1-60886-525-3, hardcover; 978-1-93450-683-7.
City of Incredibles. 2010. 112pp. 978-1-60886-529-1, hardcover; 978-1-60886-503-1.

© 2009 Disney•Pixar

Revenge from Below. 2010. 112pp. 978-1-60886-518-5.
Secrets and Lies. 2010. 112pp. 978-1-60886-583-3.
Truth and Consequences. 2011. 128pp. 978-1-60886-603-8.

Jack Kirby's Fourth World Omnibus. Written and Illustrated by **Jack Kirby** and various. DC Comics 2007–2012. T

© 2016 DC Comics

In the 1970s Jack Kirby went from Marvel to DC Comics where he created what is known as The Fourth World in which the good New Gods of New Genesis battle the forces of Darkseid, ruler of Apokolips. These omnibusses collect the complete runs of the 1970s editions of *Mister Miracle, The Forever People* and *The New Gods* as well as issues of *Superman's Pal Jimmy Olsen* and the *Hunger Dogs* graphic novel.

Vol. 1. 2007. 396pp. 978-1-4012-1344-2, hardcover; 2011. 978-1-4012-3241-2.
Vol. 2. 2007. 396pp. 978-1-4012-1357-2, hardcover; 2012. 978-1-4012-3440-9.
Vol. 3. 2007. 396pp. 978-1-4012-1485-2, hardcover; 2012. 978-1-4012-3535-2.
Vol. 4. 2008. 424pp. 978-1-4012-1583-5, hardcover; 2012. 978-1-4012-3746-2.

Justice League Dark. Written by **Peter Milligan**, **J.M. DeMatteis**, and **Jeff Lemire**. Illustrated by **Mikel Janin**, **Ray Fawkes**, and various. 2012–2015. T 🎬 🖥

© 2016 DC Comics

After the New 52 began, there were a number of Justice League teams. While two had the traditional super-heroes, a third took on supernatural threats. Members included John Constantine, Black Orchid, Frankenstein, and Deadman. Their main base was in the House of Mystery. This League worked with the others during the crossover event "Trinity War." They were also involved in the "Forever Evil" story. A direct-to-DVD animated film premiered in 2017.

Vol. 1: In the Dark. 2012. 144pp. 978-1-4012-3704-2.
Vol. 2: The Books of Magic. 2013. 224pp. 978-1-4012-4024-0.
Vol. 3: The Death of Magic. 2014. 192pp. 978-1-4012-4245-9.
Vol. 4: The Rebirth of Evil. 2014. 208pp. 978-1-4012-4725-6.
Vol. 5: Paradise Lost. 2015. 160pp. 978-1-4012-5007-2.
Vol. 6: Lost in Forever. 2015. 192pp. 978-1-4012-5481-0.

Justice League of America (JLA)

DC Comics, 2006– . T 🎬 🖥 🎮

The greatest heroes of the DC Comics Universe, Superman, Batman, Wonder Woman, Cyborg, Green Lantern, Flash, and Aquaman, are also part of the greatest super-hero team. They're a dedicated force out to fight for truth and justice whenever the Earth is threatened. Below are listed the collected graphic novel editions of the extremely popular monthly comic book series as well as a variety of graphic novel stories and miniseries featuring the heroes. An animated *Justice League* series (later called *Justice League Unlimited*) aired from 2001 to 2006, and a new series of animated shorts, *Justice League Action*, began in 2017. The team has also appeared in direct-to-DVD animated films and a live-action feature film of the *Justice League* came out in 2017.

Justice. Written by **Jim Krueger** and **Alex Ross**. Illustrated by **Doug Braithwaite** and **Alex Ross**. DC Comics, 2012. 384pp. 978-1-4012-3526-0.

Collecting the 12-volume self-contained maxi-series. The Justice League discovers that they're not the only ones well organized. A league of the greatest villains has set a plan in motion that is setting out to achieve more good than the JLA could ever accomplish. Can the heroes actually trust the criminal masterminds and is their plan really that benevolent or is there a hidden agenda to their reform?

Justice League (New 52). Written by **Geoff Johns**. Illustrated by **Jim Lee**, **Scott Williams**, **Tony Daniel**, and various. DC Comics, 2013– . T 🏃 ◎ 🎬

© 2016 DC Comics

Relaunched in 2011 as a monthly comic book, the <u>Justice League</u> series begins with the first meeting of the heroes coming together under a common enemy. Brought together by Batman when a dark evil is too much for him to handle alone, he must trust a speedster, Amazon, alien, teenage cyborg, a space cop, and an undersea ruler. Volume 3 was adapted into a direct-to-DVD animated film. A new <u>Justice League</u> series began in 2016, written Bryan Hitch.

Vol. 1: Origin. 2013. 192pp. 978-1-4012-3788-2.
Vol. 2: The Villain's Journey. 2013. 176pp. 978-1-4012-3765-3.
Vol. 3: Throne of Atlantis. 2014. 192pp. 978-1-4012-4698-3.
Vol. 4: The Grid. 2014. 176pp. 978-1-4012-5008-9.
Vol. 5: Forever Heroes. 2015. 168pp. 978-1-4012-5419-3.
Vol. 6: Injustice League. 2015. 272pp. 978-1-4012-5852-8.
Vol. 7: The Darkseid War, Part 1. 2016. 176pp. 978-1-4012-5977-8.
Vol. 8: The Darkseid War, Part 2. 2016. 176pp. 978-1-4012-6341-6.

Justice League of America. Written by **Brad Meltzer**, **Geoff Johns**, **Dwayne McDuffie**, and **James Robinson**. Illustrated by **Ed Benes**, **Mark Bagley**, and various. DC Comics, 2008–2012. T

Launched by writer Brad Meltzer in 2006, this title featured the League of an earlier continuity, continuing a tradition dating back to the 1960s. Originally this team featured a roster which included Superman, Batman, Wonder Woman, Green Lantern (Hal Jordan), Black Canary, Red Arrow, Red Tornado, Vixen, Black Lightning, and Hawkgirl.

Vol. 1: The Tornado's Path. 2008. 224pp. 978-1-4012-1580-4.
Vol. 2: The Lightning Saga. 2009. 224pp. 978-1-4012-1869-0.
Vol. 3: The Injustice League. 2009. 144pp. 978-1-4012-2050-1.
Vol. 4: Sanctuary. 2009. 128pp. 978-1-4012-2010-5.
Vol. 5: The Second Coming. 2010. 144pp. 978-1-4012-2253-6.
Vol. 6: When Worlds Collide. 2010. 176pp. 978-1-4012-2423-3.
Vol. 7: Team History. 2011. 192pp. 978-1-4012-3260-3.

Vol. 8: The Dark Things. 2012. 192pp. 978-1-4012-3193-4.
Vol. 9: Omega. 2012. 200pp. 978-1-4012-3356-3.
Vol. 10: The Rise of Eclipso. 2012. 192pp. 978-1-4012-3413-3.

Justice League of America (New 52). Written by **Geoff Johns**, **Matt Kindt**, and **Bryan Hitch**. Illustrated by **Brett Booth**, **David Finch**, **Doug Mahnke**, and **Bryan Hitch**. DC Comics, 2013– .

There have been several ***Justice League of America*** titles since the New 52 period began. The first in 2013 featured a team that worked for the U.S. government as opposed to the independent League. This series came out of *Justice League International* (2011–2012) and led into the short-lived *Justice League United* (2014–2015). Its run included a tie-in to the inter-title "Trinity War" and helped to set up the Forever Evil storyline. The second ran from 2015 to 2016 and was written and drawn by fan-favorite Bryan Hitch. A third series began in 2016 following DC's "Rebirth" event.

First series

Vol. 1: World's Most Dangerous. 2013. 224pp. 978-1-4012-4236-7, hardcover; 978-1-4012-4689-1, paperback.
Vol. 2: Survivors of Evil. 2014. 160pp. 978-1-4012-4726-3, hardcover; 978-1-4012-5047-8, paperback.

Second series

Vol. 1.: Power and Glory. 2017. 296pp. 978-1-4012-5976-1, hardcover.

Justice Society of America (JSA). Written by **James Robinson** and **Bill Willingham**. Illustrated by various. DC Comics, 2008–2015. T ◉

© 2016 DC Comics

Before the JLA, the first super-hero team was the Justice Society of America. Created by DC Comics, in 1940 in the pages of *All-Star Comics, #3*, the JSA's original members included the earliest incarnations of the Flash, Green Lantern, Dr. Fate, the Atom, Black Canary, Hawkman, the Sandman and Starman. Flash forward 70 years and the JSA is still as popular as ever. Featuring a mix of original founding members as well as the newest generation of classic JSA members, they're still out fighting evil in the name of justice. The hardcover Omnibus collections reprint the original JSA series by writer Geoff Johns in its entirety beginning with the 1999 series through the entirety of his writing through 2009.

Vol. 1: The Next Age. 2008. 144pp. 978-1-4012-1585-9.
Vol. 2: The Lightning Saga. 2009. 224pp. 978-1-4012-1869-0.
Vol. 3: Thy Kingdom Come, Part 1. 2009. 160pp. 978-1-4012-1741-9.
Vol. 4: Thy Kingdom Come, Part 2. 2009. 192pp. 978-1-4012-1946-8.
Vol. 5: Thy Kingdom Come, Part 3. 2010. 224pp. 978-1-4012-2167-6.
Vol. 6:Black Adam and Isis. 2010. 160pp. 978-1-4012-2531-5.
Vol. 7:The Bad Seed. 2010. 128pp. 978-1-4012-2714-2.
Vol. 8: Axis of Evil. 2010. 168pp. 978-1-4012-2901-6.

Vol. 9: Super Town. 2011. 144pp. 978-1-4012-3284-9.
Vol. 10: Monument Point. 2012. 144pp. 978-1-4012-3368-6.
JSA Omnibus, Vol. 1. 2014. 1224pp. 978-1401247614, hardcover.
JSA Omnibus, Vol. 2. 2014. 1408pp. 978-1401251383, hardcover.
JSA Omnibus, Vol. 3. 2015. 1248pp. 978-1401255305, hardcover.

League of Extraordinary Gentlemen. Written by **Alan Moore**. Illustrated by **Kevin O'Neill**. Vertigo/DC Comics/Top Shelf/IDW Publishing, 2001– . M 🎗 ◎ ▰

© 2016 Alan Moore and Top Shelf/
IDW Publishing

Set at the end of the 19th century, when grave danger arrives from those who wish to threaten England, a team made up of some of the most extraordinary individuals is there. Called the League of Extraordinary Gentlemen, the team is comprised of the heroes and oddities from some of English literature's finest Victorian-age fictional characters: Mina Murphy, the Invisible Man, Alan Quartermain, Dr. Jekyll/Mr. Hyde, and Captain Nemo. Together the misfit team of beasts, oddities, and drug abusers must use their talents to save England from its most deadly enemies both on Earth and in outer space. Later books in the series jump in time to other versions of the team made up of literary heroes throughout history and stand-alone stories focusing on Nemo's daughter, Janni. The series has won multiple awards including Eisner Awards and Harvey Awards over the years. The first graphic novel was also adapted into a dreadful motion picture in 2004 that many comic book fans and viewers of cinema in general have tried to forget.

Volume 1. 2001. 176pp. 978-1-56389-858-7. DC Comics.
Volume 2. 2011. 228pp. 978-1-4012-0118-0. DC Comics.
The League of Extraordinary Gentlemen Omnibus. 2011. 416pp. 978-1-4012-3321-1, hardcover; 2013. 416pp. 978-1-4012-4083-7. DC Comics.
The Black Dossier. 2008. 200pp. 978-1-4012-0307-8.
Volume 3: Century. 2014. 256pp. 978-1-60309-329-3, hardcover.
Nemo: Heart of Ice. 2013. 56pp. 978-1-60309-274-6, hardcover.
Nemo: The Roses of Berlin. 2014. 56pp. 978-1-60309-320-0, hardcover.
Nemo: River of Ghosts. 2015. 56pp. 978-1-60309-355-2, hardcover.

Red Hood and the Outlaws. Written by **Scott Lobdell**. Illustrated by various. DC Comics, 2012–2016. T

In the 1980s, Dick Grayson, the original Robin, gave up that role and soon became Nightwing. Batman soon found a new Robin, Jason Todd, who was killed by the Joker (see *Batman: A Death in the Family*). Years later he returned to life working both with and against the Batman in various identities including the Red Hood, a name once used by the Joker. In the "New 52" continuity, Jason, as the Red Hood, teams up with two former Titans, the alien princess Starfire and Green Arrow's ex-partner Arsenal to form the Outlaws.

Vol. 1: REDemption. 2012. 160pp. 978-1-4012-3712-7.
Vol. 2: The Starfire. 2013. 160pp. 978-1-4012-4090-5.
Vol. 3: Death of the Family. 2013. 176pp. 978-1-4012-4090-5.

Vol. 4: League of Assassins. 2014. 232pp. 978-1-4012-4636-5.
Vol. 5: The Big Picture. 2014. 160pp. 978-1-4012-5048-5.
Vol. 6: Lost and Found. 2015. 144pp. 978-1-4012-5342-4.
Vol. 7: Last Call. 2016. 144pp. 978-1-4012-5856-6.

Runaways: The Complete Collection. Written by **Brian K. Vaughan**, **Joss Whedon**, **Terry Moore**, **Kathyrn Immonen**, and various. Illustrated by **Adrian Alphona**, **Michael Ryan**, **Humberto Ramos**, **Sara Pichelli**, and various. Marvel Comics, 2014–2015. T 🏃 ◎

© 2016 Marvel Comics

All teenagers think that their parents are evil—but what if they really were? That's what a group of teenagers find out when they accidentally discover that their parents are secretly a group of super-powered villains known as The Pride. When the teens discover the shock of their lives, they must find the courage, strength, and power within themselves to strike out on their own and ultimately confront their parents and an enemy from within their own team. The hardcover collections reprint all of the entire series. The series was also recognized by YALSA in 2006 and 2009 for Best Books for Young Adults. The series also won Brian K. Vaughan an Eisner Award in 2005 and a Harvey Award in 2006 for Best New Series. The series was put in hiatus in 2009 after a series of creative team changes, but the highly regarded series has yet to be continued.

Vol. 1. 2014. 978-0-7851-8558-1, hardcover.
Vol. 2. 2014. 978-0-7851-8784-4, hardcover.
Vol. 3. 2015. 978-0-7851-8917-6, hardcover.
Vol. 4. 2015. 978-0-7851-8905-3, hardcover.

Sailor Moon. Written and Illustrated by **Naoko Takeuchi**. Kodansha Comics, 2011–2013. Y あ Japanese manga.

A schoolgirl and her friends turn into a super-hero group called the Sailor Warriors, and high school will never be the same again! Klutzy 14-year-old junior high school student Usagi Tsukino is recruited by a talking black cat to be a fighter for love and justice against the dark, ever-evil that is reemerging. Usagi also discovers that she is the reincarnation of Princess Serenity, a princess of the ancient moon kingdom and defender against evil. As the protector of the solar system, Usagi calls herself Sailor Moon when in costume. Along the way she meets other reincarnations of female sailor warriors like herself, including Rei Hino (Sailor Mars), Makoto Kino (Sailor Jupiter), Ami Mizuno (Sailor Mercury), and Minako Aino (Sailor Venus), as they work together as a team to defeat evil at all costs. There is one other mysterious savior of Sailor Moon, a dashing young man who is known as Tuxedo Mask. In reality he is Usagi's boyfriend Mamoru Chiba, and they find they have a lot more in common with each other than they thought: they're both the reincarnations of each other's true love.

Kodansha Comics began reprinting the series in 2011, featuring a new translation as well as reprinting the series in the original right-to-left Japanese format. The manga inspired a hit anime television series, movies, and other spin-offs.

Vol. 1. 2011. 240pp. 978-1-935429-74-6.
Vol. 2. 2011. 244pp. 978-1-935429-75-3.
Vol. 3. 2012. 248pp. 978-1-935429-76-0.
Vol. 4. 2012. 248pp. 978-1-612620-00-8.
Vol. 5. 2012. 260pp. 978-1-612620-01-5.
Vol. 6. 2012. 248pp. 978-1-612620-02-2.

Vol. 7. 2012. 240pp. 978-1-612620-03-9.
Vol. 8. 2012. 232pp. 978-1-61262-004-6.
Vol. 9. 2012. 264pp. 978-1-612620-05-3.
Vol. 10. 2013. 240pp. 978-1-612620-06-0.
Vol. 11. 2013. 240pp. 978-1-612620-07-7.
Vol. 12. 2013. 240pp. 978-1-612620-08-4.

Secret Six. Written by **Gail Simone**. Illustrated by **Dale Eaglesham**, **Brad Walker**, **Jim Calafiore**, and various. DC Comics, 2014–2016. O

Spinning out the Villains United limited series from 2005, the Secret Six is a group of super-villains who undertake dangerous projects for high reward. Members have included Deadshot, Catman, and Bane. A "New 52" rebooted version of the team debuted in late 2014, and the first volume was released in 2016. The New 52 team currently consists of Catman, Black Alice, Strix, Ventriloquist, Big Shot, and Porcelain. DC Comics is reprinting both the 2006 series and the New 52 series concurrently.

Vol. 1: Villains United. 2014. 328pp. 978-1-4012-5075-1.
Vol. 2: Money for Murder. 2015. 336pp. 978-1-4012-5537-4.
Vol. 3: Cat's Cradle. 2015. 264pp. 978-1-4012-5861-0.
Vol. 4: Caution to the Wind. 2016. 200pp. 978-1-4012-6090-3.
New 52: Vol. 1: Friends in Low Places. 2016. 144pp. 978-1-4012-5485-8.
Vol. 2: The Gauntlet. 2017. 144pp. 978-1-4012-6453-6.

Suicide Squad

DC Comics. 🎬 🖥

Also known as Task Force X, the Suicide Squad is a covert team of anti-heroes on death row. The super-villains form a black-ops squad who undertake high-risk missions in exchange for commuted prison sentences for the United States. The group operates under the directorship of Amanda Waller. Spun out of the 1987 miniseries called Legends (recollected in 2016, ISBN 978-1-4012-6316-4), the team was led by Rick Flag Jr.; the regular members of the squad included The Bronze Tiger, Captain Boomerang, and Deadshot. In the "New 52" DC Universe the Squad has been brought back together with new members including Harley Quinn and Black Manta. While the new team's adventures have all been collected, the 1980s team's stories are finally being properly collected. Various incarnations of the Squad have been seen on various DC Comics animated series, including the highly regarded *Batman: Assault on Arkham* animated film from 2014, the live-action series Smallville and Arrow, and a feature film *Suicide Squad* released in 2016.

Suicide Squad, 1st series. Written by **John Ostrander**. Illustrated by **Luke McDonnell**. DC Comics, 2008– . T

Vol. 1: Trial by Fire. 2015. 232pp. 978-1-4012-5831-3.
Vol. 2: The Nightshade Odyssey. 2015. 264pp. 978-1-4012-5831-3.
Vol. 3: Sea of Troubles. 2016. 280pp. 978-1-401-26091-0.
Vol. 4: The Janus Directive. 2016. 264pp. 978-1-4012-6261-7.

Vol. 5: Apokolips Now. 2016. 200pp. 978-1-4012-6542-7.
From the Ashes. 2008. 192pp. 978-1-4012-1866-9.

Suicide Squad, 2nd series (New 52). Written by **Adam Glass**, **Ales Kot**, and **Matt Kindt**. Illustrated by **Federico Dallocchio** and **Patrick Zircher**. 2012–2014. T

© 2016 DC Comics

Vol. 1: Kicked in the Teeth. 2012. 160pp. 978-1-4012-3544-4.
Vol. 2: Basilisk Rising. 2013. 192pp. 978-1-4012-3844-5.
Vol. 3: Death Is for Suckers. 2013. 144pp. 978-1-4012-4316-6.
Vol. 4: Discipline and Punish. 2014. 144pp. 978-1-4012-4701-0.
Vol. 5: Walled In. 2014. 208pp. 978-1-4012-5012-6.

New Suicide Squad, 3rd series (New 52). Written by **Sean Ryan**. Illustrated by various. 2015– .

Vol. 1: Pure Insanity. 2015. 978-1-4012-5238-0.
Vol. 2. Monsters. 2016. 144pp. 978-1-4012-6152-8.
Vol. 3: Freedom. 2016. 144pp. 978-1-4012-6264-8.
Vol. 4: Kill Anything. 2016. 168pp. 978-1-4012-7000-1.

Teen Titans (New 52)

Written by **Scott Lobdell** and **Will Pfeifer**. Illustrated by **Brett Booth**, **Norm Rapmund**, **Eddy Barrows**, and **Kenneth Rocafort**. DC Comics, 2012– . T 🏃

One of the most popular teen team books in the 1980s alongside Marvel Comics' *X-Men* and the inspiration for the hit cartoon television show on Cartoon Network. A team of young teen heroes, the Teen Titans first appeared in the Silver Age of comics in 1964 and has featured many youth-oriented heroes in their rotating team of heroes including Robin, Starfire, Cyborg, Aqualad, Speedy, Kid Flash, Troia, Beast Boy, Raven, Terra, Wonder Girl, Nightwing, and Superboy. Together they have battled villains over the years, the most popular being the mercenary-for-hire Deathstroke the Terminator. Collected below is the New 52 relaunch of the series, which had a re-relaunch in 2014 with Will Pfeifer as the writer, with Kenneth Rocafort featuring a more classic team comprised of Beast Boy, Wonder Girl, Red Robin, Bunker, and Raven. An additional series began in 2016 as part of the "DC Rebirth." DC has also begun collecting the second <u>New Teen Titans</u> series from the 1980s that was written by Marv Wolfman and initially drawn by George Perez.

Teen Titans, first series, 2012–2015.

Vol. 1: It's Our Right to Fight. 2012. 168pp. 978-1-4012-3698-4.
Vol. 2: The Culling. 2013. 192pp. 978-1-4012-4103-2.

Vol. 3: Death of the Family. 2013. 160pp. 978-1-4012-4321-0.
Vol. 4: Light and Dark. 2014. 144pp. 978-1-4012-4624-2.
Vol. 5: The Trial of Kid Flash. 2015. 256pp. 978-1-4012-5053-9.

Teen Titans, second series, 2015–2016

Vol. 1: Blinded by the Light. 2015. 176pp. 978-1-40125-237-3.
Vol. 2: Rogue Targets. 2016. 192pp. 978-1-4012-6162-7.
Vol. 3: The Sum of Its Parts. 2016.144pp. 978-1-4012-6520-5.
Vol. 4: When Titans Fall. 2017. ??pp. 978-1-4012-6977-7.

The Watchmen

Written by **Alan Moore**. Illustrated by **Dave Gibbons**. DC Comics, 2013–2014. O 🏅 ◎ 🎬

In an alternate world where the threat of the Cold War still looms over an America still run by President Nixon, the super-heroes of old have all but have been outlawed and only vigilante and registered heroes remain. When the soldier-of-fortune hero known as The Comedian is murdered, a complex plot to eliminate heroes and murder innocent humans is uncovered by the vigilante hero known as Rorschach. After reuniting his old Watchmen teammates back out of their retirement and self-banishment, not even the combined powers of Rorschach, Ozymandias, Nite Owl, and Dr. Manhattan can solve the mystery of their murdered companion and stop Armageddon. The story has been regarded by many fans as one of the most influential comic book stories from the 1980s. The series has won multiple awards including Eisner Awards for Best Finite/Limited Series (1988), Best Graphic Album (1988), Best Writer (1988), and Best Writer/Artist (1988), and Harvey Awards for Best Writer (1988), Best Artist or Penciller (1988), Special Award for Excellence in Production/Presentation (1988), Best Continuing or Limited Series (1988), Best Single Issue of Story (1988), and Best Graphic Album (1988), as well as recognition in YALSA's Popular Paperbacks for Young Adults in 2002. The graphic novel was also adapted into a live-action movie which was released in 2009 by director Zack Snyder.

© 2016 DC Comics

Watchmen, reprint edition. 2014. 448pp. 978-1-4012-4525-2.
Watchmen: Deluxe Edition. 2013. 448pp. 978-1-4012-3896-4, hardcover.

Before Watchmen. DC Comics, 2014. M

Inspired by the 1986 comic book series, DC Comics revisited the world of *The Watchmen*. The stand-alone stories focus on popular characters from the original series including The Comedian, Rorschach, Nite Owl, and Dr. Manhattan. The collections were well regarded but were done without the consent of Alan Moore, the original writer of the series.

© 2016 DC Comics

Minutemen/Silk Spectre. 2014. Written by **Darwyn Cooke**. Illustrated by **Amanda Conner**. 2014. 288pp. 978-1-4012-4512-2.

Comedian/Rorschach. Written by **Brian Azzarello**. Illustrated by **J.G. Jones** and **Lee Bermejo**. 2014. 256pp. 978-1-4012-4513-9.

Nite Owl/Dr. Manhattan. Written by **J. Michael Straczynski**. Illustrated by **Adam Hughes** and **Joe Kubert**. 2014. 288pp. 978-1-4012-4514-6.

Ozymandias/Crimson Corsair. Written by **Len Wein**. Illustrated by **Jae Lee** and **John Higgins**. 2014. 288pp. 978-1-4012-4515-3.

Young Avengers

Marvel Comics, 2006–2014. T 🎗

© 2016 Marvel Comics

After the Avengers are in disarray following the events of the *Avengers: Disassembled* storyline, a young group of heroes, each reminiscent of an Avenger, have mysteriously appeared: Iron Lad, the Asgardian, Patriot, and Hulkling. When Captain America and Iron Man investigate the strange appearance of these four young heroes, their connection to the original Avengers is revealed. Meanwhile, several more members, Titan and Knightress, joined this fledgling team as they continued to take on villains under the guidance of an Avenger once believed to be dead. The series was relaunched in 2012 with members including Wiccan, Hulkling, and Hawkeye, as well as new members Kid Loki, Marvel Boy, Prodigy, and Miss America. The original series won the 2006 GLAAD Media Award for Outstanding Comic Book and the 2006 Harvey Award for Best New Series. The second volume by Kieron Gillen also received the award for Outstanding Comic Book at the 25th GLAAD Media Awards in 2014.

Young Avengers, 1st series. Written by **Allan Heinberg** and various. Illustrated by **Jim Cheung**, **John Dell**, and various. 2006–2012. T

> *Vol. 1: Sidekicks*. 2006. 144pp. 978-0-7851-2018-6.
> *Vol. 2: Family Matters*. 2007. 184pp. 978-0-7851-1754-4.
> *Civil War: Young Avengers & Runaways*. 2007. 112pp. 978-0-7851-2317-0.
> *Young Avengers Presents*. 2008. 144pp. 978-0-7851-2975-2.
> *Secret Invasion: Runaways/Young Avengers*. 2009. 96pp. 978-0-7851-3266-0.
> *Dark Reign: Young Avengers*. 2010. 120pp. 978-0-7851-3909-6.
> *Ultimate Collection*. 2010. 352pp. 978-0-7851-4907-1.
> *Avengers: The Children's Crusade*. 2012. 248pp. 978-0-7851-3638-5.

Young Avengers, 2nd series. Written by **Kieron Gillen**. Illustrated by **Jamie McKelvie**. 2013–2014.

> *Vol. 1: Style > Substance*. 2013. 128pp. 978-0-7851-6708-2.
> *Vol. 2: Alternative Cultures*. 2014. 112pp. 978-0-7851-6709-9.
> *Vol. 3: Mic-Drop at the Edge of Time and Space*. 2014. 112pp. 978-0-7851-8530-7.
> *Young Avengers Omnibus*. 2014. 360pp. 978-0-7851-9171-1, hardcover.

X-Men

Created by **Stan Lee** and **Jack Kirby**. Marvel Comics, 2006– . T 🎬 🖥 🎮

In a world where a genetic evolution is on the horizon, *Homo sapiens'* time is ending and the dawn of the Homo superior—the mutants—is now upon us. Born with strange powers, the mutants live in a world that both hates and fears them for their differences and powers. In these troubling times of racial discourse, Professor Charles Xavier (Professor X) created a school for children of the atom where they could live and learn to accept their powers, control them, and use them for good. The original team was made up of Cyclops (Scott Summers), Marvel Girl (Jean Grey), Iceman (Bobby Drake), Angel (Warren Worthington), and Beast (Hank McCoy). Called X-Men, they're protectors of humanity against evil in its many forms, including such villains as the evil Magneto, Apocalypse, and the Brotherhood of Evil Mutants. Created in 1961, they've continued to be one of the most popular comic book series of titles in the United States since the late 1970s when the second generation of X-Men including Wolverine, Colossus, Storm and Nightcrawler joined the team. Though the roster of team members has changed continuously over the years, their popularity has still remained. Currently, the adventures of the X-Men are published by Marvel Comics through three main comic book monthly titles *Astonishing X-Men*, *Uncanny X-Men*, and adjectiveless *X-Men*, plus numerous spin-offs, miniseries, and more. Recommend trade paperback collections and various titles featuring the tales of the X-Men are listed below. Please visit Marvel Comics' web site at http://www.marvel.com for many more titles featuring this extremely popular team of heroes.

Classic Collected X-Men Stories

Below are listed some of the more popular X-Men storylines over the decades. Some of the stories were adapted into the live-action X-Men movies—especially the *Dark Phoenix Saga* (*X-Men: The Last Stand—2006*) and *X-Men: Days of Future Past* (*X-Men: Days of Future Past—2014*).

X-Men: Days of Future Past. Written by **Chris Claremont** and **Louise Simonson**. Illustrated by **John Byrne**, **Alan Davis**, and **Walter Simonson**. Marvel Comics, 2014. 392pp. 978-0-7851-8442-3, hardcover. ◎

© 2016 Marvel Comics

Collecting the epic storyline from *Uncanny X-Men* #141–142 (1981) as well as other stories featuring a dark future for the X-Men where mutants were enslaved by the Sentinel robots. The X-Men collection was the first to feature a look at a possible bleak future for mutantkind where the world is under the control of the mutant-hunting Sentinels and most heroes—including the X-Men—are dead. Kitty Pryde's mind is taken over by a time-traveling Katherine Pryde from the future and she warns the X-Men that the only way to prevent this dark and foreboding future for mutants and the world is to thwart the assassination of Senator Robert Kelly by Mystique and the new Brotherhood of Evil Mutants. The X-Men must try and stop Mystique from killing the senator and try to change the future for the better at all costs.

The original storyline was also the inspiration for the 2014 X-Men movie of the same name.

X-Men: The Dark Phoenix Saga. Written by **Chris Claremont**. Illustrated by **John Byrne**. Marvel Comics, 2012. 200pp. 978-0-7851-6421-0. ◎

The epic Dark Phoenix saga focuses on Jean Grey (aka Marvel Girl) who, after nearly dying while saving the team, is merged with a mysterious cosmic entity called the Phoenix force. Now Jean, like the myth of the firebird, is reborn with augmented power and she rejoins the X-Men as Phoenix. When she's played as a pawn by the mysterious mutant organization the Hellfire Club, the dark side of the Phoenix force is unleashed. After rampaging throughout the galaxy and destroying a planet, the Phoenix is put on trial for her crimes and the X-Men must try and save her life in a contest of might. Ultimately, Jean Grey knows she can't hold onto the destructive power of the Phoenix and sacrifices herself to save the lives of the entire solar system. The *Dark Phoenix Saga* is one of the most highly regarded X-Men storylines of all time, and a partial inspiration for the film *X-Men: The Last Stand* (2006).

X-Men by Chris Claremont and Jim Lee Omnibus. Written by **Chris Claremont**. Illustrated by **Jim Lee**, **Marc Silvestri**, and **Rob Liefeld**. Marvel Comics, 2011–2012.

© 2016 Marvel Comics

A collection reprinting the popular debut of artist Jim Lee to the *Uncanny X-Men* comics as well as the work of Marc Silvestri from the late 1980s to the early 1990s. The collection also includes the debut of the second X-Men monthly comic book series, the adjectiveless *X-Men* from 1991. The X-Men members divide into two teams, Blue and Gold, to better fight for the rights of mutants and the preservation of humanity. In the first adventure the Blue team (comprised of Beast, Psylocke, Rogue, Gambit, Cyclops, and Wolverine) faces a grand battle against Magneto and his minions, the Acolytes.

Vol. 1. 2011. 720pp. 978-0-7851-5822-6, hardcover.
Vol. 2. 2012. 832pp. 978-0785159056, hardcover.

Recent Collected X-Men Stories

The X-Men were originally published in the series Uncanny X-Men but due to their popularity spun off into a wide variety of X-Men series—including *Astonishing X-Men*, *X-Men*, *New X-Men*, *All-New X-Men*, and *Wolverine and the X-Men*. Listed below are some of the collections of the more popular stories featuring the X-Men teams.

All-New X-Men. Written by **Brian Michael Bendis**. Illustrated by **Stuart Immonen** and various. Marvel Comics, 2013– . T

Launched by fan-favorite writer Brian Michael Bendis in 2012, the *All-New X-Men* features the time-displaced original X-Men team of Cyclops, Beast,

Iceman, Angel, and Jean Grey, who are transported to the present day and encounter a future more dangerous than they could ever dream. The series replaced the Uncanny X-Men series. The series was relaunched in 2015 but still renamed All-New X-Men (though the collections have the subtitle "Inevitable") and features the time-displaced Cyclops, Beast, Iceman, and Angel—as well as the All-New Wolverine, Kid Apocalypse, and Oya striking out on their own.

All-New X-Men, 1st series, 2013–2015. T

Vol. 1: Yesterday's X-Men. 2013. 136pp. 978-0-7851-6637-5.
Vol. 2: Here to Stay. 2013. 136pp. 978-0-7851-6638-2.
Vol. 3: Out of Their Depth. 2013. 136pp. 978-0-7851-6639-9.
Vol. 4: All-Different. 2014. 144pp. 978-184653585-7.
Vol. 5: One Down. 2014. 152pp. 978-0-7851-8968-8.
Vol. 6: The Ultimate Adventure. 2015. 136pp. 978-0-7851-8969-5.
Vol. 7: The Utopians. 2015. 136pp. 978-0-7851-9235-0.
Guardians of the Galaxy/All-New X-Men: The Trial of Jean Grey. 2014. 144pp. 978-1-8465-3608-3.
All-New X-Men/Indestructible Hulk/Superior Spider-Man: The Arms of the Octopus. 2014. 96pp. 978-0-7851-8438-6.
X-Men: Battle of the Atom. 2014. 224pp. 978-0-7851-8907-7.

All-New X-Men Oversized Collections, 2014– .

Vol. 1. 2014. 272pp. 978-0-7851-9115-5, hardcover.
Vol. 2. 2015. 272pp. 978-0-7851-9822-2, hardcover.
Vol. 3. 2015. 288pp. 978-0-7851-9823-9, hardcover.
Vol. 4. 2016. 240pp. 978-0-7851-9989-2, hardcover.

All-New X-Men, 2nd series, 2016– .

Vol. 1: Ghost of the Cyclops. 2016. 112pp. 978-0-7851-9630-3,
Vol. 2: Apocalypse Wars. 2016. 144pp. 978-0-7851-9631-0.
Vol. 3: Hell Hath So Much Fury. 2017. 112pp. 978-1-302-90291-9.

Astonishing X-Men by Joss Whedon & John Cassaday. Written by **Joss Whedon**. Illustrated by **John Cassiday**. Marvel Comics, 2012. T ◎ 🕴

Written by popular *Buffy the Vampire Slayer* creator and *Avengers* movie director Joss Whedon, Professor X has left the school to help rebuild the mutant haven island of Genosha and the School for Gifted Students is now in the hands of Scott Summers (Cyclops) and Emma Frost (White Queen). The X-Men have formed three squads, ironically with Wolverine being in all three of them at the same time. The core group of X-Men— Cyclops, White Queen, Kitty Pryde, Wolverine, and Beast—are teaching the students how to both control their powers and save the world. Back in spandex costumes, the X-Men are out to quell the fear that they're a "mutant menace" and prove to the world at large that they're heroes. Meanwhile, a new menace threatens to destroy mutantkind. When a doctor announces she's devised a cure for mutantkind, what effect will it have on mutants, and does it really work? The series also features the much-welcomed return of a fan-favorite X-Man. The hardcover *Vol. 1* edition reprints the entire original 12 issues of the first series. In 2006 when the series debuted, the series received several Eisner Awards including Best Continuing Series and Best Artist for John Cassaday's artwork.

Book 1. 2012. 320pp. 978-0785161943.
Book 2. 2012. 344pp. 978-0785161950.

2

***Extraordinary X-Men*.** Written by **Jeff Lemire**. Illustrated by **Humberto Ramos**. Marvel Comics, 2016– . T

Following the events of the *Secret Wars* mega event, the X-Men teams are split into three groups—with this series focusing on the team leader of Storm as well as members Nightcrawler, Colossus, Iceman, Magik, Jean Grey, and an elderly Wolverine from the future.

3

Vol. 1: X-Haven. 2016. 136pp. 978-0-7851-9934-2.
Vol. 2: Apocalypse Wars. 2016. 160pp. 978-0-7851-9935-9.
Vol. 3: Kingdoms Fall. 2017. 128pp. 978-0-7851-9936-6.
Vol. 4: IvX. 2017. 112pp. 978-0-7851-9937-3.

4

Uncanny X-Men

The <u>Uncanny X-Men</u> series was the flagship title of the X-Men since the original series began in 1963. The series has had many changes to the creative team over the years, mostly under the influence of writer Chris Claremont, but other talented writers have also written for the series. <u>Uncanny X-Men</u> ended in 2011 with issue #544, but was relaunched several other times in the last several years by writers Kieron Gillan, Brian Michael Bendis, and most recently with Cullen Bunn. Below are listed a sampling of key titles over the last 10 years.

5

6

***Uncanny X-Men, 1st series*.** Written by **Matt Fraction**, **Ed Brubaker**, and **Kieron Gillen**. Illustrated by **Terry Dodson**, **Carlos Pacheco**, **Greg Land**, and various. 2013–2015.

The Complete Collection by Matt Fraction. Marvel Comics, 2013.

Vol. 1. 2013. 384pp. 978-0-7851-6593-4.
Vol. 2. 2013. 368pp. 978-0-7851-6594-1.
Vol. 3. 2013. 336pp. 978-0-7851-8450-8.

7

Breaking Point. 2011. 120pp. 978-0-7851-5226-2.
Fear Itself. 2012. 120pp. 978-0-7851-5227-9.

8

***Uncanny X-Men, 2nd series*.** Written by **Kieron Gillen**. Illustrated by **Carlos Pacheco**. 2012.

Vol. 1: Everything Is Sinister. 2012. 112pp. 978-0-7851-5994-0.
Vol. 2: Tabula Rasa. 2012. 136pp. 978-0-7851-5996-4.
Vol. 3: AvX: Book 1. 2012. 104pp. 978-0-7851-5998-8.
Vol. 4: AvX: Book 2. 2012. 136pp. 978-0-7851-6530-9.

9

Uncanny X-men, 3rd series. Written by **Brian Michael Bendis**. Illustrated by **Chris Bachalo**. 2014–2016. T

> *Vol. 1: Revolution.* 2014. 136pp. 978-0-7851-6702-0.
> *Vol. 2: Broken.* 2014. 144pp. 978-0-7851-6703-7.
> *Battle of the Atom.* 2014. 248pp. 978-0-7851-8906-0.
> *Vol. 3: The Good, the Bad, the Inhuman.* 2015. 136pp. 978-0-7851-8937-4.
> *Vol. 4: Vs. S.H.I.E.L.D.* 2015. 168pp. 978-0-7851-8938-1.
> *Vol. 5: The Omega Mutant.* 2015. 136pp. 978-0-7851-8939-8.
> *Vol. 6: Storyville.* 2016. 136pp. 978-0-7851-9231-2.

Uncanny X-Men, 4th series. Written by **Cullen Bunn**. Illustrated by **Greg Land** and **Ken Lashley**. 2016– . (Note: each volume of this series has an additional subtitle of "Superior.")

> *Vol. 1: Survival of the Fittest.* 2016. 136pp. 978-0-7851-9607-5.
> *Vol. 2: Apocalypse Wars.* 2016. 112pp. 978-0-7851-9608-2.
> *Vol. 3: Waking from the Dream.* 2017. 112pp. 978-1-302-90313-8.
> *Vol. 4: IvX.* 2017. 128pp. 978-1-302-90525-5.

Wolverine and the X-Men. Written by **Jason Aaron** and **Jason Latour**. Illustrated by **Chris Bachalo** and various. Marvel Comics, 2012–2015. T

After a schism erupts between members of the X-Men, Wolverine, Storm, Iceman, and others return to Westchester, New York, to restore one of Professor X's works—a school for young mutants. The Jean Grey School for Higher Learning is formed with Wolverine as headmaster and new and previously introduced students are taught in the use of their powers. The series restarted in 2014 and, after The Death of Wolverine (at least for now), was briefly replaced by *Spider-Man and the X-Men* in which Spider-Man came to teach at the school. There are no subtitles in the collections of the first series and at time the "and" is written as "&." Some collections are also listed with "By Jason Aaron" in the title. A few issues not collected in the listed volumes appear in the collection *X-Men: Battle of the Atom*. There is no direct connection between the Wolverine and the X-Men comics and the animated series of the same name.

Wolverine and the X-Men, 1st series. *2012–2014.*

> *Vol. 1.* 2012. 112pp. 978-0-7851-5680-2.
> *Vol. 2.* 2012. 104pp. 978-0-7851-5682-6.
> *Vol. 3.* 2012. 112pp. 978-0-7851-6000-7.
> *Vol. 4.* 2013. 112pp. 978-0-7851-6543-9.
> *Vol. 5.* 2013. 136pp. 978-0-7851-6577-4.
> *Vol. 6.* 2013. 112pp. 978-0-7851-6599-6.
> *Vol. 7.* 2013. 136pp. 978-0-7851-6600-9.
> *Vol. 8.* 2013. 152pp. 978-0-7851-6601-6.
> *Wolverine and the X-Men: Alpha & Omega.* 2012. 112pp. 978-0-7851-6400-5, hardcover; 978-0-7851-6401-2.
> *Wolverine & the X-Men by Jason Aaron Omnibus.* 2014. 936pp. 978-0-7851-9024-0.

Wolverine and the X-Men, 2nd series. *2014–2015.*

> *Vol. 1: Tomorrow Never Learns.* 2014. 144pp. 978-0-7851-8992-3.
> *Vol. 2: Death of Wolverine.* 2015. 144pp. 978-0-7851-8993-0.
> *Spider-Man and the X-Men.* 2015. 144pp. 978-0-7851-9700-3.

X-Men Spin-Offs

The success of the X-Men has spun off into a wide variety of series featuring X-Men characters and other mutants branching off into their own team of heroes. Below are some highlights of the spin-offs published by Marvel Comics.

New Mutants. Written by **Zeb Wells**, **Andy Lanning**, **Dan Abnett**, and various. Illustrated by **Diogenes Neves**, **Leonard Kirk**, **Leandro Fernandez**, and various. Marvel Comics, 2010–2012. T

© 2016 Marvel Comics

Recruited after the success of the X-Men, Professor Xavier opened the doors to his School for Gifted Youngsters to the next generation of mutants and the New Mutants were born. Originally debuting in 1982, one of the most popular adventures for the team was the *Demon Bear Saga,* which was reprinted. In time a second generation of New Mutants came to attend Professor Xavier's Institute for Higher Learning. Taught by the X-Men as well as Moonstar, Karma, Magma, and Wolfsbane, members of the original band of New Mutants, the latest teens are about to find out what a difficult life they have ahead of them for being feared for who they are and what powers they can control. The original series was renamed X-Force in the early 1990s and was a best-selling title for Marvel Comics. The third New Mutants series was originally released in 2009 and ended in 2012. Below are listed the complete New Mutants collections featuring the team from the third series.

Vol. 1: Return of Legion. 2010. 144pp. 978-0-7851-4064-1.
Vol. 2: Necrosha. 2010. 160pp. 978-0-7851-4065-8.
X-Necrosha. 2010. 448pp. 978-0-7851-4675-9.
X-Men: Second Coming. 2011. 392pp. 978-0-7851-5705-2.
Vol. 3: Fall of the New Mutants. 2011. 144pp. 978-0-7851-4583-7.
X-Men: Age of X. 2011. 256pp. 978-0-7851-5290-3.
Vol. 4: Unfinished Business. 2011. 112pp. 978-0-7851-5230-9.
Fear Itself: Wolverine/New Mutants. 2012. 152pp. 978-0-7851-5808-0.
Vol. 5: A Date with the Devil. 2012. 112pp. 978-0-7851-5233-0.
Vol. 6: De-Animator. 2012. 96pp. 978-0-7851-6160-8.
Journey into Mystery/New Mutants: Exiled. 2012. 120pp. 978-0-7851-6540-8.
Vol. 7: Fight the Future. 2012. 144pp. 978-0-7851-6161-5.

X-Factor. Marvel Comics, 2005– . T

Originally launched in 1985 and published until 1998, the series originally featured all five original members of the X-Men: Cyclops (Scott Summers), Beast (Hank McCoy), Iceman (Bobby Drake), Angel (Warren Worthington III), and a resurrected Marvel Girl (Jean Grey). The series featured the return of Jean Grey, the first appearance of the X-Men villain Apocalypse, and the dark transformation of Angel into Apocalypse's minion Death, and subsequently Archangel. The series was relaunched in 1991 by writer Peter David and featured a second string of Marvel mutant heroes who worked for the U.S. government, including Havok, Polaris, Strong Guy, Wolfsbane, Madrox

© 2016 Marvel Comics

the Multiple Man, and Quicksilver. This run has been highly regarded by X-Men fans for Peter David's use of humor in the series. The series was relaunched in 2006, with writer Peter David following the events of the *Madrox: Multiple Choice* storyline, and features the core members from Peter David's original run including Madrox the Multiple Man, Wolfsbane, and Strong Guy, plus Siryn, Rictor, and Monet working as an investigative mutant agency. Later volumes include additional teammates Longshot and Shatterstar, both extra-dimensional heroes from the Mojoverse, the latter of which began a relationship with Rictor. The third series concluded in 2013. In 2014, X-Factor was relaunched again as *All-New X-Factor* written by Peter David and featured the team of Polaris, Quicksilver, Gambit, Danger, Cypher, and Warlock. The series concluded in 2015.

X-Factor, 3rd series. Written by **Peter David**. Illustrated by various. Marvel Comics, 2007–2014. T

> *Vol. 0: Madrox—Multiple Choice*. 2010. 120pp. 978-0-7851-3031-4, hardcover.
> *Vol. 1: The Longest Night*. 2007. 144pp. 978-0-7851-1817-6.
> *Vol. 2: Life and Death Matters*. 2007. 136pp. 978-0-7851-2146-6.
> *Vol. 3: Many Lives of Madrox*. 2007. 120pp. 978-0-7851-2359-0.
> *Vol. 4: Heart of Ice*. 2008. 168pp. 978-0-7851-2360-6.
> *Vol. 5: The Only Game in Town*. 2009. 144pp. 978-0-7851-2863-2.
> *Vol. 6: Secret Invasion*. 2009. 168pp. 978-0-7851-2865-6.
> *Vol. 7: Time and a Half*. 2009. 168pp. 978-0-7851-3836-5.
> *Vol. 8: Overtime*. 2009. 168pp. 978-0-7851-3837-2.
> *Vol. 9: The Invisible Woman Has Vanished*. 2010. 128pp. 978-0-7851-4656-8.
> *Vol. 10: Second Coming*. 2010. 112pp. 978-0-7851-4369-7.
> *Vol. 11: Happenings in Vegas*. 2011. 144pp. 978-0-7851-4655-1.
> *Vol. 12: Scar Tissue*. 2011. 168pp. 978-0-7851-5284-2.
> *Vol. 13: Hardcover Labor*. 2011. 112pp. 978-0-7851-5286-6.
> *Vol. 14: Super Unnatural*. 2012. 112pp. 978-0-7851-6059-5.
> *Vol. 15: They Keep Killing Jamie Madrox*. 2012. 112pp. 978-0-7851-6061-8.
> *Vol. 16: Together Again for the First Time*. 2012. 112pp. 978-0-7851-6063-2.
> *Vol. 17: The Road to Redemption*. 2012. 96pp. 978-0-7851-6413-5.
> *Vol. 18: Breaking Points*. 2013. 112pp. 978-0-7851-6512-5.
> *Vol. 19: Short Stories*. 2013. 96pp. 978-0-7851-6699-3.
> *Vol. 20: Hell on Earth War*. 2013. 160pp. 978-0-7851-6700-6.
> *Vol. 21: The End of X-Factor*. 2014. 136pp. 978-0-7851-6701-3.
> *X-Men Messiah Complex*. 2008. 352pp. 978-0-7851-2320-0.
> *The Complete Collection. Vol. 1*. 2014. 400pp. 978-0-7851-5438-9.
> *The Complete Collection. Vol. 2*. 2014. 464pp. 978-0-7851-5439-6.

All-New X-Factor, 4th series. Written by **Peter David**. Illustrated by **Giuseppe Camuncoli** and **Pop Mhan**. Marvel Comics, 2014–2015. T

> *Vol. 1: Not Brand X*. 2014. 136pp. 978-0-7851-8816-2.
> *Vol. 2: Change of Decay*. 2014. 136pp. 978-0-7851-8817-9.
> *Vol. 3: Axis*. 2015. 176pp. 978-0-7851-8818-6.

X-Force. Marvel Comics, 2006–2015. T

© 2016 Marvel Comics

In early 1991, the *New Mutants* (see above) was relaunched as the team book called *X-Force*. The team served as a proactive military-like strike team led by the enigmatic Cable — the time-displaced son of Cyclops, leader of the X-Men. Team members included Domino, Cannonball, Shatterstar, Warpath, Feral, Boom Boom, Siryn, Rictor, and Sunspot. A second series featured a brand new X-Force team as a covert black-ops team and was comprised of Wolverine, Archangel, Domino, Warpath, Psylocke, and eventually Deadpool and Fantomex. Other team members joining the group over time included Puck, Spiral, Cluster, Marrow, and Bishop. The last version of the X-Force team included Marrow, Domino, Psylocke, Fantomex, and Cable as a secret spy organization for mutantkind. Collected below are book reprinting some of the original stories from the first X-Force team as well the second X-Force team. Also included are the stories featuring Cable from his stand-alone series.

X-Force, 1st series. Written by **Fabian Nicieza**, **Louise Simonson**, and various. Illustrated by **Rob Liefeld** and various. Marvel Comics.

The original team from the 1990s comic book series featuring the former members of the New Mutants team and led by Cable.

Assault on Graymalkin. 2011. 216pp. 978-0-7851-5899-8.
Cable and the New Mutants. 2011. 264pp. 978-0-7851-4970-5.
A Force to Be Reckoned With. 2011. 248pp. 978-0-7851-4984-2.
Under the Gun. 2011. 280pp. 978-0-7851-4985-9.
Child's Play. 2012. 248pp. 978-0-7851-6269-8.
Toy Soldiers. 2012. 232pp. 978-0-7851-6219-3.
Cable and X-Force Classic. Vol. 1. 2013. 344pp. 978-0-7851-8432-4.
The Phalanx Covenant. 2013. 256pp. 978-0-7851-6271-1.
X-Force Omnibus. Vol. 1. 2013. 848pp. 978-0-7851-6595-8.

X-Force, 2nd series. Written by **Craig Kyle** and **Christopher Yost**. Illustrated by **Clayton Crain**, **Mike Choi**, and various. Marvel Comics, 2008–2014.

Stories featuring the Cyclops-sanctioned black-ops team of X-Force featuring the team members of Wolverine, Warpath, X-23, and Wolfsbane.

Vol. 1: Angels and Demons. 2008. 144pp. 978-0-7851-2976-9.
Vol. 2: Old Ghosts. 2009. 120pp. 978-0-7851-2977-6.
Vol. 3: Not Forgotten. 2010. 152pp. 978-0-7851-3540-1.
X-Force/Cable: Messiah War. 2010. 368pp. 978-0-7851-3173-1.
X-Force: Sex and Violence. 2011. 120pp. 978-0-7851-4434-2.
X-Force by Craig Kyle & Chris Yost: The Complete Collection. 2014.

    Vol. 1. 2014. 384pp. 978-0-7851-8966-4.
    Vol. 2. 2014. 384pp. 978-0-7851-9000-4.

Uncanny X-Force, 3rd series. Written by **Rick Remender**. Illustrated by **Jerome Opena**. Marvel Comics, 2011–2014. T

The second series featured Wolverine as the team leader and members Deadpool, Archangel, Psylocke, and Fantomex.

Vol. 1: Apocalypse Solution. 2011. 120pp. 978-0-7851-4855-5.
Vol. 2: Deathlok Nation. 2011. 112pp. 978-0-7851-4857-9.
Vol. 3: The Dark Angel Saga, Book 1. 2011. 144pp. 978-0-7851-4661-2.
Vol. 4: The Dark Angel Saga, Book 2. 2012. 112pp. 978-0-7851-5888-2.
Vol. 5: Otherworld. 2012. 136pp. 978-0-7851-6182-0.
Vol. 6: Final Execution, Book 1. 2012. 112pp. 978-0-7851-6184-4.
Vol. 7: Final Execution, Book 2. 2013. 160pp. 978-0-7851-6186-8.
Uncanny X-Force by Rick Remender: The Complete Collection. 2014.

> *Vol. 1.* 2014. 520pp. 978-0-7851-8823-0.
> *Vol. 2.* 2014. 408pp. 978-0-7851-8824-7.

Uncanny X-Force by Rick Remender Omnibus. 2014. 928pp. 978-0-7851-8571-0, hardcover.
Fear Itself: Uncanny X-Force/The Deep. 2012. 152pp. 978-0-7851-5741-0.

Uncanny X-Force, 4th series. Written by **Sam Humphries**. Illustrated by **Ron Garney**. Marvel Comics, 2013–2014.

The fourth version of the team features Storm as the leader with team members Puck, Spiral, Cluster, and Psylocke.

Vol. 1: Let It Bleed. 2013. 136pp. 978-0-7851-6739-6.
Vol. 2: Torn and Frayed. 2013. 136pp. 978-0-7851-6740-2.
Vol. 3: The Great Corruption. 2014. 160pp. 978-0-7851-8985-5.

Cable and X-Force, 5th series. Written by **Dennis Hopeless**. Illustrated by **Gabriel Hernandez Walta**. Marvel Comics, 2013–2014.

© 2016 Marvel Comics

Cable creates his own X-Force team with members Colossus, Domino, Forge, Doctor Nemesis, and Tabitha Smith.

Vol. 1: Wanted. 2013. 136pp. 978-0-7851-6690-0.
Vol. 2: Dead or Alive. 2013. 96pp. 978-0-7851-6691-7.
Vol. 3: This Won't End Well. 2014. 112pp. 978-0-7851-8882-7.
Vol. 4: Vendettas. 2014. 152pp. 978-0-7851-8946-6.

X-Force, 6th series. Written by **Si Spurrier**. Illustrated by **Rock-He Kim** and **Jorge Molina**. Marvel Comics, 2014–2015.

Cable, Marrow, Fantomek, and Psylocke form a black-ops team created to spy on the other deadly organizations out there.

Vol. 1: Dirty/Tricks. 2014. 136pp. 978-0-7851-9026-4.
Vol. 2: Hide/Fear. 2015. 120pp. 978-0-7851-9027-1.
Vol. 3: Ends/Means. 2015. 112pp. 978-0-7851-9391-3.

Team-Ups and Epic Events

Team-Ups

When a large-scale threat occurs, many times heroes and super-teams join together to face the common enemy or adversary in what is called a crossover or a team-up. The team-ups can be made up of normally lone crime fighters working together (e.g., Batman and Superman) or can be large-scale team-ups featuring several heroes or a team working alongside another team (e.g., when the JLA teams up with the JSA). Part of the fun of the team-up crossovers is for readers to see how their favorite heroic characters interact with each other, especially in publications featuring heroes from several publishing companies.

Avengers vs X-Men. Written by **Brian Michael Bendis**, **Jonathan Hickman**, **Matt Fraction**, and **Ed Brubaker**. Illustrated by **John Romita Jr.**, **Frank Cho**, and various. Marvel Comics, 2013. 384pp. 978-0-7851-6318-3. T

Two of the most powerful super-hero teams collide when the deadly Phoenix Force returns and wreaks havoc on the Earth. Soon the heroes from both sides are at war, and the fate of the world hangs in the balance. The series was noted for featuring the death of Professor Charles Xavier as well as the launching point for the Uncanny Avengers team.

© 2016 Marvel Comics

The Batman/Judge Dredd Collection. Written by **John Wagner** and **Alan Grant**. Illustrated by **Simon Bisley** and various. DC Comics, 2014. 304pp. 978-1-4012-3678-6. T

A collection of three tales in which Mega City One's toughest policeman from the future has teamed up with the legendary Batman. The crossover collection features the two anti-heroes teaming up against fan-favorite arch-villains including the Joker, Judge Death, and the Riddler. The collection includes the story *Batman: Judgment in Gotham,* for which Simon Bisley won an Eisner Award in 1992 for Best Artist.

© 2016 DC Comics

Batman/Superman (New 52). Written by **Greg Pak**. Illustrated by **Jae Lee**. DC Comics, 2014–2016. T

The <u>Batman/Superman</u> series features the very first encounter between the Dark Knight Detective and the Man of Steel as played out in the New 52 reboot of DC Comics continuity. The series is set before the formation of the Justice League as well as the two heroes learn to trust each other and become allies in the war against evil.

Vol. 1: Cross World. 2014. 144pp. 978-1-4012-4509-2, hardcover.
Vol. 2: Game Over. 2014. 224pp. 978-1-4012-4935-9, hardcover.
Vol. 3: Second Chance. 2015. 160pp. 978-1-4012-5424-7, hardcover.
Vol. 4: Siege. 2015. 200pp. 978-1-4012-5755-2, hardcover.
Vol. 5: Truth Hurts. 2016. 168pp. 978-1-4012-6369-0, hardcover.

Batman/Teenage Mutant Ninja Turtles. Written by **James Tynion IV**. Illustrated by **Freddie Williams II**. DC Comics and IDW Publishing, 2016. 192pp. 978-1-4012-6278-5, hardcover. T

DC Comics and IDW Publishing team up to bring one of the most anticipated team-ups of 2016—when the Dark Knight himself teams up with the Teenage Mutant Ninja Turtles! When the Foot Clan invades Gotham City, Batman is soon on the chase to stop their crimes. Meanwhile, Michelangelo, Raphael, Donatello, and Leonardo trace the Foot Clan from their world and realize they've entered another dimension—a reality where Batman rules Gotham City. And what happens when the Shredder teams up with some of Gotham City's notorious criminals?

Batman/Teenage Mutant Ninja Turtles Adventures. Written by **Matthew K. Manning**. Illustrated by **Jon Sommariva**. DC Comics and IDW Publishing, 2017. 144pp. 978-1-63140-909-7. A 🖥

The sequel to the first Batman/Teenage Mutant Ninja Turtles team-up is a wonderful team-up of the animated versions of the characters—Batman from the *Batman: The Animated Series* and the Ninja Turtles from the new *Nickelodeon TMNT* animated series. When Batman's villains are disappearing from Arkham Asylum in Gotham City completely, he discovers that they've gone to New York City—home of the Teenage Mutant Ninja Turtles!

Deadpool and Cable. Written by **Fabian Nicieza**. Illustrated by **Patrick Zircher**, **Shane Law**, and **Mark Brooks**. Marvel Comics, 2010–2015. T

The bullets and the black humor fly in this series lampooning the "big gun" comic books of the 1990s where every hero was armed to the teeth carrying impossibly large weaponry. Featuring Cable, the son of Scott Summers (Cyclops) and a clone of Jean Grey, he's a powerful mutant with psychokinetic powers, and following the death of his adversary Apocalypse, he's lost his place in the world. Luckily he's taken up a new role of savior for the Earth. After being reluctantly teamed up with Wade Wilson (Deadpool), a mentally unstable masked mercenary for hire with an odd sense of humor, they're taking a proactive stance against the evils in the world with guns ablaze. The series was originally published from 2004 to 2008.

Ultimate Collection 1. 2010. 424pp. 978-0-7851-4313-0.
Ultimate Collection 2. 2010. 416pp. 978-0-7851-4821-0.
Ultimate Collection 3. 2010. 424pp. 978-0-7851-4920-0.
Omnibus. 2014. 1272pp. 978-0-7851-9276-3, hardcover.

Deadpool Team-Up. Written by **Adam Glass**, **Cullen Bunn**, **Rob Williams**, and **David Lapham**. Illustrated by **Frank Tieri**, **James Parker**, **Stuart Moore**, **Shane McCarthy**, and various. Marvel Comics, 2013–2015. O

The Merc with the Mouth teams up with a ridiculous amount of Marvel's heroes and oddball characters as well including Thor, the Thing, Wolverine, Galactus, and even a vampire cow!

Vol. 1: Good Buddies. 2010. 176pp. 978-0-7851-4529-5.
Vol. 2: Special Relationship. 2011. 192pp. 978-0-7851-4712-1.
Vol. 3: BFFs. 2011. 168pp. 978-0-7851-5140-1.

© 2016 Marvel Comics

Guardians Team Up. Written by **Brian Michael Bendis**, **Bill Willingham**, **Paul Scheer**, and various. Illustrated by **Shawn Crystal**, **Javier Pulido**, **Mike Norton**, and various. Marvel Comics, 2015–2016.

The various members of the Guardians of the Galaxy team up with a wide variety of Marvel Universe's heroes including the Avengers, the Ronan the Accuser, She-Hulk, and even Deadpool.

Vol. 1: Guardians Assemble. 2015. 144pp. 978-0785197140.
Vol. 2: Unlikely Story. 2016. 136pp. 978-0-7851-9911-3.

JLA/Avengers. Written by **Kurt Busiek**. Illustrated by **George Pérez**. DC Comics/Marvel Comics, 2008. 208pp. 978-1-4012-1957-4. T ◎

A crossover of epic proportions as Marvel Comics and DC Comics' favorite super-teams team up in one of the most eagerly awaited company crossovers of all time. The Avengers and the Justice League of America are brought together by two cosmic entities from different realities using the teams in a contest that will decide the fate of one of the realities. Featuring appearances by every member of both teams including Superman, Captain America, Batman, Iron Man, Wonder Woman, Thor, and many more in an astonishing battle. Both teams must set aside their differences to defeat the schemes of Krona and his devious ally the Grandmaster.

© 2016 DC Comics and Marvel Comics

Superman/Batman. Written by **Jeph Loeb**, **Alan Burnett**, **Dan Abnett**, **Andy Lanning**, and various. Illustrated by **Ed McGuinness**, **Michael Turner**, **Carlos Pacheco**, and various. DC Comics, 2005–2012. T ◎ 🎞

For years, DC Comics has featured storylines teaming up its classic characters Superman and Batman. This newest series written by fan-favorite Jeph Loeb continues that trend. After accusing Superman of crimes against

humanity, U.S. president Lex Luthor sends a squadron of heroes against Superman and Batman, including Captain Atom, Hawkman, Captain Marvel, Power Girl, and Green Lantern John Stewart. But the team of Superman and Batman are more than a match for the heroes and expose President Luthor for the fraud he's always been. When President Luthor falls from grace, just what depths he'll go to get revenge on Superman and Batman? The collection *Public Enemies* received recognition by YALSA's Quick Picks for Reluctant Readers committee in 2006. Several storylines from the series were adapted into direct-to-DVD animated movies by Warner Bros. including *Public Enemies* and *Supergirl*.

Vol. 1: Public Enemies. 2005. 160pp. 978-1-4012-0220-0.
Vol. 2: Supergirl. 2005. 168pp. 978-1-4012-0250-7.
Vol. 3: Absolute Power. 2006. 128pp. 978-1-4012-0714-4.
Vol. 4: Vengeance. 2008. 160pp. 978-1-4012-1043-4.
Vol. 5: Enemies Among Us. 2009. 160pp. 978-1-4012-1243-8.
Vol. 6: Torment. 2011. 160pp. 978-1-4012-1740-2.
Vol. 7: The Search for Kryptonite. 2009. 160pp. 978-1-4012-2012-9.
Vol. 8: Finest Worlds. 2010. 192pp. 978-1-4012-2332-8.
Vol. 9: Night & Day. 2011. 176pp. 978-1-4012-2808-8.
Vol. 10: Big Noise. 2010. 128pp. 978-1-4012-2914-6.
Vol. 11: Worship. 2011. 160pp. 978-1-4012-3032-6.
Vol. 12: Sorcerer Kings. 2012. 168pp. 978-1-4012-3446-1.
Absolute Superman/Batman Vol. 1. 978-1401240967, hardcover.
Absolute Superman/Batman Vol. 2. 978-1401248178, hardcover.

Superman/Wonder Woman. Written by **Charles Soule** and **Peter J. Tomasi**. Illustrated by **Tony S. Daniel** and **Doug Mahnke**. DC Comics, 2014– . T

Superman and Wonder Woman are two of the strongest heroes in the DC Comics Universe—and they're also an item! Can their love last when they're up against some of the most powerful villains out to get them?

Vol. 1: Power Couple. 2014. 192pp. 978-1-4012-4898-7, hardcover. 978-1-4012-5346-2.
Vol. 2: War and Peace. 2015. 224pp. 978-1-4012-5347-9, hardcover. 978-1-4012-5767-5.
Vol. 3: Casualties of War. 2015. 144pp. 978-1-4012-5768-2, hardcover. 978-1-4012-6321-8.
Vol. 4: Dark Truth. 2016. 192pp. 978-1-4012-6322-5, hardcover, 978-1-4012-6544-1.
Vol. 5: A Savage End. 2016. 208pp. 978-1-4012-6545-8, hardcover. 978-1-4012-6878-7.

Epic Events

Epic events are crossovers that feature a massive group of heroes working together against a typically grand-scale event such as a deadly villain, a worldwide crisis, or a galaxy-shaking event. Some of the earliest epic events include DC Comics' *Crisis on Infinite Earths* (originally published in 1985–1986) and Marvel Comics' original *Secret Wars* (1984–1985)—the repercussions of both series we are still experiencing to this day. Below are listed some of the better-known epic battles collected. Note that epic events featuring Marvel Comics' mutant heroes, the X-Men, are listed in their own section in this chapter.

Civil War. Written by **Mark Millar**. Illustrated by **Steve McNiven**. Marvel Comics, 2016. 256pp. 978-0-7851-9448-4, hardcover. 🎬

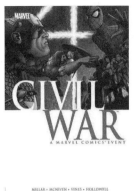

© 2016 Marvel Comics

An epic series originally published from 2006 to 2007. When the U.S. government passes the Superhero Registration Act, all heroes must register with the government with their powers and be considered as a type of law enforcement. Soon heroes are divided on the issue—with Iron Man supporting registration and Captain America opposing it. Heroes are caught in the middle, and in the end which group of heroes will win? The series also spread through the entire Marvel Comics line of titles, which are not included here for space considerations. The storyline of the series—the eternal struggle for freedom and security—was also the inspiration for the 2016 movie *Captain America: Civil War*.

Civil War II. Written by **Brian Michael Bendis**. Illustrated by **David Marquez**. Marvel Comics, 2017. 296pp. 978-1-302-90156-1, hardcover. 🎬

A sequel to the popular original Civil War series, when an Inhuman named Ulysses Cain has a vision of a dystopian future and tells the Avengers of his ability. Some members of the team want to use his powers to be proactive and take out dangers before they happen, it costs the team dearly. Factions on both sides fight for control of Ulysses's powers as heroes die and battle lines are drawn.

Convergence. Written by **Dan Jurgens**, **Jeff King**, **Tom King**, and **Scott Lobdell**. Illustrated by **Carlo Pagulayan** and various. DC Comics, 2015. T

In DC's big event for 2015, Brainiac collects characters and places from former DC realities, allowing readers to revisit versions of characters who have not been seen for years. Besides the main limited series, various two-issue limited series were collected in four, two-part collections each set during or just prior to two major DC events.

Convergence. 2015. 320pp. 978-1-4012-5686-9, hardcover.
Convergence: Crisis. 2015.

> *Book 1*. 2015. 272pp. 978-1-4012-5808-5.
> *Book 2*. 2015. 272pp. 978-1-4012-5834-4.

Convergence: Flashpoint. 2015.

> *Book 1*. 2015. 272pp. 978-1-4012-5835-1.
> *Book 2*. 2015. 272pp. 978-1-4012-5836-8.

Convergence: Infinite Earths. 2015.

> *Book 1*. 2015. 272pp. 978-1-4012-5837-5.
> *Book 2*. 2015. 272pp. 978-1-4012-5838-2.

Convergence: Zero Hour. 2015.

> *Book 1*. 2015. 272pp. 978-1-4012-5839-9.
> *Book 2*. 2015. 272pp. 978-1-4012-5840-5.

Crisis on Infinite Earths. Written by **Marv Wolfman**. Illustrated by **George Pérez**. DC Comics, 2007. 320pp. 978-1-5968-7343-8. T ◉

© 2016 DC Comics

Our planet Earth is just one of many other infinite Earths, each with its own separate history and protected by its own brand of heroes. One by one the Earths are being systematically destroyed by a planet-killing wave of Anti-Matter, culled by the vicious being known as the Anti-Monitor. As Earth after Earth is destroyed, the heroes of all the Earths are called by the mysterious man known only as the Monitor to combine forces against the Anti-Monitor and his legion of shadow-demons. Together in one monumental book, all the heroes of the DC Universe are joined together in a massive battle to save the multiple Earths against the most dangerous adversary their worlds have ever seen. As sacrifices are made and heroes die, the fate of the multiple Earths will be decided by the strength and determination of the Superman of Earth-2, the original Man of Steel, and all the brave heroes who were inspired by him. Originally published in comic book form from 1985 to 1986, the series was a monumental storyline that helped to clean house at DC Comics of many characters.

DC Comics: Rebirth. Written by **Geoff Johns**. Illustrated by **Gary Frank, Ivan Reis, Ethan Van Sciver**, and **Phil Jimenez**. DC Comics, 2016. 96pp. 978-1-4012-7072-8. T

The age of the New 52 is over! Wally West, the Flash from the DC Comics universe prior to the New 52 era, is trapped out of time and space. Missing due to the Flashpoint caused by his mentor, Barry Allen, he alone is able to witness the great mystery pervading the universe—everything is about to change for the DC Comics universe and only the Flash holds the key. The book is a new launching point for DC Comics from 2016 on out and greatly affected every DC Comics title.

Final Crisis. Written by **Grant Morrison**. Illustrated by **Doug Mahnke**. DC Comics, 2014. 352pp. 978-1-4012-4517-7. T

Darkseid, the ruler of the planet Apokolips, has finally done it and won—he's using the Anti-Life Equation to destroy the universe with his death and the heroes can't do anything to stop it. Batman and Green Lantern have been removed from the playing field, and Superman is subdued and by the bedside of his love, Lois Lane. How can the heroes win when the universe's strings are being pulled by Darkseid? The series also featured the return of Barry Allen—the Silver Age Flash, who had been killed in the Crisis on Infinite Earths. The series was originally released in 2008–2009.

Flashpoint. Written by **Geoff Johns**. Illustrated by **Andy Kubert**. DC Comics, 2012. 176pp. 978-1-4012-3338-9. T ◼

Barry Allen—the Flash—wakes up from a dream and finds himself where his family is alive, loved ones are strangers, and his closest friends are gone or worse. When Barry finds this new world on the brink of a cataclysmic war, the only hope is Cyborg who has gathered this world's version of heroes. Meanwhile, the Flash seeks to find the elusive villain responsible for the changed timeline. The storyline was adapted into the 2013 DC Comics animated film *Justice League: The Flashpoint Paradox*.

Infinite Crisis. Written by **Geoff Johns**. Illustrated by **Phil Jimenez** and **Andy Lanning**. DC Comics, 2008. T ◎

> A groundbreaking event borne from the ashes of the classic DC Comics' story *Crisis on Infinite Earths*. When the original Superman, a gray-haired aging hero, reenters our world, he finds the current heroes in disarray, the JLA disbanded, and he intends to fix it and return the world to the more peaceful Earth-2 of old from before the original crisis. What happens when the Superman of Earth-2 finally confronts the much-younger Man of Steel of Earth-1? Meanwhile, a new disaster is coming that will forever change the heroes of the DC Comics universe as heroes die, lives are changed, and a world will never be the same again. The *Superman: Infinite Crisis* collection features the back story of the original Superman and the events that lead into the series Infinite Crisis.

> *Infinite Crisis*. 2006. 264pp. 978-1-4012-0959-9, hardcover. 2008. 264pp. 978-1-4012-1060-1.
> *Infinite Crisis Companion*. 2006. 168pp. 978-1-4012-0922-3.
> *Superman: Infinite Crisis*. 2006. 128pp. 978-1-4012-0953-7.

The Infinity Gauntlet. Written by **Jim Starlin**. Illustrated by **George Pérez** and **Ron Lim**. Marvel Comics, 2011–2014. T ◎ 🎬

© 2016 Marvel Comics

Thanos, the power-hungry servant of Death, has acquired the Infinity Gems, six gems that give the wielder of the gauntlet seemingly god-like powers. As Thanos erases nearly half of the universe from existence, the Silver Surfer races to Earth to warn the heroes of the danger, especially Doctor Strange. With an army of Marvel heroes aligned with the Silver Surfer including Spider-Man, Thor, and Captain America, the heroes must try to wrest the gauntlet from Thanos before more innocent lives are killed by his devotion to Death. But there is only one man who can defeat Thanos and take possession of the glove, the resurrected hero known as Adam Warlock. For other stories featuring Thanos, please see the section below on Villains. The storyline of the Infinity Gems is a major theme through all of the Marvel Comics live-action feature films, culminating with the highly anticipated release of the *Avengers: Infinity War* movies coming out in 2018 and 2019. The sequels to the Infinity Gauntlet are listed in the record below as well.

> *The Infinity Gauntlet*. 2011. 256pp. 978-0-7851-5659-8.
> *The Infinity Gauntlet Omnibus*. 2014. 1248pp. 978-0-7851-5468-6, hardcover.
> *The Infinity Gauntlet Aftermath*. 2013. 352pp. 978-0-7851-8486-7.
> *The Infinity War*. 2006. 400pp. 978-0-7851-2105-3.
> *The Infinity Crusade*. 2008–2009.
>
> > *Vol. 1*. 2008. 248pp. 978-0-7851-3127-4.
> > *Vol. 2*. 2009. 240pp. 978-0-7851-3128-1.

The Judas Coin. Written and Illustrated by **Walter Simonson**. DC Comics, 2012. 104pp. 978-1-4012-1541-5, 2012. T

© 2016 DC Comics

A historical adventure that spans through the history of the DC Comics universe. Judas betrayed Jesus for 30 pieces of silver. Now see how that silver affects those throughout DC Comics history including the Golden Gladiator, the Viking Prince, Batman, Two-Face, and even Manhunter in the year 2070. A grand adventure as only the legendary creator Walter Simonson can tell.

Kingdom Come (20th Anniversary Deluxe Edition). Written by **Mark Waid**. Illustrated by **Alex Ross**. DC Comics, 2016. 344pp. 978-1-4012-6082-8. T 🌳 ◎

© 2016 DC Comics

A gorgeous fully painted story of the last days of the DC Comics super-heroes by writer Mark Waid and illustrator Alex Ross. Many years in the future the classic DC Comics heroes of old are retiring and making way for a new generation. When rebellion strikes the hearts of the young and corruptible, Superman and other heroes of old return to instill order and put them back in their place. Two camps, one led by Batman and the other by Superman, must decide the best way to handle the crisis. As a war breaks out, old allies must take on the armies of the young and corrupt, and an elderly Protestant minister named Norman McCay is caught up in the event to witness the end of the reign of the super-heroes. The story won several Eisner Awards in 1997 for Best Finite Series/Limited Series and Best Cover Artist, and Best Painter/Multimedia Artist (Interior), as well as two Harvey Awards in 1997 as well for Best Penciller or Artist and Best Cover Artist. The Anniversary edition includes sketches and bonus material.

Marvel 1602. Marvel Comics, 2010–2016. T ◎

In the year 1602, Europe is at a crossroads as enemies of England vie for the crown and seek to end Queen Elizabeth's life. In England, Sir Nicholas Fury and Doctor Stephen Strange, both servants of Queen Elizabeth, have been instructed by her to retrieve a holy relic en route from Jerusalem and to solve the mystery of the strange storms in the sky. Meanwhile the Spanish Inquisition is executing individuals with strange powers, including an angel with wings and other "witchbreed," and Virginia Dare, the first-born child of the Colonies, is en route to England with her Native American protector on an important mission. A unique chain of events of seemingly unrelated events is imploding: the Marvel Universe has arrived 400 years earlier and the world might not survive another day. Written by *Sandman* creator Neil Gaiman. There have been several follow-up stories to the series as well and included below.

Marvel 1602. Written by **Neil Gaiman**. Illustrated by **Andy Kubert**. 2013. 264pp. 978-0785153689, hardcover (tenth anniversary edition); 2010. 248pp. 978-0-7851-4134-1.

Marvel 1602: New World/Fantastick Four. Written by **Greg Pak** and **Peter David**. Illustrated by **Greg Tocchini** and **Pascal Alixe**. 2009. 120pp. 978-0-7851-4136-5, hardcover; 2010. 120pp. 978-0-7851-4137-2.

Marvel 1602: Spider-Man. Written by **Jeff Parker**. Illustrated by **Ramon Rosanas**. 2010. 120pp. 978-0-7851-4603-2, hardcover; 2010. 120pp. 978-0-7851-2817-5.

Marvel 1602: Witch Hunter Angela. 2016. Written by **Marguerite Bennett** and **Kieron Gillen**. Illustrated by **Stephanie Hans**. 128pp. 978-0-7851-9860-4.

Secret Wars, 1st series. Written by **Jim Shooter**. Illustrated by **Mike Zeck**. Marvel Comics. T ◉

© 2016 Marvel Comics

A mysterious god-like being called The Beyonder whisks away the Marvel heroes and villains to fight a battle for the ultimate price. When allegiances are tested and the battle lines have been drawn, only one is triumphant, and it isn't the heroes. When Doctor Doom carries within himself the power of a god, what hero can stop him? The series was originally released in comic book form as a 12-issue limited series from 1984 to 1985. The series inspired a sequel as well as the 2015 limited series of the same name.

Secret Wars Omnibus. 2008. 496pp. 978-0-7851-3110-6, hardcover.
Secret Wars. 2011. 376pp. 978-0-7851-5868-4.
Secret Wars II. 2011. 264pp. 978-0-7851-5830-1.
Secret Wars II Omnibus. 1184pp. 978-0-7851-3111-3, hardcover.

Secret Wars, 2nd series. Written and Illustrated by various. Marvel Comics, 2015–2016. T ◉

© 2016 Marvel Comics

Marvel Comics' big event for 2015 was named after the groundbreaking 1980s limited series and marked a turning point in the Marvel Universe including the end of the Ultimate Universe and changes for the main one. At one point a new "Battleworld" was created, with many realms mostly based on past storylines and events. Around 40 collections were made out of the limited series and one-shots that told that stories set on that world.

Secret Wars. Written by **Jonathan Hickman**. Illustrated by **Esad Ribic**. 2016. 224pp. 978-0-7851-9884-0, hardcover.

Secret Wars Tie-In Stories, 2015–2016

Listed below are the various tie-in stories from the 2015 Secret Wars main storyline. All of the stories feature alternate histories of popular heroes as well as tribute issues to popular storylines over the course of Marvel Comics history. The stories take place in the re-created Battleworld and are out of place of mainstream

Marvel Comics continuity, but some elements from the books have bled into the current Marvel continuity. A few of these titles have continued as ongoing series include A-Force and Old Man Logan.

1602 Witch Hunter/Siege. Written by **Kieron Gillen** and **Marguerite Bennett**. Illustrated by **Stephanie Hans**. 2016. 128pp. 978-0-7851-9860-4.

A-Force Vol. 0: Warzones. Written by **G. Willow Wilson** and **Marguerite Bennett**. Illustrated by **Jorge Molina**. 2015. 112pp. 978-0-7851-9861-1.

The Age of Apocalypse: Warzones. Written by **Fabian Nicieza**. Illustrated by **Gerardo Sandoval**. 2015. 120pp. 978-0-7851-9862-8.

Age of Ultron Vs. Marvel Zombies. Written by **James Robinson**. Illustrated by **Steve Pugh**. 2015. 128pp. 978-0-7851-9863-5.

The Amazing Spider-Man: Renew Your Vows. Written by **Dan Slott**. Illustrated by **Adam Kubert**. 2015. 136pp. 978-0-7851-9886-4.

Armor Wars. Written by **James Robinson**. Illustrated by **Marcio Takara**, and **Mark Bagley**. 2016. 112pp. 978-0-7851-9864-2.

Captain Marvel & the Carol Corps. Written by **Kelly Sue DeConnick**. Illustrated by **David Lopez**. 2015. 120pp. 978-0-7851-9865-9.

Civil War: Warzones. Written by **Charles Soule**. Illustrated by **Leinil Yu**. 2016. 120pp. 978-0-7851-9866-6.

Deadpool's Secret Secret Wars. Written by **Cullen Bunn**. Illustrated by **Matteo Lolli** and **Jacopo Carmagni**. 2016. 128pp. 978-0-7851-9867-3.

E Is for Extinction: X-Tinction Agenda. Written by **Chris Burnham**. Illustrated by **Ramon Villalobos**. 2016. 120pp. 978-0-7851-9868-0.

Future Imperfect: Warzones. Written by **Peter David**. Illustrated by **Greg Land**. 2016. 128pp. 978-0-7851-9869-7.

Ghost Racers. Written by **Felipe Smith**. Illustrated by **Juan Gedeon**. 2016. 120pp. 978-0-7851-9921-2.

Giant-Size Little Marvels AvX. Written and Illustrated by **Skottie Young**. 2016. 120pp. 978-0-7851-9870-3.

Guardians of Knowhere. Written by **Brian Michael Bendis**. Illustrated by **Mike Deodato**. 2015. 120pp. 978-0-7851-9844-4.

Hail Hydra. Written by **Rick Remender**. Illustrated by **Roland Boschi**. 2015. 112pp. 978-0-7851-9871-0.

House of M: Warzones. Written by **Dennis Hopeless**. Illustrated by **Jorge Molina**. 2016. 120pp. 978-0-7851-9872-7.

Inferno: Warzones. Written by **Dennis Hopeless**. Illustrated by **Javier Garron**. 2015. 112pp. 978-0-7851-9873-4.

Infinity Gauntlet: Warzones. Written by **Gerry Duggan**. Illustrated by **Dustin Weaver**. 2015. 112pp. 978-0-7851-9874-1.

Inhumans: Attilan Rising. Written by **Charles Soule**. Illustrated by **John Timms**. 2015. 112pp. 978-0-7851-9875-8.

Korvac Saga: Warzones. Written by **Dan Abnett**. Illustrated by **Nico Leon**, and **Otto Schmidt**. 2015. 160pp. 978-0-7851-9313-5.

M.O.D.O.K. Assassin. Written by **Christopher Yost**. Illustrated by **Amilcar Pinna**. 2015. 112pp. 978-0-7851-9876-5.

Marvel 1872. Written by **Gerry Duggan**. Illustrated by **Evan Shaner**. 2015. 112pp. 978-0-7851-9877-2.

Marvel Zombies: Battleworld. Written by **Simon Spurrier**. Illustrated by **Kevin Walker**. 2015. 112pp. 978-0-7851-9878-9.

Master of Kung Fu: Battleworld. Written by **Haden Blackman**. Illustrated by **Dalibor Talajic**. 2016. 112pp. 978-0-7851-9879-6.

Planet Hulk: Warzones! Written by **Sam Humphries**. Illustrated by **Marc Laming**. 2016. 120pp. 978-0-7851-9881-9.

Red Skull. Written by **Joshua Williamson**. Illustrated by **Luca Pizzari**. 2016. 112pp. 978-0-7851-9846-8.

Runaways: Battleworld. Written by **Noelle Stevenson**. Illustrated by **Sandford Greene**. 2015. 112pp. 978-0-7851-9882-6.

Secret Wars 2099. Written by **Peter David**. Illustrated by **Will Sliney**. 2015. 112pp. 978-0-7851-9883-3.

Secret Wars Journal/Battleworld. Written by various. 2016. 240pp. 978-0-7851-9580-1.

Siege: Battleworld. Written by **Kieron Gillen**. Illustrated by **Filipe Andrade**. 2016. 136pp. 978-0-7851-9549-8.

Spider-Island: Warzones! Written by **Christos Gage**. Illustrated by **Paco Diaz**. 2015. 120pp. 978-0-7851-9885-7.

Spider-Verse: Warzones! Written by **Mike Costa**. Illustrated by **Andre Arauio**. 2015. 120pp. 978-0-7851-9887-1.

Squadron Sinister. Written by **Marc Guggenheim**. Illustrated by **Carlos Pacheco**. 2015. 136pp. 978-0-7851-9888-8.

Star Lord & Kitty Pryde. Written by **Sam Humphries**. Illustrated by **Alti Firmansyah**. 2015. 128pp. 978-0-7851-9843-7.

Thors. Written by **Jason Aaron**. Illustrated by **Chris Sprouse**. 2016. 136pp. 978-0-7851-9889-5.

Ultimate End. Written by **Brian Michael Bendis**. Illustrated by **Mark Bagley**. 2015. 128pp. 978-0-7851-9890-1.

Weirdworld Vol. 0: Warzones! Written by **Jason Aaron**. Illustrated by **Mike Del Mundo**. 2015. 112pp. 978-0-7851-9891-8.

Where Monsters Dwell: The Phantom Eagle Flies the Savage Skies. Written by **Garth Ennis**. Illustrated by **Russ Braun**. 2016. 112pp. 978-0-7851-9892-5.

Wolverine: Old Man Logan Vol. 0: Warzones. Written by **Brian Michael Bendis**. Illustrated by **Andrea Sorrentino**. 2015. 136pp. 978-0-7851-9893-2.

X-Men '92. Written by **Chris Sims**. Illustrated by **Chad Bowers** and **Scott Koblish**. 2016. 128pp. 978-0-7851-9894-9.

X-Men: Years of Future Past. Written by **Marguerite Bennett**. Illustrated by **Mike Norton**. 2016. 128pp. 978-0-7851-9830-7.

X-Tinction Agenda: Warzones! Written by **Marc Guggenheim**. Illustrated by **Carmine Di Giandomenico**. 2016. 112pp. 978-0-7851-9550-4.

X-Men Epic Events

The X-Men, due to their plethora of titles, routinely feature epic storylines that cross over into several monthly series. Featured below are some of the highlights and a brief description of each crossover series. They are featured in this section due to the crossovers featuring mostly mutant characters with the occasional super-hero team such as the Avengers. Epic Event titles that include most major Marvel Comics characters including the X-Men, Spider-Man, the Fantastic Four, the Avengers are listed above.

House of M. Written by **Brian Michael Bendis**. Illustrated by **Oliver Coipel**. Marvel Comics, 2006. 224pp. 978-0-7851-1721-6. T

> The Avengers and the X-Men discover they have a common enemy with the Scarlet Witch—a former hero who has a mental breakdown—and the world as we know it is at stake. Now her mutant-born hex powers have gone out of control and reality has changed to one where the mutants have been granted her heart's desire—to be in the majority. Meanwhile, Wolverine senses that reality isn't right and sets out to restore it. Also collected in various ways were additional stories set in the House of M universe.

X-Men: Fall of the Mutants. Written by **Chris Claremont** and **Louise Simonson**. Illustrated by **Walter Simonson** and **Marc Silvestri**. Marvel Comics, 2011. ◎

A dark period in X-Men history where tragedy strikes all three X-Men teams comprised of the X-Men, X-Factor, and the New Mutants. The New Mutants battle against Cameron Hodge and lose one of their own in the battle; X-Factor faces betrayal from the former X-Man called Angel who is now Death, the fourth horseman of the Apocalypse, and the X-Men battle an ancient evil called the Adversary and pay the ultimate cost with their own lives.

Vol. 1. 2013. 432pp. 978-0-7851-6744-0.
Vol. 2. 2013. 400pp. 978-0-7851-6685-6.
Fall of the Mutants Omnibus. 2011. 824pp. 978-0-7851-5312-2, hardcover.

© 2016 Marvel Comics

X-Men: Inferno. Written by **Chris Claremont** and **Louise Simonson**. Illustrated by **Marc Silvestri**, **John Bogdanove**, and **Walter Simonson**. Marvel Comics, 2014–2016. ◎

Realizing that she's been a pawn of the villain Mr. Sinister, Madelyne Pryor, a genetic clone of Jean Grey created by Sinister and wife of Scott Summers (aka Cyclops), aligns herself with a demonic realm called Limo that has been infected with a techno-organic virus. As hell on Earth erupts, the forces of the X-Men, X-Factor, and the New Mutants try to save New York from this demonic menace and prevent Madelyne from sacrificing her infant son Nathan Christopher Summers in a plot to become the Goblin Queen of Limbo and Earth.

X-Men: Inferno Prologue. 2014. 824pp. 978-0785192732, hardcover.
X-Men: Inferno. 2016.

> *Vol. 1*. 2016. 432pp. 978-0-7851-9511-5.
> *Vol. 2*. 2016. 368pp. 978-0-7851-9544-3.

© 2016 Marvel Comics

X-Men: Inferno. Crossovers. 2016. 432pp. 978-0-7851-9551-1.

X-Men: Messiah Complex. Written by **Ed Brubaker**, **Mike Carey**, **Craig Kyle**, **Chris Yost**, and **Peter David**. Illustrated by **Marc Silvestri**, **Chris Bachalo**, **Humberto Ramos**, and **Scot Eaton**. Marvel Comics, 2008. 254pp. 978-0785123200, hardcover. T

© 2016 Marvel Comics

The X-Men teams are sent to track an infant named Hope who may be the key for the survival of the mutant race in the future. The first mutant born after the House of M crossover, she's considered precious, not just by the X-Men but by many X-Men villains too including Mr. Sinister.

X-Men: Mutant Massacre. Written by **Chris Claremont**. Illustrated by **John Romita Jr.**, and various. Marvel Comics, 2013. 320pp. 978-0-7851-6741-9. ◎

© 2016 Marvel Comics

When the villain Mister Sinister sends a group of hunters called the Marauders into the Morlock tunnels to destroy the mutants living in the sewers, the X-Men are all that stand in their way. The Morlocks are brutally hunted down by the Marauders, and when the day is over the X-Men and their allies will never be the same again. The story also features appearance by Power Pack, Thor, and X-Factor.

X-Men: Second Coming. Written by **Craig Kyle**, **Christopher Yost**, **Matt Fraction**, **Zeb Wells**, and **Mike Carey**. Illustrated by **David Finch**, **Terry Dodson**, **Ibraim Roberson**, **Greg Land**, and **Mike Choi**. Marvel Comics, 2011. T

Cable, on the run from Bishop, has with him the last hope for mutantkind—a child by the name of Hope. Set in the far future and in the present at the same time, the last remaining X-Men stage a last ditch battle against Bastion and the Nimrod killer Sentinels in the name of preserving the future of mutantkind.

X-Men: Second Coming. 2011. 392pp. 978-0-7851-5705-2.
X-Men: Second Coming Revelations. 2011. 208pp. 978-0-7851-5706-9.

X-Men: X-Cutioner's Song. Written by **Fabian Nicieza**, **Scott Lobdell**, and **Peter David**. Illustrated by **Andy Kubert** and **Adam Kubert**. Marvel Comics, 2011. 368pp. 978-0-7851-5610-9, hardcover.

Stryfe, the mad genetic clone of Cable, seeks revenge on the villain Apocalypse as well as Cyclops and Jean Grey for abandoning their son to the far future. Meanwhile, several X-teams including the X-Men, X-Force, and X-Factor rush in to rescue Scott and Jean.

X-Men/Avengers: Onslaught Omnibus. Written by various. Illustrated by various. Marvel Comics, 2015. 1296pp. 978-0-7851-9262-6, hardcover. T

When the fury of Magneto is combined with the psionic power of Professor X, both the combined might of the X-Men and the Avengers might not be enough to defeat the entity known as Onslaught. The series featured also the temporary "death" of the Avengers and the Fantastic Four as they were actually temporarily saved in an alternate universe created by Franklin Richards, the child of Mr. Fantastic and the Invisible Woman.

Villains: Archenemies and Rogues Galleries

A continuing theme in comic books as well as most heroic tales is an archenemy for the hero. Every hero needs a good villain as a foible for the character as well as a rogues gallery of colorful villains. Sherlock Holmes had his Professor Moriarty, and in the superhero world Superman has his Lex Luthor, Batman has his Joker, and Spider-Man has his Green Goblin. Below are listed the collected stories featuring the villains in the spotlight. Many more titles featuring appearances of the villains can be found in the sections featuring the main heroes in this chapter.

Dark Avengers. Written by **Brian Michael Bendis** and **Jake Parker**. Illustrated by **Mike Deodato**, **Neil Edwards**, **Mirco Pierfederici**, and various. Marvel Comics, 2009–2013. T

When the government gives Norman Osborn (the apparently reformed Green Goblin, now calling himself Iron Patriot) the control of the Avengers after a disastrous Skrull invasion, he molds the team known as the Thunderbolts in his own version of the Avengers. Some members were already part of the existing Thunderbolts, many of whom were villains in disguise, and many of the team played the role as their heroic counterparts (Venom as Spider-Man, Daken as Wolverine, Ragnarok as Thor, Bullseye as Hawkeye, Skaar as the Hulk, etc.). Following Osborn's defeat, a new government controlled Dark Avengers was formed, consisting of controlled villains as well as government-recruited heroes including Luke Cage and U.S. Agent. The *Dark Avengers Omnibus* collection collects all of Brian Michael Bendis's stories in one hardcover book.

Dark Avengers Assemble! 2009. 160pp. 978-0785138525.
Dark Avengers/Uncanny X-Men: Utopia. 2010. 368pp. 978-0-7851-4234-8.
Molecule Man. 2010. 112pp. 978-0-7851-3854-9.
Dark Avengers: Siege. 2011. 136pp. 978-0785148128.
Dark Avengers Omnibus. 2011. 400pp. 978-0-7851-5650-5, hardcover.
The End Is the Beginning. 2013. 192pp. 978-0-7851-6172-1.
Masters of Evil. 2013. 160pp. 978-0-7851-6847-8.

Empire. Written by **Mark Waid**. Illustrated by **Barry Kitson**. IDW Publishing. 2015. O

The gold-armored tyrant called Golgoth has done the unthinkable: he's defeated his planet's heroes and has conquered the Earth. In the bleak society where deception rules the day, what does a villainous monarch do after he's already accomplished all he can? A look at a world in which the villains do win, seen from the perspective of Golgoth's super-powered lieutenants as the monarch is surrounded by conspirators and backstabbers who fear him.

Empire. 2015. 258pp. 978-1-63140-305-7.
Empire: Uprising. 2015. 104pp. 978-1-63140-441-2.

Incorruptible. Written by **Mark Waid**. Illustrated by **Jean Diaz**, **Horacio Domingues**, **Marcio Takara**, and **Damian Couceiro**. Boom Studios, 2009–2012. O
> What does it take for a villain to redeem himself? Spilling out of the pages of Mark Waid's <u>Irredeemable</u> series (see listing in this chapter), Max Damage is a changed man. The villain has returned after being presumed dead after the rampage by the former hero named Plutonium, and precedes to undo all of his past wrongs by capturing his old gang and destroying all of the stolen goods and money he had stolen and he's even sworn off having sex with his underage lover named Jailbait. Max may be a changed man, but has he really changed his ways for good?

Vol. 1. 2010. 128pp. 978-1-60886-015-9.
Vol. 2. 2010. 128pp. 978-1-60886-028-9.
Vol. 3. 2011. 128pp. 978-1-60886-039-5.
Vol. 4. 2011. 128pp. 978-1-60886-056-2.
Vol. 5. 2011. 128pp. 978-1-60886-057-9.
Vol. 6. 2012. 128pp. 978-1-60886-084-5.
Vol. 7. 2012. 128pp. 978-1-60886-085-2.

Irredeemable. Written by **Mark Waid**. Illustrated by **Peter Krause**, **Diego Barreto**, **Eduardo Barreto**, **Paul Azaceta**, **Howard Chaykin**, and **Emma Rios**. Boom Studios, 2009–2012. O 🏆

© 2016 Boom! Studios

> What makes a hero become a villain? The super-strong hero known as Plutonian has turned evil. Once the savior of mankind, he's destroyed Sky City—the metropolis he once called home—and murdered millions of people across the world. Can his former teammates from the super-group the Paradigm save him, or is he lost beyond all hope? The first collection of *Irredeemable* was recognized as a Great Graphic Novel for Teens in 2011.

Vol. 1. 2009. 112pp. 978-1-934506-90-5.
Vol. 2. 2010. 112pp. 978-1-60886-000-5.
Vol. 3. 2010. 112pp. 978-1-60886-008-1.
Vol. 4. 2010. 112pp. 978-1-60886-029-6.
Vol. 5. 2011. 128pp. 978-1-60886-040-1.
Vol. 6. 2011. 128pp. 978-1-60886-054-8.
Vol. 7. 2011. 128pp. 978-1-60886-055-5.
Vol. 8. 2011. 128pp. 978-1-60886-082-1.
Vol. 9. 2012. 128pp. 978-1-60886-083-8.
Vol. 10. 2012. 128pp. 978-1-60886-275-7.

Joker. Written by **Brian Azzarello**. Illustrated by **Lee Bermejo**. DC Comics, 2008. 128pp. 978-1-4012-1581-1. O

When the Joker is released from Arkham Asylum, he begins to disorganize the criminal element of Gotham City and rebuild the city from the ashes that they left it in. The Joker is accompanied by a young hood named Johnny Frost who stumbles into becoming the Joker's henchman but over time sees that there's a bleak life ahead of him idolizing a sociopathic killer. A dark look at a dark villain.

Sex Criminals. Written by **Matt Fraction**. Illustrated by **Chip Zdarsky**. Image Comics, 2014– . M 🎖

Suzie and Jon hook up at a party and discover when they both orgasm, they have the unique super-power to freeze time. After their sexual histories are explored, they decide to rob the bank where Jon and Suzie use the money to save Suzie's endangered library. A unique take on superpowers to say the least! The series received an Eisner Award in 2014 for Best New Series.

Vol. 1: One Weird Trick. 2014. 128pp. 978-1-60706-946-1.
Vol. 2: Two Worlds, One Cop. 2015. 128pp. 978-1-63215-193-3.
Vol. 3: Three the Hard Way. 2016. 128pp. 978-1-63215-542-9.
Big Hard Sex Criminals, Vol. 1. 2015. 256pp. 978-1-63215-243-5, hardcover.

Super-Villains Unite: The Complete Super-Villain Team-Up. Written by **Roy Thomas**, **Tony Isabella**, **Jim Shooter**, and **Bill Mantlo**. Illustrated by **John Buscema**, **Mike Sekowsky**, **George Evans**, and **Sal Buscema**. Marvel Comics, 2015. 464pp. 978-0-7851-9406-4. Y

A collection of team-ups Marvel-style—but this time featuring the villains! The collection includes stories from the Super-Villains Team-Up series from the 1970s and features the team-ups of villains including Namor, Doctor Doom, and the Red Skull.

The Superior Foes of Spider-Man. Written by **Nick Spencer**. Illustrated by **Steve Lieber**. Marvel Comics, 2014–2016. T

The Sinister Six has often been made up of Spider-Man's deadliest and greatest foes, but perhaps not this incarnation made up of The Shocker, Speed Demon, Overdrive, and the new Beetle (and yes there are only five). When Boomerang finds himself in jail and needs a way out, he makes a deal with the shape-changing villain known as the Chameleon, and soon the doublecross is on! Who will kidnap the head of Silvermanne, the literal head of the crime families, and become the new kingpin of crime in New York? Meanwhile, can any of the members of the Sinister Six stay out of jail or stay out of trouble? A heist story with much humor and heart as villains are out to do the heist of the century!

© 2016 Marvel Comics

Vol. 1: Getting the Band Back Together. 2014. 136pp. 978-0-7851-8494-2.

Vol. 2: The Crime of the Century. 2014. 112pp. 978-0-7851-8495-9.

Vol. 3: Game Over. 2015. 136pp. 978-0-7851-9170-4.

Omnibus. 2016. 376pp. 978-0-7851-9837-6, hardcover.

Superior Spider-Man. Written by **Dan Slott** with **Christos Gage**. Illustrated by **Humberto Ramos**, **Ryan Stegman**, **Giuseppe Camuncoli**, and various. Marvel Comics, 2012–2014. T ◉

© 2016 Marvel Comics

The unthinkable has happened—Doctor Octopus, the long-time Spider-Man villain has won! He switched his mind with Spider-Man's and has taken over Peter Parker's life both in mind and in body! So what does a villain do when he's the new Peter Parker? Why, show the world that he's better at being Spider-Man than Spider-Man ever was and show that he's the Superior Spider-Man. He's upgraded Spider-Man's costume and got his doctorate too! But evil doesn't rest and Spider-Ock has his hands full against rampaging Venom, and the deadly Goblin War. No one ever said being a hero was easy.

Vol. 1: My Own Worst Enemy. 2013. 120pp. 978-0-7851-6704-4.

Vol. 2: A Troubled Mind. 2013. 140pp. 978-0-7851-6705-1.

Vol. 3: No Escape. 2013. 136pp. 978-0-7851-8472-0.

Vol. 4: Necessary Evil. 2014. 112pp. 978-0-7851-8473-7.

Vol. 5: Superior Venom. 2014. 152pp. 978-0-7851-8796-7.

Vol. 6: Goblin Nation. 2014. 168pp. 978-0-7851-8797-4.

Thanos

Created by **Jim Starlin**. Marvel Comics. T 🎬

Since his debut in the pages of *Iron Man* in 1973, Thanos has been one of the major "cosmic" villains. A demi-god from Saturn's moon Titan, Thanos has often attempted genocide on a galactic level, coming close many times. It was only due to the Avengers, Spider-Man, Adam Warlock, Captain Marvel and other heroes that he was stopped. The titles below offer a chronological listing of his major appearances, including a few occasions in which he has helped stop a greater threat. Thanos has been appearing in several films of the "Marvel Cinematic Universe," including the first *Avengers* film and *Guardians of the Galaxy*. He will be the big climatic villain in the *Avengers: Infinity War* movies coming out in 2018 and 2019. See also the earlier entry for The Infinity Gauntlet.

Avengers vs. Thanos. Written by **Jim Starlin**. Illustrated by various. Marvel Comics, 2013. 472pp. 978-0-7851-6850-8.

> Collects the earliest Thanos stories from the 1970s where he went up against Iron Man, Captain Marvel, Adam Warlock, the Thing, and others. From his first appearance to his temporary "death."

Avengers: The Legacy of Thanos. Written by **Roger Stern** and **John Byrne**. Illustrated by **John Byrne** and **John Buscema**. Marvel Comics, 2014. 256pp. 978-0-7851-8891-9.

> From the pages of The Avengers, this collection includes stories in which they fight Nebula, who claims to be Thanos's granddaughter.

Silver Surfer: Rebirth of Thanos. Written by **Jim Starlin**. Illustrated by **Ron Lim**. Marvel Comics, 2010. 224pp. 978-0-7851-4478-6, hardcover.

> After Thanos died, he is brought back once more from death to bring more destruction to the universe and not even the Silver Surfer can stop him!

Thor vs. Thanos. Written by **Dan Jurgens**. Illustrated by **John Romita Jr**. Marvel Comics, 2013. 256pp. 978-0-7851-8465-2.

The God of Thunder battles the God of Death! When Thanos acquires ancient artifacts that threaten Earth's existence and only Thor can stop him!

© 2016 Marvel Comics

Thanos: Infinity Abyss. Written and Illustrated by **Jim Starlin**. Marvel Comics, 2013. 176pp. 978-0-7851-8512-3.

> Collects the 2002 limited series where Thanos has mixed his genetic DNA with other beings including Professor X, Doctor Strange, Gladiator, Iron Man, and Galactus. The five beings try to kill Thanos, but are eventually defeated by him with the assistance of Adam Warlock, Doctor Strange, Spider-Man, Captain Marvel, and Moondragon.

Thanos: Redemption. Written by **Jim Starlin** and **Keith Giffen**. Illustrated by **Ron Lim**. Marvel Comics, 2013. 304pp. 978-0-7851-8506-2.

> Collects the 12-issue 2003–2004 Thanos ongoing series where Thanos may have turned over a new leaf. Scorned by Death, he must face Galactus, the unimaginably powerful Beyonder, and the mysterious threat only known as the Fallen One!

The Thanos Imperative. Written by **Dan Abnett** and **Andy Lanning**. Illustrated by **Brad Walker**. Marvel Comics, 2011. 200pp. 978-0-7851-4902-6.

When a rift in space called the Fault opens, alternate dimensions are unleashed, including a realm called the Cancerverse where life is preserved and there is no death. Thanos must team up with his enemies, the Guardians of the Galaxy and the Nova Corps, to save the galaxy. Collects the 2010 limited series tied into the massive *Annihilation*, *War of Kings*, and *Realm of Kings* events listed elsewhere in this chapter.

Thanos: The Infinity Revelation. Written by **Jim Starlin**. Illustrated by **Andy Smith** and **Frank D'Amata**. Marvel Comics, 2014. 112pp. 978-0-7851-8470-6, hardcover.

An original graphic novel where Thanos the Mad Titan feels a void in his life and attempts to find meaning in a universe where he is neither hero or villain. After visiting the Death's domain and the Infinity Wall, he goes on a journey with his greatest enemy, Adam Warlock.

Thanos: A God Up There Listening. Written by **Jim Starlin** and **Rob Williams**. Illustrated by **Ron Lim**. Marvel Comics, 2014. 120pp. 978-0-7851-9158-2, hardcover.

Thane, the son of Thanos, seeks to discover the history of his powerful father. Meanwhile, Thanos must face the wrath of Mephisto, the Avengers, his future self, and more.

Thanos Rising. Written by **Jason Aaron**. Illustrated by **Simone Bianci**. Marvel Comics, 2014. 120pp. 978-0-7851-9047-9, hardcover; 978-0-7851-8400-3.

The origin of Thanos is revealed as the Mad Titan's life from a youth to adulthood is finally revealed as his passion for death is unleashed at an early age and consumes him beyond a mere obsession.

© 2016 Marvel Comics

Thanos: Cosmic Powers. Written by **Ron Marz**. Illustrated by **Scot Eaton**, **Ron Lim**, and various. Marvel Comics, 2015. 344pp. 978-0-7851-9817-8.

Thanos must work with other cosmic characters including Jack of Hearts, Terrax the Tamer, and Legacy, the son of Captain Marvel, to defeat the menace of Tyrant.

Thanos vs. Hulk. Written and Illustrated by **Jim Starlin**. Marvel Comics, 2015. 978-0-7851-9712-6.

The Hulk is captured by Pip the Troll and traded to Annihilus, lord of the Negative Zone. As Annihilus plots to exploit the Hulk's power in an unexpected way, Thanos enters the fray with plots of his own. Can the Hulk survive in the Negative Zone and will Thanos be able to take on the immense strength of the Hulk?

Thanos: The Infinity Relativity. Written and Illustrated by **Jim Starlin**. Marvel Comics, 2015. 112pp. 978-0-7851-9303-6, hardcover.

Annihilus, lord of the Negative Zone, has entered the positive universe, and only a group of warriors, The Guardians of the Galaxy, Gladiator, Majestor of the Shi'ar, and Adam Warlock, can stop him. When the battle seems lost, the positive universe's greatest hope rests in the hands of Thanos.

Thanos: The Infinity Finale. Written by **Jim Starlin**. Illustrated by **Ron Lim**. Marvel Comics, 2016. 978-0-7851-9305-0.

The epic ending to the story that ran through *The Infinity Revelation* and *The Infinity Relativity*.

Alternate Time Lines, Elseworlds, and What-If Worlds

Many people might have wondered what life would be like if they hadn't made the choices they've made in life and it's the same for super-heroes, too. What would happen to our heroes and villains if they did one thing different? How would it have affected them? It could be a small change or something larger—but the possibilities of these situations are endless, and the end result can sometimes be more entertaining than the original stories. For Marvel Comics this has been shown through the various *What If?* ongoing series, limited series, and one-shots. DC Comics has published similar works under its *Elseworlds* banner, most of which feature Batman and Superman. The ideas for the stories are virtually unlimited and include such scenarios as "What if Batman fought Jack the Ripper," "What if Peter Parker's Aunt May died instead of Uncle Ben?" and "What if Superman was raised in the Soviet Union instead of the United States?" Please note that some stories based on speculative events of the future or alternative time lines including *Batman: The Dark Knight Returns*, *The Incredible Hulk: Future Imperfect*, and *Kingdom Come* are not listed here and are featured elsewhere in this chapter.

Batman: Earth One. Written by **Geoff Johns**. Illustrated by **Gary Frank**. DC Comics, 2012–2015.

A new reinterpretation of the Dark Knight by fan-favorite creators Geoff Johns and Gary Frank. Set early in Batman's career, Bruce Wayne is an impatient man setting out to solve the crime of his parents' murder and find his way as a crime fighter. The story features brand new takes on common Batman heroes and villains and is not tied in with current DC Comics Batman mythos.

Vol. 1. 2012. 144pp. 978-1-4012-3208-5, hardcover; 2014. 978-1-4012-3209-2.
Vol. 2. 2015. 160pp. 978-1-4012-4185-8, hardcover.

DC: The New Frontier. Written and Illustrated by **Darwyn Cooke**. DC Comics, 2004–2006. T 🗡 ◎ 🎬

© 2016 DC Comics

Even before the heroes of old put on costumes, they were always heroes. Joined together in an epic adventure spanning from World War II and lasting until the dawn of the Cold War, the heroes of the Silver Age of comics must band together to face an ancient foe threatening to take over the entire world; Hal Jordan (Green Lantern), The Flash, Martian Manhunter, Superman, Aquaman, Wonder Woman, Batman, Adam Strange, the Challengers of the Unknown, the Blackhawks, the Suicide Squad, and many more—the Silver Age heroes of yesterday—must work together to save mankind from extermination. The series won several Eisner Awards in 2005 for Best Finite Series/Limited Series and Best Colorist/Coloring as well as Harvey Awards for Best Artist or Penciller (2005) and Best Continuing or Limited Series (2005). In 2008 a direct-to-DVD adaptation of the story was released titled *Justice League: The New Frontier*.

Vol. 1. 2004. 208pp. 1-4012-0350-7.
Vol. 2. 2005. 208pp. 1-4012-0461-9.
Absolute DC: The New Frontier. 2006. 464pp. 1-4012-1080-5, hardcover.
DC: The New Frontier, Deluxe Edition. 2015. 520pp. 978-1-4012-4888-8, hardcover; 2016. 978-1-4012-6378-2.

DC Comics Bombshells. Written by **Marguerite Bennett**. Illustrated by **Marguerite Sauvage**. DC Comics, 2016– . T

A reimagining of the women of DC Comics set in the 1940s. Meet Supergirl, Batgirl, Wonder Woman, Harley Quinn, Hawkgirl, and more like you've never seen them before as they fight World War II on the front lines and at home! The series was inspired by artwork and statues design by Ant Lucia and DC Collectibles.

Vol. 1. 2016. 144pp. 978-1-4012-6132-0.
Vol. 2. 2016. 144pp. 978-1-4012-6448-2.
Vol. 3. 2017. 200pp. 978-1-4012-6877-0.

Elseworlds: Batman. Written by **Byron Preiss, Doug Moench, Mike W. Barr, Howard Chaykin**, and various. Illustrated by **P. Craig Russell, Kelley Jones, Norm Breyfogle, Bo Hampton, Howard Chaykin**, and various. DC Comics, 2016– . A

The Elseworlds series from DC Comics transplants familiar characters into brand-new adventures that is both familiar and fresh. Stories collected in these volumes *Batman: Holy Terror Robin 3000, Batman: Brotherhood of the Bat, Batman: Scar of the Bat,* and a trilogy of stories in which Batman becomes a vampire. Collections of Elseworlds stories with Superman will begin to be published in 2018.

Vol. 1. 2016. 524pp. 978-1-4012-6074-3.
Vol. 2. 2016. 286pp. 978-1-4012-6982-1.
Vol. 3. 2017. 288pp. 978-1-4012-6596-0.

2

3

4

5

6

7

8

9

Elseworlds: Justice League. Written by **Chuck Dixon**, **J.H. Williams III**, and various. Illustrated by various. DC Comics, 2016– . A

An anthology of alternate setting stories featuring the Justice League. The stories in these collection include *Justice Riders Elseworlds Finest, Superman's Metropolis*, and *Batman: Nosferatu*.

Vol. 1. 2016. 500pp. 978-1-4012-6377-5.

Vol. 2. 2017. 432pp. 978-1-4012-6855-8.

Injustice: Gods among Us. Written by **Tom Taylor** and **Brian Buccellato**. Illustrated by **Jheremy Raapack**, **Bruno Redondo**, **Mike S. Miller**, and various. DC Comics, 2014–2017. T 🎮

© 2016 DC Comics

Based on the storyline from the hit video game of the same name! When Superman is tricked into destroying the one thing he's loved the most, he decides to no longer be the pawn and sets out to take over the world. Heroes now and the countries of the world must decide if they are with him or against him. But not every country is willing to give in to Superman's new world order and neither is Batman! The still-ongoing series spans years in the war of Superman versus those that resist him. Who will win the ultimate battle for the world?

Vol. 1. 2013. 192pp. 978-1401245009, hardcover; 2014. 192pp. 978-1401248437.

Vol. 2. 2014. 232pp. 978-1401246013, hardcover; 2015. 232pp. 978-1401250454.

Year One: The Complete Collection. 2016. 424pp. 978-1-4012-6279-2.

Year Two: Vol. 1. 2014. 144pp. 978-1-4012-5071-3, hardcover; 2015. 144pp. 978-1-4012-5340-0.

Year Two: Vol. 2. 2015. 176pp. 978-1-4012-5341-7, hardcover; 2015. 176pp. 978-1-4012-5850-4.

Year Three: Vol. 1. 2015. 144pp. 978-1-4012-5851-1, hardcover. 2016. 144pp. 978-1-4012-6314-0.

Year Three: Vol. 2. 2016. 160pp. 978–1401259754, hardcover; 2016. 160pp. 978-1-4012-6129-0.

Year Four: Vol. 1. 2016. 160pp. 978-1-4012-6130-6, hardcover. 978-1-4012-6267-9.

Year Four: Vol. 2. 2016. 160pp. 978-1-4012-6268-6, hardcover. 978-1-4012-6737-7.

Year Five: Vol. 1. 2016. 160pp. 978-1-4012-6768-1, hardcover. 978-1-4012-6883-1.

Year Five: Vol. 2. 2017. 144 pp. 978-1-4012-6884-8, hardcover. 978-1-4012-7247-0.

Year Five: Vol. 3. 2017. 144pp. 978-1-4012-7246-3 hardcover.

Marvel Universe: The End. Written and Illustrated by **Jim Starlin**. Marvel Comics, 2011–2013. 168pp. 978-0-7851-4571-4, hardcover; 2013. 978-0-7851-6784-6. T

An epic "What If" story that tells the last tale of Thanos. When the ancient Egyptian pharaoh Akhenaten is corrupted by a power source called the Heart of the Universe, he arrives in the present day to use his power to control the Earth. All attempts to defeat him are thwarted. Thanos must gather a remaining squadron of heroes to defeat the mad pharaoh. Will they be in time to save the universe from destruction, or is it too late?

Superman & Batman: Generations. Written and Illustrated by **John Byrne**. DC Comics, 2017 160pp. 978-1-4012-6859-6. A

Have you ever wondered what would really have happened if Superman and Batman had aged in normal years since their first appearances in the comic books in the 1930s? How would life go on for them, their loved ones, and their bitter enemies? Old heroes would retire and be replaced by the younger generation of heroes, and family would live and die. As an elderly Bruce Wayne treks the Himalayas in search of the fabled Lazarus back into a frail body, a disheartened Superman finds solace after tragedy has struck his peaceful family. Can the two archetypes of heroism re-find the strength they need to battle their earliest of foes, or will they become lost in the perils of old age and the ravages of time? This volume collects Byrne's first two Generations limited series.

Superman: Earth One. Written by **J. Michael Straczynski**. Illustrated by **Shane Davis** and **Ardian Syaf**. DC Comics, 2010– . T ◉

A reinterpretation of the Man of Steel set separately from the current comic book's continuity. Superman finds his way as a protector of Earth and upholder of his fallen home planet of Krypton, battling against villains including the alien Tyrell, the Parasite, and Lex Luthor.

Vol. 1. 2010. 136pp. 978-1-4012-2468-4, hardcover.
Vol. 2. 2012. 136pp. 978-1-4012-3196-5, hardcover.
Vol. 3. 2015. 128pp. 978-1-4012-4184-1, hardcover.

Teen Titans: Earth One. Written by **Jeff Lemire**. Illustrated by **Rachel Dodson, Terry Dodson,** and **Andy MacDonald.** DC Comics, 2015– . T

An alternate-Earth version of the super-hero teen group. When four seemingly normal teens in Oregon gain superpowers, they band together to learn the secret behind them and why they've been all having similar visions. A new look at Changeling (Beast Boy), Cyborg, Jericho, Terra, and Raven as you've never seen them before!

Vol. 1 2015. 144pp. 978-1-4012-5908-2, hardcover, 978-1-4012-5908-2.
Vol. 2. 2016. 14pp. 978-1-4012-5906-8, hardcover. 978-1-4012-7153-4.

Wonder Woman: Earth One. Written by **Grant Morrison**. Illustrated by **Yanick Paquette**. DC Comics, 2016. 144pp. 978-1401229788, hardcover. T

A new retelling of Diana, Princess of the Amazons. Longing to be free of the shackles of her upbringing on Paradise Island, Diana finds her chance when she rescued Air Force pilot Steve Trevor. The first man she's ever seen, with his life in the balance she risks the oldest law of the island: to stay hidden from the world that wronged the Amazons. Brought back to the island in chains, Diana risked everything to save the life of a man, but will she pay for it with her own life?

X-Men: The Age of Apocalypse. Written by **Scott Lobdell**, **Jeph Loeb**, and various. Illustrated by **Ian Churchill**, **Andy Kubert**, **Chris Bachalo**, and various. Marvel Comics, 2015–2016. T ◉

Set in an alternate time line in which Professor X was accidentally killed before he could form the X-Men, the evil genetic villain Apocalypse has the entire world in his grasp and humanity has been nearly exterminated. Only

Erik Lensherr (Magneto) continues to fulfill Professor X's dreams and with his team of X-Men and the help of the time-displaced Bishop, they're out to set things right: to change the past to make sure that this abomination of a world never existed. Some characters introduced here made their way into the "regular" Marvel Universe.

Alpha. 2015. 400pp. 978-0-7851-9364-7.
Reign. 2015. 408pp. 978-0-7851-9365-4.
Dawn. 2016. 424pp. 978-0-7851-9350-0.
Omega. 2016. 400pp. 978-0-7851-9379-1.
Twilight. 2016. 432pp. 978–0785193449.
X-Men: The Age of Apocalypse Omnibus. 2016. 1072pp. 978-0-7851-9509-2, hardcover.

Slice-of-Life/Common Man Perspectives

Stories that tell of what it's like to live in a city where super-heroes walk the Earth from the perspective of an average person on the street to police officers working alongside the costumed heroes. The stories can also focus on the heroes before or after they became super-heroes.

Astro City. Written by **Kurt Busiek**. Illustrated by **Brent Anderson**. Covers by **Alex Ross**. DC Comics, 1999– . T 🏆 ◎

Welcome to Astro City, a city unlike any other where everyday folks and the fantastic world of super-heroes interact and work together in the shining silver city. Rebuilt in 1947, Astro City has been protected by an ever-changing array of heroes, including the super-strong Samaritan, the female warrior-hero Winged Victory, the dark and brooding vampire The Confessor, the buffoonish Crackerjack, the clown-themed Jack-in-the-Box, the mythic Old Soldier, the super-team the First Family, the Honor Guard, the Christian-based team the Crossbreed, and the Irregulars. The boroughs of Astro City including City Center, Old Town, Chesler, and Shadow Hill are protected by its own neighborhood guardian hero from any evil that would dare to commit a crime in the city. When villains such as Demolitia and the Unholy Alliance, Infidel, Mock Turtle, and the Living Nightmare attack, the heroes of Astro City will be there. Each "slice of life" story in *Astro City* is told in a unique and personal view, varying each time in perspective showing the city through the eyes of a hero, a citizen of the city, a down and out reformed criminal, and more. The series has won numerous awards including several Eisner Awards for Best Single Issue/Single Story (1996–1998), Best Serialized Story (1998), Best Continuing Series (1997–1998), Best New Series (1996), and Best Writer (1999). The series also won several Harvey Awards for Best Single Issue or Story (1996), Best Writer (1997) for Kurt Busiek's body of work including this series as well as Best New Series (1996), Best Graphic Album of Previously Published Work (1997), and Best Continuing or Limited Series

(1998). The collection *Volume 1: Life in the Big City*, originally published in 1999, received recognition by YALSA's Popular Paperbacks for Young Adults committee in 2002.

Vol. 1: Life in the Big City (new edition). 2011. 978-1-4012-3261-0, hardcover; 978-1-4012-3262-7.

Vol. 2: Confession (new edition). 2015. 192pp. 978-1-4012-5830-6, hardcover.

Vol. 3: Family Album (new edition). 2015. 224pp. 978-1-4012-3531-4.

Vol. 4: Tarnished Angel. 2001. 256pp. 978-1-5638-9653-8, hardcover; 978-1-5638-9663-7.

Vol. 5: Local Heroes. 2005. 256pp. 978-1-4012-0281-1, hardcover; 978-1-4012-0284-2.

Vol. 6: The Dark Age Book One: Brothers and Other Strangers. 2008. 256pp. 978-1-4012-1868-3, hardcover; 2015. 978-1-4012-5922-8.

Vol. 7: The Dark Age Book Two: Brothers in Arms. 2010. 240pp. 978-1-4012-2843-9, hardcover; 2011. 978-1-4012-2844-6.

Vol. 8: Shining Stars. 2011. 208pp. 978-1401229849, hardcover; 2014. 978-1-4012-2991-7.

Vol. 9: Through Open Doors. 2014. 176pp. 978-1-4012-4752-2, hardcover; 978-1-4012-4996-0.

Vol. 10: Victory. 2015. 176pp. 978-1401250577, hardcover; 978-1-4012-5460-5.

Vol. 11: Private Lives. 2015. 176pp. 978-1-4012-5459-9, hardcover; 978-1-4012-5824-5.

Vol. 12: Lovers Quarrel. 2015. 176pp. 978-1-4012-5825-2, hardcover; 978-1-4012-6134-4.

Vol. 13: Honor Guard. 2016. 176pp. 978-1-4012-6387-4, hardcover. 978-1-4012-6828-2.

Vol.14: Reflections. 2017. 176pp. 978-1-4012-6829-9, hardcover.

Demo. Written by **Brian Wood**. Illustrated by **Becky Cloonan**. Dark Horse Comics, 2015. 496pp. 978-1-6165-5682-2. O

This black and white title features multiple stories about young people, some of whom have some sort of special power, who are having to make a life-altering decision. Demo began as an Eisner-nominated 12-issue limited series published and later collected by AiT/PlanetLar. DC reprinted the book in 2008, and this was followed by the six-part *Demo 2*. The 2015 collection features all 18 stories.

Hero Happy Hour. Written by **Dan Taylor** and various. Illustrated by various. Arcana Studios, 2012. 100pp. 978-1-926914-71-8. O

Where do all the heroes of First City go after a hard day's work of fighting crime? They all go to The Hideout Bar and Grill watering hole for the best drinks in town. Run by retired hero Rupert "Rusty" Russell, it's the best place to go when you're in the mood to drown your blues. Capes and tights are more than welcome. As "regulars" including Guardian, Night Ranger, and his sidekick Scout, Feline, Knightingale, and more stop in for a brew or two, find out what it's like when the heroes are off-duty, and the trials, tribulations, and hilarities of being a hero in First City.

Kick-Ass. Written by **Mark Millar**. Illustrated by **John Romita Jr**. Marvel/Icon, 2010–2014. M

Set in the "real world," Dave Lizewski decides to create a costume and become a crime fighter called Kick-Ass. He eventually gets in over his head and encounters others including Big Daddy and his young, violent daughter Hit-Girl. His activities lead to trouble for both him and his loved ones as where there are super-heroes there must also be super-villains. The Kick-Ass books have been adapted into two feature films, Kick-Ass (2010) and Kick-Ass 2 (2013), starring Aaron Taylor-Johnson as Kick-Ass and Chloë Grace Moretz as Hit-Girl.

Kick-Ass. 2013. 240pp. 978-0-7851-8401-0, hardcover.
Kick-Ass 2 Prelude: Hit Girl. 2013. 136pp. 978-0-7851-6597-2, hardcover.
Kick-Ass 2. 2012. 208pp. 978-0-7851-5245-3, hardcover.
Kick-Ass 3. 2014. 232pp. 978-0-7851-8488-1, hardcover.

Marvels. Written by **Kurt Busiek**. Illustrated by **Alex Ross**. Marvel Comics, 2010. 248pp. 978-0-7851-4286-7. T 🎗 ◎

© 2016 Marvel Comics

See the Marvel Universe in a whole new way—through the eyes of the average man on the street in New York City. This is a look at over 35 years of Marvel Comics, history told from the perspective of *Daily Bugle* newspaper photographer Phil Sheldon. From the earliest days during World War II with Captain America and the Invaders to the salvation of the world by the Fantastic Four and the Silver Surfer from the world-devouring giant called Galactus to the persecution of an innocent little mutant girl who is protected by the X-Men to Spider-Man's greatest heartache, the Marvel Universe will never look the same way again. The story won Eisner Awards in 1994 for Best Finite Series/Limited Series, Best Painter/Multimedia Artist (Interior), and Best Publication Design as well as Harvey Awards for Best Artists or Penciller (1994), Special Award for Excellence in Production/Presentation (1994), Best Continuing or Limited Series (1994), Best Single Issue or Story (1994), and Best Graphic Album of Previously Published Work (1995).

Plutona. Written by **Jeff Lemire**. Illustrated by **Emi Lenox**. Image Comics, 2016. 152pp. 978-1-63215-601-3. T 🎗

Five teenagers find the body of the world's greatest heroine in the woods. How did the heroine Plutona get there and what affects will her death have on them all? The book was recognized by YALSA's Great Graphic Novels for Teens Top Ten list in 2017.

Powers. Written by **Brian Michael Bendis**. Illustrated by **Michael Avon Oeming**. Marvel Comics/ICON, 2001– . M 🎗 ◎ ⌨

Detectives Christian Walker and his new partner, the no-nonsense and loud-spoken Deena Pilgrim, work in a homicide department that handles cases involving "Powers" (people with super-powers). Walker himself used to be the Powers known as Diamond, but he gave it up long ago when he lost his super-powers. Today he walks a beat with a badge but still maintains close tie to the Powers community. Their first case together involves the murder of the media darling heroine known as Retro Girl, a close friend of Walker. As they continue their investigations into the world of Powers,

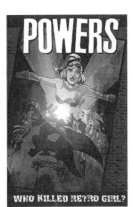

© 2016 Marvel Comics

they're exposed to the gritty, violent, and seedier aspects of the lives of these so-called heroes, including cases involving stalkers, role-playing fans, kinky sex acts, spontaneous combustion, and the obligatory scene of monkeys fighting and fornicating. After a hero goes insane and destroys most of the world, the opposition to Powers grows, resulting in the president declaring a ban on all super-powered activity. What side will Walker take and where does his allegiance lie—with his hero friends from his past or his officers and partners on the force? The series won an Eisner Award in 2001 for Best New Series as well as Eisners in 2002–2003 for Best Writer. The series was also adapted into a live-action television series which debuted on the Sony Playstation Network in 2015 starring Sharlto Copley as Christian Walker.

Powers, Volume 1, 2001–2004.

Vol. 1: Who Killed Retro Girl. 2011. 240pp. 978-0-7851-5671-0, hardcover; 2014. 978-0-7851-9274-9.
Vol. 2: Roleplay. 2011. 112pp. 978-0-7851-5983-4, hardcover; 2014. 978-0-7851-9275-6.
Vol. 3: Little Deaths. 2011. 192pp. 978-0-7851-5984-1, hardcover; 2015. 978-0-7851-9308-1.
Vol. 4: Supergroup. 2012. 176pp. 978-0-7851-6016-8, hardcover; 2015. 978-0-7851-9309-8.
Vol. 5: Anarchy. 2012. 128pp. 978-0-7851-6017-5, hardcover; 2015. 978-0-7851-9307-4.
Vol. 6: The Sellouts. 2012. 192pp. 978-0-7851-6018-2, hardcover; 2004. 978-0-7851-1582-3.
Vol. 7: Forever. 2013. 272pp. 978-0-7851-6602-3, hardcover; 2004. 978-0-7851-1656-1.

Powers, Volume 2, 2005–2009.

Vol. 8: Legends. 2005. 208pp. 978-0-7851-1742-1.
Vol. 9: Psychotic. 2006. 200pp. 978-0-7851-1743-8.
Vol. 10: Cosmic. 2007. 200pp. 978-0-7851-2260-9.
Vol. 11: Secret Identity. 2008. 200pp. 978-0-7851-2261-6.
Vol. 12: The 25 Coolest Dead Superheroes of All Time. 2009. 240pp. 978-0-7851-2262-3.

Powers, Volume 3, 2010–2012.

Vol. 13: Z. 2010. 224pp. 978-0-7851-4593-6.
Vol. 14: Gods. 2012. 168pp. 978-0-7851-4594-3.

Powers: The Bureau, 2014–2015.

Vol. 1: Undercover. 2014. 168pp. 978-0-7851-6602-3.
Vol. 2: Icons. 2015. 176pp. 978-0-7851-8918-3.

Powers, Volume 4, 2015– .

Vol. 1: All the New Powers. 2015. 200pp. 9780785197454, hardcover.
Powers Omnibus, Vol. 1. 2015. 1296pp. 978-0-7851-9827-7, hardcover.
Definitive Hardcover Collection. 2005–2014.

> *Vol. 1.* 2005. 488pp. 978-0-7851-1805-3, hardcover.
> *Vol. 2.* 2009. 480pp. 978-0-7851-2440-5, hardcover.
> *Vol. 3.* 2009. 496pp. 978-0-7851-3309-4, hardcover.
> *Vol. 4.* 2011. 600pp. 978-0-7851-5316-0, hardcover.
> *Vol. 5.* 2012. 464pp. 978-0-7851-6612-2, hardcover.
> *Vol. 6.* 2014. 424pp. 978-0-7851-9275-6, hardcover.

Top 10. Written by **Alan Moore**. Illustrated by **Gene Ha** and **Zander Cannon**. Vertigo/DC Comics, 2005–2013. M 🏃 ◎

© 2016 DC Comics

The city of Neopolis was built as a haven for science heroes and villains shortly after World War II. Since that time more and more super-powered individuals, gods, and space aliens have come to call Neopolis their home. In order to police the powered populace, the city agreed to be under the jurisdiction of a multidimensional peacekeeping force spread across many parallel Earths. Located in Neopolis is precinct 10 (nicknamed Top 10), workplace to a colorful cast of cops. Enter Robyn "Toybox" Slinger, a rookie on the force, with partner Jeff Smax, a sulky and gruff blue-skinned giant. Other colorful cops include a near-retirement classic hero Captain "Jetman" Traynor, a dog desk sergeant named Caesar, lesbian ghost girl Jackie Phantom, the armored walking weapon Irma Geddon, a Satanist named King Peacock, and high-tech cowboy Duane Dust Devil. The cases are fantastic and often humorous, ranging from an alien serial killer who murders prostitutes and bar brawls fought by gods to a giant Godzilla-sized drunken lizard named Gograh. You can be sure that the streets are much safer with them on the beat. Also features numerous inside jokes and appearances from many popular culture icons. *Top 10: The Forty-Niners* presents for the first time the origins of Neopolis as a young science hero named Jetman, and heroic companions create the beginnings of what will later become to be known as Precinct 10. Beyond the Farthest Precinct is a spin-off written by Paul Di Filippo and illustrated by Jerry Ordway. The original printing of the series received an Eisner Award in 2001 for Best Continuing Series and *Top Ten: The Forty-Niners* received several Eisner Awards in 2006 for Best Graphic Album: New and Best Writer. The entire series was reprinted in a massive *Absolute Top 10* collection by DC Comics in 2013.

The Forty-Niners. 2005. 112pp. 978-1563897573, hardcover; 978-1-4012-0573-7.
Beyond the Farthest Precinct. 2006. 136pp. 978-1-4012-0991-9.
Absolute Top 10. 2013. 576pp. 978-1-4012-3825-4, hardcover.
Top 10. 2013. 352pp. 978-1-4012-5493-3.

Anthologies

Collections of super-hero stories featuring highlights from one creator's career or stories written by a showcase of creators for the Super-Hero genre.

DC Universe by Alan Moore. Written by **Alan Moore**. Illustrated by various. DC Comics, 2013. 464pp. 978-1-4012-3340-2. T ◉

> Alan Moore has been highly praised in the comic book industry for his outstanding writing and creativity for decades. Now, collected together for the first time, are some of his best-known stories created for DC Comics. Highlights include the stories *Superman: Whatever Happened to the Man of Tomorrow?* "Mogo Doesn't Socialize", and "For the Man Who Has Everything" which has been adapted both on the Justice League cartoon and on the live-action Supergirl show. Other stories feature Swamp Thing, the Vigilante, the Omega Men, and the Green Lantern Corps.

The Simon and Kirby Library: Superheroes. Written and Illustrated by **Joe Simon** and **Jack Kirby**. Titan Books, 2010. 480pp. 978-1-84856-365-0, hardcover. Y

> The first volume of Titan Books' extensive collection of comics featuring two legendary creators focuses on some of the lesser-known heroes by the team that created Captain America. These include The Fly, The Fighting American, Black Owl, Stuntman, Vagabond Prince, and Captain 3-D.

Strange Tales. Written and Illustrated by various. Marvel Comics, 2010–2011. T

© 2016 Marvel Comics

> *Strange Tales* is what happens when new and alternative artists are given free range with the iconic super-heroes within Marvel's canon. Artists like James Stokoe, Harvery Pekar, Paul Pope, Kate Beaton, Peter Bagge, Los Bros. Hernandez, Terry Moore, Nick Gurewitch, Nick Bertozzi, and Stan Sakai all contribute their take on characters like the Hulk, Spider Man, the Avengers, and the X-Men.
>
> *Vol. 1*. 2010. 160pp. 978-0-7851-2802-1.
> *Vol. 2*. 2011. 152pp. 978-0-7851-4823-4.

Chapter 2

Action and Adventure

The Action and Adventure genre in comic books and graphic novels finds its roots in the classic tales of adventure prose from the 19th-century adventure writers such as Robert Louis Stevenson and from speculative fiction writers Jules Verne, H.G. Wells, and Sir Arthur Conan Doyle, as well as the pulp fiction novels from the early 20th century which told the exploits of such colorful heroes including Tarzan, Doc Savage, Conan the Barbarian, and the Shadow. With the expansion of the comic book industry, the original Action and Adventure tales were reprints of newspaper comic strips including such popular characters as Terry and the Pirates, Little Orphan Annie, Dick Tracy, Flash Gordon, and Tarzan. Publishers also began to create all-new adventure stories with such characters as Dr. Occult, from Jerry Siegel and Joe Shuster, the creators of the most popular super-hero character ever, Superman.

Very similar to the prose Action and Adventure books and movies, the graphic novels in this genre feature themes such as classic tales of good guys versus bad guys, exotic locations, brave heroes, dastardly villains, and plenty of danger. The stories feature heroes as rugged adventurers, jungle warriors, cowboys, samurai, spies, fighters, soldiers, and more. Due to the illustrated nature of the format, unlike prose adventure fiction, the medium of the comic book readily lends itself to showing more heroic feats and is more closely related to motion pictures in this respect. Other traditional prose adventure themes, including political intrigue and industrial adventure, have not been widely published in a comic book or graphic novel format. Note that though the Super-Hero genre is directly related to this genre, the colorful heroes are featured in their own chapter in this publication.

What is daily life like for the animals that share the Earth with us? For most animals, it's a grueling day-by-day struggle where death is around at every corner and you have to struggle to survive. The main character of this type of book is the animals themselves. Human companions may serve in a supportive role, but the focus is clearly on the animal.

For books that feature anthropomorphic animal character, they are mixed within this book in their appropriate genre. For titles featuring humorous animals, they are featured in the humor chapter of this book.

Dogs of War. Written by **Sheila Keenan** and **Nathan Fox**. Illustrated by **Nathan Fox**. Graphix/Scholastic, 2013. 208pp. 978-0-545-12888-9. Y

> Three historical fiction stories featuring three conflicts in which service dogs have played a role alongside their soldier companions. The first conflict is set during World War I; a medic and his companion dog named boots are lost deep in the trenches. The second conflict is World War II; a dog named Loki and his companion are trying to save a downed pilot. And last, a vet who has returned from the Vietnam War has flashbacks about his companion Sheba.

Laika. Written and Illustrated by **Nick Abadzis**. First Second Books, 2007. 208pp. 978-1-59643-101-0. T ◉

> A fictionalized account of Laika, the famous Samoyed-husky, who in November 1957 became the first living being to leave Earth's orbit aboard the Sputnik II satellite. Told from the perspective of Laika, she was a dog who had survived on the tough streets of Russia, was rescued by scientists, and made the ultimate sacrifice in order to further the Soviet space program. A poignant look at the cruel life in the Soviet Union and the politics that drove the space race at that time in history.

© 2016 First Second and Nick Abadzis

Love. Written by **Frédéric Brrémaud**. Illustrated by **Federico Berolucci**. Magnetic Press, 2015– . Y 🎗

> A gorgeously illustrated silent graphic novel series. Each volume tells the tale of a specific wild animal and the challenges and rewards it has in a day. The collection *Love: The Fox* was recognized by YALSA's Great Graphic Novels for Teens annual selection list in 2017.

> *The Fox*. 2015. 80pp. 978-1-94236-706-2, hardcover.
> *The Tiger*. 2015. 80pp. 978-0-9913324-4-1, hardcover.
> *The Lion*. 2016. 80pp. 978-1-94236-709-3, hardcover.
> *The Dinosaur*. 2017. 80pp. 978-1-94236-736-9, hardcover.

Mr. Big: A Tale of Pond Life. Written by **Carol Dembicki** and **Matt Dembicki**. Illustrated by **Matt Dembicki**. Sky Dog Press, 2012. 160pp. 978-1-61608-967-2. Y

> Mr. Big is a snapping turtle which is terrorizing the small pond where many smaller fish and reptiles live. The small critters plot to get rid of Mr. Big and make a deal with the crows, but if they do take out Mr. Big what else much worse will replace him? A look at the life cycle in nature and why sometimes larger predators are needed.

The Pride of Baghdad. Written by **Brian K. Vaughan**. Illustrated by **Niko Henrichon**. Vertigo/DC Comics, 2006. 136pp. 978-1-4012-0315-3. M ◎

> Based on a true story. In the early days of the Iraq war in 2003, a pride of lions escaped from the Baghdad Zoo. Confused and hungry, they wandered around the streets of the decimated city searching for food and struggling to survive. Told as a metaphor for the cost of freedom, is it better to live in the security of captivity or to die free of tyranny?

Xoc: The Journey of a Great White. Written and Illustrated by **Matt Dembicki**. Oni Press, 2012. 120pp. 978-1-934964-85-9. T

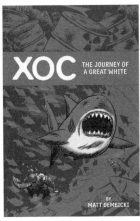

© 2016 Matt Dembicki

> The life of a Great White shark is realized in this graphic novel as it looks for prey, struggles for survival from predators of the ocean, and encounters other denizens of the deep while on a journey from the waters of California to warmer climates in Hawaii.

Prehistoric Adventure

What was life like in prehistoric times? These stories sometimes accurately and sometimes inaccurately portray prehistoric life from the age of the dinosaurs and the age of the earliest mammals onward. Some stories are definitely not scientifically accurate and may feature worlds where dinosaurs, prehistoric mammals, and mankind interact together. The protagonist may even be a dinosaur, prehistoric animal, or caveman. Although the setting for the stories is set in the past, some of these tales are set in the present or even the future. Scientific accuracy is optional, with some authors taking liberties taken for the sake of a good story. Film and television examples of this subgenre include the <u>Jurassic Park</u> series of movies, *King Kong*, *Beast from 20,000 Fathoms*, television classic *Land of the Lost* and *The Good Dinosaur*. This theme closely borders and overlaps the realm of science fiction, horror, and historical fiction.

Age of Reptiles: Ancient Egyptians. Written and Illustrated by **Ricardo Delgado**. Dark Horse Comics, 2016. 120pp. 978-1-61655-820-8. A

> Brought to life by dinosaur aficionado Ricardo Delgado, see the silently told tale of one of the most vicious dinosaurs from the Cretaceous Period: the *Spinosaurus aegyptiacus*. Set in Africa during the heyday of the dinosaurs,

Age of ReptilesTM and all its
characters, their names, and their
distinctive likenesses are TM and
© 2016 Ricardo Delgado

villains, victims, and violence rule the day as a lone Spinosaurus struggles to survive in a harsh environment with danger at every turn.

Age of Reptiles Omnibus. Written and Illustrated by **Ricardo Delgado**. Dark Horse Comics, 2011. 400pp. 978-1-59582-683-1. A 🎗 ◎

The ancient world of the dinosaurs comes alive again in three silent stories collected in one omnibus collection. In *Tribal Warfare*, a carnivorous Tyrannosaurus Rex must fight for survival against the quick-footed scavenging pack of Deinonychus. In *The Hunt*, an orphaned Allosaurus must trek across the desert of Jurassic Period North America or share the fate of his mother: a bloody death at the hands of a ferocious pack of Ceratosaurs. The third collection, *The Journey*, features the migration of the dinosaurs when changing climates force them to migrate. In 1997, Ricardo Delgado received an Eisner Award in the category of Talent Deserving of Wider Recognition.

Barry Sonnenfeld's Dinosaurs vs. Aliens. Written by **Grant Morrison** and **Barry Sonnenfeld**. Illustrated by **Mukesh Singh**. Liquid Comics/Dynamite Entertainment, 2012. 96pp. 978-1-60690-345-2, hardcover. T

From the mind behind the hit *Men in Black* movies and comic book creator Grant Morrison—meets the very first alien encounter on Earth that was 65 million years in the making! When an alien race comes to the "blue planet" in hopes of saving their race, they presume that the life-forms on Earth are unintelligent and docile animals—but little do they realize that the ultimate clash will soon begin when the dinosaurs attack to protect their world. The story is a subtle retelling of the plight of Native Americans versus the Western expansion.

Captain Raptor. Written by **Kevin O'Malley**. Illustrations by **Patrick O'Brien**. Walker Publishing Company, 2005–2007. Y

When the inhabitants of planet Jurassica needs saving, there's one dinosaur who can save the day—Captain Raptor! With his able crew of dinosaurs, they're out to save the day whenever danger rears its ugly head. In *The Moon Mystery*, when a mysterious object crashes to the nearby moon called Eon, Captain Raptor and his crew fly out in their spaceship the Megatooth to discover its secrets. In *The Space Pirates*, the crew must face their toughest battle yet against a horde of pirates who have stolen the Jewels of Jurassica.

Vol. 1: Captain Raptor and the Moon Mystery. 2005. 32pp. 978-0-8027-8935-8.
Vol. 2. Captain Raptor and the Space Pirates. 2007. 32pp. 978-0-8027-9571-7.

Devil Dinosaur. Created by **Jack Kirby**. Written by **Jack Kirby**, **Amy Reeder**, and **Brandon Montclare**. Illustrated by **Jack Kirby** and **Natacha Bustos**. Marvel Comics, 2014– . A

© 2016 Marvel Comics

Created by Jack "King" Kirby for Marvel Comics in 1978, Devil Dinosaur is a crimson-colored Tyrannosaurus Rex from an alternate world called Dinosaur World. One of the most powerful of dinosaurs, his red devil-colored skin, tough hide, and great strength were caused by a mutagenic reaction when he was a young dinosaur. His companion in the original series is Moon Boy, a primitive ape-like companion, where the two of them defy the laws of the savage land and fought together against dinosaurs, aliens, and warring tribes. In 2015, a new series called Moon Girl and Devil Dinosaur was released, which features Lunella Lafayette, a brilliant girl, whose life is turned upside down when Devil Dinosaur is teleported from Dinosaur World to the present day.

Devil Dinosaur by Jack Kirby: The Complete Collection. 2014. 184pp. 978-0-7851-9037-0.
Moon Girl and Devil Dinosaur.
Vol. 1: BFF. 2016. 136pp. 978-1-3029-0005-2.
Vol. 2: Cosmic Cooties. 2017. 136pp. 978-1-3029-0208-7.
Vol. 3: The Smartest There Is. 2017. 136pp. 978-1-3029-0534-7.

Dinosaur Hour. Written and Illustrated by **Hitoshi Shioya**. VIZ Media, 2009. 200pp. 978-1-4215-2648-5. Y

KYORYU NO JIKAN © Hitoshi Shioya/POPLAR Publishing Co., Ltd.

Meet the dinosaurs in a whole new way in this collection of short educational lessons, but the stories also incorporate plenty of humor. The story is presented for younger readers in the standard Japanese right-to-left format.

Dinosaur King. Written and Illustrated by **Yohei Sakkai**. VIZ Media, 2010. A 🎮 Japanese anime

Based off the popular Sega arcade card game of the same name. Max, a die-hard dinosaur fan, finds himself transported to the age of the dinosaurs via a magical tablet. Soon he befriends a baby triceratops he names King and finds that he's not alone there. There's an evil mastermind named Dr. Z who has enslaved the dinosaurs to use their hidden powers to take over the world!

Now Max must find a way to defeat Dr. Z and his Alpha Gang and save the dinosaurs! The popular game was also adapted into an animated series in Japan.

Vol. 1. 2010. 192pp. 978-1-4215-3253-0.
Vol. 2. 2010. 192pp. 978-1-4215-3254-7.

Dinosaurs. Written by **Arnaud Plumeri**. Illustrated by **Bloz**. Papercutz, 2014–2015. Y

A historical as well as hysterical look at the world of dinosaurs. Told in short story vignettes mixed with humor, the lives of the dinosaurs are fleshed out for the reader in an entertaining and fun format.

Vol. 1: In the Beginning. 2014. 64pp. 978-1-59707-490-2.
Vol. 2: Bite of the Albertosaurus. 2014. 54pp. 978-1-59707-515-2.
Vol. 3: Jurassic Smarts. 2014. 54pp. 978-1-59707-732-3.
Biggest Battles in 3-D! 2015. 48pp. 978-1-62991-188-5.
Vol. 4: Sea Monsters. 2015. 54pp. 978-1-62991-282-0.

© 2016 Arnaud Plumeri and Bloz

Dinosaurs and Prehistoric Predators. Written and Illustrated by various. Discovery Channel Books/Zenescope, 2011. 120pp. 978-0-9827507-4-2. Y

A collection of short stories featuring a day in the life of a variety of dinosaurs from the Triassic, Jurassic, and Cretaceous periods. The collection features short stories about the following dinosaurs: Allosaurus, Akylosaurus, Apatasaurus, Pteranodon, Sarcosuchus, Spinosaurus, Stegosaurus, Tyrannosaurus, Triceratops, and Velociraptor. The chapters all include scientific facts on the dinosaurs as well.

Dinosaurs in Space. Written and Illustrated by **Pranas T. Naujokaitis**. Balloon Toons/Blue Apple Books, 2012. 40pp. Y

It turns out the asteroid did actually wipe out the dinosaurs—they invented space travel and escaped into outer space! Includes three charming short stories of dinosaurs and space travel including *Burgers vs. Salad*—where the inhabitants of the planets Plant and Meat decide what's the best food on the menu at the local space diner; *Scary Alien from Another Planet*—the dinosaurs meet up with a scary alien: an astronaut; *The Great Space Race*—a T-Rex and Stegosaurus compete to see who can make it first to a planet in a friendly game of reckless space travel.

© 2016 Blue Apple Books

Jurassic Park. Written and Illustrated by various. IDW Publishing, 2011–. T

In 1993 *Jurassic Park* debuted in movie theaters across the world and became one of the top grossing movies of all time. Based on the original 1990 novel by Michael Crichton, the main story is set in a world where a genetics company named InGen, under the direction of its founder, John Hammond, has found a way to clone dinosaurs. The dinosaurs are kept at a soon-to-be opened theme park called Jurassic Park, located on the scenic tropical island of Isla Nubar. Naturally, science goes amok and

the dinosaurs break free. The film series had three sequels—most recently with the 2015 film *Jurassic World*. The story has been continued in comic book form since the 1990s with Topps Comics and most recently with IDW Publishing. Most of the stories are not in canon with the movies but are still entertaining.

© Universal Studios Licensing, LLLP

Classic Jurassic Park. Written by **Walter Simonson** and **Steve Englehart**. Illustrated by **George Perez**, **Gil Kane**, **Dell Barras**, **Joe Staton**, and various. 2010–2013.

Features the adaptation of the 1993 film as well as stories taking place after the events of the film. The stories were originally published by Topps Comics in the 1990s.

Vol. 1. 2010. 104pp. 978-1-60010-760-3.
Vol. 2: Raptor's Revenge. 2011. 192pp. 978-1-60010-885-3.
Vol. 3: Amazon Adventures. 2011. 124pp. 978-1-61377-042-9.
Vol. 4: Return to Jurassic Park, part 1. 2012. 128pp. 978-1-61377-117-4.
Vol. 5: Return to Jurassic Park, part 2. 2013. 108pp. 978-1-61377-533-2.

Jurassic Park: Redemption. Written by **Bob Schreck**. Illustrated by **Nate Van Dyke**. 2011. 120pp. 978-1-60010-850-1.

A tie-in to the movie as a now grown-up Lex and Tim Murphy have inherited their grandfather's park.

Jurassic Park: The Devils in the Desert. Written and Illustrated by **John Byrne**. 2011. 104pp. 978-1-60010-923-2.

Fan-favorite creator John Byrne tells the story about a small town invaded by escaped dinosaurs from Jurassic Park.

Jurassic Park: Dangerous Games. Written by **Greg Bear** and **Erik Bear**. Illustrated by **Jorge Jimenez**. 2012. 112pp. 978-1-61377-002-3, hardcover.

Famed dinosaur writer Greg Bear tells the story about an undercover CIA agent who is attempting to bring in a drug lord who has taken over the Isla Nublar site as the location for his drug empire. When his cover is blown, he has both dinosaurs and armed thugs after him!

© Universal Studios Licensing, LLLP

Kitty and Dino. Written and Illustrated by **Sara Richard**. Yen Press, 2012. 48pp. 978-0-316-13351-7. A

A beautifully silent graphic novel in which a household cat has a new unwelcomed permanent guest when a dinosaur egg hatches in the house and out of it pops out a baby Tyrannosaurus Rex! Soon the fast-growing dinosaur has a partner in crime as they love to create mischief around the house.

© 2016 Yen Press

Neozoic. Written by **Paul Ens**. Illustrated by **J. Korim**. Red Five Comics, 2009–2014. T

Set in a world where the dinosaurs never became extinct, mankind has evolved alongside the great beasts. The best hunters of the giant dinosaurs are the Predator Defense League. When a gesture of goodwill turns into a disaster after thousands of dinosaurs destroy the walls of Monanti City, it creates a feud between man and dinosaur, friend and friend, and father and daughter as the clans take sides in an all-out war.

Vol. 1. 2009. 216pp. 978-0-9809302-3-8.
Vol. 2. 2014. 216pp. 978-0-9868985-8-7.

Paleo: The Complete Collection. Written and Illustrated by **Jim Lawson**. Dover Graphic Novels, 2016. 336pp. 978-0-486-80356-2. T ◉

The savage and deadly ancient past comes alive in this exciting look at the Cretaceous Period, a time when real monstrous beasts roamed the land. From the traumatic experience of a female Triceratops chased out of her herd by a pack of flesh-eating Daspletosaurs, and that of a pack of Dromeosaurs looking for a new leader after the death of the herd's alpha male, to a day in the life of an Albertasaur, and more. Take a journey back to the past where the eaters and the eaten battle for survival and where day-to-day life was a struggle between the jaws of death of a fierce carnivorous dinosaur and the ever-changing landscape in a dangerous world.

© 2016 Jim Lawson

Super Dinosaur. Written by **Robert Kirkam**. Illustrated by **Jason Howard**. Image Comics, 2012–2015. Y

Far beneath the surface of the Earth lies a hidden land where dinosaurs still exist, and the evil Max Maximus wants the fantastic but unstable mineral called DynOre that exists only there for evil purposes. Luckily 10-year-old genius Derek Dynamo and his friend, Super Dinosaur—a 9-foot-tall intelligent Tyrannosaurus Rex in a cybernetic power suit—are there to save the day and foil Max Maximus's schemes and battle

© 2016 Robert Kirkham

against his army of mutant humanoid dinosaurs and other bad guys. Along with Derek's brilliant scientist dad Doctor Dynamo and a husband and wife team of technicians who help create Super Dinosaur's weapons and cybernetic suits, the Earth's best hope for fighting evil is the least likely team ever made: a boy and his dinosaur.

Vol. 1. 2012. 128pp. 978-1-60706-420-6.
Vol. 2. 2012. 112pp. 978-1-60706-568-5.
Vol. 3. 2013. 112pp. 978-1-60706-667-5.
Vol. 4. 2015. 128pp. 978-1-60706-843-3.

Terra Tempo. Written by **David R. Shapiro**. Illustrated by **Christopher Herndon**. Craigmore Creations, 2010– . Y

© 2016 Craigmore Creations

Jenna, Caleb, and Ari are three young explorers who stumble across a time machine to the past and are able to explore over 4.5 billion years of life on planet Earth! After nearly being eaten alive by ferocious beasts, can they learn about history without being part of the main course? Now they're part historians and part paleontologists and full-fledged Time Explorers learning about plant life, animal life, and earth-shaking events as well as famous people throughout history that have helped to shape the planet we live on!

Vol. 1: Ice Age Cataclysm! 2010. 143pp. 978-0-9844422-1-8.
Vol. 2: The Four Corners of Time. 2013. 264pp. 978-0-9844422-6-3.
Vol. 3. The Academy of Planetary Evolution. 2014. 182pp. 978-1-9400520-9-0.

Terrible Lizard. Written by **Cullen Bunn**. Illustrated by **Drew Moss**. Oni Press, 2015. 10+978-1-62010-236-7. Y

© 2016 Cullen Bunn and Drew Moss

The story of a girl and her T-Rex. When a time-travel experiment brings a live Tyrannosaurs Rex to the present, the dinosaur imprints itself on the first human it comes in contact with: a teenager named Jessica. Soon the scientists realize that the dinosaur wasn't the only thing that came through as other prehistoric mutated beasts are coming through and attacking Earth. Now Jessica and her dinosaur must do what's right and send the beasts back where they belong! A loving tribute to giant monster movies like Godzilla.

1

3

4

5

6

7

8

9

Tiger Lung. Written and Illustrated by **Simon Roy** with **Jason Wordie**. Dark Horse Comics, 2014. 88pp. 978-1-61655-543-6, hardcover. O

Set 35,000 years in the past, when ancient gods and beasts roamed the lands, death was an instant away for the Paleolithic people and the shaman warriors were the protectors. Join three tales of the shamans as they battle ancient evil, magic, death, and monstrous beasts in a struggle for human survival in the darkest of days.

Tommysaurus Rex. Written and Illustrated by **Doug TenNapel**. Graphix/Scholastic Books, 2013. 144pp. 978-0-545-48382-7, hardcover; 978-0-545-48383-4. Y ◉

Ten-year-old Ely is spending the summer at his grandfather's farm to help with the chores and to recuperate following the tragic death of Tommy, his pet golden retriever. After being chased by Randy, the local school bully, Ely finds a real Tyrannosaurus Rex buried in a cave behind his grandfather's farm. Soon, Ely and Tommysaurus Rex are inseparable and are the best of friends; but after Tommysaurus Rex has a brief rampage through town, the mayor declares that dinosaur must be declared "safe" or else he'll have to leave. When tragedy strikes, can Tommy and Randy, sworn enemies, find friendship with the healing power of forgiveness? The graphic novel also features a guest appearance by the late legendary stop-motion animator Ray Harryhausen.

© Scholastic Inc

Turok: Son of Stone. Dark Horse Comics, 2009–2012, and Dynamite Entertainment, 2014–2016. T

Turok originally appeared in 1954 in *Four Color Comics* #596 from Dell; Turok appeared in his own popular series published by Dell and then Gold Key from 1956 to 1982. The character was also published by Valiant Comics, Dark Horse Comics, and Dynamite Comics in the last several decades. The long-running series, reprinted by Dark Horse Comics, told the ongoing adventures of Turok, a pre-Columbian Native American who is trapped in a mysterious valley populated by dinosaurs and other prehistoric beasts. He's joined on his journey with Andar, his younger brother, as they escape from the dinosaurs (called by Turok as "honkers") and search for a way back home. The title was adapted by several different publishers beginning with Valiant Comics in the 1990s, which still kept the overall premise of the series, but added tweaks to the basic plot. In the Valiant series from 1992, Turok was stranded in a lost land where time has no meaning and aliens and dinosaurs interact and then was stranded in a post-apocalyptic future with biomechanical dinosaurs. Dark Horse Comics also released a single graphic novel released in 2010 and written by former Valiant Comics writer Jim Shooter. The recent Dynamite Entertainment series, which lasted three volumes, is closely associated with the original Gold Key characters. The original Valiant Entertainment and Acclaim Comics titles have yet to be released as graphic novels. The character also inspired a line of First-Person Shooter video games, beginning with Acclaim Entertainment's *Turok: Dinosaur Hunter* in 1997. Several sequels were released as well for various consoles. The character also appeared in a stand-alone animated movie in 2008 by Classic Media.

Turok: Son of Stone, 1st series and 4th series. Dark Horse Comics, 2009–2013. Dark Horse Comics reprinted many of the classic Dell/Gold Key comic books in hardcover collected editions as well as a stand-alone story.

Turok: Son of Stone Archives. Written by **Paul S. Newman** and various. Illustrated by **Alberto Giolitti**, **Matthew H. Murphy**, and various. Dark Horse Comics, 2009–2012. Y

Vol. 1. 2009. 224pp. 978-1-59582-155-3, hardcover.
Vol. 2. 2009. 224pp. 978-1-59582-275-8, hardcover.
Vol. 3. 2009. 224pp. 978-1-59582-281-9, hardcover.
Vol. 4. 2009. 216pp. 978-1-59582-343-4, hardcover.
Vol. 5. 2010. 224pp. 978-1-59582-442-4, hardcover.
Vol. 6. 2010. 216pp. 978-1-59582-484-4, hardcover.
Vol. 7. 2010. 216pp. 978-1-59582-565-0, hardcover.
Vol. 8. 2011. 232pp. 978-1-59582-641-1, hardcover.
Vol. 9. 2010. 232pp. 978-1-59582-789-0, hardcover.
Vol. 10. 2012. 248pp. 978-1-59582-861-3, hardcover.

Turok: Son of Stone: Aztlan. Written by **Jim Shooter**. Illustrated by **Eduardo Francisco** and **James Harren**. Dark Horse Comics, 2012. 96pp. 978-1-59582-690-9.

Turok: Dinosaur Hunter, 5th series. Dynamite Entertainment, 2013–2015.

Turok: Dinosaur Hunter. Written by **Greg Pak**. Illustrated by **Mirko Colak**, **Cory Smith**, and **Takeshi Miyazawa**. Dynamite Entertainment, 2014–2015.

© 2016 Dynamite Entertainment

Vol. 1: Conquest. 2014. 128pp. 978-1-60690-520-3.
Vol. 2: West. 2015. 120pp. 978-1-60690-598-2.
Vol. 3: Raptor Forest. 2015. 104pp. 978-1-60690-693-4.

Heroic Adventure

Tales of high adventure featuring true heroes against unbeatable odds in settings ranging from the Seven Seas, desert wastelands, sparse jungles to even urban jungles. The heroes featured include classics such as Tintin, aquatic heroes of the sea, and bad-boy heroes stuck in dangerous environments and lifestyles. The stories in this genre at times may closely resemble the Super-Hero genre (see Chapter 1 on super-heroes), but the heroes in these stories have subtle differences. Like the super-heroes, they have a high moral code, but typically these heroes do not have secret identities, a staple in super-hero stories. The heroes may have skills or powers that help to make them stand out above the common man to help them reach their goal. Typically the adventurous heroes are the common man striving to be the best people they can be under trying times, on a quest to receive an item or object, or to even solve a mystery.

The Adventures of Tintin. Written and Illustrated by **Hergé**. Little Brown & Company, 1994–1997, hardcover collected editions; 2011–2014, softcover stand-alone editions. Y

One of the most popular European comics published worldwide and published in over 47 languages. *Tintin* was created by Belgian writer and artist Georges Remi who went by the pen name Hergé. A young traveling reporter named Tintin, the main character, and his faithful dog companion Snowy travel around the world and even into outer space to solve many mysteries and adventures. He's also joined in his adventures by the gruff but loyal Captain Haddock, the bright but hearing-impaired Professor Calculus, and the bumbling police inspectors Thompson and Thomson. The adventures combine riveting adventure with a dash of humor that have proven to be as popular now as they've been since Hergé created the character in 1929. Little Brown has collected the series in seven volumes and has also recently released the stories in sell-contained paperback collections listed below that are aimed for younger readers with supplemental background material. In 2011, a full-length feature film called *The Adventures of Tintin* was directed by Steven Spielberg and produced by Peter Jackson, which was released in theaters. The film was based off of three stories: *The Crab with the Golden Claws* (1941), *The Secret of the Unicorn* (1943), and *Red Rackham's Treasure* (1944). A new feature film, *The Adventures of Tintin: Prisoners of the Sun*, has been announced but does not have a release date.

Collected Vol. 1: Tintin in America/Cigars of the Pharaoh/The Blue Lotus. 1994. 192pp. 978-0-316-35940-5, hardcover.
Collected Vol. 2: The Broken Ear/The Black Island/King Ottokar's Sceptre. 1994. 192pp. 978-0-316-35942-9, hardcover.
Collected Vol. 3: The Crab with the Golden Claws/The Shooting Star/The Secret of the Unicorn. 1994. 192pp. 978-0-316-35944-3, hardcover.
Collected Vol. 4: Red Rackham's Treasure/The Seven Crystal Balls/Prisoners of the Sun. 1995. 192pp. 978-0-316-35814-9, hardcover.
Collected Vol. 5: Land of the Black Gold/Destination Moon/Explorers on the Moon. 1995. 192pp. 978-0-316-35816-3, hardcover.
Collected Vol. 6: The Calculus Affair/The Red Sea Sharks/Tintin in Tibet. 1997. 192pp. 978-0-316-35724-1, hardcover.
Collected Vol. 7: The Castafiore Emerald/Flight 714/Tintin and the Picaros. 1997. 192pp. 978-0-316-35727-2, hardcover.
The Black Island. 2011. 96pp. 978-0-316-13387-6.
The Blue Lotus. 2011. 96pp. 978-0-316-13382-1.
The Broken Ear. 2011. 96pp. 978-0-316-13385-2.
Cigars of the Pharaoh. 2011. 978-0-316-13388-3.
King Ottokar's Sceptre. 2011. 978-0-316-13383-8.
Red Rackham's Treasure. 2011. 96pp. 978-0-316-13384-5.
The Secret of the Unicorn. 2011. 96pp. 978-0-316-13386-9.
Tintin in America. 2011. 96pp. 978-0-316-13380-7.

The Crab with the Golden Claws. 2012. 96pp. 978-0-316-19876-9.
The Shooting Star. 2012. 96. 978-0-316-19875-2.
Prisoners of the Sun. 2014. 96pp. 978-0-316-40917-9.
The Seven Crystal Balls. 2014. 96pp. 978-0-316-40918.

Aqua Leung. Written by **Paul Maybury**. Illustrated by **Mark Andrew Smith**. Image Comics, 2008. 208pp. 978-1-58240-863-7. O

© 2016 Paul Maybury and Mark Andrew Smith

The lost royalty to Atlantis has been found in Aqua—a boy raised on land by adopted parents far away from the bloody conflict and war. When his adoptive parents are killed, he's brought back to his undersea world. Under the tutelage of Sonny, a fighting fish, Aqua learns that his destiny to lead Atlantis awaits him and no false ruler of Atlantis will stand in his way.

Bad Island. Written and Illustrated by **Doug TenNapel**. Graphix/Scholastic, 2011. 220pp. 978-0-545-31480-0; 978-0-545-31479-4, hardcover. T ◎

© 2016 Scholastic Inc

In need of a family vacation whether they want it or not, Lyle takes his family on a boat trip to get away from it all. But when a storm destroys their boat, the castaways find themselves on a mysterious island filled with weird plant life, dangerous animals, and technology that doesn't look like it's from anywhere on Earth. On the run from the strangest inhabitants ever known to man, the family have to rely on each other more than they've ever done before if they want to escape the bad island.

Cardboard. Written and Illustrated by Doug TenNapel. Graphix/Scholastic, 2012. 288pp. 978-0-545-41873-7; 978-0-545-41872-0, hardcover. 🏃 T ◎

© 2016 Scholastic Inc

Cam's father Mike has been down on his luck and can't afford to get his son anything for his birthday. Mike brings home the worst present ever for his son: a cardboard box. Together at home they build a boxer out of the cardboard and it magically turns to life! When the neighborhood jerk steals the cardboard for himself and sets out to create an army of cardboard creations, Cam and Mike must find a way to save the neighborhood before the cardboard constructions destroy them all. The book was selected for the Great Graphic Novels for Teens selection list in 2013.

City of Spies. Written by **Susan Kim** and **Laurence Klavan**. Illustrated by **Pascal Dizin**. First Second, 2010. 176pp. 978-1-59643-262-8. Y

> Set in New York City in 1942, young Evelyn has been sent by her father to live with her bohemian Aunt Lia. Not much of a caretaker, Evelyn finds herself befriending the superintendent's son, Tony. Both in the mood to sniff out trouble, they accidentally uncover a real Nazi plot. A fun tribute to Hergé's *Tintin* books.

Compass South. Written by **Hope Larson**. Illustrated by **Rebecca Mock**. Farrar, Straus and Giroux, 2016. 224pp. 978-0-374-30043-2, hardcover. Y 🏆

© 2016 Hope Larson and Rebecca Mock

> In 1860 America, 12-year-old twins Alex and Cleo Dodge find adventure around every turn as they search for their lost father. After joining the Black Hook Gang, they get arrested but make a bargain with the police chief to leave town and start a new life. Along the way the twins get separated from each other and both have their own adventure across America as they encounter pirates, swindlers, and other set of twins. They travel from New York to New Orleans to San Francisco on an adventure both of them won't soon forget! Will Alex and Cleo meet up again in San Francisco? Will the twins be reunited with their long-lost father? The answer and the adventure awaits! In 2017 the book was recognized by YALSA's Great Graphic Novels for Teens annual selection list.

Delilah Dirk. Written and Illustrated by **Tony Cliff**. First Second Books, 2013– . T 🏆 ◎

© 2016 First Second and Tony Cliff

> Set in the 19th century, Delilah Dirk is like no other woman in her day. Adventurous, impetuous, and full of charm, her mind is as sharp as her blades she carries. In her first adventure she rescues Turkish tea-master Erdemoglu Selim, and he becomes duty-bound to follow her across Turkey, struggling to repay the debt he owes her. In the second volume, Delilah is called home to England where she finds herself seeking to clear her name for a crime she didn't commit. Highly recommended, the adventure series is full of charm with fantastic art to boot. In 2014, YALSA's Great Graphic Novels for Teens recognized the first collection as a Great Graphic Novel for Teens and in 2017 the second volume was recognized by the outstanding committee as well. In 2016 the first book was optioned by Disney to be adapted into a live-action film.

> *Vol. 1: Delilah Dirk and the Turkish Lieutenant*. 2013. 176pp. 978-1-59643-813-2.
> *Vol. 2: Delilah Dirk and the King's Shilling*. 2016. 272pp. 978-1-62672-155-5.

Five Ghosts. Written by **Frank J. Barbiere**. Illustrated by **Chris Mooneyham**. Image Comics, 2013–2015. O ◎

> Treasure hunter Fabian Gray is quite a unique adventurer. Among his travels he came across a rare artifact called The Dreamstone. Since his encounter with the artifact Fabian can now harness the power of five literary ghosts—a wizard, archer, samurai, vampire, and detective. The ghosts are five primal archetypes of fiction from which countless stories are derived—and by tapping into their essence he can channel their power.

Vol. 1: The Haunting of Fabian Gray. 2013. 978-1-60706-790-0.
Vol. 2: Lost Coastlines. 2014. 184pp. 978-1-60706-981-2.
Vol. 3: Monsters and Men. 2015. 184pp. 978-1-63215-311-1.
Deluxe Edition Vol. 1. 2015. 344pp. 978-1-63215-288-6, hardcover.

© 2016 Frank J. Barbiere and
Chris Mooneyham

Goliath. Written and Illustrated by **Tom Gauld**. Drawn and Quarterly, 2012. 96pp. 978-1-77046-065-2, hardcover. O

> Goliath of Gath works behind the lines for the Philistine army. He transcribes orders to the front lines because he is a terrible swordsman and does not have much heart for battle. Unluckily for Goliath, he is also the largest man in the army. He is recruited by higher-ups in a plan to end the stalemate with the Israelite army. Goliath is forced to act the part of the Philistine champion to scare their enemies into submission. The only thing Goliath can do now is count down the days until he is sent back to his paperwork since no one seems to accept his challenge.

Hikaru no Go. Written and Illustrated by **Yumi Hotta**. VIZ Media, LLC., 2004–2011. A. Japanese manga. あ

> Sixth-grader Hikaru Shindo was never one for his grandfather's board games, but when he finds a blood-stained board of the classic Japanese game GO, that's all about to change. Hikaru unknowingly releases the spirit of Fujiwara-no-Sai, the ghost of an ancient GO master who was the instructor to the emperor of Japan many centuries ago and has not been able to ascend to Heaven until he achieves the "Divine Move." Fujiwara teams up with Hikaru and together they make a formidable team, taking on the best GO players the world has ever seen, to free Fujiwara's spirit. The hit manga series has also spawned an anime series released in 2001 in Japan as well as reinvigorated interest in the classic game worldwide.

Vol. 1. 2004. 192pp. 978-1-59116-222-3.
Vol. 2. 2004. 194pp. 978-1-59116-496-8.
Vol. 3. 2005. 208pp. 978-1-59116-687-0.
Vol. 4. 2005. 200pp. 978-1-59116-688-7.
Vol. 5. 2005. 208pp. 978-1-59116-689-4.
Vol. 6. 2006. 208pp. 978-1-4215-0275-5.
Vol. 7. 2006. 208pp. 978-1-4215-0641-8.
Vol. 8. 2006. 208pp. 978-1-4215-0642-5.
Vol. 9. 2007. 208pp. 978-1-4215-1066-8.
Vol. 10. 2007. 208pp. 978-14215-1067-5.
Vol. 11. 2008. 194pp. 978-14215-1068-2.
Vol. 12. 2008. 200pp. 978-14215-1508-3.

Vol. 13. 2008. 210pp. 978-14215-1509-0.
Vol. 14. 2009. 216pp. 978-14215-1510-6.
Vol. 15. 2009. 216pp. 978-14215-2192-3.
Vol. 16. 2009. 200pp. 978-14215-2584-6.
Vol. 17. 2009. 208pp. 978-14215-2585-3.
Vol. 18. 2010. 216pp. 978-14215-2823-6.
Vol. 19. 2010. 200pp. 978-14215-2824-3.
Vol. 20. 2010. 208pp. 978-14215-2825-0.
Vol. 21. 2010. 200pp. 978-14215-2826-7.
Vol. 22. 2011. 200pp. 978-14215-2827-4.
Vol. 23. 2011. 200pp. 978-14215-2828-1.

Adventurers, Explorers, Pirates, and Soldiers of Fortune

In these adventure stories the main character searches for an item as part of a quest for noble reasons, or is hired for his or her exceptional skills. Sometimes the hero is even kidnapped against his or her will and forced to enslavement but ultimately breaks free. Traps, hidden dangers, and deadly archenemies are commonplace in these gripping stories, and they owe a lot of their storytelling technique to pulp adventure stories and classic pirate adventures. Comedy and romance sometimes alleviate tension that can be dark and scary at times. Comparable movies including the *Indiana Jones* films and <u>Pirates of the Caribbean</u> series of films exemplify this genre. Stories may also include influences from other genres as well including Science Fiction, Super-Heroes, and other genres.

Alison Dare. Written by **J. Torres**. Illustrated by **J. Bone**. Oni Press, 2010. Y

Twelve-year-old Alison isn't your typical "tween." She's the daughter of a famous archaeologist/adventurer. Her dad's a hero known as the Blue Scarab, so adventure is in her blood whether her divorced parents like it or not. Unfortunately for her, her parents want something a little bit more normal for her, so she's been enrolled at the strict St. Joan of Arc Academy for Girls. But curfews and rules aren't enough to keep Alison and her friends Wendy and Dot out of danger from globe-trotting the world and finding magic lamps (with wish-granting genies), confronting her parents' archenemies, hanging out with her super-spy uncle and more.

Heart of the Maiden. 2010. 104pp. 978-0-88776-935-1.
Little Miss Adventures. 2010. 96pp. 978-0-88776-934-4.

Blackbeard: Legend of the Pyrate King. Written by **Greg Hale**, **Jamie Nash**, **Eduardo Sanchez**, and **Robert Place Napton**. Illustrated by **Mario Guevara**. Dynamite Entertainment, 2011. 200pp. 978-1-60690-121-2. O

The life of Edward Teach, aka Blackbeard, is revealed in comic book form for the first time! From his birth in 1680, his youth growing up, to his bitter end in 1718, see how the man became the legendary pirate infamous pirate! The graphic novel also includes biographical information about the pirate.

© 2016 Dynamite Entertainment

Blackjack. Written by **Alex Simmons**. Illustrated by **Joe Bennett**. Dover Graphic Novels, 2015. T ◉

Set in the 1930s, Arron Day, alias Blackjack, is an African American soldier of fortune who faces danger and deception at every turn! In *Second Bite of the Cobra*, Blackjack returns to his boyhood home in Cairo and joins forces with a martial-arts expert and mercenaries to seek revenge on a charismatic Bedouin warlord known as The Cobra. In *There Came a Dark Hunter*, Blackjack is alone to face treachery at

© 2016 Alex Simmons

every turn on three countries against a heavily armed strike-force, hill raiders, and a mysterious killer. A suave but rough and tough warrior, Arron is out to fight the good fight.

Second Bite of the Cobra. 2015. 112pp. 978-0-486-79852-3.
There Came a Dark Hunter; the Further Adventures of Aaron Day. 2015. 64pp. 978-1-5192-0698-5.

Blacklung. Written and Illustrated by **Chris Wright**. Fantagraphics, 2012. 128pp. 978-1-60699-587-7. M

Life on the high seas with a crew of pirates can be measured in minutes. When a school teacher stumbles into the wrong part of town, he is shanghaied into the service of the deadliest pirate captain. The only thing that is keeping the teacher safe from the rest of the crew is his ability to read books to the captain. The stories he reads do not even compare to the massacres he sees at the side of his new crewmates. Is there any hope for salvation when the person your life depends on is hell bent on securing his spot in Hell?

The Crogan Adventures. Written and Illustrated by **Chris Schweizer**. Oni Press. T ◎

© 2016 Oni Press and Chris Schweizer

Adventures don't just last for a lifetime—the last for generations! Each volume is a look at the generation of the Crogan family throughout history. The series has been recognized as Great Graphic Novels for Teens on many selection lists. The original black and white editions are being colorized, and additional adventures are being created.

Catfoot's Vengeance. 2015. 224pp. 978-1-62010-203-9.

Set in the 18th century aboard a pirate ship, "Catfoot" Crogan is forced onto a pirate ship but soon earns the favor of the notorious pirate captain, but makes an enemy with the first mate named D'or. Can the new recruits find a way to save the ship from D'or's foolish maneuver which will result in the entire navy of the West Indies down on their heads? Color reprint edition.

Last of the Legion. 2015. 224pp. 978-1-62010-243-5.

Legionnaire Peter Crogan has served almost five years in the French Foreign Legion and his tour is almost done. Peter may have to forgo leaving when his rag-tag band of volunteers find themselves under attack by the warring Tuaregs, besieged by the relentless heat, and the brutal command of a brutally strict sergeant and a dashing commander who is too brave for his own good. Color reprint edition.

Crogan's Loyalty. 2012. 150pp. 978-1-934964-40-8.

Set during the American Revolution, two brothers, Charlie and Will, are on opposite sides of the war. When their loyalty to each other is tested against mercenaries, they need to decide what is more important—love for family or love for country? Black and white edition.

Cursed Pirate Girl. Written and Illustrated by **Jeremy Bastian**. Archaia Entertainment/ Boom! Studios, 2013. 152pp. 978-1-936393-60-2. O ◉

The Cursed Pirate Girl's life has certainly been rough. She has been cursed by a pirate witch. She has also been searching her whole life for the father she never knew. The only thing she knows about her father is that he is one of the deadly pirate captains on the unhallowed Omerta Seas and that he teaches her fencing in her dreams. The Cursed Pirate Girl goes on a topsy-turvy quest to find out which one of these captains is her father. Done in the style of period woodcuts, this book has fantastic amounts of detail in it that have to be seen.

© 2016 Archaia/Boom! Studios
and Jeremy Bastian

Destiny's Hand. Written by **Nunzio DeFilippis** and **Christina Weir**. Illustrated by **Mel Calingo**. Seven Seas Entertainment, 2006–2009. T 🏴 ◉

Destiny's Hand is a pirate ship that cannot be sunk. She's captained by Captain Blaine, an honorable pirate who's dying wish is to find the Devil's Eye, a huge legendary gem of untold value. Who does Captain Blaine appoint to lead his loyal fearless crew in search of the lost treasure? Olivia Soldana, a brash 16-year-old girl, who can outdo any man! The *Ultimate Pirate Collection* was one of YALSA's Great Graphic Novels for Teens in 2011.

Vol. 1. 2006. 192pp. 978-1-933164-11-3.
Vol. 2. 2007. 192pp. 978-1-933164-52-6.
Ultimate Pirate Collection. 2009. 512pp. 978-1-934876-73-2.

© 2016 Seven Seas and Nunzio
DeFilippis and Christina Weir.

Disney's Pirates of the Caribbean Comics Collection. Written by **Chris Schweizer**. Illustrated by **Joe Flood**. Joe Books, 2017. 96pp. 978-1-77275-335-6. T. 📹

Disney's popular ride-turned-movie series starring Johnny Depp as Captain Jack Sparrow comes to comics! Captain Sparrow's ship, the Black Pearl is stuck at Port Royal. With no wind to fill the sails, Jack and the crew are listless with no wind to set them to sea. But Jack knows of an ancient object rumored to call up the wind. With the wind at their sails, the crew of the Black Pearl's troubles may soon be over, as Jack Sparrow's good fortunes have proven time and time again, that's when their troubles are bound to get worse!

Gary the Pirate. Created and Written by **Scott Christian Sava**. Illustrated by **Tracy Bailey**. IDW Publishing, 2009. 112pp. 978-1-60010-312-4. A

Gary may not be the best pirate ever to soar the skies—in fact the teenage pirate is downright clumsy and not very good at stealing anything but junk. But when he spies

13-year-old Judy and a golden broach she got from her grandmother, Gary thinks he's found the perfect jewel to easy street. Little does he know he's going to get something else stolen instead—his heart.

Glacial Period. Written and Illustrated by **Nicolas De Crécy**. NBM Publishing, 2007. 80pp. 978-1-56163-483-5. O

In the far future when mankind has entered a new ice age, a team of scientists and a talking, genetically engineered dog are setting out on an expedition to what they believe is the South Pole. While exploring, the team comes across an entrance in what seems to be a tower or obelisk. Within the structure they see paintings and statues from ages long past and forgotten. The archaeologists theorize on the culture that could have created such bawdy and grandiose iconography. Hulk, one of the dogs, gets separated from the group. While deep within the structure, he finds out the secret of the building. They are in a museum. They are in The Louvre. Only with the help of the art can all of them find their way out before the snow swallows them up.

Hunter x Hunter. Written and Illustrated by **Yoshihiro Togashi**. VIZ Media, LLC., 2005– . T. Japanese manga. あ

Gon Freecss is a boy who discovers that his father, long thought to be dead, is actually a world-renowned hunter—a licensed professional who tackles many fantastic exploits including locating rare animal species, discovering uncharted lands, hunting for treasure, or as a bounty hunter. Gon decides to follow in his father's footsteps and pass the rigorous Hunter Examination with the hopes of one day finding his father. Along the way he encounters many other hunters, odd monsters, and even the paranormal! The manga series was also adapted into a popular animated series. The series is still being published but is currently on extended hiatus at the time of printing.

Vol. 1. 2005. 184pp. 978-1-5911-6753-2.
Vol. 2. 2005. 192pp. 978-1-5911-6785-3.
Vol. 3. 2005. 192pp. 978-1-5911-6849-2.
Vol. 4. 2005. 192pp. 978-1-5911-6992-5.
Vol. 5. 2005. 192pp. 978-1-421-50184-0.
Vol. 6. 2006. 208pp. 978-1-4215-0185-7.
Vol. 7. 2006. 208pp. 978-1-4215-0332-5.
Vol. 8. 2006. 208pp. 978-1-4215-0643-2.
Vol. 9. 2006. 208pp. 978-1-4215-0644-9.
Vol. 10. 2006. 208pp. 978-1-4215-0645-6.
Vol. 11. 2006. 208pp. 978-1-4215-0646-3.
Vol. 12. 2007. 208pp. 978-1-4215-0647-0.
Vol. 13. 2007. 200pp. 978-1-4215-1069-9.
Vol. 14. 2007. 208pp. 978-1-4215-1070-5.
Vol. 15. 2007. 208pp. 978-1-4215-1071-2.
Vol. 16. 2007. 208pp. 978-1-4215-1072-9.
Vol. 17. 2007. 208pp. 978-1-4215-1073-6.
Vol. 18. 2008. 208pp. 978-1-4215-1471-0.
Vol. 19. 2008. 208pp. 978-1-4215-1786-5.
Vol. 20. 2008. 208pp. 978-1-4215-1787-2.
Vol. 21. 2008. 198pp. 978-1-4215-1788-9.
Vol. 22. 2008. 208pp. 978-1-4215-1789-6.
Vol. 23. 2008. 210pp. 978-1-4215-1790-2.
Vol. 24. 2009. 210pp. 978-1-4215-2216-6.
Vol. 25. 2009. 216pp. 978-1-4215-2588-4.
Vol. 26. 2009. 216pp. 978-1-4215-3068-0.
Vol. 27. 2011. 200pp. 978-1-4215-3862-4.
Vol. 28. 2012. 216pp. 978-1-4215-4260-7.
Vol. 29. 2013. 216pp. 978-1-4215-4261-4.
Vol. 30. 2013. 216pp. 978-1-4215-5267-5.
Vol. 31. 2013. 208pp. 978-1-4215-5887-5.
Vol. 32. 2014. 208pp. 978-1-4215-5912-4.

Indiana Jones

Dark Horse Comics, 2008–2010. 🎬

Archaeologist Dr. Henry "Indiana" Jones has seen a lot of unexplainable things in his quest for ancient artifacts and the elusive "fortune and glory." He's discovered the Lost Ark of the Covenant, the Holy Grail, but there are many more stories of the famous adventure made famous in the Indiana Jones series of films starring Harrison Ford beginning with *Raiders of the Lost Ark* (1981), *Indiana Jones and the Temple of Doom* (1984), *Indiana Jones and the Last Crusade* (1989), and *Indiana Jones and the Kingdom of the Crystal Skull* (2008). A fifth Indiana Jones film is planned to be released in 2019. Below are listed the various collection of books published by Dark Horse Comics featuring the most famous movie archaeologist of all time.

Indiana Jones Adventures. Written by **Phillip Gelatt** and **Mark Evanier**. Illustrated by **Ethen Beavers**. Dark Horse Comics, 2008–2009. Y

An all-ages graphic novel featuring the famous archaeologist. Both volumes' artworks are based on the animated style of the Star Wars Adventures series and features classic Indiana Jones adventures but suitable for younger adventurers.

Vol. 1. 2008. 80pp. 978-1-59307-905-5.
Vol. 2. 2009. 88pp. 978-1-59582-402-8.

Indiana Jones and Kingdom of the Crystal Skull. Written **John Jackson Miller**. Based off a script by **George Lucas** and **David Koepp**. Illustrated by **Luke Ross**. Dark Horse Comics, 2008. 96pp. 978-1-59307-952-9. T

The official adaptation of the fourth Indiana Jones movie released in 2008. Set in 1957, an older Indiana Jones is pitted against Soviet agents in the hunt for a rumored telepathic crystal skull.

Indiana Jones and the Tomb of the Gods. Written by **Rob Williams**. Illustrated by **Steve Scott**. Dark Horse Comics, 2009. 120pp. 978-1-59582-247-5. T

Indiana Jones is entrusted by preeminent archaeologists who have been trying to keep a secret of ancient primeval power from falling into the wrong hands. Soon Indiana must travel the globe to prevent a group of Hitler Nazi elite from harnessing power that should have remained hidden in the mysterious Tomb of the Gods.

Indiana Jones Omnibus. Written by **William Messner-Loebs**, **Gary Gianni**, **Dan Barry**, **Lee Mars**, and various. Illustrated by **Dan Barry**, **Gary Gianni**, **Leo Duranona**, **Ken Hooper**, and various. T

The collection reprinting the entire Dark Horse Comics stories created from the 1990s beginning with *Indiana Jones and the Fate of Atlantis* (1991). The other stories collected in the omnibus books include *Thunder in the Orient* (1994), *Indiana Jones and the Arms of Gold* (1994), *Indiana Jones and the Golden Fleece* (1994), *Indiana*

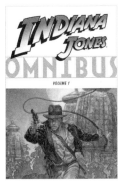

Jones and the Shrine of the Sea Devil (1994), *Indiana Jones and the Iron Phoenix* (1995), *Indiana Jones and the Spear of Destiny* (1995), *and Indiana Jones and the Sargasso Pirates* (1996).

Vol. 1. 2008. 352pp. 978-1-59307-887-4.
Vol. 2. 2008. 352pp. 978-1-59307-953-6.

Indiana Jones Omnibus © 2016
Lucasfilm Ltd & TM. All Rights
Reserved. Used under Authorization.

Indiana Jones Omnibus: The Further Adventures. Written by **Archie Goodwin** and **David Michelinie**. Illustrated by **Walter Simonson**, **Steve Ditko**, **David Mazzuc-chelli**, **Herb Trimpe**, and **Jackson Guice**. Dark Horse Comics, 2009–2010. T

The collection reprints the entire run of the original Marvel Comics Indiana Jones comic book series originally published in the 1980s. The original series lasted for 34 issues, and the collection includes the adaptations for all three original Indiana Jones films.

Vol. 1. 2009. 368pp. 978-1-59582-246-8.
Vol. 2. 2009. 368pp. 978-1-59582-336-6.
Vol. 3. 2010. 368pp. 978-1-59582-437-0.

Isle of 100,000 Graves. Written by **Fabien Vehlmann**. Illustrated by **Jason**. Fantagraphics, 2011. 56pp. 978-1-60699-442-9. O

Gwenny has found the same map in a bottle for the Isle of 100,000 Graves. The same map her father found long ago which set him off on a quest to find the legendary treasure, from which he did not return. Gwenny trickily hires a pirate crew on her own quest to locate her lost father to the island with a dark atmosphere. While on the island they are ambushed by the local residents, all students of the art of torture and execution. They have been dumping the bottles filled with maps to lure treasure hunters for their experiments. Gwenny, with the help of her newfound dangerous partners, discovers what had happened to her father. This book is filled with harrowing escapes and the darkest of dark humor.

The Museum Vaults: Excerpts from the Journal of an Expert. Written and Illustrated by **Marc-Antoine Mathieu**. NBM Publishing, 2007. 60pp. 978-1-56163-514-6. O

The Louvre has hired Mr. Volumer and an assistant to index and appraise the many treasures that are in the many vaults of the museum. Here they travel to different departments and speak with people who have spent their life working with the ancient artifacts. Mr. Volumer is soon finding out that this will become his life's work as the museum has more levels, vaults, passageways, and pieces than previously thought.

Oyster War. Written and Illustrated by **Ben Towle**. Oni Press, 2015. 168pp. 978-1-62010-262-6, hardcover. T

© 2016 Oni Press and Ben Towle

The coastal town of Blood's Haven thrives on oysters as its main source of income for the local economy. It's a dangerous trade—and not just because of the dangerous weather conditions: pirates roam the waters! When Captain Davidson Bulloch is tasked with hunting down pirates, he and his motley crew have found an adversary in the dread pirate Treacher Fink. Not only is he a force to be reckoned with, but he's got command of an ancient artifact that lets him command an ancient spirit that has complete control of the sea and everything in it!

Poppy! and the Lost Lagoon. Written by **Matt Kindt**. Illustrated by **Brian Hurtt**. Dark Horse Comics, 2016. 144pp. 978-1-61655-943-4. A

© 2016 Matt Kindt

Poppy Pepperton is a spunky 10-year-old who is the world's greatest explorer—next to her grandfather Pappy, of course. When a shrunken mummy head speaks to Poppy, she's called to an adventure across the globe in search of an exotic fish. Joined with her sidekick/guardian Colt Winchester, the two of them set out for adventure in search of clues to find the fish as well as perhaps find out what happened to her long-lost Pappy.

Prince of Persia. Written by **Jordan Mechner** and **A.B. Sina**. Illustrated by **LeUyen Pham** and **Alex Puvilland**. First Second Books, 2008. 208pp. 978-1-59643-365-6, hardcover; 978-1-59643-207-9. T

A tie-in to the popular video game series created by Jordan Mechner. Told through interweaving tales set between the 9th and 13th centuries, once long ago there was a legendary man—his name forgotten in time—who is known as the Prince of Persia. See two tales of princes—separated by centuries but connected by the notion that history repeats itself—who seek to claim their rightful thrones.

Prince of Persia: Before the Sandstorm. Written **Jordan Mechner**. Illustrated by **Bernard Chang**, **Niko Henrichon**, and **David Lopez**. Disney Press, 2010. 128pp. 978-1-4231-2429-0, hardcover; 978-1-4231-2582-2. T

When a group of five men are arrested for throwing a lavish party with stolen treasure, they must plead their case to the governor to persuade him of their innocence. A collection of five short stories featuring characters from the film Disney movie *The Prince of Persia: The Sands of Time* (2010), which is based on the popular video game series.

The Red Seas. Written by **Ian Edginton**. Illustrated by **Steve Yeowell**. Rebellion Comics, 2005–2007. T

> Originally published in the pages of *2000 AD*, meet Captain Jack Dancer and his pirate crew! With their ship, the Red Wench, they're out on the run from the British Navy and also find high adventure on the seas fighting against the zombie pirates reanimated by the villainous Doctor Orlando Doyle as well as other mythological and magical phenomena including werewolves, the hollow Earth, and wizards. Only two collections have been issued so far although the series was originally printed in comic book form from 2002 to 2013.

> *Under the Banner of King Death.* 2005. 64pp. 978-1-904265-68-9.
> *Twilight of the Idols.* 2007. 64pp. 978-1-904265-68-9.

ReMind. Written and Illustrated by **Jason Brubaker**. Coffeehouse Books, 2011–2013. T 🎗

> When Sonja's cat, Victuals, goes missing, he's found days later in her sleepy coastal town washed up on the shore with stitches in his head and the ability to speak to her! Together they set off to find out the mystery of his disappearance and his new condition. Little do they realize that they must travel to a strange kingdom underwater where a royal power struggle is brewing—and Victuals's true identity will be revealed. The first volume was recognized by YALSA's Great Graphic Novels for Teens on its 2012 selection list.

> *Vol. 1.* 2011. 152pp. 978-0-9831149-0-1.
> *Vol. 2.* 2013. 176pp. 978-0-9831149-1-8.

Salvatore. Written and Illustrated by **Nicolas De Crécy**. NBM Publishing, 2011. O

> Salvatore is a legendary mechanic and he's also part dog! His dog senses let him find out what exactly is going on inside vehicles and also let him know which parts are unnecessary. Salvatore hopes to build a super-vehicle to take him halfway around the world to the arms of the only other dog that has loved him. Joined with his reluctant assistant, a miniscule human who communicates through only a PC, they're on their way in the name of love.

> *An Eventful Crossing.* 2011. 112pp. 978-1-56163-613-6.
> *Transports of Love.* 2011. 96pp. 978-1-56163-593-1.

Set to Sea. Written and Illustrated by **Drew Weing**. Fantagraphics, 2010. 978-1-60699-368-2, hardcover; 2014. 978-1-60699-771-0. 🎗 ◎

> A lumbering poet discovers hardship and wisdom on the high seas after he is kidnapped and forced into sailor life. A beautifully written and illustrated work, the book was recognized in 2011 on YALSA's Great Graphic Novels for Teens list.

Tomb Raider. Written by **Gail Simone, Rhianna Pratchett**, and **Mariko Tamaki** Illustrated by **Nicholas Daniel Selma, Derlis Santacruz**, and **Phillip Sevy**. Dark Horse Comics, 2014– . T

> Based on the popular adventure video game phenomenon, Lara Croft is an extraordinary young woman. With a thirst for high adventure and travel, the captivating Lara is trained in archaeology, martial arts, hand-to-hand combat, and firearms to become one of the most dangerous and highly skilled adventurers. Coming from a British family of great wealth and aristocracy, she's dedicated her life in search of the most unattainable treasures and antiquities from the ancient world. Naturally, her search for adventure and treasures has pitted her against terrifying dangers, including ancient mythical forces and heavily armed opponents, yet she has always returned victorious. The current series of graphic novels are inspired by the recent video game titles since 2013 which features a younger Lara Croft on her first adventures. Beginning in 2016, the series is written by Mariko Tamaki and is set after the video game *Rise of the Tomb Raider*.

> *First Series, 2014–2015*

> *Vol. 1: Season of the Witch*. 2014. 152pp. 978-1-61655-491-0.
> *Vol. 2: Secrets and Lies*. 2015. 144pp. 978-1-61655-639-6.
> *Vol. 3: The Serpent Queen*. 2015. 144pp. 978-1-61655-818-5.

> *Second Series, 2016–*

> *Vol. 1: Spore*. 2016. 144pp. 978-1-50670-010-1.
> *Vol. 2: Choices and Sacrifice*. 2017. 144pp. 978-1-50670-162-2.

Treasure Island. Written by **Robert Louis Stevenson**. Adapted by **Roy Thomas**. Illustrated by **Mario Gulley**. Marvel Comics, 2008. 160pp. 978-0-7851-2594-5. T

© 2016 Marvel Comics

> Adaptation of the classic adventure novel first published in 1883. Set in the 18th century, young Jim Hawkins becomes entangled in a quest for buried treasure after discovering a map from an old sea captain named Billy Bones. The map is rumored to tell the whereabouts of the buried treasure of the infamous pirate Captain Flint. An expedition is put together to find the treasure, and Jim discovers that the cook, Long John Silver, was actually a shipmate of Flint's, and most of the crew on board are, too. Will the pirate mutineers get Flint's treasure before Jim and Captain Smollet's crew does, and what other secrets lie on the island?

A Trip to the Bottom of the World with Mouse. Written and Illustrated by **Frank Viva**. Toon Books, 2012. 32pp. 978-1-935179-19-1. A

> Mouse and his human friend are on a trip to the Antarctic. The only thing problem is that Mouse is very anxious about getting there and all the stuff there is to see. This is a fun story for the young comic fans just starting off to read.

The Unsinkable Walker Bean. Written and Illustrated by **Aaron Renier**. First Second Books, 2010. 192pp. 978-1-59643-453-3. Y 🎯 ◎

Walker Bean was just a meek, unobtrusive boy, who loved tinkering with his grandfather's workshop of strange inventions. But when his grandfather is struck by an ancient curse, Walker must step up and take an accursed red pearl skull made by witches back to them. Along the way of his quest are many dangers including pirates, monsters, magical machines, and danger at every turn! The book was recognized in 2011 by YALSA's Great Graphic Novels for Teens' selection list.

© 2016 First Second and Aaron Renier

Fists of Fury and Sword of Steel—Fighting Adventure Stories

Pure action defines this subgenre. The stories in this section involve a main character or characters testing their skills in a combat competition as a rite of passage, for monetary goals, for personal glory, or to survive. Combat may consist of bare-knuckle brawls, weapons combat, or even inexplicable superpowers as a natural extension of fighting prowess or mysterious powers the combatant has received. Romance and comedy may be involved but typically aren't the main focus of the storyline, where action remains supreme and characters are reduced to the sum of their own strengths—both mental and physical.

Archer and Armstrong. Valiant Entertainment, 2013– . T

The team of Archer and Armstrong were created in 1992 by Barry Windsor-Smith, Jim Shooter, and Bob Layton. Obadiah Archer is a master of martial arts and an expert with the bow and arrow. Armstrong, born Aram, is 10,000 years old, has super-strength, and is nearly invulnerable. Their enemies include the organization known as the Sect. In the 2012 Valiant Entertainment relaunch, elements of their past have been changed, including changing the part of Archer's origin where he was trained by Buddhist monks to being trained as a child to be an assassin. One of Archer's assigned targets was Armstrong, one of three immortal brothers, but he learns that those who trained him worked for the Sect. The original 1990s' series by Windsor-Smith, Mike Baron, Bob Layton, and others has been collected in an omnibus edition. The new 2013 series written by Fred Fan Lente with art by Clayton Henry, Emanuela Lupacchino, and others, has been nominated for a number of Harvey Awards, and has been collected in a series of trades, with some issues then recollected in "Deluxe Editions."

Archer and Armstrong, 1st series.

The Complete Classic Omnibus. Written by **Barry Windsor-Smith** and **Jim Shooter**. Illustrated by **Mike Baron**, **Bob Layton**, and various. 2016. 736pp. 978-1-9393-4687-2, hardcover.

© 2016 Valiant Entertainment

Archer and Armstrong, 2nd series. Written by **Fred Van Lente**. Illustrated by **Clayton Henry** and **Emanuela Lupacchino**. 2013– .

Vol. 1: The Michelangelo Code. 2013. 112pp. 978-0-97964098-8.
Vol. 2: Wrath of the Eternal Warriors. 128pp. 2013. 978-1-9393-4604-9.
Vol. 3: Far, Faraway. 2013. 128pp. 978-1-9393-461-8.
Vol. 4: Sect Civil War. 2014. 112pp. 978-1-9393-4625-4.
Vol. 5: Mission: Improbable. 2014. 128pp. 978-1-9393-4635-3.
Vol. 6: American Wasteland. 2015. 112pp. 978-1-9393-4642-1.
Vol. 7: The One Percent and Other Tales. 2015. 112pp. 978-1-9393-4653-7.

Hardcover Deluxe Edition, 2014– .

Vol. 1. 2014. 300pp. 978-1-9393-4622-3, hardcover.
Vol. 2. 2016. 400pp. 978-1-9393-4695-7, hardcover.

© 2016 Valiant Entertainment

Dragon Ball. Written and Illustrated by **Akira Toriyama**. VIZ Media, LLC., T. Japanese manga. あ 🐾

A loose retelling of the Chinese folktale "Journey to the West." Son Goku is a monkey-tailed boy and the <u>Dragon Ball</u> series follows his adventures of his youth to becoming a father. Throughout Goku's lifetime he fights many battles and over time becomes the most powerful martial artist in the universe in his quest for the Dragon Balls of power as well as his true origin as a powerful force of destruction as a member of the super-powered group of aliens known as Saiyans. The series has also featured a large and colorful cast of supporting characters of heroes and villains to supply the conflict of the story, which was originally published in Japan from 1984 to 1995 and spun off a wildly popular animated series and many video games. The other spin-offs in the <u>Dragon Ball</u> series are not done by the original creator, Akria Toriyama. In the VIZ Media translations, the series was divided into the *Dragon Ball* and *Dragon Ball Z* titles. The collections listed below are VIZ Media's three in one and VIZBIG collections which reprints three volumes in one new collection.

Dragon Ball. 2013–2016.

The adventures of Son Goku as a youth through his early adulthood as he hones his martial arts skills and searches for the legendary Dragon Balls that are able to grant wishes.

Vol. 1. 2013. 576pp. 978-1-4215-5564-5.
Vol. 2. 2013. 576pp. 978-1-4215-5565-2.
Vol. 3. 2013. 568pp. 978-1-4215-5566-9.
Vol. 4. 2014. 576pp. 978-1-4215-5612-3.
Vol. 5. 2014. 560pp. 978-1-4215-6470-8.
Vol. 6. 2014. 552pp. 978-1-4215-6471-5.
Vol. 7. 2014. 552pp. 978-1-4215-6472-2.

Vol. 8. 2015. 552pp. 978-1-4215-6473-9.
Vol. 9. 2015. 552pp. 978-1-4215-7875-0.
Vol. 10. 2015. 568pp. 978-1-4215-7876-7.
Vol. 11. 2015. 560pp. 978-1-4215-7877-4.
Vol. 12. 2016. 552pp. 978-1-4215-7878-1.
Vol. 13. 2016. 568pp. 978-1-4215-8211-5.
Vol. 14. 2016. 674pp. 978-1-4215-8212-2.

Dragon Ball Z. 2008–2012.

Five years after the events in the first series, Goku is married and has a son named Gohan. When an adversary arrives from outer space, Goku's true origin is revealed and he must team up with his old enemy, Piccolo, to save the Earth from Goku's own brother. The collection reprints the original 26 volumes in larger-sized volumes.

Vol. 1. 2008. 528pp. 978-1-4215-2064-3.
Vol. 2. 2008. 520pp. 978-1-4215-2065-0.
Vol. 3. 2008. 528pp. 978-1-4215-2066-7.
Vol. 4. 2009. 568pp. 978-1-4215-2067-4.
Vol. 5. 2009. 560pp. 978-1-4215-2068-1.

Vol. 6. 2010. 560pp. 978-1-4215-2069-8.
Vol. 7. 2010. 560pp. 978-1-4215-2070-4.
Vol. 8. 2010. 560pp. 978-1-4215-2071-1.
Vol. 9. 2012. 476pp. 978-1-4215-2072-8.

Infinite Kung-Fu. Written and Illustrated by **Kagan McLeod**. Top Shelf Productions/IDW Publishing, 2011. 464pp. 978-1-891830-83-9. O 🕱

© 2016 Top Shelf and Kagan McLeod

In the future when disease and war made Hell overflow with the dead, those that could not stay in Hell came back to the mortal plane as the walking undead. Over time the bullets ran out and mankind was forced to use more primitive weapons and to focus its skills on martial arts to fight off the zombies. One warrior, a man named Lei Kung, is trying to redeem himself after taking the life of an innocent man. Now he's tasked with bringing down the all-powerful emperor as penance for his deed. An homage to martial arts films as well as a healthy dose of Blaxsploitation influences. The book was recognized as a Great Graphic Novel for Teens for YALSA's 2012 selection list.

Kill La Kill. Written by **Kazuki Nakashima**. Illustrated by **Ryo Akizuki**. UDON Entertainment, 2015–2016. M. Japanese manga.

At the prestigious Honnouji Academy, the student council president Satsuki Kiryuin rules over the school alongside her underlings called the Elite Four. Augmented by the powerful Goku Uniforms they wear, they are a formidable force and rule the school. Only transfer student Ryuki Matoi, who is the

wielder of the fabric-slicing Scissor Blade, is the only one who can put the student council president and her foul force in their place.

Vol. 1. 2015. 180pp. 978-1-927925-49-2.
Vol. 2. 2016. 164pp. 978-1-927925-54-6.

© 2016 UDON Entertainment

The Last Man. Written and Illustrated by **Yves "Balak" Bigerel**, **Michaël Sanlaville**, and **Bastien Vivës**. First Second, 2015–2016. T 🎯 ◎

One of the greatest places a man can make his mark in the world is the Games—an annual gladiatorial contest for magic users. For Adrian Velba, it's a chance of a lifetime for him. When his partner falls ill, Adrian's chances to compete are bleak, but when a mysterious partner named Richard Ridana appears as his teammate with all brawns, bravado, and muscle, in a realm where fighting magic is the only way to win, Ridana is mopping up the floor with his fists. Who is the mysterious Ridana and can the team of Velba and Ridana come out on top to become the top contenders for the Game?

Vol. 1: The Stranger. 2015. 208pp. 978-1-62672-046-6.
Vol. 2: The Royal Cup. 2015. 208pp. 978-1-62672-047-3.
Vol. 3: The Chase. 2015. 208pp. 978-1-62672-048-0.

© 2016 First Second and Balak,
Michaël Sanlaville, and Bastien Vivës.

Vol. 4: The Show. 2016. 208pp. 978-1-62672-049-7.
Vol. 5: The Order. 2016. 208pp. 978-1-62672-050-3.

Project Arms. Written by **Ryoji Minagawa**. Illustrated by **Kyoichi Nanatsuki**. VIZ Media, 2003–2009. O. Japanese manga.

Ryo Takahashi's normal life as a high school student takes an unexpected and dramatic change when he discovers that a cybernetic arm has actually replaced his right arm, which he injured when he was young. Utilizing the latest in nanotechnology, his arm can transform into nearly any deadly shape at will, and soon he finds that he's been hunted by a mysterious fellow student and a secret organization for the secret that he carries inside of him. The series is heavily inspired by the Lewis Carol's *Alice's Adventures in Wonderland*.

Vol. 1. 2003. 208pp. 978-1-56931-889-8.
Vol. 2. 2003. 224pp. 978-1-59116-058-8.
Vol. 3. 2004. 216pp. 978-1-59116-101-1.
Vol. 4. 2004. 216pp. 978-1-59116-165-3.
Vol. 5. 2004. 200pp. 978-1-59116-338-1.
Vol. 6. 2004. 202pp. 978-1-59116-488-3.
Vol. 7. 2004. 200pp. 978-1-59116-522-4.
Vol. 8. 2005. 216pp. 978-1-59116-732-7.

Vol. 9. 2005. 216pp. 978-1-59116-733-4.
Vol. 10. 2005. 216pp. 978-1-4215-0073-7.
Vol. 11. 2006. 216pp. 978-1-4215-0194-9.
Vol. 12. 2006. 208pp. 978-1-4215-0386-8.
Vol. 13. 2006. 208pp. 978-1-4215-0502-2.
Vol. 14. 2006. 208pp. 978-1-4215-0503-9.
Vol. 15. 2007. 208pp. 978-1-4215-0504-6.
Vol. 16. 2007. 216pp. 978-1-4215-0916-7.

Vol. 17. 2007. 200pp. 978-1-4215-0917-4.   *Vol. 20.* 2008. 200pp. 978-1-4215-1698-1.
Vol. 18. 2007. 192pp. 978-1-4215-0918-1.   *Vol. 21.* 2009. 210pp. 978-1-4215-1699-8.
Vol. 19. 2008. 200pp. 978-1-4215-1697-4.   *Vol. 22.* 2009. 224pp. 978-1-4215-1700-1.

Samurai Deeper Kyo. Written and Illustrated by **Kamijyo Akimine**. TOKY-OPOP, 2003–2009; Kodansha/Del Rey Manga, 2009–2010. O. Japanese manga.

Set four years after the bloody Battle of Sekigahara at the dawn of the 17th century, a peaceful medicine peddler named Kyoshiro is joined by a young female bounty hunter named Yuya to hunt down criminals after she mistakes him for Demon Eyes Kyo, a vicious samurai whom Kyoshiro resembles. But after bandits attack Kyoshiro, his eyes turn red, and the man of peace gives way to Demon Eyes Kyo, the slayer of a thousand men. Now Kyoshiro is out to discover the mystery of the two souls inhabiting his body and Yuya is waiting for the right time to claim her reward on Kyo, the man who killed her brother. The Del Rey Manga published the final four volumes in the series after TOKYOPOP Publishing filed for bankruptcy.

Vol. 1. 2003. 208pp. 978-1-59182-225-7.   *Vol. 19.* 2006. 192pp. 978-1-59532-459-7.
Vol. 2. 2003. 208pp. 978-1-59182-226-4.   *Vol. 20.* 2006. 192pp. 978-1-59532-460-3.
Vol. 3. 2003. 208pp. 978-1-59182-227-1.   *Vol. 21.* 2007. 192pp. 978-1-59532-461-0.
Vol. 4. 2003. 208pp. 978-1-59182-249-3.   *Vol. 22.* 2007. 192pp. 978-1-59532-462-7.
Vol. 5. 2004. 200pp. 978-1-59182-541-8.   *Vol. 23.* 2007. 192pp. 978-1-59532-463-4.
Vol. 6. 2004. 208pp. 978-1-59182-542-5.   *Vol. 24.* 2007. 200pp. 978-1-59532-464-1.
Vol. 7. 2004. 208pp. 978-1-59182-543-2.   *Vol. 25.* 2007. 200pp. 978-1-59532-465-8.
Vol. 8. 2004. 200pp. 978-1-59182-544-9.   *Vol. 26.* 2008. 192pp. 978-1-59532-466-5.
Vol. 9. 2004. 216pp. 978-1-59182-545-6.   *Vol. 27.* 2008. 200pp. 978-1-59532-633-1.
Vol. 10. 2004. 216pp. 978-1-59532-450-4.   *Vol. 28.* 2008. 200pp. 978-1-59816-188-5.
Vol. 11. 2005. 192pp. 978-1-59532-451-1.   *Vol. 29.* 2008. 192pp. 978-1-59816-189-2.
Vol. 12. 2005. 200pp. 978-1-59532-452-8.   *Vol. 30.* 2008. 192pp. 978-1-59816-190-8.
Vol. 13. 2005. 200pp. 978-1-59532-453-5.   *Vol. 31.* 2008. 192pp. 978-1-59816-191-5.
Vol. 14. 2005. 192pp. 978-1-59532-454-2.   *Vol. 32.* 2008. 208pp. 978-1-4278-0222-4.
Vol. 15. 2005. 192pp. 978-1-59532-455-9.   *Vol. 33.* 2009. 192pp. 978-1-4278-0223-1.
Vol. 16. 2005. 192pp. 978-1-59532-456-6.   *Vol. 34.* 2009. 208pp. 978-1-4278-0224-8.
Vol. 17. 2006. 192pp. 978-1-59532-457-3.   *Vol. 35/36.* 2009. 384pp. 978-0-345-52026-5.
Vol. 18. 2006. 192pp. 978-1-59532-458-0.   *Vol. 37/38.* 2010. 432pp. 978-0-345-52155-2.

Street Fighter. Written by **Jim Zub**, **Chris Sarracini**, **Joe Galloway**, **Ken Siu-Chong**, and various. Illustrated by **Arnold Tsang**, **Alvin Lee**, **Joe Ng**, and various. Udon Entertainment, T 🎮

Udon Entertainment has released many collections based on the cast of the extremely popular video game *Street Fighter* video games series which was originally released in 1987. The game series has had many sequels and updates over the years and is still a popular series for Capcom to this day. The main heroes are Ryu and Ken, but the series features a massive list of hero and villain fighters the players can control, including favorites like Guile, Chun-Li, M. Bison, Blanka, Sagat, and Zangief (who made an appearance in the Disney *Wreck It Ralph* 2012 movie). The series features the heroes as what happens in between the sequels to the games as well as flesh-out origins and stories of the heroes and villains and what ultimately leads them to the next Street Fighter tournament.

© 2016 UDON Entertainment

Street Fighter Classic. 2013–2014.

Vol. 1: Hadoken. 2013. 304pp. 978-1-926778-75-4, hardcover.
Vol. 2: Canon Strike. 2014. 304pp. 978–1926778846, hardcover.
Vol. 3: Psycho Crusher. 2014. 304pp. 978-1-927925-02-7, hardcover.

Street Fighter IV: Wages of Sin. 2014. 152pp. 978-1-927925-14-0, hardcover.

Street Fighter Legends: Chun-Li. 2015. 120pp. 978-1-927925-45-4, hardcover.

Street Fighter Legends: Akuma. 2013. 120pp. 978-1-926778-78-5, hardcover.

Super Street Fighter. 2013–2015.

Vol. 1: New Generation. 2013. 144pp. 978-1-926778-54-9, hardcover.
Vol. 2: Hyper-Fighting. 2015. 144pp. 978-1-926778-85-3, hardcover.

War Stories

War stories have long been a part of comic book history, especially during World War II and shortly thereafter when comic book readership among GIs was at an all-time peak. Though the genre has declined in popularity over the years, like the Western genre, there still are a variety of titles that have focused on all aspects of war from battles in ancient times up to and including the current conflicts such as the Iraq war. War, with its stories of life and death, intense action, and high visual impact, provides a dramatic backdrop for heroics and has historically been a common theme in comic books and graphic novels. The first comic book devoted entirely to war stories was Dell's *War Comics* (May 1940), which appeared a year before America's entry into World War II. Since the 1940s, the genre's popularity has drifted, but some excellent collections on the subject have been released within the last decade. Tales here are broken down into modern and ancient warfare.

Ancient Warfare

Tales of ancient battles from centuries before the invention of modern weapons. The stories include tales of the great warriors of Sparta, the battlefields of Troy, the Viking warriors, and the Crusades.

Age of Bronze. Written and Illustrated by **Eric Shanower**. Image Comics, 2001– . O 🎋 ◎
A retelling of the epic saga of the War of Troy. Based on the accounts by the poet Homer in his epic poem The Iliad as well as a wide range of researched sources. The story of the Trojan War is played out as Paris, the long-thought dead son of King Priam of Troy, discovers his true heritage that he truly is a prince of Troy. To thwart a prophecy that Paris would destroy Troy someday, the King and Queen had abandoned Paris as an infant to die in order to save their kingdom. Now Paris has been reunited, but the prophets once again foresee that the kingdom is doomed at Paris's hand. Reunited with his father now, Paris unwillingly sets a chain of events that will doom the entire kingdom when on a rescue mission to return King Priam's sister from the kingdom of Salamis, he decides to capture someone even more fair than his aunt: the beautiful wife of Melenaus of Sparta called Helen. Agamemnon, Melenaus's brother, intends to attack Troy to free his brother's wife and he will amass the greatest army ever combining the might of the

other Achaean kingdoms. As the coming battle is prepared to rescue Helen, the stage is set for a classic tale of ancient warfare all for the beautiful Helen. The epic series is planned to be released in a total of seven collected volumes. Eric Shanower won an Eisner Award in 2001 and 2003 in the category of Best Writer/Artist for his work on this series.

Vol. 1: A Thousand Ships. 2001. 224pp. 978-1-58240-200-0.
Vol. 2: Sacrifice. 2005. 224pp. 978-1-58240-399-1.
Vol. 3: Betrayal, Part 1. 2007. 176pp. 978-1-58240-845-3, hardcover; 978-1-58240-755-5.
Vol. 3B: Betrayal, Part 2. 2013. 176pp. 978-1-60706-757-3, hardcover; 978-1-60706-758-0.

Northlanders. Written by **Brian Wood**. Illustrated by **Davide Gianfelice**, **Leandro Fernandez**, **Riccardo Burchielli**, **Becky Cloonan**, and various. Vertigo/DC Comics, 2008–2016. M ◎

© 2016 DC Comics

Set in the 11th century; witness the stories of those who lived in the harsh age of the Vikings. Though fictional, the stories tell of an age of brutality and a cruel life that is true of the age. In the first volume, Sven, a self-exiled Viking warrior prince, returns from the pleasures of Constantinople to reclaim the throne after the death of his father. Each story arc tells another tale of the Viking Age set in the harshest of conditions. The series was reprinted in 2016 in two deluxe editions which collects multiple volumes in one edition.

Vol. 1: Sven the Returned. 2008. 200pp. 978-1-4012-1918-5.
Vol. 2: The Cross + The Hammer. 2009. 144pp. 978-1-4012-2296-3.
Vol. 3: Blood in the Snow. 2010. 144pp. 978-1-4012-2620-6.
Vol. 4: The Plague Widow. 2010. 144pp. 978-1-4012-2850-7.
Vol. 5: Metal. 2011. 192pp. 978-1-4012-3160-6.
Vol. 6: Thor's Daughter. 2012. 128pp. 978-1-4012-3366-2.
Vol. 7: Icelandic Trilogy. 2013. 200pp. 978-1-4012-3691-5.

Deluxe Edition. 2016.

Vol. 1: The Anglo-Saxon Saga. 2016. 464pp. 978-1-4012-6331-7.
Vol. 2: The Icelandic Saga. 2016. 296pp. 978-1-4012-6508-3.

Solomon's Thieves. Written by **Jordan Mechner**. Illustrated by **LeUyen Pham** and **Alex Puvilland**. First Second Books, 2010. 144pp. 978-1-59643-391-5. O ◎

© 2016 First Second and Jordan Mechner

The life of a Templar Knight can be dull—lots of bread and beans, and lots of walking. When a Templar named Martin stumbles across his old girlfriend (now married), Martin learns of a plot to destroy the Templar Knights order and steal their vast treasure. Fortunately, he's one of the only knights not in jail and can seek revenge. The book is the first in a planned trilogy of Templar Knight books. The second is *Templar*, listed below.

Templar. Written by **Jordan Mechner**. Illustrated by **LeUyen Pham** and **Alex Puvilland**. First Second Books, 2013. 480pp. 978-1-59643-393-9, hardcover. O ◎

> The Knights of Templar, the sacred order who served in the Crusades and were among the bravest of fighters for over two centuries, is betrayed by King Phillip IV of France and Pope Clement V of the Catholic Church in the early 14th century. The king wishes to frame the order for heresy, torture the knights into false confessions and burn them at the stake, and then plunder the treasures of the Templar Knights. Their order disbanded and in ruins, only a handful of knights survived the purge and are in hiding. But Martin and the remaining knights are about to stage a counterattack and take back what is rightfully theirs!

Vinland Saga. Written and Illustrated by **Makoto Yukimura**. Kodansha Comics, 2013– . T. Japanese manga. 🎖

> This manga series is set in early 11th-century England and dramatizes the successful invasion of Danish Vikings including the future King Canute. Selected as one of YALSA's Great Graphic Novels for Teens. Over 16 volumes have been published so far in Japan.

> *Vol. 1*. 2013. 470pp. 978-1-61262-420-4, hardcover.
> *Vol. 2*. 2014. 432pp. 978-1-61262-421-1, hardcover.
> *Vol. 3*. 2014. 454pp. 978-1-61262-422-8, hardcover.
> *Vol. 4*. 2014. 432pp. 978-1-61262-423-5, hardcover.
> *Vol. 5*. 2014. 448pp. 978-1-61262-424-2, hardcover.
> *Vol. 6*. 2015. 400pp. 978-1-61262-803-5, hardcover.
> *Vol. 7*. 2015. 400pp. 978-1-63236-009-0, hardcover.

Modern Warfare

Tales of combat and bravery from the point of view of the soldiers during modern-era conflicts including the world wars, Viet Nam, and the war against terrorism. War doesn't affect the soldiers too—included herein are stories of how war also casts its shadow on the innocent. The tales may also feature old soldiers who are drawn back into a conflict once again as old habits die hard.

The Activity. Written by **Nathan Edmondson**. Illustrated by **Mitch Gerads**. Image Comics, 2012–2015. M

> Global warfare is escalating, and a special strike team with the finesse of a doctor's scalpel is needed to cut through the red tape and clean up the messes made. The United States' most advanced and secret special operations group is needed to clean up jobs that are botched. Armed with the latest technology, they strike secretly with deadly lethal force in countries far away protecting the United States without us ever knowing it.

> *Vol. 1*. 2012. 136pp. 978-1-60706-561-6.
> *Vol. 2*. 2013. 168pp. 978-1-60706-719-1.
> *Vol. 3*. 2015. 160pp. 978-1-60706-759-7.

Any Empire. Written and Illustrated by **Nate Powell**. Top Shelf Productions, 2011. 304pp. 978-1-60309-077-3. O

> The effects of war and violence are explored and how it trickles down to Middle America. Lee like many kids his age likes to play war. Lee unlike the others keeps the violence out

© 2016 Top Shelf and Nate Powell

of real life. When a string of turtle mutilations happen, Sarah, the sister of one of the boys, tries to figure out who is committing these acts of violence. The boss of the group of boys, Purdy, tries to include Lee in the club but comes off too forceful. While the passing of time leads our three characters down very different paths in life, Sarah and Lee lead more traditional lives while Purdy becomes a cybernetic soldier for the army, much like his toys when they were young. Things get more surreal when Purdy's next mission requires the three characters to all meet again. Not only do they come face to face with each other, but they meet their child selves. Once and for all the truth about the turtle abuser gets what they deserve.

Battle Lines: A Graphic History of the Civil War. Written by **Jonathan Fetter-Vorm** and **Ari Kelman**. Illustrated by **Jonathan Fetter-Vorm**. Hill and Wang, 2015. O

A brutal look at the conflicts of the American Civil War, a war that nearly tore the country apart. Join famous historical figures as well as a cast of soldiers, farmers, and slaves in a fascinating narrative of our nation's history that should never be forgotten.

Boxers and Saints. Written and Illustrated by **Gene Luen Yang**. First Second, 2013. Historical Fiction. T ◉

© 2016 First Second and Gene Luen Yang

In 1899 an uprising began in China aimed at Western influence, including Christian missionaries. Known as the Boxer Rebellion it would last until 1901. In this connected pair of original graphic novels, Yang tells the story of two individuals whose lives were affected by it. *Boxers* is about Bao who becomes a rebel leader when his village is slaughtered by Imperial Forces working for foreign powers. He feels that the Gods are working through him to rid China of the Foreign Devils as well as the native "Secondary Devils" who have converted to Christianity. *Saints* features a girl known simply as "Four-Girl" until she converts to Catholicism and takes the name Vibiana. She feels that Joan of Arc is guiding her. At certain points in both books, their stories intersect. The two volumes can be purchased separately or in a box set.

Boxers. 2013. 336pp. 978-1-5964-3359-5.
Saints. 2013. 176pp. 978-1-5964-3689-3.
Boxed Set. 978-1-5964-3924-5.

Call of Duty: Black Ops III. Written by **Larry Hama**. Illustrated by **Marcelo Ferreira**. Dark Horse Comics, 2016. 144pp. 978-1-61655-966-3. M 🐾

Based on the hit video game series by Activision and a tie-in to the November 2015 hit game. Set in the year 2060, America is in the middle of a new Cold

War and a covert black ops team under the authority of the Winslow Accord has been sent into enemy territory with one goal: to assassinate important political targets. Meet leader of Black Cyber Ops Division, Jacob Hendricks, and his team of specialists as they wage war around the globe against the enemies of the Common Defense Pact in futuristic foreign lands ruined by war and ravaged by environmental changes.

Civil War Adventure. Written by **Chuck Dixon**. Illustrated by **Gary Kwapisz**. Dover Publishing, 2015–2016. T ◉

A collection of short stories focusing on different time lines during the American Civil War. The stories focus on both sides of the conflict from the sharpshooters of the Union at the Battle of Gettysburg to a journey down the Mississippi aboard the Union Ram Fleet as readers experience the grueling war that took many lives on both sides. The stories are inspired by true tales of the Civil War.

Book One. 2015. 144pp. 978-0-486-79509-6.
Book Two. 2016. 168pp. 978-0-486-81111-6.

© 2016 Dover Books and Chuck
Dixon and Gary Kwapisz

The Divine. Written by **Boaz Lavie**. Illustrated by **Asaf Hanuka** and **Tomer Hanuka**. First Second Books, 2015. 160pp. 978-1-59643-674-9. O

A former military man, Mark's now working civilian job, but the war never really leaves you. An old army buddy gives him a chance for a lucrative military contract for a mining job in an obscure South-East Asian country called Quanlom in the midst of a civil war. But this country is unlike anything he's ever seen as ancient magics and the modern age vies for control of a shattered country and where 10-year-old twins brandish what looks to be magic and lead an army of what appears to be gods.

© 2016 First Second Books

Exit Wounds. Written and Illustrated by **Rutu Modan**. Drawn and Quarterly, 2008. 168pp. 978-1-897299-83-8. M 🎗

In this Israeli work, a man joins with his father's soldier girlfriend to discover if the unidentified body in a suicide bombing is indeed his estranged father. *Exit Wounds* won the Eisner Award for Best New Graphic Novel.

G.I. Combat: The War That Time Forgot. Written by **J.T. Krul**, **Justin Gray**, **Peter J. Tomasi**, and **Jimmy Palmiotti**. Illustrated by **Ariel Olivetti**, **Dan Panosian**, and **Howard Chaykin**. DC Comics, 2013. 256pp. 978-1-4012-3853-7. T

A series homage to the original weird war DC Comics series which features soldiers lost in the past and fighting for their lives against dinosaurs. The series also showcases the Haunted Tank as well as the third version of the Unknown Soldier—who is in Afghanistan and fighting for the Americans. After the series was canceled, the

Unknown Soldier became a member of the Suicide Squad. The original "War That Time Forgot" stories have been collected in a Showcase volume.

G.I. Joe

Written by various. Illustrated by various. IDW Publishing, 2008– . T

When the evil forces of COBRA are ready to strike against the free people of the world, there's only one force that can take them on and win the day: G.I. Joe! A military branch of the United States, the soldiers all use codenames to protect their identities. Join Duke, Snake Eyes, and more as they wage their battle against COBRA Commander, Destro, Serpentor, and the rest of COBRA. The current G.I. Joe continuity includes the monthly series G.I. Joe, Though there is a sampling of the titles listed below including the classic Marvel Comics series reprinted by IDW Publishing, the complete list of titles can be found at IDW Publishing's web site.

Classic G.I. Joe. Written by **Larry Hama**. Illustrated by **Herb Trimpe** and various. 2009– . T

© Hasbro. All Rights Reserved

A collection of the original Marvel Comics titles originally published from 1982 to 1994 as well as new material beginning with *Vol. 16* that continues where the original series ended.

Vol. 1. 2009. 240pp. 978-1-60010-345-2.
Vol. 2. 2009. 240pp. 978-1-60010-379-7.
Vol. 3. 2009. 240pp. 978-1-60010-423-7.
Vol. 4. 2009. 240pp. 978-1-60010-462-6.
Vol. 5. 2009. 240pp. 978-1-60010-519-7.
Vol. 6. 2009. 240pp. 978-1-60010-545-6.
Vol. 7. 2010. 232pp. 978-1-60010-598-2.
Vol. 8. 2010. 256pp. 978-1-60010-655-2.
Vol. 9. 2010. 252pp. 978-1-60010-706-1.

Vol. 10. 2011. 240pp. 978-1-60010-791-7.   *Vol. 15*. 2012. 248pp. 978-1-61377-274-4.
Vol. 11. 2011. 240pp. 978-1-60010-875-4.   *Vol. 16*. 2015. 268pp. 978-1-63140-318-7.
Vol. 12. 2011. 240pp. 978-1-60010-972-0.   *Vol. 17*. 2016. 244pp. 978-1-63140-506-8.
Vol. 13. 2011. 236pp. 978-1-61377-082-5.   *Vol. 18*. 2016. 244pp. 978-1-63140-654-6.
Vol. 14. 2012. 256pp. 978-1-61377-153-2.   *Vol. 19*. 2017. 244pp. 978-1-63140-812-0.

G.I. Joe. Written by **Chuck Dixon**. Illustrated by **Robert Atkins** and **S.L. Gallant**. IDW Publishing, 2009–2011.

The first IDW Publishing relaunch of G.I. Joe from IDW Publishing. If you want to read from the ground floor, this is the best place to start.

Vol. 1. 2009. 160pp. 978-1-60010-467-1
Vol. 2. 2010. 152pp. 978-1-60010-609-5.
Vol. 3. 2010. 152pp. 978-1-60010-692-7.

G.I. Joe Origins. Written by **Chuck Dixon**, **Larry Hama**, and **J.T. Krul**. Illustrated by **Mike Hawthorne** and **Agustin Padilla**. IDW Publishing, 2014–2015. T

Collects the original series by IDW Publishing which focuses on the origins of the G.I. Joe team, backstories of the characters, and their motivations to join the team.

Omnibus, Vol. 1. 2014. 296pp. 978-1-61377-867-8.
Omnibus, Vol. 2. 2014. 268pp. 978-1-63140-118-3.

G.I. Joe: The IDW Collection. Written and Illustrated by various. 2013– . T. IDW Publishing, 2013– . T

A collection in chronological reading order of the IDW relaunch of G.I. Joe from 2008 to the present. The series collection includes the various series including <u>G.I. Joe: Origins</u> and <u>G.I. Cobra</u>, as well as a variety of miniseries and special issues in the preferred reading order.

Vol. 1. 2013. 352pp. 978-1-61377-549-3, hardcover.
Vol. 2. 2013. 348pp. 978-1-61377-655-1, hardcover.
Vol. 3. 2013. 384pp. 978-1-61377-793-0, hardcover.
Vol. 4. 2014. 344pp. 978-1-61377-931-6, hardcover.
Vol. 5. 2015. 364pp. 978-1-63140-103-9, hardcover.
Vol. 6. 2016. 352pp. 978-1-63140-533-4, hardcover.
Vol. 7. 2017. 292pp. 978-1-63140-799-4, hardcover.

G.I. Joe: A Real American Hero. Written by **Larry Hama**. Illustrated by **Will Rosado**, **Ron Wagner**, and various. IDW Publishing, 2011– . T

An alternate-universe <u>G.I. Joe</u> series published by IDW Publishing. The series still has fan-favorite writer Larry Hama tell the tales of G.I. Joe against the terrorist threat of COBRA. The series continues from the original Marvel Comics series published as *Classic G.I. Joe*.

Vol. 1. 2011. 152pp. 978-1-60010-864-8.
Vol. 2. 2011. 132pp. 978-1-60010-941-6.
Vol. 3. 2011. 124pp. 978-1-61377-105-1.
Vol. 4. 2011. 128pp. 978-1-61377-202-7.
Vol. 5. 2012. 124pp. 978-1-61377-486-1.
Vol. 6. 2013. 128pp. 978-1-61377-582-0.
Vol. 7. 2013. 128pp. 978-1-61377-677-3.
Vol. 8. 2013. 124pp. 978-1-61377-826-5.
Vol. 9. 2014. 132pp. 978-1-61377-955-2.
Vol. 10. 2014. 124pp. 978-1-63140-154-1.
Vol. 11. 2015. 124pp. 978-1-63140-273-9.
Vol. 12. 2015. 124pp. 978-1-63140-406-1.
Vol. 13. 2015. 116pp. 978-1-63140-483-2.
Vol. 14. 2016. 116pp. 978-1-63140-554-9.
Vol. 15. 2016. 116pp. 978-1-63140-622-5.
Vol. 16. 2016. 120pp. 978-1-63140-732-1.
Vol. 17. 2017. 120pp. 978-1-63140-852-6.
Vol. 18. 2017. 128pp. 978-1-63140-959-2.

G.I. Joe: Hearts and Minds. Written by **Max Brooks**. Illustrated by **Howard Chaykin**. IDW Publishing, 2010. 132pp. 978-1-60010-776-4, hardcover. T 🎗

A self-contained story focusing on 10 members of G.I. Joe and Cobra. The 10 short stories focus on both sides of the conflict where they reveal more out themselves and what made them motivated to become members of an armed force or a terrorist organization. The book by *World War Z author* Max Brooks gives a more humanizing portrait of the heroes and villains and adds great depth to the mythology of the series. The book was recognized by YALSA's Great Graphic Novels for Teens committee in 2011.

G.I. Joe: Snake Eyes. Written by **Chuck Dixon** and **Mike Costa**. Illustrated by **Robert Atkins**, **Paolo Villanelli**, and various. IDW Publishing, 2011–2015. T

> The silent black-clad ninja-like G.I. Joe soldier named Snake Eyes is one of the most popular G.I. Joe characters. Featured below are storylines featuring the character. His main adversary from Cobra is the white-clad ninja called Snake Eyes.

> *Cobra Civil War*, 2011–2012.
> *Vol. 1*. 2011. 104pp. 978-1-61377-032-0.
> *Vol. 2*. 2012. 104pp. 978-1-61377-159-4.
> *Snake Eyes and Storm Shadow*. 2012. 124pp. 978-1-61377-419-9.
> *Agent of Cobra*. 2015. 120pp. 978-1-63140-371-2.

Goddamn This War! Written and Illustrated by **Jacques Tardi**. Fantagraphics, 2013. 152pp. 978-1-60699-582-2, hardcover. M

© 2013 Jacques Tardi and Fantagraphics

> A brutal look at a six-year period set during World War II. Each chapter represents a year that a soldier fights in the war—with each year getting more and more bleak as the war progresses.

The Harlem Hellfighters. Written by **Max Brooks**. Illustrated by **Caanan White**. Broadway Books, 2014. 272pp. 978-0-307-46497-2. O

> The 369th infantry regiment was the first African American regiment to fight in World War I, achieving great feats while also facing discrimination from their own side. This is their story. A fictionalized look at a great fighting force from history.

It Was the War of the Trenches. Written and Illustrated by **Jacques Tardi**. Fantagraphics, 2010. 120pp. 978-1-60699-353-8, hardcover. M

> War is pointless and trivial to the soldier on the front lines. Jacques Tardi illustrates in horrific straightforwardness the many short-lived lives of the soldiers in the tragic trenches of World War I and the effect that the war held on those not just in the trenches but their families back home.

Onward towards Our Noble Deaths. Written and Illustrated by **Shigeru Mizuki**. Drawn and Quarterly, 2011. 368pp. 978-1-77046-041-6. O. Japanese manga.

© Drawn and Quarterly and
Shigeru Mizuki

Onwards Towards Our Noble Deaths is the first story by criti-cally acclaimed Shigeru Mizuki to be published in English. This is the story of Japanese soldiers stationed on an island of Papua New Guinea. It recounts the comical tales of living in a foreign land while in sharp contrast with grim reminders of the horrors of war. When the soldiers are confronted with the direst of circum-stance—a suicide attack—how do men faced with the end react? What happens to those men if they actually survived the slaughter? The desperation of war is truly conveyed through the characters within.

The Property. Written and Illustrated by **Rutu Modan**. Drawn and Quarterly, 2013. 232pp. 978-1-77046-115-4. O

A woman accompanies her grandmother from Israel to Warsaw, Poland, in part to recover family property lost during World War II. There, some elements of her grand-mother's past come to light and secrets are revealed. A heartbreaking look at the hor-rors of war, painful memories, and what is really the truth.

Rebels: A Well-Regulated Militia. Written by **Brian Wood**. Illustrated by **Andrea Mutti**. Dark Horse Comics, 2016. T ◎

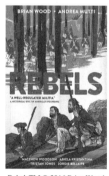

RebelsTM © 2016 Brian Wood
and Andrea Mutti

A look at the war of independence in the year 1775 from a new per-spective not from the heroes of the American Revolution, but through the eyes of the people who lived there. The brave men on the front line, their wives, the traders, trappers, farmers, volunteer soldiers, sons, and daughters who were brought together at a turbulent time in our country's founding.

Resistance. Written by **Carla Jablonski**. Illustrated by **Leland Purvis**. First Second, 2010–2012. T 🖋

© First Second.

The occupation of France by Nazi Germany had brought out many secretive qualities of the French people. Some people corroborated with the Nazis; many others did not. Paul and Marie, children from a small town in the south of France, turn to join the Resistance in order to help their Jewish friend Henri. What will these two do in order to get their country back from the Nazis? The first collection was recognized by YALSA as a Great Graphic Novel for Teens in 2011.

Resistance. 2010. 128pp. 978-1-59643-291-8.
Defiance. 2011. 128pp. 978-1-59643-292-5.
Victory. 2012. 128pp. 978-1-59643-293-2.

Sgt. Rock. Written by **Brian Azzarello**, **Robert Kanigher**, **Billy Tucci**, and various. Illustrated by **Joe Kubert**, **Russ Heath**, **Billy Tucci**, and various. DC Comics, 2002–2015. T-M

Debuting in Our Army at War comics in 1959, Sgt. Rock is one of the most iconic war heroes in comic books. He was the platoon leader of Easy Company, an outfit that faced some of the most dangerous action in World War II. Joining Rock was the ever-changing cast of soldiers in the Easy Company platoon including Ice Cream, Wild Man, Solider, and Four Eyes as they trudged on through the front lines experiencing firsthand the cost of freedom. *Sgt. Rock: Between Hell & a Hard Place* is a Vertigo title that reunited famed artist Joe Kubert with the iconic character he illustrated. The story tells of Rock and Easy Company trying to solve a mystery after four high-ranking German officials they captured are found murdered.

Sgt. Rock Archives, 2002–2012.
Vol. 1. 2002. 240pp. 978-1-5638-9841-9, hardcover.
Vol. 2. 2003. 216pp. 978-1-4012-0146-3, hardcover.
Vol. 3. 2004. 224pp. 978-1-4012-0410-5, hardcover.
Vol. 4. 2012. 248pp. 978-1401237264, hardcover.
Sgt. Rock: Between Hell & a Hard Place. Vertigo/DC Comics, 2003. 140pp. 1-4012-0053-2. M
Sgt. Rock's Combat Tales. 2005. 128pp. 1-4012-0794-4. T
Sgt. Rock: The Prophecy. 2007. 144pp. 978-1-4012-1248-3. O

Sgt. Rock: The Last Battalion. 2009. 160pp. 978-1-4012-2533-9, hardcover; 978-1-4012-2534-6.

© DC Comics

Showcase Presents: Sgt. Rock. 2007–2013.
Vol. 1. 2007. 544pp. 978-1-4012-1713-6.
Vol. 2. 2008. 520pp. 978-1-4012-1984-0.
Vol. 3. 2010. 496pp. 978-1-4012-2771-5.
Vol. 4. 2013. 520pp. 978-1-4012-3811-7.
Showcase Presents: Men of War. Written and Illustrated by various. DC Comics, 2014. 496pp. 978-1-4012-4388-3. T

A collection of the 1970s' war tales starring German World War I pilot Enemy Ace and Codename: Gravedigger, an African American soldier undercover behind enemy lines.

Showcase Presents the Unknown Soldier. Written and Illustrated by various. DC Comics, 2006–2014. T

Set during World War II, the Unknown Soldier is an intelligence agent whose head and face were so severely injured that he is forced to wear bandages. However, he is also a master of disguise, infiltrating the enemy in order to stop them. Creators of the series include Robert Kanigher, Joe Kubert, and Bob Haney. See the next two entries for other incarnations of the character.

Vol. 1. 2006. 544pp. 978-1-4012-1090-8.
Vol. 2. 2014. 552pp. 978-1-4012-4081-3.

Unknown Soldier. Written by **Joshua Dysart**. Illustrated by **Alberto Ponticelli**. Vertigo/ DC Comics, 2009–2011. M

> Set in the war-torn country of northern Uganda, Moses Lwanga is a pacific doctor who realizes after his life is threatened that he may be a sleeper agent with a deep dark secret. When his life is threatened, Moses kills his opponents with almost unabashed efficiency. Inexplicably the pacifist knows how to kill and a voice in his head that tells him that the only way to fix his country is to slaughter those responsible for his country's horrors. This is the second Unknown Soldier in DC Comics continuity.
>
> *Vol. 1: Haunted House*. 2009. 144pp. 978-1-4012-2311-3.
> *Vol. 2: Easy Kill*. 2010. 200pp. 978-1-4012-2600-8.
> *Vol. 3: Dry Season*. 2010. 144pp. 978-1-4012-2855-2.
> *Vol. 4: Beautiful World*. 2011. 128pp. 978-1-4012-3176-7.

Unknown Soldier. Written by **Garth Ennis**. Illustrated by **Kilian Plunkett**. Vertigo/DC Comics, 2014. 112pp. 978-14012-4417-0. M

© DC Comics

> Originally published in 1997, a CIA agent slowly pieces together the clues that point to the Unknown Soldier, a master of disguise from World War II who is still alive. Meanwhile, the old soldier is looking for a replacement.

Far East Adventure—Code of the Warrior: Samurai, Ninja, and Other Asian Influences

The samurai, ninja, and other Asian cultures have been explored in great detail in comic books, especially in Japanese manga, which has crossed in American markets and inspired American creators, too. The quintessential samurai epic is the 28-volume epic *Lone Wolf and Cub*, which has inspired Western illustrators and writers for many years. In typical samurai stories, the main character or characters fight with a code of honor or a sense of discipline. This is exemplified in the samurai code of Bushido as created by samurai legend Miyamoto Musashi. Thus, the subgenre can be compared to the American Western, where the cowboy code of honor is integral to the story. The samurai or ninja adventure usually takes the protagonist on a quest of discovery or search for hidden truths, but of utmost importance is that the character retains his sense of discipline throughout the task. Because of the discipline of the character, the personality may even be considered by others as arrogant or out of touch with the rest of humanity, but it is the strict adherence to his principles that enables the protagonist to succeed. In the end the hero's discipline and teamwork with his companions overcome all obstacles. Of course, fighting and swordplay are musts in these tales. Though the settings typically are set in feudal Japan or other ancient Asian countries, the story may take place as well during current times, the far future, to even a fantasy-like Asia which may have elements of the fantastic as part of the plot. Romance may be involved, but is not usually essential to the plot. Film comparisons include samurai films by Akira Kurosawa such as *Seven Samurai* (1954) and *Hidden Fortress* (1958), and the Lone Wolf and Cub films.

47 Ronin. Written by **Mike Richardson**. Illustrated by **Stan Sakai**. Dark Horse, 2014. 152pp. 978-1-59582-954-2. T 🎗 ◎

> Dark Horse publisher Richardson and award-winning creator Sakai retell the classic story of the 47 former samurai who avenged the death of their master in the early 1700s. The hardcover collection of the five-issue limited series was on the list of YALSA Best Books for Young Adults, was nominated for an Eisner Award, and won Sakai an Inkwell Award.

365 Samurai and a Few Bowls of Rice. Written and Illustrated by **J.P. Kalonji**. Dark Horse Comics, 2009. 392pp. 978-1-59582-412-7. O ◎

> A lone samurai named Ningen leaves his dojo at the request of his master to continue his search for enlightenment, but the path to peace and purity along the way is filled with danger at every turn. Each page is a full panel that helps to tell the tale of the Edo-era swordsman.

365 Samurai and a Few Bowls of Rice © 2016 J.P. Kalonji. 365 Samurai word mark and logo are registered trademarks owned by Kalonji/Gill - 11th Hour Artists Management, London 2008. Registered in the EU and other countries. And any use of such mark is under license and prohibited without permission

Avatar: The Last Airbender. Created by **Michael Dante DiMartino** and **Bryan Konietzko**. Dark Horse Comics, 2011– . Y ◎ ▱

> A follow-up to the popular animated series from Nickelodeon Animation Studio, which originally aired from 2005 to 2008. In a world reminiscent of ancient China, human civilization is divided into four nations: the Water Tribes, the Earth Kingdom, the Fire Nation, and the Air Nomads. In these lands, some people of each of the corresponding nations known as "benders" can manipulate and control the element of their nation using the physical motions of martial arts. The series focuses on Aang, the last of the Airbenders and the current Avatar—one who can master all four elements (Earth, Water, Fire, and Air). Only one Avatar is born at a time and upon his or her death, the next Avatar is reincarnated somewhere across the world. On his journey to complete his training as the Avatar, Aang befriended Katara, a Southern Water Tribe water bender and her older brother Sokka; Toph, a

Nickelodeon's "Avatar: The Last Airbender"
used with permission by Nickelodeon.
© Viacom Media Networks. All Rights
Reserved. Nickelodeon, all related titles,
characters and logos are trademarks owned
by Viacom Media Networks, a division of
Viacom International Inc.

blind Earth-bender, and ultimately befriended Prince Zuko, the son of the Fire Nation leader and enemy of the Avatar. *The Lost Adventures* collection tells of tales set during the original three seasons of the show, while the series afterward is set directly after the animated series and features the continuing adventures of Aang, Katara, Sokka, Toph, and Prince Zuko as they try to rebuild the world after the defeat of the Fire Warlord. The series has been highly regarded by fans and continues to be published by Dark Horse Comics, with the new ongoing series written by Gene Luen Yang and illustrated by the artistic team from Japan known as Gurihiru.

The Lost Adventures. Written by **Aaron Ehasz, Josh Hamilton, Tim Hedrick, Dave Roman**, and **J. Torres**. Illustrated by **Joaquim Dos Santos, Elsa Garagarza, Gurihiru**, and others. 2011. 240pp. 978-1-59582-748-7.

> *The Promise*. Written by **Gene Luen Yang**. Illustrated by **Gurihiru**.
>
>> *Book 1*. 2012. 80pp. 978-1-59582-811-8.
>> *Book 2*. 2012. 80pp. 978-1-59582-875-0.
>> *Book 3*. 2012. 80pp. 978-1-59582-941-2.
>> *Library Edition*. 2013. 240pp. 978-1-61655-074-5, hardcover.
>
> *The Search*. Written by **Gene Luen Yang**. Illustrated by **Gurihiru**.
>
>> *Book 1*. 2013. 80pp. 978-1-61655-054-7.
>> *Book 2*. 2013. 80pp. 978-1-61655-190-2.
>> *Book 3*. 2013. 80pp. 978-1-61655-184-1.
>> *Library Edition*. 240pp. 978-1-61655-226-8, hardcover.
>
> *The Rift*. Written by **Gene Luen Yang**. Illustrated by **Gurihiru**. 2014.
>
>> *Book 1*. 2014. 80pp. 978-1-61655-295-4.
>> *Book 2*. 2014. 80pp. 978-1-61655-296-1.
>> *Book 3*. 2014. 80pp. 978-1-61655-297-8.
>> *Library Edition*. 240pp. 978-1-61655-550-4, hardcover.
>
> *Smoke and Shadow*. Written by **Gene Luen Yang**. Illustrated by **Gurihiru**. 2015.
>
>> *Book 1*. 2015. 80pp. 978-1-61655-761-4.
>> *Book 2*. 2015. 80pp. 978-1-61655-790-4.
>> *Book 3*. 2016. 80pp. 978-1-61655-838-3.
>> *Library Edition*, 2016. 240pp. 978-1-50670-013-7, hardcover.
>
> *North and South*. Written by **Gene Luen Yang**. Illustrated by **Gurihiru**. 2016–2017.
>
>> *Book 1*. 2016. 80pp. 978-1-50670-022-9.
>> *Book 2*. 2017. 80pp. 978-1-50670-129-5.
>> *Book 3*. 2017. 80pp. 978-1-50670-130-1.
>> *Library Edition*, 2017. 240pp. 978-1-50670-195-0, hardcover.

Beyond the Western Deep. Written by **Alex Kain**. Illustrated by **Rachel Bennett**. Action Lab Entertainment. Y

> The first volume in a planned epic series. In a world populated by anthropomorphic warrior mammal clans, after 100 years of peace in a kingdom governed by four kingdoms, peace is about to be shattered as the Ermehns (tigers), a northern clan, are about to break the peace and reclaim their lands taken from them forcefully by the Canid (wolves) clan. Meanwhile, emissaries from the peaceful Lutren (otters) and Tamian (red squirrels) clans have been charged with speaking with the Canids to try and prevent the inevitable war.
>
> *Vol. 1*. 2015. 80pp. 978-1-63229-103-5.

Blade of the Immortal. Written and Illustrated by **Hiroaki Samura**. Dark Horse Comics, 1997–2015. M. Japanese manga. 🏃 ◎

> In feudal Japan, Manji, a fallen Ronin (wandering samurai), has been cursed with life everlasting with mystical bloodworms that will heal his every wound. The curse will end on one condition: he must slay 1,000 evil men in battle. Now immortal, no matter how many times he gets cut, stabbed, slit, burnt, or gouged, he will always heal. Joined with Rin, a female companion who is out to seek revenge on those who killed her parents, they're on the path to redeem Rin's family honor and to give her eternal rest. The series won an Eisner Award in 2000 in the category of Best U.S. Edition of Foreign Material.
>
> *Vol. 1: Blood of a Thousand*. 1997. 136pp. 978-1-56971-239-9.
> *Vol. 2: Cry of the Worm*. 1998. 176pp. 978-1-56971-300-6.
> *Vol. 3: Dreamsong*. 1999. 208pp. 978-1-56971-357-0.
> *Vol. 4: On Silent Wings*. 1999. 176pp. 978-1-56971-412-6.
> *Vol. 5: On Silent Wings II*. 2000. 184pp. 978-1-56971-444-7.
> *Vol. 6: Dark Shadows*. 2000. 192pp. 978-1-56971-469-0.
> *Vol. 7: Heart of Darkness*. 2001. 192pp. 978-1-56971-531-4.
> *Vol. 8: The Gathering*. 2001. 208pp. 978-1-56971-546-8.
> *Vol. 9: The Gathering II*. 2001. 216pp. 978-1-56971-560-4.
> *Vol. 10: Secrets*. 2002. 232pp. 978-1-56971-746-2.
> *Vol. 11: Beasts*. 2002. 192pp. 978-1-56971-741-7.
> *Vol. 12: Autumn Frost*. 2003. 232pp. 978-1-56971-991-6.
> *Vol. 13: Mirror of the Soul*. 2004. 256pp. 978-1-59307-218-6.
> *Vol. 14: Last Blood*. 2005. 256pp. 978-1-59307-321-3.
> *Vol. 15: Trickster*. 2006. 224pp. 978-1-59307-468-5.
> *Vol. 16: Shortcut*. 2006. 200pp. 978-1-59307-723-5.
> *Vol. 17: On the Perfection of Anatomy*. 2007. 184pp. 978-1-59307-782-2.
> *Vol. 18: The Sparrow Net*. 2008. 208pp. 978-1-59307-871-3.
> *Vol. 19: Badger Hole*. 2008. 168pp. 978-1-59307-969-7.
> *Vol. 20: Demon Lair*. 2008. 280pp. 978-1-59582-199-7.
> *Vol. 21: Demon Lair II*. 2009. 232pp. 978-1-59582-323-6.
> *Vol. 22: Footsteps*. 2010. 232pp. 978-1-59582-443-1.
> *Vol. 23: Scarlet Swords*. 2011. 232pp. 978-1-59582-671-8.
> *Vol. 24: Massacre*. 2011. 216pp. 978-1-59582-751-7.
> *Vol. 25: Snowfall at Dawn*. 2012. 232pp. 978-1-59582-883-5.
> *Vol. 26: Blizzard*. 2013. 224pp. 978-1-61655-098-1.

Vol. 27: Mist on the Spider's Web. 240pp. 978-1-61655-215-2.
Vol. 28: Raining Chaos. 2014. 216pp. 978-1-61655-321-0.
Vol. 29: Beyond Good and Evil. 2014. 216pp. 978-1-61655-337-1.
Vol. 30: Vigilance. 2014. 216pp. 978-1-61655-484-2.
Vol. 31: Final Curtain. 2015. 288pp. 978-1-61655-626-6.

Flame of Recca. Written and Illustrated by **Nobuyuki Anzai**. VIZ Media, 2003–2009. O. Japanese manga. あ

Recca Hanabishi is a typical high school student. He lives with his father, he's a tough scrapper of a fighter, he enjoys playing with fireworks—and he's also a ninja with the mysterious ability to shoot fire! Maybe he's not so typical. With his friends including the dumb-but-strong brute Domon, the pretty-boy Mikagami, and the ninja girl Fuuko who has the ability to control the wind, he must rescue Yanagi Sakoshita, his "princess" whom he has sworn to protect. Yanagi has the magical power to heal and has been kidnapped by an evil madman who wants to harness her powers for immortality and more. When another villain with powers similar to Recca's control of flames offers the group a chance to participate in a tournament of death, they begrudgingly accept, and through the fighting they learn more about themselves, the price of friendship, and the true secret of Recca's past. The series also inspired a hit Japanese anime television show.

Vol. 1. 2003. 180pp. 978-1-59116-066-3.
Vol. 2. 2003. 184pp. 978-1-59116-067-0.
Vol. 3. 2003. 184pp. 978-1-59116-094-6.
Vol. 4. 2004. 200pp. 978-1-59116-125-7.
Vol. 5. 2004. 200pp. 978-1-59116-193-6.
Vol. 6. 2004. 200pp. 978-1-59116-316-9.
Vol. 7. 2004. 200pp. 978-1-59116-448-7.
Vol. 8. 2004. 200pp. 978-1-59116-480-7.
Vol. 9. 2004. 192pp. 978-1-59116-481-4.
Vol. 10. 2005. 200pp. 978-1-59116-636-8.
Vol. 11. 2005. 200pp. 978-1-59116-741-9.
Vol. 12. 2005. 192pp. 978-1-59116-796-9.
Vol. 13. 2005. 192pp. 978-1-59116-858-4.
Vol. 14. 2005. 184pp. 978-1-42150-014-0.
Vol. 15. 2005. 200pp. 978-1-42150-131-4.
Vol. 16. 2006. 208pp. 978-1-42150-250-2.
Vol. 17. 2006. 208pp. 978-1-42150-381-3.

Vol. 18. 2006. 208pp. 978-1-42150-454-4.
Vol. 19. 2006. 208pp. 978-1-42150-455-1.
Vol. 20. 2006. 208pp. 978-1-42150-456-8.
Vol. 21. 2006. 192pp. 978-1-42150-457-5.
Vol. 22. 2007. 192pp. 978-1-42150-893-1.
Vol. 23. 2007. 192pp. 978-1-42150-894-8.
Vol. 24. 2007. 192pp. 978-1-42150-895-5.
Vol. 25. 2007. 200pp. 978-1-42150-896-2.
Vol. 26. 2008. 200pp. 978-1-42150-897-9.
Vol. 27. 2008. 184pp. 978-1-42150-898-6.
Vol. 28. 2008. 200pp. 978-1-42151-680-6.
Vol. 29. 2008. 210pp. 978-1-42151-681-3.
Vol. 30. 2009. 192pp. 978-1-42152-201-2.
Vol. 31. 2009. 192pp. 978-1-42152-202-9.
Vol. 32. 2009. 200pp. 978-1-42152-203-6.
Vol. 33. 2009. 192pp. 978-1-42152-204-3.

Gin Tama. Written and Illustrated by **Hideaki Sorachi**. VIZ Media, 2007–2011. O あ

Set in feudal Japan during the Edo period, samurai Gintoki Sakata works as a freelance alongside his friends Shinpachi Shimura and Kaguara just to pay the monthly rent where he lives. The series also incorporates humor and science fiction elements to the show after aliens arrive from outer space, and Gintoki has to fight them as well as the Yakuza. After the aliens take over all the jobs and then confiscate all the swords, what else can Gintoki do? The manga began in Japan in 2003, and 62 volumes have been published so far. The series was also adapted into an anime series.

Vol. 1. 2007. 192pp. 978-1-42151-358-4.
Vol. 2. 2007. 192pp. 978-1-42151-359-1.
Vol. 3. 2007. 200pp. 978-1-42151-360-7.

Vol. 4. 2008. 192pp. 978-1-42151-361-4.
Vol. 5. 2008. 192pp. 978-1-42151-618-9.
Vol. 6. 2008. 192pp. 978-1-42151-619-6.

Vol. 7. 2008. 192pp. 978-1-42151-620-2.
Vol. 8. 2008. 192pp. 978-1-42151-621-9.
Vol. 9. 2008. 210pp. 978-1-42151-622-6.
Vol. 10. 2010. 210pp. 978-1-42151-623-3.
Vol. 11. 2009. 200pp. 978-1-42152-395-8.
Vol. 12. 2009. 200pp. 978-1-42152-396-5.
Vol. 13. 2009. 200pp. 978-1-42152-397-2.
Vol. 14. 2009. 200pp. 978-1-42152-398-9.
Vol. 15. 2009. 200pp. 978-1-42152-399-6.

Vol. 16. 2010. 192pp. 978-1-42152-814-4.
Vol. 17. 2010. 200pp. 978-1-42152-815-1.
Vol. 18. 2010. 200pp. 978-1-42152-816-8.
Vol. 19. 2010. 208pp. 978-1-42152-817-5.
Vol. 20. 2010. 192pp. 978-1-42152-818-2.
Vol. 21. 2011. 200pp. 978-1-42152-819-9.
Vol. 22. 2011. 200pp. 978-1-42152-820-5.
Vol. 23. 2011. 192pp. 978-1-42152-821-2.

House of Five Leaves. Written and Illustrated by **Natsume Ono**. VIZ Media, 2010–2012. O Japanese manga. 🎏 あ

Set during the feudal period of Japan, Akitsu Masanosuke is a Ronin, a masterless samurai, who is hired as a bodyguard for a group called The Five Leaves. Though Akitsu is unsure of the group's intentions, getting good work as a bodyguard is difficult for the often-shy Ronin. Slowly Akitsu learns of the Five Leaves' less-than-honorable intentions, and he must soon make a choice where his loyalty lies. The series was turned into an anime and was selected as one of YALSA's Great Graphic Novels for Teens.

Vol. 1. 2010. 208pp. 978-1-4215-3210-3.
Vol. 2. 2010. 200pp. 978-1-4215-3211-0.
Vol. 3. 2011. 200pp. 978-1-4215-3212-7.
Vol. 4. 2011. 208pp. 978-1-4215-3213-4.

Vol. 5. 2011. 208pp. 978-1-4215-3214-1.
Vol. 6. 2012. 200pp. 978-1-4215-3542-5.
Vol. 7. 2012. 200pp. 978-1-4215-4201-0.
Vol. 8. 2012. 280pp. 978-1-4215-4202-7.

Kaze Hikaru. Written and Illustrated by **Taeko Watanabe**. VIZ Media, LLC, 2006– . T. Japanese manga.

Set during the Bakumatsu revolution held at the end of the Tokugawa era and the beginning of the Meiji era, a young woman named Sei Tominaga seeks to avenge the deaths of her father and brother. Disguising herself as a young boy, Sei—now called Seizaburo Kamiya, joins the special police force called the Shinsengumi to seek revenge, but also finds true love in Okita Souji, one of the premiere Shinsengumi swordsmen. The series is still currently being published in Japan with over 37 collected volumes.

KAZE HIKARU © 1997 Taeko WATANABE/SHOGAKUKAN

Vol. 1. 2006. 200pp. 978-1421501895.
Vol. 2. 2006. 208pp. 978-1-4215-0581-7.
Vol. 3. 2006. 208pp. 978-1-4215-0582-4.

Vol. 4. 2007. 200pp. 978-1-4215-1017-0.
Vol. 5. 2007. 208pp. 978-1-4215-1018-7.
Vol. 6. 2007. 208pp. 978-1-4215-1163-4.
Vol. 7. 2007. 208pp. 978-1-4215-1164-1.
Vol. 8. 2008. 208pp. 978-1-4215-1537-3.
Vol. 9. 2008. 200pp. 978-1-4215-1734-6.
Vol. 10. 2008. 188pp. 978-1-4215-1735-3.
Vol. 11. 2008. 210pp. 978-1-4215-1736-0.
Vol. 12. 2009. 200pp. 978-1-4215-2415-3.
Vol. 13. 2009. 200pp. 978-1-4215-2416-0.
Vol. 14. 2009. 200pp. 978-1-4215-2417-7.

Vol. 15. 2009. 200pp. 978-1-4215-2418-4.
Vol. 16. 2010. 200pp. 978-1-4215-2801-4.
Vol. 17. 2010. 200pp. 978-1-4215-2802-1.
Vol. 18. 2010. 192pp. 978-1-4215-2803-8.
Vol. 19. 2010. 192pp. 978-1-4215-2804-5.
Vol. 20. 2010. 192pp. 978-1-4215-3584-5.
Vol. 21. 2013. 192pp. 978-1-4215-3585-2.
Vol. 22. 2013. 192pp. 978-1-4215-3586-9.
Vol. 23. 2015. 192pp. 978-1-4215-3587-6.
Vol. 24. 2016. 192pp. 978-1-4215-3588-3.

LEGO Ninjago. Written by **Greg Farshtey** and various. Illustrated by **Jolyon Yates** and various. Papercutz, 2011–2013; Little, Brown Books for Young Readers, 2015– . Y ☐ ⚑
Based on the hit LEGO property. Jay, Cole, Zane, and Kai are ninja masters of the mystical art of Spinjitsu. With their sacred weapons of power (Fire, Lighting, Earth, and Ice), together the four ninja are the protectors of the mystic island of Ninjago. Taught by their master Sensei Wu, they're all that separates the island from the threat of the evil Lord Garmadon and his skeleton army, Serpentine race of snake-men, and pirates that threaten the land. The series is also a hit video game as well and has made appearances in the *LEGO Dimensions* game. A feature-length film will be released in movie theaters as well in 2017. A new LEGO Ninjago series was published through LEGO and Little, Brown Books for Young Readers in late 2015.

Papercutz, 2011–2014.

Vol. 1: Challenge of the Samukai. 2011. 64pp. 978-1-59707-297-7.
Vol. 2: Mask of the Sensei. 2012. 64pp. 978-1-59707-310-3.
Vol. 3: Rise of the Serpentine. 2012. 64pp. 978-1-59707-325-7.
Vol. 4: Tomb of the Fangpyre. 2012. 64pp. 978-1-59707-329-5.
Vol. 5: Kingdom of the Snakes. 2012. 64pp. 978-1-59707-356-1.
Vol. 6: Warriors of Stone. 2013. 64pp. 978-1-59707-378-3.
Vol. 7: Stone Cold. 2013. 64pp. 978-1-59707-410-0.
Vol. 8: Destiny of Doom. 2013. 64pp. 978-1-59707-481-0.
Vol. 9: Night of the Nindroids. 2014. 64pp. 978-1-59707-707-1.
Vol. 10: The Phantom Ninja. 2014. 64pp. 978-1-59707-718-7.
Vol. 11: Comet Crisis. 2014. 64pp. 978-1-62991-046-8.

Little Brown Books for Young Readers, 2015– .

Vol. 1: Tournament of Elements. 2015. 80pp. 978-0-316-26608-6.
Vol. 2: Ghost Ninja. 2016. 80pp. 978-0-316-26611-6.
Dark Island Trilogy, Part 1. 2016. 144pp. 978-0-316-35702-9.
Dark Island Trilogy, Part 2. 2016. 144pp. 978-0-316-35706-7.
Dark Island Trilogy, Part 3. 2016. 144pp. 978-0-316-35708-1.

Lone Wolf and Cub. Written by **Kazuo Koike**. Illustrated by **Goseki Kojima**. Dark Horse Comics, 2014–2016. O. Japanese manga. 🎬 ◎ 🎞
The classic and epic journey of a widowed and disgraced Ronin (wandering samurai) Itto Ogami and his infant son Daigoro on their long and bloody road to revenge and redemption by the sword. Set firmly with the code of Bushido and honor, they sell their "special services" to people in need as "assassins-for-hire" while traveling the Japanese countryside to confront those who framed Itto and to destroy the assassins who killed his wife. As the body count rises, Itto walks the path of the assassin to become the perfect killer-for-hire, but after miles and miles of wandering, can he finally clear his name and find a way out of the darkness and bloodshed? The series won an Eisner Award in 2001 in the category of Best U.S. Edition of Foreign Material and Harvey Award for Best Graphic Album of Previously Published Work (2002), as well as Best American Edition of Foreign Material (2001–2003). The manga series was adapted into six live-action films and released in 1972–1974. This is a second printing of the series, collecting the original 28 volumes into larger-sized editions.

Vol. 1. 2013. 712pp. 978-1-61655-134-6.
Vol. 2. 2013. 700pp. 978-1-61655-135-3.
Vol. 3. 2013. 720pp. 978-1-61655-200-8.
Vol. 4. 2014. 694pp. 978-1-61655-392-0.
Vol. 5. 2014. 712pp. 978-1-61655-393-7.
Vol. 6. 2014. 696pp. 978-1-61655-394-4.
Vol. 7. 2015. 680pp. 978-1-61655-569-6.
Vol. 8. 2015. 672pp. 978-1-61655-584-9.
Vol. 9. 2015. 672pp. 978-1-61655-585-6.
Vol. 10. 2015. 696pp. 978-1-61655-806-2.
Vol. 11. 2016. 736pp. 978-1-61655-807-9.
Vol. 12. 2016. 720pp. 978-1-61655-808-6.

New Lone Wolf and Cub. Written by **Kazuo Koike**. Illustrated by **Hideki Mori**. Dark Horse Comics, 2014–2016. M. Japanese manga. ◎

A sequel to one of the highly regarded manga of all time by its original creator Kazuo Koike. Set immediately after the events of the conclusion of the original series, young Daigoro, the son of the Ronin, Itto Ogami, is rescued by the mysterious bearded samurai, Shigetada Tōgō, who takes in the boy and seeks to continue his training. Soon the two of them become embroiled in a plot by the Shogunate to topple the Satsuma clan. The series was originally published in Japan beginning from 2003 through 2006.

Vol. 1. 2014. 216pp. 978-1-59307-649-8.
Vol. 2. 2014. 208pp. 978-1-61655-357-9.
Vol. 3. 2014. 240pp. 978-1-61655-358-6.
Vol. 4. 2015. 248pp. 978-1-61655-359-3.
Vol. 5. 2015. 232pp. 978-1-61655-360-9.
Vol. 6. 2015. 264pp. 978-1-61655-361-6.
Vol. 7. 2015. 248pp. 978-1-61655-362-3.
Vol. 8. 2016. 232pp. 978-1-61655-363-0.
Vol. 9. 2016. 232pp. 978-1-61655-364-7.
Vol. 10. 2016. 232pp. 978-1-61655-365-4.
Vol. 11. 2016. 232pp. 978-1-61655-366-1.

The Nameless City. Written and Illustrated by **Faith Erin Hicks**. First Second Books, 2016– . Y 🦌 ◎

© Faith Erin Hicks and
First Second

There exists a city that has been conquered since time immeasurable. Though the city is now in the hands of the Dao clan, the true inhabitants of the city could care less. There were men before who took over the city and there will be more after the Dao. Kaidu is a Dao, but he's not the warrior in training he was meant to be. More interested in books than blades, he befriends Rat, a young native of the city his people have conquered. Though she's considered to be less than human, with her aid, Kaidu sees the city and the role his people have played in it in a whole new light. The series is still ongoing at the time of printing and is planned to be a trilogy. In 2017 the first volume was recognized by YALSA's Great Graphic Novels for Teens annual selection list.

Vol. 1. 2016. 240pp. 978-1-62672-157-9, hardcover; 978-1-62672-156-2.
Vol. 2: The Stone Heart. 2017. 256pp. 978-1-62672-159-3, hardcover; 978-1-62672-158-6.

Naruto. Written and Illustrated by **Masashi Kishimoto**. VIZ Media, LLC., 2003–2015. T. Japanese manga. ◎ あ 🦌

Naruto is set in a world much like our own where ninja clans and their magic are commonplace. Twelve years ago a nine-tailed demon fox appeared in the Konohagakure village and was defeated only after one Shinobi—the Fourth

NARUTO © 1999 by Masashi
Kishimoto/SHUEISHA Inc.

Hokage—sacrificed his life to seal the demon inside an infant boy named Uzumaki Naruto. Now, Naruto has grown into a 12-year-old orphan ruffian who is reckless and obscene, but also skilled and confident that he will be the greatest Hokage ever. Though the village is fearful that his powers as the nine-tailed fox may one day return, the village elder Hokage has faith in him. With the help of his teachers Iruka and Kakashi and his newfound friends (and sometimes rivals) Sasuke and Sakura, Naruto continues to fight against the prejudices of the townsfolk and does whatever it takes to prove he's going to be the best Hokage ever. Volume 28 heralded a change in the series as the manga skipped several years into the future with Naruto now an older teenager. The manga series also inspired a hit Japanese anime television show currently airing in North America. The new launch of the series earned recognition by the Great Graphic Novels for Teens selection list in 2009. VIZ Media has also begun issuing the books in their three in one format, but it is not included in this listing. After the conclusion of the original series, a single special was released in Japan called *Naruto: The Seventh Hokage and the Scarlet Spring*, which features an older Naruto now a Hokage in his village. A new series called <u>Boruto</u> debuted in 2016 and features the son of Naruto.

Vol. 1. 2003. 192pp. 978-1-56931-900-0.
Vol. 2. 2003. 216pp. 978-1-59116-178-3.
Vol. 3. 2004. 208pp. 978-1-59116-187-5.
Vol. 4. 2004. 200pp. 978-1-59116-358-9.
Vol. 5. 2004. 200pp. 978-1-59116-359-6.
Vol. 6. 2005. 192pp. 978-1-59116-739-6.
Vol. 7. 2005. 192pp. 978-1-59116-875-1.
Vol. 8. 2005. 192pp. 978-1-4215-0124-6.
Vol. 9. 2006. 208pp. 978-1-4215-0239-7.
Vol. 10. 2006. 208pp. 978-1-4215-0240-3.
Vol. 11. 2006. 208pp. 978-1-4215-0241-0.
Vol. 12. 2006. 208pp. 978-1-4215-0242-7.
Vol. 13. 2007. 192pp. 978-1-4215-1087-3.
Vol. 14. 2007. 184pp. 978-1-4215-1088-0.
Vol. 15. 2007. 184pp. 978-1-4215-1089-7.
Vol. 16. 2007. 200pp. 978-1-4215-1090-3.
Vol. 17. 2007. 200pp. 978-1-4215-1652-3.
Vol. 18. 2007. 200pp. 978-1-4215-1653-0.
Vol. 19. 2007. 200pp. 978-1-4215-1654-7.
Vol. 20. 2007. 200pp. 978-1-4215-1655-4.
Vol. 21. 2007. 200pp. 978-1-4215-1855-8.
Vol. 22. 2007. 200pp. 978-1-4215-1858-9.
Vol. 23. 2007. 200pp. 978-1-4215-1859-6.
Vol. 24. 2007. 200pp. 978-1-4215-1860-2.
Vol. 25. 2007. 200pp. 978-1-4215-1861-9.
Vol. 26. 2007. 200pp. 978-1-4215-1862-6.
Vol. 27. 2007. 200pp. 978-1-4215-1863-3.

Vol. 28. 2008. 200pp. 978-1-4215-1864-0.
Vol. 29. 2008. 192pp. 978-1-4215-1865-7.
Vol. 30. 2008. 192pp. 978-1-4215-1942-5.
Vol. 31. 2008. 192pp. 978-1-4215-1943-2.
Vol. 32. 2008. 184pp. 978-1-4215-1944-9.
Vol. 33. 2008. 192pp. 978-1-4215-2001-8.
Vol. 34. 2009. 192pp. 978-1-4215-2002-5.
Vol. 35. 2009. 192pp. 978-1-4215-2003-2.
Vol. 36. 2009. 192pp. 978-1-4215-2172-5.
Vol. 37. 2009. 192pp. 978-1-4215-2173-2.
Vol. 38. 2009. 192pp. 978-1-4215-2174-9.
Vol. 39. 2009. 192pp. 978-1-4215-2175-6.
Vol. 40. 2009. 192pp. 978-1-4215-2841-0.
Vol. 41. 2009. 192pp. 978-1-4215-2842-7.
Vol. 42. 2009. 192pp. 978-1-4215-2843-4.
Vol. 43. 2009. 192pp. 978-1-4215-2929-5.
Vol. 44. 2009. 192pp. 978-1-4215-3134-2.
Vol. 45. 2009. 192pp. 978-1-4215-3135-9.
Vol. 46. 2009. 192pp. 978-1-4215-3304-9.
Vol. 47. 2010. 200pp. 978-1-4215-3305-6.
Vol. 48. 2010. 208pp. 978-1-4215-3474-9.
Vol. 49. 2010. 200pp. 978-1-4215-3475-6.
Vol. 50. 2011. 208pp. 978-1-4215-3497-8.
Vol. 51. 2011. 200pp. 978-1-4215-3498-5.
Vol. 52. 2011. 192pp. 978-1-4215-3957-7.
Vol. 53. 2011. 216pp. 978-1-4215-4049-8.
Vol. 54. 2012. 200pp. 978-1-4215-4102-0.

Vol. 55. 2012. 200pp. 978-1-4215-4152-5.
Vol. 56. 2012. 200pp. 978-1-4215-4207-2.
Vol. 57. 2012. 192pp. 978-1-4215-4306-2.
Vol. 58. 2012. 208pp. 978-1-4215-4328-4.
Vol. 59. 2012. 192pp. 978-1-4215-4942-2.
Vol. 60. 2013. 208pp. 978-1-4215-4943-9.
Vol. 61. 2013. 224pp. 978-1-4215-5248-4.
Vol. 62. 2013. 192pp. 978-1-4215-5619-2.
Vol. 63. 2013. 192pp. 978-1-4215-5885-1.

Vol. 64. 2014. 192pp. 978-1-4215-6139-4.
Vol. 65. 2014. 192pp. 978-1-4215-6455-5.
Vol. 66. 2014. 192pp. 978-1-4215-6948-2.
Vol. 67. 2014. 192pp. 978-14215-7384-7.
Vol. 68. 2014. 192pp. 978-14215-7682-4.
Vol. 69, 2015. 192pp. 978-14215-7856-9.
Vol. 70. 2015. 192pp. 978-14215-7975-7.
Vol. 71. 2015. 208pp. 978-14215-8176-7.
Vol. 72. 2015. 205pp. 978-14215-8284-9.

Naruto: The Seventh Hokage and the Scarlet Spring. 2016. 216pp. 978-1-42158-493-5. T. Japanese manga.

A spin-off from the original <u>Naruto</u> series featuring an older Naruto who is now a Hokage in his peaceful village. The main focus is on Sarada, an 11-year-old girl, who is looking for more information from her father and comes across Lord Seventh (Naruto) who helps her on Sarada's quest to find her lost father.

Ninjak. Valiant Entertainment, 2013– . T

In the original 1994 Valiant Comics version of Ninjak written by Mark Moretti with art by Joe Quesada and Jimmy Palmiotti, the main character was the son of a master spy who trained as a ninja to avenge his father's death. The 1997 Acclaim version from Kurt Busiek turned him into a teenager who gained powers from a video game. The recent Valiant Entertainment version by Matt Kindt with art by Butch Guice, Clay Mann, and others went back to the spy aspect but also tied him into the X-O Manowar storyline. Issues of the Moretti title were collected in a Valiant Masters book, with the Kindt stories being collected in softcover editions.

Ninjak, 1st series. Written by **Mark Moretti**. Illustrated by **Joe Quesada**, **Jimmy Palmiotti**, and **Kevin VanHook**. Valiant Entertainment, 2013. T

Valiant Masters: Ninjak. 2013. 184pp. 978-1-9393-4601-8.

Ninjak, 3rd series. Written by **Matt Kindt**. Illustrated by **Butch Guice** and various. Valiant Entertainment.

© Valiant Entertainment

Vol. 1: Weaponeer. 2015. 176pp. 978-1-9393-4666-7.
Vol. 2: The Shadow Wars. 2015. 144pp. 978-1-9393-4694-0.

Ningen's Nightmares. Written and Illustrated by **J.P. Kalonji**. Dark Horse Comics, 2013. 120pp. 978-1-59582-859-0. O

A follow-up to *365 Samurai and a Few Bowels of Rice*, an ancient Japanese witch named Hannya seeks to use the samurai warrior-monk Ningen's enlightened body and spirit to resurrect the demon-samurai named Atsumori and unleash a dark age in Japan ruled by chaos. Now Ningen must protect the innocent and himself from bounty hunters on his trail and prevent the evil from resurrecting.

Ningen's Nightmares © 2016
J.P. Kalonji.

Okko. Written and Illustrated by **Hub**. Archaia Entertainment, 2007– . M

Set in fictional medieval Japan called the Pagan Empire, the series focuses on the adventures of a samurai named Okko and his faithful companions—the mysterious masked Noburo, Noshin the monk, and young Tikku—as they roam the empire hunting demons. The series was originally published in France in five cycles. The final volume has yet to be published in English at the time of this printing.

Vol. 1: Cycle of Water. 2007. 112pp. 978-1-932386-45-5, hardcover.
Vol. 2: Cycle of Earth. 2010. 128pp. 978-1-932386-55-4, hardcover.
Vol. 3: Cycle of Air. 2011. 104pp. 978-1-932386-92-9, hardcover.
Vol. 4: Cycle of Fire. 2014. 136pp. 978-1-608864-10-2, hardcover.

Orphan Blade. Written by **M. Nicholas Almand**. Illustrated by **Jake Myler**. Oni Press, 2014. 160pp. 978-1-620101-209. O

Set in a world where animal life isn't sacred and revered, a young orphaned teenager named Hadashi loses his hand in a battle against a monstrous beast and is kicked out of his dojo where he grew up. He's taken in by Katz, a young ninja boy, and a young woman named Soyako, where he earns his keep. When Hadashi sees the Five Fingers of Death battling, he is merged with the mysterious weapon called the Orphan Blade—a special weapon that is controlling him as well to a new destiny to fight evil!

Samurai. Written by **Jean-Francois Di Giorgio**. Illustrated by **Frederic Genet**. Soleil/ Marvel Comics, 2009; Titan Comics, 2015. M

Reprinted from the French, Takeo had a mysterious past—he was abandoned by his brother years earlier and grew up alone in a monastery, but now as a man he's become a noble samurai and a defender of the Emperor. When General Akuma is revealed to betray the Emperor, Takeo must seek to undo the plot. Little does he know that his past is tied into the mysteries person known as the 13th prophet and their destinies are intertwined.

Vol. 1: Legend. 2009. 192pp. 978-0-7851-3235-6, hardcover.
Collected Edition Vols. 1–4: The Heart of the Prophet. 2015. 192pp. 978-1-78276-337-6, hardcover.
Vol. 5: The Unnamed Island. 2016. 48pp. 978-1-78276-541-7, hardcover.

© Titan Comics

Samurai: Heaven and Earth. Written by **Ron Marz**. Illustrated by **Luke Ross**. Dark Horse Comics, 2005–2007. T

In the year 1704, when his beloved is captured by his enemies, a lone samurai warrior risks everything to rescue her. Traveling from his native Japan to distant lands in the empire of China, across Europe, to the streets of Paris, his swords are tested against the best blades of the lands, but neither Heaven nor Earth can stop him from his epic journey to be reunited with his beloved.

Vol. 1. 2005. 120pp. 978-1-59307-388-6.
Vol. 2. 2007. 144pp. 978-1-59307-839-3.

© 2007 Ron Marz and Luke Ross

Samurai: The Graphic Novel. Written and Illustrated by various. Hyperwerks, 2011. 64pp. 978-0-9770213-5-2. O

An anthology collection telling short stories of the feudal age of Japan and the honorable path of the samurai.

Samurai Jack. Written by **Jim Zub**. Illustrated by **Andy Suriano**. IDW Publishing, 2013–2016. Y ◎ ▯

Based on the hit Cartoon Network animated series created by Genndy Tartakovsky which originally aired from 2002 to 2004. When the fearsome embodiment of evil, Aku, conquered his home in feudal Japan, a lone samurai warrior who wielded his father's enchanted katana stepped forth to oppose Aku. Before the final blow was struck, Aku hurtled the samurai into the far distant future, where Aku now rules supreme. Now the samurai—known in the far future as "Jack"—roams a bizarre future where robots, cyborgs, aliens, and bounty hunters roam. In search of a way back in time, Jack seeks to return to the past and under the future created by Aku. In 2017 a new <u>Samurai Jack</u> animated series debuted and seeks to conclude the battle between Jack and Aku. The *Classics* two-volume collections reprint short *Samurai Jack* stories originally published by DC Comics, while the 2016 collection *Tales of the Wandering Warrior* collects the entire IDW series by Jim Zub and Andy Suriano.

© TM & © Cartoon Network. © IDW Publishing, a division of Idea and Design Works, LLC

Vol. 1. 2014. 120pp. 978-1-61377-894-4.
Vol. 2: The Scotsman's Curse. 2014. 120pp. 978-1-63140-131-2.
Vol. 3. The Quest for the Broken Blade. 2015. 120pp. 978-1-63140-245-6.
Vol. 4. The Warrior-King. 2015. 120pp. 978-1-63140-380-4.
Tales of the Wandering Warrior. 2016. 444pp. 978-1-63140-709-3.

Samurai Jack Classics. **2013–2014**

Vol. 1. 2013. 132pp. 978-1-61377-781-7.
Vol. 2. 2014. 148pp. 978-1-61377-937-8.

Teenage Mutant Ninja Turtles. Written and Illustrated by **Kevin Eastman**, **Peter Laird**, and various. IDW Publishing, 2012– . T ▢ ▤ 🐾

> When four baby turtles are splashed by radioactive waste, they mutate into humanoid-like reptiles. Named after the masters of art—Leonardo, Donatello, Michelangelo, and Raphael—by their wise master Splinter, a sewer rat who was also mutated by the goo, they're also known as the Teenage Mutant Ninja Turtles. Trained in the martial arts and each skilled in the ways of a specialized weapon of choice, the Turtles are a fierce and disciplined fighting force against their arch-enemy Oroku Saki—otherwise known as the Shredder—and his ninja clan known as The Foot, as well as other villains including the dinosaur-like Triceratons and the mutant Krang. Their adventures take them to different realms, worlds, time lines, and more as they team up with characters such as the masked vigilante Casey Jones, the robot Fugitoid, and even the samurai rabbit Ronin Usagi Yojimbo. The series was originally created by Kevin Eastman and Peter Laird in 1984. The series has been adapted into many animated series over the years, most recently in 2012 on Nickelodeon as well as many feature films and video games. Other <u>Teenage Mutant Ninja Turtles</u> series not listed here can be found on the IDW Publishing web site.

Teenage Mutant Ninja Turtles (***original series***). Written and Illustrated by **Kevin Eastman**, **Peter Laird**, and **Michael Dooney**. IDW Publishing, 2012–2016. T

> IDW Publishing reprinted the original Teenage Mutant Ninja Turtles comic books by the original creators from their first appearance in 1984. The first few issues were originally more of a dark homage to Frank Miller's *Daredevil* stories. The original series was published from 1984 to 1993. The *Ultimate Collection* books are printed in their original black and white format, while the collections called *The Works* are reprinted in recolored full color editions.

> ### *Ultimate Collection*, 2012–2016
>
> *Vol. 1*. 2012. 312pp. 978-1-61377-007-8, hardcover.
> *Vol. 2*. 2012. 256pp. 978-1-61377-088-7, hardcover.
> *Vol. 3*. 2012. 288pp. 978-1-61377-138-9, hardcover.
> *Vol. 4*. 2013. 248pp. 978-1-61377-496-0, hardcover.
> *Vol. 5*. 2013. 204pp. 978-1-61377-553-0, hardcover.
> *Vol. 6*. 2016. 256pp. 978-1-63140-389-7, hardcover.
>
> ### *The Works*. 2013–2016
>
> *Vol. 1*. 2013. 308pp. 978-1-61377-625-4, hardcover.
> *Vol. 2*. 2013. 256pp. 978-1-61377-763-3, hardcover.
> *Vol. 3*. 2014. 276pp. 978-1-63140-083-4, hardcover.
> *Vol. 4*. 2015. 240pp. 978-1-63140-473-3, hardcover.
> *Vol. 5*. 2016. 240pp. 978-1-63140-635-5, hardcover.

Teenage Mutant Ninja Turtles, 2nd series. Written by **Kevin Eastman**, and **Tom Waltz**. Illustrated by **Kevin Eastman**, **Dan Duncan**, **Mateus Santolouco**, **Cory Smith**, and various. IDW Publishing, 2012– . T

> Beginning in 2012, IDW Publishing began its own take on the <u>Teenage Mutant Ninja Turtles</u>. The series features input by original TMNT creator Kevin Eastman and has

incorporated many elements from the series, gaining inspiration from the various incarnations of the animated series, films, and the original comics.

Vol. 1: Change Is Constant. 2012. 104pp. 978-1-61377-139-6.

Vol. 2: Enemies Old, Enemies New. 2012. 104pp. 978-1-61377-288-1.

Vol. 3: Shadows of the Past. 2012. 104pp. 978-1-61377-405-2.

Vol. 4: Sins of the Fathers. 2013. 104pp. 978-1-61377-568-4.

Vol. 5: Krang War. 2013. 104pp. 978-1-61377-640-7.

Secret History of the Foot Clan. 2013. 104pp. 978-1-61377-609-4.

Vol. 6: City Fall, Part 1. 2013. 104pp. 978-1-61377-783-1.

Vol. 7: City Fall, Part 2. 2014. 104pp. 978-1-61377-876-0.

Vol. 8: Northhampton. 2014. 104pp. 978-1-61377-984-2.

Vol. 9: Monsters, Misfits, and Madness. 2014. 104pp. 978-1-6314-0132-9.

Vol. 10: New Mutant Order. 2015. 104pp. 978-1-63140-233-3.

Vol. 11: Attack on Technodrome. 2015. 104pp. 978-1-63140-341-5.

Vol. 12: Vengeance, Part 1. 2015. 104pp. 978-1-63140-450-4.

Vol. 13: Vengeance, Part 2. 2016. 104pp. 978-1-63140-523-5.

Vol. 14: Order from Chaos. 2016. 104pp. 978-1-63140-612-6.

Vol. 15: Leatherhead. 2016. 120pp. 978-1-63140-746-8.

Vol. 16: Chasing Phantoms. 2017. 120pp. 978-1-63140-859-5.

Vol. 17: Desperate Measures. 2017. 120pp. 978-1-63140-968-4.

Micro Series, Vol. 1. 2012. 104pp. 978-1-61377-232-4.

Micro Series, Vol. 2. 2012. 104pp. 978-1-61377-415-1.

Villains Micro Series, Vol. 1. 2013. 104pp. 978-1-61377-799-2.

Villains Micro Series, Vol. 2. 2014. 104pp. 978-1-61377-925-5.

Teenage Mutant Ninja Turtles: New Animated Adventures. Written by **Kenny Byerly**, **Scott Tipton**, **David Tipton**, and various. Illustrated by **Dario Brizuela** and various. IDW Publishing, 2014–2016. Y

Debuting on the Nickelodeon cable channel in 2012, the animated series has been a tremendous hit for the cable network. Now in its fourth season, the animated adventures of Mike, Leo, Don, and Raph are as strong as ever. The comic book series by IDW Publishing is directly tied into the show and features a more humorous take on the Ninja Turtles.

Vol. 1. 2014. 104pp. 978-1-61377-856-2.

Vol. 2. 2014. 104pp. 978-1-61377-962-0.

Vol. 3. 2014. 104pp. 978-1-63140-112-1.

Vol. 4. 2015. 104pp. 978-1-63140-209-8.

Vol. 5. 2015. 104pp. 978-1-63140-326-2.

Vol. 6. 2015. 104pp. 978-1-63140-396-5.

Omnibus Vol. 1. 2016. 256pp. 978-1-63140-599-0.

Omnibus, Vol. 2. 2016. 268pp. 978-1-63140-806-9.

Usagi Yojimbo. Written and Illustrated by **Stan Sakai**. Fantagraphics (Books 1–7), Dark Horse Comics (Books 8–up), 1987– . T 🌱 ◎

In a story loosely based on the life of Miyamoto Musashi, one of Japan's best-known and beloved samurai, Miyamoto Usagi is a rabbit Ronin (masterless samurai) warrior roaming an anthropomorphized feudal Japan following the death of his lord. Kind-hearted and noble as the most honorable samurai yet deadly with a blade, Usagi is on a journey across Japan that is marked with death, suffering, danger, heartache, yet also great humor and joy. His journey is not easy. It's lined with conspirators, mysteries, murder, deceptive ninja clans, demonic assassins, and more. But with a colorful cast of companions including the stubborn rhinoceros samurai Gen, the fox thief Kitsune, Usagi's lion-like Master Katsuichi, Chizu of the Neko Ninja clan, the dog-like Inspector Ishida, and Usagi's "nephew," the young and brave Jotaro, it is not a lonely road but one paved with friendship. *Space Usagi* is the adventures of Usagi Yojimbo's descendant in the far future, and the publication *Yokai* (2009) is the first Usagi Yojimbo story hand painted in honor of the 25th anniversary of the series. The hardcover special *Senso* (2015) tells a tale of an alien invasion set 15 years in the future. The series has won numerous awards including Eisner Awards for Best Lettering (1993), Talent Deserving of Wider Recognition (1996), and Best Serialized Story (1999). The collections *Grasscutter* and *Duel at Kitanoji* received recognition by YALSA's Popular Paperbacks for Young Adults committee in 2002 and 2004, respectively.

Book 1: Samurai. 1987. 152pp. 978-0-930193-35-5.
Book 2: Ronin. 1989. 144pp. 978-0-930193-88-1.
Book 3: The Wanderer's Road. 1989. 152pp. 978-1-56097-009-5.
Book 4: The Dragon Bellow Conspiracy. 1990. 179pp. 978-1-56097-063-7.
Book 5: Lone Goat and Kid. 1992. 160pp. 978-1-56097-088-0.
Book 6: Circles. 1994. 144pp. 978-1-56097-146-7.
Book 7: Gen's Story. 1996. 184pp. 978-1-56097-304-1.
Book 8: Shades of Death. 1997, 2nd edition. 200pp. 978-1-59582-278-9.
Book 9: Daisho. 1998, 2nd edition. 216pp. 978-1-59582-279-6.
Book 10: The Brink of Life and Death. 1998, 2nd edition. 216pp. 978-1-59582-280-2.
Book 11: Seasons. 1999. 208pp. 978-1-56971-375-4.
Book 12: Grasscutter. 1999. 256pp. 978-1-56971-413-3.
Book 13: Grey Shadows. 2000. 208pp. 978-1-56971-459-1.
Book 14: Demon Mask. 2001. 224pp. 978-1-56971-523-9.
Book 15: Grasscutter II—Journey to Atsuta Shrine. 2002. 184pp. 978-1-56971-660-1.
Book 16: The Shrouded Moon. 2003. 184pp. 978-1-56971-883-4.
Book 17: Duel at Kitanoji. 2003. 224pp. 978-1-56971-973-2.
Book 18: Travels with Jotaro. 2004. 208pp. 978-1-59307-220-9.
Book 19: Fathers and Sons. 2005. 184pp. 978-1-59307-319-0.
Book 20: Glimpses of Death. 2006. 184pp. 978-1-59307-549-1.
Book 21: The Mother of Mountains. 2007. 184pp. 978-1-59307-783-9.
Book 22: Tomoe's Story. 2008. 184pp. 978-1-59307-947-5.
Book 23: Bridge of Tears. 2009. 248pp. 978-1-59582-298-7.
Book 24: Return of the Black Soul. 2010. 192pp. 978-1-59582-472-1.
Book 25: Fox Hunt. 2011. 192pp. 978-1-59582-726-5.
Book 26: Traitors of the Earth. 2012. 978-1-59582-910-8.
Book 27: A Town Called Hell. 2013. 208pp. 978-1-59582-970-2.

Book 28: Red Scorpion. 2014. 184pp. 978-1-61655-398-2.
Book 29: Two Hundred Jizo. 2015. 208pp. 978-1-61655-840-6.
Book 30: Thieves and Spies. 2016. 208pp. 978-1-50670-048-9.
Book 31: The Hell Screen. 2017. 208pp. 978-1-50670-187-5.
Space Usagi. 1998. 296pp. 978-1-56971-290-0.
Yokai. 2009. 64pp. 978-1-59582-362-5.
Senso. 2015. 168pp. 978-1-61655-709-6, hardcover.

The Usagi Yojimbo Saga. 2014– .

Usagi Yojimbo™ © 2016
Stan Sakai

Beginning in 2014, Dark Horse Comics has reprinted its entire collection of Usagi Yojimbo volumes in its catalog in larger-sized massive collections. Seven volumes are currently in print.

Vol. 1. 2014. 632pp. 978-1-61655-671-6, hardcover; 978-1-61655-609-9.

Vol. 2. 2015. 672pp. 978-1-61655-672-3, hardcover; 978-1-61655-610-5.

Vol. 3. 2015. 616pp. 978-1-61655-673-0, hardcover; 978-1-61655-611-2.

Vol. 4. 2015. 616pp. 978-1-61655-674-7, hardcover; 978-1-61655-612-9.

Vol. 5. 2015. 552pp. 978-1-61655-918-2, hardcover; 978-1-61655-613-6.
Vol. 6. 2016. 600pp. 978-1-61655-915-1, hardcover; 978-1-61655-614-3.
Vol. 7. 2016. 600pp. 978-1-5067-0046-5, hardcover; 978-1-61655-615-0.
Legends. 2017. 600pp. 978-1-50670-323-7.

Vagabond. Written and Illustrated by **Takehiko Inoue**. VIZ Media, 2002–2015. M. Japanese manga. ◎

© 1998-2008 I.T. Planning, Inc.

The epic life of Miyamoto Musashi (1584–1645), one of Japan's best-known and beloved samurai and creator of bushido: the code of the samurai. From his humble beginnings as a dishonored 17-year-old soldier named Takezô, he's on a long, violent, and bloody path to find spiritual enlightenment by the sword. Based on the Japanese fictionalized biography "Musashi" by Eiji Yoshikawa, 37 volumes of this highly regarded series were published in Japan. Beginning in 2008, VIZ Media has reprinted the series in its VIZ BIG editions which reprint three volumes in one edition.

Vol. 1. 2002. 248pp. 978-1-59116-034-2.
Vol. 2. 2002. 240pp. 978-1-59116-035-9.
Vol. 3. 2002. 228pp. 978-1-59116-049-6.
Vol. 4. 2002. 228pp. 978-1-56931-854-6.
Vol. 5. 2002. 208pp. 978-1-56931-893-5.
Vol. 6. 2002. 216pp. 978-1-56931-894-2.
Vol. 7. 2003. 200pp. 978-1-59116-073-1.
Vol. 8. 2004. 200pp. 978-1-59116-119-6.
Vol. 9. 2004. 216pp. 978-1-59116-256-8.

Vol. 10. 2004. 208pp. 978-1-59116-340-4.
Vol. 11. 2004. 224pp. 978-1-59116-396-1.
Vol. 12. 2004. 216pp. 978-1-59116-434-0.
Vol. 13. 2004. 216pp. 978-1-59116-451-7.
Vol. 14. 2004. 200pp. 978-1-59116-452-4.
Vol. 15. 2004. 200pp. 978-1-59116-453-1.
Vol. 16. 2004. 200pp. 978-1-59116-454-8.
Vol. 17. 2004. 192pp. 978-1-59116-455-5.
Vol. 18. 2004. 200pp. 978-1-59116-642-9.

Vol. 19. 2005. 200pp. 978-1-59116-643-6.
Vol. 20. 2005. 224pp. 978-1-59116-583-5.
Vol. 21. 2006. 208pp. 978-1-4215-0741-5.
Vol. 22. 2006. 200pp. 978-1-4215-0818-4.
Vol. 23. 2006. 208pp. 978-1-4215-0826-9.
Vol. 24. 2007. 208pp. 978-1-4215-0827-6.
Vol. 25. 2007. 208pp. 978-1-4215-0975-4.
Vol. 26. 2007. 208pp. 978-1-4215-1983-8.
Vol. 27. 2008. 208pp. 978-1-4215-2008-7.
Vol. 28. 2008. 208pp. 978-1-4215-2708-6.

Vol. 29. 2009. 200pp. 978-1-4215-3148-9.
Vol. 30. 2009. 200pp. 978-1-4215-3438-1.
Vol. 31. 2010. 200pp. 978-1-4215-3631-6.
Vol. 32. 2010. 208pp. 978-1-4215-3813-6.
Vol. 33. 2010. 208pp. 978-1-4215-3814-3.
Vol. 34. 2013. 200pp. 978-14215-4930-9.
Vol. 35. 2014. 240pp. 978-1-4215-6445-6.
Vol. 36. 2014. 224pp. 978-1-4215-6953-6.
Vol. 37. 2015. 200pp. 978-1-4215-7744-9.

VIZBIG Edition printings, 2008–2015

Vol. 1. 2008. 728pp. 978-1-4215-2054-4.
Vol. 2. 2008. 632pp. 978-1-4215-2244-9.
Vol. 3. 2009. 616pp. 978-1-4215-2245-6.
Vol. 4. 2009. 648pp. 978-1-4215-2246-3.
Vol. 5. 2009. 624pp. 978-1-4215-2247-0.
Vol. 6. 2010. 584pp. 978-1-4215-2280-7.

Vol. 7. 2010. 640pp. 978-1-4215-2281-4.
Vol. 8. 2010. 624pp. 978-1-4215-2282-1.
Vol. 9. 2010. 600pp. 978-1-4215-2313-2.
Vol. 10. 2011. 612pp. 978-1-4215-2915-8.
Vol. 11. 2012. 632pp. 978-1-4215-4929-3.
Vol. 12. 2015. 632pp. 978-1-4215-7334-2.

Spies/Espionage

Graphic novel tales involving spies, secret agents, and more, typically out to stop some fiendish James Bond–type villain out to control the world. Like the prose tales, spy films and television shows such as the *James Bond* film series that have helped to inspire the subgenre, the tales feature fast pacing, suspense, dangerous escapes, exotic locations, a dash of romance, and a heaping amount of dastardly villains.

XIII. Written by **Jean Van Hamme**. Illustrated by **William Vance**. Cinebook, 2010– . T
📖 🎮

A man wakes up on a beach on the East Coast of the United States, but is suffering from amnesia. With no memory of his life, his only clues are a tattoo of the Roman numeral XIII and a picture of him with the widow of a U.S. Army captain. Soon he finds himself on the run from a contract killer who was hired by a mysterious organization known only as XX. Conspiracies and adventure are around every corner as XIII seeks to find out his real identity and uncover out to get him. The series was originally published in Belgium and is still ongoing. The series was adapted as a hit video game as well as a television series in Canada.

Vol. 1: The Day of the Black Sun. 2010. 48pp. 978-1-84918-039-9.
Vol. 2: Where the Indian Walks. 2010. 48pp. 978-1-84918-040-5.
Vol. 3: All the Tears of Hell. 2010. 48pp. 978-1-84918-051-1.
Vol. 4: SPADS. 2010. 48pp. 978-1-84918-058-0.
Vol. 5: Full Red. 2011. 48pp. 978-1-84918-065-8.
Vol. 6: The Jason Fly Case. 2011. 48pp. 978-1-84918-073-3.
Vol. 7: The Night of August Third. 2011. 48pp. 978-1-84918-078-8.
Vol. 8: Thirteen to One. 2011. 48pp. 978-1-84918-089-4.
Vol. 9: For Maria. 2011. 48pp. 978-1-84918-093-1.
Vol. 10: El Cascador. 2011. 48pp. 978-1-84918-102-0.
Vol. 11: Three Silver Watches. 2012. 48pp. 978-1-84918-109-9.

Vol. 12: The Trial. 2012. 48pp. 978-1-84918-114-3.
Vol. 13: Top Secret. 2012. 48pp. 978-1-84918-121-1.
Vol. 14: Release the Hounds. 2012. 48pp. 978-1-84918-128-0.
Vol. 15: Operation Montecristo. 2012. 48pp. 978-1-84918-134-1.
Vol. 16: Maximilian's Gold. 2012. 48pp. 978-1-84918-139-6.
Vol. 17: The Irish Version. 2013. 48pp. 978-1-84918-145-7.
Vol. 18: The Last Round. 2013. 48pp. 978-1-84918-151-8.
Vol. 19: The Day of the Mayflower. 2014. 48pp. 978-1-84918-221-8.
Vol. 20: The Bait. 2015. 48pp. 978-1-84918-238-6.
Vol. 21: Return to Green Falls. 2016. 48pp. 978-1-84918-301-7.

Amazing Agent Jennifer. Written by **Nunzio Defilippis** and **Christina Weir**. Illustrated by **Kriss Sison**. Seven Seas Entertainment, LLC, 2011–2012. T. Neo-manga.

A prequel to the <u>Amazing Agent Luna</u> series featuring Control—Luna's tough-as-nails boss in her younger and less-experienced days. All secret agents no matter how good they are still were novices once. Meet Jennifer Kajiwara—a rookie who aspires to become a master secret agent, but she's got a lot to learn to prove she can be one of the best!

Vol. 1. 2011. 192pp. 978-1-934876-85-5.
Vol. 2. 2012. 192pp. 978-1-935934-09-7.
Complete Collection. 2012. 352pp. 978-1-935934-82-0.

Amazing Agent Luna. Written by **Nunzio Defilippis** and **Christina Weir**. Illustrated by **Shiei**. Seven Seas Entertainment, LLC., 2005–2015. T. Neo-manga. ◎

© 2016 Seven Seas Entertainment

The world's best spy has just taken on her most difficult case of all: high school! Meet Luna, a 15-year-old secret agent, who was created from the best genetic material to be the ultimate spy for the United States. Sent to a prestigious high school to unveil a plot by the devious Count Von Brucken, she's finding that being a typical teen isn't as easy as it sounds, especially when she finds herself falling for Jonah, the Count's son!

Vol. 1. 2005. 192pp. 978-1-933164-00-7.
Vol. 2. 2005. 192pp. 978-1-626920-12-5.
Vol. 3. 2006. 192pp. 978-1-933164-10-6.
Vol. 4. 2007. 192pp. 978-1-933164-50-2.

Vol. 5. 2008. 192pp. 978-1-934876-39-8.
Vol. 6. 2010. 192pp. 978-1-934876-89-3.
Vol. 7. 2011. 192pp. 978-1-934876-46-6.
Vol. 8. 2012. 192pp. 978-1-935934-19-6.

Vol. 9. 2013. 192pp. 978-1-626920-12-5.
Vol. 10. 2014. 192pp. 978-1-937867-80-5.
Vol. 11. 2015. 192pp. 978-1-626920-90-3.

Omnibus Collection, 2008–2015.

Vol. 1. 2008. 496pp. 978-1-933164-74-8.
Vol. 2. 2009. 496pp. 978-1-934876-66-4.
Vol. 3. 2012. 496pp. 978-1-935934-15-8.
Vol. 4. 2014. 496pp. 978-1-937867-73-7.
Vol. 5. 2015. 320pp. 978-1-626921-34-4.

Casanova. Written by **Matt Fraction**. Illustrated by **Gabriel Bá**. Image Comics, 2014–2015. M

Casanova Quinn is an excellent thief, but when his secret agent sister is murdered, he joins the agency known as E.M.P.I.R.E., which is run by his father. But secrets come out involving, among other things, parallel worlds and Casanova finds himself working both for and against E.M.P.I.R.E. The first volume was originally published by Image and then reprinted by Marvel, which published the next two volumes. As this is a creator-owned work, it went back to Image which printed all three volumes in hardcover editions.

Vol. 1: Luxuria. 2014. 168pp. 978-1-6321-5161-2, hardcover.
Vol. 2: Gula. 2015. 168pp. 978-1-6321-5181-0, hardcover.
Vol. 3: Avaritia. 2015. 176pp. 978-1-6321-5191-9, hardcover.

Danger Girl. Written by **Andy Hartnell** and **J. Scott Campbell**. Illustrated by **J. Scott Campbell**. IDW Publishing, 2011– . O

Who says that spying is only for dashing men like James Bond? Enter the Danger Girls, a sexy trio of lady super-spies guaranteed to break men's hearts and save the world at the same time. Join up with explorer Abbey Chase and her fellow Danger Girl team of Sydney Savage, Natalia Kassle, and Silicon Valerie as they fight the evil Hammer Empire, a neo-fascist regime with delusions of world conquest, with plenty of Indiana Jones–like treasure hunts, car chases, gun fights, kung-fu, and light-hearted humor. Lead by the mysterious elder spy named 'Deuce,' there's nothing the ultra-secret spy group can't do.

Deluxe Edition. 2011. 262pp. 978-1613770-62-7.
Destination Danger. 2011. 208pp. 978-1600108-76-1.
Revolver. 2012. 104pp. 978-1613772-15-7.
Trinity. 2013. 104pp. 978-1613777-36-7.
Back in Black. 2014. 104pp. 978-1631400-75-9.
The Chase. 2014. 104pp. 978-1613779-04-0.
Mayday. 2014. 104pp. 978-1631400-48-3.

Gunslinger Girl. Written and Illustrated by **Yu Aida**. Seven Seas Entertainment, 2011–2013. O あ Japanese manga.

© 2016 Seven Seas Entertainment

The Social Welfare Agency is not what it seems—it's a place where injured and battered young girls are given a second chance at life. . . and are programmed to be the most lethal assassins. Henrietta is one such girl. Given a second chance at life, she's now a cyborg killer with the mind of a young girl. Assigned a handler named Giuseppe to whom she is devoted, will Henrietta be able to balance being a cold-blooded killer with her emotions? The manga was also adapted into an anime, which originally aired in Japan. The six omnibus collections collect the first 14 volumes with volume 15 providing a finale.

Omnibus Collection, **2011–2013**.

Vol. 1. 2011. 576pp. 978-1-934876-92-3.
Vol. 2. 2011. 576pp. 978-1-934876-97-8.

Vol. 3. 2011. 320pp. 978-1-935934-22-6.
Vol. 4. 2012. 352pp. 978-1-935934-14-1.
Vol. 5. 2012. 352pp. 978-1-935934-83-7.
Vol. 6. 2013. 352pp. 978-1-937867-07-2.
Vol. 15: Finale. 2013. 224pp. 978-1-937867-28-7.

Iron: Or, the War After. Written and Illustrated by **S.M. Vidaurri**. Archaia Entertainment, LLC., 2013. 152pp. 978-1-936393-28-2, hardcover. T

> Sometimes the preceding generations burden their young with the issues they could not see to completion. In a bleak wintery world where anthropomorphic animals live, a horrible war was fought by the animals to decide the fate of their country. Unfortunately, Hardin was on the losing side. He and his rabbit family now live under the rule of the opposition. Hardin and his former comrades go underground to spy and sabotage the government. When Hardin is unexpectedly killed, his son feels as if it is his duty to fill his father's shoes as a spy and complete the mission.

James Bond. Written by **Warren Ellis**. Illustrated by **Jason Masters**. Dynamite Entertainment, 2016– . O

> The return of Ian Fleming's master spy, James Bond, Special Agent 007! After a mission in Helsinki, James Bond returns to London where he picks up a mission of a fallen 00 Section agent in Berlin. Bond thinks he's there to break up a particularly nasty drug-trafficking operation, but what he finds there is far deadlier than he could ever expect. In Volume 2, Bond takes on a SPECTRE ghost cell that has been waiting in the wings to strike. The series is still ongoing.

© 2016 Dynamite Entertainment

> *Vol. 1: VARGR.* 168pp. 978-1-60690-901-0, hardcover.
> *Vol. 2: Eidolon.* 978-1-5241-0272-2, hardcover.

Queen and Country: The Definitive Edition. Written by **Greg Rucka**. Illustrated by **Steve Lieber**, **Carla Speed McNeil**, **Jason Alexander**, and various. Oni Press, 2008–2009. O

> There's a top-secret organization in the United Kingdom dedicated to handling worldwide espionage in the name of the Queen. Lead agent/operative Tara Chace is the best sharpshooter in the agency, and together with her crew, they're the best offense defending England. Every action has a consequence, and for every hit they perform, another more dire circumstance can rise in its place and cost them their very lives. The series won an Eisner Award in 2002 for Best New Series.

© 2016 Oni Press and Greg Rucka

> *Vol. 1.* 2008. 376pp. 978-1-932664-87-4.
> *Vol. 2.* 2008. 376pp. 978-1-932664-89-8.
> *Vol. 3.* 2008. 276pp. 978-1-932664-96-6.
> *Vol. 4.* 2009. 320pp. 978-1-934964-13-2.

Red. Written by **Warren Ellis**. Illustrated by **Cully Hamner**. DC Comics, 2009. 128pp. 978-1-4012-2346-5. M

> When the new director of the CIA ordered a hit on one of its retired hitmen, he bit off more than he could chew. Paul Moses has done some terrible things in the name of his government, but now he is trying to enjoy what life he has left in retirement. After surviving an assassination attempt, Agent Moses comes out of retirement to get revenge on his former employers for ruining his peace. This book is bloody, action packed, and a very quick read. The graphic novel was adapted into the hit 2010 movie starring Bruce Willis, Helen Mirren, and Morgan Freeman, and it inspired the 2013 sequel *Red 2*.

The Secret Service: Kingsman. Written by **Mark Millar** and **Matthew Vaughn**. Illustrated by **Dave Gibbons**. Marvel Comics, 2014. 176pp. 978-0-7851-6545-3, hardcover; 978-0-7851-9277-0. M

> Eggsy is a young Londoner delinquent on the verge of ending up in jail. That is until his Uncle Jack recruits him into the world of Secret Agents. Can Eggsy change his ways in time to save the world? The graphic novel was translated on the big screen in 2015 as *Kingsman: The Secret Service*, which was followed in 2017 by *Kingsman: The Golden Circle*.

© 2016 Marvel Comics

S.H.I.E.L.D. Written by **Mark Waid**. Illustrated by **Carlos Pacheco** and **Greg Smallwood**. Marvel Comics, 2015– . T

> A tie-in to the *Marvel's Agents of S.H.I.E.L.D*. TV show. Special Agent Phil Coulson and his team of agents are on the field ready to handle the human and superhuman bad buys that normal law enforcement can't handle.
>
> *Vol. 1: Perfect Bullets*. 2015. 144pp. 978-0-7851-9362-3.
> *Vol. 2: A Man Called D.E.A.T.H*. 2016. 136pp. 978-0-7851-9363-0.

S.H.I.E.L.D. *by Jim Steranko: The Complete Collection*. Written by **Jim Steranko**, **Stan Lee**, and **Roy Thomas**. Illustrated by **Jim Steranko** and **Jack Kirby**. Marvel Comics, 2013. 352pp. 978-0-7851-8536-9. T

> Originally published in the Marvel 1960s title Strange Tales, Nick Fury, the one-eyed, cigar-chomping former super-soldier from World War II, is now an agent for the Supreme Headquarters, International Espionage, Law-Enforcement Division (S.H.I.E.L.D.), the United States' premiere department of espionage. In their floating Helicarrier in the sky, they're constantly thwarting the terrorist organizations of HYDRA and A.I.M. and playing the spy game one bullet at a time. The series is the inspiration for the ongoing Marvel television show *Marvel's Agents of S.H.I.E.L.D*.

© 2016 Marvel Comics

The Sleeper Omnibus. Written by **Ed Brubaker**. Illustrated by **Sean Phillips**. Vertigo/DC Comics, 2013. 720pp. 978-1-4012-3803-2. M

> Holden Carver is a double agent working for the vicious, super-powered criminal organization called Tao. Tired of the escalating body count, Holden longs to cut his ties, but the only man who can acquit him is in a coma. What can Holden do to escape the game when it becomes harder and harder to differentiate the good guys from the bad guys?

Velvet. Written by **Ed Brubaker**. Illustrated by **Steve Epting**. Image Comics, 2014–2016. M

> When the world's best secret agent is killed, all the evidence points that the personal secretary to the director of the agency, Vanessa Templeton, committed the unthinkable crime! But Vanessa has a dark secret of her own: she's also one of the world's best secret agents and she's not being framed for a crime she didn't commit!

> *Vol. 1: Before the Living End.* 2014. 128pp. 978-1-60706-964-5.
> *Vol. 2: Secret Lies of Dead Men.* 2015. 128pp. 978-1-63215-234-3.
> *Vol. 3: The Man Who Stole the World.* 2016. 128pp. 978-1-63215-727-0.

Westerns

The American cowboy has been a major entertainment figure ever since 19th-century pulp magazines first dramatized the untamed setting of the Old West. Tales featuring rugged cowboys roaming an untamed landscape and settling their differences with fists and guns were instantly popular with readers. Tales of good and evil where the good guys wore white hats and the bad guys wore black were in such demand that their popularity continued into other media including films, television, and comic books. Western comic books were in their heyday from the late 1930s through the mid-1960s with tie-ins to popular television shows and musicians including the Lone Ranger, Roy Rogers, Gene Autry, and the Durango Kid. Today publishers occasionally revisit the genre, but not with the frequency or zest of its earlier days. Some of the most recent Westerns are of old once-popular DC Comics (*Jonah Hex*) and the genre-crossing horror/Western series such as Image Comics' *Pretty Deadly* and the *Sixth Gun* from Oni Press. Note that several of the titles such as *Daisy Kutter* combine elements of science fiction with it to make them futuristic Western stories, while other titles blend the horror genre with tales set in the Old West.

Big Thunder Mountain Railroad. Written by **Dennis Hopeless**. Illustrated by **Tigh Walker**. Disney Kingdoms/Marvel Comics, 2015. 128pp. 978-0-7851-9701-0, hardcover. Y

> Based on the hit roller-coaster ride at Disney Parks in Anaheim and Orlando, the "wildest ride in the wilderness" is a look back at what made the dangerous gold mine the haunted legend it became. Abigail is the sheltered daughter of Barnabas T. Bullion, and he will do anything to preserve her from the dangers of the Wild Wild West. Abby has other plans—she wants to get away from her maleficent father even if she has to rob her own father's train full of gold!

But she finds that she's over her head when she enters the mine and discovers the truth about it and her father. Will a daughter do whatever it takes to save her family's name even if it means becoming a bandit?

© 2016 Marvel Comics

Cow Boy: A Boy and His Horse. Written by **Nate Cosby**. Illustrated by **Chris Eliopoulos**. Archaia/Boom! Studios, 2014. 112pp. 978-1-60886-419-5. A ✿

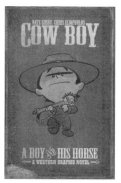

Set in the Old West, a (very) young bounty hunter sets out to send his entire outlaw family to jail! His father, brother, grandfather, and more are all awaiting justice. Also included are short stories by the likes of Roger Langridge, Brian Clevinger, Scott Wegener, Mike Maihack, and Colleen Coover.

© 2016 BOOM! Studios

Django/Zorro. Written by **Quentin Tarantino** and **Matt Wagner**. Illustrated by **Esteve Polls**. Dynamite Entertainment, 2015. 192pp. 978-1-60690-759-7, hardcover. O

The official sequel to the cult-classic Western film *Django Unchained* (2012). Set several years after the movie, Django is roaming the West as a bounty hunter, while in the Southwest he encounters an older Diego de la Vega. Diego hires Django as a bodyguard and together they become involved in a fight to free the local indigenous people from brutal servitude. The original film was adapted in 2013 as a graphic novel by DC Comics.

Gus and His Gang. Written and Illustrated by **Chris Blain**. First Second, 2008. 176pp. 978-1-59643-170-6. M

Gus and his gang, Clem and Gratt, rob anything from trains to banks. Their outlaw lifestyle allows these three stooges to pursue their interests in their downtime, and those interests always seem to be related to women. Gus uses his quick wits to come up with plans not only for their next heist but to also for chasing another lady. Gratt uses his charm and luck to always have his next catch. Clem is the most mature of the bunch as he has to think about his wife and daughter back on the prairie. Only when he is seduced by a red-headed photographer does his straight and narrow path veer drastically. Clem now carries a huge guilty conscience but cannot refuse his attraction to the wild-eyed jezebel. His affair outshines any exploits his two friends could ever hope for.

Jonah Hex

Created by **John Albano** and **Tony DeZuniga**. DC Comics, 2005–2015. T

Jonah Hex is perhaps DC Comics' best-known Western character. A scarred-faced bounty hunter in the American West of the 1870s, Hex has encountered all sorts of criminals, occasionally teamed up with other Western adventurers, and even time-traveled. The *Showcase* editions and *Welcome to Paradise* collections feature some of his earlier adventures by such creators as Michael Fleisher, John Albano, and Tony DeZuniga. *Shadow West* is one of several Hex stories written for DC's Vertigo line, while the two series by Palmiotti and Gray are more recent works. Hex has appeared in various cartoons and television programs as well as a 2010 film where he was played by Josh Brolin.

© 2016 DC Comics

Showcase Presents Jonah Hex. Written and Illustrated by various. 2005–2014.

    Vol. 1. 2005. 528pp. 978-1-4012-0760-1.
    Vol. 2. 2014. 544pp. 978-1-4012-4106-3.

Jonah Hex: Welcome to Paradise. 2010. 168pp. 978-1-4012-2757-9.

Jonah Hex: Shadows West. Written by **Joe Landsdale**. Illustrated by **Tim Truman**. 2014. 392pp. 978-1-4012-4715-7.

Jonah Hex. Written by **Jimmy Palmiotti** and **Justin Gray**. Illustrated by 2006–2011.

    Vol. 1: Face Full of Violence. 2006. 144pp. 978-1-4012-1095-3.
    Vol. 2: Guns of Vengeance. 2007. 144pp. 978-1-4012-1249-0.
    Vol. 3: Origins. 2007. 144pp. 978-1-4012-1490-6.
    Vol. 4: Only the Good Die Young. 2008. 144pp. 978-1-4012-1689-4.
    Vol. 5: Luck Runs Out. 2008. 144pp. 978-1-4012-1960-4.
    Vol. 6: Lead Poisoning. 2009. 144pp. 978-1-4012-2485-1.
    Vol. 7: Bullets Don't Lie. 2009. 144pp. 978-1-4012-2157-7.
    Vol. 8: Six Gun War. 2010. 144pp. 978-1-4012-2587-2.
    Vol. 9: Counting Corpses. 2010. 160pp. 978-1-4012-2899-6.
    Vol. 10: Tall Tales. 2011. 144pp. 978-1-4012-3009-8.
    Vol. 11: No Way Back. 2011. 136pp. 978-1-4012-2550-6, hardcover; 978-1-4012-2551-3.
    Vol. 12: Bury Me in Hell. 224pp. 2011. 978-1-4012-3249-8.

All-Star Western. Written by **Jimmy Palmiotti** and **Justin Gray**. Illustrated by **Moritat** and **Staz Johnson**. 2012–2015.

    Vol. 1: Guns and Gotham. 2012. 192pp. 978-1-4012-3709-7.
    Vol. 2: The War of Lords and Owls. 2013. 192pp. 978-1-4012-3851-3.

Vol. 3: The Black Diamond Probability. 2013. 224pp. 978-1-4012-4399-9.
Vol. 4: Gold Standard. 2014. 176pp. 978-1-4012-4626-6.
Vol. 5: Man Out of Time. 2014. 192pp. 978-1-4012-4993-9.
Vol. 6: End of the Trail. 2015. 144pp. 978-1-4012-5413-1.

The Lone Ranger. Written by **Brett Matthews**, **Ande Parks**, and **Chuck Dixon**. Illustrated by **Sergio Cariello** and **Esteve Polls**. Dynamite Entertainment, 2008– . T

© 2016 Dynamite Entertainment

The Lone Ranger was created by George W. Trendle and developed by writer Fran Striker originally as a radio show in 1933. He quickly gained fame and spawned books, a 1949–1957 TV show series starring Clayton Moore, films, and comic books. The man who became the Lone Ranger was John Reid, a Texas ranger who was left for dead when chasing down a villainous group alongside his fellow rangers. Rescued by his old friend, a Native American named Tonto, Reid was healed back to health and vowed to avenge the death of the innocents and his fellow rangers. He honors his Rangers past and wears a black mask and white cowboy hat. Calling himself the Lone Ranger, both he and Tonto set the tone for justice in the Old West.

Lone Ranger, 2008– .

Vol. 1: Now and Forever. 2008. 160pp. 978-1-93330-539-4, hardcover.
Vol. 2: Lines Not Crossed. 2008. 128pp. 978-1-93330-566-0, hardcover.
Vol. 3: Scorched Earth. 2009. 200pp. 978-1-60690-031-4, hardcover.
Vol. 4: Resolve. 2010. 140pp. 978-1-60690-118-2, hardcover.
Vol. 5: Hard Country. 2012. 136pp. 978-1-60690-346-9.
Vol. 6: Native Ground. 2013. 144pp. 978-1-60690-401-5.
Vol. 7: Back East. 2014. 144pp. 978-1-60690-478-7.
Vol. 8. Long Road Home. 2014. 160pp. 978-1-60690-563-0.
Lone Ranger and Tonto. 2011. 128pp. 978-1-60690-123-6.
The Lone Ranger/Zorro: The Death of Zorro. 2012. 128pp. 978-1-60690-157-1.
Snake of Iron. 2013. 92pp. 978-1-60690-396-4.
Vindicated. 2015. 112pp. 978-1-60690-699-6.
Lone Ranger/Green Hornet: Champions of Justice. 2017. 148pp. 978-1-52410-294-4.

Lone Ranger Omnibus. 2013– .

Vol. 1. 2013. 632pp. 978-1-60690-352-0.

The Man with No Name. Dynamite Entertainment, 2009–2010. O

© 2016 Dynamite
Entertainment

Based on the mysterious anti-hero from the classic Sergio Leone Spaghetti Western films—*A Fistful of Dollars* (1964), *For a Few Dollars More* (*1965*), and *The Good, the Bad and the Ugly* (1966). The role was played by actor Clint Eastwood, and he was a nameless bounty hunter roaming the Old West. The Dynamite Entertainment series is set after the events of the last film as the nameless anti-hero nicknamed as "Blondie" travels from town to town always finding trouble.

The Man with No Name. Written by **Christos N. Gage**. Illustrated by **Wellington Dias**. Dynamite Entertainment, 2009–2010. T

> *Vol. 1: Sinners and Saints*. 2009. 168pp. 978-1-60690-012-3.
> *Vol. 2: Holiday in the Sun*. 2010. 144pp. 978-1-60690-131-1.

The Good, the Bad, and the Ugly. Written by **Chuck Dixon**. Illustrated by **Esteve Polls**. Dynamite Entertainment, 2010. 168pp. 978-1-60690-124-3.

Zorro. Written by **Matt Wagner** and **Don MacGregor**. Illustrated by **Matt Wagner**, **Francesco Francavilla**, **Mike Mayhew**, and **Cezar Razek**. Dynamite Entertainment, 2009– . O 🎬

© 2016 Dynamite Entertainment

Before Batman, there was a masked hero who came before all others: Zorro! Created in 1919 by pulp writer Johnston McCulley, the hero is Don Diego de la Vega, a nobleman and master swordsman living in the Spanish colonial era of California. His signature look is a black costume with a flowing Spanish cape, a flat-brimmed Andalusian-style hat, and a black cowl mask that covers the top of the head to protect his identity. His preferred weapon is a rapier—which he uses to mark his signature letter Z with three quick slashes—but he is also known to use a bullwhip and a gun on occasion. He is one of the most enduring Western heroes and has been in film, television, and books for almost a century.

Zorro, *first series*. 2009–2010.

Vol. 1: Year One: Trail of the Fox. 2009. 208pp. 978-1-60690-026-0.
Vol. 2: Clashing Blades. 2010. 152pp. 978-1-60690-116-8.
Vol. 3: Tales of the Fox. 2011. 144pp. 978-1-60690-236-3.

Zorro Rides Again. 2012–2014.

Vol. 1. 2012. 144pp. 978-1-60690-271-4.
Vol. 2: Wrath of Lady Zorro. 2014. 152pp. 978-1-60690-454-1.

Zorro: Matanzas. 2010. 104pp. 978-1-60690-147-2.
Zorro Omnibus, *Vol. 1*. 2015. 544pp. 978-1-60690-506-7.

Western Genre Blends: The Weird West

Tales of the Old West but with a twist. Some of the most popular takes on Westerns involve blending other genres with the common themes found in Western tales. Two of the most popular blended genres of Westerns are Western Horror and Science Fiction Westerns.

Western Horror stories of the Old West feature a hero, typically a mysterious cowboy, who comes to a town that has been overrun by an evil presence and only a six-shooter can take care of the horrific menace. Readers who enjoy this subgenre may also enjoy titles listed in Chapter 5.

Scientific Westerns features a setting in the Old West, but the story featuring other tropes of science fiction as part of the story such as robots, spaceships, and aliens is commonplace among the cowboys. Readers of this subgenre may enjoy other titles listed in Chapter 3.

Black Jack Ketchum. Written by **Brian Schirmer**. Illustrated by **Jeremy Saliba** and **Claudia Balboni**. Image Comics, 2016– . O

> Set in the Weird West, a man named Thomas Ketchum is mistaken for Black Jack Ketchum, a notorious outlaw. With his talking sidearm, Thomas is accompanied by a mute girl with a Winchester rifle, and a mysterious gambler as they evade the law and their faceless supernatural enforcers called The Dusters. Is Thomas really Black Jack Ketchum, or is he going insane?
>
> *Vol. 1*. 2016. 128pp. 978-1-63215-703-4.

Copperhead. Written by **Jay Faerber**. Illustrated by **Scott Godlewski** and **Ron Riley**. Image Comics, 2015– . O

> Set on another planet, Clara Bronson is the new sheriff of Copperhead, a grimy mining town on the edge of a backwater planet. A single mother, life on the far frontier isn't easy—and she'll have to deal with a resentful deputy, alien hillbillies, a shady mining tycoon, and a massacre that she'll have to solve. No one said life in the West would be easy! The series is still ongoing.
>
> *Vol. 1*. 2015. 128pp. 978-1-63215-221-3.
> *Vol. 2*. 2015. 128pp. 978-1-63215-471-2.

Cowboys and Aliens. Written by **Fred Van Lente** and **Andrew Foley**. Illustrated by **Luciano Lima**. Platinum Studios, 2006. 112pp. 978-0-06-164665-2. T 🎬

> Set in the Wild West in 1873, the prairie was home to many skirmishes between the Native Americans and Western settlers. But when an alien invasion from outer space sees all the humans as slaves, all of mankind must come together to defeat the strange outer space visitors. The book was the original source material for the 2011 movie of the same name starring Daniel Craig and Harrison Ford.

Daisy Kutter: The Last Train. Written and Illustrated by **Kazu Kibuishi**. Bolt City Productions, 2013. 192pp. 978-0-615-39952-2. T 🎗 ◎

In a futuristic Old West where bandits, robots, and bounty hunters roam the land, Daisy Kutter, ex-bandit extraordinaire of the town of Middleton, has been plagued by boredom. A former gunfighter, she's put away her six-shooters for a legitimate lifestyle and a lonely dead-end job at a general store. When she loses her store in a game of cards, she's offered one last chance to win back her money and her pride—all she has to do is what she did best: rob her very last train. Are the cards in her favor this time—or has Daisy's luck just run out? YALSA's Best Books for Young Adults list recognized the story in 2006. The book was reprinted in 2013 after a successful Kickstarter campaign to reprint it.

Gun Blaze West. Written and Illustrated by **Nobuhiro Watsuki**. VIZ Media, 2008. T. Japanese manga.

> Set in the West, Viu Bannes is a young gunfighter ready to prove he's the best at the Gun Blaze West—a location where every 10 years gunfighters go to prove their mettle—a place that is free of violence. Viu, a fighter at the peak of his game, sets out with a map to the secret location where the competition will be held. Along the way he makes allies and they hope to earn the title while fighting evil along the way.

> *Vol. 1*. 2008. 192pp. 978-1-42151-806-0.
> *Vol. 2*. 2008. 232pp. 978-1-42151-807-7.
> *Vol. 3*. 2008. 216pp. 978-1-42151-808-4.

Pretty Deadly. Written by **Kelly Sue DeConnick**. Illustrated by **Emma Rios**. Image Comics, 2014– . M

© 2016 Image Comics

> When a beautiful bride is locked away in a tower by her husband to keep her from the covetous eyes of other men, she longed for death rather than imprisonment. Death came to her and he fell in love with the woman and she had a child with him—a baby girl named Ginny. The husband, a man named Mason, tried to atone for his mistreatment of his wife and begged Death for her back, but instead a bargain was made at the cost of his eyesight that ultimately Mason could not do. Now he roams the West with a young girl named Foxy who may be the key to the world's salvation or damnation. Meanwhile, Ginny roams the countryside in the name of death as a bringer of justice for women who have been wronged. A Western tale with deep fantasy undertones.

> *Vol. 1: The Shrike*. 2014. 120pp. 978-1-60706-962-1.
> *Vol. 2: The Bear*. 2016. 136pp. 978-1-63215-694-5.

The Sixth Gun. Written by **Cullen Bunn**. Illustrated by **Brian Hurtt** and **Tyler Crook**. Oni Press, 2011–2015. M ◎

© 2016 Oni Press

> Set after the Civil War, a legend tells of six pistols imbued with dark powers. For every owner of that gun, the weapon bestows upon it a powerful but dark power. The wielder carries that power until his or her death. Each gun is numbered one through six—and the sixth gun becomes the property of Becky Montcrief, an innocent girl who was only defending her family. When vile men thought long dead set their sights on retrieving the gun and killing Becky, only a mysterious gunfighter named Drake Sinclair—who wields one of the other six cursed guns—stands in their way.

> *Vol. 1: Cold Dead Fingers*. 2011. 160pp. 978-1-934964-60-6.
> *Vol. 2: Crossroads*. 2011. 160pp. 978-1-934964-67-5.

Vol. 3: Bound. 2012. 120pp. 978-1-934964-78-1.
Vol. 4: A Town Called Penance. 2012. 120pp. 978-1-934964-95-8.
Vol. 5: Winter Wolves. 2013. 160pp. 978-1-620100-77-6.
Vol. 6: Ghost Dance. 2014. 140pp. 978-1-620100-16-5.
Vol. 7: Not the Bullet, but the Fall. 2014. 160pp. 978-1-620101-41-4.
Vol. 8: Hell and High Water. 2015. 160pp. 978-1-620102-46-6.

Wynonna Earp: Strange Inheritance. Written by **Beau Smith**. Illustrated by **Joyce Chin**, **Luis Diaz**, and **Carlos Ferreira**. IDW Publishing, 2016. 300pp. 978-1-63140-602-7. O ▭
Wynonna Earp is following in the footsteps of her famous lawman descendant. A U.S. marshal, she's after capturing a whole new type of villain—she brings the unnatural to justice! From redneck drug-dealing vampires, ancient mummy hitman, and the Egyptian mafia to biker werewolves to name a few! The collection reprints previous stories "Home on the Strange," "Blood Is the Harvest," and "The Yeti Wars." The heroine was adapted into a TV show on the SyFy cable network in 2016.

Chapter 3

Science Fiction

Ever since the days of such classic prose authors such as Mary Shelley and Jules Verne to the works of authors Ray Bradbury and Robert Heinlein, readers have long been interested in speculative fiction tales. With the release of the comic strip adventures of Buck Rogers in 1929, the comic book format soon proved to be an excellent vehicle for this genre. For the first time a science fiction story could be told visually where the only limit was the writer's and illustrator's imagination. Since that time, comic books—and later graphic novels—have been a popular format for telling speculative fiction. Stories ranging from mankind's future both on and off Earth, space exploration, and contacts with alien life to concepts including mind control and telepathy, space operas, robots, science fiction action, and even the funny side of science fiction have all appeared in comic books for decades. Featured here are some of the most recent popular science fiction tales for all ages, including the subjects mentioned above as well as the equally popular variety of media tie-ins such as the *Star Wars* films to toy properties such as the *Transformers*. Note that titles that are a mix of humor and science fiction are listed in the humor chapter.

Space Opera/Space Fantasy

Science fiction stories where epic adventure, romance, action, space battles, and grand interstellar conflicts have prominence in the plot. The central characters' relationships with each other and a conflict that the protagonists must face are more central to the plot than scientific accuracy. The subgenre also is a blending of sorts of the Science Fiction and Fantasy genres. Tales feature stories where common themes from both genres blend together. Science fiction tales including starships, strange new worlds, and space exploration can easily be found alongside themes common in fantasy tales such as wizards, heroes, dragons, quests, and other fantastic elements. This unique vision of a fantastic future or of a technological long ago easily appeals to many for its unique ability to combine the best of both genres. The *Star Wars* movies and Frank Herbert's classic <u>Dune</u> series of novels are some of the best examples of the Space Opera/Space Fantasy subgenre.

The Last Days of an Immortal. Written by **Fabien Velhmann**. Illustrated by **Gwen de Bonneval**. Archaia Entertainment/BOOM! Studios, 2012. 152pp. 978-1-936393-44-2. O

> In the distant future humans have become immortal through the use of "Echoes" or copies of one's self that act autonomously and can be merged with the original so that they both share the same experiences. Through age and experience, immortality has given some humans the unique job of Philosophical Police. It is their job to mediate and understand why aliens throughout the galaxy do certain things. To one alien race something might be taboo or illegal, while in another race it is celebrated and encouraged. Elijah is one of the best Philosophical Police on the force. It is up to him to figure out why two alien races living on the same planet for thousands of years in peace are suddenly on the brink of war. A crime from centuries past may be the key Elijah needs to unraveling what is happening now. The cultural memories of both races may need to be reevaluated. As Elijah helps with their memory, he is beginning to question the value of his own memories.

The Metabarons: Ultimate Collection. Written by **Alexandro Jodorowsky**. Illustrated by **Juan Gimenez**. Humanoids Publishing, 2011. 544pp. 978-1-59465-064-2, hardcover. M

> In a universe where greed, corruption, and terror rule the day, there exist ruthless warriors called the Metabarons, a clan that values blood, self-sacrifice, cybernetic implants, and defeating your own father in battle to secure yourself a right of title as a Metabaron. An epic storyline spanning generations of the Metabarons as they battle against each other for supremacy and the right of title, might, and power.

Micronauts. Written by **Cullen Bunn**. Illustrated by **David Baldeon** and **Max Dunbar**. IDW Publishing, 2016– . T.

> Acroyear, Space Glider, Biotron, and others are on the run from the evil dark-armored Baron Karza. Their world being under threat from an entropy cloud consuming it, the Micronauts are on a quest to try to prevent their universe from dying. The series is based on the original characters based on the Mego Micronauts toy line which originally appeared from 1976 to 1980 which also inspired an original Marvel Comics series 1979–1986. The new IDW series takes a new approach to the source material due to copyright issues with Marvel Comics.
>
> *Vol. 1: Entropy*. 2016. 152pp. 978-1-63140-755-0.
> *Vol. 2: Earthbound*. 2017. 120pp. 978-1-63140-881-6.

The Moon Moth. Written by **Jack Vance**. Adapted and Illustrated by **Humayoun Ibrahim**. First Second, 2012. 128pp. 978-1-59643-367-0. O

> Life on the planet Sirene is dictated by social customs. Everyone must wear a mask, indicating their social status. They also communicate with musical instruments that fit specific social requirements. Therefore, when Edwer Thissell from Earth is sent to Sirene as a political appointee, he must quickly adapt to the unique social life on this planet. Just as Edwer starts to get the hang of everything, he is informed that he must

© 2016 First Second.

stop a murderer arriving on the planet. Just how is Edwer supposed to catch an elusive criminal on a planet where everyone hides behind masks?

Phoenix. Written and Illustrated by **Osamu Tezuka**. VIZ Media, 2002–2008. O. Japanese manga.

> From the legendary manga creator Osamu Tezuka comes an epic tale spanning 12 volumes that was in the making from 1954 and was never completed when Tezuka died in 1989. *Phoenix* is a moral parable spanning centuries, dipping far into the future and then to the past and back again in an exploration of man's quest for immortality, the struggles and strengths of faith, the ridiculousness of war, and the endearing hope for mankind.
>
> *Vol. 1: Dawn*. 2002. 200pp. 978-1-59116-608-5.
> *Vol. 2: A Tale of the Future*. 2002. 200pp. 978-1-59116-026-7.
> *Vol. 3: Yamato/Space*. 2003. 336pp. 978-1-59116-100-4.
> *Vol. 4: Karma*. 2004. 368pp. 978-1-59116-300-8.
> *Vol. 5: Resurrection*. 2004. 200pp. 978-1-59116-593-4.
> *Vol. 6: Nostalgia*. 2006. 208pp. 978-1-4215-0258-8.
> *Vol. 7: Civil War, Part 1*. 2006. 208pp. 978-1-4215-0517-6.
> *Vol. 8: Civil War, Part 2*. 2006. 208pp. 978-1-4215-0518-3.
> *Vol. 9: Strange Beings/Life*. 2006. 208pp. 978-1-4215-0519-0.
> *Vol. 10: Sun, Part 1*. 2007. 344pp. 978-1-4215-0972-3.
> *Vol. 11: Sun, Part 2*. 2007. 344pp. 978-1-4215-0973-0.
> *Vol. 12: Early Works*. 2008. 188pp. 978-1-4215-0974-7.

Rave Master. Written and Illustrated by **Hiro Mashima**. TOKYOPOP, 2003–2009; Kodansha, 2011. T. Japanese manga. あ

> Fifty years ago a dark, evil power known as the Dark Bring was vanquished with the aid of the fabled Rave stones. The blast was so powerful that the Rave stones were scattered into five pieces all around the globe. Now, a sinister society called the Demon Card has once again planned to harness the power of the Dark Bring stones, and the only one who can save the world is Haru Glory, a fun-loving adventuresome 16-year-old boy living on the peaceful Garage Island. He's the only one who can wield the power of the Rave stones and the Rave-powered sword called the "Ten Commandments." Joined with the bizarre-looking snowman dog called Plue who is the only one capable of detecting the missing Rave stones, he's out to retrieve the

missing pieces of the Rave stones, or else the powers of Demon Card and the Dark Bring will engulf the world. An anime series was also released and was based off of the manga.

Vol. 1. 2003. 176pp. 978-1-59182-064-2.

Vol. 2. 2003. 200pp. 978-1-59182-065-9.

Vol. 3. 2003. 192pp. 978-1-59182-210-3.

Vol. 4. 2003. 200pp. 978-1-59182-211-0.

Vol. 5. 2003. 200pp. 978-1-59182-212-7.

Vol. 6. 2003. 208pp. 978-1-59182-213-4.

Vol. 7. 2004. 200pp. 978-1-59182-517-3.

Vol. 8. 2004. 192pp. 978-1-59182-518-0.

Vol. 9. 2004. 208pp. 978-1-59182-519-7.

Vol. 10. 2004. 224pp. 978-1-59182-520-3.

Vol. 11. 2004. 208pp. 978-1-59182-521-0.

Vol. 12. 2004. 208pp. 978-1-59182-522-7.

Vol. 13. 2005. 192pp. 978-1-59532-018-6.

Vol. 14. 2005. 200pp. 978-1-59532-019-3.

Vol. 15. 2005. 192pp. 978-1-59532-020-9.

Vol. 16. 2005. 192pp. 978-1-59532-021-6.

Vol. 17. 2005. 192pp. 978-1-59532-022-3.

Vol. 18. 2005. 192pp. 978-1-59532-023-0.

Vol. 19. 2006. 192pp. 978-1-59532-024-7.

Vol. 20. 2006. 200pp. 978-1-59532-025-4.

Vol. 21. 2005. 192pp. 978-1-59532-026-1.

Vol. 22. 2006. 192pp. 978-1-59532-626-3.

Vol. 23. 2007. 200pp. 978-1-59532-627-0.

Vol. 24. 2007. 208pp. 978-1-59532-628-7.

Vol. 25. 2007. 208pp. 978-1-59532-629-4.

Vol. 26. 2007. 208pp. 978-1-59532-630-0.

Vol. 27. 2008. 208pp. 978-1-59532-631-7.

Vol. 28. 2008. 208pp. 978-159532-632-4.

Vol. 29. 2008. 208pp. 978-159532-809-0.

Vol. 30. 2008. 208pp. 978-159816-192-2.

Vol. 31. 2008. 208pp. 978-159816-193-9.

Vol. 32. 2009. 208pp. 978-159816-194-6.

Vol. 33/34/35. 2011. 576pp. 978-1-935429-73-9.

The Red Star. Written by **Christian Gossett** and **Bradley Kayl**. Illustrated by **Christian Gossett** and **Team Red Star**. IDW Publishing, 2014– . T

© 2016 Team Red Star.

An epic science fiction and sorcery story set in an alternate Earth version of the Soviet Union and Afghanistan conflict. Struggling to free their country of the legacy of the insane wizard Imbohl, the heroes of the Red Star continue on after their personal losses and the deaths of millions of their countrymen. Little do they know that there is something more in play here and the ghosts of the living still participate in a grand battle for the soul of a nation. A complex and awe-inspiring look at a future world where technology and magic go hand in hand and the horrors of war are ever-present. The collections also include URL links to more background information and are more accessible on the company's web site. Beginning in 2014, the series was reprinted in a deluxe format by IDW Publishing.

Deluxe Edition, Vol. 1. 2014. 328pp. 978-1-61377-807-4, hardcover.

Deluxe Edition, Vol. 2. 2016. 324pp. 978-1-63140-176-3, hardcover.

Saga. Written by **Brian K. Vaughan**. Illustrated by **Fiona Staples**. Image Comics. M

In a galaxy far away there is a planet with a moon, each inhabited by a different alien race. Two warring civilizations' ongoing conflict has spread to the reaches of the galaxy. In the middle of this galaxy-wide war are two star-crossed lovers from each side. They must escape persecution while they try to raise their newborn daughter and

© 2016 Brian K. Vaughan and
Fiona Staples.

keep their love together. The series has won many awards including an Eisner, Harvey, and Hugo award.

Vol. 1. 2012. 160pp. 978-1-60706-601-9.
Vol. 2. 2013. 144pp. 978-1-60706-692-7.
Vol. 3. 2014. 144pp. 978-1-60706-931-7.
Vol. 4. 2014. 144pp. 978-1-63215-077-6.
Vol. 5. 2015. 152pp. 978-1-63215-438-5.
Vol. 6. 2016. 152pp. 978-1-63215-711-9.
Vol. 7. 2017. 152pp. 978-1-5343-0060-6.
Deluxe Edition, Vol. 1. 2014. 504pp. 978-1-63215-078-3, hardcover.
Deluxe Edition, Vol. 2. 2017. 504pp. 978-1-63215-903-8, hardcover.

Serenity. Written by **Joss Whedon**, **Zack Whedon**, and **Brett Mathews**. Illustrated by **Will Conrad**. Dark Horse Comics, 2006– . T 🎬

Tie-ins to the cult-hit 2005 science fiction movie based on the television show *Firefly* (2002) from Joss Whedon, creator of *Buffy the Vampire Slayer* and *Angel* and director of *The Avengers* (2012 and 2015) films. In the far future, Captain Malcolm Reynolds is a hardened veteran from the losing side of an interplanetary civil war. He makes a living as a smuggler and transporter of good aboard his ship, *Serenity*. At his side is a loyal crew that is the closest thing he has to family. When Mal takes on two new passengers, a young doctor and his telepathic younger sister, the crew finds they've taken on more than they bargained for. Caught between both the Alliance's military might and the cannibalistic fury of a space-faring band called the Reavers, the crew of the *Serenity* finds that the biggest threat to the galaxy may be a passenger in their own ship. Stories take place both before and after the events of the film, with *The Shepherd's Tale* telling the secret origin of Shepherd Book that was hinted at in the series.

Vol. 1: Those Left Behind. 2006. 104pp. 978-1-59307-449-4.
Vol. 2: Better Days and Other Stories. 2011. 128pp. 978-1-59582-739-5, hardcover.
Vol. 3: The Shepherd's Tale. 2010. 56pp. 978-1-59582-561-2, hardcover.
Vol. 4: Leaves on the Wind. 2014. 152pp. 978-1-61655-489-7, hardcover.

7 Billion Needles. Written and Illustrated by **Nobuaki Tadano**. Vertical, 2010–2011. O. 🎌 Japanese manga.

Inspired by the Hal Clement novel *Needle*, in this Eisner-nominated series, Hikaru Takabe is a teenage girl who is secretly also being used as a host to a being called Horizon. Together they are on the hunt for an interstellar killer bent on killing all of humanity. The series was also selected as one of YALSA's Great Graphic Novels for Teens.

Vol. 1. 2010. 192pp. 978-1-934287-87-3.
Vol. 2. 2010. 180pp. 978-1-934287-95-8.

Vol. 3. 2011. 192pp. 978-1-932234-27-5.
Vol. 4. 2011. 204pp. 978-1-935654-16-2.

Star Wars

Dark Horse Comics, 2006–2014; Marvel Comics, 2015– . A–T 🎬 🖥

In 1977, George Lucas's *Star Wars: Episode IV: A New Hope* was released in theaters to an enthusiastic audience and became a worldwide phenomenon becoming a multimedia juggernaut selling millions of books, action figures, collectibles, and, of course, comic books as well movie tickets. The space fantasy film series continues to be as popular today as ever with the recent release of new *Star Wars* movies starting with *Star Wars: Episode VII: The Force Awakens*, in 2015 shattering box office records. The future also looks bright with the ongoing Rebels animated series which debuted in 2014. The further adventures of Luke Skywalker, Darth Vader, Kylo Ren, Darth Maul, Obi-Wan Kenobi, Ezra Bridger, and more have also been successfully continued in comic book form by both Marvel and Dark Horse Comics. Marvel Comics originally published Star Wars comics from 1977 to 1986, with Dark Horse Comics carrying the license from 1991 to 2014. Beginning in 2015 the license reverted to Marvel Comics after Disney (which owns Marvel) bought both Star Wars and Indiana Jones properties from George Lucas in 2012. Though fans were skeptical of Marvel Comics taking over the line after Dark Horse Comics had done a stellar job for decades, the content published since 2015 has continued to be outstanding. It should be noted that since Marvel Comics now publishes Star Wars, all Star Wars comics published by Marvel Comics as of 2015 are considered to be canon, and all material published prior is not. All material of Dark Horse Comics now being reprinted under Marvel Comics has the imprint title of *Star Wars Legends—Epic Collection*. Due to the high volume of recommended titles, those not listed below can be viewed at www.marvel.com. Older but still relevant Dark Horse Comics titles are also included unless they have been completely reprinted by Marvel Comics. Titles that are highly recommended are listed with brief annotations.

Star Wars *Film Adaptations*

Below are listed the adaptation of the *Star Wars* films. Some adaptations by the publishers have been just a single film only, while others include most of them in a single publication.

The Star Wars. Written by **Jonathan Rinzler**. Illustrated by **Mike Mayhew**. Dark Horse Comics, 2014. 184pp. 978-1-61655-425-5. T

You may be familiar with some of the names and characters, but you've never seen *Star Wars* like this before! For the first time ever, see an adaptation of the first screenplay of *Star Wars* that George Lucas ever created!

Star Wars: The Original Trilogy—A Graphic Novel. Written by **Lucasfilm Book Group**. Illustrated by various. Disney Book Group, 2016. 208pp. 978-1-4847-3784-2, hardcover. A ◎

A kinetic adaptation of the original trilogy of *Star Wars* films. The look of the artwork is reminiscent of a Disney animated film, and the result is a story that leaps off

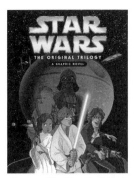

Cover art of Star Wars: The Original Trilogy—A Graphic Novel © 2016 Lucasfilm Ltd. & TM. All Rights Reserved. Used under authorization.

the page with excitement showing Star Wars in a way it's never been shown before.

Star Wars: The Prequel Trilogy—A Graphic Novel. Written by **Lucasfilm Book Group**. Illustrated by various. Disney Book Group, 2017. 208pp. 978-1-368-00274-5, hardcover. A ◎

A follow-up by the Lucasfilm Book Group's adaptation of the original trilogy. Once again while adapting the prequel trilogy of *Star Wars* films, the look of the artwork is reminiscent of a Disney animated film, and the end result is a story that is fresh and exciting look at the rise and fall of Anakin Skywalker.

Star Wars: Episode I: The Phantom Menace. Written by **Henry Gilroy**. Illustrated by **Rodolfo Damaggio**. Marvel Comics, 2016. 120pp. 978-1-302-90074-8, hardcover. A

A reprinting of the original adaptation published by Dark Horse Comics in 1999.

Star Wars: Episode II: The Attack of the Clones. Written by **Henry Gilroy**. Illustrated by **Jan Duursema**. Marvel Comics, 2016. 152pp. 978-1-302-90075-5, hardcover. A

A reprinting of the original adaptation published by Dark Horse Comics in 2002.

Star Wars: Episode III: Revenge of the Sith. Written by **Miles Land**. Illustrated by **Doug Wheatley**. Marvel Comics, 2016. 104pp. 978-1-302-90106-6, hardcover. A

A reprinting of the original adaptation published by Dark Horse Comics in 2005.

Star Wars: Episode IV: A New Hope. Written by **Roy Thomas**. Illustrated by **Howard Chaykin**. Marvel Comics, 2015. 128pp. 978-0-7851-9348-7, hardcover. A

A reprinting of the original adaptation published by Marvel Comics in 1978.

Star Wars: Episode V: The Empire Strikes Back. Written by **Archie Goodwin**. Illustrated by **Al Williamson**. Marvel Comics, 2015. 144pp. 978-0-7851-9367-8, hardcover. A

A reprinting of the original adaptation published by Marvel Comics back in 1983.

Star Wars: Episode VI: The Return of the Jedi. Written by **Archie Goodwin**. Illustrated by **Al Williamson**, **Carlos Garzón**, and **Ron Frenz**. Marvel Comics, 2015. 112pp. 978-0785193692, hardcover. A

> The adaptation by Marvel Comics originally from 1983.

Star Wars: Episode VII: The Force Awakens. Written by **Chuck Wendig**. Illustrated by **Luke Ross**. Marvel Comics, 2016. 144pp. 978-1-302-90178-3, hardcover. A

> A brand-new adaptation of the new film from 2015.

Star Wars Omnibus: Episodes I–VI—The Complete Saga. Written by **Bruce Jones**, **Archie Goodwin**, **Henry Gilroy**, and **Miles Land**. Illustrated by **Eduardo Barreto**, **Al Williamson**, **Rodolfo Damaggio**, **Jan Duursema**, and **Doug Wheatley**. Dark Horse Comics, 2011. 608pp. 978-1-59582-832-3. A

> A reprinting of the original adaptations published by Dark Horse Comics and includes its own adaptation of *A New Hope: The Special Edition*.

Star Wars. Written by **Brian Wood**, **Zack Whedon**, and **Matt Kindt**. Illustrated by **Carlos D'Anda**, **Ryan Odagawa**, **Stéphane Créty**, **Gabe Eltaeb**, and **Marco Castiello**. Dark Horse Comics, 2013–2014. T

> Written by fan-favorite writer Brian Wood, the series is set almost immediately after *A New Hope*. Leia believes there's a spy in their ranks and sets up a secret X-Wing squadron to expose it. Meanwhile, Han Solo and Chewbacca are on a covert mission. Rebel Heist is a stand-alone adventure featuring Han, Luke, and Leia as they, alongside new recruits, pull off a heist right under the noses of the Empire.
>
> *Vol. 1: In the Shadow of Yavin*. 2013. 128pp. 978-1-61655-170-4.
> *Vol. 2: From the Ruins of Alderaan*. 2014. 144pp. 978-1-61655-311-1.
> *Vol. 3: Rebel Girl*. 2014. 96pp. 978-1-61655-483-5.
> *Vol. 4: Shattered Hope*. 2014. 96pp. 978-1-61655-554-2.
> *Rebel Heist*. 2014. 96pp. 978-1-61655-500-9.

Star Wars (current series). Written by **Jason Aaron**. Illustrated by **John Cassaday**, **Mike Mayhew**, and **Leinil Yu**. Marvel Comics, 2015– . T

> The new Marvel Comics series debuted in 2015 and launched to much fanfare. The series also takes place during the time line between A New Hope and The Empire Strikes Back and focuses on the main characters of Han, Luke, and Leia and their struggles against Darth Vader and the Empire. The series is still ongoing and continues to be one of Marvel Comics' most popular titles.
>
> *Vol. 1: Skywalker Strikes*. 2015. 160pp. 978-0-7851-9213-8.
> *Vol. 2: Showdown on the Smuggler's Moon*. 2016. 144pp. 978-0-7851-9214-5.
> *Vol. 3: Rebel Jail*. 2016. 144pp. 978-0-7851-9983-0.
> *Vol. 4: Last Flight of the Harbinger*. 2017. 144pp. 978-0-7851-9984-7.
> *Vol. 5: Yoda's Secret War*. 2017.144pp. 978-1-302-90265-0.

Star Wars Adventures. Written and Illustrated by various. Dark Horse Comics, 2009–2014. A

> A collection of short stories geared for all ages. Each story is self-contained and focuses on a different character from the original trilogy.
>
> *Vol. 1: Han Solo and the Hollow Moon of Khorya.* 2009. 80pp. 978-1-59582-198-0.
> *Vol. 2: Princess Leia and the Royal Ransom.* 2009. 80pp. 978-1-59582-147-8.
> *Vol. 3: Luke Skywalker and the Treasure of the Dragonsnakes.* 2010. 80pp. 978-1-59582-347-2.
> *Vol. 4: The Will of Darth Vader.* 2010. 80pp. 978-1-59582-435-6.
> *Vol. 5: Boba Fett and the Ship of Fear.* 2011. 80pp. 978-1-59582-436-3.
> *Vol. 6: Chewbacca and the Slavers of the Shadowlands.* 2011. 80pp. 978-1-59582-764-7.
> *Omnibus.* 2014. 456pp. 978-1-61655-250-3.

Star Wars: Agent of the Empire. Written by **John Ostrander**. Illustrated by **Stéphane Roux**. Dark Horse Comics, 2012–2013. T ◉

Cover art of Star Wars: Agent of the Empire © 2016 Lucasfilm Ltd. & TM. All Rights Reserved. Used under authorization.

> Not all of the Empire's dealings involve brutal force of Stormtroopers and destruction—some of them require a little bit more finesse. Meet Imperial Intelligence agent Cross, Jahan Cross. Sent on select missions for the Empire, he's a one-man army and ready to go to the most exotic locales on special undercover espionage assignments. With his trusty droid IN-GA 44, there's nothing that he can't handle! James Bond's *Moonraker* has nothing on this master spy!
>
> *Vol. 1: Iron Eclipse.* 2012. 128pp. 978-1-59582-950-4.
> *Vol. 2: Hard Targets.* 2013. 128pp. 978-1-61655-167-4.

Star Wars: Chewbacca. Written by **Gerry Duggan**. Illustrated by **Phil Noto**. Marvel Comics, 2016. 112pp. 978-0-7851-9320-3. T

> Everyone's favorite Wookiee copilot, Chewbacca, gets the spotlight. After the Battle of Yavin, Chewbacca's ship crashes on a planet under Imperial control and needs to get back to the Rebellion. When he finds a young girl named Zarro in need of help on the planet to free her family from enslavement, Chewbacca becomes a one-Wookiee army and comes to her aid.

Star Wars: The Clone Wars. Written by **John Ostrander**, **Haden Blackman**, and various. Illustrated by **Jan Duursema**, **Brian Ching**, and various. 2012. T ◉

> Set between the events of the films *Episode II: Attack of the Clones* (2002) and *Episode III: Revenge of the Sith* (2005), the Clone Wars is the civil war period that will eventually lead to the rise of the evil Galactic Empire as seen in the original trilogy of *Star Wars* films. The Separatists, led by the fallen Jedi Count Dooku and the cyborg General Grievous, battle against the Old

Republic's clone army commanded by the Jedi Knights Yoda, Mace Windu, Obi-Wan Kenobi, and Anakin Skywalker. Meanwhile, the real manipulator of the plot, the Sith Lord called Darth Sidious, waits for the right time to strike and conclude his goal to destroy the Jedi Knights and create a Galactic Empire. The final volume takes place during and immediately after the events of the hit movie *Episode III: Revenge of the Sith*. In 2012, Dark Horse collected the volumes in its popular Omnibus format.

Omnibus Vol. 1: The Republic Goes to War. 2012. 408pp. 978-1-59582-927-6.
Omnibus Vol. 2: Enemy on all Sides. 2012. 398pp. 978-1-59582-958-0.
Omnibus Vol. 3: The Republic Falls. 2012. 416pp. 978-1-59582-980-1.

Star Wars: Clone Wars Adventures. Written by **Haden Blackman** and **Welles Hartley**. Illustrated by **Ben Caldwell**, **Matt Fillbach**, and **Shawn Fillbach**. 2004–2007. A
Short stories from the battlefields as the Republic's army of clone troopers and Jedi Knights including Anakin Skywalker and Obi-Wan Kenobi battle against Count Dooku, General Grievous, and the Separatist droid armies during the epic struggle known as the Clone Wars. Based on the Emmy Award–winning animated microseries by Genndy Tartovsky name that originally aired from 2003 to 2005.

Vol. 1. 2004. 96pp. 978-1-59307-243-8.
Vol. 2. 2004. 96pp. 978-1-59307-271-1.
Vol. 3. 2005. 96pp. 978-1-59307-307-7.
Vol. 4. 2005. 96pp. 978-1-59307-402-9.
Vol. 5. 2006. 96pp. 978-1-59307-483-8.

Vol. 6. 2006. 96pp. 978-1-59307-567-5.
Vol. 7. 2006. 80pp. 978-1-59307-678-8.
Vol. 8. 2007. 80pp. 978-1-59307-680-1.
Vol. 9. 2007. 80pp. 978-1-59307-832-4.
Vol. 10. 2007. 80pp. 978-1-59307-878-2.

Star Wars: The Clone Wars. Written by **Henry Gilroy**, **Ryder Windham**, and various. Illustrated by various. Dark Horse Comics, 2009–2014. ▢ A

Features stories inspired by the popular Clone Wars animated series which originally aired on the Cartoon Network from 2008 to 2014. The series focuses on Obi-Wan Kenobi and Anakin Skywalker, both Jedi Generals in the Clone Wars against the Separatist armies. Anakin has a Padawan apprentice, Ahsoka Tano, a Togruta alien, who is a central character to the series. The story the *Slaves of the Republic* was eventually adapted into a three-part episode of the show.

Crash Course. 2008. 96pp. 978-1-59582-230-7.
Shipyards of Doom. 2008. 96pp. 978-1-59582-207-9.
Colossus of Destiny. 2009. 80pp. 978-1-59582-416-5.

Cover art of Star Wars: Clone Wars Adventures: Vol. III © 2006 Lucasfilm Ltd. & TM. All Rights Reserved. Used under authorization.

Slaves of the Republic. 2009. 144pp. 978-1-59582-349-6.
The Wind Raiders of Taloraan. 2009. 96pp. 978-1-59582-231-4.
Deadly Hands of Shon-Ju. 2010. 80pp. 978-1-59582-545-2.
Hero of the Confederacy. 2010. 80pp. 978-1-59582-552-0.
In the Service of the Republic. 2010. 80pp. 978-1-59582-487-5.
The Starcrusher Trap. 2011. 80pp. 978-1-59582-714-2.
Strange Allies. 2011. 80pp. 978-1-59582-766-1.
The Enemy Within. 2012. 80pp. 978-1-59582-845-3.
The Sith Hunters. 2012. 80pp. 978-1-59582-949-8.
Defenders of the Lost Temple. 2013. 80pp. 978-1-61655-058-5.
Smuggler's Code. 2013. 80pp. 978-1-61655-108-7.

Star Wars: Crimson Empire Saga. Written by **Mike Richardson** and **Randy Stradley**. Illustrated by **Paul Gulacy**. Dark Horse Comics, 2012. 504pp. 978-1-59582-947-4, hardcover. T

Kir Kanos is an Imperial Royal Guard. Clad in a red mask and cloak a pike, he's one of the most loyal bodyguards to Emperor Palpatine and after the fall of the Empire, he's the last. Join Kir as on his journey to become a Royal Guard, his betrayal at the hands of a rogue Royal Guard named Carnor Jax, and Kir's struggle to seek revenge for the death of the Emperor against the hero known as Luke Skywalker. The collection includes the three stories *Crimson Empire*, *Crimson Empire II*, *Crimson Empire III*, plus supplemental material.

Star Wars: Dark Empire Trilogy. Written by **Tom Veitch**. Illustrated by **Cam Kennedy** with **Jim Baikie**. Dark Horse Comics, 2010. 352pp. 978-1-59582-612-1, hardcover. T 🏅 ◎

Cover art of Star Wars: Dark Empire © 2016 Lucasfilm Ltd. & TM. All Rights Reserved. Used under authorization.

Set six years after the destruction of the second Death Star, Luke Skywalker turns to the dark side of the Force to see why his father, Anakin Skywalker, was seduced by it. While embraced in the shadow of the dark side, he joins the reborn Sith Master, Emperor Palpatine, as his new Sith apprentice. The collection includes the stories *Dark Empire*, *Dark Empire II*, and *Empire's End*. The original story *Dark Empire* was the first Star Wars comic book published by Dark Horse Comics in 1991. The collected edition received recognition by YALSA's Quick Picks for Reluctant Readers committee in 1996 and was the first graphic novel fiction title ever recognized by YALSA.

Star Wars: Darth Maul. Written by **Tom Taylor** and **Jeremy Barlow**. Illustrated by **Bruno Redondo** and **Juan Frigeri**. Dark Horse Comics, 2013–2014. T

If you thought that the story of Darth Maul ended with him cut in two by Obi-Wan Kenobi, then you only know half the story! As seen in the *Clone Wars* animated series as well as in the new animated series *Rebels*, the fallen Sith apprentice lived and wrecked havoc across the galaxy. Death Sentence features Maul alongside his brother, Savage Opress, as they deal with a bounty brought on their heads. Son of Dathomir was based off of an unused script for the final season of *The Clone Wars* as Darth Maul and his army comprised of the crime syndicate Black Sun, the Mandalorians known as Death Watch, and the Hutt crime families wage war against the power of Darth Sidious, Darth Tyrannus (aka Count Dooku), and General Grievous.

Death Sentence. 2013. 96pp. 978-1-61655-077-6.
Son of Dathomir. 2014. 96pp. 978-1-61655-551-1.

Star Wars: Darth Vader. 2011–2017. Dark Horse Comics, 2011–2014; Marvel Comics, 2015–2016. T 🏅

Darth Vader, the black-masked Sith Lord, has always been one of the most popular characters in the *Star Wars* films. Formerly a Jedi Knight called

Anakin Skywalker, he was seduced by the Dark Side of the Force and became an apprentice to Darth Sidious—aka Emperor Palpatine. Included below are the various Dark Horse Comics stories focusing on the evil Sith Lord as well as the popular Marvel Comics series written by Kieron Gillen. The latter series from Marvel Comics was recognized on YALSA's 2017 Great Graphic Novels for Teens list.

Cover art of Star Wars: Darth Vader, Vol. 1: Vader © 2016 Lucasfilm Ltd. & TM. All Rights Reserved. Used under authorization.

Darth Vader and the Lost Command. Written by **Haden Blackman**. Illustrated by **Rick Leonardi**. Dark Horse Comics, 2011. 128pp. 978-1-59582-778-4, hardcover.

Darth Vader and the Ghost Prison. Written by **Haden Blackman**. Illustrated by **Agustin Alessio**. Dark Horse Comics, 2013. 120pp. 978-1-61655-059-2, hardcover.

Darth Vader and the Ninth Assassin. Written by **Tim Siedell**. Illustrated by **Stephen Thompson** and **Iván Fernández**. Dark Horse Comics, 2013. 128pp. 978-1-61655-207-7, hardcover.

Darth Vader and the Cry of Shadows. Written by **Tim Siedell**. Illustrated by **Gabriel Guzman**. Dark Horse Comics, 2014. 120pp. 978-1-61655-382-1, hardcover.

Darth Vader. Written by **Kieron Gillen**. Illustrated by **Salvador Larroca**. Marvel Comics, 2015–2017. ◎

>*Vol. 1: Vader.* 2015. 160pp. 978-0-7851-9255-8.
>*Vol. 2. Shadows and Secrets.* 2016. 136pp. 978-0-7851-9256-5.
>*Vol. 3: The Shu-Torun War.* 2016. 120pp. 978-0-7851-9977-9.
>*Vol. 4: End of Games.* 2016. 152pp. 978-0-7851-9978-6.
>*Vol. 1.* 2016. 296pp. 978-1-302-90195-0, hardcover.
>*Vol. 2.* 2017. 432pp. 978-1-302-90220-9, hardcover.

Star Wars: Vader Down. Written by **Jason Aaron**. Illustrated by **Mike Deodato**. Marvel Comics, 2016. 152pp. 978-0-7851-9789-8.

>When Darth Vader is forced to face the Rebel fleet on his own and crash lands on a planet, the Rebels have a chance to destroy one of the most powerful of the symbols of the Empire. But can the Rebels take down one man by themselves, or will Vader show them why he is a Dark Lord of the Sith?

Star Wars: Dark Times. Written by **Randy Stradley**, **Welles Hartley**, and **Mick Harrison**. Illustrated by **Doug Wheatley**, **Dave Ross**, **Gabriel Guzman**, and **Lui Antonio**. Dark Horse Comics, 2008–2014. T

Set after the events of *Revenge of the Sith*, witness the last days of the few remaining Jedi Knights now in hiding as Darth Vader enforces the rule of his master, Emperor Palpatine. The art by Doug Wheatley is one of the highlights of the series as well, and his pencils are featured in the *Dark Times Gallery Edition*.

Vol. 1: The Path to Nowhere. 2008. 120pp. 978-1-59307-792-1.

Vol. 2: Parallels. 2008. 120pp. 978-1-59307-945-1.

Vol. 3: Vector. 2009. 144pp. 978-1-59582-226-0.

Vol. 4: Blue Harvest. 2010. 136pp. 978-1-59582-264-2.

Vol. 5: Out of the Wilderness. 2011. 120pp. 978-1-59582-926-9.

Vol. 6: Fire Carrier. 2012. 128pp. 978-1-61655-173-5.

Vol. 7: Spark Remains. 2014. 128pp. 978-1-61655-262-6.

Omnibus, Vol. 1. 2013. 344pp. 978-1-61655-251-0.

Omnibus, Vol. 2. 2014. 456pp. 978-1-61655-252-7.

Dark Times Gallery Edition. 2014. 248pp. 978-1-61655-675-4, hardcover.

Star Wars: The Force Unleashed. Written by **Haden Blackman**. Illustrated by **Brian Ching** and **Omar Francia**. Dark Horse Comics, 2008–2010. T 🎮

A tie-in to the popular video game series created by LucasArts in 2008 and its sequel in 2010. The story revolves around Galen Marak, a son of a Jedi, during the Jedi purge. Powerful in the Force, he was raised by Darth Vader as his secret apprentice. Codenamed Starkiller, Galen was used to handle secret missions unbeknownst to the Emperor. Over time, Galen becomes a sympathizer to the Rebellion and defects against his master, Darth Vader.

Vol. 1. 2008. 104pp. 978-1-59307-891-1.

Vol. 2. 2010. 88pp. 978-1-59582-553-7.

Star Wars: Han Solo. Written by **Marjorie Liu**. Illustrated by **Mark Brooks**. Marvel Comics, 2017. 112pp. 978-0-7851-9321-0. T

The infamous smuggler is working for the Rebellion on a secret mission to rescue various informants and spies. His cover for the assignment is none other than the biggest race of all time in the galaxy—the Dragon Void. Can Han keep his head in the game and still find a way to win the biggest race in the galaxy, serve the Rebellion, and find the traitor in the Rebellion?

Star Wars: Infinities. Written by **Chris Warner**, **Dave Land**, and **Adam Gallardo**. Illustrated by **Drew Johnson**, **Davide Fabri**, and **Ryan Benjamin**. Dark Horse Comics, 2013; Marvel Comics, 2015. T

A collection of imaginary stories showcasing what could have happened in the original trilogy movies if one thing had changed. What if Luke Skywalker had not destroyed the Death Star in *A New Hope*, what if Luke had died on Hoth and Leia instead became a Jedi Knight in *The Empire Strikes Back*, and what if C-3P0 never was able to serve as a translator droid for Jabba the Hutt?

The stories are familiar to the big screen counterparts but create a unique opportunity for events wished for but never before seen. The Marvel reprinting includes *The Star Wars* adaptation of George Lucas's original screenplay for Star Wars.

Omnibus. 2013. 280pp. 978-1-61655-078-3.
Legends—Epic Collection. 2015. 504pp. 978-0-7851-9725-6.

Star Wars: Invasion. Written by **Tom Taylor**. Illustrated by **Colin Wilson**. Dark Horse Comics, 2009–2011. T

A tie-in to the New Order series of Star Wars novels. Set decades after *Return of the Jedi*, Luke and his Jedi Order must face the threat of the Yuuzhan Vong.

Vol. 1: Refugees. 2010. 144pp. 978-1-59582-479-0.
Vol. 2: Rescues. 2011. 144pp. 978-1-59582-630-5.
Vol. 3: Revelations. 2012. 128pp. 978-1-59582-882-8.

Star Wars: Kanan. Written by **Greg Weisman**. Illustrated by **Pepe Larraz**. Marvel Comics, 2015–2016. T

A tie-in to the Star Wars: Rebels (2014–) show airing on Disney XD. On Rebels, Kanan Jarrus is a smart-mouthed renegade on the run from the Galactic Empire. Before the Jedi purge, Kanan was known as Caleb Dume, Padawan to Jedi Master Depa Billaba. See how Caleb survived the Jedi purge and became the man known as Kanan. The book was on YALSA's 2017 Great Graphic Novels for Teens list.

Vol. 1: The Last Padawan. 2015. 144pp. 978-0-7851-9366-1.
Vol. 2: First Blood. 2016. 144pp. 978-0-7851-9603-7.
Omnibus. 2016. 272pp. 978-1-302-90222-3.

Cover art of Star Wars: Kanan
© 2016 Lucasfilm Ltd. & TM.
All Rights Reserved. Used under
authorization.

Star Wars: Lando. Written by **Charles Soule**. Illustrated by **Alex Maleev**. Marvel Comics, 2016. 112pp. 978-0-7851-9319-7. T

Scoundrel and smooth-talking hero Lando Calrissian is back! Before he was a general in the Rebellion and the administrator of Cloud City, Lando was a swindler and a con man. When Lando has the opportunity to steal a fast ship—but has his luck run out? The book was on YALSA's 2017 Great Graphic Novels for Teens list.

Star Wars: Legacy. Written by **John Ostrander**. Illustrated by **Jan Duursema** and various. Dark Horse Comics, 2007–2012; Marvel Comics, 2016–2017. T ◉

Set 150 years after the events of the film *Return of the Jedi*, the Sith have overtaken the galaxy, but peace is far from over. Luke Skywalker's relative, Cade Skywalker, is a fallen Jedi who has walked away from his heritage and works as a smuggler alongside Delilah Blue and Jariah Syn. With the galaxy in shambles and with a shattered empire vying for control from Darth Krayt, will Cade succumb to the temptations of the dark side of the Force or will he embrace his Skywalker destiny and save the galaxy? In late 2016 the series began to be reprinted by Marvel Comics under its Star Wars: Epic Collection—Legends edition.

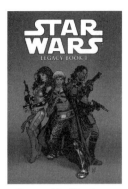

Cover art of Star Wars: Legacy
© 2016 Lucasfilm Ltd. & TM.
All Rights Reserved. Used under
authorization.

Vol. 1: Broken. 2007. 144pp. 978-1-59307-716-7.
Vol. 2: Shards. 2008. 176pp. 978-1-59307-879-9.
Vol. 3: Claws of the Dragon. 2008. 144pp. 978-1-59307-946-8.
Vol. 4: Alliance. 2008. 104pp. 978-1-59582-223-9.
Vol. 5: The Hidden Temple. 2009. 104pp. 978-1-59582-224-6.
Vol. 6: Vector, Vol. 2. 2009. 144pp. 978-1-59582-227-7.
Vol. 7: Storms. 2009. 128pp. 978-1-59582-350-2.
Vol. 8: Tatooine. 2010. 104pp. 978-1-59582-414-1.
Vol. 9: Monster. 2010. 128pp. 978-1-59582-485-1.
Vol. 10: Extremes. 2010. 104pp. 978-1-59582-631-2.
Vol. 11: War. 2012. 144pp. 978-1-59582-802-6.
Vol. 1. 2013. 440pp. 978-1-61655-178-0, hardcover.
Vol. 2. 2013. 424pp. 978-1-61655-209-1, hardcover.
Vol. 3. 2014. 440pp. 978-1-61655-260-2, hardcover.
Star Wars Legends: Epic Collection: Legacy, Vol. 1. 2016. 464pp. 978-1-302-90012-0.

Star Wars: Legacy II. Written by **Corinna Bechko** and **Gabriel Hardman**. Illustrated by **Gabriel Hardman**. Dark Horse Comics, 2013–2014. T

Set generations in the future, meet Ania Solo, the distant relative of Han and Leia Organa Solo. When she discovers a broken communications droid and a lost lightsaber, she's on her way to adventure just like her family before her.

Vol. 1: Prisoner of the Floating World. 2013. 144pp. 978-1-61655-208-4.
Vol. 2: Outcasts of the Broken Ring. 2014. 128pp. 978-1-61655-310-4.
Vol. 3: Wanted: Ania Solo. 2014. 128pp. 978-1-61655-381-4.
Vol. 4: Empire of One. 2014. 112pp. 978-1-61655-553-5.

Star Wars: Obi-Wan and Anakin. Written by **Charles Soule**. Illustrated by **Marco Checchetto**. Marvel Comics, 2016. 112pp. 978-0-7851-9679-2. T

Set in the early days of Anakin's padawan training—Obi-Wan and Anakin journey to a remote planet to aid a native who requested help, but with primitive technology and no way to communicate with the natives, they have come into a situation that may be the breaking point for the Jedi master and his padawan apprentice.

Star Wars: Poe Dameron. Written by **Charles Soule**. Illustrated by **Phil Noto**. Marvel Comics, 2016– . T

A tie-in to the film *The Force Awakens!* Poe Dameron is one of the best X-Wing fighter pilots for the Resistance. See how he went from a pilot with the Republic to following in his parents' footsteps as a leading pilot for the Resistance! Set on a mission by General Leia to seek out locations with historical importance to the Force, he's on a top-secret mission to put the puzzle together and locate the long-absent Luke Skywalker.

Vol. 1: Black Squadron. 2016. 144pp. 978-1-302-90110-3.
Vol. 2: The Gathering Storm. 2017. 144pp. 978-1-302-90111-0.

Star Wars: Princess Leia. Written by **Mark Waid**. Illustrated by **Terry Dodson**. 2015. 120pp. 978-0-7851-9317-3. T

What is a princess without a world? Grieving the loss of her adopted home planet of Alderaan after if it was destroyed by the Death Star, Leia princess is not one to back out of a fight. While doing undercover work on the planet of Sullust, Leia discovers the Empire is rounding up fugitive Alderaanians and that doesn't sit well at all with their princess!

Cover art of Star Wars: Princess Leia © 2016 Lucasfilm Ltd. & TM. All Rights Reserved. Used under authorization.

Star Wars: Purge. Written by **Haden Blackman**, **Alexander Freed**, and **John Ostrander**. Illustrated by **Jim Hall**, **Chris Scalf**, and **Doug Wheatley**. Dark Horse Comics, 2013. 120pp. 978-1-61655-143-8. T ⊚ T

Set during the rise of the Empire, Palpatine is the ruler over the galaxy. The Jedi Knight once known as Anakin Skywalker has now embraced the Dark Side of the Force and has become Palpatine's Sith Apprentice as the black-clad Darth Vader. But there are few Jedi who have escaped the purge known as Order 66—and Darth Vader is there hunting the remaining Jedi.

Cover art of Star Wars: Purge © 2016 Lucasfilm Ltd. & TM. All Rights Reserved. Used under authorization.

Star Wars: The Original Marvel Years. Written and Illustrated by various. Marvel Comics, 2015– . A

A collection of the entire Marvel Comics series that was published originally in comic book form from 1977 through 1986. The stories feature the adventures of Luke, Han, and Leia and the Rebel Alliance in their struggle against the Sith Lord Darth Vader and the evil Galactic Empire. A paperback reprinting of the series was also released beginning in 2016.

Vol. 1. 2015. 880pp. 978-0-7851-9106-3, hardcover.
Vol. 2. 2015. 848pp. 978-0-7851-9342-5, hardcover.
Vol. 3. 2015. 1138pp. 978-0-7851-9346-3, hardcover.
The Original Marvel Years, Vol. 1. 2016. 496pp. 978-1-302-90221-6.
The Original Marvel Years, Vol. 2. 2017. 448pp. 978-1-302-90680-1.

Cover art of Star Wars: The Original Marvel Years © 2016 Lucasfilm Ltd. & TM. All Rights Reserved. Used under authorization.

Star Wars: Shattered Empire. Written by **Greg Rucka**. Illustrated by **Marco Checchetto**. Marvel Comics, 2015. 136pp. 978-0-7851-9781-2. T

Set shortly after the destruction of the second Death Star, see how the early days of the newly built Republic and how the time period slowly gave rise to the events seen decades later in *The Force Awakens*.

Cover art of Star Wars: Shattered Empire © 2016 Lucasfilm Ltd. & TM. All Rights Reserved. Used under authorization.

Star Wars: Tag & Bink Were Here. Written by **Kevin Rubio**. Illustrated by **Lucas Marangon**. Dark Horse Comics, 2007. 104pp. 978-1-59307-641-2. ◎ T

When Tag Greenley and Bink Otauna, two Rebels trapped on a captured freighter carrying a certain Princess Leia, chose life over death and disguised themselves as Stormtroopers, little did they know the trouble they'd see. Now they're reluctant Stormtroopers for the Empire getting into one fine mess after another. Relive the greatest moments from the original trilogy of *Star Wars* films as the hidden heroes in disguise get into disastrous adventure after another and the Star Wars galaxy has never been more fun. A comical take on William Shakespeare's Rosencrantz and Guildenstern, two background characters from *Hamlet*.

Star Wars: Tales of the Jedi. 2007–2014. T

A collection of Star Wars adventures set 4,000 years in the past before the events of *Star Wars: A New Hope*. The stories feature the early conflicts of the Jedi Knights and their original encounters with the Sith.

Star Wars: Tales of the Jedi. Written by **Tom Veitch** and various. Illustrated by **Chris Gossett** and various. Dark Horse Comics, 2007–2008.

Set 4,000 years before the rise of the Empire, a young Jedi Knight named Ulic Quel-Droma falls to the Dark Side of the Force and a galaxy is changed forever as the epic Sith War erupts.

Omnibus, Vol. 1. 2007. 400pp. 978-1-59307-830-0.
Omnibus, Vol. 2. 2008. 496pp. 978-1-59307-911-6.

Knights of the Old Republic. Written by **John Jackson Miller**. Illustrated by **Brian Ching**. Dark Horse, 2007–2014.

A second series called <u>Knights of the Old Republic</u> was released in 2007–2010. Inspired by the classic LucasArts video game, the series continues the adventures of the Jedi Order thousands of years before Luke Skywalker and focuses on a young Jedi Padawan named Zayne Carrick who must clear his name after being framed for murdering all of his fellow Jedi-in-training.

Vol. 1: Commencement. 2007. 144pp. 978-1-59307-640-5.
Vol. 2: Flashpoint. 2007. 144pp. 978-1-59307-761-7.
Vol. 3: Days of Fear, Nights of Anger. 2008. 144pp. 978-1-59307-867-6.
Vol. 4: Daze of Hate, Knights of Suffering. 2008. 144pp. 978-1-59582-208-6.
Vol. 5: Vector. 2009. 144pp. 978-1-59582-226-0.
Vol. 6: Vindication. 2009. 168pp. 978-1-59582-274-1.
Vol. 7: Dueling Ambitions. 2009. 144pp. 978-1-59582-348-9.
Vol. 8: Destroyer. 2010. 120pp. 978-1-59582-419-6.
Vol. 9: Demon. 2010. 96pp. 978-1-59582-476-9.
Vol. 10: War. 2012. 120pp. 978-1-59582-959-7.
Omnibus, Vol. 1. 2013. 424pp. 978-1-61655-206-0.
Omnibus, Vol. 2. 2013. 440pp. 978-1-61655-213-8.
Omnibus, Vol. 3. 2014. 416pp. 978-1-61655-227-5.

Star Wars: The Old Republic. Written by **Alexander Freed** and **Rob Chestney**. Illustrated by **Dave Ross**, **Mark McKenna**, and **Alex Sanchez**. Dark Horse Comics, 2011–2013. T 🐦
Based on the popular MMORPG, after hundreds of years, the Sith Empire has returned to the galaxy, determined to crush the Republic that sent it into exile. A young Sith named Teneb Kel who has risen from the ranks and seeks favor with the Dark Council of Sith is given a mission of great importance—to hunt down the Emperor's apprentice. Meanwhile a spy for the Republic has his hands full on a mission that might restart the never-ending conflict between the Sith and the Jedi.

Vol. 1: Blood of the Empire. 2011. 96pp. 978-1-59582-646-6.
Vol. 2: Threat of Peace. 2011. 96pp. 978-1-59582-642-8.
Vol. 3: The Lost Sons. 2012. 96pp. 978-1-59582-637-4.

Star Wars: Dawn of the Jedi. Written by **John Ostrander**. Illustrated by **Jan Duursema**. Dark Horse Comics, 2012–2014. T

Set thousands of years before the birth of Luke and Leia Skywalker, meet the earliest of the Je'daii as they face off against the threat of the Rakata, powerful users of the dark side of the Force.

Vol. 1: Force Storm. 2012. 128pp. 978-1-59582-979-5.
Vol. 2: Prisoner of Bogan. 2013. 128pp. 978-1-61655-144-5.
Vol. 3: Force War. 2014. 128pp. 978-1-61655-379-1.

Cover art of Star Wars: Dawn of
the Jedi © 2016 Lucasfilm Ltd.
& TM. All Rights Reserved.
Used under authorization.

Miscellaneous Recommended Titles Prequel Trilogy. 2001–2006. T
Miscellaneous *Star Wars* tales that occur before and during Episodes I–III, the prequel trilogy of *Star Wars* films. The stories tend to focus Obi-Wan Kenobi, Anakin

Skywalker, Yoda, and Mace Windu, as well as other Jedi Knights including Ki-Adi-Mundi, Quinlan Vos, and Aayla Secura in their battle against the coming tide of war created by Darth Sidious.

Star Wars: Jedi—The Dark Side. Written by **Scott Allie**. Illustrated by **Mahmud Asrar**. Dark Horse Comics, 2012. 120pp. 978-1-59582-840-8. T

Star Wars: Rise of the Sith (Legends: Epic Collection). Written and Illustrated by various. Marvel Comics, 2015– . T
>   *Vol. 1*. 2015. 488pp. 978-0-7851-9722-5.

Star Wars: Blood Ties—A Tale of Jango Fett and Boba Fett. Written by **Tom Taylo**r. Illustrated by **Chris Scalf**. Dark Horse Comics, 2011. T
>   *Vol. 1*. 2011. 96pp. 978-1-59582-627-5.
>   *Vol. 2*. 2013. 96pp. 978-1-61655-001-1.

Star Wars: The Clone Wars Vol. 1 (Marvel Epic Collection). Written and Illustrated by various. Marvel Comics, 2017. 424pp. 978-0-7851-9553-5.

Star Wars Omnibus. 2008–2010. T
>   *Rise of the Sith*. Written by **Ron Marz**, **Ryder Windham**, and various. Illustrated by **Jan Duursema** and various. Dark Horse Comics, 2008. 448pp. 978-1-59582-172-0.
>   *Quinlan Vos—Jedi in Darkness*. Written by **John Ostrander**. Illustrated by **Jan Duursema**. Dark Horse Comics, 2010. 504pp. 978-1-59582-555-1.

Star Wars: Miscellaneous Recommended Titles Original Trilogy. 2006– . T
Miscellaneous recommended *Star Wars* titles that take place during and after the events seen in Episodes IV–VI and feature tales of characters including Luke Skywalker, Han Solo, Princess Leia, Chewbacca, Darth Vader, and Boba Fett.

Star Wars: The Empire (Legends: Epic Collection). Written and Illustrated by various. Marvel Comics, 2015– . T
>   *Vol. 1*. 2015. 432pp. 978-0-7851-9398-2.
>   *Vol. 2*. 2015. 440pp. 978-0-7851-9724-9.
>   *Vol. 3*. 2017. 472pp. 978-1-302-90375-6.

Star Wars: The New Republic (Legends: Epic Collection). Written and Illustrated by various. Marvel Comics, 2015– . T
>   *Vol. 1*. 2016. 488pp. 978-0-7851-9716-4.
>   *Vol. 2*. 2016. 512pp. 978-0-7851-9723-2.

Star Wars: The Old Republic (Legends Epic Collection). Written and Illustrated by various. Marvel Comics, 2015– . T
>   *Vol. 1*. 2015. 440pp. 978-0-7851-9717-1.
>   *Vol. 2*. 2017. 480pp. 978-1-302-90377-0.

Star Wars: The Rebellion (Legends: Epic Collection). Marvel Comics, 2016– . Written and Illustrated by various. 2016– . T

Vol. 1. 2016. 504pp. 978-0-7851-9546-7.

Star Wars Omnibus. Dark Horse Comics, 2008–2013.

Boba Fett. Written by **Mike Kennedy**, **Ron Marz**, and **John Ostrander**. Illustrated by **Cam Kennedy** and **Francisco Ruiz Velasco**. 2010. 496pp. 978-1-59582-418-9. T
Early Victories. Written and Illustrated by various. Dark Horse Comics, 2008. 336pp. 978-1-59582-172-0.
At War with the Empire. Written and Illustrated by various. Dark Horse Comics, 2011. T
A collection of stories focusing on the early days of the Galactic Empire around the days before and after *Star Wars: A New Hope*. The series focuses on Darth Vader, Emperor Palpatine, Princess Leia, and more.

Vol. 1. 2011. 408pp. 978-1-59582-699-2.
Vol. 2. 2011. 464pp. 978-1-59582-777-7.

Shadows of the Empire. Written by **Steve Perry**, **Michael A. Stackpole**, **John Wagner**, and **Timothy Zahn**. Illustrated by **Carlos Ezquerra**, **John Nadeau**, **Kilian Plunkett**, and various. Dark Horse Comics, 2010. 408pp. 978-1-59582-434-9. T
Wild Space. Written and Illustrated by various. Dark Horse Comics, 2013–2014. A
A collection of long out-of-print comic book short stories from the United Kingdom—including a story by Alan Moore—as well as the rare *Star Wars* 3-D comics, and miscellaneous mini-comics, plus the Sergio Stomps Star Wars special by Mark Evanier and Sergio Aragones and much more.

Vol. 1. 2013. 480pp. 978-1-61655-146-9.
Vol. 2. 2013. 488pp. 978-1-61655-147-6.

Star Wars: The Thrawn Trilogy. Written by **Timothy Zahn**. Adapted by **Mike Baron**. Illustrated by **Olivier Vatine**, **Fred Blanchard**, **Edvin Biukovic**, and various. Dark Horse Comics, 2009. 420pp. 978-1-59582-417-2, hardcover. T

Tegami Bachi: Letter Bee. Written and Illustrated by **Hiroyuki Asada**. VIZ Media, 2009–2016. T. Japanese manga あ

TEGAMIBACHI © 2006 by Hiroyuki Asada/SHUEISHA Inc.

In the land of AmberGround, where the only light comes from an artificial sun, Lag Seeing is a 12-year-old with the ability to see the past memories and history of people and items. He's a Letter Bee—a delivery boy who must take precious packages from town to town. Along the way he must try to avoid or fight the *Gaichuu*, giant armoured insects who try to steal the precious packages along the way. Lag is accompanied on his deliveries with his Dingo named Niche, a silent girl who protects Lag from the Gaichuu. Meanwhile, packages from other Letter Bees are being stolen from a resistance movement called the Reverse. The first volume of the series was recognized by YALSA's Great Graphic Novels for Teens selection list in 2010. The series was also adapted into an animated series in Japan.

Vol. 1. 2009. 200pp. 978-1-4215-2913-4.
Vol. 2. 2010. 200pp. 978-1-4215-2950-9.
Vol. 3. 2010. 178pp. 978-1-4215-2951-6.
Vol. 4. 2011. 184pp. 978-1-4215-2952-3.
Vol. 5. 2011. 184pp. 978-1-4215-3180-9.
Vol. 6. 2011. 184pp. 978-1-4215-3339-1.
Vol. 7. 2011. 184pp. 978-1-4215-3604-0.
Vol. 8. 2012. 200pp. 978-1-4215-3820-4.
Vol. 9. 2012. 200pp. 978-1-4215-3821-1.
Vol. 10. 2012. 200pp. 978-1-4215-4145-7.

Vol. 11. 2012. 200pp. 978-1-4215-4146-4.
Vol. 12. 2013. 200pp. 978-1-4215-4181-5.
Vol. 13. 2013. 200pp. 978-1-4215-5159-3.
Vol. 14. 2013. 192pp. 978-1-4215-5160-9.
Vol. 15. 2013. 200pp. 978-1-4215-5616-1.
Vol. 16. 2014. 200pp. 978-1-4215-6452-4.
Vol. 17. 2014. 192pp. 978-1-4215-7525-4.
Vol. 18. 2015. 200pp. 978-1-4215-7969-6.
Vol. 19. 2016. 232pp. 978-1-4215-8516-1.
Vol. 20. 2017. 256pp. 978-1-4215-9046-2.

Space Exploration

Stories that tell the tales of mankind's urge to explore the stars as well as what speculative wonders they find while in outer space. The stories tend to focus at a time near our present as the explorers have just invented the technology to explore outer space, or they may be set in the far future as mankind explores outer space and colonizes other worlds. The subgenre has much in common with the Science Action subgenre, but the focus is more on a spaceship crew or specific crewman as they explore the unknown.

The Midas Flesh. Written by **Ryan North**. Illustrated by **Braden Lamb** and **Shelli Paroline**. Boom! Studios, 2014–2015. O

The small space crew made up of captain Joey, her copilot Fatima, and Cooper the sentient Utahraptor are on a return mission to Earth—a planet completely sectioned off, abandoned, and covered in gold—to find out exactly what happened to this once-thriving planet and see if they can use that knowledge against the evil empire that's tracking them down. As luck would have it, they've just landed the most powerful weapon in the universe: some ancient dead guy's body. A unique retelling of the story of King Midas.

Vol. 1. 2014. 128pp. 978-1-60886-455-3.
Vol. 2. 2015. 128pp. 978-1-60886-727-1.

© 2016 by Ryan North, Braden Lamb,
and Shelli Paroline.

Planetes. Written and Illustrated by **Makoto Yukimura**. Dark Horse Comics, 2015–2016. T. Japanese manga. 🕴 あ ◎

In a time when mankind has reached for the stars, the spaceways around Earth are littered with debris. It's up to the crew of the Toy Box to help clean the spaceways free of space junk, but crew members Yuri, Hachimaki, Fee, and Pops all have their reasons for being in one of the worst jobs in the galaxy. Sure, it's not the most glamorous of jobs in outer space, but who else will clean up the space junk? The series was adapted into an anime series in Japan.

The original printing of the series was recognized by YALSA's Popular Paperbacks for Young Adults Science Fiction list in 2004.

Vol. 1. 2015. 528pp. 978-0-439-29819-3.
Vol. 2. 2016. 528pp. 978-1-61655-922-9.

Planetoid. Written and Illustrated by **Ken Garing**. Image Comics, 2013. 164pp. 978-1-60706-813-6. O

Stranded on a mysterious planet far in enemy alien territory when his ship crash lands, an ex-soldier-turned-pirate named Silas must fight off against various mechanical creatures, cyborg militias, and the alien military that has a bounty on him. Can he bring together scattered nomadic tribes from the planet's surface together and fight an evil force that await them?

Prophet. Written and Illustrated by **Brandon Graham** and **Simon Roy**, **Farel Dalrymple**, and **Giannis Milonogiannis**. Image Comics, 2012–2015. O

John Prophet was the Earth Empire's greatest warrior. He sired an entire army of replicas to protect the Star Mothers and other Earth Empire interests. But now thousands of years have passed, and there are only ruins of the mighty Earth Empire. Multiple alien creatures now dominate the human home planet. From the depths of the planet, a pod digs toward the surface to begin the rebirth of the Earth Empire and it is up to this John Prophet to reawaken his brethren throughout the universe. With the call of the Father Prophet it will be up to the hundreds of John Prophets to adventure back to reclaim humanity's place in this universe. *Prophet* is a reimagining of Rob Liefeld's series by the same name.

Vol. 1: Remission. 2012. 136pp. 978-1-60706-611-8.
Vol. 2: Brothers. 2013. 172pp. 978-1-60706-749-8.
Vol. 3: Empire. 2014. 128pp. 978-1-60706-858-7.
Vol. 4: The Joining. 2015. 168pp. 978-1-63215-254-1.
Vol. 5: Earth War. 2017.168pp. 978-1-63215-836-9.

Space Dumplins. Written and Illustrated by **Craig Thompson**. Graphix/Scholastic Books, 2015. 320pp. 978-0-545-56541-7, hardcover; 978-0-545-56543-1. A ◎

Family is everything for young Violet. She and her parents, hard blue-collar workers, are a tight-knit family getting by in outer space. When her father goes missing on a dangerous job in space, Violet does what any plucky young girl would do and sets out to find him. Joined along the way by some misfit friends, Violet soon realizes that her father is trapped in the middle of one of the most dangerous situations ever—but Violet's on a mission of her own to do whatever it takes to save her family.

Cover © Scholastic Inc.

Star Trek

IDW, 2007– . T 🖳 🎬

Since its debut in 1966, Star Trek has become a worldwide phenomenon with multiple spin-offs, movies, merchandising, and, of course, comic books. Over the years various publishers—including Gold Key, Marvel, and DC—have put out comic books based on not only the original series but also most of the spin-offs as well as the adventures of minor characters and even some created just for the comics. The current license holder, IDW, has produced both limited and ongoing series based on the various Star Trek shows, reprinted comics from previous publishers, and even had the crews of the various Enterprises meet the Legion of Super-Heroes, The Doctor, Green Lantern, and even visited the Planet of the Apes. Following the 2009 theatrical "Reboot," IDW has published adventures of the original crew based on both their original appearances and those of the newer actors, so that in some adventures Captain Kirk looks like William Shatner and in others he looks like Chris Pine.

Classic Star Trek Titles Reprinted by IDW Publishing, 2014– .

Star Trek: Gold Key Archives. Written by **Len Wein**, **John David Warner**, **Arnold Drake**, and various. Illustrated by various. 2014– .

> A reprint of the classic *Star Trek* Gold Key comic books published from 1967 to 1979.
>
> *Vol. 1.* 2014. 168pp. 978-1-61377-922-4, hardcover.
> *Vol. 2.* 2014. 168pp. 978-1-63140-108-4, hardcover.
> *Vol. 3.* 2015. 168pp. 978-1-63140-231-9, hardcover.
> *Vol. 4.* 2015. 164pp. 978-1-63140-449-8, hardcover.
> *Vol. 5.* 2016. 160pp. 978-1-63140-598-3, hardcover.
> *Vol. 6.* 2017. 160pp. 978-1-63140-742-0. hardcover.

Star Trek Classics. Written by **Kevin J. Anderson**, **Rebecca Moesta**, **Keith R.A. DeCandido**, **Christopher Golden**, **Nathan Archer**, **Dan Abnett**, **Andy Lanning**, **Mike Carlin**, **Peter David**, and various. Illustrated by **Igor Kordey**, **Tom Sniegoski**, **Scott Ciencin**, **Andrew Currie**, **Jeff Moy**, **Pablo Marcos**, **Gordon Purcell**, and various. 2011–2013.

> A collection of many of DC Comics stories featuring both the original series characters and the crew from *Star Trek: The Next Generation*.
>
> *Vol. 1: The Gorn Crisis.* 2011. 104pp. 978-1-61377-129-7.
> *Vol. 2: Enemy Unseen.* 2012. 224pp. 978-1-61377-131-0.
> *Vol. 3: Encounters with the Unknown.* 2012. 284pp. 978-1-61377-211-9.
> *Vol. 4: Beginnings.* 2013. 152pp. 978-1-61377-671-1.
> *Vol. 5: Who Killed Captain Kirk?* 2013. 172pp. 978-1-61377-831-9.

Star Trek Archives. Written by **Peter David**, **Michael Jan Friedman**, **Paul Jenkins**, **Howard Weinstein**, and **Mike W. Barr**. Illustrated by **Curt Swan**, **Gordon Purcell**, **Steve Erwin**, **Peter Krause**, **Sam de la Rosa**, **Rod Wigham**, **Marshall Rogers**, **James W. Fry**, **Ricardo Villagran**, and **Tom Sutton**.

> Collects various stories originally by DC Comics, grouped together with a common theme, as well as issues from Malibu's Star Trek: Deep Space Nine series.

Vol. 1: The Best of Peter David. 2008. 144pp. 978-1-60010-242-4.
Vol. 2: Best of the Borg. 2008. 160pp. 978-1-60010-265-3.
Vol. 3: The Gary Seven Collection. 2009. 184pp. 978-1-60010-278-3.
Vol. 4: DS9. 2009. 144pp. 978-1-60010-290-5.
Vol. 5: The Best of Kirk. 2009. 152pp. 978-1-60010-571-5.
Vol. 6: The Mirror Universe Saga. 2009. 196pp. 978-1-60010-522-7.

© Paramount Pictures Corporation.
© CBS Studios Inc.

IDW Publishing Star Trek. 2010– .

IDW Publishing series based on the original series.

© Paramount Pictures Corporation. © CBS Studios Inc.

Star Trek: Burden of Knowledge. Written by **Scott Tipton** and **David Tipton**. Illustrated by **Federica Manfredi**. 2010. 104pp. 978-1-60010-803-7.

Star Trek: Mission's End. Written by **Ty Templeton**. Illustrated by **Stephen Molnar**. 2009. 124pp. 978-1-60010-540-1.

Star Trek: Kahn—Ruling in Hell. Written by **Scott Tipton** and **David Tipton**. Illustrated by **Fabio Montovani**. 2011. 104pp. 978-1-60010-909-6.

Star Trek: The John Byrne Collection. Written and Illustrated by **John Byrne**. 2013. 488pp. 978-1-61377-612-4, hardcover; 978-1-63140-491-7.

Collects the various Star Trek limited series and one-shots that Byrne has written for IDW, most of which have appeared in their own collections.

Star Trek: New Visions. Written by **John Byrne**. 2014– .

In a "photonovel" type of format, Byrne takes images from episodes of the original series and uses them to create brand new stories.

Vol. 1. 2014. 140pp. 978-1-63140-039-1.
Vol. 2. 2015. 144pp. 978-1-63140-367-5.
Vol. 3. 2016. 136pp. 978-1-63140-536-5.
Vol. 4. 2017. 128pp. 978-1-6314-0805-2.

Based on Star Trek: The Next Generation *and* Star Trek: Deep Space Nine

Star Trek: The Next Generation Omnibus. Written by **David Tishman**. Illustrated by **Casey Maloney**. 2012. 480pp. 978-1-61377-537-0.

    Collects four previous collected limited series.

Star Trek: The Next Generation—Hive. Written by **Brannon Braga**, **Terry Matalas**, and **Travis Fickett**. Illustrated by **Joe Corroney**. 2013. 204pp. 978-1-61377-566-0.

Star Trek: Deep Space Nine—Fools Gold. Written by **Scott Tipton** and **David Tipton**. Illustrated by **Fabio Montovani**. 2010. 104pp. 978-1-60010-699-6.

Miscellaneous Spotlight Series and Crossover Titles, 2009– .

Star Trek: Alien Spotlight. Written and Illustrated by various. 2009–2010.

    Vol. 1. 2008. 152pp. 978-1-60010-179-3.
    Vol. 2. 2010. 128pp. 978-1-60010-612-5.

Star Trek: Captain's Log. Written by **Scott Tipton**, **David Tipton**, **Stuart Moore**, and various. Illustrated by **Frederica Manfredi**, **Andrew Currie**, and **J.K. Woodward**. 2011. 104pp. 978-1-60010-887-7.

Star Trek: The City on the Edge of Forever. Written by **Harlan Ellison**. Adapted by **Scott Tipton** and **David Tipton**. Illustrated by **J.K. Woodward**. 2015. 128pp. 978-1-63140-206-7.

    Harlan Ellison's award-winning script for this classic episode had many differences from what actually aired. Presented here is the original story.

Star Trek: Mirror Images. Written by **Scott Tipton** and **David Tipton**. Illustrated by **David Messina**. 2009. 132pp. 978-1-60010-293-6.

Star Trek: The Next Generation/Doctor Who: Assimilation². Written by **Scott Tipton** and **David Tipton**. Illustrated by **J.K. Woodward**.

The Next Generation crew teams up with the Eleventh Doctor, Rory, and Amy to fight the joint threats of the Borg and the Cybermen.

Vol. 1. 2012. 104pp. 978-1-61377-403-8.
Vol. 2. 2013. 104pp. 978-1-61377-551-6.

Star Trek/Legion of Super-Heroes. Written by **Chris Roberson**. Illustrated by **Jeffrey Moy**. 2013. 156pp. 978-1-61377-660-5.

> The 23rd century meets the 30th and the original series crew teams up to fight the multiversal threat of Vandal Savage.

Star Trek/Planet of the Apes: Primate Directive. Written by **Scott Tipton** and **David Tipton**. Illustrated by **Rachel Slott**. 2015. 120pp. 978-1-63140-362-0.

> A rift in space sends Captain Kirk and the Enterprise crew to a new Universe—one in which Earth is controlled by the Apes. The time-displaced Col. George Taylor is also there and he wants Kirk's help.

Star Trek/Green Lantern: Spectrum War. Written by **Mike Johnson**. Illustrated by **Angel Hernandez**. 140pp. 2016. 978-1-63140-559-4.

> After their universe is destroyed, the Green Lanterns find themselves in the Star Trek Universe, but other ring bearers—friends and foes—have traveled there as well. A sequel limited series came out in 2016–2017.

Star Trek (The New Films), 2009–2016

In 2012, IDW Publishing continued the *Star Trek* adventures based on the 2009 film series created by J.J. Abrams and then continued in the film *Star Trek: Into Darkness* (2013) and *Star Trek: Beyond* (2016). The ongoing series retells some of the classic stories and creates new ones. Only some of the volumes have subtitles. Several of the limited series act as prequels or sequels to the films. The series restarted in 2016 as *Star Trek: To Boldly Go*. *Star Trek: Starfleet Academy* was on YALSA's 2017 Great Graphic Novels for Teens list.

Star Trek. Written by **Mike Johnson**. Illustrated by **Tim Bradstreet**, **Steve Molnar**, **Joe Phillips**, and various. 2012–2016. Teen.

© Paramount Pictures Corporation.
© CBS Studios Inc.

Vol. 1. 2012. 104pp. 978-1-61377-150-1.
Vol. 2. 2012. 104pp. 978-1-61377-286-7.
Vol. 3. 2012. 104pp. 978-1-61377-515-8.
Vol. 4. 2013. 104pp. 978-1-61377-590-5.
Vol. 5. 2013. 104pp. 978-1-61377-687-2.
Vol. 6: After Darkness. 2013. 104pp. 978-1-61377-796-1.
Vol. 7. 2014. 104pp. 978-1-61377-882-1.
Vol. 8. 2014. 152pp. 978-1-63140-021-6.
Vol. 9: The Q Gambit. 2015. 152pp. 978-1-63140-276-0.
Vol. 10. 2015. 120pp. 978-1-63140-381-1.
Vol. 11. 2016. 120pp. 978-1-63140-521-1.
Vol. 12. 2016. 124pp. 978-1-63140-664-5.
Vol. 13. 2016. 140pp. 978-1-63140-775-8.

Star Trek: Countdown. Written by **Robert Orci**, **Alex Kurtzman**, **Mike Johnson**, and **Tim Jones**. Illustrated by **David Mesinna**. 2009. 104pp. 978-1-60010-420-6.

Star Trek: Spock-Reflections. Written by **Scott Tipton** and **David Tipton**. Illustrated by **David Messina** and **Federica Manfredi**. 2010. 104pp. 978-1-60010-590-6.

Star Trek: Nero. Written by **Mike Johnson** and **Tim Jones**. Illustrated by **David Messina**. 2010. 104pp. 978-1-60010-603-3.

Star Trek: Countdown to Darkness. Written by **Mike Johnson**. Illustrated by **David Messina**. 2013. 104pp. 978-1-61377-623-0.

Star Trek: Kahn. Written by **Mike Johnson**. Illustrated by **Claudia Balboni**. 2014.124pp. 978-1-61377-895-1.

Star Trek: Manifest Destiny. Written by **Mike Johnson** and **Ryan Parrot**. Illustrated by **Angel Hernandez**. 2016. 136pp. 978-1-63140-634-8.

Star Trek: Starfleet Academy. Written by **Mike Johnson** and **Ryan Parrot**. Illustrated by **Derek Charm**. 2016. 120pp. 978-1-63140-663-8. 🎗

Twin Spica. Written and Illustrated by **Kou Yaginuma**. Vertical, 2010–2012. T 🎗 Japanese manga. ◎ あ

> Japan's first human-manned spaceflight ended in catastrophe with civilian casualties. Years later a new generation of high school students train to become astronauts. The series was adapted into an anime and selected as one of YALSA's Great Graphic Novels for Teens.
>
> | | |
> |---|---|
> | *Vol. 1*. 2010. 192pp. 978-1-934287-84-2. | *Vol. 7*. 2011. 294pp. 978-1-935654-12-4. |
> | *Vol. 2*. 2010. 192pp. 978-1-934287-86-6. | *Vol. 8*. 2011. 294pp. 978-1-935654-13-1. |
> | *Vol. 3*. 2010. 192pp. 978-1-934287-90-3. | *Vol. 9*. 2011. 272pp. 978-1-935654-23-0. |
> | *Vol. 4*. 2010. 208pp. 978-1-934287-93-4. | *Vol. 10*. 2011. 272pp. 978-1-935654-24-7. |
> | *Vol. 5*. 2011. 192pp. 978-1-935654-02-5. | *Vol. 11*. 2012. 400pp. 978-1-935654-33-9. |
> | *Vol. 6*. 2011. 192pp. 978-1-935654-03-2. | *Vol. 12*. 2012. 400pp. 978-1-935654-34-6. |

Science Action

Action is the main focus of these stories with science fiction settings that can include the far future, tales of alien civilizations, and even a steampunk look at the past where 19th-century technology has some futuristic influences. It can even be set at the present with a dash of future technology thrown in. Readers who enjoy these titles will also enjoy those listed in the Action and Adventure genre.

50 Girls 50. Written by **Al Feldstein**. Illustrated by **Frank Frazetta**, **Al Williamson**, and various. Fantagraphics Books, 2013. 2540pp. 978-1-60699-577-8, hardcover.

> Part of the EC Comics Library, this volume collects the classic stories Feldstein wrote for *Weird Science*, *Weird Fantasy*, and other 1950s' titles. Artists include Frank Frazetta and Al Williamson.

100 Girls. Written by **Adam Gallardo**. Illustrated by **Todd Demong**. 978-1-4169-6109-3. Simon Pulse, 2008. T ◎

> Thirteen-year-old Sylvia Mark always knew she didn't quite fit in. It's not only that she's in two grades higher than anyone her age—but she's also

tremendously strong. At night Sylvia constantly has dreams of other girls who look exactly like her. In reality, Sylvia is one of 100 girls cloned in a genetics breeding experiment to give normal humans super-human powers. Thirteen years ago four of the cloned girls were kidnapped from the facility where they were created and sent to families around the country to adopt. Now Sylvia is on a journey to find her other counterparts and find out why she was kidnapped all those years ago. Meanwhile the organization that created the girls will stop at nothing to retrieve Sylvia and her counterparts at any cost.

Anomaly. Written by **Skip Brittenham**. Illustrated by **Brian Haberlin**. Anomaly Publishing, 2012. 356pp. 978-0-9853-3420-8, hardcover. M

In the year 2717 humanity lives above a depleted Earth and is ruled by the Conglomerate and its enforcers. A first-contact mission with a new planet finds itself endangered by a corrupt official, and a former enforcer and the woman he has to protect have to deal with his sinister plot.

Black Harvest. Written and Illustrated by **Josh Howard**. Image Comics, 2010. 144pp. 978-1-60706-315-5. M

Jericho, Texas, has a yearly phenomenon known as the Jericho Lights that brings tourists and UFO enthusiasts to the area every year. The origin of the lights is still a mystery to the community. When 19-year-old Zaya Vahn mysteriously returns after missing for three years, she is a changed young woman with the words "repent" etched into her skin. Caught in the middle of the mystery is Daniel Webster, a blogger who seeks to find out the truth of the lights and how it could be related to Zaya's return — but the answer is bigger than even he could have realized.

Borderlands. Written by **Mikey Neumann**. Illustrated by **Agustin Padilla**. IDW Publishing, 2013–2015. O 🎮

A tie-in with the popular video game by Gearbox Studio. On the planet Pandora is a vault of treasure like no planet-goer has ever seen, and the best bounty hunters off planet have come to the run-down city of Fyrestone to claim it! See the origins of the how Roland met his companions Mordecai, Lilith, and the Brick, as the soldiers-of-fortune continue their quest to ultimately find the vault and what treasures lie inside of it.

Vol. 1: Origins. 2013. 104pp. 978-1-61377-601-8.
Vol. 2: The Fall of Fyrestone. 2015. 104pp. 978-1-63140-195-4.
Vol. 3: Tannis & the Vault. 2015. 104pp. 978-1-63140-271-5.

Cleopatra in Space. Written and Illustrated by **Mike Maihack**. Graphix/Scholastic Books, 2014– . Y ◉

Cover © Scholastic Inc.

When a young Cleopatra is mysteriously transported to the far future, she finds that she's been destined to save the galaxy from the tyrannical Xaius Octavian. Wanting to know all that she can, she enrolls in the Yasiro Academy; Cleo learns all about biology, algebra, fighting skills, and even all about alien languages from her instructor, the talking cat named Khensu. Now the future ruler of Egypt must save the galaxy, conquer homework, and make new friends and avoid getting in detention! The series is still ongoing from Scholastic.

Vol. 1: Target Practice. 2014. 176pp. 978-0-545-52842-9, hardcover; 978-0-545-52843-6.

Vol. 2: The Thief and the Sword. 2015. 192pp. 978-0-545-52844-3, hardcover; 978-0-545-52845-0.

Vol. 3: Secret of the Time Tablets. 2016. 192pp. 978-0-545-83868-9, hardcover; 978-0-545-83867-2.

Vol. 4: The Golden Lion. 2017. 208pp. 978-0-545-83871-9, hardcover; 978-0-545-83872-6.

Dr. Grordbort Presents. Written and Illustrated by **Greg Broadmore**. WetaNZ/Dark Horse Comics/Titan Books, 2008–2014. O

© 2016 Titan Comics.

A humorous and blustery collection of steampunk-based war propaganda for other planets. Gaze with awe at the bizarre aliens from Venus! Witness the amazing weaponry mankind will use on those rapscallion aliens and the wildlife on Venus! Be in awe as Lord Bockswain, hunter extraordinaire, is able to single-handedly take on the aliens across the galaxy and save the day in time for a cuppa. The books are created by Greg Broadmore, a designer for Weta Workshop in New Zealand and visualizer for many fantastic films including *Lord of the Rings* trilogy, *District 9*, *King Kong* (2005), and the *Lion, the Witch, and the Wardrobe*.

Contrapulatronic Dingus Directory. 2008. 32pp. 978-1-59307-876-8, hardcover.
Victory: Scientific Adventure Violence. 2009. 64pp. 978-1-59582-463-9, hardcover.
Triumph. 2014. 176pp. 978-1-78276-153-2, hardcover.
Onslaught. 2014. 176pp. 978-1-78276-191-4, hardcover.

Echo. Written and Illustrated by **Terry Moore**. Abstract Studio, 2008–2011. T
🏵 ◉

Photographer Julie Martin finds herself bonded to a metallic suit that was part of a failed military battle suit. When she is bathed in liquid metal from the explosion of a prototype battle suit test being done in the desert, the metallic rain drops merge on her body to make an almost impervious suit of liquid armor. The suit is bonded to her nervous system and has given her heightened

healing abilities to herself and those she is close with as well as the ability to channel lightning to protect herself. On the run from the government and the organization that devised the battle suit, Julie finds help by a park ranger who has connections to the previous wearer of the battle suit. The book won a Harvey Award for Best New Series in 2009 as well as a Great Graphic Novels for Teens title in 2009.

Vol. 1: Moon Lake. 2008. 120pp. 978-1-892597-40-3.
Vol. 2: Atomic Dreams. 2009. 104pp. 978-1-892597-41-0.
Vol. 3: Desert Run. 2009. 104pp. 978-1-892597-43-4.
Vol. 4: Collider. 2010. 104pp. 978-1-892597-44-1.
Vol. 5: Black Hole. 2010. 104pp. 978-1-892597-46-5.
Vol. 6: Last Day. 2011. 104pp. 978-1-892597-47-2.
Echo Complete Edition. 2011. 600pp. 978-1-892597-48-9.

Fullmetal Alchemist. Written and Illustrated by **Hiromu Arakawa**. VIZ Media, 2005–2011. T. Japanese manga. 🏃 ◎ あ

In a city where steam power still exists, two teenage brothers Edward and Alphonse Elric are apprentices in the art of alchemy, the art of manipulating matter and transforming it to another state. After a tragic mistake Edward lost a leg and an arm, but his younger brother lost much more: his body. Now Alphonse's soul is grafted into a suit of armor and Edward has mechanical appendages. They both work for the state as military alchemists on dangerous missions as they continue their search for the Philosopher's Stone, a magical item with the power to restore Edward's body and even return something even more precious to them both: their mother. The series received recognition by YALSA's Quick Picks for Reluctant Readers list in 2006.

Vol. 1. 2005. 192pp. 978-1-59116-920-8.
Vol. 2. 2005. 192pp. 978-1-59116-923-9.
Vol. 3. 2005. 192pp. 978-1-59116-925-3.
Vol. 4. 2005. 200pp. 978-1-59116-929-1.
Vol. 5. 2006. 192pp. 978-1-4215-0175-8.
Vol. 6. 2006. 208pp. 978-1-4215-0319-6.
Vol. 7. 2006. 208pp. 978-1-4215-0458-2.
Vol. 8. 2006. 208pp. 978-1-4215-0459-9.
Vol. 9. 2006. 208pp. 978-1-4215-0460-5.
Vol. 10. 2006. 208pp. 978-1-4215-0461-2.
Vol. 11. 2007. 208pp. 978-1-4215-0838-2.
Vol. 12. 2007. 192pp. 978-1-4215-0839-9.
Vol. 13. 2007. 192pp. 978-1-4215-1158-0.
Vol. 14. 2007. 192pp. 978-1-4215-1379-9.
Vol. 15. 2007. 192pp. 978-1-4215-1380-5.
Vol. 16. 2008. 208pp. 978-1-4215-1381-2.
Vol. 17. 2008. 210pp. 978-1-4215-2161-9.
Vol. 18. 2009. 192pp. 978-1-4215-2536-5.
Vol. 19. 2009. 200pp. 978-1-4215-2568-6.
Vol. 20. 2009. 200pp. 978-1-4215-3034-5.
Vol. 21. 2009. 192pp. 978-1-4215-3232-5.
Vol. 22. 2010. 192pp. 978-1-4215-3413-8.
Vol. 23. 2010. 192pp. 978-1-4215-3630-9.
Vol. 24. 2011. 200pp. 978-1-4215-3812-9.
Vol. 25. 2011. 192pp. 978-1-4215-3924-9.
Vol. 26. 2011. 194pp. 978-1-4215-3962-1.
Vol. 27. 2011. 200pp. 978-1-4215-3984-3.

Gears of War. Written by **Joshua Ortega** and **Karen Traviss**. Illustrated by **Liam Sharp**, **Mike Caps**, and **Pop Mhan**. DC Comics. M 🐾

A graphic novel adaptation of the popular video game series for the Xbox consoles. Set in the far future on Sera, a planet colonized by humans eons ago. Marcus Fenix and Delta Squad are members of the Coalition of Ordered Governments (COG) tasked with trying to save Sera from the underground-dwelling aliens known as the Locust Horde. The combat is brutal against the vicious reptilian-like Locust, but Marcus and his crew of Delta Squad are there to turn the tide by any means necessary.

Book 1. 2010. 160pp. 978-1-4012-2541-4.
Book 2. 2012. 176pp. 978-1-4012-3392-1.
Book 3. 2013. 256pp. 978-1-4012-3696-0.

HALO. Written by various. Illustrated by various. Marvel Comics, 2006–2013; Dark Horse Comics, 2014– . O 🎮

© 2016 Microsoft Studios. Used with permission from Microsoft.

Based off of the characters and events from the cult-hit Xbox video game first-person shooter series <u>HALO</u> that started with the game *HALO: Combat Evolved* in 2001. The popular video game series was created originally by Bungie Studios has continued with a variety of sequels (HALO 2, 3, 4, and 5), prequels (*HALO Wars*, *HALO: ODST*, *HALO: Reach*), with many more to come. The current developer of the <u>HALO</u> series is 343 Industries. The main series focuses on the adventures of faceless armor-clad Spartan warrior called the Master Chief. Set in the 26th century, Master Chief is the last super-soldier ever created. He's the pinnacle of the Spartan soldier program that engineered humans to the tip-top of mental and physical evolution in the Earth's bid to fight against a fierce alien race. Awakened from cryogenic sleep, he's joined with the United Nations Space Command (UNSC) Marine Helljumpers as they take on the alien warrior race empire called the Covenant as well as the mutating killing parasites called the Flood. Storylines in the series focus on the Master Chief as well as other various characters including Orbital Drop Ship Troopers (ODST), other Spartan soldiers created before Master Chief, the Helljumpers, and more in this ever-expanding science fiction universe.

HALO *Graphic Novels Published by Marvel Comics*, 2006–2013. O
Marvel Comics received the license for HALO from 2006 through 2013 and published a variety of stories by some top-name creators including Peter David, Brian Michael Bendis, and Fred Van Lente. The material covered the HALO games including the final Bungie-created game, *HALO: Reach*.

HALO Graphic Novel. Written by **Brett Lewis, Lee Hammock, Tsutomu Nihei**, and **Jay Faerber**. Illustrated by **Moebius, Phil Hale, Ed Lee, Tsutomu Nihei, Jay Faerber, Andrew C. Robinson, Simon Bisley**, and **Lee Hammock**. 2006. 128pp. 0-7851-2372-5, hardcover; 2010. 978-0-7851-2378-1.

HALO: Uprising. Written by **Brian Michael Bendis**. Illustrated by **Alex Maleev**. 2009. 168pp. 978-0-7851-2838-0, hardcover; 2010. 978-0-7851-2839-7.

HALO: Helljumper. Written by **Peter David**. Illustrated by **Eric Nguyen**. 2010. 120pp. 978-0-7851-4023-8, hardcover; 2011. 978-0-7851-4051-1.

HALO: Blood Line. Written by **Fred Van Lente**. Illustrated by **Frances Portela**. 2010. 120pp. 978-0-7851-4022-1, hardcover; 2011. 978-0-7851-4050-4.

HALO: Fall of Reach. 2011–2013.

> *Boot Camp*. Written by **Eric Nylund**. Adapted by **Brian Reed**. Illustrated by **Felix Ruiz**, 2011. 112pp. 978-0-7851-5146-3, hardcover; 2011. 978-0-7851-5147-0.
> *Covenant*. Written by **Brian Reed**. Illustrated by **Felix Ruiz**. 2011. 112pp. 978-0-7851-5148-7, hardcover; 2012. 112pp. 978-0-7851-5149-4.
> *Invasion*. Written by **Brian Reed**. Illustrated by **Felix Ruiz**. 2012. 104pp. 978-0-7851-5150-0, hardcover; 2013. 978-0-7851-5151-7.

HALO Oversized Collection. Written by **Brian Michael Bendis**, **Peter David**, and **Fred Van Lente**. Illustrated by **Alex Maleev, Eric Nguyen**, and **Francis Portela**. 2013. 416pp. 978-0-7851-6570-5, hardcover.

HALO Graphic Novels Published by Dark Horse Comics, 2014– . O
In 2014, the license for HALO was transferred to Dark Horse Comics and includes brand new stories as well as collected editions of previously published material. The lead writer for *HALO 5: Guardians*, Brian Reed, is a leading writer for many of the stories.

HALO: Initiation. Written by **Brian Reed**. Illustrated by **Marco Castiello**. 2014. 72pp. 978-1-61655-325-8, hardcover.

HALO: Escalation. Written by **Chris Schlerf**. Illustrated by **Juan Castro** and **Rob Lean**. 2014– .

> *Vol. 1*. 2014. 72pp. 978-1-61655-325-8, hardcover.
> *Vol. 2*. 2015. 52pp. 978-1-61655-628-0, hardcover.
> *Vol. 3*. 2014. 140pp. 978-1-61655-759-1, hardcover.
> *Vol. 4*. 2016. 144pp. 978-1-61655-881-9, hardcover.

HALO: Fall of Reach. Written by **Brian Perry**. Illustrated by **Felix Ruiz**. 2016. 288pp. 978-1-50670-077-9.

Halo Library Edition. Written by various. Illustrated by various. 2016–2017.

> *Vol. 1*. 2016. 368pp. 978-1-61655-907-6, hardcover.
> *Vol. 2*. 2017. 296pp. 978-1-50670-234-6, hardcover.

HALO: Tales from Slipspace. Written by various. Illustrated by various. 2016. 96pp. 978-1-50670-072-4.

The Hypernaturals. Written by **Dan Abnett** and **Andy Lanning**. Illustrated by **Brad Walker**. BOOM! Studios, 2013–2014. O
It is the year 100 A.Q.—a century after the artificial intelligence called The Quantinium achieved the Singularity and changed and expanded humanity and its culture. Now humanity spans the galaxy, but there are still threats to its safety. To combat them super-powered individuals are recruited into the Hypernaturals, a team whose

membership changes every five years. But now the new "Centennial Year Iteration" has vanished and earlier members must come out of retirement to confront a threat that can expose hidden truths about their civilization.

Vol. 1. 2013. 128pp. 978-1-6088-6298-6.
Vol. 2. 2013. 144pp. 978-1-6088-6319-8.
Vol. 3. 2014. 144pp. 978-1-6088-6349-5.

Juice Squeezers: The Great Bug Elevator. Written and Illustrated by **David Lapham**. Dark Horse Comics, 2014. 128pp. 978-1-61655-438-5. T ◉

When a California town is being overrun by really big bugs burrowing small tunnels under the city, there's only one group who can take on the bugs: the Juice Squeezers! A covert group of scrawny tweens, they're the only ones small enough to fit through the tunnels and try to finish the bugs once and for all!

Judge Dredd

2000 AD, Titan Books, and IDW Publishing, 2010– . T 🎬

© 2016 Titan Books.

In a post-nuclear world, the Earth's population has been crammed into sprawling, crime-ridden Mega-Cities. A new breed of justice—the Judges—were created to police the cities and render verdicts on the spot, including executions. In Mega-City One, one Judge stands above all others and takes no prisoners: Judge Dredd! The adventures of Dredd and other characters including Psi-Judge Anderson and Judge Death have been told since Dredd's first appearance in the pages of *2000 AD* in 1977. Listed below is just a small sample of Judge Dredd stories published. Many more graphic novel collections of Judge Dredd and his cast of Judges, oddballs, and mutants can be found at Titan Book site at www.titanbooks.com, 2000 AD's web site at www.2000adonline.com, and IDW Publishing site at www. idwpublishing.com. Dredd has also appeared in a wide variety of crossovers with a variety of U.S. comic book characters including Batman, Aliens, and Predators and these are listed throughout this publication. A feature film adaptation starring Karl Urban was released in theaters in 2012 called *Dredd* to mostly positive reviews.

Judge Dredd: The Complete Case Files. Written by **Pat Mills**, **John Wagner**, **Alan Grant**, and various. Illustrated by **Mike McMahon**, **Brian Bolland**, **Steve Dillon**, **Carlos Ezquerra**, and various. 2000 AD, 2010– .

Book 1. 2010. 320pp. 978-1-906735-87-6.
Book 2. 2010. 336pp. 978-1-906735-99-9.
Book 3. 2011. 240pp. 978-1-907519-77-2.
Book 4. 2011. 384pp. 978-1-907992-53-7.
Book 5. 2012. 400pp. 978-1-78108-028-3.
Book 6. 2013. 336pp. 978-1-78108-134-1.
Book 7. 2014. 368pp. 978-1-78108-217-1.
Book 8. 2014. 352pp. 978-1-78108-244-7.
Book 9. 2015. 400pp. 978-1-78108-329-1.
Book 10. 2015. 384pp. 978-1-78108-369-7.
Book 11. 2016. 400pp. 978-1-78108-427-4.
Book 12. 2016. 332pp. 978-1-78108-479-3.
Book 13. 2017. 272pp. 978-1-78108-498-4.
Book 14. 2017. 272pp. 978-1-78108-547-9.

Judge Dredd. Written by **Duane Swierczynski**. Illustrated by **Paul Gulacy**, **Nelson Daniel**, **Andrew Currie**, **Kyle Hotz**, and various. IDW Publishing, 2013–2015. T

Vol. 1. 2013. 120pp. 978-1-61377-596-7.
Vol. 2. 2013. 104pp. 978-1-61377-757-2.
Vol. 3. 2014. 104pp. 978-1-61377-850-0.
Vol. 4. 2014. 104pp. 978-1-61377-957-6.
Vol. 5. 2014. 104pp. 978-1-63140-117-6.
Vol. 6. 2015. 104pp. 978-1-63140-199-2.
Vol. 7. 2015. 152pp. 978-1-63140-358-3.

Judge Dredd: Cursed Earth Uncensored. Written by **Pat Mills** and **John Wagner**. Illustrated by **Mike McMahon** and **Brian Bolland**. 2000 AD, 2016. 208pp. 978-1-78108-444-1, hardcover.

Judge Dredd: Dead Zone. Written by **John Wagner**. Illustrated by **Henry Flint** and **Richard Elson**. Titan Comics, 2016. 96pp. 978-1-78108-426-7.

Judge Dredd: Titan. Written by **Rob Williams**. Illustrated by **Henry Flint**. Titan Comics, 2016. 144pp. 978-1-78108-441-0.

Knights of Sidonia. Written and Illustrated by **Tsutomu Nihei**. Vertical, 2013–2016. O 🏃 Japanese manga. あ

It is the year 3394, 1,000 years after the Earth was destroyed. *Sidonia* is one of the ships containing the remnants of humanity. Nagate Tanikaze was raised in the poorer sections of the ships but now he is a Guardian, one of the mechanized warriors defending the ship from the creatures who destroyed the Earth. An anime series has also been made. Selected as one of YALSA's Great Graphic Novels for Teens.

Vol. 1. 2013. 186pp. 978-1-935654-80-3.
Vol. 2. 2013. 186pp. 978-1-935654-81-0.
Vol. 3. 2013. 186pp. 978-1-935654-82-7.
Vol. 4. 2013. 186pp. 978-1-935654-89-6.
Vol. 5. 2013. 186pp. 978-1-935654-99-5.
Vol. 6. 2013. 186pp. 978-1-932234-91-6.
Vol. 7. 2014. 184pp. 978-1-939130-02-0.
Vol. 8. 2014. 200pp. 978-1-93913021-1.
Vol. 9. 2014. 200pp. 978-1-939130-22-8.
Vol. 10. 2014. 210pp. 978-1-939130-90-7.
Vol. 11. 2014. 210pp. 978-1-939130-91-4.
Vol. 12. 2014. 212pp. 978-1-939130-99-0.
Vol. 13. 2015. 192pp. 978-1-941220-32-0.
Vol. 14. 2015. 192pp. 978-1-941220-86-3.
Vol. 15. 2016. 192pp. 978-1-942993-13-1.

Leo Geo and His Miraculous Journey through the Center of the Earth. Written and Illustrated by **Jon Chad**. Roaring Brook Press, 2012. 40pp. 978-1-59643-661-9. A

The scientist Leo Geo intends to drill, dig, and climb his way to the center of the planet for science. On his descent through the different layers of the planet, Leo discovers more than a few rocks and fossils. Leo must battle monsters and a surface-hating invading army to get back to the top. *Leo Geo*, besides the great story and art, must be seen purely on its presentation. The story is told as one long continuous descent, with the book flipped sideways.

Leo Geo and the Cosmic Crisis. Written and Illustrated by **Jon Chad**. Roaring Brook Press, 2013. 40pp. 978-1-59643-822-4. A

At the Fizzmont Institute for Rad Science, rad scientist Leo Geo is alarmed to hear that his brother, Matt Data, is in danger. Matt is aboard the Fizzmont Orbital Science facility and a comet has been sighted to be heading straight for the facility. In an inventive flip book format, Matt Data discovers his brother's computer has a bug and he and his trusty dog Maff leave the space station to try and fix it.

Library Wars: Love and War. Written by **Hiro Arikawa**. Illustrated by **Kiiro Yumi**. VIZ Media, 2010–2016. O 🌟 Japanese manga. あ

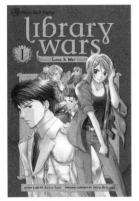

In the year 2019 Iku Kasahara joins the Library Defense Force which protects books from government censors. This was a dream for her since childhood, but the reality may not be what she expected. The manga series is based on a light novel and has also appeared in animated form. The series was selected as one of YALSA's Great Graphic Novels for Teens in 2011.

Library Wars © 2007–2014 Hakusensha, Inc.

Vol. 1. 2010. 200pp. 978-1-4215-3488-6.
Vol. 2. 2010. 192pp. 978-1-4215-3489-3.
Vol. 3. 2010. 200pp. 978-1-4215-3490-9.
Vol. 4. 2011. 200pp. 978-1-4215-3689-7.
Vol. 5. 2011. 200pp. 978-1-4215-3844-0.
Vol. 6. 2011. 200pp. 978-1-4215-3977-5.
Vol. 7. 2012. 200pp. 978-1-4215-4123-5.

Vol. 8. 2012. 200pp. 978-1-4215-4268-3.
Vol. 9. 2013. 200pp. 978-1-4215-5158-6.
Vol. 10. 2013. 200pp. 978-1-4215-5376-4.
Vol. 11. 2014. 200pp. 978-1-4215-6431-9.
Vol. 12. 2014. 200pp. 978-1-4215-6951-2.
Vol. 13. 2015. 200pp. 978-1-4215-7742-5.
Vol. 14. 2015. 200pp. 978-1-4215-8172-9.
Vol. 15. 2016. 200pp. 978-1-4215-8585-7.

Maoh: Juvenile Remix. Written and Illustrated by **Kotara Isaka**. VIZ Media, 2010–2012. O 🌟 Japanese manga.

High school student Ando has a special power—he has a long-suppressed and long-forgotten ability to make other people speak his thoughts out loud. But is it enough to stop the leader of a local vigilante group? Based on a novel and selected as one of YALSA's Great Graphic Novels for Teens in 2011.

Vol. 1. 2010. 200pp. 978-1-4215-3428-2.
Vol. 2. 2010. 200pp. 978-1-4215-4039-9.
Vol. 3. 2010. 192pp. 978-1-4215-4039-9.
Vol. 4. 2011. 200pp. 978-1-4215-3431-2.
Vol. 5. 2011. 200pp. 978-1-4215-3432-9.
Vol. 6. 2011. 200pp. 978-1-4215-3433-6.
Vol. 7. 2011. 200pp. 978-1-4215-3495-4.
Vol. 8. 2011. 200pp. 978-1-4215-3496-1.
Vol. 9. 2012. 200pp. 978-1-4215-4038-2.
Vol. 10. 2012. 200pp. 978-1-4215-4039-9.

Mass Effect. Written by **Mac Walters** and **John Jackson Miller**. Illustrated by **Matthew Clark**, **Tony Parker**, **Omar Francia**, and various. Dark Horse Comics, 2010–2017. O 🎮

Based on the exciting video game trilogy where your actions set the outcomes of the entire game. The stories were written by the original writers for the hit video game series. When Commander Shephard goes missing, it's up to his alien companion Dr. Liara T'Soni to take on a mission of great importance. Also, see the origin of the mysterious figure known as the Illusive Man and more!

Vol. 1. Redemption. 2010. 96pp. 978-1-59582-481-3.
Vol. 2: Evolution. 2011. 112pp. 978-1-59582-759-3.

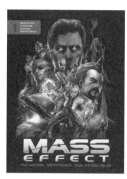

Vol. 3: Invasion. 2012. 112pp. 978-1-59582-867-5.
Vol. 4: Homeworlds. 2012. 96pp. 978-1-59582-955-9.
Foundation, Vol. 1. 2014. 96pp. 978-1-61655-270-1.
Foundation, Vol. 2. 2014. 120pp. 978-1-61655-349-4.
Foundation, Vol. 3. 2014. 120pp. 978-1-61655-488-0.
Library Edition, Vol. 1. 2013. 416pp. 978-1-61655-111-7, hardcover.
Library Edition, Vol. 2. 2015. 312pp. 978-1-61655-636-5, hardcover.
Omnibus, Vol. 1. 2016. 400pp. 978-1-50670-276-6.
Omnibus, Vol. 2. 2017. 328pp. 978-1-50670-277-3.

Mass Effect used with permission of
Electronic Arts Inc.

Maximum Ride. Written by **James Patterson**. Illustrated by **NaRae Lee**. Yen Press, 2009–2012. T. Neo-manga.

Max and her friends are a heterogeneous family. They have the same ability and background. They all have wings on their backs, which let them fly. All they know is that they were raised and trained at The School. The School is where other teens with fantastical and horrific mutations are created. Max and her friends escaped The School and the experiments performed on them. Now The School is looking to get them back at any cost. The one person they trusted at The School has informed Max that she was created to save the world. With so much pressure, staying together is all Max and her winged friends can count on. An adaptation of James Patterson's teen novel series.

Vol. 1. 2009. 256pp. 978-0-7595-2951-9.
Vol. 2. 2009. 256pp. 978-0-7595-2968-7.
Vol. 3. 2010. 240pp. 978-0-7595-2969-4.
Vol. 4. 2011. 224pp. 978-0-7595-2970-0.
Vol. 5. 2011. 240pp. 978-0-7595-2971-7.
Vol. 6. 2012. 208pp. 978-0-7595-2972-4.

Missile Mouse. Written and Illustrated by **Jake Parker**. Graphix/Scholastic Books, 2009–2011. A ◎

Missile Mouse is a secret agent for the Galactic Security Agency in its battle against the Rogue Imperium of Planets. In The Star Crusher, Missile Mouse must reluctantly team up with a hotshot young agent to rescue brilliant scientist Ulrich Vondorf, creator of the black hole–creating Star Crusher, from the hands of their enemy. In Rescue on Tankium3, Missile Mouse must free a planet from slavery at the hands of the evil king Bognarsh.

Vol. 1: The Star Crusher. 2010. 176pp. 978-0-545-11714-2, hardcover; 978-0-545-11715-9.
Vol. 2: Rescue on Tankium3. 2011. 160pp. 978-0-545-11716-6, hardcover; 978-0-545-11717-3.

Cover © Scholastic Inc.

Nnewts. Written and Illustrated by **Doug TenNapel**. Graphix/Scholastic, 2015– . A
Welcome to the world of Nnewts—where amphibian-like humanoids live alongside other races of creatures based on various real-world animals. When young Herk's

Cover © Scholastic Inc.

Nnewt village is destroyed by the devastating reptilian Lizzarks, alone and lost, Herk begins the hero's journey to self-discovery where friends are few and danger awaits at every turn.

Vol. 1: Escape from the Lizzarks. 2015. 192pp. 978-0-545-67647-2, hardcover; 978-0-545-67646-5.

Vol. 2: Rise of the Herk. 2016. 208pp. 978-0-545-67652-6, hardcover; 978-0-545-67654-0.

Paper Girls. Written by **Brian K. Vaughan**. Illustrated by **Cliff Chiang**. Image Comics, 2016– . T 🎗 ◎

© Brian K. Vaughan.

Set in 1988 on the early morning after Halloween, Erin and three of her 12-year-old friends are on their paper route, and they discover something that will forever change their world. As strange things begin to occur and weird monster-like aliens appear, the future is opened up to four girls from a sleepy Ohio town who will never see their world the same way ever again. The series is still ongoing. *Paper Girls* won the 2016 Eisner Award for Best New Series, with Chiang getting the award for Best Penciler. The first volume was also in the Top Ten of YALSA's 2017 Great Graphic Novels for Teens list.

Vol. 1. 2016. 144pp. 978-1-63215-674-7.
Vol. 2. 2016. 128pp. 978-1-63215-895-6.

Rocketo: Journey to the Hidden Sea. Written and Illustrated by **Frank Espinosa**. Image Comics, 2006–2007. T ◎

Set 2,000 years into mankind's future after the Earth that we know is gone and its magnetic field shattered by a deadly alien life-form with only fragments remaining. Only the Mappers, heroic men who have compasses fused onto their right arms, can help rebuild and map the planet. There's only one Mapper brave enough to navigate through the remnants of Earth—Rocketo Garrison! An explorer of the unknown and mapmaker, he's following in his missing father's footsteps to explore the unknown as he remaps the Earth in search of adventure. The graphic novel series is reminiscent of classic science fiction pulp stories including Flash Gordon and Buck Rogers.

Vol. 1. 2006. 256pp. 978-1-58240-585-8.
Vol. 2. 2007. 212pp. 978-1-58240-735-7.

Runners. Written and Illustrated by **Sean Wang**. Serve Man Press, 2005– . T ◎

In the ungoverned sectors of intergalactic space called "Roguespace," smuggler Roka Nostaco and his alien crew have had a tough time making it as runners of all sorts of cargo. When a simple cargo pickup goes wrong, they

discover that pirates have hijacked their rendezvous freighter ship and Roka's crew has to protect the goods. After chasing the pirates away, they discover that the freighter crew is dead, the cargo is mostly intact, and one canister has released something they're not prepared to deal with: a beautiful young girl lying unconscious on the cargo hold floor. Are they really running slaves? They hate to think of it, but a job is a job. Meanwhile, the crew find themselves in more danger than they ever realized after finding the girl as they take on bounty hunters, revenge-seeking pirates, local galactic police, a possible blossoming romance, and cliffhanger escapes.

Vol. 1: Bad Goods. 2005. 168pp. 978-0-9768517-0-7.
Vol. 2: The Snow Job. 2013. 176pp. 978-0-9768517-1-4.

Shockrockets: We Have Ignition. Written by **Kurt Busiek**. Illustrated by **Stuart Immonen**. IDW Publishing, 2010. 160pp. 978-1-60010-784-9, hardcover. O

In the year 2071 the Earth is rebuilding after defeating an alien invasion. The skies above Earth are protected by the Shockrockets, a group of flying fighters made from captured alien technology and human ingenuity and flown by the best pilots on the planet. Alejandro Cruz, a daredevil teenager who's always wanted to become a Shockrocket, accidentally becomes bonded with a Shockrocket ship. Although he's reluctantly accepted into the elite fighter pilot squadron, his unique skills may be the key to defeating the Shockrocket's most deadly adversary: a military genius who helped win the war against the alien invaders over 10 years ago.

Showcase Presents: Strange Adventures. Written by **John Broome**, **Gardner Fox**, and various. Illustrated by **Edmond Hamilton** and various others. DC Comics, 2008–2013.

Vol. 1. 2009. 512pp. 978-1-4012-1544-6.
Vol. 2. 2013. 520pp. 978-1-4012-3846-9.
These volumes collect issues 54–73 and 74–93 of the classic 1950s' science fiction series. The writers and artists include major names in the history of both comics and science fiction. Like all Showcase titles, these are reprinted in black and white.

Star Slammers: The Complete Collection. Written and Illustrated by **Walt Simonson**. IDW Publishing, 2015. 300pp. 978-1-63140-230-2, hardcover. T

A reprinting of some of the earliest professional comic book work by legendary creator Walt Simonson. Set in the far future, there was a group of men who could out-shoot, out-fight, and out-kill anybody. They went into business as mercenaries and became known as the Star Slammers, taking on contract after contract as the best warriors that money could buy. But there is an ancient secret on the planet that could destroy them all! The series reprints the original Marvel graphic novel as well as the 1990s' miniseries in one collection.

Starlight. Written by **Mark Millar**. Illustrated by **Goran Parlov**. Image Comics, 2015. 152pp. 978-1-6321-5017-2. T

Duke McQueen once traveled into outer space and saved the planet Tantalus. But when he got back to Earth no one believed him. Now it's 40 years later, Duke is a widower with grown sons, and a ship from Tantalus just landed in his front yard seeking his help.

© Mark Millar and Goran Parlov.

Trigun. Written and Illustrated by **Yasuhiro Nightow**. Dark Horse Comics, 2003–2009. T あ

In the far future on desert planet there walks a man nicknamed the "Humanoid Typhoon." Meet Vash the Stampede, a spikey blonde-haired man known for his trademarked red coat and for being an expert marksman. A slightly goofy and light-hearted man, he's become known as a walking one-man human disaster, bringing trouble wherever he goes. There's a $$60,000,000,000 bounty on his head, which will always guarantee that he'll be chased by those foolish enough to try to bring him in. Those who try soon find out that they don't stand a chance against Vash as he wanders across a dusty western landscape in search of understanding and helping those in need while reconciling with his enigmatic past. The manga was adapted into a 26-episode anime series in Japan.

Trigun. 2003.

> *Vol. 1*. 2003. 360pp. 978-1-59307-196-7.
> *Vol. 2*. 2003. 344pp. 978-1-59307-053-3.

Trigun Maximum. 2003–2009.

> *Vol. 1: The Hero Returns*. 2004. 192pp. 978-1-59307-196-7.
> *Vol. 2: Death Blue*. 2004. 200pp. 978-1-59307-197-4.
> *Vol. 3: His Life as A. . . .* 2004. 192pp. 978-1-59307-266-7.
> *Vol. 4: Bottom of the Dark*. 2005. 192pp. 978-1-59307-314-5.
> *Vol. 5: Break Out*. 2005. 208pp. 978-1-59307-344-2.
> *Vol. 6: The Gunslinger*. 2005. 208pp. 978-1-59307-351-0.
> *Vol. 7: Happy Days*. 2005. 192pp. 978-1-59307-395-4.
> *Vol. 8: Silent Run*. 2006. 224pp. 978-1-59307-452-4.
> *Vol. 9: LR*. 2006. 200pp. 978-1-59307-527-9.
> *Vol. 10: Wolfwood*. 2006. 240pp. 978-1-59307-556-9.
> *Vol. 11: Zero Hour*. 2007. 192pp. 978-1-59307-674-0.
> *Vol. 12: The Gunslinger*. 2008. 240pp. 978-1-59307-881-2.
> *Vol. 13: Double Duel*. 2008. 224pp. 978-1-59582-167-6.
> *Vol. 14: Mind Games*. 2009. 272pp. 978-1-59582-262-8.

Naoki Urasawa's 20th Century Boys/21st Century Boys. Written and Illustrated by **Naoki Urasawa**. VIZ Media, LCC, 2009–2013. O. Japanese manga.

20 SEIKI SHONEN © 2000 Naoki URASAWA/Studio Nuts Story Co-produced with Takashi NAGASAKI Original Japanese edition published by SHOGAKUKAN.

Kenji and a bunch of his friends formed a secret group in their secret hideout, where they came up with their own manga story after reading a bunch of their favorites. About 20 years later Kenji and his friends have all grown up. Kenji takes over the family corner store, while others become teachers and businessmen. Mysterious events begin happening around the world. A disease causing people to lose all their blood is breaking out across the globe. Prominent landmarks are being targeted by terrorist bombs. At the center of all this, a cult is gaining influence and followers in Japan. Soon Kenji and his friends realize that all these events are following the story they had written so long ago. Who could be behind all these events? It is up to Kenji and his friends to try to stay one step ahead and stop what happens at the end of their story, the end of the world. The conclusion to the series occurs in the two-volume series 21st Century Boys included below.

Naoki Urasawa's 20th Century Boys. 2009–2012.

Vol. 1. 2009. 216pp. 978-1-59116-922-2.
Vol. 2. 2009. 216pp. 978-1-59116-926-0.
Vol. 3. 2009. 200pp. 978-1-4215-1922-7.
Vol. 4. 2009. 200pp. 978-1-4215-1923-4.
Vol. 5. 2009. 216pp. 978-1-4215-2340-8.
Vol. 6. 2009. 216pp. 978-1-4215-2341-5.
Vol. 7. 2010. 224pp. 978-1-4215-2342-2.
Vol. 8. 2010. 204pp. 978-1-4215-2343-9.
Vol. 9. 2010. 216pp. 978-1-4215-2344-6.
Vol. 10. 2010. 216pp. 978-1-4215-2345-3.
Vol. 11. 2010. 232pp. 978-1-4215-2346-0.

Vol. 12. 2010. 232pp. 978-1-4215-2365-1.
Vol. 13. 2011. 200pp. 978-1-4215-3531-9.
Vol. 14. 2011. 200pp. 978-1-4215-3532-6.
Vol. 15. 2011. 232pp. 978-1-4215-3533-3.
Vol. 16. 2011. 216pp. 978-1-4215-3534-0.
Vol. 17. 2011. 208pp. 978-1-4215-3535-7.
Vol. 18. 2011. 208pp. 978-1-4215-3536-4.
Vol. 19. 2012. 230pp. 978-1-4215-3537-1.
Vol. 20. 2012. 200pp. 978-1-4215-3538-8.
Vol. 21. 2012. 200pp. 978-1-4215-3539-5.
Vol. 22. 2012. 256pp. 978-1-4215-4277-5.

Naoki Urasawa's 21st Century Boys. 2013.

Vol. 1. 2013. 200pp. 978-1-4215-4326-0.
Vol. 2. 2013. 200pp. 978-1-4215-4327-7.

X-O Manowar

Valiant Entertainment, 2012– . T

© 2016 Valiant Entertainment.

The armored hero of the Valiant universe, the original incarnation of the character, was created by Jim Shooter and Bob Layton and was Aric of Dacia, a fifth-century Visigoth kidnapped by aliens. When escaping them, he acquired the X-O Manowar armor (which had its own sentience) and made his way back to Earth, finding, that due to time dilation, it was now the 20th century. The Acclaim Comics reboot from Mark Waid and Brian Augustyn made the armor ancient and mysterious and worn by a modern scientist. The recent series started by Robert Venditti and Cary Nord has many of the elements of the original. The Layton version has been collected and available in an omnibus, while the Vendetti series has been collected in a series of softcover volumes and larger, hardcover, Deluxe Editions. The Mark Waid second series has yet to be collected.

X-O Manowar, 1st series. 2015.

X-O Manowar Classic Omnibus. 2015. 800pp. 978-1-9393-4630-8.

X-O Manowar, 3rd series. 2012– .

Vol. 1: By the Sword. 2012. 112pp. 978-0-97964094-0.
Vol. 2: Enter Ninjak. 2013. 112pp. 978-0-97964099-5.
Vol. 3: Planet Death. 2013. 144pp. 978-1-9393-4608-7.
Vol. 4: Homecoming. 2014. 112pp. 978-1-9393-4617-9.
Vol. 5: At War with Unity. 2014. 112pp. 978-1-9393-4624-7.
Vol. 6: Prelude to Armor Hunters. 2014. 104pp. 978-1-9393-4640-7.
Vol. 7: Armor Hunters. 2015. 112pp. 978-1-9393-4647-6.
Vol. 8: Enter: Armorines. 2015. 112pp. 978-1-9393-4655-1.
Vol. 9: Dead Hand. 2015. 144pp. 978-1-9393-4665-0.
Vol. 10: Exodus. 2016. 160pp. 978-1-9393-4693-3.
Vol. 11: The Kill List. 2016. 116pp. 978-1-68215-127-3.
Vol. 12: Long Live the King. 2016. 978-1-68215-165-5.
Vol. 13: Succession and Other Tales. 2017. 978-1-68215-177-8.
Hardcover Deluxe Edition. 2013–2015.
Book 1. 2013. 384pp. 978-1-9393-4610-0.
Book 2. 2015. 320pp. 978-1-9393-4652-0.
Book 3. 2016. 304pp. 978-1-6821-5131-0.
Book 4. 2017. 400pp. 978-1-6821-5183-9.

Zot! Written and Illustrated by **Scott McCloud**. HarperCollins Publishing, 2008. 576pp. 978-0-06-153727-1. O

> Zachary T. Paleozog is a teen from the far future of "1965"—a utopian Earth where rocket boots, robot butlers, laser guns, and plenty of world peace. He comes to our world and meets Jenny, a teenage girl, who befriends him. The series, which mixed aspects of manga, super-heroes, and action, focuses on Zot as he fights various villains, but also the travels with Zot and Jenny between worlds. Jenny loves the peaceful alternate Earth, while Zot loves the challenges of our world. The last few chapters of the series focused on more of the relationship of Zot and Jenny and her friends on Earth. The series was also one of the first of its kind to address homosexuality and frank discussions about sex—of which the specific issue was nominated for an Eisner Award. In 2008 the collection reprinted issues 1–36 of the series in one collection, reprinting all the original material from 1987 to 1991. The series was heavily inspired by Osaku Tezuka's *Astro Boy*.

New Wave Science Fiction

This subgenre takes a radical alternative look at science fiction. Prose pioneers in the field include the writings of Ray Bradbury, Phillip K. Dick, Ursula LeGuin, Harlan Ellison, and Michael Moorcock. In new wave science fiction the literate writing quality of the story tends to be more important than the scientific accuracy of occurrences in the plot. Generally difficult to categorize, the subgenre can include facets of religion, thought-provoking topics on the nature of the soul, and psychological rides of fantasy that flow alongside common science fiction themes including—but limited to—time travel, alien races, space travel to other planets, and alternative looks into the far future. Carla Speed McNeil's genre-busting series <u>Finder</u> is an excellent example of this subgenre.

Children of the Sea. Written and Illustrated by **Daisuke Igarashi**. VIZ Media, 2009–2010. O. Japanese manga.

> The world's fish are acting strangely. Deep sea fish are found near the surface. Whales are migrating to areas in the wrong seasons. And a variety of fish in aquariums are disappearing out of thin air. This mystery seems to focus around two boys named Sora and Umi who were raised by a pack of dugongs. It is up to a girl named Ruka to find out why Sora and Umi are able to swim unlike any human, and communicate with whales, and where the fish are disappearing to.

Vol. 1. 2009. 320pp. 978-1-4215-2914-1.
Vol. 2. 2009. 320pp. 978-1-4215-2919-6.
Vol. 3. 2010. 320pp. 978-1-4215-2920-2.
Vol. 4. 2010. 200pp. 978-1-4215-3541-8.

Finder. Written and Illustrated by **Carla Speed McNeil**. Lightspeed Press, 1999–2006; Dark Horse Comics, 2011– . M ⚲ ◎

© 2016 Carla Speed McNeil.

In the domed city of Anvard where various alien and familiar cultures coexist, there exist Finders, mysterious hunters and trackers, who are able to eat the sin from someone's life before they die. Jaeger Ayers is one such Finder. A shaman-like charming rogue, he's come to the city to the aid of Emma Grosvenor and her three children. Her ex-husband is Brig, a member of the Medawar clan and a vicious homicidal maniac, and Jaegar once served in the army under his command. Can Jaeger resolve the family conflict without causing any bloodshed? Through each storyline, Jaeger and other Finders travel around the planet in search of a connection with other humans and aliens, taking on their sins for the good of the world. The complex science fiction story was awarded an Ignatz Award in 2004 and 2005 for Outstanding Series and is still ongoing. Beginning in 2011, Dark Horse Comics became the home for Finder, and the series was reprinted in two Library Editions which reprint the first eight volumes, and newer material has continued to be published by Dark Horse Comics.

Sin-Eater, Part I. 1999. 168pp. 978-0-9673691-0-5.
Sin-Eater, Part II. 2000. 184pp. 978-0-9673691-1-2.
King of the Cats. 2001. 120pp. 978-0-9673691-2-9.
Talisman. 2002. 104pp. 978-0-9673691-3-6.
Dream Sequence. 2003. 104pp. 978-0-9673691-4-3.
Mystery Date. 2004. 160pp. 978-0-9673691-5-0.
The Rescuers. 2005. 160pp. 978-0-9673691-6-7.
Five Crazy Women. 2006. 136pp. 978-0-9673691-7-4.
Voice. 2011. 208pp. 978-1-59582-651-0.
Talisman. 2012. 96pp. 978-1-61655-027-1, hardcover.
Third World. 2014. 184pp. 978-1-61655-467-5.*Library Edition Vol. 1*. 2011. 616pp. 978-1-59582-652-7.*Library Edition Vol. 2*. 2011. 640pp. 978-1-59582-653-4.

Here. Written and Illustrated by **Richard McGuire**. Pantheon Books, 2014. 320pp. 0-375-40650-6. M

> *Here* started out as a six-page story in *Raw* Vol. 2 #1 (1989), which garnered critical and academic acclaim. In 2015 McGuire expanded it to a 300+ page full-color story. *Here* takes place in one corner of one room of a house. The panels show that spot at various points in time, including the distant past and centuries in the future as well as different years that the house actually existed. On some pages the time lines overlap with, for example, an image from the 1980s sharing the page with images from other times.

Aliens from Outer Space

Ever since science fiction classic novels such as H.G. Wells's *War of the Worlds*, writers have been telling tales of alien visitors from outer space and the horrors (or blessings) that their interaction with mankind would bring. The stories listed below focus on tales of alien races both benign and monstrous and their interaction with mankind. The aliens can be portrayed as the protagonists, antagonists, or supporting characters.

Alien Legion. Created by **Carl Potts**. Written by **Chuck Dixon**, **Alan Zelenetz**, and various. Illustrated by **Larry Stroman**, **Frank Cirocco**, and various. Dark Horse Comics, 2009–2010. T

> Soldiers for the Tophan Galactic Union, a rag-tag group of misfits, outcasts, criminals, and soldiers of fortune, are the main fighting force against the ruthless and hostile race known as the Harkilon Empire. Led by the blue-skinned snake-like humanoid Major Sarigar, the Legion is the best there is when it comes to taking on the toughest assignments in the galaxy. The Dark Horse collections reprint the original Epic Comics series.
>
> *Omnibus, Vol. 1*. 352pp. 2009. 978-1-59582-394-6.
> *Omnibus, Vol. 2*. 352pp. 2010. 978-1-59582-494-3.

Aliens

Dark Horse Comics, 1996– . T-O

> These acid-spewing, insectoid Aliens first appeared in Ridley Scott's film *Alien* in 1979 and have been scaring audiences ever since with three sequels, as well as the 2004 *Aliens versus Predator* film. Dark Horse Comics tales of the Aliens delve deeper into the science fiction world of facehuggers, chestbursters, Alien Queens, and the unlucky humans who find themselves face-to-face with the deadliest species in the galaxy. Note that other tie-ins featuring the Aliens and popular characters from other comic books including Superman, Green Lantern, and Judge Dredd are listed below.

Aliens, 2010– . O

> Tales spun off directly from the events seen in the Alien quadrilogy of films. The stories feature a variety of characters from the movies, including Ripley, and plenty of acid-spewing aliens and deadly facehuggers.

More Than Human. 2010. Written by **John Arcudi**. Illustrated by **Zach Howard**. 96pp. 978-1-59582-490-5.

Fast Track to Heaven. 2011. Written and Illustrated by **Liam Sharp**. 40pp. 978-1-59582-495-0, hardcover.

Inhuman Condition. Written by **John Layman**. Illustrated by **Sam Kieth**. 2013. 56pp. 978-1-59582-618-3.

Fire and Stone. Written by **Chris Robertson**. Illustrated by **Patric Reynolds**. 2015. 104pp. 978-1-61655-655-6.

Salvation. Written by **Dave Gibbons**. Illustrated by **Mike Mignola**. 2015. 56pp. 978-1-61655-755-3, hardcover.

Defiance. Written by **Brian Wood**. Illustrated by **Tristan Jones**. 2017. 160pp. 978-1-50670-126-4.

Life and Death. Written by **Dan Abnett**. Illustrated by **Moritat**. 2017. 96pp. 978-1-50670-125-7.

Aliens Omnibus. Written by **Mark Verheiden**, **Mike Richardson**, **Jerry Prosser**, **Dave Gibbons**, and various. Illustrated by **Mark A. Nelson**, **Denis Beauvais**, **Sam Keith**, **Kelley Jones**, **Mike Mignola**, **Paul Johnson**, and various. 2007–2008. O

A reprinting of most of the classic Dark Horse Comics' <u>Aliens</u> series of books in a massive omnibus format!

Vol. 1. 2007. 384pp. 978-1-59307-727-3.

Vol. 2. 2007. 448pp. 978-1-59307-828-7.

Vol. 3. 2008. 376pp. 978-1-59307-872-0.

Vol. 4. 2008. 376pp. 978-1-59307-926-0.

Vol. 5. 2008. 364pp. 978-1-59307-991-8.

Vol. 6. 2008. 376pp. 978-1-59582-214-7.

DC/Dark Horse: Aliens. Written by various. Illustrated by various. 2016. 400pp. 978-1-4012-6636-3. T

A collection of the various crossovers of DC Comics heroes and their battle against the deadly xenomorphs. The highlights include the series <u>Batman/Aliens</u> as well as <u>Superman/Batman vs. Aliens/Predator</u> as well as the long out-of-print <u>WildC.A.T.S./Aliens</u>.

Superman/Aliens. Written by **Dan Jurgens** and **Chuck Dixon**. Illustrated by **Kevin Nowlan** and **Jon Bogdanove**. DC Comics and Dark Horse Comics, 2016. T ◎

While investigating a possible signal that deviated from his home planet of Krypton, a depowered Superman finds himself face-to-face against one of the deadliest creatures in space. In the sequel, the villain Darkseid of the planet Apokolips has use for the deadly Aliens, and Superman and his allies must try and defeat the horde of Apokolips-Alien hybrids.

Aliens vs. Predator

Dark Horse Comics, 2007–2011. O 🎬

A science fiction movie fan's dream comes true; the first collection pairing up two of Hollywood's most horrific and fearsome aliens appeared in 1991, 13 years before the long-awaited Fox film based on the premise of the two alien races' battle against each other was released in 2004. Many film buffs feel that the graphic novel stories featuring the Aliens against the Predators were better-done treatments than the film could ever hope to be. The Omnibus collections reprint material originally published beginning in 1991.

Aliens vs. Predator Omnibus. Written and Illustrated by various. 2007.

> *Vol. 1. 2007.* 456pp. 978-1-59307-735-8.
> *Vol. 2.* 2007. 464pp. 978-1-59307-829-4.

Aliens vs Predator: World War Three. Written by **Randy Stradley**. Illustrated by **Rick Leonardi**. 2011. 144pp. 978-1-59582-702-9.

Creature Tech. Written and Illustrated by **Doug TenNapel**. Image Comics, 2010. 224pp. 978-1-60706-282-0. T 🏵 ◎

© 2016 Doug TenNapel.

One hundred and fifty years ago the evil Dr. Jameson wanted to destroy the world by using giant space eels. He messed up and died—but that didn't stop him. Resurrected by the Shroud of Turin, the now zombified Doctor wants to reset his evil scheme in motion. Only Doctor Ong, a young scientist at the top-secret "Creature Tech" facility, and the strangest assortment of allies including a CIA-trained praying mantis, rednecks, alien symbiotes, and a little Christian faith can save the day. The original printing of the book received recognition by YALSA's Popular Paperbacks for Young Adults committee in 2004 on the *Simply Science Fiction* list.

Meteor Man. Written by **Jeff Parker**. Illustrated by **Sandy Jarrell**. Oni Press, 2014. 128pp. 978-1-62010-151-3. T 🏵

After a meteorite crashes on his land, teenager Alden Baylor has a close encounter with an alien, which will change his life forever. Can he find out the alien's true intent and communicate with it in time? The book was recognized by YALSA as a Great Graphic Novel for Teens selection in 2016.

Parasyte. Written and Illustrated by **Hitoshi Iwaaki**. Kodansha Comics, 2011–2013. M. Japanese manga. あ

Shin seems to be a typical high school student and an all-around normal boy, but he discovers a plot by parasitic aliens to dominate the world. The aliens take over the human body and appear on the outside to blend in well with other humans, but their faces detach to reveal a sharp-toothed horror. How does Shin know of this invasion? He's got one living inside his body! He was able to trap his own attacker in his left arm before it could take over the rest of his body. Now the parasite, nicknamed "Lefty," has become an inquisitive sort and Shin must decide what he can do to prevent the invasion. Should he go public with this startling information or will it place him in even more danger, and will more innocents die by the vicious and gory aliens before it's too late? The manga inspired a Japanese anime as well.

Vol. 1. 2011. 288pp. 978-1-61262-073-2.
Vol. 2. 2011. 288pp. 978-1-61262-074-9.
Vol. 3. 2011. 288pp. 978-1-61262-075-6.
Vol. 4. 2011. 304pp. 978-1-61262-076-3.
Vol. 5. 2012. 304pp. 978-1-61262-310-8.
Vol. 6. 2012. 288pp. 978-1-61262-311-5.
Vol. 7. 2013. 288pp. 978-1-61262-341-2.
Vol. 8. 2013. 288pp. 978-1-61262-312-2.

Predator

Dark Horse Comics, 2007–2015. T 🎬

Continuing the success of Dark Horse Comics' treatment of Fox's *Aliens* license, the hunter warriors from another world that originally plagued Arnold Schwarzenegger way back in the 1987 *Predator* film also successfully translated into the comic book format. The Predators are a race of warriors who hunt the deadliest known prey across the galaxy for their own sport. The tales serve as sequels of sorts to the first *Predator* film and expand on the original concept. For other tales featuring the Predator, please see the series title of Aliens vs. Predator listed in this chapter.

Predator. 2007–2009. O

Predator: Omnibus. Written by **Mark Verheiden** and various. Illustrated by **Chris Warner** and various. 2007–2008.

Vol. 1. 2007. 440pp. 978-1-59307-732-7.
Vol. 2. 2008. 360pp. 978-1-59307-733-4.
Vol. 3. 2008. 344pp. 978-1-59307-925-3.
Vol. 4. 2008. 352pp. 978-1-59307-990-1.

Predator: Prey to the Heavens. Written by **John Arcudi**. Illustrated by **Javier Saltares**. 2010. 96pp. 978-1-59582-492-9.
Predator: Fire and Stone. Written by **Joshua Williamson**. Illustrated by **Christopher Mooneyham**. 2015. 104pp. 978-1-61655-695-2.

Archie vs. Predator. Written by **Alex de Campi**. Illustrated by **Fernando Ruiz**. 2015. 128pp. 978-1-61655-805-5. T ◎

One of the most offbeat crossovers ever! What happens when Archie Andrews and the Riverdale gang are trapped in the most dangerous game with one of the fiercest alien warriors the galaxy has ever known? Will they survive, or do they even know they're in danger? Like *Afterlife with Archie* this collected limited series is definitely not for younger readers.

Predator vs. Judge Dredd vs. Aliens. Written by **John Wagner** and **Andy Diggle**. Illustrated by **Henry Flint**, **Enrique Alcatena**, **Brian Bolland**, **Greg Staples**, and various. Dark Horse Comics and 2000 AD, 2014. 184pp. 978-1-61655-479-8, hardcover. O

What happens when the no-nonsense Judge Dredd from Mega City One meets up with the deadly Aliens and Predators? In Mega City One, the law is enforced by the toughest lawman on Earth: Judge Dredd—but when a deadly infestation of Aliens threatens to destroy the city, Dredd and a team of bug-hunters called the Verminators are there to take on the vicious killing machines from outer space. And when a rogue Predator finds its way to the far-future world of Mega City One, it's out for the biggest trophy of all—the head of Judge Dredd, the toughest lawman of Mega City One.

Scarlet Traces. Written by **Ian Edginton**. Illustrated by **D'Israeli**. Dark Horse Comics, 2003–2007. T

At the dawn of the 20th century, spider-like machines roam the dark streets of London. It's been 10 years since the failed Martian invasion when the invaders were infected by Earth germs (as seen in the classic H.G. Wells novel *War of the Worlds*), and now England is the ultimate super-power and in control of the Martian technology. When girls begin turning up dead with their throats punctured, Major Robert Autumn and his manservant Sergeant Archibald Currie are on the hunt to solve the murders. At first the culprits are thought to be vampires, but the truth is far, far worse. In the follow-up, when British citizens are disappearing in legions, Major Autumn discovers a lone Martian as the culprit and even more subterfuge is needed when a larger-scale war against Mars is discovered. In 2005 the creative team also adapted H.G. Wells's classic novel *War of the Worlds*.

H.G. Wells' War of the Worlds. 2005. 72pp. 978-1-59307-474-6, hardcover.
Vol. 1. 2003. 88pp. 978-1-56971-940-4, hardcover.
Vol. 2: The Great Game. 2007. 104pp. 978-1-59307-717-4, hardcover.

The Squidder. Written and Illustrated by **Ben Templesmith**. IDW Publishing, 2015. 128pp. 978-1-63140-205-0. O

When a squid-like race of aliens invades the Earth, a genetically modified soldier long forgotten and a priestess may be all that remain to save mankind from the tentacled aliens.

Ultraman. Written by **Eiichi Shimizu**. Illustrated by **Tomohiro Shimoguchi**. VIZ Media, 2015– . T. Japanese manga. ◉

©2012 Eiichi Shimizu and Tomohiro Shimoguchi/TPC Originally published by HERO'S INC.

Shinjiro Hayata grew up thinking that he was an ordinary kid with an ordinary father who was once part of the Science Patrol, the group who helped the alien hero Ultraman who fought the alien kaiju monsters intent on taking over the world. Now a teenager, Shinjiro learns not only that his father was the human host for Ultraman but also that he has inherited the "Ultraman Factor," giving him incredible powers. And just in time too, as the alien kaiju appears to be returning for another round! The series is still ongoing in Japan.

Vol. 1. 2015. 240pp. 978-1-4215-8182-8.
Vol. 2. 2015. 212pp. 978-1-4215-8183-5.
Vol. 3. 2016. 188pp. 978-1-4215-8184-2.
Vol. 4. 2016. 188pp. 978-1-4215-8185-9.
Vol. 5. 2016. 200pp. 978-1-4215-8186-6.   *Vol. 7*. 2017. 196pp. 978-1-4215-9060-8.
Vol. 6. 2016. 200pp. 978-1-4215-8647-2.   *Vol. 8*. 2017. 200pp. 978-1-4215-9272-5.

The Twilight Children. Written by **Gilbert Hernandez**. Illustrated by **Darwyn Cooke**. Vertigo/DC Comics. 2016. 144pp. 978-1-4012-6245-7. M

On a quiet, beachside village, mysterious orbs are floating in the sky. They blind the children and give them psychic abilities; they make families disappear and burn down homes; they inflame passions and hatred around the community and bring it to a fever pitch. Scientists and the government are drawn to this place but can't explain it. Then, just as mysterious as the orbs appears Ela: a beautiful woman who is silent but holds unspeakable power. Is she created by the orbs, or is she something entirely different? The book is the last one completed by Darwyn Cooke's before his death in 2016.

Alternate Worlds, Time Travel, and Dimensions

Stories featuring the adventures of explorers from our world transported to other worlds or dimensions. The worlds or dimensions can be very similar to our own with subtle differences that may not even be perceptible to the human eye, or they can be a vastly different world or dimension that makes the alternate world seem almost like an alien planet. The plots can even involve the protagonists exploring alternate histories of famous historical events, alternate pasts, and futures, to even worlds so abstract that it defies common thought.

All You Need Is Kill. Original story by **Hiroshi Sakurazaka**. Adapted by **Ryosuke Takeuchi**. Illustrated by **Takeshi Obata**. VIZ Media, 2014. 554pp. 978-1-4215-7601-5. O. Japanese manga.

A soldier for the United Defense Force, Keiji Kiriya wears a suit of battle armor called a Jacket and is sent out to kill an alien menace called the Mimics who have decimated the Earth. Keiji dies on the battlefield, only to be reborn each day. Stuck in a time loop, he's repeating the same day over and over again and fully aware that he is dying every day. How can Keiji get out of the time loop created by the Mimics, and will he have the guts to do what needs to be done or die one final time? The manga is adapted from the original 2004 novel by writer Hiroshi Sakurazaka which was published in Japan. The book was also adapted into the 2014 U.S. feature film *Edge of Tomorrow: Live. Die. Repeat.*

ALL YOU NEED IS KILL © 2014 by Hiroshi Sakurazaka, Ryosuke Takeuchi, yoshitoshi ABe, Takeshi Obata/SHUEISHA Inc.

The Arrival. Written and Illustrated by **Shaun Tan**. Arthur A. Levine Books, 2007. 128pp. 978-0-439-89529-3, hardcover. T

A silently told story of an immigrant who leaves his familiar to a new world—a world like none we have ever seen. Everything from the world is foreign to the man—the language, birds, buildings, and more are foreign. As he wanders in his new home, he's followed everywhere by a strange cat-sized tadpole who over time helps give him a feeling of peace in such a strange and bizarre land.

Back to the Future. Written by **Bob Gale**, **John Barber**, and **Erik Burnham**. Illustrated by **Alan Robinson**, **Corin Howell**, and various. IDW Publishing, 2016– . A

Cowritten by Bob Gale, the original writer of the *Back to the Future* movies, go back to 1985 and see how Marty McFly and Doc Brown first met. Also, take a trip in the flying Delorean and see how Doc Brown played a part in the Manhattan Project as well as other time-travel adventures! The IDW series continues the adventures of Marty and Doc from similar situations from the original film trilogy and beyond.

Untold Tales and Alternate Timelines. 2016. 120pp. 978-1-63140-570-9.
Continuum Conundrum. 2016. 136pp. 978-1-63140-727-7.

Citizen Brown. 2017. 120pp. 978-1-63140-793-2.
Who is Marty McFly?. 2017. 132pp. 978-1-63140-876-2.
Biff to the Future. 2017. 128pp. 978-1-63140-974-5.

Black Science. Written by **Rick Remender**. Illustrated by **Dean White** and **Matteo Scalera**. Image Comics, 2014– . M

Grant McKay is a past member of the Anarchistic Order of Scientists, and he's done the impossible: he has deciphered Black Science and discovered the access point to alternate realities. When Grant and his team enter through the veil, what they discover is pure chaos—an unmanageable place where alien worlds and dark realms collide. Lost in realities they couldn't begin to fathom, Grant and his crew push forward against impossible odds and try to find their way back home. The Premiere Hardcover reprints the material from the first three volumes plus supplemental material.

Vol. 1: How to Fall Forever. 2014. 152pp. 978-1-60706-967-6.
Vol. 2: Welcome, Nowhere. 2015. 128pp. 978-1-63215-018-9.
Vol. 3: Vanishing Pattern. 2015. 128pp. 978-1-63215-395-1.
Vol. 4: Godworld. 2016. 128pp. 978-1-63215-686-0.
Vol. 5: True Atonement. 2016. 104pp. 978-1-5343-0033-0.
Premiere Hardcover. 2016. 432pp. 978-1632154934, hardcover.

Chrononauts. Written by **Mark Millar**. Illustrated by **Sean Murphy**. Image Comics, 2015. 120pp. 978-1-63215-406-4. O

Corbin Quinn and Danny Reilly are two young scientists who are about to embark on the first-ever time-travel experiment. With the world watching them, Corbin and Danny jump into the time-stream with disastrous results! Diverted and lost from their originally planned course, the two must hop from ancient history and back as they both have a front row to some of history's greatest events and make a mess of everything. What will the world and their bosses say with the mess they've made?

Doctor Who

IDW Publishing, 2008–2013; Titan Comics, 2015– . T

© 2016 Titan Comics.

A Time Lord from the planet Gallifrey, The Doctor—the main character of the television series Doctor Who—travels through time and space in a vessel called the TARDIS, which due to a broken "chameleon circuit" looks like a 1960s' British police box. The show ran in the United Kingdom from 1963 to 1989, with episodes being shown in the United States beginning in the 1970s. There was a failed revival in 1996, with an American TV movie and a successful revival beginning in 2005. As a Time Lord, the Doctor has the ability to regenerate when fatally injured, changing in both appearance and personality. The Doctors are referred to by fans according to their number, with the Twelfth Doctor being on the air as of this writing. While there have long been Doctor Who comics in the United Kingdom—some of which had been reprinted in American comics—the show was not regularly seen in America until IDW began doing so in 2007. Besides the adventures of the Tenth and Eleventh Doctors, they reprinted the adventurers of the Fourth through Seventh Doctors, which were published in the United Kingdom in the 1980s and whose creators included such people as Grant Morrison and Dave Gibbons. In 2014 Titan took over the license and has published an ongoing series, with all of the modern doctors as well as limited series featuring the earlier ones. Titan has also repackaged and reprinted most of the new IDW stories. See the Star Trek entry in this chapter for The Doctor's meeting with the crew of the Enterprise.

IDW Publishing, 2008–2013

Collections of *Doctor Who* British comics finally made available in North America:

Doctor Who Classics. Written by **Pat Mills**, **John Wagner**, **Grant Morrison**, and various. Illustrated by **Dave Gibbons**, **Joe Corroney**, **Bryan Hitch**, and various. T

Vol. 1. 2008. 112pp. 978-1-60010-189-2.
Vol. 2. 2008. 120pp. 978-1-60010-289-9.
Vol. 3. 2009. 128pp. 978-1-60010-425-1.
Vol. 4. 2009. 152pp. 978-1-60010-534-0.
Vol. 5. 2010. 104pp. 978-1-60010-608-8.
Omnibus Vol. 1. 2010. 356pp. 978-1-60010-6224.
Omnibus Vol. 2. 2011. 496pp. 978-1-60010-9980.

Vol. 6. 2010. 148pp. 978-1-60010-793-1.
Vol. 7. 2011. 128pp. 978-1-61377-045-0.
Vol. 8. 2012. 152pp. 978-1-61377-484-7.
Vol. 9. 2013. 140pp. 978-1-61377-806-7.

Doctor Who: The Dave Gibbons Collection. Written by **Pat Mills**, **Steve Moore**, and various. Illustrated by **Dave Gibbons**. IDW Publishing, 2011. 372pp. 978-1-61377-063-4, hardcover.

From Titan Comics, 2015– .

Third Doctor

Jon Pertwee portrayed the Third Doctor from 1970 to 1974.

Doctor Who: The Third Doctor—The Heralds of Destruction. Written by **Paul Cornell**. Illustrated by **Christopher Jones**. Titan Comics. 2017. 128pp. 978-1-78585-731-7.

Fourth Doctor

Tom Baker portrayed the Fourth Doctor from 1974 to 1981.

Doctor Who: The Fourth Doctor—Gaze of the Medusa. Written by **Gordon Rennie** and **Emma Beeby**. Illustrated by **Brian Williamson**. Titan Comics, 2016. 128pp. 978-1-78276-755-8.

Eighth Doctor

Paul McGann first portrayed the Eighth Doctor in a 1996 television movie.

Doctor Who: The Eighth Doctor: A Matter of Life and Death. Written by **George Mann**. Illustrated by **Emma Vieceli**. Titan Comics, 2016. 128pp. 978-1-78276-753-4.

Ninth Doctor

Christopher Eccleston portrayed the Ninth Doctor in 2005 in the first season of the modern revival. After a 2015 limited series, an ongoing series began in 2016.

Doctor Who: The Ninth Doctor: Written by **Cavan Scott**. Illustrated by **Blair Shedd**. Titan Comics, 2016– .

> *Vol. 1: Weapons of Past Destruction*. 2016. 128pp. 978-1-78276-336-9, hardcover; 978-1-78585-105-6.
> *Vol. 2: Doctormania*. 2016. 128pp. 978-1-78586-022-5, hardcover. 978-1-78586-110-9.
> *Vol. 3: Official Secrets*. 2017. 128pp. 978-1-78586-111-6, hardcover.

Tenth Doctor

David Tennant portrayed the Tenth Doctor from 2005 to 2010. The omnibus editions collect the IDW stories.

Doctor Who Archives: The Tenth Doctor Omnibus. Written by **Gary Russell**, **Tony Lee**, **Matthew Dow Smith**, and various. Illustrated by **Nick Roche**, **Pia Guerra**, **Kelly Yates**, and various.

> *Vol. 1*. 2016. 288pp. 978-1-78276-770-1.
> *Vol. 2*. 2016. 288pp. 978-1-78276-771-8.
> *Vol. 3*. 2016. 288pp. 978-1-78276-772-5.

© 2016 Titan Comics.

Doctor Who: The Tenth Doctor. Written by **Robbie Morrison**, **Daniel Indro**, **Nick Abadzis**, and various. Illustrated by **Elena Casagrande**, **Arianna Florean**, and **Eleonora Carlini**.

> *Vol. 1: Revolutions of Terror.* 2015. 128pp. 978-1-728276-3840, hardcover; 978-1-78585-178-0.
> *Vol. 2: The Weeping Angels of Mons.* 2015. 128pp. 978-1-728276-1754, hardcover; 978-1-78276-657-5.
> *Vol. 3: The Fountains of Forever.* 2016. 136pp. 978-1-728276-3024, hardcover.
> *Vol. 4: The Endless Song.* 2016. 128pp. 978-1-728276-7459, hardcover; 978-1-78276-740-4.
> *Vol. 5: Arena of Fear.* 2016. 128pp. 978-1-78585-428-6, hardcover; 978-1-78585-322-7.
> *Vol. 6: Sins of the Father.* 112pp, 978-1-78585-358-6, hardcover. 978-1-78585-680-8.

Eleventh Doctor

Matt Smith portrayed the Eleventh Doctor from 2010 to 2013. The omnibus editions collect the IDW stories.

Doctor Who: The Eleventh Doctor Archives Omnibus. Written by **Tony Lee**, **Andy Diggle**, **Paul Cornell**, and various. Illustrated by **Matthew Dow Smith**, **Mark Buckingham**, **Tim Hamilton**, and various. 2015–2016.

> *Vol. 1.* 2015. 336pp. 978-1-78276-768-8.
> *Vol. 2.* 2015. 336pp. 978-1-78276-769-5.
> *Vol. 3.* 2016. 272pp. 978-1-78276-773-2.

© 2016 Titan Comics.

Doctor Who: The Eleventh Doctor. Written by **Al Ewing**, **Rob Williams**, and **Simon Spurrier**. Illustrated by **Simon Frasier**, **Warren Pleece**, **Gary Caldwell**, and various.

> *Vol. 1: After Life.* 2015. 128pp. 978-1-78276-174-7, hardcover; 978-1-78276-385-7.
> *Vol. 2: Serve You.* 2015. 128pp. 978-1-78276-176-1, hardcover; 978-1-78276-658-2.
> *Vol. 3: Conversion.* 2015. 136pp. 978-1-78276-303-1, hardcover; 978-1-78276-743-5.
> *Vol. 4: The Then and the Now.* 2016. 128pp. 978-1-78276-746-6, hardcover; 978-1-78276-746-6.
> *Vol. 5: The One.* 2016. 128pp. 978-1-78585-351-7, hardcover; 978-1-78585-323-4.
> *Vol. 6: The Malignant Truth.* 2017. 128pp. 978-1-78585-730-0, hardcover.

Twelfth Doctor

Peter Capaldi portrayed the Twelfth Doctor from 2013 to 2017 and is the current Doctor as of this writing.

Doctor Who: The Twelfth Doctor. Written by **Robbie Morrison** and **George Mann**. Illustrated by **Dave Taylor**, **Alice X. Zhang**, **Brian Williamson**, and various.

Vol. 1: Terrorformer. 2015. 128pp. 978-1-78276-177-8, hardcover; 978-1-78585-361-6.
Vol. 2: Fractures. 2015. 128pp. 978-1-78276-301-7, hardcover; 978-1-78276-659-9.
Vol. 3: Hyperion. 2016. 128pp. 978-1-78276-747-3, hardcover.
Vol. 4: The School of Death. 2016. 128pp. 978-1-78585-108-7, hardcover; 978-1-78585-107-0.
Vol. 5: The Twist. 2016. 128pp. 978-1-78585-355-5, hardcover. 978-1-78585-321-0.
Vol. 6: Sonic Boom. 2017. 112pp. 978-1-78586-012-6, hardcover.

© 2016 Titan Comics.

Multiple Doctors

The titles below feature stories in which multiple incarnations of the Doctor appear, and on occasion even team up. The first volume of *Doctor Who Archives: The Tenth Doctor Omnibus* collects the multiple Doctor story from IDW, *Doctor Who: The Forgotten*. The *Prisoners of Time Omnibus* also collects a limited series originally published by IDW.

Doctor Who Archives: Prisoners of Time Omnibus. Written by **Scott Tipton** and **David Tipton**. Illustrated by **Simon Fraser**, **Lee Sullivan**, and **Mike Collins**. 2016. 304pp. 978-1-78276-774-9.

Doctor Who: Four Doctors. Written by **Paul Cornell**. Illustrated by **Neil Edwards**. 2016. 128pp. 978-1-78276-596-7, hardcover.

Doctor Who: The Supremacy of the Cybermen. Written by **George Mann** and **Cavan Scott**. Illustrated by **Alessandro Vitti**. 2017. 128pp. 978-1-78585-684-6, hardcover.

© 2016 Titan Comics.

Five Fists of Science. Written by **Matt Fraction**. Illustrated by **Steven Sanders**. Image Comics, 2006. 112pp. 978-1-58240-605-3. T

In 1899, Mark Twain, Bertha von Suttner, and Nicholas Tesla vow to end war forever. With their connections and inventions (and a little bit of trickery), they went into business selling world peace and a new glorious future arrived for the world. The three are soon confronted by dark forces led by the dastardly Thomas Edison, John Pierpont Morgan, Andrew Carnegie, and Guglielmo Marconi, and the fate of the world rests in a climactic battle amid the skyscrapers of New York City.

Manhattan Projects. Written by **Jonathan Hickman**. Illustrated by **Nick Pitarra**. 2012– . O

Set in an alternate Earth where the Manhattan Project was a front for more esoteric scientific experiments, join scientists Oppenheimer, Feynman, Enrico Fermi, Wernher Von Braun, Einstein, Yuri Gagarin, and more as they tackle the strange and the stranger. Alternate realities, aliens, parallel dimensions, exotic energy sources, theoretical physics, and more.

Vol. 1: Science Bad. 2012. 144pp. 978-1-60706-608-8.
Vol. 2: Above Beyond. 2013. 152pp. 978-1-60706-726-9.
Vol. 3: Building. 2013. 152pp. 978-1-60706-753-5.
Vol. 4: The Four Disciplines. 2014. 144pp. 978-1-60706-961-4.
Vol. 5: The Cold War. 2015. 144pp. 978-1-63215-184-1.
Vol. 6: Sun Beyond the Stars. 2016. 152pp. 978-1-63215-628-0.

Patience. Written and Illustrated by **Daniel Clowes**. Fantagraphics, 2016. 180pp. 978-1-60699-905-9. M

In 2012 Jack's wife Patience was murdered and the killer never caught. Seventeen years later, Jack meets a man who has discovered time travel, and goes back to several points prior to 2012 in the hopes that he can figure out the identity of the killer. But things do not go exactly as planned.

© 2016 Daniel Clowes.

Pax Romana. Written and Illustrated by **Jonathan Hickman**. Image Comics, 2009. 144pp. 978-1-58240-873-6. O

In 2045, Islam has enslaved Europe and monotheism isn't yet embraced. When time travel is discovered by a Vatican-funded CERN Laboratories, a small army comprised of cardinals and hand-picked recruits are sent back in time to AD 312 to the reign of the first Christian emperor. Can the men change the future for the better, or will they make it even worse?

RASL. Written and Illustrated by **Jeff Smith**. Cartoon Books, 2013. 472pp. 978-1-888963-37-3, hardcover. O 🎖 ◎

When Rasl, an art thief and ex-military designer, discovers the lost journals of Nicholas Tesla, he finds that Tesla nearly perfected a device that lets him travel between parallel Earth dimensions. First done as a way to steal famous versions of paintings from alternative dimensions, Rasl (Dr. Robert Joseph Johnson) finds himself further

and further lost as he is chased by a government agency known as The Compound and haunted by the ghosts of his past. Can Rasl make amends to his corrupt past as his dimension hopping further sends his life into a spiral of madness, corruption, and danger? RASL was recognized by an Eisner Award for Best Graphic Novel: Reprint category in 2014.

© 2016 Jeff Smith and Cartoon Books.

The Red Wing. Written by **Jonathan Hickman**. Illustrated by **Nick Pitarra**. Image Comics, 2011. 140pp. 978-1-60706-479-4. T

In the far future, mankind's been taken over by a mysterious invasion force from an alternate reality. In order to fight the enemy, not only are fighter pilots needed to master their aircraft to combat the enemy, but they need to be able to travel back in time to combat the enemy before the invasion! Now the second generation of temporal pilots must travel in the past to fix the mistakes their temporal fighter pilot parents made and help to save mankind no matter what the cost.

Revolver. Written and Illustrated by **Matt Kindt**. Vertigo/DC Comics, 2010–2011. 2010. 192pp. 978-1-4012-2241-3, hardcover; 2011. 978-1-4012-2242-0. M

Each night when Sam falls asleep, he finds himself in a different reality. In the first, things are normal, but in the other massive terrorist attacks have caused chaos. He must use what he learns in both worlds to survive—and does he have the choice in which one to stay in permanently?

© 2016 DC Comics.

Space Mountain. Written by **Bryan Q. Miller**. Illustrated by **Kelley Jones**. Disney Press/Hyperion Books, 2014. 176pp. 978-1-4231-6229-2. T

Set in the year 2125 near the Cygnus X-1 colony, the students at the Magellan Science Academy are visiting the Visionarium—a living museum that allows people to study the past on Earth safely thanks to technology deposited in the past. A raffle picks two names to participate in a time-travel experiment with the time-travel experts—Stella Macri, a 12-year-old science whiz, and Tommy Ford, a good-hearted troublemaker. When the time-travel experiment goes horribly wrong, Tommy, Stella, and a robot

© 2014 Disney.

named Artie must rescue the crew who have been sent back in time throughout Earth's history and repair the fractured time line. The book is inspired by the popular roller coaster that is a mainstay at Disney Parks across the world.

Underwater Welder. Written and Illustrated by **Jeff Lemire**. Top Shelf Productions, 2012. 224pp. 978-1-60309-074-2. O

© 2016 Jeff Lemire.

Working under the water is like working in a different world. Jack Joseph thrives in this solitary world. Jack is drawn to the water his whole life. His father was an underwater salvager and was very important to Jack. Even though Jack and his wife are expecting their first baby any week, Jack cannot resist diving down to his own world. When Jack finds an old watch at the bottom of the ocean, a rush of memories flood his mind. That watch has taken him back in time to help him understand what is truly important in the real world.

Dystopian and Utopian Worlds

Stories where society has peaked and things seem perfect—or are they? Utopian fiction focuses on the idea of a perfect world as the basis of the plot. Dystopian fiction showcases an alternate look at the world, with the protagonist trying to cope against a totalitarian form of government—typically a fascist state. A good example of this would be the graphic novel *V for Vendetta* that transports readers to a bleak and moody fascist England where a masked vigilante out-stirs the citizens from their somber life to bring freedom and individuality back to the masses.

Afterschool Charisma. Written by **Kumiko Suekane**. VIZ Media, 2010–2016. T 🏃 Japanese manga.

You are forced to live someone else's life. Ever since you were born people have been guiding what you do and what you will become. This is the life of those who attend St. Kleio Academy. The students at this school are clones of famous and important people—all except for student Shiro Kamiya. Walk into a class and you can find Elizabeth I chatting with Mozart or Einstein playing chess of Ghandi. These clones are tutored in the ways of their predecessor so that they may pick up the mantle where they left off for the betterment of the world or the highest bidder. When the clone of John F. Kennedy is killed, the Shiro and the other students wonder if the clones

HOKAGO NO CHARISMA © 2009
Kumiko SUEKANE/SHOGAKUKAN.

all share the same fate as their original progenitors. The series was selected as one of YALSA's Great Graphic Novels for Teens in 2011.

Vol. 1. 2010. 208pp. 978-1-4215-3397-1.
Vol. 2. 2011. 200pp. 978-1-4215-3398-8.
Vol. 3. 2011. 200pp. 978-1-4215-3726-9.
Vol. 4. 2011. 208pp. 978-1-4215-4021-4.
Vol. 5. 2012. 208pp. 978-1-4215-4080-1.
Vol. 6. 2012. 208pp. 978-1-4215-4217-1.
Vol. 7. 2013. 208pp. 978-1-4215-4922-4.
Vol. 8. 2013. 200pp. 978-1-4215-5891-2.
Vol. 9. 2014. 208pp. 978-1-4215-6236-0.
Vol. 10. 2014. 208pp. 978-1-4215-7347-2.
Vol. 11. 2015. 208pp. 978-1-4215-8126-2.
Vol. 12. 2016. 208pp. 978-1-4215-8392-1.

Biomega. Written and Illustrated by **Tsutomu Nihei**. VIZ Media, 2010–2011. M Japanese manga.

Set in the far future of mankind, Zoichi Kanoe is a synthetic human who works as an agent for TOA Heavy Industries. His mission for their company is to retrieve those humans who have the ability to resist and transmute the deadly N5S virus—a deadly communicable disease where the infected become zombie-like "drones." The six-volume manga was selected as one of YALSA's Great Graphic Novels for Teens.

Vol. 1. 2010. 220pp. 978-1-4215-3184-7.
Vol. 2. 2010. 216pp. 978-1-4215-3185-4.
Vol. 3. 2010. 216pp. 978-1-4215-3186-1.
Vol. 4. 2010. 192pp. 978-1-4215-3187-8.
Vol. 5. 2011. 200pp. 978-1-4215-3188-5.
Vol. 6. 2011. 200pp. 978-1-4215-3277-6.

Bitch Planet. Written by **Kelly Sue DeConnick**. Illustrated by **Valentine De Landro**. Image Comics, 2015– . M

© 2016 Kelly Sue DeConnick and
Valentine De Landro.

A feminist-lead tribute to the exploitation and women in prison films of the 1970s. In a dystopian future, noncompliant women are sentenced to jail on a prison off planet. Noncompliant can be anything—too fat—too outspoken—and they are all sentenced to a jail all the women prisoners call Bitch Planet.

Vol. 1: Extraordinary Machine. 2015. 136pp. 978-1-63215-366-1.
Vol. 2: President Bitch. 2016. 144pp. 978-1-63215-717-1.

Black Bullet. Written by **Shiden Kanzaki**. Illustrated by **Morinohon**. Yen Press, 2015–2016. O. Japanese manga. あ

In a post-apocalypse world, mankind has been ravaged by the Gastrea virus. Those who have survived are in large communities surrounded by Monolith walls made of Varanium, a metal that is immune to the virus. Children who were born with the virus are called "Cursed Children" and have gained super-human powers. Rentaro and Enju are a team of workers from the Tendo Civil Security Agency, one of several groups dedicated to fighting Gastrea. Rentaro has half of his limbs rebuilt out of Varanium, and Enju is a "Cursed Child"—and together they do what they can to fight back against the crippling virus as well as criminals causing havoc. The series started out as a light novel series in Japan and was adapted as a manga series and an anime series as well.

Vol. 1. 2015. 160pp. 978-0-316-34503-3.
Vol. 2. 2015. 160pp. 978-0-316-34513-2.
Vol. 3. 2016. 160pp. 978-0-316-34532-3.
Vol. 4. 2016. 160pp. 978-0-316-27236-0.
Vol. 5. 2016. 256pp.978-0-316-34492-0.

Concrete Park. Written by **Tony Puryear** and **Erica Alexander**. Illustrated by **Tony Puryear**. Dark Horse, 2014– . O

Taken from stories published in *Dark Horse Presents* with new material added, Concrete Park is about a group of outcasts who have been exiled from Earth and sent off to a distant planet where they must learn to survive.

Vol. 1: You Send Me. 2014. 136pp. 978-1-6165-5530-6.
Vol. 2: R-E-S-P-E-C-T. 2015. 136pp. 978-1-6165-5633-4.

Concrete Park TM and © Tony Puryear and Erika Alexander.

Curveball. Written and Illustrated by **Jeremy Sorese**. Nobrow, 2015. 420pp. 978-1-910620-05-2. O 🎋

© 2016 Jeremy Sorese.

Against the backdrop of an apocalyptic future, technological failures are ever present, and where robots and beasts coexist with mankind, Avery is a waiter on a cruise ship for wealthy individuals. A good-hearted man, he's dealing with the end of a long and difficult relationship, which he's attempting to move on from. He has plenty of support from his coworkers on the ship and his best friend Jacqueline. When his indecisive lover, a sailor named Christophe, returns from his tour of duty, Avery's confidence wavers and the emotions of being in and out of a relationship take its toll on Avery. But can he make the heartbreaking journey to move on from a relationship that has ended and find some hope? The book was recognized as being a finalist for the LAMBDA Literary Award for Best LGBT Graphic Novel in 2016.

The East of West. Written by **Jonathan Hickman**. Illustrated by **Nick Dragotta**, **Rus Wooton**, and **Frank Martin**. Image Comics, 2013– . O

Set in a dystopian future of the United States where the Civil War never ended and the Confederacy and the Union are still fighting each other as well as black slaves, Chinese exiles, Texas separatists, and Native Americans. When a comet hits Kansas in 1908, all factions reached an accord and set up seven nations. Soon a prophecy foretells of the End of Times led by the Four Horsemen of the Apocalypse (Death, War, Famine, and Conquest), and the seven nations all have a Chosen who are tasked with the goal of bringing about the Apocalypse.

Vol. 1. 2013. 96pp. 978-1-60706-770-2.
Vol. 2. 2014. 144pp. 978-1-60706-855-6.
Vol. 3. 2014. 144pp. 978-1-63215-114-8.
Vol. 4. 2015. 144pp. 978-1-63215-381-4.
Vol. 5. 2016. 152pp. 978-1-63215-680-8.
Vol. 6. 2016. 144pp. 978-1-63215-879-6.
Vol. 7. 2017. 128pp. 978-1-5343-0214-3.

Ray Bradbury's Fahrenheit 451: The Authorized Adaptation. Written by **Ray Bradbury**. Adapted and Illustrated by **Tim Hamilton**. Hill and Wang, 2009. 160pp. 978-0-8090-5100-7, hardcover; 978-0-8090-5101-4. 🎗

An adaptation of the seminal dystopian story of Guy Montag, a fireman whose job isn't to put out fires, but to burn books, for the totalitarian government orders them to be destroyed. When Guy realizes that there's merit in preserving the books, he soon finds himself on the run from those that wish to abolish free thought and the power of words.

FreakAngels. Written by **Warren Ellis**. Illustrated by **Paul Duffield**. Avatar Press, 2008–2011. M

Twenty-three years ago, 23 children were born at exactly the same time across England. When they were all 18 years old, they unleashed their psychic powers at the same time and accidentally flooded the world. Now living in the soggy remains of Whitechapel, the "Freakangels" must save themselves one of their most dangerous enemies: one of their own. But as evil as he may be, there may be something even darker waiting the shadows.

Vol. 1. 2008. 144pp. 978-1-59291-056-4.
Vol. 2. 2009. 144pp. 978-1-59291-071-7.
Vol. 3. 2009. 144pp. 978-1-59291-078-6.
Vol. 4. 2010. 144pp. 978-1-59291-094-6.
Vol. 5. 2011. 144pp. 978-1-59291-115-8.
Vol. 6. 2011. 144pp. 978-1-59291-133-2.

Lazarus. Written by **Greg Rucka**. Illustrated by **Michael Lark**. Image Comics, 2013– . O

Set in a dystopian world where governments have long since collapsed, resources are hard to find and those who possess them hold the key to salvation. Only certain families rule the resources which are protected by a

© 2016 Greg Rucka and
Michael Lark.

representative called a Lazarus. Forever Carlyle is the Lazarus from her family and she'll do whatever she can to protect what her family owns—even if it might kill her.

Vol. 1. 2013. 96pp. 978-1-60706-809-9.
Vol. 2: Lift. 2014. 104pp. 978-1-60706-871-6.
Vol. 3: Conclave. 2015. 144pp. 978-1-63215-225-1.
Vol. 4: Poison. 2016. 144pp. 978-1-63215-523-8.
Vol. 5: Cull. 2017. 128pp. 978-1-5343-0024-8.
The First Collection. 2014. 248pp. 978-1-63215-183-4, hardcover.
The Second Collection. 2016. 320pp. 978-1-63215-722-5, hardcover.

Low. Written by **Rick Remender**. Illustrated by **Greg Tocchini**. Image Comics, 2015– . O
In the far future mankind has gone under the water to escape from the harsh planet surface. When a probe returns from outer space promising hope of a new planet which mankind can repopulate, Stel Cain tasks himself with the task of retrieving the probe on behalf of all of mankind. Meanwhile, another in his family, Stel's long-lost daughter Della, is a Hope Hunter—one tasked with destroying all the false promises of hope that the probe may provide.

Vol. 1: The Delirium of Hope. 2015. 144pp. 978-1-63215-194-0.
Vol. 2: Before the Dawn Burns Us. 2015. 112pp. 978-1-63215-469-9.
Vol. 3: Shore of the Dying Light. 2016. 128pp. 978-1-63215-708-9.

No. 6. Written by **Atsuko Asano**. Illustrated by **Hinoki Kino**. Kodansha Comics, 2013–2014. T 🏅 Japanese manga. あ
Based on a series of novels, the series is set in the city known as No. 6 and deals with Shion, a teenage boy whose "perfect" life changes when he helps an injured boy named "Rat." An anime series has also been made. Selected as one of YALSA's Great Graphic Novels for Teens in 2014.

Vol. 1. 2013. 160pp. 978-1-61262-355-9.
Vol. 2. 2013. 160pp. 978-1-61262-356-6.
Vol. 3. 2013. 160pp. 978-1-61262-357-3.
Vol. 4. 2013. 176pp. 978-1-61262-358-0.
Vol. 5. 2014. 192pp. 978-1-61262-359-7.
Vol. 6. 2014. 192pp. 978-1-61262-360-3.
Vol. 7. 2014. 176pp. 978-1-61262-553-9.
Vol. 8. 2014. 192pp. 978-1-61262-578-2.
Vol. 9. 2014. 192pp. 978-1-61262-794-6.

Saturn Apartments. Written and Illustrated by **Hisae Iwaoka**. VIZ Media, 2010–2013. T 🏅 Japanese manga.

DOSEI MANSION © 2006 Hisae
IWAOKA/SHOGAKUKAN.

In the far future, humanity lives in an artificial ring high above the Earth. Mitsu is a window washer whose work allows him to see the lives of the various social classes and investigate the disappearance of his father. This manga was selected as one of YALSA's Great Graphic Novels for Teens.

Vol. 1. 2010. 192pp. 978-1-4215-3364-3.
Vol. 2. 2010. 192pp. 978-1-4215-3373-5.
Vol. 3. 2011. 200pp. 978-1-4215-3374-2.
Vol. 4. 2011. 192pp. 978-1-4215-3375-9.
Vol. 5. 2012. 192pp. 978-1-4215-4129-7.
Vol. 6. 2012. 192pp. 978-1-4215-4130-3.
Vol. 7. 2013. 264pp. 978-1-4215-5268-2.

Shadoweyes. Written and Illustrated by **Ross Campbell**. SLG Publishing, 2010–2011. T 🎗

Scout and Kyisha live in the futuristic, dystopian city of Dranac—where crime is high, drugs are abundant, and garbage is literally everywhere. They try what they can to help clean up their city by joining a neighborhood crime watch. After a run-in with a mugger where Scout was hit in the head with a brick, she finds that she can now change into a beastly creature with superpowers—Shadoweyes. Scout then uses her newfound abilities to fight crime and do what she thinks is right, even if that can be questionable at times. With her new body and abilities will Scout lose the life and friends that she once had if it means helping everyone out in the end? The first volume was recognized by YALSA as a Top Ten Popular Paperback for Young Adults in 2011.

Shadoweyes. 2010. 204pp. 978-1-59362-189-6.
Shadoweyes in Love. 2011. 160pp. 978-1-59362-208-4.

Snowpiercer. Titan Books, 2014–2016. 🎬

Translated from the French title *Le Transperceneige*, Snowpiercer is set in the near-future where a disastrous experiment has resulted in a global ice age and what's left of humanity lives on two gigantic trains. But even in this new world there are class distinctions that can lead to chaos. Snowpiercer was adapted into a feature film in 2014.

Vol. 1: The Escape. Written by **Jacques Lob**. Illustrated by **Jean-Marc Rochette**. 2014. 110pp. 978-1-78276-133-4, hardcover; 978-1-78276-143-3.
Vol. 2: The Explorers. Written by **Benjamin Legrand**. Illustrated by **Jean-Marc Rochette**. 2014. 140pp. 978-1-78276-136-5, hardcover.
Vol. 3: Terminus. Written by **Oliver Bocqet**. Illustrated by **Jean-Marc Rochette**. 2016. 232pp. 978-1-78276-715-2, hardcover.

We Stand on Guard. Written by **Brian K. Vaughan**. Illustrated by **Matt Hollingsworth** and **Steve Skroce**. Image Comics, 2016. 160pp. 978-1-63215-702-7, hardcover. M 🎗

Set 100 years in our future, Canada is under threat by a larger power that is better armed and ready to attack: the United States. Join a heroic band of Canadian civilians-turned-freedom fighters against a highly technologically advanced force the like of which has never been seen before. The book was on the top ten list of YALSA's 2017 Great Graphic Novels for Teens.

© 2016 Brian K. Vaughan.

Post-Apocalypse

Examines what life would be like after a planet-wide disaster strikes the Earth. In the tales there may be an ecological change, civilization is nearly made extinct, and strange life-forms may now inhabit the Earth. The subgenre is closely related to dystopian science fiction, but takes it one step further by showcasing the entire collapse of society following a nuclear holocaust or other devastating effect.

Apocalyptigirl. Written and Illustrated by **Andrew MacLean**. Dark Horse Comics, 2015. 96pp. 978-1-61655-566-5. T

A lone girl named Aria is on a mission at the end of time in an apocalyptic world with her pet cat Jelly Beans as her only companion. She's on a quest to find an ancient item with immeasurable power. After an encounter with a creepy savage, Aria might just have found the path to the relic that can finally help her find her way back home.

Attack on Titan. Written and Illustrated by **Hajime Isayama**. Kodansha Comics, 2012– . O. Japanese manga. あ🎞

In the world of Attack on Titan, people live inside enormous walled cities to protect themselves against giant creatures called Titans. The main characters include those fighting the Titans. "Junior High" is a humorous take on the series, while the other spin-offs are adaptations of "light novels" that have been inspired by the manga. There have also been both animated and live-action adaptations. Selected as one of YALSA's Great Graphic Novels for Teens.

Vol. 1. 2012. 208pp. 978-1-61262-024-4.
Vol. 2. 2012. 192pp. 978-1-61262-025-1.
Vol. 3. 2012. 208pp. 978-1-61262-026-8.
Vol. 4. 2013. 192pp. 978-1-61262-253-8.
Vol. 5. 2013. 192pp. 978-1-61262-254-5.
Vol. 6. 2013. 208pp. 978-1-61262-255-2.
Vol. 7. 2013. 192pp. 978-1-61262-256-9.
Vol. 8. 2013. 192pp. 978-1-61262-547-8.
Vol. 9. 2013. 192pp. 978-1-61262-548-5.
Vol. 10. 2013. 192pp. 978-1-61262-676-5.
Vol. 11. 2014. 192pp. 978-1-61262-677-2.
Vol. 12. 2014. 192pp. 978-1-61262-678-9.
Vol. 13. 2014. 192pp. 978-1-61262-679-6.
Vol. 14. 2014. 192pp. 978-1-61262-680-2.
Vol. 15. 2015. 192pp. 978-1-61262-979-7.
Vol. 16. 2015. 192pp. 978-1-61262-980-3.
Vol. 17. 2015. 192pp. 978-1-63236-112-7.
Vol. 18. 2016. 192pp. 978-1-63236-211-7.
Vol. 19. 2016. 192pp. 978-1-63236-259-9.
Vol. 20. 2016. 192pp. 978-1-63236-309-1.
Vol. 21. 2017. 192pp. 978-1-63236-327-5.
Vol. 22. 2017. 200pp. 978-1-63236-425-8.

Attack on Titan: Junior High. Written and Illustrated by **Saki Nakagawa**. 2014– . T. Japanese manga.

Vol. 1. 2014. 336pp. 978-1-61262-916-2.
Vol. 2. 2014. 352pp. 978-1-61262-918-6.
Vol. 3. 2015. 336pp. 978-1-61262-961-2.
Vol. 4. 2015. 336pp. 978-1-63236-113-4.
Vol. 5. 2017. 512pp. 978-1-63236-410-4.

Attack on Titan: Before the Fall. Written and Illustrated by **Ryo Suzukaze**. 2014–. O. Japanese manga.

Vol. 1. 2014. 192pp. 978-1-61262-910-0.
Vol. 2. 2014. 208pp. 978-1-61262-912-4.
Vol. 3. 2014. 192pp. 978-1-61262-914-8.
Vol. 4. 2015. 192pp. 978-1-61262-981-0.
Vol. 5. 2015. 224pp. 978-1-61262-982-7.
Vol. 6. 2015. 192pp. 978-1-63236-224-7.

Vol. 7. 2016. 192pp. 978-1-63236-225-4.
Vol. 8. 2016. 192pp. 978-1-63236-260-5.
Vol. 9. 2016. 192pp. 978-1-63236-320-6.
Vol. 10. 2016. 192pp. 978-1-63236-381-7.
Vol. 11. 2017. 192pp. 978-1-63236-382-4.

Attack on Titan: No Regrets. Written by **Gun Snark**. Illustrated by **Hikaru Suruga**. Kodansha Comics, 2014. O. Japanese manga.

Vol. 1. 2014. 192pp. 978-1-61262-941-4.
Vol. 2. 2014. 192pp. 978-1-61262-943-8.

DMZ. Written by **Brian Wood**. Illustrated by **Riccardo Burchielli** and various. Vertigo/DC Comics, 2014–2015. M

In the near-future, America is in the grip of a Civil War between the U.S. government and the soldiers of the "Free States." Manhattan is a demilitarized zone stuck between the two sides filled with people who couldn't or wouldn't leave and now are surviving however they can. Matty Roth is a journalist for Liberty News stuck in New York, trying to tell the real story of the DMZ, and at times becoming part of it. The 72-issue series was originally collected in 12 paperback volumes and has since been recollected into the five hardcover collections listed below.

Book 1. 2014. 304pp. 978-1-4012-4300-5, hardcover.
Book 2. 2014. 406pp. 978-1-4012-4765-2, hardcover.
Book 3. 2014. 392pp. 978-1-4012-5000-3, hardcover.
Book 4. 2015. 384pp. 978-1-4012-5411-7, hardcover.
Book 5. 2015. 206pp. 978-1-4012-5843-6, hardcover.

Eden: It's an Endless World! Written and Illustrated by **Hiroki Endo**. Dark Horse Comics, 2006–2014. M. Japanese manga.

In the near-future, a virus has devastated much of mankind. The terrible disease has killed untold millions of people by hardening the skin and eventually turning the innards to mush. Those who were not immune to the virus survived only by replacing their organs with cybernetic robotic parts. Meanwhile, in this barren landscape, a paramilitary organization known as Propater has toppled the crumbling United Nations and a young boy named Elijah, who is immune to the virus, is joined on his travels with an artificial intelligent combat robot. Together the two of them roam the crumbling run-down cities in search of love and companionship in a dog-eat-dog world of tomorrow. The series ran for 18 volumes in Japan.

Vol. 1. 2006. 216pp. 978-1-59307-406-7.
Vol. 2. 2006. 208pp. 978-1-59307-454-8.
Vol. 3. 2006. 224pp. 978-1-59307-529-3.
Vol. 4. 2006. 208pp. 978-1-59307-544-6.

Vol. 5. 2006. 216pp. 978-1-59307-634-4.
Vol. 6. 2007. 240pp. 978-1-59307-702-0.
Vol. 7. 2007. 216pp. 978-1-59307-765-5.
Vol. 8. 2007. 224pp. 978-1-59307-787-7.

Vol. 9. 2007. 232pp. 978-1-59307-851-5.   *Vol. 12.* 2009. 224pp. 978-1-59582-296-3.
Vol. 10. 2008. 232pp. 978-1-59307-957-4.   *Vol. 13.* 2011. 224pp. 978-1-59582-763-0.
Vol. 11. 2009. 240pp. 978-1-59582-244-4.   *Vol. 14.* 2014. 232pp. 978-1-61655-288-6.

Fog Mound. Written by **Susan Schade**. Illustrated by **Jon Buller**. Simon & Schuster Books for Young Readers, 2006–2008. Y

The human occupation has long ended. It has been centuries since the last human has wreaked destruction on this planet. In their absence animals have evolved into their own civilizations with their own cultures and language. Thelonious is a young chipmunk who just moved out of his parents' house. He is an amateur mythology aficionado on humans. What he knows of humans, he learns from postcards of their ancient civilization. After a flash flood Thelonious is washed away from his comfortable home in the untamed forest. He is thrust into danger and adventure when he awakes in the heart of an abandoned human city. Here he finds that there are other animals who have adopted human artifacts for their own use. Porcupines have bookstores, bears ride airplanes, and lizards run the crime underworld. Thelonious and his new friends are on an adventure to find humanities' last safe havens and to figure out what exactly happened to all of them. This hybrid book will please children who like both comics and chapter books.

Travels of Thelonious. 2006. 214pp. 978-0-689-87685-1.
Faradawn. 2007. 195pp. 978-0-689-87686-8.
Simon's Dream. 2008. 198pp. 978-0-689-87688-2.

From the Ashes. Written and Illustrated by **Bob Fingerman**. IDW Publishing, 2010. 176pp. 978-1-60010-600-2. M

In this "Speculative Memoir" Fingerman and his wife are survivors of a nuclear war and find themselves in a world of mutants and crazies (some of whom are parodies of real-life people).

The Girl Who Owned a City. Written by **Dan Jolley** and **O.T. Nelson**. Illustrated by **Joelle Jones**. Graphic Universe, 2012. 128pp. 978-0-7613-5634-9. T

When a virus kills off every human over the age of 12, in the town of Glen Ellyn, Illinois, 10-year-old Lisa and her younger brother Todd are surviving day to day, scavenging for food. When rival gangs begin to vie for the city, Lisa has become the leader of a group of children and together they must figure out how to forge ahead and survive in a dark time that no child should over have to face. An adaptation of the 1975 novel by O.T. Nelson.

Ôoku: The Inner Chambers. Written and Illustrated by **Fumi Yoshinaga**. VIZ Media, 2009–2016. M  Japanese manga.

Set in the Edo period of feudal Japan, a mysterious disease known as the Redface Pox has begun to kill the male population. Now 80 years later, the disease has decimated over 75 percent of the men, and a new society has emerged from the old in which women do most of the chores that men used to do and the men are carefully protected. Only the most beautiful men are sent to serve under the female Shogun. Meanwhile schemes are afoot as many are still attracted to power and corruption still remains supreme as many vie for the Shogun's throne to rule Japan. The series is still ongoing in Japan. The first volume received accolades from YALSA's Great Graphic Novels for Teens in 2009.

Ôoku © Fumi Yoshinaga 2005/
HAKUSENSHA, Inc.

Vol. 1. 2009. 216pp. 978-1-4215-2747-5.   *Vol. 7.* 2012. 224pp. 978-1-4215-4220-1.
Vol. 2. 2009. 200pp. 978-1-4215-2748-2.   *Vol. 8.* 2013. 256pp. 978-1-4215-5482-2.
Vol. 3. 2010. 232pp. 978-1-4215-2749-9.   *Vol. 9.* 2013. 232pp. 978-1-4215-5877-6.
Vol. 4. 2010. 232pp. 978-1-4215-3169-4.   *Vol. 10.* 2014. 264pp. 978-1-4215-7242-0.
Vol. 5. 2010. 200pp. 978-1-4215-3669-9.   *Vol. 11.* 2015. 232pp. 978-1-4215-7979-5.
Vol. 6. 2011. 224pp. 978-1-4215-3961-4.   *Vol. 12.* 2016. 240pp. 978-1-4215-8643-4.

Showcase Presents: The Great Disaster Featuring the Atomic Knights. Written and Illustrated by various. DC Comics, 2014. 576pp. 978-1-4012-4290-9. T

Life after atomic wars and other disasters are featured in this 576-page volume. Besides the adventures of the Atomic Knights—fighters for law and order in a postwar world—other stories include the adventures of Hercules, Atlas, and even Superman. Creators include Arnold Drake, Murphy Anderson, Walter Simonson, and Jack Kirby.

Sweet Tooth. Written and Illustrated by **Jeff Lemire**. Vertigo/DC Comics, 2010–2013. M 🏵

© 2016 DC Comics.

In the aftermath of an apocalyptic pandemic, children are being born, who are human/animal hybrids. One of them is nine-year-old Gus, who has antlers. After being orphaned he is taken in by a drifter named Tommy Jepperd, who first endangers him but later becomes an ally. In the six volumes the secrets of the plague and the hybrids are revealed. Beginning in 2015 the issues are also being collected in larger, hardcover editions. Sweet Tooth was recognized by the American Library Association with an Alex Award.

Vol. 1: Out of the Deep Woods. 2010. 128pp. 978-1-4012-2696-1.
Vol. 2: In Captivity. 2010. 144pp. 978-1-4012-2854-5.
Vol. 3: Animal Armies. 2011. 144pp. 978-1-4012-3170-5.
Vol. 4: Endangered Species. 2012. 176pp. 978-1-4012-3361-7.
Vol. 5: Unnatural Habitats. 2012. 160pp. 978-1-4012-3723-3.
Vol. 6: Wild Game. 2013. 200pp. 978-1-4012-4029-5.
Deluxe Edition Book One. 2015. 296pp. 978-1-4012-5871-9, hardcover.
Deluxe Edition Book Two. 2016. 256pp. 978-1-4012-6146-7, hardcover.

Y: The Last Man. Written by **Brian K. Vaughan**. Illustrated by **Pia Guerra**. Vertigo/DC Comics, 2003–2008; Deluxe editions, 2008–2011. ; Absolute Editions, 2015–. M 🏵 ◎

A deadly plague instantaneously kills every single male human and animal on the entire planet with a Y chromosome except for one young man and his male pet monkey. How does society survive when 48 percent of the Earth's population has died? Joined by a mysterious female African American agent known only as Agent 355, young Yorrick must travel the United States in search of the mysterious cause of the man-killing plague and try to find out why he and his pet monkey Ampersand were the only males to survive in a world now ruled by women. The writer of the series, Brian K. Vaughan, received an Eisner Award for Best Writer in 2005 for his body of work including this series, while artist Pia Guerra and inker Jose Marzan Jr. won the Eisner Award for Best Penciller/Inker Team in 2008, the same year the series won as well. The series and its creators also won a Harvey Award and

© 2016 Brian K. Vaughan and
Pia Guerra.

was nominated for a Hugo. The first volume collection, *Unmanned*, received recognition by YALSA's Popular Paperbacks for Young Adults committee in 2006 on the *What Ails You* list.

Vol. 1: Unmanned. 2003. 128pp. 978-1-56389-980-5.
Vol. 2: Cycles. 2003. 128pp. 978-1-4012-0076-3.
Vol. 3: One Small Step. 2004. 168pp. 978-1-4012-0201-9.
Vol. 4: Safeword. 2004. 144pp. 978-1-4012-0232-3.
Vol. 5: Ring of Truth. 2005. 192pp. 978-1-4012-0487-7.
Vol. 6: Girl on Girl. 2005. 128pp. 978-1-4012-0501-0.
Vol. 7: Paper Dolls. 2006. 144pp. 978-1-4012-1009-0.
Vol. 8: Kimono. 2006. 144pp. 978-1-4012-1010-6.
Vol. 9: Motherland. 2007. 144pp. 978-1-4012-1351-0.
Vol. 10: Whys and Wherefores. 2008. 168pp. 978-1-4012-1813-3.

Deluxe Edition, 2008–2011.

Book 1. 2008. 256pp. 978-1-4012-1921-5, hardcover; 2014. 256pp. 978-1-4012-5151-2.
Book 2. 2009. 320pp. 978-1-4012-2235-2, hardcover; 2015. 320pp. 978-1-4012-5439-1.
Book 3. 2010. 320pp. 978-1-4012-2578-0, hardcover; 2015. 320pp. 978-1-4012-5880-1.
Book 4. 2011. 296pp. 978-1-4012-2888-0, hardcover.
Book 5. 2011. 320pp. 978-1-4012-3051-7, hardcover.

Absolute Edition, 2015– .

Vol. 1. 2015. 512pp. 978-1-4012-5429-2, hardcover.
Vol. 2. 2016. 256pp. 978-1-4012-6491-8, hardcover.
Vol. 3. 2017. 544pp. 978-1-4012-7100-8, hardcover.

Wasteland. Written by **Antony Johnston**. Illustrated by **Christopher Mitten**. Oni Press, 2007–2015. M

One hundred years after the "Big Wet" is a world where mankind's coastlines have been destroyed and the former United States is now a large dustbowl where every day is a fight for survival. A scavenger named Michael fights for his future and tries to retrace his past in a world with mutants, strange religions, and religious persecution.

Vol. 1: Cities in Dust. 2007. 160pp. 978-1-932664-59-1.
Vol. 2: Shades of God. 2007. 136pp. 978-1-932664-90-4.
Vol. 3: Black Steel in the Hour of Chaos. 2008. 128pp. 978-1-934964-08-8.
Vol. 4: Dog Tribe. 2009. 104pp. 978-1-934964-17-0.
Vol. 5: Tales of the Uninvited. 2009. 120pp. 978-1-934964-29-3.
Vol. 6: The Enemy Within. 2011. 136pp. 978-1-934964-30-9.
Vol. 7: Under the God. 2012. 136pp. 978-1-934964-94-1.
Vol. 8: Lost in the Ozone. 2013. 120pp. 978-1-620100-13-4.
Vol. 9: A Thousand Lies. 2014. 136pp. 978-1-620101-18-6.
Vol. 10: Last Exit for the Lost. 2014. 104pp. 978-1-620101-31-5.
Vol. 11: Floodland. 2015. 208pp. 978-1-620101-48-3.

The Apocalyptic Edition, 2009–2015.

Vol. 1. 2009. 384pp 978-1-934964-19-4, hardcover.
Vol. 2. 2010. 360p. 978-1-934964-46-0, hardcover.
Vol. 3. 2013. 344pp. 978-1-620100-93-6. hardcover.

Vol. 4. 2014. 352pp. 978-1-620101-70-4, hardcover.
Vol. 5. 2015. 304pp. 978-1-620102-76-3, hardcover.

Computers and Artificial Intelligence

Science fiction stories where computers play a pivotal role in the plot. Typically the fictionalized computers are much more sophisticated than any type of computer currently available in the real world. In the fictionalized world of computers, artificial intelligence (A.I.), is commonplace and surfing the Internet or online gaming can literally be a life-and-death situation for people. The tales can range from the humorous, the light-hearted to a struggle for survival against an evil computer. Films such as Walt Disney's movie *Tron* as well as the *Matrix* trilogy of films are excellent examples of the type of stories found in the subgenre.

MegaMan NT Warrior. Written and Illustrated by **Ryo Takamisaki**. VIZ Media, 2004–2008. A Japanese manga.

> Loosely based on the popular video game character. Set in a near-future where everyone is connected to the Internet Cyber Network via their PET (Personal Terminal) and artificial program called a NetNavi. Though on the outside the world seems peaceful, danger in the Internet is always only a step away. To save the day is Lan Hikari, an active fifth grader with a talent for surfing the Internet. Joined with his NetNavi, he becomes known as MegaMan, a dynamic super-powered fighting force in cyberspace against the continuous threat of the world-conquering organization known as World Three and rampant viruses out to destroy the Internet.

Vol. 1. 2004. 192pp. 978-1-59116-465-4.
Vol. 2. 2004. 192pp. 978-1-59116-466-1.
Vol. 3. 2004. 200pp. 978-1-59116-414-2.
Vol. 4. 2004. 200pp. 978-1-59116-501-9.
Vol. 5. 2004. 200pp. 978-1-59116-561-3.
Vol. 6. 2005. 200pp. 978-1-59116-755-6.
Vol. 7. 2005. 184pp. 978-1-4215-0003-4.
Vol. 8. 2005. 192pp. 978-1-59116-981-9.
Vol. 9. 2005. 192pp. 978-1-4215-0132-1.
Vol. 10. 2006. 208pp. 978-1-4215-0749-1.
Vol. 11. 2007. 184pp. 978-1-4215-1141-2.
Vol. 12. 2007. 200pp. 978-1-4215-1325-6.
Vol. 13. 2008. 184pp. 978-1-4215-1785-8.

Summer Wars. Written by **Mamoru Hosoda**. Illustrated by **Igura Sugimoto**. Vertical, Inc., 2013. T Japanese manga.

> An adaptation of the 2009 animated film in which 11th grader Kenji must help to defeat a malevolent artificial intelligence that is threatening the world. The two-volume series was on the 2015 YALSA Great Graphic Novels for Teens list.

Vol. 1. 2013. 354pp. 978-1-939130-15-0.
Vol. 2. 2013. 320pp. 978-1-939130-16-7.

Sword Art Online. Written by **Reki Kawahara**. Illustrated by **Tamako Nakamura**. Yen Press, 2014– . T

> In the year 2022, a Virtual Reality Massively Multiplayer Online Role-Playing Game (VRMMORPG) is released called Sword Art Online. The

© 2016 Yen Press.

game allows players to be immersed in a fantasy world environment. By wearing a NerveGear helmet, all of the users' five senses make the gaming experience very realistic as they control the character with their mind. Once 10,000 players log in, they discover that there is no way to log out. In order to finish the game, they must reach the 100th floor of the game's castle and defeat the final boss if they wish to be free. Anyone who removes the helmet during the game or die in the game will die in real life. The series' main character is Kazuto "Kirito" Kirigaya, a beta tester who plays the game alone, but finds a friend in a girl named Asuna Yūki, and eventually escapes. The other volumes in the series continue Kirito's battle with other online virtual reality worlds as he tries to free others trapped within other games. The series began as a series of light novels in Japan and then was adapted into a manga series as well as an anime.

Aincrad. 2014.

> *Vol. 1.* 2014. 384pp. 978-0-316-37123-0.
> *Vol. 2.* 2014. 256pp. 978-0-316-37681-5.

Fairy Dance, 2014–2015.

> *Vol. 1.* 2014. 224pp. 978-0-316-40738-0.
> *Vol. 2.* 2014. 224pp. 978-0-316-33655-0.
> *Vol. 3.* 2015. 336pp. 978-0-316-38373-8.

Girls Ops. 2015–2016.

> *Vol. 1.* 2015. 240pp. 978-0-31634-205-6.
> *Vol. 2.* 2016. 192pp. 978-0-316-26899-8.
> *Vol. 3.* 2016. 192pp. 978-0-316-55267-7.

Phantom Bullet. 2016.

> *Vol. 1.* 2016. 160pp. 978-0-316-26888-2.
> *Vol. 2.* 2016. 176pp. 978-0-316-31495-4.

Mother's Rosary. 2016.

> *Vol. 1.* 2016. 160pp. 978-0-316-27033-5.
> *Vol. 2.* 2016. 176pp. 978-0-316-27235-3.

Psychic Powers and Mind Control

The ability to control thoughts and manipulate matter is also a common theme in science fiction. The ability endows the characters with extraordinary power, allowing them the gift to read minds and use telekinesis, clairvoyance, and other powers. Typically the characters receive their powers through experimental procedures or genetically at birth. The appeal of these stories centers on the protagonist or antagonist who is an extraordinary being who uses the powers given to them for either good or evil purposes. See the super-heroes chapter featuring mutant heroes such as the X-Men for more tie-ins to characters genetically born with strange powers.

Harbinger

Valiant Entertainment, 2013– . T

A comic about super-powered teens with such abilities as psionics, flight, and pyrokinesis. The original 1990s' series was collected in a Valiant Masters collection, while the Harvey-nominated recent series written by Joshua Dysart with art by Khari Evans has been collected as both regular paperback and larger hardcover Deluxe Editions. The *Harbinger Wars Deluxe Edition* by Dysart and Duane Swierczynski with art by Clayton Henry and others collects a crossover storyline.

© Valiant Entertainment.

Harbinger, 1st series. Written by **Jim Shooter**. Illustrated by **David Lapham**. Valiant Entertainment, 2015.

> *Valiant Masters: Harbinger—Children of the Eighth Day*. 2015. 200pp. 978-1-9393-4648-3.

Harbinger, 2nd series. Written by **Joshua Dysart** and **Duane Swierczynski**. Illustrated by **Khari Evans** and **Arturo Lozzi**. Valiant Entertainment, 2013–2015.

> *Vol. 1: Omega Rising*. 2013. 128pp. 978-0-97964095-7.
> *Vol. 2: Renegades*. 2013. 128pp. 978-1-9393-4602-5.
> *Vol. 3: Harbinger Wars*. 2013. 128pp. 978-1-9393-4611-7.
> *Vol. 4: Perfect Day*. 2014. 128pp. 978-1-9393-4615-5.
> *Vol. 5: Death of a Renegade*. 2014. 160pp. 978-1-9393-4633-9.
> *Vol. 6: Omegas*. 2015. 112pp. 978-1-9393-4638-4.

> ***Hardcover Deluxe Edition***. 2013–2015.

> *Vol. 1*. 2013. 400pp. 978-1-9393-4613-1.
> *Vol. 2*. 2015. 400pp. 978-1-9393-4677-3.
> *Harbinger Wars Deluxe Edition*. 2014. 368pp. 978-1-9393-4632-2.

They're Not Like Us. Written by **Eric Stephenson**. Illustrated by **Simon Gane**. Image Comics, 2015– . M

A young woman named Syd attempts to commit suicide by jumping off a building to silence the voices in her head, but she survives the fall and finds herself in a hospital bed. She's rescued by a group of young adults who all have powers—some very similar to hers and others quite different such as pyrokinetics, speed, empaths, invulnerability, and strength. The leader is a suave but deadly young man called The Voice. His choices for her are clear: live with us and abide by our rules—you can't wear anything revealing (tattoos/bright hair/piercings), you must dress your best, and third, you must kill your parents and reject all of your past life. When Syd can't stand the cold-hearted world of blunt violence the group thrives on, she and others like her leave the influence of The Voice and strike out on their own in a world that doesn't understand them.

Vol. 1: Black Holes for the Young. 2015. 144pp. 978-1-63215-314-2.
Vol. 2: Us Against You. 2016. 144pp. 978-1-63215-665-5.

Robots, Androids, and Cyborgs

Humans have had a long fascination with robots, androids, cyborgs, and other robotic life-forms. Tales featuring metal men who were created to serve humanity but have the capability for so much more—even one day to surpass humankind—have long been a staple in science fiction books and films. Listed here are a wide variety of titles featuring robots from both Western and Eastern cultures, from human-sized robots to pint-sized cyborg saviors.

Man-Sized Robots

Stories featuring robots, cyborgs, and more that are roughly the size of humans. Central themes in titles featuring human-sized robots include mankind's paranoia of nonhuman life-forms, whether a robot can be more than just wiring and become human as told in such tales as *Astro Boy* and *Battle Angel Alita*, and tales of the dangers of robots for the future of mankind.

Astro Boy. Written and Illustrated by **Osamu Tezuka**. Dark Horse Comics, 2015–. T Japanese manga. あ

Created by the legendary manga creator Osama Tezuka in 1952, Astro Boy has been considered by many to be the launching point of the manga craze, inspiring artists and storytellers for years to come. Astro Boy is also one of the most recognizable characters from Japan. Set in a future where androids coexist with humans, Astro Boy was created in the year 2003 by the Ministry of Science's Dr. Tenma in Japan. His designs were based off of Tobio, Dr. Tenma's son who was killed in a car accident. The good doctor loved him as if he were his own son but realized that he could never truly replace his son. Though his upbringing was hard and sometimes cruel, Astro Boy was raised by Professor Ochanomizu, the new Minister of Science, who rescued him from a life in the circus. In Dr. Ochanomizu, Astro Boy finds a new father figure and proves to all of Japan that he's a hero with a 100,000 horsepower motor. Commonly facing off against bad guys ranging from robot-hating humans to giant evil robots to invaders from outer space, with his super-strength, jet-powered books, laser-tipped fingers, and more, Astro Boy is sure to win the day. The manga inspired the popular anime series, which first aired in Japan in 1963. The series was collected in 23 volumes by Dark Horse Comics from 2002 to 2004. In 2015 Dark Horse Comics began to reprint Omnibus collections of the series collecting two to three volumes in one collection. The original listings for this series can be located in the first edition of this book.

Omnibus, 2015– .

Vol. 1. 2015. 688pp. 978-1-61655-860-4.
Vol. 2. 2015. 680pp. 978-1-61655-861-1.
Vol. 3. 2016. 696pp. 978-1-61655-893-2.
Vol. 4. 2016. 688pp. 978-1-61655-956-4.
Vol. 5. 2016. 688pp. 978-1-50670-016-8.
Vol. 6. 2017. 696pp. 978-1-50670-041-0.
Vol. 7. 2017. 712pp. 978-1-50670-128-8.

Atomic Robo. Written by **Brian Clevinger**. Illustrated by **Scott Wegener** and various. Red 5 Comics, 2008–2014; IDW Publishing, 2015– . T 🎋 ◎

Atomic Robo, the Atomic Robo logo, all characters and their distinctive likenesses featured herein are trademarks and/or registered trademarks of Brian Clevinger and Scott Wegener.

Atomic Robo is a self-aware robot created by Nicola Tesla in 1923, who has spent decades fighting all sorts of threats including Nazi scientists, talking dinosaurs, government agencies, and even Thomas Edison. Each collection was originally released as a self-contained limited series set in a different time period. There was also an additional "Real Science Adventures" spin-off title. Following the last issue published by Red 5 Comics, the series became a webcomic. IDW has begun reprinting the original collections with three "old" volumes collected in each new one. IDW will also publish any collection of new material. Atomic Robo has twice been nominated for a Best Limited Series Eisner Award as well as a nomination for Best Colorist. The first storyline was recognized as a Top Ten selection for the 2009 Great Graphic Novels for Teens annual selection list.

Vol. 1: Atomic Robo and the Fightin' Scientists of Tesladyne. 2008. 180pp. 978-0-9809302-0-7.

Vol. 2: Atomic Robo and the Dogs of War. 2009. 160pp. 978-0-9868985-6-3.

Vol. 3: Atomic Robo and the Shadow from Beyond Time. 2010. 152pp. 978-0-9809302-5-2.

Vol. 4: Atomic Robo and Other Strangeness. 2010. 140pp. 978-0-9809302-8-3.

Vol. 5: Atomic Robo and the Deadly Art of Science. 2011. 152pp. 978-0-9809302-4-5.

Vol. 6: Atomic Robo and the Ghost of Station X. 2012. 152pp. 978-0-9868985-0-1.

Vol. 7: Atomic Robo and the Flying She-Devils of the Pacific. 2013. 152pp. 978-0-9868985-2-5.

Vol. 8: Atomic Robo and the Savage Sword of Dr. Dinosaur. 2014. 152pp. 978-0-9868985-6-3.

Vol. 9: Atomic Robo and the Knights of the Golden Circle. 2015. 152pp. 978-1-926513-00-3.

Vol. 10: Atomic Robo and the Ring of Fire. 2016. 120pp. 978-1-63140-569-3.

Vol. 11: Atomic Robo and the Temple of Od. 2017. 136pp. 978-1-63140-863-2.

Atomic Robo: Real Science Adventures. Written by **Brian Clevinger**. Illustrated by **John Broglia**, **Scott Wegener**, and various.

Vol. 1. 2012. 136pp. 978-0-9868985-1-8.

Vol. 2. 2014. 136pp. 978-0-9868985-5-6.

IDW Publishing is now collecting the original Red 5 Comic collections into three-volume deluxe editions.

Atomic Robo: The Everything Explodes Collection. 2015. 354pp. 978-1-63140-423-8.

Atomic Robo: The Crystals Are Integral Collection. 2016. 420pp. 978-1-63140-528-0.

Atomic Robo: The Hell and Lightning Collection. 2016. 424pp. 978-1-63140-680-5.

Battle Angel Alita. Written and Illustrated by **Yukito Kishiro**. VIZ Media, 2004–2005; Kodansha Comics, 2013–2014. O. Japanese manga. 🌳 あ ◎

In a post-apocalyptic world, Doctor Ido discovers a badly damaged cyborg in a junk heap beneath the floating city of Tiphares and renames her "Alita." Now reactivated with no memory of her past life, she discovers that she is much more than meets the eye and must seek out her hidden past. Working part-time with Ido as "hunter-warrior" bounty hunters, she's out to find the truth about her past among the fighting and bloodshed. The hit series' second editions were reprinted in the traditional right-to-left format and the follow-up to the first series, *Battle Angel Alita—Last Order*, is printed in that format as well. The second series was published in Japan in 19 volumes but was reprinted in five omnibus editions listed below. The manga helped to inspire an anime series. A live-action version of the manga is planned but has yet to be released. The collection for *Volume 1: Rusty Angel* received recognition by YALSA's Popular Paperbacks for Young Adults committee in 2004 on the *Simply Science Fiction* list.

Battle Angel Alita, 2004–2005.

> *Vol. 1: Rusty Angel*. 2004. 240pp. 978-1-56931-945-1.
> *Vol. 2: Tears of an Angel*. 2004. 216pp. 978-1-56931-951-2.
> *Vol. 3: Angel of Victory*. 2004. 216pp. 978-1-59116-274-2.
> *Vol. 4: Killing Angel*. 2004. 216pp. 978-1-59116-275-9.
> *Vol. 5: Angel of Redemption*. 2004. 208pp. 978-1-59116-276-6.
> *Vol. 6: Angel of Death*. 2004. 200pp. 978-1-59116-277-3.
> *Vol. 7: Angel of Chaos*. 2004. 216pp. 978-1-59116-278-0.
> *Vol. 8: Fallen Angel*. 2005. 232pp. 978-1-59116-280-3.
> *Vol. 9: Angel's Ascension*. 2005. 256pp. 978-1-59116-280-3.

Battle Angel Alita: Last Order Omnibus, 2013–2014.

> *Vol. 1*. 2013. 672pp. 978-1-61262-291-0.
> *Vol. 2*. 2013. 672pp. 978-1-61262-292-7.
> *Vol. 3*. 2004. 672pp. 978-1-61262-293-4.
> *Vol. 4*. 2014. 640pp. 978-1-61262-294-1.
> *Vol. 5*. 2014. 592pp. 978-1-61262-295-8.

Bloodshot

Valiant Entertainment, 2012– . T

Former soldier Angelo Mortalli has had his memories erased and his blood injected with nanites which allows him to use his body at peak efficacy, heal, and control electronic devices. Looking for the truth about himself, he goes against both criminals and the government agency that made him what he was. Bloodshot later became part of the HARD Corps. The character debuted in 1992, had a second title in 1996 when Valiant became Acclaim, and was one of the Valiant/Acclaim characters to be revived and revised in their own title for the 2012 Valiant relaunch. Issues of the original series, written by Kevin VanHook with art by Don Perlin, were collected as a Valiant Masters title, while the modern series written primarily by Duane Swierczynski with art by Manuel Garcia, Barry Kitson, Arturo Lozzi, and others has been collected in both regular and deluxe editions. A second series by Jeff Lemire and Mico Suayan, <u>Bloodshot Reborn</u>, is also being collected.

Valiant Masters: Bloodshot—Blood of the Machine, 1st series. Written by **Kevin VanHook**. Illustrated by **Don Perlin**, **Ted Halsted**, and **Andrew Wendel**. Valiant Entertainment, 2012. 200pp. 978-0-9796-4093-3, hardcover.

Bloodshot, 2nd series. Written by **Duane Swierczynski**. Illustrated by **Manuel Garcia**, **Barry Kitson**, **Arturo Lozzi**, and various. Valiant Entertainment, 2012–2015.

Vol. 1: Setting the World on Fire. 2013. 112pp. 978-0-97964096-4.
Vol. 2: The Rise and the Fall. 2013. 128pp. 978-1-9393-4603-2.
Vol. 3: Harbinger Wars. 128pp. 2013. 978-1-9393-4612-4.
Vol. 4: H.A.R.D. Corps. 2014. 128pp. 978-1-9393-4619-3.
Vol. 5: Get Some and Other Stories. 2014. 128pp. 978-1-9393-4631-5.
Vol. 6: The Glitch and Other Tales. 2015. 112pp. 978-1-9393-4671-1.

Hardcover Deluxe Edition, 2014–2015.

Book 1. 2014. 368pp. 978-1-9393-4621-6, hardcover.
Book 2. 2015. 416pp. 978-1-9393-4681-0, hardcover.

Chobits. Written and Illustrated by **CLAMP**. Dark Horse Comics, 2010. O. Japanese manga. あ

In the 22nd century, where there are no longer any females, men find companionship in persocom (personal computers) robots. Never able to afford one, young Hideki finds a discarded persocom in the trash and takes her home with him. There he begins to learn that his new robot companion, Chi, is more than he ever bargained for, and he's doing something illegal: he's falling for his persocom. The manga helped to inspire the anime series which originally debuted in Japan in 2002. The series was originally published by TOKYOPOP and was reprinted in an omnibus format by Dark Horse Comics.

Book 1. 2010. 752pp. 978-1-59582-451-6.
Book 2. 2010. 774pp. 978-1-59582-514-8.

Deathlok

Marvel Comics, 2010– . T 💻

© 2016 Marvel Comics.

Deathlok is the name of various cybernetic characters in the Marvel Universe. The first character known as Deathlok appeared in *Astonishing Tales* #25 (1974) and was created by Rich Buckler and Doug Moench. The adventures of the first, Luther Manning, took place in the post-apocalyptic future of the 1990s. Michael Collins was a contemporary Deathlok. The Jack Truman Deathlok was an agent of S.H.I.E.L.D. A hybrid of Manning and Mike Travers appeared in a limited series set in the near-future. Henry Hayes is the current version of the character though other versions have appeared elsewhere. The character has also made appearances in the ABC show *Marvel's Agents of S.H.I.E.L.D.* (2013–) as a new character named Mike Peterson as played by actor J. August Richards who becomes the cybernetically enhanced entity called Deathlok.

Deathlok (Luther Manning)

Deathlok the Demolisher: The Complete Collection. Written by **Doug Moench** and **Rich Buckler**. Illustrated by **Mike Zeck** and various. 2014. 368pp. 978-0-7851-9112-4.

Deathlok (Michael Collins). Written by **Dwayne McDuffie**. Illustrated by **Gregory Wright**, **Jackson Guice**, and various. 2012–2015.

> *The Living Nightmare of Michael Collins*. 2012. 216pp. 978-0-7851-5988-9, hardcover.
> *The Souls of Cyber-Folk*. 2015. 400pp. 978-0-7851-9334-0.

Deathlok (Jack Truman). Written by **Joe Casey**, **Alan Davis**, and **Terry Kavanagh**. Illustrated by **Jose Ladronn**, **Jim Cheung**, **Andrew Robinson**, **Rick Leonardi**, and **Leonardo Manco**.

> *Rage against the Machine*. 2015. 456pp. 978-0-7851-9291-6.

Deathlok (Luther Manning and Mike Travers). Written by **Charlie Huston**. Illustrated by **Lan Medina**.

> *Deathlok: The Demolisher*. 2010. 176pp. 978-0-7851-4365-9, hardcover; 2011. 176pp. 978-0-7851-2828-1.

Deathlok (Henry Hayes). Written by **Nathan Edmondson**. Illustrated by **Mike Perkins**.

> *Vol. 1: Control. Alt. Delete*. 2015. 120pp. 978-0-7851-9278-7.
> *Vol. 2: Man versus Machine*. 2015. 112pp. 978-0-7851-9279-4.

Descender. Written by **Jeff Lemire**. Illustrated by **Dustin Nguyen**. Image Comics, 2015– . O 🎏

© 2016 Jeff Lemire and Dustin Nguyen.

In the far future a horrific attack by giant robots called Harvesters destroyed most of the known universe's populations of the Core Planets of the Megacosm. Distrustful of all robots, the United Galactic Council in command of the nine planets has declared all androids be outlawed to try and prevent another attack from the mysterious Harvesters. On the run from bounty hunters is TIM-21, an android boy recently awakened from sleep. He may be the key to the Harvesters, but meanwhile, he's on the run from bounty hunters in a galaxy that hates his kind. Nguyen won an Eisner Award for Best Painter/Multimedia artist. Volume 2 was on YALSA's 2017 Great Graphic Novels for Teens list.

Vol. 1: Tin Stars. 2015. 160pp. 978-1-63215-426-2.
Vol. 2: Machine Moon. 2016. 116pp. 978-1-63215-676-1.
Vol. 3: Singularities. 2016. 128pp. 978-1-63215-878-9.

Electropolis: The Infernal Machine, *a Menlo Park Mystery*. Written and Illustrated by **Dean Motter**. Dark Horse Comics, 2009. 152pp. 978-1-59582-363-2. T

Once a janitorial robot, Menlo Park was reprogrammed to be a private eye in Electra City, a city created to generate massive amounts of electricity. Sixteen years after the death of his former human partner, Menlo discovers that all may not have been all that it seemed, and this new information will lead to trouble as the fate of the city soon hangs in the balance.

Ferro City: The Medusa Key. Written and Illustrated by **Jason Armstrong**. Image Comics, 2007. 160pp. 978-1-58240-738-8. O

> Private Investigator Cyrus Smithe's partner is killed and he's being accused. His only hope is a small device that could give freedom to 10 million sentient robots.

LBX. Written and Illustrated by **Hideaki Fujii**. Perfect Square/VIZ Media, 2014–2015. A. Japanese manga.

> This manga series is based on a video game that features small plastic model robots called Little Battler eXperience or LBXs. Set in the year 2050, young Van Yamano discovers that his LBX Achilles has secret data hidden inside of him that a secret organization is after.
>
> *Vol. 1: New Dawn Raisers*. 2014. 192pp. 978-1-4215-7695-4.
> *Vol. 2: Artemis Begins*. 2014. 184pp. 978-1-4215-7696-1.
> *Vol. 3: World Changer*. 2015. 192pp. 978-1-4215-7697-8.
> *Vol. 4: The Super LBX*. 2015. 192pp. 978-1-4215-7698-5.
> *Vol. 5: New Hope*. 2015. 184pp. 978-1-4215-7699-2.
> *Vol. 6: World Battle*. 2015. 152pp. 978-1-4215-7700-5.

Leave It to PET. Written and Illustrated by **Kenji Sonishi**. VIZ Media, 2009–2010. Y

> In this children's manga series, PET—polyethylene terephthalate—started off as a plastic bottle until a nine-year-old named Noboru Yamada turned him into a super-robot who at times is not that super.
>
> *Vol. 1*. 2009. 200pp. 978-1-4215-2649-2.
> *Vol. 2*. 2009. 192pp. 978-1-4215-2650-8.
> *Vol. 3*. 2009. 192pp. 978-1-4215-2651-5.
> *Vol. 4*. 2009. 192pp. 978-1-4215-2652-2.

Little Robot. Written and Illustrated by **Ben Hatke**. First Second Books, 2015. 144pp. 978-1-62672-080-0, hardcover. Y 🌳

A young girl who is handy with tools finds a robot abandoned in the woods. She fixes him up and turns him on for the first time and they become fast friends. When bad robots come to collect the little robot for nefarious purposes, the little girl armed only with her wrench is all that stands between them. The book won the 2016 Eisner Award for Best Publication for Early Readers.

© 2016 Ben Hatke and First Second.

Magnus Robot Fighter

Created by **Russ Manning**. Dark Horse Comics, 2004–2013; Dynamite Entertainment, 2014– . T

© 2016 Dynamite Entertainment.

Created by Russ Manning in 1963 the earliest Magnus stories were set in the year 4,000 where Magnus fought evil robots. Though many publishers have created Magnus comic books over the years including Gold Key, Valiant, Acclaim, Dark Horse Comics, and Dynamite Entertainment, the basic core of the character of Magnus remains. Subsequent versions have been set both in the future and in the present.

Magnus, Robot Fighter 4000 A.D. Archives. Written and Illustrated by **Russ Manning** and various. Dark Horse Comics, 2004–2006.

The original Magnus stories published by Gold Key Comics beginning in 1963.

Vol. 1. 2004. 200pp. 978-1-59307-269-8, hardcover; 2011. 978-1-59582-599-5.
Vol. 2. 2005. 200pp. 978-1-59307-290-2, hardcover; 2013. 978-1-61655-294-7.
Vol. 3. 2006. 200pp. 978-1-59307-339-8, hardcover; 2014. 978-1-61655-322-7.

Magnus, Robot Fighter. Vol. 1: Metal Mob. Written by **Jim Shooter**. Illustrated by **Bill Reinhold**. Dark Horse Comics, 2011. 104pp. 978-1-59582-604-6.

A revival of the hero published by Dark Horse Comics in 2010.

Magnus, Robot Fighter. Written by **Fred Van Lente**. Illustrated by **Cory Smith**, **Joe Cooper**, and others. 2014– .

Vol. 1: Flesh and Steel. 2014. 120pp. 978-1-60690-528-9.
Vol. 2: Uncanny Valley. 2015. 120pp. 978-1-60690-664-4.
Vol. 3: Cradle and Grave. 2015. 120pp. 978-1-60690-698-9.

Mega Man. Written by **Ian Flynn**. Illustrated by **Pat Spaz Spaziante**. Archie Comics, 2011– . A 🎮

Based off the popular video game series. Set in the near-future where robots are sentient and work alongside humans, an evil scientist named Dr. Wily sets out to conquer the Earth by stealing advanced automatons known as Robot Masters. Wily has reprogrammed them to do his evil bidding and also has duplicated the technology to make his own Robot Masters. Meanwhile, a robot named DLN-001: (Rock Light) volunteers to be augmented by his creator, Dr. Light, to help fight against Dr. Wily and his evil scenes. Reborn as Mega Man, Rock sets out to defeat Dr. Wily and other antagonists including Copy Robot, Ra Moon, and other evil Robot Masters. The series features many characters and plot points from the series of video games.

Vol. 1: Let the Games Begin. 2011. 120pp. 978-1-879794-85-6.
Vol. 2: Time Keeps Slipping. 2012. 112pp. 978-1-879794-95-5.
Vol. 3: Return of Dr. Wily. 2012. 112pp. 978-1-936975-11-2.
Vol. 4: Spiritus Ex Machina. 2013. 112pp. 978-1-936975-27-3.
Vol. 5: Rock of Ages. 2013. 104pp. 978-1-936975-48-8.
Vol. 6: Breaking Point. 2014. 104pp. 978-1-936975-78-5.

Vol. 7: Blackout: The Curse of Ra Moon. 2014. 104pp. 978-1-936975-95-2.
Vol. 8: Redemption. 2015. 104pp. 978-1-619889-44-6.

Sonic/Mega Man: When Worlds Collide. Written by **Ian Flynn**. Illustrated by various. Archie Comics, 2016. 336pp. 978-1-627389-51-8. Y

> A massive crossover of two legendary video game properties! When the evil Dr. Wily gets in contact with the equally evil Dr. Eggman, they combine their might, and seek to use the power of the Chaos Emeralds to construct an unstoppable army of Robot Masters and Roboticized Masters—Sonic's corrupted friends! Together Mega Man and Sonic the Hedgehog and their friends must team up to defeat the dynamic duo of dastardly evil doctors before the world is doomed!

O Human Star. Written and Illustrated by **Blue Delliquanti**. Blue Delliquanti Comics, 2015–. M 🏴

> Alastair Sterling was the inventor who sparked the rise of the robot revolution. When he died before his time, he didn't get to fully see what he had created. That is, until 16 years later, when he comes back in a robot body exactly like the one he left behind. Now he's in a world where robots and humans coexist and Al needs to find his old partner and learn who's behind his robot resurrection. *O Human Star* is a 2015 Ignatz nominee for Outstanding Online Comic and one of the winners of the 2012 Prism Comics Queer Press Grant.

> Vol. 1. 2015. 190pp. 978-0-9909956-0-9.

Showcase Presents: The Metal Men. Written by **Robert Kanigher**. Illustrated by **Ross Andru** and **Mike Espisito**. DC Comics, 2007–2008.

> Created by Dr. Will Magnus robots Gold, Iron, Lead, Mercury, Tin, and Platinum aka Tina use the properties of their metals to help humanity. These collections collect over 40 classic stories.

> Vol. 1. 2007. 528pp. 978-1-4012-1559-0.
> Vol. 2. 2008. 528pp. 978-1-4012-1976-5.

Monster Motors. Written by **Brian Lynch**. Illustrated by **Nick Roche**. IDW Publishing, 2015. 104pp. 978-1-63140-337-8. T

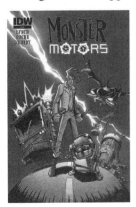

> A whole new look at the classic movie monsters—done as tricked-out cars! Vic Frankenstein isn't like all of the other mechanics in Transylvania, Kentucky. He invented a robot companion named iGOR (intelligent Garage-Operated Robot) and together they build a tricked-out semi-tractor called Frankenride. Soon Vic is teamed up with April Van Helsing (who rides Minivan Helsing) as they must thwart the hordes of gaz-sucking vampire car known as Cadillacula before the town is overrun with car monsters!

Pluto. Urasawa x Tezuka. Written and Illustrated by **Naoki Urasawa**. VIZ Media, 2009–2010. T Japanese manga. 🏆 ◎

© 2003 Naoki URASAWA/Shog-akukan.

In a reimagining of one of Osamu Tezuka's Astro Boy stories, a robot detective attempts to solve the mystery behind the deaths of both robots and humans. Other Tezuka characters also make appearances. The series has won a number of international awards and been nominated for an Eisner Award. It has also appeared in the Top Ten portion of the Great Graphic Novels for Teens list in 2010.

Vol. 1. 2009. 200pp. 978-1-4215-1918-0.
Vol. 2. 2009. 200pp. 978-1-4215-1919-7.
Vol. 3. 2009. 200pp. 978-1-4215-1920-3.
Vol. 4. 2009. 200pp. 978-1-4215-1921-0.
Vol. 5. 2009. 200pp. 978-1-4215-2583-9.
Vol. 6. 2009. 200pp. 978-1-4215-2721-5.
Vol. 7. 2010. 200pp. 978-1-4215-3267-7.
Vol. 8. 2010. 256pp. 978-1-4215-3343-8.

Rust. Written and Illustrated by **Royden Lepp**. Archaia/BOOM! Studios, 2012– . T

© 2016 BOOM! Studios.

Set in a period reminiscent around the early 1900s but with more technology, a young boy on a backpack, named Jet Jones, crashes into a farm after being pursued by a giant robot. Rescued by Roman Taylor, the oldest son at the farm struggling to survive in the closing days of the war, Jet may be the key to the family's survival in these dark times. Meanwhile, there are other robots who have set their sites on Jet. What makes the boy a target for the robots and is Jet even human?

Visitor in the Field. 2011. 192pp. 978-1-936393-27-5, hardcover; 2016. 176pp. 978-1-60886-894-0.
Secrets of the Cell. 2012. 200pp. 978-1-936393-58-9, hardcover.
Death of the Rocket Boy. 2014. 224pp. 978-1-60886-413-3, hardcover.
The Boy Soldier. 2016. 128pp. 978-1-60886-806-3.

Frank Miller's RoboCop. Written by **Frank Miller**. Adapted by **Steven Grant**. Illustrated by **Juan Jose Ryp**. BOOM! Studios, 2013–2016. M 💀

© 2016 BOOM! Studios

When superstar comic book creator Frank Miller wrote the screenplays for the two sequels to the cult-classic science fiction film *RoboCop* (1987), his original script was cut apart by Hollywood. The sequels *RoboCop 2* (1990) and *RoboCop 3* (1993) bore little—if any—resemblance to Frank Miller's original draft. Now for the first time Frank Miller's original scripts have been adapted by Steven Grant and Juan Jose Ryp, and fans can finally see what could have been. The story features RoboCop (Officer Murphy) as Frank Miller has always intended combining the violence, humor, and robotic action that made the original movie a cult classic.

Vol. 1. 2013. 208pp. 978-1-60886-375-4.
Vol. 2: Last Stand, Part 1. 2014. 112pp. 978-1-60886-374-7.
Vol. 3: Last Stand, Part 2. 2014. 128pp. 978-1-60886-429-4.

RoboCop vs. Terminator. Written by **Frank Miller**. Illustrated by **Walter Simonson**. Dark Horse Comics, 2014. 128pp. 978-1-61655-008-0, hardcover. T 🎬 ◎

© 2016 Dark Horse Comics

A cross-over of two of the most popular cyborgs in science fiction motion picture history! Cyborg Detroit police officer Murphy (RoboCop) learns a terrible secret from a time-traveler from the future: mankind will be hunted down like dogs by the year 2029 by Skynet and their killer robots called Terminators, and he's the reason for it. In the bleak future, the human-killing Terminators are the grunts. Created by the evil computer system known as Skynet, and it becomes clear to Murphy that the only way to make sure the future never happens is that he must die to ensure the secrets of his cyborg mind are never revealed. But the Terminators from the future are sent back to the past to prevent Murphy from dying again and again. Each time Murphy destroys himself, another horde of Terminators jumps back to the past to rescue him. How can the robotic supercop of today outsmart the evil technology of the future and save mankind?

Robot City Adventures. Written and Illustrated by **Paul Collicutt**. Candlewick/ Templar, 2009–2010. Y

City in Peril © 2009 by Paul Collicutt. Reproduced by permission of the publisher, Candlewick Press, Somerville, MA.

Robot City is a city where humans and robots work together in peace. Robots of all kinds live in the city, and each separate volume introduces readers to new robots who work around the city. *City in Peril* introduces readers to Curtis the Colossal Robot, who has to defend the city from a giant squid while injured. *Rust Attack* features a sleuth team of Robot City Confidential Investigations in the case to investigate robot rusting. Indestructible Metal Men features a mad scientist who plans to make an army from the remains of giant robots. A conductor must solve a mystery before a train meets its final destination in *Murder on the Robot City Express*.

Vol. 1: City in Peril. 2009. 48pp. 978-0-7636-4120-7.
Vol. 2: Rust Attack! 2009. 48pp. 978-0-7636-4594-6.
Vol. 3: Indestructible Metal Men. 2010. 48pp. 978-0-7636-5014-8.
Vol. 4: Murder on the Robot City Express. 2010. 48pp. 978-0-7636-5015-5.

Robot Dreams. Written and Illustrated by **Sara Varon**. First Second Books, 2007. 208pp. 978-1-59643-108-9. Y

A robot and a dog are the best of friends. They love to do everything together—even a day on the beach. When it rains at the beach, the robot is rusted and can't move and the dog, heartbroken, leaves his friend behind. As the seasons pass, the dog still misses his friend while the robot sits and dreams of better

days. A loving tribute to the power of friendship even as time passes and friends move on.

Rom. Written by **Chris Ryall** and **Christos Gage**. Illustrated by **David Messina**. IDW Publishing, 2017– . T

> In the furthest of galaxies, the armored knights of the Solstar Order have defended the worlds against the shape-changing magicians known as the Dire Wraiths. Though the battles were difficult, the Solstar Order prevailed and the scattered remnants of the Dire Wraiths spread to other galaxies. Now the bravest and most feared of the knights has come to Earth to vanquish the Dire Wraiths. His name is Rom. The series is based on the original Parker Brothers toy from the late 1970s which also inspired a popular Marvel Comics series called Rom: Spaceknight from 1979-1986. The new IDW series takes a new approach to the source material due to copyright issues with Marvel Comics.
>
> *Vol. 1: Earthfall.* 2017. 132pp. 978-1-63140-817-5.
> *Vol. 2.* 2017. 132pp. 978-1-63140-906-6.

Surrogates. Written by **Robert Venditti**. Illustrated by **Brett Weldele**. Top Shelf, 2006–2009. ▰ O

> In 2054 most people prefer to use Surrogates, robotic versions of themselves controlled via Telepresence. Police Lt. Harvey Greer must solve a crime with ties to an anti-surrogate group. The original volume was adapted into a 2009 film with Bruce Willis as (Tom) Greer. A prequel volume, Flesh and Blood later came out, and the two volumes have been collected into a hardcover deluxe edition.
>
> *Vol. 1.* 2006. 208pp. 978-1-891830-87-7.
> *Vol. 2: Flesh and Bone.* 2009. 144pp. 978-1-6030901-86.
> *The Surrogates Operator's Manual Special Hardcover Edition.* 2009. 304pp. 978-1-603090-45-2, hardcover.

WE3, Deluxe Edition. Written by **Grant Morrison**. Illustrated by **Frank Quitely**. Vertigo/DC Comics, 2011–2014. 2011. 144pp. 978-1-4012-3067-8, hardcover; 2013. 144pp. 978-1-4012-4302-9. M ◉

> The U.S. Air Force has created the most lethal weapons to annihilate the small-time drug cartels—the Animal Weapon 3 project. Code-named WE3, three stray pets—a dog, cat, and rabbit—are enhanced with cybernetic components giving the animals the ability to use a variety of lethal weapons and even the ability to speak basic English. Working as a close-knit team, WE3 were created as the perfect prototype weapons to

© 2016 Grant Morrison and
Frank Quitely.

fight in the future wars of America. When the project is terminated and the pets are ordered to be destroyed, the animals escape into a confusing outside world, with the only thing leading them on being a place where they distantly remember called "home."

Mecha and Giant Robots

Stories that focus on giant robots (mecha) that protect humankind on Earth or on other civilizations from alien invaders. The robots usually are humanoid in shape, but sometimes take the shape of familiar animal shapes including dinosaurs, lions, and horses. In most cases giant mecha are typically not sentient and are usually piloted by a person or team. Many Japanese manga and anime series feature stories with this popular theme.

Bokurano: Ours. Written and Illustrated by **Mohiro Kitoh**. VIZ Media, 2010–2014. O 🌱 Japanese manga. あ

A group of middle-school students find themselves having to pilot a giant mecha in battles where losing means the end of the world. The series was turned into an anime and was selected as one of YALSA's Great Graphic Novels for Teens in 2011.

Vol. 1. 2010. 200pp. 978-1-4215-3361-2. *Vol. 7*. 2012. 192pp. 978-1-4215-3394-0.
Vol. 2. 2010. 216pp. 978-1-4215-3389-6. *Vol. 8*. 2013. 200pp. 978-1-4215-3395-7.
Vol. 3. 2011. 200pp. 978-1-4215-3390-2. *Vol. 9*. 2013. 208pp. 978-1-4215-3396-4.
Vol. 4. 2011. 192pp. 978-1-4215-3391-9. *Vol. 10*. 2014. 208pp. 978-1-4215-3540-1.
Vol. 5. 2012. 200pp. 978-1-4215-3392-6. *Vol. 11*. 2014. 224pp. 978-1-4215-6532-3.
Vol. 6. 2012. 200pp. 978-1-4215-3393-3.

Doug TenNapel's Gear. Written and Illustrated by **Doug TenNapel**. Image Comics, 2007. 160pp. 978-1-58240-680-0. T

© 2016 Doug TenNapel.

Welcome to a darkly humorous and violent world where cats from the "armpit" state of Newton fight for dominance in a four-way struggle against both the dogs from Dogtown, their alliance with the cats from North Plate, and praying mantis-like insects from South Plate. Utilizing their giant robot Guardians as weapons, all sides are on the brink of war to retrieve a fabled secret gear called the Forbidden Mechanism. The gear, once placed inside a Guardian, will give the user omnipotent power and its secret location in Newton has brought all the enemies together on one battlefield. Meanwhile, four bumbling cats from the state of Newton are sent on a mission of importance to steal a giant robot Guardian from the enemy state of Dogtown.

Heroman. Written by **Stan Lee**. Illustrated by **Tamon Ohta**. Vertical, 2012–2013. Y Japanese manga. あ

Orphan Joey Jones found a broken robot which he names Heroman. He unsuccessfully tries to repair it, but after being struck by lightning, Heroman transforms into a giant robot and protects Earth against the alien Skrugg. The manga series has been adapted into an anime series.

Vol. 1. 2012. 192pp. 978-1-935654-58-2.
Vol. 2. 2012. 192pp. 978-1-935654-59-9.
Vol. 3. 2013. 192pp. 978-1-935654-66-7.
Vol. 4. 2013. 192pp. 978-1-935654-67-4.
Vol. 5. 2013. 192pp. 978-1-935654-68-1.

Incredible Change-Bots. Written and Illustrated by **Jeffrey Brown**. Top Shelf, 2007–2014. O

In these original stories that might just sound a little familiar to a popular series based on another licensed property. The shape-changing alien "Awesomebots" come to Earth to escape from their war-torn planet, but their old foes the "Fantasticons" are right behind. The series is both a black-humored parody and a loving tribute to the Transformers stories of old.

Incredible Change-Bots. 2007. 144pp. 978-1-891830-91-4.
Incredible Change-Bots Two. 2011. 144pp. 978-1-60309-067-4.
Incredible Change-Bots Two Point Something Something. 2014. 224pp. 978-1-60309-348-4.

© 2016 Jeffrey Brown.

Kill All Monsters: Ruins of Paris. Written by **Michael May**. Illustrated by **Jason Copland**. Dark Horse Comics, 2017. 232pp. 978-1-61655-827-7. T

When giant monsters have taken over the Earth, mankind may be knocked down, but they're not out for the count! In the ruins of Paris three soldiers track down another anti-monster resistance fighting group and discover a horrifying nest of giant monsters living in the City of Lights. Luckily mankind has giant robot-like vehicles to take them on!

© 2016 Michael May and Jason Copland.

Mobile Suit Gundam: The Origin. Written and Illustrated by **Yoshikazu Yasuhiko**. Vertical, 2013– . T. Japanese manga. あ

A retelling of the classic <u>Mobile Suit Gundam</u> anime series. In the future, war has broken out between the Earth Federation and the Principality of Zeon, a former Earth colony. The crew of the ship White Base must transport the new Gundam mobile suit. Selected as one of YALSA's Great Graphic Novels for Teens in 2014. The series was published in Japan in 23 volumes.

Vol. 1: Activation. 2013. 456pp. 978-1-935654-87-2, hardcover.
Vol. 2: Garma. 2013. 432pp. 978-1-935654-88-9, hardcover.
Vol. 3: Ramba Ral. 2013. 480pp. 978-1-935654-97-1, hardcover.
Vol. 4: Jaburo. 2013. 504pp. 978-1-935654-98-8, hardcover.
Vol. 5: Char & Sayla. 2014. 440pp. 978-1-939130-19-8, hardcover.
Vol. 6: To War. 2014. 440pp. 978-1-939130-20-4, hardcover.
Vol. 7: Battle of Loum. 2014. 420pp. 978-1-939130-67-9, hardcover.
Vol. 8: Operation Odessa. 2014. 460pp. 978-1-939130-68-6, hardcover.
Vol. 9: Lalah. 2015. 420pp. 978-1-941220-15-3, hardcover.
Vol. 10: Solomon. 2015. 480pp. 978-1-941220-16-0, hardcover.
Vol. 11: A Cosmic Glow. 2015. 372pp. 978-1-941220-46-7, hardcover.
Vol. 12: Encounters. 2015. 400pp. 978-1941220474, hardcover.

Pacific Rim. Written by **Travis Beacham**. Illustrated by **Mark McKenna, Sean Chen, Yvel Guichet, Pericles Junior, Joshua Fialkov**, and **Marcos Marz**. Legendary Comics, 2013–2016. T 🎬

A prequel to the events from the popular 2013 Legendary Pictures summer movie directed by Guillermo del Toro. Mankind learns it's not alone in the world when the Earth's major cities are all attacked by giant beasts that leave nothing but destruction in their wake. Called "Kaiju" (the Japanese term for giant monsters), one by one they come out of the Pacific coast waters from their interdimensional portal and mankind must find a way to neutralize and destroy the Kaiju threat. Witness the creation of the Jaeger fighting robot program where two pilots can join together and control the ultimate weapon against the Kaiju and cancel the impending apocalypse. The second volume, *Tales from the Drift*, focuses on more encounters with the Jaegers versus all new Kaiju.

Tales from Year Zero. 2013. 112pp. 978-0-7851-5394-8, hardcover.
Tales from the Drift. 2016. 112pp. 978-1-68116-008-5.

Transformers. IDW Publishing, 2006– . T 🖥 🎬

From the distant planet of Cyberton, where all life is computer-based, a never-ending battle for the planet rages between two races of cybernetic giant-sized robots called Transformers that are more than meets the eye. Each robot can transform into another form such as a car, dinosaur, and gun. After a long and weary battle between the good Autobots led by Optimus Prime and the evil Decepticons ruled by the vicious Megatron, the Autobots have fled to Earth to evade slavery by the Decepticons. Sworn to fight to the end to defeat the Decepticons and to ultimately reclaim Cybertron, the Autobots fight on against the Decepticons as well as other foes including the planet-devouring transformer known as Unicron. Inspired by the hit action figure line by Hasbro that's been popular since the 1980s, the stories feature a huge cast of characters. The series has been published by IDW since 2006. Not all of the titles are included below. For more titles please visit IDW Publishing's web site at www.idwpublishing.com.

Transformers: The IDW Collection. Written by **Simon Furman**, **Eric Holmes**, **Nick Roche**, **Zander Cannon**, and various. Illustrated by **Shane McCarthy**, **M.D. Bright**, **E.J. Su**, **Alex Milne**, and various.

The first phase of IDW Publishing's <u>Transformers</u> series collects the majority of materials published by the company from 2005 through 2009. The second phase begins with the ominous storyline "The Death of Optimus Prime." The series is also being reprinted in the massive IDW Collection Compendium. The first volume was published in 2016.

Vol. 1. 2010. 392pp. 978-1-60010-667-5, hardcover.
Vol. 2. 2010. 392pp. 978-1-60010-751-1, hardcover.
Vol. 3. 2011. 300pp. 978-1-60010-856-3, hardcover.
Vol. 4. 2011. 352pp. 978-1-60010-938-6, hardcover.
Vol. 5. 2011. 352pp. 978-1-61377-052-8, hardcover.
Vol. 6. 2012. 364pp. 978-1-61377-183-9, hardcover.
Vol. 7. 2012. 358pp. 978-1-61377-406-9, hardcover.
Vol. 8. 2013. 384pp. 978-1-61377-627-8, hardcover.

Transformers: The IDW Collection Compendium. 2016. 764pp. 978-1-63140-637-9.

Transformers: IDW Collection, Phase 2. Written by **James Roberts**, **John Barber**, and various. Illustrated by **Livio Ramondelli**, **Casey W. Coller**, **Andrew Griffith**, **Nick Roche**, and various.

The second phase of IDW Publishing's Transformers line begins with the Death of Optimus Prime and spins off into the two main series <u>More Than Meets the Eye</u> and <u>Robots in Disguise</u> as well as various miniseries.

Vol. 1. 2014. 272pp. 978-1-63140-040-7, hardcover.
Vol. 2. 2015. 332pp. 978-1-63140-364-4, hardcover.
Vol. 3. 2016. 332p. 978-1-63140-540-2, hardcover.
Vol. 4. 2016. 356pp. 978-1-63140-715-4, hardcover.
Vol. 5. 2017. 344pp. 978-1-63140-844-1, hardcover.

Transformers: More Than Meets the Eye. Written by **James Roberts**. Illustrated by **Alex Milne** and various. IDW Publishing, 2012–2016. T

A series focusing on Rodimus and a crew of over 200 Transformers aboard a vessel called the Last Light. They're on a journey to quest for the mythical Knights of Cybertron. Other main cast members include Ultra Magnus, Drift, Swerve, Ratchet, and the villainous Megatron. The series concluded and the storyline continues in the new series *Transformers: The Lost Light*.

Vol. 1. 2012. 128pp. 978-1-61377-235-5.
Vol. 2. 2012. 124pp. 978-1-61377-498-4.
Vol. 3. 2013. 148pp. 978-1-61377-592-9.
Vol. 4. 2013. 128pp. 978-1-61377-691-9.
Vol. 5. 2013. 128pp. 978-1-61377-802-9.
Vol. 6. 2014. 152pp. 978-1-63140-184-8.

Vol. 7. 2015. 132pp. 978-1-63140-327-9.
Vol. 8. 2015. 152pp. 978-1-63140-452-8.
Vol. 9. 2016. 132pp. 978-1-63140-615-7.
Vol. 10. 2016. 152pp. 978-1-63140-716-1.

Transformers: Robots in Disguise. Written by **John Barber**. Illustrated by **Andrew Griffith** and various. 2012–2016. T

Set after the Cybertron War, Bumblebee and his fellow Autobots, Decepticons, and NAILS (**N**on-**A**ligned **I**ndigenous **L**ife-forms) as they attempt to work together to rebuild Cybertron without Optimus Prime. Later issues in the series feature the return of Optimus Prime as he resumes command and as they work together to rebuild a world good for all cybernetic life-forms. In later volumes the Autobots come into conflict with the deadly Galvatron and more. The series was renamed without the subtitle to not confuse it with the new Hasbro animated series of the same name. The storyline continues with a new ongoing series simply called Transformers: Optimus Prime.

Vol. 1. 2012. 120pp. 978-1-61377-291-1.
Vol. 2. 2013. 104pp. 978-1-61377-541-7.
Vol. 3. 2013. 104pp. 978-1-61377-626-1.
Vol. 4. 2013. 124pp. 978-1-61377-765-7.
Vol. 5. 2013. 152pp. 978-1-61377-836-4.
Vol. 6. 2014. 128pp. 978-1-63140-164-0.
Vol. 7. 2015. 152pp. 978-1-63140-285-2.
Vol. 8. 2016. 104pp. 978-1-63140-585-3.
Vol. 9. 2016. 104pp. 978-1-63140-668-3.
Vol. 10. 2016. 152pp. 978-1-63140-748-2.

Transformers Classics/Regeneration, 2011–2014

Transformers Classics. Written by **Bob Budiansky**, **Bill Mantlo**, **Ralph Macchio**, **Jim Salicrup**, **Simon Furman**, and various. Illustrated by **Herb Trimpe**, **Don Perlin**, and various. IDW Publishing, 2011–2013.

A reprinting of the classic Marvel Comics Transformers series which was published in comic book form for 80 issues from 1984 to 1991.

Vol. 1. 2011. 348pp. 978-1-60010-935-5.
Vol. 2. 2012. 276pp. 978-1-61377-091-7.
Vol. 3. 2012. 276pp. 978-1-61377-163-1.
Vol. 4. 2012. 276pp. 978-1-61377-497-7.
Vol. 5. 2013. 276pp. 978-1-61377-633-9.
Vol. 6. 2013. 284pp. 978-1-61377-764-0.
Vol. 7. 2014. 276pp. 978-1-61377-987-3.

Transformers: Regeneration. Written by **Simon Furman**. Illustrated by **Stephen Baskerville** and **Andrew Wildman**. IDW Publishing, 2013–2014.

Marvel Comics originally published a wildly popular comic book series from 1984 to 1991 and ended with issue #80. Now years later, popular Transformers scribe Simon Furman tells the ongoing adventures of the original Marvel Comics series set outside of normal Transformers continuity.

Vol. 1. 2013. 132pp. 978-1-61377-555-4.
Vol. 2. 2013. 128pp. 978-1-61377-642-1.

Vol. 3. 2014. 152pp. 978-1-61377-857-9.
Vol. 4. 2014. 132pp. 978-1-61377-963-7.

Transformers Miniseries

Listed below are various short series featuring the Transformers by various creators. The first several series, Transformers Prime, focus on fan-favorite Transformers—the Dinobots! Robots that can transform into dinosaurs including the leader, Grimlock, one of the most popular Transformers ever created.

Transformers Prime: Rage of the Dinobots. Written by **Mike Johnson** and **Mairghread Scott**. Illustrated by **Agustin Padilla**. 2013. 104pp. 978-1-61377-606-3.

Transformers Prime: Beast Hunters. Written by **Mike Johnson** and **Mairghread Scott**. Illustrated by **Beni Lobel** and **Michael Gaydos**. 2013–2014.

© Hasbro. All Rights Reserved.

Vol. 1. 2013. 104pp. 978-1-61377-743-5.
Vol. 2. 2014. 104pp. 978-1-61377-926-2.

Transformers: Combiner Wars. Written by **Mairghread Scott** and **John Barber**. Illustrated by **Livio Ramondelli** and **Sarah Stone**. 2015. 152pp. 978-1-63140-386-6.

Transformers: Drift—Empire of Stone. Written by **Shane McCarthy**. Illustrated by **Guido Guidi**. 2015. 132pp. 978-1-63140-269-2.

Transformers: Sins of the Wreckers. Written and Illustrated by **Nick Roche**. 2016. 120pp. 978-1-63140-669-0.

Transformers: Distant Stars. Written by **Mairghread Scot**t. Illustrated by **Sara Pitre-Durocher** and **Corin Howell**. 2016. 120pp. 978-1-63140-600-3.

Transformers and G.I. Joe Crossovers

Since both licensed properties are owned by Hasbro, they've had a long history of meeting up. Listed below are collected stories featuring both licensed properties.

G.I. Joe/Transformers. Written by **Michael Higgins**, **Larry Hama**, **Josh Blaylock**, **Dan Jolley**, and **Tim Seeley**. Illustrated by **Jesse d'Orozco**, **Guido Guidi**, **William Rosado**, **Steve Lieber**, **Chris Batista**, and various. IDW Publishing, 2012–2013.

An anthology collection of various crossover events between both properties as the sinister Megatron aligns with the evil organization known as Cobra.

Vol. 1. 2012. 192pp. 978-1-61377-352-9.
Vol. 2. 2012. 248pp. 978-1-61377-535-6.
Vol. 3. 2013. 208pp. 978-1-61377-620-9.

Transformers/G.I. JOE: Tyrants Rise, Heroes Are Born. Written by **John Ney Rieber**. Illustrated by **Jae Lee**. IDW Publishing, 2016. 152pp. 978-1-63140-495-5.

Reprints the series which is set during the heyday of World War II in the 1940s.

Transformers vs. G.I. Joe. Written by **Tom Scioli** and **John Barber**. Illustrated by **Tom Scioli**. IDW Publishing, 2015–2016. T

The most recent series is set in an entirely self-contained universe separate from the continuities of both properties. The series was highly praised for the storytelling and retro artwork of Tom Scioli that harkens back to simpler comic book days of Jack Kirby and the classic Marvel Comics Transformers and G.I. Joe series.

Vol. 1. 2015. 152pp. 978-1-63140-190-9.
Vol. 2. 2015. 132pp. 978-1-63140-270-8.
Vol. 3. 2016. 120pp. 978-1-63140-693-5.
The Quintessential Collection. 2017. 420pp. 978-1-63140-860-1, hardcover.

Voltron. Dynamite Entertainment, 2012–2016; Lion Forge Comics, 2016– . あ

Based on the popular Japanese anime series and toy line, in the future, the planets Arus and Earth are under the constant threat of the evil King Zarkon and his gigantic beasts. The best defense is the Voltron Force—five courageous pilots from the interplanetary Galaxy Garrison patrol the skies of Arus and beyond in five giant lion robots that were recovered by ancient magics. Each lion robot is powered by a different elemental magic: the Black Lion by Lightning, the Red Lion by Fire, the Green Lion by Cyclone, the Blue Lion by Water, and the Yellow Lion by Magma. When the struggle is too great, the five lion robots transform into one giant sword-wielding defender known as Voltron: The

Defender of the Universe. The collection From the Ashes tells of a new team 200 years later in time who become the pilots of Voltron. Beginning in 2016 Netflix in conjunction with DreamWorks Animation released a new animated series called Voltron: Legendary Defender to rave reviews. The new series by Lion Forge Comics continues the adventures of the new animated series which is a new take on the old classic tale as 5 humans from Earth, Shiro, Keith, Lance, Pidge, and Hunk are recruited by Princess Allura to become the new Voltron team and to defeat Emperor Zarkon of the ruthless Galra Empire.

Voltron, Written by **Tommy Yune**, **Bill Spangler**, **Brandon Thomas** and **Cullen Bunn**. Illustrated by **Ariel Padilla**, **Craig Cermak**, **Elmer Damaso**, and **Steven Harris**. Dynamite Entertainment, 2012–2016. T

> *Vol. 1: The Sixth Pilot.* 2012. 152pp. 978-1-60690-334-6.
> *Vol. 2: Ten Lions.* 2013. 144pp. 978-1-60690-411-4.
> *Year One.* 2013. 144pp. 978-1-60690-365-0.
> *From the Ashes.* 2016. 144pp. 978-1-60690-857-0.
> *Robotech/Voltron.* 2015. 128pp. 978-1-60690-744-3.

Voltron: Legendary Defender. Written by **Tim Hedrick** and **Mitch Iverson**. Illustrated by **Digital Arts Chefs**. Lion Forge Comics, 2016– . Y

> *Vol 1.* 2017. 136pp. 978-1-941302-21-7.

Science Fiction Anthologies

Beta Testing the Apocalypse. Written and Illustrated by **Tom Kaczynski**. Fantagraphics, 2013. 136pp. 978-1-60699-541-9. M

> Secret knowledge, different outlooks, and sterilized environments are some of the recurring themes in Kaczynski's book of short stories. Often the main characters come to the realization that their controlled suburban life is just a fragile reality.

From Now On: Short Comic Tales of the Fantastic. Written and Illustrated by **Malachi Ward**. Alternative Comic, 2016. 144pp. 978-1-934460-91-7. O

> A collection of short science fiction stories that cover a broad spectrum of science fiction. A shaman predicts doom for a planet; a time-travel mission goes south when one of the travelers goes rogue; a scout encounters another version of himself while exploring a planet. Twelve short stories in all are included.

The Simon and Kirby Library: Science Fiction. Written and Illustrated by **Joe Simon** and **Jack Kirby**. Titan Books, 2013. 320pp. 978-1-84856-961-4, hardcover. T

> Known as the co-creators of characters such as Marvel Comics' Captain America, the team of Joe Simon and Jack Kirby worked on many genres and characters during their careers. The third volume of this extensive library anthology by Titan Books collects Simon and Kirby stories from various titles of the 1940s, 1950s, and 1960s. Additional writers and artists in this volume include such award-winning greats as Wallace Wood, Reed Crandall, and Al Williamson.

Strange Science Fantasy. Written by **Scott Morse**. Illustrated by **Scott Morse** and **Paul Pope**. IDW Publishing, 2011. 196pp. 978-1-60010-888-4. T

> A collection of short story collections by Scott Morse with six 1-page short story contributions by Paul Pope. The stories are told in the vein of classic Silver Age Marvel Comics series like Tales to Astonish and Amazing Fantasy. The collection tells stories that are self-contained stories that have an overall arcing connection. Behold the

© 2016 Scott Morse.

tales of the Headlight, the Shogunaut, the Projectionist, G.I. Gantic, and the Foolish Fling!

1

2

The Tipping Point. Written and Illustrated by various. Humanoids Publishing, 2016. 132pp. 978-1-59465-136-6, hardcover. M ◉

An anthology collection by some of the creme de la creme of creators across the world, including John Cassaday, Frederik Peeters, Naoki Urasawa, Boulet, Bastien Vivès, Emmanuel Lepage, Katsuya Terada, Taiyo Matsumoto, Paul Pope, Atsushi Kaneko, Keiichi Koike, Eddie Campbell, Bob Fingerman, and Enki Bilal. Each short story focuses on a certain point where a dramatic split occurs—it could be a mutation, a personal revolt, a full-fledged revolution, to a simple change in direction.

4

Valve Presents: The Sacrifice and Other Steam-Powered Stories. Written by various. Dark Horse Comics, 2011. 208pp. 978-1-59582-869-9. O 🎮

5

This omnibus collects comics from three of Valve's popular video games *Left 4 Dead 2*, *Team Fortress 2*, and *Portal 2* that were previously published through game updates and single issues. *Left 4 Dead 2: The Sacrifice* tells the tale of how the four survivors are actually the ones spreading the zombie infection. What are these four people willing to give up for each other in the end? The *Team Fortress 2*'s section collects the pieces of story told through the game updates. The story for *Portal 2* tells a bit more about the scientist who left many clues and doodles that are within the game world. What is he doing in this world and what is he going to do next? This omnibus is a great way to give fans more background on the games that they play.

6

7

8

9

Chapter 4

Fantasy

Fantasy is commonly understood as literature that portrays a fanciful realm where magic and imagination are commonplace. Many people consider a fantasy to be stories about a world where dragons, orcs, goblins, and wizards reside and where fair maidens in kingdoms languish in need of rescue. In comic books and graphic novels, the genre is no different, except that the medium aids visually in conjuring up the setting and the creatures that inhabit it. Over the last several decades, a renewed interest in fantasy fiction has erupted with the release of the *Harry Potter* novels and the popularity in books and television with George R.R. Martin's Game of Thrones, as well as the big-screen adaptations of that series as well as the *Lord of the Rings* and *The Hobbit* feature films. Graphic novels too have had their share of fantasy titles conclude with the completion of major fantasy series including Neil Gaiman's *Sandman*, Jeff Smith's *Bone*, and Bill Willingham's *Fables*. In their place have been a continued spring of new titles including Jim Zub's *Wayward*, Luke Pearson's *Hildafolk* series, and Kurtis J. Wiebe's *RatQueens*. The chapter is organized according to subgenres and common themes, which include adaptations, dark fantasy, and high fantasy. For the subgenre on Humorous Fantasy, see humor chapter for a list of highlighted titles.

Sword and Sorcery Fantasy

One of the most popular subgenres of Fantasy, tales of Sword and Sorcery generally feature battles between good and evil, as well as an individual or fellowship undertaking a monumental task or quest. Plenty of action with swordplay and magic is common and practically required. The subgenre is further broken down into subcategories of Epic, Heroic, and Quest.

Epic/Quest Fantasy

The epic or quest tale is archetypal of traditional fantasy. Set in a timeless ancient world, these sweeping tales mixed feature-strong characters, fantastical settings, and, on occasion, a quest or journey that needs to be undertaken to save the realm from certain doom. The *Lord of the Rings* books and movies are excellent examples of this type of theme in fantasy.

Adventure Time

KaBOOM!/Boom! Studios, 2012– . A 🖵

The graphic novels based on the extremely popular animated series on the Cartoon Network. A boy named Finn and his adopted brother Jake—a dog with magical powers—and their journey through the post-apocalyptic and surreal Land of Ooo.

© 2016 BOOM! Studios.

Adventure Time. Written by **Ryan North**. Illustrated by **Shelli Paroline**, **Braden Lamb**, and various. KaBOOM!/BOOM! Studios, 2012– .

Fans of the super-popular cartoon will feel as if they never left the Land of Ooo. Finn and Jake go on some epic adventures like fighting off The Lich, saving new princess, and exploring dungeons. This series takes everything that is great about the show and then uses the comic format to make it work well on paper. There are comics that use a choose-your-own-adventure-style way to tell the story. On more than one occasion the characters are drawn with pixel art when they are transported into video games. At the bottom of the page there is an omniscient narrator there telling inside jokes, sharing other humorous stories about what is on that page, or just showing a completely different contiguous mini comic.

Vol. 1. 2012. 128pp. 978-1-60886-280-1.
Vol. 2. 2013. 112pp. 978-1-60886-323-5.
Vol. 3. 2013. 112pp. 978-1-60886-317-4.
Vol. 4. 2014. 128pp. 978-1-60886-351-8.
Vol. 5. 2014. 128pp. 978-1-60886-401-0.
Vol. 6. 2015. 128pp. 978-1-60886-482-9.
Vol. 7. 2015. 128pp. 978-1-60886-746-2.
Vol. 8. 2016. 128pp. 978-1-60886-795-0.
Vol. 9. 2016. 128pp. 978-1-60886-843-8.
Vol. 10. 2016. 112pp. 978-1-60886-909-1.
Vol. 11. 2017. 112pp. 978-1-60886-946-6.

Adventure Time: The Original Graphic Novels. KaBOOM!/Boom! Studios, 2013– .

The Original Graphic Novels series are longer-form self-contained *Adventure Time* stories. These tales are often stories exploring more in depth the side characters within the universe. The earlier volumes are done in black and white with screen tones. Combined with the smaller size of the book, compared to the other series, it looks like a manga-style book.

Vol. 1: Playing with Fire. Written by **Danielle Corsetto**. Illustrated by **Zack Sterling**. 2013. 160pp. 978-1-60886-832-2.

Vol. 2: Pixel Princess. Written by **Danielle Corsetto**. Illustrated by **Zack Sterling**. 2013. 160pp. 978-1-60886-329-7.

Vol. 3: Seeing Red. Written by **Kate Leth**. Illustrated by **Zack Sterling**. 2014. 160pp. 978-1-60886-356-3.

Vol. 4: Bitter Sweets. Written by **Kate Leth**. Illustrated by **Zack Sterling**. 2014. 160pp. 978-1-60886-430-0.

Vol. 5: Graybles Schmaybles. Written by **Danielle Corsetto**. Illustrated by **Bridget Underwood**. 2015. 160pp. 978-1-60886-484-3.

Vol. 6: Masked Mayhem. Written by **Kate Leth**. Illustrated by **Bridget Underwood**. 2015. 160pp. 978-1-60886-764-6.

Vol. 7: The Four Castles. Written by **Josh Trujillo**. Illustrated by **Zack Sterling**. 2016. 144pp. 978-1-60886-797-4.

Vol. 8: President Bubblegum. Written by **Josh Trujillo**. Illustrated by **Phil Murphy**. 2016. 144pp. 978-1-60886-846-9.

Vol. 9: The Brain Robbers. Written by **Josh Trujillo**. Illustrated by **Phil Murphy and Zack Sterling**. 2017. 144pp. 978-1-60886-875-9.

The Autumnlands. Written by **Kurt Busiek**. Illustrated by **Benjamin Dewey**. Image Comics, 2015– . M

© 2016 Kurt Busiek.

In a world of anthropomorphic animals, a crisis in brewing—the magic is fading. The warthog wizard Gharta devises a plan in which she and other wizards bring a great champion from the past in the hope of bringing the magic back. But when this strange creature—a human—appears, things may change for the worse.

Vol. 1: Tooth and Claw. 2015. 184pp. 978-1-6321-5277-0.
Vol. 2: Woodland Creatures. 2017. 184pp. 978-1-6321-5713-3.

Bastard!! Written and Illustrated by **Kazushi Hagiwara**. VIZ Media, 2003–present, 2nd edition. M Japanese manga. あ

When the magical kingdom of Metallicana is under attack from the forces of Osbourne, a secret weapon can save the day. One kiss from the virgin girl named Tia to the lips of 15-year-old Lucien transforms him into the banished foul-mouthed wizard known throughout the land as Dark Schneider. One more kiss will turn him back. When the attacking army is defeated with the help of the wizard, is the solution to Metallicana's problems worse than the invading army? Loaded with references to classic Heavy Metal bands as well as fantasy role-playing games (the "Bastard" in the title refers to a weapon called a "Bastard Sword"), the series is still being published in Japan in the manga publication *Ultra Jump*, with over 27 volumes in print. Currently there are no plans to print the rest of the series in the United States. A six-part anime was also released to tie in with the manga when it debuted in Japan in 1992.

Vol. 1. 2003. 200pp. 978-1-56931-952-9.
Vol. 2. 2003. 208pp. 978-1-56931-968-0.
Vol. 3. 2003. 208pp. 978-1-56931-861-4.
Vol. 4. 2003. 208pp. 978-1-56931-826-3.
Vol. 5. 2004. 208pp. 978-1-59116-506-4.
Vol. 6. 2004. 208pp. 978-1-59116-134-9.
Vol. 7. 2005. 192pp. 978-1-59116-742-6.
Vol. 8. 2005. 200pp. 978-1-59116-837-9.
Vol. 9. 2005. 184pp. 978-1-4215-0050-8.
Vol. 10. 2006. 184pp. 978-1-4215-0219-9.

Vol. 11. 2006. 208pp. 978-1-4215-0379-0.
Vol. 12. 2006. 208pp. 978-1-4215-0434-6.
Vol. 13. 2006. 208pp. 978-1-4215-0435-3.
Vol. 14. 2007. 208pp. 978-1-4215-0436-0.
Vol. 15. 2007. 184pp. 978-1-4215-0878-8.
Vol. 16. 2008. 184pp. 978-1-4215-0879-5.
Vol. 17. 2008. 200pp. 978-1-4215-0880-1.
Vol. 18. 2008. 210pp. 978-1-4215-1600-4.
Vol. 19. 2009. 200pp. 978-1-4215-2195-4.

Beowulf. Adapted and Illustrated by **Gareth Hinds**. Candlewick Press, 2007. 128pp. 978-0-7636-3022-5, hardcover; 978-0-7636-3023-2. T

An adaptation of the epic tale of the great hero Beowulf and his triumphant battle against the great monster called Grendel, and Grendel's mother, and the final battle against a great dragon that claims the warrior-hero's life. The poem is edited but retains its overall rhythm and feel to accompany the beautiful epic illustrated.

Berserk. Written and Illustrated by **Kentaro Miura**. Dark Horse Comics, 2003– . M あ Japanese manga.

When demons and their ilk begin to destroy the medieval land of Midland and terrorize the countryside, only a fearless lone warrior named Guts, alias the Black Swordsman, is tough enough to take on the monsters and send them back to Hell in a casket. Carrying his long black sword and wearing the scars of many bloody battles and a rough and abusive upbringing, Guts is the only one capable of taking the beasts down, even if the cost is his own soul. Reluctantly accompanied by the wisecracking but kind fairy named Puck, he roams the land in search of the beasts that shed innocent blood, and no one will stand in Guts' way as he walks the path of death, mutilation, and destruction. Currently 37 volumes have been published in Japan, and the series in on hiatus. The manga was adapted into an anime series in Japan that aired from 1997 to 1998 in Japan.

Vol. 1. 2003. 224pp. 978-1-59307-020-5.
Vol. 2. 2004. 240pp. 978-1-59307-021-2.
Vol. 3. 2004. 240pp. 978-1-59307-022-9.
Vol. 4. 2004. 240pp. 978-1-59307-203-2.
Vol. 5. 2004. 240pp. 978-1-59307-251-3.

Vol. 6. 2005. 224pp. 978-1-59307-252-0.
Vol. 7. 2005. 232pp. 978-1-59307-328-2.
Vol. 8. 2005. 232pp. 978-1-59307-329-9.
Vol. 9. 2005. 240pp. 978-1-59307-330-5.
Vol. 10. 2006. 240pp. 978-1-59307-331-2.

Vol. 11. 2006. 240pp. 978-1-59307-470-8.
Vol. 12. 2006. 232pp. 978-1-59307-484-5.
Vol. 13. 2006. 240pp. 978-1-59307-500-2.
Vol. 14. 2006. 240pp. 978-1-59307-501-9.
Vol. 15. 2007. 240pp. 978-1-59307-577-4.
Vol. 16. 2007. 240pp. 978-1-59307-706-8.
Vol. 17. 2007. 240pp. 978-1-59307-742-6.
Vol. 18. 2007. 240pp. 978-1-59307-743-3.
Vol. 19. 2007. 232pp. 978-1-59307-744-0.
Vol. 20. 2007. 232pp. 978-1-59307-745-7.
Vol. 21. 2008. 248pp. 978-1-59307-746-4.
Vol. 22. 2008. 248pp. 978-1-59307-863-8.
Vol. 23. 2008. 208pp. 978-1-59307-864-5.
Vol. 24. 2008. 208pp. 978-1-59307-865-2.

Vol. 25. 2008. 224pp. 978-1-59307-921-5.
Vol. 26. 2008. 224pp. 978-1-59307-922-2.
Vol. 27. 2009. 216pp. 978-1-59307-923-9.
Vol. 28. 2009. 224pp. 978-1-59582-209-3.
Vol. 29. 2009. 216pp. 978-1-59582-210-9.
Vol. 30. 2009. 208pp. 978-1-59582-211-6.
Vol. 31. 2009. 208pp. 978-1-59582-366-3.
Vol. 32. 2009. 232pp. 978-1-59582-367-0.
Vol. 33. 2010. 232pp. 978-1-59582-372-4.
Vol. 34. 2010. 240pp. 978-1-59582-532-2.
Vol. 35. 2011. 224pp. 978-1-59582-695-4.
Vol. 36. 2012. 208pp. 978-1-59582-942-9.
Vol. 37. 2013. 232pp. 978-1-59582-205-3.

Bird Boy. Written and Illustrated by **Anne Szabla**. Dark Horse Comics, 2016. Y

Bali is a 10-year-old boy in a tribe; he seeks to prove his worth in his northern tribe even though he's short in stature. Eager to prove he has what it takes even though he is not considered an adult by his people, he sets out on his own where he comes across an ancient weapon of great power. Along the journey, Bali fights his way across a dangerous land encountering gods, men, and monsters to keep the coveted sword of Mali Mani from dark forces known as the Rooks.

Vol. 1: The Sword of Mali Mani. 2016. 88pp. 978-1-61655-930-4.
Vol. 2: The Liminal Wood. 2016. 88pp. 978-1-61655-968-7.

© 2016 Anne Szabla.

Bone. Written and Illustrated by **Jeff Smith**. Cartoon Books, 2004–2010; Graphix/
Scholastic Books, 2005–2015. A 🏃 ◎ 🐾

After being run out of Boneville, the Bone cousins—Fone Bone, Phoney Bone, and Smiley Bone—are lost in a mysterious valley far from home. Stuck in a strange land, they befriend the tough and craggy Grandma Ben, her beautiful and tough granddaughter Thorn, Grandma Ben's friend—a burly tavern keeper named Lucius, and a giant red dragon. Together the three Bone cousins become embroiled on an epic and sometimes humorous journey to end the reign of the mysterious Hooded One, the Lord of Locusts, and the fierce-but-stupid Rat Creatures. With a blend of Tolkien-esque adventure with loads of charm, humor, and a dash of *Star Wars* as inspiration, Jeff Smith's award-winning <u>Bone</u>

BONE is a ® and © 2016 Jeff Smith.

series has been well received by many comic book readers from its creation in 1992 through its completion in 2004. The series won numerous awards over the years. Bone has won Eisner Awards for Best Humor Publication (1993–1995), Best Serialized Story (1994), Best Continuing Series (1994–1995), Best Writer/Artist (1994), Best Writer/Artist: Humor (1995, 1998), and Best Graphic Album—Reprint (2005). The series has also been awarded many Harvey Awards including Best Cartoonist (1994–1997, 1999–2000, 2003, 2005), Best Graphic Album of Previously Published Work (1994, 2005), and Special Award for Humor in 1994 for Jeff Smith. The collection *Out from Boneville* received recognition by YALSA's Popular Paperbacks for Young Adults committee in 2002 on the *Graphic Novels: Superheroes and Beyond* list. The series has also spun off into two books, *Tall Tales*, which tells the humorous tale of why rat creatures don't have tails, and *Rose*, a look at the youth of Grandma Ben and her sister.

Bone (Original Black and White Graphic Novels). Cartoon Books, 1996–2016. A
  A collection of the classic fantasy series in their original black and white format. The *One Volume Edition* released in 2004 collects the entire original nine-volume arc in one inexpensive volume with over 1,300 pages of revised text and illustrations. To celebrate the 20th anniversary of Bone, a full-color *One Volume Edition* was released in 2011, with color done by Steve Hamaker. In 2016 it was announced that a special volume called Coda would be released to celebrate the 25th anniversary of Bone. The collection includes a new story as well as a concise history by librarian Stephen Weiner.

  Bone: The Complete Cartoon Epic on One Volume. 2004. 1344pp. 978-1-888963-14-4, softcover.
  20th Anniversary Full Color One Volume Edition. 2011. 1344pp. 978-1-888963-27-4.
  Bone: Coda. 2016. 128pp. 978-1-888963-54-0.

Bone (Full Color Edition Graphic Novels). Graphix/Scholastic Books, 2005–2009. A
  Beginning in 2005, Scholastic Books' Graphix imprint line reprinted the entire nine-volume series in full color by Steve Hamaker.

  Vol. 1: Out from Boneville. 2005. 144pp. 978-0-439-70623-0, hardcover; 978-0-439-70640-7.
  Vol. 2: The Great Cow Race. 2005. 144pp. 978-0-439-70624-7, hardcover; 978-0-439-70639-1.
  Vol. 3: Eyes of the Storm. 2006. 192pp. 978-0-439-70625-4, hardcover; 978-0-439-70638-4.
  Vol. 4: Dragonslayer. 2006. 176pp. 978-0-439-70626-1, hardcover; 978-0-439-70637-7.
  Vol. 5: Rock Jaw, Master of the Eastern Border. 2007. 128pp. 978-0-439-70627-8, hardcover; 978-0-439-70636-0.
  Vol. 6: Old Man's Cave. 2007. 128pp. 978-0-439-70628-5, hardcover; 978-0439-70635-3.
  Vol. 7: Ghost Circles. 2008. 160pp. 978-0-439-70629-2, hardcover; 978-0-439-70634-6.
  Vol. 8: Treasure Hunters. 2008. 144pp. 978-0-439-70630-8, hardcover; 978-0-439-70633-9.
  Vol. 9: Crown of Thorns. 2009. 224pp. 978-0-439-70631-5, hardcover; 978-0-439-70632-2.

Bone Spin-Offs

The Bone series has spun off in several other stories featuring a look at the world of *Bone* from other inhabitants from the past. The tales include familiar characters such as the rat creatures and Grandma Ben as a young woman known as Rose.

Bone: Tall Tales. Written by **Tom Sniegoski**. Illustrated by **Jeff Smith** and **Stan Sakai**. Graphix/Scholastic Books, 2010. 128pp. 978-0-545-14095-9, hardcover; 978-0-545-14096-6. A

A Bone spin-off, the book features the tall tales of Boneville settler Big Johnson Bone and tall-tale reason why rat creatures don't have any tails. A humorous fantasy tale full of adventure, humor, and one big giant rat creature. The book features a bookended tale with Smiley Bone and his three nephews—a tribute to Donald Duck's nephews Huey, Dewey, and Louie.

Bone: Tall Tales is a ® and ©
2016 Jeff Smith.

Bone: Rose. Written by **Jeff Smith**. Illustrated by **Charles Vess**. Graphix/Scholastic Books, 2009. 144pp. 978-0-545-13542-9, hardcover; 978-0-545-13543-6. T 🌱

A spin-off of Jeff Smith's <u>Bone</u> series detailing the early years of a young Grandma Ben. After inadvertently releasing a vile water dragon that is laying siege to small towns in the Northern Valley, Princess Rose vows to defeat the dragon and undo the evil she's accidentally unleashed. Unable to defeat the monster at first, Rose seeks the advice of the great Red Dragon, who tells the princess that to balance the water dragon's death, Rose victory must be balanced at a terrible cost: the life of her elder sister, Briar. Can Rose make the ultimate sacrifice to save the town? Meanwhile, the vile Lord of the Locusts has been released from the dreaming world prison and finds a willing host. Charles Vess was awarded an Eisner Award in 2002 for Best Painter/Multimedia Artist for his artwork in the series when it was originally printed.

Broxo. Written and Illustrated by **Zack Giallongo**. First Second Books, 2012. 240pp. 978-1-59643-551-3. A 🌱

Zora and Broxo make up an unlikely team. Zora is a warrior princess from a faraway land. Broxo is the last surviving member of his tribe. These two unlikely heroes are tasked by Broxo's ghostly grandmother to summon the tribal guardian to put the walking dead that plagues the mountain to rest once and for all. With the return of a deadly beast, a fickle witch, and their own desire to run away summoning the guardian will certainly be the hardest thing these two teenagers have done. *Broxo* was a selection in 2013 for YALSA's Great Graphic Novels for Teens.

© 2016 First Second.

Dawn of the Arcana. Written and Illustrated by **Rei Toma**. VIZ Media, 2011–2014. T. Japanese manga. 🎖

Princess Nakaba of the kingdom of Senan is being forced to marry Prince Caesar from an enemy kingdom of Belquat. But what will it mean when she discovers she has a strange and feared power called the Arcana which allows her to see backwards and forwards in time? This shojo manga was selected as one of YALSA's Great Graphic Novels for Teens.

Vol. 1. 2011. 192pp. 978-1-4215-4104-4.
Vol. 2. 2012. 192pp. 978-1-4215-4105-1.
Vol. 3. 2012. 192pp. 978-1-4215-4106-8.
Vol. 4. 2012. 200pp. 978-1-4215-4107-5.
Vol. 5. 2012. 192pp. 978-1-4215-4213-3.
Vol. 6. 2012. 192pp. 978-1-4215-4214-0.
Vol. 7. 2012. 184pp. 978-1-4215-4215-7.

Vol. 8. 2013. 192pp. 978-1-4215-4314-7.
Vol. 9. 2013. 184pp. 978-1-4215-4920-0.
Vol. 10. 2013. 192pp. 978-1-4215-5245-3.
Vol. 11. 2013. 192pp. 978-1-4215-5889-9.
Vol. 12. 2014. 184pp. 978-1-4215-6457-9.
Vol. 13. 2014. 192pp. 978-1-4215-5245-3.

Dragons: Defenders of Berk. Written by **Simon Furman**. Illustrated by **Iwan Nazif** and various. Titan Comics, 2014– . A 🎬 🖥

© 2016 Titan Comics.

Based off of the *How to Train Your Dragon* films and the animated series <u>The Dragon Riders of Berk</u>. The story continues the adventures of the gentle Viking son Hiccup and his companion dragon named Toothless. The adventures also include the continuing cast from the films and show including Hiccup's father Stoick, as well as the other young band of dragon riders in the village including Hiccup's friends Gobber, Snotlout, Tuffnut, and Ruffnut—and the lovely Astrid.

Dangers of the Deep. 2014. 64pp. 978-1-78276-077-1.
Dragon Down. 2014. 64pp. 978-1-78276-076-4.
The Ice Castle. 2015. 64pp. 978-1-78276-078-8.
The Legend of Ragnarok. 2015. 64pp. 978-1-78276-080-1.
The Stowaway. 2015. 64pp. 978-1-78276-079-5.
Underworld. 2015. 64pp. 978-1-78276-081-8.
Endless Night. 2016. 64pp. 978-1-78276-214-0.

ElfQuest. Written by **Wendy** and **Richard Pini**. Illustrated by **Wendy Pini**. Dark Horse Comics, 2014– . T

Created in 1977, Wendy and Richard Pini's <u>ElfQuest</u> series was one of the first independent comic book series ever created and has become one of the best-loved fantasy series in the last 40 years. Spanning centuries in time, the series tells the tales of the Wolfrider clan of elves and how they came to be a part of Earth from their extraterrestrial origins. Elves who have a close relationship with the native wolves of the region, the Wolfriders led by tribe leader Cutter, must learn to live among the fearful humans, the cave-dwelling troll civilizations, and various other tribes of elves that populate the land. Soon the Wolfrider clan discovers that what they thought of humans, trolls, and the other tribes is put to the ultimate test. Recently Dark Horse Comics reprinted the original run in a complete collection, which is still ongoing. A new series, called <u>The</u>

Final Quest, is currently ongoing and should conclude in 2017 for the anniversary of the series' beginnings.

The Complete Elfquest. 2014– .

    Vol. 1. 2014. 720pp. 978-1-61655-407-1.
    Vol. 2. 2005. 552pp. 978-1-61655-408-8.
    Vol. 3. 2016. 432pp. 978-1-5067-0080-9.
    Vol. 4. 2017. 492pp. 978-1-5067-0158-5.

Elfquest: The Final Quest. 2015– .

    Vol. 1. 2015. 192pp. 978-1-61655-409-5.
    Vol. 2. 2016. 132pp. 978-1-61655-410-1.

Fantasy Sports. Written and Illustrated by **Sam Bosma**. Nobrow Books, 2015– . T 🎗 ◎

© 2016 Sam Bosma and Nobrow.

Teenager Wiz is an intern at the United and Ancient Order of Mages. After filing a grievance with the archmage about her internship under the bull-headedly brutish but strong wizard known as Mug, she is denied reassignment. Instead Wiz and Mug are sent once again on an assignment as raiders to retrieve magical artifacts. Their next job they need to claim a treasure from a mummy's tomb. In order to get the treasure, they'll need to obey the rules of the land and best the mummy in a game of basketball! The second volume, Wiz and Mug are accidentally teleported to a ruined beach town and must best the amphibious inhabitants in a game of beach volleyball! The first volume was recognized by YALSA as a Great Graphic Novel for Teens in 2016.

Vol. 1. 2015. 56pp. 978-1-907704-80-2, hardcover.
Vol. 2: The Bandit of Barbel Bay. 2016. 56pp. 978-1-910620-10-6, hardcover.
Vol. 3: The King in Green. 2017. 56pp. 978-1-910620-18-2, hardcover.

Head Lopper. Written and Illustrated by **Andrew MacLean**. Image Comics, 2016– . O

© 2016 Andrew MacLean.

Norgal the Head Lopper has come to the island of Barra. A brute of a man with long white hair and beard, he's the son of the minotaur and the executioner of monsters. He's accompanied on his journey with the talking severed head of Agatha Blue Witch, and together they search for beasts to kill and there's plenty to kill on an island overrun with beasts who are minions of the Sorcerer of the Black Bog. When Norgal is hired by Queen Abigail to kill the wizard, Norgal has plenty of heads to lop on his way toward the sinister sorcerer.

Vol. 1: The Island or a Plague of Beasts. 2016. 128pp. 978-1-63215-886-4.

The Last Unicorn. Written by **Peter S. Beagle**. Adapted by **Peter Gillis**. Illustrated by **Renae De Liz** and **Ray Dillon**. IDW Publishing, 2011. 152pp. 978-1-60010-851-8, hardcover. T
   Adaptation of the original 1968 beloved whimsical fantasy novel by Peter S. Beagle. A lone unicorn frets that it is the last of its kind and strays from its woods in hopes of finding more of its kin. Along the way she finds a bumbling magician as a traveling companion, encounters silly bandits, and must confront a red bull and a cold-hearted king.

Mice Templar. Written by **Bryan J.L. Glass**. Illustrated by **Michael Avon Oeming** and **Victor Santos**. Image Comics, 2008–2014. T 🐭 ◎

© 2016 Bryan J.L. Glass and Michael Avon Oeming.

Once the Templar order preserved the order of the natural world and maintained the balance of life and death. But that was long ago, and both the order and world descended into chaos. Now a young mouse named Karic may be the key to restoring things the way they were. Writer Bryan J.L. Glass won the Harvey Award in 2009 for Best New Talent for his work on Mice Templar, and the series also won the Harvey Award in 2010 for Best Graphic Album of Previously Published Work.

Vol. 1: The Prophecy. 2008. 180pp. 978-1-58240-871-2, hardcover; 978-1-60706-127-4.

Vol. 2.1: Destiny Part 1. 2010. 208pp. 978-1-60706-257-8, hardcover; 978-1-60706-284-4.

Vol. 2.2: Destiny Part 2. 2010. 200pp. 978-1-60706-289-9, hardcover; 978-1-60706-313-1.
   Vol. 3: A Midwinter's Night Dream. 2012. 248pp. 978-1-60706-457-2, hardcover.
   Vol. 4.1: Legend Part 1. 2013. 248pp. 978-1-60706-822-8, hardcover.
   Vol. 4.2: Legend Part 2. 2014. 248pp. 978-1-63215-198-8, hardcover.

Monster Hunter: Flash Hunter. Written by **Keiichi Hikami**. Illustrated by **Shin Yamamoto**. VIZ Media, 2016–2017. T Japanese manga. 🐾
   In an age where monsters live in the earth, seas, and skies, there's one special hero who can dispatch the beasts: the Monster Hunter! Raiga, Keres, and Torche are three Hunters on their way to becoming the best Hunters, but they need to work together as a team to fight the beasts. When they need to overcome their differences—and fast! If they don't they're sure to be eaten by a monster before they have a chance to finish it off! The manga is based on the best-selling video game series by Capcom.

Vol. 1. 2016. 224pp. 978-1-4215-8425-6.
   Vol. 2. 2016. 224pp. 978-1-4215-8426-3.
   Vol. 3. 2016. 224pp. 978-1-4215-8427-0.
   Vol. 4. 2016. 224pp. 978-1-4215-8428-7.
   Vol. 5. 2016. 224pp. 978-1-4215-8430-0.
   Vol. 6. 2017. 224pp. 978-1-4215-8431-7.
   Vol. 7. 2017. 224pp. 978-1-4215-8432-4.

Mouse Guard. Written and Illustrated by **David Petersen**. Archaia Studios/Boom! Studios, 2007– . T 🐾 ◎ 🐭
   Life can be hard for Mice in the wild, so the Mouse Guard was formed. Not only do these sword-wielding protectors fight off intruders, but they also act as guides

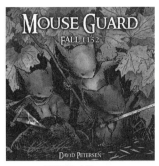

© 2016 David Petersen.

to mice traveling the land. In the first volume, set in the fall of 1152, three Guardsmice must find a missing merchant and discover a greater threat. In the next volume, set in winter, the Guardsmice must combat a food and supply shortage, as well as new dangers. The third series, The Black Axe, is a prequel set in 1115. A fourth comic series The Weasel War of 1149 is currently being worked on. The Mouse Guard comics and books have won Eisner and Harvey Awards and been on the *New York Times* best-seller lists. A spin-off anthology. *Legends of the Mouseguard* has also won an Eisner Award. Besides Petersen, other creators on that project have included Ted Naifeh, Terry Moore, Gene Ha, and Bill Willingham. An additional spin-off *Baldwin the Brave and Other Tales* features several short stories by Peterson. A related work *The Art of Mouse Guard* has come out and there is a related Role Playing Game. The series was recognized in 2008 on YALSA's Great Graphic Novel for Teens selection list as well as won two Eisner Awards for Best Publication for Kids and Best Graphic Album, Reprint, for *Mouse Guard: Fall 1152* and *Mouse Guard: Winter 1152*.

Fall 1152. 2007. 192pp. 978-1-932386-57-8, hardcover.
Winter 1152. 2009. 192pp. 978-1-932386-74-5, hardcover.
The Black Axe. 2013. 192pp. 978-1-936393-06-0, hardcover.
Legends of the Mouseguard Vol. 1. 2010. 144pp. 978-1-932386-94-3, hardcover.
Legends of the Mouseguard Vol. 2. 2013. 144pp. 978-1-936393-26-8, hardcover.
Legends of the Mouseguard Vol. 3. 2015. 128pp. 978-1-608867-67-7, hardcover.
Baldwin the Brave and Other Tales. 2014. 96pp. 978-1-608864-77-5, hardcover.

Orc Stain. Written and Illustrated by **James Stokoe**. Image Comics, 2010. 168pp. 978-1-60706-295-0. O

© 2016 James Stokoe.

The orc world is one of instability and power lust. An orc will kill another orc for looking at his love nymph in the wrong way. Where most orcs smash everything in their paths, One-Eye opens them up to find the secrets they hide beneath. He has a unique talent to see where he must strike an object to make it fall apart for plundering. This ability has made him the prime target of the Great Orktzar so that he can use this ability for his own nefarious schemes. One-Eye is constantly hounded in this crazy colorful world by crazier monsters, orcs, and poison witches.

Orcs: Forged for War. Written by **Stan Nichols**. Illustrated by **Joe Flood**. First Second Books, 2011. 208pp. 978-1-5964-3455-4. O

An original graphic novel tied into the popular Orcs series of fantasy novels by British author Stan Nichols. A group of warrior Orcs working for the dark

© 2016 First Second.

sorceress Jennesta are charged with protecting Goblins, who have their own, dangerous agenda.

Overlord. Written by **Satoshi Ōshio**. Illustrated by **Hugin Miyama**. Yen Press, 2016– . O ◎ あ Japanese manga.

© 2016 Yen Press.

Set in 2138 where the once-popular game *Yggdrasil* was once the leading virtual reality fantasy action game. When the game finally announces it will shut down for good, everyone was supposed to be logged out automatically. Momonga was once a member of a great clan—his friends all logged off on the last day of the game being shut down—and when the game doesn't shut down and the NPCs under his command in the game begin talking to him, Momonga realizes he's trapped in the game and there's no way to log out. Trapped in the persona of his undefeatable skeletal sorcerer and unable to log out, he may not have a clan of online friends anymore, but he has a plethora of evil servants who still serve his whim as the ruler of the Great Tomb of Nazarick. Now Momonga and his servants roam the lands in the guise of a bounty hunter and try to accomplish good instead of evil in a land in which he is the only human still online—but is he? The legends of Momonga and his guild begin here! The series was originally begun in Japan as a series of light novels and was adapted into a manga and animated series.

Vol. 1. 2016. 176pp. 978-0-316-27227-8.
Vol. 2. 2016. 192pp. 978-0-316-39766-7.
Vol. 3. 2016. 192pp. 978-0-316-43425-6.

Rat Queens. Written by **Kurtis J. Wiebe**. Illustrated by **Roc Upchurch**, **Stjepan Sejic**, and **Tess Fowler**. Image Comics, 2015– . M ◎

Meet Betty, Dee, Hannah, and Violet—four of the bawdiest battle maidens-for-hire in all the land! A mage, fighter, healer, and smidgen, they can drink, cavort, and kill their way through any enemy. When they find out that their latest quest is actually a plot to kill them, they're on their guard and on the hunt for whomever put a price on their head. A new twist on a classic adventure story, think of the series as *Dungeons and Dragons* with a healthy dose of *Tank Girl* and you're in for a raucous and fun ride. The *Deluxe Edition* collection reprints the material in the first two volumes in one hardcover collection.

Vol. 1: Sass and Sorcery. 2014. 128pp. 978-1-60706-945-4.
Vol. 2: The Far Reaching Tentacles of N'Rygoth. 2015. 136pp. 978-1-63215-040-0.

© 2016 Kurtis J. Wiebe.

Vol. 3: Demons. 2016. 160pp. 978-1-63215-735-5.
Deluxe Edition, Vol. 1. 2015. 304pp. 978-1-63215-492-7, hardcover.

Red Moon. Written by **Carlos Trillo**. Translation by **Zeliko Medic**. Illustrated by **Eduardo Risso**. Dark Horse, 2014. 248pp. 978-1-61655-447-7. A

In this fantasy story young acrobat Antolin encounters Moon, the red-haired daughter of a local lord (and her invisible friend), and helps her save her father and land. In this, and in other adventures, they encounter fairies, witches, monsters, and friends and foes with amazing abilities. *Red Moon* was originally published in 2005–2006 by SAF Comics in Europe.

Spera. Written by **Josh Tierney**. Illustrated by **Kyla Vanderklugt** and various. Archaia Entertainment/Boom! Studios, 2012–2013. O

The lives of the princesses Pira and Lono change forever when Pira's mother slays the visiting king and father of Lono. The two friends must escape if they want their friendship to last beyond the queen's invasion into Lono's kingdom. The two set of for the magical lands of Spera where no one knows them and they can start their lives anew. Pira and Lono travel with their other friends Yonder the shapeshifting fire spirit and Chobo the Warrior Cat. Their adventures are dangerous but rewarding as they make a new way for themselves. Each chapter of the book is handed off to a different artist, so the book looks widely different but nonetheless great.

Vol. 1. 2012. 176pp. 978-1-936393-30-5.
Vol. 2. 2013. 168pp. 978-1-936393-76-3.

Spice & Wolf. Written by **Isuna Hasekura**. Illustrated by **Keito Koume**. Yen Press, 2012– . O Japanese manga. あ

Kraft Lawrence is a 25-year-old traveling merchant in a remote village, who peddles his wares from town to town. With dreams of one day having his own storefront, one day Kraft comes across a curiosity: a 600-year-old pagan god named Holo. Though she appears like a 15-year-old girl with wolf ears, she's the goddess of the harvest and soon she becomes his traveling companion. Forsaken by the village she is in, she wishes to travel to Yoitsu, her homeland in the north and to explore the changing world. Her knowledge helps Kraft in his journey in becoming a better merchant, though her true nature draws the ire from the Church. The series is unique in that the series focuses more on the lives of trade and commerce instead of the normal themes' common tropes in fantasy stories. The series was adapted from the original light novels from Japan, and also adapted into an anime series. The series is still ongoing in Japan.

Vol. 1. 2010. 192pp. 978-0-316-07339-4.

Vol. 2. 2010. 192pp. 978-0-316-10232-2.

Vol. 3. 2010. 176pp. 978-0-316-10234-6.

Vol. 4. 2011. 192pp. 978-0-316-17826-6.

Vol. 5. 2011. 192pp. 978-0-316-19447-1.

Vol. 6. 2012. 192pp. 978-0-316-21032-4.

Vol. 7. 2012. 192pp. 978-0-316-22911-1.

Vol. 8. 2013. 192pp. 978-0-316-25085-6.

Vol. 9. 2014. 176pp. 978-0-316-29487-4.

Vol. 10. 2014. 176pp. 978-0-316-33660-4.

Vol. 11. 2015. 176pp. 978-0-316-30505-1.

Vol. 12. 2015. 176pp. 978-0-316-31476-3.

Three Thieves. Written and Illustrated by **Scott Chantler**. Kids Can Press, 2010–2016. A 🎗 ◎

© 2016 Scott Chantler and Kids Can Press.

Dessa Redd is a 14-year-old acrobat who is desperately seeking to find any clues about her long-lost brother, Jared, who was kidnapped years ago. She's accompanied in the traveling circus by Topper, a blue-skinned norker who is a juggler at the circus as well as one of the best thieves in all the lands. When they pull into the kingdom of Kingsbridge, Dessa and Topper along with a strongman named Fisk set out to steal the treasury of the evil Queen Magda and Dessa discovers clues to the whereabouts of her long-lost brother, Jared, who was kidnapped from their family years ago. Soon the chase is on across six kingdoms as Captain Drake from the queen's guard has been tasked with capturing Dessa. Meanwhile, Dessa, Topper, and Fisk follow the clues across the kingdoms that will finally reunite her with her long-lost brother Jared. Great Graphic Novels for Teens recognized both *The King's Dragon* and *Pirates of the Silver Coast* for their 2015 selection list. The series recently concluded with the final volume published in 2017.

Vol. 1: Tower of Treasure. 2010. 112pp. 978-1-55453-414-2, hardcover.

Vol. 2: Sign of the Black Rook. 2011. 112pp. 978-1-55453-416-6, hardcover.

Vol. 3: Captive Prince. 2012. 112pp. 978-1-55453-776-1, hardcover.

Vol. 4: The King's Dragon. 2014. 112pp. 978-1-55453-778-5, hardcover.

Vol. 5: Pirates of the Silver Coast. 2015. 112pp. 978-1-89478-653-9, hardcover.

Vol. 6: The Dark Island. 2016. 112pp. 978-1-89478-655-3, hardcover.

Vol. 7: The Iron Hand. 2016. 112pp. 978-1-77138-052-2, hardcover.

The Wizard's Tale. Written by **Kurt Busiek**. Illustrated by **David Wenzel**. IDW Publishing, 2010. 144pp. 978-1-60010-595-1. A 🎗

A charming and beautifully illustrated story about Bafflerog Rumplewhisker, an evil wizard from a long line of really evil wizards, who really wasn't that evil after all. In the land of Ever-Night, evil ruled and good had been driven out. But before good left, they had managed to steal and hide the spell book called the Book of Worse, and prevented the casting of the spell that would ensure evil's supremacy forever. Bafflerog is charged to find the Book of Worse and to ensure the ultimate supremacy of evil, so he reluctantly leaves his comfortable castle and journeys with his toad Gumwort and Muddle, the third son of a woodcutter, to find the book and complete the spell to destroy all the good from Ever-Night. The journey takes him to various places

© 2010 Kurt Busiek and David
Wenzel.

including a strange place called New York. The collection received recognition by YALSA's Popular Paperbacks for Young Adults committee in 2003 on the *Flights of Fantasy: Beyond Harry and Frodo* list when it was originally published by Wildstorm/DC Comics.

World of Warcraft. Written by **Walter Simonson, Louise Simonson, Micky Neilson,** and various. Illustrated by **Ludo Lullabi, Sandra Hope, Jon Landry, Jerome K. Moore,** and various. DC Comics, 2007–2013. T 🎮

The World of Warcraft, a massively multiplayer online role-playing game (MMORPG) where people can play online as warrior orcs druids, paladins, shamans, wizards, death knights, and more, has continually been a favorite online PC game since its creation in 2004 by Blizzard Entertainment. In 2008, DC Comics partnered with Blizzard to bring to life the adventures and settings from the popular game and its expansion sets to the world of comics. A feature-length movie adaptation of the hit game was released as well in 2016. Below are listed the various series written by fan-favorite writers Walter and Louise Simonson, as well as others including Blizzard Entertainment staff.

Vol. 1. 2008. 176pp. 978-1-4012-1836-2, hardcover.
Vol. 2. 2009. 176pp. 978-1-4012-2370-0, hardcover.
Vol. 3. 2010. 176pp. 978-1-4012-2810-1, hardcover.
Vol. 4. 2010. 144pp. 978-1-4012-2857-6, hardcover.
Ashbringer. 2010. 128pp. 978-1-4012-2341-0, hardcover.
Pearl of Pandaria. 2012. 112pp. 978-1401226992, hardcover.
Bloodsworn. 2013. 152pp. 978-1-4012-3029-6, hardcover.
Dark Riders. 2013. 144pp. 978-1401230272, hardcover.

World of Warcraft: The Essential Sunwell Collection. Written by **Richard Knaak**. Illustrated by **Jae Hwan Kim**. TOKYOPOP, 2010. 608pp. 978-1-4278-1897-3. T Neo-manga. 🎮

Based on the best-selling fantasy role-playing PC games by Blizzard Entertainment, the *Sunwell Trilogy* focuses on the adventures of Kalec, a shape-shifting blue dragon able to assume human form in the battle-ravaged land of Azeroth. Together with the young maiden Anveena, he's on a quest to ensure that the fabled weapon of destruction, the dreaded Sunwell, is destroyed before falling into the wrong hands. As they travel through the Elvin kingdom of Quel'Thalas, they must battle armies of orcs, goblins, and the armies of the Undead to reach their destiny.

Heroic Fantasy

Though very similar to Epic Fantasy, Heroic Fantasy focuses on a main protagonist who typically relies on his own brain and brawn and little else in a fantasy world full of deadly creatures, sorcerers, and more. The hero may have some magical skills, but this is not typically the case. Though the heroes may live in a world of sorcery and magical beasts, the focus is on a hero who lives and dies by the sword in his hand and the bloody path of vengeance that he cleaves with it. The character of the hero—his upbringing, pure (or even less-than-pure) motives, and behavior—also plays a role in forging the hero into the man he is and the man he will become. The hero, from sometimes humble and naïve beginnings, sets out to discover who he really is and begins the hero's journey. The journey is difficult, but the reward is humbling on the road to discovery. The <u>Conan the Barbarian</u> series of books and movies fit in this subgenre.

Barbarian Lord. Written and Illustrated by **Matt Smith**. Clarion Books, 2014. 176pp. 978-0-547-85906-4, hardcover. T ◉

© 2014 by Matt Smith. Reprinted by permission of Houghton Miffin Harcourt Publishing.

All hail the Barbarian Lord! Cheated of his land in faraway Garmrland, a small spot of land once inhabited by wolves and trolls, the grim-faced but well-versed Barbarian Lord sets out on a quest for revenge to regain his farm and home from the conniving plots of the Skullmaster. These adventures lead him across the ocean to the land of a king and into fierce battles with trolls, berserkers, ghosts, and sea serpents on his quest to reconquer his home.

Basara. Written and Illustrated by **Yumi Tamura**. VIZ Media, 2003–2008. O あ Japanese manga.

Japanese manga. In a post-apocalyptic Japan, a young girl must find the strength and courage to avenge her twin brother's death and to fulfill an ancient prophecy as the "child of destiny." For years, many of her people believed that Basara's brother was the promised one who would free their people from the tyranny of the land's cruel kingdoms. Now that he's dead, who will lead them? Disguised as her late brother, Basara's finding out that she just might have what it takes to be the prophesied one and be the hero of legend. An epic 27-volume series from Japan, the series features a bold female hero in a genre-bending setting mixing fantasy, science fiction, action, and romance. A 13-episode anime series based on the manga was released in Japan.

Vol. 1. 2003. 192pp. 978-1-56931-974-1.
Vol. 2. 2003. 192pp. 978-1-56931-975-8.
Vol. 3. 2003. 200pp. 978-1-59116-091-5.
Vol. 4. 2003. 200pp. 978-1-59116-123-3.
Vol. 5. 2004. 200pp. 978-1-59116-246-9.
Vol. 6. 2004. 200pp. 978-1-59116-313-8.
Vol. 7. 2004. 200pp. 978-1-59116-367-1.
Vol. 8. 2004. 200pp. 978-1-59116-368-8.
Vol. 9. 2004. 200pp. 978-1-59116-369-5.
Vol. 10. 2005. 200pp. 978-1-59116-628-3.
Vol. 11. 2005. 200pp. 978-1-59116-746-4.
Vol. 12. 2005. 200pp. 978-1-59116-800-3.
Vol. 13. 2005. 200pp. 978-1-59116-864-5.
Vol. 14. 2005. 200pp. 978-1-4215-0017-1.

Vol. 15. 2005. 200pp. 978-1-4215-0135-2. *Vol. 22.* 2007. 192pp. 978-1-4215-0979-2.
Vol. 16. 2006. 208pp. 978-1-4215-0261-8. *Vol. 23.* 2007. 208pp. 978-1-4215-0980-8.
Vol. 17. 2006. 208pp. 978-1-4215-0391-2. *Vol. 24.* 2007. 192pp. 978-1-4215-0981-5.
Vol. 18. 2006. 208pp. 978-1-4215-0528-2. *Vol. 25.* 2007. 200pp. 978-1-4215-0982-2.
Vol. 19. 2006. 208pp. 978-1-4215-0529-9. *Vol. 26.* 2008. 192pp. 978-1-4215-0983-9.
Vol. 20. 2006. 208pp. 978-1-4215-0530-5. *Vol. 27.* 2008. 200pp. 978-1-4215-0984-6.
Vol. 21. 2006. 208pp. 978-1-4215-0531-2.

Conan the Barbarian

Dark Horse Comics, 2003– . T-O

Conan ® and © Conan Properties
International LLC.

No other barbarian in pulp fiction history can compare with Robert E. Howard's Conan. Created in the 1930s, Conan has become one of the most popular characters in literature. A brutal and cunning Cimmerian warrior born on the fields of battle, Conan was consumed by wanderlust at an early age and encountered many beasts, monsters, damsels, and wizards in his adventures as a thief, warrior, mercenary, and ultimately king. The character found renewed popularity in the monthly comic book series Conan the Barbarian by Marvel Comics in the early 1970s. Written by Roy Thomas, with art by such illustrators as Barry Windsor-Smith and John Buscema, these are some of the most memorable fantasy stories inspired by Howard's novels focusing on the early years of Conan. The classic stories are now being reprinted in the Dark Horse Comics series called Chronicles of Conan with all new coloring and text corrections. Dark Horse has also begun retelling and embellishing the classic Robert E. Howard stories in both a monthly comic book series and miniseries projects. Dark Horse Comics has helped to revitalize the Conan legacy to the delight of older as well as a new generation of fans. Not included in this list are the collections of *Savage Sword of Conan* and King Conan series originally published by Marvel Comics. More titles can be found at Dark Horse Comics' web site.

The Chronicles of Conan. Written by **Roy Thomas** and **Sandy Plunkett**. Illustrated by **Barry Windsor Smith**, **John Buscema**, **Gil Kane**, and various. Dark Horse Comics, 2003– . T

Reprints and recolors the classic Marvel Comics series that began in 1970. The character was published regularly by Marvel until early 2001.

Vol. 1: Tower of the Elephant & Other Stories. 2003. 144pp. 978-1-59307-016-8.
Vol. 2: Rogues in the House & Other Stories. 2003. 160pp. 978-1-59307-023-6.
Vol. 3: The Monster of the Monoliths and Other Stories. 2004. 168pp. 978-1-59307-024-3.
Vol. 4: The Song of Red Sonja and Other Stories. 2004. 160pp. 978-1-59307-025-0.
Vol. 5: The Shadow in the Tomb and Other Stories. 2004. 160pp. 978-1-59307-175-2.
Vol. 6: The Curse of the Golden Skull and Other Stories. 2004. 160pp. 978-1-59307-274-2.
Vol. 7: The Dweller in the Pool and Other Stories. 2005. 160pp. 978-1-59307-300-8.

Vol. 8: The Tower of Blood and Other Stories. 2005. 160pp. 978-1-59307-349-7.

Vol. 9: Riders of the River-Dragons and Other Stories. 2005. 160pp. 978-1-59307-394-7.

Vol. 10: When Giants Walk the Earth and Other Stories. 2006. 168pp. 978-1-59307-490-6.

Vol. 11: The Dance of the Skull and Other Stories. 2007. 152pp. 978-1-59307-636-8.

Vol. 12: The Beast King of Abombi and Other Stories. 2007. 184pp. 978-1-5930-7778-5.

Vol. 13: The Whispering Shadows and Other Stories. 2007. 152pp. 978-1-5930-7837-9.

Vol. 14: Shadow of the Beast and Other Stories. 2008. 160pp. 978-1-5930-7899-7.

Vol. 15: The Corridor of Mullah-Kajar and Other Stories. 2008. 200pp. 978-1-59307-971-0.

Vol. 16: The Eternity War and Other Stories. 2008. 208pp. 978-1-59582-176-8.

Vol. 17: The Creation Quest and Other Stories. 2009. 244pp. 978-1-59582-177-5.

Vol. 18: Isle of the Dead and Other Stories. 2009. 208pp. 978-1-59582-382-3.

Vol. 19: Deathmark and Other Stories. 2010. 978-1-59582-515-5.

Vol. 20: Night of the Wolf and Other Stories. 2010. 200pp. 978-1-59582-584-1.

Vol. 21: Blood of a Titan and Other Stories. 2011. 224pp. 978-1-59582-704-3.

Vol. 22: Reavers in the Borderland and Other Stories. 2012. 232pp. 978-1-59582-812-5.

Vol. 23: The Well of Souls and Other Stories. 2013. 232pp. 978-1-61655-052-3.

Vol. 24: Blood Dawn and Other Stories. 2013. 240pp. 978-1-61655-107-0.

Vol. 25: Exodus and Other Stories. 2013. 232pp. 978-1-61655-286-2.

Vol. 26: Legion of the Dead and Other Stories. 2014. 232pp. 978-1-61655-348-7.

Vol. 27: Sands Upon the Earth and Other Stories. 2014. 224pp. 978-1-61655-373-9.

Vol. 28: Blood and Ice and Other Stories. 2014. 224pp. 978-1-61655-374-6.

Vol. 29: The Shape in the Shadow and Other Stories. 2015. 224pp. 978-1-61655-375-3.

Vol. 30: The Death of Conan and Other Stories. 2015. 200pp. 978-1-61655-589-4.

Vol. 31: Empires of the Undead and Other Stories. 2016. 224pp. 978-1-61655-865-9.

Vol. 32: The Second-Coming of Shuma-Gorath and Other Stories. 2016. 240pp. 978-1-61655-866-6.

Vol. 33: The Mountain Where Crom Dwells and Other Stories. 2016. 224pp. 978-1-61655-867-3.

Vol. 34: Betrayal in Zamora and Other Stories. 2016. 232pp. 978-1-61655-868-0.

Conan (ongoing series). Written by various. Illustrated by various. 2005–present. 🏹 ◎ O
The below listed titles are currently published by Dark Horse Comics. The monthly series has been written by a wide variety of talents beginning with Kurt Busiek and illustrated by Cary Nord. Included as well are self-contained stories that are new stories and adaptations of Robert E. Howard's pulp adventures. The comic book issue #0, reprinted in Volume 1, received an Eisner Award for Best Single Issue/Single Story in 2004.

Conan. Written by **Kurt Busiek**, **Tim Truman**, **Brian Wood**, and various. Illustrated by **Cary Nord**, **Becky Cloonan**, and various. Dark Horse Comics, 2005– . T

Vol. 0: Born on the Battlefield. Written by **Kurt Busiek**. Illustrated by **Greg Ruth**. 2008. 128pp. 978-1-59307-981-9.

Vol. 1: The Frost Giant's Daughter and Other Stories. Written by **Kurt Busiek**. Illustrated by **Cary Nord**. 2005. 192pp. 978-1-59307-301-5.

Vol. 2: The God in the Bowl and Other Stories. Written by **Kurt Busiek**. Illustrated by **Cary Nord**. 2005. 176pp. 978-1-59307-403-6.

Vol. 3: The Tower of the Elephant and Other Stories. Written by **Kurt Busiek**. Illustrated by **Cary Nord**. 2006. 168pp. 978-1-59307-547-7.

Conan ® and © Conan Properties
International LLC.

Vol. 4: The Hall of the Dead. Written by **Kurt Busiek, Mike Mignola, Tim Truman, Scott Allie,** and **Haden Blackman.** Illustrated by **Cary Nord.** 2007. 200pp. 978-1-59307-775-4.

Vol. 5: Rogues in the House. Written by **Tim Truman.** Illustrated by **Cary Nord** and **Tomas Giorello.** 2008. 160pp. 978-1-59307-903-1.

Vol. 6: The Hand of Nergal. Written by **Tim Truman.** Illustrated by **Tomàs Giorello.** 2008. 152pp. 978-1-59582-178-2.

Vol. 7: Cimmeria. Written by **Tim Truman.** Illustrated by **Tomàs Giorello.** 2009. 192pp. 978-1-59582-283-3.

Vol. 8: Black Colossus. Written by **Tim Truman.** Illustrated by **Tomàs Giorello.** 2010. 152pp. 978-1-59582-533-9.

Vol. 9: Free Companions. Written by **Tim Truman.** Illustrated by **Joe Kubert, Tomas Giorello,** and **Tim Truman.** 2010. 184pp. 978-1-59582-592-6.

Vol. 10: Iron Shadows in the Moon. Written by **Tim Truman.** Illustrated by **Tomàs Giorello.** 2011. 144pp. 978-1-59582-713-5.

Vol. 11: Road of the Kings. Written by **Roy Thomas.** Illustrated by **Mike Hawthorne.** 2012. 152pp. 978-1-59582-824-8.

Vol. 12: Throne of Aquilonia. Written by **Roy Thomas.** Illustrated by **Mike Hawthorne** and **Dan Panosian.** 2013. 152pp. 978-1-59582-905-4.

Vol. 13: Queen of the Black Coast. Written by **Brian Wood.** Illustrated by **Becky Cloonan** and **James Harren.** 2013. 152pp. 978-1-61655-043-1.

Vol. 14: The Death. Written by **Brian Wood.** Illustrated by **Becky Cloonan, Vasilis Lolos,** and **Declan Shalvey.** 2013. 152pp. 978-1-61655-123-0.

Vol. 15: The Nightmare of the Shallows. Written by **Brian Wood.** Illustrated by **Andrea Mutti.** 2014. 152pp. 978-1-61655-385-2.

Vol. 16: The Song of Belit. 2015. Written by **Brian Wood.** Illustrated by **Dave Stewart.** 2015. 176pp. 978-1-61655-524-5.

Vol. 17: Shadows over Kush. Written by **Fred Van Lente.** Illustrated by **Brian Ching** and **Eduardo Francisco.** 2015. 152pp. 978-1-61655-659-4.

Vol. 18: The Damned Horde. Written by **Fred Van Lente.** Illustrated by **Brian Ching.** 2016. 152pp. 978-1-61655-799-7.

Vol. 19: Xuthal of the Dusk. 2016. Written by **Fred Van Lente.** Illustrated by **Brian Ching** and **Guiu Vilanova.** 2016. 176pp. 978-1-61655-879-6.

Vol. 20: A Witch Shall Be Born. Written by **Fred Van Lente.** Illustrated by **Jose Luis** and **Brian Ching.** 2016. 152pp. 978-1-50670-005-2.

Conan Omnibus. Written by **Kurt Busiek,** and various Illustrated by **Cary Nord** and various.

Vol. 1: Birth of a Legend. 2016. 472pp. 978-1-50670-282-7.
Vol. 2: City of Thieves. 2017. 474pp. 978-1-50670-294-0.

Conan (various miniseries and adaptations). Dark Horse Comics, 2006– .

Conan and the Jewels of Gwahlur. Written and Illustrated by **P. Craig Russell.** 2006. 88pp. 1-59307-491-3, hardcover.

Conan and the Demons of Khitai. Written by **Akira Yoshida.** Illustrated by **Pat Lee.** 2006. 96pp. 1-59307-543-X.

Conan ® and © Conan Properties International LLC.

Conan: Book of Thoth. Written by **Kurt Busiek** and **Len Wein**. Illustrated by **Kelley Jones**. 2006. 192pp. 1-59307-648-7.

Conan and the Songs of the Dead. Written by **Joe R. Lansdale** and **Tim Truman**. Illustrated by **Tim Truman**. 2007. 138pp. 978-1-59307-718-1.

Conan and the Midnight God. Written by **Joshua Dysart**. Illustrated by **Will Conrad**. 2007. 136pp. 978-1-59307-852-2.

Conan and the Daughters of Midora and Other Stories. Written by **Jimmy Palmiotti**, **Ron Marz**, **Tim Truman**, **Ben Truman**, and **Michael Avon Oeming**. Illustrated by **Bart Sears**, **Michael Avon Oeming**, **Mark Texeira**, and **Marian Churchland**. 2012. 112pp. 978-1-59582-917-7.

Conan: The Phantoms of the Black Coast. Written by **Victor Gischler**. Illustrated by **Attila Futaki**. 2014. 128pp. 978-1-61655-244-2.

Conan and the People of the Black Circle. Written by **Fred Van Lente**. Illustrated by **Ariel Olivetti**. 2014. 96pp. 978-1-61655-459-0, hardcover.

Conan/Red Sonja. Written by **Gail Simone** and **Jim Zub**. Illustrated by **Randy Green**. 2015. 96pp. 978-1-61655-651-8, hardcover.

King Conan. Written by **Tim Truman**. Illustrated by **Tomàs Giorello**. Dark Horse Comics, 2012– .

Adaptations of classic Robert E. Howard novels featuring a much older Conan now the King of Aquilonia.

The Scarlet Citadel. 2012. 112pp. 978-1-59582-838-5.
The Phoenix on the Sword. 2013. 96pp. 978-1-61655-029-5.
The Hour of the Dragon. 2014. 160pp. 978-1-61655-307-4.
The Conqueror. 2015. 160pp. 978-1-61655-514-6.
Wolves Beyond the Border. 2016. 120pp. 978-1-61655-888-8.

Ezra. Written by **Sean O'Reilly**. Illustrated by **Alfonso Ruiz** and **Master Rove**. Arcana Studios, 2005–2010. T

A spin-off from the series Kade. After watching her parents die at the hands of a barbarian and his men, the young girl called Ezra tried to fight back but was severely beaten. Left for dead, her near brush with death changed her both physically and mentally: her skin became chalky white; her strength and stamina increased significantly. Over time she also learned the ways of magic from a cruel mystic named Pediot from the Order of the Black Sun. Now Ezra is a mercenary-for-hire, stealing artifacts and other goods in exchange for a few coins. When she's hired by Barak, the head of the local thieves' guild, she soon finds she is in way over her head. A simple quest to exchange the Sword of Turin for the equally powerful amulet called Eye of the Serpent becomes much more difficult when she must take on the Egyptian goddess called Nephilila and her cadre of cat-warriors.

The Egyptian Exchange. 2005. 120pp. 978-0-9763095-4-3.
Evoked Emotions. 2010. 120pp. 978-1-897548-13-4.

The Freebooters. Written and Illustrated by **Barry Windsor-Smith**. Fantagraphics Books, 2005. 184pp. 978-1-56097-662-2. O

Axus the Great is a legendary warrior, thief, and playboy. He has slain demons and has sneaked into heavily guarded royal palaces. The story in *The Freebooters* starts many years after Axus's adventuring days. Now that he is older and fatter he runs a popular tavern where many fans come to listen to tales of his past exploits. This cushy life of booze and women comes to an end when the prophet Aran stirs Axus's wanderlust and desire for more adventure. *The Freebooters* was collected from Barry Windsor-Smith's ill-fated, yet critically acclaimed periodical *The Storyteller*. The book also contains behind-the-scenes look at the creation process. Since the magazine was canceled only after nine issues, the ending for *The Freebooters* will certainly leave readers wanting more.

Green Monk. Written and Illustrated by **Brandon Dayton**. Brandon Dayton Publishing, 2009. 978-0-615-38283-8. T 🏵 ◎

Set in a fantasy version of old Russia, a young monk with the most powerful blade of grass ever made wanders into battle with a fierce giant. The short story was recognized by YALSA as one of the top 10 titles on the 2011 Great Graphic Novels for Teens selection list.

© 2016 Brandon Dayton.

Kade. Written by **Sean O'Reilly**. Illustrated by **Allan Otero** and various. Arcana Studios, 2005–2010. T

Abandoned as an infant in a world ruled by the dark lord Apollyon, the ebony-skinned and dark-haired infant with strange tattoos on his body was rescued from death and raised in a monastery by monks. There his rescuers learned that Kade has been cursed not to feel anything physical, from the blade of a sword to the soft caress of a woman's touch. Prophesied as the Lord of the Order of the Black Sun, one who will bring down Apollyon's dark reign, he searches out those who can aid him in his quest following the murder of the monks and to destroy Apollyon once and for all.

Identity. 2005. 132pp. 978-0-9763095-1-2.
Sun of Perdition. 2008. 110pp. 978-0-9763095-6-7.
Red Sun. 2010. 120pp. 978-1-897548-75-2.
Shiva's Sun. 2010. 128pp. 978-1-897548-29-5.

Kid Beowulf. Written and Illustrated by **Alexis Fajardo**. Kid Beowulf Comics/ Andrews McMeel Publishing, 2010– . A

Inspired by the epic poem Beowulf, the Kid Beowulf series follows the adventures of 12-year-old twin brothers Beowulf and Grendel as they travel to distant lands and meet fellow epic heroes therein! They travel to Francia, war-torn Spain, on their adventures. Beginning in 2016 Andrews McMeel Publishing relaunched the series in fully recolored editions.

Kid Beowulf and the Song of Roland. 2010. 272pp. 978-0-9801419-2-4.
Kid Beowulf and the Rise of El Cid. 2013. 240pp. 978-0-9746000-6-2.

Kid Beowulf Eddas: Shild and the Dragon. 2014. 240pp. 978-0-9909505-0-9.

Kid Beowulf and the Blood-Bound Oath. 2016. 240pp. 978-1-4494-7589-5.

The Legend of Zelda. Written and Illustrated by **Akira Himekawa**. VIZ Media, 2008– . A. Japanese manga. 🎮

There is a legendary cycle of a hero reborn to restore balance to the world through a powerful artifact called the Triforce. That hero's name is Link. No matter what era, an evil force, rival to the hero, returns to wreak havoc. These two characters each have a part of the Triforce. Link possesses the Triforce of courage and Ganon possesses the Triforce of power. The third and last part needed for a complete Triforce is that of wisdom held by the Princess Zelda and her descendants. Based off the immensely popular video game series, the manga adaptations follow the stories of the specific game while adding a unique fun twist that will surely entertain. Beginning in late 2016, VIZ Media began reprinting the series in larger format Legendary Editions.

Ocarina of Time

Link is a child from the Kokiri Forest. When he travels to Hyrule he meets a princess named Zelda. She tells him that he must stop Ganondorf, the evil ambassador and king from the desert. Link becomes the Hero of Time when he obtains the Ocarina of Time and pulls the Master Sword from the Temple of Time. The Master Sword is the only weapon strong enough to stop Ganondorf. Link is sealed away from Hyrule when he pulls the sword from the stone. When Link reawakens as an adult, Hyrule is not the same as it was before. Ganondorf has taken over the world. Link must use the time-traveling abilities of the Ocarina to undo this fate.

Vol. 1. 2008. 200pp. 978-1-4215-2327-9.
Vol. 2. 2008. 200pp. 978-1-4215-2328-6.
Legendary Edition Vol. 1: Ocarina of Time, Parts 1 and 2. 2016. 378pp. 978-1-4215-8959-6.

Majora's Mask

After the events of the game *Ocarina of Time*, Link was sent back in time, and comes across a portal that leads to a parallel world called Termina. Life here is much like it is back in Hyrule. Even the people look the same. The only difference is that the moon is about to crash and obliterate the world. Link must once again travel through time to stop the moon!

Vol. 3: Majora's Mask. 2009. 216pp. 978-1-4215-2329-3.

Oracle of Seasons & Oracle of Ages

In the storyline for the game *Oracle of Seasons*, Link has been teleported to a land far away from Hyrule called Holodrum. Here he finds himself traveling with a troupe, including the beautiful dancer Din. While performing one day, Din is abducted by the evil General Onyx. After they disappeared, the bright summer day turned into frigid winter weather, flowers began to bloom, and just as suddenly the leaves from the trees turned to autumn shades. The seasons were out of order. Din was secretly the Oracle of Seasons and with her absence all life will wilt away just as the flowers did. It is up to Link to fight to free Din and defeat the General's evil plans.

For the game *Oracle of Ages*, Link is once again teleported to another faraway land called Labrynna. There he finds his friend Impa. Even though Impa is acting strangely, he travels with her to a mystical forest. There they meet Nayru, the Oracle of Ages. Upon meeting Nayru, the evil spirit of the sorceress Veran flies out of Impa and possesses the body of Nayru. With Nayru's time-traveling ability, Veran tries to take over the world in the past. It is up to Link to travel back in time and work with his ancestor to stop Veran from gaining power.

Vol. 4: Oracle of Seasons. 2009. 200pp. 978-1-4215-2330-9.
Vol. 5: Oracle of Ages. 2009. 200pp. 978-1-4215-2331-6.
Legendary Edition, Vol. 2: Oracle of Seasons and Oracle of Ages. 2017. 386pp. 978-1-4215-8960-2.

Four Swords/The Minish Cap

What is better than one Link saving the day? Four Links saving the day. Why are four Links running around Hyrule at once? That is because Zelda and other princesses have mysteriously been teleported away while they were trying to reseal the evil wizard Vaati. Link grabbed the only weapon around to stop the evil forces and that was The Four Sword which split Link into four beings. Can Link work together with his other selves to stop Vaati and save Princess Zelda?

Vol. 6: Four Swords, Part 1. 2009. 200pp. 978-1-4215-2332-3.
Vol. 7: Four Swords, Part 2. 2009. 176pp.
978-1-4215-2333-0.
Legendary Edition—Four Swords. 2017. 370pp. 978-1-4215-8963-3.

The Minish Cap

There is a myth that there are a tiny race of people called the Picori that live among the Hylians. After a sour turn of events, Link is now able to shrink to the size of a thumbtack. With his travel companion, a smart mouth-talking hat, Link must travel the world he grew up in while no bigger than a bug. What were once small are now huge. What was once easy now takes an extreme amount of energy to accomplish.

Vol. 8: The Minish Cap. 2009. 192pp. 978-1-4215-2334-7.

A Link to the Past

Link is awakened in the middle of the night by a mysterious plea to be saved. Zelda and the kingdom of Hyrule are under the influence of dark powers. The wizard Agahnim used his magical abilities to gain influence within the royal court. The king has disappeared and Princess Zelda has been captured with six other maidens. Link, while traveling to save princess Zelda, is pursued by a thief and the Royal Army. He also witnesses what would happen if the power of the Dark World would do to the Light World if Agahnim's plans are successful.

Vol. 9: A Link to the Past. 2010. 192pp. 978-1-4215-2335-4.
Legendary Edition, Vol. 3: Majora's Mask/A Link to the Past. 2017. 402pp. 978-1-4215-8961-9.

The Phantom Hourglass

Hyrule has been flooded for centuries. The peoples of Hyrule had to adapt or sank with the old world. Link and a girl named Tetra sail across the expansive ocean on a pirate ship. When Tetra explores a ghost ship, she is abducted by the evil force Bellum. Link must rely on his new friends Ciela the fairy, Oshus the old man, and Linebeck the cowardly captain to get Tetra back. Link's new friends will prove to be more powerful and troubled than he originally thought. With the power of the Phantom Hourglass and the Phantom Sword Link stop the curse of the ghost ship.

Vol. 10: Phantom Hourglass. 2010. 200pp. 978-1-4215-3724-5.
Legendary Edition, Vol. 4: The Minish Cap/Phantom Hourglass. 2017. 374pp. 978-1-4215-8962-6.

Twilight Princess

The series continues with the adaptation of the popular 2006 video game by the same name. Link must prevent Hyrule from being engulfed by a corrupted parallel dimension known as the Twilight Realm. To save Hyrule Link must take on the form of a wolf as well, and is assisted by a mysterious creature named Midna.

Vol. 11: The Twilight Princess, Vol. 1. 2017. 192pp. 978-1-4215-9347-0.
Vol. 12: The Twilight Princess, Vol. 2. 2017. 192pp. 978-1-4215-9656-3.

The Legend of Zelda: A Link to the Past. Written and Illustrated by **Shotaro Ishinomori**. VIZ Media, 2015. 196pp. 978-1-4215-7541-4. A. Japanese manga.

Originally serialized in the pages of *Nintendo Power* magazine in 1992 and collected for the first time! Meet Link, a lowly boy who is awakened in his sleep by Princess Zelda to rescue her from the vile clutches of the evil Agahnim who had her locked away in Hyrule Castle. When the Princess is recaptured by Agahnim, Link must search for a weapon powerful enough to defeat the evil wizard and bring peace to Hyrule. The manga is based on the original video game of the same name for the Super Nintendo video game console.

Princess Ugg. Written and Illustrated by **Ted Naifeh**. Oni Press, 2014. 120pp. 978-1-62010-178-0. T 🌲

© 2016 Ted Naifeh.

Princess Ülga isn't your standard princess—she's tough and fierce and ready for battle. At her mother's request she goes to the city-state of Atraesca to attend the prestigious Princess Academy where she must try and learn the other side of being a princess. The book was recognized by YALSA as a Great Graphic Novel for Teens in 2016.

Red Sonja

Dynamite Entertainment, 2014– . T

© 2016 Dynamite Entertainment.

Loosely based on the original creation by *Conan the Barbarian* creator Robert E. Howard, the famed "She-Devil with a Sword" is a warrior woman from the lands of Hyrkania. When she was 17, her parents were murdered after her father refused to join the army and Sonja was raped by the leader of the soldiers. Crying for revenge, Sonja prayed to the goddess Scathach and she was blessed with superior skill of all weapons in which she could exact her revenge on mankind. Included below are the current Dynamite Entertainment ongoing series, the reprinted omnibus editions of older Dynamite Entertainment series, and a crossover with Dark Horse Comics with Conan the Barbarian. Previous collections can be found at Dynamite Entertainment's web site.

Red Sonja (current series). Written by **Gail Simone**. Illustrated by **Walter Geovanni** and **Jenny Frison**. Dynamite Entertainment, 2014– .

> *Vol. 1: Queen of the Plagues.* 2014. 160pp. 978-1-60690-481-7.
> *Vol. 2: The Art of Blood and Fire.* 2015. 152pp. 978-1-60690-529-6.
> *Vol. 3: The Forgiving of Monsters.* 2015. 160pp. 978-1-60690-601-9.
> *Conan/Red Sonja.* Written by **Gail Simone** and **Jim Zub**. Illustrated by **Randy Green**. 2015. 96pp. 978-1-61655-651-8, hardcover.

Red Sonja: The Falcon Throne. Written by **Marguerite Bennett**. Illustrated by **Marguerite Sauvage** and **Aneke**, 2016. 978-1-5241-0115-2.

Red Sonja Omnibus. Written by **Mike Carey**, **Michael Avon Oeming**, **Brian Reed**, and various. Illustrated by **John Cassaday**, **Michael Turner**, **Stephen Sadowski**, **Pablo Marcos**, **Joyce Chin**, and various.

> *Vol. 1.* 2010. 300pp. 978-1-60690-101-4.
> *Vol. 2.* 2011. 400pp. 978-1-60690-231-8.
> *Vol. 3.* 2012. 432pp. 978-1-60690-344-5.

Vol. 4. 2013. 408pp. 978-1-60690-425-1.
Vol. 5. 2014. 328pp. 978-1-60690-488-6.

Legends of Red Sonja. Written by **Gail Simone, Nancy Collins, Devin Grayson, Meljean Brook, Tamora Pierce, Leah Moore, Nicola Scott, Rhianna Pratchett, Mercedes Lackey, Marjorie Liu, Blair Butler, Kelly Sue DeConnick**, and **Valentine De Landro**. Illustrated by **Jack Jadson, Jim Calafiore, Phil Noto, Nei Ruffino, Naniiebim, Douglas Holgate, Tula Lotay, Cassandra James, Mel Rubi, Carla Speed McNeil**, and **Noah Salonga**.

> A unique collaboration by all female writers whom all contribute short stories featuring the She-Devil with a Sword. The collection of female writers was organized by Gail Simone, and she writes the wraparound tale.

Redhand: Twilight of the Gods. Written by **Kurt Busiek** and **Sam Timel**. Illustrated by **Mario Alberti** and **Bazal**. Humanoids Publishing, 2015. 148pp. 978-1-59465-134-2. O

> A perfect warrior with no memory of his past finds himself in a barbarian landscape plagued by magic, religious corruption, and violence. Immune to the magic of the land he is in, the warrior may be the one prophesied to cleanse the land of the old gods and bring peace and order to the land.

Fairy Tales and Folklore

For generations, fairy tales have been a traditional source of fantasy for children. Presented here are adaptations, reinterpretations, and brand new fairy tales. In addition, some stories take the traditional fairy tales and expand on them to show what happened after "happily ever after" or create variations and reinterpretations of tales for a new generation. Note that other titles that play on the familiar characters and settings of fairy tales and folklore can also be found in the humor and crime and mysteries chapters.

Baba Yaga's Assistant. Written by **Marika McCoola**. Illustrated by **Emily Carroll**. Candlewick Press, 2015. T ◎

Most children are afraid of Baba Yaga—the witch from Russian folklore whose house is on giant chicken legs and enjoys eating children—but not Masha. The old witch Baba Yaga needs an assistant and Masha thinks she's learned enough from her late beloved grandmother of the importance of magic and patience to win the coveted position. All Masha has to do is pass the tricky tasks that Baba Yaga has set for her. Will Masha be up for the task? A modern twist on an old Russian fable.

Beautiful Darkness. Written by **Fabien Vehlmann**. Illustrated by **Kerascoët**. Drawn + Quarterly, 2014. 96pp. 978-1-77046-129-1, hardcover. O.

A twisted anti-fairy tale; after a young girl dies, her body lies motionless. From her mind various tiny fairy tale characters emerge, including Princess Aurora and her many friends, but they are as tiny as the small insects and field mice. As time passes and the body of the girl continues to decay in the elements, the tiny inhabitants find themselves trapped in a bleak existence in the wild that soon gives way to pettiness, jealousy, and the rise of evil.

© 2016 Fabien Vehlmann and Kerascoët.

Beauty. Written by **Hubert**. Illustrated by **Kerascoët**. NBM Publishing, 2014. 144pp. 978-1-56163-894-9, hardcover. M

Coddie is a simple and repulsive girl who lives in her village. She smells of fish and no man would have her. When she inadvertently saves a fairy, she's granted a wish to be beautiful, but the wish soon becomes a curse. Now radiantly beautiful in the eyes of all who see her, it's useless in the village where she's from. She's adored by a young lord, but even that is fleeting and Coddie is destined for something even greater. A fable for adults only, but a unique look at the nature of beauty.

Calamity Jack. Written by **Shannon Hale** and **Dean Hale**. Illustrated by **Nathan Hale**. Bloomsbury, 2010. 144pp. 978-1-59990-373-6. A. 🎖 ◎

The sequel to *Rapunzel's Revenge*, Jack and Rapunzel try to right the wrongs from Jack's past as a thief, con artist, swindler, and more. When the giant named Blunderboar controls the city of Shyport, Jack's home city, Jack and Rapunzel team up with a pixie named Pru and Freddie Sparksmith, a young journalist, to set things right. The book was recognized by the Great Graphic Novels for Teens selection list in 2011.

© 2016 Shannon Hale, Dean Hale, and Nathan Hale.

Castle Waiting. Written and Illustrated by **Linda Medley**. Fantagraphics, 2006–2013. T 🎖 ◎

The tales of what happened after everyone lived happily ever after. A pregnant princess leaves her abusive prince to be with her true lover—an ogre. Fantagraphics collected the entire series of the ongoing series including previously uncollected storylines and sets the stage for future tales from Linda Medley. Currently the series is indefinite hiatus. The series has won many awards including Eisner Awards for Best New Series (1998), and Linda Medley received an Eisner for Talent Deserving of Wider Recognition (1998). The collection *The Lucky Road* received recognition by YALSA's Popular Paperbacks for Young Adults committee in 2002 on the *Graphic Novels: Superheroes and Beyond* list.

Vol. 1. 2006. 450pp. 978-1-56097-747-6, hardcover.
Vol. 2. 2013. 456pp. 978-1-60699-633-1, hardcover.

The Courageous Princess. Written and Illustrated by **Rod Espinosa**. Dark Horse Comics, 2015. A Neo-Manga.

© 2016 Rod Espinosa.

The adventures of the spunky, smart, and self-reliant young Princess Mabelrose. The daughter of the king and queen from the small, fairy tale kingdom of New Tinsley, she's beloved by the people. Though she's a little clumsy and not the fairest of the land, she's not one to accept things the way they are. When a dragon captures the princess, she doesn't wait for a dashing knight to rescue her—she does it herself! Having escaped from the dragon and a long way from home, Princess Mabelrose and her friend Spikey, a talking porcupine, find themselves in even more adventures.

Vol. 1: Beyond the Hundred Kingdoms. 2015. 248pp. 978-1-61655-722-5, hardcover.
Vol. 2: The Unremembered Lands. 2015. 240pp. 978-1-61655-723-2, hardcover.
Vol. 3: The Dragon Queen. 2015. 192pp. 978-1-61655-724-9, hardcover.

The Encyclopedia of Early Earth. Written and Illustrated by **Isabel Greenberg**. Little Brown and Company, 2013. 176pp. 978-0-316-22581-6, hardcover. O

Two young lovers from polar opposites of the world fall in love, but the laws of physics indicate that they can attract each other but cannot touch. Cursed to be forever in love but never touch or know intimacy, they tell each other stories from far and wide from lands far away about kings, kingdoms, gods, and myths.

Fables. Written by **Bill Willingham**. Illustrated by various. Vertigo/DC Comics, 2002–2016. M 🎖 ◎

The characters from our fairy tales are alive and well and living in New York City in Fabletown. After being thrown out of their world by an enemy called the Adversary, the fairy tales characters are doing what they can to survive. When Rose Red is killed, only the Big Bad Wolf can find her killer, and all of the former residents of Fabletown are suspects. The series features a large cast of fairy tale characters including Snow White, Prince Charming, the Big Bad Wolf, Boy Blue, Bluebeard, Pinocchio, and many more in genre-defying series which features story arcs featuring murder, suspense, and more featuring classic fairy tale characters in more realistic and adult situations since their time away from Fabletown. The series has won many awards including Eisner Awards for Best Serialized Story (2003, 2005, 2006) and Best New Series (2003). The collections *Legends in Exile* and *Animal*

© 2016 DC Comics.

Farm received recognition by YALSA's Quick Picks for Reluctant Readers committee in 2004 as well as the Popular Paperbacks for Young Adults committees' 2005 *Gateway to Faerie* list for *Legends in Exile*. Beginning in 2009, DC Comics has begun reprinting the earlier volumes in hardcover Deluxe Edition formats, which include sequential paperback volumes in one edition with accompanying bonus material. The deluxe series should be completed in 2017. A prequel series—<u>Fables: The Wolf Among Us</u> which was based on a video game by Telltale Games— was published 2015–2016 and was written by Matthew Sturges.

Vol. 1: Legends in Exile (2nd printing). 2012. 144pp. 978-1-4012-3755-4.

Vol. 2: Animal Farm. 2003. 128pp. 978-1-4012-0077-0.

Vol. 3: Storybook Love. 2004. 192pp. 978-1-4012-0256-9.

Vol. 4: March of the Wooden Soldiers. 2004. 192pp. 978-1-4012-0222-4.

Vol. 5: The Mean Seasons. 2005. 168pp. 978-1-4012-0486-0.

Vol. 6: Homelands. 2006. 192pp. 978-1-4012-0500-3.

Vol. 7: Arabian Nights (and Days). 2006. 144pp. 978-1-4012-1000-7.

Vol. 8: Wolves. 2006. 160pp. 978-1-4012-1001-4.

1001 Nights of Snowfall. 2006. 144pp. 978-1-4012-0367-2.

Vol. 9: Sons of Empire. 2007. 192pp. 978-1-4012-1316-9.

Vol. 10: The Good Prince. 2008. 240pp. 978-1-4012-1686-3.

Vol. 11: War and Pieces. 2008. 192pp. 978-1-4012-1913-0.

Vol. 12: The Dark Ages. 2009. 192pp. 978-1-4012-2316-8.

Vol. 13: The Great Fables Crossover. 2010. 304pp. 978-1-4012-2572-8.

Vol. 14: Witches. 2010. 192pp. 978-1-4012-2880-4.

Vol. 15: Rose Red. 2011. 256pp. 978-1-4012-3000-5.

Vol. 16: Super Team. 2011. 144pp. 978-1-4012-3306-8.

Vol. 17: Inherit the Wind. 2012. 144pp. 978-1-4012-3516-1.

Werewolves of the Heartland. 2012. 152pp. 978-1401224790, hardcover.

Vol. 18: Cubs in Toyland. 2013. 192pp. 978-1-4012-3769-1.

Vol. 19: Snow White. 2013. 168pp. 978-1-40124-248-0.

Vol. 20: Camelot. 2014. 256pp. 978-1-4012-4516-0.

Vol. 21: Happily Ever After. 2015. 200pp. 978-1-4012-5132-1.

Vol. 22: Farewell. 2015. 160pp. 978-1-4012-5233-5.

Deluxe Edition, Vol. 1. 2009. 264pp. 978-1-4012-2427-1, hardcover.

Deluxe Edition, Vol. 2. 2010. 264pp. 978-1-4012-2879-8, hardcover.

Deluxe Edition, Vol. 3. 2011. 232pp. 978-1-4012-3097-5, hardcover.

Deluxe Edition, Vol. 4. 2012. 296pp. 978-1-4012-3390-7, hardcover.

Deluxe Edition, Vol. 5. 2012. 304pp. 978-1-4012-3496-6, hardcover.

Deluxe Edition, Vol. 6. 2013. 224pp. 978-1-4012-3724-0, hardcover.

Deluxe Edition, Vol. 7. 2013. 240pp. 978-1-4012-4040-0, hardcover.

Deluxe Edition, Vol. 8. 2014. 232pp. 978-1-4012-4279-4, hardcover.

Deluxe Edition, Vol. 9. 2014. 368pp. 978-1-4012-5004-1, hardcover.

Deluxe Edition, Vol. 10. 2015. 368pp. 978-1-4012-5521-3, hardcover.

Deluxe Edition, Vol. 11. 2015. 456pp. 978-1-4012-5826-9, hardcover.

Deluxe Edition, Vol. 12. 2016. 320pp. 978-1-4012-6138-2, hardcover.
Deluxe Edition, Vol. 13. 2016. 300pp. 978-1-4012-6449-9, hardcover.
Deluxe Edition, Vol. 14. 2017. 264pp. 978-1-4012-6856-5.
Fables: The Wolf among Us. 2015–2016.

> *Vol. 1.* 2015. 256pp. 978-1-4012-5684-5.
> *Vol. 2.* 2016. 288pp. 978-1-4012-6137-5.

Fable Comics. Written and Illustrated by various. First Second Books, 2015. 128pp. 978-1-62672-107-4, hardcover. A ◉

A collection of 28 classic and obscure fables by a wonderful variety of comic book creators that retell classics like the "The Tortoise and the Hare" and "The Grasshopper and the Ant." Contributors include Graham Annable, Greg Benton, R.O. Blechman, Vera Brosgol, Graham Chaffee, Eleanor Davis, Tom Gauld, Sophie Goldstein, Charise Harper, Jaime Hernandez, John Kerschbaum, James Kochalka, Simone Lia, Liniers, Jennifer Meyer, Corinne Mucha, Mark Newgarden, George O'Connor, Shelli Paroline and Braden Lamb, Israel Sanchez, Robert Sikoryak, Maris Wicks, and Keny Widjaja.

Fairest. Written by **Bill Willingham**, **Lauren Beukes**, **Sean E. Williams**, **Marc Andreyko**, and **Mark Buckingham**. Illustrated by **Inaki Miranda**, **Stephen Sadowski**, **Phil Jimenez**, **Russ Braun**, and **Shawn McManus**. Vertigo/DC Comics, 2012–2015. M

Spun off from the main Fables series (see above) comes a variety of short story collections featuring the women from Fabletown. The series focuses on Cinderella, Rose Red, Snow White, and more. Cinderella has also been featured in two collected limited series Cinderella: From Fabletown with Love (2010) and Cinderella: Fables Are Forever (2012).

Vol. 1: Wide Awake. 2012. 160pp. 978-1-4012-3550-5.
Vol. 2: Hidden Kingdom. 2013. 160pp. 978-1-4012-4021-9.
Vol. 3: The Return of the Maharaja. 2014. 144pp. 978-1-4012-4593-1.
Vol. 4: Cinderella: Of Mice and Men. 2014. 144pp. 978-1-4012-5005-8.
Vol. 5: The Clamour for Glamour. 2015. 160pp. 978-1-4012-5426-1.
Fairest in All the Land. 2013. 160pp. 978-1-4012-3900-8, hardcover.

Fairy Tale Comics: Classic Tales Told by Extraordinary Cartoonists. Written and Illustrated by various. First Second Books, 2013. 128pp. 978-1-59643-823-1, hardcover. A ◉

A collection of 17 fairy tales by a wonderful variety of comic book creators that take "Once Upon a Time" to new heights of creativity. Works include stories by Raina Telgemeier, David Mazzucchelli, Joseph Lambert, Emily Carroll, and many more.

Fairy Tales of Oscar Wilde. Adapted by **P. Craig Russell** from the works of Oscar Wilde. NBM Publishing, 2004– . A 🏵 ◎

Adaptations of the classic fairy tales by Oscar Wilde. Each volume includes two fairy tales adapted by P. Craig Russell for children. The series has won several Eisner Awards, including Best Artist/Penciller/Inker for P. Craig Russell's body of work in 1993, as well in 1995 for the category of Best Graphic Album: New for Volume 2. The series was also awarded a Harvey Award in 1993 for Best Graphic Album of Original Work for Volume 1.

Vol. 1: The Selfish Giant and the Star Child. 1992. 32pp. 978-1-56163-056-1, hardcover.
Vol. 2: The Young King and the Remarkable Rocket. 1994. 32pp. 978-1-56163-085-1, hardcover.
Vol. 3: The Birthday of the Infanta. 1998. 32pp. 978-1-56163-213-8, hardcover.
Vol. 4: The Devoted Friend, The Nightingale, and the Rose. 2004. 32pp. 978-1-56163-391-3, hardcover.
Vol. 5: The Happy Prince. 2012. 32pp. 978-1-56163-626-6, hardcover.

A Flight of Angels. Written by **Holly Black**, **Louise Hawes**, **Bill Willingham**, **Alisa Kwitney**, and **Todd Mitchell**. Illustrated by **Rebecca Guay**. Vertigo/DC Comics, 2012. 128pp. 978-1-4012-2147-8. O

An angel has fallen into the forgotten woods of the fairy and other Fair Folk. The inhabitants are drawn to look at the unconscious heavenly being. Some of them want to help it, but others want to kill it. Since these creatures are creatures of habit and tradition, each creature gets to tell a story about angels to try to persuade the others. After all is said and done, will the fairies nurse the angel back to life or will they extinguish the heavenly creature? The story was conceived and illustrated by Rebecca Guay, with each different story about an angel written by a different author. This book works very much like a quilt, the different pieces come together to form a greater whole.

Jack of Fables. Written by **Bill Willingham** and **Matthew Sturges**. Illustrated by **Tony Akins**. Vertigo/DC Comics, 2007–2011. M

Spun off from the pages of Bill Willingham's <u>Fables</u> series from DC Comics are the adventures of Jack—the most famous Fable of all as he wanders around the heartland of America and gets into one wrong adventure after the next.

Vol. 1: The (Nearly) Great Escape. 2007. 128pp. 978-1-4012-1222-3.
Vol. 2: Jack of Hearts. 2007. 144pp. 978-1-4012-1455-5.
Vol. 3: The Bad Prince. 2008. 128pp. 978-1-4012-1854-6.
Vol. 4: Americana. 2008. 128pp. 978-1-4012-1979-6.
Vol. 5: Turning Pages. 2009. 144pp. 978-1-4012-2138-6.
Vol. 6: The Big Book of War. 2009. 128pp. 978-1-4012-2500-1.
Vol. 7: The New Adventures of Jack and Jack. 2010. 128pp. 978-1-4012-2712-8.
Vol. 8: The Fulminate Blade. 2011. 128pp. 978-1-4012-2982-5.
Vol. 9: The End. 2011. 144pp. 978-1-4012-3155-2.
Deluxe Edition, Vol. 1. 2016. 400pp. 978-1-4012-6463-5.

Jim Henson's The Storyteller. Written and Illustrated by various. Archaia Entertainment/ BOOM! Studios. 2011–2013. 120pp. 978-1-936393-24-4, hardcover; 2013. 120pp. 978-1-936393-98-5. A 🖵 ◎

Great talent like Paul Tobin, Roger Langridge, Katie Cook, and Chris Eliopoulos contribute their talents in retelling classic folktales. To an old man and his dog most everyday occurrences remind them of fairy tales and other stories that they tell each other. In this collection they recount stories from across the globe. Some of these stories tell how a peddler tricked the devil, how a frog saved his country, and why a cat turned into a human.

© 2016 Archaia/BOOM! Studios.

Jim Henson's The Storyteller: Dragons. Written and Illustrated by various. Archaia Entertainment/BOOM! Studios, 2016. 144pp. 978-1-60886-874-2, hardcover. A 🖵 ◎

Based off the classic Jim Henson show, see four tales involving dragons and the brave men and woman willing to confront them. Contributors to the stories include Daniel Bayliss, Nathan Pride, Hannah Christenson, and Jorge Corona.

© 2016 Archaia/BOOM! Studios.

Jim Henson's The Storyteller: Giants. Written and Illustrated by **Brandon Dayton**, **Conor Nolan**, and various. Archaia Entertainment/BOOM! Studios, 2017. 128pp. 978-1-68415-001-4, hardcover. A 🖵 ◎

Four tales of the mythical giants that roamed the Earth, inspired by the folk tales of them from around the world.

Jim Henson's The Storyteller: Witches. Written and Illustrated by various. Archaia Entertainment/BOOM! Studios, 2015. 112pp. 978-1-60886-747-9, hardcover. A 🖵 ◎

A collection of four tales involving witches and witchcraft from all over the world. Some are brand new, while one is based off of a never completed screenplay for the Storyteller show. Contributors to the collection include Kyla Vanderklugt, S.M. Vidaurri, Matthew Dow Smith, and Jeff Stokely.

© 2016 Archaia/BOOM! Studios.

Marvel Fairy Tales. Written by **C.B. Cebulski**. Illustrated by **Kyle Baker** and various. Marvel Comics, 2010. 144pp. 978-0-7851-4316-1. T

In this collection many classic Marvel characters are put into the roles of many classic fairy tales and myths. The cast of The Avengers are the lost boys from Peter Pan, while characters from Spider-Man retell the story of Little Red Riding Hood. Other tales include X-Men, Alice in Wonderland, and Pinocchio.

Mighty Jack. Written and Illustrated by **Ben Hatke**. First Second Books, 2016–2017. A 🏅 ◎

© 2016 Ben Hatke.

Jack is a normal boy who dreads summer time. While other kids may like it, for Jack it means he has to babysit for his younger sister who is autistic and never says a word. When Jack's sister one day while at a flea market miraculously tells Jack to sell the family car for a few magic beans, Jack does just that! Though the beans started out as a small garden soon becomes much more with onion babies, biting pink pumpkins, and then it gets really surreal when on a moonlit night a dragon arrives. A retelling of the classic Jack and the Beanstalk fairy tale. In 2017 the first volume was recognized by YALSA's Great Graphic Novels for Teens Top Ten selection list.

Vol. 1. 2016. 208pp. 978-1-62672-265-1, hardcover; 978-1-62672-264-4.
Vol. 2: Mighty Jack and the Goblin King. 2017. 208pp. 978-1-62672-267-5, hardcover; 978-1-62672-266-8.

Nursery Rhyme Comics: 50 Timeless Rhymes from 50 Celebrated Cartoonists. Written and Illustrated by various. First Second Books, 2011. 128pp. 978-1-59643-600-8, hardcover. ◎

© 2016 First Second.

A collection of 50 of some of your nursery rhymes and some perhaps not so familiar to you by some of the best creators of comic books today! Contributors include Nick Abadzis, Kate Beaton, Vera Brosgol, Jules Feiffer, Ben Hatke; Gilbert Hernandez, Jaime Hernandez, Mike Mignola, Tony Millionaire, Tao Nyeu, George O'Connor, Mo Oh, Eric Orchard, Laura Park, Cyril Pedrosa, Lark Pien, Aaron Renier, Dave Roman, Stan Sakai, Mark Siegel, Raina Telgemeier, Craig Thompson, Sara Varon, Jen Wang, and Gene Luen Yang!

Pinocchio. Written and Illustrated by **Winshluss**. Last Gasp, 2011. 192pp. 978-0-86719-751-8. M

Geppetto has constructed a robotic boy with deadly powers with the intent on selling him to the army. While he is away a depressed cockroach nests into the automaton's head triggering a kind of self-awareness. Pinocchio, the robotic war boy, wanders off on a dangerous journey. Along the way other stories of perversion, murder, betrayal, and depression intertwine with Pinocchio's march forward.

Pinocchio, Vampire Slayer Complete Edition. Written by **Van Jensen**. Illustrated by **Dusty Higgins**. Top Shelf/IDW Publishing, 2014. 528pp. 978-1-60309-347-7. T 🌶

Inspired more by the original Carlo Collodi novel than the Disney movie, these books feature the "little wooden boy" fighting the forces of the undead after Geppetto is murdered. With his allies including the Blue Fairy and a theater troupe of living puppets, Pinocchio stakes vampires, creating his own weapons by lying and then breaking off his extended nose. The story was originally published in four volumes by SLG between 2009 and 2012. The four SLG volumes were later collected in an omnibus by Top Shelf. The first part of the original collection was recognized by YALSA in 2010 as a Great Graphic Novel for Teens and was a top 10 title for the selection list.

© 2016 Van Jensen and Dusty Higgens.

Princeless. Written by **Jeremy Whitley**. Illustrated by **M. Goodwin** and **Emily Martin**. Action Lab Comics, 2012– . A ◉

Princeless plays with traditional fairy tale elements, including a dragon, a princess in a tower, and a dramatic rescue. In this case, however, the princess is the fighter who saves her brother. By playfully skewering the gender stereotypes embedded in fairy tales with incisive wit and plenty of action, *Princeless* is a delight for older kids through younger teens. Particularly lovely to see is that the entire main cast are people of color, a rarity in comics in general, and the full-color, vibrant art really brings the title to life. The series has also spun off into a miniseries featuring the heroine Raven as she sets out on a quest for revenge against her brothers. She leads an all-female crew of pirates on her journey.

© 2016 Jeremy Whitley.

Vol. 1: Save Yourself. 2014. 128pp. 978-1-939352-54-5, 2nd edition.
Vol. 2: Get Over Yourself. 2013. 128pp. 978-0-985965-24-2.
Vol. 3: The Pirate Princess. 2015. 128pp. 978-1-632291-02-8.
Vol. 4: Be Yourself. 2015. 128pp. 978-1-632291-16-5.
Vol. 5: Make Yourself, Part 1. 2016. 128pp. 978-1-632291-68-4.
Vol. 6: Make Yourself, Part 2. 2017. 128pp. 978-1-632291-38-7.
Princeless Short Stories, Vol. 1. 2014. 128pp. 978-1-939352-49-1.

Raven the Pirate Princess. 2016.

Book 1: Captain Raven and the All-Girl Pirate Crew. 2016. 128pp. 978-1-632291-19-6.
Book 2: Free Women. 2016. 128pp. 978-1-632291-29-5.
Bool 3: Two Boys, Five Girls, and Three Love Stories. 2017. 128pp. 978-1-632291-40-0.
Deluxe Edition, Vol. 1. 2015. 168pp. 978-1-632291-20-2, hardcover.

Princess Princess Ever After. Written and illustrated by **Katie O'Neill**. Oni Press, 2016. 56pp. 978-1-62010-340-1, hardcover. T 🌶

After the brave princess Amira rescues the kind-hearted princess Sadie from castle prison, the two of them must learn to work with their differences to defeat an evil sorceress out to destroy Sadie. The two princesses discover along the way that their friendship and own views of "happily ever after" can include the both of them together. The book was awarded by YALSA's Great Graphic Novels for Teens selection list in 2017.

Rapunzel's Revenge. Written by **Shannon Hale** and **Dean Hale**. Illustrated by **Nathan Hale**. Bloomsbury, 2008. 144pp. 978-1-59990-288-3. A 🏹 ◎

A retelling of the classic story of Rapunzel with a Wild West twist and lots of heart. Young Rapunzel lived in the greenest of green lands in a castle that was surrounded by a huge wall. Raised by Mother Gothel—whom she always assumed was her real mother—Rapunzel was always curious about what was beyond the walls and when her curiosity gets the best of her, she's banished in a tower far away from the palace where her red hair magically grows and grows. After years of solitude, Rapunzel discovers she has the talent to use her hair as a whip and even more. Soon after she escapes, she's joined by a con artist named Jack and the two of them will take on the entire kingdom righting wrongs and bringing joy to everyone who is against the evil rule of Mother Gothel. The book was awarded by YALSA's Great Graphic Novels for Teens selection list.

© 2016 Shannon Hale, Dean Hale, and Nathan Hale.

The Secret of the Stone Frog. Written and Illustrated by **David Nytra**. Toon Books, 2012. 80pp. 978-1-935179-18-4. Y

Leah and her younger brother Alan wake up in a different place than they went to bed. They are now in a magical dreamlike world. The only thing around their bed is a statue of a frog. The frog gives them only one instruction on how to get back to their room. They simply have to stay on the path till the end. The people and places Leah and Alan see are both fantastical and absurd.

© 2016 Toon Books.

Sharaz-De: Tales from the Arabian Nights. Written and Illustrated by **Sergio Toppi**. Boom! Studios, 2013. 224pp. 978-1-936393-48-0, hardcover. O

When a king grows mad with his adulterous wife he commands that she is to be beheaded. He also commands that each night he will sleep with a new lady and in the morning they will suffer the same fate as his late wife. This is how we find the storyteller Sharaz-De though she does not plan on being executed come the morning. With tales so fantastical and wild about faraway kingdoms, genies, other monsters, and unimaginable riches, does Sharaz-De buy life each night?

Snow White: A Graphic Novel. Written and Illustrated by **Matt Phelan**. Candlewick Press, 2016. 216pp. 978-0-7636-7233-1, hardcover. A 🌹 ◎

> Set in the heyday of the Roaring Twenties, against the backdrop of the stock market crash of 1929, a beautiful but wicked queen of the stage from the Ziegfeld Follies finds that her beauty and fame is under the threat of a new beauty—a young girl named Snow. When Snow's life is threatened, seven street urchins take her in and seek to take on the evil queen and save the beautiful young woman before it's too late. A new twist on the classic tale of Snow White. In 2017 the graphic novel was recognized by YALSA's Great Graphic Novels for Teens annual selection list.

Trickster: Native American Tales, a Graphic Collection. Edited by **Matt Dembicki**. Written and Illustrated by various. Fulcrum Publishing, 2010. 232pp. 978-1-55591-724-1. T 🌹

> The role of the trickster is a pivotal character throughout many mythologies and religions—and especially in Native American Indian myths. Collected are over 20 tales illustrated by a fantastic collection of creators highlighting tales of the cunning mischief makers of Native American myths. The collection was recognized by YALSA's Great Graphic Novels for Teens committee in 2011.

Walt Kelly's Fairy Tales. Written and Illustrated by **Walt Kelly**. IDW Publishing, 2015. 308pp. 978-1-63140-365-1, hardcover. A

> A collection of classic fairy tales adapted by Walt Kelly, a pioneering animator who worked on Walt Disney classic films *Dumbo*, *Fantasia*, *Snow White*, and *Pinocchio* and the creator of the extremely influential *Pogo* comic strip. Classic adaptation includes "The Emperor's New Clothes," "The Gingerbread Man," "The Wise Men of Gotham," "The Lost Prince," and "Cinderella."

© 2016 Walt Kelly Estate.

Mythological Fantasy

Fantasy tales that are highly influenced by the traditional world myths and legends are enjoyed by many graphic novel fans. Some tales include and feature the gods of old, while others are merely inspired by ancient myths. Tales feature prominent heroes, villains, gods, and goddesses from ancient and modern mythologies from all over the world.

The Dark Crystal: Creation Myths. Written by **Brian Holguin**. Illustrated by **Alex Sheikman** and **Lizzy John**. Archaia Entertainment/BOOM! Studios, 2011–2013. T 🎬

> Based off the fantastical 1982 movie by Jim Henson this graphic novel enriches the already-deep narrative and mythology of this world. What is Aughra and how did she come to get such mystical powers? The urSkeks are an interplanetary traveling race

of aliens that came to Thra for a purpose. The workings of the Crystal within the planet is central to all life and purpose within Thra. *Creation Myths* delves deeper into the mythology of the world of *The Dark Crystal*.

Vol. 1. 2011. 96pp. 978-1-936393-00-8, hardcover.
Vol. 2. 2013. 96pp. 978-1-936393-80-0, hardcover.
Vol. 3. 2015. 96pp. 978-1-60886-435-5, hardcover.

© 2016 BOOM! Studios.

God of War. Written by **Marv Wolfman**. Illustrated by **Andrea Sorrentino**. DC Comics, 2011. 144pp. 978-1-4012-2972-6. M 🎮

Long before Kratos became the new god of war and slayed Ares, he was once a Spartan soldier bound by the cruel code of Sparta. When his infant daughter was fated to die per the laws of Spartan society, Kratos sought out the Ambrosia of Asclepius to save her. Now years later Kratos must once again seek it out and may no man, beast, or god stand in his way. Based on the hit video game series by Sony Entertainment.

Gods of Asgard. Written and illustrated by **Erik A. Evensen**. Jetpack Press, 2012. 168pp. 978-0-9769025-2-2. T

Inspired by the original Norse myths, award-winning illustrator Erik Evensen gives us a glimpse into the legendary adventures of Thor, Odin, Loki, and the rest of the Norse gods with his graphic novel adaptation of the classic Norse myths.

Hammer of the Gods. Written by **Michael Avon Oeming** and **Mark Wheatley**. Illustrated by **Michael Avon Oeming**. Image Comics, 2005; IDW Publishing, 2010. T

Ever since he was born, Modi was blessed by the Norse Valkyries to be phenomenally strong after his parents made a deal with them. But every deal has a catch: if Modi should ever use a weapon, he would lose his soul. Modi sets sail for a life of adventure and excitement and to travel around the world to become a hero. After returning home to find his parents murdered by frost giants, he must confront the Norse gods of old to ask them why his parents were allowed to die at the hands of such vile beasts and why the gods of old seemingly abandoned him.

Vol. 1: Mortal Enemy. 2009. 184pp. 978-1-60010-631-6.
Vol. 2: Back from the Dead. 2005. 160pp. 978-1-58240-508-7.

TM Michael Avon Oeming and © Michael Avon Oeming & Mark Obie Wheatley.

The Hero. Written and Illustrated by **David Rubin**. Dark Horse Comics, 2015. M ◉

A modern retelling of the rise of Heracles, the strongest hero of all the Greek myths and the son of Zeus, ruler of the Greek gods. Born at the same time as Eurystheus, the eventual ruler of Tiryns, fate was decided that whoever was born first between the two would be a cruel tyrant king, while the other a great hero. The goddess Hera, betrayed by Zeus's philandering ways, ensures that Eurystheus was born first on condition that when he was made ruler, he would have Heracles eliminated. Now a cruel and petty boy king, Eurystheus is a vain tyrant, while Heracles is the darling of the media and beloved by all. Vowing to have the demigod son of Zeus killed in return for Hera's favor, King Eurystheus plots ways to defeat Heracles with 12 great labors—but each one seems to cause Heracles's fame to continue to soar. Now Heracles is the media darling with his face appearing in the media 24/7, while Hera and her pawn King Eurystheus plot to finally have their revenge. Updated to include modern sensibilities and technologies, we see Heracles's rise in fame since his youth to be the greatest hero known throughout all of history.

Book 1. 2015. 288pp. 978-1-61655-670-9, hardcover.
Book 2. 2015. 288pp. 9781-61655-791-1, hardcover.

Heroes of Olympus. Written by **Rick Riordan** and **Robert Venditti**. Illustrated by **Nate Powell**. Disney-Hyperion, 2014–2017. Y

The adaptation of the first book from Rick Riordan's popular Heroes of Olympus series. A boy named Jason wakes up on a school bus with no memory of himself or his friends. He's joined by a girl named Piper, who says she is his girlfriend, and Leo, a boy who has a way with tools. Soon they realize that they are the sons and daughters of Greek and Roman gods, and their group finds that a bigger destiny awaits them all! The second adaptation of the popular fantasy series, *The Son of Neptune* was released in 2017.

Book 1: The Lost Hero. 2014. 192pp. 978-1-4231-6279-7, hardcover; 978-1-4231-6325-1.
Book 2: The Son of Neptune. 2017. 192pp. 978-1-4847-1621-2, hardcover; 978-1-4847-2303-6.

Immortals: Gods and Heroes. Written by **Jim McCann** et al. Illustrated by **Dennis Calero** et al. Archaia Black Label, 2011. 112pp. 978-1-936393-32-9. M▰

Immortals: Gods and Heroes provides background to the movie *Immortals*. The book is separated into two sections, one for the gods and one for heroes. The gods have fought for their right to rule against the Titans. Zeus and his brothers have devised a way to imprison the Titans forever so that they may never torment mankind again. Aeons, later the gods of Olympus, have sworn not to interfere with the world of mankind. King Hyperion, a human tyrant, has been wreaking havoc across the known world in the absence of the gods. Zeus must break his own law to not interfere so that he may train Theseus, a champion, to defeat King Hyperion and thwart the Titan influences upon the world.

Loki: Agent of Asgard. Written by **Al Ewing**. Illustrated by **Lee Garbett**. Marvel Comics, 2014–2015. T

A spin-off from the Marvel Comics <u>Thor</u> series, Loki, the god of mischief and overall trickster, is featured in his own series. Sent on missions from the All-Mother, Loki is a one-god agent for Asgard as he lies, cheats, and steals his way to get out of any situation. The history of the character is explored with that as well as his half-brother Thor and features many references to Marvel Comics' continuity over the years.

Vol. 1: Trust Me. 2014. 120pp. 978-0-7851-8931-2.
Vol. 2: I Cannot Tell a Lie. 2015. 112pp. 978-0-7851-9331-9.
Vol. 3: Last Days. 2015. 136pp. 978-0-7851-9332-6.

© Marvel Comics.

Misfits of Avalon. Written and Illustrated by **Kel McDonald**. Dark Horse Comics, 2014–2016. T

When four modern teen girls from different walks of life are forced to work together by a magical fairy, Morgan, Elsie, Kimber, and Rae find themselves imbued with magical powers from the goddess Morrigan and sent on a quest to stop the rise of a returned King Arthur and save the realm of Avalon. Can they be up to the task when they can't even work together? And they may not realize it, but they may be the bad guys! The series mixes Irish mythology with the Arthurian Legend.

Vol. 1: The Queen of Air and Delinquency. 2014. 172pp. 978-1-61655-538-2.
Vol. 2: Ill-made Guardian. 2016. 172pp. 978-1-61655-748-5.
Vol. 3: Future in the Wind. 2017. 216pp. 978-1-61655-749-2.

Noragami: Stray God. Written and Illustrated by **Adachitoka**. Kodansha Comics, 2014– . T Japanese manga. あ

When Yato, a minor god of calamity, no longer has a shrine or any worshippers, what's a lonely god to do? He decides he's going to help those in need—for a small fee. Yato has a dream that if he makes enough money he can build a new temple for himself and then he'll be worshipped once again. To do this, he'll need a lot of money—so no feat is beneath him as he helps rescue kittens from trees, to protecting students from bullies in school to even taking out a few demons. With a teenage girl named Hiyori (who has a habit of falling asleep and having her soul enter the afterlife), the Yukine, his Regalia (a living embodiment of a weapon Yato wields), just maybe Yato will find a way to become a well-respected god once again. The series was originally published in Japan beginning in 2010 and is still being published in Japan. The series was also adapted into an anime series.

Vol. 1. 2014. 200pp. 978-1-61262-906-3.
Vol. 2. 2014. 200pp. 978-1-61262-907-0.
Vol. 3. 2015. 200pp. 978-1-61262-908-7.
Vol. 4. 2015. 200pp. 978-1-61262-994-0.
Vol. 5. 2015. 200pp. 978-1-61262-995-7.
Vol. 6. 2015. 200pp. 978-1-61262-996-4.
Vol. 7. 2015. 200pp. 978-1-63236-102-8.
Vol. 8. 2015. 200pp. 978-1-63236-103-5.

Vol. 9. 2015. 200pp. 978-1-63236-128-8.   *Vol. 15.* 2016. 200pp. 978-1-63236-256-8.
Vol. 10. 2016. 200pp. 978-1-63236-213-1.   *Vol. 16.* 2016. 200pp. 978-1-63236-257-5.
Vol. 11. 2016. 200pp. 978-1-63236-252-0.   *Vol. 17.* 2016. 200pp. 978-1-63236-301-5.
Vol. 12. 2016. 200pp. 978-1-63236-253-7.   *Vol. 18.* 2017. 200pp. 978-1-63236-345-9.
Vol. 13. 2016. 200pp. 978-1-63236-254-4.   *Vol. 19.* 2017. 200pp. 978-1-63236-439-5.
Vol. 14. 2016. 200pp. 978-1-63236-255-1.

The Odyssey. Written by **Homer**. Adapted and Illustrated by **Ben Caldwell**. All-Action Classics/Sterling Childrens Publishing, 2010. T

When Odysseus and his crew set sail for their home of Ithaca following the brutal battle of Troy, fate has a different trial for Odysseus and the crew become lost far away from home. Though shipwrecks, angry gods, magical lands, beautiful nymphs, and siren songs, Odysseus will stop at nothing to return home to his family and take back what is rightfully his.

The Odyssey. Written by **Homer**. Adapted and Illustrated by **Gareth Hinds**. Candlewick Press, 2010. 248pp. 978-0-7636-4266-2, hardcover; 978-0-7636-4268-6. T

An adaptation of the epic poem by Homer. When the mighty Odysseus and his crew head back to their home in Ithaca following the bloody battle of Troy, fate intervenes and keeps Odysseus from his loving wife and son for many years. After adventure and adventure, and thought for dead after years of being away, his wife has many suitors who want the kingdom of Ithaca, but the true leader is finally coming home.

© 2010 by Gareth Hinds. Reproduced by permission of the publisher, Candlewick Press, Somerville, MA.

The Olympians. Written and Illustrated by **George O'Connor**. First Second, 2010– . T ◎

O'Connor tells the stories of the Greek Gods and the classic myths in a vibrant and adventure-filled format. While each volume concentrates on one particular god, the stories also cover additional myths. For example, Hades discusses Persephone, Hera deals in part with her feud with her namesake Heracles, and Poseidon's book includes the story of Theseus and the Minotaur. The three remaining volumes will cover Demeter, Hephaestus, and Dionysus. Several of the series were recognized by YALSA's Great Graphic Novels for Teens.

Athena: Grey-Eyed Goddess. 2010. 80pp. 978-1-59643-649-7, hardcover; 978-1-59643-432-5.

*Zeus: King of the Gods. 2010. 80pp. 978-1-59643-625-1, hardcover; 978-1-59643-431-8.

© 2017 Geroge O'Connor and First Second Books.

*Hera: The Goddess and Her Glory. 2011. 80pp. 978-1-59643-724-1, hardcover; 978-1-59643-433-2.

Hades: Lord of the Dead. 2012. 80pp. 978-1-59643-761-6, hardcover; 978-1-59643-434-9.

Aphrodite: Goddess of Love. 2013. 80pp. 978-1-59643-947-4, hardcover; 978-1-59643-739-5.

Poseidon: Earth Shaker. 2013. 80pp. 978-1-59643-828-6, hardcover; 978-1-59643-738-8.

Ares: Bringer of War. 2015. 80pp. 978-1-62672-014-5, hardcover; 978-1-62672-013-8.

Apollo: The Brilliant One. 2016. 80pp. 978-1-62672-016-9, hardcover; 978-1-62672-015-2.

Artemis: Goddess of the Hunt. 2017. 80pp. 978-1-62672-521-8, hardcover; 978-1-62672-522-5.

Percy Jackson and the Olympians. Written by **Rick Riordan** and **Robert Venditti**. Illustrated by **Attila Futaki**, **Jose Villarrubia**, and **Tamas Gaspar**. Disney-Hyperion Books. 2010– . Y

This is the graphic novel adaptation of the popular <u>Percy Jackson and the Olympians</u> series. Percy Jackson is a troubled teen for unlikely reasons. He is the son of the Greek god Poseidon. It is up to Percy and his friends to stop the gods from starting a war that will affect the whole world. The series is still being adapted into graphic novels at this time.

The Lightning Thief. 2010. 128pp. 978-1-4231-1710-0.
The Sea of Monsters. 2013. 128pp. 978-1-4231-4550-9.
The Titan's Curse. 2013. 128pp. 978-1-4231-4551-6.

Ragnarok. Written and Illustrated by **Walter Simonson**. IDW Publishing, 2015–. T

Walt Simonson's spiritual successor to his classic Thor stories from Marvel Comics in the 1980s. When Ragnarok, the Twilight of the Norse gods, has run its course, 300 years later, Thor, the Norse thunder god, has returned from death and seeks to return to the tree of knowledge to return the spark of life back to an evil world filled with monsters and madness. Meanwhile, a dark elf is on her own personal mission to assassinate the dead god to ensure her bloodline has earned immortality.

Vol. 1: Last Man Standing. 2015. 148pp. 978-1-63140-068-1, hardcover.
Vol. 2: The Lord of the Dead. 2017. 160pp. 978-1-63140-883-0, hardcover.

Stickman Odyssey. Written and Illustrated by **Christopher Ford**. Philomel Books, 2011–2012. Y

Zozimos is set on a quest to retake the kingdom of Sticatha that was stolen from him when he was just a baby by his witch of a stepmother. Now that

Zozimos is of age, his wrath will be unleashed, just as soon as he can catch that butter-fly. Zozimos, on his voyages, meets many zany and crazy characters that balance out his bullheadedness. Slap stick humor, pun intended, is strong with this series.

An Epic Doodle. 2011. 208pp. 978-0-399-25426-0.
The Wrath of Zozimos. 2012. 224pp. 978-0-399-25427-7.

Thor. Created by **Stan Lee** and **Jack Kirby**. Marvel Comics, 2011– . T

The thunder god of Norse mythology and the son of Odin, the lord of Asgard, home of the Norse gods, giants, and dwarves. With his enchanted hammer Mjolnir, Thor is one of the strongest and most powerful warriors who has ever lived and a defender of both Midgard (Earth) and Asgard. For times, Thor has assumed a dual identity when on Earth including Dr. Donald Blake, EMS Technician Jake Olson, and construction worker Sigurd Jarlson, but the identities have been only temporary. The thunder god also is a founding and still active member of the super-hero team called The Aveng-ers and has defended both Asgard and Earth against threats including his half-brother Loki, the god of lies, the goddess Hel, the demon Surtur, the Enchantress, the Midgard Serpent, and human foes including the Absorbing Man. Joined alongside allies from Asgard including Thor's beloved Sif, the Warriors Three, Balder the Brave, and the alien Beta Ray Bill and his equally powerful hammer called Storm Breaker, he's ready to protect the realms from evil. Recently Thor has mysteriously become unworthy to carry the hammer Mjolnir and a new hero has risen up to wield the hammer. That person is none other than Jane Foster, a nurse and former love interest to Thor. How-ever, Jane carries a heavy burden since she is suffering from cancer, and when she transforms into Thor, it hastens the return of her cancer with a vengeance. She is also a member of the All-New Avengers squadron. The original Thor, since he is now unwor-thy, goes by the name of Odinson, and wields a powerful battle axe named Jarnbjor.

Thor by Walter Simonson. Written by **Walt Simonson**. Illustrated by **Walt Simonson** with **Sal Buscema**. 2013– . T ◎

A collection reprinting the classic stories from the 1980s of one of the most popular chapters in Thor's history. Written and illustrated by Walt Simonson. Many fans of the Marvel series consider Walt Simonson's tale of Thor to be the definitive take on the character, blending stories and characters from Norse myths and introducing the character of Beta Ray Bill. The god of thunder meets his match against a monstrous cybernetically enhanced horse-faced alien called Beta Ray Bill. After defeating Thor in battle, Beta Ray Bill claims Thor's hammer and Thor's power, to save his space-faring people from a demonic menace. There are very few who are pure in heart and mind who can lift the hammer of Thor, and in return Thor discovers a unique ally in the alien. Odin, proud of Beta Ray Bill and his honorable character, forges a new Uru hammer, Stormbreaker, for Bill, and together with Thor and the Lady Sif they set out to save Bill's alien race from a horde of demons. Other highlights from Walt Simonson's tales include the epic battle against Surtur the giant fire demon and his army, the coming of the dark elf Kurse, Thor's magical transformation into a frog, and the epic battle against the Midgard Ser-pent. At the time of printing Marvel Comics has yet to complete this highly regarded collection of tales by Walt Simonson.

Vol. 1. 2013. 232pp. 978-0-7851-8460-7.
Vol. 2. 2013. 240pp. 978-0-7851-8461-4.
Vol. 3. 2013. 264pp. 978-0-7851-8462-1.
Vol. 4. 2014. 240pp. 978-0-7851-8463-8.
Vol. 5. 2014. 248pp. 978-0-7851-8464-5.
Thor by Walter Simonson Omnibus. 2011. 1192pp. 978-0-7851-4633-9, hardcover.

Thor: God of Thunder. Written by **Jason Aaron**. Illustrated by **Esad Ribic**. Marvel Comics, 2014–2015. T

Set shortly before Thor Odinson lost his weapon Mjolnir, Thor must battle against a threat that has hunted gods across eons as he confronts Gorr, the God Butcher. Also, the dark elf Malekith has returned to threaten Earth. Meanwhile, in the far future, King Thor and his granddaughters battle to save Earth from the threat of Galactus. The series was reprinted in two large hardcover collections as well.

Vol. 1: The God Butcher. 2014. 136pp. 978-0-7851-6697-9.
Vol. 2: Godbomb. 2014. 136pp. 978-0-7851-6698-6.
Vol. 3: The Accursed. 2014. 160pp. 978-0-7851-8556-7.
Vol. 4: The Last Days of Midgard. 2015. 168pp. 978-0-7851-8991-6.
Deluxe Edition, Vol. 1. 2014. 272pp. 978-0-7851-9113-1, hardcover.
Deluxe Edition, Vol. 2. 2015. 320pp. 978-0-7851-9800-0, hardcover.

Thor (current series). Written by **Jason Aaron**. Illustrated by **Russell Dauterman** and **Jorge Molina**. Marvel Comics, 2015– . T 🔥

The new Thor isn't the original God of Thunder; instead, it's Jane Foster, a longtime love interest of Thor Odinson. Dying of cancer, she is miraculously able to wield Mjolnir and has become the new Thor, while Thor Odinson has temporarily become unworthy to hold the enchanted mallet. He now goes by the name Odinson and wields the battle axe Jarnbjorn. In 2016 the series was relaunched again as *The Mighty Thor*. In 2017 the volume *Thunder in Her Veins* was recognized by YALSA's Great Graphic Novels for Teens annual selection list.

© 2016 Marvel Comics.

Vol. 1: The Goddess of Thunder. 2015. 136pp. 978-0-7851-9238-1; 2016. 978-0-7851-9239-8.
Vol. 2: Who Holds the Hammer? 2015. 136pp. 978-07851-9784-3, hardcover; 2016. 978-0-7851-9785-0.
Vol. 1: Thunder in Her Veins. 2016. 136pp. 978-0-7851-9522-1, hardcover; 978-0-7851-9965-6.
Vol. 2: Lords of Migard. 2016. 160pp. 978-0-7851-9523-8, hardcover.
Vol. 3: The Asgard/Shi'ar War. 2017. 160pp. 978-1-3029-0308-4, hardcover.

Miscellaneous Thor Collections and Spin-Offs

Thor: Godstorm. Written by **Kurt Busiek**. Illustrated by **Steve Rude** and **Mike Royer**. Marvel Comics, 2011. 128pp. 978-0-7851-4976-7, hardcover. T

Told in the past and the present, an ancient sentient storm threatens the world thanks to the machinations of Loki, and only Thor can prevent it from unleashing its evil.

The Mighty Thor Omnibus. Written by **Stan Lee**. Illustrated by **Jack Kirby**. Marvel Comics, 2011–2013. A

An omnibus collection of the original stories featuring Thor from his first comic book appearances in Journey into Mystery #83 (1962) and a wide variety of appearances during the Silver Age of comics in chronological order.

Vol. 1. 2011. 768pp. 978-0-7851-4973-6, hardcover.
Vol. 2. 2013. 768pp. 978-0-7851-6783-9, hardcover.

Thor. Written by **J. Michael Straczynski**. Illustrated by **Marko Djurdjevic** and **Olivier Coipel**. Marvel Comics, 2008–2010. T

A collection of J. Michael Straczynski's Thor run originally published from 2007 to 2009 where Thor returns from a long absence. Straczynski brought back the persona of Donald Blake and reintroduces the pantheon of Asgardian gods who have been brought back following Ragnarok, the Twilight of the Gods.

Vol. 1. 2008. 160pp. 978-0-7851-1722-3.
Vol. 2. 2009. 200pp. 978-0-7851-1760-5.
Vol. 3. 2010. 112pp. 978-0-7851-2950-9.
Omnibus. 2010. 520pp. 978-0-7851-4029-0, hardcover.

The Mighty Thor. Written by **Matt Fraction**. Illustrated by **Pasqual Ferry**, **Olivier Coipel**, and **Barry Kitson**. Marvel Comics, 2011–2013. T

Continuing from J. Michael Straczynski's run, Thor battles against the Grey Gargoyle, the safety of Asgard is threatened by Galactus, and Donald Blake makes a deal with the Enchantress Amora, and Thor must battle against an ancient race of creatures that invades dreams.

The World Eaters. 2011. 216pp. 978-0-7851-4839-5.*Vol. 1*. 2012. 144pp. 978-0-7851-5624-6.
Vol. 2. 2012. 160pp. 978-0-7851-5625-3.
Vol. 3. 2013. 136pp. 978-0-7851-6167-7.

Thor: Ages of Thunder. Written by **Matt Fraction**. Illustrated by **Patrick Zircher**, **Clay Mann**, **Doug Braithwaite**, **Dan Brereton**, and **Marko Djurdjevic**. Marvel Comics, 2009. 160pp. 978-0-7851-3567-8, hardcover; 978-0-7851-3568-5. T

A look at the tragedies and triumphs in the long life of Thor, the God of Thunder. From vicious opponents on the battlefield to his own dealings with his father, Odin, the history of Thor's life is told by a variety of artists.

Thor: The Mighty Avenger. Written by **Roger Langridge**. Illustrated by **Chris Samnee**. Marvel Comics, 2010–2013. A ◎

Written by Roger Langridge and illustrated by Chris Samnee, the short-lived but highly praised series was a simple approach to Thor that all ages can enjoy. The series focuses on his relationship with Jane Foster, as well as short but accessible tales where Thor must fight Fing Fang Foom, robots, and his stepbrother Loki, and features appearances by Mr. Hyde, Giant-Man, the Warriors-Three, Captain Britain, Namor, Iron Man, and Captain America. The first volume was recognized by YALSA as a Great Graphic Novel for Teens.

Vol. 1. 2010. 128pp. 978-0-7851-4121-1.
Vol. 2. 2011. 128pp. 978-0-7851-4122-8.
The Complete Collection. 2013. 216pp. 978-0-7851-8381-5.

© 2016 Marvel Comics.

Beta Ray Bill. Created by Walter Simonson. Marvel Comics, 2005–2009. T

Beta Ray Bill is an honorable horse-faced Korbinite alien who was biologically altered to be a protector of his people and was worthy to carry the hammer of the thunder god Thor. In return for saving his son's life, the Norse god Odin bestowed upon Beta Ray Bill a mystical uru hammer called Stormbreaker to aid his people and protect the Earth in time of need. Now following the climactic events that devastated Asgard, he is the sole survivor of all that remains of Asgard. Beta Ray Bill heads off into space to help aid his Korbinite people. Included below are two collections featuring Beta Ray Bill, the cosmic hero who has earned the mantle of Thor. With his enchanted mallet called Stormbreaker, he is a noble and heroic alien who protects the Earth and beyond with his Asgardian-given strength and might.

Stormbreaker—The Saga of Beta Ray Bill. Written by **Michael Avon Oeming** and **Dan Berman**. Illustrated by **Andrea Di Vito**. Marvel Comics, 2005. 144pp. 978-0-7851-1720-9. T

In space he encounters Stardust, a powerful creature composed of vast cosmic power sent by his master to destroy Beta Ray Bill and his people. Will the wielder of the hammer of Stormbreaker and last remaining savior of Asgard fall before the cosmic might of Stardust?

Beta Ray Bill: Godhunter. Written by **Kieron Gillen**. Illustrated by **Kano** and **Dan Brereton**. Marvel Comics, 2009. 104pp. 978-0-7851-4232-4. T

Beta Ray Bill battles against the threat of Galactus, the planet-eater. When Beta Ray Bill's home planet of Korbinite was destroyed, Bill takes it upon himself to seek revenge against the entity that destroyed his home planet.

© 2016 Marvel Comics.

Magic Portal Fantasy/Parallel Worlds

Magic portal fantasy where the main protagonist is typically from our current world and is magically transported to the magic realm. The realm can be in the past or can be an alternate reality that coincides with our time line. The lead typically goes to the world in question, but on occasion, the fantasy world's elements interact with our world.

Amulet. Written and Illustrated by **Kazu Kibuishi**. Graphix/Scholastic Books. 2008– . A

Cover © Scholastic Inc.

A massive fantasy series by creator Kazu Kibuishi. Emily, her younger brother Navin, and their mother relocate to an old family estate after the death of her father. There Emily finds a mysterious amulet which was once owned by her great-grandfather Silas Charnon. The same night that she wears the amulet, Emily's mother is kidnapped by a spider-like monster and taken from our world to the fantasy realm known as Alledia. Emily and Navin follow the monster to the magical realm where they soon become entangled in a brewing war between the humans and elves of the world. While making new allies in the war against the Elf King, Emily also learns to use the power of the mystical amulet as she battles the forces of evil. The epic series is planned to be completed after nine volumes.

Vol. 1: The Stonekeeper. 2008. 192pp. 978-0-439-84680-6, hardcover; 978-0-439-84681-3.
Vol. 2: The Stonekeeper's Curse. 2009. 224pp. 978-0-439-84682-0, hardcover; 978-0-439-84683-7.
Vol. 3: The Cloud Searchers. 2010. 208pp. 978-0-545-20884-0, hardcover; 978-0-545-20885-7.
Vol. 4: The Last Council. 2011. 224pp. 978-0-545-20886-4, hardcover; 978-0-545-20887-1.
Vol. 5: Prince of the Elves. 2012. 208pp. 978-0-545-20889-5, hardcover; 978-0-545-20889-5.
Vol. 6: Escape from Lucien. 2014. 224pp. 978-0-545-84899-2, hardcover; 978-0-545-43315-0.
Vol. 7: Firelight. 2016. 208pp. 978-0-545-83966-2, hardcover; 978-0-545-43316-7.

Birthright. Written by **Joshua Williamson**. Illustrated by **Andrei Bressan** and **Adriano Lucas**. Image Comics, 2015– . O

The Rhodes family was devastated when they lost their son Mikey—but it's when he came back that things really changed. Mikey has come back—and he's now a grown man. He claims that he had adventures in a fantasy realm and was raised as a warrior. Mike is now been charged to return back to Earth and eliminate evil wizards that are in disguise. Should Aaron and Brennan, Mike's father and older brother, trust him and is this older man claiming to be Mike telling the truth?

Vol. 1: Homecoming. 2014. 128pp. 978-1-63215-231-2.
Vol. 2: Call to Adventure. 2015. 112pp. 978-1-63215-446-0.
Vol. 3: Allies and Enemies. 2016. 112pp. 978-1-63215-683-9.
Vol. 4: Family History. 2016. 112pp. 978-1-63215-871-0.
Vol. 5: Allies and Enemies. 2017. 112pp. 978-1-53430-218-1.

Copper. Written and Illustrated by **Kazu Kibuishi**. Graphix/Scholastic Books, 2010. 96pp. 978-0-545-09893-9. Y

Cover © Scholastic Inc.

A boy and his dog—but unlike anything you've ever seen! Copper is adventurous. Fred is cautious. But when the two of them are together, there's no adventure they can't have! Together both of them travel to new worlds, build new ways to travel, and visit places that no one has ever visited. The collection features several short stories in one fantastic edition.

Coraline. Written by **Neil Gaiman**. Adapted and Illustrated by **P. Craig Russell**. HarperCollins, 2008. 192pp. 978-0-06-082543-0, hardcover; 978-0-06-082545-4. Y 🎬 ◉

© 2016 P. Craig Russell and HarperCollins.

In Coraline, a girl moves into an old house where she discovers a passageway that leads her to a strange version of the house with twisted versions of its residents. Can she escape the clutches of the button-eyed "other mother"? The prose fiction novel was also adapted into an animated film by Laika Studios in 2009.

Dream Jumper. Written by **Greg Grunberg**. Illustrated by **Lucas Turnbloom**. Graphix/Scholastic Books, 2016. A

Cover © Scholastic Inc.

Young Billy has a problem: he has trouble dreaming at night since all of his dreams turn into nightmares! Billy has discovered though that he can enter the dreams of his friends at school and rescue them from an evil dream monster that is preventing them from waking up. But the monster is smart and knows the dream realm better than Billy does. Thankfully help comes to Billy in his dreams in the form of a talking rabbit companion who has a mysterious past. Can Billy find the strength within himself to defeat the dream monster and get a good night's rest once and for all? The book is the first book in a series.

The Dreamer. Written and Illustrated by **Lora Innes**. IDW Publishing, 2009–2011. T

Beatrice Whaley is like any other teenager, except she has two different lives. Bea lives like any modern-day teenage girl. She worries about homework

and boys when she is awake. When she falls asleep she has a whole different set of worries like living through the Revolutionary War and romance. To her both worlds are very real.

Vol. 1: The Consequences of Nathan Hale. 2009. 160pp. 978-1-60010-465-7.
Vol. 2: The Kipp's Bay Affair. 2011. 152pp. 978-1-61377-031-3.
Vol. 3: The Battle of Harlem Heights. 2014. 152pp. 978-1-61377-886-9.

Fushigi Yugi: The Mysterious Play. Written and Illustrated by **Yuu Watase**. VIZ Media, 2003–2010. T Japanese manga. あ

Schoolmates Miaka Yūki and Yui Hongo discover a magical Chinese book in the National Library that transports Miaka to the Universe of the Four Gods, a fictionalized version of ancient China. There they find that they can go back home only after Miaka, who has been declared the shrine maiden of Suzaku, fulfills a prophecy by finding and befriending seven celestial warriors and summoning the god Suzaku with a treasure called the Shentso-Pao. When Miaka meets Tamahome, a 17-year-old celestial warrior, and they fall in love, will she ever want to go back? The manga series is one of the most popular Shojo manga in all of Japan. An anime series based on the manga was originally released in Japan. The VIZ Big editions reprint all the original 18 volumes in six larger-sized collections.

Vol. 1. 2003. 200pp. 978-1-56931-957-4.
Vol. 2. 2003. 200pp. 978-1-56931-958-1.
Vol. 3. 2004. 200pp. 978-1-56931-992-5.
Vol. 4. 2004. 200pp. 978-1-56931-993-2.
Vol. 5. 2004. 200pp. 978-1-59116-097-7.
Vol. 6. 2005. 200pp. 978-1-59116-098-4.
Vol. 7. 2005. 200pp. 978-1-59116-139-4.
Vol. 8. 2005. 200pp. 978-1-59116-087-8.
Vol. 9. 2003. 200pp. 978-1-59116-096-0.

Vol. 10. 2004. 200pp. 978-1-59116-138-7.
Vol. 11. 2004. 200pp. 978-1-59116-107-3.
Vol. 12. 2004. 192pp. 978-1-59116-201-8.
Vol. 13. 2004. 200pp. 978-1-59116-086-1.
Vol. 14. 2005. 200pp. 978-1-59116-737-2.
Vol. 15. 2005. 200pp. 978-1-59116-843-0.
Vol. 16. 2005. 200pp. 978-1-4215-0023-2.
Vol. 17. 2006. 200pp. 978-1-4215-0180-2.
Vol. 18. 2006. 200pp. 978-1-4215-0393-6.

VIZ Big Edition, 2009–2010.

Vol. 1. 2009. 600pp. 978-1-4215-2290-6.
Vol. 2. 2009. 600pp. 978-1-4215-2300-2.
Vol. 3. 2009. 600pp. 978-1-4215-2301-9.
Vol. 4. 2009. 600pp. 978-1-4215-2302-6.
Vol. 5. 2010. 600pp. 978-1-4215-2303-3.
Vol. 6. 2010. 600pp. 978-1-4215-2304-0.

Fushigi Yugi: Genbu Kaiden. Written and Illustrated by **Yuu Watase**. VIZ Media, 2005–2014. T. Japanese manga.

Fushigi Yugi: Genbu Kaiden is a prequel to the original hit series and focuses on the origins of the Universe of the Four Gods book and the origins of the priestess of Genbu who was drawn into the book that was written by her father.

Vol. 1. 2005. 200pp. 978-1-59116-896-6.
Vol. 2. 2005. 200pp. 978-1-59116-911-6.
Vol. 3. 2006. 200pp. 978-1-4215-0288-5.
Vol. 4. 2006. 208pp. 978-1-4215-0579-4.
Vol. 5. 2006. 208pp. 978-1-4215-0580-0.
Vol. 6. 2008. 200pp. 978-1-4215-1926-5.

Vol. 7. 2008. 210pp. 978-1-4215-2256-2.
Vol. 8. 2009. 192pp. 978-1-4215-2595-2.
Vol. 9. 2009. 192pp. 978-1-4215-3035-2.
Vol. 10. 2012. 192pp. 978-1-4215-4259-1.
Vol. 11. 2013. 192pp. 978-1-4215-5244-6.
Vol. 12. 2014. 192pp. 978-1-4215-6434-0.

Ichiro. Written and Illustrated by **Ryan Inzana**. Houghton Mifflin Harcourt, 2012. 288pp. 978-0-547-25269-8, hardcover; 978-0-547-61789-3. T ◉ ❀

© Ryan Inzana 2012.

Ichiro is a boy who never knew his American father. His father died before he was born in a war and he never had a chance to know him. Lost and not quite sure where he fits in, he lives with his Japanese mother in New York City. Ichiro takes a trip to Japan to spend time with his Japanese grandfather, a stranger to him, in a country he doesn't know. One night while in Japan, he's dragged down a hole by a monster from Japanese mythology and Ichi finds himself now in the land of the Japanese gods. Can Ichi find his way in a strange new world and will it give him the peace and direction he sorely needs to find his way in life? The book was recognized by YALSA's Great Graphic Novels for Teens selection list in 2013.

InuYasha. Written and Illustrated by **Rumiko Takahashi**. VIZ Media, 2003–2011. O Japanese manga. あ

© 1997 Rumiko TAKAHASHI/Shogakukan, Inc.

Junior high schoolgirl Kagome Higurashi travels to the distant past through a well in her own backyard and ends up in a fictionalized Sengoku period in Japan where demons roam the Earth alongside men. Bound to a tree finds the strangest companion in InuYasha, a half-man/half-wolf demon whom she frees much to the chagrin of the local village. The village priestess by the name of Kaede is shocked that Kagome is the spitting image of her oldest sister Kikyo, who died protecting a mystical jewel called the Jewel of Four Souls. Kikyo also was the one who had bound InuYasha to the tree 50 years ago. Kagome, it is revealed, is the reincarnation of Kikyo and now she's given the task by Kaede to relocate the lost pieces of the Jewel of Four Souls after Kagome accidentally shatters it. Together Kagome and InuYasha set out on their quest to prevent the power of the jewel from falling into the hands of monsters and destroying feudal Japan. Along the way they are joined by an ever-expanding cast of fantastic characters including a talking flea named Myoga, Shippo the seven-year-old fox demon, and a Buddhist priest named Miroku. The series concluded with volume 56, and the series was reprinted in VIZ Media's VIZBIG Edition format, which reprints multiple volumes in one oversized collection. An anime series based on the manga was originally released in Japan and continues to be a big hit in North America as well.

Vol. 1. 2003. 178pp. 978-1-56931-947-5.
Vol. 2. 2003. 192pp. 978-1-56931-948-2.
Vol. 3. 2003. 192pp. 978-1-56931-960-4.
Vol. 4. 2003. 184pp. 978-1-56931-961-1.
Vol. 5. 2003. 192pp. 978-1-59116-052-6.
Vol. 6. 2003. 192pp. 978-1-59116-053-3.
Vol. 7. 2004. 192pp. 978-1-59116-114-1.
Vol. 8. 2004. 192pp. 978-1-59116-115-8.
Vol. 9. 2004. 192pp. 978-1-59116-236-0.
Vol. 10. 2004. 192pp. 978-1-59116-237-7.
Vol. 11. 2004. 192pp. 978-1-59116-332-9.
Vol. 12. 2004. 192pp. 978-1-59116-333-6.
Vol. 13. 2003. 192pp. 978-1-56931-808-9.
Vol. 14. 2003. 192pp. 978-1-56931-886-7.
Vol. 15. 2003. 192pp. 978-1-56931-999-4.
Vol. 16. 2004. 192pp. 978-1-59116-113-4.
Vol. 17. 2004. 192pp. 978-1-59116-238-4.
Vol. 18. 2004. 192pp. 978-1-59116-331-2.
Vol. 19. 2004. 200pp. 978-1-59116-678-8.
Vol. 20. 2004. 200pp. 978-1-59116-626-9.
Vol. 21. 2005. 200pp. 978-1-59116-740-2.
Vol. 22. 2005. 192pp. 978-1-59116-840-9.
Vol. 23. 2005. 192pp. 978-1-4215-0024-9.
Vol. 24. 2006. 192pp. 978-1-4215-0186-4.
Vol. 25. 2006. 208pp. 978-1-4215-0383-7.
Vol. 26. 2006. 208pp. 978-1-4215-0466-7.
Vol. 27. 2006. 208pp. 978-1-4215-0467-4.
Vol. 28. 2007. 208pp. 978-1-4215-0468-1.

Vol. 29. 2007. 192pp. 978-1-4215-0900-6.
Vol. 30. 2007. 192pp. 978-1-4215-0901-3.
Vol. 31. 2007. 192pp. 978-1-4215-0902-0.
Vol. 32. 2008. 192pp. 978-1-4215-1522-9.
Vol. 33. 2008. 192pp. 978-1-4215-1828-2.
Vol. 34. 2008. 192pp. 978-1-4215-1829-9.
Vol. 35. 2008. 210pp. 978-1-4215-1830-5.
Vol. 36. 2009. 210pp. 978-1-4215-2218-0.
Vol. 37. 2009. 192pp. 978-1-4215-2219-7.
Vol. 38. 2009. 192pp. 978-1-4215-2220-3.
Vol. 39. 2009. 192pp. 978-1-4215-2221-0.
Vol. 40. 2009. 192pp. 978-1-4215-2890-8.
Vol. 41. 2009. 192pp. 978-1-4215-2891-5.
Vol. 42. 2009. 192pp. 978-1-4215-2892-2.
Vol. 43. 2010. 208pp. 978-1-4215-2893-9.
Vol. 44. 2010. 208pp. 978-1-4215-2994-3.
Vol. 45. 2010. 192pp. 978-1-4215-2995-0.
Vol. 46. 2010. 192pp. 978-1-4215-2996-7.
Vol. 47. 2010. 192pp. 978-1-4215-2997-4.
Vol. 48. 2010. 192pp. 978-1-4215-2998-1.
Vol. 49. 2010. 192pp. 978-1-4215-2999-8.
Vol. 50. 2010. 192pp. 978-1-4215-3000-0.
Vol. 51. 2010. 192pp. 978-1-4215-3001-7.
Vol. 52. 2010. 192pp. 978-1-4215-3002-4.
Vol. 53. 2010. 192pp. 978-1-4215-3003-1.
Vol. 54. 2010. 192pp. 978-1-4215-3004-8.
Vol. 55. 2010. 192pp. 978-1-4215-3005-5.
Vol. 56. 2011. 216pp. 978-1-4215-3299-8.

VIZBIG Edition. 2009–2014.

Vol. 1. 2009. 576pp. 978-1-4215-3280-6.
Vol. 2. 2010. 568pp. 978-1-4215-3281-3.
Vol. 3. 2010. 566pp. 978-1-4215-3282-0.
Vol. 4. 2010. 568pp. 978-1-4215-3283-7.
Vol. 5. 2010. 568pp. 978-1-4215-3284-4.
Vol. 6. 2011. 560pp. 978-1-4215-3285-1.
Vol. 7. 2011. 560pp. 978-1-4215-3286-8.
Vol. 8. 2011. 568pp. 978-1-4215-3287-5.
Vol. 9. 2011. 576pp. 978-1-4215-3288-2.

Vol. 10. 2012. 568pp. 978-1-4215-3289-9.
Vol. 11. 2012. 568pp. 978-1-4215-3290-5.
Vol. 12. 2012. 568pp. 978-1-4215-3291-2.
Vol. 13. 2012. 568pp. 978-1-4215-3292-9.
Vol. 14. 2013. 576pp. 978-1-4215-3293-6.
Vol. 15. 2013. 576pp. 978-1-4215-3294-3.
Vol. 16. 2013. 568pp. 978-1-4215-3295-0.
Vol. 17. 2013. 758pp. 978-1-4215-3296-7.
Vol. 18. 2014. 776pp. 978-1-4215-3297-4.

Kingdom Hearts

Written and Illustrated by **Shiro Amano**. Yen Press, 2013–2015. Y 🐾 Japanese manga. Based on the popular video game series created by Square Enix. When King Mickey from the realm of Disney has gone missing, Donald Duck and Goofy set out to rescue him. Along the way they befriend 14-year-old Sora, who has left his peaceful island home in search of his two lost friends. As they travel from magical realm to realm (featuring some of Walt Disney's most beloved characters and settings from film and television), Sora discovers that the mystical artifact he is carrying, the Keyblade, may be the key to solving King Mickey and Sora's friends' disappearances

© 2016 Yen Press

and ending the reign of the wicked Maleficent and her vile minions called the Heartless. The series <u>Kingdom Hearts 358/2 Days</u> focuses the hero Roxas and his relationship with fellow Organization XIII members Axel and Xion and is a prequel to the <u>Kingdom Hearts II</u> series.

Kingdom Hearts: Final Mix. 2013.

Vol. 1. 2013. 272pp. 978-0-316-25420-5.
Vol. 2. 2013. 304pp. 978-0-316-25421-2.

Kingdom Hearts: Chain of Memories. 2013. 432pp. 978-0-316-25562-2.

Kingdom Hearts II. 2013–2014.

Vol. 1. 2013. 496pp. 978-0-316-40114-2.
Vol. 2. 2013. 480pp. 978-0-316-40115-9.
Vol. 3. 2014. 416pp. 978-0-316-28879-8.

Kingdom Hearts 358/2 Days. 2013–2015.

Vol. 1. 2013. 192pp. 978-0-316-40118-0.
Vol. 2. 2014. 208pp. 978-0-316-40119-7.
Vol. 3. 2014. 192pp. 978-0-316-40120-3.
Vol. 4. 2014. 208pp. 978-0-316-28676-3.
Vol. 5. 2015. 240pp. 978-0-316-33626-0.

Lions, Tigers, and Bears. Written by **Mike Bullock**. Illustrated by **Jack Lawrence**. Hermes Press, 2012. Y

Young Joey Price hated when his mother had to move away to take a job in a neighboring town. The move took him away from his best friends at school and most importantly far away from his loving grandmother. Before saying good-bye, his grandmother gives Joey four stuffed animals: a lion, two tigers, and a panther. Called the Night Pride, just as the stories she told, they would protect Joey with their magical powers should he ever need them. When his worst nightmares, the Beasties, come out of the closet at night, the Night Pride, now transformed into huge regal-looking beasts, are ready to protect Joey. After journeying to the Stuffed Animal Kingdom, Joey learns that the fate of all children hangs in the balance and he must find his own destiny with the help of the Night Pride.

Vol. 1. 2012. 128pp. 978-1-61345-001-7.
Vol. 2. 2012. 128pp. 978-1-61345-002-4.
Vol. 3. 2012. 128pp. 978-1-932563-78-8.

Little Nemo: Return to Slumberland. Written by **Eric Shanower**. Illustrated by **Gabriel Rodriguez**. IDW Publishing, 2015. 120pp. 978-1-63140-059-9, hardcover; 978-1-63140-322-4. A

A sequel to the beloved whimsical story by Windsor McKay. The daughter of King Morpheus is bored looking for a new playmate. She used to play with a boy named Nemo and finds a new playmate in a young boy with Nemo as his middle name. But Jimmy isn't quite the same as the original Nemo. He'd

rather roam around Slumberland and is constantly waking up. Will the princess get to have a play date with Jimmy and find new friends? The publication was recognized with an Eisner Award for Best Limited Series in 2015.

The Lost Boy. Written and Illustrated by **Greg Ruth**. Graphix/Scholastic Books, 2013. 978-0-439-82331-9, hardcover; 978-0-439-82332-6. T

Nate and his family move into a house where a boy named Walt mysteriously disappeared from over 40 years ago. Nate discovers a journal and some discarded audio cassettes from Walt as well and after reading them and listening, he better understands what happened to Walt. The story tells two stories—the events from over 40 years ago and the present as Nate puts the clues together to solve the mystery of Walt's disappearance. Little does Nate and his friend Tabitha realize that the answer lies in a magical land hidden through woods near Nate's house called The Kingdom that is the key to Walt's disappearance.

Mangaman. Written by **Barry Lyga**. Illustrated by **Colleen Doran**. Houghton Mifflin, 2011. 144pp. 978-0-547-42315-9, hardcover. T

What happens when Ryoko, a character from a manga universe (with all that entails of that eastern art style), is transported to the "real world" of Western comic books and falls in love with a girl from the wrong comic style?

Oddly Normal. Written and Illustrated by **Otis Frampton**. Image Comics, 2015– . Y

When you come from a mixed family, it can be rough growing up belonging to neither one side—but especially when you're half human and half witch! Ten-year-old

© 2016 Otis Frampton.

Oddly's mom is a witch from the magical land of Fignation and her dad is a human, so it's hard for her to fit in on Earth. When she wishes on her 10th birthday for her parents to disappear—they do! Now she must travel to the realm of Fignation and try to find out what happened to her parents—but first she's got to enroll in the school system there where the bullies really are monsters and evil is everywhere!

Vol. 1. 2015. 128pp. 978-1-63215-226-8.
Vol. 2. 2015. 128pp. 978-1-63215-484-2.
Vol. 3. 2016. 128pp. 978-1-63215-692-1.

Oz series. Written by **Eric Shanower**. Based on the novels of **L. Frank Baum**. Illustrated by **Skottie Young**. Marvel Comics, 2009–2015; IDW Publishing, 2011–2014. A

© 2016 Marvel Comics.

Eric Shanower has written a number of stories based on L. Frank Baum's Oz stories (collected in IDW's *Adventures in Oz*), but along with artist Skottie Young he adapted six of Baum's actual Oz books. These were originally published as limited series, and besides individual collections all six limited series have been collected in one giant omnibus edition.

Little Adventures in Oz. IDW Publishing, 2010. 136pp. 978-1-60010-678-1.
The Marvelous Land of Oz. 2010. 200pp. 978-0-7851-4028-3, hardcover; 2012. 978-0-7851-6365-7.
Ozma of Oz. 2011. 200pp. 978-0-7851-4247-8, hardcover; 978-0-7851-9108-7.
Dorothy and the Wizard in Oz. 2012. 192pp. 978-0-7851-5554-6, hardcover; 2014. 978-0-7851-9114-8.
Road to Oz. 2013. 136pp. 978-0-7851-6404-3, hardcover; 978-0-7851-9111-7.
Adventures in Oz. IDW Publishing, 2014. 160pp. 978-1-63140-150-3, hardcover.
The Emerald City of Oz. 2014. 120pp. 978-0-7851-8388-4, hardcover; 978-0-7851-8389-1.
The Oz Omnibus. 2014. 1080pp. 978-0-7851-8783-7, hardcover.
The Wonderful Wizard of Oz. 2014, 2nd edition. 192pp. 978-0-7851-5447-1, hardcover; 2009. 978-0-7851-4590-5.

The Return of King Doug. Written by **Greg Erb** and **Jason Oremland**. Illustrated by **Wook-Jin Clark**. Oni Press, 2009. 184pp. 978-1-934964-15-6. T

Doug Peterson, an eight-year-old, found a well that was a portal to a magical world called Valdonia. Within Valdonia there are centaurs, fairies, elves, and other creatures. Within this world it was prophesied that Doug would save the world from the rule of the evil witch empress. That is, until he got scared and ran back through the magical well. Twenty-five years later, Doug is a down-on-his-luck single parent. He has all but forgotten Valdonia until one weekend when his son and he go back to the vacation house with the magical well. While Doug was cleaning, his son was playing in the yard and stumbled

© 2016 Greg Erb and Jason
Oremland.

into the magical realm his father had found at his age. It is up to Doug to get his son back from the realm he had once abandoned in their hour of greatest need.

Magic Knight Rayearth. Written and Illustrated by **CLAMP**. Dark Horse Comics, 2011–2012. Y Japanese manga. あ ◎

Schoolgirls Hikaru, Umi, and Fuu are transported to the magical realm of Cephiro to free the Princess Emeraude. The girls discover they are the revered Magic Knights who are foretold to free the land. Each is given a special power tied into the elements. Hikaru is the Magic Knight of Fire, Umi is the Magic Knight of Water, and Fuu is the Magic Knight of Wind. Together they begin their quest with the cute blobbish creature called Makona to free the princess from the evil entity called Zagato. The sequel takes the girls back to Cephiro to once again a year later to save the mystical realm when other nearby countries claim it in their name. Will they be able to save Cephiro before it's reduced to ashes? The series was adapted into an anime series and originally aired in Japan.

Omnibus Edition. 2011–2012.
Vol. 1. 2011. 640pp. 978-1-59582-588-9.
Vol. 2. 2012. 640pp. 978-1-59582-669-5.

Red River. Written and Illustrated by **Chie Shinohara**. VIZ Media, 2004–2010. O Japanese manga.

Fifteen-year-old Yuri Suzuki's life has never seemed so good. She just passed her college entrance exams and just kissed her boyfriend Himuro for the first time. Little does she expect her life will take a drastic change to the past! Magical hands appear out of a puddle and drag her straight down into the water. She awakens to find herself in the year 1500 BC in the heart of the Hittite Empire, Anatolia, in the ancient Middle East. Captured by the queen of Anatolia, she's to be sacrificed in a ritual that will curse five princes that come before her son so that one day he may sit on the throne. Yuri manages to escape from the queen and is rescued by Prince Kail, the third in line for the throne. Now Yuri is safe in Kail's protection, and as they look for a way to return Yuri back to the present, Yuri finds that she may have a true purpose for being there in the past—a purpose that can change the fate of the war and overthrow an empire.

Vol. 1. 2004. 192pp. 978-1-59116-429-6.   *Vol. 4*. 2004. 200pp. 978-1-59116-432-6.
Vol. 2. 2004. 188pp. 978-1-59116-430-2.   *Vol. 5*. 2005. 200pp. 978-1-59116-433-3.
Vol. 3. 2004. 200pp. 978-1-59116-431-9.   *Vol. 6*. 2005. 192pp. 978-1-59116-780-8.

Vol. 7. 2005. 192pp. 978-1-59116-847-8.
Vol. 8. 2005. 200pp. 978-1-59116-988-8.
Vol. 9. 2005. 192pp. 978-1-4215-0066-9.
Vol. 10. 2006. 208pp. 978-1-4215-0195-6.
Vol. 11. 2006. 208pp. 978-1-4215-0327-1.
Vol. 12. 2006. 208pp. 978-1-4215-0554-1.
Vol. 13. 2006. 208pp. 978-1-4215-0555-8.
Vol. 14. 2006. 208pp. 978-1-4215-0556-5.
Vol. 15. 2006. 208pp. 978-1-4215-0557-2.
Vol. 16. 2007. 208pp. 978-1-4215-0558-9.
Vol. 17. 2007. 192pp. 978-1-4215-0997-6.
Vol. 18. 2007. 192pp. 978-1-4215-0998-3.
Vol. 19. 2007. 192pp. 978-1-4215-0999-0.
Vol. 20. 2008. 200pp. 978-1-4215-1000-2.
Vol. 21. 2008. 192pp. 978-1-4215-1001-9.
Vol. 22. 2008. 192pp. 978-1-4215-1722-3.
Vol. 23. 2008. 210pp. 978-1-4215-1723-0.
Vol. 24. 2009. 210pp. 978-1-4215-1724-7.
Vol. 25. 2009. 192pp. 978-1-4215-2251-7.
Vol. 26. 2009. 200pp. 978-1-4215-2252-4.
Vol. 27. 2009. 192pp. 978-1-4215-2253-1.
Vol. 28. 2010. 200pp. 978-1-4215-2254-8.

Return to Labyrinth. Written by **Jake T. Forbes**. Illustrated by **Chris Lie**. TOKYOPOP. T 🎬

Years after the events of the Jim Henson movie *The Labyrinth*, the baby brother, Toby, has grown up. Little did he or his older sister Sarah know that after they escaped the goblins and the labyrinth, Jareth the Goblin King has secretly been watching and helping his protégé. Toby must return to the labyrinth as the new goblin king. It is up to Toby to try to run the labyrinth but also try to stop a sorceress Mizumi from taking over his newly obtained kingdom.

Vol. 1. 2006. 208pp. 978-1-59816-725-2.
Vol. 2. 2007. 192pp. 978-1-59816-726-9.
Vol. 3. 2009. 192pp. 978-1-59816-727-6.
Vol. 4. 2010. 208pp. 978-1-4278-1687-0.

Sailor Twain or the Mermaid in the Hudson. Written and Illustrated by **Mark Siegel**. First Second, 2012. 400pp. 978-1-59643-636-7. O ◉

© 2016 Mark Siegel.

Captain Twain has sailed steamboats on the Hudson River for many years. He has seen many things over the years, but by far the strangest thing he has ever seen was when he fished out a wounded mermaid from the river. Twain nurses the mermaid back to health. Twain and the mermaid share stories of what it is like under the water and her ancient curse while Twain reads her poetry he has written. Elsewhere on the boat Twain is not the only person with mermaids on their brains. The ship's owner is heavily researching mermaids and their siren's call. Only when Twain travels to the realm of the mermaid will he clearly see the part he plays on the Hudson River.

Smoke and Mirrors: Life and Death and Other Card Tricks. Written by **Mike Costa**. Illustrated by **Ryan Browne**. IDW Publishing, 2012. 978-1-61377-402-1. O

Terry Ward is a regular stage magician who finds himself in a world where real magic exists and has replaced technology. Can his slight-of-hand skills compete in a world where magic is real?

The Stuff of Legend. Written by **Mike Raicht** and **Brian Smith**. Illustrated by **Charles Paul Wilson III**. Th3rd World Studios, 2010– . T

Set in 1944, a band of toys must save their owner—a small boy—who has been captured by the Boogeyman to the Dark Realm (which is located in the boy's closet). When the toys are in the Dark Realm, they become life-size and more realistic features such as teeth in a stuffed bear's case. They must battle the Boogeyman and his army of lost and discarded toys to rescue the book. The series will conclude with Volume 6.

Book 1: The Dark. 2010. 128pp. 978-0-3455210-0-2.
Book 2: The Jungle. 2011. 144pp. 978-0-9832161-0-0.
Book 3: A Jester's Tale. 2012. 124pp. 978-0-9832161-2-4.
Book 4: The Toy Collector. 2013. 124pp. 978-0-9832161-7-9.
Omnibus One. 2012. 260pp. 0-983-21619-3, hardcover.
Omnibus Two. 2014. 270pp. 0-989-57449-0, hardcover.

Tsubasa: RESERVoir CHRoNiCLE. Written and Illustrated by **CLAMP**. Del Rey Manga/Random House, 2004–2010. T Japanese manga. あ

In the magical Kingdom of the Clow, young archaeologist named Syaoran Li is in love with Sakura, the princess of the Clow and master of a magical and so-far untapped potential. When a dig finds a mysterious artifact that knocks Sakura unconscious, no science or magic can heal her—except one. Syaoran takes her to the king's magical advisor and transports Syaoran and Sakura across dimensions and worlds to the magic shop owned by the time-space witch Yuko. Joined with Fai D. Flowright, the Wizard of Serusu and Kurogane, a cursed ninja from ancient Japan, who both have a separate desire to be fulfilled by Yuko, Syaoran journeys across dimensions to retrieve the small fragments of Sakura's memories or else she'll die. There is a cost for Yuko's aid: they must all give up their most precious item. For Fai it's his tattoo of power, for Kurogane, it's his sword, but Syaoran must give up what matters to him the most: his relationship with Sakura. The cost is high, but Sakura will do anything to get her back. Now accompanied with the magical rabbit-like creature Mokona, they're traveling dimension after dimension in search of shards of Sakura's memories and more, all along the way meeting up with other popular characters from many CLAMP titles. The manga has recently been adapted into a hit anime series currently airing in Japan.

Vol. 1. 2004. 208pp. 978-0-345-47057-7.	*Vol. 15*. 2007. 192pp. 978-0-345-49831-1.
Vol. 2. 2004. 208pp. 978-0-345-47182-6.	*Vol. 16*. 2008. 192pp. 978-0-345-50148-6.
Vol. 3. 2004. 208pp. 978-0-345-47183-3.	*Vol. 17*. 2008. 192pp. 978-0-345-50165-3.
Vol. 4. 2005. 208pp. 978-0-345-47791-0.	*Vol. 18*. 2008. 192pp. 978-0-345-50409-8.
Vol. 5. 2005. 208pp. 978-0-345-47792-7.	*Vol. 19*. 2008. 192pp. 978-0-345-50579-8.
Vol. 6. 2005. 208pp. 978-0-345-47793-4.	*Vol. 20*. 2009. 192pp. 978-0-345-50580-4.
Vol. 7. 2005. 208pp. 978-0-345-47797-2.	*Vol. 21*. 2009. 192pp. 978-0-345-50809-6.
Vol. 8. 2006. 208pp. 978-0-345-48428-4.	*Vol. 22*. 2009. 192pp. 978-0-345-51038-9.
Vol. 9. 2006. 208pp. 978-0-345-48429-1.	*Vol. 23*. 2009. 192pp. 978-0-345-51230-7.
Vol. 10. 2006. 208pp. 978-0-345-48430-7.	*Vol. 24*. 2009. 192pp. 978-0-345-51715-9.
Vol. 11. 2006. 208pp. 978-0-345-48528-1.	*Vol. 25*. 2010. 192pp. 978-0-345-51716-6.
Vol. 12. 2007. 208pp. 978-0-345-48532-8.	*Vol. 26*. 2010. 208pp. 978-0-345-52070-8.
Vol. 13. 2007. 208pp. 978-0-345-48533-5.	*Vol. 27*. 2010. 192pp. 978-0-345-52071-5.
Vol. 14. 2007. 192pp. 978-0-345-48534-2.	*Vol. 28*. 2010. 288pp. 978-0-345-52164-4.

The Wizard of Oz. Written by **L. Frank Baum**. Adapted and Illustrated by **Ben Caldwell**. All-Action Classics/Sterling Childrens Books, 2012. A

> When her Kansas house is caught in a tornado, young Dorothy Gale and her dog Toto find themselves transported from Kansas to the magical land of Oz. Heralded as a hero for accidentally killing the Wicked Witch of the East when her house drops on the witch, Dorothy's given the witch's magical silver shoes as a reward for saving the munchkins. Hoping to return home, she heads to the Emerald City to seek the Wizard of Oz. Along the way she is joined by a Tin Woodsman, a Cowardly Lion, and a Scarecrow, who are also seeking something that the wizard can provide. The four companions will have their wishes granted only if one of them can kill the Wicked Witch of the West who rules in Winkle County. Adapted from the classic 1900 children's novel.

Wonderland. Written by **Tommy Kovac**. Illustrated by **Sonny Liew**. Disney Press, 2009. 160pp. 978-1-4231-0451-3, hardcover. A

> From the pages of Lewis Carroll's *Alice in Wonderland* is the tale of Mary Ann, the White Rabbit's housemaid. In the original novel the White Rabbit mistook Alice for Mary Ann. A minor character in the books, now for the first time, she's the star! After she hits the Red Queen with her scepter, Mary Ann finds herself on the run and out on her own wondrous adventure with the White Rabbit.

A Wrinkle in Time. Written by **Madeline L'Engle**. Adapted and Illustrated by **Hope Larson**. Farrar, Straus and Giroux, 2012. 392pp. 978-0-3743-8615-3, hardcover. Y 🏃

> An adaptation of the popular Science Fiction/Fantasy novel for its 50th anniversary. When her father goes missing, Meg Murry along with her five-year-old child prodigy brother Charles Wallace as well as teenager Calvin O'Keefe are sent by the mysterious Mrs. Who, Mrs. Whatsit, and Mrs. Which via the tesseract, a way of folding time and space. Now transported across the galaxy, Meg tries to rescue her father by crossing from planet to planet to saving her father as well as her young brother from the gathering darkness that has her younger brother in its thrall. The book was recognized on YALSA's Great Graphic Novels for Teens selection list in 2013.

Contemporary Fantasy

Contemporary fantasy titles involve stories set on Earth or a very similar world where sometimes the influence of magic can be very subtle. The stories usually take place in modern or contemporary times, but can be also set in the recent past. The focus of some of the stories can be on the relationships of the cast and magic—or just the hint of it—can be just the smallest part of the story.

The Anchor. Written by **Phil Hester**. Illustrated by **Brian Churilla**. BOOM! Studios, 2009–2010. O 🏃

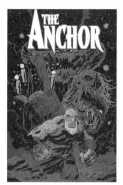

© 2016 BOOM! Studios.

Over 1,000 years ago, a Christian monk offered all he had to protect the Earth from the gates of Hell: his fists. Granted with superior strength and near-immortality, he's a prize-fighting leg-breaker who is the only one able to fight back against the beasts of Hell. After being tricked into slumbering, he's been reawakened to send the monsters back to Hell. In the vein of books like *Hellboy* and *Goon*, the first volume was recognized by YALSA as a Great Graphic Novel for Teens in 2011.

Vol. 1: Five Furies. 2010. 112pp. 978-1-60886-020-3.
Vol. 2: Black Lips. 2010. 112pp. 978-1-60886-004-3.

Bigfoot Boy. Written by **J. Torres**. Illustrated by **Faith Erin Hicks**. Kids Can Press, 2012–2014. A

© 2016 J. Torres and Faith Erin Hicks.

When 10-year-old Rufus was visiting his grandmother, he followed another child into the woods. There he found a wooden totem on cord hidden in a tree. On the totem was the word "Sasquatch," which he read aloud. Soon he finds that he is able to transform into a large, hairy creature who could talk to animals. Now he finds himself on all sorts of adventures and having to stop the plans of wolves and ravens.

Vol. 1: Into the Woods. 2012. 100pp. 978-1-5545-3713-6, hardcover; 978-1-5545-3711-2.
Vol. 2: Unkindness of Ravens. 2013. 100pp. 978-1-5545-3713-6, hardcover; 978-1-5545-3714-3.
Vol. 3: The Sound of Thunder. 2014. 100pp. 978-1-8947-8658-4, hardcover; 978-1-8947-8659-1.

The Demon Prince of Momochi House. Written and Illustrated by **Aya Shouoto**. VIZ Media, 2015– . O Japanese manga.

On her 16th birthday, orphan Himari Momochi inherits her family estate that she's never been to. It seems that the Momochi house is sitting on the barrier between two worlds and she is to be the guardian between the two worlds. That is well and all, but when Himari moves in, there are three handsome squatters living in her house! Two of them are spirits, but the last one, Aoi, is a human who has the ability to transform into a Nue (a protection spirit) and he protects the house and Himari from the bad forces from the other side.

Vol. 1. 2015. 172pp. 978-1-4215-7962-7.
Vol. 2. 2015. 172pp. 978-1-4215-7963-4.
Vol. 3. 2016. 162pp. 978-1-4215-7964-1.
Vol. 4. 2016. 172pp. 978-1-4215-8048-7.

Vol. 5. 2016. 172pp. 978-1-4215-8630-4.
Vol. 6. 2016. 172pp. 978-1-4215-8631-1.
Vol. 7. 2017. 172pp. 978-1-4215-8632-8.
Vol. 8. 2017. 172pp. 978-1-4215-8909-1.

Foiled. Written by **Jane Yolen**. Illustrated by **Mike Cavallaro**. First Second Books, 2010–2013. T

Aliera Carstairs is a regular teenage girl who loves fencing until the possession of an enchanted fencing foil that makes her the Defender of the Faerie realm of Seelie.

© 2016 Jane Yolen and
Mike Cavallaro.

Foiled. 2010. 160pp. 978-1-59643-279-6.
Curses! Foiled Again. 2013. 176pp. 978-1-59643-619-0.

The Fountain. Written by **Darren Aronofsky**. Illustrated by **Kent Williams**. Vertigo/DC Comics, 2006. 176pp. 978-1-4012-0058-9. M

True love cannot be bound by time. Two lovers are reincarnated through three time periods. Each time they find each other, their love is threatened by some tragedy. Travel back to when the Spanish Conquistadors were fighting the Mayans. Travel to present day when disease infects the one while the other rushes to find a cure. Travel to the future as the man travels the cosmos to save his star. Aronofsky wrote the graphic novel at a time when it looked like the film version of *The Fountain* would not come to pass, though production eventually restarted with the film coming out in 2006.

Four Eyes. Written by **Joe Kelly**. Illustrated by **Max Fiumara**. Image Comics, 2015– . T 🏵

© 2016 Joe Kelly and Max
Fiumara.

Originally published in 2010. Set in New York City in an alternate 1930s, a young boy's life during the Depression is turned upside down when his father is killed during an illegal dragon fighting match. Enrico learns to loathe the great beasts and hopes to kill one to get revenge for his father's death. Soon Enrico is recruited to steal a clutch of dragon eggs but fate has something else in store for the boy. The original printing of the book was recognized by YALSA on its Great Graphic Novels for Teens list in 2011.

Vol. 1: Forged in Flame. 2015. 96pp. 978-1-63215-424-8.
Vol. 2: Hearts of Fire. 2016. 104pp. 978-1-63215-806-2.

The Guild. Written by **Felicia Day**. Illustrated by **Jim Rugg**, **Jeff Lewis**, and various. Dark Horse Comics, 2010–2012. O

Cyd, Sujan, Herman, Simon, Clara, and April are all normal people with their own issues and concerns. That is when they are not logged into The Game, a massive multiplayer online role-playing game. Together they form the guild, The Knights of Good. Based off the hit web show, these graphic novels give the background for the characters. Cyd must deal with her addictive nature while using The Game as a social outlet. While managing the Knights of Good, Herman must also watch out for his grandfather. Simon, while attending high school, must also deal with his mother dating again and while trying to stay under the radar as his popular commercial model self. Each chapter shows a little more of each character, their relationship to the game, and more importantly, who they are outside of The Game. Based on the popular 2007–2013 online series created by and starring Felicia Day.

Vol. 1. 2010. 96pp. 978-1-59582-549-0.
Vol. 2. 2012. 144pp. 978-1-59582-900-9.

Hereville. Written and Illustrated by **Barry Deutsch**. Amulet Books, 2012– . Y ◎

© 2016 Barry Deutsch.

Mirka is an 11-year-old Orthodox Jewish girl with an overactive imagination whose dream is to fight dragons. When she talks to the witch at the edge of town, she is introduced to a whole different world that lives alongside the "normal" world. Mirka battles a troll, uses magic yarn, duels a meteorite, and saves her town many times all while observing Orthodox Jewish traditions. Mirka may not be the strongest or brightest girl around, but her perseverance and luck get her through some sticky situations.

How Mirka Got Her Sword. 2012. 144pp. 978-1-4197-0619-6, hardcover.
How Mirka Met a Meteorite. 2012. 128pp. 978-1-4197-0398-0, hardcover.
How Mirka Caught a Fish. 2015. 142pp. 978-1-4197-0800-8, hardcover.

Hildafolk. Written and Illustrated by **Luke Pearson**. Nobrow Press/Flying Eye Books, 2010– . Y ◎

© 2016 Luke Pearson.

Hilda is a young girl who can never sit still and loves to explore her outdoor surroundings where she's bound to encounter a creature from Scandinavian-inspired folklore like trolls, talking crows, invisible elves, Rat Kings, Salt Lions, the Nisse, and giants that tower over the largest of mountains.

Hilda and the Midnight Giant. 2012. 40pp. 978-1-907704-25-3, hardcover.
Hilda and the Bird Parade. 2013. 44pp. 978-1-9092630-60-2, hardcover.
Hilda and the Troll, 2nd edition, 2013. 40pp. 978-1-909263-14-7, hardcover.
Hilda and the Black Hound. 2014. 66pp. 978-1-909263-18-5, hardcover.
Hilda and the Bird Parade. 2016. 48pp. 978-1-911171-02-7, hardcover.
Hilda and the Stone Forest. 2016. 64pp. 978-1-909263-74-1, hardcover.

Iscariot. Written and Illustrated by **Shane Michael Vidaurri**. Archaia Press/BOOM! Studios, 2015. 160pp. 978-1-60886-761-5, hardcover. T

A dying girl named Carson receives a unique gift: the gift of magic. Given to her by Iscariot, a 400-year-old wizard. As Carson soon learns though, the power of magic comes at a great cost that can be very dangerous and causes great sacrifice, and death.

© 2016 Shane Michael Vidaurri.

What will Carson do with this gift—or is it a curse for the young girl? Meanwhile, what effects will Iscariot's gift take after he abandons the rules of the wizarding order to gives magic to a dying girl?

Jellaby. Written and Illustrated by **Kean Soo**. Stone Arch Books, 2014. Y

Ten-year-old Portia Bennett hates her new school, and family life is no better as they are adjusting to life without her dad. But no matter how bad things are, she just discovered something hiding in the deep dark woods that is better than anything she's ever had: a silent giant purple monster with wings named Jellaby who is lost and far from home. Together she and her friend Jason take a perilous journey through Toronto to take Jellaby to where he belongs.

Vol. 1: The Lost Monster. 2014. 160pp. 978-1-4342-6420-6.
Vol. 2: Monster in the City. 2014. 160pp. 978-1-4342-6421-3.

Joe the Barbarian. Written by **Grant Morrison**. Illustrated by **Sean Murphy**. Vertigo/DC Comics, 2011. 224pp. 978-1-4012-2971-9. M

Joe does not fit in at school. His mother is about to lose the house. While his mother is away at the bank, Joe forgets to take his sugar to control his diabetes. Things could not be looking worse for him. That is until he is transported to another world filled with his toys. In this world created by his diabetic hallucinations, he is the only person who can save the world. Can Joe save the world and his home while he gets a bottle of soda?

Korgi. Written and Illustrated by **Christian Slade**. Top Shelf Productions, 2007–2011. Y

Sprout and Ivy are an adventuring team that travels around the Korgi Hollow. Sprout is a young fire-breathing Korgi pup and Ivy is a young girl who has wings. With their powers no adventure is too great. There are strange and diabolical things stirring in Korgi Hollow, and they all seem to find their way toward these two.

Sprouting Wings. 2007. 80pp. 978-1-891830-90-7.
Cosmic Collector. 2008. 88pp. 978-1-60309-010-0.
A Hollow Beginning. 2011. 96pp. 978-1-60309-062-9.
The Problem with Potions. 2016. 120pp. 978-1-60309-403-0.

The Kurdles. Written and Illustrated by **Robert Goodin**. Fantagraphics, 2015. 60pp. 978-1-60699-832-8, hardcover. A

When a stuffed teddy bear named Sally gets separated from its owner while in the woods, she stumbles upon a fantastic group of creatures who live in the woods called the Kurdles. Sally soon finds out her new friends have problems of their own when their home, known as Kurdleton, has sprouted hair, eyes, and a mouth! Can they keep the house from sprouting legs and running away?

The Life After. Written by **Joshua Hale Fialkov**. Illustrated by **Gabo**. Oni Press, 2015. O

Jude's life is just the same old thing every day, but when he meets a woman, that changes his life forever—he can literally see into her past. Jude comes to a startling revelation: he's dead and his soul is in Purgatory for people who have committed suicide. Now teams up with Ernest Hemingway, can Jude change the rules of the afterlife and find happiness?

Vol. 1. 2015. 136pp. 978-1-62010-214-5.
Vol. 2. 2015. 144pp. 978-1-62010-254-1.
Vol. 3: Exodus. 2016. 136pp. 978-1-62010-321-0.

Natsume's Book of Friends. Written and Illustrated by **Yuki Midorikawa**. VIZ Media, 2010–2016. T Japanese manga. 🎗 あ

Takashi Natsume has inherited two things from his grandmother—the ability to see spirits and The Book of Friends that contains the names of the spirits who served her. The series was turned into an anime and was selected as one of YALSA's Great Graphic Novels for Teens.

Vol. 1. 2010. 208pp. 978-1-4215-3243-1.
Vol. 2. 2010. 208pp. 978-1-4215-3244-8.
Vol. 3. 2010. 208pp. 978-1-4215-3245-5.
Vol. 4. 2010. 208pp. 978-1-4215-3246-2.
Vol. 5. 2011. 208pp. 978-1-4215-3247-9.
Vol. 6. 2011. 208pp. 978-1-4215-3248-6.
Vol. 7. 2011. 192pp. 978-1-4215-3274-5.
Vol. 8. 2011. 192pp. 978-1-4215-3592-0.
Vol. 9. 2011. 192pp. 978-1-4215-3887-7.

Natsume Yujincho © Yuki Midorikawa 2005/HAKUSEN-SHA, Inc.

Vol. 10. 2011. 192pp. 978-1-4215-3939-3.
Vol. 11. 2012. 192pp. 978-1-4215-4122-8.
Vol. 12. 2012. 192pp. 978-1-4215-4231-7.
Vol. 13. 2012. 192pp. 978-1-4215-4923-1.
Vol. 14. 2013. 192pp. 978-1-4215-5375-7.
Vol. 15. 2014. 192pp. 978-1-4215-5967-4.
Vol. 16. 2014. 192pp. 978-1-4215-6782-2.
Vol. 17. 2014. 192pp. 978-1-4215-7524-7.
Vol. 18. 2015. 192pp. 978-1-4215-8024-1.
Vol. 19. 2015. 192pp. 978-1-4215-8248-1.

Long Walk to Valhalla. Written by **Adam Smith**. Illustrated by **Matthew Fox**. Archaia/BOOM! Studios, 2015. 96pp. 978-1-60886-692-2. O

Rory grew up in a sleepy town in Arkansas, but he'd rather forget all of it. The pain from his youth hurts too much to forget. He wishes he could also forget his older mentally challenged brother, Joe. They were close growing up, but after an unforgiveable incident, some things you can't forgive. When a young girl shows up telling Rory that she's a Valkyrie, charged by Odin the all-father to bring him today to Valhalla, the

home of the heroes, Rory finds that he will have to look back at his life and set free what's been haunting him for so long.

Peter Panzerfaust. Written by **Kurtis Wiebe**. Illustrated by **Tyler Jenkins**. Image Comics, 2013–2015. M

A retelling of Peter Pan set amid the ruins of war-torn France. When the city of Calais falls to Germany in 1940, a plucky American boy named Peter rallies a group of French orphans. Together they must try and survive against France's darkest hour against horrible odds.

Vol. 1: The Great Escape. 2013. 128pp. 978-1-60706-582-1.
Vol. 2: Hooked. 2013. 128pp. 978-1-60706-728-3.
Vol. 3: Cry of the Wolf. 2014. 136pp. 978-1-60706-864-8.
Vol. 4. The Hunt. 2015. 136pp. 978-1-63215-062-2.

The Rime of the Modern Mariner. Written and Illustrated by **Nick Hayes**. Viking Press, 2012. 336pp. 978-0-670-02580-0. M

Adapted from the 18th-century poem, Nick Hayes twists the tale as a commentary on the current relationship between humanity and nature. The Modern Mariner tells his sea tale to a modern businessman so that he may warn modern society of the horrors he saw. While out at sea the Modern Mariner brazenly shot and killed an albatross while he was bored at sea. His fellow shipmates told him that they cursed them all as he had killed their lucky bird. Soon the ocean would turn against the Mariner and the ship. As they entered the North Pacific Gyre, pollution surrounded the ship as far as the eye could see and stalled the engines. The Modern Mariner saw the error of man's ways all too late.

Rumble. Written by **John Arcudi**. Illustrated by **James Harren**. Image Comics, 2015– . O

The ancient gods and beasts of old are all around us—we only have to listen to hear them—but one of them just happened to crash into the front door. That's what happens when an ancient Scarecrow God walks into a bar and proceeds to get into a fight with gods and beasts in the heart of a metropolitan American city.

Vol. 1: What Color of Darkness? 2015. 144pp. 978-1-63215-383-8.
Vol. 2: A Woe That Is Madness. 2016. 160pp. 978-1-6321-5604-4.
Vol. 3: Immortal Coil. 2016. 160pp. 978-1-6321-5928-1.

The Sleepwalkers. Written and Illustrated by **Viviane Schwarz**. Candlewick Press, 2013. 96pp. 978-0-7636-6230-1. Y

If you have a bad dream that won't go away, or afraid to sleep at night? Just write a letter to the Sleepwalkers and put it under your pillow and they will come and save you so you can have a good night! Join the animal team of Sleepwalkers as they take on the weird and wild dreams in the dream world to save little children from their bedtime fears.

The Story of Saiunkoku. Written by **Sai Yukino**. Illustrated by **Yura Kairi**. VIZ Media, 2010–2013. T 🌸 Japanese manga. あ

This adaptation of a series of "light novels" from Japan takes place in the fictional empire of Saiunkoku where Shurei Hong, who is part of a noble family that has fallen on hard times, wishes to work as civil servant in the imperial court, something that is forbidden to women. But now she has an opportunity to be close to the emperor in a way she never imagined. Selected as one of YALSA's Great Graphic Novels for Teens in 2011. The series was also adapted into an animated series as well.

Vol. 1. 2010. 176pp. 978-1-4215-3834-1.
Vol. 2. 2011. 200pp. 978-14215-3835-8.
Vol. 3. 2011. 200pp. 978-1-4215-3836-5.
Vol. 4. 2011. 192pp. 978-1-4215-3837-2.
Vol. 5. 2011. 176pp. 978-1-4215-3842-6.
Vol. 6. 2012. 200pp. 978-1-4215-4179-2.
Vol. 7. 2012. 170pp. 978-1-4215-4180-8.
Vol. 8. 2012. 168pp. 978-1-4215-4946-0.
Vol. 9. 2013. 176pp. 978-1-4215-5083-1.

The Unwritten. Written by **Mike Carey**. Illustrated by **Peter Gross**. Vertigo/DC Comics, 2010–2015. 🌸 M ◎

© 2016 DC Comics.

Tommy Taylor is the boy wizard in an incredibly popular series of novels. Tom Taylor is the son of the series' missing creator who earns money by making appearances at conventions and other events. But when questions about his past arise, Tom and his new allies find links into both magic and the world inside fiction, and face the threat of an organization out to control things. The series, as well as a subsequent limited series, has been collected in its entirety, and there has also been one original graphic novel. Additional cowriters and artists on the series have included Brian Talbot and Bill Willingham, the latter of which worked on a storyline that tied in with *Fables*. *The Unwritten* received several Eisner Award nominations including one for best series. It also was nominated for a Hugo Award.

Vol. 1: Tommy Taylor and the Bogus Identity. 2010. 144pp. 978-1-4102-2565-0.
Vol. 2: Inside Man. 2010. 168pp. 978-1-4102-2873-6.
Vol. 3: Dead Man's Knock. 2011. 160pp. 978-1-4102-3046-3.
Vol. 4: Leviathan. 2011. 144pp. 978-1-4102-3292-4.
Vol. 5: On to Genesis. 2012. 144pp. 978-1-4102-3359-4.
Vol. 6: Tommy Taylor and the War of Words. 2012. 240pp. 978-1-4102-3560-4.
Vol. 7: The Wound. 2013. 144pp. 978-1-4102-3806-3.
Vol. 8: Orpheus in the Underworld. 2014. 176pp. 978-1-4102-4301-2.
Vol. 9: The Unwritten Fables. 2014. 144pp. 978-1-4102-4694-5.
Vol. 10: War Stories. 2014. 128pp. 978-1-4102-5055-3.
Vol. 11: Apocalypse. 2015. 176pp. 978-1-4102-5348-6.
The Unwritten: Tommy Taylor and the Ship That Sunk Twice. 2013. 160pp. 978-1-4012-2976-4, hardcover; 978-1-4102-2977-1, softcover.

War at Ellsmere. Written and Illustrated by **Faith Erin Hicks**. Slave Labor Graphics, 2008. 156pp. 978-1-59362-140-7. T 🎋

> Juniper has just been accepted at the Ellsmere Academy, a prestigious boarding school. An outsider in a school overrun by pompous spoiled girls, she finds comfort and friendship with Cassie, her roommate, who insists there's a mythical beast just outside the school grounds. Jun is going to have a lot on her plate this year between the princesses of the school and the great beast just outside in the woods. The book was recognized by YALSA as a Great Graphic Novel for Teens in 2009.

The Wicked + The Divine. Written by **Kieron Gillen**. Illustrated by **Jamie McKelvie** and **Kate Brown**. Image Comics, 2014– . M 🎋

© 2016 Kieron Gillen.

> The most popular group of stars in the media is The Pantheon—a group of 12 people who claimed to be gods who are mortal on Earth for a limited time and then they die again. But their story isn't fiction—they really are all gods from various sects including Baal, Lucifer, Amaterasu, Baphomet, Inanna, Minerva, and Wōden. The gods are born as humans but then are inhabited by the deities and then die after two years. The Pantheon are worshiped on Earth as rock stars and 17-year-old Laura Wilson is the biggest fan of them all. A follower of the deity Amaterasu, Laura soon becomes embroiled by the doings of the manipulative gods and those that wish to have them killed and discovers that she may be the 13th member of the Pantheon, Persephone. The series explores the myth of rock stars as gods in the public eye, who are worshipped on a daily basis by the media and their fans. In 2017 the fourth volume was recognized by YALSA Great Graphic Novels for Teens annual selection list.

Vol. 1: The Faust Act. 2014. 144pp. 978-1-63215-019-6.
Vol. 2: Fandemonium. 2015. 168pp. 978-1-63215-327-2.
Vol. 3: Commercial Suicide. 2016. 200pp. 978-1-63215-631-0.
Vol. 4: Rising Action. 2016. 144pp. 978-1-63215-913-7.
Vol. 5: Imperial Phase 1. 2017. 144pp. 978-1-5343-0185-6.

Windmill Dragons: A Leah and Alan Adventure. Written and Illustrated by **David Nytra**. Toon Books, 2015. 120pp. 978-1-935179-88-7, hardcover. Y

© 2016 David Nytra.

> A sequel to the *Secret of the Stone Frog*, Leah and Alan take a break from playing to read a story, but they end up putting themselves into the adventure where windmills turn into dragons! Looking for a way to save the villagers and their dog Rowdy, too, they encounter a knight who is captured by an ogre, a wizard who rides a giant chicken, and a meat-eating boat before they can find the origin of the magical disturbance and save their land.

Witch and Wizard. Written by **James Patterson**. Adapted by **Gabrielle Charbonnet** and **Ned Rust**. Illustrated by **Svetlana Chmakova**. Yen Press, 2011–2012. T Neo-manga.

An adaptation of the prose novel, two siblings, Whit and Wisty Allgood, are arrested from the homes and accused of being a wizard and a witch and sentenced to execution at the command of an upstart new political party called the New Order. Little do they realize that they both have a connection to magic as they become part of a larger battle to use their powers to take down the New Order.

Vol. 1. 2011. 256pp. 978-0-316-11989-4.
Vol. 2. 2012. 256pp. 978-0-316-11991-7.
Vol. 3. 2013. 240pp. 978-0-316-11984-9.

Dark Fantasy

An overshadowing, almost gothic darkness sets the mood for these atmospheric stories. Realms of angels, demons, and the faerie can all interact with the protagonist; and magic is the overall presiding force at work. The mood and setting play as much as a role here as the main characters. This subgenre is closely akin to the genre of Horror and can often be indistinguishable from it. Standout titles in this subgenre include Neil Gaiman's Sandman series.

The Ancient Magus' Bride. Written and Illustrated by **Kore Yamazak**i. Seven Seas Entertainment, 2015– . O Japanese Manga.

© 2016 Kore Yamazaki.

Chise Hator is a teenage orphan whose life is just about to get stranger! She's become the apprentice and future bride to Elias Ainsworth, the mystical Child of Thorns. With a face that resembles the skeleton of a buck, he's not a handsome man to say the least. Part fairy and part human, he takes Chise on an odyssey and encounters fairies, magical beasts, and other realms. The still ongoing series has also been adapted into an animated series.

Vol. 1. 2015. 180pp. 978-1-62692-187-0.
Vol. 2. 2015. 180pp. 978-1-62692-192-4.
Vol. 3. 2015. 180pp. 978-1-62692-224-2.
Vol. 4. 2016. 180pp. 978-1-62692-255-6.
Vol. 5. 2016. 180pp. 978-1-62692-284-6.
Vol. 6. 2017. 180pp. 978-1-62692-350-8.
Vol. 7. 2017. 180pp. 978-1-62692-499-4.

Black Butler. Written and Illustrated by **Yana Toboso**. Yen Press, 2010– . O Japanese manga. 🏃 あ

The demon Sebastian Michaelis is the demon butler of the Phantomhive household. Sebastian is the servant of Ciel Phantomhive, an egotistical business-savvy 12-year-old who is in charge of his family since the death of his parents. Sebastian became Ciel's servant after Ciel was to be sacrificed in a cult ritual. A Faustian contract was made to save Ciel's life and Sebastian commanded the demon to eliminate all those who were to have him killed. From that day forth Ciel serves as the Queen's Watchdog, whose task is to eliminate criminals and solve mysterious cases in the underworld for

© 2016 Yana Toboso and
Yen Press.

Queen Victoria. Meanwhile, Sebastian serves as the head of Ciel's staff, assisting Ciel at every turn against conspiring forces but waiting patiently for the day when he can collect on Ciel's promise and have his soul. The first volume was recognized by YALSA's Great Graphic Novels for Teens committee in 2011. The still ongoing series was also adapted as an anime series in Japan.

Vol. 1. 2010. 192pp. 978-0-316-08084-2.
Vol. 2. 2010. 192pp. 978-0-316-08425-3.
Vol. 3. 2010. 192pp. 978-0-316-08426-0.
Vol. 4. 2011. 192pp. 978-0-316-08428-4.
Vol. 5. 2011. 176pp. 978-0-316-08429-1.
Vol. 6. 2011. 176pp. 978-0-316-08430-7.

Vol. 7. 2011. 176pp. 978-0-316-18963-7.
Vol. 8. 2012. 176pp. 978-0-316-18965-1.
Vol. 9. 2012. 176pp. 978-0-316-18967-5.
Vol. 10. 2012. 176pp. 978-0-316-18988-0.
Vol. 11. 2012. 176pp. 978-0-316-22533-5.
Vol. 12. 2013. 176pp. 978-0-316-22534-2.
Vol. 13. 2013. 176pp. 978-0-316-24429-9.
Vol. 14. 2013. 176pp. 978-0-316-24430-5.
Vol. 15. 2013. 176pp. 978-0-316-25419-9.

Vol. 16. 2014. 176pp. 978-0-316-36902-2.
Vol. 17. 2014. 176pp. 978-0-316-37670-9.
Vol. 18. 2014. 176pp. 978-0-316-33622-2.
Vol. 19. 2015. 176pp. 978-0-316-25940-8.
Vol. 20. 2015. 176pp. 978-0-316-30501-3.
Vol. 21. 2015. 176pp. 978-0-316-35209-3.
Vol. 22. 2016. 176pp. 978-0-316-27226-1.
Vol. 23. 2016. 176pp. 978-0-316-50277-1.

Black Metal. Written by **Rick Spears**. Illustrated by **Chuck BB**. Oni Press, 2008–2014. T ◎

© 2016 Rick Spears and
Chuck BB.

Twin brothers, Shawn and Sam, love death metal and are dark and brooding, but they really aren't your typical kids—but their mysterious parentage is! When the twins are empowered by the legendary sword of Atoll, the boys thrash out like any metal-loving headbanger and take on demon after demon to fulfill an ancient prophecy and assume their rightful position as Hell Baron of the Pit. Rock on you demon hellspawns. Rock on.

Vol. 1. 2007. 160pp. 978-1-93266-472-0.
Vol. 2. 2011. 136pp. 978-1-93266-499-7.
Vol. 3. 2014. 160pp. 978-1-93496-482-8.
Omnibvs. 2014. 464pp. 978-1-62010-143-8.

Courtney Crumrin. Written and Illustrated by **Ted Naifeh**. Oni Press, 2012–2015. T 🎗 ◎

Courtney isn't like all those stuck-up girls who like to play with their dolls and talk about fashion and boys—she likes the creepier side of things. When she and her family move in with her elderly Uncle Aloysius in his old mansion, she's bored silly. She hates the town and the kids at school, and misses her old life. But after meeting the odd denizens of the Night Things, a dark world that her uncle is quite familiar with where witches, fairies, trolls, werewolves, and other monsters roam, the precocious 12-year-old Goth finds that

maybe things aren't so bad here after all. The original printing of *Courtney Crumrin and the Night Things* received recognition by YALSA's Popular Paperbacks for Young Adults committee in 2005 on the *Own Your Freak* list. The series was reprinted in a new hardcover format beginning in 2012 with new content, with volume 7 in full color.

Vol. 1: The Night Things. 2012. 144pp. 978-1-934964-77-4, hardcover.

Vol. 2: The Coven of Mystics. 2012. 144pp. 978-1-934964-80-4, hardcover.

Vol. 3: The Twilight Kingdom. 2013. 144pp. 978-1-934964-86-6, hardcover.

Vol. 4: Monstrous Holiday. 2013. 128pp. 978-1-934964-92-7, hardcover.

Vol. 5: The Witch Next Door. 2014. 144pp. 978-1-934964-96-5, hardcover.

Vol. 6: The Final Spell. 2014. 152pp. 978-1-62010-018-9, hardcover.

Vol. 7: Tales of a Warlock as a Young Man. 2015. 128pp. 978-1-62010-019-6, hardcover.

Death: The Deluxe Edition. Written by **Neil Gaiman**. Illustrated by **Chris Bachalo**, **Mark Buckingham**, and **Dave McKean**. Vertigo/DC Comics, 2012. 320pp. 978-1-4012-3548-2, hardcover; 2014. 978-1-4012-4716-4. M 🏆 ◎

A spin-off of Neil Gaiman's award-winning <u>Sandman</u> series, Dream's older sister Death takes the spotlight. In between the here and the hereafter, each century she walks the Earth for one day to better understand those that she must take. The collection reprints the material in the story *Death: The High Cost of Living* from 1994 in which in the guise of a girl named Didi, she helps Mad Hattie, a 250-year-old homeless woman, find her missing heart. The collection also includes the story *Death: The Time of Your Life* (1996) as well as several other appearances of the character from the <u>Sandman</u> comic book series as well as Death story from the graphic novel *Sandman: Endless Nights*. *Death: The High Cost of Living* received recognition by YALSA's Popular Paperbacks for Young Adults committee in 2002 on the *Graphic Novels: Superheroes and Beyond* list.

Edward Scissorhands. Written by **Kate Leth**. Illustrated by **Drew Rausch**. IDW Publishing, 2015–2016. T 🎬

A sequel to the cult 1990 Tim Burton-director film starring Johnny Depp. Set two generations after the film, Edward was created by his master, but was never completed. With deadly sharp scissors as his hands, Edward is still living at the top of the hill. Thought to be a myth or even a murderer by the children in town, a young girl named Meg, the granddaughter of Kim, the girl who originally befriended the creation decades earlier, seeks out the myth of Edward Scissorhands. Meanwhile, another creation has been discovered by Edward named Eli—but is he friend or foe? *The Final Cut* collection reprints all of the material in one deluxe hardcover collection.

Vol. 1: Parts Unknown. 2015. 124pp. 978-1-63140-260-9.

Vol. 2: Whole Again. 2015. 148pp. 978-1-63140-440-5.

The Final Cut. 2016. 280p. 978-1-63140-682-9, hardcover.

Elric: The Making of a Sorcerer. Written by **Michael Moorcock**. Illustrated by **Walter Simonson**. DC Comics, 2007. 208pp. 978-1-4012-1334-3. O

> *Elric: The Making of a Sorcerer* is a prequel to the renowned Elric Saga. Elric must be tested through dream quests before his father sees him as the capable heir to the Melniboné Empire. Elric must face the challenges of his heirs in the dream realm to gain knowledge of sorcery and ancient alliances. The quests Elric embarks on are not the only dangers he faces, but he must also thwart attacks from his cousin the usurper.

Feathers. Written and Illustrated by **Jorge Corona**. Archaia/BOOM! Studios, 2015. 160pp. 978-1-60886-753-0, hardcover. Y

© 2016 Jorge Corona.

> A recluse boy born covered in feathers is found abandoned on the streets. Adopted by a kind man named Gabriel and named Poe. Eleven years later, Poe spends his time helping the Mice, a band of orphans, from the darker forces around them in the slums known as the Maze. When Poe makes his first-ever friend, a young girl named Bianca who has escaped her pampered life to seek out adventure in the Maze, he hopes to return her back home. Meanwhile, darker forces are at play, snatching children from the Maze. Can Poe help Bianca escape the Maze, solve the mystery of the missing children, and perhaps find something about Poe's mysterious past as well?

The Good Neighbors. Written by **Holly Black**. Illustrated by **Ted Naifeh**. Graphix/ Scholastic Books, 2008–2011. T 🏵

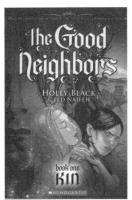

Cover © Scholastic Inc.

> Have you ever felt different from everyone else? Did you think your parents were the most embarrassing people you knew? For Rue, this is true on both occasions. She seems to see unimaginable creatures out of the corner of her eye, and her mother is always spacing off talking to plants. After an incident, her mother disappears and her father is charged with the murder of her and one of the local college students. Rue's world is turned upside down when the grandfather she never knew shows up to tell her that she is part faerie and he is going to take over the city. Rue must figure out what is really going on with her mother and stop her grandfather she just met from another world. The first volume was recognized by YALSA's Great Graphic Novels for Teens selection list in 2009.

Kin. 2008. 117pp. 978-0-439-85562-4.
Kith. 2009. 111pp. 978-0-439-85563-1.
Kind. 2011. 128pp. 978-0-439-85567-9.

Kill Shakespeare. Written by **Anthony Del Col** and **Connor McCreery**. Illustrated by **Andy Belanger**. IDW Publishing, 2010–2015. O

> William Shakespeare's characters come together in these three stories. In the original 12-part tale, Hamlet encounters Juliet, Othello, and Falstaff

© Kill Shakespeare Entertainment.

fighting the forces of Richard III and Lady Macbeth. The villain's goal—the wizard known as Shakespeare. Various other characters appear, including Romeo and Iago, with the loyalties of the latter being in doubt. In the first sequel, The Tide of Blood, the heroes must defeat the plans of the wizard, Prospero, while in The Mask of Night they are aboard a ship captained by the masked pirate Captain Cesario (and his first mate Viola), which has problems with the warship of Titus Andronicus. The series has been nominated for the Joe Shuster and Harvey Awards, has been adapted for a dramatic reading, and has been turned into a board game. The 12-issue first series has been collected in two volumes, a regular one volume edition and a "Backstage Edition" which includes additional art and story as well as annotations by Shakespearean scholars.

Vol. 1. 2010. 148pp. 978-1-60010-781-8.
Vol. 2. 2011. 148pp. 978-1-61377-025-2.
Vol. 3: Tide of Blood. 2013. 140pp. 978-1-61377-732-9.
Vol. 4: The Mask of Night. 2013. 120pp. 978-1-63140-058-2.
Complete. 2014. 352pp. 978-1-61377-130-3, hardcover.
Backstage Edition, Vol. 1. 2015. 344pp. 978-1-61377-851-7, hardcover.

Lucifer. Written by **Mike Carey** and **Holly Black** (2nd series). Illustrated by **Scott Hampton, Peter Gross**, and various. Vertigo/DC Comics, 2013– . M 🖳

© 2016 DC Comics.

A spin-off from the events from Neil Gaiman's award-winning Sandman series (see entry below). Lucifer Morningstar, the former Lord of Hell, is called back from semi-retirement by Heaven and is promised a prize of his own choosing upon completion of a task that only he can accomplish. The Prince of Darkness' request for the completion of the task rocks the foundations of Heaven and Hell and reignites Lucifer's role in the universe once again. The original series was released in 2001–2007; it was reprinted in a five-volume collection beginning in 2013. A second series was released in 2015 with Holly Black as the writer as Lucifer must solve the mystery about the death of God. Overall, though replacing Neil Gaiman's Sandman is a tall order, Mike Carey's Lucifer series was a smart and well-written spin-off; the plot was loosely adapted into the live-action procedural television show which debuted in 2016 on FOX.

Book 1. 2013. 392pp. 978-1-4012-4026-4.
Book 2. 2013. 416pp. 978-1-4012-4260-2.
Book 3. 2014. 400pp. 978-1-4012-4260-2.
Book 4. 2014. 392pp. 978-1-4012-4605-1.
Book 5. 2014. 352pp. 978-1-4012-4945-8.
Vol. 1. 2016. 144pp. 978-1-4012-6193-1.
Vol. 2. 2016. 144pp. 978-1-4012-6541-0.
Vol. 3. 2017. 128pp. 978-1-4012-7139-8.

Murder Mysteries. Written by **Neil Gaiman**. Adapted and Illustrated by **P. Craig Russell**. Dark Horse Comics, 2014. 112pp. 978-1-61655-330-2, hardcover. O

Adapted from the short story by Neil Gaiman. An elderly man recounts an old tale to a young Englishman while sharing a park bench in the city of Los Angeles. Borrowing

a cigarette from the young man, he tells him a story of God's city of angels and the first death that ever occurred. Raguel, the Angel of Vengeance, is sent to investigate the brutal murder of the angel Carasel who was in charge of handling the concept of death. The angel was stabbed in the back and God has assigned Raguel to discover who committed the crime. Like any good crime detective, Raguel questions several angelic suspects including the angels Seraquel, Phanuel, and Lucifer, the Captain to the Host, to solve the crime. Will the Angel of Vengeance be able to exact revenge, or was the murder of Carasel preordained by someone in the city of angels? The deluxe second edition of this book includes bonus material from P. Craig Russell.

Miss Peregrine's Home for Peculiar Children: The Graphic Novel. Written by **Ransom Riggs**. Illustrated by **Cassandra Jean**. Yen Press, 2013. 272pp. 978-0-316-24528-9, hardcover. T 🎬

> An adaptation of the 2011 novel. Sixteen-year-old Jacob Portman travels to Wales to learn more about his late grandfather who was recently killed by what could best be described as a monster. He finds out that his grandfather was raised at an orphanage home for "peculiar children." Jacob meets Emma, a pretty girl who can manipulate fire and is able to use time travel to take Jacob back to the 1940s and meet Miss Peregrine, the orphanage director. He discovers that the location is stuck in a time loop and meets the other fascinating children at the orphanage who all have special abilities. Jacob, it seems, has a special ability too—and he is the only one who can see the monstrous beasts called "Hollows"—the same beasts that killed his grandfather. The book was adapted into a live-action movie released in 2016 by director Tim Burton.

Nightmares & Fairy Tales. Written by **Serena Valentino**. Illustrated by **FSc**, **Crab Scrambly**, and **Camilla d'Errico**. SLG Publishing, 2004–2008. O

> Annabelle is a creepy doll that has the history of falling into different children's laps throughout time. She has the unfortunate luck of being a bystander in unspeakable horrors. Ghosts, vampires, and witches are some of the more tame monstrosities Annabelle's keepers have run-ins with. These stories are loosely based off of urban legends and other fairy tales. Unlike most modern renditions of these stories, the ones told through Annabelle rarely end happily.

> *Once Upon a Time*. 2004. 160pp. 978-0-943151-87-8.
> *Beautiful Beasts*. 2005. 24pp. 978-1-59362-018-9.
> *1140 Rue Royale*. 2007. 176pp. 978-1-59362-065-3.
> *Dancing with the Ghosts of Whales*. 2008. 144pp. 978-1-59362-132-2.

Promethea. Written by **Alan Moore**. Illustrated by **J.H. Williams III**. America's Best Comics/WildStorm Productions/DC Comics, 2009–2011. O 🎗

> Drawn into the mystery of the mythical warrior called Promethea, college student Sophie Bangs uncovers its secret and is magically transformed into

Promethea, the living embodiment of imagination. One in a long line of women bonded through the magical realm called the Immateria, she must learn to focus her power and to fight the ancient evil that has plagued Prometheas before her for centuries. The short story "Sex, Stars, and Serpents" (collected in Volume 2) was awarded an Eisner Award for the category of Best Single Issues/Best Short Story. The series has also won a Harvey Award for Best Writer in 2001 and 2003. The collection *Book 1* received recognition by YALSA's Popular Paperbacks for Young Adults committee in 2002 on the *Graphic Novels: Superheroes and Beyond* list. In 2009 the first of three Absolute Edition collections of the series was released, with the last volume published in late 2011.

Absolute Promethea. 2009–2011.
Book One. 2009. 328pp. 978-1-4012-2372-4.
Book Two. 2010. 328pp. 978-1-4012-2842-2.
Book Three. 2011. 328pp. 978-1-4012-2947-4.

The Sandman. Written by **Neil Gaiman**. Illustrated by various. Vertigo/DC Comics, 2010–2012, new printings. M 🎬 ◎

© 2016 DC Comics.

Dream, the lord of the mystical dream realm we all share at night time (aptly called "The Dreaming"), is one of the few god-like beings known as The Endless. His brothers and sisters are Death, Destruction, Delirium, Destiny, Despair, and Desire. Morpheus, as Dream is also called, rebuilds his realm after a long imprisonment and then takes the path of redemption, rescuing his once-beloved from Hell and saving his only son, Orpheus, from a fate far worse than death. Sacrifices are made, hard decisions are handed down, and Dream must make a choice in the end that will shake his realm. Gaiman's series is a literate and groundbreaking exercise in storytelling and one of the most highly praised graphic novel series published. The series was originally published in comic book form from 1989 to 1995. The series has won numerous awards and recognition. The series has won Eisner Awards for Best Continuing Series (1991–1993), Best Single Issue/Single Story (1992), Best Graphic Album—Reprint (1991) for *The Doll's House*, Best Writer (1991–1994), and Best Artist/Penciller/Inker (1993, 1997) for P. Craig Russell's and Charles Vess's work in the series. The series has also won Harvey Awards for Best Writer (1991–1992) and for Best Continuing or Limited Series (1993). The series has also been recognized by YALSA's Popular Paperbacks for Young Adults committee in 1997 for the collections of *Dream Country* and *World's End*. In 2006, DC Comics reprinted the original 10-volumes series in its Absolute hardcover format that included new coloring and a slipcase for all five volumes, and in 2010 the paperback editions of the series were also reissued and recolored. In addition, a four-volume *Annotated Sandman* was published, reprinting the stories in black and white alongside annotations by Leslie S. Klinger, but it is not included in this annotation.

Vol. 1: Preludes and Nocturnes. Illustrated by **Sam Kieth**, **Mike Dringenberg**, and **Malcolm Jones III**. 2010. 240pp. 978-1-4012-2575-9.
Vol. 2: The Doll's House. Illustrated by **Mike Dringenberg** and **Malcolm Jones III**. 2010. 232pp. 978-1-4012-2799-9.

Vol. 3: Dream Country. Illustrated by **Kelley Jones**, **Colleen Doran**, **Charles Vess**, and **Malcolm Jones III**. 2010. 160pp. 978-1-4012-2935-1.

Vol. 4: Season of Mists. Illustrated by **Kelley Jones** and **Mike Dringenberg**. 2011. 224pp. 978-1-4012-3042-5.

Vol. 5: A Game of You. Illustrated by **Shawn McManus**, **Colleen Doran**, and **Bryan Talbot**. 2011. 192pp. 978-1-4012-3043-2.

Vol. 6: Fables and Reflections. Illustrated by **P. Craig Russell**, **Bryan Talbot**, **Shawn McManus**, **Jill Thompson**, and others. 2011. 168pp. 978-1-4012-3123-1.

Vol. 7: Brief Lives. Illustrated by **Jill Thompson** and **Vince Locke**. 2011. 168pp. 978-1-4012-3263-4.

Vol. 8: Worlds' End. Illustrated by **Mike Allred**, **Gary Amano**, **Mark Buckingham**, **Dick Giordano**, **Tony Harris**, **Steve Leialoha**, **Vince Locke**, **Shea Anton Pensa**, **Alec Stevens**, **Bryan Talbot**, **John Watkiss**, and **Michael Zulli**. 2012. 168pp. 978-1-4012-3402-7.

Vol. 9: *The Kindly Ones*. Illustrated by **Marc Hempel**. 2012. 320pp. 978-1-4012-3545-1.

Vol. 10: *The Wake*. Illustrated by **Michael Zulli**, **John J. Muth**, and **Charles Vess**. 2012. 192pp. 978-1-4012-3754-7.

Absolute Sandman, 2007–2011.

Vol. 1. 2007. 612pp. 978-1-4012-1082-3, hardcover.
Vol. 2. 2007. 616pp. 978-1-4012-1083-0, hardcover.
Vol. 3. 2008. 616pp. 978-1-4012-1084-7, hardcover.
Vol. 4. 2008. 608pp. 978-1-4012-1085-4, hardcover.
Vol. 5. 2011. 520pp. 978-1-4012-3202-3, hardcover.

The Sandman: Dream Hunters. Written by **Neil Gaiman**. Adapted and Illustrated by **P. Craig Russell**. Vertigo/DC Comics, 2009–2010. 2009. 144pp. 978–1401224240, hardcover; 2010. 978-1-4012-2428-8. M 🏅

An adaptation of a prose short story written by Neil Gaiman and originally illustrated by Yoshitako Amano in 1999. Handled by the incomparable P. Craig Russell, the adaptation tells the tale of a fox and a badger who seek to drive a monk from his temple. When both lose, the fox instead falls in love with the monk. When the monk's life is in danger, the fox asks for help from the King of All Night's Dreaming to save the monk. The adaptation was recognized by YALSA as a 2010 Great Graphic Novel for Teens.

The Sandman: Endless Nights. Written by **Neil Gaiman**. Illustrated by various. 2013. 168pp. 978-1-4012-4233-6. M 🏅

A collection of short stories each focusing on a member of the Endless. The collection features the work of Glenn Fabry, Milo Manara, Dave McKean, Miguelanxo Prado, Frank Quitely, P. Craig Russell, Bill Sienkiewicz, and

Barron Storey. Each artist was handpicked by Neil Gaiman to match the corresponding Endless family member with breathtaking results. The short story "Death" won several 2004 Eisner Awards for Best Short Story and Best Anthology.

The Sandman: Overture. Written by **Neil Gaiman**. Illustrated by **J.H. Williams III**. Vertigo/DC Comics, 2015. 224pp. 978-1401248963. M ◉

In the first few pages of *The Sandman* #1 published in 1988, Dream was first introduced as being imprisoned by an occultist who had sought to capture Death, but instead captured her brother, Dream. Now 27 years later, Neil Gaiman finally tells the tale that led to Morpheus's imprisonment.

© 2016 DC Comics.

Three Shadows. Written and Illustrated by **Cyril Pedrosa**. First Second Books, 2008. 272pp. 978-1-59643-239-0. O ◉

The idyllic country life is filled with fun and adventurous days for young Joachim and his parents, Louis and Lise. They tend the orchards but enjoy spending their time together as a family. When three fates appear on the horizon, Louis knows who they have come for, Joachim. Louis is on the run with his son, desperately trying to stay one step ahead of the deathly shadows and save his boy. The story was inspired by the death of a close friend's young child.

Troll Bridge. Written by **Neil Gaiman**. Adapted and Illustrated by **Colleen Doran**. Dark Horse Comics, 2016. 64pp. 978-1-5067-0008-3, hardcover. O

An adaptation of the short story by Neil Gaiman. When a young boy full of imagination wanders in his woods near his home he comes across a troll under the bridge. The troll demands his soul but the boy convinces him to wait until he's older and has experienced life more. As the years pass, he meets the troll again and again – staving off having his soul supped in order to experience life more. In the end though, can a man avoid his destiny and will he go willingly after a lifetime of regrets?

Wayward. Written by **Jim Zub**. Illustrated by **Steve Cummings**. Image Comics, 2015– . M

When Rori Lane decides to leave her life in Ireland behind and start a new life with her mother in Japan, she unknowingly attracts the interest of ancient creatures from Japanese mythology. After being rescued by a powered girl named Akane, Rori discovers she has a super-power and soon falls in with a small band of teenage "misfits" who possess other incredible powers. As Rori learns to cope and deal with her emerging powers, Rori realized that there's more to the mysterious land of Japan than Rori ever dreamt.

Vol. 1: String Theory. 2015. 144pp. 978-1-63215-173-5.

Vol. 2. Ties That Bind. 2015. 136pp. 978-1-63215-403-3.
Vol. 3: *Out of the Shadows*. 2016. 128pp. 978-1-63215-701-0.
Vol. 4: Threads and Portents. 2017. 136pp. 978-1-5343-0053-8.
Deluxe Edition, Vol. 1. 2016. 300pp. 978-1-63215-473-6, hardcover.
Deluxe Edition, Vol. 2. 2017. 320pp. 978-1-5343-0217-4, hardcover.

Will o' the Wisp. Written by **Tom Hammock**. Illustrated by **Megan Hutchison**. Archaia/Boom! Studios, 2013. 216pp. 978-1-936393-78-7, hardcover. T

Young Aurora Grimeon is sent to live with her estranged grandfather after her parents die from a mushroom poisoning. Her grandfather's home is deep in the southern swamps at Ossuary Isle, where many graves and mausoleums are kept nearby. While on the island she befriends her grandfather's pet raccoon Missy and witnesses the odd assortment of characters and Hoodoo magic practitioners that maintain the tombstones and mausoleums. When ghostly disturbances start to happen and the island residents are starting to disappear, Aurora must solve the mystery before more disturbing secrets are revealed.

Chapter 5

Horror

The horror comic book, the crown prince of comic books in the 1950s, has had a huge resurgence in the last few decades. Readers love a good scare, and publishers, writers, and artists love to delve into that bloody, rich pool of horrific inspiration that was once one of the most popular genres in comic book history. Horror Comics, once a thriving source of imagination in the 1950s with titles like EC Comics' *Tales from the Crypt* and *Vault of Horror*, was shunned during the rise of the self-governing Comics Code of Authority (CCA) in 1954. After that, comics were forbidden the depictions of "excessive violence" as well as "lurid, unsavory, gruesome illustrations." Vampires, werewolves, ghouls, and zombies could not be portrayed, and comics could not use the words "horror" or "terror" in their titles. It took time, but comic books found ways to work around the CCA—books like DC Comics' *Swamp Thing* #29 in 1984 was one of the first horror comics to circumvent needing approval for a mainstream comic and by issue #30, DC Comics had not bothered to have the CCA approve its more mature titles. This move helped to pave way for DC Comics' mature line of titles under its Vertigo imprint, which became the home to titles like *John Constantine: Hellblazer* and Neil Gaiman's *Sandman* (see the fantasy chapter). The Vertigo imprint's rise in sophisticated storytelling embracing elements of horror and fantasy helped to give rise to the large influx of creative publishing companies from Dark Horse Comics, Image Comics, Oni Press, and newer companies including Boom! Studios and IDW Publishing. Soon, many companies bit by bit ignored the CCA until it was defunct in 2011. Image Comics' runaway hit zombie series The Walking Dead (2003) by Robert Kirkman is a prime example of an independently published comic book series becoming so popular that it was one of the first in a wave of zombie genre fiction alongside prose fiction titles like Max Brooks's *Zombie Survival* Guide (2003) that helped pave the way for the glut of zombie fandom of the last decade. The Walking Dead, of course, is the king and has been adapted into a runaway horror show with a spin-off on the AMC cable network. Since then, many other publishers have embraced the horror format with the same intensity as that of Kirkman's series. Nowadays, many publishers large and small have incorporated horror titles into their catalog where you're almost bound to find a story involving a vampire, zombie, or ghoul and able to cater it to a wide variety of age levels. Included in this section are many titles for a wide level of age groups that have incorporated many of the elements common in a horror series.

Note that the Horror genre has much in common with the Dark Fantasy subgenre of the fantasy chapter, and many titles listed in that subgenre will easily appeal to horror readers. Also note that tales featuring genre-blending titles are listed in other chapters. A section on "Weird Westerns" in which some Western horror titles are listed in the "Westerns" section of the action/adventure chapter and the humor chapter features a genre-blend subgenre on Humorous Horror.

Supernatural Heroes

Heroes can come in all shapes and sizes. Some heroes even are vampires, devils, demons, ghosts, or other beasties from the supernatural world. Despite how they may appear on the outside, their hearts are still pure and good. Below are listed titles featuring paranormal fighters who battle against the forces of evil. Though tied closely with the Super-Hero genre, the tales focus on individuals or a group of heroes who typically are either born or gifted with superhuman or even inhuman power and use it to fight monsters, ghosts, the forces of the occult, common criminals on occasion, and more. Mike Mignola's *Hellboy* series is an excellent example of this genre.

Abe Sapien. Written by **Mike Mignola**, **Scott Allie**, and **John Arcudi**. Illustrated by **Jason Shawn Alexander**, **Sebastian Fiumara**, and **Max Fiumara**. Dark Horse Comics, 2008– . O

Abe Sapien TM © Mike Mignola.

Spun off from the pages of *Hellboy*, Abe Sapien is a man like no other. Born Langdon Everett Caul over 220 years ago in Victorian England, a mystical encounter with an aquatic deity transformed him into a fish-human hybrid. Near immortal, he was recovered by the Bureau for Paranormal Research and Defense (BPRD) where he became a trusted ally of Hellboy and the other paranormal members of the team. Striking on his own, Abe continues to fight against the paranormal and those strange things that go bump in the night.

Vol. 1: The Drowning. 2008. 144pp. 978-1-59582-185-0.
Vol. 2: The Devil Does Not Jest. 2012. 144pp. 978-1-59582-925-2.
Vol. 3: Dark and Terrible and the New Race of Man. 2013. 144pp. 978-1-61655-284-8.
Vol. 4: The Shape of Things to Come. 2014. 144pp. 978-1-61655-443-9.
Vol. 5: Sacred Places. 2015. 144pp. 978-1-61655-515-3.
Vol. 6: A Darkness So Great. 2016. 144pp. 978-1-61655-656-3.
Vol. 7: The Secret Fire 2016. 168pp 978-1-61655-891-8.
Vol. 8: The Desolate Shore. 2017. 168pp. 978-1-5067-0031-1.
Vol. 9: Lost Lives and Other Stories. 2017. 144pp. 978-1-5067-0220-9.

The Amazing Screw-On Head and Other Curious Objects. Written and Illustrated by **Mike Mignola.** Dark Horse. 2010. 104pp. 978-1-59582-501-8. T 🎗️

There are dark forces threatening the United States of America during the Civil War, and the most dangerous threats did not come from the Confederates. Abraham Lincoln sends out his most trusted hero, the Amazing Screw-On Head, to fight the forces of evil. Screw-On Head chooses the right robotic body to be screwed onto for the right type of job. Screw-On Head must stop the evil emperor Zombie from obtaining a powerful ancient artifact that grants supernatural powers to the holder. The other short stories include a tale of a world conqueror before he had the supernatural artifact, a witch, and a ghost who thwarts a Martian invasion. A YALSA Great Graphic Novels for Teens title in 2011.

Baltimore. Written by **Mike Mignola** and **Christopher Golden**. Illustrated by **Ben Stenbeck** and **Peter Bergting**. Dark Horse Comics, 2011– . T

Baltimore TM and © 2016 Mike Mignola and Christopher Golden.

Captain Lord Henry Baltimore led his men on a night attack during the height of World War I. When his entire squad is killed in battle by enemy fire and he's left for dead, Baltimore finds himself face to face with a giant bat feeding off the dead and promptly wounds the creature, scaring it with his bayonet. Little does Baltimore realize that the bat was a vampire known as the Red King, who unleashes a plague of vampirism across England that has claimed Baltimore's wife and loved one. Now Baltimore becomes a man hell-bent on destroying the vampire plague that has destroyed his life and no vampire will stand in his way.

Vol. 1: The Plague of Ships. 2011. 144pp. 978-1-59582-673-2, hardcover.

Vol. 2: The Curse Bells. 2012. 144pp. 978-1-59582-674-9, hardcover.

Vol. 3: The Passing Stranger and Other Stories. 2013. 152pp. 978-1-61655-182-7, hardcover.

Vol. 4: Chapel of Bones. 2014. 144pp. 978-1-61655-328-9, hardcover.

Vol. 5: The Apostle and the Witch of Harju. 2015. 144pp. 978-1-61655-618-1, hardcover.

Vol. 6: The Cult and the Red King. 2016. 144pp. 978-1-61655-821-5, hardcover.

Vol. 7: Empty Graves. 2016. 144pp. 978-1-5067-0042-7, hardcover.

Beasts of Burden: Animal Rites. Written by **Evan Dorkin**. Illustrated by **Jill Thompson**. Dark Horse Comics, 2010. T 🎗️ ◎

The picturesque sleepy town of Burden Hill has a dark secret. Behind the white picket fences and green grasses lurks a disturbing secret—evil is alive and well hanging in the shadows of the quaint houses, and only the unique paranormal team of dogs—and one cat—are all that stands in their way. Pugs, Ace, Jack, Whitey, Red, and the Orphan—whose early experiences with the paranormal have led them to become members of the Wise Dog Society, official animal agents sworn to protect their town from evil. Will the four-legged heroes be enough to take on the growing supernatural menaces threatening

© 2013 Evan Dorkin and Jill Thompson).

their town of Burden Hill? The series received many accolades including Eisner Awards for Best Short Story, Best Painter, Best Publication for Teens, as well as a Harvey Award for Best Graphic Album Previously Published.

B.P.R.D. Written by **Mike Mignola** and **John Arcudi**. Illustrated by various. Dark Horse Comics, 2003– . T 🎬 ◎

B.P.R.D.™ © 2016 Mike Mignola.

When things go bump in the night, the Bureau for Paranormal Research and Defense (B.P.R.D) is the secret government organization that is there to bump back. Spun off from the pages of Mike Mignola's *Hellboy*, the team features the aquatic creature Abe Sabien, Roger the Homunculus, firestarter Liz Sherman, psychic Johann Kraus, Lobster Johnson, and other odd agents to confront the mysterious paranormal and the monstrous evils that are out there. The bureau was featured in the *Hellboy* films from 2004 and 2008 as well as two Hellboy animated specials. The *Plague of Frogs* omnibus collections reprint the original 14 volumes in 4 voluminous collections. The series was renamed <u>B.P.R.D.: Hell on Earth</u> in 2011.

Vol. 1: Hollow Earth and Other Stories. 2003. 120pp. 978-1-56971-862-9.
Vol. 2: The Soul of Venice and Other Stories. 2004. 128pp. 978-1-59307-132-5.
Vol. 3: A Plague of Frogs. 2005. 144pp. 978-1-59307-288-9.
Vol. 4: The Dead. 2005. 152pp. 978-1-59307-380-0.
Vol. 5: The Black Flame. 2006. 168pp. 978-1-59307-550-7.
Vol. 6: The Universal Machine. 2006. 144pp. 978-1-59307-710-5.
Vol. 7: The Garden of Souls. 2008. 146pp. 978-1-59307-882-9.
Vol. 8: Killing Ground. 2008. 140pp. 978-1-59307-956-7.
Vol. 9: 1946. 2008. 144pp. 978-1-59582-191-1.
Vol. 10: The Warning. 2009. 152pp. 978-1-59582-304-5.
Vol. 11: Black Goddess. 2009. 152pp. 978-1-59582-411-0.
Vol. 12: War on Frogs. 2010. 144pp. 978-1-59582-480-6.
Vol. 13: 1947. 2010. 160pp. 978-1-59582-478-3.
Vol. 14: King of Fear. 2010. 144pp. 978-1-59582-564-3.
Being Human. 2011. 152pp. 978-1-59582-756-2.
B.P.R.D.: 1946–1948. 2015. 472pp. 978-1-61655-646-4, hardcover.
B.P.R.D.: 1948. 2013. 144pp. 978-1-61655-183-4.
Hell on Earth, Vol. 1: New World. 2011. 144pp. 978-1-59582-707-4.

Hell on Earth, Vol. 2: Gods and Monsters. 2012. 978-1-59582-822-4.
Hell on Earth, Vol. 3: Russia. 2012. 160pp. 978-1-59582-946-7.
Hell on Earth, Vol. 4: The Devil's Engine and the Long Death. 2012. 176pp. 978-1-59582-981-8.
Hell on Earth, Vol. 5: The Pickens County Horror and Others. 2013. 152pp. 978-1-61655-140-7.
Hell on Earth, Vol. 6: The Return of the Master. 2013. 144pp. 978-1-61655-193-3.
Hell on Earth, Vol. 7: A Cold Day in Hell. 2014. 144pp. 978-1-61655-199-5.
Hell on Earth, Vol. 8: Lake of Fire. 2014. 144pp. 978-1-61655-402-6.
Hell on Earth, Vol. 9: Reign of the Black Flame. 2014. 144pp. 978-1-61655-471-2.
Hell on Earth, Vol. 10: The Devil's Wings. 2014. 144pp. 978-1-61655-617-4.
Hell on Earth, Vol. 11: Flesh and Stone. 2015. 144pp. 978-1-61655-762-1.
Hell on Earth, Vol. 12: Metamorphosis. 2015. 144pp. 978-1-61655-794-2.
Hell on Earth, Vol. 13: End of Days. 2016. 144pp. 978-1-61655-910-6.
Hell on Earth, Vol. 14: The Exorcist. 2016. 144pp. 978-1-5067-0011-3.
Hell on Earth, Vol. 15: Cometh the Hour. 2017. 144pp. 978-1-5067-0131-8.
Hellboy and the B.P.R.D.: 1952. 2015. 144pp. 978-1-61655-660-0.
Hellboy and the B.P.R.D.: 1953. 2016. 160pp. 978-1-61655-967-0.
Plague of Frogs, Vol. 1. 2014. 408pp. 978-1-59582-675-6, hardcover.
Plague of Frogs, Vol. 2. 2015. 456pp. 978-1-59582-676-3, hardcover.
Plague of Frogs, Vol. 3. 2015. 456pp. 978-1-61655-622-8, hardcover.
Plague of Frogs, Vol. 4. 2015. 456pp. 978-1-61655-641-9, hardcover.
Vampire. 2013. 144pp. 978-1-61655-196-4.

Buffy the Vampire Slayer/Angel/Spike

Created by **Joss Whedon**. Written and Illustrated by various. Dark Horse Comics, 2006–; IDW Publishing, 2006–2011. T 🎭 🖥

Listed below are adaptations of the hit TV series <u>Buffy the Vampire Slayer</u> that aired from 1997 to 2003 as well as the spin-off series <u>Angel</u> (1999–2004) featuring the vampire with a soul named Angel. "In every generation there is a Chosen One. She alone will stand against the vampires, the demons, and the forces of darkness. She is the Slayer." In this generation, the slayer is Buffy Summers, a hip high school cheerleader now saddled with a bigger responsibility than setting fashion trends. She puts her life on the line every night to save the world from bloodsuckers and other demons, while trying to be a normal teenager by day. Once the series ended, Dark Horse Comics continued with new "seasons" authorized and occasionally written by Buffy creator Joss Whedon. Listed below are the collections up through "Season 10." "Season 11" began in comic book form in late 2016, with collections beginning in 2017. The spin-off series <u>Angel</u> was first licensed by Dark Horse and then went to IDW, where, along with various limited series, there was an ongoing series originally subtitled <u>After the Fall</u> which told what happened after the series finale. Angel then returned to Dark Horse Comics, teaming up with the other slayer, Faith. There have also been collections of comics from IDW and Dark Horse featuring bad-vampire-turned-good Spike.

Buffy the Vampire Slayer. Dark Horse Comics, 2006– .

Below are listed the various Buffy the Vampire Slayer comic books published by Dark Horse Comics. The series is still ongoing even though the original show has been off the air since 2003.

Buffy the Vampire Slayer Omnibus. Written by **Andi Watson**, **Christopher Golden**, and various. Illustrated by various. 2007–2009.

These collect the original <u>Buffy the Vampire Slayer</u> series as well as several limited series, one-shots, and original graphic novels. The stories are told in the chronology of the stories, which is not always the same order as when the original comics were released.

Vol. 1. 2007. 408pp. 978-1-59307-784-6.
Vol. 2. 2007. 408pp. 978-1-59307-826-3.
Vol. 3. 2008. 320pp. 978-1-59307-885-0.
Vol. 4. 2008. 408pp. 978-1-59307-968-0.
Vol. 5. 2008. 408pp. 978-1-59582-225-3.
Vol. 6. 2009. 368pp. 978-1-59582-242-0.
Vol. 7. 2009. 408pp. 978-1-59582-331-1.

Buffy the Vampire Slayer: Season Eight. Written by **Joss Whedon**, **Brian K. Vaughan**, **Karl Moline**, and **Jane Espenson**. Illustrated by **Georges Jeanty** and various. 2008–2011.

Vol. 1: The Long Way Home. 2008. 136pp. 978-1-59307-822-5.
Vol. 2: No Future for You. 2008. 136pp. 978-1-59307-963-5.
Vol. 3: Wolves at the Gate. 2008. 136pp. 978-1-59582-165-2.
Vol. 4: Time of Your Life. 2009. 136pp. 978-1-59582-310-6.
Vol. 5: Predators and Prey. 2009. 136pp. 978-1-59582-342-7.
Vol. 6: Retreat. 2010. 136pp. 978-1-59582-415-8.
Vol. 7: Twilight. 2010. 136pp. 978-1-59582-558-2.
Vol. 8: Last Gleaming. 2011. 136pp. 978-1-59582-610-7.

Buffy the Vampire Slayer: Season Eight Library Edition. 2012–2013.

Vol. 1. 2012. 320pp. 978-1-59582-888-0, hardcover.
Vol. 2. 2012. 320pp. 978-1-59582-935-1, hardcover.
Vol. 3. 2012. 320pp. 978-1-59582-978-8, hardcover.
Vol. 4. 2013. 320pp. 978-1-61655-127-8, hardcover.

Buffy the Vampire Slayer: Season Nine. Written by **Joss Whedon**, **Andrew Chamblis**, **Jane Espenson** and various. Illustrated by **George Jeanty** and various. 2012–2014.

> *Vol. 1: Freefall.* 2012. 136pp. 978-1-59582-922-1.
> *Vol. 2: On Your Own.* 2012. 136pp. 978-1-59582-990-0.
> *Vol. 3: Guarded.* 2013. 136pp. 978-1-61655-099-8.
> *Vol. 4: Welcome to the Team.* 2013. 136pp. 978-1-61655-166-7.
> *Vol. 5: The Core.* 2014. 136pp. 978-1-61655-254-1.

Buffy the Vampire Slayer: Season Nine Library Edition. 2015.

> *Vol. 1.* 2015. 304pp. 978-1-61655-715-7, hardcover.
> *Vol. 2.* 2015. 288pp. 978-1-61655-716-4, hardcover.
> *Vol. 3.* 2015. 304pp. 978-1-61655-717-1, hardcover.

Buffy the Vampire Slayer: Season Ten. Written by **Christos Gage**, **Nicholas Brendon**, and various. Illustrated by **Rebekah Isaacs** and various. 2015–2016.

> *Vol. 1: New Rules.* 2015. 136pp. 978-1-61655-490-3.
> *Vol. 2: I Wish.* 2015. 136pp. 978-1-61655-600-6.
> *Vol. 3: Love Dares You.* 2015. 136pp. 978-1-61655-758-4.
> *Vol. 4: Old Demons.* 2016. 136pp. 978-1-61655-802-4.
> *Vol. 5: In Pieces on the Ground.* 2016. 136pp. 978-161655-944-1.
> *Vol. 6: Own It.* 2016. 136pp. 978-1-5067-0034-2.

Buffy the Vampire Slayer: The High School Years. Written by **Faith Erin Hicks** and **Kel McDonald.** Illustrated by **Yishan Li**. Dark Horse Comics, 2016– . 🦃

A new Buffy series that is set during the first season of the show. Buffy Summers must balance being the slayer as well as a high school student! The series is written by fan-favorite creator Faith Erin Hicks. The first volume was on YALSA's 2017 Great Graphic Novels for Teens list.

> *Vol. 1: Freaks & Geeks.* 2016. 80pp. 978-1-61655-667-9.
> *Vol. 2: Glutton for Punishment.* 2016. 80pp. 978-1-50670-115-8.
> *Vol. 3: Parental Parasite.* 2017. 80pp. 978-1-50670-304-6.

Angel. Created by **Joss Whedon**. Written and Illustrated by various. Dark Horse Comics, 2000–2002, 2011–; IDW Publishing, 2006–2011. T

An adaptation of the hit TV series. Who says vampires have no souls? Angelus, a vampire feared like no other, was cursed by gypsies with the return of his soul. Now he lives in torment over the pain he caused to countless innocent people while he was enjoying the art of the kill. Still with vampire strength and immortality, his new mission is to save as many victims of demonic crime as he can, and possibly himself as well. In 2006, IDW Publishing took over the license for the character, but it has since reverted back to Dark Horse Comics in 2011.

Angel (1st series). Written by **Jeff Marriotte**, **Scott Lobdell**, **John Byrne**, **Scott Tipton**, **Mariah Huehne**r, and various. Illustrated by **David Messina**, **Elena Casagrande**, **John Byrne**, and **Franco Urru**. IDW Publishing, 2006–2011.

> *The Curse.* 2006. 120pp. 978-1-93323-979-8.
> *Auld Lang Syne.* 2007 128pp. 978-1-60010-063-5.

Angel Omnibus. 2008–2011.

> *Vol. 1.* 2008. 488pp. 978-1-60010-270-7.
> *Vol. 2.* 2011. 442pp. 978-1-60010-968-3.

Smile Time. 2009. 184pp. 978-1-60010-481-7.
Only Human. 2010. 152pp. 978-1-60010-597-5.
Illyria Haunted. 2011. 104pp. 978-1-60010-933-1.
The John Byrne Collection. 2011. 160pp. 978-1-60010-892-1, hardcover.
Barbary Coast. 2010. 88pp. 978-1-60010-769-6.
A Hole in the World. 2010. 120pp. 978-1-60010-704-7.

Angel: *After the Fall/Angel* (2nd series). Written by **Mariah Huehner**, **Joss Whedon**, **Brian Lynch**, **Bill Willingham**, and various. Illustrated by **Franco Urru**, **Stephen Mooney**, **Nick Runge**, **Brian Denham**, and various. IDW Publishing, 2008–2011. Note: Due to a title change the last three volumes were listed as *Angel*, vols. 1–3.

> *Angel: After the Fall.* 2008–2010.
>
> > *Vol. 1.* 2008. 192pp. 978-1-60010-181-6, hardcover; 2009. 978-1-60010-343-8.
> > *Vol. 2. First Night.* 2008. 104pp. 978-1-60010-231-8, hardcover; 2009. 978-1-60010-393-3.
> > *Vol. 3.* 2009. 192pp. 978-1-60010-377-3, hardcover; 2011. 978-1-61377-059-7.
> > *Vol. 4.* 2009. 132pp. 978-1-60010-461-9, hardcover; 2011. 978-1-61377-100-6.
> > *Vol. 5. Aftermath.* 2009. 132pp. 978-1-60010-516-6, hardcover.
> > *Vol. 6. Angel in Hell.* 2010. 192pp. 978-1-60010-732-0, hardcover.
>
> *Angel.* 2010–2011.
>
> > *Vol. 1: Immortality for Dummies.* 2010. 132pp. 978-1-60010-689-7, hardcover.
> > *Vol. 2: The Crown Prince Syndrome.* 2010. 152pp. 978-1-60010-789-4, hardcover.
> > *Vol. 3: The Wolf, the Ram, and the Heart.* 2011. 152pp. 978-1-60010-944-7, hardcover.

Angel & Faith (3rd series). Written by **Christos Gage**. Illustrated by **Dan Jackson** and **Rebekah Isaacs**. Dark Horse Comics, 2012–2014.

> *Vol. 1: Live through This.* 2012. 136pp. 978-1-59582-887-3.
> *Vol. 2: Daddy Issues.* 2012. 136pp. 978-1-59582-960-3.
> *Vol. 3: Family Reunion.* 2013. 136pp. 978-1-61655-079-0.
> *Vol. 4: Death and Consequences.* 2013. 136pp. 978-1-61655-165-0.
> *Vol. 5: What You Want, Not What You Need.* 2014. 136pp. 978-1-61655-253-4.

> **Angel & Faith, Season 9: Library Edition.**
>
> *Vol. 1.* 2015. 280pp. 978-1-61655-712-6, hardcover.
> *Vol. 2.* 2015. 280pp. 978-1-61655-713-3, hardcover.
> *Vol. 3.* 2015. 288pp. 978-1-61655-714-0, hardcover.

Angel & Faith Season Ten (4th series). Written by **Victor Gischler**. Illustrated by **Will Conrad**. Dark Horse Comics, 2015–2016.

> *Vol. 1: Where the River Meets the Sea.* 2015. 136pp. 978-1-61655-503-0.
> *Vol. 2: Lost and Found.* 2015. 136pp. 978-1-61655-601-3.

Vol. 3: United. 2015. 136pp. 978-1-61655-766-9.
Vol. 4: A Little More Than Kin. 2016. 136pp. 978-1-61655-890-1.
Vol. 5: A Tale of Two Families. 2016. 136pp. 978-1-61655-965-6.

Angel Omnibus. Written by **Joss Whedon** and various. Illustrated by various. Dark Horse, 2011. 480pp. 978-1-59582-706-7.

Collects Dark Horse's original *Angel* series published by Dark Horse Comics plus additional one-shots.

Spike (1st series). Written by **Peter David**, **Scott Tipton**, **Bill Williams**, **Brian Lynch**, and various. Illustrated by **Fernando Goni**, **Joe Corroney**, **Franco Urru**, **ChrisCross**, and various. IDW Publishing, 2006–2012.

Spike. 2006. 152pp. 978-1-60010-030-7.
Spike vs. Dracula. 2006. 120pp. 978-1-60010-012-3.
Spike: Asylum. 2008. 120pp. 978-1-60010-061-1.
Spike: Shadow Puppets. 2008. 104pp. 978-1-60010-112-0.
Spike: Omnibus. 2009. 444pp. 978-1-60010-539-5.
Spike: After the Fall. 2009. 104pp. 978-1-60010-368-1, hardcover; 978-1-60010-665-1.
Spike: The Devil You Know. 2011. 104pp. 978-1-60010-764-1.
Spike: Alone Together Now. 2011.

Vol. 1. 2011. 104pp. 978-1-60010-908-9, hardcover.
Vol. 2. 2011. 104pp. 978-1-61377-006-1, hardcover.

Spike: The Complete Series. 2012. 200pp. 978-1-61377-285-0.

Spike (2nd series). Dark Horse Comics, 2013– . T

Spike Season Nine: A Dark Place. Written by **Victor Gischler**. Illustrated by **Paul Lee**. 2013. 144pp. 978-1-61655-109-4.
Spike: Into the Light. Written by **James Marsters** and **Laura Martin**. Illustrated by **Steve Morris**. 2014. 72pp. 978-1-61655-421-7.

Criminal Macabre: The Cal McDonald Mysteries. Written by **Steve Niles**. Dark Horse Comics and IDW Publishing, 2003–2012. O

Criminal Macabre: A Cal McDonald Mystery © 2016 Steve Niles.

Cal McDonald, an L. A. private eye with a knack for handling supernatural cases and an equal knack for booze and drugs, finds himself in a world of trouble when a simple job of trailing a vagrant vampire leads to a bigger problem than he ever expected: a secret pact between the demonic races and a mystery involving a stolen vial of the deadly bubonic plague and many more hard-boiled horrific adventures. Cal, a skeptical police officer, and the undead ghouls who live in the sewers are all that stand in the way of the total annihilation of humankind. When vampires, zombies, werewolves, and more are at war with humans, there's only one way out: a 12-gauge shotgun, plenty of silver bullets, and a wooden cross.

Dial M for Monster: A Cal McDonald Collection. Illustrated by various. IDW Publishing, 2003. 200pp. 978-1-932382-05-1.

Criminal Macabre: A Cal McDonald Mystery. Written by **Steve Niles**. Illustrated by **Ben Templesmith**. Dark Horse Comics, 2004. 168pp. 978-1-56971-935-0. O.

Last Train to Deadsville: A Cal McDonald Mystery. Illustrated by **Kelley Jones**. Dark Horse Comics, 2005. 144pp. 978-1-59307-107-3.

Two Red Eyes. Illustrated by **Kyle Hotz**. 2007. Dark Horse Comics, 2007. 104pp. 978-1-59307-843-0.

My Demon Baby. Illustrated by **Nick Stakal**. Dark Horse Comics, 2008. 104pp. 978-1-59307-908-6.

Cell Block 666. Illustrated by **Nick Stakal**. Dark Horse Comics, 2009. 104pp. 978-1-59582-408-0.

Criminal Macabre Omnibus. Illustrated by various. Dark Horse Comics, 2011–2012.

>	*Vol. 1*. 2011. 392pp. 978-1-59582-746-3.
>	*Vol. 2*. 2012. 368pp. 978-1-59582-747-0.

Freddy vs. Jason vs. Ash. Written by **Jeff Katz** and **James Kuhoric**. Illustrated by **James Craig**. WildStorm/DC Comics. 2008–2010. M ◼

Based on the screenplay for the abandoned sequel to the 2003 horror film *Freddy vs. Jason*, the battle is under way in three ways when Army of Darkness anti-hero Ash Williams encounters Freddy Krueger and Jason Voorhees. When Crystal Lake's notorious hockey-masked killer Jason is lured by a depowered Freddy Krueger to seek out the infamous book of the dead, the Necronomicon, Ash must battle both villains and try to save the world against the unkillable slasher and the equally powerful nightmare master.

Vol. 1. 2008. 144pp. 978-1-4012-2004-4.

Vol. 2: The Nightmare Warriors. 2010. 144pp. 978-1-4012-2752-4.

Hellboy. Written and Illustrated by **Mike Mignola**. Dark Horse Comics, 2004– . T 🗡 ◼ ◎

Hellboy™ © 2016 Mike Mignola.

Near the end of World War II, the Nazis were trying desperately to gain ground and win the war by any means necessary—including through the occult. In 1944, an infant demon was brought to Earth in order to carry out a fiendish plot by Nazis and a resurrected Rasputin to bring forth chaos and destroy the world. Instead, it was rescued by American soldiers and named "Hellboy." A true red-tailed devil, with horns and all, but raised on Earth by humans, Hellboy is a unique champion—a paranormal hunter with the ethics of a working-class bruiser. With his shaved horn look (to better fit in) and a large stone right hand, Hellboy fights the good fight for the secret government organization known as the Bureau for Paranormal Research and Defense, tackling oddities, monsters, mysteries, ancient myths, and more, alongside his fellow B.P.R.D. companions Liz Sherman, Abe Sapien, Roger the Homunculus, and more. The series has won numerous awards and recognition including several Eisner Awards for Best Graphic Album: Reprint (1995) for *Seed of Destruction*, Best Writer/Artist (1995, 1997–1998), Best Anthology (1998) for the *Hellboy Christmas Special* (reprinted in the collection *The Chained Coffin and Other Stories*), as well as Best Finite Series/Limited Series for the collection *Conqueror Worm*. The series has also received Harvey Awards for Best Artist or Penciller (1995–1996, 2000) and Best Graphic Album of Previously Published Work (1996). The series was also adapted into two Hellboy films *Hellboy*

(2004) and *Hellboy II: The Golden Army* (2008) by director Guillermo del Toro, starring Ron Perlman as Hellboy. For a twisted take on Hellboy and his fellow cast members as kids, see the humor chapter for the *Itty Bitty Hellboy* graphic novel.

Vol. 1: Seed of Destruction. 2004. 128pp. 978-1-59307-094-6.
Vol. 2: Wake the Devil. 2004. 144pp. 978-1-59307-095-3.
Vol. 3: The Chained Coffin and Other Stories. 2004. 168pp. 978-1-59307-091-5.
Vol. 4: The Right Hand of Doom. 2004. 144pp. 1-59307-093-4.
Vol. 5: Conqueror Worm. 2004. 144pp. 978-1-59307-092-2.
Vol. 6: Strange Places. 2006. 128pp. 978-1-59307-475-3.
Vol. 7: The Troll Witch and Others. 2007. 144pp. 978-1-59307-860-7.
Vol. 8: Darkness Calls. 2008. 192pp. 978-1-59307-896-6.
Vol. 9: The Wild Hunt. 2010. 192pp. 978-1-59582-431-8.
Vol. 10: The Crooked Man and Others. 2010. 160pp. 978-1-59582-477-6.
Vol. 11: The Bride of Hell and Others. 2011. 200pp. 978-1-59582-740-1.
Vol. 12: The Storm and the Fury. 2012. 176pp. 978-1-59582-827-9.
House of the Living Dead. 2011. 56pp. 978-1-59582-757-9.
The Midnight Circus. 2013. 56pp. 978-1-61655-238-1.
Hellboy in Hell, Vol. 1: The Descent. 2014. 152pp. 978-1-61655-444-6.
Weird Tales. 2014. 256pp. 978-1-61655-510-8.
Hellboy and the B.P.R.D.: 1952. 2015. 144pp. 978-1-61655-660-0.
Hellboy in Mexico. 2016. 152pp. 978-1-61655-897-0.
Hellboy and the B.P.R.D. 1953. 2016. 160pp 978-1-61655-967-0.
Hellboy in Hell, Vol. 2: The Death Card. 2016. 96pp. 978-1-5067-0113-4.
Into the Silent Sea. 2017. 56pp. 978-1-50670-143-1, hardcover.

Hellboy Animated. Written by **Jim Pascoe**, **Tad Stones**, **Jason Hall**, and **Nate Piekos**. Illustrated by **Rick Lacy** and **Fabio Laguna**. Dark Horse Comics, 2007. Y 🖳

The title *Hellboy Animated* is inspired by a direct-to-DVD animated series, which was originally released in 2006–2007 with two direct-to-DVD animated specials featuring Hellboy, a demon raised by humans, and other members of the Bureau for Paranormal Research including Liz Sherman, Abe Sapien, and Dr. Broom. The team is an unlikely but determined group of agents who must investigate and eliminate the evil beasts and dark forces that haunt our world. The animated series was produced by *Hellboy* creator Mike Mignola and *Hellboy* movie director Guillermo del Toro.

Vol. 1: The Black Wedding. 2007. 80pp. 978-1-59307-700-6.
Vol. 2: The Judgment Bell. 2007. 80pp. 978-1-59307-799-0.
Vol. 3: The Menagerie. 2007. 80pp. 978-1-59307-861-4.

Hoax Hunters. Written by **Michael Moreci** and **Steve Seeley**. Illustrated by **J. M. Ringuet**. Image Comics, 2012–2014. O

Monsters, aliens, cryptids—they aren't real, and the reality show Hoax Hunters is out to prove to their viewers that what goes bump in the night isn't real. Little do the viewers know that the Hoax Hunters are really there to cover up the dark disturbances across the world and keep the world safe from the creeps hiding in the dark.

Vol. 1: Murder, Death, and the Devil. 2012. 160pp. 978-1-60706-657-6.
Vol. 2: Secrets and Lies. 2013. 112pp. 978-1-60706-740-5.
Vol. 3: The Book of Mothman. 2014. 128pp. 2014. 978-1-60706-839-6.

Lobster Johnson. Written by **Mike Mignola** and **John Arcudi**. Illustrated by **Jason Armstrong**, **Tonci Zonjic**, and various. Dark Horse Comics, 2008–2014. T

Spun off from the pages of *Hellboy* and *B.P.R.D.* comes Lobster Johnson! A pulp-style hero reminiscent of novels from the 1920s and 1930s, the gun-blazing vigilante takes on mad scientists, monsters, and threats from the world beyond.

Vol. 1: Iron Prometheus. 2008. 140pp. 978-1-59307-975-8.
Vol. 2: The Burning Hand. 2012. 144pp. 978-1-61655-031-8.
Vol. 3: Satan Smells a Rat. 2014. 144pp. 978-1-61655-203-9.
Vol. 4: Get the Lobster. 2014. 144pp. 978-1-61655-505-4.

The Perhapanauts. Written by **Todd DeZago**. Illustrated by **Craig Rousseau**. Image Comics, 2012–2014. T

When the fabric of reality on Earth shatters and great beasts beyond description break free of their dimensions and enter ours, the organization called Bedlam is there to save the day. Lucky for us Earth's own monsters, Bigfoot, Ghosts, Aliens, Faeries, and Chupacabras, are on our own side. Working for Bedlam, they're called the Perhapanauts, and they're ready to save the Earth from one monster at a time.

Vol. 0: Dark Days. 2010. 240pp. 978-160706-312-4.
Vol. 1: Triangle. 2009. 208pp. 978-1-60706-016-1.
Vol. 2: Treasure Obscura. 2012. 128pp. 978-160706-658-3.
Vol. 3: Danger down Under. 2014. 160pp. 978-160706-849-5.

© 2016 Todd DeZago and Image
Comics

Soul Eater. Written and Illustrated by **Atsushi Ohkubo**. Yen Press, 2009–2015. O Japanese manga. あ ◎

At the Death Weapon Meister Academy, students are called meisters and have demon weapon companions to aid them in combat. The demons are in human form but can transfer their shape into a weapon. The meisters, Maka Albarn, Black Star, and Death the Kid, are in competition to turn their weapons, Soul Eater, Tsubaki, and the Thompson sisters, respectively, into "death scythes" for Lord Death, the Grim Reaper, and the head of the DWMA. The only way the meisters can have their weapons become death scythes is by having their weapons consume the souls of 99 evil humans and one witch.

© 2016 Yen Press and Atsushi
Ohkubo

Vol. 1. 2009. 208pp. 978-0-75953-001-0.
Vol. 2. 2010. 192pp. 978-0-75953-048-5.
Vol. 3. 2010. 192pp. 978-0-75953-064-5.

Vol. 4. 2010. 208pp. 978-0-75953-127-7.
Vol. 5. 2011. 192pp. 978-0-31607-107-9.
Vol. 6. 2011. 192pp. 978-0-31607-109-3.
Vol. 7. 2011. 208pp. 978-0-31607-110-9.

Vol. 8. 2012. 208pp. 978-0-31607-112-3.
Vol. 9. 2012. 208pp. 978-0-31607-113-0.
Vol. 10. 2012. 192pp. 978-0-31607-114-7.
Vol. 11. 2012. 192pp. 978-0-31607-115-4.

Vol. 12. 2013. 192pp. 978-0-31607-293-9.
Vol. 13. 2013. 192pp. 978-0-31623-057-5.
Vol. 14. 2013. 208pp. 978-0-31623-192-3.
Vol. 15. 2013. 192pp. 978-0-31623-490-0.
Vol. 16. 2013. 192pp. 978-0-31624-431-2.
Vol. 17. 2013. 192pp. 978-0-31624-432-9.
Vol. 18. 2014. 192pp. 978-0-31636-899-5.

Vol. 19. 2014. 192pp. 978-0-31640-694-9.
Vol. 20. 2014. 192pp. 978-0-31640-695-6.
Vol. 21. 2014. 192pp. 978-0-31640-696-3.
Vol. 22. 2014. 208pp. 978-0-31640-697-0.
Vol. 23. 2014. 208pp. 978-0-31640-698-7.
Vol. 24. 2015. 192pp. 978-0-31637-793-5.
Vol. 25. 2015. 248pp. 978-0-31637-795-9.

Spawn. Written by **Todd McFarlane**. Illustrated by **Todd McFarlane**, **Greg Capullo**, and various. Image Comics, 2009– . O 🎬 🖥 🎮

Al Simmons was a soldier for the U.S. government but was killed in the line of duty and found his soul in Hell. Given a second chance at life, he made a pact with a devil called Malbolgia and was able to roam the Earth but at a great cost. Now a Hellspawn, a solider with demonic powers and superior strength, he's back on Earth to try to right wrongs of his own past while trying to resist the temptations of a throne in Hell made for him. Spawn debuted in 1992 and remains one of the most popular independent comics since its creation. The series was reprinted in the *Origins* collections and a new direction for the series, called *Resurrection*, debuted in 2015. Spawn has been seen in a 1997 feature film, an animated television show, and various video games.

Origins, 2009–2014

Vol. 1. 2009. 160pp. 978-1-60706-071-0.
Vol. 2. 2009. 192pp. 978-1-60706-489-3.
Vol. 3. 2009. 160pp. 978-1-60706-119-9.
Vol. 4. 2010. 160pp. 978-1-60706-120-5.
Vol. 5. 2010. 160pp. 978-1-60706-224-0.
Vol. 6. 2010. 160pp. 978-1-60706-225-7.
Vol. 7. 2010. 160pp. 978-1-60706-226-4.
Vol. 8. 2010. 184pp. 978-1-60706-230-1.
Vol. 9. 2011. 160pp. 978-1-60706-236-3.
Vol. 10. 2011. 152pp. 978-1-60706-238-7.

Vol. 11. 2011. 152pp. 978-1-60706-239-4.
Vol. 12. 2011. 152pp. 978-1-60706-443-5.
Vol. 13. 2012. 160pp. 978-1-60706-445-9.
Vol. 14. 2012. 160pp. 978-1-60706-519-7.
Vol. 15. 2012. 160pp. 978-1-60706-567-8.
Vol. 16. 2012. 160pp. 978-1-60706-599-9.
Vol. 17. 2013. 160pp. 978-1-60706-663-7.
Vol. 18. 2013. 160pp. 978-1-60706-688-0.
Vol. 19. 2013. 160pp. 978-1-60706-796-2.
Vol. 20. 2014. 160pp. 978-1-60706-862-4.

Resurrection, 2015–

Vol. 1. 2015. 120pp. 978-1-63215-563-4.
Vol. 2: *Satan Saga Wars.* 2016. 184pp. 978-1-63215-807-9.

The Spectre. Written by **John Ostrander**, Illustrated by **Tom Mandrake**. DC Comics, 2014. T

© 2016 DC Comics.

The Spectre is the one of the most powerful beings in the universe and one of the original members of the Justice Society of America. The Wrath of God merged with a human soul, he has roamed the Earth for thousands of years smiting evil by avenging those who have died unavenged and punishing evildoers as penance for his past misdeeds. The current human host of the Spectre is Jim Corrigan, a hardnose police officer who died at the hands of the mob in the 1930s. Now as the Spectre, he must avenge the deaths of the innocent and learn the true nature of evil. Only then will the Spectre be free of his task and given peace in Heaven. The books collect the popular 1990s' series. Jim Corrigan has been the ghostly avenger, the Spectre, since his murder decades earlier. Now his mission of vengeance may be getting out of hand as he continues his role as not only hero but as the wrath of God.

Vol. 1: Crimes and Judgements. 2014. 320pp. 978-1-4012-4718-8.
Vol. 2: Wrath of God. 2014. 240pp. 978-1-4012-5150-5.

Witchfinder. Written by **Mike Mignola**, **John Arcurdi**, **Kim Newman**, and **Maura McHugh.** Illustrated by **Ben Stenbeck**, **John Severin**, and **Tyler Crook**. Dark Horse Comics, 2010–2015. O

From the pages of *Hellboy* and *B.P.R.D.* meet 19th-century occult investigator Edward Grey! Facing evil not just in the streets of London but across the globe, Edward confronts occult conspiracies, rampaging monsters, secret societies, evil witches, bloodthirsty criminals, and zombie cowboys!

Vol. 1: In the Service of Angels. 2010. 160pp. 978-1-59582-483-7.
Vol. 2: Lost and Gone Forever. 2012. 136pp. 978-1-59582-794-4.
Vol. 3: Mysteries of Unland. 2015. 144pp. 978-1-61655-630-3.

A Beastiary

Stories of monstrous beasts have long had a place in humankind's stories. Listed here are graphic novel tales of vampires, werewolves, the undead, muck monsters, and gigantic beasts that can crush cities. Note that humorous takes on these popular creatures can also be found in the Humorous Horror subgenre in the humor chapter.

Vampires and Werewolves

Vampires and werewolves are one of the universally recognized creatures of the night. Featured here are graphic novel tales focusing on both creatures of the night as well as the beasts as protagonists, antagonists, and antiheroes.

American Vampire. Written by **Scott Snyder** with **Stephen King**. Illustrated by **Rafael Albuquerque**. Vertigo/DC Comics, 2010– . M 🜚 ◎

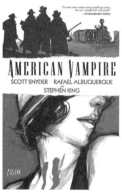
© 2016 DC Comics.

Skinner Sweet, notorious outlaw of the Wild West from the late 19th century, has died but has awakened from death and transformed into a vampire. But Skinner's a new kind of vampire—impervious to sunlight, fast, and stronger than his kind. Now Skinner and his only progeny—a young woman named Pearl Jones—are a new breed of vampire travelling through the decades across America and taking on the vampires of old and those that try to harm them. The series jumps back and forth through decades exploring Skinner and Pearl's complex relationship against the backdrop of American history. The series was recognized with an Eisner Award for Best New Series in 2011.

Vol. 1. 2010. 200pp. 978-1-4012-2830-9, hardcover; 978-1-4012-2974-0.
Vol. 2. 2011. 160pp. 978-1-4012-3069-2, hardcover; 978-1-4012-3070-8.

Vol. 3. 2012. 288pp. 978-1-4012-3333-4, hardcover; 978-1-4012-3334-1.
Vol. 4. 2012. 288pp. 978-1-4012-3718-9, hardcover; 978-1-4012-3719-6.
Vol. 5. 2013. 280pp. 978-1-4012-3770-7, hardcover; 978-1-4012-3771-4.
Vol. 6. 2014. 144pp. 978-1-4012-4708-9, hardcover; 978-1-4012-4929-8.
Vol. 7. 2015. 144pp. 978-1-4012-4882-6, hardcover; 978-1-4012-4882-6.
Vol. 8. 2016. 168pp. 978-1-4012-5433-9, hardcover; 978-1-4012-6258-7.
Vol. 9. 2017. 144pp. 978-1-4012-5965-5, hardcover.

Astounding Wolf-Man. Written by **Robert Kirkman**. Illustrated by **Jason Howard**. Image Comics, 2008–2011. T 🐾

Gary Hampton is mauled by a wolf and left for dead—but his life takes a drastic turn! Gary soon discovers that when the moon is full, he transforms into a werewolf! But Gary has vowed that the curse will be used for evil, but as a source of good, and a new superhero is born! The first volume was recognized by YALSA's Great Graphic Novels for Teens selection committee in 2009.

Vol. 1. 2008. 96pp. 978-1-58240-862-0.
Vol. 2. 2009. 160pp. 978-1-60706-007-9.
Vol. 3. 2010. 166pp. 978-1-60706-111-3.
Vol. 4. 2011. 160pp. 978-1-60706-249-3.

© 2016 Robert Kirkman and Image Comics.

Dracula. Written by **Bram Stoker**. Adapted and Illustrated by **Ben Caldwell**. All-Action Classics/Sterling Children's Books, 2008. 128pp. 978-1-4027-3152-5. T
Wonderful adaptation of the classic 1897 gothic horror novel by Bram Stoker. Jonathan Harker, intrepid estate agent, travels to distant Transylvania. He's there to handle the business of moving house for his eccentric client, Count Dracula. When the reality of the Count's true nature dawns on young Harker, he escapes from Dracula's ramshackle castle, only to have the vampire follow him to London.

Dracula. Written by **Bram Stoker**. Adapted by **Roy Thomas.** Illustrated by **Dick Giordano.** Marvel Comics 2010. 208pp. 978-0-7851-4905-7, hardcover. 978-0-7851-4906-4. T
This adaptation of Stoker's tale began in 1975 as an unfinished serialized story appearing in the black-and-white magazines *Dracula Lives!* and *Legion of Monsters*. It was finally finished in the 2004 comic book limited series <u>Stoker's Dracula</u> and collected under that title. In 2010, the series was colorized and published in both comic and book form under the Marvel Illustrated line.

Dracula Everlasting. Written by **Nunzio DeFilippis** and **Christina Weir**. Illustrated by **Rhea Silvan**. Seven Seas Entertainment, 2011–2013. T Neo-manga.
Teenager Nicholas Harker, an orphan since his parents died tragically, discovers he's the heir to a vast estate owned by none other than Lord Dracula.

Nicholas is a direct descendent from the vampire lord, and his power soon enthralls Nicholas. Old habits die hard as he attempts to rebuild Castle Dracula stone by stone in Boston. His new girlfriend, Jill Hawthorne, attempts to free Nicholas, while there are others who want him to embrace his destiny.

Vol. 1. 2011. 192pp. 978-1-935934-03-5.
Vol. 2. 2012. 192pp. 978-1-935934-95-0.
Vol. 3. 2013. 192pp. 978-1-937867-69-0.

© 2016 Seven Seas Entertainment.

Done to Death. Written by **Andrew Foley**. Illustrated by **Fiona Staples**. IDW Publishing, 2011. 144pp. 978-1-61377-055-9. M

Editor Shannon Wade is sick of receiving submissions that are nothing more than Twilight knockoffs, so she decides the proper course of action is to kill the worst of the authors. Her path soon crosses with Andy, an actual vampire who does not fit the stereotypical vampire look and is going after those writers who perpetuate that myth.

Drain. Written by **C. B. Cebulski.** Illustrated by **Sana Takeda**. Image Comics, 2008. 184pp. 978-1-58240-752-4. O

Centuries ago Chinatsu was a ninja whose family was slain by vampires and sought nothing but revenge against the vile villain vampires. Today she is vampire herself tracking vampires across the world, seeking revenge on those that dishonored her family.

Empire of the Wolf. Written by **Michael Kogge**. Illustrated by **Dan Parsons** and **David Rabbitte**. Alterna Comics, 2014. 128pp. 978-1-934985-39-7. M

Set in the early days of Rome's conquest of Britain, two centurions and friends, Lucius and Canisius, are attacked by a brute of a werewolf, and both of them are infected. Now the fate of the woman they both love as well as the empire is threatened by their bloody conflict. This comic is based both on the historical fact of the origins of the Roman Empire as well as the tale of Romulus and Remus and the foundation of Rome.

© 2016 Michael Kogge.

Hellsing. Written and Illustrated by **Kohta Hirano**. Dark Horse Comics, 2003–2010. T Japanese manga. 🐾 あ

There's a secret Protestant organization in England called Hellsing that's ready to take down the minions of darkness and the creatures of the night. A centuries-old group, currently led by Integral Van Hellsing, they're all that stands between the vampires overtaking England. Integral's tough as nails and so is her organization, but no one is as tough as Alucard, a centuries-old vampire with the skill and wit that's needed to eradicate evil. With his shotgun in hand and accompanied by his newly turned vampire Victoria Ceres as backup, he's the only weapon they'll ever need to take out the trash and rescue the world from evil. YALSA's Quick Picks for Reluctant Readers list featured the series in 2005. The hit manga was adapted into a popular 13-episode anime series in Japan.

Vol. 1. 2003. 208pp. 978-1-59307-056-4.
Vol. 2. 2004. 180pp. 978-1-59307-057-1.
Vol. 3. 2004. 192pp. 978-1-59307-202-5.
Vol. 4. 2004. 192pp. 978-1-59307-259-9.
Vol. 5. 2004. 208pp. 978-1-59307-272-8.
Vol. 6. 2005. 192pp. 978-1-59307-302-2.
Vol. 7. 2005. 192pp. 978-1-59307-348-0.
Vol. 8. 2007. 208pp. 978-1-59307-780-8.
Vol. 9. 2008. 208pp. 978-1-59582-157-7.
Vol. 10. 2010. 192pp. 978-1-59582-498-1.

He's My Only Vampire. Written and Illustrated by **Aya Shouoto**. Yen Press, 2014– . O

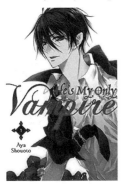

© 2016 Yen Press and Aya Shouoto.

Kana is a student who attends the St. Agatha Academy. One day while in the city, she runs into a long-lost childhood friend, a boy named Aki. Soon after, Kana is in a life-threatening accident and is rescued by none other than a vampire—Aki. Now she's the thrall of Aki—in both mind and soul. And that's not all—she's also been thrust into a dangerous game that could cost her life again when demonic powers called "STIGMA" are up for grabs. The shojo manga was published in Japan originally from 2010 to 2014.

Vol. 1. 2014. 176pp. 978-0-316-33666-6.
Vol. 2. 2015. 176pp. 978-0-316-38271-7.
Vol. 3. 2015. 160pp. 978-0-316-26055-8.
Vol. 4. 2015. 160pp. 978-0-316-26168-5.
Vol. 5. 2015. 160pp. 978-0-316-30219-7.
Vol. 6. 2016. 176pp. 978-0-316-34581-1.
Vol. 7. 2016. 176pp. 978-0-316-34582-8.
Vol. 8. 2016. 176pp. 978-0-316-34583-5.
Vol. 9. 2016. 176pp. 978-0-316-34584-2.
Vol. 10. 2017. 176pp. 978-0-316-34582-8.

Honey Blood. Written and Illustrated by **Miko Mitsuki**. VIZ Media, 2014–2015. O Japanese manga.

When a girl at a high school is attacked by what authorities can only deduce to be from a vampire, Hinata Sorazono, a student in the high school can't believe such nonsense. But when her new next-door neighbor turns out to be a young author of a popular vampire romance novel, she begins to suspect that he's not only a vampire, but the culprit!

Vol. 1. 2014. 192pp. 978-1-4215-7337-3.
Vol. 2. 2014. 192pp. 978-1-4215-7338-0.
Tale Zero. 2015. 192pp. 978-1-4215-7339-7.

I, Vampire. Written by **Joshua Hale Fialkov**. Illustrated **Andrea Sorrentino**. DC Comics. O

There is going to be a bloody war in the New 52 DC Universe. Mary, Queen of Blood, the leader of vampires, is starting her conquest to take over the planet. Andrew Bennett is the only person who can stop her. As her former lover and the one who turned her into a vampire, he is the only one strong enough to stand up to her. Andrew gets a little help fighting his fellow vampires from DC's biggest heroes. This is an updated version of a character from the 1980s, whose adventures were collected in 2012's *I, Vampire* (ISBN 978-1-4012-3371-6).

Tainted Love. 2012. 144pp. 978-1-4012-3687-8.
Rise of the Vampires. 2013. 192pp. 978-1-4012-3783-7.
Wave of Mutilation. 2013. 192pp. 978-1-4012-4278-7.

Life Sucks. Written by **Jessica Abel** and **Gabriel Soria**. Illustrated by **Warren Pleece**. First Second Books, 2008. 192pp. 978-1-59643-107-2. T 🎗

> You'd think that being a teenage vampire—one of the undead who can never die or age, it would be really cool—right? But, for Dave Marshall, it really does suck being a vampire. The girl he likes doesn't notice him at all, and ever since his boss at the local convenient store turned him into a vampire, he can't go out in daylight without getting a major sunburn—a look at the minuses about being a vampire. The book was recognized by YALSA's Great Graphic Novels for Teens committee in 2010 as a Top Ten title.

Seraph of the End: Vampire Reign. Written by **Takaya Kagami**. Illustrated by **Yamato Yamamoto**. VIZ Media, 2014– . O Japanese manga. あ

> In 2012, the world is destroyed by a virus created by humankind. The deadly virus kills all humans over the age of 13 while the children remain unharmed. At this time, vampires arise as well as other dark beasts of legend. The vampires "rescue" the children and enslave them under the Earth—their only penance is to supply the vampires with fresh blood in exchange for protection. A 12-year-old boy named Yuichiro and others from the Hyakuya Orphanage plotted an escape, but their revolution was thwarted with only Yuichiro as the lone survivor, who was rescued by the Moon Demon Company—an extermination branch of the Japanese Imperial Demon Army. Now four years later, Yuichiro dedicates his life to destroy vampires and seek revenge against them for murdering his "family." The series is still ongoing in Japan and also adapted into an anime series.

Vol. 1. 2014. 200pp. 978-1-4215-7150-8.
Vol. 2. 2014. 208pp. 978-1-4215-7151-5.
Vol. 3. 2014. 192pp. 978-1-4215-7152-2.
Vol. 4. 2015. 200pp. 978-1-4215-7153-9.
Vol. 5. 2015. 192pp. 978-1-4215-7869-9.
Vol. 6. 2015. 192pp. 978-1-4215-8030-2.
Vol. 7. 2015. 192pp. 978-1-4215-8264-1.
Vol. 8. 2016. 200pp. 978-1-4215-8515-4.
Vol. 9. 2016. 200pp. 978-1-4215-8704-2.
Vol. 10. 2016. 200pp. 978-1-4215-8854-4.
Vol. 11. 2017. 208pp. 978-1-4215-9133-9.
Vol. 12. 2017. 200pp. 978-1-4215-9439-2.

Sherlock Holmes and the Vampires of London. Written by **Sylvain Cordurie**. Illustrated by **Laci**. Dark Horse Comics, 2014. 96pp. 978-1-61655-266-4. O

> During the period when he was thought to be dead, famous detective Sherlock Holmes must work under duress for a vampire to stop another one who is threatening the safety of both humans and vampires in Victorian England. Originally published in France.

Silver. Written and Illustrated by **Stephan Franck**. Dark Planet Comics. 2014– . O

> Set in the 1930s, a con artist, James Finnegan, has partnered up with Rosalyn Sledge, the granddaughter of Abraham van Helsing. Together they, along with a team of

talented thieves, are out to steal a trove of silver from Dracula's castle. The only problem is that there's a horde of vampire kin in the way! A tribute to pulp novels and the lore of Bram Stoker's original *Dracula* novel.

Vol. 1. 2014. 112pp. 978-0-9890386-0-7.
Vol. 2. 2015. 112pp. 978-0-9890386-1-4.

The Strain. Written by **Guillermo del Toro** and **Chuck Hogan**. Adapted by **David Lapham**. Illustrated by **Mike Huddleston**. Dark Horse Comics, 2012–2016. O ⌨

The adaptation of the popular book trilogy by Guillermo del Toro and Chuck Hogan. When a Boeing 777 lands at JFK International Airport and goes dark, the Center for Disease and Control is sent to investigate. Fearing a terrorist attack, the investigators, led by Dr. Ephraim Goodweather and his team, find all the passengers dead with no markings aside from a small puncture wound to their necks. Only an old pawnbroker knows the true meaning of what is happening, and soon the world will be engulfed in the flames at the hands of the Master and his army of undead vampires. The books were also adapted into a TV series on FX channel in 2014.

Vol. 1. 2012. 152pp. 978-1-61655-032-5.
Vol. 2. 2013. 144pp. 978-1-61655-156-8.
Vol. 3: The Fall. 2014. 144pp. 978-1-61655-333-3.
Vol. 4: The Fall. 2014. 136pp. 978-1-61655-449-1.
Vol. 5: The Night Eternal. 2015. 152pp. 978-1-61655-638-9.
Vol. 6: The Night Eternal. 2015. 160pp. 978-1-61655-787-4.
Book One: The Strain. 2014. 272pp. 978-1-61655-548-1, hardcover.
Book Two: The Fall. 2015. 272pp. 978-1-61655-836-9, hardcover.
Book Three: The Night Eternal. 2016. 304pp. 978-1-61655-977-9, hardcover.

30 Days of Night. Written by **Steve Niles** and various. Illustrated by **Ben Templesmith** and various. IDW Publishing, 2011–2012. M 🧍 🎬

For 30 days a year, Barrow, Alaska, the northernmost town in North America, is covered in total darkness. When husband and wife sheriff team Eben and Stella investigate a bizarre crime wave involving a pile of burned cell phones, they connect the dots and realize it's a ploy by someone or something trying to disable all communication. They soon realize that, isolated in pitch blackness, Barrow's become the prime hunting ground for vicious vampires who savor the 30 days of eternal darkness in their hunt for blood. The self-titled collection received recognition by YALSA's Popular Paperbacks for Young Adults committee in 2005 on the *All Kinds of Creepy* list. Listed below are the Omnibus collections, which include the original story as well as the multiple follow-up stories published that continued the tale of the vampires against the backdrop of the darkest corner of the Earth in Barrow, Alaska, and beyond. The original story was adapted as a feature film in 2007.

© 2016 Steve Niles and Ben Templesmith.

Omnibus, Vol. 1. 2011. 360pp. 978-1-61377-040-5.
Omnibus, Vol. 2. 2012. 408pp. 978-1-61377-480-9.

Vampire Knight. Written and Illustrated by **Matsuri Hino**. VIZ Media, 2007–2014. O. Japanese manga. あ

Vampire Knight © Matsuri Hino 2004/HAKUSENSHA, Inc.

Yuki Cross is a girl who was rescued by a pureblood vampire at an early age from a rogue vampire. Now a teenager, she's attending the Cross Academy—a school that serves as a haven for vampires who have claimed to have reformed. Yuki's adopted parents are vampires and run the Cross Academy, and she and a childhood friend Yuki Cross protect the vampires from public knowledge. But are the vampires really cured of their lust for blood, and what other secrets will be revealed that will change Yuki's life forever? The series was adapted into an animated series in Japan in 2008.

Vol. 1. 2007. 208pp. 978-1-4215-0822-1.
Vol. 2. 2007. 208pp. 978-1-4215-1130-6.
Vol. 3. 2007. 200pp. 978-1-4215-1324-9.
Vol. 4. 2008. 200pp. 978-1-4215-1563-2.

Vol. 5. 2008. 208pp. 978-1-4215-1954-8.
Vol. 6. 2009. 200pp. 978-1-4215-2353-8.
Vol. 7. 2009. 200pp. 978-1-4215-2676-8.
Vol. 8. 2009. 208pp. 978-1-4215-3073-4.
Vol. 9. 2010. 208pp. 978-1-4215-3172-4.
Vol. 10. 2010. 200pp. 978-1-4215-3569-2.
Vol. 11. 2010. 200pp. 978-1-4215-3790-0.
Vol. 12. 2011. 192pp. 978-1-4215-3938-6.

Vol. 13. 2011. 200pp. 978-1-4215-4081-8.
Vol. 14. 2012. 200pp. 978-1-4215-4218-8.
Vol. 15. 2012. 200pp. 978-1-4215-4947-7.
Vol. 16. 2013. 200pp. 978-1-4215-5154-8.
Vol. 17. 2013. 208pp. 978-1-4215-5701-4.
Vol. 18. 2013. 208pp. 978-1-4215-6433-3.
Vol. 19. 2014. 208pp. 978-1-4215-7391-5.

Vampire Cheerleaders. Written by **Adam Arnold**. Illustrated by **Shiei** and **Comipa**. Seven Seas Entertainment, 2011–2015. O Neo-manga.

The cheerleaders of Bakertown High School have a secret behind all of the makeup and attitude—they're all vampires! When one of their five-vampire squad goes missing, they need to add a new recruit for the team and Heather Hartley from the B squad fits the bill—but can they stop her before she tries to drain the blood from the entire football team?

Vol. 1. 2011. 192pp. 978-1-934876-84-8.
Vol. 2. 2011. 192pp. 978-1-935934-06-6.
Vampire Cheerleaders/Paranormal Mystery Squad Monster Mash Collection. 2012. 416pp. 978-1-935934-74-5.
Vampire Cheerleaders Must Die!. 2013. 192pp. 978-1-937867-19-5.
Vampire Cheerleaders in Space . . . and Time?!. 2015. 192pp. 978-1-626920-98-9.

The Undead

Zombies, skeletons, golems, the reanimated dead—stories of those brought back to life from the land of the dead by humankind's own folly, mad scientists, or the dead's own will continue to exist. The Walking Dead series published by Image Comics is an excellent example of this popular genre.

Afterlife with Archie. Written by **Roberto Aguirre-Sacasa**. Illustrated by **Francesco Francavilla**. Archie Comics 2014– . O ◎

After his dog is killed by a car, Jughead asks teenage witch Sabrina to bring him back to life. But her spell leads to the walking dead invading Riverdale, and not even some of the regular characters will survive! A horror twist to a classic humor series.

Escape from Riverdale. 2014. 160pp. 978-1-61988-908-8.
Betty R.I.P. 2017. 176pp. 978-1-61988-948-4.

Chopper Zombie. Written by **Todd Livingston** and **Thom Beers**. Illustrated by **Scott Keating**. Devil's Due Publishing, 2008. 144pp. 978-1-934692-37-0. M

When a motorcycle builder is killed by a greedy corporation for refusing to sell his innovative fuel formula, even death can't stop a man set on revenge. Downed in and set aflame in the fuel that he invented, he walks among the living as a zombie out for vengeance against those who stole what was rightfully his!

Daybreak. Written and Illustrated by **Brian Ralph**. Drawn & Quarterly, 2011. 160pp. 978-1-77046-055-3. M

© 2016 Drawn + Quarterly and Brian Ralph

After a zombie apocalypse has arrived, you are a silent observer witnessing the struggle to survive in a land where the dead walk and life is shattered, dangerous, and deadly. With a unique take as you are watching the events through silent eyes, you watch your ragged, one-armed protector rescue you; fights hordes of the undead; seeks shelter; and fights against other survivors. Every moment is a life-and-death struggle and you are right in the middle of it all. A unique tale about zombies that almost plays out like a first-person perspective from a video game.

Dead@17: The Complete Collection. Written and Illustrated by **Josh Howard**. Image Comics, 2015. 760pp. 978-1-63215-325-8. M

In the small town of Darlington Hills, teenagers Nara Kilday and Hazy Foss are best friends stuck in a town going nowhere. Nara is horribly murdered inside her house by an intruder, and now something dark and sinister is afoot as demonic zombies begin to tear apart the town. Hazy, meanwhile, finds herself attacked by the zombies and rescued by the most unlikely hero: Nara. Now while the fate of the town hangs in the balance, an axe-wielding Nara finds herself as a key figure in the climactic battle of good versus evil. Even worse, she might be prophesied to be on the bad guys' side!

Death Valley. Written by **Johanna Stokes** and **Andrew Cosby**. Illustrated by **Rhoald Marcellus**. Boom! Studios, 2007. 128pp. 978-1-934506-08-0. M

When a group of high school students plan the biggest rave party ever in the San Fernando Valley, they put out all the stops and host it in a bomb shelter. When they open the doors to the shelter after the party ends, they find much more than they ever expected, with the entire valley crawling with zombies!

Fanboys vs. Zombies. Written by **Sam Humphries** and **Shane Houghton**. Illustrated by **Jerry Gaylord**. Boom! Studios, 2013–2014. M

An unlikely band of nerds use their skills at video games and hours of watching horror movies to try and survive a plague of zombies that have attacked the west coast!

Vol. 1. 2013. 128pp. 978-1-60886-289-4.
Vol. 2. 2013. 128pp. 978-1-60886-307-5.
Vol. 3. 2013. 112pp. 978-1-60886-335-8.
Vol. 4. 2014. 112pp. 978-1-60886-358-7.
Vol. 5. 2014. 112pp. 978-1-60886-395-2.

High School of the Dead. Written by **Daisuke Sato**. Illustrated by **Shouji Sato**. Yen Press, 2011–2013. M Japanese manga. あ

© 2016 Yen Press and Daisuke Sato and Shouji Sato.

A mysterious illness is spreading in Fujimi High School, and within hours, the entire campus is transformed from a place of learning to a hallowed hall of horror. Students are turning into zombies, and the students are now out for blood. Only a small group of students have survived so far. Among them is Takashi Komuro and his childhood friend, Rei. They've managed to survive so far, but how long can they last when the entire school is out for their blood?

Vol. 1. 2011. 160pp. 978-0-316-13225-1.
Vol. 2. 2011. 160pp. 978-0-316-13239-8.
Vol. 3. 2011. 160pp. 978-0-316-13242-8.
Vol. 4. 2011. 160pp. 978-0-316-13245-9.
Vol. 5. 2012. 160pp. 978-0-316-13246-6.
Vol. 6. 2012. 160pp. 978-0-316-20943-4.
Vol. 7. 2012. 160pp. 978-0-316-20944-1.

Full-Color Omnibus, 2011–2013.

Vol. 1. 2011. 704pp. 978-0-316-20104-9, hardcover.
Vol. 2. 2013. 608pp. 978-0-316-25-086-3, hardcover.

Hour of the Zombie. Written and Illustrated by **Tsukasa Saimura**. Seven Seas Entertainment, 2016– . O Japanese manga.

© 2016 Yen Press and Tsukasa Saimura.

A horrible zombie breakout has happened at a high school—one moment everything is normal and then suddenly half of the school is transformed into flesh-eating zombies, tearing the place apart with their cravings for flesh. Then suddenly they stop and revert back to normal humans. How does the school carry on past a tragedy like this where the turned and the unbitten must try to trust each once more? And what caused the students to transform, and will it happen again?

Vol. 1. 2016. 180pp. 978-1-62692-306-5.
Vol. 2. 2016. 180pp. 978-1-626923-13-3.
Vol. 3. 2016. 180pp. 978-1-626923-54-6.

iZombie Omnibus. Written by **Chris Roberson**. Illustrated by **Mike Allred**. Vertigo/DC Comics. 2015. 672pp. 978-1-4012-6203-7. M 🖳

© 2016 DC Comics.

In this basis for the popular CW television series, Gwen Dixon is a gravedigger who also happens to be a revenant, having come back from the dead. While she can pass for normal, if she does not eat a brain each month she can lose her intelligence and sense of self. After eating a brain, she gains access to the memories of its "owner." Supporting characters include the ghost of a woman who died in the 1960s and a were-terrier along with other human and supernatural individuals. Four collections of this Eisner-nominated series were published between 2011 and 2012, and the omnibus edition collects all 28 issues plus some short stories.

Junior Braves of the Apocalypse. Written by **Greg Smith** and **Michael Tanner**. Illustrated by **Zach Lehner**. Oni Press, 2015– . T

When the young Junior Braves Tribe 65 goes out camping with no contact with the outside world for seven days, they left behind all their comforts of home. Gone are cell phones, video games, parents, and the easy life. Now it was time for the boys to do a little bit of character building and find out just what they had to survive. Little did they expect that after a week full of campfire stories, survival training, and braving it in the Pacific Northwest, wilderness would await them when they returned home to find their city taken over by zombies. With their parents missing, the boys must rely on each other, their survival skills, and teamwork to survive.

Vol. 1: A Brave is Brave. 2015. 216pp. 978-1-62010-144-5.

The Last of Us: American Dreams. Written by **Faith Erin Hicks** and **Neil Druckmann**. Illustrated by **Faith Erin Hicks**. Dark Horse Comics, 2013. 112pp. 978-1-61655-212-1. M 🎮

A tie-in to the popular Sony Playstation game of the same name. Nineteen years ago, a parasitic fungus killed most of the world's population. To protect the rest of humankind, quarantine zones were set up, but it's a hard life in the post-pandemic world. For thirteen-year-old Ellie, the hard life is all she's ever known. When she's gotten on the bad side of the military-run boarding school she attends, she finds a friend in a fellow rebel named Riley—and together they heard outside of the quarantine zone into the great unknown.

The Mammoth Book of Zombie Comics. Edited by **David Kendall**. Running Press, 2008. 564pp. 978-0-7624-3398-8. M

A large collection of zombie comics and graphic short stories featuring stories from Vincent Locke, Steve Niles, Hideshi Hino, Joe Lansdale, and many more!

Marvel Zombies. Written by **Robert Kirkman, Fred Van Lente, Jonathan Maberry, David Wellington, Seth Grahame-Smith, Reginald Hudlin, Frank Marraffino, Peter David, Mark Millar**, and **Simon Spurrier**. Illustrated by **Sean Phillips, Kev Walker, Fernando Blanco, Nick Dragotta, Jason Shawn Alexander, Andrea Mutti**, and **Richard Elson**. Marvel Comics, 2006–2015. O

© 2016 Marvel Comics.

A dark twist on fan-favorite heroes from Marvel Comics. In a world very similar to where Marvel Comics heroes such as Spider-Man, Captain America, and the X-Men call home, an alien virus has turned the entire world into zombies. The super-heroes of the world are all still heroes—they're just dead zombies, too. As the zombies continue to crave human flesh, are there any heroes or villains who can repel the zombified costumed monstrosities, or are humankind's days numbered? An over-the-top romp through the Marvel Universe with a dash of good old horror mixed in. The first two collections were written by fan-favorite zombie expert Robert *The Walking Dead* Kirkman, with other creators handling the continuing stories.

Vol. 1. 2006. 136pp. 978-0-7851-2277-7, hardcover; 2007. 978-0-7851-2014-8.
Vol. 2. 2008. 120pp. 978-0-7851-2545-7, hardcover; 2009. 978-0-7851-2546-4.
Vol. 3. 2009. 112pp. 978-0-7851-3526-5.
Vol. 4. 2010. 128pp. 978-0-7851-3918-8.
Vol. 5. 2011. 120pp. 978-0-7851-4744-2.
Marvel Zombies vs. Army of Darkness. 2007. 128pp. 978-0-7851-2743-7, hardcover.
Marvel Zombies: Dead Days. 2009. 272pp. 978-0-7851-3563-0.
Marvel Zombies Return. 2010. 160pp. 978-0-7851-4238-6.
Marvel Zombies Supreme. 2011. 120pp. 978-0-7851-5167-8, hardcover; 2012. 978-0-7851-5168-5.
Marvel Zomnibus. 2012. 1200pp. 978-0-7851-4026-9, hardcover.
Marvel Zombies Destroy! 2012. 112pp. 978-0-7851-6384-8, hardcover; 2013. 978-0-7851-6385-5.
The Complete Collection. 2013–2014.
　　Vol. 1. 2013. 464pp. 978-0-7851-8538-3.
　　Vol. 2. 2014. 464pp. 978-0-7851-8829-2.
　　Vol. 3. 2014. 464pp. 978-0-7851-8899-5.

Age of Ultron vs. Marvel Zombies. 2015. 128pp. 978-0-7851-9863-5.
Marvel Zombies: Battleworld. 2015. 112pp. 978-0-7851-9878-9.

Pride and Prejudice and Zombies: The Graphic Novel. Written by **Jane Austen** and **Seth Grahame-Smith**. Adapted by **Tony Lee**. Illustrated by **Cliff Richards**. Del Rey, 2010. 176pp. 978-0-345-52068-5. T

The adaptation of Jane Austen's *Pride and Prejudice*, which cleverly adds in zombies into the overall plot as a strange plague takes over England. All of England's best families must train their daughters in the art of combat. Elizabeth Bennet is trained with the sword that is as sharp as her quick wit and even sharper tongue. Amid the battlefield of the unmentionable undead, Elizabeth finds an ally and occasional foe in the attractive Mister Darcy. When the undead rise, can true love still find its way into the heart of a British girl sworn to never stop fighting against the zombie hordes? The book was also adapted into a feature film in 2016.

Rot & Ruin: Warrior Smart. Written by **Jonathan Maberry**. Illustrated by **Tony Vargas**. IDW Publishing, 2015. 120pp. 978-1-63140-186-2. O

> Benny Imura and his friends, Nix, Lilah, and Chong, travel the country 14 years after the zombie apocalypse, looking for a safe place and hoping for a better world. The story is a tie-in to the popular series of novels written also by Jonathan Maberry.

Tokyo Ghoul. Written and Illustrated by **Sui Ishida**. VIZ Media. 2015– . T 🎋 Japanese manga あ

TOKYO GHOUL © 2011 by Sui Ishida/SHUEISHA Inc.

Set in an alternate world where ghouls exist among humans and survive in the shadows and consume human flesh to survive, Ken Kaneki is a college student who barely survives an encounter with a ghoul while on a date with her. After an operation to save his life after the attack, Ken inexplicably has the organs of the ghoul in his body. Now Ken is transformed into a half-ghoul and must consume the flesh of humans or die! With no one else to turn to, Ken is taken in by a group of ghouls who run a coffee shop. There they teach him how to cope with his new craving, the factions within the ghoul society, and how to keep his identity safe from humans. The manga was originally published in Japan in 14 volumes from 2011 to 2014 and inspired an anime series as well. Multiple volumes of this series were on YALSA's 2017 Great Graphic Novels for Teens list.

Vol. 1. 2015. 224pp. 978-1-4215-8036-4.
Vol. 2. 2015. 208pp. 978-1-4215-8037-1.
Vol. 3. 2015. 192pp. 978-1-4215-8038-8.
Vol. 4. 2015. 192pp. 978-1-4215-8039-5.
Vol. 5. 2015. 200pp. 978-1-4215-8040-1.
Vol. 6. 2015. 200pp. 978-1-4215-8041-8.
Vol. 7. 2016. 200pp. 978-1-4215-8042-5.
Vol. 8. 2016. 216pp. 978-1-4215-8043-2.
Vol. 9. 2016. 200pp. 978-1-4215-8044-9.
Vol. 10. 2016. 216pp. 978-1-4215-8045-6.
Vol. 11. 2017. 216pp. 978-1-4215-8046-3.
Vol. 12. 2017. 216pp. 978-1-4215-8047-0.
Vol. 13. 2017. 216pp. 978-1-4215-9042-4.
Vol. 14. 2007. 224pp. 978-1-4215-9043-1.

Victorian Undead. Written by **Ian Edginton**. Illustrated by **Davide Fabbri**. Wildstorm Productions/DC Comics, 2010–2011. O

© 2016 DC Comics.

In 1854 a meteor streaked across the London skies, bringing it a plague like no other: zombies! For over 20 years the threat has been under control, but when the fiendish Professor Moriarity starts to use zombies as ways to overtake Victorian-era England, Sherlock Holmes and Doctor Watson must fight against the combined might of the undead and their greatest archenemy. *Vol. 2* features Sherlock Holmes against the dreaded power of Count Dracula.

Vol. 1: 2010. 144pp. 978-1-4012-2840-8.
Vol. 2: Sherlock Holmes vs. Dracula. 2011. 160pp. 978-1-4012-3268-9.

The Walking Dead. Written by **Robert Kirkman**. Illustrated by **Tony Moore** and **Charlie Adlard**. Image Comics, 2004– . M ◉ ▭

© 2006 Robert Kirkman.

Police officer Rick Grimes was injured in the line of duty and woke from his coma to a world much harsher than he left it. Civilization has been nearly destroyed by an unknown epidemic, and now flesh-eating zombies have overrun entire cities and it's unknown how far the damage has spread. Civilization, as we know it, has collapsed and the streets are deserted. Lost and confused, he's rescued by a small band of humans who've escaped the collapse of civilization and are now hunkered down outside of Atlanta. Reunited with his family and his partner from the police force, the small band of brothers has formed a struggling family that must support itself or die. In a time when there's little hope for any rescue, a tragedy of epic proportions has done the impossible—brought people even closer to one another, but how long can they survive when the threat of zombies lurking around every corner? *The Walking Dead* has been made into a popular television show and has resulted in additional spin-off material including novels, video games, and a second TV series, <u>Fear the Walking Dead</u> (2015), which is not tied into the events of the comic books.

Vol. 1: Days Gone Bye. 2004. 144pp. 978-1-58240-358-8.
Vol. 2: Miles Behind Us. 2004. 136pp. 978-1-58240-413-4.
Vol. 3: Safety behind Bars. 2005. 136pp. 978-1-58240-487-5.
Vol. 4: The Heart's Desire. 2005. 136pp. 978-1-58240-530-8.
Vol. 5: The Best Defense. 2006. 136pp. 978-1-58240-612-1.
Vol. 6: This Sorrowful Life. 2007. 144pp. 978-1-58240-684-8.
Vol. 7: The Calm Before. 2008. 136pp. 978-1-58240-828-6.
Vol. 8: Made to Suffer. 2008. 136pp. 978-1-58240-883-5.
Vol. 9: Here We Remain. 2009. 136pp. 978-1-60706-022-2.
Vol. 10: What We Become. 2009. 136pp. 978-1-60706-075-8.
Vol. 11: Fear the Hunters. 2010. 136pp. 978-1-60706-181-6.
Vol. 12: Life among Them. 2010. 144pp. 978-1-60706-254-7.
Vol. 13: Too Far Gone. 2010. 136pp. 978-1-60706-329-2.
Vol. 14: No Way Out. 2011. 136pp. 978-1-60706-392-6.
Vol. 15: We Find Ourselves. 2011. 136pp. 978-1-60706-440-4.
Vol. 16: A Larger World. 2012. 136pp. 978-1-60706-559-3.
Vol. 17: Something to Fear. 2012. 136pp. 978-1-60706-615-6.
Vol. 18: What Comes After. 2013. 136pp. 978-1-60706-687-3.
Vol. 19: March to War. 2013. 136pp. 978-1-60706-818-1.
Vol. 20: All Out War (Part One). 2014. 136pp. 978-1-60706-882-2.
Vol. 21: All Out War (Part Two). 2014. 136pp. 978-1-63215-030-1.
Vol. 22: A New Beginning. 2014. 136pp. 978-1-63215-041-7.
Vol. 23: Whispers into Screams. 2015. 136pp. 978-1-63215-258-9.
Vol. 24: Life and Death. 2016. 136pp. 978-1-63215-402-6.
Vol. 25: No Turning Back. 2016. 136pp. 978-1-63215-659-4.
Vol. 26: Call to Arms. 2016. 136pp. 978-1-63215-917-5.
Vol. 27: The Whisperer War. 2017. 136pp. 978-1-5343-0052-1.
Compendium 1. 2009. 1088pp. 978-1-60706-076-5.
Compendium 2. 2012. 1088pp. 978-1-60706-596-8.

Compendium 3. 2015. 1088pp. 978-1-63215-456-9.
Book 1. 2006. 304pp. 978-1-58240-619-0, hardcover.
Book 2. 2007. 304pp. 978-1-58240-698-5, hardcover.
Book 3. 2007. 304pp. 978-1-58240-825-5, hardcover.
Book 4. 2008. 304pp. 978-1-60706-000-0, hardcover.
Book 5. 2010. 304pp. 978-1-60706-171-7, hardcover.
Book 6. 2010. 304pp. 978-1-60706-327-8, hardcover.
Book 7. 2011. 304pp. 978-1-60706-439-8, hardcover.
Book 8. 2012. 304pp. 978-1-60706-593-7, hardcover.
Book 9. 2013. 304pp. 978-1-60706-798-6, hardcover.
Book 10. 2014. 304pp. 978-1-63215-034-9, hardcover.
Book 11. 2015. 304pp. 978-1-63215-271-8, hardcover.
Book 12. 2016. 296pp. 978-1-63215-451-4, hardcover.
Book 13. 2016. 296pp, 978-1-63215-916-8, hardcover.

Zombie Tales. Written by **Mark Waid**, **William Messner-Loebs**, **Karl Kesel**, **Brian Augustyn**, **Michael Alan Nelson**, and various. Illustrated by **Keith Giffen**, **Jon Schnepp**, **Toby Cypress**, and various. Boom! Studios, 2011. M

Two massive collections of zombie stories by a variety of comic book creators sure to scare you to death!

Omnibus Vol. 1. 2011. 224pp. 978-1-60886-074-6.
Omnibus Vol. 2. 2011. 224pp. 978-1-60886-076-0.

Zombies Calling. Written and Illustrated by **Faith Erin Hicks**. Slave Labor Graphics, 2007. 978-1-59362-079-0. O

University student Joss loves zombie movies. She has even pieced together the rules for surviving a zombie outbreak from all the movies she's seen. When an actual zombie outbreak happens, it is up to Joss to use her knowledge of the zombie rules to keep her and her friends Sonnet and Robyn alive.

The Zombie Survival Guide: Recorded Attacks. Written by **Max Brooks**. Illustrated by **Ibraim Roberson**. Three Rivers Press, 2009. 144pp. 978-0-307-40577-7. M

Written by the author of *The Zombie Survival Guide* and *World War Z*, a look at the history of zombies throughout history. From the birth of man in the Stone Age, and many periods in human history, the undead have continued to plague mankind. Witness this lost history brought to life and know that we have always been plagued by the living dead!

Rampant Animals and Other Eco-Monsters Big and Small

Monsters and beasts both large and small outside of the traditional vampire, werewolf, or undead zombie that strike back against man. The beasts can be human-made, from unknown origins, or even created by Mother Nature to exact revenge on humankind.

Beast of Wolfe's Bay. Written and Illustrated by **Erik A. Evensen**. Evensen Creative, 2013. 96pp. 978-0-9890104-0-5. T

Brian Wegman, a perpetual college student with a passion for paleoanthropology, is called in to assist in a mysterious homicide at his lakeside college town of Wolfe's Bay. Brian is accompanied by the no-nonsense sheriff and his brilliant daughter to solve the homicide but instead finds them face to face with an urban legend. A modern retelling of *Beowulf* with lots of humor, Sasquatch, and nerdy goodness.

Brain Camp. Written by **Susan Kim** and **Laurence Klavan**. Illustrated by **Faith Erin Hicks**. First Second Books, 2010. 978-1-59643-366-3. T 🎗

Jenna and Lucas, two wayward teens stuck at a camp aimed to convert teen delinquents into child prodigies, discover there is something far more sinister than nature hikes going on at their summer camp! Soon the campers are disappearing, and many others are being turned into docile brainiacs—and Jenna and Lucas discover there's much to be afraid of at Camp Fielding. The collection was recognized by YALSA on their 2011 Great Graphic Novels for Teens' top-ten graphic novels list.

© 2016 First Second.

Dear Creature. Written and Illustrated by **Jonathan Case**. Dark Horse Comics, 2016. 192pp. 978-1-50670-095-3, hardcover. T

Deep in the ocean, a creature named Grue has a change of heart after coming across the love poems and plays of William Shakespeare. No longer a monster who wants to eat lusty teenage beachgoers, he wants instead to follow matters of the heart and fall in love! After one bad experience, Grue's found love in the form of the beautiful Giulietta. When his past catches up with him, can a monster truly stop being a monster?

Enormous. Written by **Tim Daniel**. Illustrated by **Mehdi Cheggour**. 215 Ink, 2015. 176pp. 978-0-692-32730-2. M

In the wake of a worldwide global catastrophe, the Enormous—giant-sized beasts—have emerged from Earth, causing rampant destruction in their wake. Humankind survives, but it's a cruel world where humankind at times can be the worst beast of all. As humankind fights to stave off extinction, Ellen Grace, a former school teacher who lost everything in the monstrous attacks, leads a search and rescue operation, finding children orphaned in the wake of the massive destruction.

Flink. Written and Illustrated by **Doug TenNapel**. Image Comics, 2007. 112pp. 978-1-58240-891-0. T 🎗

A boy survives a plane crash and is rescued by a Bigfoot named Flink. Both learn about loss and create a bond when they learn about the loss of each other's family members.

Giant Monster. Written by **Steve Niles**. Illustrated by **Nat Jones**. Boom! Studios, 2008–2011. 128pp. 978-1-934506-29-5; 2010. 128pp. 978-1-608860-02-9, hardcover. M

A tribute to B-monster movies from the 1950s and 1960s. When astronaut Don Maggart is infected with a mysterious substance on his reentry to Earth, his body is

transformed into a hungry monstrosity that gets bigger and bigger the more he consumes. Only a retired Nazi scientists' Super-Attack-Bot may be the key to ending the carnage!

Godzilla. IDW Publishing, 2011– . T 🎬 ◎

One of the most famous and beloved monsters in Japanese film, the atomic-breathing tyrannosaur-like dinosaur Godzilla has been a constant threat to the world for over 60 years since his first appearance in 1954 in the film *Godzilla: King of the Monsters*. After nearly destroying Japan numerous times and creating a wake of destruction in his path, destroying entire cities with his atomic breath and brute strength, the world community's out to put an end to the giant behemoth. In 2011, IDW Publishing took over the publishing of Godzilla comics, and for the first time the stories feature all the other popular monsters from the Japanese Toho Pictures kaiju films including Rodan, Anguirus, Mothra, Mechagodzilla, and more. Note that all of the separate stories featuring Godzilla are not connected and are self-contained interpretations of the giant kaiju. Highlights from the series include the epic <u>Rulers of Earth</u> series, the <u>Half-Century War</u>, and <u>Godzilla in Hell</u>.

Godzilla: Kingdom of Monsters. Written by **Eric Powell** and **Tracy Marsh**. Illustrated by **Phil Hester**. 2011–2012.

> *Vol. 1*. 2011. 104pp. 978-1-61377-016-0.
> *Vol. 2*. 2012. 104pp. 978-1-61377-122-8.
> *Vol. 3*. 2012. 104pp. 978-1-61377-205-8.

Godzilla: Gangsters and Goliaths. Written by **John Layman**. Illustrated by **Alberto Ponticelli**. 2011. 120pp. 978-1-61377-033-7.

Godzilla: Half Century War. Written and Illustrated by **James Stokoe**. 2011. 120pp. 978-1-61377-033-7; 2015. 152 pp. 978-1-63140-321-7, hardcover.

Godzilla: Legends. Written by **Chris Mowry**, **Matt Frank**, **Jeff Prezenkowski**, **Jonathan Vankin**, and **Bobby Curnow**. Illustrated by **Matt Frank**, **Dean Haspiel**, and **E.J. Su**. 2012. 128pp. 978-1-61377-223-2.

Godzilla: History's Greatest Monster. Written by **Duane Swierczynski**. Illustrated by **Simon Gane**. 2012–2013.

> *Vol. 1*. 2012. 104pp. 978-1-61377-413-7.
> *Vol. 2*. 2013. 104pp. 978-1-61377-584-4.
> *Vol. 3*. 2013. 104pp. 978-1-61377-658-2.
> *Complete Edition*. 2014. 324pp. 978-1-61377-948-4.

Godzilla: Catacalysm. Written by **Cullen Bunn**. Illustrated by **Dave Wachter**. 2015. 124pp. 978-1-63140-242-5.

Godzilla: Rulers of Earth. Written by **Chris Mowry**. Illustrated by **Matt Frank**. 2014–2017.

© Toho Co., Ltd. All Rights Reserved. GODZILLA®, Gojira, the related characters and the Character Designs are trademarks of Toho Co., Ltd. © Idea and Design Works, LLC. All Rights Reserved.

> *Vol. 1*. 2014. 124pp. 978-1-61377-749-7.
> *Vol. 2*. 2014. 104pp. 978-1-61377-933-0.
> *Vol. 3*. 2014. 104pp. 978-1-63140-009-4.
> *Vol. 4*. 2015. 104pp. 978-1-63140-172-5.
> *Vol. 5*. 2015. 104pp. 978-1-63140-281-4.
> *Vol. 6*. 2015. 148pp. 978-1-63140-407-8.
> *Complete Rulers of the Earth*.
> *Vol. 1*. 2016. 280pp. 978-1-63140-626-3.
> *Vol. 2*. 2017. 312pp. 978-1-63140-813-7.

Godzilla in Hell. Written by **James Stokoe**, **Bob Eggleton**, and various. Illustrated by **James Stokoe**, **Dave Wachter**, and various. 2016. 120pp. 978-1-63140-534-1.

Godzilla: Oblivion. Written by **Joshua Hale Fialkov.** Illustrated by **Brian Churilla.** 2016. 120pp. 978-1-63140-733-8.

Godzilla: Rage Across Time. Written by **Ulises Farinas**, **Erick Freitas**, and **Ryan Ferrier**. Illustrated by **Matt Frank** and **Tadd Galusha**. 2017. 120pp. 978-1-63140-853-3.

Godzilla: Awakening. Written by **Max Borenstein** and **Greg Borenstein**. Illustrated by **Eric Battle**. Legendary Comics/DC Comics. 2014. T 🎬

> A prequel tie-in comic book to the hit 2014 Legendary Pictures' Godzilla movie. When a giant monster seeking nuclear energy is awakened in 1954, up from the depths of the ocean awakens a towering dinosaur-like beast whose sole purpose is to fight the monster to the death and protect the Earth. Let them fight!

Gyo. Written and Illustrated by **Junji Ito**. VIZ Media, 2007–2008, 2nd edition. M Japanese manga. ◉

> The terrors of the deep sea are doing the unthinkable: they're creeping, clanking, and walking in droves on land, spreading a path of undead stench, decay, and rotting flesh. The walking and rotting sea creatures infest a seaside town of Okinawa, infecting and killing the residents one by one and spreading the infection across Japan. When a teenage boy, Tadachi, finds himself seemingly immune to the disease, all he can

do is watch in horror as his loved ones take a maddening turn from illness to transformation into walking, bloated, man-machine hybrid corpses.

Vol. 1. 2007. 200pp. 978-1-4215-1387-4.
Vol. 2. 2008. 208pp. 978-1-4215-1388-1.

Hybrid. Written by **Peter Kwong**. Illustrated by **Pablo Churin**. Studio 407, 2009. 120pp. 978-1-935385-00-4. O

College students out on a cruise of the Gulf of Mexico stumble upon an old dilapidated ship with a frightened little girl on board. Little do they know but the little girl is not alone on the vessel. When they go to save the girl, they are attacked by an intelligent deadly monstrous aquatic humanoid.

Kong of Skull Island. Written by **James Asmus.** Illustrated by **Carlos Magno.** BOOM! Studios, 2017. 112pp. 120pp. 978-1-60886-941-1. T

A prequel to the 2017 movie Kong: *Skull Island*. Two civilizations are forced to work together after their island home is destroyed. Forced to work together, they find themselves trapped on Skull Island – a home of giant beasts and dinosaurs. The only hope for their possible survival is a giant beast known as Kong.

Manifest Destiny. Written by **Chris Dingess**. Illustrated by **Matthew Roberts**. Image Comics, 2014– . T

Captain Meriwether Lewis and Second Lieutenant William Clark set out in 1804 from St. Louis, Missouri, to explore the uncharted American frontier, but little know of their true goal—they weren't just out to map uncharted territory—they were under direct orders by President Thomas Jefferson to catalog exotic life and to clear the paths for the western expansion of the monsters that roam the American wilderness.

Vol. 1: Flora and Fauna. 2014. 128pp. 978-1-60706-982-9.
Vol. 2: Amphibia & Insecta. 2015. 128pp. 978-1-63215-052-3.
*Vol.3.Chiroptera & Carniformaves.*2016.128pp.978-1-63215-397-5.
Vol. 4: Sasquatch. 2016. 128pp. 978-1-63215-890-1.

© Image Comics and Chris Dingess and Matthew Roberts.

Monster Zoo. Written and Illustrated by **Doug TenNapel**. Image Comics, 2008. 144pp. 978-1-58240-911-5. T

A teenage boy discovers that his local zoo may be more frightening than he could have ever imagined as an ancient tribal curse has transformed the zoo animals to frighteningly mutated beasts! The graphic novel was recognized by YALSA as a Great Graphic Novel for Teens on its 2009 selection list.

© Doug TenNapel and Image Comics.

Monstress. Written by **Marjorie M. Liu**. Illustrated by **Sana Takeda**. Image Comics, 2016– . M 🏺

© Image Comics and Marjorie M. Liu & Sana Takeda.

Set in an Asian steampunk in the 1900s with elements of magic, a teenage girl named Maika has a psychic connection to a giant kaiju of tremendous power. They are caught in the middle of a devastating war between humankind and otherworldly forces in which both sides have lost a tremendous amount of lives. Who will survive in cataclysmic battle for supremacy and will Maika's monster destroy both sides in the war? This Eisner Award–nominated series is still ongoing. The first volume was on YALSA's 2017 Great Graphic Novels for Teens list.

Vol. 1: Awakening. 2016. 192pp. 978-1-63215-709-6.
Vol. 2. 2017. 144pp. 978-1-53430-041-5.

Muck Monsters

Tales of horror and suspense featuring plant-like muck monsters, elementals, and creatures made from the Earth. The legends of muck monsters date back to England's history with the tales of the Jack-in-the-Green or bogie monsters. Over the history of the American comic books, there have been many tales of muck monsters spawned from the popularity of horror titles over the years including creatures such as The Heap, The Man-Thing, and Swamp Thing. Those collected in a graphic novel format are listed here. The most popular muck monster published in comic books and graphic novels is DC Comics' Swamp Thing.

Breath of Bones: A Tale of the Golem. Written by **Steve Niles**. Illustrated by **Dave Wachter**. Dark Horse Comics, 2014. 80pp. 978-1-61655-344-9. T 🏺 ◎

Breath of Bones TM © 2016 Steve Niles, Matt Santoro, and Dave Wachter.

Set in Europe during the height of World War II, when a British warplane crashes near a Jewish village, it sparks an invasion of Nazi German soldiers to the village. The Jewish residents, fearing for their lives, combine mud and clay from the nearby river to bring to life the ancient protector known as the Golem. The monstrous beast is all the stands against a Nazi horde, and the villagers fight for their lives against the greatest threat they've ever known. The book was recognized by YALSA as a Great Graphic Novel for Teens in 2015 on its annual selection list.

Swamp Thing. Created by **Len Wein** and **Bernie Wrightson**. Vertigo/DC Comics, 1987– . M 📽 🖥 ◎

Biologist Alec Holland died in a ball of flames after he was doused in chemicals in the Louisiana swamps. As his body died, his consciousness encoded itself into something more. Alec became something else: a wandering muck man, a green monster, a plant elemental, a defender of the green, a creature known as Swamp Thing. The current plant elemental from a long line of guardians of

© 2016 DC Comics.

the Green Earth, his journeys take him from not only the backwater greens of Earth, but even beyond to outer space, Heaven, and Hell where werewolves, vampires, demons, archnemesis Anton Arcane, and more are out there waiting in the hidden shadows of suspense. He is occasionally joined by his true love Abby Arcane, the dark grifter-magician John Constantine, and even DC Comics heroes including Batman and Green Lantern. The sophisticated suspense of Swamp Thing helped to make it one of the most influential comic book series in the 1980s, helped to make Alan Moore a premiere comic book writer, and paved the way for the Vertigo imprint from DC Comics. Below are listed in chronological order the tales of the muck monster called Swamp Thing both before and after Alan Moore's classic tales of the walking plant elemental. In 2012, DC Comics relaunched Swamp Thing as a New 52 title no longer under the Vertigo imprint under writer Scott Snyder as well as Jeff Lemire and Charles Soule, where Swamp Thing has also played a role as a member of Justice League Dark superhero team.

Roots of the Swamp Thing. Written by **Len Wein**. Illustrated by **Bernie Wrightson**. 2009. 320pp. 978-1-40122-236-9, hardcover. O

A collection of the first appearance of the Swamp Thing from *House of Secrets* #92 in 1971 and the first 13 issues of the original Swamp Thing series in the 1970s before Alan Moore took over the series in 1984. The series introduced classic Swamp Thing villains of Anton Arcane and the Un-Men and bore a resemblance in pacing to more classic horror comics than Alan Moore's take of Swamp Thing as a plant elemental.

Saga of the Swamp Thing. Written by **Alan Moore**, **Steve Bissette**, and **John Totleben**. DC Comics, 2009–2014. O ◎

The collection reprints all of Alan Moore's Swamp Thing run from *Saga of the Swamp Thing* #21 (1984) to his departure from the series with #64 (1987).

Book 1. 2009. 208pp. 978-1-4012-2082-2, hardcover; 2012. 978-1-4012-2083-9.
Book 2. 2009. 224pp. 978-1-4012-2532-2, hardcover; 2012. 978-1-4012-2544-5.
Book 3. 2010. 208pp. 978-1-4012-2766-1, hardcover; 2013. 978-1-4012-2767-8.
Book 4. 2011. 224pp. 978-1-4012-3018-0, hardcover; 2013. 978-1-4012-4046-2.
Book 5. 2011. 168pp. 978-1-4012-3095-1, hardcover; 2013. 978-1-4012-3096-8.
Book 6. 2011. 208pp. 978-1-4012-3298-6, hardcover; 2014. 978-1-4012-4692-1.

Swamp Thing (New 52 edition). Written by **Scott Snyder**, **Jeff Lemire**, and **Charles Soule**. Illustrated by **Yanick Paquette**, **Kano**, **Jesus Saiz**, and **Javi Pina**. DC Comics, 2012–2016. O

Relaunched in 2011 as part of DC Comics' New 52, the series features Alec Holland resurrected as a human where he finds himself haunted by a past life as a plant elemental. He can't escape his destiny though and is still part of The Green—and he must join forces with The Red (flesh and blood) against a vicious enemy known as The Black (AKA The rot), the return of Anton Arcane, and Jason Woodrue (the Floronic Man).

Vol. 1: Raise Them Bones. 2012. 168pp. 978-1-4012-3462-1.
Vol. 2: Family Tree. 2013. 160pp. 978-1-4012-3843-8.
Vol. 3: Rotworld: The Green Kingdom. 2013. 208pp. 978-1-4012-4264-0.
Vol. 4: Seeder. 2014. 144pp. 978-1-4012-4639-6.
Vol. 5: The Killing Field. 2014. 136pp. 978-1-4012-5052-2.
Vol. 6: The Sureen. 2015. 176pp. 978-1-4012-5490-2.
Vol. 7: Season's End. 2016. 200pp. 978-1-4012-5770-5.

The Old Ones

Horror that is based on or inspired by the writings of H. P. Lovecraft from his story "At the Mountains of Madness" originally published in 1936. The stories feature great ancient behemoths and gods of evil who existed before the age of man. The elder beings wait in the wings and bide their time to take over the world once again.

Alabaster Shadows. Written by **Matt Gardner**. Illustrated by **Rashad Doucet**. Oni Press, 2015. 186pp. 978-1-62010-264-0. Y

Carter Normandy's family just moved into a new community, but something isn't quite right. Maybe it's the way the adults glare at them—or maybe it's that there's another world just alongside his new community—a world where terrifying monsters still roam. Now Carter and a group of new friends he's met will try and keep the monsters out of our world before it's too late!

Arkham Woods. Written by **Christopher Rowley**. Illustrated by **Jhomar Soriano**. Seven Seas Entertainment, 2009. 200pp. 978-1-934876-36-7. O Neo-manga.

Teenager Kirsti is a fish out of water after relocating from Los Angeles to a small New England town called Arkham Woods. Kirsti and her mother are tasked with cleaning out the old house left to them by her eccentric uncle Silas. In the basement of the house Kirsti and her friends unwittingly unleash an ancient evil unless Kirsti can stop it.

Batman: The Doom That Came to Gotham. Written by **Mike Mignola**. Illustrated by **Troy Nixey**. DC Comics, 2015. 176pp. 978-1-4012-5806-1. T 🏵

Set in the 1920s, in this alternate world Batman finds himself returning to Gotham after being away for many years, and he's forced to confront Ra's al Ghul who is plotting to bring dark entities to Batman's beloved city. The book was recognized on YALSA's 2017 Great Graphic Novels for Teens list.

Colder. Written by **Paul Tobin**. Illustrated by **Juan Ferreyra**. Dark Horse Comics, 2013– . O

> Declan Thomas's body temperature is cold. It dropped from 98.6 to a current average in the high 50s. Since then, he never gets sick and he's never in any pain. He also realizes that his low body temperature gives him power to enter the broken minds of psychiatric patients, seeing their insanity and even fixing them. When a mysterious creature known as Nimble Jack arrives ready to feast on the insane, can Declan conquer his own insanity and defeat the monster of madness?

> *Vol. 1*. 2013. 152pp. 978-1-61655-136-0.
> *Vol. 2: The Bad Seed*. 2015. 144pp. 978-1-61655-647-1.
> *Vol. 3: Toss the Bones*. 2016. 136pp. 978-1-61655-776-8.

The Courtyard. Written by **Alan Moore**. Illustrated by **Jacen Burrows**. Avatar Press, 2009. 56pp. 978-1-59291-060-1. M

> Aldo Sax, a famed FBI agent, is on the trail of disturbing dismemberments. When the usual suspects are eliminated, Aldo discovers that there's something more at work—something sinister and evil. All signs for the truth lay in the location only known as the Courtyard.

Cthulhu Tales. Written by **Mark Waid**, **Steve Niles**, and **Michael Alan Nelson**. Illustrated by various. Boom Studios. O

> A wide range of short stories based on the works of H. P. Lovecraft.

> *Omnibus: Delirium*. 2011. 224pp. 978-1-60886-073-9.
> *Omnibus: Madness*. 2011. 224pp. 978-1-60886-075-3.

Fall of Cthulhu. Written by **Michael Alan Nelson**. Illustrated by various. Boom Studios. O

> Inspired by the worlds of H. P. Lovecraft. After his uncle's unexpected suicide, Cy seeks to find out why his uncle took his life. Obsessed by the truth, Cy discovers notes and scribbling of a mysterious word called Cthulhu and an ancient evil awakens. When the gods of old battle, how will humankind survive?

> *Vol. 1: The Fugue*. 2008. 128pp. 978-1-934506-19-6.
> *Vol. 2: The Gathering*. 2008. 128pp. 978-1-934506-49-3.
> *Vol. 3: The Grey Man*. 2008. 112pp. 978-1-934506-50-9.
> *Vol. 4: Godwar*. 2009. 112pp. 978-1-934506-57-8.
> *Vol. 5: Apocalypse*. 2010. 112pp. 978-1-934506-93-6.
> *Omnibus*. 2015. 500pp. 978-1-60886-404-1.

Necronomicon. Written by **William Messner-Loebs**. Illustrated by **Andrew Ritchie**. Boom! Studios, 2009. 112pp. 978-1-934506-67-7. O

> Set in the 1920s a young Arab student is drawn into a semisecret society of theosophists and asked to translate the dreaded Necronomicon into English. Terrible things begin to happen once the text has been read and the translator eventually finds himself confronted with horrors from beyond.

Neonomicon. Written by **Alan Moore**. Illustrated by **Jacen Burrows**. Avatar Press, 2011. 176pp. 978-1-59291-130-1. M

> Two young FBI agents investigate a fresh series of ritualistic murders, and during their investigation they discover the murders are connected to a former FBI agent who went mad and ended up in a maximum security prison for murder. As the trail intensifies, nothing can prepare them for the creeping insanity and unspeakable terrors they will face in the small harbor town of Innsmouth.

Nightmare World. Written by **Dirk Manning**. Illustrated by various. Image Comics, 2009–2011. O

> A collection of short stories in the vein of H.P. Lovecraft. As each short story slowly builds through the third volume, a cohesive narrative is revealed.
>
> *Vol. 1: 13 Tales of Terror.* 2009. 128pp. 978-1-60706-156-4.
> *Vol. 2: Leave the Light On.* 2010. 128pp. 978-1-60706-276-9.
> *Vol. 3: Demon Days.* 2011. 128pp. 978-1-60706-433-6.

Uzumaki: Spiral into Horror. Written and Illustrated by **Junji Ito**. VIZ Media, 2007–2013. O Japanese manga. 🎬 ◎

> In the provincial seaside town of Korozu-cho, the residents are slowly being seduced into the never-ending world of the spiral. Some are obsessed to death by it and curl up into self-made spirals, and some are slowly turned into human-sized snails. As the town slowly goes mad with their obsessions, teenager Kirie and her boyfriend must learn the terrible secret to try and survive a nightmarish world that no one can escape. The series was adapted into a live-action film in Japan.
>
> *Vol. 1.* 2007. 208pp. 978-1-4215-1389-8.
> *Vol. 2.* 2007. 208pp. 978-1-4215-1390-4.
> *Vol. 3.* 2008. 264pp. 978-1-4215-1391-1.
> *Uzimaki 3-In-1 Deluxe Edition.* 2013. 648pp. 978-1-4215-6132-5.

UZUMAKI © 2010 Junji ITO /
SHOGAKUKAN.

The Wake. Written by **Scott Snyder**. Illustrated by **Sean Murphy**. Vertigo/DC Comics, 2016. 256pp. 978-1-4012-5491-9; 978-1-4012-4523-8, hardcover. M

> A crew of an ocean-floor laboratory complex is stalked by ominous sea creatures that make them hallucinate into an even-worse madness. Inspired by the stories of H. P. Lovecraft.

Ghosts and Spirits

Curiosity about what lies after death is natural, and many people believe in spirits of the undead that have yet to find their way to the peace. Graphic novel ghost stories tend to feature protagonists who can speak with the dead, spirits that have come back to exact revenge, or even those that serve as guides to the recently deceased in the afterlife. Though ghost stories can be terrifying, the stories can also be adventurous, comical, or peaceful connections with the dead. Ghost stories that are based on humor are in the humor chapter in this book.

Anya's Ghost. Written and Illustrated by **Vera Brosgol**. First Second Books/Squarefish Books, 2011–2014. 2011. 224pp. 978-1-59643-713-5, hardcover; 2014. 978-1-25004-001-5. T 🏃 ◎

© 2017 Vera Brosgol and First Second Books.

When teenager Anya falls into a deep well, she discovers that she's not alone—there's a body of a young girl lost and forgotten for over 100 years down there with her! The ghost of the girl follows her home, and Anya soon thinks it's a great idea—especially since her family life is awful, she doesn't fit in at school, and she's too self-conscious about her body. But as Anya soon finds out, having a new friend who is a ghost maybe isn't the best idea after all. The book received many awards and accolades when it was released including being an *ALSC* Notable Book, by YALSA as a Popular Paperback for Young Adults and a Quick Pick for Reluctant Readers in 2011.

Bleach. Written and Illustrated by **Tite Kubo**. VIZ Media, 2004– . T Japanese manga. あ

BLEACH © 2001 by Tite Kubo/
SHUEISHA Inc.

Red-haired high school student Ichigo Kurosaki has always had the ability to see ghosts and spirits, but his life changes forever when he meets Rukia Kuchiki, a member of the mysterious Soul Society. Rukia is a shinigami, or soul reaper, who has the power to fight against evil spirits called Hollowers as well as the power to send the wandering souls of the dead to the Soul Society. When Ichigo's family is threatened, Rukia attempts to lend him some of her power, but instead Ichigo absorbs all of her powers. Now a shinigami himself, he's able to see the Hollowers. Together with Rukia, who is slowly regaining her own powers, they're out to save the world from Hollowers and to allow the spirits of ghosts to find peace. The series is still ongoing in Japan and has even been adapted as an anime series. VIZ Media is also beginning to reprint the series in their three-in-one edition, but it is not listed in this publication.

Vol. 1. 2004. 192pp. 978-1-5911-6441-8.
Vol. 2. 2004. 192pp. 978-1-5911-6442-5.
Vol. 3. 2004. 192pp. 978-1-5911-6443-2.
Vol. 4. 2004. 192pp. 978-1-5911-6444-9.
Vol. 5. 2005. 192pp. 978-1-5911-6445-6.
Vol. 6. 2005. 200pp. 978-1-5911-6728-0.
Vol. 7. 2005. 200pp. 978-1-5911-6807-2.
Vol. 8. 2005. 200pp. 978-1-5911-6872-0.
Vol. 9. 2005. 200pp. 978-1-5911-6924-6.
Vol. 10. 2005. 208pp. 978-1-4215-0081-2.
Vol. 11. 2006. 208pp. 978-1-4215-0271-7.
Vol. 12. 2006. 208pp. 978-1-4215-0403-2.
Vol. 13. 2006. 208pp. 978-1-4215-0611-1.
Vol. 14. 2006. 208pp. 978-1-4215-0612-8.
Vol. 15. 2006. 208pp. 978-1-4215-0613-5.
Vol. 16. 2006. 208pp. 978-1-4215-0614-2.
Vol. 17. 2007. 208pp. 978-1-4215-1041-5.
Vol. 18. 2007. 208pp. 978-1-4215-1042-2.
Vol. 19. 2007. 216pp. 978-1-4215-1043-9.
Vol. 20. 2007. 216pp. 978-1-4215-1044-6.
Vol. 21. 2007. 200pp. 978-1-4215-1165-8.
Vol. 22. 2008. 216pp. 978-1-4215-1179-5.
Vol. 23. 2008. 208pp. 978-1-4215-1541-0.
Vol. 24. 2008. 208pp. 978-1-4215-1603-5.
Vol. 25. 2008. 210pp. 978-1-4215-1796-4.
Vol. 26. 2009. 216pp. 978-1-4215-2384-2.

Vol. 27. 2009. 200pp. 978-1-4215-2385-9.
Vol. 28. 2009. 200pp. 978-1-4215-2386-6.
Vol. 29. 2009. 208pp. 978-1-4215-2387-3.
Vol. 30. 2010. 192pp. 978-1-4215-2388-0.
Vol. 31. 2010. 208pp. 978-1-4215-2809-0.
Vol. 32. 2010. 200pp. 978-1-4215-2810-6.
Vol. 33. 2010. 200pp. 978-1-4215-2811-3.
Vol. 34. 2011. 200pp. 978-1-4215-2812-0.
Vol. 35. 2011. 208pp. 978-1-4215-3312-4.
Vol. 36. 2011. 200pp. 978-1-4215-3313-1.
Vol. 37. 2011. 216pp. 978-1-4215-3314-8.
Vol. 38. 2012. 200pp. 978-1-4215-3597-5.
Vol. 39. 2012. 200pp. 978-1-4215-3598-2.
Vol. 40. 2012. 200pp. 978-1-4215-4137-2.
Vol. 41. 2012. 192pp. 978-1-4215-4138-9.
Vol. 42. 2012. 192pp. 978-1-4215-4139-6.
Vol. 43. 2012. 192pp. 978-1-4215-4296-6.
Vol. 44. 2012. 192pp. 978-1-4215-4297-3.
Vol. 45. 2012. 192pp. 978-1-4215-4298-0.
Vol. 46. 2012. 192pp. 978-1-4215-4299-7.
Vol. 47. 2012. 192pp. 978-1-4215-4300-0.
Vol. 48. 2012. 216pp. 978-1-4215-4301-7.

Vol. 49. 2012. 192pp. 978-1-4215-4302-4.
Vol. 50. 2012. 192pp. 978-1-4215-4303-1.
Vol. 51. 2012. 192pp. 978-1-4215-4304-8.
Vol. 52. 2012. 192pp. 978-1-4215-4305-5.
Vol. 53. 2012. 192pp. 978-1-4215-4949-1.
Vol. 54. 2013. 192pp. 978-1-4215-5138-8.
Vol. 55. 2013. 192pp. 978-1-4215-5236-1.
Vol. 56. 2013. 192pp. 978-1-4215-5476-1.
Vol. 57. 2013. 192pp. 978-1-4215-5882-0.
Vol. 58. 2013. 192pp. 978-1-4215-6135-6.
Vol. 59. 2014. 192pp. 978-1-4215-6237-7.
Vol. 60. 2014. 192pp. 978-1-4215-6458-6.
Vol. 61. 2014. 192pp. 978-1-4215-7383-0.
Vol. 62. 2014. 192pp. 978-1-4215-7681-7.
Vol. 63. 2015. 192pp. 978-1-42-157855-2.
Vol. 64. 2015. 192pp. 978-1-4215-7973-3.
Vol. 65. 2015. 216pp. 978-1-4215-8084-5.
Vol. 66. 2016. 192pp. 978-1-4215-8262-7.
Vol. 67. 2016. 192pp. 978-1-4215-8506-2.
Vol. 68. 2016. 208pp. 978-1-4215-8583-3.
Vol. 69. 2017. 192pp. 978-1-4215-8701-1.
Vol. 70. 2017. 200pp. 978-1-4215-8867-4.

Brody's Ghost. Written and Illustrated by **Mark Crilley**. Dark Horse Comics, 2010–2016. T 🌹

Brody is a man who has lost everything—his girlfriend, his job, and his apartment. When things couldn't get any worse for him, he sees the ghost of a young girl. In disbelief, the ghost tells him that he is the one who must stop a dangerous killer. The ghost also instructs Brody that he must undergo training by a 1,000-year-old samurai ghost to learn how to better use his ghost talker powers. When Brody discovers that his ex-girlfriend is destined to be the next victim by the killer, Brody must race against the clock and find out the identity of the killer before it's too late! The first volume was recognized by YALSA's Great Graphic Novels for Teens selection list in 2011.

Vol. 1. 2010. 96pp. 978-1-59582-521-6.
Vol. 2. 2011. 96pp. 978-1-59582-665-7.
Vol. 3. 2012. 96pp. 978-1-59582-862-0.
Vol. 4. 2013. 96pp. 978-1-61655-129-2.
Vol. 5. 2014. 96pp. 978-1-61655-460-6.
Vol. 6. 2015. 96pp. 978-1-61655-461-3.
Collected Edition. 2016. 600pp. 978-1-61655-901-4.

Death Note. Written and Illustrated by **Tsugumi Ohba**. VIZ Media, 2005–2011. O Japanese manga. ◎ ▰ あ

The Shinigami all own notebooks called "Death Notes," which grant the grim reaper-like spirits the ability to decide the fate of man. Whoever's name is written in the Death Note will die in the manner and time written (a heart attack in 40 seconds

DEATH NOTE © 2003 by Tsugumi Ohba, Takeshi Obata/SHUEISHA Inc.

being the default). When the Shinigami named Ryuk misplaces his notebook on the Earthly realm, it's recovered by a teenage boy named Light. Now the teen has command over death, and after becoming a quick study, Light has decided to remake the world the way he wants to. Now one by one Light kills off all the criminals in the world. When the countries of the world notice the large loss of life of criminals, they hired a master detective to bring this murderer. But is Light—known to the world as the mysterious Kira—really committing a crime or will someone stop him from finishing the good he's accomplished even though it's causing the deaths of some not-so-innocent men? The series was also adapted as several live-action films in Japan as well as an anime series and a live-action television show. An American film adaptation came out in 2017. The *Black Edition* volumes reprint two volumes in each of the popular series.

Vol. 1. 2005. 200pp. 978-1-4215-0168-0.
Vol. 2. 2005. 200pp. 978-1-4215-0169-7.
Vol. 3. 2006. 200pp. 978-1-4215-0170-3.
Vol. 4. 2006. 200pp. 978-1-4215-0331-8.
Vol. 5. 2006. 208pp. 978-1-4215-0626-5.
Vol. 6. 2006. 208pp. 978-1-4215-0627-2.
Vol. 7. 2006. 208pp. 978-1-4215-0628-9.
Vol. 8. 2006. 208pp. 978-1-4215-0629-6.
Vol. 9. 2006. 208pp. 978-1-4215-0630-2.
Vol. 10. 2007. 208pp. 978-1-4215-1155-9.
Vol. 11. 2007. 208pp. 978-1-4215-1178-8.
Vol. 12. 2007. 216pp. 978-1-4215-1327-0.

Black Edition. 2010–2011.

Vol. 1. 2010. 400pp. 978-1-4215-3964-5.
Vol. 2. 2011. 400pp. 978-1-4215-3965-2.
Vol. 3. 2011. 400pp. 978-1-4215-3966-9.
Vol. 4. 2011. 416pp. 978-1-4215-3967-6.
Vol. 5. 2011. 384pp. 978-1-4215-3968-3.
Vol. 6. 2011. 424pp. 978-1-4215-3969-0.

Ghostopolis. Written and Illustrated by **Doug TenNapel**. Graphix/Scholastic Books, 2010. T 🎖

Cover © Scholastic Inc.

Teenager Garth has a pretty grim look at life. He's sick with an incurable disease and, unlike most teens his age, has death on his mind. To make matters worse, he's accidentally zapped into the spirit world by Frank Gallows, a washed-out ghost wrangler from the Supernatural Immigration Task Force! Now stuck in the land of the dead where ghosts are everywhere, he finds he has latent abilities special to the realm of Ghostopolis, and the evil ruler of the land will stop at nothing to get Garth's powers. Can Garth, with the help of his deceased grandfather, rescue Ghostopolis, and can he find a way back to the land of the living? The book was recognized by YALSA's Great Graphic Novels for Teens on its 2011 selection list.

Ghost Rider. Marvel Comics, 2006– . T 📖

© 2016 Marvel Comics.

There have been several heroes to go by the name of Ghost Rider. The first is Johnny Blaze—a daredevil motorcycle stunt performer for a traveling circus. He made a deal with the devil Mephisto to save his mentor's life, and in making this pact he was bound with the demon called Zarathos. After the merging of both man and devil, at night Blaze's skin would magically melt away to reveal a leather-clad skeleton with a flaming skull, and his will could conjure a vehicle of vengeance: a motorcycle with flaming wheels that was conjured by hellfire. Now transformed into Ghost Rider, he is cursed to walk the Earth as a spirit of vengeance. The most recent Ghost Rider, introduced in 2015, is Robbie Reyes, a teenager who is killed during a street race by a drug cartel. Robbie is given a new lease on life when his body is merged with the spirit of Eli Morrow. Now a Ghost Rider for a new generation, he helps to protect his neighborhood and beyond from evils both criminal and supernatural. Ghost Rider first appeared in the Marvel comic book series Marvel Spotlight #5 in 1972. Two feature film versions of the Ghost Rider were released in 2007 and 2014, both starring Nicholas Cage as Johnny Blaze. In 2016 the Robbie Reyes incarnation appeared on the television show *Marvel's Agents of S.H.I.E.L.D.*

Ghost Rider (as Johnny Blaze). 2006– .

> *The Road to Damnation.* Written by **Garth Ennis**. Illustrated by **Clayton Crain**. 2006–2007. 144pp. 978-0-7851-1592-2, hardcover; 2007. 978-0-7851-2122-0. M.
> *Trail of Tears.* Written by **Garth Ennis**. Illustrated by **Clayton Crain**. 2007–2008. 144pp. 978-0-7851-2003-2, hardcover; 2008. 978-0-7851-2004-9.
> *Ghost Rider Omnibus.* Written by **Jason Aaron**. Illustrated by **Tony Moore**, **Tan Eng Huat**, and **Roland Boschi**. 2010. 536pp. 978-0-7851-4367-3.
> *Ghost Rider by Daniel Way Ultimate Collection.* Written by **Daniel Way**. Illustrated by **Javier Saltares**, **Mark Texeira**, and **Richard Corben**. 2012. 448pp. 978-0-7851-6447-0.

All-New Ghost Rider (as Robbie Reyes). Written by **Felipe Smith**. Illustrated by **Damion Scott**. Marvel Comics, 2014–2016. T

> *Vol. 1: Engines of Vengeance.* 2014. 112pp. 978-0-7851-5455-6.
> *Vol. 2: Legend.* 2016. 160pp. 978-0-7851-5456-3.

Ghosts. Written and Illustrated by **Raina Telgemeier**. Graphix/Scholastic Books, 2016. 256pp. 978-0-545-54062-9. Y ◉

Cover © Scholastic Inc.

When her little sister Maya is diagnosed with cystic fibrosis, Catrina and her family relocate to Bahía de la Luna in Northern California. There the air climate and the sea should help her little sister. At her new home, Catrina learns a secret from the neighbor—there are ghosts that roam around Bahía de la Luna. Maya desperately wants to see a ghost, but Catrina wants nothing to do with them. When the time of the year comes where the ghosts are believed to reunite with their families, will Catrina set aside her fears for her sister's sake—as well as her own?

The Graveyard Book. Written by **Neil Gaiman**. Adapted by **P. Craig Russell**. Illustrated by **P. Craig Russell**, **Kevin Nowlan**, **Tony Harris**, **Scott Hampton**, **Jill Thompson**, **Stephen B. Scott**, and **Galen Showman**. HarperCollins, 2014. T

The Graveyard Book tells the story of young Nobody Owens who, as an infant when his family was murdered, crawled to a nearby graveyard where he's adopted by the ghosts there and given "freedom of the graveyard." But as he gets older he is still in danger from the members of the "Jack of All Trades" that killed his family.

Vol. 1. 2014. 192pp. 978-0-06-219481-7, hardcover; 978-0-06-219482-4.

Vol. 2. 2014. 176pp. 978-0-06-219483-1, hardcover; 978-0-06-219484-8.

Cover © 2014 HarperCollins.

Haunted Mansion. Written by **Joshua Williamson**. Illustrated by **Jorge Coelho**. Disney Kingdoms/Marvel Comics, 2016. 128pp. 978-1-3029-0076-2, hardcover. T ◉

There exists a haunted house on top of a hill against the backdrop of New Orleans that is haunted like no other. Some say the ghost of a widowed bride seven times over resides there. Others say it is haunted by a pirate. And there are those who think a powerful psychic used to conjure up spirits in the old mansion. No one knows the truth for sure. Young Danny made a promise to his adventuring grandfather that they would explore the mansion together when he came back from his trip to the Matterhorn. When his beloved grandfather dies in an avalanche on top of the Matterhorn (a site for another famous Disneyland ride), Danny receives a strange message from a spirit from the mansion that warns Danny that his grandfather's spirit is in trouble and is trapped in the Haunted Mansion. Now Danny must get the courage to face the Haunted Mansion alone and confront the ghosts and ghouls, spirits, and sprites that await him at every corner in the mansion of 999 happy haunts. The series is based on the extremely popular Disney Parks' attraction that has been a hit at every Disney Park in the world since it first debuted at Disneyland in 1969.

© Marvel Comics.

Haunted Mansion: Welcome Foolish Mortals. Written by **Roman Dirge**. Illustrated by various. Slave Labor Graphics, 2007. 184pp. 978-1-59362-098-1. T

Since 1969 the Haunted Mansion at Disneyland has had a frighteningly good time where 999 happy ghosts eagerly wait for one more permanent resident to their happy haunt. Now for the first time learn some of the stories of the ghosts and ghouls from the classic ride in an anthology collection by some of Slave Labor Graphic's finest contributors.

Heathentown. Written by **Corinna Sara Bechko**. Illustrated by **Gabriel Hardman**. Image Comics. 2010. 96pp. 978-1-60706-305-6. O

> A small town near the swamps of Florida holds a dark secret. A girl named Anna finds out first hand what this town is hiding when her friend is buried after she dies. After the funeral Anna swears she saw her friend alive and walking around. While trying to catch up with her, Anna stumbles upon the secret the swamp holds. The town offers sacrifices to the undead denizens who live within the swamp.

Lola: A Ghost Story. Written by **J. Torres**. Illustrated by **Elbert Orr**. Oni Press, 2009. 114pp. 978-1-934964-33-0, hardcover. T 🏃

© Oni Press.

> Jesse's grandmother (called "Lola" in Tagalog) has just died at her home in the Philippines. He's dreading the visit since she was known to have the ability to see ghosts—and he thinks she was trying to drown him once—but that's a story for another day. Over time, Jesse learns that he has indeed inherited her gift of sight, and with the help of his cousin Maritess maybe things will be all right after all—ghosts or not. The book was recognized by YALSA as a Great Graphic Novel for Teens on its 2011 selection list.

The New Ghost. Written and Illustrated by **Robert Hunter**. Nowbrow, 2011. 24pp. 978-1-907704-14-7. T

> Everyone has a first day on the job—witness the first day at work for a newly departed man who has to get used to his new afterlife job of being a ghost.

Rin-ne. Written and Illustrated by **Rumiko Takahashi**. VIZ Media, 2009– . T Japanese manga. あ

© VIZ Media

> High school student Sakura Mamiya gained the power to see ghosts after an incident as a child. Now years later, Sakura wants to get rid of her extrasensory perception and stop seeing ghosts. Sakura might have a change of heart though when she meets classmate Rinne Rokudo, a boy of mixed human and shinigami heritage who helps lingering spirits finally pass on to be reincarnated. Together the two of them work together to help the restless spirits find their way to peace. The manga was also adapted into an anime series in Japan in 2015 that is still ongoing.
>
> *Vol. 1*. 2009. 200pp. 978-1-4215-3485-5.
> *Vol. 2*. 2010. 192pp. 978-1-4215-3486-2.
> *Vol. 3*. 2010. 192pp. 978-1-4215-3487-9.
> *Vol. 4*. 2011. 192pp. 978-1-4215-3621-7.
> *Vol. 5*. 2011. 200pp. 978-1-4215-3622-4.

Vol. 6. 2011. 200pp. 978-1-4215-4097-5.　　*Vol. 9*. 2012. 192pp. 978-1-4215-4317-8.
Vol. 7. 2011. 180pp. 978-1-4215-4173-4.　　*Vol. 10*. 2012. 192pp. 978-1-4215-4317-8.
Vol. 8. 2012. 176pp. 978-1-4215-4316-8.　　*Vol. 11*. 2013. 192pp. 978-1-4215-4981-1.

Vol. 12. 2013. 192pp. 978-1-4215-5163-0.
Vol. 13. 2013. 192pp. 978-1-4215-5379-5.
Vol. 14. 2014. 192pp. 978-1-4215-5617-8.
Vol. 15. 2014. 192pp. 978-1-4215-6644-3.
Vol. 16. 2014. 192pp. 978-1-4215-6645-0.
Vol. 17. 2015. 192pp. 978-1-4215-7679-4.
Vol. 18. 2015. 192pp. 978-1-4215-8092-0.

Vol. 19. 2015. 192pp. 978-1-4215-8093-7.
Vol. 20. 2016. 192pp. 978-1-4215-8094-4.
Vol. 21. 2016. 192pp. 978-1-4215-8382-2.
Vol. 22. 2016. 192pp. 978-1-4215-8383-9.
Vol. 23. 2017. 192pp. 978-1-4215-8384-6.
Vol. 24. 2017. 192pp. 978-1-4215-9446-0.

Shaman King. Written and Illustrated by **Hiroyuki Takei**. VIZ Media, 2003–2011. T Japanese manga. あ

In our world there are a select few individuals called shamans who are able to speak with the dead. The shamans also have the gift to have their bodies temporarily inhabited by the spirits of the dead. Yoh Asakura, a recent transfer student to Shinra Private Junior High, is a shaman-in-training. Though he appears to be a careless slacker, he is anything but. Joined with the hyper but inquisitive fellow student Manta Oyamada, his fiancée Anna Kyoyama, and the spirit of the fallen samurai Amidamaru, Yoh is ready to take on his arch-enemy, the Chinese shaman Ren, and to participate in the Great Shaman Fight in Tokyo to decide who can communicate with the Great Spirit and become the Shaman King. The series was also adapted as an anime series.

Vol. 1. 2003. 208pp. 978-1-56931-902-4.
Vol. 2. 2004. 208pp. 978-1-59116-182-0.
Vol. 3. 2004. 192pp. 978-1-59116-252-0.
Vol. 4. 2004. 200pp. 978-1-59116-253-7.
Vol. 5. 2004. 200pp. 978-1-59116-254-4.
Vol. 6. 2005. 192pp. 978-1-59116-788-4.
Vol. 7. 2005. 192pp. 978-1-59116-996-3.
Vol. 8. 2006. 192pp. 978-1-4215-0198-7.
Vol. 9. 2006. 192pp. 978-1-4215-0676-0.
Vol. 10. 2006. 192pp. 978-1-4215-0677-7.
Vol. 11. 2006. 192pp. 978-1-4215-0678-4.
Vol. 12. 2007. 200pp. 978-1-4215-1100-9.
Vol. 13. 2007. 200pp. 978-1-4215-1101-6.
Vol. 14. 2008. 200pp. 978-1-4215-1475-8.
Vol. 15. 2008. 200pp. 978-1-4215-1657-8.
Vol. 16. 2008. 200pp. 978-1-4215-1658-5.

Vol. 17. 2008. 192pp. 978-1-4215-1659-2.
Vol. 18. 2008. 192pp. 978-1-4215-1881-7.
Vol. 19. 2008. 210pp. 978-1-4215-1940-1.
Vol. 20. 2009. 210pp. 978-1-4215-2004-9.
Vol. 21. 2009. 192pp. 978-1-4215-2005-6.
Vol. 22. 2009. 192pp. 978-1-4215-2006-3.
Vol. 23. 2009. 200pp. 978-1-4215-2176-3.
Vol. 24. 2009. 200pp. 978-1-4215-2177-0.
Vol. 25. 2009. 192pp. 978-1-4215-2178-7.
Vol. 26. 2010. 200pp. 978-1-4215-2179-4.
Vol. 27. 2010. 200pp. 978-1-4215-2180-0.
Vol. 28. 2010. 192pp. 978-1-4215-2181-7.
Vol. 29. 2010. 192pp. 978-1-4215-2182-4.
Vol. 30. 2010. 192pp. 978-1-4215-2183-1.
Vol. 31. 2010. 192pp. 978-1-4215-2184-8.
Vol. 32. 2011. 224pp. 978-1-4215-2185-5.

Yu Yu Hakusho. Written and Illustrated by **Yoshihiro Togashi**. VIZ Media, 2003–2010. T Japanese manga. あ

When delinquent 14-year-old Yusuke Urameshi is killed while saving a child from a speeding car, he's given a new lease in the after-life for his honorable, selfless act. Under the guidance of Botan, the cute guide to River Styx, and Koenma, the junior Lord of the Underworld, he's been given a second chance by acting as a guardian spirit guide helping those in need. Meanwhile, his body has been brought back from the dead and kept in a coma, and Yusuke can become human for one day a month. If Yusuke can save enough lives—both the living and the dead—through good deeds, he can earn a permanent reunion with his body. The popular series was also adapted into an anime series.

Vol. 1. 2003. 200pp. 978-1-56931-904-8.
Vol. 2. 2003. 200pp. 978-1-59116-082-3.
Vol. 3. 2004. 200pp. 978-1-59116-183-7.
Vol. 4. 2004. 192pp. 978-1-59116-325-1.
Vol. 5. 2004. 200pp. 978-1-59116-521-7.
Vol. 6. 2004. 200pp. 978-1-59116-668-9.
Vol. 7. 2005. 200pp. 978-1-59116-812-6.
Vol. 8. 2005. 192pp. 978-1-4215-0026-3.
Vol. 9. 2006. 208pp. 978-1-4215-0278-6.
Vol. 10. 2006. 208pp. 978-1-4215-0695-1.

Vol. 11. 2006. 208pp. 978-1-4215-0696-8.
Vol. 12. 2007. 192pp. 978-1-4215-1118-4.
Vol. 13. 2007. 192pp. 978-1-4215-1119-1.
Vol. 14. 2008. 208pp. 978-1-4215-1120-7.
Vol. 15. 2008. 202pp. 978-1-4215-1516-8.
Vol. 16. 2008. 210pp. 978-1-4215-1517-5.
Vol. 17. 2009. 208pp. 978-1-4215-2448-1.
Vol. 18. 2009. 192pp. 978-1-4215-2449-8.
Vol. 19. 2010. 192pp. 978-1-4215-2450-4.

Demonic Possession, Black Magic, Witches, and the Occult

Here are tales featuring those who have made deals with the devil, those possessed or visited by demons, as well as tales featuring witches, warlocks, and mages. Not all magicians portrayed in graphic novels are black magic users, though some may use the dark arts to defeat evil. These tales featuring magicians closely resemble those found in the Fantasy subgenre, but here the focus is not on the more traditional focuses of magic including the faerie realm. The antihero black magician John Constantine, from the <u>Hellblazer</u> series of books, is an excellent example of a dark magician.

Black Bird. Written and Illustrated by **Kanoko Sakurakoji**. VIZ Media, 2009–2014. O. Japanese manga.

A Japanese supernatural shojo manga, Misao Harada, is a teenager who has always had the gift to see the supernatural, but the demons have never bothered her until now. Once she turned 16 all bets are off, and now the supernatural are out to get her. Her one friend when she was a child, Kyo Usui, rescues her from a supernatural attack, and he has a secret of his own: he's a demon! Misao is the "bride of the prophecy," a title of an arranged marriage to the head of the Tengu clan—which is now Kyo. Originally she was to marry Kyo's older brother, but Kyo loved Misao since they were children and promised he would marry her. Now Misao's powers are growing as well as her love for a demon.

Vol. 1. 2009. 194pp. 978-1-4215-2764-2.
Vol. 2. 2009. 200pp. 978-1-4215-2765-9.
Vol. 3. 2010. 200pp. 978-1-4215-2766-6.
Vol. 4. 2010. 200pp. 978-1-4215-2767-3.
Vol. 5. 2010. 200pp. 978-1-4215-2768-0.
Vol. 6. 2010. 192pp. 978-1-4215-3066-6.
Vol. 7. 2011. 192pp. 978-1-4215-3311-7.
Vol. 8. 2011. 200pp. 978-1-4215-3580-7.
Vol. 9. 2011. 200pp. 978-1-4215-3774-0.

Vol. 10. 2011. 200pp. 978-1-4215-3843-3.
Vol. 11. 2011. 200pp. 978-1-4215-3937-9.
Vol. 12. 2012. 200pp. 978-1-4215-4052-8.
Vol. 13. 2012. 200pp. 978-1-4215-4177-8.
Vol. 14. 2012. 194pp. 978-1-4215-4275-1.
Vol. 15. 2012. 200pp. 978-1-4215-4921-7.
Vol. 16. 2013. 192pp. 978-1-4215-5243-9.
Vol. 17. 2013. 192pp. 978-1-4215-5890-5.
Vol. 18. 2014. 200pp. 978-1-4215-6009-0.

Black Magick. Written by **Greg Rucka**. Illustrated by **Nicola Scott**. Image Comics, 2016– . M

Rowan Black is not only a tough detective with the Portsmouth PD—she's also a witch! She's been covering up her past for years, but when her life is being threatened

© Image Comics and Greg Rucka and
Nicola Scott.

by someone who knows her secret, she has to put matters into her own hands by any means necessary!

Vol. 1. 2016. 128pp. 978-1-63215-675-4.

Blue Exorcist. Written and Illustrated by **Kazue Kato**. VIZ Media, 2011– . O 🎋 Japanese manga. あ

AO NO EXORCIST © 2009 by
Kazue Kato/SHUEISHA Inc.

Teenager Rin Okumura has found out that his father is like no other—he's really the devil, Satan! When Satan kills Rin's guardian, Rin sets on the road to becoming a full-fledged exorcist at the True Cross Academy. There he'll learn the skills he needs to control his powers and take on his father himself! The manga was also adapted into an animated series in Japan. The first several volumes were recognized by YALSA's Great Graphic Novels for Teens selection list in 2012. The series is still ongoing in Japan.

Vol. 1. 2011. 202pp. 978-1-4215-4032-0.
Vol. 2. 2011. 210pp. 978-1-4215-4033-7.
Vol. 3. 2011. 200pp. 978-1-4215-4034-4.
Vol. 4. 2011. 200pp. 978-1-4215-4047-4.

Vol. 5. 2011. 202pp. 978-1-4215-4076-4.
Vol. 6. 2012. 200pp. 978-1-4215-4174-7.
Vol. 7. 2012. 200pp. 978-1-4215-4262-1.
Vol. 8. 2012. 200pp. 978-1-4215-5084-8.
Vol. 9. 2013. 192pp. 978-1-4215-5477-8.
Vol. 10. 2013. 192pp. 978-1-4215-5886-8.
Vol. 11. 2014. 210pp. 978-1-4215-6547-7.

Vol. 12. 2014. 202pp. 978-1-4215-7536-0.
Vol. 13. 2015. 202pp. 978-1-4215-7974-0.
Vol. 14. 2015. 202pp. 978-1-4215-8263-4.
Vol. 15. 2016. 202pp. 978-1-4215-8507-9.
Vol. 16. 2016. 216pp. 978-1-4215-9041-7.
Vol. 17. 2017. 186pp. 978-1-4215-9333-3.

Chilling Adventures of Sabrina. Written by **Roberto Aguirre-Sacasa**. Illustrated by **Francesco Francavilla**. Archie Comics 2016. 160pp. 978-1-62738-987-7. T 🎋

A terrifying twist on the classic Sabrina the Teenage Witch comic book series. Sabrina Spellman is approaching her 16th birthday and must choose to embrace her witch heritage or her mortal boyfriend, Harvey. But when an old family foe, Madame Satan, arrives in Greendale, she wants revenge on the Spellman family no matter who else is hurt. Other Archie characters also make appearances including Betty and Veronica who are also studying witchcraft. The book was on YALSA's 2017 Great Graphic Novels for Teens list.

The Death-Defying Doctor Mirage. Written by **Jen Van Meter**. Illustrated by **Roberto de la Torre**. Valiant Entertainment, 2015–2016. T

© 2016 Valiant Entertainment.

Doctor Mirage talks to the dead, but the only spirit Shan Fong can't find is that of her late husband, Hwen. She's solved homicides and has brought peace to the recently bereaved, but for four years, Shan's still struggling to come to grip with her own loss. When a wealthy eccentric billionaire seeks her aid, Shan discovers she might finally find a lead to reuniting with Hwen's spirit. While roaming the land of the dead, Doctor Mirage also uncovers a demon invasion that she must find a way to stop at any cost even if it may be the soul of her beloved husband.

Vol. 1. 2015. 128pp. 978-1-939346-49-0.
Vol. 2. 2016. 112pp. 978-1-682151-29-7.
Deluxe Edition. 2016. 272pp. 978-1-682151-53-2.

Doctor Strange. Marvel Comics, 2013– . T 🎞️ 📽️

© 2016 Marvel Comics.

Originally created by Stan Lee and Steve Ditko in 1963, he's the Sorcerer Supreme of Earth in the Marvel Comics Universe. The protector of our world from supernatural villains including the dreaded Dormammu, Baron Mordo, and other evil magical threats, Doctor Stephen Strange is a man who came from humble beginnings to become the chief magic user on the planet. Once an arrogant surgeon, he learned the art of magic from the fabled Ancient One and now uses his mastery over the mystic arts as a protector of Earth, a consultant to Marvel heroes in time of mystical catastrophes, and as a member of the hero group called the Defenders. *The Doctor Strange Omnibus*, *A Separate Reality*, and *What Is It That Disturbs You, Stephen?* collections highlight early stories from the 1960s and early 1970s. *Strange: Strange Origin* is a retelling of the origin of Strange's emergence as the Sorcerer Supreme. Doctor Strange and Doctor Doom is a unique team-up with one of the deadliest villains in the entire Marvel Universe. Also included is the current ongoing series as well as other highlights recently of the Sorcerer Supreme. *Doctor Strange* was also released as a feature film by Disney in 2016 starring Benedict Cumberbatch as Doctor Stephen Strange. In 2017 the title *Doctor Strange, Vol. 1: Way of the Weird* was recognized as a Great Graphic Novel for Teens by YALSA.

Doctor Strange Omnibus. Written by **Stan Lee**. Illustrated by **Steve Ditko**. 2016.

Vol. 1. 2016. 456pp. 978-0-7851-9924-3, hardcover.

Doctor Strange. (2015–) Written by **Jason Aaron**. Illustrated by **Chris Bachalo**. 2016– .

Vol. 1: The Way of the Weird. 2016. 136pp. 978-0-7851-9516-0, hardcover; 2016. 978-0-7851-9932-8.
Vol. 2: The Last Days of Magic. 2016. 168pp. 978-0-7851-9517-7, hardcover.
Vol. 3: Blood in the Ether. 2017. 136pp. 978-1-3029-0299-5.

Doctor Strange: The Flight of Bones. Written by **Tony Harris**, **Daniel Jolley**, **Ray Snyder**, and **Kieron Gillen**. Illustrated by **Paul Chadwick**, **Frazer Irving**, **Frank Brunner**, and **Ted McKeever**. 2016. 192pp. 978-1-302-90167-7.

Doctor Strange Epic Collection: A Separate Reality. Written by **Stan Lee**, **Roy Thomas**, **Steve Englehart**, and **Gardner Fox**. Illustrated by **Gene Colan**, **Frank Brunner**, **Barry Windsor-Smith**, and **Herb Trimpe**. 2016. 472pp. 978-0-7851-9444-6.

Doctor Strange: The Oath. Written by **Brian K. Vaughan**. Illustrated by **Marcos Martin**. Marvel Comics, 2013. 128pp. 978-0-7851-8786-8.

Doctor Strange: What Is It That Disturbs You, Stephen? Written by **P. Craig Russell**, **Marc Andreyko**, **Marv Wolfman**, **Gardner Fox**, **Ralph Macchio**, **Roger Stern**, **Chris Claremont**, **Mike W. Barr**, **Peter Gillis**, **George Alec Effinger**, and **Steve Gerber**. **Illustrated by P. Craig Russell**, **Tom Sutton**, **Michael Golden**, **Marshall Rogers**, **Sandy Plunkett**, **Carmine Infantino**, and **Dan Adkins**. Marvel Comics, 2016. 224pp. 978-1-30290-168-4.

Doctor Strange and Doctor Doom: Triumph and Torment. Written by **Roger Stern** and **Gerry Conway**. Illustrated by **Mike Mignola**, **Kevin Nowlan**, and **Gene Colan**. Marvel Comics, 2013. 160pp. 978-0-7851-8454-6.

Doctor Strange: Strange Origin. Written by **Greg Pak**. Illustrated by **Emma Rios**. Marvel Comics, 2016. 144pp. 978-0-7851-6391-6.

Harrow County. Written by **Cullen Bunn**. Illustrated by **Tyler Crook**. Dark Horse Comics, 2015– . O 🎗 ◎

> Emmy has always known that the woods near her home of Harrow County are haunted and filled with monsters. On the eve of her 18th birthday, she discovers that she has a strange connection to the land and the creatures that reside there. Join Emmy as she discovers the truth about her strange connection to the haunting and creepy town of Harrow County. The first volume was recognized by YALSA as a Great Graphic Novel for Teens in 2017.
> *Vol. 1: Countless Haints*. 2015. 152pp. 978-1-61655-780-5.
> *Vol. 2: Twice Told*. 2016. 120pp. 978-1-61655-900-7.
> *Vol. 3: Snake Doctor*. 2016. 136pp. 978-1-5067-0071-7.
> *Vol. 4: Family Tree*. 2017. 136pp. 978-1-5067-0141-7.
> *Vol. 5: Abandoned*. 2017. 136pp. 978-1-5067-0190-5.

John Constantine: Hellblazer/Constantine

Vertigo/DC Comics, 2011– . O-M. 🎗 🎬 💻 ◎

> A trench coat-wearing smooth-talking British grifter-magician, John Constantine is anything but a simple man. His roots began in DC Comics' Swamp Thing series where the Sting look-alike first appeared. Neck-deep in the occult ever since he was a teen in Newcastle, England, Constantine's not a powerful sorcerer by any means, but his presence alone can intimidate magic practicers and humble the demons. Traveling all around the globe to wherever he's needed, he's smart enough to trick the Devil (even though he's been known to damn some of his friends in the process) and is one of the only men on Earth capable of confronting demons, devils, and horrors of the supernatural world and our own. The first series, Hellblazer (1988–2013), was one of Vertigo's longest-running and successful imprint in its

© 2016 DC Comics

line. The series was relaunched in 2013 as <u>Constantine</u> and for the first time as a non-Vertigo title under the New 52 relaunch. The series was once again revived as <u>Constantine: The Hellblazer</u> in 2015 and then again in 2016 as *The Hellblazer*. Listed below are the original *John Constantine: Hellblazer* titles that have been recently released in chronological order by Vertigo/DC Comics as well as the newer New 52 edition of Constantine released in 2013. For many more titles featuring John Constantine, check out www.dccomics.com. In 2005, a feature film adaptation of the series was released as <u>Constantine</u>, starring Keanu Reeves and Rachel Weisz. In 2014, a short-lived adaptation of the character aired on NBC starring Matt Ryan. The series received favorable reviews, but unfortunately lasted only 13 episodes. Ryan has reprised the role on other comic-based shows as well as in animation. Core issues are listed below as well as the New 52 relaunch of the series by DC Comics. Volume one of *Constantine the Hellblazer* book was recognized on YALSA's 2017 Great Graphic Novels for Teens list.

John Constantine: Hellblazer. Vertigo/DC Comics, 2011– . M

Vol. 1. Original Sins. Written by **Jamie Delano** and **Rick Veitch**. Illustrated by **John Ridgway** and **Alfredo Alcala**. 2011. 304pp. 978-1-4012-3006-7.

Vol. 2: The Devil You Know. Written by **Jamie Delano** and **David Lloyd**. Illustrated by **Mark Buckingham**, **Bryan Talbot**, and **Richard Piers Rayner**. 2012. 304pp. 978-1-4012-3302-0.

Vol. 3: The Fear Machine. Written by **Jamie Delano**. Illustrated by **Dave McKean** and **Kent Williams**. 2012. 240pp. 978-1-4012-3519-2.

Vol. 4: The Family Man. Written by **Jamie Delano**. Illustrated by various. 2012. 288pp. 978-1-4012-3690-8.

Vol. 5: Dangerous Habits. Written by **Jamie Delano** and **Garth Ennis**. Illustrated by **William Simpson**. 2012. 352pp. 978-1-4012-3802-5.

Vol. 6: Bloodlines. Written by **Garth Ennis**. Illustrated by **William Simpson**, **Steve Dillon**, and various. 2013. 400pp. 978-1-4012-4043-1.

Vol. 7: Tainted Love. Written by **Garth Ennis**. Illustrated by **Steve Dillon**. 2014. 320pp. 978-1-4012-4303-6.

Vol. 8: Rake at the Gates of Hell. Written by **Garth Ennis**. Illustrated by **Steve Dillon**. 2014. 384pp. 978-1-4012-4749-2.

Vol. 9: Critical Mass. Written by **Paul Jenkins** and **Eddie Campbell**. Illustrated by **Sean Phillips**. 2014. 328pp. 978-1-4012-5072-0.

Vol. 10: In the Line of Fire. Written by **Paul Jenkins**. Illustrated by **Sean Phillips**. 2015. 288pp. 978-1-4012-5137-6.

Vol. 11: Last Man Standing. Written by **Paul Jenkins**. Illustrated by **Sean Phillips**. 2015. 336pp. 978-1-4012-5529-9.

Vol. 12: How to Play with Fire. Written by **Paul Jenkins**, Illustrated by **Warren Pleece**. 2016. 304pp. 978-1-4012-5810-8.

Vol. 13: Haunted. Written by **Warren Ellis**. Illustrated by **John Higgins** and **Frank Teran**. 2016. 336pp. 978-1-4012-6141-2.

Vol. 14: Good Intentions. Written by **Brian Azzarello**. Illustrated by **Marcelo Frusin**. 2016. 384pp. 978-1-4012-6373-7.

Vol. 15: Highwater. Written and Illustrated by Various. 2017. 320pp. 978-1-4012-6579-3.
Vol. 16: The Wild Card. Written and Illustrated by Various. 2017. 320pp. 978-1-4012-6909-8.

Constantine (New 52, 1st series). Written by **Robert Venditti**, **Jeff Lemire**, and **Ray Fawkes**. Illustrated by **Renato Guedes**. DC Comics, 2014–2015. O

Vol. 1: The Spark and the Flame. 2014. 144pp. 978-1-4012-4323-4.
Vol. 2: Blight. 2014. 144pp. 978-1-4012-4747-8.
Vol. 3: The Voice in the Fire. 2015. 144pp. 978-1-4012-5085-0.
Vol. 4: The Apocalypse Road. 2015. 144pp. 978-1-4012-5470-4.

Constantine: the Hellblazer (New 52, 2nd series). Written by **Ming Doyle** and **James Tynion IV**. Illustrated by **Riley Rossmo**. DC Comics, 2016. O

Vol. 1: Going Down. 2016. 144pp. 978-1-4012-5972-3.
Vol. 2: The Art of the Deal. 2016. 160pp. 978-1-4012-6371-3.

Locke and Key. Written by **Joe Hill**. Illustrated by **Gabriel Rodriguez**. IDW Publishing, 2008–2016. O ◎ 🌳

© Joe Hill, art © Idea and Design Works, LLC.

After the gruesome murder of their father, the Locke family leaves their lives on the west coast behind to begin anew in their father's childhood home in Lovecraft, Massachusetts. The children, Tyler and Kinsey, attempt to cope at their new high school, while their smaller brother Bode explores the many doorways within the Keyhouse Mansion. Bode soon finds out that many of the fantastical stories his father told him of the house seems to be true. The Locke children discover several magical keys—one of which opens a doorway that turns anyone that walks through it into a ghost—are the least of the troubles the Locke family will face in their new home as they become embattled in a war between good and evil. The six volumes contain the entire story, with the Master Editions collecting two volumes in one. The series received many accolades including recognition for YALSA's 2010 Great Graphic Novels for Teens selection list as well as an Eisner Award in 2011 for Best Writer. The series was also nominated for Best Series and Best Writer in 2009. Plans for a television adaptation were announced in 2016.

Vol. 1: Welcome to Lovecraft. 2008. 152pp. 978-1-60010-237-0, hardcover; 978-1-60010-384-1.
Vol. 2: Head Games. 2009. 156pp. 978-1-60004-831-1, hardcover. 978-1-60010-761-0.
Vol. 3: Crown of Shadows. 2010. 156pp. 978-1-60010-695-8, hardcover; 978-1-60010-953-9.
Vol. 4: Keys to the Kingdom. 2011. 152pp. 978-1-60010-886-0, hardcover; 978-1-61377-207-2.
Vol. 5: Clockworks. 2012. 152pp. 978-1-61377-227-0, hardcover; 978-1-61377-699-5.
Vol. 6: Alpha and Omega. 2014. 212pp. 978-1-61377-853-1, hardcover; 978-1-63140-144-2.
Master Edition, Vol. 1. 2015. 328pp. 978-1-63140-224-1, hardcover.

Master Edition, Vol. 2. 2016. 328pp. 978-1-63140-374-3, hardcover.

Master Edition, Vol. 3. 2016. 352pp. 978-1-63140-686-7, hardcover.

Nightschool: The Weirn Books. Written and Illustrated by **Svetlana Chmakova**. Yen Press, 2009–2011. T Neo-manga 🏃 ◎

© Yen Press and Svetlana Chmakova.

When all the other schools are closed for the night—one is open late at night—but the students are not like anyone you've ever known! Welcome to the Nightschool—a special school made for the monsters of the night—where the vampires, witches (weirns), and werewolves go to school to learn calculus as well learn about spellcasting. A young weirn named Alex enters the Nightschool to search for clues about her missing sister who seems to have had all traces of her existence removed! Will she be able to find her lost sister and survive the strangest school of them all? The first volume of *Nightschool* was recognized by YALSA as a Great Graphic Novel for Teens recommendation in 2010.

Vol. 1. 2009. 192pp. 978-0-7595-2859-8.

Vol. 2. 2009. 192pp. 978-0-7595-2860-4.

Vol. 3. 2010. 208pp. 978-0-7595-2861-1.

Vol. 4. 2010. 224pp. 978-0-3160-9126-8.

Rasputin. Written by **Alex Grecian**. Illustrated by **Riley Rossmo**. Image Comics, 2015– . M

© Alex Grecian & Riley Rossmo and Image Comics.

What if Rasputin, the "Mad Monk" from Russian history, was more than just an enigmatic influence on the Russian royal family? What if Rasputin was gifted with the power to heal the sick and dying? In this eerie retelling of Rasputin's life told in flashbacks and foresight, Rasputin's gift of healing comes at a great cost—whenever he heals, he loses a little bit of himself in the process and gains a little bit of whomever—and whatever he heals. Given foresight into his death, thanks to his healing ability, can a man who was so influential in Russia and was in one night stabbed, poisoned, beaten, shot, and then drowned in a frozen river—can he ever truly die?

Vol. 1: The Road to the Winter Palace. 2015. 184pp. 978-1-63215-267-1.

Vol. 2: The Road to the White House. 2016. 136pp. 978-1-63215-633-4.

Rachel Rising. Written and Illustrated by **Terry Moore**. Abstract Studio. 2012–2016. M

Rachel Rising is a © and TM Terry Moore and Abstract Studio.

Rachel Beck was strangled and left for dead in a shallow grave in the city of Manson—but that wasn't the end of her. Barely alive with no memory of what happened to herself, Rachel has returned from the dead. With the help of her Aunt Johnnie and her friend Jet, Rachel tries to find who killed her, and slowly Rachel realizes that the old city is cursed by Lilith, the mother of witches, who has sought revenge against the city that wronged her in the past. Meanwhile, a demon named Malus has his sights on the city as well. Can humanity survive under the onslaught of two dark entities, or will they destroy each other in their conflict?

Vol. 1: The Shadow of Death. 2012. 128pp. 978-1-892597-51-9.

Vol. 2: Fear No Malus. 2012. 128pp. 978-1-892597-52-6.

Vol. 3: Cemetery Songs. 2013. 128pp. 978-1-892597-55-7.
Vol. 4: Winter Graves. 2014. 128pp. 978-1-892597-56-4.
Vol. 5: Night Cometh. 2014. 128pp. 978-1-892597-57-1.
Vol. 6: Secrets Kept. 2015. 128pp. 978-1-892597-58-8.
Vol. 7: Dust to Dust. 2016. 128pp. 978-1-892597-60-1.

Spell Checkers. Written by **Jamie S. Rich**. Illustrated by **Joëlle Jones**. Oni Press, 2010–2013. O

Three teenage witches who have abused their powers for ill and using it for popularity, good grades, and the good life. When their cozy witch lives are threatened by another witch and her demon companion, can these shallow and pretentious witches with no redeeming qualities whatsoever work together for good? And can Cynthia win the Prom Queen contest without resorting to magic, after all the horrible things she's done to her classmates this year? *Mean Girls* with magic.

Vol. 1. 2010. 148pp. 978-1-934964-32-3.
Vol. 2: Sons of a Preacher Man. 2011. 152pp. 978-1-934964-72-9.
Vol. 3. Careless Whisper. 2013. 144pp. 978-1-620100-94-3.

Wytches. Written by **Scott Snyder**. Illustrated by **Jock**. Image Comics, 2015– . M

The Rooks family has escaped to Litchfield, New Hampshire, after a family trauma, but little do they realize that in the nearby woods is a dark and ancient horror biding their time to strike with a horror unseen in eons. These are witches much darker and horrifying than you've ever dared to dream.

Vol. 1. 2015. 144pp. 978-1-63215-380-7.

© Scott Snyder & Jock and
Image Comics.

Slasher/Thriller

Slasher stories are inspired by the film genre of the same name in which people are violently killed, usually with knives, resulting in a bloody mess. The villain can be a normal human, or he can be imbued with supernatural abilities and can be unkillable. Thrillers often share similar qualities of the Slasher genre, where heightened feelings of suspense, anticipation, or anxiety build as the mood keeps the reader on the edge of his or her seats to the climax. Gore may play a role in the story, but plot over blood is the main focus of a Thriller in Horror Fiction.

Friday the 13th. Written by **Jimmy Palmiotti**. Illustrated by **Adam Archer**. WildStorm Productions/DC Comics. 2007–2008. M

In 1980, *Friday the 13th* introduced moviegoers to a new kind of terror! With over 12 films in the franchise, the hockey masked character of "Jason" has become known worldwide as the first name in evil. When a group of teens come to Camp Crystal Lake for a summer clean-up job, they once again reawaken the terrifying Jason Voorhees. As the slaughter begins and Jason closes in, they formulate a desperate plan to survive—but whom, if anyone will make it out in just the one piece?

Vol. 1. 2007. 144pp. 978-1-4012-2004-4.
Vol. 2. 2008. 160pp. 978-1-4012-2003-7.

Hack/Slash. Written by **Tim Seeley**, **Michael Moreci**, **Steve Seeley**, and various. Illustrated by **Stefano Caselli**, **Federica Manfredi**, and various. Image Comics, 2007– . O

© Tim Seeley and Image Comics.

Everyone's seen those slasher movies in which there's only one last survivor. Cassie Hack is one such girl. Years ago she was the last one alive after a deadly encounter with the Lunch Lady slasher—who turned out to be her own mother! She got away and has made it her personal mission to prevent anyone else from sharing the same fate as she and her friends by going after the Slashers before they can kill again. She's joined on her journey with Vlad, a monstrous beast of a companion, but she may have met her match in the form of an undead killer and the army of zombie killer pets, a killer who strikes college kids on spring break, and a comic book convention killer. Slashers beware: your days are numbered! The series was originally published by Devil's Due Publishing, but moved to Image Comics in 2007. The five Omnibus collections reprint the original 13 volumes. In 2014 a special crossover collection teaming Cassie up with Ash from the *Army of Darkness* comic books was co-published with Dynamite Entertainment.

Vol. 0: My First Maniac. 2011. 112pp. 978-1-60706-338-4.
Vol. 1: First Cut 2005. 160pp. 1-932796-42-8.
Vol. 2: Death by Sequel. 2007. 160pp. 978-1-932796-75-9.
Vol. 3: Friday the 31st. 2010. 152pp. 978-1-60706-286-8.
Vol. 4: Revenge of the Return Part 4. 2008. 144pp. 978-1-934692-18-9.
Vol. 5. 2009. 184pp. 978-1-934692-44-8.
Vol. 6: In Revenge and in Love. 2009. 160pp. 978-1-934692-68-4.
Vol. 7: New Blood, Old Wounds. 2010. 160pp. 978-1-934692-83-7.
Vol. 8: Super Sidekick Sleepover Slaughter. 2010. 152pp. 978-1-60706-291-2.
Vol. 9: Torture Prone. 2011. 160pp. 978-1-60706-409-1.
Vol. 10: Dead Celebrities. 2012. 160pp. 978-1-60706-508-1.
*Vol. 11: Marry, F**k, Kill*. 2013. 160pp. 978-1-60706-656-9.
Vol. 12: Dark Sides. 2013. 160pp. 978-1-60706-731-3.
Vol. 13: Final. 2013. 160pp. 978-1-60706-747-4.
Omnibus, Vol. 1. 2010. 300pp. 978-1-60706-273-8.
Omnibus, Vol. 2. 2010. 300pp. 978-1-60706-274-5.
Omnibus, Vol. 3. 2010. 300pp. 978-1-60706-275-2.
Omnibus, Vol. 4. 2012. 300pp. 978-1-60706-526-5.
Omnibus, Vol. 5. 2013. 300pp. 978-1-60706-741-2.
Son of Samhain, Vol. 1. 2015. 128pp. 978-1-63215-244-2.
Army of Darkness vs. Hack/Slash. 2014. 160pp. 978-1-60690-497-8.

Hellbound. Written by **Victor Gischler**. Illustrated by **Riccardo Birchielli**. Dark Horse Comics, 2015. 144pp. 978-1-61655-815-4. M

When two disgraced FBI agents are sent to investigate a series of gruesome murders on Route 5, they discover that there's more than just a simple string of bodies being left by some simple serial killer. There's something very evil that is rising in power, and the only thing left to fight against the monsters is a man in junkyard-forged armor who is waiting to keep the beasts away.

Morning Glories. Written by **Nick Spencer**. Illustrated by **Joe Eisma**. Image Comics, 2010– . O

© Nick Spencer and Joe Eisma and Image Comics.

Six trouble teenage students begin their studies at the prestigious prep school called Morning Glory Academy, but they soon discover that they are trapped in a school that is far deadlier than even in their wildest dreams. Separated by their loved ones and trapped in the school, together the teens must band together or die trying against unspeakable terror.

Vol. 1. 2010. 192pp. 978-1-60706-307-0.
Vol. 2. 2011. 168pp. 978-1-60706-407-7.
Vol. 3. 2012. 240pp. 978-1-60706-558-6.
Vol. 4. 2013. 216pp. 978-1-60706-727-6.
Vol. 5. 2013. 136pp. 978-1-60706-774-0.
Vol. 6. 2013. 144pp. 978-1-60706-823-5.
Vol. 7. 2014. 120pp. 978-1-60706-943-0.
Vol. 8. 2015. 120pp. 978-1-63215-140-7.
Vol. 9. 2015. 104pp. 978-1-63215-560-3.
Vol. 10. 2016. 136pp. 978-1-63215-732-4.
Vol. 1 Deluxe Edition. 2011. 352pp. 978-1-60706-430-5, hardcover.
Compendium Vol. 1. 2014. 1048pp. 978-1-63215-213-8.

Anthologies and Short Story Collections

These collections of short stories and anthologies present the horror genre in a graphic novel format. The stories are either made for the collections or adapted from prose work.

The Chilling Archives of Horror Comics! Written and Illustrated by various. Edited by Craig Yoe. IDW Publishing, 2010– . T

From IDW's Yoe! Books imprint, this Archives series collects various horror titles from various creators and titles from the 1940s onward ranging from the well known to the obscure.

Dick Briefer's Frankenstein. 2010. 148pp. 978-1-60010-722-1, hardcover.
Bob Powell's Terror. 2011. 148pp. 978-1-61377-067-2, hardcover.
Zombies. 2012. 148pp. 978-1-61377-213-3, hardcover.
Jack Cole's Deadly Horror. 2013. 148pp. 978-1-61377-656-8, hardcover.
Haunted Horror: Banned Comics from the 1950s. 2013. 148pp. 978-1-61377-788-6, hardcover.
The Worst of Eerie Publications. 2014. 148pp. 978-1-63140-114-5, hardcover.
Haunted Horror: Comics Your Mother Warned You About. 2014. 148pp. 978-1-63140-126-8, hardcover.
Howard Nostrand's Nightmares. 2014. 148pp. 978-1-63140-151-0, hardcover.
Haunted Horror: Pre-Code Comics So Good, They're Scary. 2015. 160pp. 978–1-63140-4252.

Tom Sutton's Creepy Things. 2015. 148pp. 978-1-63140-183-1, hardcover.
The Complete Voodoo, Vol. 1. 2015. 208pp.978-1-63140-455-9.
Ghosts and Girls of Fiction House. 2015. 152pp. 978–1-63140-404-7.
Horror by Heck! 2016. 152pp. 978-1-63140-463-4, hardcover.
Devil Tales. 2016. 148pp. 978–1-63140-504-4.
Haunted Horror: Candles for the Undead and More. 2016. 144pp. 978–1-63140-671-3.
The Return of the Zombies. 2016. 148pp. 978–1-63140-630-0.
The Complete Voodoo Vol. 2. 2016. 184pp. 978–1-63140-681-2.
Snake Tales. 2016. 144pp. 978–1-63140-631-7.
The Complete Voodoo Vol. 3. 2017. 184pp. 978-1-63140-910-3.
Lou Cameron's Unsleeping Dead. 2017.144pp. 978-1-63140-931-8.

Fragments of Horror. Written and Illustrated by **Junji Ito**. VIZ Media, 2015. 224pp. 978-1-4215-8079-1, hardcover. M Japanese manga.

> A brand new anthology collection by the Japanese master of horror manga. The stories range from the spooky, erotic, terrifying, to the comedic.

Graphic Classics. Adapted and Illustrated by various. Eureka Productions, 2003– . T

> Collected works retranslating classic horror prose works by classic horror authors in a graphic novel format. The collections by Eureka Productions feature tales by the authors in both prose and graphic novel formats.

> *Vol. 1: Edgar Allan Poe*. 4th edition. 2010. 144pp. 978-0-9825630-0-7.
> *Vol. 4: H. P. Lovecraft*, 2nd edition. 2007. 144pp. 978-0-9746648-9-7.
> *Vol. 7: Bram Stoker*. 2007. 144pp. 978-0-9787919-1-9.
> *Vol. 10: Horror Classics*. 2004. 144pp. 978-0-9746648-1-1.
> *Vol. 14: Gothic Classics*. 2007. 144pp. 978-0-9787919-0-2.
> *Vol. 21: Poe's Tales of Mystery*. 2011. 144pp. 978-0-9825630-2-1.
> *Vol. 23: Halloween Classics*. 2012. 144pp. 978-0-9825630-5-2.

Joe Hill: The Graphic Novel Collection. Written by **Joe Hill**, **Stephen King**, **Jason Ciaramella**, and **Chris Ryall**. Illustrated by **Zach Howard**, **Nelson Dániel**, **Charles Paul Wilson III**, and **Vic Malhotra**. IDW Publishing, 2017. 472pp. 978-1-63140-768-0, hardcover. M

> An anthology collection by the *New York Times* best-selling author and creator of IDW Publishing's Locke and Key series. The collection includes comics, graphic novels, and short stories. Included are: *Kodiak* (2010) with illustrations by Nat Jones, *The Cape* (2010) and *The Cape* 1969 (2011) illustrated by Zach Howard, *Thumbprint* (2013) illustrated by Vic Malhotra, *Wraith* (2014) with illustrations by Charles Paul Wilson III, plus the short stories "Throttle" (2009) from the Road Rage collection and "By the Silver Water of Lake Champlain" (2012) taken from 2016 Bram Stoker Award Winner Shadow Show.

In the Dark: A Horror Anthology. Written and Illustrated by various. IDW Publishing, 2014. 336pp. 978-1-61377-934-7, hardcover. O

> A massive collection of horror stories by Rachel Deering, George Sturt, Justin Jordan, Cullen Bunn, Paul Tobin, Duane Swierczynski, Tom Taylor, F. Paul Wilson, Tim Seeley, Marguerite Bennett, Brian Keene, Christopher Sebela, Matthew Dow Smith, James Tynion IV, Sean E. Williams, Michael Moreci, Steve Seeley, Jody

© Idea and Design Works, LLC.

LeHeup, Ed Brisson, Mike Oliveri, Nate Southard, Valerie D'Orazio, Tradd Moore, Dalibor Talajić, Andy Belanger, Patric Reynolds, Chris Mooneyham, Garry Brown, Marc Laming, Christian Wildgoose, Douglas Holgate, Brian Level, Chris Dibari, Mike Henderson, Mack Chater, Alison Sampson, Jonathan Brandon Sawyer, Drew Moss, Thomas Boatwright, David James Cole, Eryk Donovan, and Tadd Galusha. The book also includes a history of the rise, decline, and rise again of horror comics by comic book historian Mike Howlett. The book started off as a successful Kickstarter campaign and was published through IDW Publishing.

Monstrosity. Written and Illustrated by various. Alterna Comics. 2013–2014. O

An anthology collection of horror stories from monsters from outer space, serial killers who hop through dimensions, robot rampages, and more!

Vol. 1. 2013. 200pp. 978-1-934985-33-5.
Vol. 2. 2014. 240pp. 978-1-934985-41-0.

Museum of Terror. Written and Illustrated by **Junji Ito**. Dark Horse Comics, 2006. M Japanese manga.

An anthology collection of short horror stories by Japan's foremost creator of horror manga. The first volume includes the story "Tomie"—about an eternally beautiful high school girl whose admirers are obsessed with her beauty that they murder her. Much to their dismay, she comes back from the dead again and again causing death in her wake.

Vol. 1. 2006. 376pp. 978-1-59307-542-2.
Vol. 2. 2006. 376pp. 978-1-59307-612-2.
Vol. 3. 2006. 392pp. 978-1-59307-639-9.

The Simon and Kirby Library: Horror. Written and Illustrated by **Joe Simon** and **Jack Kirby**. Titan Books, 2014. 320pp. 978-1-84856-959-1, hardcover. T

Known as the co-creators of characters such as Marvel Comics' Captain America, the team of Joe Simon and Jack Kirby worked on many genres and characters during their careers. This is the third volume of this extensive library anthology by Titan Books. The fourth volume of the library collects horror stories produced by Simon and Kirby for the early 1950s' titles *Black Magic* and *The Strange World of Our Dreams*.

Through the Woods. Written and Illustrated by **Emily Carroll**. Margaret K. McElderry Books/Simon and Schuster, 2014. 208pp. 978-1-4422-6595-4, hardcover; 2014. 208pp. 978-1-4422-6596-1. T 🏃 ◎

Monsters, ghosts, and death await you in a collection of five haunting short stories guaranteed to make you afraid of the dark. The stories included are "Our Neighbors House"; "A Lady's Hands Are Cold"; "My Friend Janna";

and "His Face All Red." The collection was recognized by YALSA in 2015 for the Quick Picks for Reluctant Readers selection list as well as Great Graphic Novels for Teens.

Time and Again. Written and Illustrated by **JiUn Yun**. Yen Press, 2009–2011. T Korean manhwa.

> This Korean title deals with exorcists-for-hire Baek-On and Ho-Yeon, whose work fighting spirits occasionally reflects a tragedy in their own lives. Each encounter they find retells tales of horror and possession, where sometimes the worst monsters encountered aren't the demons, but humans themselves. The series was selected as one of YALSA's Great Graphic Novels for Teens.
>
> *Vol. 1*. 2009. 160pp. 978-0-7595-3058-4.
> *Vol. 2*. 2010. 160pp. 978-0-7595-3059-1.
> *Vol. 3*. 2010. 160pp. 978-0-7595-3060-7.
> *Vol. 4*. 2010. 160pp. 978-0-7595-3061-4.
> *Vol. 5*. 2011. 160pp. 978-0-7595-3062-1.
> *Vol. 6*. 2011. 160pp. 978-0-7595-3063-8.

Trick 'r Treat. Written by **Marc Andreyko**. Illustrated by **Mike Huddleston**, **Grant Bond**, **Christopher Gugliotti**, and **Fiona Staples**. Wildstorm Press/DC Comics, 2009. 96pp. 978-1-4012-2588-9. M

> A tie-in with the 2009 cult horror movie *Trick 'r Treat*. Short stories are interconnected revolving around a young boy named Sam. Dressed in orange footy pajamas with his burlap sack head covering, he is being stalked by a stranger on Halloween night.

XxxHOLiC. Written and Illustrated by **CLAMP**. Del Rey Manga/Random House, 2004–2012. O Japanese manga. あ

> Watanuki Kimihiro's always been plagued by spirits. He can't seem to get rid of them, and they're starting to drive him crazy. By chance he stumbles into the beautiful and mysterious witch Yuko's store for a cure to his ailment but expectedly becomes her unpaid servant in the process. Now customer after customer comes into the store seeking that special aid that only Yuko knows, and her payments can cost someone his or her dearest possessions. But will being Yuko's assistant really solve his ghostly problem? Only time will tell. The manga was adapted as an anime film as well an anime television series.
>
> *Vol. 1*. 2004. 192pp. 978-0-345-47058-4.
> *Vol. 2*. 2004. 192pp. 978-0-345-47119-2.
> *Vol. 3*. 2004. 192pp. 978-0-345-47181-9.
> *Vol. 4*. 2005. 192pp. 978-0-345-47788-0.
> *Vol. 5*. 2005. 192pp. 978-0-345-47789-7.
> *Vol. 6*. 2005. 192pp. 978-0-345-47790-3.
> *Vol. 7*. 2006. 192pp. 978-0-345-48335-5.
> *Vol. 8*. 2006. 192pp. 978-0-345-48336-2.
> *Vol. 9*. 2007. 192pp. 978-0-345-49639-3.
> *Vol. 10*. 2007. 192pp. 978-0-345-49683-6.
> *Vol. 11*. 2008. 192pp. 978-0-345-50163-9.
> *Vol. 12*. 2008. 192pp. 978-0-345-50565-1.
> *Vol. 13*. 2009. 192pp. 978-0-345-50566-8.
> *Vol. 14*. 2009. 192pp. 978-0-345-51843-9.
> *Vol. 15*. 2010. 192pp. 978-0-345-52112-5.
> *Vol. 16*. 2010. 192pp. 978-0-345-52412-6.
> *Vol. 17*. 2011. 192pp. 978-0-345-53071-4.
> *Vol. 18*. 2011. 192pp. 978-0-345-53072-1.
> *Vol. 19*. 2012. 192pp. 978-0-345-53126-1.

Chapter 6

Crime and Mysteries

Crime and mystery graphic novels feature stories—both fiction and nonfiction—about criminals, police detectives, mystery cases of murder, disappearances, and much more. Crime and mystery stories have long been some of the most maligned of comic-book genres. In the mid-1950s, along with the horror genre, crime comics were singled out as a possible cause for juvenile delinquency. This claim came from Dr. Frederick Wertham, a noted psychiatrist and author of the notorious anti-comic book nonfiction title *Seduction of the Innocent* that spoke on the harmful effects of the mass media on children, and which was a factor in the comic book industry being subjected to a congressional investigation. Despite the accusations that portrayed crime comics as little more than "how-to" manuals for murder and mayhem, no clear connection ever was established between reading crime comics and committing deviant social behavior. After the Comic Code Authority's crackdown on crime and horror titles, the majority of titles slowly faded from popularity unlike other mediums including fictional works, television, and film. Within the last decade, interest in crime comic books has been renewed. With suspenseful titles such as *Sin City*, *Torso*, *100 Bullets*, and *Powers*, *Gotham Central*, the Victorian-age true crime stories by Rick Geary, and many more, it seems that the crime genre is back in full form and here to stay.

Detectives

Crime stories focusing on the police departments, detectives, and special crime units that take on criminal element, showing how they solve cases against ruthless criminals with finesse, brute force, or any other means necessary. As in mystery fiction, the emphasis here is generally on the character of a single detective or team of investigators.

Professional Detectives and Police Officers

Public investigators and city police forces that take on the criminal element play central roles in these stories. The focus may be on several partners in a police department, a specific division of the police department, or of a detective investigating a case.

Chew. Written by **John Layman**. Illustrated by **Rob Guillory**. Image Comics, 2009–2017. O 🎣

John Layman • Rob Guillory

© 2016 John Layman & Rob Guillory
and Image Comics

When Tony Chu has to investigate murder, just about anything can end up down the hatch in order to solve the crime. Tony's unique — he is cibopathic, which means he gets psychic impressions from whatever he eats. Tony's one of the best detectives on the beat, but it doesn't hurt that he can solve a murder by nibbling on the victim to figure out whodunit, and why. The collection was recognized by YALSA on its 2011 Great Graphic Novels for Teens top-10 graphic novels list. The series has won two Eisner and two Harvey awards as well. See Chapter 7 for more food-themed graphic novels.

Vol. 1: Taster's Choice. 2009. 128pp. 978-1-60706-159-5.
Vol. 2: International Flavor. 2010. 128pp. 978-1-60706-260-8.
Vol. 3: Just Desserts. 2010. 128pp. 978-1-60706-335-3.
Vol. 4: Flambe. 2011. 128pp. 978-1-60706-398-8.
Vol. 5: Major League Chew. 2012. 128pp. 978-1-60706-523-4.
Vol. 6: Space Cakes. 2013. 156pp. 978-1-60706-621-7.
Vol. 7: Bad Apples. 2013. 128pp. 978-1-60706-767-2.
Vol. 8: Family Recipes. 2014. 128pp. 978-1-60706-938-6.
Vol. 9: Chicken Tenders. 2015. 128pp. 978-1-63215-289-3.
Vol. 10: Blood Puddin. 2015. 128pp. 978-1-63215-396-8.
Vol. 11: Last Suppers. 2016. 128pp. 978-1-63215-681-5.
Vol. 12: Sour Grapes. 2017. 160pp. 978-1-5343-0031-6.

Chew Omnivore Edition. 2010–2017

Vol. 1. 2010. 264pp. 978-1-60706-293-6, hardcover.
Vol. 2. 2011. 264pp. 978-1-60706-426-8, hardcover.
Vol. 3. 2013. 288pp. 978-1-60706-426-8, hardcover.
Vol. 4. 2014. 272pp. 978-1-63215-031-8, hardcover.
Vol. 5. 2015. 304pp. 978-1-63215-623-5, hardcover.
Vol. 6. 2017. 344pp. 978-1-5343-0180-1, hardcover.

Chew Smorgasbord Edition, 2013–2017

Vol. 1. 2013. 576pp. 978-1-60706-805-1, hardcover.
Vol. 2. 2015. 576pp. 978-1-63215-428-6, hardcover.
Vol. 3. 2017. 640pp. 978-1-5343-0212-9, hardcover.

The Frankenstein Mobster: The Made Man. Written and Illustrated by **Mark Wheatley**. IDW Publishing, 2009. 264pp. 978-1-60010-632-3. O

In a city filled with supernatural creatures, a policeman is killed and reanimated in a body patched together with him and three mobsters. Now his daughter, also a cop, must save the city from him and other threats.

Happy! Written by **Grant Morrison**. Illustrated by **Darick Robertson**. Image Comics, 2013. 96pp. 978-1-60706-677-4. M

> Former detective Nick Sax is on the run from the mob due to a hit gone wrong. Years of abuse with drugs, alcohol, and worse have made this foul-mouthed, violent detective-turned down-on-his-luck-hit man a lost soul drifting amid the corrupt and the fallen. When a little girl needs Nick's help from a serial killer dressed up like Santa Claus, lucky for her he's on the case along with the little blue horse fairy that only he can see called Happy. Uh oh!

Hit. Written by **Bryce Carlson**. Illustrated by **Vanesa R. Del Rey**. Boom! Studios, 2014–2016. M

> A crime noir series focusing on a group of LAPD officers on the side who have taken up some extra jobs as hitmen. When the criminal element need to "disappear" forever, Detective Harvey Slater and his men are the ones to do it. When Slater has a run-in with his former flame—Captain Blair's daughter Bonnie—trouble is soon on the way with plenty of action, booze, dames, and guns.

> *1955*. 2014. 128pp. 978-1-60886-403-4.
> *1957*. 2016. 112pp. 978-1-60886-817-9.

© 2016 BOOM! Studios

Gotham Central. Written by **Greg Rucka** and **Ed Brubaker**. Illustrated by **Michael Lark** and various. DC Comics, 2009–2011. T 🎖 ◎

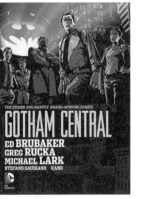

The Batman may get all the glory as the defender of the corrupt Gotham City, but the Gotham City Police Department is there to help clean up. Led by Commissioner Akins and his Major Crimes Unit commander Maggie Sawyer, the streets are kept safe with the aid of dedicated officers including Detectives Renee Montoya and Harvey Bullock. They inevitably find themselves on the lookout for some of Batman's villains, including a deadly Mr. Freeze, the pyrotechnic Firebug, the dastardly Joker, and the Penguin. The series is a realistic look at a police department working day to day against both common criminals and super-villains. The earlier collections of the series received an Eisner Award in 2004 for Best Serialized Story, a Harvey Award in 2004 for Best Single Issue or Story, as well as recognition from YALSA's Popular Paperbacks for Young Adults selection list in 2005. Collections list below is the first time all volumes of the popular and highly regarded series have been collected.

© 2016 DC Comics

Vol. 1: In the Line of Duty. 2009. 240pp. 978-1-4012-1923-9, hardcover; 2011. 978-1-4012-2037-2.

Vol. 2: Jokers and Madmen. 2009. 288pp. 978-1-4012-2521-6, hardcover; 2011. 978-1-4012-2543-8.

Vol. 3: On the Freak Beat. 2010. 224pp. 978-1-4012-2754-8, hardcover; 2011. 978-1-4012-3232-0.

Vol. 4: Corrigan. 2011. 224pp. 978-1-4012-3003-6, hardcover.

Gotham Central Omnibus. 2016. 968pp. 978-1-4012-6192-4, hardcover.

Grandville. Written and Illustrated by **Bryan Talbot**. Dark Horse Comics, 2009–2014. O 🏹 ◎
Set in a steampunk-like alternate world where France rules the world, Paris is known as Grandville, and animals roam the streets like humans. In the small country known as the Socialist Republic of Britain, Detective-Inspector Archie LeBrock of Scotland Yard—a badger with a badge—has to solve murders, hunt for escaped psychotic killers, and try have help prevent the empire from heading into war! As the creator of the series, Bryan Talbot says, "It's like Jules Verne and Sherlock Holmes directed by Quentin Tarantino—with animals!" The first volume of Grandville was recognized by YALSA as a Great Graphic Novel for Teens in 2011, and the series has been nominated for an Eisner and Hugo Award in 2012.

Grandville. 2009. 108pp. 978-1-59582-397-7, hardcover.
Grandville Mon Amour. 2010. 108pp. 978-1-59582-574-2, hardcover.
Grandville Bete Noire. 2012. 104pp. 978-1-59582-890-3, hardcover.
Grandville Noël. 2014. 104pp. 978-1-61655-572-6, hardcover.

Liar's Kiss. Written by **Eric Skillman**. Illustrated by **Jhomar Soriano**. Top Shelf Productions. 2011. 120pp. 978-1-60309-070-4. M
A private eye is hired to watch on a suspicious millionaire's wife. That same private eye is hired by the wife to prove that she remains faithful, even though she fools around with our gumshoe. Nick Archer, the private eye, seems to be over his head when the millionaire is murdered and his wife is the prime suspect. These people's destinies are tangled together more than what appears on the surface.

Old City Blues. Written and Illustrated by **Giannis Milonogiannis**. Archaia/Boom Studios. 2011–2013. O
After a cataclysmic flood destroyed much of what was Greece, many high-tech corporations swooped in to help rebuild the country. Thanks to the corporations and the government being so friendly, New Athens has become one of the most high-tech cities in the world. With the arrival of the tech companies, corruption, crime, and low lives soon followed. With a string of cyborg murders, it is up to Solano and the rest of the New Athens police force to figure out who is behind these ghastly murders.

Vol. 1. 2011. 120pp. 978-1-936393-20-6.
Vol. 2. 2013. 200pp. 978-1-939867-02-5.

Red Handed: The Fine Art of Strange Crimes. Written and Illustrated by **Matt Kindt**. First Second, 2013. 272pp. 978-1-59643-662-6, hardcover. T

© 2016 First Second and Matt Kindt

The famed Detective Gould has caught many a criminal in the city of Red Wheelbarrow. When there's a rash of crimes that are so random that the great detective is baffled, will he be able to find all the clues to find out the random culprit or has the great detective met his match?

Ruse: The Victorian Guide to Murder. Written by **Mark Waid**. Illustrated by **Jackson Guice**. Marvel Comics, 2011. 96pp. 978-0-7851-5586-7. T

© 2016 Marvel Comics

Set on the world of Arcadia, a planet similar to our own in late 19th-century Victorian England, bat-like gargoyles fly high above the streets of the city called Partington. Master sleuth Simon Archard has gotten bored with the criminals of the day. A brilliant but abrasive and distant detective able to infer clues from the ordinary to solve crimes, Archard and his assistant, the lovely but equally brilliant Emma Bishop, can solve any mystery! The comic book was originally a CrossGen comic series that was acquired by Marvel Comics after the company went bankrupt.

Sam and Twitch: The Complete Collection. Written by **Brian Michael Bendis**. Illustrated by **Angel Medina**. Image Comics, 2011–2012. M

New York City detectives Sam Burke and Max "Twitch" Williams have seen a lot of strange cases in their time on the force, but when they investigate the first of many mafia murders in the Sangiacomo mob family, they find something odd left behind at the scene of the crime: four severed thumbs, none of them belonging to any of the victims. Even more strange, the thumbs are all genetically identical to each other except that each one is more and more genetically unstable. As the body count rises and more genetically engineered body appendages are popping up, Sam and Twitch need to figure out who or what the mysterious Udaku is and what its connection is to a bioengineered virus before more innocents die.

Vol. 1. 2011. 320pp. 978-1-60706-240-0, hardcover.
Vol. 2. 2012. 320pp. 978-1-60706-242-4, hardcover.

Scalped. Written by **Jason Aaron**. Illustrated by **R. M. Guera**. Vertigo/DC Comics, 2015. M ◎ ▭

FBI agent Dash Bad Horse has returned undercover to the South Dakota Reservation where he grew up to investigate past mysteries. But while doing this he also must deal with organized crime and the tribe's issues with poverty and drug addiction. Scalped was nominated for several awards including

© 2016 DC Comics

the Eisner, the Harvey, and the Spinetingler. A television series has been in development but to date has not been made. The 60 issues of this highly acclaimed series were originally collected in 10 paperback volumes but has since been recollected in five hardcover-volume deluxe editions.

Vol. 1. 2015. 296pp. 978-1-4012-5091-1, hardcover.
Vol. 2. 2015. 320pp. 978-1-4012-5425-4, hardcover.
Vol. 3. 2015. 256pp. 978-1-4012-5858-0, hardcover.
Vol. 4. 2016. 200pp. 978-1-4012-6144-3, hardcover.
Vol. 5. 2016. 200pp. 978-1-4012-6363-8, hardcover.

Sheriff of Babylon. Written by **Tom King**. Illustrated by **Mitch Gerads**. Vertigo/DC Comics, 2016–. M

© 2016 DC Comics

A former Florida cop-turned-military consultant, Chris Henry, goes to Baghdad in 2003, two years after the fall of the city. Returning to bring some semblance of order, he hopes to retrain a new group of cadets who will become the police of the city. When one of his recruits is found dead, he is teamed up with Nassir, the last police-man in Baghdad to try and unravel the murder, but find themselves caught between more sinister forces at hand.

Vol. 1: Bang. Bang. Bang. 2016. 160pp. 978-1-4012-6466-6.
Vol. 2: Pow. Pow. Pow. 2017. 144 p. 978-1-4012-6726-1.

Will Eisner's the Spirit. Written by **Will Eisner**, **Darwyn Cooke**, **Walter Simonson**, **Kyle Baker**, **Sergio Aragones**, **Mark Evanier**, **Mark Schultz**, **Mark Waid**, **Neil Gaiman**, **Paul Chadwick**, **Alan Moore**, **Kurt Busiek**, and various. Illustrated by **Will Eisner**, **Chris Sprouse**, **J. Bone**, **Moritat**, **Darwyn Cooke**, **Paul Smith**, **Eddie Campbell**, **Dave Gibbons**, **Mike Ploog**, and various. DC Comics, 2007–2015; IDW Publishing, 2014; Dark Horse Comics, 2015. T

THE SPIRIT and WILL EISNER are Registered Trademarks of Will Eisner Studios, Inc. Used with Permission

Debuting in the newspapers in June 1940, Will Eisner's The Spirit Is Denny Colt, a policeman who is presumed dead and goes into hiding at the Wildwood Cemetery. Realizing he can fight crime anonymously, he begins a life of fighting crime wearing only a small domino mask, blue business suit, red necktie, fedora hat, and gloves for a costume—and *The Spirit* is born! Will Eisner's series mixed crime-fighting, action, humor, and mystery as *The Spirit* faces a Rogues Gallery of villains including The Octopus, femme fatale P'Gell, Dr. Cobra, and Sand Saref. The DC Comics series features a rotating cast of creators who all put their own take on Will Eisner's classic hero. The first book from DC Comics collects the highly praised *Batman/The Spirit* crossover as well. DC Comics has also published a 75-year retrospective that includes original Will Eisner stories and new adventures. In 2013, IDW

Publishing featured a fun crossover with The Rocketeer by Mark Waid and Paul Smith. Dark Horse Comics also collected an anthology of creators doing their own takes on *The Spirit,* featuring creators Alan Moore, Dave Gibbons, Kurt Busiek, Neil Gaiman, Paul Chadwick, and Eddie Campbell. In 2015, Dynamite Entertainment took over the license and will be collecting editions of *The Spirit* in the near future.

The Spirit. DC Comics, 2007–2011.
> *Book 1*. 2007. 192pp. 978-1-4012-1461-6, hardcover; 2009. 978-1-4012-1618-4.
> *Book 2*. 2008. 176pp. 978-1-4012-1920-8, hardcover; 2009. 978-1-4012-2220-8.
> *Book 3*. 2009. 168pp. 978-1-4012-2186-7.
> *Book 4*. 2009. 128pp. 978-1-4012-2505-6.
> *Book 5*. 2010. 168pp. 978-1-4012-2642-8.
> *Book 6*. 2011. 168pp. 978-1-4012-3026-5.

Rocketeer/Spirit: Pulp Friction. IDW Publishing, 2014. 104pp. 978-1-61377-881-4.
Will Eisner's The Spirit: A Celebration of 75 Years. DC Comics, 2015. 480pp. 978-1-4012-5945-7, hardcover.
Will Eisner's The Spirit: The New Adventures. Dark Horse Comics, 2016. 248pp. 978-1-61655-948-9, hardcover.

Sweets: A New Orleans Crime Story. Written and Illustrated by **Kody Chamberlain**. Image Comics, 2011. 120pp. 978-1-60706-413-8. O.

When a killer is loose in the Big Easy just a few days before Hurricane Katrina makes landfall, Detective Curt Delatte must put aside his own personal grief after losing his only daughter to try and solve the mystery before any more lives are lost.

Private Detectives

Stories featuring a detective-for-hire as featured in the classic noir fiction stories by Raymond Chandler and Mickey Spillane. The private detective is generally a tougher type than the typical "armchair detective" (or amateur) and handles tougher crimes in seedier places.

Alias. Written by **Brian Michael Bendis**. Illustrated by **Bill Sienkiewicz**, **Michael Gaydos**, and various. MAX/Marvel Comics, 2009–2015. M ◎ ▭

© Marvel Comics

Jessica Jones is barely making a living as a private investigator for her own company Alias Investigations, but it's much more fulfilling than what she used to do. She used to be a small-time superhero, but she's outgrown the costume and the spotlight and has a hard time dealing with her temper and her super strength. Now working out of a crummy office with some of the crummiest cases around, Jessica's taking on jobs that deal with infidelity, missing persons, and more in the back alleys in a seedier part of the Marvel Universe. This comic features guest appearances from some of Marvel's heroic characters, including Captain America, Luke Cage, and Daredevil. In 2015, Netflix

released a *Jessica Jones* 13-episode television show starring Krysten Ritter in the lead role, and a new *Jessica Jones* comic book series began in 2016.
Alias Ultimate Collection. 2009–2010.

> *Vol. 1.* 2009. 360pp. 978-0-7851-3732-0.
> *Vol. 2.* 2010. 360pp. 978-0-7851-4490-8.

Jessica Jones—The Pulse: The Complete Collection. 2014. 360pp. 978-0-7851-9086-8.
Alias Omnibus. 2014. 720pp. 978-0-7851-9091-2, hardcover.
Jessica Jones: Alias. 2015– .

> *Vol. 1.* 2015. 216pp. 978-0-7851-9855-0.
> *Vol. 2.* 2015. 128pp. 978-0-7851-9856-7.
> *Vol. 3.* 2015. 160pp. 978-0-7851-9857-4.

Blacksad. Written by **Juan Diaz Canales**. Illustrated by **Guarnido**. Dark Horse Comics, 2003–2010–2014. M 🏃 ◎

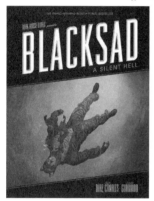

© Dark Horse Comics

Set in an anthropomorphized crime noir setting, Private Investigator John Blacksad, a humanoid black panther, finds that his past has just caught up to him as an old flame, a movie starlet, has been murdered. John decides to get to the bottom of Natalia's murder despite urgings by the police department to drop the case. The hard-boiled alley cat soon uncovers a trail of betrayal, intrigue, sex, and violence. In Volume 2: *Arctic Nation*, John investigates a child's disappearance in a racially divided small town. As tempers flare and a race war erupts, a dark conspiracy is revealed that engulfs the entire town, with John stuck in the middle. The series received a Harvey Award in 2005 for Best Graphic Album of Original Work when it was published by the late company I-Books. The series is now reprinted by Dark Horse Comics.

Vol. 1. 2010. 184pp. 978-1-59582-393-9, hardcover.
Vol. 2: A Silent Hell. 2012. 112pp. 978-1-59582-931-3, hardcover.
Vol. 3: Amarillo. 2014. 72pp. 978-1-61655-525-2, hardcover.

The Creep. Written by **John Arcudi**. Illustrated by **Jonathan Case**. Dark Horse Comics, 2013. 144pp. 978-1-61655-061-5, hardcover. M

When a young teenage boy commits suicide with a gun, the grieving mother involves her ex-boyfriend, a private detective with a gruesome appearance, onto the case that gets stranger and stranger. When a friend of the boy also commits suicide, it's no longer a coincidence and the detective must solve what terrible secret the two boys took to their graves.

Cousin Joseph: A Graphic Novel. Written and Illustrated by **Jules Feiffer.** Liveright Publishing/W.W. Norton, 2016. 118pp. 978-1-63149-065-1. M ◎

Set during the tumultuous time of the Depression, Sam Hannigan is a good-hearted bare-knuckle detective in Bay City and head of the Red Squad. He spends his days taking down union strikes, disruptions, and anything distinctly un-American. He's taken on a side job taking bribes to Hollywood producers to make only good-natured American movies courtesy of a mysterious Cousin Joseph who pulls the strings around the city. Meanwhile, a union strike is planned against the local canning factory, and Hannigan is in the thick of it, but other forces are at work in this tribute to noir fiction. The book is the second book in a planned trilogy that began with *Kill My Mother*. The final book, *The Ghost Script*, will be the last book in the trilogy.

Hawaiian Dick. Written by **B. Clay Moore**. Illustrated by **Steven Griffen**. Image Comics, 2003–2008. O

© 2016 B. Clay Moore and Image Comics

Set in 1953 Hawaii, exiled detective Byrd's trying to get over a dark past that drove him to the island with some Mai Tai drinks and odd jobs on the side. When Byrd's been asked to retrieve a stolen car with something very valuable inside, he needs help on the case. Joined with Honolulu detective Mo Kalama, he finds that this is no simple retrieval—it's a kidnapping case involving the girlfriend of the eccentric crime lord Bishop Masaki. Just when things couldn't get any worse, the psychic Madame Chan, zombies, the ghosts of ancient Hawaiian warriors, and more are all in the way to solving one of the strangest cases that Byrd's ever seen. In the second volume, Byrd is caught in the middle of two warring gangs as well as a few ghosts along the way. In the final volume, Byrd meets a World War II fighter squadron, but they soon find themselves up against a Japanese fighter plane—in 1954.

Vol. 1: Byrd of Paradise. 2003. 136pp. 978-1-58240-317-5.
Vol. 2: The Last Resort. 2006. 144pp. 978-1-58240-664-0.
Vol. 3: Screaming Black Thunder. 2008. 152pp. 978-1-58240-988-7.

Private Eye: The Cloudburst Edition. Written by **Brian K. Vaughan**. Illustrated by **Marcos Martin**. Image Comics, 2015. 300pp. 978-1-63215-572-6, hardcover. O 🎖

© 2016 Brian K. Vaughan and Image Comics

In the year 2076, there is no Internet, and everyone's secrets are out in the open following a time after the "cloud has burst"—a time when everyone's search histories and downloads were revealed to everyone else. Lives were ruined and since then to protect their identities, everyone wears a mask. When an unlicensed private investigator is hired by a femme fatale to dig up information, he soon finds himself over his head and conspiracies are all abound. The series won an Eisner and Harvey Award in 2015 for Best Web Comic.

Richard Stark's Parker. Written by **Richard Stark**. Adapted and Illustrated by **Darwyn Cooke**. IDW Publishing, 2009–2013. O 🏹 ◎

© The Estate of Donald E. Westlake. Artwork © Darwyn Cooke.

The books are based on the classic series of crime novels by author Donald Westlake who wrote under the pseudonym of Richard Stark. Originally appearing in the 1962 book *The Hunter*, Parker appeared in over 24 books by the author through 2008. The series by the late Darwyn Cooke won many Eisner and Harvey awards over the course of its publication history and has perfected the grit of the original novels in graphic novel form. The Martini Edition reprints the first two collections—*The Hunter* and *The Outfit* in one deluxe edition.

The Hunter. 2009. 144pp. 978-1-60010-493-0, hardcover; 2012. 978-1-61377-399-4.
The Outfit. 2010. 160pp. 978-1-60010-762-7, hardcover. 978-1-63140-740-6.
The Martini Edition. 2011. 360pp. 978-1-60010-980-5, hardcover.
The Score. 2012. 160pp. 978-1-61377-208-9, hardcover.
Slayground. 2013. 96pp 978-1-61377-812-8, hardcover.

You Have Killed Me. Written by **Jamie S. Rich**. Illustrated by **Joëlle Jones**. Oni Press, 2009. 184pp. 978-1-932664-88-1, hardcover. M

© 2016 Oni Press and Jamie S. Rich

Set in the 1930s, P. I. Antonio Mercer takes on a missing person's case that is nothing but simple. When his ex-girlfriend disappears, her beautiful sister hires Mercer for the case. But true to form, the gumshoe is soon on the run from the mob, the police, gamblers, knife-wielding musicians and more as he tries to solve the baffling case.

Amateur Detectives

Mysteries featuring a novice detective protagonist are popular with many fans. Like their mainstay fictional counterparts, the amateur detective can be someone who has stumbled onto a case by accident and tries to solve the mystery, or an up-and-coming detective or detective agency out to prove they can handle any case that comes their way. They tend to have less in common with traditional "cozies" in fiction due to the visual medium showcasing more action and gore and tend to be more brutal along the lines of Hard-boiled detective novels.

Arisa. Written and Illustrated by **Natsumi Ando**. Kodansha Comics, 2011–2014. T Japanese manga.

After her estranged twin sister's failed suicide event, teenager Tsubasa Uehara goes undercover to find the identity of the person known only as "King" who may have coaxed her sister Arisa to violence. Disguised as her twin sister, Tsubasa must find out the identity of King before more students in Arisa's class are hurt or worse. The series was selected as one of YALSA's Great Graphic Novels for Teens.

Vol. 1. 2011. 208pp. 978-1-61262-335-1.   Vol. 7. 2012. 176pp. 978-1-61262-114-2.
Vol. 2. 2011. 176pp. 978-1-93542-916-6.   Vol. 8. 2012. 176pp. 978-1-61262-162-3.
Vol. 3. 2011. 176pp. 978-1-93542-917-3.   Vol. 9. 2012. 176pp. 978-1-61262-240-8.
Vol. 4. 2011. 176pp. 978-1-93542-918-0.   Vol. 10. 2013. 160pp. 978-1-61262-251-4.
Vol. 5. 2011. 176pp. 978-1-93542-919-7.   Vol. 11. 2013. 160pp. 978-1-61262-252-1.
Vol. 6. 2012. 176pp. 978-1-61262-039-8.   Vol. 12. 2014. 160pp. 978-1-61262-439-6.

Bandette. Written by **Paul Tobin**. Illustrated by **Colleen Coover**. Dark Horse Comics, 2013– . T 🎗

Bandette © 2016 Paul Tobin and Colleen Coover

The greatest thief in all of Paris is a costumed teenage girl! She's the best at what she does—and what she does best is being a thorn in the side of the police as well as the criminal underworld. Can a teenager balance being neither good nor evil—especially when an international crime syndicate wants her dead? The first and third volumes were recognized by YALSA's Great Graphic Novels for Teens selection list in 2014 and 2017, respectively. In 2013 and 2016 the series was recognized with an Eisner Award for Best Digital/Webcomic.

Vol. 1: Presto. 2013. 136pp. 978-1-61655-279-4, hardcover.
Vol. 2: Stealers Keepers. 2015. 136pp. 978-1-61655-668-6, hardcover.
Vol. 3: The House of the Green Mask. 2016. 128pp. 978-1-5067-0219-3, hardcover.

Codeflesh: The Definitive Edition. Written by **Joe Casey** and **Charlie Adlard**. Illustrated by **Richard Starkings**. Image Comics, 2009. 128pp. 978-1-60706-077-2. M

A gritty look at what it takes to become a vigilante. Antihero Cam Daltrey is a bail bondsman who takes his job a little too seriously. When he severely injures a super-villain who skipped out on his court date, he's court-ordered to stop and proceeds to take it out as the barcode-masked vigilante known as Codeflesh. As both his private and public lives are being destroyed by his crime-fighting, he steps back and sees the villains for what they truly are: individuals with hopes, dreams, responsibilities, and families just like him. Has Cam done the right thing striking back at these people and losing touch with what really matters in life?

The Dare Detectives! Collected Edition: The Snowpea Plot. Written and Illustrated by **Ben Caldwell**. Archaia Entertainment/Boom! Studios, 2011. 208pp. 978-1-936393-41-1, hardcover. T

Maria Dare is young and tough reformed crook out to redeem her name. She's created the Dare Detective Agency, a group made up of the oddest assortment of crime-fighters including Toby, the naive and ignorant muscle, and Jojo, the

© 2017 Ben Caldwell.

irritable and sarcastic-talking rabbit. Together the energetic team takes on the most bizarre cases in the world. After destroying half the city in their reckless chase of the simian criminal Furious George, with their license suspended and rent due, they inadvertently find themselves on a new case chasing Madame Bleu, a new villain with the dastardly plot to steal the city's supply of snow peas. Can they stop Madame Bleu and her snowpea-swiping gang of abominable snowmen and panda bears before it's too late?

The Fade Out. Written by **Ed Brubaker**. Illustrated by **Sean Phillips**. Image Comics, 2015–2016. M

© 2016 Ed Brubaker and Sean Phillips

Set in Hollywood during the heyday of the 1950s, a struggling Hollywood writer stumbles into a grizzly scene where a leading actress is dead. Afraid of being blamed, he leaves the scene, but realizes that the crime was staged to look like a suicide and there are darker forces in play in the land where nothing is real. The *Fade Out* won a 2016 Eisner Award for best limited series.

Vol. 1. 2015. 120pp. 978-1-63215-171-1.
Vol. 2. 2015. 120pp. 978-1-63215-447-7.
Vol. 3. 2016. 128pp. 978-1-63215-629-7.
Deluxe Edition 2016. 384pp. 978-1-63215-911-3.

Kill My Mother: A Graphic Novel. Written and Illustrated by **Jules Feiffer.** Liveright Publishing/W.W. Norton, 2014. 160pp. 978-0-87140-314-8. M ◎

With locations ranging from depression-era California to World War II, South Pacific and a cast of characters that includes drunken PIs, boxers, soldiers, actors, three femme fatales, people with secrets, and an estranged mother and daughter, Feiffer tells a compelling noir story. The book is the first book in a planned trilogy. The second book, *Cousin Joseph*, was published in 2017.

Louise Brooks: Detective. Written and Illustrated by **Rick Geary**. NBM Publishing, 2015. 80pp. 978-1-56163-952-6, hardcover. T

A fictional mystery featuring a real actress. Louise Brooks was a smoldering actress who popularized the short hair look from the Roaring Twenties. The story is set up when Brooks, a native of Wichita, Kansas, returns home and becomes intrigued by a mystery involving a friend, a reclusive writer, and a distrustful beau. Can an actress with no skills in detective work be able to solve a mystery that has baffled the police?

Master Keaton. Written by **Hokusei Katsushika**, **Takashi Nagasaki**, and **Naoki Urasawa**. Illustrated by **Naoki Urasawa**. VIZ Media, LLC, 2014– . O Japanese manga. 🎋 あ

Taichi Hiraga-Keaton is quite an unorthodox insurance investigator. A background in archaeology and a former soldier for the British Army's SAS, he works for the prestigious Lloyd's of London where he's known as one of the best investigators. On the side, Taichi his friend Daniel O'Connell operate their own insurance investigation business as well. Life is certainly not dull for Taichi as he's called to take on murder investigations, terrorist attacks, the Mafia, and more! The series was published in Japan from 1988 to 1994 and published in 18 volumes. A sequel to the series, written and illustrated by Naoki Urasawa, was released in 2012–2014. The first three volumes were recognized by YALSA on its 2016 Great Graphic Novels for Teens selection list.

MASTER KEATON © 1989 Naoki URASAWA/Studio Nuts, Hokusei KATSUSHIKA, Takashi NAGASAKI. Original Japanese edition published by SHOGAKUKAN

Vol. 1. 2014. 338pp. 978-1-4215-7589-6.
Vol. 2. 2015. 338pp. 978-1-4215-7591-9.
Vol. 3. 2015. 320pp. 978-1-4215-7592-6.
Vol. 4. 2015. 320pp. 978-1-4215-7593-3.
Vol. 5. 2016. 352pp. 978-1-4215-7594-0.
Vol. 6. 2016. 298pp. 978-1-4215-7595-7.

Vol. 7. 2016. 320pp. 978-1-4215-7596-4.
Vol. 8. 2016. 320pp. 978-1-4215-7597-1.
Vol. 9. 2016. 322pp, 978-1-4215-8377-8.
Vol. 10. 2017. 322pp. 978-1-4215-8526-0.
Vol. 11. 2017. 322pp. 978-1-4215-8379-2.
Vol. 12. 2017. 322pp. 978-1-4215-8380-8.

Mind Mgmt. Written and Illustrated by **Matt Kindt**. Dark Horse Comics, 2013–2016. O ◎

While investigating a flight in which everyone lost their memories, Meru, an investigative journalist, discovers the existence of the government-run Mind Management program. The organization is a spy agency made of people with psychic abilities. As Meru investigates even deeper into the mystery of a missing Mind Management agent, she realizes that her mind is at risk. Can anything she uncovers be real?

Vol. 1: The Manager. 2013. 200pp. 978-1-59582-797-5, hardcover.
Vol. 2: The Futurist. 2013. 176pp. 978-1-61655-198-8, hardcover.
Vol. 3: The Homemaker. 2014. 176pp. 978-1-61655-390-6, hardcover.
Vol. 4: The Magician. 2014. 184pp. 978-1-61655-391-3, hardcover.
Vol. 5. The Eraser. 2015. 168pp. 978-1-61655-696-9, hardcover.

Mind MGMT™ and © Matt Kindt

Vol. 6: The Immortals. 2016. 192pp. 978-1-61655-798-0, hardcover.

Miss Don't Touch Me. Written by **Hubert**. Illustrated by **Kerascoet**. NBM Publishing. M

The dances of Paris in the 1930s had young people out all night. Blanche, a young Parisian lady, preferred not to go dancing with her friends as there is a murderer on the loose targeting women. When Blanche's best friend becomes

© 2016 Hubert & Kerascoet and NBM
Publishing

one of the victims she is determined to find out who the murderer is and get revenge. Her detective work leads her to one of Paris's "classy" brothels. She starts working within this establishment to find out who has perpetrated these murders.

Vol. 1. 2008. 96pp. 978-1-56163-544-3.
Vol. 2. 2010. 96pp. 978-1-56163-592-4.
Complete. 2011. 192pp. 978-1-56163-621-1, hardcover.

Naoki Urasawa's Monster: *The Perfect Edition*. Written and Illustrated by **Naoki Urasawa.** VIZ Media LLC. 2014–2016. 🕯 O Japanese manga. あ ◎

MONSTER KANZENBAN © 2008
Naoki URASAWA/Studio Nuts.
Story Coproduced with Takashi
NAGASAKI. Original Japanese edition published by SHOGAKUKAN

Kenzō Tenma is a Japanese brain surgeon living in Germany. His life is turned upside down after he rescues a young boy named Johan Liebert that has a gunshot wound to the head. Johan is saved, but he and his twin sister mysteriously disappear shortly after the hospital director and other doctors are murdered. Nine years later, Tenma is chief of surgery at Eisler Memorial and he finds himself embroiled in a deadly race against time from a coldhearted killer revealed to be none other than Johan Liebert. Now Tenma seeks to find the origin of Liebert's coldhearted past and to save the "monster" before others may die at his hands. The series was originally reprinted into 18 volumes but were reprinted again in a two-in-one volume Perfect collections that condensed the series into nine volumes. The series was adapted into an anime series, and *Monster* has also received numerous awards in Japan as well as recognition from YALSA for the 2007 Great Graphic Novels for Teens list.

Vol. 1. 2014. 426pp. 978-1-4215-6906-2.
Vol. 2. 2014. 402pp. 978-1-4215-6907-9.
Vol. 3. 2015. 434pp. 978-1-4215-6908-6.
Vol. 4. 2015. 438pp. 978-1-4215-6909-3.
Vol. 5. 2015. 410pp. 978-1-4215-6910-9.
Vol. 6. 2015. 406pp. 978-1-4215-6911-6.
Vol. 7. 2016. 416pp. 978-1-4215-6912-3.
Vol. 8. 2016. 432pp. 978-1-4215-6913-0.
Vol. 9. 2016. 482pp. 978-1-4215-6914-7.

The New Deal. Written and Illustrated by **Jonathan Case**. Dark Horse Comics, 2015. 112pp. 978-1-61655-731-7, hardcover. O

A mystery set in Depression-era New York City in 1936 at the famous Waldorf Astoria hotel. Frank, a bellhop, and Theresa, a maid, become embroiled in a series of mysterious thefts involving a beautiful young woman named Nina, a member of high society. Social and racial classes are pushed to the limit as Frank and Theresa try to solve the mystery of the stolen jewels and break out of their own social settings of their own.

The New Deal © 2016 Jonathan
Case

Rex Mundi. Written by **Arvid Nelson**. Illustrated by **Eric Johnson**. Dark Horse Comics, 2006–2010. O

> Set in an alternate version of 1933 Paris, where the Catholic Church controls much of Europe with an iron fist. A secret manuscript entrusted to Father Gerard Martin by the church has gone missing, and the priest can only turn to his good friend Doctor Julien Saulniere for help. When Father Martin and a prostitute who knew of his secret are found ritualistically murdered, all signs point to something more disturbing than just a common theft: someone or something using magic is behind all of this. Meanwhile, the French government has its own plans for conquest, Julien discovers the identity of Father Martin's murderer—a white-suited man with magical powers, and the scroll and its secrets are still lost.

> *Vol. 1: The Guardian of the Temple.* 2006, 2nd edition. 176pp. 978-1-59307-652-8.
> *Vol. 2: The River Underground.* 2007, 2nd edition. 176pp. 978-1-59307-682-5.
> *Vol. 3: The Lost Kings.* 2006. 176pp. 978-1-59307-651-1.
> *Vol. 4: Crown and Sword.* 2007. 192pp. 978-1-59307-824-9.
> *Vol. 5: The Valley at the End of the World.* 2008. 208pp. 978-1-59582-192-8.
> *Vol. 6: Gate of God.* 2010. 248pp. 978-1-59582-403-5.

Junior Sleuths

Adults aren't the only ones capable of solving crimes. Listed here are some of the best junior sleuths in print, including adaptations of Nancy Drew and the Hardy Boys and other young detectives. They are listed separately from the Amateur Detectives subcategory because many of the Junior Detectives are more skilled at solving the murders and crimes than their Amateur Detective counterparts, and, of course, they're younger.

Case Closed. Written and Illustrated by **Gosho Aoyama**. VIZ Media, LLC., 2004– . O Japanese manga. あ ◎

MEITANTEI CONAN © 1994 Gosho
AOYAMA/SHOGAKUKAN

> High school student Jimmy Kudo is an 11th-grade legend around Japan. He's a brilliant crime-solver, handling disturbing cases that have perplexed the Japanese police. His hero is the fictional creation of Sir Arthur Conan Doyle: the super-sleuth Sherlock Holmes. Like Holmes, Jimmy uses the art of deduction and reasoning to be one step ahead of the crime. One day he is poisoned from behind, and while the poison doesn't kill him, it mysteriously turns him into a grade-schooler. The school and police (and Jimmy's would-be girlfriend Rachel) all believe that Jimmy has vanished. Determined to still fight crime, he takes on the pseudonym of Conan Edogawa and continues to live up to his personal hero in his pint-sized adventures with the hopes of one day finding a cure for his condition. The series is a huge hit in Japan and has been collected into over 88 volumes so far and has also spawned a hit animated series.

Vol. 1. 2004. 192pp. 978-1-59116-327-5.
Vol. 2. 2004. 184pp. 978-1-59116-587-3.
Vol. 3. 2005. 200pp. 978-1-59116-589-7.
Vol. 4. 2005. 200pp. 978-1-59116-632-0.
Vol. 5. 2005. 200pp. 978-1-59116-633-7.
Vol. 6. 2005. 184pp. 978-1-59116-838-6.
Vol. 7. 2005. 184pp. 978-1-59116-978-9.
Vol. 8. 2005. 192pp. 978-1-4215-0111-6.
Vol. 9. 2006. 184pp. 978-1-4215-0166-6.
Vol. 10. 2006. 194pp. 978-1-4215-0316-5.
Vol. 11. 2006. 208pp. 978-1-4215-0441-4.
Vol. 12. 2006. 208pp. 978-1-4215-0442-1.
Vol. 13. 2006. 208pp. 978-1-4215-0443-8.
Vol. 14. 2006. 208pp. 978-1-4215-0444-5.
Vol. 15. 2007. 208pp. 978-1-4215-0445-2.
Vol. 16. 2007. 192pp. 978-1-4215-0881-8.
Vol. 17. 2007. 208pp. 978-1-4215-0882-5.
Vol. 18. 2007. 192pp. 978-1-4215-0883-2.
Vol. 19. 2007. 192pp. 978-1-4215-0884-9.
Vol. 20. 2007. 192pp. 978-1-4215-0885-6.
Vol. 21. 2008. 200pp. 978-1-4215-1456-7.
Vol. 22. 2008. 200pp. 978-1-4215-1674-5.
Vol. 23. 2008. 200pp. 978-1-4215-1675-2.
Vol. 24. 2008. 208pp. 978-1-4215-1676-9.
Vol. 25. 2008. 200pp. 978-1-4215-1677-6.
Vol. 26. 2008. 210pp. 978-1-4215-1678-3.
Vol. 27. 2009. 210pp. 978-1-4215-1679-0.
Vol. 28. 2009. 200pp. 978-1-4215-2196-1.
Vol. 29. 2009. 200pp. 978-1-4215-2197-8.
Vol. 30. 2009. 200pp. 978-1-4215-2198-5.
Vol. 31. 2009. 200pp. 978-1-4215-2199-2.
Vol. 32. 2009. 192pp. 978-1-4215-2200-5.

Vol. 33. 2010. 200pp. 978-1-4215-2884-7.
Vol. 34. 2010. 200pp. 978-1-4215-2885-4.
Vol. 35. 2010. 200pp. 978-1-4215-2886-1.
Vol. 36. 2010. 192pp. 978-1-4215-2887-8.
Vol. 37. 2011. 200pp. 978-1-4215-2888-5.
Vol. 38. 2011. 200pp. 978-1-4215-2889-2.
Vol. 39. 2011. 200pp. 978-1-4215-3499-2.
Vol. 40. 2011. 184pp. 978-1-4215-3500-5.
Vol. 41. 2012. 200pp. 978-1-4215-3607-1.
Vol. 42. 2012. 200pp. 978-1-4215-3608-8.
Vol. 43. 2012. 200pp. 978-1-4215-3609-5.
Vol. 44. 2012. 200pp. 978-1-4215-3610-1.
Vol. 45. 2013. 192pp. 978-1-4215-3611-8.
Vol. 46. 2013. 200pp. 978-1-4215-3612-5.
Vol. 47. 2013. 192pp. 978-1-4215-3613-2.
Vol. 48. 2013. 184pp. 978-1-4215-3614-9.
Vol. 49. 2014. 192pp. 978-1-4215-5506-5.
Vol. 50. 2014. 192pp. 978-1-4215-5507-2.
Vol. 51. 2014. 192pp. 978-1-4215-6507-1.
Vol. 52. 2014. 192pp. 978-1-4215-6507-1.
Vol. 52. 2014. 192pp. 978-1-4215-6508-8.
Vol. 53. 2014. 192pp. 978-1-4215-6509-5.
Vol. 54. 2015. 192pp. 978-1-4215-6510-1.
Vol. 55. 2015. 192pp. 978-1-4215-7783-8.
Vol. 56. 2015. 192pp. 978-1-4215-7784-5.
Vol. 57. 2016. 192pp. 978-1-4215-7785-2.
Vol. 58. 2016. 192pp. 978-1-4215-7786-9.
Vol. 59. 2016. 192pp. 978-1-4215-8385-3.
Vol. 60. 2016. 192pp. 978-1-4215-8386-0.
Vol. 61. 2017. 192pp. 978-1-4215-8684-7.
Vol. 62. 2017. 192pp. 978-1-4215-8685-4.
Vol. 63. 2017. 192pp. 978-1-4215-9444-6.

Cat Burglar Black. Written and Illustrated by **Richard Sala.** First Second, 2009. 128pp. 978-1-59643-144-7. A 🌻

K. Westree is a cat burglar attending Bellsong Academy, a boarding school that has many mysteries. An orphan at a young age, she was raised in an orphanage by Mother Claude, who turned the orphanage into a breeding ground for thieving children. Now one of the most skilled burglars, she uses her talents to unlock the secrets of the school—one of which has a tie to her own father! The book is an homage to European comics and is one Part Tin-Tin/Oliver Twist and one part Nancy Drew. The book was recognized by YALSA on its Great Graphic Novels for Teens list in 2010.

Chicagoland Detective Agency. Written by **Trina Robbins**. Illustrated by **Tyler Page**. Graphic Universe, 2010–2014. Y

Megan is a vegan and loves to write haiku and read manga. Raf is a full-time geek and the son of a local pet shop owner. When trouble is afoot they're joined up with Bradley, a talking dog. Together they set up the Chicagoland Detective Agency to solve the hilarious and bizarre mysteries from zombies, aliens, and more!

Vol. 1: The Drained Brains Caper. 2010. 60pp. 978-0-7613-5635-6.
Vol. 2: The Maltese Mummy. 2011. 60pp. 978-0-7613-5636-3.
Vol. 3: Night of the Living Dogs. 2012. 60pp. 978-0-7613-5637-0.
Vol. 4. The Big Flush. 2012. 60pp. 978-0-8225-9161-0.
Vol. 5: The Bark in Space. 2013. 60pp. 978-1-4677-0725-1.
Vol. 6: A Midterm Night's Scheme. 2014. 60pp. 978-1-4677-1499-0.

Goldie Vance. Written by **Hope Larson**. Illustrated by **Brittney Williams**. BOOM! Studios, 2016– . Y

Move over Nancy Drew, there's a new sleuth in town! Meet Marigold "Goldie" Vance, a junior sleuth with dreams of being the in-house detective for her father's Florida resort. When Charles, the current detective, encounters a case he can't crack, he agrees to mentor Goldie in exchange for her help solving the mystery.

Vol. 1. 2016. 112pp. 978-1-60886-898-8.
Vol. 2. 2017. 112pp. 978-1-60886-974-9.

© 2016 Boom! Studios

Gotham Academy. Written by **Becky Cloonan** and **Brenden Fletcher**. Illustrated by **Karl Kerschel**. DC Comics, 2015– . T 🏆 ◎

The most prestigious school in Gotham is now open! Olive Silverlock is a new student at the prestigious Gotham Academy. She's soon befriended by Mia "Maps" Mizoguchi—the sister of Olive's ex-boyfriend, Kyle. A group of friends is soon formed, and soon the "Detective Club" is on their way to solving the riddles of the ghost of *Millie Jane Cobblepot*, the mysterious beast in the sewers, and the truth behind Olive's hatred for the Dark Knight himself. Boasting influences from a variety of Batman-related properties including the 1960s' *Batman* TV show and *Batman: The Animated Series*, the collection is a treat for old and young Batman fans. The characters also teamed up with the characters from *Lumberjanes* (see later in this chapter). The first two volumes in the series were recognized by YALSA's Great Graphic Novels for Teens selection list in 2016 and 2017, respectively.

© 2016 DC Comics

Vol. 1: Welcome to Gotham Academy. 2015. 160pp. 978-1-4012-5472-8.

Vol. 2: Calamity. 2016. 144pp. 978-1-4012-5681-4.

Vol. 3: Yearbook. 2016. 144pp. 978-1-4012-6478-9.

Second Semester, Vol. 1. 2017. 144pp. 978-1-4012-7119-0.

The Hardy Boys. Written by **Scott Lobdell**. Illustrated by **Lea Hernandez**, **Daniel Rendon**, **Paulo Henrique**, and various. Papercutz, 2005– . Y

© 2016 NBM Publishing

Frank and Joe Hardy are America's best teen detectives. Members of a secret organization called ATAC (American Teens against Crime), there's no mystery they can't solve: stolen art, diamond-smuggling skydivers, identity thefts, murders, and more. Now the classic series of teen novels is back in all-new graphic novel stories. A new series, <u>The Hardy Boys Adventures</u>, debuted in 2016 and reprints several previously released volumes on one economic collection.

The Hardy Boys. 2005–2010.

Vol. 1: The Ocean of Osyria. 2005. 96pp. 978-1-59707-005-8, hardcover; 978-1-59707-001-0.

Vol. 2: Identity Theft. 2005. 96pp. 978-1-59707-007-2, hardcover; 978-1-59707-003-4.

Vol. 3: Mad House. 2005. 96pp. 978-1-59707-011-9, hardcover; 978-1-59707-010-2.

Vol. 4: Malled. 2006. 96pp. 978-1-59707-015-7, hardcover; 978-1-59707-014-0.

Vol. 5: Sea You, See Me! 2006. 96pp. 978-1-59707-023-2, hardcover; 978-1-59707-022-5.

Vol. 6: Hyde & Shriek. 2006. 96pp. 978-1-59707-029-4, hardcover; 978-1-59707-028-7.

Vol. 7: The Opposite Numbers. 2006. 96pp. 978-1-59707-035-5, hardcover; 978-1-59707-034-8.

Vol. 8: Board to Death. 2007. 96pp. 978-1-59707-053-9.

Vol. 9: To Die or Not to Die. 2007. 112pp. 978-1-59707-063-8, hardcover; 978-1-59707-062-1.

Vol. 10: A Hardy's Day Night. 2007. 112pp. 978–1597070713, hardcover; 978-1-59707-070-6.

Vol. 11: Abracadeath. 2008. 112pp. 978-1-59707-081-2, hardcover; 978-1-59707-080-5.

Vol. 12: Dude Ranch O'Death! 2008. 112pp. 978-1-59707-089-8, hardcover; 978-1-59707-088-1.

Vol. 13: The Deadliest Stunt! 2008. 112pp. 978-1-59707-103-1, hardcover; 978-1-59707-102-4.

Vol. 14: Haley Danelle's Top Eight! 2008. 96pp. 978-1-59707-114-7, hardcover; 978-1-59707-113-0.

Vol. 15: Live Free, Die Hardy! 2008. 96pp. 978-1-59707-124-6, hardcover; 978-1-59707-123-9.

Vol. 16: Shhhhhhh! 2009. 96pp. 978-1-59707-139-0, hardcover; 978-1-59707-138-3.

Vol. 17: Word Up! 2009. 96pp. 978-1-59707-148-2, hardcover; 978-1-59707-147-5.

Vol. 18: D.A.N.G.E.R. Spells the Hangman. 2009. 96pp. 978-1-59707-161-1, hardcover; 978-1-59707-160-4.

Vol. 19: Chaos at 30,000 Feet! 2010. 96pp. 978-1-59707-170-3, hardcover; 978-1-59707-169-7.

Vol. 20: Deadly Strategy. 2010. 96pp. 978-1-59707-183-3, hardcover; 978-1-59707-182-6.

Hardy Boys Adventures, 2016–

Vol. 1. 2016. 384pp. 978-1-62991-607-1.
Vol. 2. 2017. 384pp. 978-1-62991-651-4.

Lumberjanes. Written by **Noelle Stevenson, Grace Ellis** and **Shannon Watters**. Illustrated by **Brooke Allen**. Boom! Studios, 2015– . Y 🎖

© 2016 BOOM! Studios.

Part of Boom! Studios Boom! Box imprint for "experimental titles," Lumberjanes is set at Miss Quinzella Thiskwin Penniquiqul Thistle Crumpet's Camp for Hardcore Lady Types, which is attended by Lumberjane Scouts who work on their various scout badges. The main characters are the girls of Roanoke Cabin—Jo, April, Molly, Mal, and Ripley, who have adventures, sometimes without the knowledge of cabin scout-leader Jen and scout-master Rosie. These adventures often involve monsters, magical beings, and other mysteries. The series has appeared on the top-10 list of the YALSA Great Graphic Novels for teens, won multiple Eisner Awards, and was nominated for a GLAAD Media Award for Outstanding Comic Book. The "To the Max" editions reprint two previously published volumes plus extra content. In 2016 the Lumberjanes teamed up with the cast from *Gotham Academy* in a company crossover special.

Vol. 1: Beware the Kitten Holy. 2015. 128pp. 978-1-6088-6687-8.
Vol. 2: Friendship to the Max. 2015. 112pp. 978-1-6088-6737-0.
Vol. 3: A Terrible Plan. 2016. 112pp. 978-1-6088-6803-2.
Vol. 4: Out of Time. 2016. 128pp. 978-1-6088-6860-5.
Vol. 5: Band Together. 2016. 112pp. 978-1-6088-6919-0.
Vol. 6: Sink or Swim. 2017. 112pp. 978-1-6088-6954-1.

To the Max Edition, 2015– .

Vol. 1. 2015. 272pp. 978-1-6088-6809-4, hardcover.
Vol. 2. 2016. 272pp. 978-1-6088-6889-6, hardcover.
Vol. 3. 2017. 256pp. 978-1-68415-003-8, hardcover.
Lumberjanes/Gotham Academy. Written by **Chynna Clugston-Flores**. Illustrated by **Rosemary Valero-O'Connell**. 2017. 160pp. 978-1-6088-6945-9.

Nancy Drew. Written by **Stefan Petrucha** and **Vaughn Ross**. Illustrated by **Sho Murase**. Papercutz, 2005– . Y

Based on the original series created 75 years ago by Carolyn Keene, America's favorite girl detective is back. From tackling cases involving urban legends and a stolen child, to a mysterious doll house that predicts murder, there's not a case that Nancy, with the aid of some of her best friends from

© 2016 NBM Publishing

River Heights, can't handle. The second series, <u>Nancy Drew Diaries</u>, is the current series and debuted in 2014.

Nancy Drew. 2005–2009.

Vol. 1: The Demon of River Heights. 2005. 96pp. 978-1-59707-004-1, hardcover; 978-1-59707-000-3.

Vol. 2: Writ in Stone. 2005. 96pp. 978-1-59707-006-5, hardcover; 978-1-59707-002-7.

Vol. 3: The Haunted Dollhouse. 2005. 96pp. 978-1-59707-009-6, hardcover; 978-1-59707-008-9.

Vol. 4: The Girl Who Wasn't There. 2006. 96pp. 978-1-59707-013-3, hardcover; 978-1-59707-012-6.

Vol. 5: The Fake Heir. 2006. 96pp. 978-1-59707-025-6, hardcover; 978-1-59707-024-9.

Vol. 6: Mr. Cheeters Is Missing. 2006. 96pp. 978-1-59707-031-7, hardcover; 978-1-59707-030-0.

Vol. 7: The Charmed Bracelet. 2006. 96pp. 978-1-59707-037-9, hardcover; 978-1-59707-036-2.

Vol. 8: Global Warning. 2007. 112pp. 978-1-5970-7052-2, hardcover; 978-1-59707-051-5.

Vol. 9: Ghost in the Machinery. 2007. 112pp. 978-1-59707-061-4, hardcover; 978-1-59707-058-4.

Vol. 10: The Disoriented Express. 2007. 112pp. 978-1-59707-067-6, hardcover; 978-1-59707-066-9.

Vol. 11: Monkey Wrench Blues. 2007. 112pp. 978-1-59707-077-5, hardcover; 978-1-59707-076-8.

Vol. 12: Dress Reversal. 2008. 112pp. 978-1-59707-087-4, hardcover; 978-1-59707-086-7.

Vol. 13: Doggone Town. 2008. 112pp. 978-1-59707-099-7, hardcover; 978-1-59707-098-0.

Vol. 14: Sleight of Dan. 2008. 112pp. 978-1-59707-108-6, hardcover; 978-1-59707-107-9.

Vol. 15: Tiger Counter. 2008. 96pp. 978-1-59707-119-2, hardcover; 978-1-59707-118-5.

Vol. 16: What Goes Up. 2009. 96pp. 978-1-59707-135-2, hardcover; 978-1-59707-134-5.

Vol. 17: Night of the Living Chatchke. 2009. 96pp. 978-1-59707-144-4, hardcover; 978-1-59707-143-7.

Vol. 18: City under the Basement. 2009. 96pp. 978-1-59707-155-0, hardcover; 978-1-5970-7154-3.

Vol. 19: Cliffhanger. 2009. 96pp. 978-1-59707-166-6, hardcover; 978-1-59707-165-9.

Nancy Drew Diaries. 2014–.

Vol. 1. 2014. 176pp. 978-1-59707-501-5.
Vol. 2. 2014. 176pp. 978-1-59707-778-1.
Vol. 3. 2014. 176pp. 978-1-62991-054-3.
Vol. 4. 2015. 176pp. 978-1-62991-158-8.
Vol. 5. 2015. 176pp. 978-1-62991-193-9.
Vol. 6. 2015. 176pp. 978-1-62991-293-6.
Vol. 7. 2016. 176pp. 978-1-62991-462-6.
Vol. 8. 2016. 176pp. 978-1-62991-593-7.

Sam and Friends Mysteries. Written by **Mary Labatt**. Illustrated by **Jo Rioux**. Kids Can Press, 2009–2011. Y

Samantha the Sheepdog isn't your ordinary dog—she loves to solve mysteries! After moving to a small town with her owners, she bonds with Jennie, a 10-year-old

© 2016 Kids Can Press

next-door neighbor, who has the unique ability to hear Sam's thoughts. Now Sam, Jennie, and Jennie's best friend Beth are out trying to solve mysteries of the supernatural—or do they? The stories are based off of the prose novels in the <u>Dog Detective Sam</u> mystery series by Mary Labatt.

Vol. 1: Dracula Madness. 2009. 96pp. 978-1-55337-303-2.
Vol. 2: Lake Monster Mix-Up. 2009. 96pp. 978-1-55337-302-5.
Vol. 3: Mummy Mayhem. 2010. 96pp. 978-1-55453-471-5.
Vol. 4: Witches' Brew. 2011. 96pp. 978-1-55453-473-9.

Secret Coders. Written by **Gene Luen Yang.** Illustrated by **Mark Holmes**. First Second Books, 2015– . Y

© 2016 First Second and Gene Luen Yang

The first book in a series by Yang (whose past employment includes teaching computers science to high school students), *Secret Coders* is set in the mysterious Statley Academy in which 12-year-old Hopper is a new student. She soon makes friends but discovers odd things about the school including robot birds and mysterious caretakers. Many of the mysteries can be solved with the knowledge of coding.

Vol. 1. 2015. 96pp. 978-1-62672-276-7, hardcover; 978-1-62672-075-6.
Vol. 2: Paths and Portals. 2016. 96pp. 978-1-62672-340-5, hardcover; 978-1-62672-076-3.
Vol. 3: Secrets and Sequences. 2017. 112pp. 978-1-62672-618-5.
Vol. 3: Robots & Repeats. 2017. 96pp. 978-1-62672-606-2.

Crime and the Criminal Underworld

Graphic novel stories focusing the criminal element including tales of murder and the world of ex-cons, thieves, pimps, gangsters, and hitmen. Here the focus is on the darker side of crime, with the antagonist receiving the spotlight instead of the police and detectives. The tales can range from life as a gang member on the streets, to a group of criminals planning to rob the biggest payload of their lives, to other darker looks at the criminal element. The stories are reminiscent of television shows such as *The Sopranos* and movies such as *Ocean's 11*, *The Godfather*, and *Pulp Fiction*. The comic books have also inspired movies as well, as seen with the 2005 release of Frank Miller's *Sin City*, which is adapted from his graphic novel series.

Catwoman: Selina's Big Score. Written and Illustrated by **Darwyn Cooke**. DC Comics, 2003. 96pp. 978-1-56389-922-5. T ◎

Selina Kyle, better known as the thief called Catwoman, has temporarily put away her costume and is laying low in Gotham City after being presumed

© 2016 DC Comics

dead. Desperate for some serious money after a failed international heist and the closing of her personal accounts, she hears of a money train loaded with $24 million in mob money heading north. She recruits a team of specialists, including her ex-lover Stark, and together they're going to take that train. Sounds like an easy job, right? Meanwhile a private eye by the name of Slam Bradley (a character who has been around longer than Superman) has figured out that Selina isn't as dead as was rumored and is determined to catch her any way he can. See the super-heroes chapter for more title recommendations featuring Catwoman.

The Couriers: The Complete Series. Written **Brian Wood**. Illustrated by **Rob Goodridge** and **Brett Weldele**. Image Comics, 2012. 360pp. 978-1-60706-641-5. M

A collection of creator Brian Wood's early work includes the series *Couscous Express* and three tales of the *Couriers*. When you absolutely need something dangerous delivered around New York City, there's only one group you can trust: the Couriers. Anything you need done, they can do—assassinations, money transactions, protection, or intelligence gathering. In the first Couriers story, Moustafa and Special reluctantly deal with an odd biological package: a deaf/mute Nepalese girl. When the Chinese Red Army Brigade will stop at nothing to get her back, it's up to them to finish the job. In the second story, when a gun-run goes wrong, Moustafa and Special travel to upstate New York to get what's coming to them: money. The third story is a flashback story of how Moustafa and Special met.

Criminal*.* Written by **Ed Brubaker**. Illustrated by **Sean Phillips**. Image Comics, 2015. M

© 2016 Ed Brubaker

Originally published from 2007 to 2011, Leo is a pickpocket and master heist planner and thief who has one rule for his heists: he calls the shots. That means no guns and there's always a quick exit if things turn south. When he's lured into a heist that goes horribly wrong, he finds himself on the run from the law and those that double-crossed him. Unfortunately for them, Leo has to dig deep and unleash a violence that he's kept in check for years.

Vol. 1: Coward. 2015. 128pp. 978-1-63215-170-4.
Vol. 2: Lawless. 2015. 128pp. 978-1-63215-203-9.
Vol. 3: The Dead and the Dying. 2015. 104pp. 978-1-63215-233-6.
Vol. 4: Bad Night. 2015. 144pp. 978-1-6321-5260-2.
Vol. 5: The Sinners. 2015. 144pp. 978-1-63215-298-5.
Vol. 6: Last of the Innocent. 2015. 144pp. 978-1-63215-299-2.

Fatale*.* Written by **Ed Brubaker**. Illustrated by **Sean Phillips** and **Dave Stewart**. Image Comics, 2012–2015. M 🍸

A crime story that blends crime noir with influences of Lovecraftian horror. Josephine is the pinnacle of beauty—reminiscent of the classic femme fatale from the 1930s. She cannot age and has the power to hypnotize men whether she likes it or not. The series focuses on Jo's travels and the men that she ensnares in her

© 2016 Ed Brubaker

escapades. Meanwhile, while Jo is trying to understand her powers, a violent cult of worshippers wants her for something sinister. The series received many nominations for Eisner Awards in 2013 for Best New Series, Best Continuing Series, Best Writer, and more. The series won an Eisner Award that year for Best Coloring by Dave Stewart.

Book 1: Death Chases Me. 2012. 144. 978-1-60706-563-0.
Book 2: The Devil's Business. 2013. 136pp. 978-1-60706-618-7.
Book 3: West of Hell. 2013. 128pp. 978-1-60706-743-6.
Book 4: Pray for Rain. 2014. 144pp. 978-1-60706-835-8.
Book 5: Curse of the Demon. 2014. 144pp. 978-1-63215-007-3.
Deluxe Edition, Book 1. 2014. 288pp. 978-1-60706-942-3, hardcover.
Deluxe Edition, Book 2. 2015. 440pp. 978-1-63215-503-0, hardcover.

Goldfish. Written and Illustrated by **Brian Michael Bendis**. Marvel Comics, 2012. 272pp. 978-0-7851-6396-1, hardcover. M

A con artist named David "Goldfish" Gold has realized that sometimes you can't come back home, but he's not about to leave without his young son. After returning to his home town of Cleveland, the grifter discovers that things have drastically changed since he left. His former partner-in-crime Izzy is now a detective, and his ex-girlfriend Lauren is leading the city's crime bosses. All he wants to do is get out of town with his young son, but will they let him leave?

Incognito. Written by **Ed Brubaker**. Illustrated by **Sean Phillips**. Icon/Marvel Comics, 2009–2012. M

When a reformed super-villain has been entered into a Witness Protection program, life becomes dull and mundane for Zack Overkill. Depowered and made to work as an office clerk, he longs for the days when the rules didn't apply for him. When he discovers that getting high causes his powers to come back, he decides to use his powers for good and to take justice into his own hands. A thrilling mix of noir with super-heroes.

Vol. 1. 2009. 176pp. 978-0-7851-3979-9.
Vol. 2: Bad Influences. 2011. 144pp. 978-0-7851-5155-5.
The Classified Edition. 2012. 368pp. 978-0-7851-6574-3, hardcover.

Jinx: The Essential Collection. Written and Illustrated by **Brian Michael Bendis**. Marvel Comics, 2011. 480pp. 978-0-7851-5672-7, hardcover. M ◎

Bounty hunter Jinx Alameda has had it rough being one of the only female headhunters in a male-dominated business. Capturing bail jumpers hasn't been quite the romantic life she imagined, and it's starting to wear her down. Petty criminal David Gold AKA "Goldfish" can't stand his partner-in-crime, the chrome-domed Columbia, and they're at each other's throats following a nearly botched game of dice. When a dying man gives them clues to where $3 million is hidden somewhere in the dark alleys of Cleveland, the two must

try to work together one last time to find the stolen mob cash. After a chance meeting in a diner, Jinx and David find themselves attracted to each other even though he's a criminal and she could take him in at any time for a cash reward. But when David dumps Colombia and tells Jinx about the hidden cash, they have to learn to trust each other so they both can leave their pasts behind and recover the mob money.

Kill or Be Killed. Written by **Ed Brubaker**. Illustrated by **Sean Phillips**. Image Comics, 2017– . M

> A young NYU grad student's life is turned upside down when he's forced to become a vigilante and murder a bad person once a month. Can a man who has such a heavy burden to bare keep ramifications of his deep and dark secret from destroying his life?
>
> *Vol. 1*. 2017. 128pp. 978-1-5343-0028-6.

Lady Killer. Written by **Jamie S. Rich**. Illustrated by **Joelle Jones**. Dark Horse Comics, 2015– . M

Josie Schuller isn't just a happy homemaker living in Seattle in the1960s with a loving husband, and kids: she's also a deadly assassin for hire! When her employer wants to terminate her contract permanently, Josie's on the run out to figure out who wants her dead and why? A humorous twisted take on domestic bliss by way of *Dexter*. The series was nominated for an Eisner Award for Best Limited Series, Best Penciller/Inker, Best Cover Artist, and Best Coloring in 2016. More stories featuring Josie will be released in 2017.

Vol. 1. 2015. 136pp. 978-1-61655-757-7.
Vol. 2. 2017. 136pp. 978-1-5067-0029-8.

Like a Sniper Lining up His Shot. Written by **Jean-Patrick Manchette**. Illustrated by **Jacques Tardi**. Fantagraphics, 2011. 104pp. 978-1-60699-448-1. M

> Martin Terrier is a hired killer, but he's ready to retire. He's got one last job to do, and then he's planning on going back home, reuniting with his childhood sweetheart, and retire. The only problem is his last job is a setup. Now on the run from the authorizes, those that double-crossed him, as well as another crime syndicate who want him from a previous hit, Martin's retirement is looking more and more less likely.

New York Mon Amour. Written by **Benjamin Legrand** and **Dominique Grange**. Illustrated by **Jacques Tardi**. Fantagraphics Books. 2012. 64pp. 978-1-60699-524-2. M

New York is a giant rough city: the type of city where one wrong step off of an elevator can get you in over your head. This happens to Walter, a cockroach exterminator, who got off on the 13th floor and was swooped up in a giant conspiracy. Other stories collected in this book tell different tales of murder and revenge in the Big Apple.

100 Bullets. Written by **Brian Azzarello**. Illustrated by **Eduardo Risso**. Vertigo/ DC Comics, 2000–2016. M 🏃 ◎

© 2016 DC Comics

If you were given 100 forensically untraceable bullets to exact revenge and get away with it, would you do it? The mysterious Agent Graves is in a position to give any person this gift and to make the user above the law. Handling personal conflicts isn't his only concern—there are much bigger fish to fry. Graves is out to put an end to a shadow organization called The Trust, a wealthy and powerful 13-family organization with connections into nearly all of organized crime. At his aid are the Minutemen, a squad of specialists trained to beat the odds and to get the job done no matter how many bullets it takes. As the bullets, bloodshed, double-crosses, morality issues, and street lingo fly, Agent Graves' plan is put in motion for revenge, but can the Minutemen and their new recruits really take down The Trust? The series has won several Eisner Awards including Best Serialized Story (2001) for *Hang Up on the Hang Low* and Best Continuing Series (2002, 2004), and Best Artist/Penciller/ Inker (2002) for Eduardo Risso's illustrations. The series has also won Harvey Awards for Best Writer (2002), Best Artist (2002–2003), and Best Continuing or Limited Series (2002). The complete series was reprinted in into five deluxe-sized volumes from 2014 to 2016. The *Brother Lono* collection is a brand new story arc not part of the original series. A film adaptation has been planned but as of this writing has not been officially announced.

Vol. 1. 2014. 456pp. 978-1-4012-5056-0.
Vol. 2. 2015. 416pp. 978-1-4012-5431-5.
Vol. 3. 2015. 512pp. 978-1-4012-5795-8.
Vol. 4. 2016. 512pp. 978-1-4012-5794-1.
Vol. 5. 2016. 356pp. 978-1-4012-6133-7.
Brother Lono. 2014. 192pp. 978-1-4012-4506-1.

The One Trick Rip-Off and Deep Cuts. Written and Illustrated by **Paul Pope**. Image Comics, 2013. 288pp. 978-1-60706-775-7. M

Two young lovers, Tubby and Vim want to escape from their past mistakes they've made and start fresh. But in order to do that, they need to make one

worse mistake and try and rip-off the One-Tricks—the toughest street gang in Los Angeles. The book also includes some short story collections and artwork originally published in Japan.

Run Like Crazy, Run Like Hell. Written by **Jean-Patrick Manchette**. Illustrated by **Jacques Tardi**. Fantagraphics, 2015. 104pp. 978-1-60699-620-1, hardcover. M

> A wealthy industrialist named Michel Hartog hires a young woman named Julie as a nanny for his bratty nephew, Peter. It seems like an altruistic gesture since Julie has been in a psychiatric asylum for several years, but his motive is to far sinister: he wishes to stage a fake kidnapping and frame Julie. When the kidnapping plot goes horribly wrong, Julie and Peter are on the run from the police, Hartog's goons, and an almost terminator-like contract killer named Thompson who will not stop his pursuit. The collection intermixes the tense story with humor and social commentary as well.

The Simon and Kirby Library: Crime. Written and Illustrated by **Joe Simon** and **Jack Kirby**. Titan Books, 2011. 320pp. 978-1-84856-960-7. T

> The second volume of the anthology collection by famed comic book icons Joe Simon and Jack Kirby collects 32 stories originally published in the 1940s and 1950s from such titles as *Clue Comics* and *Justice Traps the Guilty*.

Frank Miller's Sin City. Written and Illustrated by **Frank Miller**. Dark Horse Comics, 2010. M 🏶 ◎ 🎬

If you like your crime hard-boiled, then welcome to Basin City aka Sin City, the toughest, seediest city ever, where everyone's a cut-throat or worse. Each volume, in black and white with accentuated colors, tells a different hard-hitting crime noir story guaranteed to shock the reader with tales of revenge, over-the-top violence, and occasional nudity. Featuring a strong cast of tough guys, killers, strippers, and prostitutes, including Marv, Goldie, Dwight, and many more unforgettable noir characters. The series was won numerous awards including Eisner Awards for Best Writer/Artist (1993), Best Artist/Penciller/Inker (1993), Best Graphic Album: Reprint for *The Hard Goodbye* (1993) and *That Yellow Bastard* (1998), Best Short Story (1995), and Best Finite Series/Limited Series for *A Dame to Kill For* (1995) and *The Big Fat Kill* (1996). In 2005 director Robert Rodriguez with Frank Miller released a film version of Frank Miller's stories, adapting the stories included in *The Hard Goodbye*, *The Big Fat Kill*, and *That Yellow Bastard*.

A 2014 sequel, *Sin City: Dame to Kill For* was also from Rodriguez and Miller, and was primarily based on that collection. A sequel is planned to tell other tales of Sin City. The series also won a Harvey Award in 1996 for Best Continuing or Limited Series and Best Graphic Novel of Original Work for *Sin City: Family Values* in 1998.

Vol. 1: The Hard Goodbye. 2010. 3rd edition. 280pp. 978-1-59307-293-3.

Tough-but-simple Marv finds true love in a hooker named Goldie, but when she's found murdered he'll stop at nothing to take on a serial killer and get his revenge.

Vol. 2: A Dame to Kill For. 2010. 3rd edition. 208pp. 978-1-59307-294-0.

Dwight McCarthy, a down-on-his-luck photojournalist, can't resist his femme fatale ex-girlfriend's pleas for help and is drawn back into her world of corruption, deceit, and lies.

Vol. 3: Big Fat Kill. 2010. 3rd edition. 184pp. 978-1-59307-295-7.

Dwight and a group of Old City prostitutes try to salvage the red light district from the corrupt mob and the police.

Vol. 4: That Yellow Bastard. 2005. 3rd edition. 240pp. 978-1-59307-296-4.

Hartigan, a cop on the verge of retirement, must save an 11-year-old girl from the clutches of a lunatic before it's too late.

Vol. 5: Family Values. 2010. 3rd edition. 128pp. 978-1-59307-297-1.

Dwight and Miho take on the mob after a hooker is killed and her lover demands revenge.

Vol. 6: Booze, Broads, and Bullets. 2010. 3rd edition. 160pp. 978-1-59307-298-8.

A vignette collection of short stories in Sin City, including stories of Marv, Dwight, and Delia.

Vol. 7: Hell and Back. 2010. 3rd edition. 320pp. 978-1-59307-299-5.

Wallace, a brooding artist with a knack for hurting people, saves a beautiful actress from killing herself. A tale of true love with twists and turns and deadly conspiracies.

Big Damn Sin City. 2014. 1360pp. 978-1-61655-237-4, hardcover.
A collection of all seven *Sin City* stories in one omnibus collection.

Southern Bastards. Written by **Jason Aaron**. Illustrated by **Jason Latour**. Image Comics, 2014– . M

© 2016 Jason Aaron & Jason Latour and Image Comics

Craw County, Alabama, is full of some of the biggest bastards you've ever met. And old Earl Tubb aims to take down those bastards one by one. After coming back to town and finding that Euless Boss, the high school football coach, has taken over the town and has buried half of his enemies under the bleachers of the football stadium, Earl decides to take it upon himself to brandish a big stick struck by lightning from a tree near his dearly departed father's grave and to bring some good old fashioned justice back to Craw County one head at a time. The book won the Eisner Award for best Continuing Series in 2016 and was among the titles that earned Aaron a Best Writer Eisner.

Vol. 1: Here Was a Man. 2014. 128pp. 978-1-63215-016-5.
Vol. 2: Gridiron. 2015. 128pp. 978-1-63215-269-5.
Vol. 3: Homecoming. 2016. 128pp. 978-1-63215-610-5.
Deluxe Hardcover Edition. 2015. 256pp. 978-1-63215-444-6.

Stray Bullets. Written and Illustrated by **David Lapham**. El Capitan Books, 2014– . M
🎗 ◎

Begun originally in comic book format in 1995, David Lapham's series spans from the 1980s through the mid-1990s and features a sprawling cast of lowlifes, con artists, deadbeats, criminals, and other people caught in circumstances beyond their control and the repercussions that follow. Though the graphic novels were originally published earlier, they were recently reprinted in 2014. In 1996 David Lapham won an Eisner for Best Writer/Artist and in 1997 the first collection received an Eisner Award for Best Graphic Album: Reprint. The series has continued to be published but is on an irregular schedule.

Vol. 1: Innocence of Nilhilism. 2014. 224pp. 978-1-63215-113-1.
Vol. 2: Somewhere Out West. 2015. 224pp. 978-1-63215-377-7.
Vol. 3: Other People. 2015. 256pp. 978-1-63215-482-8.
Vol. 4: Dark Days. 2015. 224pp. 978-1-63215-553-5.
Vol. 5: Hi-Jinx and Derring-Do. 2016. 264pp. 978-1-63215-733-1.
Vol. 6: Killers. 2015. 248pp. 978-1-63215-215-2.

Torpedo. Written by **Enrique Sánchez Abulí**. Illustrated by **Jordi Bernet**. IDW Publishing, 2012–2014. M

Originally published in Italy in the 1980s comes a dark and humorous look at the crime industry. The series' main antagonist is Luca Torelli, a heartless hitman who is a part of organized crime in New York City during the depression. After fleeing Sicily and making his way up the crime industry in New York participating in armed robberies, he's joined with his sidekick, a Polish American named Rascal, and begin their careers as hit men.

Vol. 1. 2012. 144pp. 978-1-61377-516-5.
Vol. 2. 2013. 144pp. 978-1-61377-569-1.
Vol. 3. 2013. 144pp. 978-1-61377-641-4.
Vol. 4. 2013. 144pp. 978-1-61377-713-8.
Vol. 5. 2014. 144pp. 978-1-61377-801-2.

West Coast Blues. Written by **Jean-Patrick Manchette**. Illustrated by **Jacques Tardi**. Fantagraphics, 2009. 80pp. 978-1-60699-295-1, hardcover. M

George Gerfaut is a Parisian businessman who has little time for his family and would rather spend it smoking cigarettes, drinking booze, and listening to jazz. When George becomes an accidental witness to a murder, he finds his life is in danger by a pair of romantically linked hitmen who want to rub him out, but George isn't going down without a fight. The story is based on the original novel by Jean-Patrikc Manchette written in 1976.

True Crime

Whether it's the historical aspects, morbid details or the psychological questions surrounding the crime, tales of real-life murders have fascinated people for ages. Collected here is a small but excellent collection of true-life crime in a graphic novel format.

Fist Stick Knife Gun. Written by **Geoffrey Canada**. Illustrated by **Jamar Nicholas**. Beacon Press. 2010. 124pp. 978-0-8070-4449-0. T 🏹 ◎

As a kid growing up in the Bronx, violence was a part of daily life for Geoffrey. As a little kid, Geoffrey and his friends would fight each other for fun and to establish their pecking order. When he was a little older he had his first run in with guns. A neighborhood man had almost shot him. When Geoffrey was old enough to buy a pocket knife he carried it around to feel strong. He only ended up mutilating his own finger. Would he fall into the same trap when he travels away for college? Mr. Canada's story is an inspiring tale of breaking the cycle of violence. The book was recognized by YALSA's Great Graphic Novels for Teens selection list in 2011.

From Hell. Written by **Alan Moore**. Illustrated by **Eddie Campbell**. Top Shelf Productions/IDW Publishing, 2012. 572pp. 978-0-9585783-4-9. M 🏹 ◎ 🎬

© 2016 Alan Moore and Campbell

"Jack the Ripper" is one of the most infamous murderers in modern history. From 1888 to 1891 he terrorized London's East End in the highly publicized London's Whitechapel murders, where five prostitutes were brutally murdered. To this day no one really knows his true identity. In this in-depth, well-researched, and annotated tome, writer Alan Moore surmises who the killer was—Queen Victoria's personal physician Dr. William Gull. By compiling facts, rumors, and speculation along with detailed information of the gruesome murders, Moore sets up a fantastical story in which the doctor is portrayed as a leader of a Masonic plot to eliminate Queen Victoria's illegitimate grandson's prostitute mother. Though it is never certain who 'Jack the Ripper' really was, it makes for a thrilling and well-researched bloody tale that also helped to inspire the 2001 movie starring Johnny Depp. The series won an Eisner Award for Best Serialized Story (1993), Best Writer (1995–1997), and Best Graphic Novel: Reprint (2000). The series also received several Harvey Awards including Best Writer (1995–1996, 1999), Best Continuing or Limited Series (1995), and Best Graphic Album of Previously Published Work (2000).

Green River Killer: A True Detective Story. Written by **Jeff Jensen**. Illustrated by **Jonathan Case**. Dark Horse Comics, 2015. 248pp. 978-1-61655-812-3. M

In the 1980–1990s in the Seattle area, over 48 women were brutally murdered by a mysterious killer. Detective Tom Jensen was assigned the case and through DNA evidence was able to implicate Gary Leon Ridgway of the murders. Join Jeff Jensen, the son of the detective on a journey into the darkness of man and see the face of evil.

In the Days of the Mob. Written and Illustrated by **Jack Kirby**. DC Comics, 2013. 108pp. 978-1-4012-4079-0, hardcover. T

© 2016 DC Comics

In this reprint of a 1971 work, the legendary Jack Kirby tells true stories of mobsters from the 1930s.

Torso. Written by **Brian Michael Bendis** and **Marc Andreyko**. Illustrated by **Brian Michael Bendis**. Marvel Comics, 2012. 280pp. 978-0-7851-5356-6. M ◎ ⌨

© 2016 Brian Michael Bendis and
Marc Andreyko

Heavily researched by Bendis and Andreyko, the story is based on the true unsolved story of the very first serial killer in the United States, which claimed at least 12 to possibly 30 murder victims in Cleveland in the mid-1930s. Elliot Ness, fresh from his success at cleaning out notorious gangster Al Capone from Chicago, became the safety director in Cleveland to clamp down on corruption on the streets and in his own police force. When body parts wash ashore that are so badly mutilated that the victims' remains are mostly headless torsos, there are few clues to go on. As the body count rises by the media-dubbed "Torso Murderer," Ness does what he can to catch the real killer.

A Treasury of Victorian Murder. Written and Illustrated by **Rick Geary**. NBM Publishing, 1990– . T 🏃 ◎

© 2016 Rick Geary

A collection of true crime graphic novels, each focusing on a particular event in crime history from Lincoln's assassination, the mystery of Jack the Ripper, to the murders by Lizzy Borden. Geary takes the reader on a meticulously researched journey to each well-known murder and includes minute-by-minute accounts of the famous murders, the events leading up the events, and what happened afterwards. The collection *Jack the Ripper* was featured on YALSA's Best Books for Young Adults list in 1996, while *The Bloody Benders* was on YALSA's Great Graphic Novel for Teens list in 2008.

Vol. 1: A Treasury of Victorian Murder. 2002, reprint edition. 64pp. 978-1-56163-309-8.

An anthology collection looking at three different murders that occurred during the Victorian era. After an introduction that sets the stage of the time period, the reader is taken on an accurate and uncomfortable journey into the dark recesses of the criminal mind and how they committed murder.

Vol. 2: Jack the Ripper. 2001, reprint edition. 64pp. 978-1-56163-308-1.

At look at the notorious butcher of White Chapel, known as "Jack the Ripper," as told from the perspective of an English commoner fascinated by the horrendous killings during 1888–1889. Seven women, all prostitutes, were horrifically mutilated by a mysterious murderer whose identity remains unknown to this day.

Vol. 3: The Borden Tragedy. 1997. 80pp. 978-1-56163-189-6.

The tale of Lizzy Borden, famous for being accused of committing the double murder in her own home in 1892 of her father and stepmother. Through the meticulous notes of a friend of Lizzie, Geary attempts to figure out the facts of what led up to and what occurred after this family tragedy.

Vol. 4: The Fatal Bullet: The Assassination of President Garfield. 1999. 80pp. 978-1-56163-228-2.

On July 2, 1881, popular U.S. president James A. Garfield was shot by con-man Charles Guiteau, and the president later died from complications on September 19. The book takes a look at the lives of both James and Charles, two men from very similar upbringings but who walked very different paths in life, proving how one man can rise so high and yet another can sink so low.

Vol. 5: The Mystery of Mary Rogers. 2001. 80pp. 978-1-56163-228-2, hardcover.

A detail of the 1840 disappearance and murder of New York City native Mary Cecilia Rogers who sold cigars and tobacco in a shop frequented by many of the time period's authors including Edgar Allan Poe. When her bruised and broken body was found in the Hudson River, her death inspired Poe and people have never fully accepted the cause of her death.

Vol. 6: The Beast of Chicago. 2004. 80pp. 978-1-56163-365-4.

The tale of H.H. Holmes, a seemingly mild-mannered young man, but who was in actuality a con-man murderer who became one of America's first serial killers. His brutal murders in Chicago from 1886 to 1891 in his "murder castle"—a boarding house that drew in newcomers to the city, including those come to visit the World's Fair—shocked the nation.

Vol. 7: The Murder of Abraham Lincoln. 2005. 80pp. 978-1-56163-425-5, hardcover; 978-1-56163-426-2.

An in-depth look at the stages leading up to and after of the assassination of Abraham Lincoln and the life of his murderer, John Wilkes Booth.

Vol. 8: The Case of Madeleine Smith. 2006. 80pp. 978-1-56163-467-5, hardcover; 978-1-56163-468-2.

A look at the life of Madeleine Smith, a Glasgow socialite that some people were convinced was a murderess by killing her lover with arsenic. Though she was proven not guilty, many believed that she escaped the noose by the sheer luck that there were no witnesses to the murder.

Vol. 9: The Saga of the Bloody Benders. 2007. 80pp. 978-1-56163-498-9, hardcover.

In early 1870s the Bender clan, a family of German origins, sets up a combination home/grocery store/inn for weary travelers along the Osage Trail in Kansas. But patrons check in, but they don't check out.

A Treasury of Victorian Murder Compendiums. 2013–2015.
A collection of all the Victorian Murder stories in two massive collections.

A Treasury of Victorian Murder Compendium I. 2013. 228pp. 978-1-56163-704-1, hardcover.
A Treasury of Victorian Murder Compendium II. 2015. 400pp. 978-1-56163-907-6, hardcover.

A Treasury of XXth Century Murder. Written and Illustrated by **Rick Geary**. NBM Publishing, 2010– . T ✿ ◎

© 2016 Rick Geary

Continuing Rick Geary's true crime graphic novels, each collection focuses on a particular event in crime history from the 20th century. The events are once again very well-researched with Geary's impeccable detail. *The Lives of Sacco & Vanzetti* and *Black Dhalia* were recognized by YALSA as Great Graphic Novel for Teens in 2011 and 2017, respectively.

Vol. 1: The Lindbergh Child. 2010. 80pp. 978-1-56163-529-0, hardcover; 978-1-56163-530-6.

In 1932, famous aviator Charles Lindbergh's baby, Charles Jr., was kidnapped from his home. The baby's body was found two months later and became the crime of the century. How was the baby kidnapped and did the police find and execute the right suspect?

Vol. 2: The Terrible Ax-Man of New Orleans. 80pp. 978-1-56163-581-8, hardcover.

Set in New Orleans from 1918 to 1919, immigrant Italian grocers and their families were found murdered by an ax within their own homes. What was the motive for such heinous crimes, and was the culprit ever caught?

Vol. 3: Famous Players: The Mysterious Death of William Desmond Taylor. 2010. 80pp. 978-1-56163-555-9, hardcover; 978-1-56163-559-7.

During the early heyday of Hollywood, when the film director William Desmond Taylor is found dead in his bungalow of a gunshot wound in 1922, tinseltown is forever changed by his mysterious death. Suspects come out of the woodwork, but a motive and a murderer were never found.

Vol. 4: The Lives of Sacco and Vanzetti. 2011. 80pp. 978-1-56163-605-1, hardcover; 2015. 978-1-56163-936-6.

When anarchists Ferdinando Nicola Sacco and Bartolomeo Vanzetti were convicted of murdering two men in an armed robbery, the Italian immigrants were sentenced to die and were executed in 1927. To this day there isn't consensus of their guilt, and Geary examines their case to see if they were framed and if they received a fair trial.

Vol. 5: Lovers' Lane: The Hall-Hills Mystery. 2012. 80pp. 978-1-56163-628-0, hardcover.

In 1922, a respected reverend and a married woman from the church choir were found shot to death in a park in New Brunswick, New Jersey. Love letters between the two were scattered by their bodies. The church community knew of the affair as well as the spouses, but who was the killer?

Vol. 6: Madison Square Tragedy: The Murder of Stanford White. 2013. 80pp. 978-1-56163-762-1, hardcover.

In 1901 celebrated architect Stanford White was murdered by young millionaire Harry Thaw. Thaw has done this to avenge the honor of his wife, showgirl Evelyn Nesbit, who had had an affair with White before their marriage. The murder scene was at Madison Square Garden, one of White's best-known structures. The case led to one of the earliest "Trials of the Century."

Vol. 7: Black Dhalia. 2016. 80pp. 978-1-68112-052-2, hardcover.

On January 14, 1947, a body was found on the road in Los Angeles, which was drained of its blood, meticulously scrubbed, and cut in two. The woman was identified as Elizabeth Short, and the case became known as the "Black Dahlia" due to the woman's striking features. How did a woman who wanted to be in show business end up this way? Days later an anonymous letter was delivered to a newspaper and claimed to be from the murderer of Miss Short, and many more taunted the LAPD. Join Geary in a look at one of the most baffling unsolved cases of the 20th century.

A Treasury of XXth Murder Compendium I. 2017. 240pp. 978-1-68112-063-8, hardcover.

A collection featuring the first three volumes in the 20th-century crime stories.

Yummy: The Last Days of a Southside Shorty. Written by **G. Neri**. Illustrated by **Randy Duburke**. Lee & Low Books, 2010. 96pp. 978-1-58430-267-4. T 🏵

The life, death, and aftermath of an 11-year-old gangbanger. The story is based on a true tragedy. The collection was recognized by YALSA on its 2011 Great Graphic Novels for Teens top-10 graphic novels list.

Chapter 7

General Fiction

While graphic novels feature characters that readers can relate to are listed throughout this book (the most popular being the down-on-his-luck real-life issues of teenager Peter Parker and his alter-ego as Spider-Man), included here are stories that for the most part describe real-life situations featuring teenagers, young adults, and adults as well. The focus is on common issues that readers can readily identify with, including tales of romance, friendships, slice-of-life stories, teen issues, and even activities such as playing sports. This genre finds its origins in the Romance comic book stories published by American comic book publishers during the golden age of comics until the early 1970s, as well as in the plethora of teen and adult prose fiction being published today. Though mainstream publishers including Marvel Comics and DC Comics have not published romance comic books and graphic novels on a regular basis for several decades, there has been a resurgence of graphic novels in the United States featuring slice-of-life tales. Many smaller publishing companies in North America including Dark Horse Comics, Oni Press, Fantagraphics, Top Shelf Productions, and Abstract Studios have published stories that deal with the everyday, but the current popular trend has been mostly spurred by the popularity of Asian romance titles being reprinted in English. The tales from Asia are striking a chord with nontraditional U.S. graphic novel readers, mostly comprised of teenage girls and adults, drawn into the strong focus on romantic comedies, sympathetic characters, lighthearted romances, and heartbreaking stories of teenage and adult life.

Romance

Stories dealing with the love, confusion, heartache, hilarity, and ups and downs of teenage and young adult romance. Romance comic books have had a long-standing history in the United States when they were published during the 1940s until their decline in the

1970s. It has only been within the last decade with the popularity of Asian graphic novels and North American independent publishers that there have been significant graphic novel titles published with a strong focus on teens and young adults. Like most teen romance fiction as well as adult romance, the focus for a graphic novel romance title is the blossoming relationship between two individuals. Romance knows no boundaries, so titles may include off-beat couples, same-sex couples, far away settings, and even a heavy helping of comedy. Listed below are several subgenres of romance including Romantic Comedy and Romantic Fantasy.

Baby's in Black: Astrid Kirchherr, Stuart Sutcliffe, and The Beatles. Written and Illustrated by **Arne Bellstorf.** First Second Books, 2013. 208pp. 978-1-59643-771-5, hardcover; 2014. 978-1-59643-918-4. O

© 2016 First Second.

A fictionalized account of the love story between Stuart Sutcliffe, the original bassist for the Beatles, and Astrid Kirchherr, a German photographer. Stuart was the original "Fifth Beatle" but he eventually left the band to pursue an art career. Astrid was one of the original photographers who helped to put the Beatles on the map and she and Stu's friendship (and then eventually more than that) is touched upon here as well as Stuart's untimely death from an aneurysm. The book appropriately features plenty of Beatles music in the book as well, to help put you in the mood for the time period and the romance of Astrid and Stuart.

Blue Is the Warmest Color. Written and Illustrated by **Julie Maroh**. Arsenal Press, 2013. 160pp. 978-1-55152-514-3. M 🎬

In this prize-winning French work, Emma goes to the home of the parents of her lover Clementine after the latter's death. There she follows Clementine's wishes and reads her diary entries of their time together starting from the moment Clementine first saw her. The graphic novel is the source of the award winning 2013 film of the same name.

Boys Over Flowers: Hana Yori Dango. Written and Illustrated by **Yoko Kamio**. VIZ Media, 2003–2009. T あ ◎

Japanese manga middle-class girl Tsukusi Makino has just been accepted to the prestigious Eitoku Academy, a school for the snobbish elite, but she is no meek conformist. The school is ruled by the "F4" (or Flower Four), a group of prissy and pompous rich boys who enjoy wreaking havoc and ruining lives at school. When a friend of hers accidentally trips into one of the F4, Tsukusi stands up to them and becomes their main enemy. Now no one at school wants to be her friend for fear of retribution of the F4 and she must try to remain one step ahead of the boorish bullies. Strangely, she does feel some attraction to Rui, a sometimes-helpful yet aloof member of the F4. Is there really some chemistry there? Does she even want to be a part of this horrid clique? The series was also adapted into an anime series.

Vol. 1. 2003. 216pp. 978-1-56931-996-3.   *Vol. 3*. 2003. 192pp. 978-1-56931-998-7.
Vol. 2. 2003. 184pp. 978-1-56931-997-0.   *Vol. 4*. 2004. 192pp. 978-1-59116-112-7.

Vol. 5. 2004. 192pp. 978-1-59116-141-7.
Vol. 6. 2004. 192pp. 978-1-59116-314-5.
Vol. 7. 2004. 200pp. 978-1-59116-370-1.
Vol. 8. 2004. 200pp. 978-1-59116-371-8.
Vol. 9. 2004. 200pp. 978-1-59116-372-5.
Vol. 10. 2005. 176pp. 978-1-59116-629-0.
Vol. 11. 2005. 184pp. 978-1-59116-747-1.
Vol. 12. 2005. 176pp. 978-1-59116-801-0.
Vol. 13. 2005. 176pp. 978-1-59116-865-2.
Vol. 14. 2005. 192pp. 978-1-4215-0018-8.
Vol. 15. 2005. 192pp. 978-1-4215-0136-9.
Vol. 16. 2006. 208pp. 978-1-4215-0262-5.
Vol. 17. 2006. 208pp. 978-1-4215-0392-9.
Vol. 18. 2006. 208pp. 978-1-4215-0532-9.
Vol. 19. 2006. 208pp. 978-1-4215-0533-6.
Vol. 20. 2006. 208pp. 978-1-4215-0534-3.
Vol. 21. 2006. 208pp. 978-1-4215-0535-0.
Vol. 22. 2006. 208pp. 978-1-4215-0985-3.
Vol. 23. 2006. 192pp. 978-1-4215-0986-0.
Vol. 24. 2007. 192pp. 978-1-4215-0987-7.
Vol. 25. 2007. 184pp. 978-1-4215-0988-4.
Vol. 26. 2007. 192pp. 978-1-4215-0989-1.
Vol. 27. 2007. 192pp. 978-1-4215-0990-7.
Vol. 28. 2008. 216pp. 978-1-4215-1533-5.
Vol. 29. 2008. 192pp. 978-1-4215-1716-2.
Vol. 30. 2008. 192pp. 978-1-4215-1717-9.
Vol. 31. 2008. 162pp. 978-1-4215-1718-6.
Vol. 32. 2008. 210pp. 978-1-4215-1719-3.
Vol. 33. 2008. 210pp. 978-1-4215-1720-9.
Vol. 34. 2009. 184pp. 978-1-4215-2248-7.
Vol. 35. 2009. 192pp. 978-1-4215-2249-4.
Vol. 36. 2009. 200pp. 978-1-4215-2250-0.
Jewelry Box. 2009. 176pp. 978-1-4215-3087-1.

Idol Dreams. Written and Illustrated by **Arina Tanemura**. VIZ Media, 2015–2016. T Japanese manga.

Chikage Deguchi is 31 years old and feels that life and success has passed her by. Unmarried and still a virgin, she wishes that she could turn back time to when she was young and popular. When she takes an experimental drug that makes her look a teenager again, Chikage decides to do all the things she missed out in those years—including being a pop music star!

Vol. 1. 2015. 192pp. 978-1-4215-8256-6.
Vol. 2. 2016. 184pp. 978-1-4215-8257-3.
Vol. 3. 2016. 184pp. 978-1-4215-8856-8.

Long Distance. Written and Illustrated by **Thom Zahler**. IDW Publishing, 2016. 188pp. 978-1-63140-486-3. O.

© Thomas F. Zahler.

When you fall in love, distance is no object, right? What happens when you find your soul mate at of all places in an airport and you live in Columbus and she lives two states away in Chicago? Can love find a way when you're separated by the state of Indiana?

The Nao of Brown. Written and Illustrated by **Glyn Dillon**. Harry N. Abrams, 2012. 208pp. 978-1-906838-42-3, hardcover. M

Nao Brown is a young woman fighting to find balance with all her relationships. A hafu (half Japanese/half English) Nao suffers from obsessive-compulsive disorder and intrusive thoughts of hurting people around her. She just got out of a relationship, and she is just starting a job at a high-end toy store with an old college friend who had a crush on her. She wants to pursue a career in design and also fine true love. The only stable relationship she has held is the one with her mother. After two men come into her life—Gregory—a washing-machine repairman, and Ray, an art teacher at the Buddist center, Nao finally may have the key to happiness and discovers that life is neither black or white but instead is a lot like brown.

The New York*.* Written by **Brian Wood**. Illustrated by **Ryan Kelly**. Minx/Vertigo/DC Comics, 2008–2011. O

Going to college can be an exciting time. There are so many new people to meet, new places to see, and things to experience. This is true for Riley Wilder. She has lived in Brooklyn, New York, her life but when she decides to attend NYU she gets a taste of the Manhattan life. Here she runs into her older sister, the black sheep of the family. Riley's sister introduces her to many aspects of living within the city. She goes to social events, finds three great friends who are in many of her classes, and gets a great job because she is doing so well in school. All this is threatened when she becomes obsessed with her mysterious long-distance boyfriend whom she met by finding a random e-mail address in her coat pocket. Who could this guy be for whom she is willing to throw away all the great stuff she just got?

The New York Four. 2008. 176pp. 978-1-4012-1154-7.
The New York Five. 2011. 144pp. 978-1-4012-3291-7.

The Professor's Daughter. Written by **Joann Sfar**. Illustrated by **Emmanuel Guibert**. First Second. 2007. 80pp. 978-1-59643-130-0. T

The daughter of the head professor at the London museum takes her friend Imhotep IV out for a walk around town. The only issue is that Imhotep IV is the ancient pharaoh from ancient Egypt and he is not supposed to leave the museum for his safety. Things get complicated when Lillian gets kidnapped by Imhotep IV's father. The London police get involved, and it becomes very hard for Lillian and Imhotep IV to enjoy their day out.

Sand Chronicles. Written and Illustrated by **Hinako Ashihara**. VIZ Media, 2008–2011. O Japanese manga. 🎗

SUNADOKEI © 2003 Hinako ASHIHARA/SHOGAKUKAN.

Can time heal all wounds? When 12-year-old Ann Uekusa and her mother moved to the peaceful town of Shimane, she makes friends with boys named Daigo and Fuji. After her mother commits suicide, Ann falls in love with Daigo, but he urges her to go back to Tokyo with her estranged father. Meanwhile, love gets more complicated when over time, Fuji falls in love with Ann. As the years pass, can Ann find love again with Daigo after so much has passed between the both of them? The first two volumes were recognized by the 2009 Great Graphic Novels for Teens selection committee.

Vol. 1. 2008. 200pp. 978-1-4215-1477-2.
Vol. 2. 2008. 200pp. 978-1-4215-1478-9.
Vol. 3. 2008. 200pp. 978-1-4215-1479-6.

Vol. 4. 2009. 210pp. 978-1-4215-1480-2.
Vol. 5. 2009. 192pp. 978-1-4215-2463-4.
Vol. 6. 2009. 200pp. 978-1-4215-2464-1.
Vol. 7. 2010. 192pp. 978-1-4215-2805-2.

Vol. 8. 2010. 192pp. 978-1-4215-2806-9.
Vol. 9. 2010. 200pp. 978-1-4215-2807-6.
Vol. 10. 2011. 200pp. 978-1-4215-2808-3.

Skip Beat. Written and Illustrated by **Yoshiki Nakamura**. VIZ Media, 2006– . T Japanese manga. あ

Kyoko Mogami is a 16-year-old girl who learns that her childhood friend and romantic goal, Sho Fuwa, is only using her as a personal maid and source of income while he works his way up the top of the pop music charts. Vowing revenge, Kyoko will do anything to beat him in show business! The manga was originally released in 2002 in Japan is still being published. The manga was also adapted into an anime series.

Vol. 1. 2006. 184pp. 978-1-4215-0585-5.
Vol. 2. 2006. 208pp. 978-1-4215-0586-2.
Vol. 3. 2006. 208pp. 978-1-4215-0587-9.
Vol. 4. 2007. 208pp. 978-1-4215-0588-6.
Vol. 5. 2007. 208pp. 978-1-4215-1022-4.
Vol. 6. 2007. 208pp. 978-1-4215-1023-1.
Vol. 7. 2007. 200pp. 978-1-4215-1024-8.
Vol. 8. 2007. 200pp. 978-1-4215-1025-5.
Vol. 9. 2007. 200pp. 978-1-4215-1026-2.
Vol. 10. 2008. 200pp. 978-1-4215-1399-7.
Vol. 11. 2008. 200pp. 978-1-4215-1751-3.
Vol. 12. 2008. 200pp. 978-1-4215-1752-0.
Vol. 13. 2008. 208pp. 978-1-4215-1753-7.
Vol. 14. 2008. 200pp. 978-1-4215-1754-4.
Vol. 15. 2008. 210pp. 978-1-4215-1952-4.
Vol. 16. 2008. 210pp. 978-1-4215-2040-7.
Vol. 17. 2009. 200pp. 978-1-4215-2352-1.
Vol. 18. 2009. 200pp. 978-1-4215-2598-3.
Vol. 19. 2009. 200pp. 978-1-4215-2780-2.

Vol. 20. 2010. 200pp. 978-1-4215-3072-7.
Vol. 21. 2010. 200pp. 978-1-4215-3270-7.
Vol. 22. 2010. 192pp. 978-1-4215-3508-1.
Vol. 23. 2011. 192pp. 978-1-4215-3692-7.
Vol. 24. 2011. 192pp. 978-1-4215-3833-4.
Vol. 25. 2011. 184pp. 978-1-4215-3923-2.
Vol. 26. 2012. 184pp. 978-1-4215-3999-7.
Vol. 27. 2012. 200pp. 978-1-4215-4108-2.
Vol. 28. 2012. 200pp. 978-1-4215-4219-5.
Vol. 29. 2012. 192pp. 978-1-4215-4334-5.
Vol. 30. 2013. 200pp. 978-1-4215-5061-9.
Vol. 31. 2013. 192pp. 978-1-4215-5479-2.
Vol. 32. 2013. 192pp. 978-1-4215-6234-6.
Vol. 33. 2014. 192pp. 978-1-4215-6952-9.
Vol. 34. 2015. 192pp. 978-1-4215-7743-2.
Vol. 35. 2015. 200pp. 978-1-4215-8034-0.
Vol. 36. 2016. 200pp. 978-1-4215-8450-8.
Vol. 37. 2016. 200pp. 978-1-4215-8714-1.
Vol. 38. 2017. 192pp. 978-1-4215-9161-2.

The Story of Saiunkoku. Written by **Sai Yukino**. Illustrated by **Kairi Yura**. VIZ Media, 2010–2013. T Japanese manga. 🌳 あ

This adaptation of a series of "light novels" takes place in the fictional empire of Saiunkoku where Shurei Hong, who is part of a noble family that has fallen on hard times, wishes to work as civil servant in the imperial court, something that is forbidden to women. But now she has an opportunity to be close to the emperor in a way she never imagined. Selected as one of YALSA's Great Graphic Novels for Teens in 2011.

Vol. 1. 2010. 176pp. 978-1-4215-3834-1.
Vol. 2. 2011. 200pp. 978-1-4215-3835-8.
Vol. 3. 2011. 200pp. 978-1-4215-3836-5.
Vol. 4. 2011. 192pp. 978-1-4215-3837-2.
Vol. 5. 2011. 176pp. 978-1-4215-3842-6.

Vol. 6. 2012. 200pp. 978-1-4215-4179-2.
Vol. 7. 2012. 170pp. 978-1-4215-4180-8.
Vol. 8. 2012. 168pp. 978-1-4215-4946-0.
Vol. 9. 2013. 176pp. 978-1-4215-5083-1.

Strangers in Paradise. Written and Illustrated by **Terry Moore**. Abstract Studio, Incorporated, 2005–2013. O 🎋 ◎

© 2016 and TM Abstract Studio and
Terry Moore.

The complex story of three friends, Katina "Katchoo" Choovanski, Francine Peters, and David Qin, and their turbulent experiences of love, life, and sorrow with the ones they fall in and out of love with—including each other. The emotional dynamite Katchoo and "All-American Girl" Francine have been best friends since high school and Katchoo, despite her aggressive tendencies and dark past, loves Francine dearly. David loves Katchoo through all her highs and lows, and sweet Francine is caught awkwardly in the middle, not sure of where or who she really belongs with. The romantic triangle between Katchoo, Francine, and David started in comic book form in 1993, and *Strangers in Paradise* has been regarded as one of the best-known independent comic books. The series has won multiple awards including an Eisner Award for Best Serialized Story (1996), as well as recognition on YALSA's Popular Paperbacks for Young Adults in 2002 and 2005. The series came to its conclusion in 2007. The pocket book editions of the titles include the contents of several normal-sized graphic novel collections and reprints all 90 issues of the single issue series. An omnibus edition was released for the 20th anniversary of the series' debut. The series will return in 2018 for the 25th anniversary of the series.

Pocket Book 1. 2005. 360pp. 978-1-892597-26-7.
Pocket Book 2. 2005. 344pp. 978-1-892597-29-8.
Pocket Book 3. 2005. 372pp. 978-1-892597-30-4.
Pocket Book 4. 2005. 360pp. 978-1-892597-31-1.
Pocket Book 5. 2005. 376pp. 978-1-892597-38-0.
Pocket Book 6. 2007. 272pp. 978-1-892597-39-7.
Strangers in Paradise Omnibus Edition. 2013. 2128pp. 978-1-892597-54-0.

Strobe Edge. Written and Illustrated by **Io Sakisaka**. VIZ Media, 2012–2014. T Japanese manga. 🎋 🎬

Teenager Ninako Kinoshita has fallen in love with popular fellow student Ren Ichinose, but Ren already has a girlfriend. A live-action film was made in 2015. Selected as one of YALSA's Great Graphic Novels for Teens.

Vol. 1. 2012. 200pp. 978-1-4215-5068-8.	*Vol. 6.* 2013. 216pp. 978-1-4215-5314-6.
Vol. 2. 2013. 200pp. 978-1-4215-5069-5.	*Vol. 7.* 2013. 216pp. 978-1-4215-5315-3.
Vol. 3. 2013. 192pp. 978-1-4215-5070-1.	*Vol. 8.* 2014. 184pp. 978-1-4215-5316-0.
Vol. 4. 2013. 192pp. 978-1-4215-5270-5.	*Vol. 9.* 2014. 200pp. 978-1-4215-5317-7.
Vol. 5. 2013. 216pp. 978-1-4215-5313-9.	*Vol. 10.* 2014. 184pp. 978-1-4215-6448-7.

Romantic Comedy

Like today's television and movies, romantic comedy is one of the more common forms of romance stories being published as graphic novels. Typically the romance is depicted as a clumsy and awkward relationship that blossoms, falters, resurges, and then fully blooms by the conclusion of the story. The stories tend to be lighthearted in nature, and though there usually is some conflict that can possibly destroy the love relationship, there is almost always guaranteed a happy ending unless the protagonist is totally inept at finding love.

Ares & Aphrodite: Love Wars. Written by **Jamie S. Rich**. Illustrated by **Megan Levens**. Oni Press. 2015. 168pp. 978-1-62010-208-4. O

A divorce lawyer named Will Ares finds himself working alongside a wedding planner named Gigi Averelle when both of their clients—a movie producer and a Hollywood starlet—plan to get married. When the movie producer's ex-wives come out of the woodwork, Will and Gigi make a deal: if their clients get married, then Will and Gigi will go out on a date. However, if the couple breaks up, then Will must post a full-page ad revealing how many marriages he's ruined. Will this be the start of a beautiful relationship, or is Will's part going to haunt him?

© 2016 and Oni Press and Jamie S. Rich.

Dengeki Daisy. Written and Illustrated by **Kyousuke Motomi**. VIZ Media, 2010–2015. O Japanese manga.

When 16-year-old orphan Teru Kurebayashi loses her beloved older brother, one of the only solaces she has is a cell phone her brother owned. There's a mysterious person on the other end known only as the enigmatic DAISY whom she texts back and forth with and makes her feel closer to her late brother. Meanwhile, a mysterious 24-year-old janitor at the school known as Tasuku Kurosaki always seems to be around whenever Teru needs help. One day at school, Teru accidentally breaks a window and agrees to pay for it by helping Tasuku with chores around school. But he is a ridiculously impossible boss, but he seems to be hiding a secret from Teru. Is he really DAISY?

DENGEKI DAISY © 2007 Kyousuke MOTOMI/SHOGA-KUKAN.

Vol. 1. 2010. 192pp. 978-1-4215-3727-6.
Vol. 2. 2010. 200pp. 978-1-4215-3728-3.

Vol. 3. 2010. 200pp. 978-1-4215-3729-0.	*Vol. 10*. 2012. 192pp. 978-1-4215-4267-6.
Vol. 4. 2011. 192pp. 978-1-4215-3730-6.	*Vol. 11*. 2013. 192pp. 978-1-4215-5060-2.
Vol. 5. 2011. 200pp. 978-1-4215-3739-9.	*Vol. 12*. 2013. 192pp. 978-1-4215-5242-2.
Vol. 6. 2011. 192pp. 978-1-4215-3826-6.	*Vol. 13*. 2013. 192pp. 978-1-4215-5966-7.
Vol. 7. 2011. 192pp. 978-1-4215-3941-6.	*Vol. 14*. 2014. 192pp. 978-1-4215-6944-4.
Vol. 8. 2012. 192pp. 978-1-4215-3997-3.	*Vol. 15*. 2014. 192pp. 978-1-4215-7343-4.
Vol. 9. 2012. 200pp. 978-1-4215-4176-1.	*Vol. 16*. 2015. 192pp. 978-1-4215-7771-5.

Empire State: A Love Story (or Not). Written and Illustrated by **Jason Shiga**. Abrams Comicarts, 2011. 144pp. 978-0-8109-9747-9, hardcover. O

Jimmy works at the Oakland library and hasn't quite yet experienced the world at his age and grown up. His best friend, Sara, moves to New York

City, and Jimmy longs to profess his feelings for her, so he takes a bus ride across the country to surprise her—but he's the one in for a surprise when he meets her older boyfriend! From dealing with ex-cons on the bus ride, to dealing with Sara's boyfriend, Mark, Jimmy's got a lot of learning to do and maybe he's finally ready to make that leap. Or not. The story is told in stark colors—red is for the flashback scenes and blue is for the present time.

Hana-Kimi: For You in Full Blossom. Written and Illustrated by **Hisaya Nakajo**. VIZ Media, 2004–2008. O Japanese manga.

Teenager Mizuki Ashiya, a female Japanese-American track-and-field star, will do anything to be close to her idol, high-jump star Izumi Sano. Anything. So when the opportunity comes to be near him, she transfers to an exclusive school in Japan—an all-male high school. Now Izumi is closer than ever—he's in her classes and also her roommate! How long can her secret remain safe, and can it be she's falling in love with Izumi?

Vol. 1. 2004. 184pp. 978-1-59116-329-9.
Vol. 2. 2004. 200pp. 978-1-59116-398-5.
Vol. 3. 2004. 200pp. 978-1-59116-399-2.
Vol. 4. 2005. 188pp. 978-1-59116-458-6.
Vol. 5. 2005. 200pp. 978-1-59116-497-5.
Vol. 6. 2005. 200pp. 978-1-59116-498-2.
Vol. 7. 2005. 200pp. 978-1-59116-499-9.
Vol. 8. 2005. 192pp. 978-1-4215-0007-2.
Vol. 9. 2005. 192pp. 978-1-4215-0138-3.
Vol. 10. 2006. 208pp. 978-1-4215-0264-9.
Vol. 11. 2006. 208pp. 978-1-4215-0394-3.
Vol. 12. 2006. 208pp. 978-1-4215-0542-8.
Vol. 13. 2006. 208pp. 978-1-4215-0543-5.
Vol. 14. 2006. 208pp. 978-1-4215-0544-2.
Vol. 15. 2006. 208pp. 978-1-4215-0545-9.
Vol. 16. 2007. 184pp. 978-1-4215-0991-4.
Vol. 17. 2007. 184pp. 978-1-4215-0992-1.
Vol. 18. 2007. 200pp. 978-1-4215-0993-8.
Vol. 19. 2007. 200pp. 978-1-4215-0994-5.
Vol. 20. 2007. 200pp. 978-1-4215-0995-2.
Vol. 21. 2007. 184pp. 978-1-4215-0996-9.
Vol. 22. 2008. 192pp. 978-1-4215-1534-2.
Vol. 23. 2008. 192pp. 978-1-4215-1721-6.

High School Debut. Written and Illustrated by **Kazune Kawahara**. VIZ Media, 2014–2015. T Japanese manga.

When Haruna has no luck with boys in her school, she asks the upperclassman Yoh to give her tips on how to make herself more appealing to the boys at school. Yoh agrees on one condition—she must not fall for him! Is this an easy arrangement or the most difficult thing Haruna has ever done? The series was originally published in 15 volumes from 2008 to 2010, but was recently collected in five three-in-one edition collections. The original collections of the series were recognized in 2009 on the Great Graphic Novels for Teens selection list.

Vol. 1. 2014. 544pp. 978-1-4215-6588-0.
Vol. 2. 2014. 544pp. 978-1-4215-6589-7.
Vol. 3. 2014. 544pp. 978-1-4215-6624-5.
Vol. 4. 2014. 560pp. 978-1-4215-6625-2.
Vol. 5. 2015. 560pp. 978-1-4215-6626-9.

KOKO DEBUT © 2003 by Kazune Kawahara/SHUEISHA Inc.

Itazura Na Kiss. Written and Illustrated by **Kaoru Tada**. Digital Manga Publishing, 2009–2016 T Japanese manga あ

High school student Kotoko Aihara has finally told the boy she has a crush on how she feels only to be rejected. But when her home is damaged in an earthquake, she and her father move in with his best friend who also happens to be the father of guess who! This original 23-volume Japanese manga from the 1990s was collected by DMP publishing as a 12-volume omnibus collection. The series has been adapted into multiple live-action series as well as an anime and was selected as one of YALSA's Great Graphic Novels for Teens for its 2010 list.

Vol. 1. 2009. 300pp. 978-1-56970-131-7.
Vol. 2. 2010. 300pp. 978-1-56970-136-2.
Vol. 3. 2010. 376pp. 978-1-56970-171-3.
Vol. 4. 2010. 328pp. 978-1-56970-191-1.
Vol. 5. 2011. 328pp. 978-1-56970-192-8.
Vol. 6. 2011. 344pp. 978-1-56970-197-3.
Vol. 7. 2012. 200pp. 978-1-56970-228-4.
Vol. 8. 2012. 200pp. 978-1-56970-246-8.
Vol. 9. 2012. 200pp. 978-1-56970-252-9.
Vol. 10. 2014. 250pp. 978-1-56970-277-2.
Vol. 11. 2016. 350pp. 978-1-56970-306-9.
Vol. 12. 2016. 350pp. 978-1-56970-319-9.

Kamisama Kiss. Written and Illustrated by **Julietta Suzuki**. VIZ Media, 2010–2017. T Japanese manga. あ

Nanami Momozono has found herself homeless, but a man who she has helped has offered her a place to stay. The only problem is that the place turns out to be a shrine, and by living there she has taken his place as the local deity. The series was adapted into an anime series and has been selected as one of YALSA's Great Graphic Novels for Teens in 2011. The series is expected to end after volume 25.

Vol. 1. 2010. 200pp. 978-1-4215-3638-5.
Vol. 2. 2011. 200pp. 978-1-4215-3639-2.
Vol. 3. 2011. 200pp. 978-1-4215-3640-8.
Vol. 4. 2011. 200pp. 978-1-4215-3658-3.
Vol. 5. 2011. 200pp. 978-1-4215-3823-5.
Vol. 6. 2011. 200pp. 978-1-4215-3886-0.
Vol. 7. 2012. 200pp. 978-1-4215-4025-2.
Vol. 8. 2012. 200pp. 978-1-4215-4082-5.
Vol. 9. 2012. 200pp. 978-1-4215-4198-3.
Vol. 10. 2012. 200pp. 978-1-4215-4269-0.
Vol. 11. 2012. 200pp. 978-1-4215-4924-8.
Vol. 12. 2013. 200pp. 978-1-4215-5082-4.
Vol. 13. 2013. 200pp. 978-1-4215-5266-8.
Vol. 14. 2014. 200pp. 978-1-4215-5586-7.
Vol. 15. 2014. 200pp. 978-1-4215-6308-4.
Vol. 16. 2014. 200pp. 978-1-4215-6764-8.
Vol. 17. 2015. 200pp. 978-1-4215-7725-8.
Vol. 18. 2015. 200pp. 978-1-4215-7970-2.
Vol. 19. 2015. 200pp. 978-1-4215-8033-3.
Vol. 20. 2016. 200pp. 978-1-4215-8261-0.
Vol. 21. 2016. 200pp. 978-1-4215-8522-2.
Vol. 22. 2016. 200pp. 978-1-4215-8712-7.
Vol. 23. 2017. 200pp. 978-1-4215-9047-9.
Vol. 24. 2017. 200pp. 978-1-4215-9221-3.

Love Hina, Omnibus Edition. Written and Illustrated by **Akamatsu Ken**. Kodansha Comics, 2011–2012. O Japanese manga. あ

Keitaro Urashima has failed his entrance exams to Tokyo University twice, he's been unlucky at love, and his parents have kicked him out of their home! Rejected and unemployed, his grandmother has the perfect job to tide him over until he can pass his entrance exams: to be the landlord at the beautiful Hinata House. What his grandmother neglected to mention that it's an all-girl college dorm, and now he's living a life that most men would kill for. But after spending time with five beautiful women, he's not sure he's going to survive the experience much less have time to study for his entrance exams! Meanwhile, Keitaro finds out that Naru, one of the girls living at the dorm, might be his very first crush when he was a child. Will they end up together like they promised as kids, or will Keitaro's accidental antics destroy that chance forever? The series was adapted into an anime series in Japan.

Vol. 1. 2011. 592pp. 978-1-935429-47-0.
Vol. 2. 2011. 592pp. 978-1-935429-48-7.
Vol. 3. 2012. 592pp. 978-1-61262-020-6.
Vol. 4. 2012. 576pp. 978-1-61262-021-3.
Vol. 5. 2013. 500pp. 978-1-61262-022-0.

Lucky Penny. Written by **Ananth Hirsh**. Illustrated by **Yuko Ota**. Oni Press, 2016. 208pp. 978-1-62010-287-9. O

© Oni Press and Anath Hirsh.

Penny's lucky—but just not the good kind of luck! She lost her job and her apartment—and all in the same day! Luckily she's got a friend who has a cozy storage unit she can crash. Can Penny's luck improve enough to get a new job and to stop sounding like a dork in front of the cute guy who works at the community center? Penny, this may be your day! Or not.

My Little Monster. Written and Illustrated by **Robico**. Kodonsha Comics, 2014–2016. T 🐾 Japanese manga.

The high school relationship between two students Shizuku Mizutani and Haru Yoshida is explored in this manga series that has also been turned into an anime. Shizuku wants nothing to do but study and is known for being emotionless and cold. Haru is known for being violent and uncontrollable, but after he meets her, they begin a gentle relationship that how only two previously unsocial people can be. The series was on the 2015 YALSA Great Graphic Novels for Teens List.

Vol. 1. 2014. 176pp. 978-1-61262-597-3.
Vol. 2. 2014. 176pp. 978-1-61262-598-0.
Vol. 3. 2014. 176pp. 978-1-61262-599-7.
Vol. 4. 2014. 176pp. 978-1-61262-600-0.
Vol. 5. 2014. 176pp. 978-1-61262-601-7.
Vol. 6. 2015. 176pp. 978-1-61262-800-4.
Vol. 7. 2015. 176pp. 978-1-61262-991-9.

Vol. 8. 2015. 176pp. 978-1-61262-992-6.
Vol. 9. 2015. 176pp. 978-1-61262-993-3.
Vol. 10. 2015. 176pp. 978-1-63236-106-6.
Vol. 11. 2015. 208pp. 978-1-63236-108-0.
Vol. 12. 2016. 208pp. 978-1-63236-127-1.
Vol. 13. 2016. 224pp. 978-1-63236-208-7.

Otomen. Written and Illustrated by **Aya Kanno**. VIZ Media, 2009–2014. T Japanese manga.

This best-selling romantic comedy manga is about high school student Asuka Masamune. A manly teenager, he excels in martial arts and is the captain of the school's Kendo team. But he secretly prefers cooking, sweets, sewing, and shojo manga. Then he meets Ryo Miyakozuka who needs his help with those sorts of things. *Otomen* was a very high-selling manga in America and was turned into a live-action program in Japan.

Vol. 1. 2009. 208pp. 978-1-4215-2186-2.
Vol. 2. 2009. 192pp. 978-1-4215-2187-9.
Vol. 3. 2009. 200pp. 978-1-4215-2472-6.

Vol. 4. 2009. 200pp. 978-1-4215-2537-2.
Vol. 5. 2010. 192pp. 978-1-4215-2737-6.
Vol. 6. 2010. 200pp. 978-1-4215-2930-1.

Vol. 7. 2010. 200pp. 978-1-4215-3236-3.   *Vol. 13.* 2012. 192pp. 978-1-4215-4265-2.
Vol. 8. 2010. 200pp. 978-1-4215-3591-3.   *Vol. 14.* 2013. 192pp. 978-1-4215-4925-5.
Vol. 9. 2011. 200pp. 978-1-4215-3690-3.   *Vol. 15.* 2013. 192pp. 978-1-4215-5271-2.
Vol. 10. 2011. 208pp. 978-1-4215-3830-3.   *Vol. 16.* 2013. 192pp. 978-1-4215-5480-8.
Vol. 11. 2011. 200pp. 978-1-4215-3978-2.   *Vol. 17.* 2014. 192pp. 978-1-4215-5968-1.
Vol. 12. 2012. 200pp. 978-1-4215-4109-9.   *Vol. 18.* 2014. 200pp. 978-1-4215-6309-1.

Romantic Fantasy

Romance titles where magic or a fantasy-based incident plays a key role in giving the protagonist with the means to finding true love, sometimes with someone that person least expects. The appeal of a fantasy-based romance is that it drops two lovers into the make-believe setting of a fantasy world where magic is real, knights in shining armor do exist, as well as true love. The setting may take place in a fantasy world or in the present day wish subtle hints of science fiction, but it is through magic that love is possible. For other fantasy titles, see the fantasy chapter.

Fruits Basket. Written and Illustrated by **Natsuki Takaya**. TOKYOPOP, 2004–2009; Yen Press, 2016–2017. T Japanese manga. 🎐 あ ◉

© Yen Press and Natsuki Takaya.

After losing her mother in a car accident, young orphaned high school student Tohru Honda is living in a tent in a forest near her school. Headstrong and positive despite her family's misfortunes, she's neighbors with the odd but generous Sohma family, who have a special secret. The Sohma family members are possessed by the spirits of the Chinese Zodiac. When hugged by a member of the opposite sex, they will turn into the animal sign of the Zodiac that they represent. Taken in by the Sohma family in return for helping around the house, Honda's found a new family—but can she keep the animals running around the house from destroying it? The series received recognition by YALSA's Popular Paperbacks for Young Adults committee in 2006 as well as the Quick Picks for Reluctant Readers in 2005. Twenty-three original volumes were published in Japan and were originally published in North America by Tokyopop. The complete series was reprinted in 2016 by Yen Press in Collector's Editions. A sequel series is currently being published in Japan.

Tokyopop volumes, 2004–2009.

Vol. 1. 2004. 216pp. 978-1-59182-603-3.   *Vol. 8.* 2005. 208pp. 978-1-59532-403-0.
Vol. 2. 2004. 200pp. 978-1-59182-604-0.   *Vol. 9.* 2005. 208pp. 978-1-59532-404-7.
Vol. 3. 2004. 200pp. 978-1-59182-605-7.   *Vol. 10.* 2005. 192pp. 978-1-59532-405-4.
Vol. 4. 2004. 216pp. 978-1-59182-606-4.   *Vol. 11.* 2005. 192pp. 978-1-59532-406-1.
Vol. 5. 2004. 208pp. 978-1-59182-607-1.   *Vol. 12.* 2005. 192pp. 978-1-59532-407-8.
Vol. 6. 2004. 208pp. 978-1-59182-608-8.   *Vol. 13.* 2006. 192pp. 978-1-59532-408-5.
Vol. 7. 2005. 208pp. 978-1-59532-402-3.   *Vol. 14.* 2006. 192pp. 978-1-59532-409-2.

Vol. 15. 2006. 192pp. 978-1-59816-023-9.   *Vol. 20.* 2008. 192pp. 978-1-4278-0009-1.
Vol. 16. 2006. 192pp. 978-1-59816-024-6.   *Vol. 21.* 2008. 224pp. 978-1-4278-0682-6.
Vol. 17. 2007. 224pp. 978-1-59816-799-3.   *Vol. 22.* 2009. 216pp. 978-1-4278-0683-3.
Vol. 18. 2007. 216pp. 978-1-59816-862-4.   *Vol. 23.* 2009. 210pp. 978-1-4278-0827-1.
Vol. 19. 2008. 216pp. 978-1-59816-863-1.

Yen Press Collector's Edition, 2016–2017.

Vol. 1. 2016. 400pp. 978-0-316-36016-6.   *Vol. 7.* 2016. 400pp. 978-0-316-36072-2.
Vol. 2. 2016. 400pp. 978-0-316-36018-0.   *Vol. 8.* 2016. 400pp. 978-0-316-36073-9.
Vol. 3. 2016. 400pp. 978-0-316-36064-7.   *Vol. 9.* 2017. 400pp. 978-0-316-50162-0.
Vol. 4. 2016. 400pp. 978-0-316-36065-4.   *Vol. 10.* 2017. 400pp. 978-0-316-50164-4.
Vol. 5. 2016. 400pp. 978-0-316-36066-1.   *Vol. 11.* 2017. 400pp. 978-0-316-50168-2.
Vol. 6. 2016. 400pp. 978-0-316-36071-5.   *Vol. 12.* 2017. 400pp. 978-0-316-50176-7.

Coming of Age/Slice of Life

Included here are interpersonal graphic novels focusing on the drama, relationships, love, hard choices, heartaches, and occasion humorous look at growing up as a teen and as an adult and the choices they make. Some of the titles listed may include a plot point that may not normally occur in everyday life like a gift of time travel, mystical beings, or magical boyfriends, but the overall story focuses on the emotional choices that the main character makes to get through the situation.

The Alcoholic. Written by **Jonathan Ames**. Illustrated by **Dean Haspiel**. Vertigo/DC Comics, 2009. 136pp. 978-1-4012-1057-1. M

Jonathan has always been chasing after something or someone. He has been trying to get into contact with his old best friend for years. He chases any skirt that will look his way in an attempt to forget his past girlfriend who left him. He attempts to write that one book that will seal his fame. Jonathan is chasing the ghosts of his past while he shoulders the two things that are constant in his life, caring for his great aunt and his addiction to alcohol. Every time things seem to start working in Jonathan's favor, he messes everything up by tipping the bottle and falling into self-destruction.

American Born Chinese. Written and Illustrated by **Gene Luen Yang**. First Second, 2007–2008. 2007. 240pp. 978-1-59643-373-1, hardcover; 2008. 978-0-31238-448-7. T 🏆 ◎

Teenager Jin Wang, an American born Chinese, has it hard enough being an outcast at school. He's awkward around Caucasian girls he likes, he regularly gets picked on by school bullies and jocks, and he's one of the only few Asian students at school. When he befriends another Asian student, they find a kindred link in their heritage, but soon their friendship put to the ultimate test. Meanwhile, two parallel stories are played out that may be more closely related to Jin Wang's plight: the legend of the Monkey King and the stereotype exploits of Chin-Kee, an embarrassing buck-toothed relative visiting a young Caucasian boy. Can Jin Wang learn to come to terms with himself and his heritage? The book won the Michael L. Printz award from YALSA in 2007, the first graphic novel to win such an award.

© First Second and Gene Luen Yang.

Americus. Written by **M. K. Reed**. Illustrated by **Jonathan David Hill**. First Second Books, 2011. 224pp. 978-159643-601-5. T

Graduating eighth graders Neil and Danny don't quite fit in at school. They're best friends and mutually share their love for books—especially the hit fantasy series "The Chronicles of Apathea Ravenchilde." When Danny's strict Christian mother discovers that he's reading the series, she forbids him to read it and sends him off to military school. She then sets off on a crusade to ban the book from the public library from where he got the book. Now Neil is alone in ninth grade with no friends and books are his only means of escape. When the book is challenged, Neil must make a stand for his friends, what he believes, and ultimately for himself. A realistic and well-fleshed out look at life in small town America.

Ann Tenna: A Novel. Written and Illustrated by **Marisa Acocella Marchetto.** Alfred A. Knopf 2015. 978-0-307-26747-4. M

In this tale by New Yorker cartoonist Marchetto (*Cancer Vixen*), Ann Tenna runs the hottest gossip website Eyemauler and has the rich and famous fighting for her attention. But a near-death experience lets her meet her "cosmic" self SuperAnn, and learn that she can change her behavior and become a "higher power" or have to be reincarnated yet again.

Archie: The Married Life. Written by **Michael Uslan** and **Paul Kupperberg**. Illustrated by **Stan Goldberg**, **Norm Breyfogle**, and others. Archie Comics 2010–2014. T

In issues 600–606 of *Archie*, readers were treated to a look at worlds where Archie and friends were adults and Archie finally chose between Betty and Veronica. In one world he chose Betty and the other Veronica. In the pages of *Life with Archie* readers saw a continuation of those worlds and saw how things differed between the world where Archie married the "girl next door" and the one where he married the daughter of the richest man in town. The series ended after the adult Archie was killed saving the life of a friend, an event that made national news. These stories are for a slightly older readership than some of other Archie titles and have been nominated for the Eisner Award.

The Archie Wedding: Archie in Will You Marry Me? 2010. 168pp. 978-1-879794-51-1.
Book One. 2011. 320pp. 978-1-936975-01-3.
Book Two. 2012. 320pp. 978-1-879794-99-3.
Book Three. 2013. 320pp. 978-1-936975-35-8.
Book Four. 2013. 272pp. 978-1-936975-69-3.
Book Five. 2014. 272pp. 978-1-619889-02-6.
Book Six. 2014. 336pp. 978-1-619889-45-3.
The Death of Archie: A Life Remembered. 2014. 112pp. 978-1-627389-82-2.

Aya. Written by **Marguerite Abouet**. Illustrated by **Cle'ment Oubrerie**. Drawn and Quarterly, 2007–2012. O

Aya is not like the rest of her boy chasing friends. She helps her friends study for school, get jobs, prepare for a beauty pageant, and even helping take care

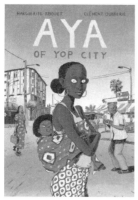

© Drawn and Quarterly and Marguerite Abouet.

of their kids. Drama is no stranger to her family and friends. Her parents must deal with an affair. Her friend gets engaged to the richest sleaze to help take care of her and her newborn child by another man. All this takes place in the author's native country the Ivory Coast. Each book also includes cultural tidbits and recipes. An award-nominated adaptation of *Aya of Yop City* was released in France in 2013. A sixth volume has not yet been translated into English.

Aya. 2007. 132pp. 978-1-894937-90-0.
Aya of Yop City. 2008. 112pp. 978-1-897299-41-8.
The Secrets Come Out. 2009. 132pp. 978-1-897299-79-1.
Life in Yop City. 2012. 384pp. 978-1-77046-082-9.
Love in Yop City. 2013. 384pp. 978-1-77046-092-8.

Bad Houses. Written by **Sara Ryan**. Illustrated by **Carla Speed McNeil**. Dark Horse Comics, 2013. 152pp. 978-1-59582-993-1. O

© 2016 Sara Ryan.

The sleepy town of Failin, Oregon, was once the home to a thriving logging industry that's dried up. Now the town's businesses are crumbling and the townsfolk are bitter and discontented with the drudgery of their lives. Teenagers Anne and Lewis, who meet at an estate sale, want to avoid the apathy and pain of the older generation and instead discover secrets about the history of the town and of their own families' lives as well.

Bakuman. Written by **Tsugumi Ohba**. Illustrated by **Takeshi Obata**. VIZ Media, 2010–2013. T あ

BAKUMAN. © 2008 by Tsugumi Ohba, Takeshi Obata/SHUEISHA Inc.

Moritaka Mashiro and his friend Akito Takagi are two ninth-grade boys who wish to become manga creators with Mashiro as the artist and Takagi as the writer. The series follows their ups and downs as creators who, under the pen name Muto Ashirogi, finally get to achieve their dream to be serialized in *Weekly Shōnen Jump*. Will Mashiro and Takagi make it big or will their manga creations just be a bust? The series was also adapted into an anime in Japan.

Vol. 1. 2010. 208pp. 978-1-4215-3513-5.
Vol. 2. 2010. 200pp. 978-1-4215-3514-2.
Vol. 3. 2011. 192pp. 978-1-4215-3515-9.
Vol. 4. 2011. 200pp. 978-1-4215-3793-1.
Vol. 5. 2011. 192pp. 978-1-4215-3794-8.
Vol. 6. 2011. 192pp. 978-1-4215-3824-2.
Vol. 7. 2011. 192pp. 978-1-4215-3888-4.

Vol. 8. 2011. 192pp. 978-1-4215-3889-1.
Vol. 9. 2012. 192pp. 978-1-4215-3958-4.
Vol. 10. 2012. 200pp. 978-1-4215-3995-9.
Vol. 11. 2012. 200pp. 978-1-4215-4103-7.
Vol. 12. 2012. 200pp. 978-1-4215-4136-5.
Vol. 13. 2012. 192pp. 978-1-4215-4208-9.
Vol. 14. 2012. 192pp. 978-1-4215-4290-4.

Vol. 15. 2012. 192pp. 978-1-4215-4291-1.
Vol. 16. 2012. 192pp. 978-1-4215-4292-8.
Vol. 17. 2012. 192pp. 978-1-4215-4293-5.
Vol. 18. 2013. 192pp. 978-1-4215-4294-2.
Vol. 19. 2013. 192pp. 978-1-4215-4295-9.
Vol. 20. 2013. 176pp. 978-1-4215-5370-2.

Barefoot Serpent. Written and Illustrated by **Scott Morse**. Top Shelf Productions, 2003. 128pp. 978-1-891830-37-2. T ◎

© 2016 Scott Morse.

Famed Japanese film director Akira Kurosawa's life and works are explored through the framework of a fictional girl and her family who come to Hawaii to heal and rediscover themselves following the death of her older brother. While on the island, the girl befriends a young local boy who, though reluctantly at first, helps to show the girl true friendship and helps to give her a personal way of healing through grief. Through their story, Kurosawa's personal life and the characters he brought to life are honored to show how we can all rise up and overcome adversity and challenge to live life to the fullest.

Blue Monday. Written and Illustrated by **Chynna Clugston Flores**. Image Comics, 2016– . T ◎

© 2016 Chynna Clugston Flores.

Bleu L. Finnegan is a spunky and fun teenage girl who has a penchant for old 1980s songs and has a crush on her history teacher Mr. Bishop as well as her favorite rocker Adam Ant. She spends her days hanging out with her best friend tough girl Clover and her two prankish guy friends, Alan and Victor, listening to their favorite songs, riding scooters, and participating in other fun foolish teen shenanigans. A love quadrangle emerges when Adam and Victor find they they're both in love with Bleu, Clover is in love with Victor, and Bleu still secretly pines for Mr. Bishop. Love, relationships, and high school are never easy, but good times, the occasional slapdash prank, and some good humor make it all worthwhile. The series was originally published in the early 2000s by Oni Press. Beginning in 2016 the series is being reprinted by Image Comics in full color as well as with a brand new story by Clugston Flores beginning with the story arc *Thieves Like Us*. Other volumes will be reprinted in color in the coming months.

Vol. 1: The Kids Are Alright. 2016. 136pp. 978-1-63215-704-1.
Vol. 2: Absolute Beginners. 2016. 128pp. 978-1-63215-873-4.

Chiggers. Written and Illustrated by **Hope Larson**. Atheneum Books for Young Readers, 2008. 172pp. 978-1-4169-3584-1, hardcover; 978-1-4169-3587-2. T 🌳

Abby is shy and nerdy and once again being sent to summer camp. Last year she was friends with Rose, but this year she's too busy. Irritated and friendless, Abby seeks friendship at camp, but who will be her friend? Will it be Shasta, the new girl whom nobody likes; Zoe, who seems to be aiming to be super-cool; or will it be Beth, who is new to camp and clinging to Abby? The hurt, jealousy, and loneliness, and hints of romance is all part of the youth experience that almost any girl who attended camp can recognize, *Chiggers* was recognized by YALSA's Great Graphic Novels for Teens committee on its selection list in 2009 as well as an Eisner Award for Special Recognition in 2007.

The Contract with God Trilogy: Life on Dropsie Avenue. Written and Illustrated by **Will Eisner**. W. W. Norton & Company, 2006. 498pp. 978-0-393-06105-5, hardcover. O ◉

A collection featuring three of Will Eisner's highly praised works set in the fictionalized South Bronx community. Partly taken from Eisner's Jewish youth growing up in New York in the early 20th century, the collections focus on a wide cross-section of cultures and span from well over 100 years of life in the same neighborhood. As time goes by, many families from a variety of cultures and nationalities help to bring their own influences to a small part of South Brooklyn—both the good and the bad. In that small space called Dropsie Avenue, nationalities clash, life-long friendships are forged, people fall in and out of love, and new communities continually rise from the ashes of old. In the end, though, the old brick buildings of Dropsie Avenue are just buildings: it is the people of the community that help to make a neighborhood. The collection includes the graphic novel collections of *A Contract with God and Other Tenement Stories*, *A Life Force*, and *Dropsie Avenue: The Neighborhood*. First published in 1978, *A Contract with God* was Eisner's earliest original graphic novel, and in some places has been mistakenly been said to have been the first graphic novel.

Curses. Written and Illustrated by **Kevin Huizenga**. Drawn and Quarterly, 2006. 144pp. 978-1-894937-86-3. O

Glenn Ganges is a very introspective middle-aged man. Through this collection of stories Glenn reflects on many aspects of everyday life in a unique way that only a theology major can. Hallucinatory visions, war refugees, birds, insomnia, and golf are some of the topics he has to deal with in his oddly mundane life.

Daytripper. Written by **Fábio Moon**. Illustrated by **Gabriel Ba**. Vertigo/DC Comics, 2010. 978-1-4012-2969-6. M ◉

© 2016 DC Comics.

Brás de Oliva Domingos always lived in the shadow of his famous father, a Brazilian writer. A writer himself, Brás finds his own voice writing obituaries. Death—that final chapter in the book of our lives—is a daily part of his life, always lurking in the recesses of his mind. Traveling backward and forward in time, we see Brás' life and the important moments of his life from his early days as a writer; monumental days with his best friend Jorge; his youth as a boy; the first kiss with a girl; his first failed marriage; to the loss of his father and more—with a twist ending to each chapter. A poignant, touching look at how we must all accept our own deaths to truly move on and live life to the fullest we can with the remaining time we all have left.

A Devil and Her Love Song. Written and Illustrated by **Miyoshi Tomari**. VIZ Media, 2012–2014. T 🎖 Japanese manga.

Maria Kawai has transferred to a new school after being expelled from her old one and things have gotten off to a rocky start. But with the help of new friends things may change. Selected as one of YALSA's Great Graphic Novels for Teens in 2013.

Vol. 1. 2012. 200pp. 978-1-4215-4164-8.
Vol. 2. 2012. 200pp. 978-1-4215-4165-5.
Vol. 3. 2012. 200pp. 978-1-4215-4166-2.
Vol. 4. 2012. 216pp. 978-1-4215-4167-9.
Vol. 5. 2012. 208pp. 978-1-4215-4182-2.
Vol. 6. 2012. 208pp. 978-1-4215-4183-9.
Vol. 7. 2013. 200pp. 978-1-4215-4184-6.
Vol. 8. 2013. 200pp. 978-1-4215-4185-3.
Vol. 9. 2013. 208pp. 978-1-4215-4186-0.
Vol. 10. 2013. 216pp. 978-1-4215-4187-7.
Vol. 11. 2013. 224pp. 978-1-4215-5134-0.
Vol. 12. 2013. 200pp. 978-1-4215-5135-7.
Vol. 13. 2014. 232pp. 978-1-4215-5136-4.

Drama. Written and Illustrated by **Raina Telgemeier**. Graphix/Scholastic Books, 2012. 240pp. 978-0-545-32699-5; 978-0-54532698-8, hardcover. T 🎖 ◎

Cover © Scholastic Inc.

Callie's love of the stage doesn't add up to any on stage talent, so she is content to work behind the scenes. There's plenty of drama to be had though off the stage—boys she likes and boys who like her. There's best friend trouble and friends coming to terms with their sexual identity all amongst the backdrop of an impending school play. Already a sure-fire hit, it captures the angst and joy of the tumultuous years of middle school.

Escapo. Written and Illustrated by **Paul Pope**. Z2 Comics, 2014. 160pp. 978-1-940878-00-3, hardcover. O

Originally printed in 1999, Paul Pope's graphic novel is about the world's greatest escape artist—the one and only Escapo! In one short story, Escapo has to confront the skeletal shadow of death. Can the escape artist escape from the inevitable? And in the second story, love may be Escapo's downfall. Dismissed by a girl of his dreams, he contemplates ending it all in one of his ludicrous devises he usually escapes from.

Essex County. Written and Illustrated by **Jeff Lemire**. Top Shelf Productions, 2007–2009. O ◎

Set in Essex County, Ontario, the series is a look at various members of the community over a span of years. First, a boy named Lester who has lost his mother and unhappy with his home life and school develops a friendship with a child-like ex hockey player who owns a gas station. Next, two brothers, former hockey players, reflect on the failures of their lives. And last, a nurse who

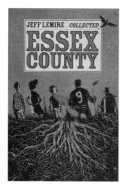

works around the county meets the players from the first two story arcs and the history of Essex County is featured as well.

Vol. 1: Tales from the Farm. 2007. 112pp. 978-1-891830-88-4.
Vol. 2: Ghost Stories. 2007. 224pp. 978-1-891830-94-5.
Vol. 3: The Country Nurse. 2008. 128pp. 978-1-891830-95-2.
The Complete Essex County. 2009. 512pp. 978-1-603090-46-9, hardcover; 978-1-60309-038-4.

© 2016 Jeff Lemire and Top Shelf.

Exquisite Corpse. Written and Illustrated by **Pénélope Bagieu**. First Second Books, 2015. 128pp. 978-1-62672-082-4, hardcover. M

Zoe is a pretty young girl who isn't exactly the most book-smart person. She's not quite sure what she wants in life, but anything beats her dead-end job working as a merchandise exhibitor at trade shows and her horrible boyfriend. When Zoe stumbles into the apartment of best-selling author, the eccentric Thomas Rocher, Zoe has no idea who he is, but she soon has the scandal of the century right in her midst! The book was originally published in France in 2010.

© Pénélope Bagieu and First
Second.

The Freddie Stories. Written and Illustrated by **Linda Barry**. Drawn and Quarterly, 2013. 72pp. 978-1-77046-090-4. M

Nothing goes right for Freddie. He lives in a dysfunctional family, where his sister is the only person that cares for him. Freddie is framed by his "friends" as an arsonist. Freddie gets very sick and begins seeing hallucinations. The kids at school tease Freddie relentlessly. It is not easy being Freddie.

Friends with Boys. Written and Illustrated by **Faith Erin Hicks**. First Second Books/ MacMillan Books, 2015. 224pp. 978-1-250-06816-3, 2nd edition. T 🎗 ◎

Maggie McKay's about the leave her sheltered life of being homeschooled into the scary world of high school. As terrifying as school can be, she's got her big brothers and her dad, but things haven't been the same since their mom left home. Alone and friendless, Maggie's trying to make real friends and fit in at school for the first time in her life. If that wasn't hard enough, there's also the small matter about the ghostly spirit of a woman that's been haunting her too. The book was originally published in 2012 and was a recipient of the Great Graphic Novels top-10 list from 2013.

© Faith Erin Hicks and First
Second.

Freshmen: Tales of 9th Grade Obsessions, Revelations, and Other Nonsense. Written and Illustrated by **Corinne Mucha**. Zest Books, 2011. 112pp. 978-0-9819733-6-4. T

> Annie's freshman year in high school isn't going as well as she had envisioned: her best former best friend now won't even talk to her, she's jealous of everyone, she just embarrassed herself in every sport imaginable, and she has a crush on her friend's older brother. What could possibly get worse? So much for this being the most important year of school ever—now she's bound for failure!

Giant Days. Written by **John Allison**. Illustrated by **Lissa Treiman** and **Max Sarin**. Boom Studios, 2015– . O

© 2016 BOOM! Studios.

> Susan, Esther, and Daisy are three girls who meet at college and become fast friends. From dealing with issues like being sick on campus with a cold, unrequited crushes, and the scary breed of males known as dudebros—college life between girls has never been so much fun. The first two volumes were in the Top Ten of YALSA's 2017 Great Graphic Novels for Teens List.
>
> *Vol. 1*. 2015. 128pp. 978-1-60886-789-9.
> *Vol. 2*. 2016. 128pp. 978-1-60886-804-9.
> *Vol. 3*. 2016. 112pp. 978-1-60886-851-3.
> *Vol. 4*. 2017. 112pp. 978-1-60886-938-1.
> *Vol. 5*. 2017. 112pp. 978-1-60886-982-4.

The Gigantic Beard That Was Evil. Written and Illustrated by **Stephen Collins**. Picador, 2013. 240pp. 978-1-250-05039-7. T 🎗

> In the isolated island known as "Here" people lived ordered lives—quiet, neat, and clean shaven—all but for one single hair, David is bald. But when Dave's beard continues to grow and grow, disorder ensues. This original work won the very first 9th Art Award at the Edinburgh International Book Festival. The book was recognized by YALSA's Great Graphic Novels for Teens selection list in 2015.

Hopeless Savages. Written by **Jen Van Meter**. Illustrated by **Christine Norrie, Chynna Clugston Flores**, **Bryan Lee O'Malley**, **Meredith McClaren**, and **Ross Campbell**. Oni Press, 2010–2015. T 🎗 ◎

© 2016 Oni Press.

> The daily lives of two hit punk rockers, who never quit the business or forgot about their ways, married and settled down. Their kids all have names like Arsenal, Skank, and Twitch. When the parents are kidnapped, the kids have to figure out how to save them, but they can't do it without the help of their estranged eldest brother Rat. What did he do to rebel when his parents were the ultimate rebels? Become a businessman, that's what. In the continuing adventures, Skank, the youngest of the family, starts considering dating as well as forming her own band, the Dust Bunnies, in the

midst of a video crew recording the family's every move for a television show. Meanwhile Twitch, the middle brother, is discovering his own sexual identity. Both he and Arsenal are dating the Shi brothers as well as participating in a kung fu tournament in Hong Kong, and the punk family follows them to Hong Kong to watch them compete, as well as to escape from their religiously converted grandmother. A humorously touching look at an anti-establishment family, the collection includes all of the original three volumes published by Oni Press as well as supplemental short stories in one complete collection. The original *Volume 1* collection story received recognition by YALSA's Popular Paperbacks for Young Adults committee in 2003 on the *On That Note . . . Music and Musicians* list.

Greatest Hits. 2000–2010. 2010. 390pp. 978-1-934964-48-4.
Break. 2015. 152pp. 978-1-62010-252-7.

How I Made It to Eighteen: A Mostly True Story. Written and Illustrated by **Tracy White**. Roaring Brook Press. 2010. 160pp. 978-1-59643-454-7. O 🌶

Stacy Black has some issues. She has anger issues, a terrible relationship, and abuses drugs on top of a bunch of other issues. Stacy has committed herself to the Golden Meadows Hospital to help her get better. With some words of advice from friends, staff, and herself she is coming to understand the issues she faces. *How I Made It to Eighteen* is a mostly true, slightly embellished, and in parts made up story of a real girl who faces many issues teens face. The book was recognized by YALSA on their Great Graphic Novels for Teens 2011's selection list.

I Kill Giants, 5th anniversary edition. Written by **Joe Kelly**. Illustrated by **J. M. Ken Niimura**. Image Comics, 2014. 232pp. 978-1-60706-985-0. T 🌶

Fifth grader Barbara Thorson tells everyone that giants are real and that she kills them with a giant norse hammer—so real that she's starting to believe it herself. For Barbara though, things aren't always what they seem—the giants in her life aren't real and she is just running away from the harsh realities of the real world to a world of magic and monsters for one dark reason. The book was recognized by YALSA as a Great Graphic Novel for Teens in 2010.

© 2016 Image Comics and Joe Kelly.

In Real Life. Written by **Cory Doctorow**. Illustrated by **Jen Wang**. First Second, 2011. 192pp. 978-1-59643-658-9. T 🌶

Teenager Anda loves playing the massively multiplayer role playing game called Coarsegold Online—it's a place for her to escape reality and be a leader of clans and a fighter against orcs and monsters and leave reality behind. When she befriends a boy from China in the game, she discovers that he is a gold farmer—he acquires hard-to-find items in the game and then resells them to others from better-developed

© 2016 First Second and Cory
Doctorow.

countries at a huge profit. This behavior is illegal in Coarse-gold Online, but Anda finds that the matters of right and wrong are tested as well as her online friendship with a boy halfway around the world. The book was based on a short story by Doctorow and was recognized by YALSA on the 2015 top-10 list for Great Graphic Novels for Teens.

Koko Be Good. Written and Illustrated by **Jen Wang**. First Second Books, 2010. 304pp. 978-1-59643-555-1. T

What happens when two very different people with two very different outlooks on life meet? Koko is a carefree, hyperactive girl with nothing to tie her down. Jon is a man who gave up everything to be with the woman he loves. These two people collide on the night Jon is at his last company party before he leaves for Peru so he can teach with his girlfriend. After these two people butt heads they realize that they may learn something from each other. Koko is forced to deal with the emotions she tries to bury. Jon must face the thought that he is running away with a fantasy. Can these two people help each other out while they try to not lose control of who they are?

Lost in NYC. Written by **Nadja Spiegelman**. Illustrated by **Sergio García Sánchez**. Toon Books, 2015. 48pp. 978-1-935179-81-8, hardcover. Y 🌳

© 2016 Toon Books.

When a student named Pablo gets separated from his class on his first field trip to New York City, he befriends a girl who helps show him around the city on one of the best forms of transportation—the subway! Learn the history of the subway and feel like you're right in the middle of the hustle and bustle of New York City. The book received recognition by ALSC in 2016 as a Notable Children's Book as well as other accolades including being selected as a School Library Journal Best Books of 2015, Texas Library Association's Little Maverick Graphic Novel Reading List for 2016, and the ABC Best Books for Young Readers 2015 List.

Marble Season. Written and Illustrated by **Gilbert Hernandez**. Drawn and Quarterly, 2013. 120pp. 978-1-77046-086-7, hardcover. T

This semiautobiographic original work features Huey, the middle child of a large family living in a California suburb in the 1960s. Huey plays with marbles, pretends to be Captain America, and has the other experiences of a typical young boy.

Meanwhile: Pick Any Path: 3,856 Story Possibilities. Written and Illustrated by **Jason Shiga**. Amulet Books, 2010. 80pp. 978-0-8109-8423-3, hardcover. T 🏵

Have you played any comics lately? Choose your own adventure in a way you've never done before. Little Jimmy wants to choose between a chocolate or vanilla ice cream cone—but after that the path is endless! The collection was recognized by YALSA on its 2011 Great Graphic Novels for Teens top-10 graphic novels list.

© 2016 Jason Shiga.

Mercury. Written and Illustrated by **Hope Larson**. Atheneum Books for Young Readers, 2010. 240pp. 978-1-4169-3585-8, hardcover; 978-1-4169-3588-9. O 🏵

A coming of age story of two generations. The parallels of two members of the same family—separated by centuries apart. Set in Nova Scotia in the present, young Tara and her mother lost everything when their old family farmhouse burns down. Tara is living with her extended family while her mother works to support both of them with hopes to rebuild again. Meanwhile in 1859, Tara's ancestor Josey wishes to marry a gold dowser, but her mother, who has supernatural sight—forbids it. The destinies of two generations intersect as Josey gains the supernatural site her mother has and Tara finds out that she has skills at dowsing and seeks to find the gold that was hidden by Josey over 150 years ago. The book was recognized on YALSA's Great Graphic Novels for Teens selection list in 2011.

Nothing Can Possibly Go Wrong. Written by **Prudence Shen**. Illustrated by **Faith Erin Hicks**. First Second Books, 2013. 288pp. 978-1-59643-659-6. T

Nate and Charlie are the unlikeliest of friends. Charlie is the laid-back captain of the basketball team and Charlie is the neurotic and scheming president of the robotics club. When Nate declares war on the cheerleaders retaliate with Nate stuck in the middle of the worst school election campaign ever. At stake is the student funding for the robotics club or new cheerleader uniforms—but not both.

© 2016 Prudence Shen & Faith Erin Hicks
and First Second.

Our Expanding Universe. Written and Illustrated by **Alex Robinson**. Top Shelf Productions, 2015. 256pp. 978-1-60309-377-4. O

Scott, Bill, and Brownie are three friends who used to do everything together—but now they're in new places in their lives: Scott just got married; Bill is trying to have

a baby with his wife; and Brownie is their divorced weed-ing-loving friend. Can their friendship survive the biggest change to their lives—the passing of time? In the tradition of Alex Robinson's *Box Office Poison* graphic novel, mar-riages are tested, babies are born, and once strong friend-ships are in doubt when lives change.

© 2016 Top Shelf and Alex Robinson.

Page by Paige. Written and Illustrated by **Laura Lee Gulledge**. Amulet Books, 2011. 192pp. 978-0-8109-9722-6. T

When teenage Paige Turner moves with her family to New York City, she uses her drawings to chronicle her new life and new friends while slowly trying to reveal her secret identity as an artist.

Part-Time Princesses. Written and Illustrated by **Monica Gallagher**. Oni Press, 2015. 168pp. 978-1-62010-217-6. O

Four teenage girls who are too stuck-up for their own good spend their sum-mers working at an Enchanted Forest theme park as the princesses. But when their life goals for the future are all up in smoke, the one place they all can't stand to work—the Enchanted Forest—may be gone for good due to decreased attendance and crime. With no future goals like they planned, the four girls resolve to get back the customers at the theme park they never wanted to work at in the first place and maybe learn something too in the process.

The Paul Series. Written and Illustrated by **Michel Rabagliati**. Drawn and Quar-terly, 2002–2008; Conundrum Press 2012– . O

In these semiautobiographical stories, Paul acts as a stand in for the French-Ca-nadian Rabagliati, telling stories from both his youth and adulthood including working as a camp councilor, his time in scouting, the attempts of his wife and himself to have a baby, and even the life and death of his father-in-law. The books were originally published in French and then in English.

Paul Has a Summer Job. 2002. 160pp. 978-1-896597-54-6, hardcover.
Paul Moves Out. 2005. 120pp. 978-1-896597-87-4, hardcover.
Paul Goes Fishing. 2008. 208pp. 978-1-897299-28-9, hardcover.
The Song of Roland. 2012. 192pp. 978-1-894994-61-3.
Paul Joins the Scouts. 2013. 144pp. 978-1-894994-69-9.
Paul up North. 2016. 184pp. 978-1-77262-001-6.

La Perdida. Written and Illustrated by **Jessica Abel**. Pantheon Press/Random House, 2008. 288pp. 978-0-375-71471-9. O

Twenty-something American slacker Carla moves to Mexico, the home of her long-lost father. She hopes to become better acquainted with her heritage; her ex-lover who lives there as well is an expat who only hangs out with other Americans. Carla tries to meet more Mexican youth, but loses her way when she begins to hang out with petty thieves and lowlifes who have higher goals in their thieving ways. Can Carla get out of her vortex of fear and violence?

Princess Jellyfish. Written and Illustrated by **Akiko Higashimura**. Kodansha Comics, 2016– . O 🎎 Japanese manga. あ

Welcome to Amamizukan, an apartment building in Tokyo where the only female tenants (who are all otaku) are allowed. Eighteen-year-old Tsukimi, the protagonist of the series, is an otaku girl wants to be an illustrator but she's awkward around beautiful people and afraid of fashionable people. As the quirks of all the other women apartment are revealed, Tsukimi is also befriended by one of the apartment renters who isn't quite what she seems. She goes by the name "Kurako" but she is really a he! His name is Kuranosuke, a cross-dressing son of a wealthy family who wants to escape the responsibilities of a traditional male and enter the world of fashion. Can Tsukimi keep Kuranosuke's secret from the rest of the apartment owners and can Amamizukan Apartments survive a bid to be demolished and turned into a metropolitan shopping complex. The series was originally was published in Japan from 2009 through 2015 and collected in 15 volumes so far. Kodansha is reprinting the series in two-in-one editions. The series was also adapted to an 11-episode anime series in 2010. The first volume was on YALSA's 2017 Great Graphic Novels for Teens list.

Vol. 1 (collects Vol. 1 & 2). 2016. 376pp. 978-1-63-236228-5.
Vol. 2. (collects Vol. 3 & 4). 2016. 400pp. 978-1-63-236229-2.
Vol. 3. (collects Vol. 5 & 6). 2016. 400pp. 978-1-63-236230-8.
Vol. 4. (collects Vol. 7&8). 2017. 400pp. 978-1-63-236231-5.

Punk Rock and Trailer Parks. Written and Illustrated by **Derf Backderf**. Slave Labor Graphics, 2008. 144pp. 978-1-59362-135-3. O

Set in the 1980s in the heyday of punk rock music, Teenager Otto "the Baron" Pizcok, lives in the local trailer park looking after his senile tractor-driving uncle and a frequent visitor to the venue The Bank—home to all the best local punk rock shows. With the glorious fury of punk rock music, Otto sheds his nerdy persona to become a tour guide to the local punk rock legends when they come to town. As the school year progresses and prom comes up, will Otto go on to college out of state or find his destiny as Akron's latest punk rock legend? A semi-autobiographical look at Derf's teenage years in a suburb of Akron, Ohio.

© 2016 Derf Backderf.

The Reason for Dragons. Written by **Chris Northrop**. Illustrated by **Jeff Stokely**. Boom! Studios, 2013. 128pp. 978-1-936393-74-9, hardcover. T

Wendell, a teen who struggles with fitting in with his rugged step-dad at home and dealing with bullies in school, is dared to go to visit the burned-out grounds of a Renaissance Faire. The place is supposedly haunted, but Wendell instead finds an old

© 2016 BOOM! Studios.

man who claims his name is Sir Habersham, a knight who is in search of the dragon that burned down the Renaissance Faire! Is Sir Habersham really who he says he is and will Wendell help the old man fulfill his quest no matter how absurd it could be—or is it?

Roller Girl. Written and Illustrated by **Victoria Jamieson**. Dial Books for Young Readers, 2015. 240pp. 978-0-525-42967-8, hardcover; 978-0-803-74016-7, softcover. Y 🎗 ◎

© 2016 Random House/Dial Books for Young Readers.

Astrid, a 12-year-old girl, falls in love with the local Roller Derby and sets out to be the best she can be at the sport—but discovers that the game is more daunting than she thought. Along the way she discovers that though she isn't quite into the same things as her best friend—that's part of the growing pains and gains of getting older and finding true friends. The book was recognized by as a Newbery Honor book, a 2016 YALSA Quick Picks for Reluctant Readers selection, as well as a 2016 YALSA Popular Paperback selection.

Sacred Heart. Written and Illustrated by **Liz Suburbia**. Fantagraphics, 2015. 312pp. 978-1-60699-841-0. O 🎗 ◎

© 2016 Liz Suburbia and Fantagraphics.

Collecting Liz Suburbia's webcomic, *Sacred Heart* is set in the small town of Alexandria in which all the adults have left on a four-year religious pilgrimage. The teenagers are in charge and trying to live a normal life but mysterious events and secrets may lead to trouble. More volumes are planned. *Sacred Heart* was a 2016 Alex Award winner and on the top-10 list of the YALSA Great Graphic Novels for teens list in 2016.

Same Difference. Written and Illustrated by **Derek Kirk Kim**. First Second Books, 2011. Reprint edition. 96pp. 978-1-59643-657-2, hardcover. O 🎗 ◎

Best friends Simon and Nancy, both 20-something Korean-Americans, have had their share of humor, heartache, and regret. When Simon spots a former

© 2016 First Second and Derek Kirk Kim.

high school classmate whom he had treated badly, he shares his own personal insecurities of when he was in high school and was embarrassed to go to the school dance with a platonic and disabled friend. Meanwhile Nancy, a chain-smoking nosy sleuth, confesses to Simon that she's been writing back love letters to a man who lives in Simon's hometown. The man was sending love letters that were addressed to the previous owner of her apartment and as a game, Nancy has been pretending to be the ex-girlfriend. As Nancy and Simon travel back to Simon's California hometown to find out just who this man is, Simon spots his old friend and gets the opportunity to tell her how he really feels. When true confessions and pent-up feelings are revealed, both Nancy and Simon find that though the truth hurts, the healing power of the heart can mend all wounds. In 2005 the creator received an Eisner Award in the category of Talent Deserving of Wider Recognition as well as an Ignatz Award in 2003 for Promising New Talent.

The Sculptor. Written and Illustrated by **Scott McCloud**. First Second Books, 2015. 496pp. 978-1-59643-573-5, hardcover. O

© 2016 Scott McCloud and First Second.

Would you trade lasting fame for only 200 days left to live? David Smith is a destitute young sculptor still looking to recapture a little bit of the promise he had years earlier. With his family all gone, he's alone, lost, and penniless. After years of losing his patron, he's still looking to make a lasting mark in the Big Apple's art scene. When he has a chance encounter with Death, he's given a choice: to live a long peaceful life in obscurity away from the art world or 200 days left to live and be famous. David chooses 200 days and as his life counts down he finds his muse in Meg, a young actor whose chance encounter with him may just be his key to finding his way in this lonely world. The book was recognized as a Great Graphic Novel for Teens selection in 2016.

Scott Pilgrim. Written and Illustrated by **Bryan Lee O'Malley**. Oni Press, 2012–2015. T

© 2016 Bryan Lee O'Malley.

Scott Pilgrim's got it good. A 23-year-old slacker, he's "in-between" jobs right now (i.e., unemployed) and on the side he plays in a so-so band called Sex Bob-omb and plays video games. He's sharing a tiny apartment with his roommate who owns most of everything in it. He's even got a girlfriend named Knives Chau who's still in high school and is really nice. Basically Scott's not that bright a guy, but he's cool. Über cool. When he meets a rollerblading delivery girl named Ramona Flowers at several parties, is she worth having a relationship with and breaking his girlfriend's heart? And just why is it that Ramona's seven evil exes want to fight him to the death? Meanwhile, the inevitable happens after Scott's cheating results in Knives and Ramona have a confrontation kung-fu style and plenty of drama, comedy, and action mixed in-between. In 2010, a feature film called *Scott Pilgrim vs. the World* was directed by Edgar Wright adapting the six volumes and has become a cult classic. The collections are the full color editions of the series reprinted in hardcover for the first time.

Vol. 1: Scott Pilgrim's Precious Little Life. 2012. 192pp. 978-1-62010-000-4, hardcover.
Vol. 2: Scott Pilgrim vs. the World. 2012. 208pp. 978-1-62010-001-1, hardcover.
Vol. 3: Scott Pilgrim and the Infinite Sadness. 2013. 160pp. 978-1-62010-002-8, hardcover.
Vol. 4: Scott Pilgrim Gets It Together. 2013. 208pp. 978-1-62010-003-5, hardcover.
Vol. 5: Scott Pilgrim vs. the Universe. 2014. 192pp. 978-1-62010-004-2, hardcover.
Vol. 6: Scott Pilgrim's Finest Hour. 2015. 280pp. 978-1-62010-005-9, hardcover.

Shoplifter. Written and Illustrated by **Michael Cho**. Pantheon Books, 2014. 96pp. 978-0-307-91173-5, hardcover. O

Corinna Park wanted to be a novelist but took a job in advertising. Now five years later she has to decide if this is what she wants to do with her life.

A Silent Voice. Written and Illustrated by **Yoshitoki Oima**. Kodansha Comics, 2015–2016. T Japanese manga.

When Shoya Ishida was in elementary school, he was known to be a bully and a delinquent along with all of his friends. He was especially cruel to a deaf girl in his class named Shoko Nishimiya—so bad, in fact, that she had to leave the school and be homeschooled due to the humiliation. As a result, Shoya lost the respect of his friends and grew up lonely and isolated. Six years later, Shoko reenters his life and Shoya resolves to make up to her how horribly he treated her. Is it too little too late to prevent further tragedies or will they both learn of the importance of forgiveness? The series was on YALSA Great Graphic Novels for Teens list in both 2016 and 2017.

Vol. 1. 2015. 192pp. 978-1-63236-056-4.
Vol. 2. 2015. 192pp. 978-1-63236-057-1.
Vol. 3. 2015. 192pp. 978-1-63236-058-8.
Vol. 4. 2015. 192pp. 978-1-63236-059-5.
Vol. 5. 2016. 192pp. 978-1-63236-060-1.
Vol. 6. 2016. 192pp. 978-1-63236-061-8.
Vol. 7. 2016. 192pp. 978-1-63236-222-3.

Sing No Evil. Written and Illustrated by **JP Ahonen** and **KP Alare**. Harry N. Abrams, 2014. 192pp. 978-1-4197-1359-0, hardcover; 978-1-4197-1360-6. O 🌳

Aksel is the frontman of the heavy metal band Perkeros, but he's got a hard time keeping the band together. Plagued with bad reviews, the band still tries to work out the kinks with Lily on keyboard; old hippie Kervinen on bass; Bear, a real bear who is the drummer; Aydin, a new singer to the band who has the voice of an angel, but wants to steal the spotlight. As if keeping a band together isn't enough, there's also this small matter about a supernatural

force that's about to take over the city! Can Aksel save the city and himself before his weird visions get the best of him? The book was recognized by YALSA's Great Graphic Novels for Teens selection list in 2015.

Skim. Written by **Mariko Tamaki**. Illustrated by **Jillian Tamaki**. Groundwood Books, 2008–2010. 2008. 140pp. 978-0-88899-753-1, hardcover; 2010. 978-0-88899-964-1. O 🎋

Kimberly Keiko Cameron (aka "Skim") is a Goth girl from a mixed race family going to an all-girls school in Toronto. Skim is best friends with fellow Goth girl Lisa, and she spends her time learning about Wiccan history and tarot cards, but something still feels missing from her life as she's burdened by thoughts of suicide, depression, love, sexual preference, high school pressures, and loneliness. Skim finds out over time that many of those at school that she has had issue with are just as lonely, hurt, and like her after all. A melancholy and quiet look at trying to make it day to day as a teen especially when everything feels like it's spinning out of control. The series was recognized by YALSA for Great Graphic Novels List in 2008, Best Book for Young Adults, as well as Quick Picks for Reluctant Readers 2008. The series also won the Eisner Award for Best Graphic Album (New) 2008, Best Publication for Tweens/Teens 2008, and a Harvey Award for Best Graphic Album 2008.

Solanin. Written and Illustrated by **Inio Asano**. VIZ Media, 2008. 432pp. 978-1-4215-2321-7. O 🎋 Japanese manga.

Meiko and Taneda graduated from college over two years ago. Meiko works as an office clerk and Taneda works as an illustrator to pay the rent and get by, but they have no focus in their lives. They both decide to change their malaise and turn their lives around—Taneda focuses on writing music for his band and Meiko quits her job—a new direction is before them, but fate has something else in mind. The story was nominated for the 2009 Eisner Award for Best U.S. Edition of International Material—Japan and was nominated for the 2009 Harvey Award for Best American Edition of Foreign Material. The book was also recognized by YALSA as a Great Graphic Novel for Teens selection list in 2010.

Sunny Side Up. Written by **Jennifer L. Holm**. Illustrated by **Matthew Holm** with **Lark Pien**. Graphix/Scholastic, 2015. 224pp. 978-0-545-74165-1, hardcover; 978-0-545-74166-8. Y ◉

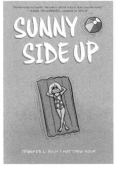
Cover © Scholastic Inc

Sunny gets to spend the entire summer away from her family and gets to stay in Florida with her retired grandfather. Spending time in the same state as Disney World sounds like a lot of fun, but where her grandfather lives it's anything but an amusement park. They people there are really really old! Luckily she's not the only kid there. She befriends Buzz, a boy who is obsessed with comic books. Soon the both of them are discovering the best comic book heroes, as well as facing off against golf-ball-eating alligators, helping to rescue runaway cats, and more. But the question remains — why is Sunny down in Florida anyway away from her family? It won't be a secret much any longer.

Swallow Me Whole. Written and Illustrated by **Nate Powell**. Top Shelf Productions, 2008. 216pp. 978-1-60309-033-9, hardcover. O 🎗 ◉

© Nate Powell and Top Shelf.

The life of two siblings, Ruth and Perry, who both have hidden adolescent personal demons that have affected them in different ways. As the siblings grow past adolescence, they both continue to have deep developmental and psychological issues. Ruth obsesses over insects and amphibians as her OCD disorder worsens, and Perry imagines a small gnome is forcing him to draw to the point of exhaustion. The idea of mental illness as a condition instilled in our DNA and is hereditary is established as the elderly matriarch of the family, the sibling's grandmother, has problems of her own in a family dealing with mental illness and schizophrenia. The book won an Eisner Award in 2009 for Best Original Graphic Novel and was recognized by YALSA on the Great Graphic Novels for Teens selection list in 2009.

This One Summer. Written by **Mariko Tamaki**. Illustrated by **Jillian Tamaki**. Groundwood Books, 2015. 320pp. 978-1-55498-152-6. T 🎗 ◉

© First Second books and Mariko Tamaki and Jillian-Tamaki.

Rose and Windy are two young teenagers who have been best summer friends for as long as they can remember. For years their parents have spent the summers in lazy Awago Beach at the summer cottages. But this year their bodies are changing, they're getting interested in boys, and learning swear words. Rose and Windy pass their time watching scary movies, and finding out stuff about sex they never learned in health class. Clinging to adolescence but not yet an adult, Rose is getting her first taste of young adulthood, but Windy is still rejoicing in being a kid. When Rose realizes that her parents' marriage is falling apart, will her summers ever be the same again?

Regardless of what happens, this will be one summer neither Rose or Windy will forget. The book received many accolades and awards including the Eisner Award for Best New Graphic Album 2015, the Michael L. Printz Award for Excellence in Young Adult Literature, Honor Book 2015, as well as the Randolph Caldecott Honor Book in 2015.

Too Cool to Be Forgotten. Written and Illustrated by **Alex Robinson**. Top Shelf Productions, 2008. 128pp. 978-1-891830-98-3, hardcover. O

Andy Wicks has been smoking for well over 25 years. He'll try anything to break the habit and one day goes under hypnosis to but instead finds himself suddenly transformed into his 15-year-old self. With a 40-something mind still intact, he is forced to relive the horrors of school including dating life, cliques, and algebra. If you could go back in time to revisit high school, what would you change knowing what you know now?

© Alex Robinson.

Toxic Planet. Written and Illustrated by **David Ratte**. Yen Press. 2009. 160pp. 978-0-7595-2928-1. M

Set in the not too distant future where everyone wears gas masks, *Toxic Planet* is a satirical parable of what living in a world may be like if pollution runs rampant. Going to the virtual zoo can be a great date. When walking through the city you better run for cover when the acid rain sirens ring. And the only time you see your significant other's face is the day after the wedding. The sad comedy of this future will hopefully remain in the colorful pages of this book.

Trashed. Written and Illustrated by **Derf Backderf**. Abrams Comic Arts, 2015. 256pp. 978-1-4197-1453-5, hardcover; 978-1-4197-1454-2. O

Inspired by Backderf's own time as a garbage man, *Trashed* originated as a 52-page, Eisner-Award Nominated book put out by Slave Labor Graphics. It was later restarted as a webcomic and now as a larger work. Three 20-something friends work as garbage men dealing with all sorts of weather and people. Trashed was on the top 10 list of the YALSA Great Graphic Novels for teens and earned Backderf an Einser Award for lettering.

© Derf Backderf.

Two Brothers. Written and Illustrated by **Gabriel Bá** and **Fabio Moon**. Dark Horse Comics, 2015. 232pp. 978-1-6165-5856-7. M

From twin brothers Bá and Moon comes the story of twin brothers Omar and Yaqub. Set in Manaus, Brazil, the story, which is based on a work by Milton Hatoum, shows the conflict and tensions between brothers, which are only made worse after Yaqub spends several years overseas. The book was a 2016 Eisner Award winner.

Will & Whit. Written and Illustrated by **Laura Lee Gulledge**. Amulet Books 2013. 192pp. 978-1-4197-0546-5. T 🌸

> Teenager Wilhelmina "Will" Huxstep creates lamps to overcome her fear of the dark and cope with the loss of her parents but when Hurricane Whitney takes away the power in her town she must find new ways to cope. The book was a 2014 Great Graphic Novel for Teens.

Wilson. Written and Illustrated by **Daniel Clowes**. Drawn and Quarterly, 2010. 80pp. 978-1-77046-007-2. M 🎬

> Sometimes nothing can go your way. For Wilson his whole life never seems to work out in his favor and he knows it. The way Wilson goes through life lets readers fully appreciate the dark humor that makes up our days. A feature film version came out in 2017 with Woody Harrelson in the title role.

The Zabime Sisters. Written and Illustrated by **Aristophane**. First Second Books, 2010. 96pp. 978-1-59643-638-1. T 🌸

> Experience the first day of summer vacation with three sisters on their island home of Guadalupe. Translated from the French graphic novel. The collection was recognized by YALSA on its 2011 Great Graphic Novels for Teens top-10 graphic novels list.

© First Second and Aristophane.

Sports

Graphic novel tales in which sports play a central role in the story to hook the reader in. Many times the sport itself serves to reinforce common issues including teamwork, working to your full potential, and playing fair. The sport itself may also serve as a backdrop to teen-related issues including relationships, friendship, and personal secrets.

Cross Game. Written and Illustrated by **Mitsuru Adachi**. VIZ Media, 2010–2012. T Japanese manga.

The story of Ko Kitamura and the four Tsukishima sisters as they deal with friendship, loss, and baseball. The storylines is divided into three parts beginning in elementary school and ending in high school. A popular anime series was based on the manga. The first volume of *Cross Game* was selected as one of YALSA's Great Graphic Novels for Teens in 2011.

Vol. 1. 2010. 576pp. 978-1-4215-3758-0.
Vol. 2. 2011. 376pp. 978-1-4215-3766-5.
Vol. 3. 2011. 376pp. 978-1-4215-3767-2.
Vol. 4. 2011. 376pp. 978-1-4215-3768-9.

CROSS GAME © 2005 Mitsuru ADACHI/SHOGA-KUKAN.

Vol. 5. 2011. 376pp. 978-1-4215-3769-6. *Vol. 7.* 2012. 376pp. 978-1-4215-3771-9.
Vol. 6. 2012. 376pp. 978-1-4215-3770-2. *Vol. 8.* 2012. 376pp. 978-1-4215-3772-6.

Eyeshield 21. Written by **Riichiro Inagaki**. Illustrated by **Yusuke Murata**. VIZ Media, 2005–2011. O Japanese manga.

A look at the sport of Football, Japanese style! Sena Kobayakawa is a pencil-neck high school student just barely getting by and being walked over by bullies. When he tries to make new friends, he reluctantly joins fellow student Kurita's American Football team (all two of them) and thinks he'll have no problem being the team's manager. When he is inadvertently spotted running by the Hiruma, the team captain, he instantly gets bumped from sidelines to the frontline. To protect his identity from rival schools and potential bullies, Sena wears a tinted eyeshield helmet so no one can see his face or know his identity. Can the "mysterious" Eyeshield 21 take the team to Japan's high school championships?

Vol. 1. 2005. 208pp. 978-1-59116-752-5. *Vol. 20.* 2008. 200pp. 978-1-4215-1625-7.
Vol. 2. 2005. 208pp. 978-1-59116-809-6. *Vol. 21.* 2008. 172pp. 978-1-4215-1626-4.
Vol. 3. 2005. 200pp. 978-1-59116-874-4. *Vol. 22.* 2008. 210pp. 978-1-4215-1955-5.
Vol. 4. 2005. 208pp. 978-1-4215-0074-4. *Vol. 23.* 2008. 208pp. 978-1-4215-1956-2.
Vol. 5. 2005. 208pp. 978-1-4215-0113-0. *Vol. 24.* 2009. 200pp. 978-1-4215-2393-4.
Vol. 6. 2006. 208pp. 978-1-4215-0274-8. *Vol. 25.* 2009. 208pp. 978-1-4215-2394-1.
Vol. 7. 2006. 208pp. 978-1-4215-0405-6. *Vol. 26.* 2009. 200pp. 978-1-4215-2621-8.
Vol. 8. 2006. 208pp. 978-1-4215-0637-1. *Vol. 27.* 2009. 200pp. 978-1-4215-2622-5.
Vol. 9. 2006. 208pp. 978-1-4215-0638-8. *Vol. 28.* 2009. 200pp. 978-1-4215-2623-2.
Vol. 10. 2006. 208pp. 978-1-4215-0639-5. *Vol. 29.* 2009. 200pp. 978-1-4215-2776-5.
Vol. 11. 2006. 208pp. 978-1-4215-0640-1. *Vol. 30.* 2010. 192pp. 978-1-4215-2813-7.
Vol. 12. 2007. 208pp. 978-1-4215-1061-3. *Vol. 31.* 2010. 192pp. 978-1-4215-2927-1.
Vol. 13. 2007. 216pp. 978-1-4215-1062-0. *Vol. 32.* 2010. 192pp. 978-1-4215-3162-5.
Vol. 14. 2007. 216pp. 978-1-4215-1063-7. *Vol. 33.* 2010. 200pp. 978-1-4215-3231-8.
Vol. 15. 2007. 208pp. 978-1-4215-1064-4. *Vol. 34.* 2011. 216pp. 978-1-4215-3306-3.
Vol. 16. 2007. 200pp. 978-1-4215-1065-1. *Vol. 35.* 2011. 200pp. 978-1-4215-3577-7.
Vol. 17. 2007. 200pp. 978-1-4215-1166-5. *Vol. 36.* 2011. 192pp. 978-1-4215-3684-2.
Vol. 18. 2008. 200pp. 978-1-4215-1544-1. *Vol. 37.* 2011. 200pp. 978-1-4215-3685-9.
Vol. 19. 2008. 200pp. 978-1-4215-1624-0.

Play Ball. Written by **Nunzio DeFilippis** and **Christina Weir**. Illustrated by **Jackie Lewis**. Oni Press, 2012. 146pp. 978-1-934964-79-8. T ◎

All Dashiell Brody ever wanted to do in high school was to be the best—and she is the best at playing softball. When her family relocates, she discovers that the new high school has a championship-level baseball team, and Dashiell wants to play. Can a girl play on a boys' baseball team? Dashiell finds out in a story that tests her family, her team, and more as she finds out where she truly belongs.

© Oni Press and Nunzio DeFilippis & Christina Weir.

The Prince of Tennis. Written and Illustrated by **Takeshi Konomi**. VIZ Media, 2004–2011. A Japanese manga. あ

Ryoma Echizen, a freshman tennis player and four-time junior champion in the United States, has returned home to Japan and enrolled in the prestigious Seishun Gakuen Middle School. Allowing seventh graders to play on the varsity tennis squad has never been done before, but Ryoma knows he has the skills and the moves to prove he's one of the best. The popular sports series manga inspired an anime spin-off as well as a live-action movie. The manga series was also adapted as a 178-episode anime series in Japan.

Vol. 1. 2004. 184pp. 978-1-59116-435-7.	*Vol. 22.* 2008. 200pp. 978-1-4215-1098-9.
Vol. 2. 2004. 200pp. 978-1-59116-436-4.	*Vol. 23.* 2008. 200pp. 978-1-4215-1473-4.
Vol. 3. 2004. 200pp. 978-1-59116-437-1.	*Vol. 24.* 2008. 200pp. 978-1-4215-1646-2.
Vol. 4. 2004. 200pp. 978-1-59116-438-8.	*Vol. 25.* 2008. 200pp. 978-1-4215-1647-9.
Vol. 5. 2004. 200pp. 978-1-59116-439-5.	*Vol. 26.* 2008. 190pp. 978-1-4215-1648-6.
Vol. 6. 2005. 200pp. 978-1-59116-440-1.	*Vol. 27.* 2008. 190pp. 978-1-4215-1649-3.
Vol. 7. 2005. 192pp. 978-1-59116-787-7.	*Vol. 28.* 2008. 210pp. 978-1-4215-1650-9.
Vol. 8. 2005. 184pp. 978-1-59116-853-9.	*Vol. 29.* 2009. 210pp. 978-1-4215-1651-6.
Vol. 9. 2005. 184pp. 978-1-59116-995-6.	*Vol. 30.* 2009. 192pp. 978-1-4215-2431-3.
Vol. 10. 2005. 184pp. 978-1-4215-0070-6.	*Vol. 31.* 2009. 184pp. 978-1-4215-2432-0.
Vol. 11. 2006. 176pp. 978-1-4215-0201-4.	*Vol. 32.* 2009. 200pp. 978-1-4215-2433-7.
Vol. 12. 2006. 208pp. 978-1-4215-0337-0.	*Vol. 33.* 2009. 200pp. 978-1-4215-2434-4.
Vol. 13. 2006. 208pp. 978-1-4215-0666-1.	*Vol. 34.* 2009. 184pp. 978-1-4215-2435-1.
Vol. 14. 2006. 208pp. 978-1-4215-0667-8.	*Vol. 35.* 2010. 192pp. 978-1-4215-2847-2.
Vol. 15. 2006. 208pp. 978-1-4215-0668-5.	*Vol. 36.* 2010. 176pp. 978-1-4215-2848-9.
Vol. 16. 2006. 208pp. 978-1-4215-0669-2.	*Vol. 37.* 2010. 192pp. 978-1-4215-2849-6.
Vol. 17. 2006. 208pp. 978-1-4215-0670-8.	*Vol. 38.* 2010. 192pp. 978-1-4215-2850-2.
Vol. 18. 2007. 208pp. 978-1-4215-1094-1.	*Vol. 39.* 2010. 192pp. 978-1-4215-2851-9.
Vol. 19. 2007. 208pp. 978-1-4215-1095-8.	*Vol. 40.* 2011. 200pp. 978-1-4215-2852-6.
Vol. 20. 2007. 192pp. 978-1-4215-1096-5.	*Vol. 41.* 2011. 200pp. 978-1-4215-2853-3.
Vol. 21. 2007. 192pp. 978-1-4215-1097-2.	*Vol. 42.* 2011. 172pp. 978-1-4215-2854-0.

Whistle! Written and Illustrated by **Daisuke Higuchi**. VIZ Media, 2004–2010. T Japanese manga. あ

After being banned from his high school soccer team for being too short, teenager Sho Kazamatsuri still won't give up his dream of becoming a top-notch player, even after a few embarrassing mishaps. Now he and the other second string soccer players at his new school will prove they've got what it takes to be the best. A tale of David vs. Goliath on the field of soccer! The manga also has an anime adaptation.

Vol. 1. 2004. 208pp. 978-1-59116-685-6.	*Vol. 8.* 2005. 208pp. 978-1-4215-0068-3.
Vol. 2. 2004. 208pp. 978-1-59116-686-3.	*Vol. 9.* 2006. 200pp. 978-1-4215-0206-9.
Vol. 3. 2004. 208pp. 978-1-59116-692-4.	*Vol. 10.* 2006. 208pp. 978-1-4215-0340-0.
Vol. 4. 2005. 200pp. 978-1-59116-727-3.	*Vol. 11.* 2006. 208pp. 978-1-4215-0685-2.
Vol. 5. 2005. 208pp. 978-1-59116-789-1.	*Vol. 12.* 2006. 208pp. 978-1-4215-0686-9.
Vol. 6. 2005. 200pp. 978-1-59116-836-2.	*Vol. 13.* 2006. 208pp. 978-1-4215-0687-6.
Vol. 7. 2005. 200pp. 978-1-59116-973-4.	*Vol. 14.* 2006. 208pp. 978-1-4215-0688-3.

Vol. 15. 2006. 208pp. 978-1-4215-0689-0.   *Vol. 20.* 2008. 200pp. 978-1-4215-1111-5.
Vol. 16. 2007. 208pp. 978-1-4215-1107-8.   *Vol. 21.* 2009. 210pp. 978-1-4215-1656-1.
Vol. 17. 2007. 200pp. 978-1-4215-1108-5.   *Vol. 22.* 2009. 200pp. 978-1-4215-2445-0.
Vol. 18. 2008. 208pp. 978-1-4215-1109-2.   *Vol. 23.* 2009. 200pp. 978-1-4215-2446-7.
Vol. 19. 2008. 200pp. 978-1-4215-1110-8.   *Vol. 24.* 2010. 208pp. 978-1-4215-2447-4.

Food

One of the trends in prose fiction are the quirky books (typically mysteries) that deal with food as a main part of the plot. There have been a great many Mystery writers such as Nancy Fairbanks' *Carolyn Blue Culinary Mystery Series* and Joanne Fluke's *Cookie Jar Cozy Mystery Series*. Many manga series from Japan as well as special titles published in North America have embraced the love of food. Some have even included recipes in their books as well. Enjoy and we hope you don't read these books on an empty stomach! Of note, a short selection of non-fiction food-related books including *Relish* and *Dirt Candy* are both included here as well instead of the non-fiction chapter. The book *Chew* is not listed below but is in the crime chapter since the main character is a police officer who psychically solves crimes by eating meat (including human body parts).

Antique Bakery. Written by **Fumi Yoshinaga**. Digital Manga Publishing, 2005–2006. T Japanese manga 📚 あ

In this Shojo Manga, Keisuke Tachibana, Yusuke Ono, Eiji Kanda, and Chikage Kobayakawa work together in small bakery. The series won the 2002 Kodansha Manga Award for shōjo manga and was nominated for an Eisner award. The series was also adapted in Japan as both a live-action and an anime television series and as a live-action film in South Korea.

Vol. 1. 2005. 200pp. 978-1-5697-0946-7.
Vol. 2. 2005. 208pp. 978-1-5697-0945-0.
Vol. 3. 2006. 208pp. 978-1-5697-0944-3.
Vol. 4. 2006. 232pp. 978-1-5697-0943-6.

Cafe Kichijouji de. Written by **Yuki Miyamoto**. Illustrated by **Kyoko Negishi**. Digital Manga Publishing. 2005–2006. O Japanese manga.

A "bishōnen" manga about five workers in a café and their manager. The volumes contain several individual stories instead of an extended storyline. The manga was first adapted into a best-selling audio performance and later into a live-action television series.

Vol. 1. 2005. 168pp. 978-1-5697-0949-8.
Vol. 2. 2006. 135pp. 978-1-5697-0948-1.
Vol. 3. 2006. 168pp. 978-1-5697-0947-4.

Death by Chocolate: Redux. Written and Illustrated by **David Yurkovich**. Top Shelf Productions, 2007. 120pp. 978-1-8918-3092-1. O

In a twist on "The Chocolate Touch," a candy store owner destroyed his town after being turned into chocolate and gaining the ability to turn things into

© Top Shelf.

chocolate as well. Now as "Agent Sweete" he works for the FBI's Food Crime Division.

Drops of God. Written by **Tadashi Agi**. Illustrated by **Shu Okimoto**. Vertical, Inc. 2011–2012. O Japanese manga.

Created by brother and sister Yuko and Shin Kibayashi under the name Tadashi Agi. Drops of God is about Kanzaki Shizuku, the son of a famous wine critic who now works for a beverage company. After his father's death he learn that in order to inherit his family fortune, he will be required to correctly identify 13 specific wines—the "Twelve Apostles" and the final bottle known as "The Drops of God." After publishing the first four volumes (covering the first two bottles), Vertical published the first "Drops of God" volume that skipped down to the seventh bottle. This was done by the request of the authors and it is not known if the missing stories will be translated.

Vol. 1: Les Gouttes de Dieu. 2011. 432pp. 978-1-9356-5427-8.
Vol. 2: Les Gouttes de Dieu. 2011. 416pp. 978-1-9356-5429-2.
Vol. 3: Les Gouttes de Dieu. 2012. 416pp. 978-1-9356-5436-0.
Vol. 4: The Second Apostle. 2012. 392pp. 978-1-9356-5439-1.
Drops of God: New World. 2012. 376pp. 978-1-9356-5452-0.

Feast of the Seven Fishes: The Collected Comic Strip and Italian Holiday Cookbook. Written by **Robert Tinnell** and **Shannon Tinnell**. Illustrated by **Alex Saviuk**, and **Ed Piskor**. Allegheny Image Factory, 2005. 96pp. 978-0-9769-2880-5. T

A collection of online comic strip dealing with popular Italian-American Christmas Eve tradition. The book includes recipes.

Food Wars! Shokugeki no Soma. Created by **Yuki Morisaki**. Written by **Yuto Tsukuda**. Illustrated by **Shun Saeki**. VIZ Media, 2014– . O Japanese manga. あ

SHOKUGEKI NO SOMA ©
2012 by Yuto Tsukuda, Shun
Saeki /SHUEISHA Inc.

Soma Yukihira's dream is to become a full-time chef in his father's neighborhood restaurant and to one day surpass his father's culinary skills. But just as Soma graduates from middle school, his father has to close his restaurant leaving Soma without a goal. Soma's father gives him a challenge: if he can attend an elite culinary school that is so difficult that only 10% of the students graduate. Meanwhile, Sōma meets many new students and culinary techniques that only help him toward his goal. The manga series is still ongoing in Japan. The manga was also adapted as a Japanese anime that debuted in 2015 in Japan.

Vol. 1. 2014. 208pp. 978-1-4215-7254-3.
Vol. 2. 2014. 200pp. 978-1-4215-7255-0.
Vol. 3. 2014. 200pp. 978-1-4215-7256-7.
Vol. 4. 2015. 192pp. 978-1-4215-7257-4.
Vol. 5. 2015. 192pp. 978-1-4215-7385-4.
Vol. 6. 2015. 192pp. 978-1-4215-7688-6.
Vol. 7. 2015. 200pp. 978-1-4215-7965-8.
Vol. 8. 2015. 208pp. 978-1-4215-7966-5.
Vol. 9. 2015. 192pp. 978-1-4215-8028-9.
Vol. 10. 2016. 192pp. 978-1-4215-8446-1.

Vol. 11. 2016. 192pp. 978-1-4215-8445-4.
Vol. 12. 2016. 192pp. 978-1-4215-8508-6.
Vol. 13. 2016. 192pp. 978-1-4215-8509-3.
Vol. 14. 2016. 192pp. 978-1-4215-8655-7.
Vol. 15. 2016. 200pp. 978-1-4215-8814-8.
Vol. 16. 2017. 192pp. 978-1-4215-9018-9.
Vol. 17. 2017. 192pp. 978-1-4215-9094-3.
Vol. 18. 2017. 192pp. 978-1-4215-9334-0.
Vol. 19. 2017. 192pp. 978-1-4215-9335-7.

Get Jiro. Written by **Anthony Bourdain** and **Joel Rose**. Illustrated by **Langdon Foss** and **Alé Garcia**. Vertigo/DC Comics, 2013–2015. M

Co-written by celebrity chef Bourdain, Get Jiro is set in a near future Los Angeles in which the city has been divided into different rings and power and control is divided into what kind of food you prepare, serve, and eat. Master Chefs control the territories. Into this world comes Jiro, a master of preparing sushi, and everyone wants him on their side. Blood and Sushi is a prequel telling how Jiro went from the son of a Yakuza-boss to what he is in book one.

Get Jiro. 2013. 160pp. 978-1-4012-2828-6.
Get Jiro: Blood and Sushi. 2015. 160pp. 978-1-4012-5226-7.

© DC Comics.

Iron Wok Jan. Written by **Shinji Saijyo**. Illustrated by **ComicsOne/DR Publishing**, 2005–2007. T Japanese manga.

At Gobancho, best Chinese restaurant in all of Tokyo, master chefs wowing customers with their signature dishes and succulent masterpieces, and Kiriko Gobancho, grand-daughter of the owner, is their most talented chef. When the arrogant but super-talented chef Jan Akiyama, grandson of Grandfather Gobancho's only real rival, is hired at Gobancho, Kiriko and Jan instantly become competitors and the fried rice flies. As they try to out-do each other with their soy sauce skills and prove who's the better prodigy in cooking competitions, Kiriko is determined to show Jan that even though he's talented and arrogant, she can talk the talk and wok the wok.

Vol. 1. 2005. 200pp. 978-1-58899-256-7.
Vol. 2. 2005. 200pp. 978-1-58899-257-4.
Vol. 3. 2005. 200pp. 978-1-58899-258-1.
Vol. 4. 2005. 200pp. 978-1-58899-259-8.
Vol. 5. 2005. 200pp. 978-1-58899-260-4.
Vol. 6. 2005. 200pp. 978-1-58899-261-1.
Vol. 7. 2005. 200pp. 978-1-58899-262-8.
Vol. 8. 2005. 200pp. 978-1-58899-263-5.
Vol. 9. 2005. 200pp. 978-1-58899-264-2.
Vol. 10. 2005. 200pp. 978-1-58899-000-6.
Vol. 11. 2005. 200pp. 978-1-58899-302-1.

Vol. 12. 2005. 200pp. 978-1-58899-303-8.
Vol. 13. 2005. 200pp. 978-1-59796-031-1.
Vol. 14. 2005. 200pp. 978-1-59796-032-8.
Vol. 15. 2006. 200pp. 978-1-59796-033-5.
Vol. 16. 2006. 200pp. 978-1-59796-034-2.
Vol. 17. 2006. 200pp. 978-1-59796-035-9.
Vol. 18. 2006. 200pp. 978-1-59796-036-6.
Vol. 19. 2006. 200pp. 978-1-59796-037-3.
Vol. 20. 2006. 200pp. 978-1-59796-038-0.
Vol. 21. 2006. 200pp. 978-1-59796-039-7.
Vol. 22. 2007. 200pp. 978-1-59796-040-3.

*Vol.23.*2007.200pp.978-1-59796-119-6.   *Vol. 26.* 2007. 200pp. 978-1-59796-049-6.
*Vol.24.*2007.200pp.978-1-59796-042-7.   *Vol. 27.* 2008. 200pp. 978-1-59796-050-2.
*Vol.25.*2007.200pp.978-1-59796-048-9.

Kitchen Princess Omnibus. Written by **Miyuki Kobayashi**. Illustrated by **Natsumi Ando**. Kondansha Comics, 2012–2013. T Japanese manga.

In this shojo manga, 13-year-old Najika Kazami hopes to become a chef someday. She also pines for her "flan prince," the mysterious boy who saved her from drowning when she was younger. This leads her to Seika Academy thanks to a clue that he left behind. Del Rey originally published Kitchen Princess as a 10-volume collection from 2007 to 2009 and that has been recollected into the four omnibus editions. Kitchen Princess was the winner of the Kodansha Manga Award for children's manga.

Vol. 1. 2012. 400pp. 978-1-9354-29449.
Vol. 2. 2012. 384pp. 978-1-9354-29456.
Vol. 3. 2013. 576pp. 978-1-6126-20640.
Vol. 4. 2013. 576pp. 978-1-6126-20657.

Mixed Vegetables. Written and Illustrated by **Ayumi Komura**. VIZ Media, 2008–2010. T Japanese manga.

A romantic comedy about two teenagers—Hanayu Ashitaba, the daughter of a famous pastry chef who herself wants to be a sushi chef and Hayato Hyuga, the son of a famous sushi chef who wants to become a pastry chef.

Vol. 1. 2008. 208pp. 978-1-4215-1967-8.   *Vol. 5*. 2009. 200pp. 978-1-4215-1971-5.
Vol. 2. 2008. 210pp. 978-1-4215-1968-5.   *Vol. 6*. 2009. 192pp. 978-1-4215-1982-1.
Vol. 3. 2009. 200pp. 978-1-4215-1969-2.   *Vol. 7*. 2010. 200pp. 978-1-4215-3199-1.
Vol. 4. 2009. 200pp. 978-1-4215-1970-8.   *Vol. 8*. 2010. 208pp. 978-1-4215-3235-6.

Not Love, but Delicious Foods Make Me so Happy. Written and Illustrated by **Fumi Yoshinaga**. Yen Press, 2010. 160pp. 978-0-7595-3187-1. O Japanese manga

A one-shot manga in which manga-ka Y-naga (most likely a stand-in for the author) goes out to restaurants with her friends. Each of the 15 stories is set a different location with the types of food including Korean, French, and Italian as well as local fare.

Nutmeg. Written by **James F. Wright**. Illustrated by **Jackie Crofts**. Action Labs, 2015– . T

Set in the 1960s, two junior high girls Poppy and Cassia hatch a plan to take down one of the mean girls at school—a girl named Saffron. Unintentionally, the girls build a criminal empire as the Patty Cakes and become known for their irresistible brownies. Will Poppy's addition to her own brownies crumble their criminal empire?

Vol. 1: Early Fall: Taste Buddies. 2015. 96pp. 978-1-63229-105-9.
Vol. 2: Late Fall: Brownie Points. 2015. 96pp. 978-1-63229-123-3.
Vol. 3: Early Winter: Femme Brûlée. 2016. 96pp. 978-1-63229-153-0.

Oishinbo a la Carte. Written by **Tetsu Kariya**. Illustrated by **Akira Hanasaki**. VIZ Media, 2009– . T Japanese manga. あ

OISHINBO A LA CARTE © 2005 Tetsu KARIYA, Akira HANASA- KI/SHOGAKUKAN.

Oishinbo is taken by combining the Japanese words for "delicious" and "someone who loves to eat/" the manga is about Shirō Yama-oka, a culinary journalist. The manga ran in Japan from 1983 to 2008 and again from 2009 to 2014 before going on hiatus. Over 100 volumes were collected in Japan, with those titles listed below representing just a random sample. The series won an award in Japan and was adapted into an anime series.

Vol. 1: Japanese Cuisine. 2009. 272pp. 978-1-4215-2139-8.
Vol. 2: Sake. 2009. 272pp. 978-1-4215-2140-4.
Vol. 3: Ramen and Gyoza. 2009. 272pp. 978-1-4215-2141-1.
Vol. 4: Fish, Sushi, and Sashimi. 2009. 276pp. 978-1-4215-2142-8.
Vol. 5: Vegetables. 2009. 268pp. 978-1-4215-2143-5.
Vol. 6: The Joy of Rice. 2009. 268pp. 978-1-4215-2144-2.
Vol. 7: Pub Food. 2010. 276pp. 978-1-4215-2145-9.

Over Easy. Written and Illustrated by **Mimi Pond.** Drawn and Quarterly, 2014. 272pp. 978-1-77046-153-6, hardcover. M

© Mimi Pond and Drawn & Quarterly.

Inspired by her own life, Pond shows the life of Margaret, an artist working in a diner in late 1970s, and the interesting characters who work there with her.

Ristorante Paradiso. Written and Illustrated by **Natsume Ono**. VIZ Media, 2010–2011. O Japanese manga.

The lives of the workers in Rome restaurant are shown in these manga. The original was just one volume but it has been followed up by a three volume series. An animated TV series based on the manga aired in Japan in 2009.

Ristorante Paradiso. 2010. 176pp. 978-1-4215-3250-9.
Gente: The People of Ristorante Paradiso. 2010–2011.
    Vol. 1. 2010. 176pp. 978-1-4215-3251-6.
    Vol. 2. 2010. 200pp. 978-1-4215-3252-3.
    Vol. 3. 2011. 200pp. 978-1-4215-3480-0.

Seconds: A Graphic Novel. Written and Illustrated by **Bryan Lee O'Malley**. Ballantine Books, 2014. 336pp. 978-0-345-52937-4, hardcover. O 🏃 ◎

Katie has a good life as the owner and chef of a restaurant. She's got big plans to open up a second restaurant—but then all of a sudden things go from good to worse: her fling with another chef falls apart, her ex-boyfriend comes back into her life, the construction on the second restaurant is getting bogged down, and she's working even harder when one of her best waitresses gets injured. Katie needs a second chance and gets just that when she is visited by a mysterious girl who gives her a grove of magical mushrooms with the power to redo a mistake. When she takes one, it works like a charm and she's back in the game. But with a dresser drawer with more mushrooms, what else can she fix to turn her life from good to great? The book was recognized by YALSA as a Great Graphic Novel for Teens on its 2015 selection list.

Space Battle Lunchtime. Written and Illustrated by **Natalie Riess**. Oni Press, 2016–2017. Y 🏆 ◎

Penny is a coffee shop worker and loved to bake desserts in her spare time. When an alien comes to her coffee shop, she's recruited to be a guest contestant in an outer space cooking show called *Space Battle Lunchtime*. Now she's millions of miles away from home surrounded by weird aliens, food she doesn't know how to prepare, and cutthroat competitors. Does Penny have what it takes to be in finalist? The first volume was recognized by YALSA's Great Graphic Novels for Teens selection list in 2017.

Vol. 1: Lights, Cameras, Snacktion!. 2016. 120pp. 978-1-62010-313-5.
Vol. 2: A Recipe for Disaster. 2017. 120pp. 978-1-62010-404-0.

Toriko. Written and Illustrated by **Mitsutoshi Shimabukuro**. VIZ Media, 2010– . T Japanese manga. あ 🖵

Still ongoing as of 2017, Toriko is about its titular character a "Gourmet Hunter" who travels the world looking for the rarest of foods in order to create his ideal full course meal. The series is set on a planet divided into the Human World and the mostly inhospitable Gourmet World, and the Gourmet Hunters have special abilities to help them survive during their quests. There have been both anime films and television shows.

Vol. 1: Gourmet Hunter Toriko!! 2010. 200pp. 978-1-4215-3509-8.
Vol. 2: Coco!! 2010. 200pp. 978-1-4215-3510-4.
Vol. 3: The Thing!! 2010. 200pp. 978-1-4215-3511-1.
Vol. 4: Sunny!! 2011. 200pp. 978-1-4215-3512-8.
Vol. 5: The Regal Plateau!! 2011. 200pp. 978-1-4215-3693-4.
Vol. 6: Ten-Fold!! 2011. 200pp. 978-1-4215-3694-1.
Vol. 7: Jewel of the Jungle!! 2011. 200pp. 978-1-4215-3798-6.
Vol. 8: Century Soup!! 2012. 200pp. 978-1-4215-3903-4.
Vol. 9: Battle below Freezing!! 2012. 200pp. 978-1-4215-4065-8.
Vol. 10: Wild Fight!! 2012. 200pp. 978-1-4215-4273-7.
Vol. 11: Race to Recovery!! 2012. 200pp. 978-1-4215-4308-6.
Vol. 12: Vegetable Sky!! 2012. 200pp. 978-1-4215-4309-3.
Vol. 13: Deadly Gourmet World. 2012. 200pp. 978-1-4215-4310-9.
Vol. 14: The "Real" Melk. 2013. 200pp. 978-1-4215-4311-6.
Vol. 15: Zebra!! 2013. 200pp. 978-1-4215-4312-3.
Vol. 16: Reunion with Terror!! 2013. 200pp. 978-1-4215-5149-4.
Vol. 17: Shining Gourami!! 2013. 200pp. 978-1-4215-5150-0.
Vol. 18: Gourmet Casino!! 2013. 200pp. 978-1-4215-5151-7.

Vol. 19: Gourmet Tasting!! 2013. 200pp. 978-1-4215-5152-4.

Vol. 20: Ichiryu and Midora!! 2014. 200pp. 978-1-4215-5369-6.

Vol. 21: Showdown at Chowlin Temple!! 2014. 200pp. 978-1-4215-5615-4.

Vol. 22: Four-Beasts!! 2014. 200pp. 978-1-4215-6481-4.

Vol. 23: Meal Fit for a King!! 2014. 200pp. 978-1-4215-6482-1.

Vol. 24: The Cooking Festival Begins!! 2014. 200pp. 978-1-4215-6483-8.

Vol. 25: Gourmet Corp. Invasion!! 2014. 200pp. 978-1-4215-6779-2.

Vol. 26: Beyond the Limit!! 2015. 200pp. 978-1-4215-7346-5.

Vol. 27: Hidden Strength!! 2015. 200pp. 978-1-4215-7345-8.

Vol. 28: The Tiger's Tale!! 2015. 200pp. 978-1-4215-7691-6.

Vol. 29: World's Greatest Gourmet Hunter!! 2015. 200pp. 978-1-4215-7782-1.

Vol. 30: Onward to the Gourmet World!! 2015. 200pp. 978-1-4215-7912-2.

Vol. 31: Hex Food World!! 2015. 200pp. 978-1-4215-8031-9.

Vol. 32: Vs. Heracles!! 2016. 200pp. 978-1-4215-8266-5.

Vol. 33: Onward to Area 7!! 2016. 200pp. 978-1-4215-8266-5.

Vol. 34: King at Play!! 2016. 200pp. 978-1-4215-8517-8.

Vol. 35: Macaque I Have This Dance!! 2016. 200pp. 978-1-4215-8642-7.

Vol. 36: Deployment!! 2016. 200pp. 978-1-4215-8705-9.

Vol. 37: Signs of Life!! 2017. 208pp. 978-1-4215-9021-9.

Vol. 38: To the Back Channel!! 2017. 200pp. 978-1-4215-9121-6.

What Did You Eat Yesterday? Written and Illustrated by **Fumi Yoshinaga**. Vertical, Inc. 2014– . M Japanese manga.

Shiro Kakei is a lawyer living with his boyfriend, salon stylist Kenji Yabuki. Their days are stressful but sitting together with Shiro's made-from-scratch meals give them a chance to relax and talk. The series was nominated for the first Manga Taisho Award and received a jury recommendation at the 13th Japan Media Arts Festival Awards. As of 2016 it is still ongoing.

Vol. 1. 2014. 200pp. 978-1-93913-038-9.

Vol. 2. 2014. 200pp. 978-1-93913-039-6.

Vol. 3. 2014. 200pp. 978-1-93913-040-2.

Vol. 4. 2014. 152pp. 978-1-93913-079-2.

Vol. 5. 2014. 172pp. 978-1-93913-080-8.

Vol. 6. 2015. 172pp. 978-1-93913-081-5.

Vol. 7. 2015. 160pp. 978-1-94122-022-1.

Vol. 8. 2015. 160pp. 978-1-94122-023-8.

Vol. 9. 2015. 180pp. 978-1-94122-050-4.

Vol. 10. 2016.160pp. 978-1-94299-324-7.

Vol. 11. 2016. 160pp. 978-1-94299-375-9.

Vol. 12. 2017. 160pp. 978-1-945054-25-9.

Wonton Soup: The Collected Edition. Written and Illustrated by **James Stokoe**. Oni Press, 2014. 224pp. 978-1-6201-0166-7. O

Johnny Boyo left cooking school to become an intergalactic space trucker, but he's still into cooking, using strange alien ingredients to make the food even better. This collection includes the two volumes originally published in 2007 and 2009.

© James Stokoe.

Yakitate!! Japan. Written and Illustrated by **Takashi Hashiguchi**. VIZ Media, 2006–2011. O Japanese manga. あ

A comedy manga in which young Kazuma Azuma wants to create "Ja-pan" a national bread for Japan. Among his skills is the possession of "Solar Hands," warmer than normal hands, which allows the yeast to ferment both faster and better. Other characters are Azuma's co-workers at the bread-making chain Pantasia. It spawned an animated television series.

Vol. 1. 2006. 978-1-4215-0719-4.	*Vol. 14*. 2008. 978-1-4215-1709-4.
Vol. 2. 2006. 978-1-4215-0720-0.	*Vol. 15*. 2009. 978-1-4215-1710-0.
Vol. 3. 2007. 978-1-4215-0721-7.	*Vol. 16*. 2009. 978-1-4215-2233-3.
Vol. 4. 2007. 978-1-4215-0921-1.	*Vol. 17*. 2009. 978-1-4215-2234-0.
Vol. 5. 2007. 978-1-4215-0922-8.	*Vol. 18*. 2009. 978-1-4215-2235-7.
Vol. 6. 2007. 978-1-4215-0923-5.	*Vol. 19*. 2009. 978-1-4215-2236-4.
Vol. 7. 2007. 978-1-4215-0924-2.	*Vol. 20*. 2009. 978-1-4215-2237-1.
Vol. 8. 2007. 978-1-4215-0925-9.	*Vol. 21*. 2010. 978-1-4215-2903-5.
Vol. 9. 2008. 978-1-4215-1457-4.	*Vol. 22*. 2010. 978-1-4215-2904-2.
Vol. 10. 2008. 978-1-4215-1705-6.	*Vol. 23*. 2010. 978-1-4215-2905-9.
Vol. 11. 2008. 978-1-4215-1706-3.	*Vol. 24*. 2010. 978-1-4215-2906-6.
Vol. 12. 2008. 978-1-4215-1706-3.	*Vol. 25*. 2011. 978-1-4215-2907-3.
Vol. 13. 2008. 978-1-4215-1708-7.	*Vol. 26*. 2011. 978-1-4215-2908-0.

Non-Fiction Food Titles

A selection of non-fiction graphic novels that also focus on foods and recipes.

The Big Skinny: How I Changed My Fattitude. Written and Illustrated by **Carol Lay**. Villard, 2008. 208pp. 978-0-3455-0404-3. O

In this graphic memoir, cartoonist Lay tells of how she finally lost weight and kept it off after years of trying.

Cook Korean!: A Comic Book with Recipes. Written and Illustrated by **Robin Ha**. Ten Speed Press, 2016. 176pp. 978-1-60774-887-8. O

Want to learn how to cook Korean but don't know where to start? Follow Robin Ha's illustrated instructions and learn how to cook Korean staples such as kimchi, soy garlic beef over rice, braised beef in white sauce, seaweed salad, and more. The book was recognized in 2016 on NPR's Best Books list.

Dirt Candy: A Cookbook: Flavor-Forward Food from the Upstart New York City Vegetarian Restaurant. Written by **Amanda Cohen** and **Grady Hendrix**. Illustrated by **Ryan Dunlavey**. Clarkson Potter 2012. 224pp. 978-0-3079-5217-2. T

Amanda Cohen is the real-life owner and Head Chef of the New York City vegetarian restaurant Dirt Candy. This original graphic novel acts as both a cookbook (with an index) and the story of how Cohen opened her restaurant.

The Manga Cookbook: Japanese Bento Boxes, Main Dishes and More! Written by **The Manga University Culinary Institute**. Illustrated by **Chihiro Hattori**. Japanime Co. Ltd. 2007. 158pp. 978-4-9212-0507-2. T Japanese manga.

This illustrated guide to provides step-by-step instructions to cooking various Japanese foods using common ingredients. Besides the foods, the books also show how to assemble bento boxed lunches and even how to use chopsticks.

Relish: My Life in the Kitchen. Written and Illustrated by **Lucy Knisley**. First Second Books. 2013. 176pp. 978-1-59643-623-7. O

For Lucy memories are recollected by taste and smell. All of her life's important moments have been linked with food. The different chapters in the book are each their own memory and how food played an important role, accompanied by a corresponding recipe. Memories like going to a foreign country, growing up in New York City, later living in the country, and going to college are all enhanced by what was on her plate. The non-fiction book was recognized by YALSA on its Great Graphic Novels for Teens selection list in 2014.

© Lucy Knisley and First Second.

Historical Fiction

Stories in which the setting is based in the past, but is based on true history from our past. The listings below include adaptations of classic works of literature originally written centuries ago as well as recently written historical fiction.

Around the World. Written and Illustrated by **Matt Phelan**. Candlewick Press, 2011. 240pp. 978-0-7636-3619-7. Y

At the end of the 19th century, when Jules Verne wrote the book "Around the World in 80 Days" the public was starved for true tales of adventure. Many rose to the challenge, but three remarkable true tales of those who dreamt of travelling around the world and succeeded: Thomas Stevens, who made the journey by bicycle; Nellie Bly, a reporter who raced around the world; and Joshua Slocum, a captain who became the first person to sail around the world alone.

© 2011 by Matt Phelan. Reproduced by permission of the publisher, Candlewick Press, Somerville, MA.

Berlin. Written and Illustrated by **Jason Lutes**. Drawn and Quarterly, 2000– . O ◎

A poignant look at pre–World War II Germany and the citizens who helped to shape and define the struggle that the Weimar Republic faced following the reconstruction after World War I. As the shadow of the Third Reich rises from the ashes of a devastated Germany, the citizens struggle to find their voice in a country plagued by poverty and sadness. Seen through the eyes of the many citizens from the famed yet impoverished city of Berlin, college students, shipyard workers, cabaret singers, and more struggle with the harsh realities of life and love amidst the ever-growing powder keg of political uprising of a 1928 Germany and the tumultuous years afterward. The series is still ongoing with a planned third volume to be released.

Book 1: City of Stones. 2000. 212pp. 978-1-896597-29-4.
Book 2: City of Smoke. 2008. 200pp. 978-1-897299-53-1.

Bluffton: ***My Summers with Buster Keaton***. Written and Illustrated by **Matt Phelan**. Candlewick Press, 2013. 240pp. 978-0-7636-5079-7, hardcover. Y ◎

Set in 1908, the sleepy town of Muskegon, Michigan that Henry lives in is visited by a travelling circus. The troupe is staying all summer in Bluffton, so for the whole summer elephants, jugglers, trapeze artists and more are relaxing nearby. Henry also meets a boy his age who is part of the troupe—an "indestructible" boy named Buster Keaton. Henry wants to learn how to take a fall like Buster does, but Buster just wants to play baseball and hang out with the kids his own age. A beautiful look at a bygone era.

© 2013 by Matt Phelan. Reproduced by permission of the publisher, Candlewick Press, Somerville, MA.

The Borgias. Written by **Alejandro Jodorowsky**. Illustrated by **Milo Manara**. Dark Horse Comics, 2014. 216pp. 978-1-61655-542-9, hardcover. M

A collection of the four semi-fictionalized graphic albums about Rodrigo Borgia (aka Pope Alexander VI) and his family from noted writer and filmmaker Jodorowsky and Italian artist Manara. Murder, plots, sex, violence, and more in this beautiful but very graphic and adult work.

A Bride's Story. Written and Illustrated by **Kaoru Mori**. Yen Press, 2011–2016. T 🎎 Japanese manga.

The lives of a rural town alongside the Caspian Sea in Turkic Central Asia is portrayed lovingly in this slice-of-life historical fiction. Set in the 19th century alongside the Silk Road, a 20-year-old bride-to-be, Amir Halgal, leaves her home to be wedded to Karluk Eihon—a boy 12 years younger than herself. The series focuses on the courtship and wedding of the two, as well as the loves and lives of the other villagers that the Eihon family resides in. The series was recognized by YALSA in 2012 as a Great Graphic Novel for Teens series.

Vol. 1. 2011. 192pp. 978-0-316-18099-3, hardcover.
Vol. 2. 2011. 192pp. 978-0-316-19446-4, hardcover.
Vol. 3. 2012. 208pp. 978-0-316-21034-8, hardcover.

© 2016 Yen Press and Kaoru Mori.

Vol. 4. 2013. 192pp. 978-0-316-23203-6, hardcover.
Vol. 5. 2013. 208pp. 978-0-316-24309-4, hardcover.
Vol. 6. 2014. 196pp. 978-0-316-33610-9, hardcover.
Vol. 7. 2015. 192pp. 978-0-316-34893-5, hardcover.
Vol. 8. 2016. 192pp. 978-0-316-31762-7, hardcover.

The Color Trilogy. Written and Illustrated by **Kim Dong Hwa**. First Second, 2009. O 🏆 Korean manhwa.

© 2016 First Second and Kim Dong Hwa.

The gentle love between a mother and daughter as the daughter grows into adulthood against the backdrop of traditional Korean society. Young teenager, Ehwa, lives with her widowed mother. Each book focuses on a different span in Ehwa's life as she learns about love, her blossoming sexuality, and grows into womanhood. The series was recognized by YALSA's Great Graphic Novels for Teens selection list in 2010.

Color of Earth. 2009. 320pp. 978-1-59643-458-5.
Color of Heaven. 2009. 320pp. 978-1-59643-460-8.
Color of Water. 2009. 320pp. 978-1-59643-459-2.

Emma. Written by **Jane Austen**. Adapted by **Nancy Butler**. Illustrated by **Janet Lee**. Marvel Comics, 2011. 120pp. 978-0-7851-5685-7, hardcover. T

© 2016 Marvel Comics.

The adaptation of the perennially popular novel by Jane Austen about 20-year-old Emma Woodhouse, the highly intelligent, spoiled, and wealthy young woman of society. Will Emma find "perfect happiness" with someone finally? Highly regarded since the novel debuted in 1815, the book is a smartly written novel about youthful hubris and the perils of misconstrued romance.

Emma. Written and Illustrated by **Kaoru Mori**. Yen Press, 2015–2016. T 🏆 Japanese manga.

© 2016 Yen Press.

A Victorian period romance, the series focuses on Emma, a poor Yorkshire girl who after being kidnapped and sold into a brothel, escapes and then becomes a maid to an elderly woman who helps her to better herself. After serving as a maid under a new family, Emma falls in love with William Jones, a member of gentry and outside of Emma's social class. The series was originally published by DC Comics' CMX imprint where it was recognized by YALSA as a Great Graphic Novel for Teens series in 2008.

Vol. 1. 2015. 388pp. 978-0-316-30223-4, hardcover.
Vol. 2. 2015. 380pp. 978-0-316-30444-3, hardcover.
Vol. 3. 2015. 368pp. 978-0-316-30445-0, hardcover.

Vol. 4. 2016. 480pp. 978-0-316-30446-7, hardcover.
Vol. 5. 2016. 384pp. 978-0-316-30447-4, hardcover.

Gaijin: American Prisoner of War. Written and Illustrated by **Matt Faulkner**. Disney-Hyperion Books, 2014. 144pp. 978-1-4231-3735-1, hardcover. T ◎

Set during the beginning days of World War II, a Japanese bi-racial family learns of the cruelty of racial bias in San Francisco. After the bombing of Pearl Harbor, no one trusts Americans who are Japanese. Koji Miyamoto, a boy whose father is Japanese, learns of oppression first hand and he experiences what it's like to be persecuted, ignored, and ultimately humiliated as he and his mother are forced to go to a relocation center for Japanese Americans. Ignored for being half-white in San Francisco, it's not any easier to be considered half-Japanese in a prison camp where you're a prisoner of war in your own country.

Habibi. Written and Illustrated by **Craig Thompson**. Pantheon/Random House, 2011. 672pp. 978-0-375-42414-4, hardcover. M 🏆 ◎

Set in an unnamed country in the Middle East, the story focuses on Dodola and Zam, two refugees from an Arab slave trade. After living nine years together, Dodola is kidnapped into the harem of the sultan, and Zam must fend for himself in the streets. Both of them undergo their own trials and tribulations in a complex world full of greed, prejudice, lust, and fear. Can their still ever-present longing for each other survive in a climate where freedom is a fragile dream? Craig Thompson received an Eisner Award in 2012 for Best Writer/Artist for *Habibi*.

Hidden: A Child's Story of the Holocaust. Written by **Loic Dauviller**. Illustrated by **Marc Lizano**. First Second, 2015. 80pp. 978-1-59643-873-6, hardcover. Y ◎

A touching look at a difficult subject. A grandmother named Dounia tells her granddaughter Elsa a reason for her sadness and she tells her the tale when she was a child in 1942 Nazi occupied Paris. The story is a view of a child's experience knowing persecution for the first time and dealing with the horrible atrocities of the Nazis at such a young age.

King Lear. Written by **William Shakespeare**. Adapted and Illustrated by **Gareth Hinds**. Candlewick Press, 2009. 978-0-7636-4343-0, hardcover; 978-0-7636-4344-7. T

Adaptation of the classic tragedy by William Shakespeare. An old King slowly descends into madness as he banishes his favorite of his three daughters and the professed loyalty of his two remaining daughters, false in love, proves to undo them all.

© 2007 by Gareth Hinds. Reproduced by permission of the publisher, Candlewick Press, Somerville, MA.

Macbeth. Written by **William Shakespeare**. Adapted and Illustrated by **Gareth Hinds**. Candlewick Press, 2015. 152pp. 978-0-7636-6943-0, hardcover; 978-0-7636-7802-9. T

The adaptation of the classic William Shakespeare play. After three witches prophesize that a general in the king's army would be the future King of Scotland, Macbeth and Lady Macbeth take matters into their own hand and usurp the throne through violence and treachery.

Manga Classics: Emma. Written by **Jane Austen**. Adapted by **Crystal Chan**. Illustrated by **Po Tse**. UDON Entertainment, 2015. 308pp. 978-1-927925-36-2, hardcover; 978-1-927925-35-5. T Japanese manga.

An adaptation of the classic 1815 Jane Austen novel as Emma Woodhouse, a young 20-something woman who enjoys her comfortable life and her matchmaking skills may have finally met her match with her friend George Knightley.

© UDON Entertainment.

Manga Classics: Great Expectations. Written by **Charles Dickens**. Adapted by **Crystal Chan**. Illustrated by **Nokman Poon**. UDON Entertainment, 2015. 308pp. 978-1-9279-2532-4, hardcover; 978-1-927925-31-7. T Japanese manga.

Adaptation of the classic rages-to-riches tale by Charles Dickens. Join the unforgettable characters of Pip, Miss Haversham, Estella, Abel Magwitch and more in one of Dicken's classic novels with an added manga twist.

Manga Classics: Les Miserables. Written by **Victor Hugo**. Adapted by **Crystal Chan**. Illustrated by **TseMei Lee**. UDON Entertainment, 2014. 336pp. 978-1-927925-15-7, hardcover; 978-1-927925-16-4. T Japanese manga.

An adaptation of Victor Hugo's classic French novel. Written in 1862, the novel is a sprawling epic look at a span of time in French history from 1815 to 1832 culminating

© UDON Entertainment.

with the June Revolution in Paris. Intermixed with a wide range of characters and social classes, the main protagonist is Jean Valjean, an ex-convict who seeks his on redemption in a turbulent time.

Manga Classics: Pride and Prejudice. Written by **Jane Austen**. Adapted by **Stacy King**. Illustrated by **Po Tse**. UDON Entertainment, 2014. 376pp. 978-1-927925-17-1, hardcover; 978-1-927925-18-8. T Japanese manga.

Set in England the 19th century, the lives of the five Mr. and Mrs. Bennett's unmarried daughters are forever changed when the rich and eligible bachelor Mr. Bingly and his friend Mr. Darcy come to town.

© UDON Entertainment.

Manga Classics: The Scarlet Letter. Written by **Nathaniel Hawthorne**. Adapted by **Crystal Chan**. Illustrated by **SunKeno Lee**. UDON Entertainment, 2015. 308pp. 978-1-927925-34-8, hardcover; 978-1-927925-33-1. T Japanese manga. ◎

An adaptation of the original 1850 novel. Set in the 17th century in Puritan Boston, Massachusetts, Hester Prynne has a daughter through an affair and though she is mocked and shamed, seeks to reclaim her dignity in an unforgiving society.

© UDON Entertainment.

Manga Classics: Sense & Sensibility. Written by **Jane Austen**. Adapted by **Stacy King**. Illustrated by **Po Tse**. UDON Entertainment, 2016. 308pp. 978-1-927925-62-1, hardcover; 978-1-927925-63-8. O 🐾 Japanese manga ◎

An adaptation of the 1811 novel by writer Jane Austen. Set in southwest England, Elinor and Marianne Dashwood, two daughters without means after their father dies and they are spurned by their half-brother's family, must endure hardships and heartbreak before ultimately finding true love. The manga adaptation was recognized by YALSA's Great Graphic Novels for Teens selection list in 2017.

Marathon. Written by **Boaz Yakin**. Illustrated by **Joe Infurnari**. First Second Books, 2012. 192pp. 978-1-59643-680-0. T

In 490 BC, a warrior named Eucles must run from Athens to Sparta and back again in order to fend off an invasion by the Persian emperor Darius. Eucles is charged with running there and back to Athens to alert the city of the Athenian army's victory over the Persians. Though the Athenians were outnumbered, they were still able to persevere. Witness the grueling 300-mile journey that Eucles ran to save his city and forever made the run a source of inspiration to runners worldwide.

© First Second and Boaz Yakin.

Moving Pictures. Written by **Kathryn Immonen**. Illustrated by **Stuart Immonen**. Top Shelf Productions, 2010. 144pp. 978-1-60309-049-0. M

The plight of a museum curator in France during the occupation of Nazi Germany and priceless collection she rescues from the country's occupiers. In charge of a minor part of the collection, Ira Gardner learns how to slowly prevent the theft of her country's treasures by having the art stored in the basement of her museum's poorly documented basement.

© Top Shelf Productions and
Kathryn & Stuart Immonen.

Northanger Abbey. Written by **Jane Austen**. Adapted by **Nancy Butler**. Illustrated by **Janet Lee**. Marvel Comics, 2013. 112pp. 978-0-7851-6440-1. O

Adapted from the original 1817 novel by Jane Austen. Seventeen-year-old Catherine Morland loves to read Gothic romance novels, but can real life be as romantic as the books she reads? When she meets both Henry Tilney, a 26-year-old clergyman, she may have found her match, but can a girl who lives more in fiction than in reality find true love?

Pride and Prejudice. Written by **Jane Austen**. Adapted by **Nancy Butler**. Illustrated by **Hugo Petrus**. Marvel Comics, 2009. 120pp. 978-0-7851-3915-7, hardcover. O

An adaptation of one of the most beloved novels in English literature. Originally published in 1813, the book focuses on Elizabeth Bennett, the second of five daughters of a country gentleman. Set in England in the early 19th century, Elizabeth's mother is trying to find suitable husbands for all of her daughters. When two young men of prominence come to Netherfield Park in the neighborhood, a Mr. Bingley and

© Marvel Comics.

Mr. Darcy, Mr. Bingley takes a liking to Elizabeth's older sister Jane. Meanwhile, Mr. Darcy and Elizabeth are at odds with each other. Will time and an openness for Elizabeth to forgive her past prejudices find her true love?

Romeo and Juliet. Written by **William Shakespeare**. Adapted and Illustrated by **Gareth Hinds**. Candlewick Press, 2013. 128pp. 978-0-7636-5948-6, hardcover; 978-0-7636-6807-5. T

An adaptation of the classic tragedy by William Shakespeare when two star-crossed lovers from two warring families come together.

Sense & Sensibility. Written by **Jane Austen**. Adapted by **Nancy Butler**. Illustrated by **Sonny Liew**. Marvel Comics, 2010. 128pp. 978-0-7851-4819-7, hardcover. O

© Marvel Comics.

An adaptation of the 1811 novel by writer Jane Austen. Set in southwest England, Elinor and Marianne Dashwood, two daughters without means after their father dies and they are spurned by their half-brother's family, must endure hardships, heartbreak before ultimately finding true love.

Storm in the Barn. Written and Illustrated by **Matt Phelan**. Candlewick Press, 2009–2011. 208pp. 978-0-7636-3618-0, hardcover; 978-0-7636-5290-6. Y ◉

© 2009 by Matt Phelan. Reproduced by permission of the publisher, Candlewick Press, Somerville, MA.

Set in Kansas in 1937 during the Dust Bowl, and 11-year-old Zack can't help his dad with the harvest and being bullied by other his age has made him feel more useless than ever before. The stories of plentiful crops and rain seems almost like a fairy tale. To pass the time he listens to tall tales and stories about a mythical Jack who confronts the King of the West Wind, the King of Blizzards, and the King of the Northeast Winds. That's well and good, but just tall tales—but when Jack discovers that the true Storm King has been hiding in an abandoned barn and holding back the rain, Jack must find the strength inside him to find his own voice and try to rescue his—and his town's—future. The book received the 2010 Scott O'Dell Award for Historical Fiction.

Tom Sawyer. Written by **Mark Twain**. Adapted by **Tim Mucci**. Illustrated by **Rad Sechrist**. All-Action Comics/Sterling Children's Publishing, 2008. T

There's no one this side of the Mississippi River other than Tom Sawyer who likes to get into trouble—except maybe his best friend Huckleberry Finn. Driving his poor Aunt Polly crazy, instead of going to school and doing his chores, Tom would rather love to going pole fishing, swimming, or hunting for buried treasure. Adapted from the 1876 novel by Mark Twain.

Short Stories and Anthologies

A collection of general titles featuring a variety of works by many writers and illustrators. The anthology stories include tales of true love, adventure, humor, horror, and many other genres and showcase a wide variety of talent in the comic book industry.

24Seven. Written and Illustrated by various. Image Comics, 2006–2007. O

An anthology collection featuring some of the best writers and artists in the industry including Phil Hester, Adam Hughes, Jim Mahfood, Tony Moore, Mike Oeming, Eduardo Risso, Gene Ha, and many more. The stories run the gamut of genres from romance, horror, comedy, science fiction, and more.

Vol. 1. 2006. 200pp. 978-1-58240-636-7.
Vol. 2. 2007. 240pp. 978-1-58240-846-0.

Abandon the Old in Tokyo. Written and Illustrated by **Yoshihiro Tatsumi**. Drawn and Quarterly, 2012. 224pp. 978-1-77046-077-5. O Japanese manga.

This is a collection of short stories about the lives of young men in modern Japan. These stories have dark undertones of modern society and the new culture of keeping up with the times, impersonalization of society, of the quick abandonment and rejection within this civilization. Not all the tales are hopeless but can be read as a warning and even a message of hope like that in the short *Eel*. People learn to adapt to the world around them.

The Best American Comics. Edited by various. Written and Illustrated by various. Houghton Mifflin Harcourt, 2006– . M

2006. Edited by **Anne Elizabeth Moore** and **Harvey Pekar**. 320pp. 978-0-618-71874-0, hardcover.

2007. Edited by **Anne Elizabeth Moore** and **Chris Ware**. 368pp. 978-0-618-71876-4, hardcover.

2008. Edited by **Linda Barry, Jessica Abel,** and **Matt Madden**. 352pp. 978-0-618-98976-8, hardcover.

2009. Edited by **Charles Burns, Jessica Abel,** and **Matt Madden**. 352pp. 978-0-618-98965-2, hardcover.

2010. Edited by **Neil Gaiman, Jessica Abel**, and **Matt Madden**. 352pp. 978-0-547-24177-7, hardcover.

2011. Edited by **Jessica Abel** and **Matt Madden**. 332pp. 978-0-547-33362-5, hardcover.

2012. Edited by **Françoise Mouly, Jessica Abel**, and **Matt Madden**. 352pp. 978-0-547-69112-1, hardcover.

2013. Edited by **Jeff Smith**, **Jessica Abel**, and **Matt Madden**. 400pp. 978-0-547-99546-5, hardcover.

2014. Edited by **Scott McCloud** and **Bill Kartalopoulos**. 400pp. 978-0-544-10600-0, hardcover.

2015. Edited by **Jonathan Lethem** and **Bill Kartalopoulos**. 400pp. 978-0-544-10770-0, hardcover.

2016. Edited by **Roz Chast** and **Bill Kartalopoulos**. 352pp. 978-0-544-75035-7, hardcover.

2017. Edited by **Ben Katchor** and **Bill Kartalopoulos.** 352pp. 978-0-544-75036-4.

The Antler Boy and Other Stories. Written and Illustrated by **Jake Parker**. Jake Parker Productions, 2012. 152pp. 978-0-615-69710-9. Y

An anthology of short stories created by Missile Mouse author Jake Parker. Ten short stories are included and were made during 2003–2012. The stories range from adventurous, funny, heartwarming, and even have an appearance by Missile Mouse himself.

Bad Karma. Written by **B. Clay Moore**, **Seth Peck**, **Alex Grecian**, and various. Illustrated by **Phil Hester**, **Brian Churilla**, and various. Dynamite Comics. 2015– . O

© 2016 Dynamite Entertainment.

The first collection of an anthology series that includes comic stories, prose, and illustrations by a variety of creators including Alex Grecian, Jeremy Haun, B. Clay Moore, and Seth Peck. Stories included in the collection are: *Hellbent*, by Peck & Tigh Walker; *The Ninth Life of Solomon Gunn*, by Grecian, Haun, Moore & Peck, with art by Haun; *Old Dog*, by Moore & Christopher Mitten; *Middleton*, by Grecian and Phil Hester; and *Chaos Agent*, by Haun and Mike Tisserand. Featuring short stories revolving around the concepts and contributions from several notable creators, including Tony Harris, Ben Templesmith, Francesco Francavilla, Rebekah Isaacs, Chris Samnee, Jenny Frison, Shane White, Shaky Kane, and Andrew MacLean.

Vol. 1. 2015. 200pp. 978-1-60690-669-9, hardcover.

De: Tales—Stories from Urban Brazil. Gabriel Bá and Fabio Moon. Dark Horse, 2010. 112pp. 978-1-5958-2557-5. M

A new edition of this collection of short stories by Moon and Bá, Some are collaborative while others were done individually.

Dirty Diamonds. Written and Illustrated by various. Dirty Diamonds, 2016. 152pp. No ISBN. M

An anthology collection edited by Kelly Phillips and Claire Folkman featuring all female creators. The collection features the first four out of print comics in one bound collection. For more issues not yet collected, visit the website at http://dirtydiamonds.storenvy.com/.

Drawn & Quarterly: 25 Years of Contemporary Cartooning, Comics, and Graphic Novels. Written and Illustrated by various. Drawn and Quarterly, 2015. 776pp. 978-1-77046-199-4, hardcover. O

A massive oversize collection of highlighted work of over 25 years' worth of stories by the Canadian publisher Drawn and Quarterly. The collection focuses on literary works ranging from all genres for comic book readers of comics and includes works from creators all across the world as well as reprints of classic comic strips.

© 2016 Drawn & Quarterly.

A Drunken Dream and Other Stories. Written and Illustrated by **Moto Hagio**. Fantagraphics. 2010. 288pp. 978-1-60699-377-4. O Japanese manga. ◉

Moto Hagio was one of the first pioneering women artists of shojo manga. The short stories that are collected in this volume deal with romance, family, belonging, and much more. Some of the stories are about a teacher helping his suicidal student that there is much more to live for, a girl who find out a dark secret about her mother than has shunned her for looking like an iguana, and tragic lovers doomed to repeat their inescapable fates as they have in all their past lives. These tales have cemented Moto Hagio as one of the founding mothers of this style of manga. Also included in the collection is a fascinating interview with the creator and a retrospective by manga scholar Matt Thorn.

Explorer. Edited by **Kazu Kibuishi**. Written and Illustrated by various. Amulet Books/ Harry N. Abrams, 2012–2014. Y ◉

A collection of short stories ranging from the adventurous, funny, mysterious, and the heartbreaking. The stories are edited by Amulet creator Kazu Kibuishi and features a whole slew of comic book talent including works by Kazu Kibuishi, Raina Telgemeier, Jason Caffoe, Stuart Livingston, Johane Matte, Rad Sechrist. Steve Hamaker, Faith Erin Hicks, Dave Roman, Jake Parker, Michel Gagné, Katie and Steven Shanahan, Chrystin Garland, Jen Wang, and Emily Carroll,

Mystery Boxes. 2012. 128pp. 978-1-4197-0010-1, hardcover; 978-1-4197-0009-5.
Lost Islands. 2013. 128pp. 978-1-4197-0881-7, hardcover; 978-1-4197-0883-1.
Hidden Doors. 2014. 129pp. 978-1-4197-0882-4, hardcover; 978-1-4197-0884-8.

© 2016 Kazu Kibuishi.

Flight. Edited by **Kazu Kibuishi**. Written and Illustrated by various. Villard/Ballantine Books, 2007–2010. T ◉

An anthology collection of short stories taking the reader to unique and creative settings with imaginative characters brought to you by some of the comic book

© 2016 Kazu Kibuishi.

and animation industries' brightest talents in a series edited by Kazu Kibuishi. The stories vary and include the adventures of a boy and his dog building a kit plane, a flying whale courier service, a young man's sentimental journey back home to India, to how two high school graduates find something in common while kite flying and many more. The stories touch a variety of subjects and themes including humor, sadness, adventure, and more and were inspired by the animated works and short stories of Hayao Miyazaki and Moebius.

Vol. 1. 2007. 208pp. 978-0-345-49636-2.
Vol. 2. 2007. 432pp. 978-0-345-49637-9.

Vol. 3. 2006. 352pp. 978-0-345-49039-1.   *Vol. 6*. 2009. 288pp. 978-0-345-50590-3.
Vol. 4. 2007. 352pp. 978-0-345-49040-7.   *Vol. 7*. 2010. 288pp. 978-0-345-51737-1.
Vol. 5. 2008. 368pp. 978-0-345-50589-7.   *Vol. 8*. 2011. 288pp. 978-0-345-51738-8.

Flight Explorer. Edited by **Kazu Kibuishi**. Villard Publishing/Random House, 2008. 112pp. 978-0-345-50313-8. Y ◎

© 2016 Kazu Kibuishi.

A younger-reader companion to the Flight anthology series, the book features an excellent collection of short stories ranging from artists and writers represented in this first volume are Kean Soo, Rad Sechrist, Jake Parker, Steve Hamaker, and Matthew S. Armstrong. Highlights includes short stories including Jake Parker's *Missile Mouse*, Kazu Kibuishi's *Copper*, and Kean Soo's *Jellaby*.

P. Craig Russell Library of Opera Adaptations. Adapted by **P. Craig Russell**. NBM Publishing, 2003–2011. T

© 2016 P. Craig Russell.

P. Craig Russell has always been a fan of opera and the classic stories of drama, love, betrayal, pathos, fantasy, and comedy that they're comprised of. Featured herein are adaptations of some of opera's greatest musical works translated into a comic book format. A three-in-one collection was published by NBM Publishing in 2011.

Vol. 1: The Magic Flute. 2003. 144pp. 978-1-56163-350-0.
Vol. 2: Parsifal, Ariane & Bluebeard, I Pigliacci, Songs by Mahler. 2003. 128pp. 978-1-56163-372-2.
Vol. 3: Pelleas & Melisande, Salome, Ein Heldentraum, Cavalleria Rusticana. 2004. 144pp. 978-1-56163-389-0.
P. Craig Russell Library of Opera Adaptations Set. 2011. 440pp. 978-1-56163-389-0.

Project: Romantic. Written and Illustrated by various. AdHouse Books, 2006. 256pp. 978-0-9770304-2-2. M

>An anthology collection of romance tales that features stories of love, relationships, and everything else in between. The collection features contributors including Big Time Attic, Randall Christopher, Joshua Cotter, Nick Craine, Brian Flynn, Doug Fraser, Jose Garibaldi, Debbie Huey, Damien Jay, Hope Larson, Mike Laughead, Adam McGovern/Paolo Leandri, Junko Mizuno, Scott Morse, Roger Peterson, Chris Pitzer, Joel Priddy, Paul Rivoche, Alberto Ruiz, Maris Wicks, and many more.

Stuck in the Middle: Seventeen Comics from an Unpleasant Age. Edited by **Ariel Schrag**. Viking Juvenile. 2007. 224pp. 978-0-670-06221-8. T

>Middle school can be a pain. From figuring out what to wear to school, to dealing with acne, dealing with peer pressure, and beginning to notice people as more than friend; middle school can be a really confusing time. Luckily this book has 17 different examples of what it was like growing up for these artists. With hindsight these events are quite comical after the fact. With enough perseverance everyone can make it through middle school to tell their own stories of when they were growing up.

Chapter 8

Humor

Consider the term "comic books." From its beginning, the comic book format has often featured comedy and humor. Though comic books can trace their origins back time, one of their closest forerunners, the comic strip, debuted in 1895 in newspapers with the first appearance of the comic strip cartoon character called The Yellow Kid in Richard F. Outcault's strip called *Hogan's Alley*. The hit character was soon followed by the *Katzenjammer Kids* by Rudolph Dirks in 1897. Decades later, the very first comic book, *Funnies on Parade* was published by the Eastern Color Printing Company in 1933. The comic book was originally a collection of reprinted comic strips and helped to launch the comic book in America. This chapter features a wide variety of graphic novels and trade collections featuring media tie-ins including Walt Disney's Mickey Mouse, Uncle Scrooge, and Donald Duck; Matt Groening's *The Simpsons*; classic comedy series collections including *Little Lulu*, *Archie*, and many more. Please note that most other genres have influences where comedy plays a role in some form. Titles that are a blended genre mix of comedy and another genre are listed at the end of this chapter.

General Humor

Here are stories of everyday life heavily interspersed with comedy. The plot lines typically border on the ridiculous and the focus is on the absurdities of the life of the protagonist and may even focus on his surroundings, friends, and families included are reprints of classic comic books, stories featuring mostly young protagonists, and the tales typically tend to be more appropriate for all ages. Included here are *Archie Comics*, *Little Lulu*, as well as a variety of new titles from both the United States and Japan.

Abigail and the Snowman. Written and Illustrated by **Roger Langridge**. KaBoom!/Boom! Studios, 2016. 112pp. 978-1-60886-900-8. Y

© 2016 BOOM! Studios.

Abigail is a young girl with a vivid imagination, but when she and her dad move to a small town, she finds it hard to fit in. All of that changes when Claude comes into her life. By the way, Claude is a Yeti who escaped from a top-secret government facility. Though he's invisible to everyone else but Abigail, he soon becomes her best friend. When the Shadow Men come to recapture Claude, Abigail and Claude are soon on the run from them and in a race to get him home — but home may not be where they quite expected.

Amelia Rules! Written and Illustrated by **Jim Gownley**. Atheneum Books for Young Readers, 2009–2012. A ◉

After her parents' divorce, sarcastic and outspoken nine-year-old Amelia Louise McBride begins to adjust to a new life away from the hustle of Manhattan. She is settling into life in small-town America with her mom and her hip Aunt Tanner. She's starting at a new school and has formed a club with her three new quirky friends Reggie, Rhonda, and Pajamaman, called G.A.S.P. (Gathering of Awesome Superpals). Life sure is different in rural America when you're the only "normal" one and everyone around you is crazy.

Vol. 1: The Whole World's Crazy. 2009. 176pp. 978-1-4169-8604-1.
Vol. 2: What Makes You Happy. 2009. 176pp. 978-1-4169-8605-8.
Vol. 3: Superheroes. 2009. 176pp. 978-1-4169-8606-5.
Vol. 4: When the Past Is a Present. 2010. 176pp. 978-1-4169-8607-2.
Vol. 5: The Tweenage Guide to Not Being Unpopular. 2010. 176pp. 978-1-4169-8608-9.
Vol. 6: True Things (Adults Don't Want Kids To Know). 2010. 176pp. 978-1-4169-8609-6.
Vol. 7: The Meaning of Life (and Other Stuff). 2011. 160pp. 978-1-4169-8612-6.
Vol. 8: Her Permanent Record. 2012. 160pp. 978-1-4169-8614-0.

Archie. Written by **Alex Simmons**, **Dan Parent**, and various. Illustrated by various. Archie Comics Publications, 2009–2015. A ▭

Archie Andrews, Betty Cooper, Veronica Lodge, Reggie Mantle and Forsythe "Jughead" Jones and the rest of the gang at Riverdale High have been entertaining comic book readers ever since their first appearance in *Pep Comics* #22 in 1941. After 75 years, Archie still hasn't graduated from high school or decided if he really loves Betty or Veronica the best, but Archie comics are as popular today as ever. Over the years they have appeared on television in both animated and live-action form including the television series <u>Riverdale</u>. Here you'll find highlights from the past decades as well as a collection featuring Betty and Veronica summertime adventures through the years as they spend time on the beach relaxing as Archie and Reggie vie for their affection. In the All-Star series the gang has various adventures, encounter the president, and even have a crossover with the characters from Glee. Archie titles elsewhere in this volume include *Archie: The Married Life* in General Fiction and *Afterlife with Archie* in Horror. The titles listed below are part of the *Archie and Friends All-Stars* series, Many other compilations of *Archie* stories can be found at www.archiecomics.com.

Vol. 1: Veronica's Passport. 2009. 96pp. 978-1-879794-43-6.
Vol. 2: The Best of Betty's Diary. 2009. 96pp. 978-1-879794-46-7.
Vol. 3: The Cartoon Life of Chuck Clayton. 2010. 96pp. 978-1-879794-48-1.
Vol. 4: Betty and Veronica Beach Party. 2010. 96pp. 978-1-879794-50-4.
Vol. 5: Archie's Haunted House. 2010. 96pp. 978-1-879794-52-8.
Vol. 6: Christmas Stocking. 2010. 96pp. 978-1-879794-57-3.
Vol. 7: Betty and Veronica Storybook. 2010. 112pp. 978-1-879794-60-3.
Vol. 8: The Archies and Josie and the Pussycats. 2010. 112pp. 978-1-879794-61-0.
Vol. 9: Best of Jughead: Crowning Achievements. 2011. 96pp. 978-1-879794-67-2.
Vol. 10: Night at the Comic Shop. 2011. 128pp. 978-1-879794-69-6.
Vol. 11: Archie's World Tour. 2011. 128pp. 978-1-879794-73-3.
Vol. 12: Archie's Weird Mysteries. 2011. 128pp. 978-1-879794-74-0.
Vol. 13: Sabrina: Based on the Animated Series. 2011. 128pp. 978-1-879794-80-1.
Vol. 14: Archie: Obama & Palin in Riverdale. 2011. 96pp. 978-1-879794-87-0.
Vol. 15: Magic of Sabrina the Teenage Witch. 2011. 128pp. 978-1-879794-75-7.
Vol. 16: Betty and Veronica: Best Friends Forever. 2011. 128pp. 978-1-879794-76-4.
Vol. 17: Archie: Clash of the New Kids. 2012. 160pp. 978-1-936975-09-9.
Vol. 18: Archie: Love Showdown. 2012. 128pp. 978-1-936975-21-1.
Vol. 19: Betty and Veronica: Prom Princesses. 2012. 128pp. 978-1-936975-30-3.
Vol. 20: Betty and Veronica's Princess Storybook. 2013. 128pp. 978-1-936975-71-6.
Vol. 21 Archie: A Rock and Roll Romance. 2014. 104pp. 978-1-936975-33-4.
Vol. 22: Betty and Veronica: Shopping Spree. 2014. 128pp. 978-1-619889-04-0.
Vol. 23: Archie: Rockin' the World. 2015. 128pp. 978-1-619889-07-1.
Vol. 24: Archie Campfire Stories. 2015. 224pp. 978-1-627389-42-6.
Vol. 25: Betty and Veronica: Girls Rule. 2016. 978-1-627389-52-5.
Vol. 26: Betty and Veronica: Fairy Tales. 2016. 978-1-627388-94-8.

Archie. (2nd series) Written by **Mark Waid**. Illustrated by **Fiona Staples**, **Annie Wu**, and **Veronica Fish**. Archie Comics, 2015– . A. 🏆 ◎

Beginning in 2015, Archie Comics did a fresh relaunch of the Archie series. Written by fan-favorite writer Mark Waid, the series and cast has remained the same for the most part. They're all still the same characters from Riverdale you love, but the look of the series has been modernized and the characters appear more realistic-looking in their designs. Archie Andrews is still America's Favorite Teenager, and he's best friends with Jughead and still head over heels with his ex-girlfriend Betty and the new girl in town, Veronica. In 2017 the first volume was recognized by YALSA's Great Graphic Novels for Teens annual selection list.

Vol. 1. 2016. 176pp. 978-1-62738-867-2.
Vol. 2. 2016. 176pp. 978-1-62738-798-9.
Vol. 3. 2017. 144pp. 978-1-68255-993-2.

Archie Meets Glee. Written by **Roberto Aguirre-Sacasa**. Illustrated by **Dan Parent**. Archie Comics, 2013. 978-1-936975-45-7. A

A science-experiment gone wrong allows Archie and company to meet the teens of TV's musical show *Glee*, but what happens when members of both groups switch worlds and can't get back?

The Best of Archie Comics: 75 Years, 75 Stories. Written and Illustrated by various. Archie Comics, 2015. 640pp. 978-1-62738-992-1. A

A compilation of classic 75 years of Archie Andrews—each story representing one year in the amazing publication history of Archie Andrews—the World's Oldest Teenager since his first appearance in 1941.

Awkward. Written and Illustrated by **Svetlana Chmakova**. Yen Press, 2015. 224pp. 978-0-316-38130-7. Y 🕯 Neo-manga. ◎

© 2016 Yen Press.

Awkward and insecure, Peppi just started middle school and already made a fool of herself by and embarrassing herself in front of Jaime, the unpopular boy in school. Months later, she's found a niche with the after-school art club, but a bitter competition with Jaime's science club springs up, and all bets are off between the rival factions as they vie for a lone spot at the school fair. And more importantly, can Peppi finally apologize to Jaime about her behavior on the first day of school? The book was recognized by YALSA as a Great Graphic Novel for Teens in 2016. The series continues in the book called *Brave* (see listing below).

The Baby-Sitters Club. Written by **Ann M. Martin**. Adapted and Illustrated by **Raina Telgemeier**. Graphix/Scholastic Books, 2015–2016. Y ◎

Cover © Scholastic Inc.

When best friends Kristy, Mary, Anne, Claudia, and Stacey start up their own baby-sitting club, they have their hands full of dirty diapers and more as the Baby-Sitters Club. As best friends, they also have to deal with their own family lives including keeping secrets, adjusting to a parent dating again following a divorce, and much more. Luckily they have each other to count on. Based on the best-selling series of novels for kids created by Ann M. Martin. Retold by fan-favorite creator Raina Telgemeier, the series was originally published in 2006 but reprinted in full color by Scholastic in 2015–2016. It was recently announced that the adaptations will continue in 2017 with the baton being handed over to the very talented Gale Galligan.

Vol. 1: Kristy's Great Idea. 2015. 192pp. 978-0-545-81386-0, hardcover; 978-0-545-81387-7.

Vol. 2: The Truth about Stacy. 2015. 144pp. 978-0-545-81388-4, hardcover; 978-0-545-81389-1.

Vol. 3: Mary Ann Saves the Day. 2015. 160pp. 978-0-545-88617-8, hardcover; 978-0-545-88621-5.

Vol. 4: Claudia and Mean Janine. 2016. 176pp. 978-0-545-88623-9, hardcover; 978-0-545-88622-2.

Bake Sale. Written and Illustrated by **Sara Varon**. First Second Books, 2011. 160pp. 978-1-59643-740-1, hardcover. A

Cupcake is living the good life—he has a bakery, loves playing in a band, and has Eggplant as his best friend. Lately though, something in the kitchen isn't right and he goes in searching for a solution to his problems—but sometimes the answer is closer than you think. The book also includes fun recipes as well!

© First Second and Sarah Varon.

Barakamon. Written and Illustrated by **Satsuki Yoshino**. Yen Press, 2014– . T Japanese manga. あ

Seishuu Handa is a handsome young calligrapher who has relocated to a remote island on the westernmost edge of Japan. A lifelong city boy, Seishuu is a fish out of water on the rural island. Will a young first grader, a girl named Naru, be the first of the many island residents to help open the heard of the Sensei calligrapher and help him soften his hardened heart? The series is still ongoing in Japan and was also adapted into an anime series.

Vol. 1. 2014. 208pp. 978-0-316-33608-6.
Vol. 2. 2014. 192pp. 978-0-316-33658-1.
Vol. 3. 2015. 208pp. 978-0-316-25943-9.
Vol. 4. 2015. 208pp. 978-0-316-34029-8.
Vol. 5. 2015. 208pp. 978-0-316-34031-1.

Cover © Yen Press.

Vol. 6. 2015. 208pp. 978-0-316-34033-5.
Vol. 7. 2015. 208pp. 978-0-316-34035-9.
Vol. 8. 2015. 224pp. 978-0-316-34037-3.
Vol. 9. 2016. 208pp. 978-0-316-26999-5.

Vol. 10. 2016. 192pp. 978-0-316-39348-5.
Vol. 11. 2016. 192pp. 978-0-316-39352-2.
Vol. 12. 2016. 192pp. 978-0-3165-4544-0.
Vol. 13. 2017. 224pp. 978-0-3165-5313-1.

Brave. Written and Illustrated by **Svetlana Chmakova**. Yen Press, 2017. 224pp. 978-0-316-36317-4, hardcover; 978-0-316-36318-1. Y 🎋 Neo-manga. ◎

Meet Jensen—in his dreams he's a hero of the day and always saves his friends, but reality is much more difficult. Middle school is hard. Math is hard. Friendship is hard, and he's always picked last for everything at school. Jensen's always taken each day one moment at a time—but can Jensen break out of his mold with the help of the school newspaper team of Jenny and Akilah, or is he doomed to forever be last in life? The book is the second volume in a middle school years by *Awkward* creator Svetlana Chmakova.

Comics Squad. Written and Illustrated by various. Random House, 2014–2017. Y

Some of the biggest names in comics for kids together in one place! The volumes include stories based around a common themes (Recess, Lunch, and

Detention). Contributors include Jennifer and Matthew Holm, Raina Telgemier, Jarrett J. Krosoczka, Dave Roman, Cece Bell, Jeffrey Brown, Jason Shiga, Eric Wight, Gene Luen Yang, Nathan Hale, Sara Varon, Cecil Castelucci, Ben Hatke, Rafael Rosado, and more!

Vol. 1: Recess. 2014. 144pp. 978-0-385-37003-5.
Vol. 2: Lunch. 2016. 144pp. 978-0-553-51264-9.
Vol. 3: Detention. 2017. 144pp. 978-0-553-51267-0.

Genshiken. Written and Illustrated by **Shimoku Kio**. Kodansha Comics, 2012–2013. T Japanese manga. あ ◎

A tongue-in-cheek look at the world of otaku fandom. A group of fellow otaku at school have their own club called the Society for the Study of Modern Visual Culture. A new membership drive starts up and new members are welcomed into the club including Kanji Sasahara and Saki Kasukabe. Kanji has been a fanboy and has eagerly awaited being a part of the club while Saki is a different beast all together. A surprisingly normal girl, she wanted her boyfriend, Kousaka, to stop watching anime and reading manga. So how the heck did she end up in a club with what she despises? Could it be she's starting to become an otaku, too? A fun look at all the stereotypes of otaku and the otaku lifestyle. The series was originally printed in nine volumes under Del Rey, but was re-collected in three omnibus editions by Kodansha in 2012. A second season of the manga was released in Japan in 2009 and is still ongoing. The series was also adapted as an anime series in Japan.

Genshiken: Omnibus Edition. 2012–2013.

Vol. 1. 2012. 528pp. 978-1-935429-36-4.
Vol. 2. 2012. 560pp. 978-1-935429-37-1.
Vol. 3. 2013. 592pp. 978-1-612620-62-6.

Genshiken: Second Season. 2012– .

Vol. 1. 2012. 208pp. 978-1-61262-237-8.
Vol. 2. 2013. 192pp. 978-1-61262-242-2.
Vol. 3. 2013. 176pp. 978-1-61262-299-6.
Vol. 4. 2014. 192pp. 978-1-61262-549-2.
Vol. 5. 2014. 192pp. 978-1-61262-576-8.
Vol. 6. 2015. 192pp. 978-1-61262-987-2.

Vol. 7. 2015. 192pp. 978-1-63236-116-5.
Vol. 8. 2016. 192pp. 978-1-63236-116-5.
Vol. 9. 2016. 192pp. 978-1-63236-316-9.
Vol. 10. 2017. 192pp. 978-1-63236-341-1.
Vol. 11. 2017. 192pp. 978-1-63236-482-1.

The Book of Grickle. Written and Illustrated by **Graham Annable**. Dark Horse Comics, 2010. 200pp. 978-1-59582-430-1. T

The quirky, mundane, melancholy, and hilarious combine in short vignettes by Graham Annable. Drawn in a simple style, the characters emote sadness, regret, fear, infatuation, love, and more while wrapped up in rich dark humor.

Johnny Hiro. Written and Illustrated by **Fred Chao**. Tor Books, 2012–2013. T

Johnny Hiro can never catch a break. When things look good, events turn to the absurd. Just as he is settling down for the night a giant monster rips through the wall and steals his girlfriend. Determined fishmongers pursue Johnny in a death defying car chase. He must fend of Japanese businessmen, in full samurai armor, just because he was in the wrong place at the wrong time while watching the opera. No matter what comes Johnny Hiro's way, he somehow manages to survive to see another day. Now only if he can pay off the debt from the monstrous hole in his apartment!

Vol. 1: Half Asian, All Hero. 2012. 192pp. 978-0-7653-2937-0.
Vol. 2: Skills to Pay the Bills. 2013. 192pp. 978-0-7653-2938-7.

Jughead. Written by **Chip Zdarsky** and **Ryan North**. Illustrated by **Erica Henderson** and **Derek Charm**. Archie Comics, 2016– . A 🎯

Spun off of the revamp of *Archie* (see listing above) is a fresh and yet still wholesome look at Archie's best friend Jughead. Jughead is laid back, easygoing, and always in the mood for food. When a new principal takes over the school, school uniforms are established, and worst of all the school lunch program is swapped out for inedible mush. When there's a fight to bring back burgers to the school lunch program, there's only one whoopee cap-wearing teen for the job and Jughead takes action as only he can! In 2017 the first volume was recognized by YALSA's Great Graphic Novels for Teens annual selection list.

Vol. 1. 2016. 168pp. 978-1-62738-893-1.
Vol. 2. 2017. 144pp. 978-1-68255-998-7.

Knights of the Lunch Table. Written and Illustrated by **Frank Cammuso**. Graphix/ Scholastic Books, 2008–2011. Y

A new twist on the Arthurian legend! At Camelot Middle School, Artie King is just getting to know the school. Percy and Wayne are his new lunch buddies, and he actually enjoys learning science thanks to his teacher, Mr. Merlyn, is pretty cool. But no school is perfect—especially when he has gotten on the bad side of Principal Dagger and big bad Joe and The Horde, the bullies who rule the school.

Vol. 1: The Dodgeball Chronicles. 2008. 144pp. 978-0-439-90322-6.
Vol. 2: The Dragon Players. 2009. 128pp. 978-0-439-90323-3.
Vol. 3: The Battling Bands. 2011. 128pp. 978-0-439-90318-9.

Cover © Scholastic Inc.

Level Up. Written by **Gene Luen Yang**. Illustrated by **Thien Pham**. First Second Books. 2011. 160pp. 978-1-59643-235-2. T

Dennis's main passions in life are video games and playing video games. When a life of study and preparing to become a doctor is pushed on him by his father he does not take to it very easily. Why study human anatomy when he can save the princess in the next castle? Dennis is so absorbed with video games that he actually gets kicked out of college. Things do not look good for Dennis and keeping his father's expectations, until four small angels appear. These angels will do anything for Dennis, so that he can keep on working toward his destiny

of becoming a gastroenterologist. After this turn of fate, Dennis gives up video games, studies hard, and finds new friends. Dennis just needs to not let all the feces and the overbearing angels burn him out. Will Dennis be able to find the balance between work and play so that he can stay sane while juggling his promises to his father and the angels?

Little Lulu. Written by **John Stanley**. Illustrated by **Irving Tripp**. Dark Horse Comics, 2004–2011. A ◎

Reprinted for the first time in a collected format comes the fun humorous adventures of Little Lulu, the sassiest girl on the block and one of the most beloved comic book heroines ever. Hailed as one of the best all ages series of comic book stories, these stories are once again available in an inexpensive format through Dark Horse Comics, which has been reprinting the classic tales that originally appeared starting in 1942. Also listed is the spin-off series featuring Lulu's friend Tubby. Little Lulu first appeared as a strip in *The Saturday Evening Post* in 1935 which was done by Marjorie Henderson Buell under the pen name "Marge."

Vol. 1: My Dinner with Lulu. 2005. 200pp. 978-1-59307-318-3.
Vol. 2: Sunday Afternoon. 2005. 208pp. 978-1-59307-345-9.
Vol. 3: In the Doghouse. 2005. 208pp. 978-1-59307-346-6.
Vol. 4: Lulu Goes Shopping. 2004. 200pp. 978-1-59307-270-4.
Vol. 5: Lulu Takes a Trip. 2005. 200pp. 978-1-59307-317-6.
Vol. 6: Letters to Santa. 2005. 200pp. 978-1-59307-386-2.
Vol. 7: Lulu's Umbrella Service. 2005. 200pp. 978-1-59307-399-2.
Vol. 8: Late for School. 2006. 200pp. 978-1-59307-453-1.
Vol. 9: Lucky Lulu. 2006. 232pp. 978-1-59307-471-5.
Vol. 10: All Dressed Up. 2006. 200pp. 978-1-59307-534-7.
Vol. 11: April Fools. 2006. 200pp. 978-1-59307-557-6.
Color Special. 2006. 208pp. 978-1-59307-613-9.
Vol. 12: Leave It to Lulu. 2006. 208pp. 978-1-59307-620-7.
Vol. 13: Too Much Fun. 2006. 200pp. 978-1-59307-621-4.
Vol. 14: Queen Lulu. 2007. 240pp. 978-1-59307-683-2.
Vol. 15: The Explorers. 2007. 240pp. 978-1-59307-684-9.
Vol. 16: A Handy Kid. 2007. 216pp. 978-1-59307-685-6.
Vol. 17: The Valentine. 2007. 232pp. 978-1-59307-686-3.
Vol. 18: The Expert. 2008. 216pp. 978-1-59307-687-0.
Vol. 19: The Alamo and Other Stories. 2009. 200pp. 978-1-59582-293-2.
Vol. 20: The Bawlplayers and Other Stories. 2009. 200pp. 978-1-59582-364-9.
Vol. 21: Miss Feeney's Folly and Other Stories. 2009. 200pp. 978-1-59582-365-6.

Vol. 22: The Big Dipper Club and Other Stories. 2010. 200pp. 978-1-59582-420-2.
Vol. 23: The Bogey Snowman and Other Stories. 2010. 200pp. 978-1-59582-474-5.
Vol. 24: The Space Dolly and Other Stories. 2010. 200pp. 978-1-59582-475-2.
Vol. 25: The Burglar-Proof Clubhouse and Other Stories. 2010. 200pp. 978-1-59582-539-1.
Vol. 26: The Feud and Other Stories. 2011. 200pp. 978-1-59582-632-9.
Vol. 27: The Treasure Map and Other Stories. 2011. 200pp. 978-1-59582-633-6.
Vol. 28: The Prize-Winner and Other Stories. 2011. 200pp. 978-1-59582-731-9.
Vol. 29: The Cranky Giant and Other Stories. 2011. 192pp. 978-1-59582-732-6.

Little Lulu's Pal Tubby, 2010–2011.

Vol. 1: The Castaway and Other Stories. 2010. 224pp. 978-1-59582-421-9.
Vol. 2: The Runaway Statue and Other Stories. 2010. 224pp. 978-1-59582-422-6.
Vol. 3: The Frog Boy and Other Stories. 2011. 216pp. 978-1-59582-635-0.
Vol. 4: The Atomic Violin and Other Stories. 2011. 208pp. 978-1-59582-733-3.

Lucy & Andy Neanderthal. Written and Illustrated by **Jeffrey Brown**. Crown Books for Young Readers/Random House, 2016– . Y

© 2016 Random House.

Meet Lucy and Andy—they're two pretty typical kids growing up—40,000 years in the past! Lucy loves to make art while Andy longs to be a mastodon hunter. Join them and their family on their humorous life 40,000 years ago when Neanderthals lived in caves. The book also intersperses historical facts on Neanderthals as well to show how different and similar they were to humans.

Vol. 1. 2016. 224pp. 978-0-385-38835-1.
Vol. 2: The Stone Cold Age. 2017. 224pp. 978-0-385-38838-2.

My Dirty Dumb Eyes. Written and Illustrated by **Lisa Hanawalt**. Drawn and Quarterly. 2013. 120pp. 978-1-77046-116-1. M

This book collects the short stories and observations of humorist Lisa Hanawalt. These stories are completely far out. Most of the characters in the stories are anthropomorphic animals in completely normal or totally absurd situations. Other stories may be about animals wearing different hats or her experiences watching other people.

My Neighbor Seki. Written and Illustrated by **Takuma Morishige**. Vertical Comics, 2015– . Y Japanese manga. あ

Rumi Yokoi is a middle school student and all she wants to do is get her work done in school, but she's constantly bothered by her neighboring classmate Toshinari Seki who is always creating elaborate hobbies at his desk and amazingly never gets caught. The series is still ongoing in Japan. The manga was also adapted into a 21-episode anime that aired in Japan in 2014.

Vol. 1. 2015. 176pp. 978-1-939130-96-9.
Vol. 2. 2015. 176pp. 978-1-939130-97-6.
Vol. 3. 2015. 176pp. 978-1-941220-48-1.
Vol. 4. 2015. 176pp. 978-1-941220-49-8.
Vol. 5. 2015. 176pp. 978-1-941220-89-4.

Vol. 6. 2016. 166pp. 978-1-942993-09-4.
Vol. 7. 2016. 170pp. 978-1-942993-10-0.
Vol. 8. 2016. 176pp. 978-1-942993-50-6.
Vol. 9. 2017. 162pp. 978-1-945054-01-3.

The Rabbi's Cat. Written and Illustrated by **Joann Sfar**. Pantheon Press/Random House, 2007–2008. ◎ O 🎖

© 2016 Random House.

Set in the 1930s, the story focuses on a rabbi, his beautiful daughter Zlabya, and their talking cat. After gaining the ability to speak after eating the family parrot, the cat begins to tell lies, and the rabbi decides to teach the cat the ways of the Torah, but can a cat become Jewish? When Zlabya falls in love with a young rabbi from France, soon the master and his cat journey to Paris to meet the in-laws after both admitting feeling jealous losing their beloved Zlabya to a dashing young man. As the master and cat experience one adventure to another, they always have a chance to philosophize and discuss the important and trivial issues in life. A tender and humorous look at a most unique pet. The story won an Eisner award in 2006 for Best U.S. Edition of Foreign Material.

The Rabbi's Cat. 2007. 152pp. 978-0-375-71464-1.
The Rabbi's Cat 2. 2008. 144pp. 978-0-375-42507-3.

The Show Must Go On. Written and Illustrated by **Roger Langridge**. Boom! Studios, 2011. 208pp. 978-1-6088-6091-3. O

A collection of various works by Langridge over the past decades with such features as *Fred the Clown*, *The Kabuki Kid*, and *Frankenstein Meets Shirley Temple*.

Snarked. Written and Illustrated by **Roger Langridge**. KaBoom/Boom! Studios, 2012–2013. A

© BOOM! Studios.

Inspired in part by the works of Lewis Carroll, *Snarked* is about Princess Scarlett, who, with her baby brother Rusty, team up with the Walrus and the Carpenter to search for her missing father, The Red King. Their destination—Snark Island. The three volumes collect the entire series along with extras.

Vol. 1: Forks and Hopes. 2012. 128pp. 978-1-6088-6095-1.
Vol. 2: Ships and Sealing Wax. 2012. 112pp. 978-1-6088-6276-4.
Vol. 3. 2013. 112pp. 978-1-6088-6295-5.

Sock Monkey Treasury. Written and Illustrated by **Tony Millionaire**. Fantagraphics, 2014. 336pp. 978-1-60699-696-6, hardcover. T 🎖 ◎

The oddly endearing but unsettling adventures of a mischievous sock monkey called Uncle Gabby and his pal, a clumsy stuffed animal bird called Drinky Crow. Home alone among the various toys, the two stuff animals discover adventures galore, sometimes with disastrous results on the chandelier, as they try to return a shrunken head to its home, burn down the house, and much more. The collection includes 12 short story collections as well as the full-length graphic novel story "The Inches Incident." The series won several Eisner Awards including Talent Deserving of Wider Recognition (2000), Best Humor Publication (2001), and creator Tony Millionaire received recognition as Best Writer/Artist: Humor (2001) for his work as well as a Harvey Award in 2004 for Special Award for Humor.

Sweaterweather and Other Stories. Written and Illustrated by **Sara Varon**. First Second, 2016. 128pp. 978-1-62672-118-0, hardcover. Y

© First Second.

A turtle and a rabbit seek refuge from a snowstorm in a turtle shell, a raccoon wins a pie-eating contest and a dog builds a robot friend, in this collection of short stories by Sara Varon originally published in 2003, the collection reprints early Sara Varon stories that are heartwarming and gentle and speaks of the power of friendship.

Teen Boat. Written by **Dave Roman**. Illustrated by **John Green**. Clarion Books, 2012–2015. Y

© Dave Roman and John Green.

"The angst of being a teen . . . the thrill of being a boat!" Teenagers have it bad—it's the awkward years of life and what could be more awkward when you're a teenager who can turn into a small yacht? Teen Boat is just that—his dad is a boat and his mom is a human (don't ask!) and he just wants to fit in and woo the girl of his dreams, Nina Pinta Santa Maria, but little does he know true love is right by his side.

Teen Boat. 2012. 144pp. 978-0-547-63669-6, hardcover.
Teen Boat: The Race to Boatlantis. 2015. 160pp. 978-0-547-86563-8, hardcover.

Voice Over! Seiyu Academy. Written and Illustrated by **Maki Minami**. VIZ Media, 2013–2015. T 🌸 Japanese manga.

Hime Kino wants nothing more than to become a voice-over performer like her idol, Sakura Aoyama. After entering the Holly Academy's voice-acting

·department, the school from which all of her idols graduated, Hime strives to make it big in the anime voiceover world even if she must pretend to be a man to do it. The series was on the 2015 YALSA Great Graphic Novels for Teens List

Vol. 1. 2013. 208pp. 978-1-4215-5970-4.   *Vol. 7*. 2014. 200pp. 978-1-4215-5976-6.
Vol. 2. 2013. 192pp. 978-1-4215-5971-1.   *Vol. 8*. 2014. 192pp. 978-1-4215-5977-3.
Vol. 3. 2014. 192pp. 978-1-4215-5972-8.   *Vol. 9*. 2015. 200pp. 978-1-4215-5978-0.
Vol. 4. 2014. 192pp. 978-1-4215-5973-5.   *Vol. 10*. 2015. 192pp. 978-1-4215-5979-7.
Vol. 5. 2014. 192pp. 978-1-4215-5974-2.   *Vol. 11*. 2015. 192pp. 978-1-4215-7342-7.
Vol. 6. 2014. 192pp. 978-1-4215-5975-9.   *Vol. 12*. 2015. 192pp. 978-1-4215-7726-5.

Yotsuba&! Written and Illustrated by **Kiyohiko Azuma**. Yen Press, 2009–2013. Y. Japanese manga. ◎

© 2016 Yen Press.

These are the charming exploits of an innocent but odd four-year-old girl named Yotsuba and how she naively reacts to the world around her. Yotsuba and her adoptive father have just moved into a new neighborhood in Japan, but is the neighborhood really ready for Yotsuba? After settling in, the exuberant little girl discovers how a swing works, the wonders of air conditioners, the horrors of global warming, the proper way to catch cicadas, and even how to enjoy a beautiful skyline view of a city. The father and her three beautiful girls who live next door may have trouble keeping up with this little ball of energy, but there's nothing in the world that can get her down.

Vol. 1. 2009. 208pp. 978-0-316-07387-5.
Vol. 2. 2009. 192pp. 978-0-316-07389-9.
Vol. 3. 2009. 176pp. 978-0-316-07390-5.
Vol. 4. 2009. 192pp. 978-0-316-07391-2.   *Vol. 9*. 2010. 224pp. 978-0-316-12679-3.
Vol. 5. 2009. 208pp. 978-0-316-07392-9.   *Vol. 10*. 2011. 224pp. 978-0-316-19033-6.
Vol. 6. 2009. 208pp. 978-0-316-07324-0.   *Vol. 11*. 2011. 224pp. 978-0-316-22539-7.
Vol. 7. 2009. 208pp. 978-0-316-07325-7.   *Vol. 12*. 2013. 224pp. 978-0-316-32232-4.
Vol. 8. 2010. 224pp. 978-0-316-07327-1.   *Vol. 13*. 2016. 224pp. 978-0-316-31921-8.

The Zoo Box. Written by **Ariel Cohn**. Illustrated by **Aron Nels Steinke**. First Second Books, 2014. 48pp. 978-1-62672-052-7, hardcover. 🐾 Y

When their parents go out, Patrick and Erika open a strange box in the attic out of which comes all sorts of animals. They follow them to the zoo where they discover the animals are walking, talking, and wearing clothes, while humans in their normal habitats are the attraction. The book was a Will Eisner Award winner in 2015 for Best Publication for Early Readers

Cartoons, Animation, and Media Tie-Ins

Humor that is adapted from popular animated films or from animated television shows. The titles include graphic novel collections based on the cable network *The Cartoon Network's* programming, classic cartoons including *Bugs Bunny* and *Mickey Mouse*, *The Simpsons*, as well as motion pictures including *The Minions*.

Angry Birds Comics. Written by **Jeff Parker**, **Paul Tobin**, **Janne Toriseva**, and various. Illustrated by **Paco Rodriques**, **Cesar Ferioli**, **Audrey Bussi**, and various. IDW Publishing, 2014– . Y

The comic book adaptation of the hit videogame series by Rovio Games in which the Bad Piggies from Piggyland try to steal bird eggs. But the pigs never counted on the birds—the birds aren't just furious about it—they're angry!

Vol. 1: Welcome to the Flock. 2014. 96pp. 978-1-6314-0090-2, hardcover.
Vol. 2: When Pigs Fly. 2015. 80pp. 978-1-6314-0248-7, hardcover.
Vol. 3: Sky High. 2015. 80pp. 978-1-6314-0368-2, hardcover.
Vol. 4: Fly of the Handle. 2016. 80pp. 978-1-6314-0653-9, hardcover.
Vol. 5: Ruffled Feathers. 2016. 80pp. 978-1-6314-0762-8, hardcover.
Vol. 6: *Wing It*. 2017. 80pp. 978-1-6314-0851-9, hardcover.
Big Movie Eggstravaganza. 2016. 80pp. 978-1-6314-0568-6.
Super Angry Birds. 2016. 100pp. 978-1-6314-0549-5.
Game Play, Vol. 1. 2017. 80pp. 978-1-6314-0973-8, hardcover.

Cars. Written by **Alan J. Porter** and **Keith R. A. DeCandido**. Illustrated by **Albert Carreres** and **Travis Hill**. BOOM! Studios, 2009–2011; Joe Books, 2017– . A

Welcome to Radiator Springs, the most scenic location in Carburetor County and accessible just off Route 66! Inspired by the hit Disney•Pixar films *Cars* (2006) and *Cars 2* (2011) films, welcome to the continuing adventures of racecar Lightning McQueen, Mater, Sally, Ramone, Luigi, Flo, Sarge, Doc Hudson, and all the rest of the cast of cars from Radiator Springs! The *Disney•Pixar Cars Comics Treasury* reprints the Boom! Studios stories as well as previously unpublished works. Joe Books has also released movie adaptations of the movies.

© 2009 Disney•Pixar.

The Rookie. 2009. 112pp. 978-1-60886-522-2, hardcover; 978-1-93450-684-4.
Radiator Springs. 2010. 112pp. 978-1-60886-528-4, hardcover; 978-1-60886-502-4.
Rally Race. 2010. 112pp. 978-1-60886-517-8.
Route 66. 2010. 112pp. 978-1-60886-585-7.
Rust Bucket Derby. 2011. 112pp. 978-1-60886-607-6.
Disney•Pixar Cars Comics Treasury. 2017. 800pp. 978-1-77275-327-1.
Disney•Pixar Cars: Movie Graphic Novel. 2017. 64pp. 978-1-77275-524-4.
Disney•Pixar Cars 3: Movie Graphic Novel. 2017. 64pp. 978-1-77275-503-9.

Dexter's Laboratory. IDW Publishing, 2014. Y

A collection of stories based off the popular Cartoon Network show that originally aired from 1996 to 2003. The show was created by Genndy Tartakovsky. The show features the adventures of mad scientist genius Dexter and his dim-witted older sister Dee Dee who always gets them in trouble. The classics collection reprints material originally published by DC Comics.

Dexter's Laboratory Classics. 2014. Written by **John Kelly**, **Chuck Kim**, **Dave Roman**, and **John Rozum**. Illustrated by **Ethen Beavers**, **Bill Alger**, and **Jeff Albrecht**. IDW Publishing, 2014. Y

> *Vol. 1*. 2014. 128pp. 978-1-61377-975-0.
> *Vol. 2*. 2014. 140pp. 978-1-63140-169-5.

Dexter's Laboratory: ***Dee's Day***. Written by **Derek Fridolfs**. Illustrated by **Ryan Jampole**. IDW Publishing, 2014. 104pp. 978-1-63140-049-0. Y

Disney Frozen Comics Collection. Written by **Georgia Ball** and various. Illustrated by **Benedetta Barone** and various. Joe Books, 2017. A 🎬

> Disney's popular 2013 animated film comes to the world of comics! Join Queen Elsa, Princess Anna, Kristoff, Sven, and Olaf the snowman on their brand new adventures in the kingdom of Arendelle.
> *Travel Arendelle*. 2017. 96pp. 978-1-77275-332-5.
> *Hearts Full of Sunshine*. 2017. 96pp. 978-1-77275-465-0.
> *Winter Wonderland Comics Collection*. 2017. 320pp. 978-1-988032-00-9.

Disney Moana Comics Collection. Written and Illustrated by various. Joe Books, 2017. 240pp. 978-1-77275-461-2. A 🎬

> After her pacific island home is in danger, a spirited teenager named Moana sails out on a daring mission to prove herself a master wayfinder and fulfill her ancestors' unfinished quest. Along the way she's joined by a strong demigod named Maui as they set out to right some wrongs from the past. The collection is an adaptation of the hit 2016 animated feature film *Moana* as well as supplemental stories featuring Moana, Maui, Heihei, and more.

Disney Princess Comics Treasury, Vol. 1. Written by **Peter David** and various. Illustrated by various. Joe Books, 2015. 800pp. 978-1-926516-02-8. A 🎬

A massive collection of Disney Princess movies adapted into the comics format and in print for the first time! Fall in love again with the movie adaptations of *Snow White and the Seven Dwarfs*, *Cinderella*, *Sleeping Beauty*, *The Little Mermaid*, *Beauty and the Beast*, *Aladdin*, *Pocahontas*, *Mulan*, *The Princess and the Frog*, *Tangled* and *Brave*. The collection also includes a variety of short stories featuring the cast of the many princess-themed films as well.

© 2015 Disney.

Disney Tangled: The Story of the Movie in Comics. Written and Illustrated by various. Joe Books, 2017. 64pp. 978-1-77275-292-2. A 🎬

Disney adaptation of the popular 2011 animated film. The dashing rogue Flynn Rider is on the run from the kingdom. After stealing the royal crown of the lost princess, he hides away in a tower and discovers he's not alone! In the tower he finds Rapunzel, a spirited teen with an unlikely superpower: 70 feet of magical golden hair! Together the two of them go on an adventure outside of the tower where Rapunzel discovers her true family heritage.

Disney's Darkwing Duck Treasury. Written by **Aaron Sparrow** and various. Illustrated by **James Silvani** and various. Joe Books, 2015. 400pp. 978-1-926516-04-2. A 📖

"I am the terror that flaps in the night!" Drake Mallard is a mild-mannered father. He loves to help with his daughter Gosalyn with her schoolwork and to pal around with his friend Launchpad McQuack. But Drake has a secret: at night he prowls the city as Darkwing Duck! The citizens of St. Canard are safe when Darkwing Duck, Launchpad and Gosalyn are there to protect the city from a hilarious group of villains that threaten the city. The series is based on the popular cartoon series that originally aired from 1991 to 1995.

© 2015 Disney.

Disney's Phineas and Ferb Colossal Comics Collection. Written by **Scott Peterson**, **Jim Bernstein**, and various. Illustrated by **John Green**, **Tom Neely**, and various. Joe Books, 2015. 354pp. 978-1-926516-08-0. A 📖

For the first time in print, read all the further adventures of Phineas and his silent step-brother Ferb as they make the most of their summer vacation days in the city of Danville! What are they going to do every day? Why they're going to build a new outrageous contraption every day—much to the frustration of their big sister Candace who desperately wants to bust her brothers and get them in trouble with mom. Meanwhile, little do they realize it, but Phineas's pet platypus is really a secret agent named Agent P who daily thwarts his evil nemesis—Dr. Heinz Doofenshmirtz and his evil plot to take over the Tri-State area! The hit show aired from 2007 to 2015 on the Disney Channel and Disney XD.

© 2015 Disney.

Disney•Pixar Finding Dory: Movie Graphic Novel. Written and Illustrated by various. Joe Books, 2017. 64pp. 978-1-77275-291-5. A 🎬

An adaptation of the hit 2016 Disney•Pixar sequel to *Finding Nemo*. Dory the blue tang has severe short term memory issues. She doesn't know anything about where she's from or who her parents are. When she suddenly recalls something from her youth, she sets out to rediscover her roots and to find out what happened to her parents.

Disney•Pixar Finding Nemo: Movie Graphic Novel. Written and Illustrated by various. Joe Books, 2017. 64pp. 978-1-77275-290-8. A 🎬

The adaptation of the popular 2003 Disney•Pixar film. In the Great Barrier Reef, an overprotective clownfish named Marlin seeks to protect his son Nemo from the dangers of the sea. But when Nemo is captured by deep sea divers where he's taken to a dentist's office in Australia, Marlin finds a friend with a forgetful blue tang fish named Dory, and together they take on the dangers of the deep sea to find and rescue his son.

Disney•PixarTreasury, Vol. 1. Written and Illustrated by various. Joe Books, 2015. 800pp. 978-1-926516-01-1. A 🎬

A fantastic collection that includes adaptations of some of Disney's Pixar great films as well as brand new stories of your favorite characters from the hit movies *Toy Story 1*, *2 & 3*, *A Bug's Life*, *Monsters, Inc.*, *Finding Nemo*, *The Incredibles*, *Cars & Cars 2*, *Ratatouille*, *Wall-E*, *Up*, *Brave*, and *Monsters University*! Many of the adaptations are in print for the first time in North America as well as reprinted items originally published by Boom! Studios.

© 2015 Disney•Pixar.

Donald Duck and Uncle Scrooge. A ◎ 🖵

Donald Duck has been appearing in comic books around the world since the 1930s. Over the years the stories have been collected in various forms by a number of publishers. The same goes for Donald's incredibly wealthy Uncle, Scrooge McDuck. Currently both Fantagraphics and IDW Publishing have been putting out collections. Fantagraphics' collections include *The Complete Carl Barks Disney Library* that collects the Donald and Uncle Scrooge works by Carl Barks, whose work was loved by readers even during the days when there was no creator credit and he was known by fans as "The Good Duck Artist." The stories also feature many beloved citizens of Duckburg including Donald's nephews Huey, Dewey, and Louie Duck, Gyro Gearloose, as well as villainous Beagle Boys, the witch Magica De Spell, as well as Uncle Scrooge's nemesis, the industrialist Flintheart Glomgold. It is Fantagraphics' plan to collect all of the stories Barks did between 1942 and 1966 in an approximately 30 volume collection. Fantagraphics are also collecting the stories featuring the Barks-created Uncle Scrooge done by legendary creator Don Rosa including some of his Eisner-Winning work. IDW Publishing is also putting out collections, first out in comic book form, that collects various stories from over the years, including translations of Donald/Scrooge stories first published in Germany, the Netherlands, and other European countries. Many of Carl Barks's and Don Rosa's stories were adapted into the popular animated series *DuckTales* that originally aired from 1987 to 1990. A new animated *DuckTales* series is planned to debut in 2017.

The Complete Carl Barks Disney Library. Written and Illustrated by **Carl Barks**. Fantagraphics, 2011– . A ***Walt Disney's Donald Duck.***

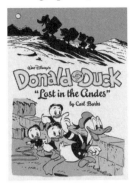

© 2011 Disney.

Lost in the Andes. 2011. 240pp. 978-1-60699-474-0, hardcover.
A Christmas for Shacktown. 2012. 240pp. 978-1-60699-574-7, hardcover.
Christmas on Bear Mountain. 2013. 216pp. 978-1-60699-697-3, hardcover.
The Old Castle's Secret. 2013. 240pp. 978-1-60699-653-9, hardcover.
Trail of the Unicorn. 2014. 216pp. 978-1-60699-741-3, hardcover.
The Pixilated Parrot. 2015. 216pp. 978-1-60699-834-2, hardcover.
Trick or Treat. 2015. 228pp. 978-1-60699-874-8, hardcover.
Terror of the Beagle Boys. 2016. 232pp. 978-1-60699-920-2, hardcover.
The Ghost Sheriff of Last Gasp. 2016. 240pp. 978-1-60699-953-0, hardcover.

Walt Disney's Donald Duck collections. 2014– .

In 2014, Fantagraphics also began reprinting Carl Barks's Donald Duck stories in a smaller paperback format as a more kid-friendly option aside from their *Complete Carl Barks Disney Library* collections. The stories will eventually all be included in the hardcover collections.

The Ghost of the Grotto. 2014. 96pp. 978-1-60699-779-6.
Sheriff of Bullet Valley. 2015. 96pp. 978-1-60699-820-5.
The Golden Helmet. 2015. 128pp. 978-1-60699-852-6.

Walt Disney's Uncle Scrooge. 2012–

© 2012 Disney.

Fantagraphics has recently begun to reprint the timeless Uncle Scrooge tales. The first collection, includes classic stories including "Only a Poor Old Man," "Back to the Klondike," "Tralla La, " and many other shorter stories. Through these humorous stories the love and the paranoia Scrooge has for his vault of money. To Uncle Scrooge each coin and greenback has a story of how he earned, fought, and out connived to earn his fortune. With the help of his nephew Donald and great nephews Huey, Dewey, and Louie they will fend off the Beagle Brothers and anything else that can pose a threat to mountain of wealth.

Only a Poor Old Man. 2012. 240pp. 978-1-60699-742-0, hardcover.
The Seven Cities of Gold. 2014. 240pp. 978-1-60699-795-6, hardcover.
The Lost Crown of Genghis Khan. 2017. 232pp. 978-1-68396-013-3, hardcover.

Walt Disney's Uncle Scrooge and Donald Duck: ***The Don Rosa Disney Library***. Written and Illustrated by **Don Rosa**. Fantagraphics, 2014– . A ◎

© 2014 Disney.

Don Rosa is a Disney artist who helped to continue to expand upon the wonderful Carl Barks stories. His first collection, The *Son of the Sun* was nominated for a Harvey Award for Best Story of the Year. Fantagraphics has begun to reprint his classic stories as well in a deluxe hardcover format.

The Son of the Sun. 2014. 208pp. 978-1-60699-742-0, hardcover.
Return to Plain Awful. 2014. 216pp. 978-1-60699-780-2, hardcover.
Treasure under Glass. 2015. 192pp. 978-1-60699-836-6, hardcover.
The Last of the Clan McDuck. 2015. 192pp. 978–1606998663, hardcover.
The Richest Duck in the World. 2016. 192pp. 978-1-60699-927-1, hardcover.
The Universal Solvent. 2016. 192pp. 978-1-60699-961-5, hardcover.
The Treasure of the Ten Avatars. 2017. 192pp. 978-1-68396-006-5, hardcover.

Walt Disney's Donald Duck. Written by **Romano Scarpa**, **Dick Kinney**, **Jonathan Gray**, and various. Illustrated by **Romano Scarpa**, **Al Taliaferro**, **Al Hubbard**, **Mau Heymans**, and various. IDW Publishing, 2015– . A

Beginning in 2015, IDW Publishing has begun to publish Disney Comics that were originally published in Italy. The works feature familiar Disney characters as well as characters created solely in the comics.

Shellfish Motives. 2015. 148pp. 978-1-63140-403-0.
Timeless Tales, Vol. 1. 2015. 256pp. 978-1-63140-572-3, hardcover.
The True Origin of the Diabolical Duck Avenger. 2015. 116pp. 978-1-63140-480-1.
Revenge of the Duck Avenger. 2016. 124pp. 978-1-63140-730-7.
Timeless Tales Vol. 2. 2016. 256pp. 978-1-63140-765-9, hardcover.
Tycoonraker. 2016. 120pp. 978-1-63140-553-2.
The Big Sneeze. 2017. 192pp. 978-1-63140-832-8.
Donald and Mickey: Timeless Tales, Vol. 3. 2017. 256pp. 978-1-63140-911-0, hardcover.
Duck Avenger, Book 1. 2017. 200pp. 978-1-63140-864-9.
Donald Quest, Hammer of Magic. 2017. 160pp. 978-1-63140-912-7.

Walt Disney's Uncle Scrooge. Written by **Jonathan Gray**, **Rodolfo Cimino**, **Jan Kruse**, **Romano Scarpa**, **Joe Torcivia**, and various. Illustrated by **Romano Scarpa**, **Tony Strobl**, **Bas Heymans**, and various. IDW Publishing, 2015– . A

A collection of classic Italian *Uncle Scrooge* stories now in print for the first time ever in North America!

The Grand Canyon Conquest. 2015. 112pp. 978-1-63140-475-7.
Pure Viewing Satisfaction. 2015. 148pp. 978-1-63140-388-0.
Eternal Knot. 2016. 120pp. 978-1-63140-639-3.
Peril of Pandora's Box. 2016. 112pp. 978-1-63140-525-9.
Scrooge's Last Adventure. 2016. 160pp. 978-1-63140-717-8.
Timeless Tales Vol. 1. 2016. 240pp. 978-1-631-40566-2, hardcover.
Timeless Tales Vol. 2. 2016. 256pp. 978-1-63140-672-0, hardcover.
Himalayan Hideout. 2017. 124pp. 978-1-63140-822-9.
Timeless Tales Vol. 3. 2017. 256pp. 978-1-63140-935-6, hardcover.
Tyrant of the Tides. 2017. 124pp. 978-1-63140-887-8.

Donald and Mickey: The Persistence of Mickey. Written and Illustrated by **Andrea Castellan**, **Giorgio Cavazzano**, **Roberto Gagnor**, **Mau Heymans**, **Byron Erickson**, **Joe Torcivia**, and **William Van Horn**. IDW Publishing, 2017. 124pp. 978-1-63140-833-5. A

> In 1946 Walt Disney and famous abstract artist Salvador Dali teamed up for a project called Destino which wasn't seen until years after its inception. What took so long? Why blame Mickey, Donald, and Goofy!

Donald and Mickey: The Walt Disney's Comics and Stories 75th Anniversary Collection. Written and Illustrated by **Carl Barks**, **Daan Jippes**, **Paul Murry**, **Fred Milton**, **William Van Horn**, **Gil Turner**, and **Walt Kelly**. IDW Publishing, 2016. 120pp. 978-1-63140-541-9. A

> A collection of classic Disney comics featuring Donald Duck and his pal Mickey Mouse by some of Disney's most famous contributors over the last 75 years.

Donald and Mickey: The Walt Disney's Comics and Stories Holiday Collection. Written by **William Van Horn**, **Mau Heymans**, and **Jonathan Gray**. Illustrated by **William Van Horn**, **Mau Heymans**, and **Giovan Battista Carpi**. IDW Publishing, 2017. 156pp. 978-1-63140-729-1. A

> A collection of classic Disney comics featuring Donald Duck, Mickey Mouse, Uncle Scrooge, Goofy, and many others as they celebrate Halloween and Christmas in their own special Disney style.

Finding Nemo. Written by **Marie Croall**, **Brian Reis Smith**, and **Mike Raicht**. Illustrated by **Erica Leigh Currey,** and **Jake Myler**. Boom! Studios, 2009–2011. A ▰

> A collection of stories featuring the cast of the hit 2003 PIXAR film *Finding Nemo*. Join Marlin, his son Nemo, and their friend Dory as they set out on new adventures underwater!

> *Reef Rescue*. 2009. 112pp. 978-1-934506-88-2.
> *Losing Dory*. 2011. 128pp. 978-1-608866-09-0.
> *Fish out of Water*. 2011. 128pp. 978-1-608866-29-8.

Fraggle Rock. Written and Illustrated by various. Archaia/BOOM! Studios, 2010–2013. A ▱

© BOOM! Studios.

Dance your cares away. Archaia has several titles featuring Jim Henson's popular characters from the 1980s. In their underground world the Fraggles (and some other creatures) have adventures and learn lessons. Archaia's books include collections of the comics put out by Marvel's Star Comics line, two recent limited series, and an original graphic novel.

Fraggle Rock. 2010–2012.

> *Vol. 1*. 2010. 136pp. 978-1-9323-8642-4, hardcover.
> *Vol. 2: Tails and Tales*. 2012. 136pp. 978-1-9363-9313-8, hardcover.

Fraggle Rock Classics. 2012–2013.

 Vol. 1. 2012. 96pp. 978-1-9363-9322-0.
 Vol. 2. 2013. 96pp. 978-1-9363-9337-4.

Fraggle Rock: Journey to the Everspring. 2015. 112pp. 978-1-6088-6694-6, hardcover.

Geronimo Stilton. Written and Illustrated by **Geronimo Stilton**. Papercutz, 2009– . Y ◎

© NBM Publishing.

Based on the popular chapter books featuring Geronimo Stilton, the editor and publisher of The Rodent's Gazette, New Mouse City's most widely read daily newspaper. A mild-mannered mouse, Geronimo would rather spend a quiet evening at home, but that never seems to happen when his sister Thea, his cousin Trap, and his favorite little nephew, nine-year-old Benjamin Stilton. When the pirate cats try to change history, it's up to Geronimo and his family to save the day! Each adventure is full of humor and history. Originally published in Italy, the series is extremely popular with young readers.

 Vol. 1: The Discovery of America! 2009. 56pp. 978-1-59707-158-1.
 Vol. 2: Secret of the Sphinx. 2009. 56pp. 978-1-59707-159-8.
 Vol. 3: The Coliseum Con. 2009. 56pp. 978-1-59707-172-7.
 Vol. 4: Following the Trail of Marco Polo. 2010. 56pp. 978-1-59707-188-8.
 Vol. 5: The Great Ice Age. 2010. 56pp. 978-1-59707-202-1.
 Vol. 6: Who Stole the Mona Lisa? 2010. 56pp. 978-1-59707-221-2.
 Vol. 7: Dinosaurs in Action. 2011. 56pp. 978-1-59707-239-7.
 Vol. 8: Play It Again, Mozart! 2011. 56pp. 978-1-59707-276-2.
 Vol. 9: The Weird Book Machine. 2012. 56pp. 978-1-59707-295-3.
 Vol. 10: Geronimo Stilton Saves the Olympics. 2012. 56pp. 978-1-59707-319-6.
 Vol. 11: We'll Always Have Paris. 2012. 56pp. 978-1-59707-347-9.
 Vol. 12: The First Samurai. 2013. 56pp. 978-1-59707-385-1.
 Vol. 13: The Fastest Train In the West. 2013. 56pp. 978-1-59707-448-3.
 Vol. 14: First Mouse on the Moon. 2014. 56pp. 978-1-5970-7-731-6.
 Vol. 15: All for Stilton, Stilton for All! 2015. 56pp. 978-1-62991-149-6.
 Vol. 16: Lights, Camera, Stilton! 2015. 56pp. 978-1-62991-208-0.
 Vol. 17: Mystery of the Pirate Ship. 2016. 56pp. 978-1-62991-451-0.
 Vol. 18: First to the Last Place on Earth. 2016. 56pp. 978-1-62991-603-3.
 Vol. 19: Lost in Translation. 2017. 56pp. 978-1-62991-758-0.

Thea Stilton. Written and Illustrated by **Thea Stilton**. Papercutz, 2013– . Y

Like her older brother Geronimo, Thea has quite an adventurous life! She's a correspondent for her brother's newspaper The Rodent's Gazette. She's inspired a group of college students from Mouseford Academy. After having Thea Stilton as their journalism professor, they now want to be just like Thea and have named themselves the Thea Sisters! Now Colette, Nicky, Pamela, Paulina, and Violet solve mysteries, eat pizza, and have fun.

 Vol. 1: The Secret of Whale Island. 2013. 56pp. 978-1-59707-403-2.
 Vol. 2: Revenge of the Lizard Club. 2013. 56pp. 978-1-59707-430-8.
 Vol. 3: The Treasure of the Viking Ship. 2014. 56pp. 978-1-59707-514-5.
 Vol. 4: Catching the Giant Wave. 2014. 56pp. 978-1-62991-050-5.
 Vol. 5: The Secret of the Waterfall in the Woods. 2016. 56pp. 978-1-62991-288-2.
 Vol. 6: The Thea Sisters and the Mystery of the Sea. 2016. 56pp. 978-1-62991-478-7.
 Vol. 7: A Song for Thea Sisters. 2017. 56pp. 978-1-62991-640-8.

Hello Kitty. Written and Illustrated by **Jacob Chabot**, **Jorge Monlongo**, **Ian McGinty**, **Susie Ghahremani**, and various. Perfect Square/VIZ Media, 2013–2015. Y

> Since 1974 Hello Kitty has been a household name. Introduced by the company Sanrio in Japan, the cat known as Kitty White in Japan become an international symbol ever since. In 2013, VIZ Media created a variety of short stories written and illustrated by a variety of creators taking Kitty White on silently told adventures all over the world to be enjoyed by all ages alongside her sister Mimmy, and her variety of friends.

> *Here We Go*. 2013. 64pp. 978-1-4215-5878-3.
> *Delicious*. 2014. 64pp. 978-1-4215-5879-0.
> *Surprise*. 2014. 64pp. 978-1-4215-5880-6.
> *Just Imagine*. 2014. 64pp. 978-1-4215-7362-5.
> *Work of Art*. 2014. 64pp. 978-1-4215-7542-1.
> *It's About Time*. 2015. 64pp. 978-1-4215-7769-2.
> *Fashion Music Wonderland*. 2015. 48pp. 978-1-4215-5903-2.

Hello Kitty, Hello 40: A 40th Anniversary Tribute. Written and Illustrated by various. Perfect Square/VIZ Media, 2014. 144pp. 978-1-4215-7141-6, hardcover. A ◎

> A collection of stories by a wonderful assortment of creators to celebrate Hello Kitty's 40th anniversary. The book also includes a foreword by Jennifer L. Holm and Matthew Holm, creators of *Babymouse*.

Invader Zim. Written by **Jhonen Vasquez** and **Eric Trueheart**, Illustrated by **Aaron Alexovich**, **Megan Lawton**, **Simon Troussellier**, and **Rikki Simons**. Oni Press, 2016. 128pp. 978-1-620102-93-0. Y ⌨

> A continuation of the popular animated TV series that originally aired from 2001 to 2006. Zim is an extraterrestrial from the planet Irk. He plans to conquer the Earth, but meets resistance from Dib, a young paranormal investigator who is out to stop Zim.

© Jhonen Vasquez.

Looney Tunes, Vol. 1: What's Up, Doc? Written and Illustrated by various. DC Comics, 2016. 144pp. 978-1-4012-6359-1. A

> A collection reprinting the ongoing Looney Tunes comic books. Featuring all of your favorite Warner Bros. characters including Bug Bunny, Daffy Duck, Elmer Fudd, Wile E. Coyote, Road Runner, and more!

Minions. Written by **Stephane Lapuss**. Illustrated by **Renaud Collin**. Titan Comics, 2015– . A 🎬

> The cute yellow Minions, the silly group of creatures who are henchmen to Gru from the films *Despicable Me* (2010), *Despicable Me 2* (2013) and *Minions* (2015), the most evil man on the planet, star in their own silent graphic

© Titan Comics.

novel collection! The collections feature short stories of the goofy Minions as they go about their daily lives in servitude to Gru and making mischief along the way.

Vol. 1: Banana! 2015. 48pp. 978-1-78276-554-7.
Vol. 2: Evil Panic. 2016. 48pp. 978-1-78276-555-4.

Mickey Mouse. Written by **Andrea Castellan**, **Giorgio Cavazzano**, **Bill Wright**, and **Jonathan Gray**. Illustrated by, **Giorgio Cavazzano**, **Bill Wright**, **Manuel Gonzales**, and **Paul Murry**. IDW Publishing. A 🖳 📟 ◎

Mickey Mouse is perhaps one of the most-recognizable characters around the world. Created by Walt Disney and Ub Iwerks in 1928 the animated short Steamboat Willie. Since they he's been an icon for the Walt Disney company and has appeared in animated shorts, newspaper comics, TV shows, films, as well as a corporate symbol for the Walt Disney Company. The stories published by IDW Publishing reprint classic tales from Italy that have never appeared in print in the United States and features many other classic Disney characters as well as ones exclusive to the comics. The *Timeless Tales* collections are hardcover editions of the books published by IDW but in a more collector-friendly format with bonus content. *The Mickey Mouse Shorts, Season One* collection adapts the award-winning short films from Disney Television Animation was created by Paul Rudish.

The Mysterious Crystal Ball. 2015. 148pp. 978-1-63140-445-0.
The Chirikawa Necklace. 2016. 120pp. 978-1-63140-575-4.
Gift of the Sun Lord. 2016. 116pp. 978-1-63140-514-3.
Shadow of the Colossus. 2016. 124pp. 978-1-63140-687-4.
Timeless Tales, Vol. 1. 2016. 260pp. 978-1-63140-580-8, hardcover.
Timeless Tales, Vol. 2. 2017. 256pp. 978-1-63140-801-4, hardcover.
Dark Mines of the Phantom Metal. 2017. 124pp. 978-1-63140-857-1.
Mickey Mouse Shorts, Season One. 2017. 132pp. 978-1-63140-814-4.
Darkenblot. 2017. 124pp. 978-1-63140-932-5.

Mickey Mouse: Mysterious Melody. Written and illustrated by **Bernard Cosey**. IDW Publishing, 2017. 64pp. 978-1-63140-777-2, hardcover. A ◎

A look at what Mickey Mouse was like before his first appearance in 1928. Set as a "what if" story—see Mickey before he became famous—when he was the writer for Oswald the Lucky Rabbit. Find out how Mickey met Minnie and more by Swiss cartoonist Bernard Cosey.

The Muppets. Written and Illustrated by **Roger Langridge**. Boom! Studios, 2009–2011; Marvel Comics, 2012–2014. A ◎ 📟 🖳

Kermit, Gonzo, Miss Piggy, Fozzie Bear, and all the rest are here in these comic book adventures. Roger Langridge's sense of humor was perfectly appropriate for

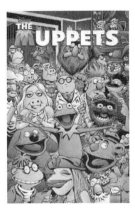

© 2014 Disney.

the zany format of the Muppets's as a comic book series. The Omnibus edition collects the Roger Langridge books previously published by Boom! Studios in a deluxe hardcover edition.

Meet the Muppets. 2009. 112pp. 978-1-60886-527-7, hardcover; 978-1-93450-685-1.
The Treasure of Peg-Leg Wilson. 2010. 112pp. 978-1-60886-530-7, hardcover; 978-1-60886-504-8.
On the Road. 2010. 112pp. 978-1-60886-516-1.
Family Reunion. 2010. 112pp. 978-1-60886-587-1.
Muppet Mash. 2011. 128pp. 978-1-60886-611-3.
The Four Seasons. 2012. 96pp. 978-0-7851-6538-5.
The Muppets Omnibus. 2014. 526pp. 978-0-7851-8792-9, hardcover.

Muppet Adaptations. Written and Illustrated by various. Boom! Studios, 2009–2011. A

In the tradition of live-action Muppet films that have adapted classic works such as *The Muppet Christmas Carol* (1992) and *Muppet Treasure Island* (1996), Boom! Studios adapted other classic works in the Muppets style.

Muppet Robin Hood. Written by **Tim Beedle**. Illustrated by **Armand Villavert Jr**. and **David Petersen**. 2009. 112pp. 978-1-60886-526-0, hardcover; 978-1-93450-679-0.
Muppet King Arthur. Written by **Paul Benjamin** and **Patrick Storck**. Illustrated by **Dave Alverez** and **James Silvani**. Boom! Studios, 2010. 112pp. 978-1-60886-556-7, hardcover; 978-1-60886-555-0.
Muppet Peter Pan. Written by **Grace Randolph**. Illustrated by **Amy Mebberson**. Boom! Studios, 2010. 112pp. 978-1-60886-531-4, hardcover; 978-1-60886-507-9.
Muppet Snow White. Written by **Jesse Blaze Snider**. Illustrated by **Shelli Paroline**. Boom! Studios, 2010. 112pp. 978-1-60886-574-1.
Muppet Sherlock Holmes. Written by **Patrick Storck**. Illustrated by **Amy Mebberson**. Boom! Studios, 2011. 128pp. 978-1-60886-613-7.

My Little Pony. IDW Publishing. 2013– . Y 🎭 ◎ 💻

Twilight Sparkle, Fluttershy, Pinky Pie, Rainbow Dash, Rarity and Applejack and the rest of the magical horses from the magical kingdom of Equestria appear in these various series from IDW. Some of these are new stories while others are based the animated cartoon series *My Little Pony: Friendship is Magic*, which debuted in 2010 and is still extremely popular today. The *Friendship is Magic* series won the Best All-Ages Comic from Diamond Comic Distributors' Gem Awards. The series has proved so popular with not only girls but boys as well, that two other books in the series were added—*Friends Forever* and *Adventures in Friendship* as well as several spin-off stories.

My Little Pony: Friendship Is Magic. Written by **Katie Cook**, **Jeremy Whitley**, **Ted Anderson**, **Christina Rice**, **Thom Zahler**, and various. Illustrated by **Andy Price, Tony Fleecs**, **Agnes Garbowska**, **Jay Fosgitt**, and various. 2013–

Vol. 1. 2013. 104pp. 978-1-61377-605-6.
Vol. 2. 2013. 104pp. 978-1-61377-760-2.
Vol. 3. 2014. 104pp. 978-1-61377-854-8.
Vol. 4. 2014. 104pp. 978-1-61377-960-6.
Vol. 5. 2014. 104pp. 978-1-63140-105-3.
Vol. 6. 2015. 104pp. 978-1-63140-203-6.
Vol. 7. 2015. 104pp. 978-1-63140-324-8.
Vol. 8. 2015. 120pp. 978-1-63140-446-7.
Vol. 9. 2016. 104pp. 978-1-63140-556-3.

Vol. 10. 2016. 124pp. 978-1-63140-688-1.
Vol. 11. 2017. 120pp. 978-1-63140-815-1.
Vol. 12. 2017. 120pp. 978-1-63140-903-5.
Omnibus Vol. 1 2014. 280pp. 978-1-63140-140-4.
Omnibus, Vol. 2. 2015. 280pp. 978-1-63140-409-2.
Omnibus, Vol. 3. 2016. 316pp. 978-1-63140-629-4.

My Little Pony: Friends Forever. Written by **Alex De Campi**, **Jeremy Whitley**, and **Ted Anderson**. Illustrated by **Carla Speed McNeil**, **Christina Rice**, **Amy Mebberson**, and others. 2014–

Vol. 1. 2014. 104pp. 978-1-61377-981-1.
Vol. 2. 2014. 104pp. 978-1-63140-159-6.
Vol. 3. 2014. 104pp. 978-1-63140-243-2.
Vol. 4. 2015. 104pp. 978-1-63140-377-4.
Vol. 5. 2015. 104pp. 978-1-63140-488-7.
Vol. 6. 2016. 104pp. 978-1-63140-596-9.
Vol. 7. 2016. 100pp. 978-1-63140-707-9.

Vol. 8. 2016. 100pp. 978-1-63140-839-7.
Vol. 9. 2017. 100pp. 978-1-63140-918-9.
Omnibus Vol. 1. 2016. 292pp. 978-1-63140-771-0.
Omnibus, Vol. 2. 2017. 292pp. 978-1-63140-882-3.

My Little Pony: Adventures in Friendship. Written by **Ryan Lindsay**, **Thom Zahler**, **Barbara Kesel**, and various. Illustrated by **Tony Fleecs**, **Agnes Garbowska**, and various. 2014–

Vol. 1. 2014. 76pp. 978-1-63140-189-3, hardcover.
Vol. 2. 2015. 76pp. 978-1-63140-225-8, hardcover.
Vol. 3. 2015. 76pp. 978-163140-360-6, hardcover.
Vol. 4. 2015. 76pp. 978-1-63140-466-5, hardcover.
Vol. 5. 2016. 76pp. 978-1-63140-610-2, hardcover.

My Little Pony: Fiendship Is Magic. Written by **Jeremy Whitley**, **Ted Anderson**, and others. Illustrated by **Brenda Hickey**, **Tony Fleecs**, and others. 2015. 124pp. 978-1-63140-339-2.

The origins of some of Equestria's greatest villains: Sombra, Tirek, Sirens, Nightmare Moon, and Queen Chrysalis!

My Little Pony: Pony Tales. Written by **Thom Zahler**, **Katie Cook**, **Ted Anderson**, **Georgia Ball**, and others. Illustrated by **Amy Mebberson**, **Ben Bates**, and others. 2013–2014.

Vol. 1. 2013. 104pp. 978-1-61377-740-4.
Vol. 2. 2014. 104pp. 978-1-61377-873-9.

Peanuts. Created by **Charles M. Schulz**. Written **Charles M. Schulz** and **Shane Houghton**. Illustrated by **Charles M. Schulz, Vicki Scott, Mona Koth**, and various. KaBoom/BOOM! Studios, 2012– . A ◎ ⌨ 🎬

© BOOM! Studios.

For 65 years, Charlie Brown, Snoopy, Linus, Lucy, and the rest of the gang have entertained readers of all ages. Now Boom's KaBoom children's line has created a new comic featuring both classic Charles Schulz strips and the first new Peanuts stories since the daily newspaper strip ended in 2000. The stories are written and drawn by various creators with reprints of classic Charles Schulz comics. Also available are original graphic novels and tie-ins to the 2015 feature film. In addition, a 65th Anniversary tribute book, *Peanuts: A Tribute to Charles M. Schulz*, was created with many of comics' greatest creators including Matt Groening, Raina Telgemeier, Jeffrey Brown, and many more. For those who want to see more of the classic Peanuts strips, collections have been put out by Fantagraphics, AMP Kids, and Titan Books.

Peanuts (ongoing series). 2012– .

Vol. 1. 2012. 112pp. 978-1-60886-260-3. *Vol. 5*. 2015. 128pp. 978-1-60886-483-6.
Vol. 2. 2013. 112pp. 978-1-60886-299-3. *Vol. 6*. 2015. 112pp. 978-1-60886-745-5.
Vol. 3. 2014. 128pp. 978-1-60886-357-0. *Vol. 7*. 2016. 112pp. 978-1-60886-790-5.
Vol. 4. 2014. 128pp. 978-1-60886-427-0. *Vol. 8*. 2016. 112pp. 978-1-60886-899-5.

Peanuts: The Beagle has Landed Charlie Brown. Written by **Paige Braddock**. Illustrated by **Vicki Scott**. 2014. 96pp. 978-1-60886-334-1.
Peanuts: A Tribute to Charles M. Schulz. 2015. 144pp. 978-1-60886-714-1, hardcover; 2016. 978-1-60886-888-9.
Peanuts: Where Beagles Dare (Movie Tie-In). 2015. 96pp. 978-1-60886-711-0.

Popeye. IDW Publishing 2013–2015. A ⌨

© King Features Syndicate. TM Hearst
Holdings, Inc.

When he first debuted in 1929, Popeye was just another character in the long-running *Thimble Theatre*. Soon he became the star and title character, and he, along with Olive Oil, Wimpy, and others, appeared in cartoons, movies, and of course, many comic books. Classic Popeye collects issues from the Dell series of the 1940s and '50s, while new stories appeared in 2012–2013 series that has been collected in three smaller volumes and one large one.

Popeye. Written by **Roger Langridge**. Illustrated by **Bruce Ozella**, **Vince Musacchia**, and **Ken Wheaton**. IDW Publishing, 2013–2014. A.

Vol. 1. 104pp. 978-1-6137-7423-6.
Vol. 2. 104pp. 978-1-6137-7587-5.
Vol. 3. 104pp. 978-1-6137-7685-8.
Popeye: The Whole Shebang. 2014. 300pp. 978-1-6137-7893-7.

Classic Popeye. Written and Illustrated by **Bud Sagendorf**. IDW Publishing, 2013–2015. A

> *Vol. 1*. 2013. 212pp. 978-1-6137-7557-8.
> *Vol. 2: Moon Goon and More*. 2013. 212pp. 978-1-6137-7652-0.
> *Vol. 3: Which Whistle and More*. 2014. 252pp. 978-1-6137-7779-4.
> *Vol. 4: King Blozo's Problem and More*. 2014. 252pp. 978-1-6137-7936-1.
> *Vol. 5: A Thousand Bucks Worth of Fun and More*. 2015. 200pp. 978-1-6314-0175-6.
> *Vol. 6: Weed Shortage and More*. 2015. 192pp. 978-1-6314-0325-5.
> *Vol. 7*. 2015. 200pp. 978-1-6314-0447-4.

Punky Brewster. Written by **Joelle Sellner**. Illustrated by **Lesley Vamos**. IDW Publishing, 2015. 112pp. 978-1-63140-314-9. Y

> A faithful adaptation of the classic 1980s sitcom but with a slightly more modern twist. Young Punky is an orphan scraping by on the streets of Chicago with her pet dog Brandon. A cheerful attitude despite her circumstances, she's having a hard time finding a foster home. When all hope seems lost, Punky may have found a true home with a cranky old curmudgeon named Henry.

Rocky and Bullwinkle. IDW Publishing, 2014. A 🖳

> Bullwinkle J. Moose and Rocky the Flying Squirrel have entertained generations, primarily with their early 1960s animated series. They have also appeared in comic book form. IDW has collected issues from the *Bullwinkle* comic series from Gold Key. There have been four volumes to date collecting four issues each, plus "Classic Adventures" which collects the first 12 issues. Recently, IDW began a new comic that has also been collected.

Rocky and Bullwinkle Classics. Written by **Jack Mendelsohn** and **Dave Berg**. Illustrated by **Al Kilgore**, **Fred Fredericks**, **Jerry Robinson**, and **Mel Crawford**. 2014–2015.

> *Vol. 1: Star Billing*. 2014. 122pp. 978-1-6137-7914-9.
> *Vol. 2: Vacational Therapy*. 2014. 124pp. 978-1-6314-0019-3.
> *Vol. 3: Mastermind Moose*. 2014. 124pp. 978-1-6314-0161-9.
> *Vol. 4: Sneezy Does It*. 2015. 104pp. 978-1-6314-0275-3.

Rocky and Bullwinkle Classics Adventures. 2015. 328pp. 978-1-6314-0490-0.

Rocky and Bullwinkle. Written by **Mark Evanier**. Illustrated by **Roger Langridge**. 2014. 104pp. 978-1-6314-0044-5.

Scooby-Doo Team Up. Written by **Sholly Fisch**. Illustrated by **Dario Brizuela**. DC Comics, 2015– . Y

> In the 1972–74 animated series *The New Scooby-Doo Movies* Scooby-Doo and the gang would meet both celebrities (Don Knotts, Sonny and Cher, etc.) and characters from TV, cartoons, and comics (Speed Buggy, Batman, and Robin, etc.). Over 40 years later, Scooby-Doo Team-Up carries on the tradition of having them work with not only heroes like Superman, Batman, and Wonder Woman, but the Jetsons, Secret Squirrel, The Flintstones, and other Warner Brothers-owned characters. DC had previously published Scooby Doo titles that have had their own collections.

Vol. 1. 2015. 128pp. 978-1-4012-4946-5.
Vol. 2. 2015. 128pp. 978-1-4012-5859-7.

The Simpsons/Futurama Infinitely Secret Crossover Crisis. Written and Illustrated by **Matt Groening et al.** Harry N. Abrams, 2010. 208pp. 978-0-81-098837-8. Y 🎗 ◎ 💻

> The comic crossover event of the century! When the casts of Matt Groening's two popular cartoon series, *The Simpsons* and *Futurama*, meet up, both worlds will never be the same again. The collection features two crossover tales including Fry's battle against the Brain Spawn as he and the rest of the Planet Express are crew up trapped in a *Simpsons* comic book as well as what happens when the citizens of Springfield are transported to New York in the year 3005. The story was recognized by YALSA's Great Graphic Novels for Teens in 2011.

The Simpsons Comics. Written and Illustrated by **Matt Groening**, **Bill Morrison**, and various. Bongo/HarperTrade/Perennial, 1994– . Y 🎗 ◎ 💻

© 2016 Matt Groening and HarperPerennial, a Division of HarperCollins Publishing.

> The longest-running prime-time television show in U.S. history (28 seasons and over 600 episodes as of this writing) since its debut on December 17, 1989. Set in the fictional U.S. town of Springfield, the comics continues the hilarious lampooning antics of well-meaning buffoon Homer, his wife Marge, trouble-maker son Bart, brainiac daughter Lisa, baby Maggie, and Grampa Simpson. Drawing from the large cast of main and supporting characters including Comic Book Guy, Barney Gumble, C. Montgomery Burns, and Bumble Bee Man, the satirical series continues to make light of middle-class living in America and popular culture topics including movies, music, and comic books. The series won an Eisner Award for Best Short Story in 1994 for "The Amazing Colossal Homer." The story is collected in the graphic novel *Simpsons Extravaganza.* The series has also won an Eisner for Best Title for Younger Readers/Best Comics Publication for a Younger Audience in 2000. The series has also received recognition by YALSA's Quick Picks for Reluctant Readers several years in a row for *Simpsons Comics a Go-Go* (2001), *Simpsons Comics Royale* (2002), *Simpsons Comics Unchained* (2003), and *Simpsons Comics Madness* (2004).

Simpsons Comics Extravaganza. 1994. 128pp. 978-0-06-095086-6.
Simpsons Comics Spectacular. 1995. 128pp. 978-0-06-095148-1.
Simpsons Comics Simpsorama. 1996. 128pp. 978-0-06-095199-3.
Simpsons Comics Strike Back. 1996. 128pp. 978-0-06-095212-9.
Simpsons Comics Wingding. 1997. 120pp. 978-0-06-095245-7.
Simpsons Comics Big Bonanza. 1999. 120pp. 978-0-06-095317-1.
Simpsons Comics On Parade. 1999. 120pp. 978-0-06-095280-8.
Simpsons Comics a Go-Go. 2000. 120pp. 978-0-06-095566-3.
Simpsons Comics Royale. 2001. 160pp. 978-0-06-093378-4.
Simpsons Comics Unchained. 2002. 176pp. 978-0-06-000797-3.

Simpsons Comics Madness. 2003. 176pp. 978-0-06-053061-7.
Simpsons Comics Belly Buster. 2004. 176pp. 978-0-06-058750-5.
Simpsons Comics Holiday Humdinger. 2004. 144pp. 978-0-06-072338-5.
Simpsons Comics Barn Burner. 2005. 160pp. 978-0-06-074818-0.
Simpsons Comics Jam-Packed Jamboree. 2006. 128pp. 978-0-06-087661-6.
Simpsons Comics Beach Blanket Bongo. 2007. 128pp. 978-0-06-123126-1.
Simpsons Comics Dollars to Donuts. 2008. 160pp. 978-0-06-143697-0.
Simpsons Comics Hit The Road! 2009. 144pp. 978-0-06-169881-1.
Simpsons Comics Get Some Fancy Book Learnin'. 2010. 128pp. 978-0-06-195787-1.
Simpsons Comics Meltdown. 2011. 144pp. 978-0-06-203653-7.
Simpsons Comics Confidential. 2012. 128pp. 978-0-06-211532-4.
Simpsons Comics Supernova. 2013. 128pp. 978-0-06-225438-2.
Simpsons Comics Colossal Compendium, Vol. 1. 2013. 176pp. 978-0-06-226775-7.
Simpsons Comics Colossal Compendium, Vol. 2. 2014. 176pp. 978-0-06-233609-5.
Simpsons Comics Shake-Up. 2014. 176pp. 978-0-06-230185-7.
Simpsons Comics Clubhouse. 2015. 128pp. 978-0-06-236060-1.
Simpsons Comics Colossal Compendium, Vol. 3. 2015. 176pp. 978-0-06-236059-5.
Simpsons Comics Chaos. 2016. 128pp. 978-0-06-241947-7.
Simpsons Comics Colossal Compendium, Vol. 4. 2016. 176pp. 978-0-06-242326-9.
Simpsons Comics Colossal Compendium, Vol. 5. 2017. 176pp. 978-0-06-256754-3.
Simpsons Comics Knockout. 2017. 128pp. 978-0-06-256891-5.

The Simpsons Treehouse of Horror. Written and Illustrated by **Matt Groening** and various. Bongo/HarperTrade/Perennial, 1999– . Y 🎖 ◎ 🖥

© 2016 Matt Groening and HarperPerennial, a Division of HarperCollins Publishing.

An annual tradition since the first Halloween episode on October 25, 1990, the comic book Treehouse of Horror stories continue to spoof the scary and spooky things that go bump in the night and features the Simpsons cast in a gore-ific theme. Anything is lampooned in the collections including tributes to giant monster movies, slasher films, classic horror novels, science fiction stories, and more. The compilations and their original issues have been nominated for comic book industry awards for years and won an Eisner Award in 2000 for Best Humor Publication. The collection *Bart Simpson's Treehouse of Horror Spine-Tingling Spooktacular* received recognition by YALSA's Popular Paperbacks for Young Adults committee in 2002 on the *Graphic Novels: Superheroes and Beyond* list.

Bart Simpson's Treehouse of Horror Heebie-Jeebie Hullabaloo. 1999. 144pp. 978-0-06-098762-6.
Bart Simpson's Treehouse of Horror Spine-Tingling Spooktacular. 2001. 144pp. 978-0-06-093714-0.
The Simpsons Treehouse of Horror: Fun-Filled Frightfest. 2003. 128pp. 978-0-06-056070-6.
The Simpsons Treehouse of Horror: Hoodoo Voodoo Brouhaha. 2006. 128pp. 978-0-06-114872-9.
The Simpsons Treehouse of Horror Dead Man's Jest, 2008. 128pp. 978-0-06-157135-0.
The Simpsons Treehouse of Horror From Beyond the Grave, 2011. 128pp. 978-0-06-206900-9.

Bart Simpson. Created by **Matt Groening**. Written and Illustrated by various. HarperPerennial. 1995–2017. A ◎ 🖥

The comic book adventures of kid troublemaker and skateboarding underachiever, Bart Simpson. The 10-year-old son of Marge and Homer Simpson, the juvenile jokester's collected short stories revolve around daily fun life in Springfield, USA where almost anything can happen. Bart's colorful cast of supporting characters include many of The Simpsons television staples including his parents, Bart's sisters Lisa and Maggie, best friend Milhouse, and many more.

Bartman: The Best of the Best! 1995. 128pp. 978-0-06-095151-1.
Big Book of Bart Simpson. 2002. 120pp. 978-0-06-008469-1.
Big Bad Book of Bart Simpson. 2003. 128pp. 978-0-06-055590-0.
Big Bratty Book of Bart Simpson. 2004. 120pp. 978-0-06-072178-7.
Big Beefy Book of Bart Simpson. 2005. 118pp. 978-0-06-074819-7.
Big Bouncy Book of Bart Simpson. 2006. 128pp. 978-0-06-112455-6.
Big Beastly Book of Bart Simpson. 2007. 128pp. 978-0-06-123128-5.
Big Brilliant Book of Bart Simpson. 2008. 128pp. 978-0-06-145022-8.
Bart Simpson: Son Of Homer. 2009. 128pp. 978-0-06-169879-8.
Bart Simpson: Class Clown. 2010. 128pp. 978-0-06-197629-2.
Bart Simpson: Prince of Pranks. 2011. 128pp. 978-0-06-204500-3.
Bart Simpson: Out to Lunch. 2012. 128pp. 978-0-06-211533-1.
Bart Simpson Big Shot. 2013. 128pp. 978-0-06-226254-7.
Bart Simpson to the Rescue. 2014. 128pp. 978-0-06-230183-3.
Bart Simpson Blastoff. 2015. 128pp. 978-0-06-236061-8.
Bart Simpson: Master of Disaster. 2016. 128pp. 978-0-06-241951-4.
Bart Simpson Sucker Punch. 2017. 128pp. 978-0-06-256893-9.

The Smurfs. Written and Illustrated by **Peyo**. Papercutz, 2010– . A

This series from Papercutz collect new translations of the classic comic by Belgian artist Peyo about the little blue creatures that were "three apples high" and have appeared in America in animation, film, and elsewhere.

Vol. 1: The Purple Smurfs. 2010. 56pp. 978-1-59707-207-6, hardcover; 978-1-59707-206-9.
Vol. 2: The Smurfs and the Magic Flute. 2010. 56pp. 9781597072090, hardcover; 978-1-59707-208-3.
Vol. 3: The Smurf King. 2010. 56pp. 978-1-59707-225-0, hardcover; 978-1-59707-224-3.
Vol. 4: The Smurfette. 2011. 56pp. 978-1-59707-237-3, hardcover; 978-1-59707-236-6.
Vol. 5: The Smurfs and the Egg. 2011. 56pp. 978-1-59707-247-2, hardcover; 978-1-59707-246-5.
Vol. 6: The Smurfs and the Howlbird. 2011. 56pp. 978-1-59707-261-8, hardcover; 978-1-59707-260-1.
Vol. 7: The Astrosmurf. 2011. 56pp. 978-1-59707-251-9, hardcover; 978-1-59707-250-2.
Vol. 8: The Smurf Apprentice. 2011. 56pp. 978-1-59707-280-9, hardcover; 978-1-59707-279-3.
Vol. 9: Gargamel and the Smurfs. 2011. 56pp. 978-1-59707-290-8, hardcover; 978-1-59707-289-2.
Vol. 10: The Return of the Smurfette. 2012. 56pp. 978-1-59707-293-9, hardcover; 978-1-59707-292-2.

Vol. 11: The Smurf Olympics. 2012. 56pp. 978-1-59707-302-8, hardcover; 978-1-59707-301-1.
Vol. 12: Smurfs Versus Smurf. 2012. 56pp. 978-1-59707-321-9, hardcover; 978-1-59707-320-2.
Vol. 13: Smurf Soup. 2012. 56pp. 978-1-59707-359-2, hardcover; 978-1-59707-381-3.
Vol. 14: The Baby Smurf. 2013. 56pp. 978-1-59707-382-0, hardcover; 978-1-59707-381-3.
Vol. 15: The Smurflings. 2013. 56pp. 978-1-59707-408-7, hardcover; 978-1-59707-407-0.
Vol. 16: The Aerosmurf. 2013. 56pp. 978-1-59707-427-8, hardcover; 978-1-59707-426-1.
Vol. 17: The Strange Awakening of Lazy Smurf. 2014. 56pp. 978-1-59707-510-7, hardcover;
978-1-59707-509-1.
Vol. 18: The Finance Smurf. 2014. 56pp. 978-1-59707-725-5, hardcover; 978-1-59707-724-8.
Vol. 19: The Jewel Smurfer. 2015. 56pp. 978-1-62991-195-3, hardcover; 978-1-62991-194-6.
Vol. 20: Doctor Smurf. 2016. 56pp. 978-1-62991-434-3, hardcover; 978-1-62991-433-6.
Vol. 21: The Wild Smurf. 2016. 64pp. 978-1-62991-576-0, hardcover. 978-1-62991-575-3.
Vol. 22: The Smurf Menace. 2017. 64pp. 978-1-62991-623-1. Hardcover. 978-1-62991-622-4.
Smurfs Christmas. 2013. 56pp. 978-1-59707-452-0, hardcover; 978-1-59707-451-3.
The Smurfs Monsters. 2015. 56pp. 978–1–629912769, hardcover; 978-1-62991-275-2.
The Smurfs: The Village Beyond the Wall. 2017. 64pp. hardcover. 978-1-62991-783-2.

The Smurfs Anthology 2013–

Vol. 1. 2013. 192pp. 978-1-59707-417-9, hardcover.
Vol. 2. 2013. 192pp. 978-1-59707-417-9, hardcover.
Vol. 3. 2014. 192pp. 978-1-59707-746-0, hardcover.
Vol. 4. 2015. 192pp. 978-1-62991-172-4, hardcover.

Steven Universe. Written by **Jeremy Sorese**. Illustrated by **Coleman Engle**. KaBOOM!/
BOOM! Studios, 2015– . Y 🖥

Created by Rebecca Sugar, the animated series debuted in 2013 and
is still in production. The series focuses on the adventures of Steve,
a boy who lives in the town of Beach City who lives with three magically powered aliens—known as "Crystal Gems"—Garnet, Ame-
thyst, and Pearl. Steven himself is part gem and the four of them go
on adventures to protect the world from others like them that want
to harm Beach City. As Steven slowly starts to figure out his powers
he inherited from his mother, Rose Quartz, he spends time with his
father Greg, as well as his best friend Connie.

Vol. 1. 2015. 128pp. 978-1-60886-706-6.
Vol. 2. 2016. 112pp. 978-1-60886-796-7.
© 2016 BOOM! Studios.   *Too Cool for School.* 2016. 978-1-60886-771-4.

Toy Story. Written by **Dan Jolley** and **Jesse "Blaze" Snider**. Illustrated by **Chris Moreno**
and **Nathan Watson**. Boom! Studios, 2009–2011; Marvel Comics, 2012. A 📽

If you thought the adventures of Buzz Lightyear and Woody ended with the Dis-
ney•Pixar *Toy Story* films, guess again! Join Woody, Buzz, Jesse, Bullseye, Hamm,
and more in all new adventures! The license switched to Marvel Comics for the 2012
Tales from the Toy Chest compilation.

Mysterious Stranger. 2009. 112pp. 978-1-608865-23-9, hardcover; 978-1-934506-91-2.
The Return of Buzz Lightyear. 2010. 978-1-608865-58-1, hardcover; 978-1-608865-57-4.
Some Assembly Required. 2010. 112pp. 978-1-608865-70-3.

Toy Overboard. 2011. 128pp. 978-1-608866-05-2.
Tales from the Toy Chest. 2012. 96pp. 978-0-7851-6506-4.

Wall-E. Written by **J. Torres** and **Bryce Carlson**. Illustrated by **Morgan Luthi**. Boom! Studios, 2010. A 🎬

© 2010 Disney•Pixar.

A collection of prequel stories to the popular 2008 Disney•Pixar movie. Wall-E is one of the last remaining cleanup robots left on the planet while mankind is in space waiting for plant life to come back to Earth. While other robots of his kind have run down, Wall-E still thrives, rebuilding himself and seeking to find companionship in the most unique of places. In Out There, an astronaut named Andy arrives on Earth and Wall-E must help him find his family in outer space.

Recharge. 2010. 112pp. 978-1-60886-554-3, hardcover; 978-1-60886-512-3.

Out There. 2010. 112pp. 978-1-60886-568-0.

Zootopia. Written and Illustrated by various. 2016. 240pp. 978-1-77275-177-2. Joe Books, 2016. A

A graphic adaptation of the hit 2016 Disney animated film. In the modern mammal metropolis of Zootopia, the optimistic police officer Judy Hopps is teamed up with a fast-talking fox con-artist named Nick Wilde to uncover a mysterious case. The collection also includes a prequel story before the events of the film.

Funny Animals

Humorous stories in which the protagonist or supporting characters are animals. The animals may appear to be normal-looking animals, typically with the ability to speak, or may be anthropomorphized animals with human qualities as well as the ability to speak. Anthropomorphized stories such as Usagi Yojimbo and the Teenage Mutant Ninja Turtles are not listed in this chapter, but are featured in the action and adventure chapter in this book since the main focus in the stories featuring those characters tends to be on the action side, though some humorous tales may occur. Other licensed anthropomorphized characters including Walt Disney's Mickey Mouse and Donald Duck are listed in the "Animated Cartoon Characters Tie-Ins" section of this chapter.

Ariol. Written by **Emmanuel Guibert**. Illustrated by **Marc Boutavant**. Papercutz, 2013– . Y

The daily life of a tween blue donkey named Ariol. The series features his school days, his best friend Ramono the pig, his crush Petula (a cute little cow with freckles), and his teacher is a dog. Basically, he's just like you and me. The series is translated from the French where it debuted in 1999.

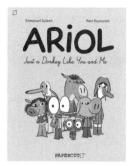

Vol. 1: Just a Donkey Like You and Me. 2013. 124pp. 978-1-59707-399-8.
Vol. 2: Thunder Horse. 2013. 124pp. 978-1-59707-412-4.
Vol. 3: Happy as a Pig. 2013. 124pp. 978-1-59707-487-2.
Vol. 4: A Beautiful Cow. 2014. 124pp. 978-1-59707-513-8.
Vol. 5: Bizzbilla Hits the Bullseye. 2014. 124pp. 978-1-59707-735-4.
Vol. 6: Where's Petula? 2015. 124pp. 978-1-62991-186-1.
Vol. 7: Top Dog. 2016. 124pp. 978-1-62991-280-6.
Vol. 8: The Three Donkeys. 2016. 124pp. 978-1-62991-439-8.
Vol. 9: The Teeth of the Rabbit. 2016. 124pp. 978-1-62991-602-6.
Vol. 10: Little Rats of the Opera. 2016. 124pp. 978-1-62991-736-8.

Babymouse. Created by **Jenni Holm** and **Matt Holm.** Illustrated by **Matt Holm**. Random House Books for Young Readers, 2005– . 🐾 Y ◉

Babymouse is a sassy middle school student who attends an all-animal school. She has curly whiskers that seem to never go straight, a school locker that is always jammed, and no matter how hard she tries, Babymouse will never be as popular as Felicia Furrypaws. But, Babymouse has the best of friends and an active imagination and always imagines herself in fun places from a rock star, mad scientist, to an Olympic gold medalist. Join her and her friends on adventure after adventure with each one as exciting as the next! The Babymouse series is extremely popular with younger readers and has been a hit since the series was created in 2005. The series is co-created by siblings Jenni and Matt Holm. In 2016, the first *Babymouse* picture book, *Little Babymouse and the Christmas Cupcakes* came out. In 2017 a new hybrid series featuring Babymouse as a middle schooler in *Babymouse: Tales from the Locker*.

Our Hero. 2005. 96pp. 978-0-375-83230-7.
Queen of the World. 2005. 96pp. 978-0-375-83229-1.
Beach Babe. 2006. 96pp. 978-0-375-83231-4.
Heartbreaker. 2006. 96pp. 978-0-375-83798-2.
Rock Star. 2006. 96pp. 978-0-375-83232-1.
Camp Babymouse. 2007. 96pp. 978-0-375-83988-7.
Puppy Love. 2007. 96pp. 978-0-375-83990-0.
Skater Girl. 2007. 96pp. 978-0-375-83989-4.
Monster Mash. 2008. 96pp. 978-0-375-84387-7.
Dragonslayer. 2009. 96pp. 978-0-375-85712-6.
The Musical. 2009. 96pp. 978-0-375-84388-4.
Burns Rubber. 2010. 96pp. 978-0-375-85713-3.
Cupcake Tycoon. 2010. 96pp. 978-0-375-86573-2.
Mad Scientist. 2011. 96pp. 978-0-375-86574-9.
A Very Babymouse Christmas. 2011. 96pp. 978-0-375-86779-8.
Babymouse for President. 2012. 96pp. Eisner Award. 978-0-375-86780-4.
Extreme Babymouse. 2013. 96pp. 978-0-307-93160-3.
Happy Birthday Babymouse. 2014. 96pp. 978-0-307-93161-0.
Bad Babysitter. 2015. 96pp. 978-0-307-93162-7.
Babymouse Goes for the Gold. 2016. 96pp. 978-0-307-93163-4.

Benny and Penny. Written and Illustrated by **Geoffrey Hayes**. Toon Books, 2008–2013. A

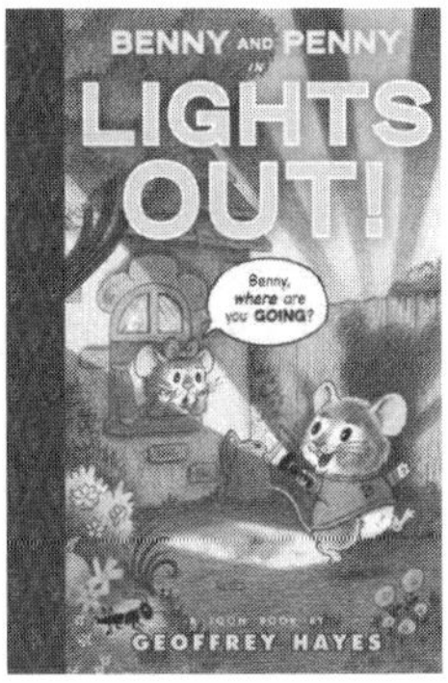

© 2016 Toon Books.

Benny and his little sister Penny are two mice who love to get into all sorts of adventures at their home. Though Benny thinks his sister is too little to play with him, they both discover they have a lot in common with each other and are the best of friends as well as siblings. The series focuses on simple dialogue accompanied by colorful illustrations that help to bring their world to life. In 2010 *Benny and Penny in the Big No-No!* was recognized with a Theodor Seuss Geisel Award presented by the Association for Library Service to Children. 1 2

Benny and Penny in Just Pretend. 2008. 32pp. 978-0-9799238-0-7, hardcover. 3
Benny and Penny and the Big No-No! 2009. 32pp. 978-0-9799238-9-0, hardcover.
Benny and Penny and the Toy Breaker. 2010. 32pp. 978-1-9351790-7-8, hardcover.
Benny and Penny in Lights Out! 2012. 32pp. 978-1-935179-20-7, hardcover.
Benny and Penny in Lost and Found. 2013. 40pp. 978-1-935179-64-1, hardcover.

Binky. Written and Illustrated by **Ashley Spires**. Kids Can Press, 2009–2013. Y 4

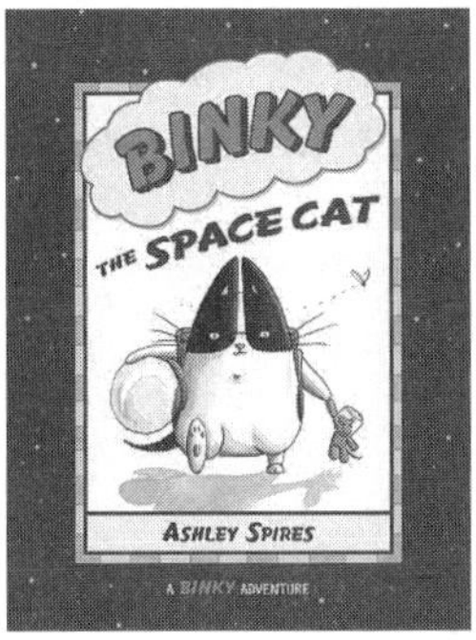

© 2016 Kids Can Press.

Binky is a cat with a very active imagination. He dreams that he's a space cat and is ready to explore outer space (his own back yard) and battle aliens (bugs). With his crew of fellow space pets, they'll be ready to explore the great vast regions of space and beyond in this fun younger reader series where every day's an adventure just waiting to happen! 5

The Space Cat. 2009. 64pp. 978-1-55453-309-1, hardcover
To the Rescue. 2010. 64pp. 978-1-55453-502-6, hardcover
Under Pressure. 2011. 64pp. 978-1-55453-504-0, hardcover. 6
Takes Charge. 2012. 64pp. 978-1-55453-703-7, hardcover.
License to Scratch. 2013. 64pp. 978-1-55453-963-5, hardcover.

Bird and Squirrel. Written and Illustrated by **James Burks**. Graphix/Scholastic Books, 2012–2015. Y

The unlikeliest of friends, Bird is carefree and reckless, while Squirrel is nervous and easily frightened. Together the two of them are the best of friends, but adventure and humor are never too far from them as they seek fun, adventure, and warmer weather (and no cats!). 7

Bird and Squirrel on the Run. 2012. 128pp. 978-0-545-31283-7.
Bird and Squirrel on Ice. 2014. 128pp. 978-0-545-56318-5.
Bird and Squirrel on the Edge. 2015. 144pp. 978-0-545-80426-4.
Bird an Squirrel on Fire. 2017. 192pp. 978-0-545-80430-1.

Chi's Sweet Home. Written and Illustrated by **Konami Kanata**. Vertical Comics, 2010– . Y Japanese manga. あ 9

The adventures of a small, adorable white and grey kitten. After she wanders away from her mother cat, a small kitten is rescued by a young boy named Youhei. He brings the kitten back to his family's apartment complex where no pets are allowed. The family tries to give the kitten away, but it proves difficult so they keep the kitten. The kitten is humorously named "Chi" after it answers mistakenly to the Japanese word for urine ("shi"—short for "shikko") and as the series progresses the kitten has many adventures in the house. The series was adapted into an anime series in Japan that originally aired from 2008 to 2009. Beginning in 2015, Vertical began re-issuing the *Chi's Sweet Home* books in three-in-one volume collections with bonus content called *The Complete Chi's Sweet Home*.

Vol. 1. 2010. 168pp. 978-1-93428-781-1.
Vol. 2. 2010. 158pp. 978-1-934287-85-9.
Vol. 3. 2010. 144pp. 978-1-934287-91-0.
Vol. 4. 2010. 146pp. 978-1-934287-96-5.
Vol. 5. 2011. 160pp. 978-1-934287-13-2.
Vol. 6. 2011. 160pp. 978-1-935654-14-8.
Vol. 7. 2011. 168pp. 978-1-935654-21-6.
Vol. 8. 2012. 160pp. 978-1-935654-35-3.
Vol. 9. 2012. 160pp. 978-1-935654-42-1.
Vol. 10. 2013. 160pp. 978-1-935654-69-8.
Vol. 11. 2014. 160pp. 978-1-939130-51-8.
Vol. 12. 2015. 160pp. 978-1-941220-25-2.

The Complete Chi's Sweet Home. 2015–2016

Vol. 1. 2015. 480pp. 978-1-942993-16-2.
Vol. 2. 2016. 480pp. 978-1-942993-17-9.
Vol. 3. 2016. 480pp. 978-1-942993-48-3.
Vol. 4. 2016. 480pp. 978-1-942993-57-5.

Congress of the Animals. Written and Illustrated by **Jim Woodring**. Fantagraphics Books, 2011. 104pp. 978-1-60699-437-5, hardcover. O

When Frank's house is destroyed in a freak accident, he takes up a job to help pay for the repairs but ultimately escapes the harshness of a factory job to escape it. He sets out to the hallucinogenic-like world of the Unifactor and falls in love with a girl named Fran in this silently told graphic novel.

Dog Man. Written and Illustrated by **Dav Pilkey**. Graphix/Scholastic Books, 2016– . Y

Cover © Scholastic Inc.

Spun off from the Adventures of Captain Underpants comes a new hero from the minds of boys Harold and George: Dog Man! When a police officer and his trusty canine Greg are in an accident, a life-saving operation is the only way to save them is done and Dog Man is born! Now can Dog Man continue to fight on the side of justice against the sinister Petey the cat while also fighting the urge to go for a walk? The adventures will continue in 2018 with the third title *A Tail of Two Kitties*.

Vol. 1: Dog Man Unleashed. 2016. 240pp. 978-0-545-58160-8, hardcover.
Vol. 2. 2017. 240pp. 978-0-545-93520-3, hardcover.

Elephant and Piggie. Written and Illustrated by **Mo Willems**. Disney Hyperion Press, 2007–2016. Y 🏆 ◎

Gerald the elephant and Piggie the pig are the best of friends in this early-reader graphic novel series by Mo Willems. Gerald gets worried a lot and Piggie is a fun-loving pig. The series features the two of them speaking in conversational style with Piggie's words appearing in pink letter bubbles and Gerald's appearing in grey letter bubbles. The stories are often very humorous and guaranteed to get a laugh out of youngsters

and their parents. *There Is a Bird on Your Head* and *Are You Ready to Play Outside?* won the Geisel Medal in 2008 and 2009 as well as five Geisel Honors (for *We Are in a Book!*, *I Broke My Trunk!*, *Let's Go for a Drive!*, *A Big Guy Took My Ball!* and *Waiting Is Not Easy!*). The series concluded in 2016 much to the chagrin of parents everywhere with the last book *The Thank You Book*.

I Am Invited to a Party! 2007. 64pp. 978-1-4231-0687-6, hardcover.

My Friend is Sad. 2007. 64pp. 978-1-4231-1347-8, hardcover.

There Is a Bird on Your Head!. 2007. 64pp. 978-1-4231-0686-9, hardcover.

Today I Will Fly!. 2007. 64pp. 978-1-4231-0295-3, hardcover.

Are You Ready to Play Outside?. 2008. 64pp. 978-1-4231-1347-8, hardcover.

I Love My New Toy!. 2008. 64pp. 978-1-4231-0961-7, hardcover.

I Will Surprise My Friend!. 2008. 64pp. 978-1-4231-0962-4, hardcover.

Elephants Cannot Dance!. 2009. 64pp. 978-1-4231-1410-9, hardcover.

Pigs Make Me Sneeze!. 2009. 64pp. 978–1423114116, hardcover.

Watch Me Throw The Ball!. 2009. 64pp. 978-1-4231-1348-5, hardcover.

Can I Play Too?. 2010. 64pp. 978-1-4231-1991-3, hardcover.

I am Going!. 2010. 64pp. 978-1-4231-1990-6. hardcover.

We Are In A Book!. 2010. 64pp. 978-1-4231-3308-7, hardcover.

Happy Pig Day!. 2011. 64pp. 978-1-4231-4342-0, hardcover.

I Broke My Trunk!. 2011. 64pp. 978-1-4231-3309-4, hardcover.

Should I Share My Ice Cream?. 2011. 64pp. 978-1-4231-4343-7, hardcover.

Let's Go for a Drive. 2012. 64pp. 978-1-4231-6482-1, hardcover.

Listen to My Trumpet. 2012. 64pp. 978-1-4231-5404-4, hardcover.

A Big Guy Took My Ball. 2013. 64pp. 978-1-4231-7491-2, hardcover.

I'm a Frog!. 2013. 64pp. 978-1-4231-8305-1, hardcover.

My New Friend Is So Fun. 2014. 64pp. 978-1-4231-7958-0, hardcover.

Waiting Is Not Easy!. 2014. 64pp. 978-1-4231-9957-1, hardcover.

I Really Like Slop!. 2015. 64pp. 978-1-4847-2262-6, hardcover.

I Will Take a Nap! 2015. 64pp. 978-1-4847-1630-4, hardcover.

The Thank You Book. 2016. 64pp. 978-1-4231-7828-6, hardcover.

Elephants Never Forget. Written and Illustrated by **Bill Slavin**. Kids Can Press, 2011–2013. Y

Otto, a sweet-natured elephant, will do anything to rescue his childhood best friend Georgie, a monkey who was kidnapped from their home in Africa and taken by a man with a wooden nose. Accompanied by a wisecracking parrot named Crackers, Otto hops on a plane and looks for Georgie in America. Now Otto is on a journey from the big city of New York, to the Circus, and to Hollywood as he searches high and low to find just what happened to Georgie.

Big City Otto. 2011. 80pp. 978-1-55453-477-7.

Big Top Otto. 2013. 80pp. 978-1-55453-807-2.

Big Star Otto. 2015. 80pp. 978-1-89478-697-3.

© 2016 Random House.

Flying Beaver Brothers. Written and Illustrated by **Maxwell Eaton III**. Knopf Books for Young Readers, 2012–2015. Y

Ace and Bub are two beavers who are nothing like each other. Ace likes extreme sports and Bub excels at napping! When their island home or their vacation plans are under threat by a new animal menace, the boys must use their wits and dry humor to save the day!

The Flying Beaver Brothers and the Evil Penguin Plan. 2012. 96pp. 978-0-375-86447-6.

The Flying Beaver Brothers and the Fishy Business. 2012. 96pp. 978-0-375-86448-3.

The Flying Beaver Brothers: Birds vs. Bunnies. 2013. 96pp. 978-0-449-81022-4.

The Flying Beaver Brothers and the Mud-Slinging Moles. 2013. 96pp. 978-0-449-81019-4.

The Flying Beaver Brothers and the Hot Air Baboons. 2014. 96pp. 978-0-385-75466-8.

The Flying Beaver Brothers and the Crazy Critter Race. 2015. 96pp. 978-0-385-75469-9.

Fran. Written and Illustrated by **Jim Woodring**. Fantagraphics Books, 2013. 120pp. 978-1-60699-661-4, hardcover. O

Frank has found newfound love in his feline counterpart named Fran. When an argument set them apart, Frank realizes his mistake and tries to make amends. Joined with his two pets Pupshaw and Pushpaw, Frank wanders a hallucinogenic landscape to lands unknown to get back his love.

FukuFuku Kitten Tales. Written and Illustrated by **Konami Kanata**. Vertical, Inc, 2016– . Y Japanese manga.

By the creator of *Chi's Sweet Home* comes a tale about a kitten named FukuFuku and her daily life. Seasons pass. Nap times. Time to Eat. Play time. More time for sleeping—that is, a look at the life of an adorable kitten.

Vol. 1. 2016. 160pp. 978-1-942993-43-8. A
Vol. 2. 2017. 160pp. 978-1-942993-63-6.

Fuzzy Baseball. Written and Illustrated by **John Steven Gurney**. Papercutz, 2016. 56pp. 978-1-62991-447-0. Y

© 2016 Papercutz.

A young possum named Blossom Honey has always dreamed of playing for the local team, the Fernwood Valley Fuzzies. When she finally joins the team, it's a dream come true! When the team is beginning to lose hope when playing against the Rocky Ridge Red Claws, can Blossom Honey help get her team on the path to victory?

Gary's Garden. Written and Illustrated by **Gary Northfield**. Scholastic Books, 2016. 64pp. 978-0-545-86183-0. A ◎

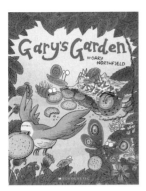

Cover © Scholastic Inc.

If you think you have a silly backyard, welcome to Gary's Garden! It's a silly but fun place where the worms think they're caterpillars, the caterpillars think they're acrobats, the birds raid the house for crackers and other snacks, the fox is giving nocturnal lesson to a hedgehog, the spider traps bugs for a captive audience to his orchestral music, and the squirrel has lost his nuts! Full of colorful creatures from the animal kingdom, they're all from the backyard of creator Gary Northfield!

Guinea Pig: Pet Shop Private Eye. Written by **Colleen AF Venable**. Illustrated by **Stephanie Yue**. Graphic Universe, 2010–2013. Y

Sasspants the guinea pig lives at Mr. Venezi's pet shop as well as a color cast of critters. When Sasspants is mistaken by Hamisher the hamster to be a private eye detective, Sasspants is roped into solving mysteries at the pet shop. Each book revolves around a short mystery with plenty of humor and heart along for the ride.

Vol. 1: Hamster and Cheese. 2010. 48pp. 978-0-7613-5479-6.
Vol. 2: And Then There Were Gnomes. 2010. 48pp. 978-0-7613-5480-2.
Vol. 3: The Ferret's a Foot. 2011. 48pp. 978-0-7613-5629-5.
Vol. 4: Fish You Were Here. 2011. 48pp. 978-0-7613-5630-1.
Vol. 5: Raining Cats and Detectives. 2012. 48pp. 978-0-7613-8541-7.
Vol. 6: Going, Going, Dragon! 2013. 48pp. 978-1-4677-0726-8.

Gon. Written and Illustrated by **Masashi Tanaka**. Kodansha Comics, 2011–2012. A Japanese manga. 🕱 ◎

Though pint-sized, he's still king of the animals and the toughest little dinosaur you'll ever meet. He's Gon, a pygmy Tyrannosaurus Rex and the last of his kind. A friend to the helpless animals of the world, if you're a vicious predator, you've been warned: even though he's silent and a little on the short side, he'll clean your clock and help the helpless. From his travels all around the world to exotic locales and habitats, Gon is the true king of the animals. In each silent story, he roams a different part of the Earth's landscape intermingling with the local animals. From Africa to Australia, he's befriending defenseless animals, looking for a good place to nap, and making the animal kingdom his own. Previous reprintings of *Gon* have won several Eisner Awards when it was originally printed for the categories of Best U.S. Edition of Foreign Material (1998) and Best Humor Publication (1998) as well as a Harvey Award for Best American Edition of Foreign Material (1997).

Vol. 1. 2011. 144pp. 978-1-935429-39-5. *Vol. 5*. 2012. 176pp. 978-1-61262-017-6.
Vol. 2. 2011. 160pp. 978-1-935429-40-1. *Vol. 6*. 2012. 192pp. 978-1-61262-018-3.
Vol. 3. 2011. 160pp. 978-1-935429-41-8. *Vol. 7*. 2012. 176pp. 978-1-61262-019-0.
Vol. 4. 2012. 176pp. 978-1-935429-42-5.

Grumpy Cat. Written by **Royal McGraw**, **Elliot Serrano**, and **Ben Fisher**. Illustrated by **Steve Uy**, **Ken Haeser**, and **Tavis Maiden**. Dynamite Entertainment, 2016– . A

One of the most popular internet sensations—the Grumpy Cat (AKA the real life cat known as Tardar Sauce), the Mistress of Grumpy Memes— is now a comic book series! Join "the World's Grumpiest Cat" and her younger brother Pokey as they get into one misadventure after another!

Misadventures. 2016. 104pp. 978-1-60690-796-2, hardcover; 978-1-60690-909-6.
Grumpus. 2017. 104pp. 978-1-5241-0246-3, hardcover.

© Grumpy Cat LTD. DYNAMITE, DYNAMITE ENTERTAINMENT and its logo are ® & © 2016 Dynamite.

Hippopotamister. Written and Illustrated by **John Green**. First Second, 2016. 96pp. 978-1-62672-200-2, hardcover. Y

When the zoo is too run down and losing customers, Hippo and his friend Red Panda decide it's time to get a new job and look elsewhere. Leaving the confines of the zoo, Hippo realizes to get a job he must act like a human. But after trying job after job, maybe what Hippo needs is to get a job where he can be himself.

© First Second and John Green.

Howard the Duck. Created by **Steve Gerber**. Marvel Comics, 2008– . O

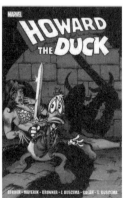

Created in 1973 by Steve Gerber, Howard the Duck is cigar-smoking three-foot tall anthropomorphic duck from another dimension. Trapped on our Earth, he's trying to make the best of it. As an outsider to our culture and way of life, he easily sees the absurdities of our lives with razor-sharp wit. The Howard the Duck collection lampooned the tumultuous 1970s and even included a run for the presidency of the United States. *Howard the Duck* was also released as a movie in 1986 and had a cameo appearance in the 2014 *Guardians of the Galaxy* film. In 2015 creators Chip Zdarsky and Joe Quinones did their own take on the classic quack with him as a private investigator.

© Marvel Comics.

Howard the Duck, 1st series. Written by **Steve Gerber**, **Marv Wolfman**, and **Mark Evanier**. Illustrated by **Val Mayerik**, **Gene Colan**, **Michael Golden**, and **John Buscema**. 2008–2016.

> *The Howard the Duck Omnibus*. 2008. 808pp. 978-0-7851-3023-9, hardcover.
> *The Complete Collection*. 2015–2016.
>
> > *Vol. 1*. 2015. 456pp. 978-0-7851-9776-8.
> > *Vol. 2*. 2016. 360pp. 978-0-7851-9686-0.
> > *Vol. 3*. 2016. 384pp. 978-1-302-90204-9.

Howard the Duck, 2nd series. Written by **Chip Zdarsky**. Illustrated by **Joe Quinones**, **Veronica Fish**, and **Kevin Maguire**. 2015– .

> *Vol. 0: What the Duck?* 2015. 112pp. 978-0-7851-9772-0.
> *Vol. 1: Duck Hunt*. 2016. 160pp. 978-0-7851-9938-0.
> *Vol. 2. Good Night and Good Duck*. 2016. 112pp. 978-0-7851-9939-7.

Little Mouse Gets Ready. Written and Illustrated by **Jeff Smith**. Toon Books, 2009. 32pp. 978-1-935179-01-6, hardcover. Y 🏅 ◎

© Toon Books.

A little mouse learns that there's a lot of this he must learn to do before going to the barn. In order to get ready he must learn how to dress himself from underwear to pants and more in this light-hearted book by *Bone* creator Jeff Smith. In 2010 the book was recognized as an honor book for the Theodor Seuss Geisel Award presented by the Association for Library Service to Children.

Long Tail Kitty. Written and Illustrated by **Lark Pien**. Blue Apple Books. 2009–2015. Y

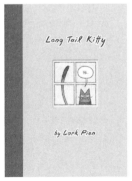
© Lark Pien and Blue Apple Books.

The daily life of a cat who lives in a community with other animal friends including Good Tall Mouse, Bernice the dog, Big E the elephant, and even visiting aliens from outer space! Long Tail Kitty gets stung by a bee, goes grocery shopping with friends,

Long Tail Kitty. 2009. 52pp. 978-1-93470-644-2, hardcover.
Long Tail Kitty: Come Out and Play. 2015. 80pp. 978-1-60905-394-9, hardcover.

March Grand Prix: Fast and the Furriest. Written and Illustrated by **Kean Soo**. Capstone Books, 2015. 978-1-62370-171-0. Y

The race is on as a rabbit named March—who loves racing cars more than anything in the world—wants to be known as the fastest race car driver around. To prove it, he'll have to compete in the streets and a race in the desert to prove his worth!

Mr. Wuffles!. Written and Illustrated by **David Wiesner**. Clarion Books, 2013. 32pp. 978-0-618-75661-2, hardcover. Y 🎗

A nearly silently told picture book about a black cat who, bored with his expensive cat toys, discovers a shiny little disc—which turns out to be the tiny spacecraft! The alien inhabitants seek aid after their ship is damaged by the gigantic feline monster, and they seek the help of the insects in the wall to help repair their ship and escape back into outer space. The book won a Caldecott Honor book in 2014.

Narwhal: Unicorn of the Sea. Written and Illustrated by **Ben Clanton**. Tundra Books, 2016. 64pp. 978-1-101-91826-5. Y

What do you get when a happy-go-lucky narwhal and a series-minded jellyfish get together and become friends? On the outside they have nothing in common, but they soon become the best of friends. Join Narwhal and Jelly on their fun adventures across the ocean in three short story adventures.

© Ben Clanton.

Odd Duck. Written by **Cecil Castellucci**. Illustrated by **Sara Varon**. First Second, 2013. 96pp. 978-1-59643-557-5, hardcover. Y ◎

Theodora is a nice, normal duck—who happens to wear a teacup on her head when she swims. And she never flies south for the winter. Her friend Chad is an odd duck. Everything he does is strange and Theodora just can't get over them. When others make fun of the "odd duck"—is it really Chad they're making fun of? A parable that reminds us all to just be yourself, to follow your own dreams, and to find like friends regardless of what others may think.

© First Second and Cecil Castellucci.

Otto. Written **Jay Lynch**. Illustrated by **Frank Cammuso**. Toon Books, 2008–2013. Y

Otto the cat, in Orange Day meets a genie and has the genie transform everything into his favorite color: orange! In Backwards Day, Otto's birthday presents have been stolen and he must go on a quest to find them. In the end is there anything better than cake and presents?

© Frank Cammuso.

Otto's Orange Day. 2008. 32pp. 978-0-979923-82-1.
Otto's Backwards Day. 2013. 32pp. 978-1-935179-33-7.

Owly. Written and Illustrated by **Andy Runton**. Top Shelf Productions/IDW Publishing, 2004–2012. A 🧍 ◎

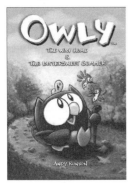

© Andy Runton.

The simple and kind adventures of an owl who is always on the lookout for new friends and fun. The simple yet beautiful stories earned creator Andy Runton an Ignatz Award for Promising New Talent in 2005. The 2011 and 2012 publications are wordless picture books in full color and published by Atheneum Books for Young Readers and stars both Owly and his tiny friend Wormie.

Vol. 1: The Way Home and the Bittersweet Summer. 2004. 160pp. 978-1-891830-62-4.
Vol. 2: Just A Little Blue. 2005. 128pp. 978-1-891830-64-8.
Vol. 3: Flying Lessons. 2005. 128pp. 978-1-891830-76-1.
Vol. 4: A Time to Be Brave. 2007. 120pp. 978-1-891830-89-1.
Vol. 5: Tiny Tales. 2008. 144pp. 978-1-603090-19-3.
Owly and Wormie: Friends All Aflutter. 2011. 40pp. 978-1-4169-5774-4, hardcover.
Owly and Wormie: Bright Lights and Starry Nights. 2012. 40pp. 978-1-4169-5775-1, hardcover.

The Portable Frank. Written and Illustrated by **Jim Woodring**. Fantagraphics Books. 2008. 200pp. 978-1-56097-978-4. O

The Portable Frank is a black and white reprint of the *Frank* comics. There are no words spoken in this graphic novel. The world within the pages of *The Portable Frank* is a bizarre alien world like ours but just enough distortion to be disturbing. Watch as the main character, Frank, lives in this hallucinatory type world as he finds a friend, fights off villains, and survives a trip to another dimension.

Rascal Raccoon's Raging Revenge. Written by **Brendan Hay**. Illustrated by **Justin Wagner**. Oni Press, 2011. 144pp. 978-1-93496-471-2, hardcover. O

After trying for years, Rascal Raccoon's has finally managed to kill his arch-nemesis, the adorable Toonie named Jumpin' Jackalope! But when you've finally fulfilled your life-long dream, what else is there for you to do? Lost and purposeless, Rascal settles on a new arch-nemesis— Pen Man, the animator who drew him! An homage to animated cartoons like Willie E. Coyote.

Sam & Max: Surfin' the Highway. Written and Illustrated by **Steve Purcell**. Telltale Games, 2008. 198pp. 978-0-9792576-2-9. T 🎮 🖥 ◎

Holy jumping mother o' God in a sidecar with chocolate jimmies and a lobster bib! Collects the cult-hit hilarious antics of private investigators Sam the dog and his long-eared rabbit partner Max. The series also inspired a hit video game from LucasArts and Telltale games as well as a cartoon show of the same name. Sam is reminiscent of a canine version of Columbo and Max is pretty much just a naked rabbit wearing a maniacal grin and packing a Colt 45. Together they take on the most absurd cases and still know how to relax by playing a fun game of fizzball, which basically entails hitting cheap beer cans with a whacking object of your choice. The characters have also been adapted into video games and a short-lived animated series.

Squish. Written by **Jenni Holm**. Illustrated by **Matt Holm**. Random House Books for Young Readers, 2011– . Y

© 2016 Jenni Holm and Matt Holm.

Have you ever wondered what life is like for amoeba? Spinning off from their appearance in Babymouse #14: Mad Scientist, meet Squish the amoeba. He loves twinkies and video games. He's best friends with the amoeba Pod, the always cheerful paramecium named Peggy. At middle school he has to deal with the bully Lynwood and his scary friends who are made of bacteria, algae, e. Coli, and more! A super fun series that focuses on the tiniest of life forms and introduces scientific discussion mixed with plenty of humor as well.

Brave New Pond. 2011. 96pp. 978-0-375-84390-7.
Super Amoeba. 2011. 96pp. 978-0-375-84389-1.
Captain Disaster. 2012. 96pp. 978-0-375-84392-1.
The Power of the Parasite. 2012. 96pp. 978-0-375-84391-4.

Game On!. 2013. 96pp. 978-0-307-98299-5.
Fear the Amoeba. 2014. 96pp. 978-0-307-98302-2.
Deadly Disease of Doom. 2015. 96pp. 978-0-307-98305-3.
Pod vs. Pod. 2016. 96pp. 978-0-307-98308-4.

Stinky Cecil. Written and Illustrated by **Paige Braddock**. Andrews McMeel Publishing, 2015–2016. Y

© 2015 Paige Braddock, published by Andrews McMeel Publishing, a division of Andrews McMeel Universal.

Stinky the toad, as well as his four friends—a fly, hamster, and two other amphibians realize their habitat is going to be steamrolled and do their best to save their home! In the second book, the 3rd grade class shows up to his pond and captures him for their classroom terrarium! Will Stinky like being the class pet?

Stinky Cecil in Operation Pond Rescue. 2015. 128pp. 978-1-4494-5711-2.
Stinky Cecil in Terrarium Terror. 2016. 128pp. 978-1-4494-7186-6.

Weathercraft: A Frank Comic. Written and Illustrated by **Jim Woodring**. Fantagraphics, 2010. 104pp. 978-1-60699-340-8, hardcover. O

> *Weathercraft* chronicles the odd, unfortunate and pathetic life of Manhog, the adversary of Frank from Jim's Woodring's ongoing series. Nothing Manhog does can lead to any positive result for Manhog as he wanders the wilderness eating most of everything he comes across and being punished heavily for it by the grinning character half-moon—faced Whim as well as the Fate-like creates called Betty and Veronica.

Black Humor/Satire

These stories feature toilet humor, dirty jokes, bawdy situations, and dark humor that sometimes teeter between comedy and tragedy. The humor may be crude, but the reader still finds the offensive and possibly inappropriate jokes to be quite funny. Readers' advisors beware: some people may not think of these comics as humorous. Also, the titles in this section tend to be more appropriate for older audiences. Films in this genre include Mel Brooks's *Blazing Saddles*, Stanley Kubrick's *Dr. Strangelove*, as well as Matt Stone and Trey Parker's *Team America* film well as their *South Park* television series. Satire Graphic novels featuring stories where the humor makes light of current subjects from within our own culture including government, entertainment, relationships, and our own way of life.

Afrodisiac. Written and Illustrated by **Jim Rugg** and **Brian Maruca**. AdHouse Books. 2010. 96pp. 978-1-935233-06-0. O

> Afrodisiac is a force that no man keep down for long, except some smoking hot ladies. Always fighting crime, aliens, super villains, dinosaurs, and much more, Afrodisiac comes out looking great and stealing all the ladies' hearts. With visuals that look to be straight out of the 1970s this book is a time capsule for anyone who loves pop culture of that era.

Assassination Classroom. Written and Illustrated by **Yusei Matsui**. VIZ Media, 2014– . O Japanese manga. あ 🎬

> A class of junior high misfit students are instructed with one task—to kill their instructor Koro-sensei! He's an octopus-shaped alien who has announced that he will destroy the world at the end of the school year. There's just one catch though—he's also the best teacher the students have ever had! The students are armed with weapons that are deadly to their alien teacher but harmless to humans, but no matter what, Koro-sensei is always able to outsmart them. Can the students kill their teacher and save the world, or will they just get the best education of their lives before time runs out? The series was published in Japan in 17 volumes and was adapted into an anime series as well as a live-action movie. A sequel to the series, *Koro-sensei Q!* was released in Japan beginning in 2015 and is still ongoing.

> *Vol. 1*. 2014. 192pp. 978-1-4215-7607-7.   *Vol. 4*. 2015. 192pp. 978-1-4215-7610-7.
> *Vol. 2*. 2015. 200pp. 978-1-4215-7608-4.   *Vol. 5*. 2015. 192pp. 978-1-4215-7611-4.
> *Vol. 3*. 2015. 192pp. 978-1-4215-7609-1.   *Vol. 6*. 2015. 192pp. 978-1-4215-7612-1.

Vol. 7. 2015. 192pp. 978-1-4215-7613-8.
Vol. 8. 2016. 192pp. 978-1-4215-8280-1.
Vol. 9. 2016. 192pp. 978-1-4215-8281-8.
Vol. 10. 2016. 192pp. 978-1-4215-8322-8.
Vol. 11. 2016. 208pp. 978-1-4215-8323-5.
Vol. 12. 2016. 200pp. 978-1-4215-8324-2.

Vol. 13. 2016. 200pp. 978-1-4215-8444-7.
Vol. 14. 2017. 200pp. 978-1-4215-8505-5.
Vol. 15. 2017. 200pp. 978-1-4215-8641-0.
Vol. 16. 2017. 200pp. 978-1-4215-9091-2.
Vol. 17. 2017. 200pp. 978-1-4215-9092-9.

Detroit Metal City. Written and Illustrated by **Kiminori Wakasugi**. VIZ Media., 2009–2014. M Japanese manga. あ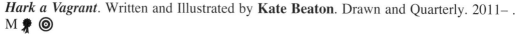

On the outside, Soichi Negishi is a nerdy and shy musician. Still a virgin, he has dreams of making it to the top of the pop music charts. But when the evening comes, Soichi puts on stage makeup and transforms into Krauser II— the lead guitarist of Detroit Metal City, the most outrageous death metal band in Japan! How did Soichi get to be in a death metal band and can he reconcile his love for pop music with his hell-spawned alter-ego? The black comedy was also adapted into an animated series as well as a live-action film in Japan.

Vol. 1. 2009. 200pp. 978-1-4215-2742-0.
Vol. 2. 2009. 200pp. 978-1-4215-2743-7.
Vol. 3. 2009. 192pp. 978-1-4215-2744-4.
Vol. 4. 2010. 208pp. 978-1-4215-2745-1.
Vol. 5. 2010. 208pp. 978-1-4215-2746-8.

Vol. 6. 2010. 208pp. 978-1-4215-2926-4.
Vol. 7. 2010. 208pp. 978-1-4215-3256-1.
Vol. 8. 2011. 208pp. 978-1-4215-3683-5.
Vol. 9. 2011. 208pp. 978-1-4215-3849-5.
Vol. 10. 2011. 216pp. 978-1-4215-3940-9.

Hark a Vagrant. Written and Illustrated by **Kate Beaton**. Drawn and Quarterly. 2011– . M 🎗 ◎

© 2016 Kate Beaton.

History does not have to be such a bore. *Hark a Vagrant* treats many topics ranging from Macbeth to Canadian history with little reverence. This book collects some of the more popular earlier strips from Kate Beaton's webcomic of the same name. Strips cover many topics of the comics cover the history in an accurate way but with humor that makes it much more entertaining. Not all comics are about historical topics; superheroes, feminism, and literature are not safe from Beaton's satirical touch. The 2015 collection was recognized by YALSA's Great Graphic Novels for Teens selection list and a 2016 Eisner Award for Best Humor Publication.

Hark! A Vagrant! 2011. 160pp. 978-1-77046-060-7, hardcover; 978-0-22409-414-6.
Step Aside, Pops: A Hark a Vagrant Collection. 2015. 160pp. 978-1-77046-208-3, hardcover; 978-1-91070-222-2.

Is That All There Is? Written and Illustrated by **Joost Swarte**. Fantagraphics Books, 2012. 144pp. 978-1-60699-628-7. M

This book collects all the underground comix of Joost Swarte from the 1980s to his recent stuff. His style is reminiscent of the light hearted comics of mainstream European comics but with a much darker twist. Crime, sex, and jazz music are some of the topics within these short comedic skits.

Marshal Law: The Deluxe Edition. Written by **Pat Mills**. Illustrated by **Kevin O'Neill**. DC Comics, 2013–2014. 2013. 480pp. 978-1-4012-3855-1, hardcover; 2014. 978-1-4012-5140-6. M ◎

© 2016. DC Comics.

Welcome to San Futuro, a rebuilt San Francisco of the near future that was decimated in a crippling earthquake and has become the haven for heroes. But when the heroes cross the line, there's only one licensed vigilante to take them down: Joe Gilmore, the leather-clad and heavily armed warrior called Marshal Law. Joe was once one of many super-soldiers who fought in "The Zone," a South American war in which the United States created the ideal super-soldiers to feel no pain, but who were also unable to feel empathy. Since returning from the war, the heroes have committed terrible atrocities without fear or mercy, and now Marshal Law is playing clean-up and doling out extremely brutal punishments on all the "heroes" that have committed violent crimes. Originally published in 1987 in Marvel Comics' Epic imprint and later by Dark Horse Comics, the series was ahead of its time and highly regarded by critics for its scathingly humorous look at the world of super-heroes as well as religion, hypocrisy, war, and establishment.

Sexcastle. Written and Illustrated by **Kyle Starks**. Image Comics, 2015. 208pp. 978-1-63215-300-5. M ◎

© 2016. Kyle Starks and Image Comics.

When Shane Sexcastle, the World's Greatest Assassin, walked away from the violence and guns, he thought he could live a peaceful life moving to a small town and working in a flower shop with a widow and her son. But a man born mean is hard to escape his past life. When a corrupt crime lord named Bradley seeks to extort the flower shop owner, Shane Sexcastle declares a one man war against Bradley and his army of goons—all homages to 1980s action heroes—and the body count rises. A perfect tribute in excess of action movies of old with biting humor.

X'ed Out. Written and Illustrated by **Charles Burns**. Pantheon, 2010–2014. M

Something happened to Doug. He awakes in a bed surrounded by images and mementos of the past. He also has a head injury and cannot remember too much of what has happened. He slowly pieced things together. He is a performance artist. He is in a troubled relationship. His father had died and left a lot for Doug to deal with. Something happened to Doug. He awakes in a bed in a ruined down room. He has a head injury and is not sure where he is. He follows a black cat through a hole in the wall. Upon exiting that room he is greeted to a world that is alien. Lizard-like people in business attire verbally assault him as he emerges from the hole in the wall. The only thing familiar and somewhat kind to him is a fat pink man wearing briefs, a backpack, and tennis shoes. All Doug has now is a job given to him from the pink man and a desire to help a lady that he finds out is being used by the lizardmen. These may be two personas of Doug struggling to get by in their own, but equally, strange worlds.

X'ed Out. 2010. 56pp. 978-0-307-37913-9.
The Hive. 2012. 56pp. 978-0-307-90788-2.
Sugar Skull. 2014. 64pp. 978-0-307-90790-5.

Genre Blends

The popularity of humor continues to this day in a variety of forms and crosses a variety of genres. Most other genres have been touched by humor in some form, even genres where one might not think comedy could flourish such as horror and science fiction. By adding a touch of humor into another genre, that genre can be reinterpreted in a new light and readers can laugh along at the plot points both familiar and new to them. The tales tend to feature mockeries of standard genre characters. Typically in a genre-bending comedy, the main characters appear the opposite of that genre's traditions. Instead of being overly brave or heroic, can appear clumsy or dim-witted, and standard plot points, locations, and more are fair game for spoofing.

Humorous Horror

Often humor can best alleviate the dread and fright of horror, and the two are often paired. Ghosts, vampires, zombies, and other beasts that would give us nightmares sometimes can be seen in a humorous light. Some of the best examples of this comparable in film are the classic films like Abbott and Costello Meet Frankenstein (1948), *Evil Dead* series of films by Sam Raimi as well as zombie movies such as *Zombieland* (2009) and *Shaun of the Dead* (2004). For other mainstream horror titles without the heaping mix of fun, see the horror chapter.

Army of Darkness. Created by **Sam Raimi** and **Ivan Raimi**. Written and Illustrated by various. Dynamite Entertainment, 2006– . O

© 2016 Dynamite Comics. Used with Permission.

Based off of director Sam Raimi's classic horror movies *Evil Dead* (1981), *Evil Dead II* (1987), *Army of Darkness* (1992) and the cable television series *Ash vs. Evil Dead* (2015) which features a buffoonish wisecracking blue collar hero named Ash who wages a one man battle against the Deadite armies of evil who escaped into our world from a powerful spell found in the Necronomicon—the book of the dead. With his severed right replaced by a chainsaw and his "boomstick" (sawed-off shotgun) in his left, there's nothing that can stop Ash from defeating the skeletal soldiers of the Deadite armies.

Shop 'til You Drop. 2005. 112pp. 978-1-933305-26-4.
Old School and More. 2006. 136pp. 978-1-933305-18-9.
Ash vs. The Classic Monsters. 2007. 160pp. 978-1-933305-41-7.

Ashes 2 Ashes. 2007. 112pp. 978-0-974963-89-1.
Ash Saves Obama. 2010. 104pp. 978-1-60690-108-3.
Hellbillies and Deadnecks. 2010. 104pp. 978-0-9749638-9-1.
Omnibus Vol. 1. 2010. 300pp. 978-1-60690-100-7.
Omnibus Vol. 2. 2012. 432pp. 978-1-60690-274-5.
Hail to the Queen, Baby! 2013. 144pp. 978-1-60690-387-2.
The King is Dead, Long Live the Queen. 2013. 168pp. 978-1-60690-423-7.
Omnibus Vol. 3. 2013. 360pp. 978-1-60690-397-1.
Ash and the Army of Darkness. 2014. 192pp. 978-1-60690-516-6.
Ash Gets Hitched. 2015. 978-1-60690-597-5.
Ash in Space. 2015. 144pp. 978-1-60690-691-0.
Furious Road. 2016. 144pp. 978-1-5241-0094-0.

Army of Darkness Crossover Collections.

The cult following of the Evil Dead/Army of Darkness hero Ash has also crossed over in the comic book world as well. Included here are some popular crossover volumes where Ash has team up with or against some popular film/TV properties as well as well-known comic book licenses.

Army of Darkness vs. Re-Animator. 2006. 112pp. 978-1-93330-513-4.
Darkman vs. Army of Darkness. 2007. 96pp. 978-1-93330-548-6.
Marvel Zombies vs. Army of Darkness. 2007. 128pp. 978-0-7851-2743-7.
Xena/Army of Darkness, Vol. 1. 2009. 104pp. 978-1-60690-008-6.
Xena/Army of Darkness, Vol. 2. 2009. 104pp. 978-1-60690-032-1.
Danger Girl and the Army of Darkness. 2013. 978-1-60690-246-2. IDW/Dynamite.
Army of Darkness vs. Hack/Slash. 2014. 160pp. 978-1-60690-497-8.
Vampirella/Army of Darkness. 2016. 96pp. 978-1-60690-837-2.
Army of Darkness / Xena, Warrior Princess: Forever and a Day. 2017. 144pp. 978-1-5241-0351-4.

Costume Quest: Invasion of the Candy Snatchers. Written and Illustrated by **Zac Gorman**. Oni Press, 2014. 54pp. 978-1-62010-190-2, hardcover. Y 🎭

© 2016 Zac Gorman and Double Fine Studios.

In the land of Repugia Grubbins are monsters that spend their time snatching trick-or-treaters from our world and eating their candy. But even among monsters, there are misfits—Klem is a Grubbin who doesn't want to kidnap kids—he loves Earth's Halloween and just wants to be liked by the other Grubbin students. Klem tries to prove he can fit in with the popular Grubbins and goes to Earth to steal candy on the dare of the popular monsters. Joined with his friends Sellie and Brolo, can three monsters fit in on the spookiest night of the year among the human kids and will they be able to find their way back home? A tie-in to the *Costume Quest* games created by Double Fine Studios.

Cowa! Written and Illustrated by **Akira Toriyama**. VIZ Media, 2008. 208pp. 978-1-4215-1805-3. Y Japanese manga.

Three young monster children Paifu (a half vampire/were-koala), José (a ghost), and a human retired sumo wrestler named Maruyama go on a quest to get medicine to save their town from a deadly flu known to kill only monsters. The book was recognized as one of the best graphic novels for kids by manga specialist Deb Aoki in 2009.

COWA! © 1997 by BIRD STUDIO/SHUEISHA Inc.

The Creeps. Written and Illustrated by **Chris Schweizer**. Amulet Books/Harry N. Abrams, 2015– . Y ◎

When there are spooky mysteries about in Pumpkin County, there's a group of kids who will solve the mystery: The Creeps! Carol, a big-city girl who just moved to the area has found kindred spirits in Rosario (a fashion expert but the muscle on the team), Jarvis (a military brat with logistics know-how), and Mitchell (the resident monster expert). The Creeps are on the case to figure out the spooky mysteries and still get to class on time. Join them as the solve the cases including the Frankenfrog attacks, hungry trolls, and attacking Jack-o-lanterns! Never fear folks, the Creeps will solve the mysterious mysteries!

© 2016 Chris Schweizer.

Vol. 1: Night of the Frankenfrogs. 2015. 128pp. 978-1-4197-1379-8, hardcover; 978-1-4197-1766-6.

Vol. 2: The Trolls will Feast. 2016. 128pp. 978-1-4197-1882-3, hardcover; 978-1-4197-1883-0.

Vol. 3: Curse of the Attack-o-Lanterns. 2016. 128pp. 978–1419721908, hardcover; 978-1-4197-2191-5.

The Goon. Written and Illustrated by **Eric Powell**. Dark Horse Comics, 2003– . T 🎖 ◎

Set in a backdrop reminiscent of 1930–1940s gangster movies with a heaping mix of humor and horror, when the Zombie Priest has come to Lonely Street to rule the neighborhood with his gang of zombies, only one bruiser of a man is tough enough to handle the job and beat the living daylights out of the hordes of undead: the Goon. Goon and his longtime buddy Franky have seen their share of weird things in the neighborhood. Whether it's zombies, ghosts, fish mobsters, spider cardsharks, reverse zombies, werewolves, harpies, and many other oddities. When you absolutely need someone to beat up the monsters, just ask for the Goon. Volume 3 features a cameo appearance by Mike Mignola's *Hellboy*. The series has won multiple Eisner

Goon TM © 2016 Eric Powell.

Awards including Best Single Issue/Single Story (2004), Best Continuing Series (2005), and Best Humor Publication (2005). The *Fancy Pants Edition* is a limited edition hardcover volume collecting key stories of the Goon. *The Goon Library* collections reprint three volumes of the series in one hardcover collection.

Vol. 0: Rough Stuff. 2010. 104pp. 978-1-5958-2468-4.

Vol. 1: Nothin' But Misery. 2013. 144pp. 978-1-5958-2624-4.

Vol. 2: My Murderous Childhood (and Other Grievous Yarns). 2010. 136pp. 978-1-5958-2616-9.

Vol. 3: Heaps of Ruination. 2011. 128pp. 978-1-5958-2625-1.

Vol. 4: Virtue and the Grim Consequences Thereof. 2006. 144pp. 978-1-5958-2617-6.

Vol. 5: Wicked Inclinations. 2011. 128pp. 978-1-5958-2626-8.

Vol. 6: Chinatown and the Mystery of Mr. Wicker. 2009. 136pp. 978-1-5958-2406-6.

Vol. 7: A Place of Heartache and Grief. 2009. 128pp. 978-1-5958-2311-3.

Vol. 8: Those That is Damned. 2009. 136pp. 978-1-5958-2324-3.

Vol. 9: Calamity of Conscience. 2009. 128pp. 978-1-5958-2346-5.

Vol. 10: Death's Greedy Comeuppance. 2011. 136pp. 978-1-5958-2643-5.

Vol. 11: The Deformed of Body and Devious of Mind. 2012. 136pp. 978-1-5958-2881-1.

Vol. 12: Them That Raised Us Lament. 2013. 120pp. 978-1-6165-5006-6.

Vol. 13: For Want of Whiskey and Blood. 2014. 128pp. 978-1-6165-5101-8.

Vol. 14: Occasion of Revenge. 2015. 136pp. 978-1-6165-5596-2.

Vol. 15: Once Upon a Hard Time. 2016. 136pp. 978-1-5067-0098-4.

The Goon Library. 2015– .

Vol. 1. 2015. 496pp. 978-1-6165-5842-0, hardcover.

Vol. 2. 2016. 416pp. 978-1-6165-5843-7, hardcover.

Vol. 3. 2016. 416pp. 978-1-6165-5986-1, hardcover.

Vol. 4. 2016. 416pp. 978-1-5067-0018-2, hardcover.

Vol. 5. 2017. 480pp. 978-1-5067-0401-2, hardcover.

Ghostbusters. IDW Publishing, 2009– . T

Based off the popular films Ghostbusters (1984) and Ghostbusters 2 (1989) starring Bill Murray, Dan Aykroyd, Harold Ramis, and Ernie Hudson. When ghosts are leaving their psychokinetic energy and ectoplasmic slime everywhere, it's time to call the professionals. Who are you going to call, why Ghostbusters, of course! The series follows the continuing adventures of the ghost-trapping team professionals of as they help clean up the ghosts creating havoc in New York City and around the country too! The Teenage Mutant Ninja Turtles/Ghostbusters crossover features the two heroic teams from New York City from alternate dimensions as they team up for the first time.

TM & © Columbia Pictures Industries, Inc.

Ghostbusters (current series). Written by **Erik Burnham**. Illustrated by **Dan Schoening**. IDW Publishing, 2012– .

Vol. 1: The Man from the Mirror. 2012. 104pp. 978-1-6137-7157-0.

Vol. 2: The Most Magical Place on Earth. 2012. 104pp. 978-1-6137-7279-9.

Vol. 3: Haunted America. 2012. 124pp. 978-1-6137-7512-7.

Vol. 4: Who You Gonna Call?. 2013. 104pp. 978-1-6137-7583-7.

Vol. 5: The New Ghostbusters. 2013. 104pp. 978-1-6137-7678-0.

Vol. 6: Trains, Brains, and Ghostly Remains. 2013. 104pp. 978-1-6137-7828-9.

Vol. 7: Happy Horror Days. 2014. 104pp. 978-1-6137-7932-3.

Vol. 8: Mass Hysteria, Part 1. 2014. 104pp. 978-1-6314-0079-7.

Total Containment Deluxe Edition. 2014. 432pp. 978-1-6137-7919-4, hardcover.

Vol. 9: Mass Hysteria, Part 2. 2014. 104pp. 978-1-6314-0171-8.

Get Real. 2015. 104pp. 978-1-6314-0484-9.

Mass Hysteria Deluxe Edition. 2015. 460pp. 978-1-6314-0336-1, hardcover.
Teenage Mutant Ninja Turtles/Ghostbusters. 2015. 104pp. 978-1-6314-0253-1.
Vol. 10: Ghostbusters International. 2016. 120pp. 978-1-6314-0623-2.

Ghostbusters (1st series). Written by **Scott Lobdell**. Illustrated by **Ilias Kyriazis** and **Nick Runge**. IDW Publishing, 2009–2012.

The Other Side. 2009. 104pp. 978-1-6001-0426-8.
Displaced Aggression. 2010. 104pp. 978-1-6001-0610-1.
Haunted Holidays. 2010. 104pp. 978-1-6001-0778-8.
Omnibus, Vol. 1. 2012. 280pp. 978-1-6137-7441-0.

The Real Ghostbusters Omnibus. Written by **James Van Hise** and **La Morris Richmond**. Illustrated by **Howard Bender**, **Evan Dorkin**, **Phil Hester**, and **John Tobias**. 2012–2013.

The Real Ghostbusters Omnibus collections reprint the comic books based on the well-regarded animated series from 1986 to 1991.
Vol. 1. 2012. 354pp. 978-1-6137-7493-9.
Vol. 2. 2013. 304pp. 978-1-6137-7657-5.

Ghostbusters. 2016. Written by **Erik Burnham**. Illustrated by **Lee Loughridge**. 2016.
The adaptation of the new 2016 *Ghostbusters* film that recasts the Ghostbusters team as an all-female team.

The New Ghostbusters. 2016. 104pp. 978-1-63140-625-6.
Who Ya Gonna Call? 2016. 104pp. 978-1-63140-624-9.

Itty Bitty Hellboy. Written by **Art Baltazar** and **Franco**. Illustrated by **Art Baltazar**. Dark Horse Comics, 2014–2016. Y
Mike Mignola's Hellboy and his friends and monsters from the B.P.R.D. get the Aw Yeah Comics treatment by the team of Art Baltazar and Franco! The series plays for laughs with the monsters and go bump in the night and the team of hero monsters who bump back.

Vol. 1. 2014. 128pp. 978-1-61655-414-9.
Vol. 2: Search for the Were-Jaguar. 2016. 194pp. 978-1-61655-801-7.

Johnny Boo. Written and Illustrated by **James Kochalka**. Top Shelf Productions/IDW Publishing. 2008– . A

© 2016 James Kolchalka.

Johnny Boo is the best little ghost in the world. He's an adorable young ghost with Ghost Power (the ability to say "Boo" really loudly) and he has lots of fun adventures with his pet ghost Squiggle, who has the ghost power called Squiggle Power (which means he can fly and do big loop-de-loops). Together they have the best ghost adventures. The *Johnny Boo's Big Boo Box* collects the first five volumes in one hardcover collection.

Vol. 1: The Best Little Ghost in the World. 2008. 40pp. 978-1-60309-013-1, hardcover.
Vol. 2: Twinkle Power. 2009. 40pp. 978-1-60309-015-5, hardcover.
Vol. 3: Happy Apples. 2009. 40pp. 978-1-60309-041-4, hardcover.
Vol. 4: The Mean Little Boy. 2010. 40pp. 978-1-60309-059-9, hardcover.
Vol. 5: Does Something. 2013. 40pp. 978-1-60309-084-1, hardcover.

Vol. 6: Zooms to the Moon. 2014. 40pp. 978-1-60309-349-1, hardcover.
Johnny Boo Meets Dragon Puncher. 2015. 40pp. 978-1-60309-368-2, hardcover.
Vol. 7: Johnny Boo Goes Like This! 2016. 48pp. 978-1-60309-384-2, hardcover.
Johnny Boo's Big Boo Box. 2016. 200pp. 978-1-60309-385-9, hardcover.

Kurosagi Corpse Delivery Service. Written by **Eiji Ōtsuka**. Illustrated by **Housui Yamazaki**. Dark Horse Comics, 2015– . M Japanese manga.

Five young college students from a Buddhist College—three guys and two girls—find they all have gifts that connect them with the recently departed dead—especially Kuro Katsuro who can "speak" to the dead and hear their last wishes. The five form the Kurosagi Corpse Delivery Service: whether suicide, murder, accident, or illness, they promise to take the soul of the deceased and make sure it gets the final rest it needs. The only problem is it's never that easy and the cases they take on range from the bizarre to the humor. The omnibus collections of the popular mature-rated horror/humor series from Japan that was originally published beginning in 2002. The series is still ongoing in Japan with over 20 volumes published. Beginning in 2015, Dark Horse Comics began publishing the series in the omnibus format, with the volumes listed below currently in print.

Vol. 1. 2015. 640pp. 978-1-61655-754-6.
Vol. 2. 2015. 664pp. 978-1-61655-783-6.
Vol. 3. 2016. 648pp. 978-1-61655-887-1.
Vol. 4. 2016. 688pp. 978-1-50670-055-7.

Little Vampire, Written by and Illustrated by **Joann Sfar**. First Second Books, 2008. 96pp. 978-1-59643-233-8. A

A young vampire, tired of being lonely in a home filled with grown up monsters, goes to school and befriends a young school boy named Michael. Collected here are three short stories of the Little Vampire and Michael—*Little Vampire Goes to School*, *Little Vampire Does Kung Fu*, and *Little Vampire and the Society of Canine Defenders.*

The Lunch Witch. Written and Illustrated by **Deb Lucke**. Papercutz, 2015–2016. Y

© 2016 Deb Lucke.

Grunhilda the witch comes from a long line of women who loved to stir up trouble in their big cauldrons. But in this day and age no one believes in witches anymore (even though they're real). In fact, the scariest thing that Grunhilda can make in her cauldron is foul-tasting brew! With things not quite the way her ancestors would like, Grunhilda gets a job at the local school at the scariest position she can get: as a lunch lady. When Grunhilda befriends a young girl at the school named Madison who needs help both at school as well as home, will Grunhilda go against everything her ancestors have taught her and learn to be a good person?

Vol. 1. 2015. 180pp. 978-1-62991-162-5.
Vol. 2: Knee-Deep in Niceness. 2016. 180pp. 978-1-62991-503-6.

Magic Trixie. Written and Illustrated by **Jill Thompson**. HarperCollins, 2008–2009. Y

The misadventures of a junior witch named Trixie. Even though Trixie's a witch, she has spooky monsters as friends, but still has to do all the annoying things kids her age has to do like brush her teeth, go to bed on time, bring something special to show and tell, and not have any fun while her baby sister gets away with everything. Maybe it's time to turn her baby sister into a dragon?

Vol. 1: Magic Trixie. 2008. 96pp. 978-0-06-117045-4.
Vol. 2: Magic Trixie Sleeps Over. 2009. 96pp. 978-0-06-117048-5.
Vol. 3: Magic Trixie and the Dragon. 2009. 96pp. 978-0-06-117050-8.

The Misadventures of Salem Hyde. Written and Illustrated by **Frank Cammuso**. Harry N. Abrams Books/Amulet Books, 2014–2015. Y ◎

Salem is a spunky, impulsive, stubborn little girl—and she's also the only one in her class that is a witch too! It's a good thing Salem's been assigned an animal companion, Lord Percival J. Whamsford III—or better known by Salem as "Whammy." Together the two of them get into plenty of hijinks and fun at school and at home with a tiny bit of magic too along the way!

Book One: Spelling Trouble. 2014. 96pp. 978-1-4197-0804-6.
Book Two: Big Birthday Bash. 2014. 96pp. 978-1-4197-1026-1.
Book Three: Cookie Catastrophe. 2014. 96pp. 978-1-4197-1199-2.
Book Four: Dinosaur Dilemma. 2015. 96pp. 978-1-4197-1535-8.
Book Five: Frozen Fiasco. 2015. 96pp. 978-1-4197-1652-2.

© 2016 Frank Cammuso.

Monsters! and Other Stories. Written and illustrated by **Gustavo Duarte**. Dark Horse Comics, 2014. 152pp. 978-1-61655-309-8. T

A collection of silently told stories featuring giant monsters who love to wreak havoc on cities as well as other stories including an alien abduction, and the story on how two business partners on the run from fate learn that you can never change the future.

© 2016 Dark Horse Comics.

My Monster Secret. Written and Illustrated by **Eiji Masuda**. Seven Seas Entertainment, 2016– . T Japanese manga. あ

How well can you keep a secret? Asahi Kuromine is just a typical boy in school who accidentally discovers that one of the girls in the school, Yōko Shiragami, sprouting wings from behind her back! She's secretly a vampire and only allowed to be in a normal school to learn provided that no one knows about her secret! Soon Asahi discovers that others in the school have hidden secrets—from a tiny alien roaming the

© 2016 Seven Seas Entertainment.

halls in a human exoskeleton, a sex-reversing werewolf, a 1,000-year-old demon who is the principal at the school and more! The ongoing series in Japan debuted in 2013 has been collected in 15 volumes so far and an anime based on the manga was released in Japan in 2015.

Vol. 1. 2016. 168pp. 978-1-62692-238-9.
Vol. 2. 2016. 180pp. 978-1-62692-259-4.
Vol. 3. 2016. 180pp. 978-1-62692-291-4.
Vol. 4. 2016. 180pp. 978-1-62692-345-4.
Vol. 5. 2017. 180pp. 978-1-62692-385-0.
Vol. 6. 2017. 180pp. 978-1-62692-455-0.
Vol. 7. 2017. 180pp. 978-1-62692-503-8.
Vol. 8. 2017. 180pp. 978-1-62692-581-6.

Plants vs. Zombies. Written by **Paul Tobin**. Illustrated by **Ron Chan**. Dark Horse Comics, 2013– . Y 🎮

Plants vs. Zombies used with permission of Electronic Arts Inc.

Based on the extremely popular video game series that has won multiple awards, a war of ridiculous proportions has arrived when zombies have gathered on Earth to conquer mankind—but the zombies have met their match thanks to Crazy Dave, a gibberish-speaking inventor who has created an unlimited army of vegetables to combat the "fun-dead." Joined by his niece, Patrice, and young adventurer Nate Timely, Crazy Dave and the plants are out to take on the zombies no matter when or where. The books are inspired by the various *Plants vs. Zombies* video games including the 2016 released *Plants vs. Zombies: Garden Warfare 2.*

Vol. 1: Lawnmageddon. 2013. 80pp. 978-1-61655-192-6, hardcover.
Vol. 2: Timepocalypse. 2015. 80pp. 978-1-61655-621-1, hardcover.
Vol. 3: Bully for You. 2015. 96pp. 978-1-61655-889-5, hardcover.
Garden Warfare. 2016. 80pp. 978-1-61655-946-5, hardcover.
Vol. 4: Grown Sweet Home. 2016. 80pp. 978-1-61655-971-7, hardcover.
Vol. 5: Petal to the Metal. 2016. 80pp. 978-1-61655-999-1, hardcover.
Vol. 6: Boom Boom Mushroom. 2017. 80pp. 978-1-5067-0037-3, hardcover.
Vol. 7: Battle Extravagonzo. 2017. 80pp. 978-1-5067-0189-9, hardcover.

Preacher. Written by **Garth Ennis**. Illustrated by **Steve Dillon** and various. Vertigo/DC Comics, 1996–2001. M 🔪 🖥

A black-humored and ultra-violent journey of one man given the power of God. Jesse Custer had dedicated his life to God as a preacher for a small town church in Texas. When he's unexpectedly joined with a half-angel/half-demon known as Genesis, he given the gift of The Word. Now he can command anyone to do his bidding, even to kill. He joins up with his gun-toting tough ex-girlfriend Tulip and a hard-drinking Irish vampire named Cassidy, and the group begins a violent and dark-humored journey across America to find God, who has left his throne in Heaven in fear of Genesis. Pursued by a secret

religious organization called the Grail and by an unkillable ultra-violent force of nature known as the Saint of Killers, Jesse, Tulip, and Cassidy's friendship is all that they have to keep them together—but even that might not be enough to get them past the horrors awaiting them in the coming conflict. The series won several Eisner Awards including Best Writer (1998) and Best Continuing Series (1999). The series was adapted in 2016 as a TV show on the cable channel AMC starring Dominic Cooper as Jesse Custer, Ruth Negga as Tulip, and Joe Gilgun as Cassidy.

Book 1. 2013. 352pp. 978-1-4012-4045-5.
Book 2. 2013. 368pp. 978-1-4012-4255-8.
Book 3. 2014. 352pp. 978-1-4012-4501-6.
Book 4. 2014. 368pp. 978-1-4012-3094-4.
Book 5. 2014. 356pp. 978-1-4012-5074-4.
Book 6. 2014. 384pp. 978-1-4012-5279-3.

Princess Decomposia and Count Spatula. Written and Illustrated by **Andi Watson**. First Second, 2015. 176pp. 978-1-62672-275-0, hardcover; 978-1-62672-149-4. T 🌶

In the underworld kingdom's ruler is ill (or just perhaps lazy) and his daughter, the Princess Decomposia has to do his job to make sure the kingdom runs accordingly. The Princess is buried in paperwork all the while she has to work with the various subjects like werewolves, ghosts, and mummies. When the castle needs a new chef since the king has fired the old one, the kingdom hires Count Spatula, a charming vampire with a sweet tooth. Soon he and the princess become fast friends and maybe more? The book was recognized as a Great Graphic Novel for Teens in 2016 by YALSA.

Rosario + Vampire. Written and Illustrated by **Akihisa Ikeda**. VIZ Media. 2008–2015. O Japanese manga. あ

Teenager Tsukune Aono enrolls at a boarding school called Yokai Academy where the monsters at school aren't jocks and popular kids, but real monsters! Monsters of all kinds roam the halls. At least all the girls have a crush on him, but that just makes all the boys at school want to eat him (or worse!). Tsukune has his eyes on the most beautiful vampire at school, the lovely Moka. Too bad she's also got the thirst for his blood! The popular horror comedy series was adapted into an anime series as well.

Vol. 1. 2008. 192pp. 978-1-4215-1903-6.
Vol. 2. 2008. 200pp. 978-1-4215-1904-3.
Vol. 3. 2008. 210pp. 978-1-4215-1905-0.
Vol. 4. 2008. 210pp. 978-1-4215-1906-7.
Vol. 5. 2009. 208pp. 978-1-4215-1907-4.

Vol. 6. 2009. 192pp. 978-1-4215-1908-1.
Vol. 7. 2009. 200pp. 978-1-4215-1909-8.
Vol. 8. 2009. 200pp. 978-1-4215-1910-4.
Vol. 9. 2009. 200pp. 978-1-4215-2354-5.
Vol. 10. 2009. 208pp. 978-1-4215-2355-2.

Season II. 2010–2012.

Vol. 1. 2010. 184pp. 978-1-4215-3136-6.	*Vol. 8.* 2012. 200pp. 978-1-4215-4050-4.
Vol. 2. 2010. 184pp. 978-1-4215-3137-3.	*Vol. 9.* 2012. 218pp. 978-1-4215-4209-6.
Vol. 3. 2010. 200pp. 978-1-4215-3268-4.	*Vol. 10.* 2012. 218pp. 978-1-4215-4879-1.
Vol. 4. 2011. 200pp. 978-1-4215-3544-9.	*Vol. 11.* 2013. 198pp. 978-1-4215-5240-8.
Vol. 5. 2011. 216pp. 978-1-4215-3691-0.	*Vol. 12.* 2013. 212pp. 978-1-4215-5702-1.
Vol. 6. 2011. 192pp. 978-1-4215-3831-0.	*Vol. 13.* 2014. 220pp. 978-1-4215-6949-9.
Vol. 7. 2012. 192pp. 978-1-4215-4026-9.	*Vol. 14.* 2015. 288pp. 978-1-4215-7967-2.

Sabrina the Teenage Witch: The Magic Within. Written and Illustrated by **Tania Del Rio**. Archie Comics, 2013–2014. Y Neo-manga.

Originally published by Archie Comics from 2004 to 2009, Tana Del Rio's story still retains the comedy and romance of the half-witch Sabrina, but the series featured a Japanese manga–like look to the characters in the series.

Vol. 1. 2013. 256pp. 978-1-936975-39-6.
Vol. 2. 2013. 240pp. 978-1-936975-54-9.
Vol. 3. 2013. 256pp. 978-1-936975-60-0.
Vol. 4. 2014. 272pp. 978-1-936975-76-1.

Scary Godmother: Comic Book Stories. Written and Illustrated by **Jill Thompson**. Dark Horse Comics, 2011. 312pp. 978-1-59582-723-4. Y 🎈 ◎ 🖥

Little Hannah Marie's spending Halloween with her rotten cousin Jimmy who is sullen because he's stuck baby-sitting her on Halloween night. To make up for it, he's making sure Hannah's scared silly. To Hannah's rescue comes the oddest fairy of all—her Scary Godmother! Dressed in a witch's costume with white and red-striped stockings and bright red hair, Scary Godmother, with a little help from her spooky friends, will give Jimmy a fright he'll never forget. Further adventures take Hannah, Jimmy, Scary Godmother, and her ghastly monstrous friends to the realm of Fright Side (where Scary Godmother comes from—and where every day is Halloween) and more. The series has won several Eisner Awards including Best Title for Younger Readers/Best Comics Publication for a Younger Audience (2001) as well as an Eisner for Jill Thompson for Best Painter/Multimedia Artist (Interior) (2001). The collection reprints various short comic book adventures separate from the original picture book series and includes the stories *Scary Godmother: Ghoul's Out for Summer*; *Scary Godmother: Holiday Spooktakular*; *Scary Godmother: Bloody Valentine Special*; *Scary Godmother Activity Book*; *Scary Godmother: Wild about Harry* and more. The story was adapted as a computer animated series of cartoons that have aired on the Cartoon Network in 2004–2005.

Sketch Monsters. Written by **Joshua Williamson**. Illustrated by **Vicente Navarrete**. Oni Press. 2011–2014. Y

> Maddie, an eight-year-old girl, has never showed her feelings—instead of expressing herself, she draws her feelings as monsters in her sketchbook. When her older sister leaves home for college, Mandy spends all day drawing her emotions as monsters. That night, all of the monsters but one has escaped and now Maddie and a monster named Happster must capture Maddie's monster feelings (and learn to express her own feelings) before it's too late!
>
> *Vol. 1: Escape of the Scribbles.* 2011. 40pp. 978-1-934964-69-9, hardcover.
> *Vol. 2: The New Kid.* 2013. 40pp. 978-1-620100-12-7, hardcover.

Stinky. Written and Illustrated by **Eleanor Davis**. Toon Books, 2008. 40pp. 978-0-9799238-4-5, hardcover. Y 🏅

> Can a lonely monster who hates people but loves pickles and possums find friendship even when he looks and smells—well, like a monster? The book was recognized by the American Library Association with an Geisel Award honor book in 2009.

Supernatural Law. Written and Illustrated by **Batton Lash**. Exhibit A Press, 2003– . T ◎

© 2016 Exhibit A Press.

> When the creatures of the night are in dire need of help, there's only one place they can trust: Alanna Wolff and Jeff Byrd, attorneys at law! At Wolf & Byrd, they can handle any case of the supernatural including a "hexual harassment" case, a teenage vampire afraid of a vampire slayer, an ex-wife of a mad scientist, a famed horror author in a coma, and a man so negative that he repels everything. There's no case too strange for Wolff & Byrd to handle. The series has been in print since 1979 in comic strip form in various publications as well as a monthly comic book series in 1994 and is still ongoing.
>
> *Mister Negativity and other tales of Supernatural Law.* 2003. 176pp. 978-0-9633954-8-1.
> *Sonovawitch! and other tales of Supernatural Law.* 2003. 176pp. 978-0-9633954-6-7.

The Vampire Brat and other tales of Supernatural Law. 2003. 176pp. 978-0-9633954-7-4.

Tales of Supernatural Law. 2005. 184pp. 978-0-9633954-9-8.
Soddyssey & Other Tales of Supernatural Law. 2008. 184pp. 978-0-9815519-0-6.
The Monsters Meet on Court Street and Other Tales of Supernatural Law. 2012. 176pp. 978-0-9815519-1-3.
The Werewolf of New York: A Supernatural Law Book. 2013. 112pp. 978-0-9815519-3-7.
Zombie Wife and Other Tales of Supernatural Law. 2014. 160pp. 978-0-9815519-5-1.
A Vampire in Hollywood and Other Tales of Supernatural Law. 2016. 192pp. 978-0-9815519-7-5.

Yamada Kun and the Seven Witches. Written and Illustrated by **Miki Yoshikawa**. Kodansha Comics, 2015– . O Japanese manga. あ

> Ryū Yamada is a delinquent student at school, but discovers accidentally that when he kisses a studious girl in his class named Urara, he swaps bodies with her! It turns out that Ryū can duplicate powers and Urara has the power to swap bodies. Soon others in the school who are special form the Supernatural Studies Club as others with powers are revealed and those who have witch powers—both female and male cause

mischievous havoc in the school swapping bodies and causing charms with Ryū caught in the middle. The manga series is still currently being published in Japan with over 21 volumes released so far. The series was also adapted into an eight-episode anime series that aired in Japan in 2013.

Vol. 1. 2015. 208pp. 978-1-63236-068-7.   *Vol. 8*. 2016. 192pp. 978-1-63236-137-0.
Vol. 2. 2015. 192pp. 978-1-63236-069-4.   *Vol. 9*. 2016. 192pp. 978-1-63236-138-7.
Vol. 3. 2015. 192pp. 978-1-63236-070-0.   *Vol. 10*. 2016. 192pp. 978-1-63236-139-4.
Vol. 4. 2015. 192pp. 978-1-63236-071-7.   *Vol. 11*. 2016. 192pp. 978-163236-140-0.
Vol. 5. 2015. 192pp. 978-1-63236-072-4.   *Vol. 12*. 2017. 192pp. 978-163236-141-7.
Vol. 6. 2016. 192pp. 978-1-63236-073-1.   *Vol. 13*. 2017. 192pp. 978-163236-142-4.
Vol. 7. 2016. 192pp. 978-1-63236-136-3.   *Vol. 14*. 2017. 192pp. 978-1-63236-354-1.

Zombillenium. Written and Illustrated by **Arthur de Pins**. NBM Publishing, 2013– . O ◉

© 2016 Arthur de Pins.

Welcome to Zombillenium—a horror-inspired theme park managed by family man (and vampire) Francis von Bloodt and staffed by actual monsters, including mummies, vampires, werewolves, witches, skeletons, zombies, and more. When park visitors are not getting scared anymore of the classic monsters (and they think they are all just actors and special effects), something needs to be done to bring back the revenue. When the newest recruit to the park—a young man named Aurelian (who just had the worst day of his life and ends up being bitten by both a vampire and a werewolf) may be just what the park needs to survive when he transforms into something monstrous.

Vol. 1: Gretchen. 2013. 48pp. 978-1-56163-734-8, hardcover.
Vol. 2: Human Resources. 2014. 52pp. 978-1-56163-850-5, hardcover.
Vol. 3: Control Freaks. 2015. 48pp. 978-1-56163-956-4, hardcover.

Humorous Science Fiction

A tongue-in-cheek look at what life could be like with androids, robots, and alien invaders. The stories can be set in present day on Earth, in the far future, or a million miles away in outer space, but an inclusion of the absurd or the off-beat is a must. Prose science fiction titles comparable to this subgenre include Douglas Adams's *Hitchhiker's Guide to the Galaxy* as well as the writings of Terry Pratchett. You may be glad to see that in the future there are plenty of laughs.

Aliens vs. Parker. Boom! Studios. Written by **Paul Scheer** and **Nick Giovannetti**. Illustrated by Manuel Bracchi. BOOM! Studios, 2014. 112pp. 978-1-60886-350-1. O

Set in the near future, a group of slacker delivery guys do nothing but slack off and play video games. When they have to deliver a package labeled "classified" to a planet more dangerous than they've ever seen before, they must use their limit skills to fight off the aliens just to stay alive.

Astronaut Academy. Written and Illustrated by **Dave Roman**. First Second Books, 2011–2013. Y ◎

© 2016 Dave Roman and First Second.

Hakata Soy is a teenager who just wants to put the past behind him and start afresh after he enrolls at Astronaut Academy—but it's hard to put the past behind him when he's the former leader of a popular super-hero super team! It's hard to get a fresh start when the most popular girl in school wants nothing to do with him, his best friend won't return his calls, and there's an evil doppleganger roaming the school halls out to kill him! In *Re-Entry*, Hakata Soy has lost his heart—literally! Someone is roaming the school halls and capturing hearts. Can the students find out who is taking their extra lives?

Zero Gravity. 2011. 192pp. 978-1-59643-756-2, hardcover; 978-1-59643-620-6.

Re-Entry. 2013. 192pp. 978-1-59643-621-3.

Dr. Slump. Written and Illustrated by **Akira Toriyama**. VIZ Media, 2005– . T Japanese manga. あ ◎

Dr. Slump is known as Dr. Senbei Norimaki (which translates in Japanese to "little rice cracker") of Penguin Village. He's a crazy inventor and has just created his finest work—a robot who appears as a cute 13-year-old girl. He names "her" Arale (which translates to "even littler cracker"), but even though she's super-strong, she's near-sighted and she's innocently constantly getting herself into trouble. From problems attending middle school, the one thing that girls have but Arale doesn't, x-ray specs, time travel, pet bears, and more, Arale and Senbei are constantly getting into calamitous trouble no matter what the situation. The series is a reprinting of the original 18-volume collection originally published in Japan. The manga series was also adapted into several anime series including several television shows and movies.

Vol. 1. 2005. 192pp. 978-1-59116-950-5.

Vol. 2. 2005. 192pp. 978-1-59116-951-2.

Vol. 3. 2005. 200pp. 978-1-59116-991-8.

Vol. 4. 2005. 200pp. 978-1-4215-0165-9.

Vol. 5. 2006. 200pp. 978-1-4215-0173-4.

Vol. 6. 2006. 200pp. 978-1-4215-0174-1.

Vol. 7. 2006. 200pp. 978-1-4215-0631-9.

Vol. 8. 2006. 208pp. 978-1-4215-0632-6.

Vol. 9. 2006. 208pp. 978-1-4215-0633-3.

Vol. 10. 2006. 208pp. 978-1-4215-0634-0.

Vol. 11. 2007. 208pp. 978-1-4215-0635-7.

Vol. 12. 2007. 192pp. 978-1-4215-1056-9.

Vol. 13. 2007. 208pp. 978-1-4215-1057-6.

Vol. 14. 2008. 192pp. 978-1-4215-1058-3.

Vol. 15. 2008. 200pp. 978-1-4215-1059-0.

Vol. 16. 2008. 204pp. 978-1-4215-1060-6.

Vol. 17. 2009. 210pp. 978-1-4215-1999-9.

Vol. 18. 2009. 248pp. 978-1-4215-2000-1.

Earthling. Written and Illustrated by **Mark Fearing**. Chronicle Books, 2012. 248pp. 978-1-4521-0906-0. Y

Bud just moved out into the middle of the desert with his father. His father works with hundreds of satellite dishes aimed to hear outer space. On what should be his first day of grade school, Bud instead gets on the wrong bus—one that is headed to the interstellar academy for students all over the galaxy. Beyond his initial reaction of seeing so many aliens, he is surprised that all the aliens are quite friendly and act like his Earth friends. When his friends find out that he is an Earthling, they warn him, legend says, that Earthlings are the most feared creatures in the galaxy. It is up to Bud and his new friends to get him home before the principal finds out who Bud truly is.

Hilo. Written and Illustrated by **Judd Winick**. Random House Books for Young Readers. 2015– . Y

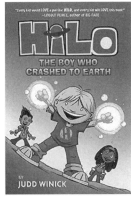

© 2016 Random House and Judd Winick.

D.J. and Gina are two normal kids, but their boring lives at school is about to change when a mysterious boy crash lands to Earth. Where did he come from? What is his mission on Earth? Can D.J. and Dina help Hilo to remember why he's on Earth and convince him to wear more than underwear to school in time to save the world together?

Vol. 1: The Boy Who Crashed to Earth. 2015. 208pp. 978-0-385-38617-3, hardcover.
Vol. 2: Saving the Whole Wide World. 2016. 208pp. 978-0-385-38623-4, hardcover.
Vol. 3: The Great Big Boom. 2017. 208pp. 978-0-385-38620-3. hardcover.

Jim Henson's The Musical Monsters of Turkey Hollow. Written by **Jim Henson** and **Jerry Juhl**. Adapted and Illustrated by **Roger Langridge**. BOOM! Studios, 2014. 96pp. 978-1-60886-434-8. A 🖳

© 2016 BOOM! Studios.

Based on an unused screenplay created by Jim Henson in 1968, the story revolves around Thanksgiving time in the picturesque town of Turkey Hollow. Unbeknownst to the town, over a hundred years ago a meteorite crashed. Meanwhile in the woods, a young boy named Timmy Henderson is playing his guitar and hears strange noises accompanying him. He discovers that the meteorite was really and an egg that contained seven goofy-looking aliens who speak only by making noises. Soon Timmy befriends them and brings the aliens back to Turkey Hollow, but residents there don't take a liking to them and it's up to Timmy to rescue the aliens and save Thanksgiving as well. The unused screenplay was finally adapted into the live-action movie called *Jim Henson's Turkey Hollow* and aired in 2015 on the Lifetime Channel

Kaijumax. Written and Illustrated by **Zander Cannon**. Oni Press, 2016– . O ◉

Welcome to Kaijumax—the largest prison ever! Set in a world where Kaiju (the Japanese word for "Giant Monster") roam the Earth, they're kept in check at Kaijumax prison after rampaging. The series focuses on the many Kaiju in the prison including Electrogor, the main Kaiju protagonist, all under the thumb of the evil warden Kang and his guards. The series features a colorful cast of Kaiju and Ultra-man-like guards with

their own problems, addictions, rivalries, and scores to settle. Cannon does impressive work creating a vast design of all different Kaiju and includes their back histories as well. Though humorous at times, the series is also a prison drama and includes brutal scenes and situations not suitable for younger ages. More volumes in the series are expected.

Season One. 2016. 168pp. 978-1-62010-270-1.
Season Two: The Seamy Underbelly. 2017. 160pp. 978-1-62010-396-8.

Mal and Chad. Written and Illustrated by **Stephen McCranie**. Philomel Books/Penguin, 2011–2014. Y

Mal is a boy genius, able to make any device like a time machine, dream-reading machine, weather machines, and more. His best friend Chad, his pet dog, can talk—but no one else seems to notice. Together the two of them get into hilarious situations and another—all the while Chad just wants to impress the girl of his dreams. Will she ever see him as more than just a dork?

Vol. 1: The Biggest, Bestest Time Ever!. 2011. 224pp. 978-0-399-25221-1.
Vol. 2: Food Fight!. 2012. 224pp. 978-0-399-25657-8.
Vol. 3: Belly Flop!. 2012. 224pp. 978-0-399-25658-5.

Poptropica. Created by **Jeff Kinney**. Written by **Jack Chabert** and **Mitch Krpata**. Illustrated by **Kory Merritt**. Amulet Books, 2016– . Y 🎮

Based on the popular online video game web site, comes a new adventure based on a concept by *Diary of a Wimpy Kid* creator Jeff Kinney. Oliver, Mya, and Jorge are stranded on a mysterious island after their pilot, the nefarious Octavian, crash lands there. The island seems like a place where time has no meaning—filled with Vikings, extinct animals, and danger! Can the three of them find a way to get off the island?

Vol. 1: Mystery of the Map. 2016. 112pp. 978-1-4197-2067-3, hardcover.
Vol. 2: The Lost Expedition. 2016. 112pp. 978-1-4197-2129-8, hardcover.

Red's Planet. Written and Illustrated by **Eddie Pittman**. Amulet Books, 2016– . Y

Red is a 10-year-old foster child who has had enough of being sent from home to home and she's ready to run away to her dream place—some place far away from her annoying foster family. While running away from her latest foster home, she's accidentally captured by an alien starcraft and taken literally farther than she ever expected—in outer space! After the ship crashes on a planet, she's marooned with a menagerie of misfit aliens. With her newfound friend, a little grey alien named Tawee, Red's got to find a way to survive on a hostile planet with angry castaways, a vicious wildfire, and more. This is like no paradise that Red ever wished for!

Vol. 1. 2016. 192pp. 978-1-4197-1907-3, hardcover; 978-1-4197-1908-0.
Vol. 2: Friends and Foes. 2017. 192pp. 978-1-4197-2315-5. hardcover. 978-1-4197-2315-5.

Sardine in Outer Space. Written by **Emmanuel Guibert**. Illustrated by **Joann Sfar**. First Second Books, 2006–2008. Y

The adventures of Sardine, a pint-sized swashbuckling heroine with a grand thirst for adventure. Joined with her cousin Louie and her pirate uncle Captain Yellow Shoulder, they fly across the galaxy in her uncle's ship, the Huckleberry, ready to take on any quest and bad guy across the galaxy no matter how big or absurd they are. From Sardine's dim-witted arch-nemesis Super-muscleman, cosmic squids, talking clouds, a dancing space queen slug, and more oddities, Sardine will be there to save the day. The series was originally published in Europe and are now being reprinted in North America

Vol. 1. 2006. 128pp. 978-1-59643-126-3.
Vol. 2. 2006. 128pp. 978-1-59643-127-0.
Vol. 3. 2007. 112pp. 978-1-59643-128-7.
Vol. 4. 2007. 112pp. 978-1-59643-129-4.
Vol. 5. 2008. 112pp. 978-1-59643-380-9.
Vol. 6. 2008. 96pp. 978-1-59643-424-0.

Secret Science Alliance and the Copycat Crook. Written and Illustrated by **Eleanor Davis**. Bloomsbury for Kids, 2009. 154pp. 978-1-59990-396-5. Y 🏅

Julian is super-smart and just started junior high at a new school. Self-conscious about showing off his nerd-cred for science, he pleasantly discovers he's not alone in his scientific interests and forms a secret science club with Ben and Greta—complete with a secret hidden lair! There the three secret scientists can create new inventions! When they discover a villain is set to rob a museum, the three must use their science skills and save the day! The book was recognized by YALSA in 2010 on the Great Graphic Novels for Teens list.

Zita the Spacegirl. Written and Illustrated by **Ben Hatke.** First Second Books, 2011– . A 🏅 ◎

© 2016 Ben Hatke and First Second.

When her best friend is kidnapped by an alien death-cult, Earth girl Zita must come to the rescue. After fighting monsters and saving the day, she finds herself the subject of intergalactic fame hampering her attempts to return home. The books in the trilogy have been among Kirkus' and School Library Journal's best books and won the Cybils Award and nominated for an Eisner.

Zita the Spacegirl. 2011. 192pp. 978-1-5964-3695-4, hardcover; 978-1-5964-3446-2.
Legends of Zita the Spacegirl. 2012. 224pp. 978-1-5964-3806-4, hardcover; 978-1-5964-3447-9.
The Return of Zita the Spacegirl. 2014. 240pp. 978-1626-72058-9, hardcover; 978-1-5964-3876-7.

Super-Hero Humor

Stories that tell the humorous side of being a super-hero. Though the story is still mainly regarding the heroes and fighting crime, often the tales focus on the absurdity of the character themselves including their silly costumes, funny instances when saving the day, to black comedies focusing on the cynical side of super-heroics. Popular characters include the comedic antics of Plastic Man, the screwball antics of a super-hero team such as the Justice League International, and even the over-the-top black comedy of such anti-heroes as Marshal Law. For more standard super-hero fare, see the super-hero chapter.

Adventures of Superhero Girl: Expanded Edition. Written and Illustrated by **Faith Erin Hicks**. Dark Horse Comics, 2017. 128pp. 978-1-61655-084-4, hardcover. T 🌶 ◎

© 2013 Faith Erin Hicks.

The quirky life of a Superhero Girl, a hero who lives in a small Canadian town who loves to buy her capes at second-hand stores, has a soft spot for rescuing kittens, and loves hanging and having conversations with her roommate. Faith Erin Hicks's trademark humor shines in this loving parody of the superhero genre complete with fighting ninjas, the downsides of not wearing sunscreen while wearing a mask, a little brotherly superhero competition, as well as plenty of cats. The only thing missing from this collection is a sequel. The collection was recognized by YALSA's Great Graphic Novels for Teens committee's annual selection list in 2014. The expanded edition collects the original comic, two new stories, and new art from creators including Tyler Crook, Ron Chan, Jake Wyatt, Paulina Ganucheau, and more.

Aw Yeah Comics! Written by **Art Baltazar** and **Franco**. Illustrated by **Art Baltazar**. Dark Horse Comics, 2014– . Y

Aw Yeah Comics. . . and Action
TM © 2016 Art Baltazar and
Franco.

The city of Skokie, Illinois is under the protection of Action Cat and Adventure Bug and their hero friends from the villainous (and silly) Evil Cat and Parallel-O-Ham! The series is an homage to the Aw Yeah Comics comic book store chain owned by the creators and has plenty of heart, humor, heroes, and pancakes!

Vol. 1: And . . . Action!. 2014. 152pp. 978-1-61655-558-0.
Vol. 2: Time For . . . Adventure!. 2015. 168pp. 978-1-61655-689-1.
Action Cat and Adventure Bug. 2016. 104pp. 978-1-50670-023-6.
Vol. 3: Make Way . . . For Awesome!. 2016. 160pp. 978-1-50670-045-8.

Batman '66. Written by **Jeff Parker** and **Ty Templeton**. Illustrated by **Jonathan Case** and **Ty Templeton**. DC Comics, 2014– . T

In 1966, television was never the same again when Batman became a cultural phenomenon with a camp hit television series starring Adam West and Burt Ward as

© 2016 DC Comics.

the Dynamic Duo of Batman and Robin. Revisit those campy and kooky days when Batman wasn't quite so grim and gritty with more whimsical plot lines and zany villains. While there are plenty of Batman-Related books out there, the characters are drawn to resemble their TV counterparts (right down to the Joker's semi-hidden mustache). Besides the usual rogues gallery there are appearances by characters who were first introduced in the show as well as new versions of characters introduced since then.

Vol. 1. 2014. 176pp. 978-1-4012-4721-8, hardcover; 2014. 978-1-4012-4931-1.

Vol. 2. 2014. 176pp. 978-1-4012-4932-8, hardcover; 2015, 978-1-4012-5461-2.

Vol. 3. 2015. 168pp. 978-1-40125-462-9, hardcover; 2015, 978-1-4012-5750-7.

Vol. 4. 2015. 176pp. 978-1-4012-5751-4, hardcover; 2015, 978-1-4012-6104-7.

Vol. 5. 2016. 176pp. 978-1-4012-6105-4, hardcover. 978-1-4012-6483-3.

Batman '66 Meets the Green Hornet. Written by **Kevin Smith** and **Ralph Garman**. Illustrated by **Ty Templeton**. 144pp. 978-1-4012-5228-1, hardcover; DC Comics, 2015. T

A crossover reunion of two of the most popular superhero shows from the 1960s is finally here! When General Gumm resurfaces, Batman and the Green Hornet must set aside their differences and together team up to defeat the sticky villain.

Batman '66 Meets the Man from U.N.C.L.E. Written by **Jeff Parker**. Illustrated by **David Hahn**. 200pp. 2016. 978-1-4012-6447-5, hardcover. 978-1-4012-6864-0. T

The Caped Crusader teams up with Agents Napoleon Solo and Illya Kuryakin to fight both Gotham's Supercriminals and the evil organization T.H.R.U.S.H.

Batman '66 Meets John Speed and Emma Peel. Written by **Ian Edginton**. Illustrated by **Matthew Dow Smith**. 2017. 136pp. 978-1-4012-6820-6. T

Batman meets the Avengers! No, not them, that pair of British adventures, as they work together to fight Catwoman, Lord Fogg, and the Cybernauts. This book was co-published with Boom Studios.

Batman: Li'l Gotham. Written and Illustrated by **Dustin Nguyen** and **Derek Fridolfs**. DC Comics, 2014–2016. A

© 2016 DC Comics.

A humor kid-ified version of the characters from Gotham City, including Batman, Robin, Nightwing, Catwoman, The Joker, The Penguin and many others! Each short story focuses on a different season or holiday of the year including Halloween, Thanksgiving, Christmas, and New Years. The series is a humorous portrait of the characters and the beautiful artwork is fully painted as well.

Vol. 1. 2014. 128pp. 978-1-4012-4494-1.

Vol. 2. 2014. 128pp. 978-1-4012-4723-2.

Batman: Li'l Gotham Deluxe Edition. 2016. 252pp. 978-1-4012-6927-2, hardcover.

Buzzboy. Written and Illustrated by **John Gallagher**. Sky Dog Press, 2002–2003; Red Giant Entertainment, 2012. Y

> After the hero of the world, Captain Ultra, declares martial law and becomes its ruler, only the last remaining hero can save the day: Buzzboy, the comic sidekick of Captain Ultra! An oddball hero with a penchant for quoting obscure pop culture references and gorging fast-food, with the power of his mysterious Buzzbelt, Buzzboy's able to fight crime one burrito at a time. He is helped in his quest to vanquish "Lord Ultra" by Doc Cyber, a former arch-nemesis who is now his weapons designer and banker; a reality-warping high school student named Becca; Dream Angel Pandora, a guardian of dreams; and Zoomer, former teen-hero like Buzzboy who has the power of super speed. Together they're able to take on any bad guys who dare to threaten New Paradise and eat free meals at the local Tastee Diner.

Vol. 1: Trouble in Paradise. 2002. 144pp. 978-0-9721831-0-9.
Vol. 2: Monsters, Dreams, & Milkshakes! 2003. 144pp. 978-0-9721831-1-6.
Vol. 3: Sidekicks Rule! 2012. 120pp. 978-0-9745645-3-1.

Franklin Richards: Son of a Genius Ultimate Collection*.* Written by **Marc Sumerak** and **Chris Eliopoulos**. Illustrated by **Chris Eliopoulos**. Marvel Comics, 2010. Y

It's The Fantastic Four meets Calvin and Hobbes as Franklin Richards, son of Mr. Fantastic and the Invisible Woman has wacky adventures much to the consternation of his robot babysitter H.E.R.B.I.E. (first seen in the 1970s Fantastic Four cartoon series). The Franklin and H.E.R.B.I.E. stories first began as strips at the end of comic books that were first collected into one comic book that was followed by 14 new comic books between 2005 and 2009. These comics were collected into various digests, the contents of which are collected in these two Ultimate Collections.

© 2016 Marvel Comics.

Vol. 1. 2010. 216pp. 978-0-7851-4924-8.
Vol. 2. 2010. 184pp. 978-0-7851-4925-5.

G-Man. Written and Illustrated by **Chris Giarrusso**. Image Comics, 2010–2013. Y.

Mikey G wants to be a hero just like his idol Captain Thunderman. They all get to save the day, but he doesn't have any powers and is just a kid in school. But one day when he puts on his family's magic blanket, he finds that he gains super strength, super endurance, and flight and G-Man is born! He soon teams up with other kid heroes including Tan Man, Billy Demon, Suntrooper, and the Spark against Kid Thunder and more! The series was also released as a hybrid novel series beginning in 2015 from AMP Comics for Kids.

© 2016 Chris Giarrusso.

Vol. 1: Learning to Fly. 2010. 96pp. 978-1-60706-270-7.
Vol. 2: Cape Crisis. 2010. 96pp. 978-1-60706-271-4.
Vol. 3: Coming Home. 2013. 96pp. 978-1-60706-571-5.

Giant-Sized Little Marvel: AvX*.* Written and Illustrated by **Skottie Young**. Marvel Comics, 2016. 120pp. 978-0-7851-9870-3. A

A collection of pint-sized stories featuring cute child-like version of the Avengers and X-Men. Set during the storyline of Secret Wars, on the Battleworld zone called Marville, the heroes and villains are all kids where elementary-school hijinx are on the order for the day. Who will win the super-dodge-ball games? Who's got the best hi-tech hideouts? And what team is the toughest kid-heroes on the block?

© 2016 Marvel Comics.

Impossible Man. Written by **Stan Lee**, **Roy Thomas**, **Chris Claremont**, and **Peter David**. Illustrated by **Jack Kirby** and various. Marvel Comics, 2011. 360pp. 978-0-7851-5520-1. A

Meet the Impossible Man. he's a shape-changing comedian from the planet Poppup. Since his first appearance in *The Fantastic Four* #11 (1963) he's been a humorous source of fun for the entire Marvel Universe. Often very lonely, he uses his shape-changing abilities to often cause chaos and often irritates all of those around him. Collected in this edition are a variety of fun appearances of the Impossible Man as he irritates the heroes and villains of the Marvel Universe!

© 2016 Marvel Comics.

Jack Staff. Written and Illustrated by **Paul Grist**. Image Comics, 2004–2010. T ◎
Twenty years ago Great Britain's favorite super-hero from Castletown disappeared from the public eye, but what really happened to him? Becky Burdock, an investigative reporter for the local tabloid newspaper, is trying to find out. While investigating a series of murders possibly caused by a vampire, she uncovers what really happened to the patriotic hero. When an ancient villain threatens the town after last being seen during the Blitzkreig, Jack Staff has to come out of retirement, face his fears, and fight alongside the heroes of today to defeat an old foe. The series is a light parody of super-hero, science fiction, and horror comic books with an indelible British style of humor.

Vol. 1: Everything Used to Be Black and White. 2011, 2nd edition. 352pp. 978-1-60706-380-3.
Vol. 2: Soldiers. 2010, 2nd printing. 160pp. 978-1-58240-392-2.
Vol. 3: Echoes of Tomorrow. 2007. 200pp. 978-1-58240-719-7.
Vol. 4: Rocky Realities. 2010. 224pp. 978-1-60706-148-9.

Justice League. Written by **Keith Giffen** and **J.M. DeMatteis**. Illustrated by **Kevin Maguire**, **Bart Sears**, **Adam Hughes**, and **Ty Templeton**. DC Comics. T 🎗 ◎

© 2016 DC Comics.

A humorous take on the classic super-team, mixing witty humor with super-heroic action collecting the earliest stories from the now-classic 1980s tales of the Justice League. Rebuilt with the guidance of financial tycoon Maxwell Lord, the team, comprised at first of Batman, Black Canary, Green Lantern Guy Gardner, Blue Beetle, Booster Gold, the Martian Manhunter, Mr. Miracle, Captain Marvel, Dr. Fate, and Dr. Light, became a United Nations-sponsored team. With a larger cast of heroes on the team. The Justice League 3001 series has the super hero team cloned by Wonder Twins Terry and Teri Magnus but the process flawed. But nonetheless, Superman, Batman, Wonder Woman, Green Lantern and the Flash are ready to save the day! For more listings that focus more on action instead of humor, see the Justice League listing in the super-hero chapter.

Justice League International, 2009–2011.

> *Vol. 1*. 2009. 192pp. 978-1-4012-1739-6.
> *Vol. 2*. 2009. 208pp. 978-1-4012-2020-4.
> *Vol. 3*. 2009. 224pp. 978-1-4012-2538-4.
> *Vol. 4*. 2010. 192pp. 978-1-4012-2197-3.
> *Vol. 5*. 2011. 240pp. 978-1-4012-3010-4.
> *Vol. 6*. 2011. 240pp. 978-1-4012-3119-4.

Justice League 3001, 2016.

> *Vol. 1: Déjà vu All Over Again*. 2016. 192pp. 978-1-4012-6148-1.
> *Vol. 2: Things Fall Apart*. 2016. 144pp. 978-1-4012-6472-7.

Love and Capes. Written and Illustrated by **Tom Zahler**. IDW Publishing 2008–2015. T

© 2016 Thomas F. Zahler.

In this funny and romantic series, bookstore owner Abby find's out that her accountant boyfriend Mark is the Superman-like hero The Crusader. Over the course of the series the couple get engaged, marry, and have a child while Abby has to accept the odder parts of her husband's life, including his past relationship with super-heroine Amazonia. The series was nominated for a Harvey Award.

> *Vol. 1: Do You Want to Know a Secret?*. 2008. 168pp. 978-1-60010 275 2.
> *Vol. 2: Going to the Chapel*. 2010. 190pp. 978-1-60010-680-4.
> *Vol. 3: Wake Up Where You Are*. 2011. 172pp. 978-1-61377-049-8.
> *Vol. 4: What to Expect*. 2013. 148pp. 978-1-61377-586-8.
> *The Complete Collection*. 2015. 676pp. 978-1-63140-000-1.

Lunch Lady. Written and Illustrated by **Jarrett J. Krosoczka**. Random House, 2009–2014. Y ◉

What do you think your lunch lady does when she's not serving food? Students Hector, Dee, and Terrence have always wondered. Does she go home and pet her cats? Where does she live? Little do they realize, she does more than serve sloppy joe—she serves a healthy dosage of dosage of justice as a super hero!

> *Vol. 1: Lunch Lady and the Cyborg Substitute*. 2009. 96pp. 978-0-375-84683-0.
> *Vol. 2: Lunch Lady and the League of Librarians*. 2009. 96pp. 978-0-375-84684-7.

© 2016 Jarrett J. Krosoczka.

Vol. 3: Lunch Lady and the Author Visit Vendetta. 2009. 96pp. 978-0-375-86094-2.

Vol. 4: Lunch Lady and the Summer Camp Shakedown. 2010. 96pp. 978-0-375-86095-9.

Vol. 5: Lunch Lady and the Bake Sale Bandit. 2010. 96pp. 978-0-375-86729-3.

Vol. 6: Lunch Lady and the Field Trip Fiasco. 2011. 96pp. 978-0-375-86730-9.

Vol. 7: Lunch Lady and the Mutant Mathletes. 2012. 96pp. 978-0-375-87028-6.

Vol. 8: Lunch Lady and the Picture Day Peril. 2012. 96pp. 978-0-375-87035-4.

Vol. 9: Lunch Lady and the Video Game Villain. 2013. 96pp. 978-0-307-98079-3.

Vol. 10: Lunch Lady and the Schoolwide Scuffle. 2014. 96pp. 978-0-385-75279-4.

Madman. Written and Illustrated by **Mike Allred**. Image Comics, 2007–2012. T

© 2016 Mike Allred.

When kooky Snap City needs rescuing from the mutant street beatniks, the evil genius Mr. Mondstadt, renegade robots, the Puke, and other oddball enemies, there's only one zany undead masked hero for the job: Madman! Alias Frank Einstein, he was reanimated and now wears a mask and costume to conceal his disfigured face and body. Only Frank's true love, the freckle-faced Joe, loves him for the man he is inside. Joined with a colorful cast of madcap and goofy characters including Dr. Flem, the Big Guy, G-Men from Hell, and more, Frank and Joe are on the wackiest and hippest adventures possible taking them back in time, to Hell, on top of a giant brain of Dr. Boiffard, and much more. With Madman here, Snap City is in good hands, but it's one groovy and wild ride. The series has been published under various publishers over the years, but the omnibus collections and the 20th anniversary celebration have been published by Image Comics. The 20th Anniversary Monster collection features contributions from many creators to celebrate Michael Allred's zany hero.

Madman (original series). 2007–2008.

Vol. 1. 2007. 268pp. 978-1-58240-810-1.
Vol. 2. 2007. 456pp. 978-1-58240-811-8.
Vol. 3. 2008. 264pp. 978-1-58240-893-4.

Madman and the Atomics. 2007. 380pp. 978-1-58240-812-5.
Madman Gargantua. 2007. 852pp. 978-1-58240-740-1, hardcover.
Madman: Atomic Comics. 2008–2010.

Vol. 1. 2008. 162pp. 978-1-58240-916-0.
Vol. 2. 2009. 200pp. 978-1-60706-014-7.
Vol. 3. 2010. 200pp. 978-1-60706-263-9.

Madman Atomica. 2011. 900pp. 978-1-60706-341-4, hardcover.
Madman 20th Anniversary Monster. 2012. 264pp. 978-1-60706-472-5, hardcover.

Magic Pickle. Written and Illustrated by **Scott Morse**. Graphix/Scholastic Books, 2008. 112pp. 978-0-439-87995-8. Y ◎

Little Jo Jo Wigman's got the strangest superhero of all living under her floorboards—the mysterious and rather short vegetable hero who dills out justice like no other hero before: Weapon Kosher! After being revived after 50 years in hibernation to track down Chili Chili Bang Bang, the Phantom Carrot, and the rest of the Brotherhood, Weapon Kosher is ready to fight with his fists and a little help from Jo Jo, and plenty of bad produce jokes all around.

Cover © Scholastic Inc.

Mini Marvels: The Complete Collection. Written and drawn by **Chris Giarrusso**. Marvel Comics, 2013. 216pp. 978-0-7851-8490-4. A

In these humorous strips, the Marvel characters are portrayed as children. The Mini Marvel strips started off as "Bullpen Bits" in the Bullpen Bulletin information pages in various Marvel Comics titles and later appeared on letter's pages and in the post-story pages in the comic books Some strips parodied events happening in the comics while other created new characters. For example, the Green and Red Hulks were joined in the strips by a Blue one. There have been various Mini Marvel Collections, the contents of which appear in this volume along with additional material.

© 2016 Marvel Comics.

One-Punch Man. Written by **ONE**. Illustrated by **Yusuke Murata**. VIZ Media, 2015–2016. T 🚹 Japanese manga. あ

The intimating young hero named Saitama is the most powerful superhero. He is so powerful that he can now defeat anyone with one punch. Imposing with a bald head and a white flowing cape, Saitama doesn't feel challenged anymore when all it takes is one punch to take out the monsters and villains. Listless since he's bored with no real opponents and no one takes him seriously because he's bald, Saitama is looking for the next big challenge. Is there anyone in the world—or elsewhere who can give him a challenge? The series was originally based on a web-comic in Japan. The series, which is still ongoing in Japan, has also been adapted into an anime series as well. The first volume in the series was recognized as a Great Graphic Novel for Teens on their 2016 selection list.

ONE-PUNCH MAN © 2012 by ONE,
Yusuke Murata/SHUEISHA Inc.

Vol. 1. 2015. 200pp. 978-1-4215-8564-2.
Vol. 2. 2015. 200pp. 978-1-4215-8565-9.

Vol. 3. 2015. 216pp. 978-1-4215-6461-6.   *Vol. 8*. 2016. 216pp. 978-1-4215-8656-4.
Vol. 4. 2016. 216pp. 978-1-4215-6920-8.   *Vol. 9*. 2016. 216pp. 978-1-4215-8657-1.
Vol. 5. 2016. 216pp. 978-1-4215-6954-3.   *Vol. 10*. 2017. 216pp. 978-1-4215-9015-8.
Vol. 6. 2016. 216pp. 978-1-4215-8527-7.   *Vol. 11*. 2017. 216pp. 978-1-4215-9226-8.
Vol. 7. 2016. 216pp. 978-1-4215-8528-4.   *Vol. 12*. 2017. 216pp. 978-1-4215-9620-4.

Pet Avengers. Written by **Chris Eliopoulos**. Illustrated by **Ig Guara**. Marvel Comics 2010–2011. A

It's the animals of the Marvel Universe ready to save the day. The Inhumans' teleporting pet Lockjaw gains possession of the Mind Gem and recruits other animals to save the day. Making up the team are Ka-Zar's sabretooth Zabu, Kitty Pryde's dragon Lockheed, the Falcon's bird Redwing, Speedball's superpowered cat Hairball, Throg, a frog with the power of Thor, and Ms. Lion, the dog first seen in the Spider-Man and His Amazing Friends cartoon series. The team would later reunite for additional adventures. The 2009 title, *Pet Avengers Classic*, reprinted earlier appearances of the animals.

Pet Avengers Classic. 2009. 208pp. 978-0-7851-3966-9.
Lockjaw and the Pet Avengers. 2010. 128pp. 978-0-7851-4123-5.
Lockjaw and the Pet Avengers Unleashed. 2010. 120pp. 978-0-7851-4304-8.
Avengers vs. Pet Avengers. 2011. 128pp. 978-0-7851-5185-2.

Pix: One Weirdest Weekend. Written and Illustrated by **Gregg Schigiel**. Hatter Entertainment, 2015. 120pp. 978-0-9905218-0-8. Y

Emaline Laurel Pixley (AKA Pix) is a good-natured and loving teenager who just happens to be a fairy princess who wants to be a superhero. She lives in a good city with great parents and fantastic friends. Her daily life is rarely boring—her kitchen sink leads to another dimension; her next-door neighbor's dog can talk; and she just rescued a celebrity from killer TV cameras! Pix is on her way to being a hero—but is she really a fairy? Pix is what would happen if Supergirl was a Disney Princess!

© 2016 Gregg Schigiel.

Powerpuff Girls. Written by **Sean Carolan**, **Abby Denson**, **Jeremy Whitley**, **Jake Goldman**, and **Haley Mancini**. Illustrated by **Derek Charm**, **Mike DeCarlo**, **Dan Fraga**, and **Phil Moy**. IDW Publishing, 2014– . A 🖵

When Professor Utonium was trying to create the perfect little girl, he added a little sugar, spice, everything nice, plus an accidental dosage of Chemical X, and Powerpuff Girls were born! Now Blossom, Bubbles, and Buttercup use their super-powers to save the city of Townsville against fiends like their simian arch-rival Mojo Jojo, Fuzzy Lumpkins, the Gangreen Gang, giant monsters, and more. The stories are based on the hit cartoon show on the Cartoon Network that originally aired from 1998 to 2005. The comic book series was relaunched in 2013 by IDW Publishing, with the classic titles originally published by DC Comics released as well under the imprint *Powerpuff Girls Classics*. A new *Powerpuff Girls* series from IDW Publishing debuted in 2016 to tie in with the release of a new animated series of *Powerpuff Girls* cartoons.

TM & © Cartoon Network. (s13). © Idea and Design Works, LLC. IDW Publishing, a division of Idea and Design Works, LLC.

Powerpuff Girls. 1st series, 2014–2015.

> *Vol. 1: Second Chances.* 2014. 152pp. 978-1-61377-906-4.
> *Vol. 2: Monster Mash.* 2014. 104pp. 978-1-63140-107-7.
> *Super Smash Up.* 2015. 120pp. 978-1-63140-378-1.

Powerpuff Girls Classics, 2014–2015.

> *Vol. 1: Power Party.* 2013. 148pp. 978-1-61377-733-6.
> *Vol. 2: Power Up.* 2013. 140pp. 978-1-61377-745-9.
> *Vol. 3: Pure Power.* 2014. 140pp. 978-1-61377-921-7.
> *Vol. 4: Picture Perfect.* 2014. 140pp. 978-1-63140-017-9.
> *Vol. 5: Bless This Mess.* 2015. 140pp. 978-1-63140-160-2.

Powerpuff Girls. 2nd series, 2016– .

> *Vol. 1: Homecoming.* 2017. 76pp. 978-1-63140-829-8, hardcover.
> *Vol. 2: Power Up My Mojo.* 2017. 76pp. 978-1-63140-871-7, hardcover.

ps238. Written and Illustrated by **Aaron Williams**. Do Gooder Press, 2004–2011. Y
Welcome to ps238, the only school designed to help train and prepare the metahumans of tomorrow. Located three miles below the surface of a seemingly normal Excelsior Public School for normal students, the special students with super-human powers train in the underground facility to prepare them for a life of crime-fighting adventure and even the occasional life of crime. While their parents fight elsewhere against the forces of evil, the students—including Captain Clarinet, Suzi Fusion, Emerald Gauntlet, evil genius Zodon, Victor VonFogg, Guardian Angel, and Tyler Marlocke, a boy whose parents are heroes but he doesn't have any powers at all—must learn to do battle against such fearsome challenges as field trips to other planets, super-hero themed homework assignments, and much more. The series reverted to an online-only format and no new collections have been printed. Fans of the books can still read online stories for free at http://ps238.nodwick.com/.

> *Vol. 1: With Liberty and Recess for All.* 2004. 160pp. 978-1-930964-69-3.
> *Vol. 2: To the Cafeteria. . . For Justice!* 2005 160pp. 978-1-933288-13-0.
> *Vol. 3: No Child Left Behind.* 2006. 160pp. 978-1-933288-24-6.
> *Vol. 4: Not Another Learning Experience!* 2007. 200pp. 978-1-933288-36-9.
> *Vol. 5: Extraterrestrial Credit.* 2008. 160pp. 978-1-933288-42-0.
> *Vol. 6: Senseless Acts of Tourism.* 2009. 160pp. 978-1-933288-49-9.
> *Vol. 7: Daughters, Sons, and Shrink-ray Guns.* 2009. 160pp. 978-1-933288-40-6.
> *Vol. 8: When Worlds Go Splat!* 2010. 160pp. 978-1-933288-41-3.
> *Vol. 9: Saving Alternate Omaha.* 2011. 160pp. 978-0-9847929-0-0.

Quantum and Woody. Valiant Entertainment, 2012– . T
In the original run of this occasionally goofy superhero adventure Eric Henderson and Woodrow Van Chelton are boyhood friends reunited in the mysterious deaths of their fathers. While investigating, the pair is affected by an industrial accident that requires them to clang metal wristbands together every day or risk turning into energy and fading away. Eric becomes to the costumed Quantum with slacker Woody finding himself in the unwanted role of sidekick. In the 2013 revival, the duo is now adoptive siblings who were investigating the death of their father when the accident happened.

© 2016 Valiant Entertainment.

In this incarnation they still have to "klang" every 24 hours but also have energy based powers. The original series by Christopher Priest and M.D. Bright was first collected as an omnibus and then in three smaller, cheaper volumes. Priest and Bright returned for a limited series set years after their final issue. The new series by James Asmus with art by Tom Fowler and Ming Doyle has been collected in regular and deluxe editions and was nominated for several Harvey awards. Asmus also worked with Steve Lieber on the *Quantum and Woody Must Die* limited series

1

2

Quantum and Woody, 1st series. Written by **Christopher Priest**. Illustrated by **M.D. Bright**. Valiant Entertainment, 2015. T

> *Vol. 1: Klang.* 2015. 208pp. 978-1-9393-4678-0.
> *Vol. 2: Switch.* 2015. 192pp. 978-1-9393-4680-3.
> *Vol. 3: And So. . .* 2015. 224pp. 978-1-9393-4686-5.
> *Q2: The Return of Quantum and Woody.* 2015. 160pp. 978-1-9393-4656-8, hardcover; 978-1-6821-5109-9.
> *Complete Quantum and Woody Classic Omnibus.* 2014. 624pp. 978-1-9393-4636-0, hardcover.

3

Quantum and Woody, 2nd series. Written by **James Asmus**. Illustrated by **Tom Fowler**, **Ming Doyle**, and **Steve Lieber**. Valiant Entertainment, 2013– .

> *Vol. 1: The World's Worst Superhero Team.* 2013. 112pp. 978-1-9393-4618-6.
> *Vol. 2: In Security.* 2014. 112pp. 978-1-9393-4623-0.
> *Vol. 3: Crooked Pasts, Present Tense.* 2014. 128pp. 978-1-9393-463-1.
> *Vol. 4: Quantum and Woody Must Die.* 2015. 144pp. 978-1-9393-4662-9.

4

5

> **Hardcover Deluxe Edition,** 2015.
> *Book 1.* 2015. 350pp. 978-1-9393-4668-1.

6

Scribblenauts Unmasked: A Crisis of Imagination. Written by **Josh Elder**. Illustrated by **Adam Archer.** DC Comics, 2015. 978-1-4012-4926-7. A 🎮

© 2016 DC Comics.

A sequel to the popular video game *Scribblenauts Unmasked: A DC Comics Adventure*, this work began as a digital comic before being printed as a nine-issue limited series. Maxwell and his sister Lilly (as well as their formally bad doppelgangers) and summoned by The Phantom Stranger and Madame Xanadu to use their magical notebook and globe to help the heroes of the DC Universe Besides fans of the game, the various cameos and Easter Eggs will delight long time comic-readers.

7

9

SMASH: Trial by Fire. Written by **Chris A. Bolton**. Illustrated by **Kyle Bolton**. Candlewick, 2013. 160pp. 978-0-7636-5596-9, hardcover. Y

When the local superhero known as Defender is killed in a blast, his powers get transferred to a boy that was caught near the explosion, 5th grader Andrew Ryan suddenly has super strength, speed, and flight! To protect his identity he makes a homemade costume and the hero known as Smash is born! But being a hero isn't easy especially when you have homework and a school bully to deal with too!

© 2016 Candlewick.

Sidekicks. Written and Illustrated by **Dan Santat**. Arthur A. Levine Books/ Scholastic Books, 2011. 224pp. 978-0-439-29819-3. Y

Captain Amazing, the aging hero of Metro City can't fight crime alone anymore. He's in need of a sidekick and will be holding try-outs in several weeks. Little does Captain Amazing realize that his home already has the best sidekicks he could ever hope for—his four pets who are ready to prove they're each the best sidekick of all. Little do they realize they'll need to get over their sibling rivalry and come together as a team to save the city in its time of need if they're going to prove they're all ready to be Captain Amazing's sidekick.

Cover © Scholastic Inc.

Squirrel Girl. Created by **Steve Ditko** and **Will Murray**. Marvel Comics, 2015– . 🌳 T

The most unlikely of heroes now in her own comic book! Doreen Green's not your typical hero—she's got the uncanny ability to speak to squirrels and has buck teeth to boot that can bite through wood—but she was able to take on and beat Wolverine, Deadpool, and Doctor Doom! Doreen can handle her quirky powers and the biggest challenge of all: college? The first collection was recognized by YALSA's Great Graphic Novels for Teens' on its top-10 titles for 2016 selection list. *The Unbeatable Squirrel Girl & the Great Lakes Avengers* collection reprints the early first appearances of Squirrel Girl before her newfound popularity.

Unbeatable Squirrel Girl. Written by **Ryan North.** Illustrated by **Erica Henderson**. 2015– .

© 2016 Marvel Comics.

Vol. 1: Squirrel Power. 2015. 128pp. 978-0-7851-9702-7.
Vol. 2: Squirrel You Know It's True. 2015. 128pp. 978-0-7851-9703-4.
Vol. 3: Squirrel You Really Got Me Now. 2016. 160pp. 978-0-7851-9626-6.
Vol. 4: I Kissed a Squirrel, and I Like It. 2016. 112pp. 978-0-7851-9627-3.
Vol. 5: Like I'm the Only Squirrel in the World. 2017. 112pp. 978-1-302-90328-2.

Vol. 1. 2016. 248pp. 978-1-302-90224-7, hardcover.
Vol. 2. 2017. 296pp. 978-1-302-90373-2, hardcover.

The Unbeatable Squirrel Girl Beats Up the Marvel Universe. 2016. 120pp. 978-1-3029-0303-9.
Unbeatable Squirrel Girl & the Great Lakes Avengers. 2016. 264pp. 978-1-3029-0066-3.

Super Diaper Baby. Written and Illustrated by **Dav Pilkey**. Scholastic Books. 2002–2015. Y ◎

George and Harold, the co-stars of the Captain Underpants series, are in trouble with Principal Krupp. He bans their comic book adventures of Captain Underpants—so what do the two boys do? Create a spin-off series adventure of a little baby named Billy Hoskins who gains the powers of Captain Underpants and now fights crime and the dastardly Deputy Doo-Doo. The sequel pits Super Diaper Baby against Rip Van Tinkle and more poop and pee puns.

The Adventures of Super Diaper Baby, 2nd printing. 2014. 144pp. 978-0-545-66544-5, hardcover.
Super Diaper Baby 2: Invasion of the Potty Snatchers. 2011. 192pp. 978-0-545-17532-6, hardcover.

Cover © Scholastic Inc.

Supermutant Magic Academy. Written and Illustrated by **Jillian Tamaki**. Drawn and Quarterly, 2015. O 🌳

Welcome to the Supermutant Magic Academy—a school where wizards, witches, and mutants in training attend to learn their skills to prepare for the future! Filled with tropes of teen coming-of-age stories, the teens—though they have powers—still have some of the same problems as other teens! A collection of the webcomic with supplemental material in the collected edition. The collection was recognized with an Eisner Award for the category of Best Publication for Teens in 2016.

© Jillian Tamaki.

Super Powers. Written by **Art Baltazar** and **Franco**. Illustrated by **Art Baltazar**. DC Comics, 2017– . A

A new all-ages series by the creator of Tiny Titans and Superman Family Adventures. Batman has gone missing and it's up to Superman to clean up Gotham City. When clues are found that show the Batman is in outer space, Wonder Woman is set to the further reaches of space to find her lost friend. The name of the comic is a homage to the original Super Powers DC Comics action figure line from the 1980s.

Vol. 1. 2017. 144pp. 978-1-4012-6842-8.

Super Secret Crisis War! Written by **Louise Simonson**, **Jim Zub**, and various. Illustrated by **Derek Charm**. IDW Publishing, 2015. A

It's a crossover of comic proportions at the Cartoon Network stars all team up when the evil Aku and the vile Vilgrax team up. It's up to the heroes from the shows *Samurai Jack*, the *Powerpuff Girls*, *Dexter's Laboratory*, *Ben 10*, and *Ed Edd, and Eddy* are here to save the day! The epic battle continues to the worlds of *Johnny Bravo*, *The Grim Adventures of Billy and Mandy*, *Foster's Home for Imaginary Friends*, *Cow & Chicken*, and *Codename Kids Next Door*!

Vol. 1. 2015. 140pp. 978-1-63140-207-4.
Vol. 2. 2015. 120pp. 978-1-63140-232-6.

2016 TM & © Cartoon Network.

Superman Family Adventures. Written by **Art Baltazar** and **Franco**. Illustrated by **Art Baltazar**. DC Comics, 2013–2014. A ◉

When the citizens of Metropolis are in trouble, there's no fear since Superman and his family of heroes—Superboy, Supergirl, Krypto, and Streaky the super-pets, and more are here! Joined with Lois Lane and even help from Batman, Superman, and Wonder Woman, they're here to help save Metropolis from silly menaces from outer space or villains from Earth like Lex Luthor, Parasite, and more.

Vol. 1. 2013. 128pp. 978-1-4012-4050-9.
Vol. 2. 2014. 128pp. 978-1-4012-4415-6.

© 2016 DC Comics.

Teen Titans Go. Written by **J. Torres**. Illustrated by **Todd Nauck**, **Tim Smith**, and **Lary Stucker**. DC Comics, 2006– . A 💻

Adapted from the hit animated series Teen Titans that aired for three seasons on the Cartoon Network from 2003 to 2006. Robin, the Boy Wonder, along with his teammates Cyborg, Beast Boy, Starfire, Raven, and more are out to fight evil, just as soon as they're done eating a slice of pizza. Recently DC Comics has begun to reprint the out of print series.

Vol. 1: Truth, Justice, Pizza!, 2nd printing. 2015. 112pp. 978-1-4012-6196-2.
Vol. 2: Heroes on Patrol, 2nd printing. 2016. 112pp. 978-1-4012-6638-7.
Vol. 3: Bring it On!, 2nd printing. 2016. 104pp. 978-1-4012-6468-0.
Vol. 4: Ready for Action. 2006. 104pp. 978-1-4012-0985-8.
Vol. 5: On the Move. 2006. 104pp. 978-1-4012-0986-5.

© 2016 DC Comics.

Teen Titans Go, 2nd series. Written by **Sholly Fisch**. Illustrated by **Lea Hernandez**. DC Comics, 2015– . A 🖵

In 2013, Cartoon Network brought back the Teen Titans animated series, but tweaked it to being purely a comedic show where all of the Teen Titans antics are more lighthearted and full of improbably but hilarious situations. The series still features Robin the Boy Wonder, Cyborg, Beast Boy, Starfire, and Raven.

Vol. 1: Party Party! 2015. 128pp. 978-1-4012-5242-7.
Vol. 2: Welcome to the Pizza Dome. 2016. 144pp. 978-1-4012-6730-8.
Vol. 3: Mumble Jumble. 2017. 128pp. 978-1-4012-6765-0.

Tiny Titans. Written by **Art Baltazar** and **Franco Aureliani**. Illustrated by **Art Baltazar**. DC Comics, 2009–2015. A 🎃

While there have been a number of Teen Titans related titles since the 1960s, the series is written for younger readers and has a lighter tone than many of the other, in-continuity comics. A multiple Eisner-Award winner, *Tiny Titans,* portrays the Titans, and other DC Universe characters and students and staff in an elementary school.

Vol. 1: Welcome to the Treehouse. 2009. 144pp. 978-1-4012-2078-5.
Vol. 2: Adventures in Awesomeness 2009. 144pp. 978-1-4012-2328-1.
Vol. 3: Sidekickin' It. 2010. 144pp. 978-1-4012-2653-4.
Vol. 4: The First Rule of Pet Club. 2010. 160pp. 978-1-4012-2892-7.
Vol. 5: Field Trippin'. 2011. 160pp. 978-1-4012-3173-6.
Vol. 6: The Treehouse and Beyond!. 2011. 144pp. 978-1-4012-3310-5.
Vol. 7: Growing Up Tiny!. 2012. 128pp. 978-1-4012-3525-3.
Vol. 8: Aw Yeah Titans! 2013. 128pp. 978-1-4012-3812-4.
Return to the Treehouse. 2015. 128pp. 978-1-4012-5492-6.

WordGirl. Written by **Chris Karwowski**, **Scott Ganz**, **Anita Serwacki**, and **Andrew Samson**. Illustrated by **Steve Young.** Boom!/Kaboom! 2011–2012. A 🖵

© 2016 BOOM! Studios.

Based on the Emmy-winning PBS show *WordGirl*—a super-heroine from the planet Lexicon whose ship crash-landed on Earth. Now when she's not student Becky Botsford, she uses her powers, including a large vocabulary, and her simian sidekick Captain Huggy Face, to fight such villains as Granny May, The Butcher, and Chuck the Evil Sandwich-Making Guy. The series was published as part of Boom's KaBoom line of graphic novels for younger readers.

Vol. 1: Coalition of Madness. 2011. 64pp. 978-1-6088-6678-6.
Vol. 2: The Incredible Shrinking Allowance. 2011. 64pp. 978-1-6088-6679-3.
Vol. 3: Word Up. 2012. 64pp. 978-1-6088-6680-9.
Vol. 4: Fashion Disaster. 2012. 64pp. 978-1-6088-6256-6.

X-Babies. Written by **Chris Claremont**, **Scott Lobdell**, and **Gregg Schigiel**. Illustrated by **Arthur Adams**, **Andy Kubert**, and **Jacob Chabot**. Marvel Comics, 2010. A

After an encounter with Mojo, the spineless bloated ruler of Mojoworld, the superhero mutant X-Men team were shrunk down to the size of toddlers and the X-Babies were born! The collections include the classic stories with the X-Babies as well as a new group of X-Babies created by Mojo to improve his television ratings on Mojoworld.

> *X-Babies Classic*. 2010. 160pp. 978-0-7851-4654-4.
> *X-Babies: Stars Reborn*. 2010. 104pp. 978-0-7851-4380-2.

© 2016 Marvel Comics.

Young Marvel: Little X-Men, Little Avengers, Big Trouble. Written by **Skottie Young, Dan Slott**, **Ruben Diaz**, and **Chris Claremont**. Illustrated by **Gurihiru**, **Mark Buckingham**, **JJ Kirby**, **Skottie Young**, and **Tom Raney**. Marvel Comics, 2013. 208pp. 978-0-7851-8498-0. A

It's an all-out super-hero-fest with the heroes as kids! It's pint-sized heroes all around as the Mitey 'Avengers fight the X-Babies. Then, the X-Men members Longshot and Dazzler travel to Mojoworld to rescue Wolverine and the X-Babies are there to help. Also, the Brotherhood of Mutant Bullies are in a contest versus the X-Babies organized by Mojo and Arcade!

(c) 2017 Marvel Comics.

Action and Adventure Humor

Tales that include heavy amounts of humor, including black comedy, slapstick, sarcasm and the like, to serve as a counter to the action and adventure in the plot. Note that the humor helps to alleviate the tension of the action and venture plot.

Axe Cop. Written by **Malachai Nicolle** and **Ethan Nicolle**. Illustrated by **Ethan Nicolle**. Dark Horse Comics, 2011– . T ▭

Axe Cop began life as a webcomic created by cartoonist Ethan Nicolle and his brother Malachai who was five when the series first started. The title character is Axey Smartist, a police officer who uses a firefighter's axe to fight crime. Besides ordinary criminals, Alex also fought zombies, aliens, and other weird things. His allies include Flute Cop, Baby Man, and Best Fairy Ever. An animated version of the series aired on Fox, moving to FXX channel for the second season. Nick Offerman provides the voice of Axe Cop.

Axe Cop TM © 2016 Malachai
Nicolle and Ethan Nicolle.

Vol. 1. 2011. 144pp. 978-1-5958-2681-7.
Vol. 2: Bad Guy Earth. 2011. 104pp. 978-1-5958-2825-5.
Vol. 3. 2012. 160pp. 978-1-5958-2911-5.
Vol. 4: President of the World. 2013. 96pp. 978-1-6165-5057-8.
Vol. 5: Axe Cop Gets Married and Other Stories. 2014. 160pp.
978-1-6165-5245-9.
Vol. 6: American Choppers. 2014. 112pp. 978-1-6165-5424-8.

Bookhunter. Written and Illustrated by **Jason Shiga**. Sparkplug Comics, 2007.
144pp. 978-0-9742715-6-9. T

The Oakland Public Library is hosting the tour of John Quincy Adams' Bible.
When it's discovered that the copy on display is a fake and the real edition
is stolen—there's only one group of librarian specialists you can call—the
Bookhunters! They must use their skills of the Dewey Decimal System,
research capabilities, and microfilm to solve the mystery of the theft find the
book before its scheduled to leave for the next destination of its tour. Plenty
of John Woo-like action and intrigue at the best place on Earth: the library!

King City. Written and Illustrated by **Brandon Graham**. Image Comics. 2012.
424pp. 978-1-60706-510-4. O

King City is a place you only go to if you are prepared for anything. The
streets are filled with gangs, ninjas, musicians, peddlers, monsters, aliens,
and other famous people. Anything you want from drugs, sex, weapons, and
much more can be gotten within King City. Joe, a Cat Master, and his mystical cat, Earthling, return to King City after some time. Small jobs need to
be done and Joe must meet up with old friends. While in King City, Joe and
Earthling must break into secret vaults, get mixed up in a gang war, and help
his friend break up an alien prostitution ring. All these events lead up to what
maybe the end of the world. It is up to Joe to decide whether to stop this
ancient demon from being resurrected or help his ex-girlfriend find her new
boyfriend. Whatever happens in *King City* it will truly be ridiculously crazy.

Ninja Baseball Kyuma. Written and Illustrated by **Shunshin Maeda**. Udon Entertainment, 2009–2010. Y Japanese manga.

A young boy named Kyuma and his dog Inui live in the mountains, where he
trains every day to be a great ninja. When he mistakes a local baseball coach
for his own ninja master he's to learn from, the world of shadow and stealth
collides with the world of bats, baseballs, and home runs. Can a ninja step up
to the plate and learn to play baseball?

Vol. 1. 2009. 200pp. 978-1-897376-86-7.
Vol. 2. 2010. 200pp. 978-1-897376-87-4.
Vol. 3. 2010. 200pp. 978-1-897376-88-1.

One Piece. Written and Illustrated by **Eiichiro Oda**. VIZ Media, 2003– . T Japanese manga. あ ◎

ONE PIECE © 1997 by Eiichiro Oda/SHUEISHA Inc.

Monkey D. Luffy has wanted to be a pirate since he was a kid after being rescued by his pirate friend, "Red Haired" Shanks. Indebted by Shanks's bravery, Monkey will do whatever it takes to be as noble and tough as his mentor, and he vows to find the hidden treasure left by the "Pirate King" Gold Roger. Luffy has also an odd power: he accidentally ate the "devil's fruit"—the gum-gum fruit—that makes the eater's body stretch like rubber. Now with his unique power and his small crew made up of the skilled swordsman Roronoa Zoro, the cute and spunky thief Nami, and more, there is nothing to stop Luffy from being the new Pirate King. The series originally debuted in Japan in 1997 and is still being published with over 81 volumes currently published overseas. The manga series has also been adapted as an anime series.

Vol. 1. 2003. 216pp. 978-1-5693-1901-7.
Vol. 2. 2003. 200pp. 978-1-5911-6057-1.
Vol. 3. 2003. 200pp. 978-1-5911-6184-4.
Vol. 4. 2004. 208pp. 978-1-5911-6337-4.
Vol. 5. 2004. 200pp. 978-1-5911-6615-3.
Vol. 6. 2005. 200pp. 978-1-5911-6723-5.
Vol. 7. 2005. 200pp. 978-1-5911-6852-2.
Vol. 8. 2005. 208pp. 978-1-4215-0191-8.
Vol. 9. 2006. 208pp. 978-1-4215-0406-3.
Vol. 10. 2006. 208pp. 978-1-4215-0406-3.
Vol. 11. 2006. 208pp. 978-1-4215-0663-0.
Vol. 12. 2006. 200pp. 978-1-4215-0664-7.
Vol. 13. 2007. 208pp. 978-1-4215-0665-4.
Vol. 14. 2007. 192pp. 978-1-4215-1091-0.
Vol. 15. 2007. 192pp. 978-1-4215-1092-7.
Vol. 16. 2008. 192pp. 978-1-4215-1093-4.
Vol. 17. 2008. 192pp. 978-1-4215-1511-3.
Vol. 18. 2008. 208pp. 978-1-4215-1512-0.
Vol. 19. 2008. 210pp. 978-1-4215-1513-7.
Vol. 20. 2009. 216pp. 978-1-4215-1514-4.
Vol. 21. 2009. 200pp. 978-1-4215-2429-0.
Vol. 22. 2009. 216pp. 978-1-4215-2430-6.
Vol. 23. 2009. 232pp. 978-1-4215-2844-1.
Vol. 24. 2009. 200pp. 978-1-4215-2845-8.
Vol. 25. 2010. 200pp. 978-1-4215-2846-5.
Vol. 26. 2010. 200pp. 978-1-4215-3442-8.
Vol. 27. 2010. 200pp. 978-1-4215-3443-5.
Vol. 28. 2010. 200pp. 978-1-4215-3444-2.
Vol. 29. 2010. 200pp. 978-1-4215-3445-9.
Vol. 30. 2010. 200pp. 978-1-4215-3446-6.
Vol. 31. 2010. 200pp. 978-1-4215-3447-3.
Vol. 32. 2010. 200pp. 978-1-4215-3448-0.

Vol. 33. 2010. 200pp. 978-1-4215-3449-7.
Vol. 34. 2010. 200pp. 978-1-4215-3450-3.
Vol. 35. 2010. 200pp. 978-1-4215-3451-0.
Vol. 36. 2010. 200pp. 978-1-4215-3452-7.
Vol. 37. 2010. 200pp. 978-1-4215-3453-4.
Vol. 38. 2010. 200pp. 978-1-4215-3454-1.
Vol. 39. 2010. 200pp. 978-1-4215-3455-8.
Vol. 40. 2010. 200pp. 978-1-4215-3456-5.
Vol. 41. 2010. 200pp. 978-1-4215-3457-2.
Vol. 42. 2010. 200pp. 978-1-4215-3458-9.
Vol. 43. 2010. 200pp. 978-1-4215-3459-6.
Vol. 44. 2010. 200pp. 978-1-4215-3460-2.
Vol. 45. 2010. 200pp. 978-1-4215-3461-9.
Vol. 46. 2010. 200pp. 978-1-4215-3462-6.
Vol. 47. 2010. 200pp. 978-1-4215-3463-3.
Vol. 48. 2010. 200pp. 978-1-4215-3464-0.
Vol. 49. 2010. 200pp. 978-1-4215-3465-7.
Vol. 50. 2010. 200pp. 978-1-4215-3466-4.
Vol. 51. 2010. 232pp. 978-1-4215-3467-1.
Vol. 52. 2010. 216pp. 978-1-4215-3468-8.
Vol. 53. 2010. 216pp. 978-1-4215-3469-5.
Vol. 54. 2010. 208pp. 978-1-4215-3470-1.
Vol. 55. 2010. 200pp. 978-1-4215-3471-8.
Vol. 56. 2011. 208pp. 978-1-4215-3850-1.
Vol. 57. 2011. 208pp. 978-1-4215-3851-8.
Vol. 58. 2011. 208pp. 978-1-4215-3926-3.
Vol. 59. 2011. 208pp. 978-1-4215-3959-1.
Vol. 60. 2012. 200pp. 978-1-4215-4085-6.
Vol. 61. 2012. 200pp. 978-1-4215-4144-0.
Vol. 62. 2012. 200pp. 978-1-4215-4196-9.
Vol. 63. 2012. 192pp. 978-1-4215-4307-9.
Vol. 64. 2012. 200pp. 978-1-4215-4329-1.

Vol. 65. 2012. 200pp. 978-1-4215-4979-8.
Vol. 66. 2012. 216pp. 978-1-4215-5237-8.
Vol. 67. 2013. 224pp. 978-1-4215-5371-9.
Vol. 68. 2013. 192pp. 978-1-4215-5881-3.
Vol. 69. 2013. 200pp. 978-1-4215-6143-1.
Vol. 70. 2013. 208pp. 978-1-4215-6460-9.
Vol. 71. 2013. 200pp. 978-1-4215-6945-1.
Vol. 72. 2014. 208pp. 978-1-4215-7344-1.
Vol. 73. 2015. 208pp. 978-1-4215-7683-1.
Vol. 74. 2015. 232pp. 978-1-4215-7867-5.

Vol. 75. 2015. 200pp. 978-1-4215-8029-6.
Vol. 76. 2015. 200pp. 978-1-4215-8260-3.
Vol. 77. 2016. 232pp. 978-1-4215-8514-7.
Vol. 78. 2016. 200pp. 978-1-4215-8584-0.
Vol. 79. 2016. 200pp. 978-1-4215-8815-5.
Vol. 80. 2016. 208pp. 978-1-4215-9024-0.
Vol. 81. 2017. 200pp. 978-1-4215-9159-9/
Vol. 82. 2017. 200pp. 978-1-4215-9269-5.
Vol. 83. 2017. 200pp. 978-1-4215-9433-0.

Pokemon: Black and White. Written by **Hidenori Kusaka**. Illustrated by **Satoshi Yamamoto**. VIZ Media, 2011–2015. Y Japanese manga. 🖥 🎮 🎬

©2011 Pokémon. ©1995-2011 Nintendo/
Creatures Inc./GAME FREAK inc. TM,
®, and character names are trademarks
of Nintendo. POCKET MONSTERS
SPECIAL © 1997 Hidenori KUSAKA,
Satoshi YAMAMOTO/SHOGAKUKAN.

Tied in with the popular video game for the Nintendo 3DS, join the adventures of Black, a young Pokemon trainer who begins his journey to become a Pokemon master. Joined with his friends Bianca and Cheren, the three of them learn how to train their pocket monsters that they can carry in small Pokeballs until they're needed for battle against an opponent. VIZ Media has published an astounding amount of other Pokemon titles featuring other heroes and Pokémon characters since the games inception over 20 years ago and they can be found on their site www.viz.com.

Vol. 1. 2011. 978-1-4215-4090-0.
Vol. 2. 2011. 978-1-4215-4091-7.
Vol. 3. 2011. 978-1-4215-4092-4.
Vol. 4. 2011. 978-1-4215-4114-3.

Vol. 5. 2012. 978-1-4215-4280-5.
Vol. 6. 2012. 978-1-4215-4281-2.
Vol. 7. 2012. 978-1-4215-4282-9.
Vol. 8. 2012. 978-1-4215-4283-6.
Vol. 9. 2013. 978-1-4215-5893-6.
Vol. 10. 2013. 978-1-4215-5894-3.
Vol. 11. 2013. 978-1-4215-5895-0.
Vol. 12. 2013. 978-1-4215-5896-7.

Vol. 13. 2013. 978-1-4215-5897-4.
Vol. 14. 2014. 978-1-4215-6766-2.
Vol. 15. 2014. 978-1-4215-6767-9.
Vol. 16. 2014. 978-1-4215-6768-6.
Vol. 17. 2014. 978-1-4215-6769-3.
Vol. 18. 2014. 978-1-4215-7602-2.
Vol. 19. 2014. 978-1-4215-7603-9.
Vol. 20. 2015. 978-1-4215-7604-6.

Polly and the Pirates. Written and Illustrated by **Ted Naifeh**. Oni Press, 2006–2012. T

Young Polly-Anne Pringle was the most refined girl at her local boarding school. Dull and proper, she's surprised one day to be kidnapped by the crew of Meg Malloy, the Pirate Queen to become their new captain. It seems that Polly-Anne's father never told her the truth about her mother. Polly-Anne's mother was not a prim and proper lady, but the rowdy and adventurous Meg Malloy! Now that Meg has gone missing, Polly-Anne is reluctantly made to lead the pirates. Can prim and proper Polly-Anne fill her mother's shoes and lead the pirates to high adventure?

Vol. 1. 2006. 168pp. 978-1-932664-46-1.
Vol. 2: Mystery of the Dragonfish. 2012. 168pp. 978-1-934964-73-6.

Reed Gunther. Written by **Shane Houghton**. Illustrated by **Chris Houghton**. Image Comics, 2011–2012. A

© Shane and Chris Houghton.

Reed Gunther is unlike any cowboy you've ever met. Instead of a horse, he rides his trusty grizzly bear steed named Sterling through the Wild West fighting all sort of interesting critters, beasts, zombies, soul-stealing demon, special government agents, and all sorts of wild monsters. With his tough partner Stella, they're bound to take out the monsters and the mysterious Idol that has been creating all the monsters before it's too late!

Vol. 1: The Bear-Riding Cowboy. 2011. 184pp. 978-1-60706-462-6.
Vol. 2: Monsters and Mustaches. 2012. 172pp. 978-1-60706-556-2.

Sabertooth Swordsman. Written by **Damon Gentry**. Illustrated by **Aaron Conley**. Dark Horse Comics, 2013. 120pp. 978-1-61655-176-6. T

A simple farmer is granted the gift of a god to save his village and free his wife from the malevolent Mastodon Mathematician. Granted the powers of the Sabertooth Swordsman by the Cloud God of Sasquatch Mountain, the hero must battle through a treacherous path to the Mastodon's fortress filled with fights, goats, vile armies, ogres, and plenty of humor.

Salt Water Taffy: The Seaside Adventures of Jack and Benny. Written and Illustrated by **Matthew Loux**. Oni Press, 2008–2011. T

Jack and Benny are dragged to Chowder Bay to spend the summer with their parents without TV or video games. Shortly after they arrive they realize they do not need any of that stuff because Chowder Bay holds many secrets and adventures. In *The Legend of Old Salty* they meet up with the old sailor Angus O'Neil who is always filled with tall tales. Jack and Benny soon find out that not all his tall tales are exactly that. A monstrous lobster is planning to steal all the taffy in the town and it is up to Jack and Benny to stop this dastardly plot. The adventure does not stop there for the brothers. They climb Mt. Barnabas to face a legendary giant eagle who stole their father's favorite hat in *A Climb Up Mt. Barnabus*. In *The Truth About Dr. True* the town finds out about the hero of Chowder Bay through ghostly apparitions. *Caldera's Revenge* parts one and two takes them on one of their most dangerous exploits, Jack and Benny set sail with ghosts to find out why an enormous whale will not let any boat within the bay to leave without getting attacked. This summer is certainly shaping up to be one to remember.

The Legend of Old Salty. 2008. 96pp. 978-1-932664-94-2.
A Climb Up MT. Barnabas. 2008. 96pp. 978-1-934964-03-3.

The Truth About Dr. True. 2009. 96pp. 978-1-934964-04-0.
Caldera's Revenge part 1. 2011. 72pp. 978-1-934964-62-0.
Caldera's Revenge part 2. 2011. 80pp. 978-1-934964-63-7.

Humorous Fantasy

Fantastic tales of dragons, barbarians, elves, wizards, gods and goddesses, and other staples of the Fantasy genre blended with a heavy helping of humor. The formulaic characters, plots, and settings are spoofed in these stories, adding a light-hearted look at the worlds of fantasy. Highlights include the clumsy mendicant barbarian called Groo, the lighthearted romance between Keiichi and the Norse goddess Belldandy in *Oh! My Goddess.*

Animal Land. Written and Illustrated by **Makoto Raiku**. Kodansha Comics, 2011–2016. T 🌺 Japanese manga.

Monoko the tanuki finds Taroza, an abandoned human baby, and decides to raise him as her own. As he grows, Taroza learns to speak all animal languages and interacts with humans and animals alike. The series ran through 14 volumes in Japan. The series was elected as one of YALSA's Great Graphic Novels for Teens in 2012.

Vol. 1. 2011. 208pp. 978-1-935429-13-5.   *Vol. 7.* 2013. 208pp. 978-1-612622-49-1.
Vol. 2. 2011. 208pp. 978-1-935429-14-2.   *Vol. 8.* 2013. 192pp. 978-1-612622-50-7.
Vol. 3. 2011. 208pp. 978-1-935429-15-9.   *Vol. 9.* 2014. 192pp. 978-1-61262546-1.
Vol. 4. 2012. 208pp. 978-1-612620-36-7.   *Vol. 10.* 2014. 192pp. 978-1-61262557-7.
Vol. 5. 2012. 208pp. 978-1-612620-37-4.   *Vol. 11.* 2016. 208pp. 978-1-61262978-0.
Vol. 6. 2012. 208pp. 978-1-612620-38-1.   *Vol. 12.* 2016. 208pp. 978-1-63236104-2.

Asterix Omnibus Written by **René Goscinny.** Illustrated by **Albert Uderzo.** Orion, 2002– . A ◎

Around the year 50 B.C. in northwest Armorica near ancient Gaul, there exists one last city that has escaped the wrath of Julius Caesar and the Roman Empire. The Gaul citizens have a secret ace up their sleeve to defeat the Romans: Getafix, a druid from the city, has concocted a magical potion that grants the villagers temporary super-strength. And when the trouble gets tough, there's only one Gaul for the job—Asterix! A short blonde-haired man with a mustache and a winged Viking helmet, he's the most cunning of all the Gauls. Joined with his companion, the oafish Obelix, together they get into many misadventures against the Roman Empire. Beloved the world over, Asterix and his friends are one of the most popular comic book characters from France since their first appearance in 1959. The list of titles below collected in Omnibus editions by Orion Publishing focuses solely on the work of Goscinny and Uderzo up until volume 33. Since the death of the original co-creator Goscinny, new stories were created by Uderzo until his retirement. Since 2013, new stories are being created by Jean-Yves Ferri and Didier Conrad.

Vol. 1. 2011. 152pp. 978-1-4440-0423-6.
Vol. 2. 2011. 156pp. 978-1-4440-0424-3.
Vol. 3. 2012. 160pp. 978-1-4440-0475-5.
Vol. 4. 2012. 156pp. 978-1-4440-0487-8.
Vol. 5. 2013. 152pp. 978-1-4440-0490-8.
Vol. 6. 2013. 152pp. 978-1-4440-0491-5.

Vol. 7. 2014. 156pp. 978-1-4440-0836-4.
Vol. 8. 2014. 152pp. 978-1-4440-0838-8.
Vol. 9. 2015. 152pp. 978-1-4440-0966-8.
Vol. 10. 2011. 156pp. 978-1-4440-0425-0.
Vol. 11. 2012. 176pp. 978-1-4440-0426-7.

The Chronicles of Claudette. Written by **Jorge Aguirre**. Illustrated by **Rafael Rosado**. First Second, 2012–2015. Y ◎

© Jorge Aguirre & Rafael Rosado and
First Second.

The city of Mont Petit Pierre sits behind its giant walls. The citizens live in fear from the dangerous world outside, but most of all a giant who marauded the town quite some time ago. The monster is known as the Baby-Feet Eating Giant. Claudette, the daughter of the tragic adventurer turned blacksmith, wants nothing more than to slay the giant who hides in the mountains. Claudette tricks her chef in training brother and her princess in training friend to sneak out of the village to kill the giant. They must travel across treacherous terrain, overcome challenges, and make it to the giant before their parents come to bring them back. Will Claudette be able to slay the Baby-Feet Eating Giant or was the whole adventure based on a misunderstanding? In the second collection, Claudette vows to get revenge on Azra the Atrocious, the dragon who swallowed her father's legs and his magical sword named Breaker! Now Claudette is ready to get the sword back, and hopefully soon since an evil wizard named Grombach who is amassing an army of gargoyles to destroy the city! Can Claudette and her brother Gaston and their perfect princess Marie save the day once again?

Giants Beware!. 2012. 208pp. 978-1-59643-582-7.
Dragons Beware!. 2015. 160pp. 978-1-59643-878-1.

Disney Fairies. Written by **Stefan Petrucha**, **Tea Orsi**, **Augusto Marchetto**, **Paola Mulazzi**, and others. Illustrated by **Giada Perissinotto**, **Sara Storino**, and others. Papercutz, 2010– . A

© Disney.

Tinker Bell and her fairy friends have new adventures in the land of Pixie Hollow in these stories originally produced by Disney Italia. The stories are inspired by and based on the Pixie Hollow series of animated films.

Vol. 1: Prilla's Talent. 2010. 64pp. 978-1-59707-187-1, hardcover; 978-1-59707-186-4.
Vol. 2: Tinker Bell and Wings of Rani. 2010. 64pp. 978-1-59707-227-4, hardcover; 978-1-59707-226-7.
Vol. 3: Tinker Bell and the Day of the Dragon. 2010. 64pp. 978-1-59707-129-1, hardcover; 978-1-59707-128-4.
Vol. 4: Tinker Bell to the Rescue. 2010. 64pp. 978-1-59707-230-4, hardcover; 978-1-59707-200-7.

Vol. 5: Tinker Bell and the Pirate Adventure. 2011. 64pp. 978-1-59707-241-0, hardcover; 978-1-59707-240-3.

Vol. 6: A Present for Tinker Bell. 2011. 64pp. 978-1-59707-257-1, hardcover; 978-1-59707-256-4.

Vol. 7: Tinker Bell the Perfect Fairy. 2012. 64pp. 978-1-59707-282-3, hardcover; 978-1-59707-281-6.

Vol. 8: Tinker Bell and Her Stories for a Rainy Day. 2012. 64pp. 978-1-59707-304-2, hardcover; 978-1-59707-303-5.

Vol. 9: Tinker Bell and Her Magical Arrival. 2012. 64pp. 978-1-59707-324-0, hardcover; 978-1-59707-323-3.

Vol. 10: Tinker Bell and the Lucky Rainbow. 2012. 64pp. 978-1-59707-368-4, hardcover; 978-1-59707-367-7.

Vol. 11: Tinker Bell and the Most Precious Gift. 2013. 64pp. 978-1-59707-395-0, hardcover; 9781597073943.

Vol. 12: Tinker Bell and the Lost Treasure. 2013. 64pp. 978-1-59707-429-2, hardcover; 978-1-59707-428-5.

Vol. 13: Tinker Bell and the Pixie Hollow Games. 2013. 64pp. 978-1-59707-447-6, hardcover; 978-1-59707-446-9.

Vol. 14: Tinker Bell and Blaze. 2014. 64pp. 978-1-59707-489-6, hardcover; 978-1-59707-488-9.

Vol. 15: Tinker Bell and the Secret of the Wings 2014. 64pp. 978-1-59707-730-9, hardcover; 978-1-59707-729-3.

Vol. 16: Tinker Bell and the Pirate Fairy. 2015 64pp. 978-1-62991-154-0, hardcover; 978-1-62991-153-3.

Vol. 17: Tinker Bell and the Legend of the NeverBeast 2015. 64pp. 978-1-62991-190-8, hardcover; 978-1-62991-189-2.

Vol. 18: Tinker Bell and her Magical Friends. 2016. 64pp. 978-1-62991-430-5, hardcover; 978-1-62991-429-9.

Vol. 19: Tinker Bell and the Flying Monster. 2016. 64pp. 978-1-62991-606-4, hardcover; 978-1-62991-605-7.

Vol. 20: Tinker Bell and the Talent Search. 2017. 64pp. 978-1-62991-785-6, hardcover; 978-1-62991-784-9.

Dragon Puncher. Written and Illustrated by **James Kochalka**. Top Shelf Productions, 2010–2011. Y

Dragon Puncher is a famous dragon fighter. With some help from his tag-along partner Spoony-e, no adversary stands a chance against them. Except maybe a butterfly. *Dragon Puncher* is done with a hybrid of photographs and crayon-esque drawings. The light hearted story mixed with interesting art and great character make this a great graphic novel for the little ones just starting to read.

Dragon Puncher. 2010. 40pp. 978-1-60309-057-5.
Dragon Puncher Island. 2011. 40pp. 978-1-60309-085-8.

© James Kochalka.

Dungeon. Written and Illustrated by **Lewis Trondheim** and **Joann Sfar**. NBM Publishing, 2004–2016. O ◉

© 2016 Lewis Trondhein and Joann Sfar.

In a fantasy world where heroic barbarian champions regularly battle hordes of monsters, there's only one place to go for your fix of fighting and prizes: the Dungeon! Run by the old bird called the Dungeon Keeper, the keep is a haven for ghouls, beasts, assorted monsters, dark labyrinths, and a large fire-breathing dragon. Like any good business, it needs to attract more customers the Dungeon does this by hiring the best monsters as well as having the best treasure trove ever to attract fresh champions. Herbert of Craftiwich, a timorous talking duck and a simple messenger for the Dungeon, is mistakenly chosen to be the new guardian of the Dungeon. With such a klutz as the hero (even with the help of a magical sarcastic sword), the Dungeon Keeper has assigned Herbert with a much more capable partner in Marvin, the vegetarian dragon, to keep the Dungeon safe. There are four main story arcs: *The Early Years, Zenith, Twilight* and *Monstres*. These story arcs cover different time periods in the world of *Dungeon*. *The Early Years* goes back in time and revisits the origins of the Dungeon when the Dungeon Keeper is barely an adult and setting out for the adventure of a lifetime with plenty of humor along the way. The series called *Twilight* focuses on an aging Marvin who realizes that the world is doomed and heads for the legendary dragon cemetery to face the end but finds himself teamed up with a rabbit warrior and a timid bat against the most vile of enemies: a much changed Herbert. *Montres* is a series that spans all the timelines but focuses on minor characters as well as appearances by the main characters such as Herbert. The stories from *Dungeon: Parade* take place in the timeline of *Dungeon: Twilight*.

Dungeon: Zenith. Illustrated by **Boulet** and **Lewis Trondheim**. 2004–2009.

> *Duck Heart.* 2004. 96pp. 978-1-56163-401-9.
> *The Barbarian Princess.* 2005. 96pp. 978-1-56163-421-7.
> *Back In Style.* 2009. 96pp. 978-1-56163-550-4.

Dungeon: The Early Years. Illustrated by **Joann Sfar**. 2005–2006.

> *The Night Shirt.* 2005. 96pp. 978-1-56163-439-2.
> *Innocence Lost.* 2009. 96pp. 978-1-56163-564-1.

Dungeon: Twilight Illustrated by **Joann Sfar**, **Kerascoët**, and **Obion**. 2006–2010.

> *Dragon Cemetery.* 2006. 96pp. 978-1-56163-460-6.
> *Armageddon.* 2006. 92pp. 978-1-56163-477-4.
> *The New Centurions.* 2010. 112pp. 978-1-56163-578-8.

Dungeon: Parade. Illustrated by **Manu Larcenet**. 2007–

> *A Dungeon Too Many.* 2007. 64pp. 978-1-56163-495-8.
> *Day of the Toads.* 2007. 64pp. 978-1-56163-507-8.

Dungeon: Monstres. Illustrated by **Mazan** and **Jean-Christophe Menu**. 2008–2016.

> *The Crying Giant.* 2008. 120pp. 978-1-56163-525-2.
> *The Dark Lord.* 2008. 94pp. 978-1-56163-540-5.

Heartbreaker. 2010. 144pp. 978-1-56163-591-7.
Night of the Lady Killer. 2011. 96pp. 978-1-56163-608-2.
My Son the Killer. 2015. 96pp. 978-1-56163-937-3.
The Great Reanimator. 2016. 96pp. 978-1-56163-998-4.

Fangbone: Third Grade Barbarian. Written and Illustrated by **Michael Rex**. G.P. Putnam's Sons Books for Young Readers, 2012. Y 🖳

Eastwood Elementary's got a new student in their third grade class and he's like no exchange student from ever before! He's Fangbone—nine-year-old barbarian from another world! He's been charged to protect a deadly weapon from the hands of Skullbania's vilest villain Venomous Drool. But can he learn to sit still in a chair and take a pop quiz? The series was also adapted into an animated series that debuted on the Disney XD cable channel in 2016.

Vol. 1. 2012. 128pp. 978-0-399-25522-9.
Vol. 2: Egg of Misery. 2012. 128pp. 978-0-399-25522-9.
Vol. 3. Birthday Party of Dread. 2012. 128pp. 978-0-39925523-6.

Glister. Written and Illustrated by **Andi Watson**. Image Comics, 2007–2008. A.

Glister Buttersworth is a young girl who lives in England and has the most curious adventures. Strange things always happen to her. It could be that she got up on the wrong side of the bed—or maybe even that when she was born the clock struck thirteen, but most of her adventures begin when there's a strange knock on the door. Join her on her adventures as she deals with a haunted teapot, a runaway house, and more!

Vol. 1. 2007. 80pp. 978-1-58240-853-8.
Vol. 2. 2007. 64pp. 978-1-58240-884-2.
Vol. 3. 2008. 64pp. 978-1-58240-925-2.

Groo. Written by **Sergio Aragonés** and **Mark Evanier**. Illustrated by **Sergio Aragonés**; lettered by **Stan Sakai**. Dark Horse Comics, 1998–2016. 🎖◎ A

© 2016 Sergio Aragonés and Mark Evanier.

People run and hide when the name "Groo the Wanderer" is mentioned. Groo is the stupidest barbarian in the world, causing destruction and mayhem wherever he goes. Ships sink when he sets one foot on them; cities burn just for taking him in; and woe be it if anyone should call Groo a 'mendicant.' He has no idea what the word means, but he can get violently angry when he hears someone call him one! A large-nosed buffoon, Groo is also a master swordsman capable of defeating entire armies for no reason at all except it's a chance to participate in a fray. With his dog companion Rufferto, together they roam the fantasy-land countryside encountering a large cast of characters including the Sage, con men Pal and Drumm, the Minstel, and many more as they search for money, cheese dip, food, and frays. Mostly food. Groo first appeared in 1981 and the series has been regarded by many fans in the comic book industry to be one of the best humorous fantasy titles. The series has won Eisner Awards for Best Humor Publication (1992, 1999), and Best

Writer/Artist: Humor (1996); Harvey Awards for Best Cartoonist (1998), and Special Award for Humor (1991–1993, 1995, 1997–2001).

The Most Intelligent Man in the World. 1998. 112pp. 978-1-56971-294-8.
The Groo Houndbook. 1999. 96pp. 978-1-56971-385-3.
The Groo Inferno. 1999. 96pp. 978-1-56971-430-0.
The Groo Jamboree. 2000. 96pp. 978-1-56971-462-1.
Sergio Aragonés' Groo and Rufferto. 2000. 112pp. 978-1-56971-447-8.
The Groo Kingdom. 2001. 96pp. 978-1-56971-478-2.
The Groo Library. 2001. 96pp. 978-1-56971-571-0.
The Groo Maiden. 2002. 96pp. 978-1-56971-756-1.
The Groo Nursery. 2002. 96pp. 978-1-56971-794-3.
Mightier Than the Sword. 2002. 112pp. 978-1-56971-612-0.
Death and Taxes. 2003. 112pp. 978-1-56971-797-4.
The Groo Odyssey. 2003. 96pp. 978-1-56971-858-2.
Hell on Earth. 2008. 112pp. 978-1-59307-999-4.
Hogs of Horder. 2010. 120pp. 978-1-59582-423-3.
Friends and Foes, Vol. 1. 2015. 112pp. 978-1-61655-814-7.
Groo vs. Conan. 2015. 104pp. 978-1-61655-603-7.
Friends and Foes, Vol. 2. 2016. 96pp. 978-1-61655-822-2.
Friends and Foes, Vol. 3. 2016. 96pp. 978-1-61655-906-9.
Fray of the Gods. 2017. 116pp. 978-1-50670-241-4.
Friends and Foes. 2017. 332pp. 978-1-50670-297-1, hardcover.

The Helm. Written by **Jim Hardison**. Illustrated by **Bart Sears**. Dark Horse Comics, 2009. 104pp. 978-1-59582-261-1. T 🏵
Slacker Matt Blurdy is far from being heroic. He's overweight, works at a video store, and still lives at home with his overbearing mother. When at an antique shop, Matt finds a magical helmet that tells him that he has a heroic destiny. When the helmet finds out that Matt is a loser, even the magical helmet begins to doubt the prophecy, but Matt will do whatever it takes to prove there's more to him than a loser. Meanwhile, a dark force is on the rise and Matt and his magical helmet may be all that stands in evil's way! The book was recognized by YALSA in 2010 as a Great Graphic Novel for Teens.

I Hate Fairyland. Written and Illustrated by **Skottie Young**. Image Comics, 2016– . O

Gert's been trapped in the magical realm of Fairyland for a long time. Thirty years ago, Gert was magically transported to the Wonderland- like world of Fairyland. Trapped in the body of a six-year-old girl when you're 40 years old will definitely mess you up. Now Gert is travelling the mad land with a giant axe and swinging it with reckless abandon because she wants to get out of Fairyland and anyone who stands in her way is going to be a bloody mess!

Vol. 1: Madly Ever After. 2016. 128pp. 978-1-63215-685-3.
Vol. 2: Fluff My Life. 2016. 144pp. 978-1-63215-887-1.

Kamisama Kiss. Written and Illustrated by **Julietta Suzuki**. VIZ Media, 2010– . T 🍖 Japanese manga. あ

Nanami Momozono has found herself homeless, but a man that she has helped has offered her a place to stay. The only problem is that the place turns out to be a shrine, and by living there she has taken his place as the local Earth deity. The series is still ongoing in Japan was has been adapted as an anime series as well. Selected as one of YALSA's Great Graphic Novels for Teens in 2011.

Vol. 1. 2010. 200pp. 978-1-4215-3638-5. *Vol. 13.* 2013. 200pp. 978-1-4215-5266-8.
Vol. 2. 2011. 200pp. 978-1-4215-3639-2. *Vol. 14.* 2014. 200pp. 978-1-4215-5586-7.
Vol. 3. 2011. 200pp. 978-1-4215-3640-8. *Vol. 15.* 2014. 200pp. 978-1-4215-6308-4.
Vol. 4. 2011. 200pp. 978-1-4215-3658-3. *Vol. 16.* 2014. 200pp. 978-1-4215-6764-8.
Vol. 5. 2011. 200pp. 978-1-4215-3823-5. *Vol. 17.* 2015. 200pp. 978-1-4215-7725-8.
Vol. 6. 2011. 200pp. 978-1-4215-3886-0. *Vol. 18.* 2015. 200pp. 978-1-4215-7970-2.
Vol. 7. 2012. 200pp. 978-1-4215-4025-2. *Vol. 19.* 2015. 200pp. 978-1-4215-8033-3.
Vol. 8. 2012. 200pp. 978-1-4215-4082-5. *Vol. 20.* 2016. 200pp. 978-1-4215-8261-0.
Vol. 9. 2012. 200pp. 978-1-4215-4198-3. *Vol. 21.* 2016. 200pp. 978-1-4215-8522-2.
Vol.10. 2012. 200pp. 978-1-4215-4269-0. *Vol. 22.* 2016. 200pp. 978-1-4215-8712-7.
Vol.11. 2012. 200pp. 978-1-4215-4924-8. *Vol. 23.* 2017. 200pp. 978-1-4215-9047-9.
Vol.12. 2013. 200pp. 978-1-4215-5082-4.

Monster on the Hill. Written and Illustrated by **Rob Harrell**. Top Shelf Productions, 2013. 186pp. 978-1-60309-075-9. A 🍖 ◎

© 2016 Rob Harrell.

What if every township in 1860s England had a giant monster to terrorize the local townfolk—and they loved it? Well, everyone loves it except for the town of Stoker-on-Avon—their monster—named Rayburn—hasn't attacked the town in years and is a bit of a disappointment to the community pride. Rayburn's been down in the dumps for years and it's up to Dr. Charles Wilkie and a street urchin named Timothy to set Rayburn right. They take Rayburn on a journey outside of the township to rediscover his monstrous roots and hopefully have him become a ferocious monster that will hopefully someday attack the town of Stoker-on-Avon. But when a deadlier beast arrives at the city before their return, can Rayburn (with a little help from his friends) be the giant monster he needs to be to beat the deadly beast called "The Murk?" The book was recognized by YALSA's Great Graphic Novels for Teens selection list in 2014.

Negima!: Magister Negi Magi. Written and Illustrated by **Akamatsu Ken**. Del Rey Manga/Random House, 2004–2012. O Japanese manga. ◎ あ

Ten-year-old Negi Springfield has just graduated the youngest in his class of apprentice wizards in England For all graduating students, there is one more trial they must pass first: each must be assigned a career in the human world until he is old enough to be bestowed the title of wizard. Negi has been assigned to be the younger-ever English teacher at an all-girl high school in Japan! Though most of his students think he's adorable, one girl, Asuna Kagurazaka, despises Negi for replacing the teacher she had a crush on. Though Negi is forbidden to use his magic powers, sometimes just can't resist, and after Asuna discovers Negi's powers, she vows to make his career as short as possible. The hit manga was also adapted as an anime series.

Vol. 1. 2004. 208pp. 978-0-345-47046-1.

Vol. 2. 2004. 208pp. 978-0-345-47120-8.

Vol. 3. 2004. 224pp. 978-0-345-47180-2.

Vol. 4. 2004. 208pp. 978-0-345-47784-2.

Vol. 5. 2005. 208pp. 978-0-345-47785-9.

Vol. 6. 2005. 208pp. 978-0-345-47786-6.

Vol. 7. 2005. 208pp. 978-0-345-47787-3.

Vol. 8. 2005. 208pp. 978-0-345-46540-5.

Vol. 9. 2006. 208pp. 978-0-345-48273-0.

Vol. 10. 2006. 208pp. 978-0-345-48441-3.

Vol. 11. 2006. 208pp. 978-0-345-49231-9.

Vol. 12. 2006. 208pp. 978-0-345-49463-4.

Vol. 13. 2007. 208pp. 978-0-345-49505-1.

Vol. 14. 2007. 208pp. 978-0-345-49614-0.

Vol. 15. 2007. 208pp. 978-0-345-49615-7.

Vol. 16. 2007. 208pp. 978-0-345-49924-0.

Vol. 17. 2008. 208pp. 978-0-345-50139-4.

Vol. 18. 2008. 192pp. 978-0-345-50202-5.

Vol. 19. 2008. 192pp. 978-0-345-50526-2.

Vol. 20. 2008. 192pp. 978-0-345-50527-9.

Vol. 21. 2009. 192pp. 978-0-345-50528-6.

Vol. 22. 2009. 192pp. 978-0-345-51030-3.

Vol. 23. 2009. 192pp. 978-0-345-51426-4.

Vol. 24. 2009. 192pp. 978-0-345-51427-1.

Vol. 25. 2010. 192pp. 978-0-345-51882-8.

Vol. 26. 2010. 192pp. 978-0-345-52111-8.

Vol. 27. 2010. 192pp. 978-0-345-52159-0.

Vol. 28. 2011. 192pp. 978-1-61262-846-2.

Vol. 29. 2011. 192pp. 978-1-935429-56-2.

Vol. 30. 2011. 192pp. 978-1-935429-57-9.

Vol. 31. 2011. 192pp. 978-1-935429-58-6.

Vol. 32. 2011. 192pp. 978-1-935429-59-3.

Vol. 33. 2012. 192pp. 978-1-61262-115-9.

Vol. 34. 2012. 192pp. 978-1-61262-116-6.

Vol. 35. 2012. 208pp. 978-1-61262-120-3.

Vol. 36. 2012. 208pp. 978-1-61262-239-2.

Vol. 37. 2013. 208pp. 978-1-61262-271-2.

Vol. 38. 2013. 208pp. 978-1-61262-243-9.

Omnibus Edition. 2011–2014.

Vol. 1. 2011. 576pp. 978-1-935429-62-3.

Vol. 2. 2011. 592pp. 978-1-935429-63-0.

Vol. 3. 2011. 560pp. 978-1-935429-64-7.

Vol. 4. 2012. 592pp. 978-1-612620-67-1.

Vol. 5. 2012. 592pp. 978-1-612620-68-8.

Vol. 6. 2013. 592pp. 978-1-612620-69-5.

Vol. 7. 2013. 592pp. 978-1-612629-99-5.

Vol. 8. 2013. 544pp. 978-1-612622-72-9.

Vol. 9. 2014. 544pp. 978-1-612622-73-6.

Nimona. Written and Illustrated by **Noelle Stevenson**. HarperTeen, 2015. 266pp. 978-0-06-227823-4, hardcover; 978-0-06-227822-7. T 🎯 ◎

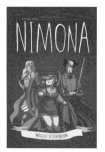

In a world filled with both magic and technology Lord Ballister Blackheart is a villain whose schemes put him up against the Institution of Law Enforcement and its champion Goldenloin. Blackheart and Goldenloin had been friends at the academy, until an incident after a joust cost Blackheart an arm and led him on another path. He has been joined by Nimona, a girl with a mysterious past and the power to change into any living thing include sharks, cats, and dragons. Together they attempt to show the world that the Institution is not as good as it seems. This graphic novel originated as a webcomic Stevenson created while at the Maryland Institute College of Art. Nimona was nominated for an Eisner Award and was a finalist for the National Book Award's Young Adult category. The book was also recognized by YALSA in 2016 as a Great Graphic Novel for Teens as well as a Quick Pick for Reluctant Readers.

Oh My Goddess! Written and Illustrated by **Kosuke Fujishima**. Dark Horse Comics, 2005– . T 🏃 ◎ あ

Oh My Goddess! © 2016 by Kosuke Fujishima. All rights reserved. New and adapted artwork and text copyright 2016. Dark Horse Comics, Inc.

What would you do if you accidentally dialed the wrong number and instead of ordering pizza, you dialed up your very own goddess? That's what college student Keiichi Morisato has done, and now the beautiful and shy Norse goddess Belldandy has been delivered to his dorm room with one wish to grant him. When Keiichi wishes for a girl just like Belldandy to stay with him forever, his wish is granted, and now the goddess is living at his place and experiencing what life is all about. When Belldandy's sisters, the techno-savvy Skuld and the vixenish Urd decide to move in, too, it's more and more hijinks as Heaven and Earth collide. As Keiichi's life gets turned upside down living with three goddesses, he learns about the pluses and minuses of getting exactly what you wished for. The first volume, originally published in 2002, received recognition by YALSA's Popular Paperbacks for Young Adults committee in 2002 on the *Graphic Novels: Superheroes and Beyond* list as well as the 2003 Quick Picks for Reluctant Readers list. In late 2005 Dark Horse Comics has proceeded to reprint the series in the original right-to-left format from Japan and have reissued the original volumes in the traditional right-to-left format. Recently Dark Horse Comics has begun to collect the series in an omnibus format.

Vol. 1. 2005. 192pp. 978-1-59307-387-9.
Vol. 2. 2006. 192pp. 978-1-59307-457-9.
Vol. 3. 2006. 192pp. 978-1-59307-539-2.
Vol. 4. 2006. 192pp. 978-1-59307-623-8.
Vol. 5. 2007. 184pp. 978-1-59307-708-2.
Vol. 6. 2007. 184pp. 978-1-59307-772-3.
Vol. 7. 2008. 184pp. 978-1-59307-850-8.
Vol. 8. 2008. 192pp. 978-1-59307-889-8.
Vol. 9. 2008. 200pp. 978-1-59307-970-3.
Vol.10. 2008. 184pp. 978-1-59582-190-4.
Vol.11. 2009. 200pp. 978-1-59582-254-3.
Vol.12. 2009. 200pp. 978-1-59582-322-9.
Vol.13. 2009. 192pp. 978-1-59582-386-1.
Vol.14. 2010. 184pp. 978-1-59582-455-4.
Vol.15. 2010. 240pp. 978-1-59582-524-7.
Vol.16. 2010. 240pp. 978-1-59582-594-0.
Vol.17. 2011. 256pp. 978-1-59582-691-6.
Vol.18. 2011. 232pp. 978-1-59582-749-4.
Vol.19. 2011. 248pp. 978-1-59582-815-6.
Vol.20. 2012. 248pp. 978-1-59582-901-6.
Vol.21. 2005. 176pp. 978-1-59307-334-3.
Vol.22. 2006. 176pp. 978-1-59307-400-5.

Vol. 23. 2006. 176pp. 978-1-59307-463-0.
Vol. 24. 2007. 176pp. 978-1-59307-545-3.
Vol. 25. 2007. 176pp. 978-1-59307-644-3.
Vol. 26. 2007. 176pp. 978-1-59307-715-0.
Vol. 27. 2007. 176pp. 978-1-59307-788-4.
Vol. 28. 2008. 160pp. 978-1-59307-857-7.
Vol. 29. 2008. 160pp. 978-1-59307-912-3.
Vol. 30. 2008. 160pp. 978-1-59307-979-6.
Vol. 31. 2009. 152pp. 978-1-59582-233-8.
Vol. 32. 2009. 144pp. 978-1-59582-303-8.
Vol. 33. 2009. 144pp. 978-1-59582-376-2.
Vol. 34. 2010. 144pp. 978-1-59582-448-6.
Vol. 35. 2010. 160pp. 978-1-59582-509-4.
Vol. 36. 2010. 152pp. 978-1-59582-581-0.
Vol. 37. 2011. 152pp. 978-1-59582-660-2.
Vol. 38. 2011. 144pp. 978-1-59582-711-1.
Vol. 39. 2011. 168pp. 978-1-59582-795-1.
Vol. 40. 2012. 128pp. 978-1-59582-870-5.
Vol. 41. 2012. 168pp. 978-1-59582-891-0.
Vol. 42. 2012. 176pp. 978-1-59582-892-7.
Vol. 43. 2013. 176pp. 978-1-61655-082-0.
Vol. 44. 2013. 168pp. 978-1-61655-131-5.

Vol. 45. 2013. 176pp. 978-1-61655-298-5.   *Vol. 47*. 2015. 160pp. 978-1-61655-733-1.
Vol. 46. 2014. 176pp. 978-1-61655-433-0.   *Vol. 48*. 2015. 168pp. 978-1-61655-855-0.

***Omnibus Editions*. 2015– .**

Vol. 1. 2015. 552pp. 978-1-61655-740-9.
Vol. 2. 2015. 548pp. 978-1-61655-784-3.
Vol. 3. 2016. 560pp. 978-1-61655-895-6.
Vol. 4. 2016. 568pp. 978-1-50670-052-6.
Vol. 5. 2016. 568pp. 978-1-50670-093-9.

***Rutabaga the Adventure Chef*.** Written and Illustrated by **Eric Colossal**. Harry N. Abrams, 2015– . Y

(c) 2017 Eric Colossal.

In a fantasy world where dragons exist even there the people have to eat—and Rutabaga along with his magic pot called Pot are there to ensure that everyone eats well! He's on a quest to discover new ingredients and new foods to try—and along the way he also has to fight dragons, giant spiders, and other beasts, but he always gets to save the day by cooking unique and fantastically fun recipes! The books also include safe recipes for kids who are really picky eaters.

Vol. 1. 2015. 128pp. 978-1-4197-1380-4, hardcover; 978-1-4197-1597-6.
Vol. 2: Feasts of Fury. 2016. 128pp. 978-1-4197-1658-4, hardcover; 978-1-4197-1659-1.

***Skullkickers*.** Written by **Jim Zub**. Illustrated by **Misty Coats** and **Edwin Huang**. Image Comics, 2011–2015. T 🏅 ◎

© 2016 Jim Zub.

Set in a sword and sorcery world, Rolf and Rex are a team of bounty hunters out for money, fame, and fortune as they battle beast after beast across the land causing as much damage and bloodshed as possible. Rex is a bald merc with a gun and Rolf is a dwarf with an axe and between the two of them there's no werewolf, goblin, skeleton, or mage that they can't take care of with over-the-top violence and a heaping spoof on fantasy tropes. The first volume was recognized by YALSA's Great Graphic Novels for Teens on its 2012 selection list.

Vol. 1: 1000 Opas and a Dead Body. 2011. 144pp. 978-1-60706-366-7.
Vol. 2: Five Funerals and a Bucket of Blood. 2011. 144pp. 978-1-60706-442-8.
Vol. 3: Six Shooter on the Seven Seas. 2012. 144pp. 978-1-60706-612-5.
Vol. 4: Eighty Eyes on an Evil Island. 2013. 160pp. 978-1-60706-766-5.

Vol. 5: A Dozen Cousins and a Crumpled Crown. 2014. 144pp. 978-1-63215-033-2.
Vol. 6: Infinite Icons of the Endless Epic. 2015. 144pp. 978-1-63215-343-2.

Treasure Trove (Deluxe Edition), 2012–2015.

Vol. 1. 2012. 300pp. 978-1-60706-374-2, hardcover.
Vol. 2. 2013. 320pp. 978-1-60706-794-8, hardcover.
Vol. 3. 2015. 320pp. 978-1-63215-398-2, hardcover.

Skylanders. Written by **Ron Marz** and **David A. Rodriguez**. Illustrated by Fico Ossio. IDW Publishing, 2014– . Y 🎮

© Activision Publishing, Inc. TM is a trademark, SM is a service mark, and ACTIVISION is a registered trademark of Activision Publishing, Inc.

Based off of the popular Toys to Life games from Activision! Welcome to the magical realm called the Skylands—where dragons, monsters, and magic interact with technology across worlds where lands float in the sky and pirate ships sail through the clouds. The realm is under the protection of heroes called Skylanders and Lord Kaos, the evil (and sometimes goofy) lord of darkness will stop at nothing to gain the magical power from the Skylands and rule the magical realm. Luckily the Skylanders are group of heroic beasts, monsters, and more who use the elements of Earth, Air, Fire, Water, Life, Undead, Magic, and Tech to protect the realm. The Skylanders are led by the small purple dragon Spyro with many other Skylanders who play a role in the game as well as the comic books including Trigger Happy, Stealth Elf, Gear Shift, Knight Light, and many more.

The Kaos Trap. 2014. 80pp. 978-1-63140-141-1, hardcover.
Champions. 2015. 80pp. 978-1-63140-229-6, hardcover.
Return of the Dragon King. 2015. 80pp. 978-1-63140-268-5, hardcover.
Rift into Overdrive. 2015. 80pp. 978-1-63140-412-2, hardcover.
Dive, Dive, Dive. 2016. 80pp. 978-1-63140-710-9. hardcover.
A Light in the Dark. 2016. 88pp. 978-1-63140-520-4, hardcover.
Secret Agent Secrets. 2016. 88pp. 978-1-63140-581-5, hardcover.

Yo-kai Watch. Written and Illustrated by **Noriyuki Konishi**. VIZ Media, 2015– . Y. Japanese manga. あ 🎮

YO-KAI WATCH © 2013 Noriyuki KONISHI/SHOGAKUKAN ©LEVEL-5 Inc.

While hunting for bugs in the woods, a boy named Nate stumbles across a capsule near a sacred tree. After opening up the capsule he frees a Yo-kai named Whisper. The Yo-kai gives Nate a special item—a Yo-kai watch that when he puts it on his arm he can see Yo-kai! Now Nate can identify the Yo-kai and see which ones are in particular creating mischief and haunting people. Nate also befriends a cat Yo-kai named Jibanyan and they befriend all sorts of odd Yo-kai around the city. With the watch Nate can summon the good Yo-kai he's befriended and use them to battle the bad and mischievous Yo-kai causing problems. The manga has also been translated into an immensely popular Nintendo video game series by Level 5 as well as an anime series.

Vol. 1. 2015. 192pp. 978-1-4215-8251-1.
Vol. 2. 2015. 192pp. 978-1-4215-8252-8.
Vol. 3. 2016. 192pp. 978-1-4215-8273-3.
Vol. 4. 2016. 192pp. 978-1-4215-8274-0.

Vol. 5. 2016. 192pp. 978-1-4215-8275-7.
Vol. 6. 2016. 192pp. 978-1-4215-9217-6.
Vol. 7. 2017. 192pp. 978-1-4215-9218-3.

Chapter 9

Non-Fiction

Though not as common as fictional graphic novels, non-fiction graphic novels are still published today and tackle a variety of topics including biographies, science, religion, and history. The majority of titles are published by smaller press companies or by mainstream book publishers rather than by the larger comic book publishers such as Marvel and DC Comics. Please note that for readers interested in graphic novels featuring tales of true crime, see Crime and Mysteries chapter for a selection of titles.

Art—Comics, Comic Books, and Graphic Novels

Several publications that use a graphic novel format to explain the medium of comic books, comic strips, and graphic novels have been released. Below are listed some of the best-known publications focusing on the intricacies that make the medium so appealing for storytelling.

Adventures in Cartooning. Written and Illustrated by **James Sturm**, **Andrew Arnold**, and **Alexis Frederick-Frost**. First Second Books. 2009–2015. A ◎

A fun interactive collection of stories that can easily inspire kids to create their own comic strips and comic books. The overall books feature a Magic Cartooning Elf and his colorful cast of friends including the Knight and a princess, as he helps to show how fun it can be to create your own comics. The *Sleepless Knight* and *Gryphons Aren't So Great* books are self-contained short stories featuring the Knight from the Adventures in Cartooning series and are intended for younger readers.

Adventures in Cartooning: How to Turn Your Doodles into Comics. 2009. 112pp. 978-1-59643-369-4.

© 2016 First Second and James Sturm.

Adventures in Cartooning Christmas Special. 2012. 64pp. 978-1-59643-730-2.

Adventures in Cartooning: Characters in Action. 2013. 64pp. 978-1-59643-732-6.

Gryphons Aren't So Great. 2015. 40pp. 978-1-59643-652-7, hardcover.

Sleepless Knight. 2015. 40pp. 978-1-59643-651-0, hardcover.

Ogres Awake. 2016.40pp. 978-1-59643-653-4, hardcover.

Hocus Focus. 2017. 40pp. 978-1-59643-654-1, hardcover.

The Comic Book History of Comics. Written by **Fred Van Lente**. Illustrated by **Fred Dunlavey**. IDW Publishing, 2012. 224pp. 978-1-61377-197-6. O

Though comic books as we know it are a relatively new media, this format has a rich and storied history. This book covers the whole history of comics in a comic format with enough information and humor to not bore the reader. The books starts with the predecessors of sequential art and stories and goes through the evolution of the art and what trends may be setting the course for the future of comics. While the book's main focus is on telling the history behind American comics, it also covers comics history from Europe and Japan. The reader will become well informed on the people and companies that shaped comics into what people now know as the diverse media.

Comics and Sequential Art. Written and Illustrated by **Will Eisner**. W.W. Norton, 2008. 192pp. 978-0-06-097625-5. T

The late legendary comic art veteran Will Eisner's guide to the basic principles of graphic storytelling. Adapted from his art class taught at the New York School of Visual Arts, the guide examines the basic anatomy of sequential art and practical applications of using the art form of words and pictures to tell a story.

Expressive Anatomy for Comics and Narrative. Written and Illustrated by **Will Eisner**. W. W. Norton, 2008. 192pp. 978-0-393-33128-8. T

The last book in Will Eisner's instructional series was published after his death in 2005, but includes his techniques for body movement, facial expressions, and posture—which are key components to graphic storytelling.

Graphic Storytelling and Visual Narrative. Written and Illustrated by **Will Eisner**. W.W. Norton, 2008. 192pp. 978-0-393-33127-1. T

A companion to Will Eisner's publication *Comics and Sequential Art*. The publication includes storytelling samples not only by Will Eisner but also by Pulitzer Prize–winner Art Spiegelman, Robert Crumb, Milton Caniff, and Al Capp.

Making Comics: Storytelling Secrets of Comics, Manga, and Graphic Novels. Written and Illustrated by **Scott McCloud**. HarperPerennial, 2006. 272pp. 978-0-06-078094-4. T

A guide for all of those interested in creating their own manga, graphic novel, or webcomic. Scott McCloud takes the beginning artist on a tour of tips and secrets found nowhere else. Topics include selecting appropriate moments for comic book panels, how to guide the reader's eye in the comic book layout, understanding body and facial language, an overview of genres, and more.

Reinventing Comics: How Imagination and Technology Are Revolutionizing an Art Form. Written and Illustrated by **Scott McCloud**. HarperPerennial, 2000. 252pp. 978-0-06-095350-8. T

A sequel to Scott McCloud's *Understanding Comics*, the publication shifts the focus to other aspects of the medium including creator's rights, comics as an art form and literature, to online potential of webcomics.

Understanding Comics: The Invisible Art. Written and Illustrated by **Scott McCloud**. HarperPerennial, 1994. 216pp. 978-0-06-097625-5. T ◎

A groundbreaking book, creator Scott McCloud offers to both professionals of the comics medium, long-time readers of comics, and even novice readers a complete overview of the comics medium illustrated in a comic book format. Hosted by Scott McCloud, the highly regarded publication dissects many facets of the comics including the origins of comics, basic facts of the medium, the secret language of comics, how a comic book is made, and other informative observations of the medium.

© 2016 Scott McCloud and HarperPerennial.

Biography/Autobiography/Memoir

A collection of biographies, autobiographies, and memoirs. The collections include tales of heroism and heartache during wartime, life on the street and everyday angst by renowned comic book artists, and people whose stories have inspired us all.

21: The Story of Roberto Clemente. Written and Illustrated by **Wilfred Santiago**. Fantagraphics, 2011. 200pp. 978-1-56097-892-3. T

Roberto Clemente was destined to be a great baseball player. Even though baseball ran through his blood, Roberto had to work hard and fight against prejudices to prove his skill in the major leagues. This graphic novel tells the stories of what he had to put up with as well as what he accomplished on and off the field. Roberto Clemente's legacy is much deeper than the titles and records he holds.

Alan's War: Memories of G.I. Alan Cope. Written and Illustrated by **Emmanuel Guibert**. First Second Books, 2008. 336pp. 978-1-59643-096-9. O

The memories of G.I. Alan C. Cope are translated into a graphic novel. After joining the army to fight against Adolf Hitler at the tender age of 18, in this book Cope chronicles his experiences in the war, the friendships and the

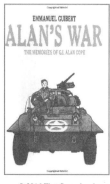

heartaches he encountered in the grueling war that made people of his time the Greatest Generation.

Amazing Fantastic Incredible: A Marvelous Memoir. Written by **Stan Lee** and **Peter David**. Illustrated by **Colleen Doran**. Marvel Comics, 2015. 192pp. 978-1-5011-0772-6, hardcover. T 🎯 ◎

Stan Lee is one of the most recognizable faces of Marvel Comics. The co-creator of many beloved characters including Spider-Man, the Fantastic Four, and the Avengers; he's helped to bring the heroes to life as well put the human in the superhuman by creating flawed heroes who greatly resonated with the readers. The book features not just Stan's work in comics, but also his upbringing on the streets of Manhattan, his early writing days in comic books, his time in World War II, and the formation of Marvel Comics to today. Excelsior! The book was on YALSA's 2017 Great Graphic Novels for Teens list.[0]

American Splendor. Written by **Harvey Pekar**. Illustrated by various. Four Walls Eight Windows, Ballantine Books, and DC Comics, 1994–2012. M ◎ 🎬

The down and out life of the late Harvey Pekar (1939–2010). The series began in 1976, when Pekar was working as a file clerk at a Veteran's Administration hospital in Cleveland, Ohio. The various collections highlight everyday life—including those of his coworkers, his daily grind, problems unclogging a toilet, relationships, how to have a car survive a Cleveland winter, his short-lived fame on the *Late Night with David Letterman* show, and even his bout with cancer. Since Pekar was not an artist, he has relied on a number of creators to tell his tales including Robert Crumb, Gary Dumm, Frank Stack, Dean Hapsiel, Kevin Brown, and Joe Zabel. The life of Harvey Pekar was also adapted into a 2003 film called *American Splendor* staring Paul Giamatti as Pekar. A few graphic novels under the "American Splendor" name are about other people, but those below are about Pekar.

The New American Splendor Anthology. Four Walls Eight Windows, 1991. 300pp. 978-0-941423-64-9.
Our Cancer Year. Four Walls Eight Windows, 1994. 252pp. 978-1-56858-011-1.

American Splendor Presents: Bob & Harv's Comics. Four Walls Eight Windows, 1996. 96pp. 978-1-56858-101-9.
American Splendor: The Life and Times of Harvey Pekar. Ballantine Books, 2003. 320pp. 978-0-345-46830-7.
American Splendor: Our Movie Year. Ballantine Books, 2004. 176pp. 978-0-345-47937-2.
Best of American Splendor. Ballantine Books, 2005. 336pp. 978-0-345-47938-9.
American Splendor: Another Day. Vertigo/DC Comics, 2008. 136pp. 978-1-4012-1235-3.
American Splendor: Another Dollar. Vertigo/DC Comics, 2009. 136pp. 978-1-4012-2173-7.

Andre the Giant: Closer to Heaven. Written by **Brandon Easton**. Illustrated by **Denis Medri**. IDW Publishing, 2015. 104pp. 978-1-6314-0400-9. O

© 2016 First Second and Box Brown.

Andre the Giant: Life and Legend. Written and Illustrated by **Box Brown**. First Second, 2014. M
Two recent biographic looks at the life and legend of Andre Roussimoff, better known across the world as Andre the Giant. Born with immense girth, he towered in his prime at almost 500 lbs and became known worldwide as not only a wrestler but also as actor beloved by many, most famously for his role as the giant Fezzik in the fairytale classic 1987 movie *The Princess Bride*. The books chronicle his life, from his youth in France (where he was driven to school by the playwright Samuel Beckett) to his career in the United States up to his untimely death in 1993. The books are full of stories and anecdotes, and no wrestling fan or fan of pop culture fanatic would be remiss to learn about the gentle giant known as Andre.

Anne Sullivan and the Trials of Helen Keller. Written and Illustrated by **Joseph Lambert**. The Center for Cartoon Studies/Disney-Hyperion Publishing, 2012. 96pp. 978-1-4231-1336-2, hardcover. Y

A graphic novel portrayal of how the blind and deaf girl called Helen Keller learned from Annie Sullivan how to communicate. Together the both of them accomplished what was once thought impossible and helped to inspire many of those with disabilities on how to persevere.

Are You My Mother? A Comic Drama. Written and Illustrated by **Alison Bechdel**. Houghton Mifflin Harcourt, 2012. 304pp. 978-0-618-98250-9, hardcover. M

There is so much more to the relationship of a mother and daughter than can be communicated. Alison Bechdel is taking on that challenge by telling of her complicated and trying relationship with her own mother. Alison chronicles so many stories in this book that it really demands the reader's attention. There is at its base the story of her and her mother, but also about her mother's relationship with her grandmother. Her relationship with her therapists, her girlfriends, and herself. Much like life there is so much going on it is hard to sort out what a relationship is about from all the surrounding noise. See *Fun Home* below.

Baggywrinkles: A Lubber's Guide to Life at Sea. Written and Illustrated by **Lucy Bellwood**. Toonhound Studios, 2016. 132pp. 978-0-9882202-9-4. A

A look at life at the sea from the eyes of creator Lucy Bellwood. She served as a volunteer deckhand aboard the tall ship *Lady Washington* and shares her experiences as well as historical seafaring tales together in one collection. Learn exactly what a baggywrinkle is! What's a turkhead? And why do sailors not count to three before doing anything? Find out inside you landlubber!

© Lucy Bellwood.

Blankets. Written and Illustrated by **Craig Thompson**. Drawn and Quarterly, 2015. New Printing. 592pp. 978-1-77046-220-5, hardcover; 978-1-77046-218-2. O 🎋 ◎

© 2016 Craig Thompson.

The autobiographical touching tale of Craig Thompson's youth growing up in his rigid fundamentalist home with his brother Phil, as well as his awkward and touching first experience with love while attending a youth church camp. Raised in a strict Midwest household where his overbearing parents often sent him and his brother to a claustrophobic storage chamber nicknamed "the cubby hole" for punishment and inappropriate schoolboy behavior, Craig emerged from his youth a shattered vulnerable teen. At a church camp he meets a kindred spirit in Raina and her friends. As their relationship blossoms, their brightly burning raw emotional, physical, and even spiritual love for each other helps to inspire Craig's future endeavors as a creator and to help erase some of the pain of his youth. The story has won many awards including two Eisner Awards for Best Graphic Novel: New (2004) and Best Writer/Artist (2004); a Harvey Award for Best Artist (2004), Best Cartoonist (2004), and Best Graphic Album of Original Work (2004); and several Ignatz Awards including Outstanding Artist (2004) and Outstanding Graphic Novel or Collection (2004). The graphic novel has also received recognition by YALSA's Best Books for Young Adults committee in 2004 as well as the Popular Paperbacks for Young Adults committee in 2005.

Blue Pills: A Positive Love Story. Written and Illustrated by **Frederik Peeters**. Houghton Mifflin Harcourt, 2008. 192pp. 978-8-1906-2413-8. O

>The touching true story about the author's romance with a woman named Cati who has a three-year-old son who both are HIV-positive. The book focuses on the author's personal struggles of the chronic condition in his loved ones as well as his own realization that living with an illness can also be a gift.

Cancer Vixen: A True Story. Written and Illustrated by **Marissa a. Marchetto**. Pantheon Books, 2009. 224pp. 978-0-375-71474-0. O

>The true story of a "terminal bachelorette" cartoonist living in New York City. She had it all—successful career as a cartoonish for the New Yorker and Glamour, and engaged to a cool restaurateur. She had the Manhattan life to dream of, until one day she found a lump on her breast.

Can't We Talk about Something More Pleasant? Written and Illustrated by **Roz Chast**. Bloomsbury, 2014. 240pp. 978-1-60819-806-1, hardcover. M

>In a mixture of text, comics, and regular art, cartoonist and illustrator Chast tells of having to deal with her elderly parents in the latter years of their lives.

Child Soldier: When Boys and Girls Are Used in War. Written by **Jessica Dee Humphreys** and **Michel Chikwanine**. Illustrated by **Claudia Davila**. Kids Can Press, 2015. 48pp. 978-1-77138-126-0. Y ◉

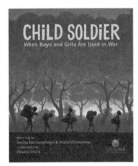

>A true life story of cowriter Michel Chikwainie of the harsh life of living in the Democratic Republic of Congo in his youth. In 1993, when Michel was only five years old and playing with his friends, rebel soldiers pulled up to his school grounds and forced them into trucks. Forced to do unspeakable acts in the name of the rebel militia, the boys are thrust into a violent world that no one should ever face.

© 2016 Kids Can Press.

Cleveland. Written by **Harvey Pekar**. Illustrated by **Joseph Remnant**. Top Shelf Productions, 2012. 128pp. 978-1-60309-091-9. O

>Harvey Pekar's *Cleveland* is a brief history of the setting of most of his stories. Harvey lays out the development of the city from its foundation, to its rise in importance, and its decline. The book is more about Harvey's relationship with the city than it is a straight history lesson. Harvey's life often mirrored the same challenges the city he could not leave behind faced. One of the high points in both Harvey's life and Cleveland's recent history was when the Cleveland Indians won the World Series. After that everything seemed to be in decline for these two for

© 2016 Harvey Pekar and Top Shelf.

some time. After some time, and a movie deal, things got better for Harvey in the early millennium. Harvey promotes some of the finer points of Cleveland, but more importantly showing that there are great things in any city. *Cleveland* is a very personal summation of Harvey Pekar's work that is befitting one of the first works that were published posthumously.

Dark Night: A True Batman Story. Written by **Paul Dini**. Illustrated by **Eduardo Risso**. Vertigo/DC Comics, 2016. 128pp. 978-1-4012-4143-8, hardcover. M 🌹 ◎

© 2016 DC Comics.

In the 1990s, Paul Dini was already regarded as a legendary writer in the field of animation. He was the main developer of *the Batman: The Animated Series* TV show and *Tiny Toon Adventures*. While walking home one evening, Paul was jumped from behind and viciously beaten within an inch of his life. His road to recovery was hard, often revisiting the attack not by the main assailant, but by the costumed villains he was writing about including the Joker, Harley Quinn, and the Penguin. Still, no matter how bleak the situation was, Paul envisioned that Batman—the Dark Knight himself was there by his side to get him through his darkest moments. A look back at a man during his darkest hour and the courage he found to come back to the light. The book was on YALSA's 2017 Great Graphic Novels for Teens list.

Dotter of Her Father's Eyes. Written by **Mary Talbot**. Illustrated by **Bryan Talbot**. Dark Horse, 2012. 96pp. 978-1-59582-850-7, hardcover. O 🌹

With the help of her husband Bryan (*Tale of One Bad Rat*, *Alice in Sunderland*, etc.), author Mary M. Talbot tells the story of her youth and her father, a noted scholar of the works of James Joyce. Talbot mixes her story with the life of Joyce's daughter Lucia and her relationship with her father. The book was the winner of the 2012 Costa Book Awards (formerly the Whitbread) in the biography category, making it the first graphic novel to do so.

Drawing from Memory. Written and Illustrated by **Allen Say**. Scholastic Books, 2011. 72pp. 978-0-545-17686-6. A 🌹

The life of Caldecott Medal winning author Allen Say is revealed in his own words and pictures. Allen grew up in Japan loving art, but his father shunned him and didn't understand his artist leanings. Instead, Allen found a second father in Noro Shinpei, one of Japan's leading cartoonists who treated Allen almost as a second father. World War II also had an effect on Allen as he began to have doubts of his country's role in the conflict. Ultimately, through hard work and perseverance, Allen finds his way in the world—not just in art, but in life as well. The book was recognized by ALSC as a notable book in 2012.

The Dumbest Idea Ever. Written and Illustrated by **Jimmy Gownley**. Graphix/Scholastic, 2014. 240pp. 978-0-545-45346-2, hardcover; 978-0-545-45347-9. A

A memoir of *Amelia Rules* creator Jimmy Gownley. Sidelined after a bad bout with chickenpox and pneumonia for a month, Jimmy rediscovers his love for comic books

Cover © Scholastic Inc.

and along the way his growing awkwardness from child-hood to adolescence. Was creating comic books the dumb-est idea ever for a teenager to have?

Edu-Manga: Anne Frank. Written by **Etsuo Suzuki**. Illustrated by **Yoko Miyawaki**. Digital Manga Publishing, 2006. 160pp. 978-1-56970-974-0. Y Japanese manga.

An illustrated look at the life of one of the most deeply moving figures from World War II. A German-born Jewish girl, she and her family escaped to Amsterdam during the Nazi occupation of Germany. After two years of hiding, she and her family were captured and Anne died of typhus in the Bergen-Belsen concentration camp at the young age of 15. Her diary chron-icling the events of her life from 1942 to 1944 was published after her death by the only surviving member of her family, her father. In English, the book is called *The Diary of a Young Girl*, and because of it Anne Frank is one of the best-known Holocaust victims. The manga is hosted by Astro Boy, the popular manga character created by Osamu Tezuka.

Edu-Manga: Helen Adams Keller. Written by **Sozo Yanagawa**. Illustrated by **Rie Yagi**. Digital Manga Publishing, 2006. 160pp. 978-1-56970-976-4. A Japanese manga.

An illustrated look at the life of one of the most inspirational people from the 20th century. Born in 1880, Helen Keller lost both her sight and hearing at the tender age of one and also lost the ability to speak. With the aid of tutor Anne Sullivan, Helen learned Braille, and eventually how to speak. Helen graduated from Radcliffe College, becoming the first deaf and blind person to earn a Bachelor of Arts degree, and continued to be an inspiration to many of those born with disabilities with her lectures and appearances across the world until her death in 1968. The manga is hosted by Astro Boy, the popular manga character created by Osamu Tezuka.

Edu-Manga: Ludwig Van Beethoven. Written by **Takayuki Kanda**. Illustrated by **Naoko Takase**. DMP Productions, 2002. 152pp. 978-1-56970-973-3. Y Japanese manga.

The life of the famous composer, Ludwing Van Beethoven is explored with the help of Osamu Tezuka's Astro Boy and his companions as a framing sequence to help draw in the reader. Beethoven led a turbulent life, dealing with the hardships of deafness but still able to create many musical master-pieces despite his setbacks in life. The manga is hosted by Astro Boy, the popular manga character created by Osamu Tezuka.

Edu-Manga: Mother Theresa. Written by **Masahide Kikai**. Illustrated by **Ren Kishida**. DMP Productions, 2003. 152pp. 978-1-56970-972-6. Y Japanese manga.

The life of Mother Theresa, an Albanian Roman Catholic religious sister who lived from 1910 to 1997. She founded the Missionaries of Charity, a Roman Catholic religious congregation, and was well known for her service to the poor and needy. The manga is hosted by Astro Boy, the popular manga character created by Osamu Tezuka.

El Deafo. Written and Illustrated by **Cece Bell**. Amulet Books, 2014. 248pp. 978-1-41971-217-3. A 🏆 ◎

While drawing the characters to look like anthropomorphic bunnies, Bell tells the story of her childhood and how she had to use a Phonic Aid hearing aid to deal with her deafness. Mainly covering her time in elementary school, Bell recounts how her deafness and the hearing aid affected her relationships with both her teachers (who wore microphones so that she could hear them) and children her own age. *El Deafo* was a 2015 Newbery Award Honor book, a Kirkus Prize finalist, and the winner of Eisner Award for Best Publication for Kids.

© Cece Bell.

Fifth Beatle: The Brian Epstein Story. Written by **Vivek J. Tiwary**. Illustrated by **Andrew C. Robinson**. Dark Horse Comics, 2013. 144pp. 978-1-61655-256-5, hardcover. O

The life of Brian Epstein, the manager of the rock band The Beatles, is revealed in graphic novel form. From the band's early days to their unprecedented international stardom, Brian was there guiding the Fab Four. Not just a look at the manager of The Beatles, it's a look at the man who was from a dirt-poor town of Liverpool, a homosexual when it was a crime in the United Kingdom, and Jewish when anti-Semitism was rampant.

The Fifth Beatle All material, unless otherwise specified, © 2016 Tiwary Entertainment Group Ltd. TM produced under license by Dark Horse Comics.

Fun Home: A Family Tragicomic. Written and Illustrated by **Alison Bechdel**. Mariner Books, 2007. 232pp. 978-0-618-87171-1. M ◎ 🏆

In this graphic memoir, Bechdel tells of her father and her youth, as well as how she came to terms with her own sexuality and the discovery that her father was hiding his. *Fun Home* was a nominee for the National Book Critics Circle Award and the winner of a number of awards including the Stonewall Award and the Eisner. Over the years the book has had some controversy with attempts to ban it from libraries and schools. It was also adapted into a musical which won a number of off-Broadway and Broadway-related awards including the Tony Award for Best Musical in 2015. See also *Are You My Mother: A Comic Drama* earlier in this section.

A Game for Swallows: To Die, To Leave, To Return. Written and Illustrated by **Zeina Abirached**. Graphic Universe, 2012. 192pp. 978-1-57505-941-9. T

The continued biography of the author and her family's life in Beirut. When Zeina's parents don't return home on a night when the city is shattered by bombings, her neighbors in their apartment complex create a separate world for Zeina and her family to make it through the dramatic night. A touching look at the importance of the community and family. See also *I Remember Beirut*.

Good Riddance: An Illustrated Memoir of Divorce. Written and Illustrated by **Cynthia Copeland**. Abrams ComicArts, 2013. 978-1-4197-0670-7. M

After 18 years, Copeland's marriage came to an end when she discovered a romantic e-mail sent to her husband. Now this mother and author of books on parenting and family must adjust to her new life as a divorced woman.

The High School Chronicles of Ariel Schrag. Written and Illustrated by **Ariel Schrag**. Touchstone/Simon & Shuster, 2008–2009. M

As a high school student, Ariel Schrag would create autobiographical comics over summer vacation, photocopy them, and sell them to her classmates. In the late 1990s, SLG published the first three as *Awkward*, *Definition*, and *Potential* each set in a different school year. They were successful with Potential getting an Eisner nomination. The books were later republished by Touchstone who combined the first two into one volume and also published the unreleased senior year story, *Likewise*. These volumes cover Schrag's high school life and include the loss of her virginity, her coming out as a lesbian, and her first girlfriend. Some of the books do contain nudity.

Awkward and Definition. 2008. 144pp. 978-1-4165-5231-4.
Potential. 2008. 232pp. 978-1-4165-5235-2.
Likewise. 2009. 400pp. 978-1-4165-5237-6.

I Remember Beirut. Written and Illustrated by **Zeina Abirached**. Graphic Universe, 2014. 96pp. 978-1-4677-4458-4. T

Abirached was born in Beirut during Lebanon's long civil war and tells of her childhood living under the threat of bombs and bullets and the people in her East Beirut apartment building that helped her family when her parents went missing. Her second book, *A Game for Swallows* (see above), has other memories of her times during the war.

Invisible Ink: My Mother's Secret Love Affair with a Famous Cartoonist. Written and Illustrated by **Bill Griffith**. Fantagraphics, 2015. 200pp. 978-1-60699-895-3. M

In this Eisner Award–winning graphic memoir, Bill Griffith, best known for his character of Zippy the Pinhead, tells of how in 1972 his mother revealed to him the truth about a secret affair. For 16 years Barbara Griffith had a romantic relationship with Lawrence Lariar, a cartoonist writer, and editor whose work included *The Best Cartoons of the Year* 1books. The books tell about that time, along with some of his mother's history, and how Griffith learned more about the affair.

Jerusalem: Chronicles from the Holy City. Written and Illustrated by **Guy Delisle**. Drawn and Quarterly, 2012. 320pp. 978-1-77046-071-3. O ◎

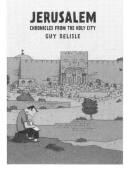

In the tradition of his other travelogues, Delisle is a stranger in a strange land in Jerusalem. See from his point of view what daily life is like in one of the holiest cities in the world.

© 2016 Drawn and Quarterly.

Junji Ito's Cat Diary: Yon and Mu. Written and Illustrated by **Junji Ito**. Kodansha Comics, 2015. 120pp. 978-1-63236-197-4. T 🕴 Japanese manga

The master of Japanese horror manga, Junji Ito, turns his talents to something else entirely—his own home experiences with his cats named Yon and Mu! The two cats were owned by Junji Ito's fiancée, A-ko, and we see firsthand the trials and tribulations of a dog owner trying to acclimate to living in a household with cats when A-ko moves in with her feline companions with hilarious results. The book was on YALSA's 2017 Great Graphic Novels for Teens list.[0]

Lewis & Clark. Written and Illustrated by **Nick Bertozzi**. First Second, 2011. 144 pp. 978-1-59643-450-9. T

In 1804, explorers Meriweather Lewis and William Clark left St. Louis, Missouri, to embark on one of the most ambitious plans of the day—to cross the untamed west and to make it to the Pacific Ocean. The journey was not easy, and the journey was full of perilous bouts with sickness, bad luck, hostile tribes of Indians, and even Lewis's chronic depression. Though their journey was long, they made it to the Pacific in 1806 and became legends of their time.

Marbles: Mania, Depression, Michelangelo, & Me: A Graphic Memoir. Written and Illustrated by **Ellen Forney**. Avery/Penguin Books, 2012. 256pp. 978-1-59240-732-3. T 🕴

Is Ellen doomed to live as a crazy artist? Who were the other great artists who dealt with being bipolar? If she were to get medication to help control her mood swings, would that be the end of her creative life? These are all questions important to Ellen in her life as an artist. Award-winning creator Forney tells of how she was diagnosed with bipolar disorder and her struggles to deal with her condition and well as her fears that any treatment would interfere with her creativity. Winner of the National Association for the Advancement of Psychoanalysis "Gradiva" winner in Art.

March. Written by **John Lewis** and **Andrew Aydin**. Illustrated by **Nate Powell**. Top Shelf Productions, 2013–2016. 🎖 O ◎

© 2016 Top Shelf and John Lewis.

A graphic biography of Congressman John Lewis, one of the most important figures in the civil rights movement. The trilogy recollects Lewis's own personal experiences in the tumultuous times of the civil rights movement of the 1960s from his days as a sharecropper to the 1963 March on Washington, D.C., to the beatings he received at the hands of state troopers, to his receiving the Medal of Freedom by President Obama. The series was recognized with multiple awards including YALSA's Great Graphics Novels for Teens lists in 2014, 2016, and 2017 as well as the Robert F. Kennedy Book Award, the Coretta Scott King Award, the Sibert Medal, the Printz Award, an ALA Notable Book, one of YALSA's Outstanding Books for the College Bound, the 2016 Eisner Award for Best Reality-Based Work, and more. In 2016, volume three became the first ever graphic novel to win a National Book Award. Lewis and his co-creators have traveled the country, discussing the series at both comic and library conventions.

Book One. 2013. 128pp. 978-1-60309-300-2.
Book Two. 2015. 192pp. 978-1-60309-400-9.
Book Three. 2016. 240pp. 978-1-60309-402-3.

A Matter of Life. Written and Illustrated by **Jeffrey Brown**. Top Shelf, 2013. 96pp. 978-1-60309-266-1. O

Brown looks upon his past and present life, with looks at the life of his father, himself both as a child and an adult, and his young son.

Maus: A Survivor's Tale. Written and Illustrated by **Art Spiegelman**. Pantheon Books/Random House Publishing, 1986–2011. O 🎖 ◎

© 2016 Art Spiegelman.

The tragic acclaimed series in which a father recounts the horrors of trying to survive through the Jewish Holocaust and an estranged family tries to mend wounds that will never heal. Vladek Spiegelman, a Jewish survivor of Hitler's Holocaust, and his cartoonist son Art have had a troubled relationship. Vladek's first wife, who also survived the camps, committed suicide years ago, and the family has always been broken. Told in flashbacks taking the reader back to Vladek's life in Poland before the war, during the Nazi concentration camps, and in the present, the story features anthropomorphized versions of humans where Jews are mice, Germans are cats, Poles are pigs, French are frogs, Americans are dogs, Swedes are reindeer, and Gypsies are moths. The story has won multiple awards including a Pulitzer Prize Special Award in 1992 for *Maus I*; an Eisner Award for Best Graphic Novel: Reprint (2002) for *Maus II*; and a Harvey Award for Best Graphic Album of

Previously Published Work for *Maus II*. Art Spiegelman has also received recognition in the Will Eisner Hall of Fame in 1999 for his contributions to the comic book industry. The series has also received recognition from YALSA: both volumes were selected for the Popular Paperbacks for Young Adults' selection list in 1997.

I: My Father Bleeds History. 1986. 160pp. 978-0-394-74723-1.
II: And Here My Troubles Began. 1992. 144pp. 978-0-679-72977-8.
The Complete Maus. 2011. Reprint edition. 298pp. 978-0-679-40641-9, hardcover.

Mike's Place: A True Story of Love, Blues, and Terror in Tel Aviv. Written by **Jack Baxter** and **Joshua Faudem**. Illustrated by **Koren Shadmi**. First Second, 2015. 192pp. 978-1-59643-857-6, hardcover. M

Jack and Joshua wanted to film all about the famous blues bar called Mike's Place. Situated on the beachfront of Tel Aviv, it's a place of refuge where religion and politics has no place and a cold beer can help you forget the conflict outside. As Jack and Joshua befriend the locals, one month into filming, tragedy struck: a suicide bomber targets Mike's Place and the family and friends of the bar will never be the same again. Meanwhile, to cope with the horror they've seen, Jack and Joshua still rolled the cameras. This is their gripping true story.

© 2016 First Second.

Mom's Cancer. Written and Illustrated by **Brian Fies**. Harry N. Abrams, Incorporated, 2006. 115pp. 0-8109-5840-6. O

Originally featured as an online webcomic, the collected features the poignant as well as uniquely humorous true story of how Fies' mother suffered and battled against advanced-stage lung cancer and the toll it takes on not just those suffering from the disease, but the stress and anguish that family and loved ones suffer as well.

My Friend Dahmer. Written and Illustrated by **Derf Backderf**. Abrams ComicArts, 2012. 224pp. 978-1-4197-0217-4. O 🎖 ◎

Derf lived in a small town outside of Akron, Ohio. Here Derf would form lifelong friendships and have many experiences here that he would always remember. One of those memories is how his friend and he became fascinated with the odd behavior of one of their classmates. Their "friend" had many mannerisms that would become his trademark during high school. He would shout in libraries when no one would look, act like he had tourettes, and just be the weirdest kid Derf and his friends ever knew. They formed a fan club of sorts around their friend. Their friend's name was Jeffrey Dahmer. Derf Backderf reflects on his friendship with Dahmer, before he became a serial murderer, and realizes that there were many clues that there was something not quite right. The book received many accolades including a YALSA Alex Award in 2013 for excellence in narrative

© 2016 Derf Backderf.

fiction, a Top Ten finalist for Quick Picks for Reluctant Readers and the Great Graphic Novels for Teens selection list as well. A film adaptation came out in 2017.

My Most Secret Desire. Written and Illustrated by **Julie Doucet**. Drawn and Quarterly, 2006. 96pp. 978-1-896597-95-9, hardcover. M

Partake in one of the most voyeuristic collections of comics as the reader gets to peek into the psyche of another person. Julie Doucet records her dreams about being a man, inanimate objects talking, sex, giving birth to animals, and much more. There is nothing hidden in her comics as she talks about masturbating with cookies, but nothing is revealed by the author in ways of possible meanings to these dreams. This collection of short comics lets the reader pick through and hypothesize about this author's most secret desires.

Ordinary People Can Change the World. Written by **Brad Meltzer**. Illustrated by **Chris Eliopoulos**. Dial Books for Young Readers, 2014–. A

There are certain individuals who have been known throughout American history to have had an immense effect on our culture—icons who will have stood the test of time and have been the pinnacle of the American way of life of rugged individualism, compassion, and doing what is right even though others may think you are wrong. Written by Brad Meltzer and illustrated in a Bill Watterson Calvin and Hobbes-inspired style comes a concise but creative focus on those who have helped to shape America forever and to inspire tomorrow's future that they can be heroes too.

I am Abraham Lincoln. 2014. 40pp. 978-0-803-74083-9, hardcover.
I am Albert Einstein. 2014. 40pp. 978-0-803-74084-6, hardcover.
I am Amelia Earhart. 2014. 40pp. 978-0-803-74082-2, hardcover.
I am Rosa Parks. 2014. 40pp. 978-0-803-74085-3, hardcover.
I am Helen Keller. 2015. 40pp. 978-0-525-42851-0, hardcover.
I am Jackie Robinson. 2015. 40pp. 978-0-803-74086-0, hardcover.
I am Lucille Ball. 2015. 40pp. 978-0-525-42855-8, hardcover.
I am George Washington. 2016. 40pp. 978-0-525-42848-0, hardcover.
I am Jane Goodall. 2016. 40pp. 978-0-525-42849-7, hardcover.
I am Martin Luther King, Jr. 2016. 40pp. 978-0-525-42852-7, hardcover.
I am Jim Henson. 2017. 40pp. 978-0-525-42850-3, hardcover.

The Osamu Tezuka Story—A Life in Manga and Anime. Written and Illustrated by **Toshio Ban**. Stone Bridge Press, 2016. 928pp. 978-1-61172-025-9. Japanese manga. T

The life of Osamu Tezuka—known throughout Japan as the "godfather of manga"—is revealed from his humble beginnings growing up in the Osaka Prefecture to his importance in being a pioneer in both comics and animation in Japan.

Perfect Example. Written and Illustrated by **John Porcellino**. Drawn and Quarterly, 2005. 144pp. 1-896597-75-0. M

A collection of the creator's King-Cat mini-comics showcasing the author's awkward years of late high school starting 1987. With college looming on the horizon, John experiences drunken rock concerts, arguments with his parents, make-out sessions, and ultimately a deteriorating relationship with his longtime girlfriend. An honest and true depiction of the life of a high school student unsure of the path that lies ahead and the challenges that await him.

Persepolis. Written and Illustrated by **Marjane Satrapi**. Pantheon Books/Random House Publishing, 2004. O 🎭 🎬 ◎

© 2016 Marjane Satrapi.

Based on the author's own life in Iran and abroad, it is her own memoir recounting her youth and the Islamic Revolution in Iran, the downfall of the Shah's regime, the deadly conflict with Iraq, and what life is like under repressive rule. At the age of 14 she was sent to live in Vienna, and where Volume II continues, she learns of love and growing up, and eventually returns to Iran. But is her homeland where Marjane wants to permanently live and go to college, or have both she and her homeland changed? The series won a Harvey Award for Best American Edition of Foreign Material in 2004. *Vol. 2: The Story of a Return* won an Ignatz Award for Outstanding Graphic Novel in 2005. The graphic novel series has also received recognition by several of YALSA's selection list committees including Best Books for Young Adults for *Volume 1* (2004) and *Volume 2* (2005), respectively, as well as Outstanding Books for the College Bound (2004) and an Alex Award (2004) for *Volume 1*. The graphic novels were also adapted into an animated film released in 2007 which was written and directed by Satrapi.

Vol. 1: The Story of a Childhood. 2004. 160pp. 978-0-375-71457-3.
Vol. 2: The Story of a Return. 2004. 192pp. 978-0-375-42288-1.

Pyongyang: A Journey in North Korea. Written and Illustrated by **Guy Delisle**. Drawn and Quarterly, 2007. 176pp. 978-1-897299-21-0. T 🎭 ◎

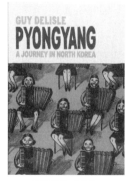

© 2016 Guy Delisle.

The true story of Guy Delisle, a Quebec-born, France-based animator, and his short time living in the bleak country of North Korea. While staying in the city of Pyongyang for two months while overseeing the production of a kids' cartoon, Delisle captures the oddities of the quirky people of North Korea from their bland customs as well as endless line of locations dedicated to North Korea's late founder Kim Il Sung and his son, current leader Kim Jong Il. A stranger in an even stranger land, Delisle's frank look at life in a sheltered country is an awakening appreciation for free countries and the beauty of free expression. The book was awarded recognition on YALSA's Best Books for Young Adults 2006 list.

The Quitter. Written by **Harvey Pekar**. Illustrated by **Dean Haspiel**. Vertigo/DC Comics, 2006. 104pp. 978-1-4012-0400-6. M ◎

The childhood and young adult life of the late Harvey Pekar, author of the ongoing series *American Splendor*. Pekar focuses on the difficult times growing up in Cleveland, Ohio, as a young Jewish boy in an increasingly African American neighborhood

and his attempts to find out where he belongs. Pekar was his own worst enemy, too. He was always too hard on himself when things didn't go his way and quitting when the push came to shove. Pekar's successes, though small, help to encourage him down his path toward eventual fame and recognition.

© 2016 DC Comics and Harvey Pekar.

Ronald Reagan: A Graphic Biography. Written by **Andrew Helfer**. Illustrated by **Steve Buccellato** and **Joe Staton**. Hill & Wang, 2007. 102pp. 978-0-8090-9507-0. T

The life of Ronald Reagan, a modest acting talent who rose to become one of the gold standards for American governance as the governor of California from 1967 to 1975 and as the 40th president of the United States.

Rosalie Lightning: A Graphic Memoir. Written and Illustrated by **Tom Hart**. St. Martin's Press, 2016. 272pp. 978-1-250-04994-0, hardcover. O ◉

A poignant reflection on the undying love a parent has for a child as the author retells of the life, untimely death of his two-year-old daughter, Rosalie. The book is heartbreaking as it shows the love the author and his wife shared for Rosalie, the grief they shared, as well as the eventual hope for the future as a family that, though shattered, continues to thrive through the grief.

Shackleton: Antarctic Odyssey. Written and Illustrated by **Nick Bertozzi**. First Second Books, 2014. 128 pp. 978-1-59643-451-6. T

One of the last great Antarctic explorers, Ernest Shackleton was never one to quit. After being a crewmember of two failed missions to explore the frozen Antarctic region, Ernest and his crew aboard the *Endurance* vowed to complete the first ever trans-Antarctic exploration in 1914. Two years later through bitter weather. Shackleton and his crew beat all the odds: amazingly not one crew member was lost in their two-year journey across the vast snow-covered continent. Join "Shacks" and his crew for an engrossing journey across one of the most inhospitable regions of the Earth.

Cover © First Second.

Shenzhen: A Travelogue from China. Written and Illustrated by **Guy Delisle**. Drawn and Quarterly, 2012, new printing. 152pp. 978-1-77046-079-9. T ◉

It is a follow-up to the highly recognized *Pyongyang: A Journey in North Korea* and continues the true-life tales of Guy Delisle, a Quebec-born animator and his experiences living in China while overseeing the production of a kids' cartoon that had been outsourced by his animation studio. Like with *Pyongyang,* Delisle shows the oddities and humorous side of life in another communist country in which he finds himself spending time. Delisle showcases the differences of Western and Eastern culture and the small moments where freedom is savored in a country where no one is truly free.

Smile and Sisters. Written and Illustrated by **Raina Telgemeier**. Graphix/Scholastic Books.

Smile. 2010. 224pp. 978-0-545-13206-0; 978-0-545-13205-3, hardcover. Y🏅 ◎

Cover © Scholastic Inc.

Sisters. 2014. 208pp. 978-0545-54059-9, hardcover; 978-0-545-54060-5. Y 🏅 ◎

Cover © Scholastic Inc.

These two autobiographical books by Raina Telgemeier have become perennial *New York Times* best sellers and have appealed to children and adults alike, including many who do not usually read graphic novels. In *Smile*, Raina is like many other middle-schoolers: she is growing up and going through all the pains of puberty and finding her way in with finding true friends, and that awkward age of discovering boys. When Raina accidentally knocks out her two front teeth while out with the Girl Scouts, she has to undergo multiple dealings with headgear, fake front teeth, embarrassing headgear, and visit after visit to get her perfect smile back. A unique twist on the already abnormal days middle-schoolers put themselves through, and it's all true! The book was received numerous recognitions including a 2011 Eisner Award for Best Publication for Teens, a YALSA Great Graphic Novels for Teens top ten list finalist in 2011, and an ALSC Notable Children's Book for Middle Readers.

Sisters showcases the ups and downs of being siblings in a family. Raina always wanted to be a big sister, but when her baby sister Amara is born, they seem to have nothing in common as they get older—Amara likes to play by herself and they seldom interact. When a baby brother comes along, can the two of them find common ground? Told against the backdrop of a family road trip from San Francisco as they head to a family reunion in Colorado, the story creatively uses flashbacks to the past and present to help tell the stories of Raina's own experiences growing up with ever-changing family dynamics with heart, heartache, and humor along the way. The book was recognized as a Great Graphic Novel for Teens in 2015 as well an Eisner Award for Best Writer/Artist.

Stitches: A Memoir. Written and Illustrated by **David Small**. W.W. Norton & Company, 2009. 336pp. 978-0-393-06857-3, hardcover. O

The memoir of the Caldecott-winning creator's harsh experiences in life from his youth to adulthood while growing up in a silent and cruel family household. Since he was six, Small underwent numerous X-rays for sinus problems which resulted in him eventually developing cancer. Fourteen-year-old Small is operated on without being told what is wrong with him, and he loses his voice as a result of the cancer surgery. Now unable to communicate to the world around him, Small's feelings of helplessness is exacerbated by his loneliness in a household already barren of love. The book was a finalist for the 2009 National Book Award and finalist for two 2010 Will Eisner Comic Industry Awards.

The Story of My Tits. Written and Illustrated by **Jennifer Hayden**. Top Shelf Productions, 2015. 352pp. 978-1-60309-054-4. O

Comic book creator Jennifer Hayden's graphic novel about her own life and her experience with breast cancer.

© Top Shelf and Jennifer Hayden.

Tangles: A Story about Alzheimer's, My Mother, and Me. Written and Illustrated by **Sarah Leavitt**. Skyhorse Publishing, 2012. 128pp. 978-1-61608-639-8. O

The tragic tale of how Alzheimer's disease can affect not only a beloved family member, but an entire family. When Midge, the author's mother, begins to show signs of Alzheimer's disease, Sarah learns that even though there is heartache and pain, their love for each other endures no matter what may happen.

Thoreau: A Sublime Life. Written by **A. Dan**. Illustrated by **Maximilien Le Roy**. NBM Publishing, 2016. 88pp. 978-1-68112-025-6. T

A new biography of Henry David Thoreau, "author, philosopher and pioneering ecologist" responsible for Walden, an early proponent of civil disobedience, and one of the great figures of the transcendental movement.

Tiger! Tiger! Tiger! Written and Illustrated by **Scott Morse**. Adhouse Books, 2009. 48pp. 978-0-9774715-3-9, hardcover. O ◎ 🎖

© Scott Morse.

A poignant look at fatherhood from the eyes of animator and comics creator Scott Morse. Drawn through the persona of a tiger and his son, we see a day unfold that could be full of danger, possibilities, and full of life.

To Dance: A Ballerina's Graphic Novel. Written by **Siena Cherson Siegel**. Illustrated by **Mark Siegel**. Atheneum Books for Young Readers, 2006. 64pp. 978-1-4169-2687-0, hardcover. T

The dance career of Siena Cherson Siegel ballet dancer is revealed with beautiful illustrations by her husband, Mark Siegel. Follow Siena's love of ballet from the age of six to her time at the School of American Ballet to when she rediscovered it after completing college. The book is an honest look as a ballerina's life and not all of it is rosy. Leg injuries and foot pain are commonplace, and hard work, love for the art, and dedication are needed to succeed in a career that is like no other.

Tomboy: A Graphic Memoir. Written and Illustrated by **Liz Prince**. Zest Books, 2014. 256pp. 978-1-936976-55-3. O

The memoirs of a girl trying to figure out just who she is. Growing up, she was never a girly-girl—she preferred to play with boys and often played the role of hero instead of a princess. Her parents recognized her search for self-exploration and let her dress more like a boy—much to the ridicule of bullies when growing up. It was only when she met girlfriends like her that she realized she enjoyed the freedoms that a boy had but didn't want to be a boy. A memoir about finding your own way and being comfortable with who you are on the inside and outside.

True Story Swear to God Archives. Written and Illustrated by **Tom Beland**. Image Comics, 2008. 512pp. 978-1-58240-881-1. O

I swear to God I'm not making this up. It's all true. Tom never really believed in the power of fate and taking chances, but that's all about to change. One day when Tom goes on a work-related trip to Walt Disney World, little does he know that he'll meet the love of his life there. While at a concert he meets the fun-loving and carefree Lily, and sparks do fly. There's only one problem: they live 9,000 miles apart from each other. Can a cartoonist from California and a journalist from Puerto Rico find true love? The story of how writer/artist Tom Beland met and fell in love with his wife, Lily—and it's all true.

Woman Rebel: The Margaret Sanger Story. Written and Illustrated by **Peter Bagge**. Drawn and Quarterly, 2013. 104pp. 978-1-77046-126-0. M

> Bagge looks at the life of Margaret Sanger, the controversial carly birth control pioneer and founder of Planned Parenthood.

You'll Never Know. Written and Illustrated by **Carol Tyler**. Fantagraphics, 2009–2012. M

> Carol Tyler tells of her father's life, concentrating on his service in World War II and his early life with her mother, as well as how those experiences shaped his later life. The trilogy was nominated for several awards including multiple Eisners.
>
> *Book One*: *A Good & Decent Man*. 2009. 104pp. 978-1-60699-144-2.
> *Book Two: Collateral Damage*. 2010. 104pp. 978-1-60699-418-4.
> *Book Three: Soldier's Heart*. 2012. 104pp. 978-1-60699-548-8.

History

A look at history both old and new from an entirely new perspective—as a graphic novel. The books feature current subjects as well as ancient history. Highlights include the history of the United States and of the universe, courtesy of Larry Gonick.

A.D.: New Orleans after the Deluge. Written and Illustrated by **Josh Neufeld**. Pantheon, 2009–2010. 2009. 208pp. 978-0-307-37814-9, hardcover; 2010. 978-0-375-71488-7. O 🎖 ◎

> An oral history focusing on seven New Orleans residents as they share their experiences before, during, and after the horrific events when Hurricane Katrina hit Louisiana on August 29, 2005. The New Orleans area dealt flooding waters which crippled the city and forced people to abandon their homes. The book was a 2010 selection by YALSA's Great Graphic Novels for Teens. See also *Drowned City* below.

© Josh Neufeld and Pantheon Books.

Alice in Sunderland. Written and Illustrated by **Bryan Talbot**. Dark Horse Comics, 2007. 328pp. 978-1-59307-673-3. O

> Part fiction and part non-fiction, Bryan Talbot explores the history of England, the biography of *Alice in Wonderland* creator Lewis Carroll, and the English town of Sunderland and how they're all interrelated. The book is a merry visual chase throughout England that pinpoints various features and events in Carroll's life that may have inspired one of the world's most cherished modern fairy tales.

Cartoon History Series. Written and Illustrated by **Larry Gonick**. 1992–2002. T 🎗
An ambitious project by Larry Gonick that's still in the making today as he's explored the history of the old world, the modern world, as well as the United States. Larry has tackled many histories including the "Big Bang," the formation of the Earth, the time of the dinosaurs, the origins of world faiths, the rise of great conquerors and ancient civilizations, and the modern ages of man. Particular detail is given to showcasing perspectives from other cultures as well. Gonick's work is an impressive and thorough look at civilizations worldwide and is both educational and humorously entertaining. *Vol. III: From the Rise of Arabia to the Renaissance* received a Harvey Award for Best Graphic Album of Original Work in 2003. The graphic novel series has also received recognition by YALSA's Popular Paperbacks for Young Adults committee for the 1997 list.

Cartoon History of the Universe. Various companies, 1990–2002.

Book I: From the Big Bang to Alexander The Great. Doubleday. 1990. 368pp. 978-0-3852-6520-1.
Vol. II: From the Springtime of China to the Fall of Rome. Main Street Books/Broadway Books. 1992. 320pp. 978-0-3854-2093-8.
Vol. III: From the Rise of Arabia to the Renaissance. W. W. Norton & Company. 2002. 320pp. 978-0-3933-2403-7.

The Cartoon History of the Modern World. William Morrow, 2006–2009.

Part 1: From Columbus to the U.S. Constitution. 2006. 272pp. 978-0-0607-6004-5.
Part 2: From the Bastille to Bagdad. 2009. 272pp. 978-0-0607-6008-3.

The Cartoon History of the United States. HarperCollins. 1991. 400pp. 978-0-0627-3098-5.

The Comic Book Story of Beer. Written by **Jonathan Hennessey** and **Mike Smith**. Illustrated by **Aaron McConnell**. Ten Speed Press, 2015. 180pp. 978-1-60774-635-5. O

A history of the cause and solution to all of life's problems, the book is a historical look at the world's favorite beverage from 7000 BC to today's craft brewing revolution. Learn how early farmers learned how to preserve grains from getting spoiled in wet winters and how that resulted into malt grain and brew it into beer. The origins of beer are traced from its earliest history in Mesopotamia, through the Dark Ages, to the microbreweries of today.

© Ten Speed Press. Reprinted with permission

Drowned City: Hurricane Katrina and New Orleans. Written and illustrated by **Don Brown**. Houghton Mifflin Harcourt, 2015. 96pp. 978-0-5441-5777-4. T 🎗
On August 29, 2005, one of the greatest natural disasters to strike the United States when Hurricane Katrina hit the Gulf Coast. Among the best-known targets of the

storm was the New Orleans region which suffered massive flooding as well as other damage and loss of life. Brown's graphic novel tells about the event along with both the natural and manmade problems that came along with it. Drowned City was on the top 10 list of the YALSA Great Graphic Novels for teens, on a number of "best of" lists, and the winner of the NTCE's 2016 Orbis Pictus Award for Outstanding Nonfiction for Children. See also *A.D.* above.

Filmish: A Graphic Journey through Film. Written and Illustrated by **Edward Ross**. Self Made Hero, 2015. 200pp. 978-1-910593-03-5. T 🏆

A graphic novel look at the history and behind the scenes of the film industry from its inception to the modern movies of today. The book covers other subjects integral to the behind the scenes of the movies including set design, famous directors, and actors. The book was on the Top Ten List of YALSA's 2017 Great Graphic Novels for Teens list.

© Edward Ross.

Graphic History Series. Written by **Wayne Vansant**. Zenith Press, 2012–2015. T
These six books cover notable figures and battles of the American Civil War, World War I, and World War II. The series was originally released in softcover between 2012 and 2014 and in hardcover library binding. Vansant has a history of writing and drawing war-related comics and graphic novels including Marvel's Vietnam War fictional story *The 'Nam*, as well as an adaptation of *The Red Badge of Courage*.

Gettysburg: The Graphic History of America's Most Famous Battle and the Turning Point of the Civil War. 2013. 96pp. 978-0-7603-4406-4; 978-1-9395-8177-8, library binding.
Normandy: A Graphic History of D-Day, The Allied Invasion of Hitler's Fortress Europe. 2012. 104pp. 978-0-7603-4392-0; 978-1-9395-8179-2, library binding.
Bombing Nazi Germany: The Graphic History of the Allied Air Campaign That Defeated Hitler in World War II. 2013. 104pp. 978-0-7603-4530-6; 9781939581761, library binding.
Grant Vs. Lee: The Graphic History of The Civil War's Greatest Rivals during the Last Year of the War. 2013. 104pp. 978-0-7603-4531-3; 978-1-9395-8178-5, library binding.
Battle of the Bulge: A Graphic History of Allied Victory in the Ardennes, 1944–1945. 2014. 104pp. 978-0-7603-4622-8; 978-1-9395-8175-4, library binding.
The Red Baron: The Graphic History of Richthofen's Flying Circus and the Air War in WWI. 2014. 104pp. 978-0-7603-4602-0; 978-1-9395-8180-8, library binding.

Hit by Pitch: Ray Chapman, Carl Mays and the Fatal Fastball. Written and Illustrated by **Molly Lawless**. McFarland & Company, Inc., 2012. 196pp. 978-0-7864-4609-4. T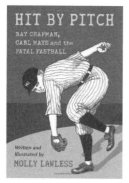

On August 16, 1920, Cleveland Indians shortstop and fan-favorite player Ray Chapman was struck by a fastball pitch by New York Yankees pitcher Carl Mays. Chapman died the next morning. Born in the same year in 1891 in Kentucky, but worlds apart in personality, Molly Lawless focuses on the lives of Mays and Chapman and the true story of two men forever bound by one fateful pitch during Americas' national pastime.

© 2012 Molly Lawless.

Journey into Mohawk Country. Written by **Harmen Meyndertsz von den Bogaert**. Adapted and Illustrated by **George O'Connor**. First Second Books, 2006. 144pp. 978-1-59643-106-5. T

Adapted from the 16th-century journals of a Dutch trader. The journals tell of a 1634 trip when Harmen Meyndertsz von den Bogaert journeyed with two companions from Fort Orange (present-day Albany, New York) into the heart of Mohawk Indian territory. There he hoped to set up a trade agreement of beaver pelts on behalf of the Dutch West India Company. The journals are a fascinating look at true Native American culture and a portrait of a country in the making.

© First Second.

A Most Imperfect Union: A Contrarian History of the United States. Written by **Ilan Stavans**. Illustrated by **Lalo Alcaraz**. Basic Books, 2014. 270pp. 978-0-465-03669-1, hardcover. O

A look at the history of American history from an alternate perspective of the American story. The book is not a rose-colored glasses look, but examines many of the lost histories that are both positive and negative but intermixed with some humor along the way.

Nathan Hale's Hazardous Tales. Written and Illustrated by **Nathan Hale**. Amulet Books. 2012–. Y ◎ ⚑

In this series of historical graphic novels, award-winning illustrator Hale tells stories from history, including the life of his Revolutionary War–namesake, the Alamo, and war stories throughout American history. The stories are hosted by the real historical hero Nathan Hale as he's accompanied a stiff serious-minded British constable and a humorous hangman as they magically journey from one historical conflict to the

© 2016 Nathan Hale.

next. Libraries carrying these titles may be keeping many of them in the 900s. The series has been recognized multiple times by YALSA's Great Graphic Novels for Teens in 2013, 2014, 2015, and 2016. The series is still ongoing.

One Dead Spy. 2012. 128pp. 978-1-4197-0396-6, hardcover.
Nathan Hale's role as America's first spy is revealed in the midst of the American Revolutionary War.

Big Bad Ironclad. 2012. 128pp. 978-1-4197-0395-9, hardcover.
Nathan Hale and company visit the period of the U.S. Civil War and see the history of the amazing ironclad steam warships used in the conflict.

Donner Dinner Party. 2012. 128pp. 978-1-4197-0856-5, hardcover.
Nathan Hale and company visit one of the harrowing true tales of western expansion hardship and bad decisions that lead to the Donner party's predicament in the Sierra Nevada Mountains.

Treaties, Trenches, Mud, and Blood. 2014. 128pp. 978-1-4197-0808-4, hardcover.
World War I's grueling skirmishes were the first introduction to modern warfare the world had ever known in the 20th century. Travel back to the time when battles were fought by trench warfare, tanks, and great sacrifice.

The Underground Abductor: An Abolitionist Tale. 2015. 128pp. 978-1-4197-1536-5, hardcover.
The life of Araminta Ross, a slave born in Delaware in the early 19th century, is revealed. Once she became free, she changed her name to Harriet Tubman, and spent her life freeing other slaves.

Alamo All-Stars. 2016. 128pp. 978-1-4197-1902-8, hardcover.

The Texas Revolution is revealed with the help of Vicente Guerrero. See how the state of Texas came to be as well as the lives of the "Alamo All-Stars" like William Travis, Jim Bowie, Davy Crockett, and Juan Seguin and how they met their end.

© 2016 Nathan Hale.

The Photographer. Written by **Didier Lefevre**. Illustrated by **Emmanuel Guibert**. First Second Books, 2009. 288pp. 978-1-59643-375-5. O 🎖️ ◎

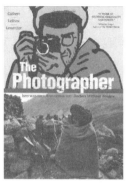

A documentary graphic novel that combines artwork and photographs of the photographer, Didier Lefevre in his experiences of traveling in the mid-1980s with Doctors Without Borders in Afghanistan. A heartbreaking look at war-torn country using a combination of photographs and art. The book was a winner of the 2010 Eisner Award for Best US Edition of International Material.

© 2016 First Second.

The Plot: The Secret Story of the Protocols of the Elders of Zion. Written and Illustrated by **Will Eisner**. W.W. Norton and Co., 2005. 978-0-3930-6045-4, hardcover. O

First published in 1903, *The Protocols of the Elders of Zion* are a forgery that aimed to show that Jews are part of an international conspiracy of global domination. It has been used to justify anti-Semitism in many countries and material from it has been adapted into anti-Semitic speeches and writings from people ranging from Adolf Hitler to Henry Ford. In this, his final work, completed shortly before his death and published posthumously, Will Eisner explores the history of the *Protocols* and how, despite frequent debunking over the decades, it still pops up to spread hatred.

Tetris: The Games People Play. Written and Illustrated by **Box Brown**. First Second Books, 2016. 256pp. 978-1-62672-315-3. O 🎖️

In 1984, the gaming world was forever transformed with the release of Alexey Pajitnov's endless puzzle game called Tetris. Though he worked for the Dorodnitsyn Computing Centre of the Soviet Academy of Sciences in the Soviet Union, once the game hit beyond the Iron Curtain, it was a smash hit—everyone wanted the game—including Atari, Nintendo, Sega, and more. Now for the first time, learn about the bidding wars, the back-door deals, and outright theft of a cultural phenomenon. The book was on YALSA's 2017 Great Graphic Novels for Teens list.

© 2016 First Second.

The United States Constitution: A Graphic Adaptation. Written by **Jonathan Hennessey**. Illustrated by **Aaron McConnell**. Hill and Wang, 2008. 160pp. 978-0-8090-9487-5, hardcover. T

An illustrated guide to the U.S. Constitution—it's the blueprint to the United States of America—our military defends it, our leaders swear to uphold it, but do you truly know the Constitution?

Walking Wounded: Uncut Stories from Iraq. Written by **Oliver Morel**. Illustrated by **Mael**. NBM Publishing, 2015. 120pp. 978-1-56163-982-3. O

> A look at those who those who bravely served their country and had difficulty coping on their return home.

Science and Math

The world of science comes alive as graphic novels. What could be thought of by some as stodgy and difficult to understand takes on a whole new light. The majority of books in this chapter can be credited to three individuals: Larry Gonick for his guides to such principles as physics and chemistry; Jim Ottaviani for his dedication to a wide range of scientific history including the life of Niels Bohr and the history of early dinosaur bone hunters; and Jay Hosler and his whimsical looks at science including the life cycle of a bee and the theories of Charles Darwin.

Bone Sharps, Cowboys, and Thunder Lizards: A Tale of Edwin Drinker Cope, Othniel Charles Marsh, and the Gilded Age of Paleontology. Written by **Jim Ottaviani**. Illustrated by **Zander Cannon** and **Shad Petosky**. GT Labs, 2005. 176pp. 978-0-9660106-6-4. T ◎

© 2016 Jim Ottaviani and GT Labs.

An embellished account of the controversial early years of paleontology in the late 19th century where scientists Edwin Drinker Cope and Othniel Charles Marsh scrambled to one-up the other in their search to discover the of the bones of "thunder lizards." Both scientists came from wealthy families and were able to fund their very competitive expeditions out west, which became known as the Bone Wars. Competition was so fierce that expeditions in search of Cretaceous fossils were also accompanied by sensationalized accounts of thievery, bribery, and spying that sullied the name of American paleontology for years to come.

Larry Gonick's Cartoon Guides. Illustrated by **Larry Gonick**. Various Publishers. 1991–. T

> Larry Gonick has also covered a great many other non-fiction subjects from science such as Chemistry to math concepts including statistics, algebra, and calculus. On occasion he's worked with others on the books and they are listed below as well.
>
> *The Cartoon Guide to Algebra*. Written by **Larry Gonick**. William Morrow, 2015. 240pp. 978-0-0622-0269-7.
> *The Cartoon Guide to Calculus*. Written **Larry Gonick**. 2011. 256pp 978-0-0616-8909-3.
> *The Cartoon Guide to Chemistry*. Written by **Larry Gonick** and **Craig Criddle**. HarperCollins, 2005. 256pp. 978-0-0609-3677-8.

The Cartoon Guide to Genetics. Written by **Larry Gonick** and **Mark Wheelis**. HarperCollins. 1991. 224pp. 978-0-0627-3099-2.

The Cartoon Guide to Physics. Written by **Larry Gonick** and **Art Huffman**. HarperCollins, 1991. 224pp. 978-0-0627-3100-5.

The Cartoon Guide to Sex. Written by **Larry Gonick** and **Christine Devault**. HarperCollins, 1999. 256pp. 978-0-0627-3431-0.

The Cartoon Guide to Statistics. Written by **Larry Gonick** and **Woollcott Smith**. HarperCollins, 1993. 230pp. 978-0-0627-3102-9.

The Cartoon Guide to the Environment. Written by **Larry Gonick** and **Alice Outwater**. William Morrow, 1996. 240pp. 978-0-0627-3274-3.

Charles Darwin's On the Origin of Species. Written by **Michael Keller**. Illustrated by **Nicole Fuller**. Rodale Books, 2009. 192pp. 978-1-60529-948-8. T

A graphic adaptation of Darwin's *On the Origin of Species*, one of the most famously contested books written of all time.

Clan Apis. Written and Illustrated by **Jay Hosler**. Active Synapse, 2013–2014. 2013. 160pp. 978-1-4823-4745-6; 2013. 160pp. 978-0-9906171-0-5, hardcover. A 🌸

A unique look at the life cycle of the honey bee from a humorous, charming, and informative point of view: as a biography. Join honey bee Nyuki from the earliest stages of her life as a larvae to her role in the overall relationship with her hive and the flowers and insects that live in her world. From her birth to her death, every aspect of a honey bee's life is given focus with added humor and attention to detail. The first printing of the graphic novel was recognized by YALSA's Popular Paperbacks for Young Adults as a 2002 pick for *Graphic Novels: Superheroes and Beyond* selection list.

© 2016 Jay Hosler.

Dignifying Science: Stories about Women Scientists. Written by **Jim Ottaviani**. Illustrated by **Donna Barr, Lea Hernandez, Carla Speed McNeil**, and various. GT Labs, 2009, 3rd edition. 144pp. 978-0-9788037-3-5. T

Science has been stereotyped as a profession for men only, but Ottaviani's collection showcases seven women who have left their indelible mark in the field of science. The profiled women include Marie Sklodovska, Hedy Lamarr, Lise Meitner, Rosalind Franklin, Barbara McClintock, Birute Galdikas, and Marie Curie. The artwork is handled by a handful of talented female artists including Marie Severin, Carla Speed McNeil, Jen Sorensen, Stephanie Gladden, Donna Barr, Roberta Gregory, Linda Medley, Lea Hernandez, and Anne Timmons.

© 2016 Jim Ottaviani and GT Labs.

Evolution: The Story of Life on Earth. Written by **Jay Hosler**. Illustrated by **Kevin Cannon** and **Zander Cannon**. Hill and Wang, 2011. 160pp. 978-0-8090-4311-8. T

>   Featuring many of the same characters seen in 2009's *The Stuff of Life: A Graphic Guide to Genetics and DNA* (by Mark Schultz and the Cannons) alien scientist Bloort-183 takes King Floorsh 727 and Prince Floorsh 418 on a tour of the new Holographic Museum of Earth Evolution. As he has done in the past Hosler used a fictional setup to convey scientific information.

Fallout: J. Robert Oppenheimer, Leo Szilard, and the Political Science of the Atomic Bomb. Written by **Jim Ottaviani**. Illustrated by **Jeff Parker**, **Janine Johnston**, **Vince Locke**, **Bernie Mireault**, **Steve Lieber**, and various. GT Labs, 2013. 240pp. 978-0-9660106-3-3. O

A look at the creation of the atomic bomb as seen from the perspectives of Leó Szilárd, a pioneering physicist who first thought of the possibility of creating the atomic weapon, and J. Robert Oppenheimer, the physicist in charge of the famed Manhattan Project, as they worked an uneasy alliance with the U.S. government. The project was created during the height of World War II and resulted in the design, production, and detonation of the atomic bombs dropped over Hiroshima and Nagasaki in Japan in 1945.

© 2016 Jim Ottaviani and GT Labs.

Feynman. Written by **Jim Ottaviani**. Illustrated by **Leland Myrick**. First Second Books, 2013. 272pp. 978-1-59643-259-8, hardcover; 978-1-59643-827-9. O

>   A graphic look at the life of Richard Feynman, the Nobel Prize–winning quantum physicist who worked on the Manhattan Project and later on such things as the *Challenger* disaster investigation and who was one of the most accomplished minds of the 20th century.

Howtoons. Written by **Nick Dragotta**, **Saul Griffith**, **Fred Van Lente**, and **Joost Bonsen**. Illustrated by **Sandy Jarrell**, **Meredith McClaren**, **Tom Fowler**, and **Nick Dragotta**. Image Comics, 2014–2015. Y ◎

Join tweens Celine and Tucker as they discover 50 DIY projects that kids can make from equipment found in a garage and the local hardware store. The second volume has a sci-fi angle as Celine and Tuck use their gadgeteering skills to survive in the far future with plenty of more DIY project to try out.

Vol. 1: Tools of Mass Destruction. 2014. 360pp. 978-1-63215-101-8. *Vol. 2: Re-Ignition.* 2015. 160pp. 978-1-63215-056-1.

© 2016 Image Comics.

Human Body Theater. Written and Illustrated by **Maris Wicks**. First Second Books, 2015. 234pp. 978-1-62672-277-4, hardcover. Y

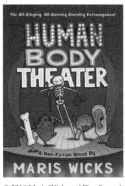

Welcome to the Human Body Theater where the master of ceremonies puts on a theater show featuring all of the organs of the human body! As the MC starts off as the skeleton, the organs are part of her "costume" as she gets dressed before your very eyes! A unique and fun theatrical look at what makes us all so special inside and out.

© 2016 Maris Wicks and First Second.

The Imitation Game. Written by **Jim Ottaviani**. Illustrated by **Leland Purvis**. Abrams, 2016. 240pp. 978-1-4197-1893-9. T 🎭

A biography of the noted scientist and mathematician whose story was told in the 2014 film of the same name. Turing's work helped to decrypt the German Enigma code during World War II, but his sexuality led to legal persecution which contributed to his death. The book was on YALSA's 2017 Great Graphic Novels for Teens list.

Last of the Sandwalkers. Written and Illustrated by **Jay Hosler**. First Second Books, 2015. 320pp. 978-1-62672-024-4. T 🎭 ◎

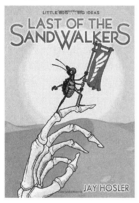

Nestled in the desert under a palm tree, an entire civilization of beetles exists. One beetle named Lucy is a scientist, and she decides to set forth from the safety of her home to explore the great wilderness where she discovers that they are definitely not alone! Jay Hosler mixes science and humor in another fun look at our world's smaller cohabitants. The book was recognized by YALSA as a Great Graphic Novel for Teens selection in 2016.

© 2016 Jay Hosler and First Second.

The Manga Guides. No Starch Press, 2009–. T Japanese manga.

These translated guides from a variety of writers and artists concentrate on various areas of science including mathematics. Most of them have a plot that involves a high school student who needs to be tutored in a particular subject with the "tutoring" explaining the subject to the readers. Over 40 volumes have been published in Japan, with only those listed below currently available in English. However, more are expected.

The Manga Guide to Biochemistry. Written by **Masaharu Takemura**. Illustrated by **Kikuyaro**. 2011. 272pp. 978-1-59327-276-0.

The Manga Guide to Calculus. Written by **Hiroyuki Kojima**. Illustrated by **Shin Togami**. 2009. 256pp. 978-1-59327-194-7.

The Manga Guide to Databases. Written by **Mana Takahashi**. Illustrated by **Shoko Azuma**. 2009. 224pp. 978-1-59327-190-9.

The Manga Guide to Electricity. Written by **Kazuhiro Fujitaki**. Illustrated by **Matsuda**. 2009. 232pp. 978-1-59327-197-8.

The Manga Guide to Linear Algebra. Written by **Shin Takahashi**. Illustrated by **Iroha Inoue**. 2012. 264pp. 978-1-59327-413-9.

The Manga Guide to Microprocessors. Written by **Michio Shubuya** Illustrated by **Takashi Tonagi.**

The Manga Guide to Molecular Biology. Written by **Masaharu Takemura**. Illustrated by **Sakura**. 2009. 256pp. 978-1-59327-202-9.

The Manga Guide to Physics. Written by **Hideo Nitta**. Illustrated by **Keita Takatsu**. 2009. 248pp. 978-1-59327-196-1.

The Manga Guide to Physiology. Written by **Etsuro Tanaka**. Illustrated by **Keiko Koyama**. 2015. 256pp. 978-1-59327-440-5.

The Manga Guide to Regression Analysis. Written by **Shin Takahashi**. Illustrated by **Iroha Inoue**. 2016. 224pp. 978-1-59327-419-1.

The Manga Guide to Relativity. Written by **Hideo Nitta** and **Masafumi Yamamoto**. Illustrated by **Keita Takatsu**. 2011. 192pp. 978-1-59327-272-2.

The Manga Guide to Statistics. Written by **Shin Takahashi**. 2008. 224pp. 978-1-59327-189-3.

The Manga Guide to the Universe. Written by **Kenji Ishikawa** and **Kiyoshi Kawabata**. Illustrated by **Yukita Hiiragi**. 2011. 256pp. 978-1-59327-267-8.

Max Axiom Super Scientist. Capstone Press, 2007–. Y

Max Axiom is a super-smart scientist with special abilities that help with his research like X-ray vision glasses, a time traveling coat, and the ability to shrink. It is up to Max Axiom to use his superintelligence to help out others and occasionally save the day while explaining the topic of the book. Max explains many aspects of science like the scientific method, volcanoes, light, ecosystems, and bacteria. These books are great jumping-off points for students to get a basic understanding of these topics they may be learning about in class or starting a science project on.

Adventures in Sound with Max Axiom, Super Scientist. Written by **Emily Sohn**. Illustrated by **Cynthia Martin** and **Anne Timmons**. 2007. 32pp. 978-0-7368-7889-0.

The Attractive Story of Magnetism with Max Axiom, Super Scientist. Written by **Andrea Gianopoulos**. Illustrated by **Cynthia Martin** and **Barbara Schulz**. 2008. 32pp. 978-1-4296-1769-7.

The Basics of Cell Life with Max Axiom, Super Scientist. Written by **Amber J. Keyser**. Illustrated by **Cynthia Martin** and **Barbara Schulz**. 2010. 32pp. 978-1-4296-3904-0.

A Crash Course in Forces and Motion with Max Axiom, Super Scientist. Written by **Emily Sohn**. Illustrated by **Steve Erwin and Charles Barnett III**. 2007. 32pp. 978-0-7368-7890-6.

Decoding Genes with Max Axiom, Super Scientist. Written by **Amber J. Keyser**. Illustrated by **Tod Smith** and **Al Milgrom**. 2010. 32pp. 978-1-4296-4862-2.

The Dynamic World of Chemical Reactions with Max Axiom, Super Scientist. Written by **Agnieszka Biskup**. Illustrated by **Cynthia Martin** and **Barbara Schulz**. 2011. 32pp. 978-1-4296-5635-1.

The Earth-Shaking Facts about Earthquakes with Max Axiom, Super Scientist. Written by **Katherine Krohn**. Illustrated by **Tod Smith** and **Al Milgrom**. 2008. 32pp. 978-1-4296-1759-8.

Engineering an Awesome Recycling Center with Max Axiom, Super Scientist. Written by **Nikole Brooks Bethea**. Illustrated by **Pop Art Studios**. 2013. 32pp. 978-1-6206-5699-0.

Engineering a Totally Rad Skateboard with Max Axiom, Super Scientist. Written by **Tammy Enz**. Illustrated by **Pop Art Studios**. 2013. 32pp. 978-1-6206-5703-4.

Exploring Ecosystems with Max Axiom, Super Scientist. Written by **Agniesezka Biskup**. Illustrated by **Tod Smith**. 2007. 32pp. 978-0-7368-7894-4.

The Explosive World of Volcanoes with Max Axiom, Super Scientist. Written by **Christopher Harbo**. Illustrated by **Tod Smith**. 2008. 32pp. 978-1-4296-1770-3.

The Illuminating World of Light with Max Axiom, Super Scientist. Written by **Emily Sohn**. Illustrated by **Nick Derington**. 2008. 32pp. 978-1-4296-1768-0.

Investigating the Scientific Method with Max Axiom, Super Scientist. Written by **Donald Lemke**. Illustrated by **Tod Smith** and **Al Milgrom**. 2008. 32pp. 978-1-4296-1760-4.

A Journey into Adaptation with Max Axiom, Super Scientist. Written by **Agniesezka Biskup**. Illustrated by **Cynthia Martin** and **Barbara Schulz**. 2007. 32pp. 978-0-7368-7892-0.

A Journey through the Digestive System with Max Axiom, Super Scientist. Written by **Emily Sohn**. Illustrated by **Cynthia Martin** and **Barbara Schulz**. 2009. 32pp. 978-1-4296-3452-6.

Lessons in Science Safety with Max Axiom, Super Scientist. Written by **Donald B. Lemke** and **Thomas K. Adamson**. Illustrated by **Tod Smith** and **Bill Anderson**. 2007. 32pp. 978-0-7368-7887-6.

The Powerful World of Energy with Max Axiom, Super Scientist. Written by **Agniesezka Biskup**. Illustrated by **Cynthia Martin** and **Anne Timmons**. 2009. 32pp. 978-1-4296-3450-2.

A Refreshing Look at Renewable Energy with Max Axiom, Super Scientist. Written by **Katherine Krohn**. Illustrated by **Cynthia Martin** and **Barbara Schulz**. 2010. 32pp. 978-1-4296-3902-6.

The Science of Baseball with Max Axium, Super Scientist. Written by **David L. Dreier**. Illustrated by **Maurizio Campidelli**. 2015. 32pp. 978-1-4914-6087-0.

The Science of Basketball with Max Axium, Super Scientist. Written by **Nikole Brooks Bethea**. Illustrated by **Caio Cacau**. 2015. 32pp. 978-1-4914-6088-7.

The Science of Football with Max Axium, Super Scientist. Written by **Nikole Brooks Bethea**. Illustrated by **Caio Cacau**. 2015. 32pp. 978-1-4914-6089-4.

The Science of Hockey with Max Axium, Super Scientist. Written by **Blake Hoena**. Illustrated by **Caio Cacau**. 2015. 32pp. 978-1-4914-6090-0.

The Shocking World of Electricity with Max Axiom, Super Scientist. Written by **Liam O'Donnell**. Illustrated by **Richard Dominguez** and **Charles Barnett III**. 2007. 32pp. 978-0-7368-7888-3.

The Solid Truth about States of Matter with Max Axiom, Super Scientist. 2009. Written by **Agniesezka Biskup**. Illustrated by **Cynthia Martin** and **Barbara Schulz**. 32pp. 978-1-4296-3451-9.

Super Cool Chemical Reaction Activities with Max Axiom. Written by **Agnieszka Biskup**. Illustrated by **Maurizio Campidelli**. 2016. 32pp. 978-1-4062-9327-2.

Super Cool Mechanical Activities with Max Axiom. Written by **Tammy Enz**. Illustrated by **Marcelo Baez**. 2015. 32pp. 978-1-4914-2284-7.

The Surprising World of Bacteria with Max Axiom, Super Scientist. Written by **Agnieszka Biskup**. Illustrated by **Tod Smith**. 2010. 32pp. 978-1-4296-4863-9.

Understanding Global Warming with Max Axiom, Super Scientist. Written by **Agniesezka Biskup**. Illustrated by **Cynthia Martin** and **Bill Anderson**. 2008. 32pp. 978-1-4296-1767-3.

Understanding Photosynthesis with Max Axiom, Super Scientist. Written by **Liam O'Donnell**. Illustrated by **Richard Dominguez** and **Charles Barnett III**. 2007. 32pp. 978-0-7368-7893-7.

Understanding Viruses with Max Axiom, Super Scientist. Written by **Agniesezka Biskup**. Illustrated by **Nick Derington**. 2009. 32pp. 978-1-4296-3453-3.

The Whirlwind World of Hurricanes with Max Axiom, Super Scientist. Written by **Katherine Krohn**. Illustrated by **Cynthia Martin** and **Al Milgrom**. 2011. 32pp. 978-1-4296-5636-8.

The World of Food Chains with Max Axiom, Super Scientist. Written by **Liam O'Donnell**. Illustrated by **Cynthia Martin** and **Bill Anderson**. 2007. 32pp. 978-0-7368-7891-3.

Primates: The Fearless Science of Jane Goodall, Dian Fossey, and Biruté Galdikas. Written by **Jim Ottaviani**. Illustrated by **Maris Wicks**. First Second Books, 2013. 144pp. 978-1-59643-865-1. T

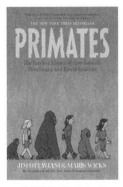

A look at three of the best-known primatologists and how they helped us to understand primates better.

© 2016 Jim Ottaviani and First Second.

Reading with Pictures: Comics That Make Kids Smarter. Edited by **Josh Elder**. Written and Illustrated by various. Andrews McMeel Publishing, 2014. 184pp. 978-1-4494-5878-2, hardcover. Y

Edited by Josh Elder, the collection features work of over a dozen creators combined with the nation's leading supporters of visual literacy to create a unique classroom tool that addresses topics in math, social studies, language arts, and science that kids will enjoy.

© 2016 Andrews McMeel Publishing

The Sandwalk Adventures. Written and Illustrated by **Jay Hosler**. Active Synapse, 2013–2014. 2013. 160pp. 978-1-4823-8500-7; 2014. 160pp. 978-0-9906171-1-2, hardcover. A

© 2016 Jay Hosler.

Ever wonder what Charles Darwin would say to a follicle mite named Mara who's living in his left eyebrow? In Jay Hosler's humorous and informative style, Charles and Mara strike up an unlikely friendship while strolling through his thinking path called the Sandwalk. After reassuring Mara that he's no deity, Charles explains to her his theories on Natural Selection, a subject he knows a great deal about, and how we all fit together in our role in the universe.

Science: A Discovery in Comics. Written and Illustrated by **Margreet De Heer**. NBM Publishing 2013. 192pp. 978-1-56163-750-8. T

An introduction to the basic concepts of Science. Included are three basic types of scientists, famous scientists, and scientific disciplines.

Science Comics. First Second Books, 2016–. Y ◎

A new series of non-fiction books for middle-grade readers that debuted in 2016. New editions should come out twice a year and include a broad amount of subjects related to science in a fresh new format.

Bats: Learning to Fly. Written and Illustrated by **Falynn Koch**. 2017. 128pp. 978-1-62672-409-9, hardcover; 978-1-62672-408-2.

After a small brown bat is injured during a nature hike, the bat is taken to a rehabilitation center where the remarkable world of bats is revealed. Come and learn how the bat flies, eats, live, and more!

Coral Reefs: Cities of the Ocean. Written and Illustrated by **Maris Wicks**. 2016. 128pp. 978-1-62672-146-3, hardcover; 978-1-62672-145-6.

© 2016 First Second.

The remarkable coral reefs of the ocean are explored as well as the creatures that live in them as home—from dolphins to coral polyps.

Dinosaurs: Fossils and Feathers. Written by **MK Reed**. Illustrated by **Joe Flood**. 2016. 128pp. 978-1-62672-144-9, hardcover; 978-1-62672-143-2. ◎

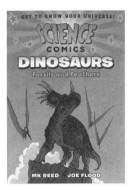

A scientific look at dinosaurs over time. From the Jurassic age to the Cretaceous age dinosaurs roam the Earth. Join the Science Comics team as they look at the dinosaurs themselves as well as the paleontologists who have tried to make sense of the fossils they've discovered. How did the dinosaurs live and die? Read and find out!

Dogs: From Predators to Protectors. Written and Illustrated by **Andy Hirsch**. 2017. 128pp. 978-1-62672-767-0, hardcover; 978-1-62672-768-7. Y

How did man's best friend evolve from the dangerous predators of the past? Are all dogs related to wolves? What's the difference between a Chihuahua and a Saint Bernard? Find all of this and more in the exciting world of dogs comes to comics!

Flying Machines: How the Wright Brothers Soared. Written by **Alison Wilgus**. Illustrated by Molly Brooks. 2017. 128pp. 978-1-62672-140-1, hardcover; 978-1-62672-139-5. Y

Ages ago mankind dreamed of flight. Stories of Icarus gave way centuries later to two men from Dayton, Ohio with a dream to fly. Join Wilbur and Orville Wright on the fields of North Carolina as they battled bad weather, fierce competition, mechanical failures in more for their quest to fly where eagles dare.

Plagues: The Microscopic Battlefield. Written and Illustrated by **Falynn Koch**. 2017. 128pp. 978-1-62672-753-3, hardcover; 978-1-62672-752-6. Y

A look at the little critters that are responsible for some of our history's worst diseases. Learn about how the body fights against infections, builds immunities to diseases, and how technology has changed how we control and treat diseases.

Volcanoes: Fire and Life. Written and Illustrated by **Jon Chad**. 128pp. 978-1-62672-361-0, hardcover; 978-1-62672-360-3.

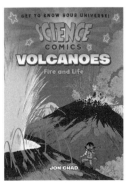

Come and see the magnificence that is located under the Earth's crust. Volcanoes have had a continuing impact on our planet for millions of years. See how they have affected continental shifts, created land masses, and play a continuing role for our planet.

Stuff of Life. Written by **Mark Schultz**. Illustrated by **Kevin Cannon** and **Zander Cannon**. Hill and Wang, 2009. 150pp. 978-0-8090-8947-5. T

> Meet the Squinch, an asexual race from the planet Glargal. When their race is at risk of extinction, interplanetary biologist Bloort 183 is sent to study Earth's long evolutionary history and scientific concepts with the hope of it helping his race. The Squinch returns in *Evolution: The Story of Life on Earth* (see earlier in this section).

Suspended in Language: Niels Bohr's Life, Discoveries, And the Century He Shaped. Written by **Jim Ottaviani**. Illustrated **by Jay Hosler, Linda Medley**, and various. GT Labs, 2009, second edition. 332pp. 978-0-9788037-2-8. O

> An ambitious look at the life of Niels Bohr, a Danish physicist who helped to define the significance of the atomic structure and quantum mechanics. His work as a scientist earned him the Nobel Prize in 1922, and after escaping from occupied Denmark during World War II, he eventually made it to America where he spent time as a consultant in the creation of the Manhattan Project.

© 2016 Jim Ottaviani and GT Labs.

The Thrilling Adventures of Lovelace and Babbage the (Mostly) True Story of the First Computer. Written and Illustrated by **Sydney Padua**. Pantheon Books, 2015. 320pp. 978-0-307-90827-8, hardcover. T

> In the 1830s mathematician and inventor Charles Babbage encountered the much younger Ada Byron later Ada King, the Countess of Lovelace (daughter of Lord Byron and historically known as Ada Lovelace). Together they came up with the idea of the building and programing of a proposed "Analytical Engine"—an early idea for a general purpose computer. After portraying the real events, Padua presents stories from a world where the machine was built. A number of historical figures appear often quoting actual things they said about the pair.

T-Minus: Race to the Moon. Written by **Jim Ottaviani**. Illustrated by **Kevin Cannon** and **Zander Cannon.** Aladdin, 2009. 128pp. 978-1-4169-4960-2. T 🏵

> A look at the space race between the United States and the Soviet Union to see who was first to get to the moon. The book was recognized by YALSA in 2010 for its Great Graphic Novels for Teens selection list.

© 2016 Jim Ottaviani and GT Labs.

Trinity: A Graphic History of the First Atomic Bomb. Written and Illustrated by **Jonathan Fetter-Vorm**. Hill and Wang/Farrar, Strauss, and Giroux, 2012. 154pp. 978-0-8090-9468-4. T 🏆

> A semi-fictionalized account of the race to create the first atomic bomb and the hard decisions facing the United States to use it. The book was recognized by YALSA's Great Graphic Novels for Teens selection list in 2013.

Two-Fisted Science: Stories about Scientists. Written by **Jim Ottaviani**. Illustrated by various. GT Labs, 2010, third edition. 128pp. 978-0-9788037-4-2. T

© 2016 Jim Ottaviani and GT Labs.

> A collection of stories of famous scientists and oddball inventors from nuclear physicists to amateur locksmiths who helped change the world in their own creative ways. The collection includes stories and funny anecdotes about Albert Einstein, Niels Bohr, and Richard Feynman that celebrate their services to science but also showcase their humanity.

When Fish Got Feet, When Bugs Were Big, and When Dinos Dawned: A Cartoon Prehistory of Life on Earth. Written and Illustrated by **Hannah Bonner**. National Geographic Kids, 2015. 128pp. 978-1-4263-2104-7. Y

> A collection of three volumes in National Geographic Kids' line of titles focusing on the early days of planet Earth and the dangerous world that the animals lived in the prehistory before man when dinosaurs walked the Earth!

Wild Ocean: Sharks, Whales, Rays, and Other Endangered Sea Creatures. Edited by **Matt Dembicki**. Written and Illustrated by various. Fulcrum Publishing, 2014. 156pp. 978-1-938486-38-8. T

> A collection of short stories by a variety of creators that focus on endangered animals of the oceans. The stories range from fiction, non-fiction, and folklore tales.

Miscellaneous Non-Fiction

A miscellaneous collection of non-fiction graphic novels that cover a broad spectrum that doesn't have an overall subgenre. Titles included here include discussions on religion, philosophy, travel, and even how radio shows are done!

Cartoon Guide to Economics. Written by **Yoram Bauman**. Illustrated by **Grady Klein**. Hill and Wang, 2010–2011. T

> A humorous, well-organized, and direct look at the general concepts of both microeconomics and macroeconomics.
>
> *Vol. 1: Microeconomics*. 2010. 224pp. 978-0-8090-9481-3.
> *Vol. 2: Macroeconomics*. 2011. 240pp. 978-0-8090-3361-4.

Cartoon Introduction to Philosophy. Written by **Michael F. Patton**. Illustrated by **Kevin Cannon**. Hill and Wang, 2015. 176pp. 978-0-8090-3362-1. T

A cartoon guide to the basic concepts of philosophy.

Cool Japan Guide: Fun in the Land of Manga, Lucky Cats and Ramen. Written and Illustrated by **Abby Denson**. Tuttle Publishing, 2015. 125pp. 978-4-8053-1279-7. T

© 2016 Abby Denson.

Have you ever wanted to go to Japan, the land of the Rising Sun? Creator Abby Denson has created a visual guide to traveling to Japan—the land anime, manga, cosplay, hot springs, and sushi! The guidebook looks at the culture of Japan, pronunciation of words, geek culture of Japan, toilets, various kinds of food unique to each area of Japan, vending machines, and even buying tickets for the Shinkansen train. A fun visual guide to a beautiful country you will want to get tickets for after reading this book.

Eat That Frog! From SmarterComics. Written by **Brian Tracy**. Illustrated by **Paul Maybury**. SmarterComics, 2012. 80pp. 978-1-61082-002-8. T

A guide for procrastinators on how to budget their time and how to be the most productive they can be. A helpful guide for those of us—including myself—who need to make the most of their busy day and to get tasks done in time.

Health Care Reform: What It Is, Why It's Necessary, and How It Works. Written by **Jonathan Gruber**. Illustrated by **Nathan Schreiber**. Hill and Wang, 2011. 160pp. 978-0-8090-5397-1. O

This is a documentary-style graphic novel about health-care reform, specifically the Affordable Care Act passed by President Obama. The author of this graphic novel, an architect of both the ACA and of Massachusetts health-care reform plan, writes this book in a sort of question-and-answer format. Through the different types of people who will be affected by the law, he answers potential question and concerns about the law to clear up misconceptions and why he believes this plan will succeed.

Information Now: A Graphic Guide to Student Research. Written by **Matt Upson** and **C. Michael Hall**. Illustrated by **Kevin Cannon**. University of Chicago Press, 2015. 128pp. 978-0-226-09569-1. O

A visually engaging research guide for undergrads, faculty, and librarians on how to succeed in the world of academic research.

Michael Townsend's Amazing Greek Myths of Wonder and Blunders. Written and Illustrated by **Michael Townsend**. Dial Books for Young Readers, 2010. 160pp. 978-0-8037-3308-4, hardcover. T 🏅

Nine retellings of the most famous of the Greek myths but with lots of chicken, stupid sheep, bunnies, and toasters thrown in. The selection was recognized as a Great Graphic Novel for Teens on YALSA's selection list in 2011.

Out on the Wire: The Storytelling Secrets of the New Masters of Radio. Written and Illustrated by **Jessica Abel**. Broadway Books, 2015. 240pp. 978-0-385-34843-0. O

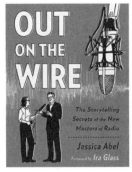

© 2016 Jessica Abel.

A unique oral history of the current masters of online radio. Join Jessica Abel, noted comic book creator and passionate devotee to narrative radio, as she looks at seven radio shows and presents an inside look at how they construct the narratives for their shows that reach audiences via podcasts for millions of listeners. The radio shows and their staff included in this retrospective are *This American Life*, *The Moth*, *Radiolab*, *Planet Money*, *Snap Judgement*, *Serial*, and *Invisibilia*.

Philosophy: A Discovery in Comics. Written and Illustrated by **Margreet De Heer**. NBM Publishing, 2012. 120pp. 978-1-56163-698-3, hardcover. T

An introduction to the complex and weighty topic of Philosophy all told in a fun and enlightening illustrated format.

Religion: A Discovery in Comics. Written and Illustrated by **Margreet De Heer**. NBM Publishing, 2015. 120pp. 978-1-56163-994-6, hardcover. T

A look at the five major world religions and at modern spirituality.

Appendix I

Recommended Additional Book Sources

General References on Comic Books and Graphic Novels

Baetens, Jan. *The Graphic Novel: An Introduction*. New York: Cambridge University Press, 2015.

Beaty, Bart H. and Stephen Weiner, eds. *Critical Survey of Graphic Novels* Series. Ipswich, MA: Salem Press, 2012.

> *Heroes and Superheroes*
> *History, Theme, and Technique*
> *Independent and Underground Classics*

Bendis, Brian Michael. *Words for Pictures: The Art and Business of Writing Comics and Graphic Novels*. Berkeley, CA: Watson-Guptill, 2014.

Booker, M. Keith, ed. *Comics through Time*. Santa Barbara, CA: Greenwood Press, 2014.

Booker, M. Keith, ed. *Encyclopedia of Comic Books and Graphic Novels*. Santa Barbara, CA: Greenwood Press, 2010.

Caputo, Tony C. *Visual Storytelling: The Art and Technique*. New York: Watson-Guptill, 2002.

Duncan, Randy and Matthew J. Smith, eds. *Icons of the American Comic Book*. Santa Barbara: CA: Greenwood, 2013.

Eisner, Will. *Comics and Sequential Art: Principles and Practices from the Legendary Cartoonist*. New York: W.W. Norton, 2008.

Eisner, Will. *Graphic Storytelling and Visual Narrative: Principles and Practices from the Legendary Cartoonist*. New York: W.W. Norton, 2008.

Forbeck, Matt. *Marvel Encyclopedia*. New York: DK, 2014.

Gertler, Nat and Steve Lieber. *Complete Idiot's Guide to Creating a Graphic Novel*. New York: Alpha Books, 2004.

Gravett, Paul. *Graphic Novels: Everything You Need to Know*. New York: Harper Design International, 2005.

Hoppenstand, Gary, ed. *The Graphic Novel*. Ipswich, MA: Salem Press, 2014.

Kan, Kat, ed. *Graphic Novels and Comic Books.* New York: H.W. Wilson, 2010.

Kannenberg, Gene. *500 Essential Graphic Novels: The Ultimate Guide.* New York: HarperCollins, 2008.

Kneece, Mark. *The Art of Comic Book Writing: The Definitive Guide to Outlining, Scripting, and Pitching Your Sequential Art Stories.* Berkeley, CA: Watson-Guptill, 2015.

McCloud, Scott. *Making Comics:* Storytelling Secrets of Comics, Manga, and Graphic Novels. New York: HarperTrade, 2006.

McCloud, Scott. *Reinventing Comics: How Imagination and Technology Are Revolutionizing an Art Form.* New York: HarperTrade, 2000.

McCloud, Scott. *Understanding Comics: The Invisible Art.* New York: HarperTrade, 1994.

Pendergast, Sara, ed. *U-X-L Graphic Novelists.* Detroit, MI: U-X-L/Thomson Gale, 2007.

Pilcher, Tim and Brad Brooks. *The Essential Guide to World Comics.* London: Collins and Brown, 2005.

Wallace, Dan, et al. *The DC Comics Encyclopedia: The Definitive Guide to the Characters of the DC Universe.* New York: DK, 2008.

Weiner, Steve. *Faster Than a Speeding Bullet: The Rise of the Graphic Novel.* New York: NBM Publishing Company, 2003.

Books about Asian Comic Books, Manga, and More

Beaty, Bart H. and Stephen Weiner, eds. *Critical Survey of Graphic Novels Manga.* Ipswich, MA: Salem Press, 2012.

Brenner, Robin. *Understanding Manga and Anime.* Westport, CT: Libraries Unlimited, 2007.

Campos, Cristian. *1,000 Ideas by 100 Manga Artists.* Beverly, MA: Rockport Publishers, 2008.

Koyama-Richard, Brigitte. *One Thousand Years of Manga.* Paris: Flammarion, 2008.

Layman, John and David Hutchison. *The Complete Idiot's Guide to Drawing Manga Illustrated.* Indianapolis, IN: Alpha Books, 2008.

Schodt, Frederick L. *Dreamland Japan: Writings on Modern Manga.* New York: DIANE Publishing Company, 2001.

Schodt, Frederick L. *Manga! Manga!: The World of Japanese Comics.* New York: Kodansha International, 1998.

Wong, Wendy Siuyi. *Hong Kong Comics: A History of Manhua.* New York: Princeton Architectural Press, 2002.

Yadeo, Jason. *The Rough Guide to Manga.* New York: Rough Guides, 2009.

Titles for Collection Development and Use in Libraries

Cornog, Martha and Timothy Perper, eds. *Graphic Novels beyond the Basics: Insights and Issues for Libraries.* Westport, CT: Libraries Unlimited, 2009.

Crawford, Philip Charles. *Graphic Novels 101: Selecting and Using Graphic Novels to Promote Literacy for Children and Young Adults*. New York: Hi Willow Research & Publishing, 2003.

Goldsmith, Francisca. *Graphic Novels Now: Building, Managing, and Marketing a Dynamic Collection*. Chicago: American Library Association, 2005.

Gorman, Michele. *Getting Graphic!: Using Graphic Novels to Promote Literacy with Teens*. New York: Linworth Publishing, Incorporated, 2003.

Miller, Steve. *Developing and Promoting Graphic Novel Collections*. New York: Neal-Schuman Publishers, Incorporated, 2005.

Robbins, Scott and Snow Wildsmith. *A Parent's Guide to the Best Kids' Comics: Choosing Titles Your Children Will Love*. Iola, WI: Krause Publishing, 2012.

Serchay, David S. *The Librarian's Guide to Graphic Novels for Adults*. Chicago: Neal-Schuman/ALA, 2009.

Serchay, David S. *The Librarian's Guide to Graphic Novels for Children and Tweens*. Chicago: Neal-Schuman/ALA, 2008.

Thompson, Jason. *Manga: The Complete Guide*. New York: Ballantine Books, 2007.

Weiner. Robert G., ed. *Graphic Novels and Comics in Libraries and Archives: Essays On Readers, Research, History and Cataloging*. Jefferson, NC: McFarland and Co, 2010.

Weiner, Stephen and Danny Fingeroth. *101 Outstanding Graphic Novels*. New York: NBM, 2015.

Titles for Using Comics and Graphic Novels in the Classroom

Bakis, Maureen. *The Graphic Novel Classroom: POWerful Teaching and Learning with Images*. New York: Skyhorse Publishing, 2014.

Brozo, William, Gary Moorman, and Carla K. Meyer. *Wham!: Teaching with Graphic Novels across the Curriculum*. New York: Teachers College Press, 2014.

Carter, James Bucky. *Building Literacy Connections with Graphic Novels: Page by Page, Panel by Panel*. Urbana, IL: National Council of Teachers of English, 2007.

Frey, Nancy and Douglas B. Fisher, eds. *Teaching Visual Literacy: Using Comic Books, Graphic Novels, Anime, Cartoons, and More to Develop Comprehension and Thinking Skills*. Thousand Oaks, CA: Corwin Press, 2008.

Lyga, Allyson A. W. with Barry Lyga. *Graphic Novels in Your Media Center: A Definitive Guide*. Englewood, NJ: Libraries Unlimited, 2004.

Monnin, Katie. *Teaching Graphic Novels: Practical Strategies for the Secondary ELA Classroom*. Gainesville, FL: Maupin House, 2013.

Novak, Ryan. *Teaching Graphic Novels in the Classroom: Building Literacy and Comprehension*. Waco, TX: Prufrock Press, 2013.

Syma, Carrye Kay and Robert G. Weiner, eds. *Graphic Novels and Comics in the Classroom: Essays on the Educational Power of Sequential Art*. Jefferson, NC: McFarland and Co., 2013.

History and General Information for Comic Books, Characters, and Creators

Arnaudo, Marco. Translated By Jamie Richards. *The Myth of the Superhero*. Baltimore, MD: Johns Hopkins University Press.

Bender, Hy. *The Sandman Companion: A Dreamer's Guide to the Award-Winning Comic Series*. New York: DC Comics, 2000.

Bongco, Mila. *Reading Comics: Language, Culture and the Concept of the Superhero in Comic Books*. New York: Garland Publishing, Incorporated, 2000.

Brod, Harry. *Superman Is Jewish?: How Comic Book Superheroes Came to Serve Truth, Justice, and the Jewish-American Way*. New York: Free Press, 2012.

Chinn, Mike. *Writing and Illustrating the Graphic Novel*. New York: Barron's Educational Series, Incorporated, 2004.

Conroy, Mike. *500 Comic Book Villains*. New York: Barron's Educational Series, Incorporated, 2004.

Conroy, Mike. *500 Great Comic Book Action Heroes*. New York: Barron's Educational Series, Incorporated, 2003.

Conversations with Comic Artists Series. Jackson: University Press of Mississippi, 2007.

Alan Moore: Conversations	*Howard Chaykin: Conversations*
Art Spiegelman: Conversations	*Michael Allred: Conversations*
Carl Barks: Conversations	*Peter Bagge: Conversations*
Chester Brown: Conversations	*Peter Kuper: Conversations*
Daniel Clowes: Conversations	*R. Crumb: Conversations*
Dave Sim: Conversations	*Seth: Conversations*
Ed Brubaker: Conversations	*Stan Lee: Conversations*
Harvey Pekar: Conversations	*Will Eisner: Conversations*

Conway, Gerry, ed. *Webslinger: SF and Comic Writers on Your Friendly Neighborhood Spider-Man*. Dallas, TX: Benbella Books, 2007.

Daniels, Les. *Batman: The Complete History*. New York: Chronicle Books, 2004.

Daniels, Les. *DC Comics: A Celebration of the World's Favorite Comic Book Heroes*. New York: Watson-Guptill, 2003.

Daniels, Les. *Marvel: Five Fabulous Decades of the World's Greatest Comics*. New York: Harry N. Abrams, Incorporated, 1993

De Haven, Tom. *Our Hero: Superman on Earth*. New Haven, CT: Yale University Press, 2010.

Duin, Steve and Mike Richardson. *Comics between the Panels*. 2nd edition. Milwaukee WI: Dark Horse Comics, 1998.

Duncan, Randy, Matthew J. Smith, and Paul Levitz. *The Power of Comics: History, Form and Culture*. 2nd edition. London: Bloomsbury Academic, 2015.

Fingeroth, Danny. *Rough Guide to Graphic Novels*. New York: Rough Guides, 2007.

Gabilliet, Jean-Paul. Translated by Bart Beaty and Nick Nguyen. *Of Comics and Men: A Cultural History of American Comic Books*. Jackson: University Press of Mississippi, 2010.

Goulart, Ron. *Comic Book Culture: An Illustrated History*. New York: Collectors Press, Incorporated, 2004.

Goulart, Ron. *Comic Book Encyclopedia: The Ultimate Guide to Characters, Graphic Novels, Writers, and Artists in the Comic Book Universe*. New York: Morrow/ Avon HarperEntertainment, 2004.

Greenberger, Robert. *The Essential Batman Encyclopedia*. New York: Del Rey, 2008.

Hajdu, David. *The Ten-Cent Plague: The Great Comic-Book Scare and How It Changed America*. New York: Farrar, Straus, and Giroux, 2008.

Hanley, Tim. *Wonder Woman Unbound: The Curious History of the World's Most Famous Heroine*. Chicago: Chicago Review Press, 2014.

Howe, Sean. *Marvel Comics: The Untold Story*. New York: Harper, 2012.

Isabella, Tony. *1,000 Comic Books You Must Read*. Iola, WI: Krause Publications, 2009.

Jones, Gerard. *Men of Tomorrow: Geeks, Gangsters, and the Birth of the Comic Book*. New York: Basic Books, 2004.

Klock, Geoff. *How to Read Superhero Comics and Why*. New York: Continuum, 2002.

Lepore, Jill. *The Secret History of Wonder Woman*. New York: Alfred A. Knopf, 2014.

Manning, Matthew K. *Iron Man: The Ultimate Guide to the Armored Super Hero*. New York: DK, 2010.

Nyberg, Amy Kiste. *Seal of Approval: The History of the Comics Code*. Jackson: University Press of Mississippi, 1998.

O'Neil, Dennis. *Batman Unauthorized: Vigilantes, Jokers, and Heroes in Gotham City*. Dallas, TX : Benbella Books, 2008.

Phillips, Nickie D. and Stacy Strobl. *Comic Book Crime: Truth, Justice, and the American Way*. New York: New York University Press, 2013.

Raphael, Jordan and Tom Spurgeon. *Stan Lee and the Rise and Fall of the American Comic Book*. Chicago: Chicago Review Press.

Ricca, Brad. *Super Boys: The Amazing Adventures of Jerry Siegel and Joe Shuster—The Creators of Superman*. New York: St. Martin's Press, 2013.

Sabin, Roger. *Comics, Comix & Graphic Novels: A History of Comic Art*. London: Phaidon Press, 2001.

Schumacher, Michael. *Will Eisner: A Dreamer's Life in Comics*. New York: Bloomsbury, 2010.

Sommers, Joseph Michael, ed. *The American Comic Book*. Ipswich, MA: Salem Press, 2014.

Talon, Durwin. *Comics above Ground: Sequential Art Affects Mainstream Media*. New York: TwoMorrows Publishing, 2004.

Talon, Durwin. *Panel Discussions: Design in Sequential Art Storytelling*. 2nd edition. New York: TwoMorrows Publishing, 2002.

Thomas, Lynne M. and Sigrid Ellis, eds. *Chicks Dig Comics: A Celebration of Comic Books by the Woman Who Loved Them*. Des Moins, IA: Man Norwegian Press, 2012.

Versaci, Rocco. *This Book Contains Graphic Language: Comics as Literature*. New York: Continuum, 2007.

Wein, Len and Leah Wilson, eds. *The Unauthorized X-Men: SF and Comic Writers on Mutants, Prejudice, and Adamantium*. Dallas, TX: Benbella Books, 2006.

Weist, Jerry. *100 Greatest Comic Books*. New York: Whitman Publishing, LLC., 2004.

Wolk, Douglas. *Reading Comics: How Graphic Novels Work and What They Mean*. Cambridge, MA: Da Capo Press, 2007.

Appendix II

Publishing Companies on the Internet

Mainstream Publishers

The comic book industry has hundreds of publishing companies—from large publishers to small independent publishing companies. Below are listed some of the most popular large publishing companies of graphic novels and comic books.

Archie Comics (www.archie.com)

The adventures of Archie Andrews and his Riverdale friends have sold continuously for nearly 60 years, and remain as popular as ever. Archie Comics are the most steadfastly kid-friendly comics on the market, and the publisher works hard to maintain its wholesome reputation. It is believed that Archie Comics is the third-largest comics publisher in America. Unlike most comic book publishers, most of Archie's revenues come from sales to "newsstand" distributors rather than comic book stores.

Dark Horse Comics (www.darkhorse.com)

Founded in 1986, Dark Horse Comics has quickly grown to being one of the best-respected publishers in the industry. Dark Horse Comics publishes one of the most consistently diverse lines of comics in America today including adult humor, detective stories, realistic fiction, fantasy, science fiction, horror, movie/television adaptations including properties such as *Aliens*, realistic drama, historical fiction, Japanese manga, and the occasional super-hero title.

DC Comics (www.dccomics.com)

Founded in 1935 DC Comics is the oldest comic book company in America and features the most widely recognized comic book characters including Superman, Batman, and Wonder Woman. DC Comics publishes the largest variety of comic books today and has branched out with several imprints including Vertigo, for fantastic horror, fantasy, and mature-adult stories.

IDW (www.idwpublishing.com)

Founded in 2000 as the publishing arm of Idea and Dream Works, IDW has grown to become one of the top five comic publishers. Some of IDW's notable original works have included *30 Days of Night, Kill Shakespeare,* and *Locke and Key.* Licensed works include *Star Trek, My Little Pony, Transformers. GI Joe,* and *Godzilla,* as well as some of the classic Disney properties. In 2015, IDW acquired Top Shelf Productions (http://www.topshelfcomix.com/), which now operates as a separate imprint. Top Shelf's titles include *March, The Essex County Trilogy,* and *Owly* as well as works by Craig Thompson, Jeffrey Brown, and Alan Moore.

Image Comics (www.imagecomics.com)

Founded in 1992, Image Comics was created and is divided into three houses—Todd McFarlane Productions (www.spawn.com), Top Cow (www.topcow.com), and Image Central. Each of the creators/owners maintains a separate studio, incorporated independently of Image and employing its own writers, artists, and editors. Image Central promotes creator-owned work under the general banner of Image Comics and includes works such as Colleen Doran's *A Distant Soil,* Erik Larsen's *Savage Dragon,* Eric Shanower's *Age of Bronze,* Robert Kirkman's *Walking Dead* and *Invincible,* plus many more.

Marvel Comics (www.marvel.com)

Marvel Comics, along with DC Comics, is one of the two powerhouses of the comic book industry. The company was founded in 1939, but it wasn't until 1961 that Marvel Comics came into its own when Stan Lee and Jack "King" Kirby created its own brand of super-heroes like the Fantastic Four, Spider-Man, the X-Men, the Hulk, Captain America, and many other memorable heroes and villains. Marvel also has an imprint called Marvel MAX, created to focus on more mature titles and themes as well as the creator-owned Icon imprint, which is the home for Brian Michael Bendis's *Powers* series. Marvel is owned by Disney and also has a line of Disney-related titles as well as several books related to the Disney-owned Star Wars.

Independent Publishers

There are many independent publishers—from those who self-publish only one comic book title to companies who publish a variety of titles in a graphic novel format. Here's a very small sample of some of the best independent publishers, and the list includes mainstream North American companies and publishers of Asian titles as well. Mind that this is just a very short list and that there are currently hundreds of other smaller publishing companies currently publishing comic books and graphic novels.

Antarctic Press (www.antarctic-press.com)

One of North America's longest-running publishers of Neo-manga titles including the cult-hit favorites *Gold Digger, Neotopia, Ninja High School, The Courageous Princess,* and many more.

Avatar Press (www.avatarpress.com)

Founded in 1996, Avatar Press is the home to such titles as *Lady Death* and comics created by Alan Moore, Warren Ellis, Garth Ennis, and others.

Bongo Comics Group (www.littlegreenman.com)

Matt Groening, creator of *The Simpsons* and *Futurama* TV shows, publishes his own line of comic books. Ongoing titles include the flagship Simpsons comic, *Bart Simpson*, *Futurama*, and the annual *Bart Simpsons' Treehouse of Horror*. The trade paperback collections are published through HarperCollins Publishers.

Boom! Studios (www.boom-studios.com)

Founded by Ross Richie in 2005, BOOM! Studios consists of four imprints—the main "Studios," which has included titles such as *Irredeemable* and *The Woods*; "BOOM! Box," which publishes "experimental" titles such as *Lumberjanes*; the All-Ages imprint "KaBOOM!" which includes *Peanuts* and *Garfield*; and the "Archaia" Imprint home of *Mouse Guard*.

Cartoon Books (www.boneville.com)

Created by Jeff Smith in 1991, Cartoon Books came into the independent comic book market with Jeff's comic book *Bone*—and became an instant hit with fans all over the world. *Bone* has won numerous awards, including the Eisner and Harvey awards, since 1993. Recent other titles collected include the <u>Rose</u> mini-series written by Jeff Smith with art by Charles Vess.

Cinebook (cinebook.co.uk)

A British-based company known for translating French comics into English.

Digital Manga Publishing (www.dmpbooks.com)

Founded as a bridge between Japan and the Western world for anime, manga, and other licenses, the company has recently expanded as a publisher of Japanese manga. Titles range from all ages including their Edu-Manga series to properties including *Berserk*, *Trigun*, *Hellsing*, and even Yaoi homosexual romance titles for older audiences.

Drawn and Quarterly (www.drawnandquarterly.com)

Based in Canada, the independent publisher was founded in 1992 and is one of the best-known publishers of literary graphic novels. The title of the company comes from the highly regarded anthology of the same name. The publisher is also known for publishing the works by such highly regarded creators as Adrian Tomine, Seth, Chester Brown, Joe Matt, Julie Doucet, James Sturm, and Debbie Drechsler.

Dynamite Entertainment (www.dynamite.com)

The publishing arm of Dynamic Forces, Dynamite publishes both original and licensed materials, including *Vamperella*, *Xena*, *Army of Darkness*, and *The Lone Ranger*.

Fantagraphics Books (www.fantagraphics.com)

Founded by the creators of the magazine *The Comics Journal* in 1976, the Seattle-based company produces some of the most striking and compelling alternative comic book titles. From the Los Hernandez Brother's *Love and Rockets* to Peter Bagge's *Hate*, to Daniel Clowes's *Ghost World*, Fantagraphics Books continues a high-standard of producing comics for an audience that appreciates comics as a serious means of expression on the same level of film, theater, or literature.

Humanoids Publishing (www.humanoids.com)

The books, comics, and trade paperbacks from Humanoids Publishing feature groundbreaking comic art from the world's finest creators. Imaginative and sophisticated, Humanoids' science-fiction and heroic fantasy stories are designed to be read and enjoyed by an audience older than that of a typical American comic book. Popular titles include *The Metabarons* and *The Incal*.

Kodansha Comics (www.kodanshacomics.com)

The American subsidiary of Japanese publisher Kodansha, this manga publisher produces such titles as *Attack on Titan*, *Fairy Tail*, and *UQ Holder*. Several of their titles were formally published in the United States by the now-defunct Del Rey Manga which was part of Random House.

NBM Publishing (www.nbmpub.com)

Among one of the first publishers to bring the graphic novel to the United States in 1976, Nantier, Beall, Minoustchine (NBM) specializes in paperback and hardcover graphic novels for a variety of ages. Genres include Realistic Fiction, Mystery, Fantasy, Science Fiction, Humor, Children's Literature, and adaptations of classic literature. Among the outstanding titles in its backlist are Vittorio Giardino's acclaimed *A Jew in Communist Prague*, P. Craig Russell's adaptation of *Fairy Tales of Oscar Wilde*, and Will Eisner's *Last Knight*.

Oni Press (www.onipress.com)

Oni Press has received critical acclaim for its diverse line of quality comics. Highlights include *The Sixth Gun*, *Invader Zim*, *Whiteout*, and *Junior Braves of the Apocalypse*.

Papercutz (www.papercutz.com)

Cofounded by NBM founder Terry Nantier, Papercutz published graphic novels for younger readers, including new adventures of *The Hardy Boys* and *Nancy Drew*, *Lego Nijango*, as well as English translations of the popular *Geronimo Stilton* comics.

Seven Seas Entertainment (www.gomanga.com)

An up-and-coming publisher of Neo-manga titles that look and feel nearly identical to Japanese manga title—including printing the books in the traditional right-to-left

Japanese manga format. Notable titles include the *Alice in. . . .* titles, *Pita-Ten*, and *Amazing Agent Luna*.

Titan Comics (www.titan-comics.com)

A British-based company, Titan's American output includes multiple *Doctor Who* titles. The same owner publishers Titan Books, which include collections of older material from Joe Simon and Jack Kirby.

Toon Books (www.toon-books.com)

Founded by Françoise Mouly, Toon Books primarily creates original graphic novels aimed at early readers. It recently began a line called Toon Graphics aimed at ages eight and up.

Udon Entertainment (www.udonentertainment.com)

A publisher of Japanese manga and Korean Manhwa, titles include the <u>Street Fighter</u> series.

Valiant Entertainment (www.valiantentertainment.com)

Valiant has gone through several incarnations since its 1989 founding, as have its characters, some of which have their origins in the Gold Key Comics in the 1960s. Characters published over the years include Ninjak, Archer and Armstrong, and X-O Manowar.

Vertical Comics (www.vertical-inc.com)

A manga publisher whose output includes many of the works of the legendary Osumu Tezuka.

VIZ Media, LLC. (www.viz.com)

VIZ Media, LLC. is the leading U.S. publisher of Japanese comics (manga) for English-speaking audiences. Founded in 1987, VIZ serves a growing market of dedicated fans of all ages. Based in San Francisco, California, VIZ publishes dozens of popular Japanese titles such as *Ranma 1/2*, *Dragon Ball Z*, *Nausicaá of the Valley of Wind*, and *Battle Angel Alita*. VIZ is a wholly owned subsidiary of Shogakukan, one of Japan's three largest publishers of manga. VIZ also distributes both dubbed and subtitled anime for English-speaking countries.

Yen Press (www.yenpress.com)

This manga publisher is co-owned by the Hachette Book Group. Its translated titles include *Black Butler*, *Durarara!!*, and the *Puella Magi Madoka Magica* titles. In addition, it has produced manga-style adaptions of *Twilight*, *Maximum Ride*, and other literary works.

Mainstream Book Publishers

Many mainstream book publishers of prose fiction and nonfiction titles also publish graphic novels. Some of those do so under their own names, while others develop special imprints specifically for the publications of graphic novels. Here are some of them.

Abrams Comicarts (www.abramsbooks.com/imprints/abramscomicarts)

The comics imprint of Abrams publishing produces graphic novels such as *The Imitation Game* and *My Friend Dahmer,* books on comics, and reprints of lesser-known works from the past. Abrams also puts out graphic novels under its main line and the young adult/middle grade line Amulet. The latter includes *Nathan Hale's Hazardous Tales* and *The Creeps*.

First Second: 01 (www.firstsecondbooks.com)

Founded in 2006 as an imprint of Roaring Brook Press, a division of Holtzbrinck Publishers. First Second Books has produced a large number of well-received and award-winning books, including *American Born Chinese*, *This One Summer*, and *Anya's Ghost*.

Graphix (www.scholastic.com/graphix)

An imprint of Scholastic Books, the graphic novel imprint launched its line of titles in 2005 with Jeff Smith's <u>Bone</u> series in full-color. Other notable titles equally suitable for tweens and teens include the award-winning *Smile* and *Sisters*, *The Baby-Sitters Club*, and adaptations of the <u>Percy Jackson</u> series.

Pantheon Press (www.randomhouse.com/pantheon/graphicnovels/home.pperl)

The imprint from Random House is best known for being the publisher of Art Spiegelman's *Maus* in a graphic novel format. Known for its serious works, it also publishes works including Marjane Satrapi's autobiographical graphic novel *Persepolis*, Jessica Abel's *La Perdida*, Chris Ware's *Acme Novelty Library*, Joann Sfar's *The Rabbi's Cat*, Charles Burns's *Black Hole*, and many more.

Other Online Sources

The Internet has greatly changed how we use information—not only as librarians but also for personal searches. Here's just a small sample of the plethora of comic book web sites.

Comic Book Industry News and Reviews

Web sites that provide daily or weekly news in the comic book industry, publisher press releases, as well as other news from the industry.

The Beat (http://www.comicsbeat.com)

Run by Heidi MacDonald the Beat has been around in various forms over the years and features news and commentary.

Bleeding Cool (www.bleedingcool.com)

Founded by British comics writer Rich Johnston, this award-winning site provides news and information.

Comic Books Resources (www.cbr.com)

Online since 1995, CBR has received a wide variety of acclaim and recognition for its well–put-together information on the comic book industry, including previews, reviews, and movie news.

Comics Continuum (www.comicscontinuum.com)

An excellent source of daily news from the comic book industry and many comic book-related media projects including television and movies.

Newsarama (www.newsarama.com)

Newsarama is one of the best sources for daily information on the comic book industry, including headline news, previews of titles, and company press releases.

Miscellaneous Online Journals and Information Sources

A listing of web sites that include basic information for beginners on graphic novels and comic books as well as well as links to a variety of miscellaneous sites.

Collected Editions (collectededitions.blogspot.com)

News and reviews about new and upcoming collected editions, helpful for knowing what to get for a library.

Comic Book Database (www.comicbookdb.com)

Grand Comic Database (www.comics.org)

These two searchable databases feature creator information, covers, and the contents of collected editions among other information.

The Comics Journal (www.tcj.com)

Official web site to the comic book magazine from the Fantagraphics publisher.

Diamond Bookshelf (www.diamondbookshelf.com)

Produced by Diamond, the main distributor of comics and graphic novels to comic book shops, the Bookshelf provides resources for educators and librarians.

Graphic Novel Reporter (www.graphicnovelreporter.com)

Part of the Book Reporter Network, the site includes reviews and interviews as well as core lists.

New Comics Releases List (www.comiclist.com)

A staple on the web for years, it's a weekly listing of all the comic book and graphic novel titles available for the coming week at your local comic book shop. The site also has links to reviews, publishers, and professionals on the Internet.

Sequential Tart (www.sequentialtart.com)

An Internet magazine published by an eclectic band of women. Interviews, articles, reviews, and commentaries are included.

Web Sites Created by Librarians

Web sites created by librarians for librarians on all sorts of comic book and graphic novel information.

Good Comics for Kids (http://blogs.slj.com/goodcomicsforkids/)

Hosted by school libray journal, this site covers comics aimed at younger readers. Many of the contributors are libarians.

No Flying, No Tights (www.noflyingnotights.com)

Created by librarian Robin Brenner, the site is a very useful and user-friendly source to a wide variety of graphic novels. The site is broken down into three divisions for kids, teens, and older audiences and features titles for a wide variety of genres. One of the best web sites for library-appropriate reviews.

Intellectual Freedom Issues

Comic Book Legal Defense Fund (www.cbldf.org)

The official site for one of the most important nonprofit organizations in the comic book industry. The CBLDF's guiding principle is that comics should be accorded the same constitutional rights as literature, film, or any other form of expression.

Comic Book and Graphic Novel Awards and Recognition

Like most mediums, there are many awards and forms of recognition given to the comic book and graphic novel industry. The awards can come from within the industry—such as the Will Eisner awards—to even recognition from fans and libraries. Below are listed some main web sites for some of the most popular awards given out to the comic book industry as well as some recognition from other outside sources. For a full list of awards listed in the publication in all the chapters, please see the introduction to this book.

Comic Book Awards Almanac (http://www.hahnlibrary.net/comics/awards/)

A website with links to all the award-winning comic books and graphic novels from American awards to non-American awards and includes all major awards from the Kirbys, Ignatz, Eisners, Harveys, and many more both from professions and from fans.

Harvey Kurtzman Awards (www.facebook.com/theharveyawards/)

Awarded at the Baltimore Comic-Con, the Harvey's are named in honor of writer and cartoonist Harvey Kurtzman, best remembered for founding *MAD* magazine. The awards recognize the best in the comic book industry in over 20 categories. The awards were originally created in 1988.

Ignatz Awards (www.spxpo.com)

Awarded at the Small Press Expo, the award recognizes *outstanding achievement in comics and cartooning.*

Will Eisner Awards (http://www.comic-con.org/awards/eisner-awards-current-info)

Awarded each year at the San Diego Comic-Con International, the award is named in honor of pioneering cartoonist Will Eisner and recognizes the best in comic book industry. The Eisners have been awarded each year since 1988.

YALSA Booklists and Book Awards (http://www.ala.org/yalsa/booklistsawards/booklistsbook)

The Young Adults Library Services Association (YALSA), a division of the American Library Association (ALA), regularly recognizes the works of graphic novels. Featured from this link includes the lists of all the titles—both prose and graphic novel—that have been recognized in such award categories, including Popular Paperbacks for Young Adults, Best Books for Young Adults, Quick Picks for Reluctant Young Adult Readers, as well as others. In 2006 a new selection group, Great Graphic Novels, was created by YALSA to recognize the best graphic novels with young adult appeal.

Mailing Lists

There are many e-mail lists dedicated to comics and graphic novels. These are some for librarians.

Graphic Novels for Libraries—Begun in 1999, the list includes public, school, and academic librarians. A great place for recommendations for both books and programs. E-mail gn4lib-subscribe@yahoogroups.com to subscribe

Comix-Acadlibs—A list for librarians in academic libraries, https://lists.columbia.edu/mailman/listinfo/comix-acadlibs

Creator Index

Aaron, Jason, 66, 98, 113, 121, 208, 212, 333, 406, 412, 427, 449
Abadzis, Nick, 134, 252, 323
Abel, Jessica, 384, 479, 506–7, 641, 655
Abirached, Zeina, 613
Abnett, Dan, 71–75, 99, 105, 112, 120, 223, 232, 244
Abouet, Marguerite, 469–70
Abulí, Enrique Sánchez, 450
Acuña, Daniel, 29, 81
Adachi, Mitsuru, 487
Adachitoka, 329
Adams, Arthur, xxxi, 54, 83, 586
Adamson, Thomas K., 634
Adkins, Dan, 413
Adlard, Charlie, 47, 392, 433
Agi, Tadashi, 491
Aguirre, Jorge, 592
Aguirre-Sacasa, Roberto, 386, 411, 514
Ahonen, J. P., 483–84
Aida, Yu, 190
Aja, David, 48, 50
Akamatsu, Ken, 465, 597
Akimine, Kamijyo, 161
Akins, Tony, 321
Akizuki, Ryo, 159
Alare, K. P., 483–84
Albano, John, 195
Alberti, Mario, 316
Albrecht, Jeff, 524
Albuquerque, Rafael, 380
Alcala, Alfredo, 414
Alcaraz, Lalo, 626
Alcatena, Enrique, 246
Alessio, Augustin, 212
Alexander, Erica, 258
Alexander, Jason Shawn, 191, 368, 390
Alexovich, Aaron, 531
Alger, Bill, 524
Alixe, Pascal, 111
Allen, Brooke, 441
Allie, Scott, 219, 309, 368
Allison, John, 475
Allred, Michael "Mike," 76, 363, 389, 577, 646

Almand, M. Nicholas, 182
Alphona, Adrian, 56, 89
Alverez, Dave, 533
Alves, Wellington, 74
Amano, Gary, 363
Amano, Shiro, 340
Amano, Yoshitako, 363
Ames, Jonathan, 468
Anderson, Bill, 634–35
Anderson, Brent, 126
Anderson, Kevin J., 223
Anderson, Murphy, 265
Anderson, Ted, 534
Ando, Natsumi, 432, 493
Andrade, Filipe, 73–74, 113
Andreyko, Marc, 27, 320, 413, 422, 452
Andru, Ross, 74, 277
Aneke, 315
Anka, Kris, 70
Annable, Graham, 320, 516
Antonio, Lui, 212
Anzai, Nobuyuki, 176
Aoyama, Gosho, 437
Aparo, Jim, 9
Aragonés, Sergio, 220, 428, 595–96
Arakawa, Hiromu, 230
Arauio, Andre, 113
Archer, Adam, 64, 417, 581
Archer, Nathan, 223
Arcudi, John, 244, 246, 353, 368, 370, 378, 380, 430
Arikawa, Hiro, 235
Aristophane, 487
Armstrong, Jason, 275, 378
Armstrong, Matthew S., 509
Arnaudo, Marco, 646
Arnold, Adam, 386
Arnold, Andrew, 603
Aronofsky, Darren, 349
Asada, Hiroyuki, 220
Asano, Atsuko, 260
Asano, Inio, 484
Ashihara, Hinako, 460
Asmus, James, 30, 397, 581
Asrar, Mahmud, 64, 77, 219
Atkins, Robert, 167, 169
Atwood, Margaret, 24
Augustyn, Brian, 240, 393

Aureliani, Franco (as Franco), 560, 572, 583–85
Austen, Chuck, 55
Austen, Jane, 390, 500, 502–5
Aydin, Andrew, 615
Azaceta, Paul, 117
Azuma, Kiyohiko, 522
Azuma, Shoko, 633
Azzarello, Brian, 15–16, 68, 93, 117, 171, 414, 447

Ba', Gabriel, 190, 472, 486, 507
Bachalo, Chris, 98, 115, 125, 358, 412
Bachs, Ramon, 60
Backderf, Derf, 480, 486, 616
Baez, Marcelo, 634
Baetens, Jan, 643
Bagge, Peter, 131, 623, 646, 652
Bagieu, Pénélope, 474
Bagley, Mark, 21, 83, 86, 112–13
Baikie, Jim, 211
Bailey, Tracy, 150
Baker, Kyle, 38, 323, 428
Bakis, Maureen, 645
Balak. *See* Bigerel, Yves "Balak"
Balboni, Claudia, 198, 227
Baldeon, David, 75, 202
Ball, Georgia, 524, 534
Baltazzar, Art, 560, 572, 583–85
Ban, Toshio, 617
Barber, John, 248, 284–87
Barbiere, Frank J., 146–47
Barks, Carl, 526–29, 646
Barlow, Jeremy, 211
Barnett, Charles III, 634–35
Baron, Mike, 157–58, 220
Barone, Bendedetta, 524
Barr, Donna, 630
Barr, Mike W., 15, 123, 223, 413
Barras, Dell, 139
Barreto, Diego, 117
Barreto, Eduardo, 117, 208
Barrows, Eddy, 13, 57, 91
Barry, Dan, 152
Barry, Linda, 474, 506
Baskerville, Stephen, 285
Bastian, Jeremy, 150
Bates, Ben, 534
Batista, Chris, 286

Battle, Eric, 396
Baum, L. Frank, 343, 347
Bauman, Yoram, 639
Baxter, Jack, 616
Baylis, Daniel, 322
Bazal, 316
BB, Chuck, 357
Beacham, Travis, 283
Beagle, Peter S., 300
Bear, Erik, 139
Bear, Greg, 139
Beaton, Kate, 131, 323, 554
Beaty, Bart H., 643–44, 647
Beatty, Scott, 27
Beauvais, Denis, 244
Beavers, Ethen, 152, 524
Bechdel, Alison, 608, 612
Bechko, Corinna Sara, 215, 408
Beck, C. C., 32
Bedard, Tony, 46, 48
Beeby, Emma, 251
Beechen, Adam, 14, 27, 60
Beedle, Tim, 533
Beers, Thom, 387
Beland, Tom, 622
Belanger, Andy, 359, 421
Bell, Cece, xxix, 516, 612
Bellegarde, Nate, 52
Bellstorf, Arne, 458
Bellwood, Lucy, 608
Bender, Howard, 560
Bender, Hy, 646
Bendis, Brian Michael, xxxi,
    20–23, 35–36, 53, 71–72,
    78–79, 95, 98, 103, 105, 107,
    112–14, 116, 128, 231–32, 427,
    429, 445, 452, 643, 650
Benes, Ed, 12, 26, 46, 86
Benjamin, Paul, 533
Benjamin, Ryan, 213
Bennett, Joe, 55, 148
Bennett, Marguerite, 77, 111–13,
    123, 315, 420
Bennett, Rachel, 175
Benton, Greg, 320
Berg, Dave, 536
Bergting, Peter, 369
Berman, Dan, 335
Bermejo, Lee, 16, 61, 93, 117
Bernet, Jordi, 450
Bernstein, Jim, 525
Berolucci, Federico, 134
Bertozzi, Nick, 131, 614, 619
Bethea, Nicole Brooks, 634
Beukes, Lauren, 320
Bianci, Simone, 121

Big Time Attic, 510
Bigerel, Yves "Balak," 160
Bilal, Enki, 289
Bingham, Jerry, 15
Birchielli, Riccardo, 418
Biskup, Agnieszka, 634–35
Bisley, Simon, 15, 103, 231
Bissette, Steve, 399
Biukovic, Edvin, 220
Black, Holly, 321, 359–60
Blackman, Haden, 27, 113,
    209–10, 212–13, 216, 309
Blain, Chris, 194
Blanchard, Fred, 220
Blanco, Fernando, 13, 390
Blaylock, Josh, 286
Blechman, R. O., 320
Bloz, 138
Boatwright, Thomas, 421
Bocqet, Oliver, 261
Bogdanove, Jon, 3, 114, 244
Bogdanovic, Viktor, 5, 14
Bolland, Brian, 16, 233–34, 246
Bolton, Chris A., 582
Bolton, Kyle, 582
Bond, Grant, 422
Bone, J., 62, 148, 428
Bongco, Mila, 646
Bonner, Hannah, 638
Bonsen, Joost, 631
Booker, M. Keith, 643
Booth, Brett, 41, 87, 91
Borenstein, Greg, 396
Borenstein, Max, 396
Boschi, Roland, 112, 406
Bosma, Sam, 299
Boulet, 289, 594
Bourdain, Anthony, 492
Boutavant, Marc, 541–42
Bowers, Chad, 38, 113
Boyd, Jordan, 24
Bradbury, Ray, 201, 241, 259
Braddock, Paige, 535, 552
Bradstreet, Tim, 226
Braga, Brannon, 225
Braithwaite, Doug, 86, 334
Braun, Russ, 113, 320
Brendon, Nicholas, 373
Brenner, Robin, 644, 659
Brereton, Dan, 334–35
Bressan, Andrei, 336
Breyfogle, Norm, 15, 27, 59,
    123, 469
Briefer, Dick, 419
Bright, M. D., 284, 581
Brisson, Ed, 421

Brittenham, Skip, 228
Brizuela, Dario, 185, 536
Broadmore, Greg, 229
Brod, Harry, 646
Broglia, John, 271
Brook, Meljean, 316
Brooks, Brad, 644
Brooks, Mark, 104, 213
Brooks, Max, 168–69, 367, 393
Broome, John, 238
Brosgol, Vera, 320, 323, 403
Brown, Box, 607, 628
Brown, Chester, 646
Brown, Don, 624
Brown, Garry, 34, 421
Brown, Jeffrey, 282, 516, 519,
    535, 615, 650
Brown, Kate, 355
Brown, Kevin, 606
Browne, Ryan, 345
Brozo, William, 645
Brrémaud, Frédéric, 134
Brubaker, Ed, 9, 30–31, 34,
    36, 50–51, 65, 80, 97, 103,
    115, 193, 425, 427, 434,
    444–46, 646
Brubaker, Jason, 155
Brunner, Frank, 412–13
Buccellato, Brian, 12, 41, 124
Buccellato, Steve, 619
Buckingham, Mark, 55, 252, 320,
    358, 363, 414, 586
Buckler, Rich, 273–74
Budiansky, Bob, 285
Buffagni, Matteo, 20
Buller, Jon, 264
Bullock, Dave, 62
Bullock, Mike, 341
Bunn, Cullen, 37, 46, 80, 97, 105,
    112, 141, 199, 202, 288, 296,
    413, 420
Burchett, Rick, 6, 18
Burchielli, Riccardo, 163, 263
Burks, James, 543
Burnett, Alan, 105
Burnham, Chris, 10, 112,
Burnham, Erik, 248, 559–60
Burns, Charles, 506, 555, 655
Burrows, Jacen, 401–2
Buscema, John, 36, 56, 70, 74, 76,
    118, 120, 307, 549
Buscema, Sal, 73–74, 118, 332
Busiek, Kurt, xxxi, 4, 105, 126,
    128, 181, 238, 293, 304–5,
    308–10, 316, 333, 428–29
Bussi, Audrey, 523

Bustos, Natacha, 137
Butler, Blair, 316
Butler, Nancy, 500, 504–5
Butters, Tara, 69–70
Byerly, Kenny, 185
Byrne, John, 55, 73, 76, 84, 94, 120, 124, 139, 224, 373–74

Cacau, Caio, 634
Caffoe, Jim, 508
Cain, Chelsea, 56
Calafiore, Jim, 90, 316
Calderon-Zurita, Victor, 54
Caldwell, Ben, 210, 330, 347, 381, 433
Caldwell, Gary, 252
Calero, Dennis, 328
Calingo, Mel, 150
Camagni, Jacopo, 54
Cameron, Lou, 420
Cammuso, Frank, 517, 550–51, 562
Campbell, Eddie, 289, 414, 428–29, 451
Campbell, J. Scott, 190
Campbell, Ross, 261, 475
Campidelli, Maurizio, 634
Campos, Cristian, 644
Campos, Jamie, 55
Camuncoli, Giuseppe, 20, 60, 100, 119
Canada, Geoffrey, 451
Canales, Juan Diaz, 430
Cannon, Kevin, 631, 638, 640
Cannon, Zander, 130, 284, 569–70, 629, 631, 638
Caps, Mike, 230
Capullo, Greg, 11–12, 379
Caputo, Tony C., 643
Carey, Mike, 115, 315, 354, 360
Cariello, Sergio, 196
Carlin, Mike, 223
Carlini, Eleonara, 252
Carlson, Bryce, 425, 541
Carmagni, Jacopo, 112
Carolan, Sean, 579
Carpi, Giovan Battista, 529
Carreres, Albert, 523
Carroll, Emily, 316, 320, 421, 508
Carter, James Bucky, 645
Casagrande, Elena, 252, 373
Case, Jonathan, 394, 430, 436, 451, 572
Caselli, Stefano, 78, 418
Casey, Joe, 4, 274, 433

Cassaday, John, 81, 96, 208, 289, 315
Castellan, Andrea, 529, 532
Castellucci, Cecil, 516, 550
Castiello, Marco, 208, 232
Castro, Juan, 232
Cavallaro, Mike, 348–49
Cavazzano, Giorgio, 529, 532
Cebulski, C. B., 72, 323, 382
Cereno, Benito, 52
Cermak, Craig, 288
Chabert, Jack, 570
Chabot, Jacob, 531, 586
Chad, Jon, 234, 637
Chadwick, Paul, 412, 428–29
Chaffee, Graham, 320
Chamberlain, Kody, 429
Chamblis, Andrew, 373
Chan, Crystal, 502–3
Chan, Ron, 563, 572
Chang, Bernard, 154
Chantler, Scott, 304
Chao, Fred, 516
Charbonnet, Gabrielle, 356
Charm, Derek, 227, 517, 579, 584
Chast, Roz, 507, 609
Chater, Mack, 421
Chaykin, Howard, 117, 123, 166, 168, 207, 646
Checchetto, Marco, 215, 217
Cheggour, Mehdi, 394
Chen, Sean, 283
Chestney, Rob, 218
Cheung, Jim, 93, 274
Chiang, Cliff, 68, 237
Chikwanine, Michel, 609
Chin, Joyce, 200, 315
Ching, Brian, 64, 209, 213, 217, 309
Chinn, Mike, 646
Chmakova, Svetlana, 356, 416, 514–15
Cho, Frank, 78, 103
Cho, Michael, 483
Choi, Mike, 83, 101, 115
Christenson, Hannah, 322
Christmas Johnnie, 24
Christopher, Randall, 510
Churchill, Ian, 125
Churchland, Marion, 310
Churilla, Brian, 347, 396, 507
Churin, Pablo, 397
Ciaramella, Jason, 420
Ciencin, Scott, 223
Cimino, Rodolfo, 528
Cirocco, Frank, 243

CLAMP, 273, 344, 346, 422
Clanton, Ben, 550
Claremont, Chris, 15, 55, 66, 71, 73, 83, 94–95, 97, 114–15, 413, 575, 586
Clark, Matthew, 235
Clark, Scott, 10
Clark, Wook-Jin, 343
Clevinger, Brian, 194, 271
Cliff, Tony, 146
Cloonan, Becky, 58, 127, 163, 308–9, 439
Clowes, Daniel, xxxi, 254, 487, 646, 652
Clugston Florres, Chynna, 441, 471, 475
Coates, Ta-Nehisi, 28
Coats, Misty, 600
Coelho, Jorge, 407
Cohen, Amanda, 497
Cohn, Ariel, 522
Coipel, Oliver, 81, 114, 334
Colak, Mirko, 143
Colan, Gene, 413, 549
Cole, David James, 421
Cole, Jack, 419
Coller, Casey W., 284
Collicutt, Paul, 279
Collin, Renaud, 531
Collins, Mike, 253
Collins, Nancy, 316
Collins, Stephen, 475
Colossal, Eric, 600
ComicsOne, 492
Comipa, 386
Conley, Aaron, 590
Conner, Amanda, 47–48, 93
Conrad, Will, 205, 310, 374
Conroy, Mike, 646
Conway, Gerry, 20, 70, 413, 646
Cook, Katie, 20, 322, 534
Cooke, Darwyn, 16, 34, 93, 123, 247, 428, 432, 443
Cooper, Joe, 276
Coover, Colleen, 194, 433
Copeland, Cynthia, 613
Copiel, Oliver, 114
Copland, Jason, 282
Corben, Richard, 406
Cordurie, Sylvain, 384
Cornell, Paul, 29, 250, 252–53
Cornog, Martha, 644
Corona, Jorge, 322, 359
Corroney, Joe, 225, 250, 375
Corsetto, Danielle, 293
Cosby, Andrew, 387

Cosby, Nate, 194
Cosey, Bernard, 532
Costa, Michael "Mike," 20, 113, 169, 346
Cotter, Joshua, 510
Couceriro, Damian, 117
Craig, James, 376
Craig, Wes, 71
Crain, Clayton, 101, 406
Craine, Nick, 510
Crandall, Reed, 288
Crawford, Mel, 536
Crawford, Philip Charles, 645
Crety, Stephanie, 208
Criddle, Craig, 629
Crilley, Mark, 404
CrisCross, 375
Croall, Marie, 529
Crofts, Jackie, 493
Crook, Tyler, 199, 380, 413, 572
Crumb, Robert (R.), 606
Crystal, Shawn, 38, 105
Cummings, Steve, 364
Curnow, Bobby, 395
Currey, Erica Leigh, 529
Currie, Andrew, 223, 225, 234
Cypress, Toby, 393

Dallocchio, Federico, 91
Dalrymple, Farel, 222
Damaggio, Rodolfo, 207–8
Damaso, Elmer, 288
D'Amata, Frank, 121
Dan, A., 621
D'Anda, Carlos, 14, 208
Daniel, Nelson, 234, 420
Daniel, Tim, 394
Daniel, Tony S., 12, 86, 106
Daniels, Les, 646
Dauterman, Russell, 333
Dauviller, Loic, 501
David, Peter, 20, 23, 49–50, 61, 67, 99–100, 111–13, 115, 223–24, 231–32, 375, 390, 524, 575, 606
Davila, Claudia, 609
Davis, Alan, 30, 55, 94, 274
Davis, Dan, 18
Davis, Eleanor, 320, 566, 571
Davis, Shane, 125
Day, Felicia, 349–50
Dayton, Brandon, 311, 322
Dazo, Bong, 72
de Bonneval, Gwen, 202
de Campi, Alex, 246, 534

DeCandido, Keith R. A, 223, 523
DeCarlo, Mike, 579
DeConnick, Kelly Sue, 70, 112, 199, 257, 316
De Créy, Nicolas, 151, 155
Deering, Rachel, 420
DeFalco, Tom, 6
DeFilippis, Nunzio, 150, 189, 381, 488
De Haven, Tom, 646
De Heer, Margreet, 636, 641
De Landro, Valentine, 257, 316
Delano, Jamie, 414
de la Rosa, Sam, 223
De La Torre, Roberto, 70, 412
Del Col, Anthony, 359
Delgado, Ricardo, 135–36
Delisle, Guy, 614, 618–20
De Liz, Renae, 300
Dell, John, 93
Delliquanti, Blue, 277
del Mundo, Mike, 113
Del Rey, Vanesa R., 425
Del Rio, Tania, 565
del Toro, Guillermo, 283, 377, 385
DeMatteis, J. M., 85, 575
Dembicki, Carol, 134
Dembicki, Matt, 134–35, 326, 639
Demong, Todd, 227
Denham, Brian, 374
Denson, Abby, 579, 640
Deodato, Mike, 78, 80, 112, 116, 212
de Pins, Arthur, 567
Derington, Nick, 634–35
D'Errico, Camilla, 361
Deutsch, Barry, 350
Devault, Christine, 630
Dewey, Benjamin, 293
DeZago, Todd, 378
DeZuniga, Tony, 195
Dias, Wellington, 197
Diaz, Jean, 117
Diaz, Luis, 200
Diaz, Paco, 113
Diaz, Ruben, 586
Dibari, Chris, 421
Dickens, Charles, 16, 502
Didier, Lefevre, 628
Diggle, Andy, 42–43, 246, 252
Di Giandomenico, Carmine, 113
Di Giorgio, Jean-Francois, 182
Digital Arts Chefs, 288

Dillon, Glyn, 459
Dillon, Ray, 300
Dillon, Steve, 58–59, 233, 414, 563–64
DiMartino, Michael Dante, 173
Dingess, Chris, 397
Dini, Paul, 10–11, 14–15, 17, 34, 46–48, 610
Dirge, Roman, 407
D'Israeli, 246
Ditko, Steve, 18, 153, 412, 582
Di Vito, Andrea, 335
Dixon, Chuck, xxxi, 27, 34, 59–60, 124, 166–67, 169, 196–97, 243–44
Dizin, Pascal, 146
Djurdjevic, Marco, 334
Doctorow, Cory, 476–77
Dodson, Rachel, 47, 125
Dodson, Terry, 47, 97, 115, 125, 216
Domingues, Horacio, 117
Dominguez, Richard, 634–35
Donner, Richard, 4
Donovan, Eryk, 421
Dooney, Michael, 184
Doran, Colleen, 342, 363–64, 606, 650
D'Orazio, Valerie, 421
Dorkin, Evan, 369–70, 560
d'Orozco, Jesse, 286
Dos Santos, Joaquim, 174
Doucet, Julie, 617, 652
Doucet, Rashad, 400
Doyle, Ming, 415, 581
Dragotta, Nick, 259, 390, 631
Drake, Arnold, 223, 265
Drechsler, Debbe, 652
Dreir, David L., 634
Dringenberg, Mike, 362–63
Druckerman, Neil, 389
Duarte, Gustavo, 562
Duburke, Randy, 455
Duce, Christian, 14
Duffield, Paul, 259
Duffy, Jo, 55
Duggan, Gerry, 37–38, 75, 81, 112, 209
Duin, Steve, 646
Dumm, Gary, 606
Dunbar, Max, 202
Duncan, Dan, 184
Duncan, Randy, 643
Dunlavey, Fred, 604
Dunlavey, Ryan, 497

Duranona, Lee, 152
Duursema, Jan, 207–9, 214, 218–19
Dysart, Joshua, 172, 269, 310

Eaglesham, Dale, 83, 90
Eastman, Kevin, 184
Easton, Brandon, 607
Eaton, Maxwell III, 546
Eaton, Scot, 30, 80, 115, 121
Edginton, Ian, 155, 246, 391, 573
Edmondson, Nathan, 29, 59, 164, 274
Edwards, Neil, 116, 254
Effinger, George Alec, 413
Eggleton, Bob, 396
Ehasz, Aaron, 174
Eisma, Joe, 419
Eisner, Will, xvii, xxxi, 428–29, 472, 604, 628, 643, 646–47, 652, 660
Elder, Josh, 581, 635
Eliopoulos, Chris, 194, 322, 574, 579, 617
Ellis, Grace, 441
Ellis, Sigrid, 647
Ellis, Warren, 53, 80, 191–92, 259, 414, 651
Ellison, Harlan, 225, 241
Elson, Richard, 234, 390
Eltaeb, Gabe, 208
Endo, Hiroki, 263
Engle, Coleman, 540
Englehart, Steve, 55, 73, 76, 139, 413
Ennis, Garth, 59, 113, 172, 406, 414, 563–64, 651
Ens, Paul, 140
Enz, Tammy, 634
Epting, Steve, 30, 193
Erb, Greg, 343–44
Erickson, Byron, 529
Erwin, Steve, 223, 634
Espenson, Jane, 372–73
Espinosa, Frank, 237
Espinosa, Rod, 318
Espisito, Mike, 277
Evanier, Mark, 152, 220, 428, 536, 549, 595
Evans, George, 118
Evans, Khari, 269
Ewing, Al, 78–79, 252, 329
Evensen, Erik A., 327, 393
Ezquerra, Carlos, 220, 233

Fabbri, Davide, 213, 391
Fabok, Jason, 12–13
Fabry, Glenn, 363
Faerber, Jay, 198, 231
Fajardo, Alexis, 311–12
Farinas, Ulises, 396
Farshtey, Greg, 178
Faudem, Joshua, 616
Faullkner, Matt, 501
Fawkes, Ray, 13, 85, 415
Fazekas, Michelle, 69–70
Fearing, Mark, 568
Feiffer, Jules, 323, 430, 434
Felder, James, 55
Feldstein, Al, 227
Ferioli, Cesar, 523
Fernandez, Ivan, 212
Fernandez, Leandro, 59, 99, 163
Ferrier, Ryan, 396
Ferreira, Carlos, 200
Ferreira, Marcelo, 165
Ferreyra, Juan, 401
Ferry, Pasqual, 55, 334
Fetter-Vorm, Jonathan, 165, 639
Fialkov, Joshua Hale, 283, 352, 383, 396
Fickett, Travis, 225
Fies, Brian, 616
Fillbach, Matt, 210
Fillbach, Shawn, 210
Finch, David, 11–12, 68, 78, 79, 87, 115
Finch, Meredith, 68
Finger, Bill, 7, 34
Fingerman, Bob, 264, 289
Fingeroth, Danny, 645
Firmansyah, Alti, 113
Fisch, Sholly, 18, 536, 585
Fish, Veronica, 513, 549
Fisher, Ben, 548, 645
Fisher, Douglas B., 645
Fiumara, Max, 349, 368
Fiumara, Sebastian, 368
Fleecs, Tony, 534
Fleisher, Michael, 195
Fletcher, Brendon, 26, 28, 439
Flint, Henry, 234, 246
Flood, Joe, 150, 301, 636
Florean, Arianna, 252
Flynn, Brian, 510
Flynn, Ian, 276–77
Foley, Andrew, 198, 382
Folkman, Claire, 507
Forbeck, Matt, 643
Forbes, Jake T., 345

Ford, Christopher, 331
Forney, Ellen, 614
Fosgitt, Jay, 534
Foss, Langdon, 492
Fowler, Tess, 302
Fowler, Tom, 581, 631
Fox, Gardner, 238, 413
Fox, Matthew, 352–53
Fox, Nathan, 134
Fraction, Matt, 48, 50, 53, 83, 97, 103, 115, 118, 190, 253, 334
Fraga, Dan, 579
Frampton, Otis, 342–43
Francavilla, Francesco, 48, 197, 386, 411, 507
Francia, Omar, 213, 235
Francisco, Eduardo, 143, 309
Franck, Stephan, 384
Franco. *See* Aureliani, Franco
Frank, Gary, 4, 6, 33, 49, 108, 122,
Frank, Matt, 395–96
Fraser, Doug, 510
Frasier, Simon, 252–53
Frazetta, Frank, 227
Frederick-Frost, Alexis, 603
Fredericks, Fred, 536
Freitas, Erick, 396
Freed, Alexander, 216, 218
Frenz, Ron, 62, 208
Frey, Nancy, 645
Fridolfs, Derek, 14, 524, 573
Friedman, Michael Jan, 223
Friedrich, Mike, 56
Frigeri, Juan, 211
Frison, Jenny, 315, 507
Frusin, Marcelo, 414
Fry, James W., 223
FSc, 361
Fujii, Hideaki, 275
Fujishima, Kosuke, 599
Fujitaki, Kazuhiro, 633
Fuller, Noele, 630
Furman, Simon, 284–85, 298
Futaki, Attila, 310, 331

Gabilliet, Jean-Paul, 647
Gabo, 352
Gage, Christos N., 20, 27, 113, 119, 197, 280, 373–74
Gagne, Michel, 508
Gagnor, Roberto, 529
Gaiman, Neil, xxxi, 10, 15, 55–56, 110, 291, 337, 356, 358, 360, 362–64, 367, 407, 428–29, 506

Gale, Bob, 248
Gallagher, John, 574
Gallagher, Monica, 479, 574
Gallant, S. L., 167
Gallardo, Adam, 213, 227
Galloway, Joe, 161
Galusha, Tadd, 396, 421
Gammill, Kerry, 55
Gan, Steve, 73
Gane, Simon, 269, 396
Ganucheau, Paulina, 572
Ganz, Scott, 585
Garagarza, Elsa, 174
Garbett, Lee, 329
Garbowska, Agnes, 534
Garcia, Ale, 492
Garcia, Manuel, 26, 29, 272–73
Gardner, Matt, 400
Garibaldi, Jose, 510
Garing, Ken, 222
Garland, Chrystin, 508
Garman, Ralph, 573
Garney, Ron, 36–37, 66, 83, 102
Garron, Javier, 73, 112
Garzon, Carlos, 208
Gaspar, Tamas, 331
Gauld, Tom, 147, 320
Gaydos, Michael, 286, 429
Gaylord, Jerry, 388
Geary, Rick, 423, 434, 452, 454
Gedeon, Juan, 112
Gelatt, Phillip, 152
Genet, Frederic, 182
Gentry, Damon, 590
Geovanni, Walter, 315
Gerads, Mitch, 59, 164, 428
Gerber, Steve, 71, 413, 548–49
Gertler, Nat, 643
Ghahremani, Suzie, 531
Giallongo, Zack, 297
Gianfelice, Davide, 163
Gianni, Gary, 15, 152
Gianopoulos, Andrea, 633
Giardano, Vittorio, 652
Giarrusso, Chris, 574, 578
Gibbons, Dave, 92, 192, 244, 250,
    428–29
Giffen, Keith, 42, 72, 120,
    393, 575
Gillen, Kieron, 67, 93, 97,
    111–13, 212, 335, 355, 412
Gillis, Peter, 300, 413
Gilroy, Henry, 207–8, 210
Gimenez, Juan, 201
Giolitti, Alberto, 143

Giordano, Dick, 34, 363, 381
Giorello, Tomas, 309–10
Giovannetti, Nick, 567
Gischler, Victor, 310, 374–75, 418
Gladden, Stephanie, 630
Glass, Adam, 91, 105
Glass, Bryan J. L., 300
Gleason, Patrick, 8, 25, 60
Godlewski, Scott, 198
Goldberg, Stan, 469
Golden, Christopher, 223,
    369, 372
Golden, Michael, 413, 549
Goldman, Jake, 579
Goldsmith, Francisca, 645
Goldstein, Sophie, 320
Goni, Fernando, 375
Gonick, Larry, 623–24, 629–30
Gonzales, Manuel, 532
Goodin, Robert, 352
Goodridge, Rob, 444
Goodwin, Archie, 15, 55, 70, 153,
    207–8
Goodwin, M., 324
Googe, Neil, 47
Gorman, Michele, 645
Gorman, Zac, 557
Goscinny, René, 590
Gossett, Christian "Chris,"
    204, 217
Goulart, Ron, 647
Gownley, Jimmy, 512, 610
Graham, Billy, 55
Graham, Brandon, 222, 587
Grahme-Smith, Seth, 390
Grange, Dominique, 447
Granov, Ari, 53
Grant, Alan, 59, 103, 233
Grant, Steven, 56, 58, 280
Gravett, Paul, 643
Gray, Jonathan, 528–29
Gray, Justin, 166, 195
Grayson, Devin, 29, 316
Grecian, Alex, 416, 507
Green, John, xi, 521, 525, 548
Green, Michael, 64
Green, Randy, 310, 315
Greenberg, Isabel, 318
Greenberger, Robert, 647
Greene, Sandford, 55, 113
Gregory, Roberta, 630
Grell, Mike, 42
Griffen, Steven, 431
Griffith, Andrew, 284–85
Griffith, Bill, 613

Griffith, Saul, 631
Grindberg, Tom, 15
Grist, Paul, 57, 575
Groening, Matt, 511, 535,
    537–38, 651
Gross, Peter, 354, 360
Gruber, Jonathan, 640
Gruenwald, Mark, 56
Grummett, Tom, 3, 84
Grunberg, Greg, 337
Guara, Ig, 579
Guarnido, 430
Guay, Rebecca, 321
Guedes, Renato, 4, 415
Guera, R. M., 427
Guerra, Pia, 251, 265–66
Guevara, Mario, 148
Guggenheim, Marc, 62, 113
Gugliotti, Christopher, 422
Guibert, Emmanuel, 460, 541–42,
    571, 605–6, 628
Guice, Jackson "Butch," 3, 65,
    153, 181, 274, 427
Guichet, Yvel, 283
Guidi, Guido, 286
Guillory, Rob, 424
Gulacy, Paul, 34, 211, 234
Gulledge, Laura Lee, 479, 487
Gulley, Mario, 156
Gurewitch, Nick, 131
Gurihiru, 174, 586
Gurney, John Steven, 546
Guzman, Gabriel, 212

Ha, Gene, 130, 301, 506
Ha, Robin, 497
Haberlin, Brian, 228
Haeser, Ken, 548
Hagio, Moto, 508
Hagiwara, Kazushi, 293
Hahn, David, 573
Hajdu, David, 647
Hale, Dean, 317, 325
Hale, Greg, 148
Hale, Nathan, 317, 325, 516,
    626, 654
Hale, Phil, 231
Hale, Shannon, 317, 325
Hall, C. Michael, 640
Hall, Jason, 377
Hall, Jim, 216
Halsted, Ted, 273
Hama, Larry, 67, 165,
    167–68, 286
Hamaker, Steve, 296, 508–9

Hamilton, Edmond, 238
Hamilton, Josh, 174
Hamilton, Tim, 252, 259
Hammock, Lee, 231
Hammock, Tom, 365
Hamner, Cully, 192
Hampton, Bo, 123
Hampton, Scott, 360, 407
Hanasaki, Akira, 494
Hanawalt, Lisa, 519
Haney, Bob, 171
Hanley, Tim, 647
Hans, Stephanie, 111–12
Hanuka, Asaf, 166
Hanuka, Tomer, 166
Hapsiel, Dean, 606
Harbo, Christopher, 634
Hardin, Chad, 47
Hardison, Jim, 596
Hardman, Gabriel, 80, 215, 408
Harper, Charise, 320
Harrell, Rob, 597
Harren, James, 143, 309, 353
Harris, Joe, 12
Harris, Steven, 288
Harris, Tony, 39, 63, 363, 407,
    412, 507
Harrison, Mick, 212
Hart, Tom, 619
Hartley, Welles, 210, 212
Hartnell, Andy, 190
Hasekura, Isuna, 303
Hashiguchi, Takashi, 497
Haspiel, Dean, 395, 468, 618
Hastings, Christopher, 54
Hatke, Ben, xi, 275, 323, 516, 571
Hattori, Chihiro, 497
Haun, Jeremy, 27, 507
Hawes, Louise, 321
Hawthorne, Mike, 38, 167, 309
Hawthorne, Nathaniel, 503
Hay, Brenden, 551
Hayden, Jennifer, 621
Hayes, Geoffrey, 543
Hayes, Nick, 353
Haynes, Rob, 61
Heath, Russ, 171
Heck, Don, 52
Heinberg, Alan, 93
Helfer, Andrew, 619
Hempel, Marc, 363
Henderson, Erika, 517, 582
Henderson, Mike, 421
Hendrick, Tim, 174, 288
Hendrix, Grady, 497

Hennessey, Jonathan, 624, 628
Henrichon, Niko, 135, 154
Henrique, Paulo, 440
Henry, Clayton 157–58, 269
Henson, Jim, 322, 326, 345, 529,
    569, 617
Hergé, 144
Hernandez, Angel, 226–27
Hernandez, Gilbert, 131, 247,
    323, 477
Hernandez, Jamie, 131, 320, 323
Hernandez, Lea, 440, 585, 630
Herndon, Christopher, 141
Hester, Phil, 42, 52, 347, 395,
    506–7, 560
Heymans, Bas, 528
Heymans, Mau, 528–29
Hickey, Brenda, 534
Hickman, Jonathan, 78–79, 83,
    103, 111, 254–55, 259
Hicks, Faith Erin, 179, 348, 355,
    373, 389, 393–94, 474, 478,
    508, 572
Higashimura, Akiko, 480
Higgins, Dusty, 324
Higgins, John, 93, 414
Higgins, Kyle, 27, 57
Higgins, Michael, 286
Higuchi, Daisuke, 489
Hiiragi, Yukita, 633
Hikami, Keiichi, 300
Hill, Joe, 415, 420
Hill, Jonathan David, 469
Hill, Travis, 523
Himekawa, Akria, 312
Hinds, Gareth, 294, 330, 502, 505
Hine, David, 20
Hino, Matsuri, 386, 389
Hirano, Kohta, 382
Hirsh, Ananth, 466
Hirsh, Andy, 637
Hitch, Bryan, 83, 87, 250
Hoena, Blake, 634
Hogan, Chuck, 385
Holgate, Douglas, 316, 421
Holguin, Brian, 326
Hollingworth, Matt, 261
Holm, Jennifer L. "Jenni," xi,
    xxxi, 485, 516, 531, 542, 552
Holm, Matthew, 485, 516, 531,
    542, 552
Holmes, Eric, 284
Holmes, Mark, 443
Homer, 162, 330
Hooper, Ken, 152

Hope, Sandra, 305
Hopeless, Dennis, 102, 112, 193
Hoppenstand, Gary, 643
Hosler, Jay, 629–32, 636, 638
Hosoda, Mamoru, 267
Hotta, Yumi, 147
Hotz, Kyle, 234, 376
Houghton, Chris, 590
Houghton, Shane, 388, 534, 590
Howard, Jason, 140, 381
Howard, Josh, xxxi, 228, 387
Howard, Robert E., 307–8,
    310, 315
Howard, Zach, 244, 420
Howe, Sean, 647
Howell, Corin, 248, 286
Howlett, Mike, 421
Huang, Edwin, 600
Huat, Tan Eng, 406
Hub, 182
Hubbard, Al, 528
Hubert, 317, 435–36
Huddleson, Mike, 385, 422
Hudlin, Reginald, 28, 390
Huehner, Mariah, 373–74
Huey, Debbie, 510
Huffman, Art, 630
Hughes, Adam, 93, 506, 575
Hugo, Victor, 502
Huizenga, Kevin, 472
Humphreys, Jessica Dee, 609
Humphries, Sam, 45, 73, 102,
    113, 388
Hunter, Robert, 408
Hurtt, Brian, 154, 199
Hurwitz, Gregg, 12
Huston, Charlie, 274
Hutchison, David, 644
Hutchison, Megan, 365
Hwa, Kim Dong, 500

Ibrahim, Humayoun, 202
Igarashi, Daisuke, 242
Ikeda, Akihisa, 564
Immonen, Kathryn, 89, 504
Immonen, Stuart, 31, 95, 238, 504
Inagaki, Riichiro, 488
Indro, Daniel, 252
Infantino, Carmine, 73–74, 413
Infurnani, Joe, 504
Innes, Lorna, 337–38
Inoue, Iroha, 633
Inoue, Takehiko, 187
Inzana, Ryan, 339
Irving, Frazer, 412

Isaacs, Rebekah, 373–74, 507
Isabella, Tony, 118, 647
Isaka, Kotara, 235
Isanove, Richard, 20
Isayama, Hajime, 262
Ishida, Sui, 391
Ishikawa, Kenji, 633
Ishinomori, Shotaro, 314
Ito, Junji, 396, 402, 420–21, 614
Iverson, Mitch, 288
Iwaaki, Hitoshi, 245
Iwaoka, Hisae, 260

Jablonski, Carla, 170
Jackson, Dan, 374
Jadson, Jack, 316
James, Cassandra, 316
Jamieson, Victoria, 481
Jampole, Ryan, 524
Janin, Mikel, 41, 85
Janson, Klaus, 15–16, 35–36
Jarrell, Sandy, 245, 631
Jason, 153
Jay, Damian, 510
Jean, Cassandra, 361
Jeanty, Georges, 372–73
Jenkins, Paul, 12, 67, 223, 414
Jenkins, Tyler, 353
Jensen, Jeff, 451–52
Jensen, Van, 41, 324
Jimenez, Phil, 108–9, 320
Jippes, Daan, 529
Jock, 43, 417
Jodorowsky, Alejandro, 202, 499
John, Lizzy, 326
Johns, Geoff, 4, 6, 25, 33, 40,
    44–45, 86–87, 108–9, 122
Johnson, Drew, 213
Johnson, Eric, 437
Johnson, Mike, 64, 226–27, 286
Johnson, Paul, 244
Johnson, Staz, 195
Johnston, Antony, 266
Johnston, Janine, 631
Jolley, Dan, 264, 286, 412, 540
Jones, Bruce, 208
Jones, Christopher, 250
Jones, Eric, 18
Jones, Gerard, 647
Jones, J. G., 29, 93
Jones, Joelle, 264, 417, 432, 446
Jones, Kelley, 123, 244, 255, 310,
    363, 376
Jones, Malcolm III, 362–63
Jones, Nat, 394, 420

Jones, Tim, 226–27
Jones, Tristan, 244
Jordan, Justin, 46, 420
Juhl, Jerry, 569
Junior, Pericles, 283
Jurgens, Dan, 3, 26–27, 42, 107,
    120, 244

Kaczynski., Tom, 288
Kagami, Takaya, 384
Kain, Alex, 175
Kalonji, J. P., 173, 182
Kamarga, Ramanda, 84
Kamio, Yoko, 458
Kan, Kat, 644
Kanata, Konami, 543, 546
Kanda,Takayuki, 611
Kane, Bob, 7, 34
Kane, Gil, 56, 139, 307
Kane, Shaky, 507
Kaneko, Atsushi, 289
Kanigher, Robert, 171, 277
Kannenberg, Gene, 644
Kanno, Aya, 466
Kano, 335, 399
Kanzaki, Shiden, 258
Kariya, Tetsu, 494
Kartalopoulos, Bill, 507
Karwowski, Chris, 585
Katchor, Ben, 507
Kato, Kazue, 411
Katsura, Masakazu, 65
Katsushika, Hokusei, 435
Katz, Jeff, 376
Kavanagh, Terry, 274
Kawabata, Kiyoshi, 633
Kawahara, Kazune, 464
Kawahara, Reki, 267
Kayl, Bradley, 204
Keenan, Shelia, 134
Keene, Brian, 420
Kieth, Sam, 244, 362
Keller, Michael, 630
Kelly, Joe, 4, 37, 64, 349, 476
Kelly, John, 524
Kelly, Ryan, 460
Kelly, Walt, 326, 529
Kelman, Ari, 165
Kendall, David, 389
Kennedy, Cam, 211, 220
Kennedy, Mike, 220
Keown, Dale, 49
Kerascoët, 317, 435–36, 594
Kerschbaum, John, 320
Kerschel, Karl, 439

Kesel, Barbara, 534
Kesel, Karl, 47, 393
Kessinger, Brian, 74
Keyser, Amber J., 633–34
Kibuishi, Kazu, xi, xxxi, 198,
    336–37, 508–9
Kieth, Sam, 244, 362
Kikai, Masahide, 612
Kikuyaro, 633
Kilgore, Al, 536
Kim, Chuck, 524
Kim, Derek Kirk, 481–82
Kim, Jae Hwan, 305
Kim, Rock-He, 102
Kim, Susan, 146, 394
Kindt, Matt, 87, 91, 154, 181, 208,
    255, 426–27, 435
King, Jeff, 107
King, Stacy, 503
King, Stephen, 380, 420
King, Tom, 11–12, 41, 107, 428
Kinney, Dick, 528
Kinney, Jeff, 570
Kino, Hinoki, 260
Kio, Shimoku, 516
Kirby, Jack, xxxi, 29, 49, 52, 73,
    75–77, 82, 84, 94, 131, 137,
    192, 265, 287–88, 332, 334,
    421, 448, 452, 575, 650, 653
Kirby, J. J., 586
Kirk, Leonard, 84, 99
Kirkham, Tyler, 46
Kirkman, Robert, 51, 140, 367,
    381, 390, 392, 650
Kishida, Ren, 612
Kishimoto, Masashi, 179–80
Kishiro, Yukito, 272
Kitoh, Mohrio, 281
Kitson, Barry, 116, 272–73, 334
Klavan, Laurence, 146, 394
Klein, Grady, 639
Klinger, Leslie S., 361
Klock, Geoff, 647
Knaak, Richard, 305
Kneece, Mark, 644
Knisley, Lucy, 498
Kobayashi, Miyuki, 493
Koblish, Scott, 38, 113
Koch, Falynn, 636–37
Kochalka, James, 320, 560, 593
Koepp, David, 152
Kogge, Michael, 382
Koike, Kazuo, 178–79
Koike, Keiichi, 289
Kojima, Goseki, 178

Kojima, Hiroyuki, 633
Komura, Ayumi, 493
Konietzko, Bryan, 173
Konishi, Noriyuki, 601
Konomi, Takeshi, 489
Kordey, Igor, 223
Korim, J., 140
Kot, Ales, 80, 91
Koth, Mona, 534
Koume, Keito, 303
Kovac, Tommy, 347
Koyama, Keiko, 633
Koyama-Richard, Brigitte, 644
Krause, Peter, 117, 223
Kreisberg, Andrew, 43
Krohn, Katherine, 634–35
Krosoczka, Jarret J., 516, 576–77
Krpata, Mitch, 570
Krueger, Jim, 86
Krul, J. T., 42–43, 166, 167
Kruse, Jan, 528
Kubert, Adam, 4–5, 10, 77, 81,
    112, 115
Kubert, Andy, 7, 15, 67, 108, 110,
    115, 125, 586
Kubert, Joe, 93, 171, 309
Kubo, Tite, 403
Kuder, Aaron, 46
Kuhoric, James, 376
Kuper, Peter, 646
Kupperberg, Paul, 469
Kurtzman, Alex, 226
Kusaka, Hidenori, 589
Kwapisz, Gary, 166
Kwitney, Alisa, 321
Kwong, Peter, 397
Kyle, Craig, 101, 115
Kyriazis, Illias, 560

Labatt, Mary, 442–43
Lackey, Mercedes, 316
Lacy, Rick, 377
Ladronn, Jose, 274
Laguna, Fabio, 377
Laird, Peter, 184
Lamb, Braden, 221, 292, 320
Lambert, Joseph, 320, 607
Laming, Marc, 113, 421
Land, Dave, 213
Land, Greg, 20, 78, 97,
    112, 115
Land, Miles, 207–8
Landridge, Roger, 62
Landry, Jon, 305
Landsdale, Joe, 195

Langridge, Roger, 194, 322,
    334, 512, 520, 532–33,
    535–36, 569
Lanning, Andy, 71–75, 99, 105,
    109, 120, 223, 232
Lansdale, Joe R., 310, 389
Lapham, David, 37–38, 105, 233,
    269, 385, 450
Lapuss, Stephanie, 531
Larcenet, Maru, 594
Lark, Michael, 36, 65,
    259–60, 425
Larosa, Lewis, 59
Larraz, Pepe, 214
Larroca, Salvador, 53, 81, 212
Larsen, Erik, 49, 650
Larson, Hope, 146, 347, 439, 471,
    478, 510
Lash, Batton, 566
Lashley, Ken, 98
Latour, Jason, 63, 98, 449
Laughead, Mike, 510
Lavie, Boaz, 166
Law, Shane, 104
Lawless, Molly, 626
Lawrence, Jack, 341
Lawson, Jim, 140
Lawton, Meagan, 531
Lay, Carol, 497
Layman, John, 12–13, 244, 395,
    424, 644
Layton, Bob, 53, 157–58, 240
Lean, Rob, 232
Leandri, Paolo, 510
Leavitt, Sarah, 621
Lee, Alvin, 161
Lee, Ed, 231
Lee, Jae, 93, 103, 287
Lee, Janet, 500, 504
Lee, Jim, 9, 15, 86, 95
Lee, NaRae, 236
Lee, Pat, 309
Lee, Paul, 375
Lee, Stacey, 62
Lee, Stan, xxxi, xxxiv, 18, 49, 52,
    75–77, 82, 84, 94, 192, 281,
    332, 334, 412–13, 575, 606,
    646–47, 650
Lee, SunKeno, 503
Lee, Tony, 251–52, 390
Lee, TseMei, 502
Legrand, Benjamin, 261, 447
LeHeup, Jody, 420–21
Lehner, Zach, 389
Leialoha, Steve, 363

Lemire, Jeff, 42–43, 67, 85, 97,
    125, 128, 256, 265, 273, 274,
    349, 399, 415, 473–74
Lemke, Donald, 634
L'Engle, Madeline, 347
Lenox, Emi, 128
Leon, Nico, 112
Leonardi, Rick, 23, 212, 245, 274
Lepage, Emmanuel, 289
Lepore, Jill, 647
Lepp, Royden, 278
Le Roy, Maximilien, 621
Leth, Kate, 58, 293, 358
Lethem, Jonathan, 507
Level, Brian, 421
Levens, Megan, 463
Lewis, Brett, 231
Lewis, Jackie, 488
Lewis, Jeff, 349
Lewis, John, 615
Levitz, Paul, 646
Li, Yishan, 373
Lia, Simone, 320
Lie, Chris, 345
Lieber, Steve, 118, 191, 286, 581,
    587, 631, 643
Lieberman, A. J., 47
Liefeld, Rob, 37–38, 95, 101, 222
Liew, Sonny, 62, 347, 505
Lim, Ron, 76, 109, 120–22
Lima, Luciano, 198
Lindsay, Ryan, 534
Liniers, 320
Liu, Marjorie, 29, 213, 316, 398
Livingston, Stuart, 508
Livingston, Todd, 387
Lizano, Marc, 501
Lloyd, David, 414
Lob, Jaques, 261
Lobdell, Scott, 4–5, 88, 91, 107,
    115, 125, 373, 440, 560, 586
Lobel, Beni, 286
Locke, Vincent "Vince," 363,
    389, 631
Loeb, Jeph, 9, 32, 35, 64, 75,
    105, 125
Lolli, Matteo, 112
Lolos, Vasillis, 309
Lopez, David, 60, 70, 112, 154
Lopresti, Aaron, 49
Lotay, Tula, 316
Loughridge, Lee, 560
Loux, Matthew, 590
Lovecraft, H. P, 400–402, 420
Loveness, Jeff, 74

Lozzi, Arturo, 269, 272–73
Lucas, Adriano, 336
Lucas, George, 152, 206, 214
Lucasfilm Book Group, 206–7
Lucke, Deb, 561
Luis, Jose, 309
Lullabi, Ludo, 305
Lupacchino, Emanuela, 157–58
Lutes, Jason, 498
Luthi, Morgan, 541
Lyga, Allsion A. W., 645
Lyga, Barry, 342, 645
Lyle, Tom, 59
Lynch, Brian, 277, 374–75
Lynch, Jay, 55

Maberrry, Jonathan, 390–91
Macchio, Ralph, 285, 413
MacDonald, Andy, 125
MacGregor, Don, 197
Mack, David, 35
MacLean, Andrew, 262, 299, 507
Madden, Matt, 506–7
Madureira, Joe, 37
Maeda, Shunshin, 587
Mael, 629
Magno, Carlos, 397
Magurie, Kevin, 549, 575
Mahfood, Jim, 506
Mahnke, Doug, 9, 45, 87,
   106, 108
Maiden, Tavis, 548
Maihack, Mike, 194, 229
Malhotra, Vic, 420
Maleev, Alex, 36, 214, 231–32
Maloney, Casey, 225
Manapul, Francis, 12, 41
Manara, Milo, 363, 499
Manchette, Jean-Patrick, 446,
   448, 450
Mancini, Haley, 579
Manco, Leonardo, 274
Mandrake, Tom, 378
Manfredi, Federica, 224, 226, 418
Manga University Culinary
   Institute, 497
Mann, Clay, 181, 334
Mann, George, 251, 253
Manning, Dirk, 402
Manning, Matthew K., 104, 647
Manning, Russ, 276
Mantlo, Bill, 73, 118, 285
Marangon, Lucas, 217
Marcellus, Rhoald, 387
March, Guillem, 34, 48

Marchetto, Augusto, 592
Marchetto, Marisa Acocella,
   469, 609
Marcos, Pablo, 223, 315
Marino, Jesus, 4
Maroh, Julie, 458
Marquez, David, 23, 53, 107
Marraffino, Frank, 390
Marriotte, Jeff, 373
Mars, Lee, 152
Marsh, Tracy, 395
Marsters, James, 375
Martin, Ann M., 514
Martin, Cynthia, 633–35
Martin, Emily, 324
Martin, Frank, 259
Martin, Laura, 375
Martin, Marcos, 27, 413, 431
Martinez, Alvaro, 13
Maruca, Brian, 553
Marx, Christy, 82
Marz, Marcos, 283
Marz, Ron, 121, 183, 219–20,
   310, 601
Marzan, Jose Jr, 265
Mashima, Hiro, 203
Masters, Jason, 191
Masuda, Eiji, 562
Matalas, Terry, 225
Mathieu, Marc-Antoine, 153
Matsuda, 633
Matsui, Yusei, 553
Matsumoto, Taiyo, 289
Matt, Joe, 652
Matte, Johane, 508
Matthews, Brett, 196, 205
May, Michael, 282
Maybury, Paul, 145, 640
Mayernik, Val, 549
Mayhew, Mike, 197, 206, 208
Mazan, 594
Mazzucchelli, David, 16, 36,
   153, 320
McCann, Jim, 328
McCarthy, Ray, 60
McCarthy, Shane, 105, 284, 286
McClaren, Meredith, 475, 631
McCloud, Scott, 6, 241, 482, 507,
   604–5, 644
McConnell, Aaron, 624, 628
McCoola, Marika, 316
McCranie, Stephen, 569
McCreery, Connor, 359
McDaniel, Scott, 60
McDonald, Kel, 329, 373

McDonnell, Luke, 90
McDuffie, Dwanye, 86, 274
McFarlane, Todd, 49, 379, 650
McGinty, Ian, 531
McGovern, Adam, 510
McGraw, Royal, 548
McGuinness, Ed, 37, 75, 105
McGuire, Richard, 243
McHugh, Maura, 380
McKean, Dave, 358, 363, 414
McKeever, Ted, 412
McKelvie, Jamie, 93, 355
McKenna, Mark, 218, 283
McLauirn, Marc, 55
McLeod, Kagan, 159
McMahon, Mike, 233–34
McManus, Shawn, 320, 363
McNeil, Carla Speed, 191, 242,
   316, 470, 534, 630
McNiven, Steve, 30, 68, 71,
   81, 107
Mebberson, Amy, 533–34
Mechner, Jordan, 154, 163–64
Medic, Zeliko, 303
Medina, Angel, 427
Medina, Lan, 274
Medina, Paco, 37–38, 73, 75
Medley, Linda, 317–18, 630, 638
Medri, Denis, 607
Meltzer, Brad, 42, 86, 617
Mendelsohn, Jack, 536
Menu, Jean-Christophe, 594
Merritt, Kory, 570
Messina, David, 34, 225–27,
   280, 373
Messner-Lobes, William, 152,
   393, 401
Meyer, Carla K., 645
Meyer, Jennifer, 320
Mhan, Pop, 60, 100, 230
Michelinie, David, 53, 153
Midorikawa, Yuki, 352
Miéville, China, 39
Mignola, Mike, 67, 73, 244, 309,
   323, 368–70, 376–78, 380, 400,
   413, 558, 560
Milgrom, Al, 634–35
Millar, Mark, 40, 67, 83, 107, 127,
   192, 239, 249, 390
Miller, Bryan Q., 255
Miller, Frank, xxxi, 15–16,
   35–36, 66, 184, 279, 443, 448
Miller, John Jackson, 152,
   217, 235
Miller, Mike S., 124

Miller, Steve, 645
Milligan, Peter, 46, 85
Millionaire, Tony, 323, 336, 520–21
Mills, Pat, 233–34, 250, 555
Milne, Alex, 284
Milonogiannis, Giannis, 222, 426
Milton, Fred, 529
Minagawa, Ryoji, 160
Minami, Maki, 521
Miranda, Inaki, 320
Mireault, Bernie, 631
Mitchell, Todd, 321
Mitsuki, Miko, 383
Mitten, Christopher, 266, 507
Miura, Kentaro, 294
Miyama, Hugin, 302
Miyamoto, Yuki, 490
Miyawaki, Yoko, 611
Miyazawa, Takeshi, 56, 143
Mizuki, Shigeru, 170
Mizuno, Junko, 510
Mock, Rebecca, 146
Modan, Rutu, 166, 170
Moebius, 76, 231, 509
Moench, Doug, 73, 123, 273–74
Moesta, Rebecca, 223
Molina, Jorge, 32, 77, 102, 112, 333
Moline, Karl, 372
Molnar, Stephen "Steve," 224, 226
Monlongo, Jorge, 531
Monnin, Katie, 645
Montclare, Brandon, 137
Montovani, Fabio, 224–25
Moon, Fabio, 472, 486, 507
Mooney, Stephen, 41, 374
Mooneyham, Christopher (Chris), 146–47, 246, 421
Moorcock, Michael, 241, 359
Moore, Alan, xxxi, 16, 55, 88, 92, 130–31, 220, 361, 399, 401–2, 428–29, 451, 646, 650–51
Moore, Anne Elizabeth, 506
Moore, B. Clay, 431, 507
Moore, Jerome K., 305
Moore, Leah, 316
Moore, Steve, 250
Moore, Stuart, 105, 225
Moore, Terry, 89, 131, 229, 301, 416, 462
Moore, Tony, 38, 392, 406, 506
Moore, Tradd, 421
Morales, Rags, 5

Moreci, Michael, 377, 418, 420
Morel, Oliver, 629
Moreno, Chris, 540
Moretti, Mark, 181
Mori, Hideki, 179
Mori, Kaoru, 499–500
Morinohon, 258
Morisaki, Yuki, 491
Morishige, Takuma, 519
Moritat, 195, 244, 428
Morris, Steve, 375
Morrison, Bill, 537
Morrison, Grant, 5–8, 10–11, 40, 61, 108, 125, 136, 250, 281, 351, 425
Morrison, Robbie, 252–53
Morse, Scott, 289, 471, 510, 578, 622
Moss, Drew, 141, 421
Motomi, Kyousuke, 463
Motter, Dean, 274
Mouly, Francoise, 506, 653
Mowry, Chris, 395–96
Moy, Jeffrey "Jeff," 223
Moy, Phil, 579
Mucci Tim, 506
Mucha, Corinne, 320, 475
Mulazzi, Paola, 592
Murase, Sho, 441
Murata, Yusuke, 488, 578
Murphy, Matthew H., 143
Murphy, Phil, 293
Murphy, Sean, 249, 351, 402
Murray, Will, 582
Murry, Paul, 529, 532
Musacchia, Vince, 535
Muth, John J., 363
Mutti, Andrea, 13, 170, 309, 390
Myler, Jake, 182, 529
Myrick, Leland, 631

Nadeau, John, 220
Nagasaki, Takashi, 435
Naifeh, Ted, 301, 315, 357–59, 589
Nakagawa, Saki, 262
Nakajo, Hisaya, 464
Nakamura, Tamako, 267
Nakamura, Yoshiki, 461
Nakashima, Kazuki, 159
Nanatsuki, Kyoichi, 160
Naniiebim, 316
Napton, Robert Place, 148
Nash, Jamie, 148
Nauck, Todd, 52, 584

Naujokaitis, Pranas T., 138
Navarrete, Vincente, 566
Nazif, Iwan, 298
Neely, Tom, 525
Negishi, Kyoko, 490
Neilson, Micky, 305
Nelson, Avrid, 437
Nelson, Michael Alan, 64, 244, 393, 401
Nelson, O. T., 264
Neri, G., 455
Neufeld, Josh, 623
Neumann, Mikey, 228
Neves, Diogenes, 99
Newgarden, Mark, 320
Newman, Kim, 380
Newman, Paul S., 143
Ng, Joe, 161
Nguyen, Dustin, 10–11, 274, 573
Nguyen, Eric, 231–32
Nguyen, Nick, 647
Nguyen, Peter, 80
Nicholas, Jamar, 451
Nichols, Stan, 301
Nicieza, Fabian, 4, 37, 60, 101, 104, 112, 115
Nicole, Ethan, 586
Nicole, Malachai, 586
Niemczyk, Kate, 56
Nightow, Yasuhiro, 239
Nihei, Tsutomu, 231, 234, 257
Niimura, J. M. Ken, 476
Niles, Steve, 375–76, 385, 389, 394, 398, 401
Nitta, Hideo, 633
Nixey, Troy, 400
Nocenti, Ann, 34–35, 42–43, 54
Nolan, Conor, 322
Nord, Cary, 240, 308–9
Norrie, Christine, 475
Norris, Paul, 25
North, Ryan, 221, 292, 517, 582
Northfield, Gary, 546–47
Northrop, Chris, 480
Norton, Mike, 43, 105, 113
Nostrand, Howard, 419
Noto, Phil, 29, 209, 215, 316
Novak, Ryan, 645
Nowlan, Kevin, 244, 407, 413
Nyberg, Amy Kiste, 647
Nyeu, Tao, 323
Nylund, Eric, 232
Nytra, David, 325, 355

Obata, Takeshi, 248, 405, 470
O'Brien, Patrick, 136
O'Connor, George, 320, 323, 330, 626
Oda, Eiichiro, 588
Odagawa, Ryan, 208
O'Donnell, Liam, 634–35
Oeming, Michael Avon, 128, 300, 310, 315, 327, 335, 506
Oh, Mo, 323
Ohba, Tsugumi, 404–5, 470
Ohkubo, Atsushi, 378
Ohta, Tamon, 281
Oima, Yoshitoki, 483
Okimoto, Shu, 491
Oliveri, Mike, 421
Olivetti, Ariel, 166, 310
Olliffe, Pat, 62
O'Malley, Bryan Lee, xxxi, 475, 482, 494
O'Malley, Kevin, 136
O'Neil, Dennis, 15, 34, 647
O'Neill, Katie, 324
O'Neill, Kevin, 88, 555
Ono, Natsume, 177, 494
Opena, Jerome, 78, 101
Orchard, Eric, 323
Orci, Robert, 226
Ordway, Jerry, 3, 130
O'Reilly, Sean, 310–11
Oremland, Jason, 343–44
Orlando, Steve, 64
Orr, Elbert, 408
Orsi, Tea, 592
Ortega, Joshua, 230
Ōshio, Satoshi, 302
Ostrander, John, xxxi, 55, 90, 209, 214, 216, 218–20, 379
Ota, Yuko, 466
Otero, Allan, 311
Otsuka, Eiji, 561
Ottaviani, Jim, 629–32, 635, 638–39
Ottley, Ryan, 51
Oubrerie, Cle'ment, 469
Outwater, Alice, 630
Ozella, Bruce, 535

Pacheco, Carlos, 31, 97, 105, 113, 192
Padilla, Agustin, 167, 228, 286
Padilla, Ariel, 288
Padua, Sydney, 638
Page, Tyler, 439
Pagulayan, Carlo, 49, 107

Pak, Greg, 5, 49, 72, 103, 111, 143, 413
Palmiotti, Jimmy, 34, 47–48, 166, 181, 195, 310, 417
Panosian, Dan, 166, 309
Paquette, Yanick, 10, 66, 125, 399
Parent, Dan, 512, 514
Park, Laura, 323
Parker, Bill, 32
Parker, Jake, 73, 116, 236, 507–9
Parker, James, 105
Parker, Jeff, 25, 111, 245, 523, 572–73, 631
Parker, Tony, 235
Parks, Ande, 42, 196, 480
Parlov, Goran, 239
Parobeck, Mike, 17
Paroline, Shelli, 221, 292, 320, 533
Parrot, Ryan, 227
Parsons, Dan, 382
Pasarin, Fernando, 26, 46
Pascoe, Jim, 377
Patterson, James, 236, 356
Patton, Michael F., 640
Pearson, Luke, 291, 350
Peck, Seth, 507
Pedrosa, Cyril, 323, 364
Peeters, Frederik, 289, 609
Pekar, Harvey, 131, 506, 606–7, 609–10, 618–19, 646
Pelletier, Paul, 25, 71–73
Pendergast, Sara, 644
Pensa, Shea Anton, 363
Percy, Benjamin, 43
Pérez, George, 4, 50, 69, 91, 105, 108–9, 139
Perez, Ramon, 48,
Perissinotto, Giada, 592
Perkins, Mike, 274
Perlin, Don, 272–73, 285
Perper, Timothy, 644
Perry, Brian, 232
Perry, Steve, 220
Petersen, David, 300–301, 533
Peterson, Brandon, 78
Peterson, Roger, 510
Peterson, Scott, 525
Petosky, Shad, 629
Petrucha, Stefan, 441, 592
Petrus, Hugo, 504
Peyo, 539
Pfeifer, Will, 25, 34, 91
Pham, LeUyen, 154, 163–64
Pham, Thien, 517

Phelan, Matt, 326, 498–99, 505
Phillips, Joe, 226
Phillips, Kelly, 507
Phillips, Nickie D., 647
Phillips, Sean, 193, 390, 414, 434, 444–46
Pichelli, Sara, 20, 23, 71, 89
Piekos, Nate, 377
Pien, Lark, 323, 485, 549
Pierce, Tamora, 316
Pierfederici, Mirco, 116
Pilcher, Tim, 644
Pilkey, Dav, 544, 583
Pina, Javiar "Javi," 46, 399
Pini, Richard, 298
Pini, Wendy, 298
Pinna, Amilcar, 112
Piskor, Ed, 491
Pitarra, Nick, 254–55
Pitre-Durocher, Sara, 286
Pittman, Eddie, 570
Pitzer, Chris, 510
Pizzari, Luca, 113
Pleece, Warren, 252, 384, 414
Ploog, Mike, 428
Plumeri, Arnaud, 138
Plunkett, Kilian, 172, 220
Plunkett, Sandy, 307, 413
Poe, Edgar Allan, 420, 453
Polls, Esteve, 194, 196–97
Pond, Mimi, 494
Ponticelli, Alberto, 39, 172, 395
Poon, Nokman, 502
Pop Art Studios, 634
Pope, Paul, 17, 28, 131, 289, 447–48, 473
Porcellino, John, 617
Portela, Frances, 232
Porter, Alan J., 523
Posehn, Brian, 37–38
Potts, Carl, 243
Powell, Bob, 419
Powell, Eric, 395, 558
Powell, Nate, 164–65, 328, 485, 615
Prado, Joe, 25
Prado, Miguelanxo, 363
Pratchett, Rhianna, 156, 316
Preiss, Byron, 123
Prezenkowski, Jeff, 395
Price, Andy, 534
Priddy, Joel, 510
Pride, Nathan, 322
Priest, Christopher, 28, 37, 581
Prince, Liz, 622

Prosser, Jerry, 244
Puckett, Kelley, 17
Pugh, Steve, 112
Pulido, Javier, 48, 105
Purcell, Gordon, 55, 223
Purcell, Steve, 552
Purvis, Leland, 170, 632
Puryear, Tony, 258
Puvilland, Alex, 154, 163–64

Quesada, Joe, 181
Quinones, Joe, 13, 548–49
Quitely, Frank, 6, 8, 281, 363

Raapack, Jheremy, 124
Rabagliati, Michel, 479
Rabbitte, David, 382
Raicht, Mike, 346, 529
Raiku, Makoto, 591
Raimi, Sam, 555
Raimi. Ivan, 555
Ralph, Brian, 387
Ramondelli, Livio, 284, 286
Ramos, Humberto, 19–20, 89, 97,
    115, 119
Randolph, Grace, 533
Randolph, Khary, 61
Raney, Tom, 29, 586
Raphael, Jordan, 647
Rapmund, Norm, 91
Ratte, David, 486
Rausch, Drew, 358
Rayner, Richard Piers, 414
Razek, Cezar, 197
Redondo, Bruno, 124, 211
Reed, Brian, 70, 232, 315
Reed, M. K., 469, 636
Reed, Scott, 72
Reeder, Amy, 137
Reinhold, Bill, 276
Reis, Ivan, 25, 44, 108
Remender, Rick, 31, 80, 101–2,
    112, 249, 260
Remnant, Joseph, 609
Renaud, Paul, 31
Rendon, Daniel, 440
Renier, Aaron, 157, 323
Rennie, Gordon, 251
Rex, Michael, 595
Reynolds, Patric, 244, 421
Ribic, Esad, 66, 76, 111, 333
Ricca, Brad, 647
Rice, Christina, 534
Rich, Jamie S., 417, 432, 446, 463
Richard, Sara, 140

Richards, Cliff, 5, 46, 390
Richardson, Mike, 173, 211,
    244, 646
Richmond, La Morris, 560
Ridgway, John, 414
Rieber, John Ney, 287
Reiss, Natalie, 495
Riggs, Ransom, 361
Riley, Ron, 198
Ringuet, J. M., 377
Rinzler, Jonathan, 206
Riordan, Rick, 328, 331
Rios, Emma, 70, 117, 199, 413
Rioux, Jo, 442
Risso, Eduardo, 303, 447,
    506, 610
Ritchie, Andrew, 401
Rivoche, Paul, 510
Robbins, Scott, 645
Robbins, Trina, 439
Roberson, Chris, 226, 389
Roberson, Ibraim, 115, 393
Roberts, James, 284
Roberts, Matthew, 397
Robertson, Chris, 244
Robertson, Darick, 59, 425
Robico, 466
Robinson, Alan, 248
Robinson, Alex, 478–79, 486
Robinson, Andrew C., 231,
    274, 612
Robinson, James, 63, 83,
    86–87, 112
Robinson, Jerry, 536
Rocafort, Kenneth, 4, 91
Roche, Nick, 251, 277, 284, 286
Rochette, Jean-Marc, 261
Rodriguez, David, 600
Rodriguez, Gabriel, 341, 415
Rodriguez, Javier, 36
Rodriguez, Robbi, 63
Rodriques, Paco, 523
Rogers, Marshall, 76, 223, 413
Roman, Dave, 174, 323, 508, 516,
    521, 524, 568
Romita, John Jr., 4–5, 13–14, 16,
    28, 31, 36, 49, 78, 103, 115,
    120, 127
Rosa, Don, 526–28
Rosado, Rafael, 516, 592
Rosado, William "Will," 168, 286
Rosanas, Ramon, 24, 111
Rose, Joel, 492
Ross, Alex, 15, 86, 110, 126, 128
Ross, Dave, 212, 218

Ross, Edward, 625
Ross, Luke, 152, 183, 208
Ross, Vaughn, 441
Rossmo, Riley, 415–16
Rousseau, Craig, 378
Roux, Stephane, 48, 209
Rove, Master, 310
Rowley, Christopher, 400
Roy, Simon, 142, 222
Royer, Mike, 333
Rozum, John, 524
Rubi, Mel, 316
Rubin, David, 328
Rubio, Kevin, 217
Rucka, Greg, 27, 29, 191, 217,
    259–60, 410–11, 425
Rude, Steve, 333
Ruffino, Nei, 316
Rugg, Jim, 349, 553
Ruiz, Alberto, 510
Ruiz, Alfonzo, 310
Ruiz, Felix, 232
Ruiz, Fernando, 246
Runge, Nick, 374, 560
Runton, Andy, 551
Russell, Gary, 251
Russell, P. Craig, 123, 309, 321,
    337, 360–63, 407, 413, 509, 652
Rust, Ned, 356
Ruth, Greg, 308, 342
Ryall, Chris, 280, 420
Ryan, Michael, 89
Ryan, Paul, 40
Ryan, Sara, 470
Ryan, Sean, 75, 91
Ryp, Juan Jose, 279

Sabin, Roger, 647
Sadowski, Stephen, 315, 320
Saeki, Shun, 491
Sagendorf, Bud, 536
Saijyo, Shinji, 492
Saimura, Tsukasa, 388
Saiz, Jesus, 31, 46, 399
Sakai, Stan, 61, 131, 173, 186–87,
    297, 323, 595
Sakakibara, Mizuki, 65
Sakisaka, Io, 462
Sakkai, Yohei, 137
Sakura, 633
Sakurakoji, Kanoko, 410
Sakurazaka, Hiroshi, 248
Sala, Richard, 438
Sale, Tim, 15, 32, 34
Saliba, Jeremy, 198

Salicrup, Jim, 285
Salonga, Noah, 316
Saltares, Javier, 246, 406
Samnee, Chris, 29, 36, 62, 334, 507
Sampson, Alison, 421
Samson, Andrew, 585
Samura, Hiroaki, 175
Sanchez, Alex, 218
Sanchez, Eduardo, 148
Sanchez, Israel, 320
Sanchez, Sergio Garcia, 477
Sanders, Steven, 253
Sandoval, Gerardo, 79, 112
Sandoval, Rafa, 34
SanGiacomo, Mike, 58
Sanlaville, Michaël, 160
Santacruz, Derlis, 156
Santacruz, Juan, 49
Santat, Dan, 582
Santiago, Wilfred, 605
Santolouco, Mateus, 39, 184
Santos, Victor, 300
Sarin, Max, 475
Sarracini, Chris, 161
Sato, Daisuke, 388
Sato, Shouji, 388
Satrapi, Marjane, 618, 655
Sauvage, Marguerite, 123, 315
Sava, Scott Christian, 150
Saviuk, Alex, 491
Sawyer, Jonathan Brandon, 421
Say, Allen, 610
Scalera, Matteo, 249
Scalf, Chris, 216, 219
Scarpa, Romano, 528
Schade, Susan, 264
Schaffenberger, Kurt, 3
Scheer, Paul, 105, 567
Schigiel, Gregg, 579, 586
Schirmer, Brian, 198
Schiti, Valerio, 72
Schlerf, Chris, 232
Schmidt, Otto, 112
Schnepp, Jon, 393
Schodt, Frederick, 644
Schoening, Dan, 559
Schrag, Ariel, 510, 613
Schreiber, Nathan, 640
Schreck, Bob, 139
Schultz, Charles M., 534–35
Schultz, Mark, 4, 428, 631, 638
Schulz, Barbara, 633–34
Schumacher, Michael, 647
Schwartz, Viviane, 354

Schweizer, Chris, xi, 149–50, 558
Scioli, Tom, 287
Scott, Cavan, 251, 253
Scott, Damion, 60, 406
Scott, Mairghread, 286
Scott, Nicola, 43, 316, 410–11
Scott, Stephen B. "Steve," 152, 407
Scott, Vicki, 534–35
Scrambly, Crab, 361
Sears, Bart, 310, 575, 596
Sebela, Christopher, 420
Sechrist, Rad, 506, 508–9
Seeley, Steve, 377, 418, 420
Seeley, Tim, 13, 41, 286, 418, 420
Sejic, Stjepan, 302
Sekowsky, Mike, 118
Sellner, Joelle, 536
Selma, Nicholas Daniel, 156
Sepulveda, Miguel, 46
Serchay, David S., 645
Serrano, Elliot, 548
Serwacki, Anita, 585
Seth, 646, 652
Severin, John, 380
Severin, Marie, 630
Sevy, Phillip, 156
Sfar, Joann, 460, 520, 561, 571, 594, 655
Shadmi, Koren, 616
Shakespeare, William, 217, 359–60, 394, 502, 505
Shalve Declan, 309
Shanahan, Katie, 508
Shanahan, Steven, 508
Shaner, Evan, 112
Shanower, Eric, 162–63, 341, 343, 650
Shapiro, David R., 141
Sharp, Liam, 230, 244
Shedd, Blair, 251
Sheikman, Alex, 326
Shen, Prudence, 478
Shiei, 189, 386
Shiga, Jason, 463, 478, 516, 587
Shimabukuro, Mitsutoshi, 495
Shimizu, Eiichi, 247
Shimoguchi, Tomohiro, 247
Shinohara, Chie, 344
Shioya, Hitoshi, 137
Shooter, Jim, 111, 118, 142–43, 157–58, 240, 269, 276
Shouoto, Aya, 348, 383
Showman, Galen, 407
Shubuya, Michio, 633

Shuster, Joe, 2, 133, 647
Siedell, Tim, 212
Siegel, Jerry, 2, 133, 647
Siegel, Mark, 323, 345, 622
Siegel, Siena Cherson, 622
Sienkiewicz, Bill, 36, 73, 363, 429
Sikoryak, Robert, 320
Silas, Thony, 27
Silvan, Rhea, 381
Silvani, James, 525, 533
Silvestri, Marc, 67, 95, 114–15
Sim, Dave, 646
Simmons, Alex, 148–49, 512
Simon, Joe, 29, 131, 288, 421, 448, 653
Simone, Gail, 26, 37, 90, 156, 310, 315–16
Simons, Rikki, 531
Simonson, Louise, 3, 83, 94, 101, 114, 305, 584
Simonson, Walter "Walt," xxxi, 15, 67, 75, 78, 83, 94, 110, 114, 139, 153, 238, 265, 279, 305, 331–33, 335, 359, 428
Simpson, William, 414
Sims, Chris, 38, 113
Sina, A. B., 154
Singh, Mukesh, 136
Sison, Kriss, 189
Siu-Chong, Ken, 161
Skillman, Eric, 426
Skroce, Steve, 261
Slade, Christian, 351
Slavin, Bill, 545
Sliney, William "Will," 23, 113
Slott, Dan, 19–20, 76, 112, 119, 586
Slott, Rachel, 226
Small, David, 621
Smallwood, Greg, 192
Smith, Adam, 352–53
Smith, Andy, 121
Smith, Beau, 200
Smith, Brian Reis, 346, 529
Smith, Cory, 75, 143, 184, 276
Smith, C. P., 66
Smith, Felipe, 70, 112, 406
Smith, Greg, 389
Smith, Jeff, xxxi, xxxv, 33, 254–55, 291, 295–97, 507, 549, 651, 654
Smith, Kevin, 35, 42, 573
Smith, Mark Andrew, 145
Smith, Matt, 306

Smith, Matthew Dow, 251, 322, 420, 573
Smith, Matthew J., 643
Smith, Mike, 624
Smith, Paul, 62, 428–29
Smith, Tim, 584
Smith, Tod, 634–35
Smith, Woollcott, 630
Snark, Gun, 263
Snider, Jesse Blaze, 533, 544
Sniegoski, Tom, 223, 297
Snyder, Ray, 412
Snyder, Scott, 11, 13, 380, 399, 402, 417
Sohn, Emily, 633–34
Sommariva, Jon, 104
Sommers, Joseph Michael, 647
Sonishi, Kenji, 275
Sonnenfeld, Barry, 136
Soo, Kean, 351, 509, 549
Sook, Ryan, 10
Sorachi, Hideaki, 176
Sorensen, Jen, 630
Sorese, Jeremy, 258, 540
Soria, Gabriel, 384
Soriano, Jhomar, 400, 426
Sorrentino, Andrea, 42–43, 67, 113, 327, 383
Soule, Charles D., 36–37, 46, 68, 106, 112, 214–15, 399
Southard, Nate, 421
Soy, Dexter, 70
Spangler, Bill, 288
Sparrow, Aaron, 525
Spaziante, Pat "Spaz," 276
Spears, Rick, 357
Spencer, Nick, 24, 31, 78, 80, 118, 419
Spiegelman, Art, xxxi, 604, 615–16, 646, 655
Spiegelman, Nadja, 477
Spires, Ashley, 543
Sprouse, Chris, 10, 113, 428
Spurgeon, Tom, 647
Spurrier, Simon "Si," 102, 113, 252, 390
Stack, Frank, 606
Stackpole, Michael A., 220
Stakal, Nick, 376
Stanley, John, 518
Staples, Fiona, 204–5, 382, 422, 513
Staples, Greg, 246
Stark, Richard, 432
Starkings, Richard, 433

Starks, Kyle, 555
Starlin, Jim, 9, 76, 109, 119–22, 124
Staton, Joe, 139, 619
Stavans, Ilan, 626
Stegman, Ryan, 81, 119
Steinke, Aron Nels, 522
Stenbeck, Ben, 369, 380
Stephenson, Eric, 269
Steranko, Jim, 192
Sterling, Zack, 293
Stern, Roger, 3, 71, 120, 413
Stevens, Alec, 363
Stevens, Dave, 61
Stevenson, Noelle, 113, 441, 598
Stevenson, Robert Louis, 133, 156
Stewart, Cameron, 10, 26, 34
Stewart, Dave, 309, 444–45
Stilton, Geronimo, 530
Stilton, Thea, 530
Stokely, Jeff, 322, 480
Stoker, Bram, 381, 385, 420
Stokes, Johanna, 387
Stokoe, James, 131, 301, 395–96, 496
Stone, Sarah, 286
Stones, Tad, 377
Storck, Patrick, 533
Storey, Barron, 364
Storino, Sara, 592
Straczynski, J. Michael, 76, 93, 125, 334
Stradley, Randy, 211–12, 245
Strobl, Staci, 647
Strobl, Tony, 528
Stroman, Larry, 243
Stucker, Larry, 584
Sturges, Matthew, 319, 321
Sturm, James, 603–4, 652
Sturt, George, 420
Su, E. J., 284, 395
Suayan, Mico, 273
Suburbia, Liz, 481
Sudžuka, Goran, 37
Suekane, Kumiko, 256–57
Sugimoto, Igura, 267
Sullivan, Lee, 253
Sumerak, Marc, 574
Sunrise, 65
Suriano, Andy, 183
Suruga, Hikaru, 263
Sutton, Tom, 223, 413, 420
Suzukaze, Ryo, 263
Suzuki, Etsuo, 611
Suzuki, Julietta, 465, 597

Swan, Curt, 223
Swarte, Joost, 554
Swierczynski, Duane, 29, 50, 82, 234, 269, 272–73, 396, 420
Syaf, Ardian, 26, 125
Syma, Carrye Kay, 645
Szabla, Anne, 295

Tada, Kaoru, 464
Tadano, Nobuaki, 205
Takahashi, Mana, 633
Takahashi, Rumiko, xxxi, 339, 408
Takahashi, Shin, 633
Takamisaki, Ryo, 267
Takara, Marcio, 84, 112, 117
Takase, Naoko, 611
Takatsu, Keita, 633
Takaya, Natsuki, 467
Takeda, Sana, 382, 398
Takei, Hiroyuki, 409
Takemura, Masaharu, 633
Takeuchi, Naoko, 34, 89
Takeuchi, Ryosuke, 248
Talajic, Dalibor, 113, 421
Talbot, Bryan, 354, 363, 414, 426, 610, 623
Talbot, Mary, 610
Taliaferro, Al, 528
Talon, Durwin, 647
Tamaki, Jillian, xxix, 484–85, 583
Tamaki, Mariko, xxix, 156, 484–85
Tamura, Yumi, 306
Tan, Billy, 45
Tan, Shaun, 248
Tanaka, Etsuro, 633
Tanaka, Massashi, 547
Tanemura, Arina, 459
Tanner, Michael, 389
Tardi, Jacques, 169, 446–48, 450
Tarentino, Quentin, 194, 426
Tarr, Babs, 26
Tatsumi, Yoshihiro, 506
Taylor, Dan, 127
Taylor, Dave, 253
Taylor, Tom, 66, 124, 211, 214, 219, 420
Team Red Star, 204
Telgemeier, Raina, xi, xxxi, 320, 323, 406, 473, 508, 514, 516, 535, 620–21
Templesmith, Ben, 247, 376, 385, 507

Templeton, Ty, 17, 224, 572–73, 575
TenNapel, Doug, 142, 145, 236, 245, 281, 394, 397, 405
Terada, Katsuya, 289
Teran, Frank, 414
Texeira, Mark, 28, 310, 406
Tezuka, Osamu, 203, 270, 278, 611–12, 617, 654
Thomas, Brandon, 288
Thomas, Lynne M, 647
Thomas, Roy, 56, 118, 156, 192, 207, 307, 309, 381, 413, 575
Thompson, Craig, xxxi, 222, 323, 501, 608, 650
Thompson, Jason, 645
Thompson, Jill, xxxi, 68–69, 363, 369–70, 407, 562, 565
Thompson, Robbie, 62
Thompson, Stephen, 212
Tieri, Frank, 105
Tierney, Josh, 303
Timel, Sam, 316
Timm, Bruce, 17, 46–47
Timmons, Anne, 630, 633–34
Timms, John, 75, 112
Tinnell, Robert, 491
Tinnell, Shannon, 491
Tipton, David, 185, 224–26, 253
Tipton, Scott, 185, 224–26, 253, 373, 375
Tishman, David, 225
Tisserand, Mike, 507
Tiwary, Vivek J., 612
To, Marcus, 60
Tobias, Jonas, 560
Tobin, Paul, 322, 401, 420, 433–34, 523, 563
Toboso, Yana, 356–57
Tocchini, Greg, 111, 260
Togami, Shin, 633
Togashi, Yoshihiro, 151, 40
Tolibao, Harvey, 43
Toma, Rei, 298
Tomari, Miyoshi, 473
Tomasi, Peter J., 8, 12, 14, 46, 61, 106, 166
Tomine, Adrian, 652
Tonagi, Takashi, 633
Toppi, Sergio, 325
Torcivia, Joe, 528–29
Toriseva, Janne, 523
Toriyama, Akira, 158, 557, 568
Torres, J., 18, 43, 148, 174, 348, 408, 541, 584
Totleben, John, 55, 399
Towle, Ben, 154

Townsend, Michael, 640
Tracy, Brian, 640
Traviss, Karen, 230
Treiman, Lissa, 475
Trillo, Carlos, 303
Trimpe, Herb, 56, 153, 167, 285, 413
Tripp, Irving, 518
Trondheim, Lewis, 594
Troussellier, Simon, 531
Trueheart, Eric, 531
Trujillo, Josh, 293
Truman, Ben, 310
Truman, Tim, 195, 308–10
Tsang, Arnold, 161
Tse, Po, 502–3
Tsukuda, Yuto, 491
Tucci, Billy, 171
Turnbloom, Lucas, 337
Turner, Dwayne, 55
Turner, Gil, 529
Turner, Michael, 64, 105, 315
Tuska, George, 55
Twain, Mark, 506
Tyler, Carol, 623
Tynion, James IV, 13, 104, 415, 420

Uderzo, Albert, 590
Udon Studios, 37
Ueno, Haruki, 82
Underwood, Bridget, 293
Upchurch, Roc, 302
Upson, Matt, 640
Urasawa, Naoki, 240, 278, 289, 435–36
Urru, Franco, 373–75
Uslan, Michael, 469
Uy, Steve, 548

Valentine, Genevieve, 34
Valentino, Jim, 71
Valentino, Serena, 361
Valero-O'Connell, Rosemary, 441
Vamos, Leslie, 536
Vance, Jack, 202
Vance, William, 188
Vanderklugt, Kyla, 303, 322
Van Dyke, Nate, 139
Van Hamme, Jean, 188
Van Hise, James, 560
VanHook Kevin, 181, 272–73
Van Horn, William, 529
Vankin, Jonathan, 395
Van Lente, Fred, 157–58, 198, 231–32, 276, 309–10, 390, 604, 631

Van Meter, Jen, 412, 475
Vansant, Wayne, 625
Van Sciver, Ethan, 12, 40, 44, 108
Vargas, Tony, 391
Varon, Sara, 280, 323, 515–16, 521, 550
Vasquez, Jhonen, 531
Vatine, Oliver, 220
Vaughan, Brian K., xxxi, 39, 89, 135, 204–5, 237, 261, 265–66, 372, 413, 431
Vaughan, Mathew, 192
Vehlmann, Fabien, 153, 317
Veitch, Rick, 25, 55, 414
Veitch, Tom, 211, 217
Velasco, Francisco Ruiz, 220
Velhmann, Fabian, 202
Venable, Colleen AF, 547
Venditti, Robert, 41, 45, 240, 280, 328, 331, 415
Verheiden, Mark, 244, 246
Versaci, Rocco, 648
Vess, Charles, 297, 362–63, 651
Vidaurri, Shane Michael "S. M.," 191, 322, 350–51
Vieceli, Emma, 251
Vilanova, Guiu, 309
Villagran, Ricardo, 223
Villalobos, Ramon, 112
Villanelli, Paolo, 169
Villarrubia, Jose, 331
Villavert, Armand Jr., 533
Vitti, Alessandro, 253
Viva, Frank, 156
Vivës, Bastien, 160, 289
von den Bogaert, Harmen Meyndertsz, 626
Von Eeden, Trevor, 55

Wachter, Dave, 396, 398
Wagner, Doug, 14
Wagner, John, 103, 220, 233–34, 246, 250
Wagner, Justin, 551
Wagner, Matt, 194, 197
Wagner, Ron, 168
Waid, Mark, xxxi, 19, 29, 32, 36–37, 40, 61–62, 77, 84, 110, 116–17, 192, 216, 240, 393, 401, 427–29, 513
Wakasugi, Kiminori, 554
Walker, Brad, 46, 71, 90, 120, 232
Walker, Cory, 51
Walker, David, 55
Walker, Kevin "Kev," 72, 113, 390
Walker, Landry Q., 18, 84
Walker, Tigh, 193, 507

Wallace, Dan, 644
Walsh, Michael, 80
Walta, Gabriel Hernandez, 102
Walters, Mac, 235
Waltz, Tom, 184
Wang, Jen, 323, 476–77, 508
Wang, Sean, 237–38
Ward, Malachi, 288
Warner, Chris, 213, 246
Warner, John David, 223
Ware, Chris, 506, 655
Watanabe, Taeko, 177
Watase, Yuu, 338
Watkiss, John, 363
Watson, Andi, 372, 564, 595
Watson, Nathan, 540
Watsuki, Nobuhiro, 199
Watters, Shannon, 441
Way, Daniel, 37–38, 406
Way, Gerard, 20
Wayne, Matt, 18
Weaver, Dustin, 112
Wegener, Scott, 194, 271
Wein, Len, 34, 69, 74, 93, 223,
    310, 398–99, 648
Weiner, Robert G., 645
Weiner, Stephen (Steve), xi, 296,
    643–44
Weing, Drew, 155
Weinstein, Howard, 223
Weir, Christina, 150, 189,
    381, 488
Weisinger, Mort, 25
Weisman, Greg, 214
Weldele, Brett, 280, 444
Wellington, David, 390
Wells, H. G., 133, 243, 246–47
Wells, Zeb, 99, 115
Wendel, Andrew, 273
Wendig, Chuck, 208
Wenzel, David, 304
Wheatley, Doug, 207–8,
    212–13, 216
Wheatley, Mark, 327, 424
Wheaton, Ken, 535
Whedon, Joss, 89, 96, 205,
    371–75
Whedon, Zack, 205, 208
Wheelis, Mark, 630
White, Caanan, 169
White, Dean, 249
White, Shane, 507
White, Tracy, 476
Whitley, Jeremy, 324, 534, 579
Wicks, Maris, 320, 510, 632,
    635–36
Wiebe, Kurtis J., 291, 302–3, 353

Wieringo, Mike, 40
Wiesner, David, 550
Weist, Jerry, 648
Widjaja, Keny, 320
Wigham, Rod, 223
Wight, Eric, 516
Wilde, Oscar, 321
Wildgoose, Christian, 421
Wildman, Andrew, 285
Wildsmith, Snow, 645
Wilgus, Alison, 637
Wilkins, Dave, 14
Willems, Mo, 544
Williams, Aaron, 580
Williams, Bill, 375
Williams, Brittney, 58, 439
Williams, Freddie E., 43, 60,
    73, 104
Williams, J. H. III, 11, 27, 124,
    361, 364
Williams, Kent, 349, 414
Williams, Rob, 105, 121, 152,
    234, 252
Williams, Scott, 86
Williams, Sean E., 320, 420
Williamson, Al, 207–8, 227, 288
Williamson, Brian, 251, 253
Williamson, Joshua, 113, 246,
    336, 407, 566
Willingham, Bill, 60, 87, 105,
    291, 301, 318, 320–21, 354, 374
Wilson, Charles Paul III,
    346, 420
Wilson, Colin, 214
Wilson, F. Paul, 420
Wilson, G. Willow, 56, 77, 112
Wilson, Leah, 648
Windham. Ryder, 210, 219
Windsor-Smith, Barry, 56,
    157–58, 307, 310–11, 413
Winick, Judd, 12, 34, 42, 569
Winshluss, 323
Wolfman, Marv, 74, 91, 108, 327,
    413, 549
Wolk, Douglas, 648
Wong, Wendy Siuyi, 644
Wood, Brian, 127, 163, 170, 208,
    244, 263, 308–9, 444, 460
Wood, Wallace, 288
Woodring, Jim, 544, 546,
    551, 553
Woods, Pete, 4
Woodward, J. K., 225
Wooton, Rus, 259
Wordie, Jason, 142
Wright, Bill, 532
Wright, Chris, 149

Wright, Gregory, 274
Wright, James F., 493
Wrigtson, Bernie, 398–99
Wu, Annie, 28, 48, 513
Wyatt, Jacob, 56, 572

Yadeo, Jason, 644
Yagi, Rie, 611
Yaginuma, Kou, 227
Yakin, Boaz, 504
Yamamoto, Masafumi, 633
Yamamoto, Satoshi, 589
Yamamoto, Shin, 300
Yamamoto, Yamato, 384
Yamazaki, Housui, 561
Yamazaki, Kore, 356
Yanagawa, Sozo, 611
Yang, Gene Luen, 5, 62, 165, 174,
    323, 443, 468, 516–17
Yasuhiko, Yoshikazu, 282
Yates, Jolyon, 178
Yates, Kelly, 251
Yeowell, Steve, 155
Yoe, Craig, 419
Yolen, Jane, 348–49
Yoshida, Akira, 309
Yoshikawa, Miki, 566
Yoshinaga, Fumi, 264, 490,
    493, 496
Yoshino, Satsuki, 515
Yost, Christopher, 60, 101,
    112, 115
Young, Skottie, 73–74, 112, 343,
    574, 586, 596
Young, Steve, 585
Yu, Leinil Frances, 78, 112, 208
Yue, Stephanie, 547
Yukimura, Makoto, 164, 221
Yukino, Sai, 354, 641
Yumi, Kiiro, 235
Yune, Tommy, 288
Yun, JiUn, 422
Yura, Kairi, 354, 461
Yurkovich, David, 490

Zabel, Joe, 606
Zahler, Thom, 459, 534, 576
Zahn, Timothy, 220
Zdarsky, Chip, 118, 517, 548–49
Zeck, Mike, 58, 111, 274
Zelenetz, Alan, 243
Zhang, Alice X., 253
Zircher, Patrick, 43, 91, 104, 334
Zonjic, Tonci, 378
Zub, Jim, 161, 183, 291, 310, 315,
    364, 584, 600
Zulli, Michael, 363

Title Index

Abandon the Old in Tokyo, 506
Abe Sapien, 368
Abigail and the Snowman, 512
Abracadeath (Hardy Boys), 440
Absolute All-Star Superman, 6
Absolute Batman and Robin: Batman Reborn, 8
Absolute Batman: Hush, 9
Absolute DC: The New Frontier, 123
Absolute Promethea, 362
Absolute Sandman, 363
Absolute Superman/Batman, 106
Absolute Top 10, 130
Absolute Y, The Last Man, 266
Action Cat and Adventure Bug, 572
Activity, The, 164
A.D.: New Orleans after the Deluge, 623
Adventure Time, 292
Adventure Time: The Original Graphic Novels,
    292–93
Adventures in Cartooning, 603–4
*Adventures in Cartooning: Characters in
    Action*, 604
Adventures in Cartooning Christmas Special, 604
*Adventures in Cartooning: How to Turn Your
    Doodles into Comics*, 603
Adventures in Oz, 343
*Adventures in Sound with Max Axiom, Super
    Scientist*, 633
Adventures of Super Diaper Baby, The, 583
Adventures of Superhero Girl, 572
Adventures of Tintin, The, 144
A-Force, 77, 112
A-Force Presents, 77
Afrodisiac, 553
Afterlife with Archie, 386–87
Afterschool Charisma, 256–57
Age of Apocalypse: Warzones, The, 112
Age of Bronze, 162–63, 650
Age of Reptiles: Ancient Egyptians, 135
Age of Reptiles Omnibus, 136
Age of Ultron vs. Marvel Zombies, 112, 390
Alabaster Shadows, 400
*Alamo All-Stars (Nathan Hale's Hazardous
    Tales)*, 627
Alan Moore: Conversations, 646
Alan's War: Memories of G.I. Alan Cope, 605–6
Alcoholic, The, 468
Alias, 429–30
Alias Omnibus, 430

Alias Ultimate Collection, 430
Alice in Sunderland, 623
Alien Legion, 243
Aliens, 243–44, 649
Aliens (2010), 243–44
Aliens: Defiance, 244
Aliens: Fast Track to Heaven, 244
Aliens: Fire and Stone, 244
Aliens: Inhuman Condition, 244
Aliens: Life and Death, 244
Aliens: More than Human, 244
Aliens Omnibus, 244
Aliens: Salvation, 244
Aliens vs. Parker, 567
Aliens vs. Predator, 244
Aliens vs. Predator Omnibus, 245
Aliens vs. Predator: World War Three, 245
Alison Dare, 148
Alison Dare: Heart of the Maiden, 148
Alison Dare: Little Miss Adventures, 148
*All for Stilton, Stilton for All (Geronimo
    Stilton)*, 530
All-New, All-Different Avengers, 77
All-New Batman: The Brave and the Bold, 18
All-New Captain America, 32
All-New Ghost Rider, 406
All-New Hawkeye, 48
All-New Wolverine, 66
All-New X-Factor, 100
All-New X-Men, 95–96
All-New X-Men (2013), 95
All-New X-Men (2016), 96
*All-New X-Men/Indestructible Hulk/Superior
    Spider-Man: The Arms of the Octopus*, 96
All-New X-Men Oversized Collections, 96
All-Star Batman, 13–14
All-Star Superman, 6
All-Star Superman Omnibus Edition, 6
All-Star Western, 195–96
All You Need Is Kill, 248
Amazing Agent Jennifer, 189
Amazing Agent Luna, 189, 653
*Amazing Fantastic Incredible: A Marvelous
    Memoir*, 606
*Amazing Screw-On Head and Other Curious
    Objects*, 369
Amazing Spider-Girl, 63
Amazing Spider-Man (2008), 19. *See also*
    Spider-Man

Amazing Spider-Man (2014), 20
Amazing Spider-Man (2016), 20
Amazing Spider-Man: Edge of Spider-Verse, 21
Amazing Spider-Man: Spider-Verse, 21
Amazing Spider-Man: Spider-Verse Prelude, 21
Amazing Spider-Man: Renew Your Vows, The, 112
Amelia Rules!, 512
American Born Chinese, xxix, 468, 654
American Comic Book, The, 647
American Splendor, 606–7
American Splendor: Another Day, 607
American Splendor: Another Dollar, 607
American Splendor Presents: Bob & Harv's
    Comics, 607
American Splendor: Our Movie Year, 607
American Splendor: The Life and Times of Harvey
    Pekar, 607
American Vampire, 380–81
Americus, 469
Amulet, 336
Anchor, The, 347–48
Ancient Magus' Bride, The, 356
Andre the Giant: Closer to Heaven, 607
Andre the Giant: Life and Legend, 607
Angel, 371, 373–74
Angel (2010 series), 374
Angel: After the Fall, 371, 374
Angel: A Hole in the World, 374
Angel & Faith, 374
Angel & Faith Season Nine Library Edition, 374
Angel & Faith: Season Ten, 374–75
Angel: Auld Lang Syne, 373
Angel: Barbary Coast, 374
Angel Catbird, 24
Angel: Illyria Haunted, 374
Angel Omnibus (2008), 374
Angel Omnibus (2011), 375
Angel: Only Human, 374
Angel: Smile Time, 374
Angel: The Curse, 373
Angel: The John Byrne Collection, 374
Angry Birds, 523
Angry Birds: Big Movie Eggstravaganza, 523
Animal Land, 591
Anne Frank (Edu-Manga), 611
Annihilation, 72
Annihilation: Conquest, 72
Annihilation: Conquest Omnibus, 72
Annihilation Omnibus, 72
Anne Sullivan and the Trials of Helen Keller, 607
Annotated Sandman. The, 362
Ann Tenna: A Novel, 469
Anomaly, 228
Antique Bakery, 490
Antler Boy and Other Stories, 507

Ant-Man, 24
Ant-Man: Second Chance Man, 24
Anya's Ghost, 403, 654
Any Empire, 164–65
Aphrodite: Goddess of Love (Olympians), 331
Apocalyptigirl, 262
Apollo: The Brilliant One (Olympians), 331
Aqua Leung, 145
Aquaman, 25
Aquaman (1st series), 25
Aquaman (2nd series), 25
Aquaman and the Others, 26
Aquaman: Sub Diego, 25
Aquaman: The Waterbearer, 25
Aquaman: To Serve and Protect, 25
Archer and Armstrong, 157–58, 653
Archer and Armstrong: The Complete Classic
    Omnibus, 158
Archie, 511, 512–14
Archie (2016 series), 513
Archie and Friends All-Stars, 513
Archie & Friends: Night at the Comic Shop
    (Archie), 513
Archie: A Rock and Roll Romance (Archie), 513
Archie Campfire Stories (Archie), 513
Archie: Clash of the New Kids (Archie), 513
Archie: Love Showdown (Archie), 513
Archie Meets Glee, 514
Archie: Obama & Palin in Riverdale (Archie), 513
Archie: Rockin' the World (Archie), 513
Archies and Josie and the Pussycats, The, 513
Archie's Christmas Stocking, 513
Archie's Haunted House, 513
Archie's Weird Mysteries, 513
Archie's World Tour, 513
Archie: The Married Life, 469
Archie vs. Predator, 246
Archie Wedding: Archie in Will You Marry Me,
    The, 469
Ares & Aphrodite: Love Wars, 463
Ares: Bringer of War (Olympians), 331
Are You My Mother? A Comic Drama, 608
Are You Ready to Play Outside (Elephant and
    Piggie), 545
Ariol, 541–42
Arisa, 432–33
Arkham Woods, 400
Armor Wars, 112
Army of Darkness, 556–57, 651, 652
Army of Darkness: Ashes to Ashes, 557
Army of Darkness: Ash Gets Hitched, 557
Army of Darkness: Ash in Space, 557
Army of Darkness: Ash Saves Obama, 557
Army of Darkness: Ash vs. the Classic
    Monsters, 556

Army of Darkness: Furious Road, 557
Army of Darkness: Hellbillies and Deadnecks, 557
Army of Darkness: Old School and More, 556
Army of Darkness Omnibus, 556
Army of Darkness: Shop 'til You Drop, 556
Army of Darkness vs. Hack/Slash, 418, 557
Army of Darkness vs. Re-Animator, 557
Army of Darkness/Xena, Warrior Princess:
   Forever and a Day, 556
Around the World, 498
Arrival, The, 248
Art of Comic Book Writing: The Definitive Guide
   to Outlining, Scripting, and Pitching Your
   Sequential Art Stories, 644
Artemis: Goddess of the Hunt (Olympians), 331
Art Spiegelman: Conversations, 646
Ash and the Army of Darkness, 557
Assassination Classroom, 553–54
Asterix Omnibus, 591–92
Astonishing Ant-Man, 24–25
Astonishing X-Men by Joss Whedon and John
   Cassaday, 96
Astounding Wolf-Man, 381
Astro Boy, 270
Astro City, 126–27
Astronaut Academy, 568
Astronaut Academy: Re-Entry, 568
Astronaut Academy: Zero Gravity, 568
Athena: Grey-Eyed Goddess (Olympians), 330
Atomic Robo, 271
Atomic Robo: Real Science Adventures, 271
Atomic Robo: The Crystals Are Integral
   Collection, 271
Atomic Robo: The Everything Explodes
   Collection, 271
Atomic Robo: The Hell and Lightning
   Collection, 271
Attack on Titan, 262, 652
Attack on Titan: Before the Fall, 263
Attack on Titan: Junior High, 262
Attack on Titan: No Regrets, 263
Attractive Story of Magnetism with Max Axiom,
   Super Scientist, The, 633
Autumlands, The, 293
Avatar: The Last Airbender, 173–74
Avatar: The Last Airbender: North and South, 174
Avatar: The Last Airbender: Smoke and
   Shadow, 174
Avatar: The Last Airbender: The Lost
   Adventures, 174
Avatar: The Last Airbender: The Promise, 174
Avatar: The Last Airbender: The Rift, 174
Avatar: The Last Airbender: The Search, 174
Avengers, 77–81
Avengers (2011), 78

Avengers (2013), 78
Avengers: Fear Itself, 80
Avengers: The Children's Crusade, 93
Avengers: The Legacy of Thanos, 120
Avengers: Time Runs Out, 80
Avengers vs. Pet Avengers, 579
Avengers vs. Thanos, 120
Avengers vs. X-Men, 103
Awkward, 514
Awkward and Definition (High School Chronicles
   of Ariel Schrag), 613
Aw Yeah Comics, 572
Axe Cop, 586–87
Aya, 469–70
Aya: Life in Yop City, 470
Aya: Love in Yop City, 470
Aya of Yop City, 470
Aya: The Secrets Come Out, 470

Baba Yaga's Assistant, 316
Babymouse, 542
Baby's in Black: Astrid Kirchherr, Stuart Sutcliffe,
   and The Beatles, 458
Baby-Sitters Club, The, 514, 654
Back to the Future, 248–49
Back to the Future: Biff to the Future, 249
Back to the Future: Citizen Brown, 249
Back to the Future: Continuum Conundrum, 248
Back to the Future: Untold Tales and Alternate
   Timelines, 248
Back to the Future: Who Is Marty McFly, 249
Bad Houses, 470
Bad Island, 145
Bad Karma, 507
Baggywrinkles: A Lubber's Guide to Life at
   Sea, 608
Bake Sale, 515
Bakuman, 470–71
Baltimore, 369
Bandette, 433
Barakamon, 515
Barbarian Lord, 306
Barefoot Serpent, 471
Barry Sonnenfeld's Dinosaurs vs. Aliens, 136
Bart Simpson, 538–39, 651
Bart Simpson Big Shot, 539
Bart Simpson Blastoff, 539
Bart Simpson: Class Clown, 539
Bart Simpson: Master of Disaster, 539
Bart Simpson: Out to Lunch, 539
Bart Simpson: Prince of Pranks, 539
Bart Simpson: Son of Homer, 539
Bart Simpson's Treehouse of Horror, 651
Bart Simpson's Treehouse of Horror *Heebie-Jeebie*
   Hullabaloo, 538

Bart Simpson's Treehouse of Horror Spine-Tingling Spooktacular, 538
Bart Simpson Sucker Punch, 539
Bart Simpson to the Rescue, 539
Bartman: The Best of the Best, 539
Basara, 306–7
Basics of Cell Life with Max Axiom, Super Scientist, The, 633
Bastard!, 293–94
Batgirl, 26
Batgirl (2013 series), 26
Batgirl (2015 series), 26
Batgirl/Robin Year One, 27
Batman, 7–18
Batman (2008 series), 7–8
Batman (2012 series), 11–12
Batman (2017 series), 12
Batman: A Death in the Family, 9
Batman Adventures, 17–18
Batman Adventures: Mad Love Deluxe Edition, 47
Batman and Robin (2010 series), 8
Batman and Robin (2012 series), 8–9
Batman and Robin Adventures, 17–18
Batman and Robin Eternal, 13
Batman and Son, 8
Batman: Arkham City, 14
Batman: Arkham Knight, 14
Batman: Arkham Knight: Genesis, 14
Batman: Arkham Origins, 14
Batman: Arkham Unhinged, 14
Batman Beyond, 27
Batman Beyond: Batgirl Beyond, 27
Batman Beyond: Hush Beyond, 27
Batman Beyond: Industrial Revolution, 27
Batman Beyond: 10,000 Clowns, 27
Batman Birth of the Demon, 15
Batman: Black and White, 15
Batman: Brave and the Bold, 18
Batman: Death and the City, 11
Batman: Detective, 11
Batman: Detective Comics (2007), 11
Batman: Detective Comics (2012), 12–13
Batman: Detective Comics (2017), 13
Batman: Earth One, 122
Batman: Ego and Other Tales, 16
Batman Eternal, 13
Batman: Harley Quinn, 47
Batman: Hush, 9
Batman: Hush Unwrapped Deluxe Edition, 9
Batman Incorporated, 10
Batman/Judge Dredd Collection, The, 103
Batman: Li'l Gotham, 573
Batman: Li'l Gotham Deluxe Edition, 573
Batman: Noel, 16
Batman: Private Notebook, 11

Batman R.I.P., 8
Batman '66, 572–73
Batman '66 Meets John Speed and Emma Peel, 573
Batman '66 Meets the Green Hornet, 573
Batman '66 Meets the Man from U.N.C.L.E, 573
Batman: Streets of Gotham, 10
Batman/Superman, 103–4
Batman/Teenage Mutant Ninja Turtles, 104
Batman/Teenage Mutant Ninja Turtle Adventures, 104
Batman: The Black Glove, 8
Batman: The Brave and the Bold, 18
Batman: The Complete History, 646
Batman: The Dark Knight, 12
Batman: The Dark Knight Returns, 15–16, 122
Batman: The Dark Knight Returns: The Last Crusade, 16
Batman: The Dark Knight Saga Deluxe Edition, 16
Batman: The Dark Knight Strikes Again, 15–16
Batman: The Doom That Came to Gotham, 400
Batman: The Killing Joke, 16
Batman: The Man Who Laughs, 9
Batman: The Return of Bruce Wayne, 10
Batman: The Resurrection of Ra's Al Ghul, 10
Batman: Time and the Batman, 8
Batman Unauthorized: Vigilantes, Jokers, and Heroes in Gotham City, 647
Batman: Whatever Happened to the Caped Crusader?, 10
Batman: Year One Deluxe Edition, 16–17
Batman Year 100, 17
Batman Year 100 and Other Tales Deluxe Edition, 17
Bats: Learning to Fly (Science Comics), 636
Battle Angel Alita, 272, 654
Battle Angel Alita: Last Order Omnibus, 272
Battle Lines: A Graphic History of the Civil War, 165
Battle of the Bulge: A Graphic History of Allied Victory in the Ardennes, 1944–1945 (Graphic History), 625
Battling Boy, 27
Batwoman, 27
Batwoman: Elegy, 27
Beast of Chicago, The (Treasury of Victorian Murder), 453
Beast of Wolfe's Bay, 393–94
Beasts of Burden: Animal Rites, 369–70
Beautiful Darkness, 317
Beauty, 317
Before Watchmen, 92
Before Watchmen: Comedian/Rorschach, 93
Before Watchmen: Minutemen/Silk Spectre, 93
Before Watchmen: Nite Owl/Dr. Manhattan, 93

Before Watchmen: Ozymandias/Crimson Corsair, 93
Benny and Penny, 543
Benny and Penny and the Big No-No!, 543
Benny and Penny and the Toy Breaker, 543
Benny and Penny in Just Pretend, 543
Benny and Penny in Lights Out, 543
Benny and Penny in Lost and Found, 543
Beowulf, 294
Berlin, 498–99
Berserk, 294–95, 652
Best American Comics, The, 506–7
Best of American Splendor, 607
Best of Archie Comics: 75 Years, 75 Stories, 514
Best of Betty's Diary, The (Archie), 513
Best of Jughead: Crowning Achievements, The (Archie), 513
Beta Ray Bill, 335
Beta Ray Bill: Godhunter, 335
Beta Testing the Apocalypse, 288
Betty and Veronica Beach Party (Archie), 513
Betty and Veronica: Best Friends Forever (Archie), 513
Betty and Veronica: Fairy Tales (Archie), 513
Betty and Veronica: Girls Rule (Archie), 513
Betty and Veronica: Prom Princesses (Archie), 513
Betty and Veronica: Shopping Spree (Archie), 513
Betty and Veronica's Princess Storybook (Archie), 513
Betty and Veronica Storybook (Archie), 513
Beyond the Western Deep, 175
Big Bad Ironclad (Nathan Hale's Hazardous Tales), 627
Big Bad Book of Bart Simpson, 539
Big Beastly Book of Bart Simpson, 539
Big Beefy Book of Bart Simpson, 539
Big Book of Bart Simpson, 539
Big Bouncy Book of Bart Simpson, 539
Big Bratty Book of Bart Simpson, 539
Big Brilliant Book of Bart Simpson, 539
Big City Otto (Elephants Never Forget), 545
Big Damn Sin City, 449
Bigfoot Boy, 348
Big Guy Took My Ball, A (Elephant and Piggie), 545
Big Hard Sex Criminals, 118
Big Hero Six, 82
Big Skinny: How I Changed My Fattitude, The, 497
Big Star Otto (Elephants Never Forget), 545
Big Thunder Mountain Railroad, 193–94
Big Top Otto (Elephants Never Forget), 545
Binky, 543
Binky: License to Scratch, 543
Binky: Takes Charge, 543
Binky: The Space Cat, 543

Binky: To the Rescue, 543
Binky: Under Pressure, 543
Biomega, 257
Bird and Squirrel, 543
Bird and Squirrel on Fire, 543
Bird and Squirrel on Ice, 543
Bird and Squirrel on the Edge, 543
Bird and Squirrel on the Run, 543
Bird Boy, 295
Birds of Prey, 82
Birthright, 336
Bitch Planet, 257
Blackbeard: Legend of the Pyrate King, 148
Black Bird, 410
Black Bullet, 258
Black Butler, 356–57, 654
Black Canary, 28
Black Dhalia (Treasury of XXth Century Murder), 455
Black Harvest, 228, 651
Black Island, The (Tintin), 144
Blackjack, 148–49
Black Jack Ketchum, 198
Blackjack: Second Bite of the Cobra, 149
Blackjack: There Came a Dark Hunter; the Further Adventures of Aaron Day, 149
Blacklung, 149
Black Magick, 410–11
Black Metal, 357
Black Panther, 28
Black Panther by Christopher Priest: The Complete Collection, 28
Black Panther: Who Is the Black Panther?, 28
Blacksad, 430
Black Science, 249
Black Widow, 29
Black Widow: Deadly Origin, 29
Black Widow: Itsy-Bitsy Spider, 29
Black Widow: Kiss or Kill, 29
Black Widow: The Name of the Rose, 29
Black Widow: Web of Intrigue, 29
Blade of the Immortal, 175–76
Blankets, 608
Bleach, 403–4
Bloodshot, 272–73
Bloodshot (2012), 273
Bloodshot—Blood of the Machine (Valiant Masters), 273
Blue Exorcist, 411
Blue Is the Warmest Color, 458
Blue Lotus, The (Tintin), 144
Blue Monday, 471
Blue Pills: A Positive Love Story, 609
Bluffton: My Summers with Buster Keaton, 499
Board to Death (Hardy Boys), 440

Bob Powell's Terror (Chilling Archives), 419
Bokurano: Ours, 281
Bombing Nazi Germany: The Graphic History of the Allied Air Campaign That Defeated Hitler in World War II (Graphic History), 625
Bone, xxxv, 33, 291, 295–96, 549, 651, 654
Bone (black & white), 296
Bone (color), 296
Bone: Coda, 296
Bone: Rose, 297
Bone Sharps, Cowboys, and Thunder Lizards: A Tale of Edwin Drinker Cope, Othniel Charles Marsh, and the Gilded Age of Paleontology, 629
Bone: Tall Tales, 297
Bone: The Complete Cartoon Epic on One Volume, 296
Bone 20th Anniversary Full Color One Volume Edition, 296
Bookhunter, 587
Book of Grickle, The, 516
Borden Tragedy, The (Treasury of Victorian Murder), 453
Borderlands, 228
Borgias, The, 499
Boxers, 165
Boys Over Flowers: Hana Yori Dango, 458–59
B.P.R.D., 370–71, 378, 380
B.P.R.D.:1946–1948, 370
B.P.R.D.: 1948, 370
B.P.R.D.: Being Human, 370
B.P.R.D: Hell on Earth, 370–71
B.P.R.D.: Plague of Frogs, 371
B.P.R.D.: Vampire, 371
Brain Camp, 394
Bram Stoker (Graphic Classics), 420
Brave, 515
Breath of Bones: A Tale of the Golem, 398
Bride's Story A, 499
Brody's Ghost, 404
Broken Ear, The (Tintin), 144
Broxo, 297
Buffy the Vampire Slayer, 371–73
Buffy the Vampire Slayer Omnibus, 372
Buffy the Vampire Slayer Season Eight, 372, 372
Buffy the Vampire Slayer Season Eight Library Edition, 372
Buffy the Vampire Slayer Season Nine, 373
Buffy the Vampire Slayer Season Nine Library Edition, 373
Buffy the Vampire Slayer Season Ten, 373
Buffy the Vampire Slayer: The High School Years, 373
Building Literacy Connections with Graphic Novels: Page by Page, Panel by Panel, 645
Buzzboy, 574

Cable and X-Force, 102
Cable and X-Force Classic, 101
Cafe Kichijouji de, 490
Calamity Jack, 317
Cal McDonald Mysteries, The
Call of Duty: Black Ops III, 165–66
Cancer Vixen: A True Story, 609
Can I Play Too? (Elephant and Piggie), 545
Can't We Talk about Something More Pleasant?, 609
Captain America, 29–32
Captain America (2005 series), 30
Captain America (2014 series, 31
Captain America and Bucky: Old Wounds, 31
Captain America and Bucky: The Life Story of Bucky Barnes, 31
Captain America and the Mighty Avengers, 78
Captain America Lives Omnibus, 31
Captain America: Man Out of Time, 32
Captain America: No Escape, 31
Captain America Omnibus, 31
Captain America: Prisoner of War, 31
Captain America: Reborn, 30
Captain America: Return of the Winter Soldier Omnibus, 31
Captain America: Road to Reborn, 30
Captain America: Sam Wilson, 32
Captain America: Steve Rogers, 32
Captain America: The Man with No Face, 30
Captain America: The Trial of Captain America, 31
Captain America: The Trial of Captain America Omnibus, 31
Captain America: Two Americas, 31
Captain America: White, 32
Captain Marvel, 69–70
Captain Marvel (2013 series), 70
Captain Marvel (2014 series), 70
Captain Marvel (2016 series), 70
Captain Marvel and the Carol Corps, 112
Captain Marvel/Shazam, 32 33
Captain Raptor, 136
Captain Raptor and the Moon Mystery, 136
Captain Raptor and the Space Pirates, 136
Cardboard, 145
Carl Barks: Conversations, 646
Cars, 523
Cars: Radiator Springs, 523
Cars: Rally Race, 523
Cars: Route 66, 523
Cars: Rust Bucket Derby, 523
Cars: The Rookie, 523
Cartoon Guide to Algebra, The, 629
Cartoon Guide to Calculus, The, 629
Cartoon Guide to Chemistry, The, 629
Cartoon Guide to Economics, 639

Cartoon Guide to Genetics, The, 630
Cartoon Guide to Physics, The, 630
Cartoon Guide to Sex, The, 630
Cartoon Guide to Statistics, The, 630
Cartoon Guide to the Environment, The, 630
Cartoon History of the Modern World, The, 624
Cartoon History of the United States, The, 624
Cartoon History of the Universe, 624
Cartoon History Series, 624
Cartoon Introduction to Philosophy, 640
Cartoon Life of Chuck Clayton, The (Archie), 513
Casanova, 190
Case Closed, 437–38
Case of Madeleine Smith, The (Treasury of
    Victorian Murder), 453
Castle Waiting, 317–18
Cat Burglar Black, 438
Catching the Giant Wave (Thea Stilton), 530
Catwoman, 33–34
Catwoman (first series), 34
Catwoman (second series), 34
Catwoman: A Celebration of 75 Years, 34
Catwoman: Selina's Big Score, 34, 443–44
Chaos at 30,000 Feet (Hardy Boys), 440
Charles Darwin's On the Origin of Species, 630
Charmed Bracelet, The (Nancy Drew), 442
Chester Brown: Conversations, 646
Chew, 424, 490
Chew Omnivore Edition, 424
Chew Smorgasbord Edition, 424
Chicagoland Detective Agency, 439
Chicks Dig Comics: A Celebration of Comic Books
    by the Woman Who Loved Them, 647
Chiggers, 471–72
Children of the Sea, 242
Child Soldier: When Boys and Girls Are Used in
    War, 609
Chilling Adventures of Sabrina, 411
Chilling Archives of Horror Comics, The, 419–20
Chi's Sweet Home, 543–44
Chobits, 273
Chopper Zombie, 387
Chronicles of Claudette, The, 592
Chronicles of Conan, The, 307–8
Chrononauts, 249
Cigars of the Pharaoh (Tintin), 144
City of Spies, 146
City under the Basement (Nancy Drew), 442
Civil War, 107
Civil War II, 107
Civil War Adventure, 166
Civil War: Warzones, 112
Civil War: Young Avengers and Runaways, 93
Clan Apis, 630
Classic G.I. Joe, 167

Classic Jurassic Park, 139
Classic Popeye, 536
Claudia and Mean Janie (Baby-Sitter's Club), 514
Cleopatra in Space, 229
Cleveland, 609–10
Cliffhanger (Nancy Drew), 442
Codeflesh: The Definitive Edition, 433
Codename: Sailor V, 34–35
Colder, 401
Coliseum Con, The (Geronimo Stilton), 530
Color of Earth, The, 500
Color of Heaven, The, 500
Color of Water, The, 500
Comic Book Crime: Truth, Justice, and the
    American Way, 647
Comic Book Culture: An Illustrated History, 647
Comic Book Encyclopedia: The Ultimate Guide to
    Characters, Graphic Novels, Writers, and Artists
    in the Comic Book Universe, 647
Comic Book History of Comics, The, 604
Comic Book Story of Beer, 624
Comics above Ground: Sequential Art Affects
    Mainstream Media, 647
Comics and Sequential Art: Principles and
    Practices from the Legendary Cartoonist, 604, 643
Comics between the Panels, 646
Comics, Comix & Graphic Novels: A History of
    Comic Art, 647
Comics Squad, 515–16
Comics through Time, 643
Compass South, 146
Complete Carl Barks Disney Library, 527
Complete Chi's Sweet Home, The, 544
Complete Elfquest, 299
Complete Essex County, 474
Complete Idiot's Guide to Creating a Graphic
    Novel, 643
Complete Idiot's Guide to Drawing Manga
    Illustrated, 644
Complete Invincible Library, 52
Complete Maus, The, 616
Complete Quantum and Woody Omnibus, 581
Complete Voodoo Vols. 1–3 (Chilling
    Archives), 420
Conan, 308–10
Conan (2005 series), 308–9
Conan and the Daughters of Midora and Other
    Stories, 310
Conan and the Demons of Khitai, 309
Conan and the Jewels of Gwahlur, 309
Conan and the Midnight God, 310
Conan and the People of the Black Circle, 310
Conan and the Songs of the Dead, 310
Conan: Book of Thoth, 310
Conan Omnibus, 309

Conan/Red Sonja, 315
Conan the Barbarian, 307–10
Conan: The Phantoms of the Black Coast, 310
Concrete Park, 258
Congress of the Animals, 544
Constantine, 413–15
Constantine (series), 415
Constantine the Hellblazer, 414–15
Contract with God Trilogy: Life on Dropsie
    Avenue, The, 472
Convergence, 107
Convergence: Crisis, 107
Convergence: Flashpoint, 107
Convergence: Infinite Earths, 107
Convergence: Zero Hour, 107
Conversations with Comic Artists, 646
Cook Korean!: A Comic Book with Recipes, 497
Cool Japan Guide: Fun in the Land of Manga,
    Lucky Cats and Ramen, 640
Copper, 337
Copperhead, 198
Coraline, 337
Coral Reefs: Cities of the Ocean (Science
    Comics), 636
Costume Quest: Invasion of the Candy
    Snatchers, 557
Courageous Princess, The, 318, 651
Couriers: The Complete Series, The, 444
Courtney Crumrin, 357–58
Courtyard, The, 401
Cousin Joseph: A Graphic Novel, 430–31, 434
Cowa!, 557–58
Cow Boy. A Boy and His Horse, 194
Cowboys and Aliens, 198
Crab with the Golden Claws, The (Tintin), 145
Crash Course in Forces and Motion with Max
    Axiom, Super Scientist, A, 634
Creature Tech, 245
Creep, The, 430
Creeps, The, 558, 654
Crime (Simon and Kirby Library), 448
Criminal, 444
Criminal Macabre: A Cal McDonald Mystery, 376
Criminal Macabre: Cell Block 666, 376
Criminal Macabre: My Demon Baby, 376
Criminal Macabre Omnibus, 376
Criminal Macabre: The Cal McDonald Mysteries,
    375–76
Criminal Macabre: Two Red Eyes, 376
Crisis on Infinite Earths, 108
Critical Survey of Graphic Novels, 643–44
Crogan Adventures, The, 149
Crogan Adventures: Catfoot's Vengeance, The, 149
Crogan Adventures: Last of the Legion, 149
Crogan's Loyalty, 150

Cross Game, 487–88
Cthulhu Tales, 401
Cursed Pirate Girl, 150
Curses, 472
Curses, Foiled Again, 349
Curveball, 258

Daisy Kutter: The Last Train, 193, 197
Danger Girl, 190
Danger Girl and the Army of Darkness, 557
Danger Girl: Back in Black, 190
Danger Girl: Deluxe Edition, 190
Danger Girl: Destination Danger, 190
Danger Girl: Mayday, 190
Danger Girl: Revolver, 190
Danger Girl: The Chase, 190
Danger Girl: Trinity, 190
D.A.N.G.E.R. Spells the Hangman (Hardy
    Boys), 440
Daniel Clowes: Conversations, 646
Dare Detectives! Collected Edition: The Snowpea
    Plot, The, 433–34
Daredevil, 35–37
Daredevil (2011/2014 series), 36–37
Daredevil (2016 series), 37
Daredevil: Born Again, 36
Daredevil by Brian Michael Bendis & Alex Maleev
    Ultimate Collection, 36
Daredevil by Ed Brubaker and Michael Lark
    Ultimate Collection, 36
Daredevil by Frank Miller Omnibus
    Companion, 36
Daredevil by Frank Miller and Klaus Janson, 36
Daredevil by Frank Miller and Klaus Janson
    Omnibus, 35
Daredevil: The Man without Fear, 36
Dark Avengers, 116
Dark Avengers: Masters of Evil, 116
Dark Avengers Omnibus, 116
Dark Avengers: Siege, 116
Dark Avengers: The End Is the Beginning, 116
Dark Avengers/Uncanny X-Men: Utopia, 116
Dark Crystal: Creation Myths, 326–27
Darkman vs. Army of Darkness, 557
Dark Night: A True Batman Story, 610
Dark Reign: Young Avengers, 93
Dave Sim: Conversations, 646
Dawn of the Arcana, 298
Daybreak, 387
Daytripper, 472
DC Comics: A Celebration of the World's Favorite
    Comic Book Heroes, 646
DC Comics Bombshells, 123
DC Comics Encyclopedia: The Definitive Guide to
    the Characters of the DC Universe, 644

DC Comics: Rebirth, 108
DC/Dark Horse Aliens, 244
DC: The New Frontier, 123
DC Universe by Alan Moore, 131
Dead@17: The Complete Collection, 387
Deadliest Stunt, The (Hardy Boys), 440
Deadly Strategy (Hardy Boys), 441
Deadpool, 37–38
Deadpool (2008 series), 38
Deadpool (2014 series), 38
Deadpool and Cable, 104
Deadpool and Cable Omnibus, 104
Deadpool: Bad Blood, 38
Deadpool by Daniel Way: The Complete Collection, 38
Deadpool Classic, 37–38
Deadpool Classic Companion, 38
Deadpool Classic Omnibus, 38
Deadpool Max, 38
Deadpool's Secret Secret Wars, 112
Deadpool Team-Up, 105
Deadpool: World's Greatest, 38
Dear Creature, 394
Death and Return of Superman Omnibus, 3
Death by Chocolate: Redux, 490–91
Death-Defying Doctor Mirage, The, 412
Deathlok, 273–74
Deathlok (2015), 274
Deathlok: Rage against the Machine, 274
Deathlok: The Demolisher, 274
Deathlok the Demolisher: The Complete Collection, 274
Deathlok: The Living Nightmare of Michael Collins, 274
Deathlok: The Souls of Cyber-Folk, 274
Death Note, 404–45
Death Note Black Edition, 405
Death of Archie: A Life Remembered, The, 469
Death of Captain America Omnibus, The, 31
Death of Captain America: The Complete Collection, The, 30
Death of Superman, The, 3
Death of Wolverine, 68
Death: The Deluxe Edition, 358
Death Valley, 387
Decoding Genes with Max Axiom, Super Scientist, 634
Defiance, 170
Delilah Dirk, 146
Delilah Dirk and the King's Shilling, 146
Delilah Dirk and the Turkish Lieutenant, 146
Demo, 127
Demon of River Heights, The (Nancy Drew), 442
Demon Prince of Momochi House, The, 348
Dengeki Daisy, 463

Descender, 274
Destiny's Hand, 150
De: Tales—Stories from Urban Brazil, 507
Detective Comics, 11
Detroit Metal City, 554
Developing and Promoting Graphic Novel Collections, 645
Devil and Her Love Song, A, 472–73
Devil Dinosaur by Jack Kirby: The Complete Collection, 137
Devil Tales (Chilling Archives), 420
Dexter's Laboratory, 523–24
Dexter's Laboratory Classics, 524
Dexter's Laboratory: Dee's Day, 524
Dial H: The Deluxe Edition, 39
Dial M for Monster: A Cal McDonald Collection, 375
Dick Briefer's Frankenstein (Chilling Archives), 419
Dignifying Science: Stories about Women Scientists, 630
Dinosaur Hour, 137
Dinosaur King, 137–38
Dinosaurs, 138
Dinosaurs and Prehistoric Predators, 138
Dinosaurs: Fossils and Feathers (Science Comics), 636–37
Dinosaurs in Action (Geronimo Stilton), 530
Dinosaurs in Space, 138
Dirt Candy: A Cookbook: Flavor-Forward Food from the Upstart New York City Vegetarian Restaurant, 490, 497
Dirty Diamonds, 507
Discovery of America, The (Geronimo Stilton), 530
Disney Fairies, 592–93
Disney Frozen Comics Collection, 524
Disney Frozen Comics Collection: Hearts Full of Sunshine, 524
Disney Frozen Comics Collection: Travel Arendelle, 524
Disney Frozen Comics Collection: Winter Wonderland Comics Collection, 524
Disney Moana Comics Collection, 524
Disney Pixar Cars Comics Treasury, 523
Disney Pixar Cars Movie Graphic Novel, 523
Disney Pixar Cars 3 Movie Graphic Novel, 523
Disney Pixar Finding Dory: Movie Graphic Novel, 525
Disney Pixar Finding Nemo: Movie Graphic Novel, 526
Disney Pixar Treasury, 526
Disney Princess Comics Treasury, 524
Disney's Darkwing Duck Treasury, 525
Disney's Phineas and Ferb Treasury, 525

Disney's Pirates of the Caribbean Comics Collection, 150
Disney Tangled: The Story of the Movie in Comics, 524–25
Disoriented Express, The (Nancy Drew), 442
Divine, The, 166
Django/Zorro, 194
DMZ, 263
Doctor Strange, 412–13
Doctor Strange (2015), 412
Doctor Strange and Doctor Doom: Triumph and Torment, 413
Doctor Strange Epic Collection: A Separate Reality, 412–13
Doctor Strange Omnibus, 412
Doctor Strange: Strange Origin, 412–13
Doctor Strange: The Flight of Bones, 412
Doctor Strange: The Oath, 413
Doctor Strange: What Is It That Disturbs You, Stephen?, 412–13
Doctor Who, 250–53, 653
Doctor Who Archives: Prisoners of Time Omnibus, 253
Doctor Who Archives: The Tenth Doctor Omnibus, 251
Doctor Who Classics, 250
Doctor Who: Four Doctors, 253
Doctor Who: The Dave Gibbons Collection, 250
Doctor Who: The Eighth Doctor: A Matter of Life and Death, 251
Doctor Who: The Eleventh Doctor, 252
Doctor Who: The Eleventh Doctor Archives Omnibus, 252
Doctor Who: The Fourth Doctor—Gaze of the Medusa, 251
Doctor Who: The Ninth Doctor, 251
Doctor Who: The Supremacy of the Cybermen, 253
Doctor Who: The Tenth Doctor, 252
Doctor Who: The Third Doctor—The Heralds of Destruction, 250
Doctor Who: The Twelfth Doctor, 252–53
Doggone Town (Nancy Drew), 442
Dog Man, 544
Dogs: From Predators to Protectors (Science Comics), 637
Dogs of War, 134
Donald and Mickey: The Persistence of Mickey, 529
Donald and Mickey: The Walt Disney's Comics and Stories 75th Anniversary Collection, 529
Donald and Mickey: The Walt Disney's Comics and Stories Holiday Collection, 529
Donald and Mickey Timeless Tales, 529
Donald Duck, 528
Donald Duck: Duck Avenger, 528

Donald Duck: Revenge of the Duck Avenger, 528
Donald Duck: Shellfish Motives, 528
Donald Duck: The Big Sneeze, 528
Donald Duck: The True Origin of the Diabolical Duck Avenger, 528
Donald Duck: Timeless Tales Vols. 1–3, 528
Donald Duck and Uncle Scrooge, 526–29
Donald Quest: Hammer of Magic, 528
Done to Death, 382
Donner Dinner Party (Nathan Hale's Hazardous Tales), 627
Dorothy and the Wizard of Oz, 343
Dotter of Her Father's Eyes, 610
Doug TenNapel's Gear, 281
Dracula (All-Action Classics), 381
Dracula (Marvel Comics), 381
Dracula Everlasting, 381–82
Dragon Ball, 158–59
Dragon Ball Z, 159, 654
Dragon Puncher, 593
Dragon Puncher Island, 593
Dragons Beware (Chronicles of Claudette, The), 592
Dragons: Defenders of Berk, 298
Drain, 382
Drama, 473
Drawing from Memory, 610
Drawn & Quarterly: 25 Years of Contemporary Cartooning, Comics, and Graphic Novels, 508
Dreamer, The (Innis), 337–38
Dream Jumper, 337
Dreamland Japan: Writings on Modern Manga, 644
Dress Reversal (Nancy Drew), 442
Dr. Grordbort's Contrapulatronic Dingus Directory, 229
Dr. Grordbort Presents, 229
Dr. Grordbort Presents Onslaught, 229
Dr. Grordbort Presents Triumph, 229
Dr. Grordbort Presents Victory: Scientific Adventure Violence, 229
Drops of God, 491
Drops of God: New World, 491
Drowned City: Hurricane Katrina and New Orleans, 624–25
Dr. Slump, 568
Drunken Dream and Other Stories, A, 508
Dude Ranch O'Death (Hardy Boys), 440
Dumbest Idea Ever, The, 610–11
Dungeon, 594–95
Dungeon: Monstres, 594–95
Dungeon: Parade, 594
Dungeon: The Early Years, 594
Dungeon: Twilight, 594
Dungeon: Zenith, 594

Dynamic World of Chemical Reactions with Max Axiom, Super Scientist, The, 634

Earthling, 568–69
Earth-Shaking Facts about Earthquakes with Max Axiom, Super Scientist, The, 634
East of West, The, 259
Eat that Frog! from SmarterComics, 640
Echo, 229–30
Echo Complete Collection, 230
Ed Brubaker: Conversations, 646
Eden: It's an Endless World, 263–64
Edgar Allan Poe (Graphic Classics), 420
Edu-Manga: Anne Frank, 611
Edu-Manga: Helen Adams Keller, 611
Edu-Manga: Ludwig Van Beethoven, 611
Edu-Manga: Mother Theresa, 612
Edward Scissorhands, 358
Edward Scissorhands: The Final Cut, 358
E Is for Extinction: X-Tinction Agenda, 112
El Deafo, xxix, 612
Electropolis: The Infernal Machine, a Menlo Park Mystery, 274–75
Elephant and Piggie, 544–45
Elephant's Cannot Dance (Elephant and Piggie), 545
Elephants Never Forget, 545
Elfquest, 298–99
Elfquest: The Final Quest, 299
Elric: The Making of a Sorcerer, 359
Elseworlds: Batman, 123
Elseworlds: Justice League, 124
Emerald City of Oz, The, 343
Emma (by Butler), 500
Emma (by Mori), 500–501
Emma (Manga Classics), 502
Empire, 116–17
Empire of the Wolf, 382
Empire State: A Love Story (or Not), 463–64
Empire: Uprising, 117
Encyclopedia of Comic Books and Graphic Novels, 643
Encyclopedia of Early Earth, The, 318
Engineering an Awesome Recycling Center with Max Axiom, Super Scientist, 634
Engineering a Totally Rad Skateboard with Max Axiom, Super Scientist, 634
Enormous, 394
Escapo, 473
Essential Batman Encyclopedia, 647
Essential Guide to World Comics, The, 644
Essential Ms. Marvel, 70
Essex County, 473–74
Evolution: The Story of Life on Earth, 631
Exit Wounds, 166
Ex Machina, 39

Explorer, 508
Exploring Ecosystems with Max Axiom, Super Scientist, 634
Explosive World of Volcanoes with Max Axiom, Super Scientist, The, 634
Expressive Anatomy for Comics and Narrative, 604
Exquisite Corpse, 474
Extraordinary X-Men, 97
Eyeshield 21, 488
Ezra, 310
Ezra: Evoked Emotions, 310
Ezra: The Egyptian Exchange, 310

Fable Comics, 320
Fables, 291, 318–20
Fables Deluxe Edition, 319–20
Fables: 1001 Nights of Snowfall, 319
Fables: The Wolf among Us, 320
Fables: Werewolves of the Heartland, 319
Fade Out, The, 434
Fairest, 320
Fairest: In All the Land, 320
Fairy Tale Comics: Classic Tales Told by Extraordinary Cartoonists, 320
Fairy Tales of Oscar Wilde, 321, 652
Fake Heir, The (Nancy Drew), 442
Fall of Cthulhu, 401
Fall of the House of West, The, 27
Fallout: J. Robert Oppenheimer, Leo Szilard, and the Political Science of the Atomic Bomb, 631
Famous Players: The Mysterious Death of William Desmond Taylor (Treasury of XXth Century Murder), 454
Fanboys vs. Zombies, 388
Fangbone: Third Grade Barbarian, 595
Fantastic Four, 82–84
Fantastic Four (2009), 83
Fantastic Four (2010), 83
Fantastic Four (2013), 83
Fantastic Four (2014), 83
Fantastic Four (by John Byrne Omnibus), 84
Fantastic Four Epic Collection: Into the Time Stream, 83
Fantastic Four Omnibus, 84
Fantasy Sports, 299
Faradawn (Fog Mound), 264
Faster than a Speeding Bullet: The Rise of the Graphic Novel, 644
Fastest Train the West, The (Geronimo Stilton), 530
Fatal Bullet: The Assassination of President Garfield, The (Treasury of Victorian Murder), 453
Fatale, 444–45
Fatale Deluxe Edition, 445
Fear Itself: Secret Avengers, 80

Fear Itself: Uncanny X-Force/The Deep, 102
Fear Itself: Wolverine/New Mutants, 99
Feast of the Seven Fishes: The Collected Comic Strip and Italian Holiday Cookbook, 491
Feathers, 359
Ferro City: The Medusa Key, 275
Feynman, 631
Fifth Beatle: The Brian Epstein Story, The, 612
50 Girls 50, 227
Filmish: A Graphic Journey through Film, 625
Final Crisis, 108
Finder, 242
Finder: Dream Sequence, 242
Finder: Five Crazy Women, 242
Finder: King of the Cats, 242
Finder Library Edition, 242
Finder: Mystery Date, 242
Finder: *Sin-Eater Vols. 1 & 2*, 242
Finder: *Talisman (2002)*, 242
Finder: *Talisman (2012)*, 242
Finder: *Third World*, 242
Finder: *The Rescuers*, 242
Finder: *Voice*, 242
Finding Nemo, 529
Finding Nemo: Fish Out of Water, 529
Finding Nemo: Losing Dory, 529
Finding Nemo: Reef Rescue, 529
First Mouse on the Moon, The (Geronimo Stilton), 530
First Samurai, The (Geronimo Stilton), 530
First to the Last Place on Earth (Geronimo Stilton), 530
Fist Stick Knife Gun, 451
Five Fists of Science, 253–54
Five Ghosts, 146–47
500 Comic Book Villains, 646
500 Essential Graphic Novels, 644
500 Great Comic Book Action Heroes, 646
Flame of Recca, 176
Flash, The, 39–41
Flash, The (2010 series), 40
Flash, The (2012 series), 41
Flash: A Celebration of 75 Years, The, 41
Flash by Grant Morrison and Mark Millar, The, 40
Flash by Mark Waid, The, 40
Flash Omnibus by Geoff Johns, The, 40
Flashpoint, 108
Flash: Rebirth, The, 40
Flight, 508–9
Flight Explorer, 509
Flight of Angels, A, 321
Flink, 394
Flying Beaver Brothers, The, 546
Flying Beaver Brothers and the Crazy Critter Race, The, 546

Flying Beaver Brothers and the Evil Penguin Plan, The, 546
Flying Beaver Brothers and the Fishy Business, The, 546
Flying Beaver Brothers and the Hot Air Baboons, The, 546
Flying Beaver Brothers and the Mud-Slinging Moles, The, 546
Flying Beaver Brothers: Birds vs. Bunnies, The, 546
Flying Machines: How the Wright Brothers Soared (Science Comics), 637
Fog Mound, 264
Foiled, 348–49
Foiled, 349
Following the Trail of Marco Polo (Geronimo Stilton), 530
Food Wars! Shokugeki no Soma, 491–92
47 Ronin, 173
Fountain, The, 349
Four Eyes, 349
Fraggle Rock, 529
Fraggle Rock Classics, 530
Fraggle Rock: Journey to the Everspring, 530
Fragments of Horror, 420
Fran, 546
Frankenstein Mobster: The Made Man, The, 424
Franklin Richards: Son of a Genius Ultimate Collection, 574
Frank Miller's Daredevil, 35–36
Frank Miller's Robocop, 278
Frank Miller's Sin City. *See* Sin City
Freakangels, 259
Freddie Stories, The, 474
Freddy vs. Jason vs. Ash, 376
Freebooters, The, 310–11
Freshmen: Tales of 9th Grade Obsessions, Revelations, and Other Nonsense, 475
Friday the 13th, 417–18
Friends and Foes (Red's Planet), 571
Friends with Boys, 474
Freshmen: Tales of Ninth Grade Obsessions, Revelations, and Other Nonsense, 475
From Hell, 451
From Now On: Short Comic Tales of the Fantastic, 288
From the Ashes, 264
Fruits Basket, 467–68
FukuFuku Kitten Tales, 546
Fullmetal Alchemist, 230
Fun Home: A Family Tragicomic, 612–13
Fury of Iron Fist, The, 51
Fushigi Yugi: Genbu Kaiden, 338–39
Fushigi Yugi: The Mysterious Play, 338
Future Imperfect: Warzones, 112
Fuzzy Baseball, 546

Gaijin: American Prisoner of War, 501
Game for Swallows: To Die, To Leave, To Return, A, 613
Gary the Pirate, 150–51
Gary's Garden, 546–47
Gear. *See Doug TenNapel's Gear*
Gears of War, 230–31
Genshiken, 516
Gente: The People of Ristorante Paradiso, 494
Geronimo Stilton, 530, 653
Geronimo Stilton Saves the Olympics (Geronimo Stilton), 530
Get Jiro!, 492
Get Jiro: Blood and Sushi, 492
Getting Graphic!: Using Graphic Novels to Promote Literacy with Teens, 645
Gettysburg: The Graphic History of America's Most Famous Battle and the Turning Point of the Civil War (Graphic History), 625
Ghostbusters, 559–60
Ghostbusters (2009 series), 560
Ghostbusters (2012 series), 559–60
Ghostbusters (2016 series), 560
Ghostbusters: Get Real, 559
Ghostbusters Mass Hysteria Deluxe Edition, 560
Ghostbusters: The New Ghostbusters, 560
Ghostbusters Total Containment Deluxe Edition, 559
Ghostbusters: Who Ya Gonna Call, 560
Ghost in the Machinery (Nancy Drew), 442
Ghost of the Grotto (Donald Duck), 527
Ghostopolis, 405
Ghost Racers, 112
Ghost Rider, 406
Ghost Rider by Daniel Way Ultimate Collection, 406
Ghost Rider Omnibus, 406
Ghost Rider: The Road to Damnation, 406
Ghost Rider: Trail of Tears, 406
Ghosts, 406
Ghosts and Girls of Fiction House (Chilling Archives), 420
Giant Days, 475
Giant Monster, 394–95
Giant-Size Little Marvel AvsX, 112, 574–75
Giants Beware (Chronicles of Claudette, The), 592
G.I. Combat: The War That Time Forgot, 166
Gigantic Beard That Was Evil, The, 475
G.I. Joe, 167–69, 650–51
G.I. Joe (2009 series), 167
G.I. Joe: A Real American Hero, 168
G.I. Joe: Hearts and Minds, 168
G.I. Joe Origins, 167
G.I. Joe: Snake Eyes, 169
G.I. Joe: Snake Eyes: Agent of Cobra, 169
G.I. Joe: Snake Eyes and Storm Shadow, 169
G.I. Joe: Snake Eyes: Cobra Civil War, 169

G.I. Joe: The IDW Collection, 168
G.I. Joe/Transformers, 286
Gin Tama, 176–77
Girl Who Owned a City, The, 264
Girl Who Wasn't There, The (Nancy Drew), 442
Glacial Period, 151
Glister, 595
Global Warning (Nancy Drew), 442
G-Man, 574
Goddamn This War!, 169
God of War, 327
Gods of Asgard, 327
Godzilla, 395–96, 650
Godzilla: Awakening, 396
Godzilla: Cataclysm, 396
Godzilla: Gangsters and Goliaths, 395
Godzilla: Half Century War, 395
Godzilla: History's Greatest Monster, 396
Godzilla in Hell, 395–96
Godzilla: Kingdom of Monsters, 395
Godzilla: Legends, 395
Godzilla: Oblivion, 396
Godzilla: Rage across Time, 396
Godzilla: Rulers of Earth, 395–96
Golden Helmet (Donald Duck), 527
Goldie Vance, 439
Goldfish, 445
Goliath, 147
Gon, 547
Good Neighbors, The, 359
Good Riddance: An Illustrated Memoir of Divorce, 613
Good, The Bad, and the Ugly, The, 197
Goon, The, 348, 558–59
Goon Library, The, 559
Gotham Academy, 439–40
Gotham Central, 423, 425–26
Gotham Central Omnibus, 426
Gotham City Sirens, 48
Gothic Classics (Graphic Classics), 420
Grandville, 426
Grandville Bete Noire, 426
Grandville Mon Amour, 426
Grandville Noël, 426
Grant Vs. Lee: The Graphic History of the Civil War's Greatest Rivals during the Last Year of the War (Graphic History), 625
Graphic Classics, 420
Graphic History Series, 625
Graphic Novel, The, 643
Graphic Novel: An Introduction, 643
Graphic Novel Classroom: POWerful Teaching and Learning with Images, The, 645
Graphic Novels 101: Selecting and Using Graphic Novels to Promote Literacy for Children and Young Adults, 645

Graphic Novels and Comic Books, 644
*Graphic Novels and Comics in Libraries and
    Archives: Essays on Readers, Research, History
    and Cataloging*, 645
*Graphic Novels and Comics in the Classroom:
    Essays on the Educational Power of Sequential
    Art*, 645
*Graphic Novels beyond the Basics: Insights and
    Issues for Libraries*, 644
*Graphic Novels: Everything You Need to
    Know*, 643
Graphic Novels in Your Media Center, 645
*Graphic Novels Now: Building, Managing, and
    Marketing a Dynamic Collection*, 645
*Graphic Storytelling and Visual Narrative:
    Principles and Practices from the Legendary
    Cartoonist*, 604, 643
Graveyard Book, The, 407
Grayson, 41
Great Expectations (Manga Classics), 502
Great Ice Age, The (Geronimo Stilton), 530
Green Arrow, 42–43
Green Arrow (first series), 42–43
Green Arrow (second series), 43
Green Arrow: A Celebration of 75 Years, 43
Green Arrow/Black Canary, 43
*Green Arrow/Black Canary: A League of Their
    Own*, 43
Green Arrow/Black Canary: Big Game, 43
Green Arrow/Black Canary: Enemies List, 43
Green Arrow/Black Canary: Five Stages, 43
Green Arrow/Black Canary: Road to the Altar, 43
*Green Arrow/Black Canary: The Wedding
    Album*, 43
*Green Arrow by Jeff Lemire and Andrea
    Sorrentino Deluxe Edition*, 43
Green Arrow: The Longbow Hunters, 42
Green Arrow: Year One, 43
Green Lantern, 44–46
Green Lantern (2006 series), 45
Green Lantern: A Celebration of 75 Years, 46
Green Lantern: Agent Orange, 45
Green Lantern: Blackest Night, 45
Green Lantern: Brightest Day, 45
Green Lantern by Geoff Johns Omnibus, 45
Green Lantern Corps, 46
Green Lantern Corps: The Lost Army, 46
Green Lantern: Lights Out, 45
Green Lantern: New Guardians, 46
Green Lantern: No Fear, 45
Green Lantern: Rage of the Red Lanterns, 45
Green Lantern: Rebirth, 45
Green Lantern: Revenge of the Green Lanterns, 45
Green Lantern: Rise of the Third Army, 45
Green Lantern: Secret Origin, 45

Green Lantern: Sinestro Corps War, 45
Green Lantern: Wanted: Hal Jordan, 45
Green Lantern: War of the Green Lanterns, 45
Green Lantern: Wrath of the First Lantern, 45
Green Monk, 311
Green River Killer: A True Detective Story, 451–52
Groo, 595–96
Groo: Death and Taxes, 596
Groo: Fray of the Gods, 596
Groo: Friends and Foes, Vols. 1–3, 596
Groo: Hell on Earth, 596
Groo: Hogs of Horder, 596
Groo Houndbook, The, 596
Groo Inferno, The, 596
Groo Jamboree, The, 596
Groo Kingdom, The, 596
Groo Library, The, 596
Groo Maiden, The, 596
Groo: Mightier than the Sword, 596
Groo Nursery, The, 596
Groo Odyssey, The, 596
Groo: The Most Intelligent Man in the Word, 596
Groo vs. Conan, 596
Groot, 74
Grumpy Cat, 548
*Gryphons Aren't So Great (Adventures in
    Cartooning)*, 604
Guardians of Knowhere, 112
Guardians of the Galaxy, 70–74
Guardians of the Galaxy (modern team 2013), 71
Guardians of the Galaxy (modern team 2015), 72
Guardians of the Galaxy (original team, 2014), 71
*Guardians of the Galaxy/All-New X-Men: The
    Trial of Jean Grey*, 72, 96
*Guardians of the Galaxy & X-Men: The Black
    Vortex*, 72
Guardians of the Galaxy by Abnett and Lanning:
    The Complete Collection, 71
*Guardians of the Galaxy: Tomorrow's
    Avengers*, 71
Guardians Team-Up, 105
Guild, The, 349–50
Guinea Pig: Pet Shop Private Eye, 547
Gun Blaze West, 199
Gunslinger Girl, 190–91
Gus and His Gang, 194–95
Gyo, 396–97

Habibi, 501
Hack/Slash, 418, 651
Hack/Slash Omnibus, 418
Hack/Slash: Son of Samhain, 418
Hades: Lord of the Dead (Olympians), 330
Hail Hydra, 112
Haley Danelle's Top Eight! (Hardy Boys), 440

Halloween Classics (Graphic Classics), 420
HALO, 231–32
HALO: Bloodline, 232
HALO: Escalation, 232
HALO: Fall of Reach (2011), 232
HALO: Fall of Reach (2016), 232
HALO: Fall of Reach: Bootcamp, 232
HALO: Fall of Reach: Covenant, 232
HALO: Fall of Reach: Invasion, 232
Halo Graphic Novel, 231
HALO: Helljumper, 231
HALO: Initiation, 232
HALO Library Edition, 232
HALO Oversized Collection, 232
HALO: Tales from Slipspace, 232
HALO: Uprising, 231
Hammer of the Gods, 327
Hana-Kimi: For You in Full Blossom, 464
Happy!, 425
Happy Pig Day (Elephant and Piggie), 545
Harbinger, 269
Harbinger (2013), 269
Harbinger—Children of the Eighth Day (Valiant Masters), 269
Harbinger Deluxe Edition, 269
Harbinger Wars Deluxe Edition, 269
Hardy Boys, The, 440–41, 653
Hardy Boys Adventures, 441
Hardy Day Night, A (Hardy Boys), 440
Hark! A Vagrant!, 554
Harlem Hellfighters, The, 169
Harley and Ivy Deluxe Edition, 47
Harley Quinn, 46–48
Harley Quinn (2009 series), 47
Harley Quinn (2014 series), 47–48
Harley Quinn and Power Girl, 48
Harrow County, 413
Harvey Pekar: Conversations, 646
Haunted Dollhouse, The (Nancy Drew), 442
Haunted Horror: Banned Comics from the 1950s (Chilling Archives), 419
Haunted Horror: Candles for the Undead and More (Chilling Archives), 420
Haunted Horror: Comics Your Mother Warned You About (Chilling Archives), 419
Haunted Horror: Pre-Code Comics So Good, They're Scary (Chilling Archives), 419
Haunted Mansion, 407
Haunted Mansion: Welcome Foolish Mortals, 407
Hawaiian Dick, 431
Hawkeye, 48–49
Hawkeye Omnibus, 49
Head Lopper, 299
Health Care Reform: What It Is, Why It's Necessary, and How It Works, 640

Heathentown, 408
Helen Adams Keller (Edu-Manga), 611
Hellblazer. *See* John Constantine: Hellblazer
Hellbound, 418–19
Hellboy, 348, 368, 370, 376–78, 380
Hellboy and the B.P.R.D., 371
Hellboy and the B.P.R.D. 1952, 377
Hellboy and the B.P.R.D. 1953, 377
Hellboy Animated, 377
Hellboy: House of the Living Dead, 377
Hellboy in Hell, 377
Hellboy in Mexico, 377
Hellboy: Into the Silent Sea, 377
Hellboy: The Midnight Circus, 377
Hellboy: Weird Tales, 377
Hello Kitty, 531
Hello Kitty: Delicious, 531
Hello Kitty: Fashion Music Wonderland, 531
Hello Kitty, Hello 40: A 40th Anniversary Tribute, 531
Hello Kitty: Here We Go, 531
Hello Kitty: It's about Time, 531
Hello Kitty: Just Imagine, 531
Hello Kitty: Surprise, 531
Hello Kitty: Work of Art, 531
Hellsing, 382–83, 652
Helm, The, 596
Hera: The Goddess and Her Glory (Olympians), 330
Her Permanent Record (Amelia Rules), 512
Here, 243
Hereville, 350
Hero, The, 328
Hero Happy Hour, 127
Heroes and Superheroes (Critical Survey of Graphic Novels), 643
Heroes of Olympus, 328
Heroman, 282
He's My Only Vampire, 383
H.G. Wells' The War of the Worlds, 247
Hidden: A Child's Story of the Holocaust, 501
High School Chronicles of Ariel Schrag, The, 613
High School Debut, The, 464
High School of the Dead, 388
High School of the Dead Omnibus, 388
Hikaru No Go, 147
Hilda and the Bird Parade, 350
Hilda and the Black Hound, 350
Hilda and the Midnight Giant, 350
Hilda and the Stone Forest, 350
Hilda and the Troll, 350
Hildafolk, 291, 350
Hilo, 569
Hippopotamister, 548

History, Theme, and Technique (Critical Survey of Graphic Novels), 643

Hit, 425

Hit by Pitch: Ray Chapman, Carl Mays and the Fatal Fastball, 626

Hive, The, 556

Hoax Hunters, 377–78

Hocus Focus (Adventures in Cartooning), 604

Honey Blood, 383

Honey Blood: Tale Zero, 383

Hong Kong Comics: A History of Manhua, 644

Hopeless Savages, 475–76

Hopeless Savages: Break, 476

Hopeless Savages Greatest Hits 2000–2010, 476

Horror (Simon and Kirby Library), 421

Horror by Heck! (Chilling Archives), 420

Horror Classics (Graphic Classics), 420

Hour of the Zombie, 388

House of Five Leaves, 177

House of M, 114

House of M: Warzones, 112

Howard Chaykin: Conversations, 646

Howard Nostrand's Nightmares (Chilling Archives), 419

Howard the Duck, 548–49

Howard the Duck (2015 series), 549

Howard the Duck Omnibus, 549

Howard the Duck: The Complete Collection, 549

How I Made It to Eighteen: A Mostly True Story, 476

Howtoons, 631

How to Read Superhero Comics and Why, 647

H.P. Lovecraft (Graphic Classics), 420

Hulk, 49–50

Hulk: Future Imperfect, 50, 122

Hulk Visionaries: Peter David, 49

Human Body Theater, 632

Hunter X Hunter, 151

Hybrid, 397

Hyde & Shriek (Hardy Boys), 440

Hypernaturals, The, 232–33

I, Vampire, 383–84

I Am Abraham Lincoln (Ordinary People Can Change the World), 617

I Am Albert Einstein (Ordinary People Can Change the World), 617

I Am Amelia Earhart (Ordinary People Can Change the World), 617

I Am George Washington (Ordinary People Can Change the World), 617

I Am Going (Elephant and Piggie), 545

I Am Helen Keller (Ordinary People Can Change the World), 617

I Am Invited to a Party (Elephant and Piggie), 545

I Am Jackie Robinson (Ordinary People Can Change the World), 617

I Am Jane Goodall (Ordinary People Can Change the World), 617

I Am Jim Henson (Ordinary People Can Change the World), 617

I Am Lucille Ball (Ordinary People Can Change the World), 617

I Am Martin Luther King, Jr (Ordinary People Can Change the World), 617

I Am Rosa Parks (Ordinary People Can Change the World), 617

I Broke My Trunk (Elephant and Piggie), 545

Ichiro, 339

Icons of the American Comic Book, 643

Identity Theft (Hardy Boys), 440

Idol Dreams, 459

I Hate Fairyland, 596

I Kill Giants, 476

Illuminating World of Light with Max Axiom, Super Scientist, The, 634

I Love My New Toy (Elephant and Piggie), 545

I'm a Frog! (Elephant and Piggie), 545

Imitation Game, The, 632, 654

Immortal Iron Fist: The Complete Collection, 50–51

Immortals: Gods and Heroes, 328

Impossible Man, The, 575

Incognito, 445

Incognito: The Classified Edition, 445

Incorruptible, 117

Incredible Change-Bots, 282

Incredible Change-Bots Two, 282

Incredible Change-Bots Two Point Something Something, 282

Incredible Hulk, 49–50

Incredible Hulk: Heart of the Monster, 50

Incredible Hulk: Planet Hulk, 49–50

Incredible Hulk: Planet Skaar, 50

Incredible Hulk: Skaar: Son of Hulk, 50

Incredible Hulks, 49–50

Incredible Hulks: Fall of the Hulks, 50

Incredible Hulks: Planet Savage, 50

Incredible Hulks: World War Hulks, 50

Incredibles, The, 84

Independent and Underground Classics (Critical Survey of Graphic Novels), 643

Indiana Jones, 151–53

Indiana Jones Adventures, 152

Indiana Jones and Kingdom of the Crystal Skull, 152

Indiana Jones and the Tomb of the Gods, 152

Indiana Jones Omnibus, 152–53

Indiana Jones Omnibus: The Further Adventures, 153

Inferno: Warzones, 112
Infinite Crisis, 109
Infinite Crisis Companion, 109
Infinite Kung-Fu, 159
Infinity Crusade, The, 109
Infinity Gauntlet, The, 109
Infinity Gauntlet Aftermath, The, 109
Infinity Gauntlet Omnibus, The, 109
Infinity Gauntlet: Warzones, The, 112
Infinity War, The, 109
*Information Now: A Graphic Guide to Student
    Research*, 640
Inhumans: Attilan Rising, 112
Injustice: Gods among Us, 124
Injustice: Gods among Us Year Five, 124
Injustice: Gods among Us Year Four, 124
Injustice: Gods among Us Year One, 124
*Injustice: Gods among Us Year One: The Complete
    Collection*, 124
Injustice: Gods among Us Year Three, 124
Injustice: Gods among Us Year Two, 124
In Real Life, 476–77
In the Dark: A Horror Anthology, 420–21
In the Days of the Mob, 452
InuYasha, 339–40
Invader Zim, 531, 653
*Investigating the Scientific Method with Max
    Axiom, Super Scientist*, 634
Invincible, 51–52, 650
Invincible Compendium, 52
Invincible Iron Man (2008), 53–54
Invincible Iron Man (2016), 53
Invincible Iron Man: Fear Itself, 54
Invincible Iron Man Omnibus, 54
Invincible Presents Atom Eve & Rex Splode, 52
Invincible Ultimate Collection, 52
Invincible Universe, 52
*Invisible Ink: My Mother's Secret Love Affair with
    a Famous Cartoonist*, 613–14
I Really Like Slop (Elephant and Piggie), 545
I Remember Beirut, 613
Iron, or the War After, 191
Iron Man, 52–54
Iron Man: Extremis, 53
Iron Man Epic Collection: Stark Wars, 53
*Iron Man: The Ultimate Guide to the Armored
    Super Hero*, 647
Iron Wok Jan, 492–93
Irredeemable, 117, 651
Iscariot, 350–51
Isle of 100,000 Graves, 153
Is That All There Is?, 554
Itazura Na Kiss, 464–65
Itty Bitty Hellboy, 377, 560
It Was the War of the Trenches, 169

*I Will Surprise My Friend (Elephant and
    Piggie)*, 545
I Will Take a Nap (Elephant and Piggie), 545
Izombie Omnibus, 389

Jack Cole's Deadly Horror (Chilling Archives), 419
Jack Kirby's Fourth World Omnibus, 85
Jack of Fables, 321
Jack Staff, 575
*Jack the Ripper (Treasury of Victorian
    Murder)*, 453
James Bond, 191
Jellaby, 351
Jerusalem: Chronicles from the Holy City, 614
Jessica Jones: Alias, 430
*Jessica Jones—The Pulse: The Complete
    Collection*, 430
*Jim Henson's The Musical Monsters of Turkey
    Hollow*, 569
Jim Henson's The Storyteller, 322
Jim Henson's The Storyteller: Dragons, 322
Jim Henson's The Storyteller: Giants, 322
Jim Henson's The Storyteller: Witches, 322
Jinx: The Essential Collection, 445–46
JLA/Avengers, 105
Joe Hill: The Graphic Novel Collection, 420
Joe the Barbarian, 351
John Constantine: Hellblazer, 367, 410, 413–15
Johnny Boo, 560–61
Johnny Boo Meets Dragon Puncher, 561
Johnny Boo's Big Boo Box, 561
Johnny Hiro, 516–17
Joker, 117–18
Jonah Hex, 193, 195
Jonah Hex (2006 series), 195
Jonah Hex: Shadows West, 195
Jonah Hex (*Showcase Presents*), 195
Jonah Hex: Welcome to Paradise, 195
*Journey into Adaptation with Max Axiom, Super
    Scientist, A*, 634
Journey into Mohawk Country, 626
Journey into Mystery/New Mutants: Exiled, 99
*Journey through the Digestive System with Max
    Axiom, Super Scientist, A*, 634
JSA Omnibus, 88
Judas Coin, The, 110
Judge Dredd, 233–34
Judge Dredd (2013 series), 234
Judge Dredd: Cursed Earth Uncensored, 234
Judge Dredd: Dead Zone, 234
Judge Dredd: The Complete Case Files, 233
Judge Dredd: Titan, 234
Jughead, 517
Juice Squeezers: The Great Bug Elevator, 233
Junior Braves of the Apocalypse, 389, 653

Junji Ito's Cat Diary: Yon and Mu, 614
Jurassic Park, 138–39
Jurassic Park: Dangerous Games, 139
Jurassic Park: Redemption, 139
Jurassic Park: The Devils in the Desert, 139
Justice, 86
Justice League, 86, 575–76
Justice League 3001, 576
Justice League Dark, 85
Justice League International, 576
Justice League of America, 85–88
Justice League of America (2008), 86
Justice League of America (2013), 87
Justice League of America (2017), 87
Justice Society of America, 87–88

Kade, 310–11
Kade: Identity, 311
Kade: Red Sun, 311
Kade: Shiva's Sun, 311
Kade: Sun of Perdition, 311
Kaijumax, 569–70
Kaijumax Season One, 570
Kaijumax Season Two, 570
Kamisama Kiss, 465, 597
Kaze Hikaru, 177
Kick-Ass, 127–28
Kick-Ass, 128
Kick -Ass 2, 128
Kick-Ass 2 Prelude: Hit Girl, 128
Kick-Ass 3, 128
Kid Beowulf, 311–12
Kid Beowulf and the Blood-Bound Oath, 312
Kid Beowulf and the Rise of El Cid, 311
Kid Beowulf and the Song of Roland, 311
Kid Beowulf Eddas: Shild and the Dragon, 312
Kill All Monsters: Ruins of Paris, 282
Kill La Kill, 159–60
Kill My Mother: A Graphic Novel, 434
Kill or Be Killed, 446
Kill Shakespeare, 359–60, 650
Kill Shakespeare Backstage Edition, 360
Kill Shakespeare: The Complete Edition, 360
Kill Shakespeare: The Mask of Night, 360
Kill Shakespeare: The Tide of Blood, 360
King City, 587
King Conan, 310
King Conan: The Conqueror, 310
King Conan: The Hour of the Dragon, 310
King Conan: The Phoenix on the Sword, 310
King Conan: The Scarlet Citadel, 310
King Conan: Wolves beyond the Border, 310
Kingdom Come, 110, 122
Kingdom Hearts, 340–41
Kingdom Hearts 358/2 Days, 341

Kingdom Hearts II, 341
Kingdom Hearts: Chain of Memories, 341
Kingdom Hearts: Final Mix, 341
King Lear, 502
King Ottokar's Sceptre (Tintin), 114
Kingsman (Secret Service), 192
Kitchen Princess Omnibus, 493
Kitty and Dino, 140
Knights of Sidonia, 234
Knights of the Lunch Table, 517
Koko Be Good, 477
Kong of Skull Island, 397
Korgi, 351
Korvac Saga: Warzones, 112
Kristy's Great Idea (Baby-Sitter's Club), 514
Kurdles, The, 352
Kurosagi Corpse Delivery Service, 561

Lady Killer, 446
Laika, 134
Larry Gonick's Cartoon Guides, 629–30
Last Days of an Immortal, 202
Last Man, The, 160
Last of the Sandwalkers, 632
Last of Us: American Dreams, The, 389
Last Train to Deadsville: A Cal McDonald Mystery, 376
Last Unicorn, The, 300
Lazarus, 259–60
Lazarus: The First Collection, 260
Lazarus: The Second Collection, 260
LBX, 275
League of Extraordinary Gentlemen, The, 88
League of Extraordinary Gentlemen: Omnibus Edition, The, 88
League of Extraordinary Gentlemen: The Black Dossier, The, 88
Leave It to Pet, 275
Legendary Star-Lord, 73
Legend of Zelda, The, 312–14
Legends of Zelda: A Link to the Past, The, 314
Legend of Zelda *Legendary Edition Four Swords*, 313
Legend of Zelda Legendary Edition: Majora's Mask/ A Link to the Past, The, 314
Legend of Zelda *Legendary Edition: Ocarina of Time*, The, 312
Legend of Zelda *Legendary Edition Oracle of Seasons and Oracle of Ages, The*, 313
Legend of Zelda *Legendary Edition: The Minish Cap/Phantom Hourglass, The*, 314
Legend of Zelda: Ocarina of Time, The, 312
Legends, 90
Legends of Red Sonja, 316
Legends of Zita the Space Girl, 571

Lego Nijango, 178, 653
Lego Ninjago (2011), 178
Lego Ninjago (2015), 178
Lego Ninjago: Dark Island Trilogy, 178
Leo Geo and His Miraculous Journey through the Center of the Earth, 234
Leo Geo and the Cosmic Crisis, 234–35
Lessons in Science Safety with Max Axiom, Super Scientist, 634
Let's Go For a Drive (Elephant and Piggie), 545
Level Up, 517–18
Lewis & Clark, 614
Liar's Kiss, 426
Librarian's Guide to Graphic Novels for Adults, The, 645
Librarian's Guide to Graphic Novels for Children and Tweens, The, 645
Library Wars: Love and War, 235
Life After, The, 352
Life Sucks, 384
Lightning Thief: The Graphic Novel, The, 331
Lights, Camera, Stilton (Geronimo Stilton), 530
Like a Sniper Lining Up His Shot, 446
Likewise (High School Chronicles of Ariel Schrag), 613
Lindbergh Child, The (Treasury of XXth Century Murder), 454
Lions, Tigers, and Bears, 341
Listen to My Trumpet (Elephant and Piggie), 545
Little Adventures in Oz, 343
Little Lulu, 511, 518–19
Little Lulu Color Special, 518
Little Lulu's Pal Tubby, 519
Little Mouse Gets Ready, 549
Little Nemo: Return to Slumberland, 341–42
Little Robot, 275
Little Vampire, 561
Live Free, Die Hardy (Hardy Boys), 440
Lives of Sacco and Vanzetti, The (Treasury of XXth Century Murder), 454
Lobster Johnson, 378
Locke and Key, 415–16, 650
Lockjaw and the Pet Avengers, 579
Lockjaw and the Pet Avengers Unleashed, 579
Loki: Agent of Asgard, 329
Lola: A Ghost Story, 408
Lone Ranger, The, 196, 652
Lone Ranger and Tonto, 196
Lone Ranger/Green Hornet: Champions of Justice, The, 196
Lone Ranger Omnibus, 196
Lone Ranger: Snake of Iron, The, 196
Lone Ranger: Vindicated, The, 196
Lone Ranger/Zorro: The Death of Zorro, The, 196
Lone Wolf and Cub, 178–79

Long Distance, 459
Longshot, 54
Longshot Saves the Marvel Universe, 54
Long Tail Kitty, 549
Long Tail Kitty: Come Out and Play, 549
Long Walk to Valhalla, 352–53
Looney Tunes, 531
Lost Boy, The, 342
Lost in NYC, 477
Lost in Translation (Geronimo Stilton), 530
Lou Cameron's Unsleeping Dead (Chilling Archives), 420
Louise Brooks: Detective, 434
Love, 134
Love and Capes, 576
Love Hina, Omnibus Edition, 465–66
Lovers' Lane: The Hall-Hills Mystery (Treasury of XXth Century Murder), 454–55
Low, 260
Lucifer, 360
Lucy & Andy Neanderthal, 519
Lucky Penny, 466
Ludwig Van Beethoven (Edu-Manga), 611
Luke Cage, Iron Fist, and the Heroes for Hire, 55
Luke Cage: Hero for Hire (Marvel Masterworks), 55
Luke Cage: Second Chances, 55
Lumberjanes, 441, 651
Lumberjanes/Gotham Academy, 441
Lumberjanes: To the Max Edition, 441
Lunch Lady, 576–77
Lunch Lady and the Author Visit Vendetta, 577
Lunch Lady and the Bake Sale Bandit, 577
Lunch Lady and the Cyborg Substitute, 576
Lunch Lady and the Field Trip Fiasco, 577
Lunch Lady and the League of Librarians, 576
Lunch Lady and the Mutant Mathletes, 577
Lunch Lady and the Picture Day Peril, 577
Lunch Lady and the Schoolwide Scuffle, 577
Lunch Lady and the Summer Camp Shakedown, 577
Lunch Lady and the Video Game Villain, 577
Lunch Witch, The, 561

Macbeth, 502
Mad House (Hardy Boys), 440
Madison Square Tragedy: The Murder of Stanford White (Treasury of XXth Century Murder), 455
Madman, 577
Madman (series), 577
Madman and the Atomics, 577
Madman Atomica, 577
Madman: Atomic Comics, 577
Madman Gargantua, 577
Madman 20th Anniversary Monster, 577

Madrox: Multiple Choice, 100
Magic Knight Rayearth, 344
Magic of Sabrina the Teenage Witch (Archie), 513
Magic Pickle, 578
Magic Trixie, 562
Magic Trixie and the Dragon, 562
Magic Trixie Sleeps Over, 562
Magnus, Robot Fighter, 276
Magnus, Robot Fighter (2011), 276
Magnus, Robot Fighter (2014), 276
Magnus, Robot Fighter 4000 A.D. Archives, 276
*Making Comics: Storytelling Secrets of
    Comics, Manga, and Graphic Novels*,
    604–5, 644
Mal and Chad, 570
Mal and Chad: Belly Flop, 570
Mal and Chad: Food Fight, 570
*Mal and Chad: The Biggest, Bestest Time
    Ever*, 570
Malled (Hardy Boys), 440
Mammoth Book of Zombie Comics, The, 389
Manga (Critical Survey of Graphic Novels), 644
Manga Classics, 502–3
Manga Classics: Emma, 502
Manga Classics: Great Expectations, 502
Manga Classics: Les Miserables, 502–3
Manga Classics: Pride and Prejudice, 503
Manga Classics: Sense and Sensibility, 503
Manga Classics: The Scarlet Letter, 503
*Manga Cookbook: Japanese Bento Boxes, Main
    Dishes and More, The*, 497–98
Manga Guide to Biochemistry, The, 633
Manga Guide to Calculus, The, 633
Manga Guide to Databases, The, 633
Manga Guide to Electricity, 633
Manga Guide to Linear Algebra, The, 633
Manga Guide to Microprocessors, The, 633
Manga Guide to Molecular Biology, The, 633
Manga Guide to Physics, The, 633
Manga Guide to Physiology, The, 633
Manga Guide to Regression Analysis, The, 633
Manga Guide to Relativity, The, 633
Manga Guide to Statistics, The, 633
Manga Guide to the Universe, The, 633
Manga Guides, 632–33
Mangaman, 342
*Manga! Manga!: The World of Japanese
    Comics*, 644
Manga: The Complete Guide, 645
Manhattan Projects, 254
Manifest Destiny, 397
Man with No Name, The, 196–97
Maoh: Juvenile Remix, 235
Marathon, 504
Marble Season, 477

*Marbles: Mania, Depression, Michelangelo, &
    Me: A Graphic Memoir*, 614
March, 615
March Grand Prix: Fast and the Furriest, 549–50
Marshall Law: The Deluxe Edition, 555
Marvel 1602, 110
Marvel 1602: New World/Fantastick Four, 111
Marvel 1602: Spider-Man, 111
Marvel 1602: Witch Hunter Angela, 111
Marvel 1872, 112
Marvel Comics: The Untold Story, 647
Marvel Encyclopedia, 643
Marvel Fairy Tales, 323
*Marvel: Five Fabulous Decades of the World's
    Greatest Comics*, 646
Marvel Masterworks Luke Cage: Hero for Hire, 55
Marvelous Land of Oz, The, 343
Marvels, 128
Marvel Universe: The End, 124
Marvel Zombies, 390
Marvel Zombies Battleworld, 113, 390
Marvel Zombies: Dead Days, 390
Marvel Zombies Destroy, 390
Marvel Zombies Return, 390
Marvel Zombies Supreme, 390
Marvel Zombies: The Complete Collection, 390
Marvel Zombies vs. Army of Darkness, 390, 557
Marvel Zomnibus, 390
Mary Ann Saves the Day (Baby-Sitter's Club), 514
Mass Effect, 235–36
Mass Effect Foundation, 236
Mass Effect Library Edition, 236
Master Keaton, 435
Master of Kung Fu: Battleworld, 113
Matter of Life, A, 615
Maus: A Survivor's Tale, 615–16, 655
Max Axiom Super Scientist series, 633–35
Maximum Ride, 236, 654
*Meaning of Life (and Other Stuff), The (Amelia
    Rules)*, 512
*Meanwhile: Pick Any Path: 3,856 Story
    Possibilities*, 478
Mega Man, 276–77
Megaman NT Warrior, 267
*Men of Tomorrow: Geeks, Gangsters, and the Birth
    of the Comic Book*, 647
Men of War (Showcase Presents), 171
Mercury, 478
Metabarons: Ultimate Collection, The, 202
Metal Men, The (Showcase Presents), 277
Meteor Man, 245
Mice Templar, 300
Michael Allred: Conversations, 646
*Michael Townsend's Amazing Greek Myths of
    Wonder and Blunders*, 640

Mickey Mouse, 532
Mickey Mouse: Darkenblot, 532
Mickey Mouse: Dark Mines of the Phantom Metal, 532
Mickey Mouse: Gift of the Sun Lord, 532
Mickey Mouse: Mysterious Melody, 532
Mickey Mouse: Shadow of the Colossus, 532
Mickey Mouse Shorts, Season One, 532
Mickey Mouse: The Chirikawa Necklace, 532
Mickey Mouse: The Mysterious Crystal Ball, 532
Mickey Mouse: Timeless Tales Vols. 1–2, 532
Micronauts, 202
Midas Flesh, The, 221
Mighty Avengers, 78
Mighty Avengers (2008), 78
Mighty Avengers (2014), 79
Mighty Jack, 323
Mighty Jack and the Goblin King, 323
Mighty Thor, The, 334
Mighty Thor Omnibus, The, 334
Mike's Place: A True Story of Love, Blues, and Terror in Tel Aviv, 616
Miles Morales: Ultimate Spider-Man, 23
Mind Mgmt, 435
Mini Marvels: The Complete Collection, 578
Minions, 531–32
Miracleman, 55–56
Miracleman: The Golden Age, 56
Misadventures of Grumpy Cat and Pokey, The
Misadventures of Salem Hyde, The, 562
Miserabes, Les (Manga Classics), 502–3
Misfits of Avalon, 329
Miss Don't Touch Me, 435–36
Miss Don't Touch Me: The Complete Set, 436
Missile Mouse, 236
Miss Peregrine's Home for Peculiar Children: The Graphic Novel, 361
Mister Negativity and Other tales of Supernatural Law, 566
Mixed Vegetables, 493
Mobile Suit Gundam: The Origin, 282–83
Mockingbird, 56
Mockingbird: Bobbi Morse, Agent of S.H.I.E.L.D., 56
M.O.D.O.K. Assassin, 112
Mom's Cancer, 616
Monkey Wrench Blues (Nancy Drew), 442
Monster Hunter: Flash Hunter, 300
Monster Motors, 277
Monster on the Hill, 597
Monsters! and Other Stories, 562
Monsters Meet on Court Street and Other Tales of Supernatural Law, The, 566
Monster: The Perfect Edition, 436
Monster Zoo, 397

Monstress, 398
Monstrosity, 421
Moon Girl and Devil Dinosaur, 137
Moon Moth, The, 202–3
Morning Glories, 419
Morning Glories Compendium, 419
Morning Glories Deluxe Edition, 419
Most Imperfect Union: A Contrarian History of the United States, A, 626
Mother Theresa (Edu-Manga), 612
Mouse Guard, 300–301, 651
Mouse Guard: Baldwin the Brave and Other Tales, 301
Mouse Guard: Fall 1152, 301
Mouse Guard: Legends of the Mouseguard, 301
Mouse Guard: The Black Axe, 301
Mouse Guard: Winter 1152, 301
Moving Pictures, 504
Mr. Big: A Tale of Pond Life, 134
Mr. Cheeters Is Missing (Nancy Drew), 442
Mr. Wuffles!, 550
Ms. Marvel (1970s), 69–70
Ms. Marvel (2006), 70
Ms. Marvel (2014), 56–57
Ms. Marvel Omnibus, 57
Mudman, 57
Muppet Adaptations, 533
Muppet King Arthur, 533
Muppet Peter Pan, 533
Muppet Robin Hood, 533
Muppets, The, 532–33
Muppet Sherlock Holmes, 533
Muppet Show Comic Book: Family Reunion, The, 533
Muppet Show Comic Book: Meet the Muppets, The, 533
Muppet Show Comic Book: Muppet Mash, The, 533
Muppet Show Comic Book: On the Road, The, 533
Muppet Show Comic Book: The Four Seasons, The, 533
Muppet Show Comic Book: The Treasure of Peg Leg Wilson, The, 533
Muppet Snow White, 533
Muppets Omnibus, The, 533
Murder Mysteries, 360–61
Murder of Abraham Lincoln, The (Treasury of Victorian Murder), 453
Museum of Terror, 421
Museum Vaults: Excerpts from the Journal of an Expert, The, 153
My Dirty Dumb Lives, 519
My Friend Dahmer, 616–17, 654
My Friend Is Sad (Elephant and Piggie), 545
My Little Monster, 466

My Little Pony, 533–34, 650
My Little Pony: Adventures in Friendship, 534
My Little Pony: Fiendship Is Magic, 534
My Little Pony: Friends Forever, 534.
My Little Pony: Friendship Is Magic, 534
My Little Pony: Pony Tales, 534
My Monster Secret, 562–63
My Most Secret Desire, 617
My Neighbor Seki, 519–20
My New Friend Is So Fun (Elephant and
    Piggie), 545
Mystery of Mary Rogers, The (Treasury of
    Victorian Murder), 453
Mystery of the Pirate Ship (Geronimo Stilton), 530
Myth of the Superhero, 646

Nameless City, The, 179
Nancy Drew, 441–42, 653
Nancy Drew Diaries, 442
Nao of Brown, The, 459–60
Naoki Urasawa's 20th Century Boys, 240
Naoki Urasawa's 21st Century Boys, 240
Naoki Urasawa's Monster: The Perfect
    Edition, 436
Naruto, 179–81
Naruto: The Seventh Hokage and the Scarlet
    Spring, 181
Narwhal: Unicorn of the Sea, 550
Nathan Hale's Hazardous Tales, 626–27, 654
Natsume's Book of Friends, 352
Necronomicon, 401
Negima!: Magister Negi Magi, 597–98
Nemo: Heart of Ice, 88
Nemo: River of Ghosts, 88
Nemo: The Roses of Berlin, 88
Neonomicon, 402
Neozoic, 140
New American Splendor Anthology, 606
New Avengers, 79–80
New Avengers (2006), 79
New Avengers (2010), 79
New Avengers (2013), 80
New Avengers (2016), 80
New Deal, The, 436
New Ghost, The, 408
New Lone Wolf and Cub, 178–79
New Mutants, 99
New Suicide Squad, 91
New York Five, The, 460
New York Four, The, 460
New York Mon Amour, 447
Nightmare World, 402
Nightmares & Fairy Tales, 361
Night of the Living Chatchke (Nancy Drew), 442
Nightschool: The Weirn Books, 416

Nightwing, 57
Nimona, 598
Ningen's Nightmares, 182
Ninja Baseball Kyuma, 587
Ninjak, 181, 653
Ninjak (2013), 181
Nnewts, 236–37
No. 6, 260
Noragami: Stray God, 329–30
Normandy: A Graphic History of D-Day, The
    Allied Invasion of Hitler's Fortress Europe
    (Graphic History), 625
Northanger Abbey, 504
Northlanders, 163
Northlanders Deluxe Edition, 163
Nothing Can Possibly Go Wrong, 478
Not Love, But Delicious Food Make Me So
    Happy, 493
Nova, 74–75
Nova (2007), 74
Nova (2013), 74–75
Nova Classic, 74
Nova the Human Rocket, 75
Nursery Rhyme Comics: 50 Timeless Rhymes from
    50 Celebrated Cartoonists, 323
Nutmeg, 493

Ocean of Osyria, The (Hardy Boys), 440
Odd Duck, 550
Oddly Normal, 342–43
Odyssey, The (All-Action Classics), 330
Odyssey, The (Candlewick Press), 330
Of Comics and Men: A Cultural History of
    American Comic Books, 647
Ogres Awake (Adventures in Cartooning), 604
Oh My Goddess, 599–600
O Human Star, 277
Oishinbo a la Carte, 494
Okko, 182
Old City Blues, 426
Olympians, The, 330–31
One Dead Spy (Nathan Hale's Hazardous
    Tales), 627
100 Bullets, 423, 447
100 Bullets: Brother Lono, 447
100 Girls, 227–28
100 Greatest Comic Books, 648
101 Outstanding Graphic Novels, 645
One Piece, 588–89
One-Punch Man, 578
1,000 Comic Books You Must Read, 647
1,000 Ideas by 100 Manga Artists, 644
One Thousand Years of Manga, 644
One Trick Rip-Off and Deep Cuts, The, 447–48
Onward towards Our Noble Deaths, 169

Ôoku: The Inner Chambers, 264–65

Opposite Numbers, The (Hardy Boys), 440

Orcs: Forged For War, 301–2

Orc Stain, 301

Ordinary People Can Change the World, 617

Orion Omnibus, 75

Orphan Blade, 182

Osamu Tezuka Story—A Life in Manga and
    Anime, 617

Otomen, 466–67

Otto, 550–51

Otto's Backward's Day, 551

Otto's Orange Day, 551

Our Cancer Year, 606

Our Expanding Universe, 478–79

Our Hero: Superman on Earth, 646

Out on the Wire: The Storytelling Secrets of the
    New Masters of Radio, 641

Over Easy, 494

Overlord, 302

Owly, 551

Owly and Wormie: Bright Lights and Starry
    Nights, 551

Owly and Wormie: Friends All Aflutter, 551

Oyster War, 154

Ozma of Oz, 343

Oz Omnibus, 343

Oz Series, 343

Pacific Rim, 283

Pacific Rim: Tales from the Drift, 283

Pacific Rim: Tales from Year Zero, 283

Page by Paige, 479

Paleo: The Complete Collection, 140

Panel Discussions: Design in Sequential Art, 647

Paper Girls, 237

Parasyte, 245

Parent's Guide to the Best Kids' Comics: Choosing
    Titles Your Children Will Love, A, 645

Part-Time Princesses, 479

Patience, 254

Patsy Walker, A.K.A. Hellcat, 58

Paul Series, 479

Paul Goes Fishing, 479

Paul Has a Summer Job, 479

Paul Joins the Scouts, 479

Paul Moves Out, 479

Paul Up North, 479

Pax Romana, 254

P. Craig Russell Library of Opera Adaptations, 509

Peanuts, 534–35, 651

Peanuts (series), 535

Peanuts: A Tribute to Charles M. Schulz, 535

Peanuts: The Beagle Has Landed Charlie
    Brown, 535

Peanuts: Where Beagles Dare, 535

Percy Jackson and the Olympians, 331, 654

Perdida, La, 479–80, 655

Perfect Example, 617–18

Perhapanauts, The, 378

Persepolis, 618, 655

Pet Avengers, 579

Pet Avengers Classic, 579

Peter Bagge: Conversations, 646

Peter Kuper: Conversations, 646

Peter Panzerfaust, 353

Phantom Jack: The Nowhere Man Agenda, 58

Philosophy: A Discovery in Comics, 641

Phoenix, 203

Photographer, The, 628

Pigs Make Me Sneeze (Elephant and Piggie), 545

Pinocchio, 323

Pinocchio, Vampire Slayer Complete Edition, 324

Pix: One Weirdest Weekend, 579

Plagues: The Microscopic Battlefield (Science
    Comics), 637

Planates, 221–22

Planet Hulk: Warzones, 113

Planetoid, 222

Plants vs. Zombies, 563

Play Ball, 488

Play It Again, Mozart! (Geronimo Stilton), 530

Plot: The Secret Story of the Protocols of the
    Elders of Zion, The, 628

Pluto. Urasawa X Tezuka, 278

Plutona, 128

Poe's Tales of Mystery (Graphic Classics), 420

Pokemon: Black and White, 589

Polly and the Pirates, 589–90

Popeye, 535–36

Popeye (series), 535

Popeye: The Whole Shebang, 535

Poppy! and the Lost Lagoon, 154

Poptropica, 570

Poptropica: Mystery of the Mask, 570

Poptropica: The Lost Expedition, 570

Portable Frank, The, 551

Poseidon: Earth Shaker (Olympians), 331

Potential (High School Chronicles of Ariel
    Schrag), 613

Powerful World of Energy with Max Axiom, Super
    Scientist, The, 634

Power Man and Iron Fist, 55

Power Man and Iron Fist Epic Collection: Heroes
    for Hire, 55

Power Man and Iron Fist Epic Collection:
    Revenge, 55

Power of Comics: History, Form and Culture, 646

Powerpuff Girls, 579–80

Powerpuff Girls (2014 series), 580

Powerpuff Girls (2016 series), 580
Powerpuff Girls Classics, 580
Powers, 128–30, 423, 650
Powers (2001 series), 129
Powers (2005 series), 129
Powers (2010 series), 129
Powers (2015 series), 130
Powers Definitive Hardcover Collection, 130
Powers Omnibus, 130
Powers: The Bureau, 129
Preacher, 563–64
Predator, 246
Predator: Fire and Stone, 246
Predator Omnibus, 246
Predator: Prey to the Heavens, 246
Predator vs. Judge Dredd vs. Aliens, 246
Pretty Deadly, 193, 199
Pride and Prejudice (by Butler), 504–5
Pride and Prejudice (*Manga Classics*), 503
Pride and Prejudice and Zombies: The Graphic Novel, 390
Pride of Baghdad, The, 135
Primates: The Fearless Science of Jane Goodall, Dian Fossey, and Biruté Galdikas, 635
Prince of Persia, 154
Prince of Persia, 154
Prince of Persia: Before the Sandstorm, 154
Prince of Tennis, The, 489
Princeless, 324
Princeless Short Stories, 324
Princess Decomposia and Count Spatula, 564
Princess Jellyfish, 480
Princess Princess Ever After, 324–25
Princess Ugg, 314
Prisoners of the Sun (Tintin), 145
Private Eye: The Cloudburst Edition, 431
Professor's Daughter, The, 460
Project Arms, 160–61
Project: Romantic, 510
Promethea, 362
Property, The, 170
Prophet, 222
PS238, 580
Punisher, The, 58–59
Punisher, The (2014 series), 59
Punisher: Circle of Blood, 58
Punisher Max: The Complete Collection, 59
Punisher: Welcome Back Frank, 59
Punk Rock and Trailer Parks, 480
Punky Brewster, 536
Pyongyang: A Journey in North Korea, 618

Q2: The Return of Quantum and Woody, 581
Quantum and Woody, 580–81
Quantum and Woody (first series), 581

Quantum and Woody (second series), 581
Queen and Country the Definitive Edition, 190
Quitter, The, 618–19

Rabbi's Cat, The, 520, 655
Rachel Rising, 416–17
Ragnarok, 331
Rapunzel's Revenge, 317, 325
Rascal Raccoon's Raging Revenge, 551
RASL, 254–55
Rasputin, 416
Rat Queens, 291, 302–3
Rat Queens Deluxe Edition, 303
Rave Master, 203–4
Raven The Pirate Princess, 324
Ray Bradbury's Fahrenheit 451: The Authorized Adaptation, 259
R. Crumb: Conversations, 646
Reading Comics: How Graphic Novels Work and What They Mean, 648
Reading Comics: Language, Culture and the Concept of the Superhero in Comic Books, 646
Reading with Pictures: Comics That Make Kids Smarter, 635
Real Ghostbusters Omnibus, The, 560
Realm of Kings, 72–73
Reason for Dragons, The, 480–81
Rebels: A Well-Regulated Militia, 170
Red, 192
Red Baron: The Graphic History of Richthofen's Flying Circus and the Air War in WWI, The (Graphic History), 625
Red Handed: The Fine Art of Strange Crimes, 426–27
Redhand: Twilight of the Gods, 316
Red Hood and the Outlaws, 88–89
Red Lanterns, 46
Red Moon, 303
Red Rackham's Treasure (Tintin), 144
Red River, 344–45
Red Robin, 60
Red Seas, The, 155
Red Seas: Twilight of the Idols, The, 155
Red Seas: Under the Banner of King Death, The, 155
Red Skull, 113
Red Sonja, 315–16
Red Sonja (2014 series), 315
Red Sonja Omnibus, 315–16
Red Sonja: The Falcon Throne, 315
Red's Planet, 570–71
Red Star, The, 204
Red Wing, The, 255
Reed Gunther, 590

Refreshing Look at Renewable Energy with Max Axiom, Super Scientist, A, 634
Reinventing Comics: How Imagination and Technology Are Revolutionizing an Art Form, 605, 644
Religion: A Discovery in Comics, 641
Relish: My Life in the Kitchen, 490, 498
ReMind, 155
Resistance, 170
Resistance, 170
Return of King Doug, The, 343–44
Return of the Zombies (Chilling Archives), 420
Return of Zita the Space Girl, The, 571
Return to Labyrinth, 345
Revenge of the Lizard Club (Thea Stilton), 530
Revolver, 255
Rex Mundi, 437
Richard Stark's Parker, 432
Richard Stark's Parker: The Martini Edition, 432
Rime of the Modern Mariner, The, 353
Rin-Ne, 408–9
Rise of Aurora West, The, 27
Ristorante Paradiso, 494
Road to Oz, 343
Robin, 59–61
Robin (1990s series), 59–60
Robin (2006), 60
Robin, Son of Batman, 60–61
Robin: Days of Fire and Madness, 60
Robin: Search for a Hero, 60
Robin: Teenage Wasteland, 60
Robin: The Big Leagues, 60
Robin: To Kill a Bird, 60
Robin: Violent Tendencies, 60
Robin: Wanted, 60
Robocop, 278
Robocop vs. Terminator, 279
Robot City Adventures, 279
Robot Dreams, 279
Robotech/Voltron, 288
Rocketeer, The, 61–62
Rocketeer Adventures, 61
Rocketeer at War!, The, 62
Rocketeer: Cargo of Doom, 62
Rocketeer: Hollywood Horror, 62
Rocketeer/Spirit: Pulp Friction, 62, 429
Rocketeer: The Complete Adventures, 61
Rocketo: Journey to the Hidden Sea, 237
Rocket Raccoon, 73
Rocket Raccoon and Groot, 73–74
Rocket Raccoon and Groot (series), 74
Rocket Raccoon and Groot: The Complete Collection, 73
Rocky and Bullwinkle, 536
Rocky and Bullwinkle, 536

Rocky and Bullwinkle Classic, 536
Rocky and Bullwinkle Classic Adventures, 536
Roller Girl, 481
Rom, 280
Romeo and Juliet, 505
Ronald Reagan: A Graphic Biography, 619
Roots of the Swamp Thing, 399
Rosalie Lightning: A Graphic Memoir, 619
Rosario + Vampire, 564–65
Rosario + Vampire Season II, 565
Rot & Ruin, 391
Rough Guide to Graphic Novels, 646
Rough Guide to Manga, 644
Rumble, 353
Run Like Crazy, Run Like Hell, 448
Runaways: Battleworld, 113
Runaways: The Complete Collection, 89
Runners, 237–38
Ruse: The Victorian Guide to Murder, 427
Rust, 278
Rutabaga the Adventure Chef, 600

Sabertooth Swordsman, 590
Sabrina: *Based on the Animated Series (Archie)*, 513
Sabrina the Teenage Witch: The Magic Within, 565
Sacred Heart, 481
Saga, 204–5
Saga Deluxe Edition, 205
Saga of the Bloody Benders, The (Treasury of Victorian Murder), 454
Saga of the Swamp Thing, 399
Sailor Moon, 89–90
Sailor Twain or the Mermaid in the Hudson, 345
Saints, 165
Salt Water Taffy: A Climb Up Mt. Barnabas, 590
Salt Water Taffy: Caldera's Revenge, pts 1–2, 591
Salt Water Taffy: The Legend of Old Salty, 590
Salt Water Taffy: The Seaside Adventures of Jack and Benny, 590–91
Salt Water Taffy: The Truth about Dr. True, 591
Salvatore, 155
Sam and Friends Mysteries, 442–43
Sam & Max: Surfin' the Highway, 552
Sam and Twitch: The Complete Collection, 427
Same Difference, 481–82
Samurai, 182
Samurai Collected Edition, 182
Samurai Deeper Kyo, 161
Samurai: Heaven and Earth, 183
Samurai Jack, 183
Samurai Jack Classics, 183
Samurai Jack: Tales of the Wandering Warrior, 183
Samurai: The Graphic Novel, 183

Sand Chronicles, 460–61
Sandman, The, 291, 358, 360, 362–64, 367
Sandman, The (series), 362–63
Sandman Companion: A Dreamer's Guide to the
    Award-Winning Comic Series, The, 646
Sandman: Endless Nights, The, 358, 363
Sandman: Overture, The, 364
Sandman: The Dream Hunters, 363–64
Sandwalk Adventures, 636
Sardine in Outer Space, 571
Saturn Apartments, 260
Scalped, 427–28
Scarlet Letter (Manga Classics), 503
Scarlet Traces, 246–47
Scary Godmother: Comic Book Stories, 565
Science: A Discovery in Comics, 636
Science Comics, 636
Science Fiction (Simon and Kirby Library), 288
Science of Baseball with Max Axiom, Super
    Scientist, The, 634
Science of Basketball with Max Axiom, Super
    Scientist, The, 634
Science of Football with Max Axiom, Super
    Scientist, The, 634
Science of Hockey with Max Axiom, Super
    Scientist, The, 634
Scooby-Doo Team-Up, 536–37
Scott Pilgrim, 482–83
Scott Pilgrim and the Infinite Sadness, 483
Scott Pilgrim Gets It Together, 483
Scott Pilgrim's Finest Hour, 483
Scott Pilgrim's Precious Little Life, 483
Scott Pilgrim vs. the Universe, 483
Scott Pilgrim vs. the World, 483
Scribblenauts Unmasked: A Crisis of
    Imagination, 581
Sculptor, The, 482
Seal of Approval: The History of the Comics
    Code, 647
Sea of Monsters: The Graphic Novel, The, 331
Sea You. See Me (Hardy Boys), 440
Seconds: A Graphic Novel, 494–95
Secret Avengers, 80
Secret Avengers (2011), 31, 80
Secret Avengers (2013a), 81
Secret Avengers (2013b), 81
Secret Avengers (2014), 81
Secret Coders, 443
Secret History of Wonder Woman, The, 647
Secret Invasion: Runaways/Young Avengers, 93
Secret of the Sphinx (Geronimo Stilton), 530
Secret of the Stone Frog, The, 325
Secret of the Unicorn, The (Tintin), 144
Secret of the Waterfall in the Woods, The (Thea
    Stilton), 530

Secret of Whale Island, The (Thea Stilton), 530
Secret Science Alliance and the Copycat
    Crook, 571
Secret Service: Kingsman, 192
Secret Six (2014), 90
Secret Six (2016), 90
Secret Wars (2011), 111
Secret Wars (2015), 111–13
Secret Wars (2016), 111
Secret Wars 2099, 113
Secret Wars II, 111
Secret Wars II Omnibus, 111
Secret Wars Journal/Battleworld, 113
Secret Wars Omnibus, 111
Sense & Sensibility, 505
Sense & Sensibility (Manga Classics), 503
Seraph of the End: Vampire Reign, 384
Serenity, 205
Sergio Aragonés' Groo. See Groo
Sergio Aragonés' Groo and Rufferto, 596
Seth: Conversations, 646
Set to Sea, 155
7 Billion Needles, 205–6
Seven Crystal Balls (Tintin), 145
Sexcastle, 555
Sex Criminals, 118
Sgt. Rock, 171
Sgt. Rock (Showcase Presents), 171
Sgt. Rock Archives, 171
Sgt. Rock: Between Hell and a Hard Place, 171
Sgt. Rock: The Last Battalion, 171
Sgt. Rock: The Prophecy, 171
Sgt. Rock's Combat Tales, 171
Shackleton: Antarctic Odyssey, 619
Shade, The, 64
Shadow Hero, The, 62
Shadoweyes, 261
Shadoweyes in Love, 261
Shaman King, 409
Sharaz-De: Tales from the Arabian Nights, 325
Shazam!, 33
Shazam! The Monster Society of Evil, 33
Shenzhen: A Travelogue from China, 619–20
Sheriff of Babylon, 428
Sheriff of Bullet Valley, The (Donald Duck), 527
Sherlock Holmes and the Vampires of London, 384
Sherlock Holmes vs. Dracula, 391
Shhhhhh! (Hardy Boys), 440
S.H.I.E.L.D, 192
S.H.I.E.L.D by Jim Sterenko: The Complete
    Collection, 192
Shocking World of Electricity with Max Axiom,
    Super Scientist, The, 634
Shockrockets: We Have Ignition, 238
Shooting Star, The (Tintin), 145

Shoplifter, 483
Should I Share My Ice Cream? (Elephant and Piggie), 545
Showcase Presents: Jonah Hex, 195
Showcase Presents: Men of War, 171
Showcase Presents: Sgt. Rock, 171
Showcase Presents: Strange Adventures, 238
Showcase Presents: The Great Disaster Featuring the Atomic Knights, 265
Showcase Presents: The Metal Men, 277
Showcase Presents: The Unknown Soldier, 172
Show Must Go On, The, 520
Sidekicks, 582
Siege: Battleworld, 113
Silent Voice, A, 483
Silk, 62
Silver, 384–85
Silver Surfer, 75–76
Silver Surfer (2014 series), 76
Silver Surfer Epic Collection, 76
Silver Surfer: Parable, 76
Silver Surfer: Rebirth of Thanos, 76, 120
Silver Surfer: Requiem, 76
Simon and Kirby Library: Crime, The, 448
Simon and Kirby Library: Horror, The, 421
Simon and Kirby Library: Science Fiction, The, 288
Simon and Kirby Library: Superheroes, The, 131
Simon's Dream (Fog Mound), 264
Simpsons, The, 511, 537–39, 651
Simpsons Comics, 537–38
Simpsons Comics a Go-Go, 537
Simpsons Comics Barn Burner, 538
Simpsons Comics Beach Blanket Bongo, 538
Simpsons Comics Belly Buster, 538
Simpsons Comics Big Bonanza, 537
Simpsons Comics Chaos, 538
Simpsons Comics Clubhouse, 538
Simpsons Comics Colossal Compendium, vols. 1–5, 538
Simpsons Comics Confidential, 538
Simpsons Comics Dollars to Donuts, 538
Simpsons Comics Extravaganza, 537
Simpsons Comics Get Some Fancy Book Learnin', 538
Simpsons Comics Hit the Road, 538
Simpsons Comics Holiday Humdinger, 538
Simpsons Comics Jam-Packed Jamboree, 538
Simpsons Comics Knockout, 538
Simpsons Comics Madness, 538
Simpsons Comics Meltdown, 538
Simpsons Comics On Parade, 537
Simpsons Comics Royale, 537
Simpsons Comics Shake-Up, 538
Simpsons Comics Simpsorama, 537
Simpsons Comics Spectacular, 537
Simpsons Comics Strike Back, 537
Simpsons Comics Supernova, 538
Simpsons Comics Unchained, 537
Simpsons Comics Wingding, 537
Simpsons/Futurama Infinitely Secret Crossover Crisis, The, 537
Simpsons Treehouse of Horror, 538
Simpsons Treehouse of Horror Dead Man's Jest, The, 538
Simpsons Treehouse of Horror From Beyond the Grave, The, 538
Simpsons Treehouse of Horror: Fun-Filled Frightfest, The, 538
Simpsons Treehouse of Horror: Hoodoo Voodoo Brouhaha, The, 538
Sin City, 423, 443, 448–49
Sin City: A Dame to Kill For, 449
Sin City: Booze, Broads, and Bullets, 449
Sin City: Family Values, 449
Sin City: Hell and Back, 449
Sin City: That Yellow Bastard, 449
Sin City: The Big Fat Kill, 449
Sin City: The Hard Goodbye, 449
Sing No Evil, 483–84
Sisters, 620–21, 654
1602 Witch Hunter/Siege, 112
Sixth Gun, The, 193, 199–200, 653
Sketch Monsters, 566
Skim, 484
Skip Beat, 461
Skullkicker, 600
Skullkicker Treasure Trove, 600
Skylanders, 601
Skylanders: A Light in the Dark, 601
Skylanders: Champions, 601
Skylanders: Dive, Dive, Dive, 601
Skylanders: Return of the Dragon King, 601
Skylanders: Rift into Overdrive, 601
Skylanders: Secret Agent Secrets, 601
Skylanders: The Kaos Trap, 601
Sleeper Omnibus, The, 193
Sleepless Knights (Adventures in Cartooning), 604
Sleepwalkers, The, 354
Sleight of Dan (Nancy Drew), 442
SMASH: Trial by Fire, 582
Smile, 620, 654
Smoke and Mirrors: Life and Death and Other Card Tricks, 345
Smurfs, The, 539–40
Smurfs Anthology, The, 540
Smurfs Christmas, 540
Smurfs Monsters, The, 540
Smurfs: The Village beyond the Wall, 540
Snake Tales (Chilling Archives), 420

Snarked, 520
Snowpiercer, 261
Snow White: A Graphic Novel, 326
Sock Monkey Treasury, 520–21
Soddyssey & Other Tales of Supernatural Law, 566
Solanin, 484
Solid Truth about States of Matter with Max Axiom, Super Scientist, The, 634
Solomon's Thieves, 163
Song for Thea Sisters (Thea Stilton), 530
Song of Roland, The, 479
Sonic/Mega Man: When Worlds Collide, 277
Sonovawitch! and Other Tales of Supernatural Law, 566
Soul Eater, 378–79
Southern Bastards, 449–50
Southern Bastards Deluxe Hardcover Edition, 450
Space Battle Lunchtime, 495
Space Dumplins, 222
Space Mountain, 255–56
Space Usagi, 186–87
Spawn, 379
Spawn: Origins, 379
Spawn: Resurrection, 379
Spectacular Spider-Girl, 63
Spectre, The, 379–80
Spell Checkers, 417
Spera, 303
Spice & Wolf, 303–4
Spider-Girl, 62–63
Spider-Gwen, 63
Spider-Island: Warzones!, 113
Spider-Man, 18–24
Spider-Man 24/7, 19
Spider-Man 2099, 23–24
Spider-Man 2099 Classic, 23
Spider-Man: American Son, 19
Spider-Man and the X-Men, 98
Spider-Man: Big Time, 19
Spider-Man: Crime and Punisher, 19
Spider-Man: Danger Zone, 19
Spider-Man: Death and Dating, 19
Spider-Man: Died in Your Arms Tonight, 19
Spider-Man: Dying Wish, 19
Spider-Man: Election Day, 19
Spider-Man: Ends of the Earth, 19
Spider-Man: Fantastic Spider-Man, The, 19
Spider-Man: Flying Blind, 19
Spider-Man: Grim Hunt, 19
Spider-Man: Kraven's First Hunt, 19
Spider-Man: Lizard—No Turning Back, 19
Spider-Man: Matters of Life and Death, 19
Spider-Man: Miles Morales, 23
Spider-Man: New Ways to Die, 19
Spider-Man: One Moment in Time, 19

Spider-Man: Origin of the Species, 19
Spider-Man: The Gauntlet, Vols. 1–5, 19
Spider-Men, 20
Spider-Verse, 20–21
Spider-Verse, 21
Spider-Verse: War-Zones!, 113
Spike, 371, 375
Spike (2006), 375
Spike: After the Fall, 375
Spike: Alone Together Now, 375
Spike: Asylum, 375
Spike: Into the Light, 375
Spike Omnibus, 375
Spike Season Nine: A Dark Place, 375
Spike: Shadow Puppets, 375
Spike: The Complete Series, 375
Spike: The Devil You Know, 375
Spike vs. Dracula, 375
Spirit, The, 429
Squadron Sinister, 113
Squidder, The, 247
Squirrel Girl. See Unbeatable Squirrel Girl
Squish, 552
Stan Lee and the Rise and Fall of the American Comic Book, 647
Stan Lee: Conversations, 646
Star Slammers: The Complete Collection, 238
Star Trek, 222–27, 650
Star Trek (2012 series), 226
Star Trek Archives, 223–24
Star Trek Classics, 223
Star Trek: Alien Spotlight, 225
Star Trek: Burden of Knowledge, 224
Star Trek: Captain's Log, 225
Star Trek: Countdown, 226
Star Trek: Countdown to Darkness, 227
Star Trek: Deep Space Nine—Fool's Gold, 225
Star Trek: Gold Key Archives, 223
Star Trek/Green Lantern: Spectrum War, 226
Star Trek: Kahn, 227
Star Trek: Kahn—Ruling in Hell, 224
Star Trek/Legion of Super-Heroes, 226
Star Trek: Manifest Destiny, 227
Star Trek: Mirror Images, 225
Star Trek: Mission's End, 224
Star Trek: Nero, 227
Star Trek: New Visions, 224
Star Trek/Planet of the Apes: Primate Directive, 226
Star Trek: Spock-Reflections, 226
Star Trek: Starfleet Academy, 227
Star Trek: The City on the Edge of Forever, 225
Star Trek: The John Byrne Collection, 224
Star Trek: The Next Generation/Doctor Who: Assimilation, 2, 225

Star Trek: The Next Generation—Hive, 225
Star Trek: The Next Generation Omnibus, 225
Star Wars, 201–2, 206–20
Star Wars (2013), 208
Star Wars (2015), 208
Star Wars, The, 206
Star Wars Adventures, 209
Star Wars Adventures: Boba Fett and the Ship of Fear, 209
Star Wars Adventures: Chewbacca and the Slavers of the Shadowlands, 209
Star Wars Adventures: Han Solo and the Hollow Moon of Khorya, 209
Star Wars Adventures: Luke Skywalker and the Treasure of the Dragonsnakes, 209
Star Wars Adventures Omnibus, 209
Star Wars Adventures: Princess Leia and the Royal Ransom, 209
Star Wars Adventures: Will of Darth Vader, 209
Star Wars: Agent of the Empire, 209
Star Wars: Blood Ties—A Tale of Jango Fett and Boba Fett, 219
Star Wars: Chewbacca, 209
Star Wars: Clone War Adventures, 210
Star Wars: Crimson Empire Saga, 211
Star Wars: Dark Empire Trilogy, 211
Star Wars: Dark Times, 212–13
Star Wars: Dark Times Gallery Edition, 213
Star Wars: Dark Times Omnibus Editions, 213
Star Wars: Darth Maul, 211
Star Wars: Darth Maul—Death Sentence, 211
Star Wars: Darth Maul—Son of Dathomir, 211
Star Wars: Darth Vader, 211–12
Star Wars: Darth Vader (2015 series), 212
Star Wars: Darth Vader and the Cry of Shadows, 212
Star Wars: Darth Vader and the Ghost Prison, 212
Star Wars: Darth Vader and the Lost Command, 212
Star Wars: Darth Vader and the Ninth Assassin, 212
Star Wars: Dawn of the Jedi, 218
Star Wars: Episode I: The Phantom Menace, 207
Star Wars: Episode II: The Attack of the Clones, 207
Star Wars: Episode III: Revenge of the Sith, 207
Star Wars: Episode IV: A New Hope, 207
Star Wars: Episode V: The Empire Strikes Back, 207
Star Wars: Episode VI: The Return of the Jedi, 208
Star Wars: Episode VII: The Force Awakens, 208
Star Wars: Han Solo, 213
Star Wars: Infinites, 213–14
Star Wars: Infinities Omnibus, 214
Star Wars: Invasion, 214

Star Wars: Jedi—The Dark Side, 219
Star Wars: Kanan, 214
Star Wars: Kanan Omnibus, 214
Star Wars: Knights of the Old Republic, 217–18
Star Wars: Knights of the Old Republic Omnibus, 218
Star Wars: Lando, 214
Star Wars: Legacy, 214–15
Star Wars: Legacy II, 215
Star Wars Legends: Epic Collection: Infinities, 214
Star Wars Legends: Epic Collection: Legacy, 215
Star Wars Legends Epic Collection: Rise of the Sith, 219
Star Wars Legends Epic Collection: The Clone Wars, 219
Star Wars Legends Epic Collection: The Empire, 219
Star Wars Legends Epic Collection: The New Republic, 219
Star Wars Legends Epic Collection: The Old Republic, 219
Star Wars Legends Epic Collection: The Rebellion, 220
Star Wars: Obi-Wan and Anakin, 215
Star Wars Omnibus: At War with the Empire, 220
Star Wars Omnibus: Boba Fett, 220
Star Wars Omnibus: Early Victories, 220
Star Wars Omnibus: Episodes I-VI—The Complete Saga, 208
Star Wars Omnibus: Quinlan Vos—Jedi in Darkness, 219
Star Wars Omnibus: Rise of the Sith, 219
Star Wars Omnibus: Shadows of the Empire, 220
Star Wars Omnibus: Wild Space, 220
Star Wars: Poe Dameron, 215
Star Wars: Princess Leia, 216
Star Wars: Purge, 216
Star Wars: Rebel Heist, 208
Star Wars: Shattered Empire, 217
Star Wars: Tag & Bink Were Here, 217
Star Wars: Tales of the Jedi, 217–18
Star Wars: Tales of the Jedi (2007), 217
Star Wars: The Clone Wars (2009), 210
Star Wars: The Clone Wars (2012), 209–10
Star Wars: The Clone Wars—Colossus of Destiny, 210
Star Wars: The Clone Wars—Crash Course, 210
Star Wars: The Clone Wars—Deadly Hands of Shon-Ju, 210
Star Wars: The Clone Wars—Defenders of the Lost Temple, 210
Star Wars: The Clone Wars—Hero of the Confederacy, 210
Star Wars: The Clone Wars—In the Service of the Republic, 210

Star Wars: The Clone Wars—Shipyards of Doom, 210

Star Wars: The Clone Wars—Slaves of the Republic, 210

Star Wars: The Clone Wars—Smuggler's Code, 210

Star Wars: The Clone Wars—Strange Allies, 210

Star Wars: The Clone Wars—The Enemy Within, 210

Star Wars: The Clone Wars—The Sith Hunters, 210

Star Wars: The Clone Wars—The Starcrusher Trap, 210

Star Wars: The Clone Wars—Wind Raiders of Taloraan, The, 210

Star Wars: The Force Unleashed, 213

Star Wars: The Old Republic, 218

Star Wars: The Original Marvel Years, 216

Star Wars: The Original Trilogy—A Graphic Novel, 206–7

Star Wars: The Prequel Trilogy—A Graphic Novel, 207

Star Wars: The Thrawn Trilogy, 220

Star Wars: Vader Down, 212

Starlight, 239

Star-Lord, 73

Star-Lord and Kitty Pryde, 113

Star-Lord: Guardian of the Galaxy, 73

Starman, 64

Step Aside, Pops: A Hark a Vagrant Collection, 554

Steve Rogers, Super Solider, 31

Steven Universe, 540

Steven Universe: Too Cool for School, 540

Stickman Odyssey, 331–32

Stinky, 566

Stinky Cecil, 552

Stinky Cecil in Operation Pond Rescue, 552

Stinky Cecil in Terrarium Terror, 552

Stitches: A Memoir, 621

Stormbreaker—The Saga of Beta Ray Bill, 335

Storm in the Barn, 505

Story of My Tits, The, 621

Story of Saiunkoku, The, 354, 461

Strain, The, 385

Strange Adventures (Showcase Presents), 238

Strangers in Paradise, 462

Strangers in Paradise Omnibus Edition, 462

Strange Science Fantasy, 288

Strange Tales, 131

Stray Bullets, 450

Street Fighter, 161–62, 651, 653

Street Fighter Classic, 162

Street Fighter IV: Wages of Sin, 162

Street Fighter Legends: Akuma, 162

Streetfighter Legends: Chun-Li, 162

Strobe Edge, 462

Stuck in the Middle: Seventeen Comics from an Unpleasant Age, 510

Stuff of Legend, The, 346

Stuff of Life, 638

Sugar Skull, 556

Suicide Squad, 90–91

Suicide Squad (2008), 90–91

Suicide Squad (2012), 91

Suicide Squad: From the Ashes, 91

Summer Wars, 267

Sunny Side Up, 485

Super Angry Birds, 523

Super Boys: The Amazing Adventures of Jerry Siegel and Joe Shuster—The Creators of Super

Cool Chemical Reaction Activities with Max Axiom, 634

Super Cool Mechanical Activities with Max Axiom, 634

Super Diaper Baby 2: Invasion of the Potty Snatchers, 583

Super Dinosaur, 140–41

Supergirl, 64–65

Supergirl (2005), 64

Supergirl (2011), 64–65

Superheroes (Amelia Rules), 512

Superheroes (Simon and Kirby Library), 131

Superman, 647

Super Powers, 583

Super Secret Crisis War, 584

Super Street Fighter, 162

Superior Foes of Spider-Man, The, 118–19

Superior Foes of Spider-Man Omnibus, 119

Superior Spider-Man, 119

Superman, 2–6

Superman (2006 series), 4

Superman (2013 series), 4–5

Superman (2016 series), 5

Superman: Action Comics, 5

Superman Adventures, 6

Superman/Aliens, 244

Superman & Batman: Generations, 124

Superman/Batman, 105–6

Superman: Brainiac, 6

Superman: Day of Doom, 3

Superman/Doomsday Omnibus, 3

Superman: Earth One, 125

Superman: Emperor Joker, 4

Superman: Ending Battle, 4

Superman Family Adventures, 584

Superman: Infinite Crisis, 109

Superman Is Jewish?: How Comic Book Superheroes Came to Serve Truth, Justice, and the Jewish-American Way, 646

Superman: Reign of Doomsday, 3

Superman: Secret Origin, 4

Superman: The Death and Return of Superman Omnibus, 3
Superman: The Death of Superman, 3
Superman: The Doomsday Wars, 3
Superman: The Last Son of Krypton, 4
Superman: The Return of Doomsday, 3
Superman: The Return of Superman, 3
Superman/Wonder Woman, 106
Superman: World without a Superman, 3
Supermutant Magic Academy, 583
Supernatural Law, 566
Super-Villains Unite: The Complete Super-Villain Team-Up, 118
Surprising World of Bacteria with Max Axiom, Super Scientist, The, 635
Surrogates, 280
Surrogates Operator's Manual Special Hardcover Edition, 280
Suspended in Language: Niels Bohr's Life, Discoveries, and the Century He Shaped, 638
Swallow Me Whole, 485
Swamp Thing, 367, 398–400
Swamp Thing (2012 series), 399–400
Sweaterweather and Other Stories, 521
Sweets: A New Orleans Crime Story, 429
Sweet Tooth, 265
Sweet Tooth Deluxe Edition, 265
Sword Art Online, 267–68
Sword Art Online: Aincrad, 268
Sword Art Online: Fairy Dance, 268
Sword Art Online: Girls Ops, 268
Sword Art Online: Mother's Rosary, 268
Sword Art Online: Phantom Bullet, 268

Tales of Supernatural Law, 566
Tangles: A Story about Alzheimer's, My Mother, and Me, 621
Teaching Graphic Novels: Practical Strategies for the Secondary ELA Classroom, 645
Teaching Graphic Novels in the Classroom: Building Literary and Comprehension, 645
Teaching Visual Literacy: Using Comic Books, Graphic Novels, Anime, Cartoons, and More to Develop Comprehension and Thinking Skills, 645
Teen Boat, 521
Teen Titans, 91
Teen Titans (2013), 91
Teen Titans (2015), 91–92
Teen Titans: Earth One, 125
Teen Titans Go, 584–85
Teen Titans Go (2006), 584
Teen Titans Go (2015), 585
Teenage Mutant Ninja Turtles, 184–85
Teenage Mutant Ninja Turtles (2012 series), 184–85

Teenage Mutant Ninja Turtles (original series), 184
Teenage Mutant Ninja Turtles/Ghostbusters, 560
Teenage Mutant Ninja Turtles Micro-Series, 185
Teenage Mutant Ninja Turtles: New Animated Adventures, 185
Teenage Mutant Ninja Turtles: The Works, 184
Teenage Mutant Ninja Turtles Ultimate Collection, 184
Teenage Mutant Ninja Turtles Villain Micro-Series, 185
Tegami Bachi: Letter Bee, 220–21
Templar, 164
Ten-Cent Plague: The Great Comic-Book Scare and How It Changed America, The, 647
Terra Tempo, 141
Terrible Ax-Man of New Orleans, The (Treasury of XXth Century Murder), 454
Terrible Lizard, 141
Tetris: The Games People Play, 628
Thank You Book, The (Elephant and Piggie), 545
Thanos, 119–22
Thanos: A God Up There Listening, 121
Thanos: Cosmic Powers, 121
Thanos Imperative, The, 120–21
Thanos: Infinity Abyss, 120
Thanos: Redemption, 120
Thanos Rising, 121
Thanos: The Infinity Finale, 122
Thanos: The Infinity Relativity, 122
Thanos: The Infinity Revelation, 121
Thanos vs. Hulk, 121
Thea Sisters and the Mystery of the Sea, The (Thea Stilton), 530
Thea Stilton, 530
There Is a Bird on Your Head (Elephant and Piggie), 545
They're Not Like Us, 269–70
30 Days of Night, 385, 650
This Book Contains Graphic Language: Comics as Literature, 648
This One Summer, xxix, 485–86, 654
Thor, 332–35
Thor (2008 series), 334
Thor (2015 series), 333
Thor: Ages of Thunder, 334
Thor by Walt Simonson, 332–33
Thor by Walt Simonson Omnibus, 333
Thoreau: A Sublime Life, 621
Thor: God of Thunder, 333
Thor: God of Thunder Deluxe Edition, 333
Thor: Godstorm, 333
Thor Omnibus, 334
Thors, 113
Thor: The Mighty Avenger, 334–35

Thor: The Mighty Avenger—The Complete Collection, 335
Thor vs. Thanos, 120
Three Shadows, 364
365 Samurai and a Few Bowls of Rice, 173
Three Thieves, 304
Thrilling Adventures of Lovelace and Babbage: The (Mostly) True Story of the First Computer, The, 638
Through the Woods, 421–22
Tiger & Bunny, 65
Tiger & Bunny Comic Anthology, 65
Tiger & Bunny: The Beginning, 65
Tiger Counter (Nancy Drew), 442
Tiger Lung, 142
Tiger! Tiger! Tiger, 622
Tightly Tangled Web, The
Time and Again, 422
Tintin, 143–45
Tintin in America (Tintin), 144
Tiny Titans, 585
Tipping Point, The, 289
Titan's Curse: The Graphic Novel, The, 331
T-Minus: Race to the Moon, 638
To Dance: A Ballerina's Graphic Novel, 622
Today I Will Fly (Elephant and Piggie), 545
To Die or Not to Die (Hardy Boys), 440
Tokyo Ghoul, 391
Tomboy: A Graphic Memoir, 622
Tomb Raider (2014 series), 156
Tomb Raider (2016 series), 156
Tommysaurus Rex, 142
Tom Sawyer, 506
Tom Sutton's Creepy Things (Chilling Archives), 420
Too Cool to Be Forgotten, 486
Top 10, 130
Top 10: Beyond the Farthest Precinct, 130
Top 10: The Forty-Niners, 130
Toriko, 495–96
Torpedo, 450
Torso: The Definitive Edition, 423, 452
Toxic Planet, 486
Toy Story, 540–41
Toy Story: Mysterious Stranger, 540
Toy Story: Some Assembly Required, 540
Toy Story: Tales from the Toy Chest, 541
Toy Story: The Return of Buzz Lightyear, 540
Toy Story: Toy Overboard, 541
Transformers, 201, 283–87, 650
Transformers Classics, 285
Transformers: Combiner Wars, 286
Transformers: Distant Stars, 286
Transformers: Drift—Empire of Stone, 286

Transformers/G.I. JOE: Tyrants Rise, Heroes Are Born, 287
Transformers: IDW Collection Phase II, 284
Transformers: More than Meets the Eye, 284–85
Transformers Prime: Beast Hunters, 286
Transformers Prime: Rage of the Dinobots, 286
Transformers: Regeneration, 285
Transformers: Robots in Disguise, 285
Transformers: Sins of the Wreckers, 286
Transformers: The IDW Collection, 284
Transformers: The IDW Collection Compendium, 284
Transformers vs. G.I. Joe, 287
Trashed, 486
Travels of Thelonious (Fog Mound), 264
Treasure Island, 156
Treasure of the Viking Ship, The (Thea Stilton), 530
Treasury of Victorian Murder, A (book), 452
Treasury of Victorian Murder, A (series), 452–54
Treasury of Victorian Murder Compendium, A, 454
Treasury of XXth Century Murder, A, 454–55
Treasury of XXth Century Murder Compendium, A, 455
Treaties, Trenches, Mud, and Blood (Nathan Hale's Hazardous Tales), 627
Trick 'r Treat, 422
Trickster: Native American Tales, a Graphic Collection, 326
Trigun, 239, 652
Trigun Maximum, 239
Trinity: A Graphic History of the First Atomic Bomb, 639
Trip to the Bottom of the World with Mouse, A, 156
Troll Bridge, 364
True Story Swear to God Archives, 622
True Things (Adults Don't Want Kids to Know) (Amelia Rules), 512
Truth About Stacy, The (Baby Sitters Club), 514
Tsubasa: RESERVoir CHRoNiCLE, 346
Turok: Dinosaur Hunter, 143
Turok: Son of Stone, 142–43
Turok: Son of Stone Archives, 143
Turok: Son of Stone: Aztlan, 143
Tweenage Guide to Not Being Unpopular, The (Amelia Rules), 512
20th Century Boys/21st Century Boys. See Naoki Urasawa's 20th Century Boys
21: The Story of Roberto Clemente, 605
24Seven, 506
Twilight Children, The, 247
Twin Spica, 227
Two Brothers, 486
Two-Fisted Science: Stories about Scientists, 639

Ultimate Comics Spider-Man (2010), 22
Ultimate Comics Spider-Man (2012), 22–23
Ultimate Comics Spider-Man Ultimate
   Collection, 23
Ultimate End, 113
Ultimate Spider-Man, 21–22
Ultraman, 247
*Unauthorized X-Men: SF and Comic Writers on
   Mutants, Prejudice, and Adamantium*, The, 648
Unbeatable Squirrel Girl, 582–83
*Unbeatable Squirrel Girl & the Great Lakes
   Avengers*, 583
*Unbeatable Squirrel Girl Beats Up the Marvel
   Universe*, The, 583
*Ultimatum: Requie*m, 22
Uncanny Avengers, 81
Uncanny Avengers (2013), 81
Uncanny Avengers (2015a), 81
Uncanny Avengers (2015b), 81
Uncanny Avengers Omnibus, 81
Uncanny X-Force, 101–2
Uncanny X-Force (third series), 101
Uncanny X-Force (fourth series), 102
Uncanny X-Force (sixth series), 102
Uncanny X-Force by Rick Remender Omnibus, 102
Uncanny X-Force by Rick Remender: The
   Complete Collection, 101
Uncanny X-Men, 97
Uncanny X-Men (first series), 97
Uncanny X-Men (second series), 97
Uncanny X-Men (third series), 98
Uncanny X-Men: Breaking Point, 97
Uncanny X-Men: Fear Itself, 97
Uncanny X-Men: The Complete Collection by Matt
   Fraction, 97
Uncle Scrooge, 528
*Uncle Scrooge and Donald Duck: The Don Rosa
   Disney Library*, 527–28
Uncle Scrooge: Eternal Knot, 528
Uncle Scrooge: Himalayan Hideout, 528
Uncle Scrooge: Peril of Pandora's Box, 528
Uncle Scrooge: Pure Viewing Satisfaction, 528
Uncle Scrooge: Scrooge's Last Adventure, 528
Uncle Scrooge: The Grand Canyon Conquest, 528
Uncle Scrooge: Timeless Tales Vols. 1–3, 528
Uncle Scrooge: Tyrant of the Tides, 528
*Underground Abductor: An Abolitionist Tale
   (Nathan Hale's Hazardous Tales)*, 627
Understanding Comics: The Invisible Art, 605, 644
*Understanding Global Warming with Max Axiom,
   Super Scientist*, 635
Understanding Manga and Anime, 644
*Understanding Photosynthesis with Max Axiom,
   Super Scientist*, 635

*Understanding Viruses with Max Axiom, Super
   Scientist*, 635
Underwater Welder, 256
*United States Constitution: A Graphic
   Adaptation*, 628
Unknown Soldier, The, 172
Unknown Soldier, The (2009 series), 172
Unknown Soldier, The (2014), 172
Unknown Soldier, The *(Showcase Presents)*, 172
Unsinkable Walker Bean, The, 157
Unwritten, The, 354
*Unwritten: Tommy Taylor and the Ship That Sunk
   Twice*, 354
Usagi Yojimbo, 186–87
Usagi Yojimbo Saga, The, 187
Uzumaki: Spiral into Horror, 402
U-X-L Graphic Novelists, 644

Vagabond, 187–88
*Valiant Masters: Bloodshot—Blood of the
   Machine*, 273
*Valiant Masters: Harbinger—Children of the
   Eighth Day*, 269
Valiant Masters: Ninjak, 181
*Valve Presents: The Sacrifice and Other
   Steam-Powered Stories*, 289
Vamperella/Army of Darkness, 557
*Vampire Brat and other tales of Supernatural Law,
   The*, 566
Vampire Cheerleaders, 386
*Vampire Cheerleaders in Space . . . and
   Time?!*, 386
Vampire Cheerleaders Must Die, 386
*Vampire Cheerleaders/Paranormal Mystery Squad
   Monster Mash Collection*, 386
*Vampire in Hollywood and Other Tales of
   Supernatural Law, A*, 566
Vampire Knight, 386
Velvet, 193
Veronica's Passport (Archie), 513
Victorian Undead, 391
Victory, 170
Vinland Saga, 164
Visual Storytelling: The Art and Technique, 643
Voice Over! Seiyu Academy, 521–22
Volcanoes: Fire and Life (Science Comics), 637
Voltron, 287–88
Voltron: From the Ashes, 288
Voltron: Legendary Defender, 288
Voltron Year One, 288

Waiting Is Not Easy (Elephant and Piggie), 545
Wake, The, 402
Walking Dead, The, 367, 386, 392–93, 650

Walking Wounded: Uncut Stories from Iraq, 629
Wall-E, 541
Wall-E: Out There, 541
Wall-E: Recharge, 541
Walt Disney's Donald Duck, 527
Walt Disney's Donald Duck: A Christmas for Shacktown, 527
Walt Disney's Donald Duck: Christmas on Bear Mountain, 527
Walt Disney's Donald Duck: Lost in the Andes, 527
Walt Disney's Donald Duck: Terror of the Beagle Boys, 527
Walt Disney's Donald Duck: The Ghost Sheriff of Last Gasp, 527
Walt Disney's Donald Duck: The Old Castle's Secret, 527
Walt Disney's Donald Duck: The Pixelated Parrot, 527
Walt Disney's Donald Duck: Trail of the Unicorn, 527
Walt Disney's Donald Duck: Trick or Treat, 527
Walt Disney's Uncle Scrooge, 527
Walt Disney's Uncle Scrooge and Donald Duck: Return to Plain Awful, 528
Walt Disney's Uncle Scrooge and Donald Duck: The Don Rosa Disney Library, 527–28
Walt Disney's Uncle Scrooge and Donald Duck: The Last of the Clan McDuck, 528
Walt Disney's Uncle Scrooge and Donald Duck: The Richest Duck in the World, 528
Walt Disney's Uncle Scrooge and Donald Duck: The Son of the Sun, 528
Walt Disney's Uncle Scrooge and Donald Duck: The Treasure of the Ten Avatars, 528
Walt Disney's Uncle Scrooge and Donald Duck: The Universal Solvent, 528
Walt Disney's Uncle Scrooge and Donald Duck: Treasure under Glass, 528
Walt Disney's Uncle Scrooge: Only a Poor Old Man, 527
Walt Disney's Uncle Scrooge: The Lost Crown of Genghis Kahn, 527
Walt Disney's Uncle Scrooge: The Seven Cities of Gold, 527
Walt Kelly's Fairy Tales, 326
War at Ellsemere, 355
War of Kings, 72
War of Kings Omnibus Edition, 72
War of the Green lanterns: Aftermath, 45
Wasteland, 266
Wasteland: The Apocalyptic Edition, 266
Watchmen, 92
Watch Me Throw the Ball (Elephant and Piggie), 545

Watchmen Deluxe Edition, 92
Wayward, 291, 364–65
We Are in A Book (Elephant and Piggie), 545
We Are Robin, 61
We'll Always Have Paris (Geronimo Stilton), 530
We Stand on Guard, 261
We3, 280
Weathercraft: A Frank Comic, 553
Webslinger: SF and Comic Writers on Your Friendly Neighborhood Spider-Man, 646
Weird Book Machine, The (Geronimo Stilton), 530
Weirdworld Vol. 0: Warzones, 113
Werewolf of New York: A Supernatural Law Book, The, 566
West Coast Blues, 450
Wham!: Teaching with Graphic Novels across the Curriculum, 645
What Did You Eat Yesterday?, 496
What Goes Up (Nancy Drew), 442
What Makes You Happy (Amelia Rules), 512
When Fish Got Feet, When Bugs Were Big, and When Dinos Dawned: A Cartoon Prehistory of Life on Earth, 639
When the Past Is a Present (Amelia Rules), 512
Where Monsters Dwell: The Phantom Eagle Flies the Savage Skies, 113
Whirlwind World of Hurricanes with Max Axiom, Super Scientist, The, 635
Whistle!, 489–90
Whole World's Crazy, The (Amelia Rules), 512
Who Stole the Mona Lisa, The (Geronimo Stilton), 530
Wicked + The Divine, The, 355
Wild Ocean: Sharks, Whales, Rays, and Other Endangered Sea Creatures, 639
Will & Whit, 487
Will Eisner: A Dreamer's Life in Comics, 647
Will Eisner: Conversations, 646
Will Eisner's The Spirit: The New Adventures, 429
Will Eisner's The Spirit, 428–29
Will Eisner's The Spirit: A Celebration of 75 Years, 429
Will o' the Wisp, 365
Wilson, 487
Windmill Dragons: A Leah and Alan Adventure, 355
Winter Soldier: The Complete Collection, 65
Witch and Wizard, 356
Witchfinder, 380
Wizard of Oz, The, 347
Wizard's Tale, The, 304–5
Wolverine, 65–68
Wolverine (by Claremont), 66
Wolverine and the X-Men, 98
Wolverine and the X-Men (2012), 98

Wolverine and the X-Men (2014), 98
Wolverine and the X-Men: Alpha & Omega, 98
Wolverine and the X-Men by Jason Aaron
   Omnibus, 98
Wolverine by Jason Aaron: The Complete
   Collection, 66–67
Wolverine by Larry Hama and Marc Silvestri, 67
Wolverine by Mark Millar Omnibus, 67
Wolverine: Old Man Logan, 67, 113
Wolverine: Origin, 67–68
Wolverine: Origin II, 68
*Woman Rebel: The Margaret Sanger
   Story*, 623
Wonder Woman, 68–69
Wonder Woman (2013), 68
Wonder Woman: Earth One, 125
Wonder Woman Omnibus by George Perez, 69
Wonder Woman: The True Amazon, 68–69
*Wonder Woman Unbound: The Curious
   History of the World's Most Famous
   Heroine*, 647
Wonderful Wizard of Oz, The, 343
Wonderland, 347
Wonton Soup: The Collected Edition, 496
Word Up! (Hardy Boys), 440
Wordgirl, 585
*Words for Pictures: The Art and Business of
   Writing Comics and Graphic Novels*, 643
*World of Food Chains with Max Axiom, Super
   Scientist*, 635
World of Warcraft, 305
World of Warcraft: Ashbringer, 305
World of Warcraft: Bloodsworn, 305
World of Warcraft: Dark Riders, 305
World of Warcraft: Pearl of Pandaria, 305
*World of Warcraft: The Essential Sunwell
   Collection*, 305
World War Hulk, 49–50
*Worst of Eerie Publications, The (Chilling
   Archives)*, 419
Wrinkle in Time, A, 347
Writing and Illustrating the Graphic Novel, 646
Writ In Stone (Nancy Drew), 442
Wynonna Earp: Strange Inheritance, 200
Wytches, 417

X-Babies, 586
X-Babies Classic, 586
X-Babies: Stars Reborn, 586
X'ed Out, 555–56
Xena/Army of Darkness, 557
X-Factor, 99–100
X-Factor (2007), 100
X-Factor: The Complete Collection, 100
X-Force, 101–102

X-Force (1st series), 101
X-Force (2nd series), 101
X-Force (6th series), 102
X-Force: A Force to Be Reckoned With, 101
X-Force: Assault on Graymalkin, 101
X-Force by Craig Kyle & Chris Yost: The Complete
   Collection, 101
X-Force: Cable and the New Mutants, 101
X-Force/Cable: Messiah War, 101
X-Force: Child's Play, 101
X-Force Omnibus, 101
X-Force: Phalanx Covenant, 101
X-Force: Sex and Violence, 101
X-Force: Toy Soldiers, 101
X-Force: Under the Gun, 101
XIII, 188–89
X-Men, 94–101
X-Men '92, 113
X-Men: Age of X, 99
X-Men/Avengers: Onslaught Omnibus, 116
X-Men: Battle of the Atom, 96, 98
X-Men by Chris Claremont and Jim Lee
   Omnibus, 95
X-Men: Days of Future Past, 94
X-Men: Fall of the Mutants, 114
X-Men: Fall of the Mutants Omnibus, 114
X-Men: Inferno, 114
X-Men: Inferno. Crossovers, 114
X-Men: Inferno Prologue, 114
X-Men: Messiah Complex, 100, 115
X-Men: Mutant Massacre, 115
X-Men: Second Coming, 99, 115
X-Men: Second Coming Revelations, 115
X-Men: The Age of Apocalypse, 125–26
X-Men: The Age of Apocalypse Omnibus, 126
X-Men: The Dark Phoenix Saga, 94
X-Men: X-Cutioner's Song, 115–16
X-Men: Years of Future Past, 113
X-Necrosha, 99
Xoc: The Journey of a Great White, 135
X-O Manowar, 240–41, 653
X-O Manowar (2012), 241
X-O Manowar Classic Omnibus, 241
X-O Manowar Hardcover Deluxe Edition, 241
X-Tinction Agenda: Warzones, 113
XxxHOLiC, 422

Yakitate!! Japan, 497
Yamada Kun and the Seven Witches, 566–67
Yo-Kai Watch, 601
Yotsuba&!, 522
You Have Killed Me, 432
You'll Never Know, 623
Young Avengers, 93
Young Avengers (2006), 93

Young Avengers (2013), 93
Young Avengers Omnibus, 93
Young Avengers Presents, 93
Young Avengers Ultimate Collection, 93
Young Marvel: Little X-Men, Little Avengers, Big Trouble, 586
Y The Last Man, 265–66
Y The Last Man Deluxe Edition, 266
Yummy: The Last Days of a Southside Shorty, 455
YuYu Hakusho, 409–10

Zabime Sisters, The, 487
Zeus: King of the Gods (Olympians), 330
Zita the Space Girl, 571
Zombies (Chilling Archives), 419

Zombies Calling, 393
Zombie Survival Guide: Recorded Attacks, The, 393
Zombie Tales, 393
Zombie Wife and Other Tales of Supernatural Law, 566
Zombillenium, 567
Zoo Box, The, 522
Zootopia, 541
Zorro, 197
Zorro (2009), 197
Zorro: Matanzas, 197
Zorro Omnibus, 197
Zorro Rides Again, 197
Zot!, 241

Subject Index

ABC Best Books for Young Readers, 477

Abstract Studio, 229, 416, 457, 462

Action and Adventure, 133–200; Adventurers, Explorers, Pirates, and Soldiers of Fortune, 147–57; Ancient Warfare, 162–64; Animals, 134–35; Far East Adventure—Code of the Warrior: Samurai, Ninja, and Other Asian Influences, 172–87; Fists of Fury and Sword of Steel—Fighting Adventure Stories, 157–62; Heroic Adventure, 143–47; Modern Warfare, 164–72; Prehistoric Adventure, 135–43; Spies/Espionage, 187–93; War Stories, 162–72; Westerns, 193–97; Western Genre Blends: The Weird West, 197–200. *See also* Humor

Action Lab Comics/Entertainment, 175, 324, 493

Active Synapse, 630, 636

Adhouse Books, 501, 553, 622

Alex Awards, 265, 481, 616, 618

Alfred A. Knopf, 469, 546, 647

Aliens (Film series), 233, 243–46, 649

All-Action Classics, 330, 347, 381, 506

Allegheny Image Factory, 491

Alterna Comics, 382, 421

Alternative Comics, 288

Amulet Books, xxx, 350, 478, 479, 487, 508, 558, 562, 570, 612, 626, 654

Anime, xxxiii, 65, 90, 137, 147, 151, 158, 176–77, 179, 190, 203, 220–21, 227, 230, 234–35, 239, 245, 258, 260, 262, 270, 272–73, 280–82, 287, 293–94, 302–3, 306, 317, 329, 338–39, 344, 346, 352, 354, 356, 378, 382, 384, 386, 388, 391, 403–4, 408–9, 422, 435–37, 458, 461, 464–65, 467, 470, 480, 489–91, 494–95, 497, 515–16, 519, 543, 553–54, 562, 564, 566, 568, 578, 588, 597, 599, 601

Anomaly Publishing, 228

Arcana Studios, 127, 310, 311

Archaia Entertainment, 150, 182, 191, 194, 202, 278, 300, 303, 322, 326, 350, 352, 359, 365, 426, 433, 529, 651; Black Label, 328

Archie Andrews (character), 246, 386, 387, 469, 512–14

Archie Comics, 276, 277, 386, 411, 469, 512–14, 517, 565, 649

Army of Darkness/Ash Williams, 376, 390, 418, 556, 557, 651, 652

Arsenal Press, 458

Arthur A. Levine Books, 248, 582

Astro Boy (character), 241, 270, 278, 611, 612

Atheneum Books for Young Readers, 471, 478, 512, 551, 622

Avatar Press, 259, 401, 402, 651

Avengers (characters), 22, 24, 29, 32, 48, 53, 55, 58, 69, 71, 77–81, 103, 105, 107, 114, 116, 119–21, 131, 323, 332, 579, 608; A-Force, 77, 112; Dark Avengers, 116; Mighty Avengers, 78; other versions, 112, 575, 579, 582–83, 586; Secret Avengers, 80; Uncanny Avengers, 81; Young Avengers, 93

Avery, 614

Award winners, xxxiii, 6, 11–12, 15–17, 19, 21, 23–24, 26–28, 30, 36, 39, 44, 47–51, 53, 56, 58, 61–62, 64–65, 67, 69, 73, 76, 85, 87–88, 91–93, 97, 110, 117–18, 123, 126, 128, 130, 134, 136, 145–46, 150, 155, 157, 159–60, 162, 164, 168–70, 173, 175, 177–79, 186, 191, 194, 197–98, 204–5, 211, 214, 221, 227, 229–30, 234–35, 237, 242, 245, 254, 256–61, 264–65, 267, 271, 274, 277–78, 280, 295, 297, 299–300, 304, 308, 311, 315, 317–18, 321, 323–26, 333, 341, 347, 349, 352, 354–59, 361–63, 369, 371, 373, 376, 378, 380–82, 384–85, 391, 394, 397–98, 400, 403–5, 408, 410, 412–13, 415–16, 421–22, 424–26, 430–33, 435–36, 438–40, 444, 447–48, 450–52, 454–55, 460, 462, 464–68, 471, 473–78, 480–85, 487, 494–96, 498–501, 503, 505, 513–14, 517, 520–22, 533, 537–38, 542–44, 547, 549–52, 554, 558, 563–66, 571–72, 575, 578, 582–83, 585, 591, 595–600, 606, 608, 610, 612, 614–16, 618–20, 621, 623–26, 628, 630, 638–40. *See also individual awards*

Ballantine Books, 494, 508, 606–7, 645

Balloon Toons, 138

Basic Books, 626, 647

Batgirl (character), 7, 12, 16, 26–27, 82, 123

Batman (characters): Bruce Wayne, 1–4, 7–18, 26–27, 33, 41–42, 46–47, 57, 59–61, 68, 82, 85–86, 88, 90, 103–6, 108, 110, 116, 122, 197, 233, 244, 399–400, 425, 428, 439, 536, 572–73, 576, 583–84, 610, 646–47, 649; other versions, 122–24; Terry McGinnis (Batman Beyond), 27

Beacon Press, 451

Best Books for Young Adults. *See* Young Adult Library Services Association (YALSA) Selection Lists

Betty and Veronica (character), 387, 411, 469, 512–13

Black Canary (character), 28, 42–43, 82, 86–87, 576

Bloomsbury, 317, 325, 571, 609, 646–47

Blue Apple Books, 138, 549

Blue Delliquanti Comics, 277

Bolt City Productions, 198

Bongo, 537–38, 651

Boom Studios, 29, 84, 117, 150, 194, 202, 221, 232, 278, 292, 300, 303, 322, 325–27, 347–48, 350, 352, 359, 365, 367, 387–88, 393–95, 397, 401, 425–26, 433, 439, 441, 475, 480–81, 512, 520, 523, 526, 529, 532–35, 540–41, 567, 569, 573, 585, 651; Boom Kids, 84; KaBoom, 292, 512, 520, 534–35, 540, 585, 651

Brandon Dayton Publishing, 311, 322

Broadway Books, 624, 641

Cable (character), 101–102, 104, 115

Caldecott Award, xxix, xxxiii, 486, 550, 610, 621

Candlewick Press, xi, 279, 294–95, 316, 326, 330, 354, 498–99, 502, 505, 582

Capstone Books, 549, 633

Captain America (character), 28–32, 53, 65, 77–81, 93, 105, 107, 109, 128, 131, 288, 344, 390, 421, 429, 477, 650; Sam Wilson version, 30–32, 77

Captain Marvel (characters): Billy Batson/Shazam, 32–33, 55, 106, 576; Carol Danvers, 56, 69–70, 77, 112 (see also Ms. Marvel); Marv-El, 119–21

Cartoon Books, xi, 254–55, 295–96, 651

Catwoman (character), 7, 16, 33–34, 48, 443–44, 573

Center for Cartoon Studies, The, 607

Chronicle Books, 568, 646

Cinebook, 188, 651

Civil War (Marvel Comics Event), 70, 79, 93, 107, 112

Civil War II (Marvel Comics Event), 24, 32, 38, 57, 66, 70, 72, 74, 78, 80, 82, 107

Clarion Books, 306, 521, 550

Clarkson Potter, 497

Coffeehouse Books, 155

Conan (character), 133, 306–10, 315, 596

Conundrum Press, 479

Core titles, xxxiii, 3, 5–6, 8–9, 11–12, 14–17, 19, 21, 23, 27–28, 30, 34–36, 39, 44, 48–51, 53, 55–56, 59, 62, 64, 66–67, 79, 82, 85, 87–88, 91, 94, 96, 105, 108–11, 114–15, 119, 123, 125–26, 128, 130–31, 134–36, 140, 142, 144, 146, 148–50, 155, 157, 160, 162–66, 170, 173–74, 178–79, 182–83, 186–87, 189, 191, 197–99, 204, 206–7, 209, 211–12, 214, 216–17, 221–22, 227, 229–30, 233, 236–37, 242, 244–47, 254, 265, 271–72, 278–79, 281, 295, 300, 302, 304, 306, 308, 311, 316–18, 320–24, 328, 330, 334, 336, 344–45, 350, 354, 357–58, 362, 364, 369–70, 376, 380, 386, 392, 395, 398–99, 402–4, 406–7,

413, 416, 421, 425–27, 429–30, 432, 434–36, 445, 447–48, 450–52, 454, 458, 462, 467–68, 471–75, 481–82, 485, 488, 494–95, 498–99, 501, 505, 508–9, 512–14, 518, 520, 526–27, 530, 532–34, 537–38, 442, 546–51, 554–55, 558, 562, 565–69, 572, 575–76, 578, 583–84, 588, 591–92, 594–95, 597–600, 602, 605–6, 608–10, 612, 615, 618–20, 622, 628, 631–32, 636

Coretta Scott King Award, 615

Costa Book Award, 610

Craigmore Creations, 141

Crime and Mysteries, 423–55; Amateur Detectives, 432–37; Crime and the Criminal Underworld, 443–50; Detectives, 423–43; Junior Sleuths, 437–43; Private Detectives, 429–32; Professional Detectives and Police Officers, 424–29; True Crime, 451–55

Crown Books for Young Adults, 519

Cybils Award, 571

Daredevil (character), 35–37, 184, 249

Dark Horse Comics, xi, xxix, 24, 127, 135–36, 142–43, 151–54, 156, 165, 170, 173–75, 178–79, 182–83, 186–87, 205–21, 229, 231–33, 235, 239, 242–44, 246, 258, 262–63, 270, 273–74, 276, 279, 282, 289, 294–95, 298, 303, 307–8, 310, 315, 318, 328–29, 344, 349, 360, 364, 367–78, 380, 382, 384–85, 389, 394, 398, 401, 404, 413, 418, 421, 426, 428–30, 433, 435–37, 446, 448, 451, 457, 470, 486, 499, 507, 516, 518, 557–58, 560–63, 565, 572, 586, 590, 595, 598–99, 610, 612, 618, 623, 646, 649

DC Comics, xi, xxix, xxxv, 1–18, 25–28, 32–34, 39–48, 57, 59–61, 64, 68–69, 75–76, 82, 85–92, 103–10, 117–18, 122–26, 130–31, 135, 163, 166, 171–72, 183, 192–95, 223, 230, 238, 244, 247, 255, 263, 265, 277, 280, 305, 318–21, 327, 349, 351, 354, 358–64, 367, 376, 379–80, 383, 389, 391, 396, 398–400, 402, 413–15, 417, 422, 425, 427–29, 439, 443 44, 447, 452, 457, 460, 468, 472, 492, 500, 524, 531, 536, 555, 563, 572–73, 575–76, 579, 581, 583–85, 603, 606–7, 610, 618–19, 644, 646, 649–50; America's Best Comics, 361; Minx, 406; Vertigo, xxxv, 39, 88, 130, 135, 163, 171–72, 193, 195, 247, 255, 263, 265, 280, 318, 320–21, 349, 351, 354, 358, 360, 362–64, 367, 380, 389, 398–99, 402, 413–14, 427–28, 447, 460, 468, 472, 492, 563, 607, 610, 618, 649; Wildstorm Productions, 305, 361, 376, 391, 417, 422

Deadpool (character), 22, 37–38, 101–102, 104–5, 112, 582

Death of the Family (Batman storyline), 8, 11, 26, 34, 57, 88, 92

Del Rey Manga, 161, 346, 390, 422, 425, 493, 516, 597, 652

Devil's Due Publishing, 387, 418, 651
Dial Books for Young Readers, 481, 617, 640
Digital Manga Press (DMP), 464–65, 490, 611–12
Dirty Diamonds, 507
Discovery Channel Books, 138
Disney Press, xi, 154, 265, 347; Hyperion, 255, 328, 331, 501, 544–45, 607
Doctor Strange (character), 54, 109, 120, 412–13
Doctor Who (The Doctor, character), 223, 225, 250–53, 653
Dover Graphic Novels/Dover Publishing, 140, 148, 166
Dracula (character), 375, 381–82, 385, 391, 443
Drawn and Quarterly, 147, 166, 169, 469–70, 472, 474, 477, 479, 487, 494, 498, 506, 508, 519, 554, 583, 608, 614, 617–19, 623, 652
Dynamite Entertainment, xxix, 136, 142–43, 148, 191, 194, 196–97, 276, 287–88, 315, 418, 429, 507, 548, 556, 652

Eisner Award, xxxii, 6, 15–17, 30, 36, 39, 49, 51, 53, 64, 76, 88, 92, 97, 110, 118, 123, 126, 128–30, 136, 163, 166, 175, 178, 186, 191, 205, 255, 265, 271, 274, 278, 295, 301, 308, 318, 321, 342, 354, 361–62, 364, 370, 376, 380, 415, 424–26, 431–34, 440, 445, 447–48, 450–51, 462, 472, 482, 484–86, 501, 520–22, 537–38, 547, 554, 558, 563, 565, 571, 583, 585, 595, 598, 608, 612, 615, 620–21, 628
El Capitan Books, 450
Eureka Productions, 420
Evensen Creative, 393
Exhibit A Press, 566

Fantagraphics, xxix, 149, 153, 155, 169, 186, 227, 254, 288, 310, 317, 352, 446–48, 450, 457, 481, 508, 520, 526–28, 535, 544, 546, 551, 553–54, 605, 613, 623, 652, 658
Fantastic Four (characters), 72, 76–77, 82–84, 114, 116, 128, 574–75, 606, 650
Fantasy, 291–365; Contemporary Fantasy, 347–56; Dark Fantasy, 356–65; Epic/Quest Fantasy, 292–305; Fairy Tales and Folklore, 316–26; Heroic Fantasy, 306–16; Magic Portal Fantasy/ Parallel Worlds, 336–47; Mythological Fantasy, 326–35; Sword and Sorcery Fantasy, 291–316. See also Humor
Farrar, Straus and Giroux, 146, 347, 639, 647
Fear Itself (Marvel Comics Event), 54, 80, 97, 99, 102
Films, xxxiii, 2–3, 6, 15–16, 24–25, 28–29, 37, 39, 44, 47–49, 52, 59, 61, 65, 68–70, 77, 84–85, 87–88, 90–91, 105–9, 119, 123, 144–45, 150–51, 154, 178, 184, 192, 195, 197–98, 205–6, 222, 233, 243–44, 246, 248, 261–62, 278–79, 283–84, 298, 326, 328, 358, 361, 370, 376, 379,

385, 395–98, 402, 404, 406, 412–13, 417, 448, 451–52, 458, 482, 487, 490, 523–26, 529, 531–32, 534, 540–41, 553–54, 556, 559, 589, 606, 616, 618
First Second Press, xi, 28, 62, 134, 146, 154, 157, 160, 163–66, 170, 179, 194, 202–3, 275, 280, 297, 301–2, 320, 323, 330, 345, 348, 364, 384, 394, 403, 426–27, 438, 443, 458, 460, 468–69, 474, 476–78, 481–82, 485–87, 498, 500, 504, 515, 517–18, 521–22, 548, 550, 561, 564, 566, 568, 571, 592, 603–7, 614, 616, 619, 626, 628, 631–32, 635–37, 654
Flash (character): Barry Allen, 39–41, 85, 108, 123; others, 41, 87, 576; Wally West, 39–41, 108
Flying Eye Books, 350
Four Walls Eight Windows, 606–7
Fulcrum Publishing, 326, 639

Gaming, xxxiii, 2, 14, 23, 25, 37, 39, 44, 52, 59, 65, 70, 74, 77, 124, 154, 158, 161, 165, 178, 184, 213, 218, 228, 230–31, 235, 267, 276, 295, 300, 305, 314, 319, 327, 340, 379, 389, 523, 552, 557, 563, 570, 581, 589, 601
Geisel Award, 543, 549, 566
Gem Awards, 533
General Fiction, 457–510; Coming of Age/Slice of Life, 468–87; Food, 490–98; Historical Fiction, 498–506; Romance, 457–68; Romantic Comedy, 462–67; Romantic Fantasy, 467–68; Short Stories and Anthologies, 506–10; Sports, 487–90
G.I. Joe (characters), 167–69, 287, 651
GLAAD Media Awards, 9, 440
G.P. Putnam's Sons Books for Young Readers, 595
Graphic Universe, 264, 439, 613
Graphix/Scholastic, xi, xxx, xxxv, 134, 142, 145, 222, 229, 236–37, 295–97, 336–37, 342, 359, 405–6, 473, 485, 514, 517, 543–44, 546–47, 578, 582–83, 610–11, 620, 654
Gravida Award, 614
Great Graphic Novels for Teens List. See Young Adult Library Services Association (YALSA) Selection Lists
Green Lantern (all versions of the character), 42, 44–46, 85–87, 106, 108, 123, 131, 223, 226, 243, 399, 576
Groundwood Books, 484–85
GT Labs, 629–31, 638–39
Guardians of the Galaxy (Characters), 70–73, 74, 96, 105, 121–22

Harley Quinn (character), 17, 46–48, 90, 123
HarperCollins Publishing, 241, 337, 407, 562, 624, 629–30, 643–44, 647, 651; HarperPerennial, 537–38, 604–5; HarperTeen, 598
Harry N. Abrams, 459, 483, 508, 537, 558, 562, 600, 632, 646; Abrams Comicart, 463, 486, 613, 616, 654

Harvey Award, xxxii, 6, 15–16, 30, 36, 88, 92–93, 110, 126, 128, 178, 205, 230, 265, 296, 300, 321, 361–62, 370, 376, 424–25, 430–32, 447, 451, 484, 521, 608, 615, 618, 624

Hatter Entertainment, 579

Hellboy, 348, 368, 370–71, 376–78, 380, 558, 560

Hermes Press, 341

Hill and Wang, 165, 259, 619, 628, 631, 638–40

Horror, 367–422; Anthologies and Short Story Collections, 419–22; Bestiary, 380–402; Demonic Possession, Black Magic, Witches, and the Occult, 410–17 (see also Witches); Ghosts and Spirits, 402–10; Muck Monsters, 398–400; Old Ones, The, 400–402; Rampant Animals and Other Eco-Monsters Big and Small, 393–98; Slasher/Thriller, 417–19; Supernatural Heroes, 368–80; Undead, The, 386–93 (see also Zombies/Walking Dead); Vampires, 380–86 (see also Vampires); Werewolves, 380–86 (see also Werewolves). See also Humor

Houghton Mifflin Harcourt, 339, 342, 506, 608–9, 624

Hugo Award, 56, 205, 266, 354, 426

Hulk (characters): Bruce Banner, 49–50, 65, 73, 96, 113, 121–22, 131, 650; other versions, 50, 78, 116, 578

Humanoids Publishing, 202, 289, 316, 652

Humor, 511–601; Action and Adventure Humor, 586–91; Black Humor/Satire, 553–56; Cartoon, Animation, and Media Tie-Ins, 522–41; Funny Animals, 541–53; General Humor, 511–22; Genre Blends, 556–601; Humorous Fantasy, 591–601; Humorous Horror, 556–67; Humorous Science Fiction, 567–71

Hyperwerks, 143

IDW Publishing, xi, xxix, 58, 61, 88, 104, 116, 138–39, 150, 159, 167–69, 183–85, 190, 200, 202, 204, 222–24, 226, 228, 233–34, 238, 247–48, 250–53, 264, 271, 277, 280, 284–87, 288, 300, 304, 324, 326–27, 331, 337–38, 341–43, 345, 358–59, 367, 371, 373–75, 382, 385, 391, 395, 415, 419–21, 424, 428–29, 432, 450–51, 459, 523–24, 526, 528–29, 532–33, 535–36, 551, 557, 559–60, 576, 579, 584, 601, 604, 607, 608, 650

Ignatz Award, xxxiii, 242, 277, 482, 551, 618

Image Comics, xi, xxix, 51–52, 57, 77, 118, 140, 145–46, 162, 164, 190, 193, 198–99, 204, 222, 228, 237, 239, 245, 249, 253–55, 257, 259–61, 269, 274, 281, 293, 299–302, 327, 336, 342, 349, 353, 355, 364, 367, 377–79, 381–82, 386–87, 392, 394, 397–98, 402, 408, 410–11, 416–19, 424–25, 427, 429, 431, 433–34, 444, 446–49, 471, 476, 506, 555, 574–75, 577, 587, 590, 595–96, 600, 622, 631, 650

Iron Man (character), 24, 29, 52–54, 77–79, 93, 105, 107, 119–20, 334, 647

Japanime Co. Ltd, 497

Jetpack Press, 327

Joe Books, 150, 523–26, 541

Judge Dredd (character), 103, 233–34, 243, 246

Justice League (all versions of team), 25, 27, 39–40, 44, 68, 77, 85–86, 104, 105, 108, 123, 124, 131, 399, 572, 575–76

Justice Society of America (characters), 76–77, 87, 379

Keller, Helen, 607, 611, 617

Kid Beowulf Comics, 311

Kids Can Press, 304, 348, 442–43, 543, 545, 609

Kirkus Prize, 612

Kodansha Comics, xxx, xxxii, 34, 90, 161, 164, 203, 245, 260, 262–63, 272, 329, 432, 465, 480, 483, 490, 493, 516, 547, 566, 591, 614, 652

LAMBDA LiteraryAward for Best LGBT Graphic Novel, 258

Last Days (Marvel Comics event), 29, 57, 59, 76, 79, 329

Last Gasp, 323

Lee & Low Books, 455

Lightspeed Press, 242

Lion Forge Comics, 287–88

Liquid Comics, 136

Literary adaptations, 156, 236, 259, 264, 268, 294, 302, 304, 307, 310, 328, 330–31, 337, 343, 347, 354, 356, 361, 385, 390, 407, 420, 432, 500, 502–6, 509, 533

Little, Brown, and Company, 144, 178, 318

Liveright Publishing, 430, 434

Magnetic Press, 134

Manga, xxxii, 34, 65, 82, 89–90, 147, 151, 158–61, 164, 169, 175–79, 181, 187, 190, 199, 203, 205, 220–21, 227, 230, 234–35, 239–40, 242, 245, 247, 256, 258, 260, 262–64, 267, 270, 272–73, 275, 278, 281–82, 293–94, 298, 300, 302–3, 306, 312, 314, 329, 338–39, 344, 346, 348, 352, 354, 356, 378, 382–84, 386, 388, 391, 402–4, 408–10, 421–22, 432, 435–37, 458–67, 470, 473, 480, 483–84, 487–88, 489–97, 499–500, 502–3, 506, 508, 515–16, 519, 521–22, 543, 546, 553–54, 558, 560, 562, 564, 566, 568, 578, 587–89, 591, 597, 599, 601, 611–12, 614, 632–33; Neo-Manga, xxxii, 18, 236, 305, 318, 381, 514

Manhwa, xxxii, 422, 500

Margaret K. McElderry Books, 421

Mariner Books, 612

Marvel Comics, xi, xxix, 18–24, 28–33, 35–38, 40, 48–50, 52–56, 58–59, 62–63, 65–67, 69–84, 89, 91–107, 109–12, 114–16, 118–22, 125–26, 128–29, 131, 137, 153, 156, 167–68, 182, 192–94, 202, 206–9, 211–17, 219–20, 231, 273–74, 280, 285, 287–88, 307, 323, 329, 331–35, 343, 381, 390, 406–7, 412–13, 421, 427, 429, 445–46, 452, 457, 500, 504, 505, 532–33, 540–48, 555, 574–75, 578–79, 582, 586, 606, 647, 650; Disney Kingdoms, 193, 407; Icon, 127–28, 445; MAX, 37–38, 59, 429, 650; Soleil, 182
Marvel Zombies, 112–13, 390, 557
McFarland & Co, 626, 645
Ms. Marvel (characters): Carol Danvers, 69–70 (*see also* Captain Marvel); Kamilla Kahn, 56–57, 76–79

National Book, 598, 615, 621
NBM Publishing, xxix, 151, 153, 155, 317, 321, 434–36, 440, 442, 452, 454, 509, 530, 567, 594, 621, 629, 636, 641, 644–45, 652
Newbery Award, xxxiii, 481, 612
Nightwing (character). *See* Robin
9th Art Award, 475
Nobrow Books, 258, 299, 350
Nonfiction, 602–41; Art—Comics, Comic Books, and Graphic Novels, 602–5; Biography/Autobiography/Memoir, 605–23; History, 623–29; Miscellaneous Nonfiction, 639–41; Science and Math, 629–39
No Starch Press, 632

Oni Press, xxix, 135, 141, 148–49, 154, 182, 191, 193, 199, 245, 266, 314, 324, 343, 352, 357, 367, 389, 400, 408, 417, 432, 457, 463, 466, 471, 475–76, 479, 482, 488, 495–96, 531, 551, 557, 566, 569–70, 589–90, 653
Orbis Pictus Award, 625
Original Sin (Marvel Comics event), 72, 75, 79, 84
Orion (Publisher), 591

Pantheon Books/Pantheon Press, 243, 483, 501, 520, 555, 609, 615, 618, 623, 638, 655
Papercutz, 133, 178, 440–41, 530, 539, 541, 546, 561, 592, 653
Penguin Books, 570, 614
Perfect Square, 275, 531
Philomel Books, 331, 570
Picador, 475
Popular Paperbacks for Young Adults. *See* Young Adult Library Services Association (YALSA) Selection Lists
Predator (characters), 233, 243–46
Printz Award, xxxiii, 468, 486, 615
Prism Comics Queer Press Grant, 277
Pulitzer Prize, 615

Quick Pick for Reluctant Readers. *See* Young Adult Library Services Association (YALSA) Selection Lists

Random House, xi, 29, 346, 422, 479, 501, 509, 515–16, 519–20, 542, 552, 569, 576, 597, 615, 618, 652, 655
Rebellion Comics, 155
Red Five Comics, 140
Red Hood (character). *See* Robin
Red Robin (character). *See* Robin
Roaring Brook Press, 234, 476, 654
Robert F. Kennedy Book Award, 615
Robin (characters): Damian Wayne, 7–8, 10, 13, 59–61; Dick Grayson/Nightwing, 7–8, 17–18, 27, 57, 59, 88, 91, 536, 572–73, 584–85; Jason Todd/Red Hood, 7, 9, 15, 59, 88; other/multiple Robins, 7, 15, 26, 61, 123, 573; Tim Drake/Red Robin, 7, 9, 13, 27, 59–60, 91
Rodale Books, 630
Running Press, 389

Sabrina (character), 387, 411, 513, 565
Sandman, The (character), xxxv, 291, 356, 358, 360, 362–64, 367, 646
Scholastic. *See* Graphix/Scholastic
School Library Journal Best Books, 477
Science Fiction, 201–89; Aliens from Outer Space, 243–47; Alternate Worlds, Time Travel, and Dimensions, 248–256; Computers and Artificial Intelligence, 267–68; Dystopian and Utopian Worlds, 256–61; Man-Sized Robots, 270–81; Mecha and Giant Robots, 281–88; New Wave Science Fiction, 241–43; Post-Apocalypse, 261–67; Psychic Powers and Mind Control, 268–70; Robots, Androids, and Cyborgs, 270–88; Science Action, 227–41; Science Fiction Anthologies, 288–89; Space Exploration, 221–27; Space Opera/Space Fantasy, 201–21. *See also under* Humor
Scott O'Dell Award, 505
Secret Invasion (Marvel Comics Event), 70, 75, 79–80, 93, 100
Secret Wars (Marvel Comics Event), 20, 53, 67, 77–78, 97, 111–13, 575
Serve Man Press, 237
Seven Seas Entertainment, xxx, xxxii, 150, 189–90, 356, 381–82, 386, 388, 400, 562–63, 653
She-Hulk (character), 77–78, 84, 105
Sherlock Holmes, 116, 384, 391, 426, 437, 533
Sibert Medal, 615
Simon & Schuster Books, 264, 421; Simon Pulse, 227
Sky Dog Press, 134, 574
Skyhorse Publishing, 621, 645

Slave Labor Graphics/SLG Publishing, 261, 324, 355, 361, 393, 407, 480, 486, 613, 653

Smarter Comics, 640

Sparkplug Comics, 587

Spider-Man (characters): Miguel O'Hara (*Spider-Man 2099*), 20, 23–24; Miles Morales, 20–23, 77; other versions, 20, 62–63, 111–13, 116, 119, 323, 390, 579; Peter Parker, xxxiv, 2, 18–20, 62, 71, 77–79, 96, 98, 109, 114, 116, 118–20, 128, 457, 606, 646, 650; Peter Parker (*Ulitmate*), 21–22

Spider-Verse (Marvel Comics Event), 20–21, 23–24, 113

Star Trek (TV/movies), 222–27, 250, 650

Star Wars (movies/TV), xxxiv, xxxv, 152, 201–2, 206–20, 295, 650

Sterling Children's Publishing, 330, 347, 506

St. Martin's Press, 619, 647

Stone Arch Books, 351

Stone Bridge Press, 617

Stonewall Award, 612

Studio, 407, 397

Supergirl (character), 64–65, 106, 123, 131, 579, 584

Super-Heroes, 1–131; Alternate Time Lines, Elseworlds, and What–If Worlds, 122–26; anthologies, 130–31; Classic and Contemporary Crime Fighters, 24–69; Cosmic Heroes, 69–76; Epic Events, 106–16; Slice-of-Life/Common Man Perspectives, 126–30; Super-Hero Icons, 2–24; Super-Hero Teams, 76–102; Team-Ups, 103–6; Villains: Archenemies and Rogues Galleries, 115–22; X-Men Epic Events, 113–15

Superman (character), 1–6, 9, 15, 25, 27, 64, 68, 85–86, 103–4, 105–6, 108–10, 116, 122–25, 131, 133, 243–44, 265, 444, 536, 576, 583–84, 646–47, 649

Teenage Mutant Ninja Turtles, 104, 184–85, 541, 559–60

Television programs, xxxiii, 2, 17–18, 25, 27, 35, 39, 42, 44, 46, 48–50, 52, 54, 58, 59, 64–65, 70, 74, 85, 90–91, 128, 173, 178, 183–84, 188, 192, 200, 206, 210, 214, 222, 250, 284, 292, 298, 322, 360, 371, 377, 379, 385, 389, 392, 398, 413, 427, 429, 495, 523, 525–26, 529, 531–38, 540, 552, 563, 565, 569, 572–73, 579, 584–86, 589, 595

Telltale Games, 319, 552

Texas Library Association Little Maverick Graphic Novel Reading List, 477

Thanos, 71, 76, 109, 119–22, 124

Thor (all versions of character), 77, 81, 105, 109, 113, 115–16, 120, 329, 332–35

Three Rivers Press, 393

Th3rd World Studios, 346

Titan Books/Titan Comics/Titan Publishing, 131, 182, 225, 229, 233–34, 250–53, 261, 288, 298, 421, 448, 531–32, 535, 653

Tokyopop, 161, 203, 273, 305, 345, 467

Toon Books, 156, 325, 355, 477, 543, 549–50, 566, 653

Toonhound Studios, 608

Top Shelf Comics, xi, xxix, 88, 159, 164–65, 256, 280, 282, 324, 351, 426, 451, 457, 471, 473–74, 478–79, 485–86, 490–91, 504, 551, 560, 593, 597, 609, 615, 621, 650

Tor Books, 516

Touchstone, 613

Transformers (characters), 201, 282, 283–287

Tundra Books, 550

215 Ink, 394

2000 AD, 233, 234, 246

UDON Entertainment, 37, 159–62, 502–3, 587, 653

Valiant Entertainment, xxix, 142, 157–58, 181, 240, 269, 272–73, 276, 412, 580–81, 653

Vampires, 105, 123, 126, 146, 200, 247, 277, 324, 361, 367–69, 371–75, 380–86, 393–99, 416, 556, 558, 561–64, 566–67, 575. *See also* Horror

Vertical Comics, xxxii, 205, 227, 234, 267, 281–82, 491, 496, 519, 543–44, 546, 654

Vertigo. *See* DC Comics

Video Games. *See* Gaming

Viking Press, 353

Villard, 508–9

Viz Media, xi, xxx, xxxii, 65, 137, 147, 151, 158, 160, 176–77, 179–80, 187–88, 199, 203, 220, 230, 235, 240, 242, 247–48, 256–57, 260, 264, 267, 272, 275, 278, 281, 293, 298, 300, 306, 312, 314, 338–40, 344, 348, 352, 354, 383–84, 386, 391, 396, 402–4, 408–11, 420, 435–37, 458–66, 470, 473, 484, 487–89, 491, 493–95, 497, 521, 531, 553–54, 557, 564, 568, 578, 588–89, 597, 601, 654

Walker Publishing Company, 136

Walt Disney characters: Donald Duck, 297, 340, 511, 526–29, 541; Mickey Mouse, 511, 522, 529, 532, 541; Tinkerbell, 592–93; Uncle Scrooge, 511, 526–29

Werewolves, 155, 200, 319, 357, 367, 375, 380–82, 393, 399, 416, 558, 563–64, 566–67, 600

Wildstorm Productions. *See* DC Comics

William Morrow, 624, 629–30

Witches, 150, 157, 182, 297, 299, 301, 303, 316, 319, 322, 342–343, 346–47, 350, 356–58, 361, 369, 377–78, 380, 387, 410–11, 416–17, 422, 443, 502, 513, 526, 561–62, 565–67, 583. *See also* Horror

Wolverine (all versions of character), 65–68, 78, 79, 81, 94, 95–96, 98–100, 101–102, 105, 113–14, 116, 582, 586

Wonder Woman (character), 25, 68–69, 85–86, 105–6, 123, 125, 536, 576, 583–84, 647, 649

W.W. Norton and Co., 430, 434, 472, 604, 621, 624, 628, 643

X-Men (characters), 66, 72, 77, 81, 91, 94–101, 103, 106, 113–16, 125–26, 128, 131, 268, 323, 390, 575, 586, 648, 650

X-Men spin-off teams: New Mutants, 79, 99–101, 114; X-Factor, 99–100, 114–16; X-Force, 99–102, 116

Yen Press, 82, 140, 236, 258, 267–68, 302–3, 340–41, 356–57, 361, 378, 383, 388, 416, 422, 467–68, 486, 493, 499–500, 514–15, 522, 654

Young Adult Library Services Association (YALSA) Selection Lists: Best Books for Young Adults, xxxii, xxxiii, 89, 198, 452, 484, 608, 618; Great Graphic Novels for Teens List, xxxiii, 6, 11, 16, 22, 24, 26–28, 36, 45, 47, 53, 56, 58, 61–62, 65–66, 70, 73, 117, 128, 134, 145–46, 150, 155, 157, 159, 168, 170, 177, 180, 205, 212, 214, 226–27, 230, 234–35, 237, 245, 257, 260–61, 264, 267, 271, 274, 278, 281, 297, 299, 301, 304, 311, 315, 317, 323–26, 333, 347, 349, 352, 354–55, 357, 359, 363, 373, 381, 384, 391, 394, 397–98, 400, 404–5, 408, 410, 412–16, 422, 424, 426, 432–33, 435–36, 438–40, 452, 454–55, 460, 462, 464–66, 472, 474–78, 480–85, 487, 495, 498–500, 503, 513–14, 517, 521, 537, 554, 564, 571–72, 578, 582, 591, 596–98, 600, 606, 610, 614–16, 620–21, 623, 625, 627–28, 632, 638–40; Popular Paperbacks for Young Adults, xxxiii, 21, 62, 64, 92, 127, 186, 222, 245, 261, 272, 295, 305, 319, 358, 362, 385, 403, 425, 462, 467, 476, 481, 538, 599, 608, 616, 624, 630; Quick Pick For Reluctant Readers, xxxiii, 51, 67, 106, 211, 230, 319, 383, 403, 422, 481, 484, 537, 598–99, 616

Zenescope, 138

Zest Books, 475, 622

Zombies/Walking Dead, 112–13, 155, 159, 289, 297, 367–69, 375, 380, 386–93, 418–20, 431, 439, 556–58, 563, 566–67, 586, 590

About the Authors

MICHAEL PAWUK is a librarian for the Cuyahoga County Public Library system. He is the author of the first edition of Libraries Unlimited's book *Graphic Novels: A Genre Guide to Comic Books, Manga, and More* published in late 2006. Michael was the chair for the 2002 YALSA all-day preconference on graphic novels which featured guest speakers Neil Gaiman, Art Spiegelman, Jeff Smith, and Colleen Doran and he regularly speaks on the subject of graphic novels at library conferences including ALA, San Diego Comic-Con, and elsewhere. Pawuk helped to create the YALSA's Great Graphic Novels for Teens selection list before it debuted in 2007 and served as a judge for the Will Eisner Awards for the comic book industry in 2009. Currently, Pawuk contributes graphic novels reviews for School Library Journal's Good Comics for Kids blog, is a moderator for the GN-4LIB graphic novel listserv, and is a co-convener for the American Library Association's Graphic Novels in Libraries Member Initiative Group.

DAVID S. SERCHAY is a librarian in the Broward County Library system, where his responsibilities include selecting graphic novels. He is the author of *The Librarian's Guide to Graphic Novels for Children and 'Tweens* and *The Librarian's Guide to Graphic Novels for Adults*. He has also contributed to various reference books on graphic novels, including *The Encyclopedia of Comic Books and Graphic Novels*, *Comics Through Time*, and *Icons of the American Comic Book*. Serchay has spoken on the topic of graphic novels and libraries at ALA conferences and the San Diego Comic-Con as well as in libraries around Florida.